ATTENTION DEFICIT HYPERACTIVITY DISORDER

STATE OF THE SCIENCE • BEST PRACTICES

Edited by
Peter S. Jensen, M.D.
James R. Cooper, M.D.

Civic Research Institute

4478 U.S. Route 27 • P.O. Box 585 • Kingston, NJ 08528

Printed in the United States of America

Library of Congress Cataloging in Publication Data
Attention deficit hyperactivity disorder: State of the science; best practices/
Peter S. Jensen, M.D. and James R. Cooper, M.D. (editors)

ISBN 1-887554-26-2

Library of Congress Control Number: 2002106887

About the Editors and Authors

Peter S. Jensen, M.D., is the Director of the Center for the Advancement of Children's Mental Health~"Putting Science to Work" and Ruane Professor of Science in Child Psychiatry at the Columbia University College of Physicians and Surgeons. Before assuming his current position in the fall of 1999, Dr. Jensen was the Associate Director of Child and Adolescent Research at the National Institute of Mental Health (NIMH). Serving at NIMH from 1989 until 1999, Dr. Jensen functioned in a range of government leadership positions, all concerned with children's mental health research. At NIMH Dr. Jensen served as the lead NIMH investigator on the six-site NIMH and Department of Education-funded study of Multimodal Treatment of ADHD (the MTA Study) and also as an investigator on other NIMH multisite studies. He serves on many editorial and scientific advisory boards (including the CHADD Professional Advisory Board), is the author of over 150 scientific articles and book chapters, and has edited or coedited five books on children's mental health research. For his research, writing, and teaching, he has received many national awards, including the Rieger Award (1990 and 1996) and the Lewis Award (2000) from the American Academy of Child and Adolescent Psychiatry, the McGavin (1996) and Ittelson Awards (1998) from the American Psychiatric Association, and Special Recognition Awards from the American Psychological Association and the Association for Child Psychiatric Nursing. In 1999 he received the Exemplary Psychiatrist Award from the National Alliance for the Mental Ill, and in 2000 he received the Outstanding Mentor Award.

James R. Cooper, M.D., received his medical degree from Jefferson Medical College, completed his residency training at Pennsylvania Hospital and is a Diplomat, American Board of Psychiatry. For most of the twenty-seven years that he worked at the National Institute on Drug Abuse (NIDA), he directed a program which developed abuse liability research information on psychoactive drugs, such as the various stimulants used to treat patients with attention deficit hyperactivity disorder (ADHD), and formulated recommendations regarding the need for federal and international drug controls. Since 1983, he served as a member of the U.S. Delegation to the United Nations Commission on Narcotic Drugs, a temporary adviser to the World Health Organization on various drug abuse consultations, and director of NIDA's World Health Organization Collaborating Center projects. Dr. Cooper retired from the NIH in 1999 and is currently practicing psychiatry and consulting on various psychotropic drug projects. His publications include chapters, monographs, and scientific journal articles on psychotropic drug abuse liability and drug abuse treatment. He has served as peer reviewer for the *Journal of the American Medical Association* and the *Archives of General Psychiatry* and an editorial board member of several medical journals.

Howard Abikoff, Ph.D., is the Pevaroff Cohn Professor of Child and Adolescent Psychiatry at New York University (NYU) School of Medicine and Director of

Research at the NYU Child Study Center. Dr. Abikoff's clinical research activities have spanned three interrelated areas: the development of novel treatment approaches, treatment evaluation, and the development of measures to quantify treatment outcome. For the past three decades, much of his work has been funded by the National Institute of Mental Health, and has centered on treatment development and treatment evaluation of children with ADHD, as well as youngsters with conduct disorder. These large clinical trials have compared the efficacy of pharmacological and psychosocial treatments, alone and in combination. Dr. Abikoff has served as a reviewer on numerous NIMH panels and study sections, and recently participated as a member of the National Advisory Mental Health Council Clinical and Services Research Workgroup, which generated the 1999 National Institute of Health Report "Bridging Science and Service."

Jennifer D. Ambroggio, M.S., is currently working on the earliest stages of child development as an embryologist at the University of Southern California's fertility clinic. She performs *in vitro* fertilization and related assisted reproductive technologies. She received a B.A. in human biology from Stanford University, where her two main topics of study were developmental biology and psychology. Her two publications about attention deficit hyperactivy disorder (ADHD) with Dr. Jensen were part of an internship for her undergraduate major. She attributes her interest in mental health to her psychiatrist parents and to her wonderfully creative and endlessly energetic brother who has ADHD.

L. Eugene Arnold, M.Ed., M.D., is Professor Emeritus of Psychiatry at Ohio State University (OSU), where he was formerly Director of the Division of Child and Adolescent Psychiatry and Vice Chair of Psychiatry. He is a co-investigator in the OSU Research Unit of Pediatric Psychopharmacology. He has more than thirty years of experience in attention deficit hyperactivity disorder (ADHD) treatment research, including the six-site National Institute of Mental Health Multimodal Treatment Study of Children with ADHD (the MTA Study), for which he continues as executive secretary of the steering committee. His publications include eight books, more than fifty chapters, and over ninety articles. His original research includes trials of alternative treatments of ADHD, the topic of his chapter.

Russell A. Barkley, Ph.D., is Distinguished University Professor in the College of Health Professions, Medical University of South Carolina, Charleston, South Carolina. He received his Ph.D. from Bowling Green State University and did internship training at the Oregon Health Sciences University. He is the author of 14 books, 7 professional videos, and more than 175 book chapters and scientific papers related to ADHD and associated disorders. He is also the founder and editor of *The ADHD Report*, a bimonthly newsletter for professionals. He was Associate Professor of Neurology at the Medical College of Wisconsin from 1977–1985 and Professor of Psychiatry and Neurology and Director of Psychology at the University of Massachusetts Medical School from 1985–2002.

Joseph Biederman, M.D., is Chief of the Joint Program in Pediatric Psychopharmacology at the Massachusetts General and McLean Hospitals, Chief of the Adult ADHD Program at the Massachusetts General Hospital, and Professor of Psychiatry at the Harvard Medical School. Dr. Biederman is board certified in general and child psychiatry. He has been the recipient of the American Psychiatric Association Blanche Ittelson Award for Excellence in Child Psychiatric Research and the American Academy of Child and Adolescent Psychiatry Charlotte Norbert Rieger Award for Scientific Achievement. He has been inducted into the CHADD "Hall of Fame." Dr Biederman has also been selected every year since its inception into the "The Best Doctors in America" compilation of the best physicians in the country. Dr. Biederman is mentor to more than ten junior investigators in the field. He is on the editorial boards of multiple journals, a reviewer for most of the psychiatric journals, and has served as a grant reviewer in the Child Psychopathology and Treatment Review Committee of the National Institue of Mental Health. Dr. Biederman is the author and coauthor of close to 300 scientific articles, 50 book chapters, and 200 scientific abstracts. During the decade of the 1990s, he was the fourth highest producer of high-impact papers in psychiatry as determined by the Institute for Scientific Information and the highest-ranked child psychiatrist (*Science*, 2000, Vol. 288, p. 959).

Hector R. Bird, M.D., received his medical degree from Yale University Medical School and his training in general and child psychiatry at the New York State Psychiatric Institute/Columbia University. He is presently Professor of Clinical Psychiatry at Columbia University, College of Physicians and Surgeons and Deputy Director of the Division of Child and Adolescent Psychiatry. Dr. Bird's major research interests are in child psychiatric epidemiology, measurement, and cross-cultural epidemiology. He is on the editorial boards of several prestigious publications including *Journal of Abnormal Child Psychology*, *Journal of the American Academy of Psychoanalysis*, and *Journal of Child and Family Studies*. Currently Dr. Bird is principal investigator of project funded by the National Institute of Mental Health to study the development of antisocial behaviors in U.S. and island Puerto Rican Youth.

William B. Carey, M.D., is a pediatrician, who graduated from the Harvard Medical School in 1954 and did his specialty training at the Children's Hospital of Philadelphia. Subsequently he spent thirty-one years in primary pediatrics care mostly in Media, Pennsylvania. While in solo practice, he began his studies of child development and behavior, in particular of children's temperament differences. With a team of psychologists he developed for ages 1 month through 12 years a series of five temperament questionnaires, which have been widely used throughout the world and translated into many languages. For the last twelve years he has been Clinical Professor of Pediatrics at the University of Pennsylvania, teaching developmental-behavioral pediatrics at the Children's Hospital of Philadelphia. His numerous publications on temperament include *Coping with Children's Temperament. A Guide for Professionals* (Basic Books, 1995) and *Understanding Your Child's Temperament* (Macmillan, 1997). His principal honors are the Aldrich Award in Child Development from the American Academy of Pediatrics and election to the Institute of Medicine of the National Academy of Sciences.

F. Xavier Castellanos, M.D., a child psychiatrist and pediatrician, is Brooke and Daniel Neidich Professor of Child and Adolescent Psychiatry and Professor of

Clinical Radiology at New York University (NYU) School of Medicine, and Director of the Institute for Pediatric Neuroscience of the NYU Child Study Center. Formerly chief of the ADHD Research Unit of the Child Psychiatry Branch at the National Institute of Mental Health, Dr. Castellanos's work has centered on understanding the pathophysiology of attention deficity hyperactivity disorder (ADHD) through longitudinal studies of brain anatomy using magnetic resonance imaging in children with ADHD and controls.

Betty Chemers, M.A., is the former Deputy Administrator of the Office for Juvenile Justice and Delinquency Prevention (ODJJDP), U.S. Department of Justice. She has spent more than twenty-five years in the public and not-for-profit sectors working on criminal and juvenile justice issues. As Deputy Administrator, she managed 800 research, statistics, demonstration and technical assistance grants designed to prevent juvenile crime and improve the juvenile justice system. Under her leadership, OJJDP identified mental health for juveniles as a priority area and supported research on attention deficit hyperactivity disorder. Ms. Chemers's specific areas of expertise include youth gangs, school violence, mentoring, and community-based crime prevention initiatives.

Diane Comer is a Senior Research Associate in the Child Services Research and Development Program at the University of Pittsburgh Medical Center.

Louis Danielson, Ph.D., is a national leader in the field of special education and has been involved in programs that improve results for students with disabilities for nearly three decades. He brings an unparalleled and unique depth of knowledge in both special education policy and research to his current position as Director of the Research to Practice Division in the Office of Special Education Programs (OSEP), U.S. Department of Education. Dr. Danielson was awarded a doctorate of philosophy in educational psychology from Pennsylvania State University in 1976. His career spans several roles in education, including secondary school science and mathematics teacher, school psychologist, and teaching at the university level. For the past twenty-three years, Dr. Danielson has held leadership roles in OSEP and is currently responsible for the discretionary grants program, including research, technical assistance and dissemination, personnel preparation, technology, and parent training priorities, national evaluation activities, and other major policy-related studies in OSEP. He has served in numerous research and policy roles across the Department and has represented OSEP in major school reform activities. A frequent contributor to professional journals, Dr. Danielson has published extensively in the literature and is a frequent speaker at national and international conferences and events focusing on special education. His particular areas of interest include policy implementation and national evaluation studies.

June K. Dunnick, Ph.D., is a toxicologist at the National Institute of Environmental Health Sciences. Dr. Dunnick was the principal investigator for the two-year carcinogenisis studies that the National Toxicology Program conducted on d-amphetamine and methylphenidate.

Michael Feil, M.B.A., M.S., is Chief Statistician of the Agricultural Marketing

Service in the U.S. Department of Agriculture. His research interests include statistical consulting, agent-based computation, and algorithmic modeling. Prior to his current position, he was a statistician with the National Institute of Mental Health.

Gretchen Feussner, **B.S.**, received her degree in chemistry from Trinity College and did graduate work in pharmacology at the State University of New York, Upstate Medical Center. She served as a research chemist for ten years at the National Institutes of Health and joined the Drug Enforcement Administration in 1991 in the Office of Diversion Control. Her primary responsibilities involve monitoring drugs of abuse and evaluating drugs for possible control under the Controlled Substances Act.

Steven R. Forness, **Ed.D.**, is a Special Educator and Professor on the faculty of the Psychiatry and Biobehavioral Sciences Department at the University of California, Los Angeles (UCLA). He is also principal of the UCLA Neuropsychiatric Hospital School and Chief of Educational Psychology Services for the hospital. He has coauthored 8 books on children with learning or behavioral disorders and published more than 200 papers in education or mental health. Dr. Forness's research has primarily focused on early detection and eligibility of children with psychiatric disorders for special education services in the public schools. He is also recipient of the Wallin Award from the Council for Exceptional Children and the Berman Award from the American Academy of Child and Adolescent Psychiatry.

Laurence L. Greenhill, **M.D.**, is a Professor of Clinical Psychiatry at Columbia University, Director of the New York State Research Unit of Pediatric Psychopharmacology at the New York State Psychiatric Institute and Medical Director of the Disruptive Behavior Disorders Clinic at Columbia Presbyterian Medical Center. Under the mentorship of Edward Sachar, M.D., he studied the psychoneuroendrocinological responses of children with attention deficit hyperactivity disorder (ADHD) to psychostimulants, in particular. He has published on the effect of stimulant medication on the growth hormone and prolactin secretion. He continued his career with funded research investigating the dose equivalency and efficacy of sustained release methylphenidate, the efficacy of molindone in the treatment of inpatient children with conduct disorder, familial pathways in offspring of adult suicide attempters, the effects of age on the cardiovascular responses to tricyclic antidepressants, and the efficacy of multimodal treatments in children with ADHD. He is the principal investigator of four National Institute of Mental Health (NIMH) Grants, including the New York Research Unit of Pediatric Psychopharmacology, the New York State Psychiatric Institute site of the Multimodal Treatment Study of Attention Deficit Hyperactivity Disorder (the MTA Study), the study of methylphenidate safety and efficacy in preschool children with ADHD, and an investigator-initiated grant to study central serotonin metabolites in depressed adolescent inpatient suicide attempters. He currently holds pharmaceutical company contracts to study the efficacy and safety of SLI381 in ADHD, ampakine treatment of adults with ADHD, and the use of long-duration Adderall and long-duration methylphenidate (Concerta) in children and adolescents with ADHD. His award of a NIMH grant to study the effects of methylphenidate in preschool children in a multisite study (Preschool ADHD Treatment Study, or PATS) places him as the lead investigator of this six-site trial. He was also awarded a contract from NIMH to follow-up the MTA sample as they now enter adolescence. Dr. Greenhill is the author of over sixty published articles and has edited three books, including a monograph on methylphenidate. He serves as the current Chair of the Program Committee of the American Academy of Child and Adolescent Psychiatry and is the coeditor of the *Journal of Attention Disorders*, with C. Keith Conners, Ph.D. While working on the MTA Study, he coordinated the development of its medication manual. He has completed a five-year term as the member of the Workgroup on Research of the Academy of Child and Adolescent Psychiatry. He serves as one of the senior investigators in the New York State Psychiatric Institute's Center for Study of Suicidal Behavior (John Mann, M.D., Director), and the Director of the Psychopharmacology Core of the New York State Psychiatric Institute Intervention Research Center (David Shaffer, M.D., Principal Investigator).

Kelly Henderson, Ph.D., is a Research Education Program Specialist in the Research to Practice division of the Office of Special Education Programs (OSEP), U.S. Department of Education. Her work at OSEP includes management of a national study on the state and local implementation of the federal special education law, several education policy research projects, as well as a technical assistance center focused on state-federal policy issues. Her research interests include characteristics of children with emotional and behavioral disorders, special education policy, and educational reforms including standards-based accountability and school choice. Dr. Henderson received her Ph.D. in special education from the University of Maryland in 1997 and was previously a public school teacher of children with emotional and behavioral disorders and learning disabilities and a policy analyst for a professional special education association.

Stephen P. Hinshaw, Ph.D., is Professor of Psychology and former Director of Clinical Science at the University at California, Berkeley. He received his B.A. from Harvard in 1974 and his doctorate in clinical psychology from the University of California, Los Angeles in 1983. He has been awarded numerous grants from the National Institute of Mental Health for his work in developmental psychopathology, and he is the author of over 120 books, articles, and chapters in the field. He is immediate past president of the International Society for Research in Child and Adolescent Psychopathology and is currently president of Division 53 of the American Psychological Association, the Society for Clinical Child and Adolescent Psychology.

Kimberly Hoagwood, Ph.D., is Director of Research on Child and Adolescent Services for the Office of Mental Health in the State of New York, and is on the faculty of Columbia University. Previously she served as Associate Director of Child and Adolescent Mental Health Research with the National Institute of Mental Health (NIMH), where she oversaw a broad range of scientific studies on child and adolescent mental health. In that capacity, she also chaired the Child and Adolescent Research Consortium, a forum for interdisciplinary scientists at the National Institutes of Health, whose mission was to set research priorities in child and adolescent mental health. Dr. Hoagwood has directed numerous research programs on children's clinical and educational services at NIMH and in the state of Texas. Prior to her appointment at NIMH, Dr. Hoagwood was Research Director at the Texas Education Agency, where she supervised a statewide, multidisciplinary program of research on community-based services for children with serious emotional, behavioral, and psychiatric disorders. Dr. Hoagwood earned her doctorate in School Psychology in 1987, and practiced clinically for nine years. She has held academic appointments at the Pennsylvania State University and the University of Maryland. She has received numerous grants and awards, including the American Psychological Association's Distinguished Contribution award and the Outstanding Scholar in Education award from the University of Maryland. Among her numerous publications are articles and books examining the clinical effectiveness of children's services, national psychotropic medication practices, research ethics, and genetic epistemology in the work of Gabriel Garcia Marquez.

Charlotte Johnston, Ph.D., received her doctorate in clinical psychology from Florida State University in 1987. She is currently Professor of Psychology at the University of British Columbia in Vancouver, Canada. She has received funding from agencies such as the Canadian Institutes for Health Research and the Social Sciences and Humanities Research Council of Canada to study children with ADHD and their families. She has published over sixty scientific articles, with a particular focus on parent characteristics and child outcomes in attention deficit hyperactivity disorder. Dr. Johnston is on the editorial boards of *The ADHD Report* and the *Journal of Clinical Child and Adolescent Psychology*, and is a scientific adviser for CHADD Canada.

Kenneth A. Kavale, Ph.D., is Professor of Special Education at the University of Iowa. His research focuses on the theoretical and conceptual foundation of the special education category of specific learning disability. He is past Editor-in-Chief of *Learning Disabilities Research and Practice* and coauthor (with Steven Forness) of *The Nature of Learning Disabilities: Critical Elements of Diagnosis and Classification* (Erlbaum, 1995).

Kelly J. Kelleher, M.D., M.P.H., is Staunton Professor of Pediatrics and Psychiatry at the University of Pittsburgh, School of Medicine. Dr. Kelleher received his B.S. (summa cum laude) and M.D. (summa cum laude) from Ohio State University. His pediatric residency was completed at the Children's Memorial Hospital of Northwestern University before receiving his M.P.H. degree (honors) from Johns Hopkins University. He also completed the National Institutes of Health Epidemiology Training Program. Dr. Kelleher has been principal or co-principal investigator on federal research grants focused primarily on health, mental health and alcohol services research for high-risk children and their families, and the impact of managed care on children and adolescents with chronic psychiatric, medical, or alcohol problems. In addition, he has completed work on failure to thrive, child abuse and neglect, and the quality of primary care services for youth.

Rachel G. Klein, Ph.D., is Professor of Psychiatry at the Child Study Center of the New York University (NYU) School of Medicine. She has been an active researcher in child psychiatry for several decades. A major aspect of her work has been the conduct of large scale clinical studies that have examined the efficacy of various medications and psychosocial treatments in children with attention deficit hyperactivity disorder. She has followed up the largest cohort of children with ADHD into adulthood, with systematic focus on the evolution of substance use and abuse. She has authored close to 200 articles and 7 books. Prior to joining the NYU Child Study Center in 1999, she was Professor in the Department of Psychiatry at Columbia University, and Director of Clinical Psychology at the New York State Psychiatric Institute and the New York Presbyterian Hospital.

John R. Kramer, Ph.D., received his doctorate in clinical psychology from the University of Iowa in 1978 after graduating from Oberlin College and completing an internship at The Children's Village in New York. Dr. Kramer's clinical interests include psychometric assessment as well as cognitive-behavioral treatment of stress and depression. His research has focused on the long-term outcome of attention deficit hyperactivity disorder, psychological aspects of diabetes, and alcoholism.

Benjamin B. Lahey, Ph.D., is Professor of Psychiatry and Chief of Psychology in the Pritzker Medical School of the University of Chicago. The aim of his program of research is to contribute to our understanding of the dimensions and types of psychopathology as they emerge and change during the course of development and to help identify causal influences on child and adolescent psychopathology using the methods of developmental and genetic epidemiology. He is Past President of the International Society for Child and Adolescent Psychopathology.

Nadine M. Lambert, Ph.D., is Professor in the Cognition and Development area in the Graduate School of Education at the University of California at Berkeley, where she has been on the faculty since 1964. Early in her career she was a member of a team of investigators for the California State Department of Education charged with establishing and evaluating an array of programs for children with educational handicaps, including those who were diagnosed as hyperactive, resulting in the first state legislation supporting educational programs for children with learning and behavior disorders. At Berkeley she became the director of the School Psychology Program which received National Institue of Mental Health support for eighteen years as a model program to prepare professional psychologists to promote academic, social, and personal development of the school age population. Her research program on the mental health problems of the school-age population resulted in the publication of measures of adaptive behavior, attention deficit disorder, and teacher, peer, and self ratings of effective school functioning. The research reported in this volume was supported by a prospective, longitudinal investigation of hyperactive children and their classmates identified from public, private, and parochial schools in 1973–1974. This research established the prevalence of hyperactivity and treatment interventions, and its longitudinal phase resulted in documenting the life histories of these community-based samples of participants over a twenty-five-year period from childhood into early adulthood Professor Lambert is a Diplomate of the American Board of Professional Psychology, and a licensed psychologist. In 1999, she was honored with the award from the American Psychological Association for Distinguished Contributions for Applications of Psychology to Education and Training.

Jan Loney, Ph.D., received her undergraduate training at Stanford University. She did an internship and postdoctoral fellowship at Langley Porter Neuropsychiatric Institute in San Francisco, and then obtained a doctorate in child clinical psychology, with a minor in mathematics, from the University of Illinois at Champaign-Urbana. Subsequently, she was Professor of Psychiatry at the University of Iowa from 1967 to 1983, and in the Department of Psychiatry and Behavioral Science at the State University of New York (SUNY) at Stony Brook from 1983 to 2000. Her research has concerned the diagnosis, treatment, and outcome of what is now called attention deficit hyperactivity disorder (ADHD). Dr Loney is currently Professor Emeritus from SUNY and Visiting Professor in the Department of Pediatrics at the University of Iowa. At Iowa, she is conducting the midlife follow-up of a large group of boys with ADHD originally referred between 1967 and 1978. She has also received federal funding to develop an automated assessment system for child attention deficit disorder.

Diane B. Miller, Ph.D., is a neurotoxicologist at the National Institute of Occupational Safety and Health in Morganton, West Virgina. Dr. Miller has been studying the neurotoxic effects of substituted amphetamines for many years.

James P. O'Callaghan, Ph.D., is a neurotoxicologist at the National Institute of Occupational Safety and Health in Morganton, West Virgina. Dr. O'Callaghan has-been studying the neurotoxic effects of substituted amphetamines for many years.

William E. Pelham, Ph.D., is a graduate of Dartmouth College and earned his doctorate in clinical psychology from the State University of New York at Stony Brook in 1976. From 1986 until 1996 he was the Director of the ADHD Clinic and Research Program and Professor of Psychiatry at Western Psychiatric Institute and Clinic, the University of Pittsburgh School of Medicine (WPIC), and he maintains a laboratory at WPIC as an Adjunct Professor of Psychiatry. He is currently Professor of Psychology, Pediatrics, and Psychiatry at the State University of New York at Buffalo and Director of the Center for Children and Families. His summer treatment program for ADHD children has been recognized by the American Psychological Association (APA) as a model program and is widely recognized as the state of the art in treatment for attention deficit hyperactivity disorder (ADHD). Dr. Pelham has authored or coauthored more than 150 professional papers dealing with ADHD and its treatment. Past President of the Division of Child Clinical Psychology of the APA (Division 53) and Past President of the International Society for Research in Child and Adolescent Psychopathology, he has had more than forty-three research grants. He has served as a consultant/adviser on ADHD and related topics to several federal agencies, including National Institute of Mental Health, National Institute of Alcoholism and Alcohol Abuse, National Institute of Drug Abuse, Institute of Medicine, Office of Medical Application of Research, and the Centers for Disease Control.

Andrew S. Rowland, Ph.D., is an epidemiologist who works at the University of New Mexico Health Sciences Center. At the time of the Consensus conference, he was a senior staff fellow at the National Institute of Environmental Health Sciences where he was conducting a large population-based study of attention deficit hyperactivity disorder (ADHD) called the Johnston County ADHD study.

Helen Salisbury, Ph.D., received her undergraduate training in psychology from the University of Rhode Island (URI), where she continued on to receive her M.A. in school psychology. During her undergraduate and graduate career at URI, she participated in a Specialty Clinic for Psychopharmacology Research and Consultation for children with attention deficit hyperacitvity disorder. Dr. Salisbury received clinical training at the State University of New York at Stony Brook, where she was awarded a doctorate in biopsychology, with an emphasis in neuropsychology, especially pertaining to children and adolescents with symptoms suggesting a bipolar-spectrum disorder. Her research interests include the clinical and neuropsychological aspects of children with symptoms of mania as well as other childhood internalizing and disruptive behavior disorders. In addition, she is actively interested in designing, programming, and evaluating computerized psychological screening and assessment techniques.

Ellen Schiller, Ph.D., is a Senior Associate at Abt Associates Inc., Bethesda, Maryland. Dr. Schiller has over twenty-five years of experience managing research programs and conducting research on issues relevant to educating children with disabilities. Dr. Schiller has concentrated her studies on special education practice and policy, the study of innovations, effective reading practices, and research syntheses. She has made contributions at the federal, national, and local levels. Her particular interests have included teaching reading to children with learning disabilities, educating children with attention deficit disorders, and technology implementation. Currently, she directs the study of State and Local Implementation of IDEA, a longitudinal and multimethod policy study of states, school districts, and schools funded by the U.S. Department of Education, Office of Special Education Programs. Dr. Schiller has worked with multiple audiences. She has testified before a congressional committee on Government Oversight and Reform and the National Academy of Sciences; appeared on *Good Morning America*; made numerous presentations to researchers and practitioners at national meetings; published in refereed journals; and written for teacher and parent magazines on special education, teaching, and learning. Most recently, Dr. Schiller, along with her colleagues, published *Contemporary Special Education Research: Syntheses of the Knowledge Base on Critical Instructional Issues* (Erlbaum, 2000), for use by graduate students in education.

Thomas J. Spencer, M.D., is an Associate Professor of Psychiatry at Harvard Medical School and the Assistant Chief of the Pediatric Psychopharmacology Research Program at Massachusetts General Hospital. Before joining Massachusetts General Hospital, Dr. Spencer was the head of the Clinical Team, Child and Adolescent Division, of the Massachusetts Department of Mental Health. His research and clinical interests have focused on the effectiveness and safety of standard and novel pharmocological treatments of attention deficit hyperactivity disorder (ADHD) throughout the life cycle. Dr. Spencer has been co-investigator in Dr. Joseph Biederman's longitudinal and family-genetic studies of ADHD. In addition, Dr. Spencer is principal investigator in a project, funded by the National Institute of Mental Health, that examines the translation of of improvement in ADHD symptoms into increased functional capacities and quality of life in adults with ADHD. Dr. Spencer has published over 100 scientific articles and over 35 book chapters and is on the editorial boards of a number of journals.

James M. Swanson, Ph.D., is a Professor of Pediatrics and Director of the Child

Development Center at the University of California, Irvine (UC Irvine). After receiving his doctorate in psychology at Ohio State University in 1970, he was an Assistant Professor of Psychology at the University of Texas, Austin until 1974 and then a Research Scientist at the Hospital for Sick Children in Toronto until 1980. He joined the faculty of UC Irvine in 1980 and until 1990 focused on the development of school-based interventions for ADHD children. He established a public school on the UC Irvine campus where clinical and educational interventions were combined and directed the development of the Irvine Paraprofessional Program for application in the regular school setting. In 1990, his research focus shifted to address etiologies of attention deficit hyperactivity disorder (ADHD), using the Posner and Raichle model to investigate neuroanatomical networks of attention, which implicated specific dopamine pathways that are involved in attentional networks and in ADHD. In 1993, Dr. Swanson initiated a program of clinical trials with various pharmaceutical companies to develop new medications for ADHD and began participation in the Multimodal Treatment Study of ADHD. In 1995, he initiated a collaborative program involving the University of Toronto and UC Irvine to investigate the molecular genetics of ADHD, using candidate dopamine genes suggested by the neuroanatomical networks of attention. In 1999, he participated in the development of the Preschool ADHD Treatment Study (PATS) that is now in progress. In 2000, he became a Senior Fellow at the Sackler Institute of Developmental Psychobiology at Cornell University in New York City, where he is participating in the development of new nonpharmacological interventions for ADHD that are being applied and evaluated at the Child Development Center at UC Irvine and in the formulation of strategies for molecular genetic studies of normal and abnormal development of attention in children.

Rosemary Tannock, Ph.D., is a Senior Scientist in the Research Institute of The Hospital for Sick Children and an Associate Professor of Psychiatry at the University of Toronto, Canada. Her interdisciplinary training undertaken in England and Canada includes physiotherapy, developmental/educational psychology, and developmental psychopathology. Her clinical research program investigates the etiology and treatment of attention deficit hyperactivity disorder (ADHD), with a specific focus on its cognitive manifestations and the overlap of ADHD with learning disabilities. Her research is funded by the Canadian Institutes of Health Research, Ontario Mental Health Foundation, National Institute of Mental Health (NIMH), and recently the Australian Research Council (for collaborative research with colleagues at the University of Western Australia). She is also a recipient of a five-year Scientist Award from the Medical Research Council of Canada and a Distinguished Visitor's Award and Visiting Professorship from University of Western Australia, where she was appointed a Research Associate. Her work is published widely in peer-reviewed psychology and psychiatry journals and academic texts and has been cited frequently in the media. She has been invited to present her work internationally: in England, the Netherlands, France, Germany, Iceland, Norway, Puerto Rico, Venezuela, Australia, and the United States, including invitations to speak at the National Institutes of Health Consensus Development Conference on ADHD and the NIMH Interdisciplinary Research Workshop on ADHD.

David M. Umbach, Ph.D., is a biostatistician at the National Institutes of

Environmental Health Sciences and co-investigator on the Johnston County ADHD study.

Timothy E. Wilens, M.D., completed his undergraduate and medical school studies at the University of Michigan and his psychiatric training at Massachusetts General Hospital. He is board certified in child, adolescent, adult, and addiction psychiatry. He is currently Director of Substance Abuse Services in the Pediatric and Adult Psychopharmacology Clinics at Massachusetts General Hospital and is Associate Professor of Psychiatry at Harvard Medical School. Dr. Wilens has extensive clinical and research experience in both pediatric and adult psychopharmacology and addictions having published over 200 articles, chapters, and abstracts. He has also recently written a popular book, *Straight Talk About Psychiatric Medications for Kids* (Guilford Press, 1999). Dr. Wilens has federal funding from National Institutes of Mental Health and Drug Abuse as well as pharmaceutical support and is currently involved in pediatric and adult-related research projects including the characterization and treatment of attention deficit hyperactivity disorder (ADHD) across the lifespan; overlap of ADHD, bipolar disorder, and addictions; the pharmacological treatment of juvenile psychiatric disorders; and studies of the children of substance-abusing parents.

Erik G. Willcutt, Ph.D., is Assistant Professor of Psychology in the Department of Psychology and Faculty Fellow in the Institute for Behavioral Genetics, University of Colorado, Boulder. His overall research interests involve the application of basic science and clinical research techniques to test and improve the validity of psychiatric disorders across the lifespan, with a specific focus on attention deficit hyperactivity disorder and learning disabilities.

Mark L. Wolraich, M.D., is the CMRI/Shaun Walters Professor of Pediatrics and the Director of the Section of Developmental and Behavioral Pediatrics at Oklahoma University Health Sciences Center and the Child Study Center. He received his B.A. from Harpur College of the State University of New York (SUNY) at Binghamton and his M.D. from SUNY Syracuse Health Sciences Center. His residency training in pediatrics was split between the SUNY Syracuse Health Sciences Center and the University of Oklahoma, followed by a fellowship in the care of handicapped children at the University of Oregon. Following his training, Dr. Wolraich joined the pediatric faculty at the University of Iowa for fourteen years where he progressed to the rank of professor. He was subsequently on the faculty at Vanderbilt University for eleven years where he was Director of the Division of Child Development and the Director of the Child Development Center, the Junior League Center for Chronic Illnesses and Disabilities of Children, and the Greater Nashville Region Tennessee Early Intervention System. In addition, he was an investigator at the John F. Kennedy Center and the Center for Mental Policy. His research has been funded by the National Institutes of Health and Mental Health, Maternal and Child Health Research Program, National Institute on Disabilities and Rehabilitation Research and the Office of Special Education and Rehabilitation. Dr. Wolraich has been active nationally in the American Academy of Pediatrics (AAP) where he chaired the Task Force on Coding Mental Health in Children, which developed *The Classification of Child and Adolescent Mental Diagnoses in Primary Care: Diagnostic and Statistical Manual for*

Primary Care (DSM-PC) Child and Adolescent Version (AAP, 1996), and the Committee on Psychosocial Aspects of Child and Family Health and the Child. He was a member of the Committee on Quality Improvement-Subcommittee on ADHD and is on the AAP ADHD Advisory Committee. He is a member of the Society for Developmental and Behavioral Pediatrics for which he is a past president. Dr. Wolraich was the coeditor of *Advances in Developmental and Behavioral Pediatrics* (1982–1992). He has authored numerous journal articles and book chapters including articles in the *New England Journal of Medicine, Pediatrics*, and the *Journal of the American Medical Association*. He has edited a number of books, including a text-book—*Disorders of Development and Learning: A Practical Guide to Assessment and Management* (Mosby and now BC Decker, 1996), now in progress for its third addition, and the *DSM-PC Child and Adolescent Version*—and coedited *Behavioral Pediatrics* (Springer-Verlag, 1992). He is a section editor for a new pediatric textbook, *Comprehensive Pediatrics* (Harcourt), for use by graduate students in education.

Preface: Attention Deficit Hyperactivity Disorder— Where Have We Come, Where Are We Going?

by C. Keith Conners, Ph.D.

It is a wonderful feeling to recognize the unity of a complex of phenomena that to direct observation appear to be quite separate things.

—Albert Einstein

This volume comes at an historic time. There is a vast amount of new data regarding the description, epidemiology, neuropsychology, neurobiology, and therapeutics of attention deficit hyperactivity disorder (ADHD). It is already a concept accepted by much of the medical, educational, and health care communities (Goldman, Fenel, Bezman, & Slanetz, 1998). The frequency of the diagnosis of ADHD in physicians' offices has more than doubled in the past five years for children and adolescents and quintupled for adults. Dozens of research articles pour out in professional journals each month regarding its prevalence, neuropsychology, comorbidities, developmental course, and response to treatments. Advances in the neurosciences are being rapidly applied to ADHD, with researchers adopting the latest methods in genetics, neuroimaging, electrophysiology, and neurochemistry. New and more rigorous definitions of caseness are encouraging developmental epidemiologists to address issues of service need, utilization of services, and community practices of diagnosis and treatment (Hoagwood, Jensen, Petti, & Burns, 1996; Jensen, Hoagwood, & Petti, 1996). New tools for enhancing assessment and diagnosis appear with increasing frequency. Educational videos and workshops on recognition, management, and research findings regarding ADHD dominate the educational, medical, and psychological conventions. After forty years of relative quiescence, the pharmaceutical industry is engaged in furious competition to develop new or improved alternatives to available drug treatments.

Despite its wide acceptance, however, ADHD is a concept that still elicits controversies within the professional and lay communities, as it has in much of its past (Gustafsson, 1993). Although a long-standing debate regarding the etiology and pathophysiology of the disorder has been largely sidestepped by taking a purely descriptive approach to definition of the syndrome, impassioned discussion still takes place regarding the validity of the syndrome, its boundaries, and its operational definition (Koriath et al., 1985). Wide variations in diagnostic practice are evident (Kwasman, Tinsley, & Lepper, 1995). The frequent revisions of the American Psychiatric Association's official definition of ADHD in the *Diagnostic and Statistical Manual of Mental Disorders* (American Psychiatric Association, 1968, 1980, 1987, 1994) attests to the rapid conceptual changes taking place, as do revisions made necessary by new empirical data.

The controversies surrounding ADHD have been couched in a variety of forms, some carefully reasoned with empirical support, others merely strident denunciations. Some of the scientific arguments come from temperament theorists. Other challenges come from those who prefer dimensional rather than categorical models of psychopathology. There are those who prefer narrower and more specific constructs. Some argue that the constructs lack adequate operational definition. Some arguments appear to reflect objections to the use of stimulant drugs, or belief in the efficacy of more "natural" or nonpharmacological treatments, rather than objections to the concept of ADHD itself (Abikoff, 1991; Arnold, Christopher, Heustis, & Smelter, 1978; Arnold et al., 1989; Borden & Brown, 1989; Boris & Mandel, 1994; Colquhoun & Bunday, 1981; Conners, 1980; Feingold, 1975; Levy et al., 1997; Lubar, 1991; Marshall, 1989; Pelham, Wheeler, & Chronis, 1998; Whalen & Henker, 1991).

In sum, ADHD is an enormously popular but controversial concept. It has been a fruitful heuristic for much empirical research. Important advances have taken place in diagnostics and therapeutics. At the same time, controversy still exists as to the nature of the concept, its operational definition, etiology, and treatment practices. Is it a medical syndrome or merely a set of continuous dimensions of behavior or temperament? If it is a syndrome, is it a monothetic class (defined by a single core criterion) or a polythetic class (formed from two or more independent characteristics) (Barkley, 1990)? Are the symptom criteria simply nonspecific features applying to many disorders? Are these criteria capable of operational definition within the broader context of neuroscience, or are they vague and multidimensional constructs (Cohen, 1993) which lead inevitably to overdiagnosis and overtreatment? What are the roles of environmental, family, nutritional and other risk factors? The changing scientific paradigms through which the concept has been viewed may shed some light on the status of the concept, and what remains to be done in future research.

This book assembles the leading experts in the field of ADHD and scientifically addresses the debates and controversies surrounding this disorder. It coalesces into a single volume for the mental health professional the research underpinning the validity of ADHD as a disorder, as well as information concerning the possible causes of ADHD. It examines the treatment options for the disorder: What do we know, what is the safety and efficacy profile of the available treatments, and what are some alternative treatments? In addition, there is a section devoted to the controversies surrounding stimulant treatment of ADHD. The volume also examines current policies and practices regarding the assessment and treatment of ADHD.

Perhaps most important, this book takes a look at what is not being done, but should be, in terms of assessment, diagnosis, treatment, the availability of resources for getting help, and the elimination of barriers to care for individuals with ADHD. And, finally, the book outlines where research needs to go from here. I trust you will enjoy reading this volume as much my colleagues and I have enjoyed contributing to it.

References

Abikoff, H. (1991). Cognitive training in ADHD children: Less to it than meets the eye. *Journal of Learning Disabilities, 24*, 205–209.

American Psychiatric Association. (1968). *Diagnostic and statistical manual of mental disorders* (DSM-II) (2nd ed.). Washington, DC: Author.

American Psychiatric Association. (1980). *Diagnostic and statistical manual of mental disorders* (DSM-III) (3rd ed.). Washington, DC: Author.

American Psychiatric Association. (1987). *Diagnostic and statistical manual of mental disorders* (DSM-III-R) (3rd ed., rev.). Washington, DC: Author.

American Psychiatric Association. (1994). *Diagnostic and statistical manual of mental disorders* (DSM-IV) (4th ed.). Washington, DC: Author.

Arnold, L. E., Christopher, J., Heustis, R. D., & Smelter, D. J. (1978). Megavitamins for minimal brain dysfunction: a placebo-controlled study. *Journal of the American Medical Association, 240,* 2642–2643.

Arnold, L. E., Kleykamp, D., Votolato, N. A., Taylor, W. A., Knotras, S. B., & Tobin, K. (1989). Gamma-linolenic acid for attention-deficit hyperactivity disorder: placebo-controlled comparison to d-amphetamine. *Biological Psychiatry, 25,* 222–228.

Barkley, R. A. (1990). *Attention deficit hyperactivity disorder: A handbook for diagnosis and treatment* (p. 747). New York: Guilford Press.

Borden, K. A., & Brown, R. T. (1989). Attibutional outcomes: the subtle messages of treatments for attention deficit disorder. *Cognitive Therapy and Research, 13,* 147–160.

Boris, M., & Mandel, F. S. (1994). Foods and additives are common causes of the attention deficit hyperactivity disorder in children. *Annals of Allergy, 72,* 462–468.

Cohen, R. A. (1993). *The neuropsychology of attention.* New York: Plenum Press.

Colquhoun, I., & Bunday, S. (1981). A lack of essential fatty acids as a possible cause of hyperactivity in children. *Medical Hypothesis, 7,* 673–679.

Conners, C. K. (1980). *Food additives and hyperactive children.* New York: Plenum Press.

Feingold, B. (1975). *Why your child is hyperactive.* New York: Random House.

Goldman, L. S., Genel, M., Bezman, R. J., & Slanetz, P. J. (1998). Diagnosis and treatment of attention-deficit/hyperactivity disorder in children and adolescents. Council on Scientific Affairs, American Medical Association. *Journal of the American Medical Association, 279,* 1100–1107.

Gustafsson, P. (1993). [From MBD to ADHD–and then? A literature review on a controversial diagnosis.] *Lakartidningen, 90,* 2979–2982.

Hoagwood, K., Jensen, P. S., Petti, T., & Burns, B. J. (1996). Outcomes of mental health care for children and adolescents: I. A comprehensive conceptual model. *Journal of the American Academy of Child and Adolescent Psychiatry, 35,* 1055–1063.

Jensen, P. S., Hoagwood, K., & Petti, T. (1996). Outcomes of mental health care for children and adolescents: II. Literature review and application of a comprehensive model. *Journal of the American Academy of Child and Adolescent Psychiatry, 35,* 1064–1077.

Koriath, U., Gualtieri, C. T., Van Bourgondien, M. E., Quade, D., & Werry, J. S. (1985). Construct validity of clinical diagnosis in pediatric psychiatry: Relationship among measures. *Journal of the American Academy of Child and Adolescent Psychiatry, 24,* 429–436.

Kwasman, A., Tinsley, B. J., & Lepper, H. S. (1995). Pediatricians' knowledge and attitudes concerning the diagnosis and treatment of attention deficit and hyperactivity disorders. A national survey approach. *Archives of Pediatric Adolescent Medicine, 149,* 1211–1216.

Levy, F., Hay, D. A., McStephen, M., Wood, C., & Waldman, I. (1997). Attention-deficit hyperactivity disorder: A category or a continuum? Genetic analysis of a large-scale twin study. *Journal of the American Academy of Child and Adolescent Psychiatry, 36,* 737–744.

Lubar, J. F. (1991). Discourse on the development of EEG diagnostics and biofeedback for attention-deficit/hyperactivity disorders. *Biofeedback and Self Regulation, 16,* 201–225.

Marshall, P. (1989). Attention deficit disorder and allergy: A neurochemical model of the relation between the illnesses. *Psychological Bulletin, 106,* 434–446.

Pelham, W. E., Jr., Wheeler, T., & Chronis, A. (1998). Empirically supported psychosocial treatments for attention deficit hyperactivity disorder. *Journal of Clinical Child Psychology, 27,* 190–205.

Whalen, C. K., & Henker, B. (1991). Therapies for hyperactive children: Comparisons, combinations, and compromises. *Journal of Consulting and Clinical Psychology, 59,* 126–137.

Introduction

Attention deficit hyperactivity disorder (ADHD) has a prevalence of approximately 5 percent among children (Shaffer et al., 1996). When full ADHD criteria are met (early onset, six-month duration, and cross-situational symptoms), substantial functional impairment accompanies the condition, with impairments including elevated risk for serious accidents, problems in peer and family functioning, and sub-average academic achievement (Lahey et al., 1994). Importantly, ADHD co-occurs with other childhood disorders far more often than it appears alone (e.g., Biederman, Newcorn, & Sprich, 1991). Further, some studies show an increased risk for substance abuse and antisocial behavior (Mannuzza, Klein, Bessler, Malloy, & LaPadula, 1993). Comorbidity with aggressive disorders, learning disabilities, and internalizing disorders appears important for prognosis and even for treatment response (Jensen et al., 2001; Klein & Mannuzza, 1991). Although some debate surrounds the question of the level of impairment in adulthood (Shaffer, 1994), long-term outcome studies with carefully diagnosed ADHD subjects indicate that the syndrome persists into adulthood in a majority of cases (Barkley et al., 1990; Mannuzza et al., 1993).

Literally thousands of studies have been conducted on ADHD and its various predecessors prior to the fourth edition of *Diagnostic and Statistical Manual of Mental Disorders* (DSM-IV; American Psychiatric Association, 1994). Despite this long research history and its well-documented prevalence and associated impairments, ADHD is not necessarily well understood among the lay public, given the many controversies and public misconceptions concerning the disorder. Even respected scientists in other fields may misunderstand the disorder and/or have biases against recognizing and accepting the disorder as a valid medical condition. To address these issues, the National Institutes of Health (NIH) sponsored a Consensus conference in November 1998 and subsequently published the consensus statement emerging from this conference on the World Wide Web (http://odp.od.nih.gov/consensus/cons/ 110/110_statement.htm) (March 1999) and in the *Journal of the American Academy of Child Psychiatry* (National Institutes of Health Consensus Development Conference Statement, 2000). The consensus conference and final statement addressed many questions, including the following: What is the scientific evidence to support ADHD as a disorder? What is the impact of ADHD on individuals, families, and society? What are the effective treatments for ADHD? What are the risks of the use of stimulant medication and other treatments? What are the existing diagnostic and treatment practices, and what are the barriers to appropriate identification, evaluation, and intervention? Is ADHD over- or underdiagnosed? What are the directions for future research?

To answer these questions in the most expert and unbiased fashion, NIH brought together many of the best scientists in the world, most of whom had spent the majority of their career studying various aspects of ADHD, ranging from its causes, its assessment, its neurobiology, its treatments and their costs, and the services and systems that care for children with ADHD. These scientists prepared careful comments as a part of scientific testimony to be delivered to a panel of independent scientific judges at the conference. In addition, policymakers representing important federal perspectives and programs related to ADHD provided testimony concerning the educational, juvenile justice, and drug enforcement agencies' perspectives on ADHD.

This volume was inspired by these scientists' and policymakers' initial written testimony. Building on the findings of the conference, the contributors to the volume have since updated each of their respective topical areas with new research findings completed in the interim. As such, it represents an up-to-date, state-of-the-art review of what is known concerning the disorder by the world's leading authorities on each of the topic areas.

The volume is organized into parts covering each of the major topical areas: Part 1 covers ADHD diagnosis, epidemiology, clinical course, associated impairments, and outcomes. Part 2 addresses the pathophysiology and causes of ADHD, reviewing genetic, neuroimaging, neurobiological, and neuropsychological studies. Part 3 focuses on ADHD treatments—psychotherapeutic, pharmacological, alternative, and combined, as well as issues related to the matching of patients to treatments. Part 4 reviews the evidence concerning whether ADHD treatments, particularly the stimulants, are related to risk for substance abuse. Part 5 examines existing practices and policies related to ADHD, including over- and underdiagnosis, service system fragmentation, costs, and ADHD's impact on educational and juvenile justice systems.

Not all authors agree with each other on all topics. Thus, various perspectives are represented, in part because they discuss respected viewpoints with substantial impact and/or weight on research, policy, or both. To address such discrepancies, and to offer a balanced perspective on such discrepancies where they exist, we have provided commentary concerning each section and have taken a clear position as to where we stand on the controversy. In some sections, our friend and colleague, C. K. Conners, Ph.D., one of the preeminent authorities on ADHD in the world, has joined us in providing commentary.

The final summary chapter outlines many of the major findings presented in this volume and identifies areas in which additional research is needed. Appendix A presents the consensus conference statement itself.

The volume is dense but packed with up-to-date information. We trust that readers will find it useful in identifying ways to apply this information to their clinical practice, to policy, or even to guide the conduct of additional research.

P.S. Jensen
J.R. Cooper
May 31, 2002

References

American Psychiatric Association. (1994). *Diagnostic and statistical manual of mental disorders* (4th ed.). Washington, DC: Author.

Barkley, R. A., Fischer, M., Edelbrock, C. S., & Smallish, L. (1990). The adolescent outcome of hyperactive children diagnosed by research criteria. I: An 8-year prospective follow-up study. *Journal of the American Academy of Child and Adolescent Psychiatry, 29*, 546–557.

Biederman, J., Newcorn, J., & Sprich, S. (1991). Comorbidity of attention deficit hyperactivity disorder with conduct, depressive, anxiety, and other disorders. *American Journal of Psychiatry, 148*, 564–577.

Jensen, P. S., Hinshaw, S. P., Kraemer, H. C., Lenora, N., Newcorn, J. H., Abikoff, H. B., March, J. S., Arnold, L. E., Cantwell, D. P., Conners, C. K., Elliott, G. R., Greenhill, L. L., Hechtman, L., Hoza, B., Pelham, W. E., Severe, J. B., Swanson, J. M., Wells, K. C., Wigal, T., & Vitiello, B. (2001). ADHD comorbidity findings from the MTA study: Comparing comorbid subgroups. *Journal of the American Academy of Child and Adolescent Psychiatry, 40*, 147–158.

Klein, R. G., & Mannuzza, S. (1991). Long-term outcome of hyperactive children: A review. *Journal of the American Academy of Child and Adolescent Psychiatry, 30*, 383–387.

Lahey, B. B., Applegate, B., McBurnett, K., Biederman, J., Greenhill, L., Hynd, G. W., Barkley, R. A., Newcorn, J., Jensen, P., Richters, J., Garfinkel, B., Kerdyk, L., Frick, P. J., Ollendick, T., Perez, D., Hart, E. L., Waldman, I., & Shaffer, D. (1994). DSM-IV Field Trials for attention deficit hyperactivity disorder in children and adolescents. *American Journal of Psychiatry, 151*, 1673–1685.

Mannuzza, S., Klein, R. G., Bessler, A., Malloy, P., & LaPadula, M. (1993). Adult outcome of hyperactive boys: Educational achievement, occupational rank, and psychiatric status. *Archives of General Psychiatry, 50*, 565–576.

National Institutes of Health Consensus Development Conference Statement. (2000). Diagnosis and treatment of attention-deficit/hyperactivity disorder (ADHD). *Journal of the American Academy of Child and Adolescent Psychiatry, 39*, 182–188.

Shaffer, D. (1994). Attention deficit hyperactivity in adults. *American Journal of Psychiatry, 151*, 633–638.

Shaffer, D., Fisher, P., Dulcan, M. K., Davies, M., Piacentini, J., Schwab-Stone, M. E., Lahey, B. B., Bourdon, K., Jensen, P. S., Bird, H. R., Canino, G., & Regier, D. A. (1996). The NIMH diagnostic interview schedule for children version 2.3 (DISC-2.3): Description, acceptability, prevalence rates, and performance in the MECA study. *Journal of the American Academy of Child and Adolescent Psychiatry, 35*, 865–877.

Table of Contents

About the Authors iii
Preface xvii
Introduction xxi

PART 1: IS ADHD A REAL DISORDER?

Chapter 1: Validity of the Diagnosis and Dimensions of Attention Deficit Hyperactivity Disorder

Introduction 1-2
Dimensions of ADHD Symptoms: Internal Validity of
  DSM-IV Model 1-3
Discriminant Validity of the Two-Dimensional Structure of ADHD 1-3
    Differential Association of the Two Dimensions of Symptoms
      With Concurrent Mental Disorders 1-3
    Differential Association of the Two Dimensions of Symptoms
      With Types of Impairment 1-4
    Developmental Course of the Two Dimensions of
      ADHD Behaviors 1-5
Correspondence of DSM-IV ADHD to DSM-III-R ADHD 1-5
Correspondence of DSM-IV ADHD to ICD-10 Hyperkinesis 1-7
Validity of the Diagnosis of ADHD 1-7
    Face Validity 1-8
    Predictive Validity of ADHD in Childhood 1-8
    Concurrent Validity of ADHD 1-8
    Validity of DSM-IV Criteria for Age of Onset and
      Cross-Situational Impairment 1-10
Discriminant Validity of the Subtypes of DSM-IV ADHD 1-11
ADHD and Comorbid Mental Disorders 1-13
ADHD in Adulthood 1-14
Assessment of ADHD 1-14
Is ADHD Better Conceptualized in Diagnostic or Dimensional
  Terms? 1-14
Recommendations for Clinical Practice, Policy, and Future
  Research 1-15
    Implications for Clinical Practice 1-15
    Implications for Public Policy 1-16
    Areas to Target in Future Research 1-16

Chapter 2: The Diagnostic Classification, Epidemiology, and Cross-Cultural Validity of ADHD

Introduction 2-1
Changes in the Nosology and Effects on Rates 2-2
     Earlier Diagnostic Definitions 2-2
     Current Diagnostic Taxonomies 2-2
     Unresolved Classification Issues 2-3
Prevalence of the Disorder 2-3
Cross-Cultural Validity of the Construct 2-6
Presence of a Syndrome of Hyperkinesis/ADHD in Different
     Settings 2-8
Analysis of Epidemiological Data 2-9
     Risk Factors and Comorbidities 2-9
     Other Outcomes 2-11
Summary 2-12

Chapter 3: Is ADHD a Valid Disorder?

Overview 3-1
The ADHD Diagnosis 3-2
     Increasingly Frequent Diagnosis 3-2
     Shortcomings of Diagnostic Criteria 3-3
An Area of Consensus 3-3
Major Diagnostic Problems 3-4
     ADHD Behaviors Not Clearly Distinguishable From
         Normal Temperament Variations 3-5
     Absence of Clear Evidence That ADHD Symptoms Are
         Related to Brain Malfunction 3-7
     Neglect of the Role of the Environment and Interactions
         With It as Factors in Etiology 3-8
     Diagnostic Questionnaires Now in Use Are Highly
         Subjective and Impressionistic 3-9
     Most Important Predisposing Factors May Be Low
         Adaptability and Cognitive Problems 3-10
     Lack of Evolutionary Perspective 3-12
     Small Practical Usefulness and Possible Harm From
         Label 3-12
     Widespread Misapplication of the Present ADHD Label 3-13
     Nonspecific Effects of Methylphenidate and Other
         Stimulants 3-14
Conclusion 3-14

Chapter 4: ADHD—Long-Term Course, Adult Outcome, and Comorbid Disorders

Introduction 4-1
Limitations of Methodology 4-2
     Lack of Consensus on Diagnostic Criteria 4-2
     Use of Different Assessment Instruments 4-2
     Unreliability of Measurement Over Time 4-3
     Developmental Issues 4-3
     Shifting Information Sources 4-4
     Attrition 4-4
Outcome at Adolescence 4-5
     Persistence of ADHD Symptoms 4-5
     Occurrence of Comorbid Disorders 4-6
Outcome at Adulthood 4-7
     Persistence of ADHD Symptoms 4-7
     Risk for Antisocial or Criminal Behavior 4-8
     Risk of Substance Abuse 4-9
     Risk of Mood Disorders 4-10
Conclusion 4-10

Chapter 5: Is ADHD an Impairing Condition in Childhood and Adolescence?

Introduction 5-2
Methodological and Conceptual Issues 5-3
     Current Definitions of ADHD May Lead to Circular Reasoning
       Regarding Impairment 5-3
     Types of Samples and Kinds of Measures Used to Appraise
       Impairment Crucial to Unbiased Definitions 5-3
     Comorbidities, Rather Than ADHD Per Se, May Explain
       Impairment 5-4
     Which Subtypes of ADHD Show Impairment? 5-5
     Does Impairment Change Across the Developmental Span
       From Preschool to Adolescence? 5-5
     Summary 5-5
ADHD-Related Impairment: Evidence 5-6
     Academic Achievement and School Functioning 5-6
       Academic Achievement 5-6
       School-Related Impairment: Special Education, Suspension,
         Expulsion 5-7
       Summary 5-7

Family Relationships and Home Life 5-8
    Impaired Family Relationship Patterns 5-8
    Escalating Pattern of Discordant
        Interchanges 5-8
    Impact of Comorbid Aggression 5-9
    Summary 5-9
Peer Relationships 5-10
    Peer Rejection 5-10
    Impact of Comorbid Aggression 5-10
    Effect of ADHD Subtype on Likelihood of
        Rejection 5-11
    ADHD Children's Social Competence 5-11
    Summary 5-12
Self-Esteem and Self-Perception 5-12
    Lower Self-Esteem 5-12
    Overconfidence 5-12
    Summary 5-12
Accidental Injury 5-13
    Personal and Familial Variables 5-13
    Developmental Factors 5-13
    Summary 5-14
Overall Adaptive Functioning 5-14
Conclusions 5-14
    Summary of Findings 5-14
    Practical Implications 5-16

Chapter 6: The Impact of Attention Deficit Hyperactivity Disorder on Social and Vocational Functioning in Adults

Introduction 6-2
Identification and Study of ADHD in Adults 6-2
    Challenges to Reliability of Diagnosis 6-3
        Lack of Consensus on Diagnostic Criteria 6-3
        Manifestation of ADHD in Adults 6-3
        Reliability of Childhood History 6-4
        Differentiation of ADHD From Other
            Disorders 6-4
    Prevalence of Adult ADHD 6-4
    Summary 6-5
Evaluating Evidence of the Impact of ADHD on Adult
    Functioning 6-6

Educational and Vocational Functioning in Adults With
   ADHD 6-7
      Montreal Longitudinal Study 6-7
      New York Longitudinal Study 6-8
      Other Findings 6-8
      Lifelong Impact of Childhood Difficulties 6-9
      Employment Discrimination Challenges 6-9
      Summary 6-10
Social Functioning in Adults With ADHD 6-10
      Impairments in Psychological Functioning 6-11
      Social Skills Deficits 6-13
      Family Functioning 6-13
         Marital Ties 6-13
         Parenting 6-14
Conclusions 6-15
Recommendations for Clinical Practice and Future Research 6-16

PART 2: WHAT CAUSES ADHD?

Chapter 7: Biological Bases of ADHD—Neuroanatomy, Genetics, and Pathophysiology

Introduction 7-1
      DSM-IV/ICD-10 Overlap 7-2
      Dopamine Theory of ADHD 7-4
Research on Neuroanatomical Abnormalities 7-4
      Differences in Neuroanatomic Structures in Children
         With ADHD 7-5
         Basal Ganglia and Cerebellum 7-5
         Frontal Regions 7-6
      Areas of Difference Among the Findings 7-6
      Overall Consistency of Findings 7-7
Research on Functional Brain Imaging and ADHD 7-7
Genetic Investigations 7-9
      Twin Studies 7-9
      Genes Associated With ADHD/HKD 7-9
      Populations and Family Studies of Candidate Genes 7-10
         DRD4 Gene 7-11
         DAT1 Gene 7-11
      Study Replications 7-12
Investigations of Nongenetic Etiologies 7-12

Neurobiological Bases for Pharmacological Treatment 7-13
    Methylphenidate as a Dopamine Blocker 7-13
    Debate Regarding Net Effect of Dopamine Blockade 7-14
Alternative Site-of-Action Hypotheses 7-14
Summary 7-15

Chapter 8: Cognitive Correlates of ADHD
Introduction 8-2
Conceptual and Methodological Challenges 8-3
    Diverse and Shifting Definitions of ADHD 8-3
    Effect of Co-Occurring Disorders, Age, and
        Gender 8-3
    State of the Science 8-4
    Impact on Current Study 8-4
General Intellectual Function 8-4
Academic Achievement 8-6
    Low Productivity 8-6
    Underachievement 8-6
    Academic Outcomes 8-7
Neuropsychological Function 8-8
    Impairments in Executive Functioning 8-8
    Other Neuropsychological Impairments 8-9
    Cognitive Functions Not Directly Affected by ADHD 8-10
    Summary 8-10
Impact of Comorbidity on Neuropsychological Profile 8-10
    Reading Disorder 8-10
    Anxiety Disorder 8-11
    Conduct Disorder 8-11
Specificity of Cognitive Correlates to Neuropsychological
    Functioning 8-12
Information Processing 8-13
    Impairments in Sustained Attention 8-13
    Response Inhibition Deficits 8-14
    Spatial Allocation of Attention 8-15
Implications for Neural Substrate and Pathophysiology of
    ADHD 8-15
Clinical Implications 8-16
    Diagnosis 8-16
    Assessment and Treatment 8-17
Implications for Future Research 8-18

PART 3: ARE ADHD TREATMENTS SAFE AND EFFECTIVE?

Chapter 9: Stimulant Medication Treatment of Children With Attention Deficit Hyperactivity Disorder

Introduction 9-2
Pharmacology 9-3
Absorption and Metabolism 9-4
Toxicology 9-6
Stimulant Adverse Events 9-6
Are There Long-Term Risks of Stimulant Use? 9-6
Short-Term Efficacy Shown in Randomized Controlled
   Trials of Stimulants 9-7
Benefits of Stimulant Medications 9-9
      Amelioration of Disruptive Behaviors 9-9
      Improvement of Cognitive Functioning 9-9
      Placebo vs. Medication Response 9-9
Efficacy of Long-Duration Stimulant Preparations 9-12
Limitations of Short-Term Stimulant Trials 9-13
Long-Term Randomized Controlled Trials of Stimulant
   Medications 9-14
      The MTA Study 9-14
         MTA Study Design 9-14
         Study Outcome 9-18
         MTA Study's Answers to Treatment
            Questions 9-18
      Other Long-Term Studies 9-19
Issues for Practitioners 9-19
      Do the Research Findings Inform Practice? 9-19
      Limitations of Available Stimulants 9-20
         Response/Dosing Issues 9-20
         Side Effects 9-21
Recommendations 9-21

Chapter 10: Public Health and Toxicological Issues Concerning Stimulant Treatment for ADHD

Introduction 10-2
Prevalence 10-2
Toxicology 10-3
      Methylphenidate 10-3

    Amphetamines 10-4

    Pemoline (Cylert) 10-5

Efficacy of Stimulant Treatment 10-5

    Short-Term Efficacy 10-5

    Long-Term Effectiveness 10-6

Safety 10-7

    Short-Term Safety 10-7

        Methylphenidate and Amphetamines 10-7

        Pemoline (Cylert) 10-7

    Long-Term Safety 10-8

        Limits of Adverse Drug-Reporting Systems 10-8

        Need for Large-Scale Cohort and Drug Surveillance

            Studies 10-9

        Phenobarbital as Analogy 10-10

Future Research Needs 10-11

    Toxicology 10-11

    Efficacy/Effectiveness 10-11

    Safety 10-12

An Opportunity and a Responsibility 10-12

Chapter 11: Nonstimulant Treatments for ADHD

Introduction 11-1

    Evolving Nosology of ADHD 11-2

    Drawbacks of Using Stimulants to Treat ADHD 11-2

Alternative Treatments for ADHD: Tricyclic

   Antidepressants 11-4

    Advantages of TCAs 11-4

    Favorable Results With Desipramine 11-4

        DMI in Treating Children 11-4

        DMI in Treating Adults 11-5

    Efficacy of Nortriptyline 11-5

    Comparison of TCAs to Stimulants 11-5

    Safety of TCAs 11-6

Non-TCA Antidepressants 11-6

    Bupropion 11-6

    MAOIs and SSRIs 11-6

    Tomoxetine 11-7

Alpha-2 Noradrenergic Agonists 11-7

    Other Drugs 11-7

    New Directions: Cholinergic Drugs 11-8

Summary and Discussion 11-9
    Viability of Nonstimulant Treatments 11-9
    Need for Further Research 11-10

Chapter 12: Psychosocial Interventions for ADHD
Introduction 12-2
Limitations of Pharmacological Interventions 12-3
    Little Effect on Interpersonal Relationships or Family
        Functioning 12-3
    Individual Differences in Response 12-3
    Long-Term Prognosis Discouraging 12-4
Psychosocial Interventions 12-4
    Cognitive-Behavioral Treatment 12-5
    Clinical Behavior Therapy 12-6
        Improved Behavior 12-8
        Impact on School Functioning 12-9
        Effect of Concurrent Medication
            Therapy 12-10
    Contingency Management 12-10
        Use of Negative Consequences 12-11
        Treatment Effects 12-11
    Intensive Treatments 12-12
        The Children's Summer Treatment Program 12-12
        Treatment Response 12-13
        Need for Comprehensive Long-Term
            Intervention 12-14
Shortcomings of Behavioral Interventions 12-14
Combined Pharmacological and Behavioral Interventions 12-15
    Advantages of Combining Behavioral and Pharmacological
        Treatments 12-15
    Long-Term Impact 12-16
    Research Findings Show Positive Results 12-16
    Long-Term Efficacy 12-18
Summary and Future Directions 12-18
    Efficacy of Behavioral Treatment Is Clear 12-18
    Open Questions 12-19
        Does Child's Age Affect Treatment Choice? 12-19
        How Should Comorbidities Affect Treatment
            Choice? 12-21
        How Do Family Factors Affect Treatment Choice? 12-21

Can Medication Dosage or Parent Training Mitigate
Treatment Intensity? 12-21
What Is Optimum Treatment Sequence? 12-22
How Long Must Treatment Continue? 12-22
Cost-Effectiveness 12-23
Exportability of Programs to Real-World Settings 12-24
Long-Term Effectiveness 12-24

Chapter 13: Treatment Alternatives for Attention Deficit Hyperactivity Disorder

Introduction 13-2
Eliminaton Diets (Few-Foods Diets/Oligoantigenic) 13-2
Recent Research Documents Efficacy 13-2
Probable Responders to Elimination Diets 13-3
Sugar Elimination Alone Unlikely to Work 13-4
Possible Risks 13-7
Immune Therapy 13-7
Nutritional Supplements 13-7
Amino Acid Supplementation 13-7
Essential Fatty Acid Supplementation 13-8
Possible L-Carnitine Effect 13-9
Glyconutritional Supplements 13-9
Dimethylaminoethanol 13-9
Vitamin Supplementation 13-10
Mineral Supplements 13-11
Iron Supplementation 13-11
Zinc Supplementation 13-11
Magnesium Supplementation 13-12
Herbal and Homeopathic Treatments 13-12
Acupuncture 13-13
EEG Biofeedback 13-13
EMG Biofeedback, Relaxation Training, and Hypnosis 13-14
Meditation 13-15
Mirror Feedback 13-15
Perceptual Stimulation/Training 13-15
Massage 13-15
Vestibular Stimulation 13-16
Channel-Specific Perceptual Training 13-17
Antifungal Treatment 13-17
Thyroid Treatment 13-17
Deleading 13-18

Recommendations for Clinical Practice 13-18
    Weighing Alternatives 13-18
        Category 1: Unproven 13-18
        Category 2: Ineffective/Unsafe 13-19
        Category 3: Indicated Only for Selected Etiologies 13-19
        Category 4: Proven Efficacy 13-19
        Category 5: Worth Trying Despite Limited Evidence
            of Efficacy 13-20
    Approach to Selecting Treatment 13-20
Recommendations for Future Research 13-20

Chapter 14: Behavioral and Medication Treatments for ADHD— Comparisons and Combinations

Background 14-2
Short-Term Treatment Studies 14-4
    Medication vs. Behavior Therapy vs. Combined
        Treatment 14-4
    Medication/Psychosocial Treatment 2 x 3 Study 14-4
    Small-Sample Studies 14-4
        Cognitive Treatment Plus Medication vs. Medication
            Alone 14-4
        Behavior Treatment With and Without Medication 14-5
        Dose-Reduction Study 14-5
        Medication With and Without Auditory Feedback or
            Contingency Management 14-6
    Durability of Treatment 14-6
    Studies Favoring Combined Treatment Over Medication
        Alone in the Minority 14-7
Long-Term Treatment Studies 14-8
    The MTA Study 14-9
        Intensive Psychosocial/Behavioral Treatment vs.
            Medication Management 14-9
        Combined Treatment vs. Unimodal Treatments 14-9
        MTA-Delivered Treatments vs. Community Standard
            Care 14-10
        Summary of MTA Findings 14-10
Research Limitations 14-10
    Small Samples 14-10
    Short Duration of Most Studies 14-11
    Insufficiently Intensive Psychosocial Treatment 14-11
    Treatments Not Adjusted to Subject-Specific Needs 14-11

Summary and Conclusion 14-12
Future Research Needs 14-12

Chapter 15: Matching Patients to Treatments

Introduction 15-1
ADHD and Disruptive Behaviors 15-2
     Response to MPH Treatment 15-2
     Stimulant vs. Psychosocial Treatment 15-3
ADHD and Anxiety Disorders 15-4
     Response to Medication 15-4
     Stimulant vs. Psychosocial Treatment 15-5
ADHD and Comorbidity Patterns 15-7
ADHD and Mood Disorders 15-7
ADHD and Mental Retardation 15-8
ADHD Subtypes 15-9
Recommendations for Clinical Practice 15-9
     Children Who Clearly Benefit From Stimulant
        Treatment 15-10
     Treatment of Children With Internalizing
        Problems 15-10
     When Psychosocial Treatment Is Indicated 15-10
     Gray Areas 15-11
Recommendations for Future Research 15-11

PART 4: DOES STIMULANT USE FOR ADHD LEAD TO SUBSTANCE ABUSE?

Chapter 16: Alcohol, Stimulants, Nicotine, and Other Drugs in ADHD

Introduction 16-1
Rationale for Hypothesis That Individuals With ADHD Are Likely to
     Abuse Drugs 16-2
Retrospective Surveys of ADHD in Substance Use Disorders
     (Adults and Adolescents) 16-3
     ADHD and Alcohol-Related Disorders 16-3
     ADHD and Cocaine Use 16-5
     ADHD and Use of Opiates 16-6
     ADHD and Mixed Substance Use Disorders 16-6
Retrospective Reports of Drug Use and Abuse in Adults With ADHD 16-7
Retrospective Report in Adolescents in the General Population 16-8
Current ADHD and Patterns of SUD 16-8
Longitudinal Studies of Children With ADHD 16-9

Clinical Studies 16-9
Community Studies 16-11
Public Health and Clinical Implications 16-12
Problems in Drawing Inferences From Multiple Studies 16-13
The Conduct Disorder Link 16-14
Conclusions 16-15

Chapter 17: Medicated vs. Unmedicated ADHD Children—Adult Involvement With Legal and Illegal Drugs

Introduction 17-2
Implicit Theories About Medication and Drug Abuse 17-3
Theories That Medication Causes or Predisposes to Drug Abuse 17-3
Pharmacological Predisposition 17-3
Psychological Predisposition 17-3
Theories That Medication Prevents or Protects Against Drug Abuse . . . 17-3
Pharmacological Protection 17-4
Psychological Protection 17-4
Findings From Early Investigations 17-4
Recent California Study 17-5
New Iowa Study 17-5
Who Was Chosen to Receive Medication, and Why 17-5
Follow-up Review of Patients' Attitudes Toward and
Experience With ADHD Medication 17-6
Central Questions About Childhood Medication and
Drug Abuse 17-7
Adult Attitudes About Medication Prescribed in
Childhood 17-7
Relationships Between Childhood Medication Status
and Adult Attitudes About Drugs 17-8
Relationships Between Childhood Medication Status
and Later Involvement With Drugs 17-8
Relationships Between Childhood Medication Status and
Adult Psychiatric Diagnoses 17-11
Implications of Newer Studies 17-11
Future Directions 17-13

Chapter 18: Stimulant Treatment as a Risk Factor for Nicotine Use and Substance Abuse

Introduction 18-2
Perspectives on ADHD as a Risk Factor for Tobacco Smoking
and Substance Use 18-3

Hypotheses Pertaining to Higher Rates of Smoking and Substance
    Use by ADHD Individuals 18-3
        Self-Medication Hypothesis 18-3
        Stimulant Treatment Sensitization Hypothesis 18-4
Other Risk Factors for Substance Use 18-5
        Tobacco as the Gateway to Substance Use 18-5
        Problem Behavior as a Risk Factor for Substance Use 18-6
Research Objectives and Methods 18-6
        Hypotheses Explored 18-6
        Study Participants 18-7
        Development of Research Diagnostic Proxies for ADHD 18-7
        DSM-IV Criteria of Onset of Symptoms 18-8
        Criteria for Severity of ADHD 18-8
        DSM-IV ADHD Classification Compared With Original
            Classification of Subjects 18-9
Procedures for Collecting Tobacco and Substance Use Data 18-9
        Variables in the Statistical Analyses 18-10
            Dependent Variables 18-10
            Independent Variables 18-11
            Statistical Analysis 18-12
Study Results 18-12
        Survival Analyses 18-12
            Survival Analysis of Delay in Onset of Regular
                Smoking by Severity of ADHD 18-12
            Survival Analysis of Delay in Onset of Regular
                Smoking by Use of CNS Stimulant
                Treatment in Childhood 18-13
        Relationship of Severity of ADHD and Childhood Stimulant
            Treatment to Adult Smoking 18-15
        Multivariate Prediction of Adult Daily Smoking and DSM-III-R
            Psychoactive Substance Use Disorders 18-15
        Support for the Self-Medicating Hypothesis 18-17
        Support for the Sensitization Hypothesis 18-18
        Partial Support for Tobacco Gateway Hypothesis 18-19
        Childhood Problem Behavior Not Supported as a Factor in PSUD . . 18-19
Conclusion 18-20

Chapter 19: Attention Deficit Hyperactivity Disorder and Substance Use Disorders—The Nature of the Relationship, Subtypes at Risk, and Treatment Issues

Introduction 19-1

Overlap Between ADHD and SUD 19-2
ADHD as a Risk Factor for SUD 19-3
    Longitudinal Studies: ADHD 19-3
    ADHD Treatment and SUD 19-3
    Longitudinal Studies of SUD 19-5
SUD Pathways Associated With ADHD 19-5
Familial Relationships Between ADHD and SUD 19-6
Implications of Current Research 19-7
    Increased Risk of SUD for ADHD Youth 19-8
    Parental SUD a Risk Factor for Juvenile ADHD/Conduct
        Disorder 19-8
    Self-Medication a Likely Factor 19-8
    Impact of Psychosocial Risk Factors 19-9
Diagnosis and Treatment Guidelines 19-10
    Evaluation 19-10
    Stabilization of the Addiction 19-10
    Psychotherapeutic Interventions 19-11
    Pharmacotherapy 19-11
Summary 19-12

Chapter 20: Diversion, Trafficking, and Abuse of Methylphenidate
Introduction 20-1
Abuse Liability Studies 20-2
    Amphetamine- and Cocaine-Like Effects 20-2
    Dose-Reinforcing Effects 20-2
    Disruptive and Stimulus Effects 20-5
    Summary 20-6
MPH Manufacture, Distribution, and Use 20-7
    Increased Production and Sale 20-7
    Disparities in Usage 20-8
Diversion and Trafficking 20-9
Issues Related to MPH Medication for ADHD 20-12
    Growing Problem of Abuse by Schoolchildren 20-12
    Increased Abuse Among Adolescents 20-12
    Diversion of Children's Prescribed Medication 20-14
    Three-State Diversion Survey Findings 20-15
        Why and How Survey Was Conducted 20-15
        MPH Diversion Not Rare 20-15
        Factors Contributing to Diversion of MPH
            Intended for ADHD Treatment 20-16
Conclusion 20-17

Chapter 21: Availability of Stimulant Medications—Nature and Extent of Abuse and Associated Harm
Introduction 21-1
Monitoring the Future 21-4
    Design and Methodology 21-4
    Sampling Procedures 21-5
    Questions Pertaining to the Medical and Nonmedical
       Use of Amphetamines 21-5
The Drug Abuse Warning Network 21-6
    Design and Methodology 21-6
    DAWN Sample 21-7
Community Epidemiology Work Group 21-8
What the Ongoing Studies Reveal About Drug Abuse 21-8
    MTF Results 21-8
    DAWN Results 21-10
    CEWG Results 21-13
Discussion 21-13

Chapter 22: Treatment Services for Children With ADHD—A National Perspective
Introduction 22-2
Prevalence of Attentional Problems and Available Services 22-3
Review of Treatment Services 22-4
    Trends in Prescription Practices 22-4
        Increasing Levels of Prescribing 22-4
        Prevalence of Medication Treatments 22-5
    Rates of Specialty Mental Health and School Services
       Received 22-5
    Variations in Treatments or Use of Services 22-6
        Gender Variations 22-6
        Racial Variations 22-6
        Geographical Variations 22-6
    Barriers to Care 22-6
    Conclusions From the Review 22-7
The National Ambulatory Medical Care Survey 22-8
    Survey Methods 22-8
        Data Set 22-8
        Data Assessment 22-8
    Increased Identification of ADHD 22-9
    Trends in Types of Treatments and Services 22-9
        Medication Management 22-10

        Diagnostic Services 22-10
        Counseling Services 22-10
        Follow-up Services 22-11
    Types of Services by Provider Type 22-11
        Medication Management 22-11
        Diagnostic Services 22-11
        Mental Health Counseling 22-11
        Other Counseling 22-11
        Psychotherapy 22-11
        Specific Follow-up 22-12
The Child Behavior Study 22-12
    Survey Methods 22-12
    Receipt of Specialty Mental Health Services and
        Stimulant Treatments 22-13
    Service Mix 22-13
    Identified Barriers to Care 22-13
Conclusions and Recommendations 22-13
    Service Patterns and Continuing Problems 22-13
    Continuing Barriers to Care 22-15
    Recommendations for Clinical Practice and
        Policy 22-15
    Recommendations for Future Research 22-16

PART 5: EXISTING PRACTICES AND POLICIES REGARDING ASSESSMENT AND TREATMENT OF ADHD

Chapter 23: Current Assessment and Treatment Practices in ADHD

Introduction 23-1
History of ADHD 23-2
    Evolving Medical Interest 23-2
    Educational Interest 23-2
    Treatment Diversity and Controversy 23-3
Role of Primary Care Physicians vs. Mental Health
    Clinicians 23-3
Diagnosis 23-4
    Importance of Multidisciplinary Communication 23-4
    Spectrum of Behavioral Symptoms 23-4
    School and Primary Care Process in Terms of Diagnosis
        and Treatment 23-5
    Presence and Diagnosis of Comorbidity With Other Cognitive
        and Behavioral Disorders 23-6

Treatment 23-7
     Use of Stimulants and Other Psychotropic Medications 23-7
     School System Concerns Regarding Treatment 23-7
     School's Role in Use of Nondrug Therapies 23-8
     Physician Follow-up and Assessment of Treatment 23-8
     Need for Systematic Methods to Provide Comprehensive Services 23-9
Summary 23-10

Chapter 24: Impact of ADHD on School Systems

Introduction 24-1
Children With ADHD in Special Education 24-3
     Learning Disabilities 24-3
     Emotional Disturbance 24-4
     Other Health Impaired 24-5
     Estimates of ADHD Eligibility in Special Education 24-7
Cost Estimates 24-8
Impact of ADHD on Schools 24-9
     Impact on Segregated Classroom 24-10
     Impact on Inclusive or Mainstream Classrooms 24-12
Conclusions and Recommendations 24-14
     Research 24-15
     Training 24-15
     School Practice and Policy 24-16

Chapter 25: The Impact of Attention Deficit Hyperactivity Disorder on the Juvenile Justice System

Introduction 25-1
Trends in Juvenile Offending 25-1
     Growth in Number of Detained Juveniles 25-1
     Prevalence of Mental Health Disorders, ADHD, and Conduct
        Disorders Among Youth in the Juvenile Justice System 25-2
     Relationship of ADHD and CD to Antisocial and Violent
        Behavior 25-3
Juvenile Justice System Response 25-3
Research Needs 25-4

Chapter 26: Educational Policy—Educating Children With Attention Deficit Hyperactivity Disorder

Introduction 26-1
Federal Policy History 26-2
     Background 26-2

Joint Federal Policy Memorandum 26-2
    IDEA Eligibility 26-2
    Rehabilitation Act Section 504 Eligibility 26-3
Federal Support for ADHD Research and Technical
   Assistance 26-3
U.S. Department of Education Activities Since 1991 26-4
Revised IDEA Regulations 26-5
State Education Agency Policies 26-6
    Background 26-6
    Adoption of Written Policies 26-6
ADHD as Part of a Disability Category 26-7
Policies Specific to Identification and Assessment
   of ADHD 26-7
Policies Regarding Medication of Students With ADHD 26-8
Prevalence of ADHD in States 26-8
Technical Assistance Needs of State and Local
   Educators 26-8
    ADHD as an "Other Health Impairment" 26-9
    Discussion and Implications 26-10

Chapter 27: Use of Services and Costs for Youth With ADHD and Related Conditions
Introduction 27-2
Prevalence of ADHD in Primary Care Settings 27-2
ADHD Increasingly Diagnosed 27-2
Demographic Factors 27-3
Frequency of Comorbidity 27-3
Summary 27-4
Use of Services 27-4
The Child Behavior Study 27-5
Setting 27-5
Sample 27-5
Procedures 27-6
Measures 27-6
    Clinician-Reported Items (Clinician Identification) 27-6
    Parent- or Guardian-Reported Items (Services Use) 27-6
Analysis 27-6
Results 27-7
    Increased Use of Many Types of Health Services 27-7
    Predictors of Receipt of Specific Treatment
       Services 27-7

Costs of Care—ADHD Cost of Services in Medicaid Study for
    Southwestern Pennsylvania 27-8
        Setting 27-9
        Sample 27-9
        Procedures 27-9
        Measures 27-10
        Analysis 27-10
Need for Cost-Benefit Analysis 27-11
Conclusion 27-12

Afterword: ADHD, Past, Present, and Future A-1

Appendix A: National Institutes of Health Consensus Statement ..... App. A-1
Appendix B: Bibliography .... App. B-1
Index I-1

Part 1

Is ADHD a Real Disorder?

One of the most basic debates surrounding attention deficit hyperactivity disorder (ADHD) is the answer to the most fundamental of questions: Is ADHD a real disorder? Among the general public, among members of the media, and even in some scientific circles, this question is posed with an explicit tone of incredulity, because so many easy answers are available to those who would answer the question in the negative. For example, those who see ADHD as a form of inherited temperamental traits argue that there is no sharp line demarcating the normal from the abnormal. Thus, temperament theorists (e.g., see Chapter 3) can point to strong evidence that the ADHD symptoms of activity, impulsivity, and inattention lie along continua having no "bumps" in the distribution to mark a dividing line between normal and abnormal, as well as genetic evidence showing that ADHD is best conceived as a continuous function. They argue that the annoyance threshold of caretaker, teacher, or peer is the real criterion being used by those believing in a "disease" of ADHD. Characteristics of ADHD are not seen as symptoms in a medical sense but outcomes of the interactions between the vectors of temperament and environment. In this view, treatment requires resolution of the misfit between the child's temperament and environmental demands: Social learning interacting with genes is the cause; therefore one must provide beneficent environments, not drugs.

Others attack the syndrome concept of ADHD on grounds that the current diagnostic criteria for ADHD lack specificity. The criteria are said to lead to a hodge-podge of disorders because hyperactivity, impulsivity, and inattention are common to many psychiatric conditions. This lack of specificity leads to a disorder with so many "comorbidities" that doubt is cast on its reality as a distinctive syndrome. Comorbidity becomes the rule, and the "pure" disorder is so rare that to study it is said to lead to nonrepresentative samples. Indeed, this criticism can easily be supported, because a continuing problem in the definition of ADHD has been identifying which symptoms are *intrinsic* to the syndrome, which are its *consequences* or *effects*, and which represent *co-occurrence* of other disorders. Relatedly, the field has struggled with the question whether ADHD is one disorder, a disorder with several subtypes, or several different disorders (see Barkley, 1990, for review). Loney and colleagues were among the first to argue for an aggressive subtype. Review of the literature suggests that perhaps there are both distinctive aggressive and anxious subtypes, which need to be included in the diagnosis of ADHD.

In an even more radical attack, doubt is cast on the meaningfulness of the core symptoms themselves because they are either poorly operationalized or multidimensional in nature. Most of the laboratory measures correlate weakly with the clinically defined constructs of attention, activity, and impulsivity. Moreover, the core symptoms invariably turn out to be multidimensional *in the laboratory*. For example, attention resolves into many specific components, ranging from early stimulus selection and preparatory motor adjustments on the input side to response selection and motor execution on the output side (Cohen, 1993). Defined by rigorous laboratory operations, concepts of sustained or selective attention may be readily linked to neuroanatomic circuits and are sometimes related to right-hemisphere deficits in ADHD. But in other studies the same measures yield opposite hemispheric deficits. Quantitative measures of motor activity and clinically defined measures of hyperactivity often have little relationship to one another, and both appear to be highly context-sensitive. This relative lack of objective laboratory criteria and operationalized measures of assessment leads to wide variation in diagnostic practices among practitioners in the community and understandable concerns among thoughtful skeptics about the validity of the core elements of the syndrome itself.

Still others believe that ADHD is a shared myth or part of the "madness of crowds," representing a conspiracy or unwitting collusion among financial interests competing for health-care dollars. They argue that the condition is vastly overdiagnosed and overtreated. In one version of the argument, authoritarian conspiracies are alleged for drugging children into submission. Dull and boring classrooms are said to elicit disruptive behavior in the brightest and most free-spirited children, who then receive their quietus with Ritalin. Others allege that drug companies conspire with psychiatry in creating a fictitious disorder, arguing further that ADHD criteria are simply used to justify the excessive use of medications or to help doctors recover income lost to managed care. Whew!

All the debates and arguments, from the level-headed to the ludicrous, can leave one's head reeling. Where does the evidence stand with respect to the validity of ADHD as a syndrome? From the finest scholars in the field, this section pulls together the best available evidence concerning the nature of the disorder, its symptomatic aspects, associated impairments, short- and long-term clinical course and outcomes, and its presence and prevalence in other cultural contexts. In Chapter 1, Lahey and Willcutt carefully dissect the issues of ADHD diagnostic reliability and validity, trace the history and overlaps between previous and current versions of ADHD, and critically analyze existing data on the validity of the various subtypes. In Chapter 2, Bird provides an excellent compilation of research summarizing what is known about the prevalence of ADHD in cross-cultural contexts—his evidence clearly shows that ADHD is not a U.S.-only phenomenon but has been found where ever it has been rigorously studied. Still in the level-headed category, in Chapter 3 Carey provides an alternative conceptualization of at least some cases of ADHD. Although the temperamental hypothesis of ADHD has not been systematically studied, many studies of normal childhood development suggest that this is a sensible line of argument, at least for some "threshold" cases of ADHD. Yet even if ADHD is "merely" the high end of a normative set of traits, the last three chapters of this section (by Barkley, Hinshaw, and Johnston, respectively) provide compelling evidence that this set of traits (temperamental or not) has serious consequences, both immediate and long term, for youth who are identified with ADHD. By way of analogy, elevated blood pressure, as seen in benign essential hypertension, may also be "normative" (i.e., the high end of a normally distributed trait), but high levels of the trait are nonetheless associated with adverse health consequences. And in the case of ADHD, such consequences cut across many domains—not just physical health (automobile accidents) but also other psychiatric illnesses (e.g., depression, substance use) as well as social and economic consequences (vocational and marital outcomes).

—**C.K. Conners**
—**P.S. Jensen**

References

Barkley, R. A. (1990). *Attention deficit hyperactivity disorder: A handbook for diagnosis and treatment.* New York: Guilford Press.

Cohen, R. A. (1993). *The neuropsychology of attention.* New York: Plenum.

Chapter 1

Validity of the Diagnosis and Dimensions of Attention Deficit Hyperactivity Disorder

by Benjamin B. Lahey, Ph.D. and Erik G. Willcutt, Ph.D.

Introduction 1-2
Dimensions of ADHD Symptoms: Internal Validity of
  DSM-IV Model 1-3
Discriminant Validity of the Two-Dimensional Structure of
  ADHD 1-3
    Differential Association of the Two Dimensions of Symptoms
    With Concurrent Mental Disorders 1-3
    Differential Association of the Two Dimensions of Symptoms
    With Types of Impairment 1-4
    Developmental Course of the Two Dimensions of
    ADHD Behaviors 1-5
Correspondence of DSM-IV ADHD to DSM-III-R ADHD 1-5
Correspondence of DSM-IV ADHD to ICD-10 Hyperkinesis 1-7
Validity of the Diagnosis of ADHD 1-7
    Face Validity 1-8
    Predictive Validity of ADHD in Childhood 1-8
    Concurrent Validity of ADHD 1-8
    Validity of DSM-IV Criteria for Age of Onset and
    Cross-Situational Impairment 1-10
Discriminant Validity of the Subtypes of DSM-IV ADHD 1-11
ADHD and Comorbid Mental Disorders 1-13
ADHD in Adulthood 1-14
Assessment of ADHD 1-14
Is ADHD Better Conceptualized in Diagnostic or Dimensional Terms? 1-14
Recommendations for Clinical Practice, Policy, and Future Research 1-15
    Implications for Clinical Practice 1-15

Implications for Public Policy 1-16
Areas to Target in Future Research 1-16

INTRODUCTION

The mental health profession's understanding of the pattern of maladaptive behavior termed "attention deficit hyperactivity disorder" (ADHD) according to the fourth edition of *Diagnostic and Statistical Manual of Mental Disorders* (DSM-IV; American Psychiatric Association, 1994) has evolved considerably over the past forty years. Few disorders have undergone as many changes in name and refinements of diagnostic criteria, perhaps because few disorders have been the subject of as much taxonomic study. For many years, researchers and clinicians used the term "minimal brain dysfunction" to refer to a syndrome of maladaptive motor hyperactivity, impulsivity, and inattention. In the second edition of *Diagnostic and Statistical Manual of Mental Disorders* (DSM-II; American Psychiatric Association, 1968), this syndrome was named hyperkinetic reaction of childhood or adolescence. By the late 1970s, the work of Virginia Douglas (Douglas & Peter, 1979) precipitated a reconceptualization of the syndrome that emphasized deficits in sustained attention, response inhibition, and self-modulation. In DSM-III (American Psychiatric Association, 1980), the name of this syndrome was changed to attention deficit disorder (ADD) and the diagnostic definition relegated motor hyperactivity to secondary importance. Indeed, in addition to providing for the diagnosis of persons with maladaptive levels of inattention, impulsivity, and motor activity (ADD with hyperactivity), the DSM-III definition allowed the diagnosis of persons with attention deficits and impulsivity whose motor activity was within the normal range (ADD without hyperactivity) (Lahey et al., 1988). The DSM-III-R (American Psychiatric Association, 1987) definition of ADHD, however, combined inattention, impulsivity, and hyperactivity in a single list of symptoms much like the DSM-II definition. Although a diagnostic category termed "undifferentiated attention deficit disorder" was included in DSM-III-R for individuals with attention deficits in the absence of motor hyperactivity, specific diagnostic criteria were not provided. Thus, DSM-III-R criteria for ADHD tacitly discouraged the diagnosis of what was defined as ADD without hyperactivity in DSM-III.

The change from the three-dimensional DSM-III definition to the single-dimension DSM-III-R definition of ADHD sparked controversy and led to extensive research on the number of dimensions of symptoms that underlie DSM-III-R ADHD. The great majority of studies (Lahey et al., 1988; Lahey, Carlson, & Frick, 1997; Bauermeister, 1992; Bauermeister et al., 1995; Pelham, Evans, Gnagy, & Greenslade, 1992; Pelham, Gnagy, Greenslade, & Milich, 1992) suggested that the symptoms of ADHD do not form a unitary dimension as implied by the DSM-III-R definition of ADHD, but that the three-dimensional approach of DSM-III (separate dimensions of inattention, impulsivity, and hyperactivity) is not consistent with the data either. Rather, most studies indicated that two dimensions of symptoms underlie parent and teacher reports of ADHD symptoms, a dimension of symptoms reflecting inattention and a dimension reflecting both hyperactivity and impulsivity.

Based on these two dimensions of symptoms, the DSM-IV definition of ADHD distinguishes between individuals who exhibit maladaptive levels of both dimensions (combined [C] type), maladaptive levels of inattention only (predominantly inattentive

[I] type), and maladaptive levels of hyperactivity/impulsivity only (predominantly hyperactive-impulsive [H-I] type). Thus, the DSM-III distinction between ADD with and without hyperactivity was essentially restored (C and I types) in DSM-IV, and the new H-I subtype was added. The H-I type was added primarily because youths in the DSM-IV field trials (Lahey et al., 1994) who met the diagnostic threshold for hyperactive-impulsive symptoms, but not inattention symptoms, were considered to be impaired by parents, interviewers, and clinicians on the same measures of impairment that characterized the C type. In addition, most of the youths who met criteria for the H-I type in the DSM-IV field trials had met DSM-III-R criteria for ADHD.

DIMENSIONS OF ADHD SYMPTOMS: INTERNAL VALIDITY OF DSM-IV MODEL

Because the decision was made to distinguish between separate dimensions of inattention and hyperactivity/impulsivity in DSM-IV, the dimensions of symptoms specified in DSM-IV have been studied using exploratory factor analysis (Conners, Sitarenios, Parker, & Epstein, 1998a, 1998b; Hudziak et al., 1998; Sherman, Iacono, & McGue, 1997), confirmatory factor analysis (Burns, Walsh, Owen, & Snell, 1997; Burns, Walsh, Patterson, et al., 1997; Conners et al., 1998a, 1998b; DuPaul et al., 1997; DuPaul et al., 1998; Pillow, Pelham, Holza, Molina, & Stultz, 1998), and latent class analysis (Hudziak et al., 1998). These studies consistently indicate that the distinction between two dimensions of inattention and hyperactivity/impulsivity symptoms in DSM-IV provides a better explanation for the pattern of covariation among symptoms than either the three-dimensional model implicit in the DSM-III definition of ADHD or the single dimension that underlies the DSM-III-R definition of ADHD. When the extensive exploratory and confirmatory factor analysis literatures are considered together, they provide substantial support for the internal validity of the two-dimensional structure of DSM-IV ADHD symptoms, even though it is clear from these studies that the two dimensions of symptoms are correlated and co-occur more often than they occur separately.

DISCRIMINANT VALIDITY OF THE TWO-DIMENSIONAL STRUCTURE OF ADHD

Although covariation among symptoms is a necessary condition for the identification of independent dimensions of symptoms, it does not provide sufficient justification for the distinction between dimensions by itself. In addition, the discriminant validity of putatively distinct dimensions of symptoms must be established by demonstrating different correlations with other variables that are conceptually related to the validity of the disorder, but are independent of its definition.

Differential Association of the Two Dimensions of Symptoms With Concurrent Mental Disorders

Currently, little evidence is available that directly compares the correlations of inattention and hyperactivity/impulsivity with other aspects of psychopathology. One recent study (Willcutt, 1998) and new regression analyses of the DSM-IV field trials data (Lahey et al., 1994) conducted for this chapter, however, both showed that hyperactivity/impulsivity was more strongly associated with both conduct disorder and oppositional defiant disorder symptoms than was inattention. In addition, inattention was associated with anxiety symptoms and with depression symptoms when hyperactivity/impulsivity was controlled, but hyperactivity/impulsivity was not associated with anxiety and depression when inattention was controlled.[1] The possible greater association between inattention and anxiety may be particularly important, as several studies suggest that children who meet criteria for ADHD and exhibit high levels of comorbid anxiety show less robust clinical response to methylphenidate (Buitelaar, Van der Gagg, Swaab-Barneveld, & Kuiper, 1995; Pliszka, 1989; Tannock & Ickowicz, 1995) and greater increases in diastolic blood pressure and heart rate (Tannock & Ickowicz, 1995; Urman, Ickowicz, Fulford, & Tannock, 1995). Thus, current findings support the external validity of the distinction between inattention and hyperactivity/impulsivity symptoms, but more evidence is needed.

Differential Association of the Two Dimensions of Symptoms With Types of Impairment

In the DSM-IV field trials for the disruptive behavior disorders of youths 4 through 17 years of age (Lahey et al., 1994), regression analyses were conducted to assess the associations of inattentive and hyperactive-impulsive behaviors with several indices of functional impairment, controlling for the number of symptoms of oppositional defiant disorder, conduct disorder, anxiety disorders, and depressive disorders. The number of inattentive behaviors was not related to parent or interviewer global ratings of adaptive functioning using the Children's Global Assessment Scale (C-GAS) (Setterberg, Bird, & Gould, 1992), but was significantly associated with parent ratings of homework problems and teacher ratings of schoolwork problems. In contrast, the number of hyperactivity/impulsivity symptoms was associated with parent and interviewer C-GAS ratings, but not with ratings of academic difficulties.

Similar regression analyses were conducted in a more extensive study of impairment associated with ADHD in a separate sample of 4–6-year-old children (Lahey et al., 1998). In addition to controlling for symptoms of other types of psychopathology, these analyses controlled family income, intelligence, and ethnicity to determine if the association between ADHD and impairment was independent of these factors. Inattention was independently associated with teacher ratings of shyness and withdrawal, lack of assertiveness, lack of cooperation, and peer rejection; underachievement in mathematics; child-reported friendship problems; enrollment in special education; and parent C-GAS ratings. In contrast, hyperactivity/impulsivity was uniquely associated with accidental injuries and with teacher-reported lack of self-control, aggression, and disruptiveness. Both ADHD dimensions were inversely associated with teacher-rated peer acceptance and prosocial behavior and with interviewer C-GAS ratings.

Combining evidence from the two studies, the inattention dimension appears to be more strongly associated with academic underachievement, use of special education services, and peer relationship problems related to shyness and social withdrawal. In contrast, hyperactivity/impulsivity is more strongly related to accidental injuries and peer relationship problems related to disruption, aggression, and low self-control. Thus, both dimensions are associated with important aspects of functional impairment in rigorously controlled analyses, and the finding that inattention and hyperactivity/impulsivity appear to be associated with different aspects of impairment validates their distinction.

Developmental Course of the Two Dimensions of ADHD Behaviors

Most studies indicate a decline in ratings over time, more so in hyperactivity/impulsivity than inattention (DuPaul et al., 1997; DuPaul et al., 1998; Conners et al., 1998a, 1998b; Hart, Lahey, Loeber, Applegate, Green, & Frick, 1995; Kanbayashi, Kakata, Fujii, Kita, & Wada, 1994; for further information on the developmental course of ADHD, see Chapter 4 of this volume).

CORRESPONDENCE OF DSM-IV ADHD TO DSM-III-R ADHD

To fully evaluate the validity of the DSM-IV diagnostic definition, it is necessary to examine the extent to which it leads to the diagnosis of the same individuals as previous definitions and, more important, the accuracy with which the DSM-IV criteria identify functionally impaired individuals. Two studies have compared the prevalence of the diagnoses of DSM-III-R and DSM-IV ADHD using symptom criteria (i.e., DSM-III-R requires eight symptoms from one list, whereas as DSM-IV requires six symptoms from one or both of two lists of symptoms), but not the age of onset or impairment criteria. In the DSM-IV field trials sample, the prevalence of any subtype of DSM-IV ADHD was 15 percent higher than the prevalence of DSM-III-R ADHD (Lahey et al., 1994). Although 97.5 percent of youths who met criteria for DSM-III-R ADHD also met criteria for DSM-IV ADHD in the field trials sample, a considerable number of children and adolescents who met DSM-IV criteria did not meet DSM-III-R criteria. This differed by DSM-IV type, with all youths who met criteria for the C type, 74 percent of youths who met criteria for the I type, and 61 percent of youths who met criteria for the H-I type also meeting DSM-III-R criteria (Lahey et al., 1994). Thus, all the increase in the prevalence of ADHD from DSM-III-R to DSM-IV in this sample was due to the new DSM-IV I and H-I types. Similarly, a large independent replication of the DSM-IV field trials (McBurnett et al., 1999) that defined ADHD using symptom criteria found that the number of youths who met criteria for DSM-IV ADHD was 15 percent higher than for DSM-III-R ADHD. Again, the increase was entirely due to youths who met criteria for either the I or H-I types who did not meet criteria for DSM-III-R ADHD, as all youths who met criteria for the C type also met criteria for DSM-III-R ADHD.

The relative prevalence of DSM-IV and DSM-III-R ADHD in clinic samples is rather different when full DSM-IV diagnostic criteria are used to define ADHD, however. In addition to changes in symptom criteria from DSM-III-R to DSM-IV, changes were made in the age of onset criterion and a new criterion was added that requires impairment in two or more settings (e.g., home and school). The revised age of onset criterion in DSM-IV (presence of impairment due to symptoms before age 7 years) influences the prevalence of each of the three subtypes of ADHD to different degrees. In the DSM-IV field trials (Lahey et al., 1994), all youths who meet DSM-IV symptom criteria for the H-I type met the age of onset criterion, but 18 percent of youths who met symptom criteria for the C type and 43 percent of youths who met criteria for the I type did not (Applegate et al., 1997). New analyses of the DSM-IV field trials sample (Lahey et al., 1994) for this chapter showed that the requirement of cross-situational impairment reduced the prevalence of the C type by 16.8 percent but reduced the prevalence of the I and hyperactive types by 35.1 percent and 34.1 percent, respectively. The greater reductions in prevalence for the I and H-I types may simply indicate that youths who meet criteria for the C type have a more severe disorder, but it could occur because impairment associated with high levels of inattention symptoms is more likely to occur in the school setting, whereas impairment associated with hyperactivity/impulsivity may be more evident in the home (Lahey et al., 1994; Lahey et al., 1998). Thus, the I and H-I types may be more likely to manifest situation-specific impairment than the C type.

Table 1.1 presents the results of new analyses of the DSM-IV field trials sample that were conducted for this chapter using full diagnostic criteria for DSM-III-R and DSM-IV ADHD. In this clinic sample, the prevalence of DSM-IV ADHD was 31.2 percent less than DSM-III-R ADHD when full diagnostic criteria were applied. All youths who met criteria for the DSM-IV C type and about three-quarters of youths who met criteria for the DSM-IV I and H-I types also met criteria for DSM-III-R ADHD, but nearly 40 percent of youths who met criteria for DSM-III-R ADHD did not meet criteria for any subtype of DSM-IV ADHD. In contrast, a comparison of 405 clinic-referred children and adolescents who met full criteria for ADHD (Biederman et al., 1997) found no difference in the prevalence of DSM-III-R and DSM-IV ADHD, with 87 percent of youths who met criteria for either definition of ADHD meeting criteria according to both definitions. Thus, although the prevalence of DSM-IV ADHD appears to be greater than DSM-III-R ADHD in clinic samples when only symptom criteria are used, the prevalence of DSM-IV ADHD appears to be equal to or less than the prevalence of DSM-III-R ADHD when full diagnostic criteria are used. For comparative purposes with Table 1.1, Table 1.2 presents the diagnoses from the DSM-IV field trials sample, according to the extent to which subjects met DSM-III versus

Table 1.1
Correspondence Between DSM-III-R and DSM-IV Definitions of ADHD Using Full Diagnostic Criteria

DSM-IV Definition	DSM-III-R Definition	
	ADHD	Not ADHD
Combined	99	0
Hyperactive	21	6
Inattentive	17	7
Not ADHD	81	148

Table 1.2
Correspondence Between DSM-III and DSM-IV Definitions of ADHD Using Full Diagnostic Criteria

DSM-IV Definition	DSM-III Definition		
	With Hyperactivity	Without Hyperactivity	Not ADHD
Combined	97	0	2
Hyperactive	15	0	12
Inattentive	9	9	6
Not ADHD	51	20	158

DSM-IV criteria for ADHD.

Unfortunately, little evidence on the relative prevalence of DSM-III-R and DSM-IV ADHD is available currently from population-based samples. Two studies of school-based samples that used only symptom criteria for ADHD found that rates of DSM-IV ADHD were nearly twice as high as those for DSM-III-R using a teacher symptom checklist (Baumgaertel, Wolraich, & Dietrich, 1995; Wolraich, Hannah, Pinnock, Baumgaertel, & Brown, 1996). Most of the increase in prevalence from DSM-III-R to DSM-IV in these community samples was due to large number of youths who met criteria for the I type who did not meet DSM-III-R criteria. Because these studies did not measure functional impairment, however, it is not possible to determine how many of these youths were impaired enough to warrant diagnosis.

CORRESPONDENCE OF DSM-IV ADHD TO ICD-10 HYPERKINESIS

The tenth edition of *International Statistical Classification of Diseases and Related Health Problems*(ICD-10; World Health Organization, 1992) uses the same list of symptoms for hyperkinesis as DSM-IV uses for ADHD but identifies only the equivalent of the C type. Unlike DSM-IV, ICD-10 requires that a minimum number of symptoms of inattention, hyperactivity, and impulsivity each be present, rather than treating hyperactivity/impulsivity as a single dimension. In addition, full ICD-10 criteria must be met independently according to both parent and teacher reports. As a result, the ICD-10 definition identifies a smaller number of children and adolescents than does the DSM-IV definition (Tripp, Luk, Schaughency, & Singh, 1999). It is not yet clear, however, if the more restrictive ICD-10 definition leads to more or less accurate identification of impaired individuals.

VALIDITY OF THE DIAGNOSIS OF ADHD

Diagnostic categories of mental disorders are social constructions (Bandura, 1969). It is essential, therefore, that the mental health field continually question whether diagnostic categories are defined in ways that serve the best interests of the diagnosed. That is, each of the many aspects of the validity of each diagnosis, including ADHD, must be thoughtfully and persistently questioned.

Face Validity

Some view ADHD as a disorder with high face validity (Goldman, Genel, Bezman, & Slanetz, 1998), whereas others conceptualize ADHD as a valid syndrome of maladaptive behavior that warrants treatment but object to its being considered a categorical mental disorder (British Psychological Society, 1996). Some researchers find the definition of ADHD to lack specificity (Prior & Sanson, 1986), and some believe that ADHD simply describes the exuberant behavior of normal children and view efforts to treat ADHD as inappropriate "mind control" (see Safer & Krager, 1992). Such varying opinions are not unique to ADHD, as all mental disorders are controversial to some extent. The controversy is perhaps more intense, however, for mental disorders such as ADHD for which the symptoms are not distinctly different from normal behavior but are defined in terms of degree of severity and impairment. Furthermore, ADHD tends not be distressing to the individual, at least during childhood. For these reasons, aspects of validity other than face validity are of great importance to an evaluation of the overall validity of the DSM-IV diagnostic category of ADHD.

Predictive Validity of ADHD in Childhood

The developmental outcomes of ADHD constitute an important aspect of the validity of the diagnosis. If children who meet criteria for the disorder have poorer functional outcomes in adolescence and adulthood than do other children, the validity of the disorder in childhood would be supported. There is substantial evidence that adverse outcomes in academic achievement, occupational attainment, and motor vehicle accidents are independently associated with childhood ADHD after controlling for childhood conduct problems and other potential confounds (Mannuzza, Klein, Bessler, Malloy, & LaPadula, 1993; McGee, Partridge, Williams, & Silva, 1991; Nada-Raja et al., 1997; Taylor, Chadwick, Heptinstall, & Danckaerts, 1996). Although antisocial behavior during adulthood has long been thought to be a key adverse outcome of childhood ADHD, a number of studies strongly suggest that this outcome is actually found only among the subgroup of children who both meet criteria for ADHD and exhibit significant childhood conduct problems and oppositional behavior (Lilienfeld & Waldman, 1990; Lahey, McBurnett, & Loeber, 2000; Satterfield & Schell, 1997). Unfortunately, most longitudinal studies that have followed children into adulthood used diagnostic criteria for ADHD predating DSM-III-R. It will be some time until evidence is available on the long-term outcomes of children who meet criteria for the DSM-IV ADHD, but at least one longitudinal study of DSM-IV ADHD has been initiated (Lahey et al., 1998; see Chapters 4, 5, and 6 for more detailed coverage of this subject).

Concurrent Validity of ADHD

A diagnostic category can be said to have concurrent validity if individuals who meet criteria for the disorder differ from individuals who do not meet criteria for the disorder on other important variables, particularly measures of functional impairment. A large empirical literature (Hinshaw, 1994) suggests that children who meet criteria for ADHD are functionally impaired, but in many studies, it is not clear whether this impairment is associated with ADHD or with other factors that tend to be related to ADHD, particularly concurrent mental disorders. In this section, we review only studies that controlled such potential confounds.

A study of 7- to 12-year-old boys who met DSM-III-R criteria for ADHD suggested that ADHD was associated with academic underachievement when differences in intelligence and concurrent conduct disorder were controlled (Frick et al., 1991). Similarly, a well-controlled study of 101 6- to 12-year-old boys who met criteria for DSM-III-R ADHD and 80 nonreferred comparison boys who did not exhibit ADHD provided evidence that the peer social status of boys who met criteria for ADHD was impaired (Hinshaw & Melnick, 1995). In a summer camp setting, the mothers and teachers of boys who met criteria for ADHD rated them as more unpopular with peers than boys who did not meet criteria for ADHD. In addition, the boys' campmates selected boys with ADHD less often as someone with whom they would like to be friends than boys without ADHD. Importantly, these differences were found not to be attributable to differences in age, intelligence, reading level, family income, or level of aggression (Hinshaw & Melnick, 1995; Tannock & Ickowicz, 1995).

Published data on the concurrent validity of DSM-IV ADHD from the DSM-IV field trials defined ADHD only in terms of DSM-IV symptom criteria (Lahey et al., 1994). Therefore, new analyses of the field trials data for this chapter compared the 175 4- through 17-year-old clinic-referred children who met both symptom and age of onset criteria for any subtype of DSM-IV ADHD to 55 nonreferred comparison children on four measures of functional impairment. The DSM-IV requirement of impairment in two or more settings was not used to define ADHD to avoid circularity in these analyses of the amount of impairment associated with ADHD. Youths who met criteria for any DSM-IV subtype of ADHD were given significantly lower global ratings of adaptive functioning by parents and interviewers, were rated as having more homework problems by parents, and were rated as performing less well in classroom academic work by teachers. These differences were significant when age, gender, ethnicity, family income, intelligence, and concurrent symptoms of oppositional defiant disorder, conduct disorder, and any anxiety or mood disorder were controlled.[2]

In a study of 4- through 6-year-old children (Lahey et al., 1998), children who met criteria for any of the subtypes of DSM-IV ADHD[3] exhibited significantly greater deficits in teacher-rated peer social relations, greater self-reported friendship problems, greater teacher-rated classroom disruption, and lower global ratings of adaptive functioning by parents and interviewers and were more likely to have used special education services than were nonreferred comparison children. In addition, children who met criteria for the C and I types had lower mean scores on standardized tests of mathematics achievement relative to intelligence. These differences were statistically significant after controlling for age, gender, ethnicity, socioeconomic status, intelligence, and concurrent symptoms of other disorders (oppositional defiant disorder, conduct disorder, anxiety disorders, and mood disorders) (Lahey et al., 1998). Two other studies of clinic-referred youths also provided evidence that youths who meet criteria for DSM-IV ADHD (particularly the C and I types) exhibit impaired social functioning and learning problems, are rated by adults as globally impaired, and are more likely than nonreferred youths to have used mental health and special education services, but fewer confounds (intelligence, socioeconomic status, etc.) were controlled in these studies (Faraone, Biederman, Weber, & Russell, 1998; Paternite, Loney, & Roberts, 1996).

In a study of adolescents and young adults, Barkley (1998) found that 105 individuals who met criteria for ADHD differed from 64 nonreferred controls on a number of important aspects of their driving history. Persons with ADHD were more likely to have driven illegally before obtaining their license, were more likely to have had their license suspended or revoked, have received more speeding tickets and citations for driving while intoxicated, had more auto accidents, caused more than three times the damage in dollar amounts when they had accidents, and were more likely to have been found to be at fault in accidents. In new analyses conducted for this chapter (R. A. Barkley, personal communiction, 1998), the two groups differed on the number of traffic violations when controlling for the number of conduct disorder symptoms, number of oppositional disorder symptoms, self-reported depression and anxiety, and intelligence.

As noted previously, some individuals have argued that the diagnosis of ADHD is a construct that inappropriately labels as abnormal variations in behavior that are upsetting to parents and teachers but that are not inherently maladaptive for children. It is of great importance, therefore, that children and adolescents who meet criteria for ADHD have been shown in several studies to be impaired in ways that do not simply reflect the wishes of adults that they sit down, be quiet, and do their work. From this perspective, the most convincing evidence that ADHD is a valid disorder are the findings of difficulties in peer relationships that are reported by the children themselves (Lahey et al., 1998) and by their peers (Hinshaw & Melnick, 1995), greater discrepancies between academic achievement and intelligence among children who meet criteria for ADHD using standardized tests (Lahey et al., 1998; Mariani & Barkley, 1997; Morgan, Hynd, Riccio, & Hall, 1996), the greater frequency of unintentional injuries (Lahey et al., 1998), the higher frequency of motor vehicle accidents (R. A. Barkley, personal communication, 1998), and reduced educational attainment and lower occupational status during adulthood (Mannuzza et al., 1993). Thus, there is now substantial evidence that the diagnosis of ADHD is associated with important aspects of functional impairment after controlling for a wide range of variables that are confounded with the diagnosis.

Validity of DSM-IV Criteria for Age of Onset and Cross-Situational Impairment

Although there is evidence that the current DSM-IV definition of ADHD is valid, it may be possible to improve its validity further by reconsidering the DSM-IV requirements for age of onset and cross-situational impairment. Several studies suggest that the DSM-IV age-of-onset criterion reduces the accuracy of identification of impaired cases and reduces agreement with clinician judgments (Applegate et al., 1997; Barkley & Biederman, 1997). There is no question that ADHD is a syndrome that begins in early childhood, but a substantial minority of youths first display impairment shortly after age 7 years (nearly half the youths who meet symptom criteria for the I type), and these children are no less likely to be impaired or to receive a clinical diagnosis of ADHD during childhood or adolescence (Applegate et al., 1997). Not allowing the diagnosis for these youths with later ages of onset of impairment may reduce the accurate identification of impaired individuals. If this requirement is dropped in the future, however, it will be necessary to strengthen rules for distinguishing ADHD from other disorders with similar symptoms, such as major depression, that tend to have later ages of onset.

To date, no studies have addressed the validity of the new requirement in DSM-IV that impairment be evident in two or more settings. The new analyses of data from the DSM-IV field trials (Lahey et al., 1994) noted previously, however, indicated that this requirement reduces the prevalence of DSM-IV ADHD, particularly for the I and H-I types. In further new analyses of these data for this chapter, the 134 youths who met full DSM-IV criteria for ADHD (including the requirement of cross-situational impairment) were compared to the 41 youths who met DSM-IV symptom and age-of-onset criteria for any subtype of ADHD (but not the requirement of cross-situational impairment) and to the 93 clinic-referred youths who did not meet criteria for DSM-IV ADHD. On two measures of impairment (parent ratings of homework problems and the interviewer's global ratings of functional impairment), both ADHD groups (those that did or did not meet the requirement of cross-situational impairment) differed significantly from the group that did not meet criteria for ADHD, but the two ADHD groups did not differ significantly from one another. On a third measure of impairment (the parent's global ratings of functional impairment), however, the ADHD group that met criteria for cross-situational impairment was rated as more impaired than youths who only met the symptom and age of onset criteria for ADHD.[4] These mixed findings only underscore the urgent need for additional research on the requirement of cross-situational impairment. In particular, new research is needed on the I and H-I types that often do not exhibit cross-situational impairment. The requirement of cross-situational impairment may preclude some youths with significant impairment in one important setting from receiving the diagnosis of these subtypes of ADHD.

DISCRIMINANT VALIDITY OF THE SUBTYPES OF DSM-IV ADHD

The distinction of subtypes of a disorder is valid only if the subtypes differ from one another in important ways (e.g., differences in demographics, patterns of comorbidity, patterns of functional impairment, and developmental course). Relatively little has been published to date on the discriminant validity of the subtypes of DSM-IV ADHD to date, but an extensive literature is available on the validity of the earlier distinction between the DSM-III subtypes. A review of this literature (Lahey, Carlson, & Frick, 1997) showed that ADD with hyperactivity had a higher male:female gender ratio, an earlier age of onset, a higher degree of comorbidity with conduct disorder, and a greater likelihood of peer rejection than ADD without hyperactivity. Youths who met criteria for ADD without hyperactivity, on the other hand, showed a different pattern of symptoms of inattention (less distractibility and more daydreaming), were equally unpopular with peers but not as actively disliked, and were somewhat more likely to exhibit academic underachievement. In addition, some studies found that youths who meet criteria for ADD without hyperactivity exhibited greater anxiety than youths who meet criteria for ADD with hyperactivity, but many studies have failed to confirm this difference (Lahey et al., 1997).

In some (Baumgaertel et al., 1995; Lahey et al., 1988; Lahey et al., 1998; Morgan et al., 1996; Wolraich et al., 1996), but not all (Ostrander, Weinfurt, Yarnold, & August, 1998), studies of clinic and population-based samples that used DSM-IV criteria, a higher proportion of girls met criteria for the I type than the C type (and the H-I type in some cases), but the difference in gender ratios was not statistically significant within most samples. This raises the possibility that a population-based study with adequate statistical power might find a significantly lower male:female ratio among the I type than the C type, but no conclusions can be reached at present. In two studies of the DSM-IV subtypes, youths who met criteria for the I type had significantly older ages of onset than youths who met criteria for the H-I type (Applegate et al., 1997; Faraone et al., 1998), and one of these studies found that the age of onset of the H-I group was significantly younger than the other two subtypes (Applegate et al., 1997).

Five studies have found that youths from clinic- and population-based samples who met full diagnostic criteria for the DSM-IV I type exhibited fewer concurrent conduct problems than did youths who met criteria for the C type (Eiraldi, Power, & Nezu, 1997; Faraone et al., 1998; Morgan et al., 1996; Ostrander et al., 1998; Paternite et al., 1996). Youths who met criteria for the H-I type tended to show levels of conduct problems intermediate between the levels of the C and the I types, but there was variation on this point across studies. Similarly, in new analyses of the DSM-IV field trials data (Lahey et al., 1994) conducted for this chapter, children who met full DSM-IV diagnostic criteria were compared on rates of concurrent diagnoses of conduct disorder and oppositional defiant disorder. Youths who met criteria for the C type were significantly more likely to meet criteria for oppositional defiant disorder and conduct disorder than were the I type.[5] Youths who met criteria for the H-I type did not differ significantly from the other two subtypes on the rate of either of these disorders.

Similarly, four studies that defined the DSM-IV ADHD subtypes in terms of symptom criteria found that there were significant differences among the three subtypes on the prevalence of comorbid oppositional defiant disorder (descending prevalence of oppositional defiant disorder among the C, H-I, and I types, respectively) (Baumgaertel et al., 1995; Gaub & Carlson, 1997a; McBurnett et al., 1999; Wolraich et al., 1996). In addition, two of these studies examined the prevalence of comorbid conduct disorder behaviors and found that both the C and H-I type exhibited more conduct disorder behaviors than did the I type (McBurnett et al., 1999; Wolraich et al., 1996). These findings from studies using DSM-IV criteria are consistent with many earlier studies that found that DSM-III ADD with hyperactivity is more strongly associated with concurrent conduct problems than ADD without hyperactivity (Lahey et al., 1997; Morgan et al., 1996). Thus, there is little doubt that the C type is more commonly comorbid with conduct problems than the I type, but more remains to be learned about patterns of comorbidity of the H-I type.

Several studies (Eiraldi et al., 1997; Faraone et al., 1998; Lahey et al., 1998; McBurnett et al., 1999; Morgan et al., 1996) suggest that the mean full-scale intelligence of clinic-referred children who meet criteria for the C and I types is somewhat lower (in the range of 5–10 points) than that of non-referred comparison children who are reasonably matched on age, gender, race-ethnicity, and socioeconomic status. The mean intelligence of children who meet criteria for the H-I type does not appear to differ significantly from that of control children, however. Unfortunately, data from population-based samples are not available on this topic to rule out the possible influence of referral bias. That is, it is possible that lower intelligence is not an inherent characteristic of ADHD, but lower intelligence may increase the likelihood of clinic referral among children who meet criteria for ADHD. Regardless of how this issue is settled, however, it is essential that studies of the impairment associated with the C and I types rule out the possibility that the apparent impairment associated with ADHD actually reflects their lower intelligence instead.

One study that controlled for intelligence and other potential confounds found that the C and H-I types were more likely to have had unintentional injuries than the other subtypes (Lahey et al., 1998). In addition, children in this study who met criteria for the C and I types were liked by fewer classmates and rated as less cooperative by teachers than children who met criteria for the H-I type; children who met criteria for the C type were disliked by more classmates than children who met criteria for the two other subtypes of ADHD (Lahey et al., 1998). Three studies suggest that the I type is particularly associated with underachievement in mathematics relative to intelligence, but underachievement is common among youths who meet criteria for the C type as well (Lahey et al., 1998; Morgan et al., 1996; Lamminaki, Narhi, Lyytinen, & Todd de Barra, 1995). No data have been published on potential differences among the DSM-IV subtypes of ADHD in response to treatment, but one study found differences in response to methylphenidate between youths who met criteria for DSM-III ADD with and without hyperactivity, suggesting that differences in response to stimulant medication among the subtypes are probable (Barkley, DuPaul, & McMurray, 1991).

It also is essential that the validity of the subtypes of DSM-IV ADHD be evaluated in longitudinal studies that can determine whether children who meet criteria for a subtype of DSM-IV ADHD continue to meet criteria for that subtype over time. If youths shift from meeting criteria for one subtype to another in a systematic way over time, such developmental changes would not necessarily invalidate the subtypes. For example, if inattention remains relatively stable with increasing age, but hyperactivity/impulsivity declines with age, many children who meet criteria for the C type in childhood may come to meet criteria for the I type as their symptoms of hyperactivity/impulsivity fall below the diagnostic threshold. Such a developmental shift would not invalidate the distinction between these two subtypes but may lead to a reconceptualization or redefinition of the I type. On the other hand, if youths shift randomly from one subtype to another over time due to fluctuations in levels of the two dimensions of symptoms, the subtyping schema would be shown to be invalid.

ADHD AND COMORBID MENTAL DISORDERS

In most sections of this chapter, mental disorders that co-occur with ADHD have been controlled in statistical analyses to determine whether each type of impairment was associated with ADHD rather than a comorbid mental disorder. This was necessary because children with ADHD have a much higher prevalence of other mental disorders, particularly oppositional defiant disorder and anxiety disorders, than do children in the general population (Lahey et al., 2000; Lahey, Miller, Gordon, & Riley,

1999). It also is important to consider this relationship between ADHD and other mental disorders in quite a different light, however. It is possible that ADHD should be considered a significant disorder precisely because it is associated with increased risk for other mental disorders. Similarly, there is evidence that children with ADHD who develop conduct disorder may do so earlier in life and continue to engage in antisocial behavior over longer periods, suggesting that the severity of some mental disorders may be greater when they co-occur with ADHD (Lahey et al., 2000).

ADHD IN ADULTHOOD

Children with ADHD become increasingly less likely to meet DSM diagnostic criteria for ADHD as they grow older, but some children continue to meet criteria for ADHD and to be impaired into adulthood (Hill & Schoener, 1996; Spencer, Biederman, Wilens, & Faraone, 1994; for further information on ADHD in adulthood, see Chapters 4 and 6).

ASSESSMENT OF ADHD

The reliability of assessments of ADHD is quite high using both structured diagnostic interviews (Biederman et al., 1992; Goldman et al., 1998; Orvaschel, 1995; Schwab-Stone et al., 1996; Shaffer et al., 1996) and parent and teacher rating scales (Conners, 1973; Quay & Peterson, 1983). In addition, many, but not all, studies using mechanical measures have found that clinic-referred children who meet criteria for ADHD exhibit significantly higher levels of motor activity and less visual attending than do comparison children (Paternite et al., 1996; Porrino et al., 1983; Teicher, Ito, Glod, & Barber, 1996). Such evidence supports the validity of interviews and rating scales. Less is known about the reliability of the assessment of ADHD in adults, but the little existing evidence is encouraging (Spencer et al., 1994).

IS ADHD BETTER CONCEPTUALIZED IN DIAGNOSTIC OR DIMENSIONAL TERMS?

Some researchers and critics have suggested that ADHD is more appropriately viewed as a dimension of maladaptive behavior than a taxonomic category (British Psychological Society, 1996; Fergusson & Horwood, 1995; Levy et al., 1997). At present, there is growing evidence that two valid dimensions of impairing ADHD behaviors can be identified, but there is no evidence of a natural threshold between ADHD and "normal" behavior. The distributions of numbers of inattention and hyperactivity/impulsivity symptoms in the general population are not bimodal, associations between numbers of ADHD symptoms and impairment are linear rather than curvilinear (Lahey et al., 1994), and a twin study of the inheritability of ADHD found no evidence of a natural diagnostic threshold based on differential inheritability (Levy, Hay, McStephen, Wood, & Waldman, 1997). Thus, there is little evidence at this time to suggest that there is a natural boundary for the diagnostic category of ADHD.

Much more evidence is needed before this issue can be meaningfully addressed, but even if ADHD proves to be naturally continuous, that would not necessarily mean that ADHD should not be treated as a diagnostic category. Many individuals with high numbers of impairing ADHD behaviors present for treatment, requiring clinicians to make dichotomous decisions to treat or not treat each individual. The clinician must decide whether the risks inherent in treating are lower than the risks inherent in not treating a person with impairing symptoms. Because all forms of treatment involve some iatrogenic risk, it seems more appropriate to adopt a well-considered diagnostic threshold than to require each clinician to make this decision individually, even if the threshold is viewed as more conventional than natural. It is important to note that similar questions can be raised about the boundaries of many mental disorders other than ADHD.

RECOMMENDATIONS FOR CLINICAL PRACTICE, POLICY, AND FUTURE RESEARCH

Although much remains to be learned, current findings on the validity of the dimensions and diagnostic category of ADHD have a number of important implications for clinical practice and public policy. Some gaps in current knowledge are discussed while summarizing the implications of the present database for clinical practice and policy, and other gaps are described at the end of this section.

Implications for Clinical Practice

There is good evidence that the symptoms of DSM-IV ADHD can be assessed reliably and validly across the lifespan using structured diagnostic interviews and symptom checklists. Because unstructured diagnostic assessment by clinicians is notoriously unreliable, clinicians should consider adopting these simple and cost-effective methods of assessment as part of their standard diagnostic procedures. A considerable amount of evidence suggests that ADHD is independently associated with significant impairment in at least three areas: social relationships, educational and occupational attainment, and unintentional injuries. Because impairment is required for the diagnosis of DSM-IV ADHD, clinicians must assess functional impairment in ways that are as reliable and valid as their assessment of the symptoms of ADHD. Many recent studies of the validity of the diagnosis of ADHD cited in this chapter used psychometrically strong measures of peer social status, academic achievement, homework and classwork performance, unintentional injuries, and other aspects of impairment that are appropriate for clinical applications. Although different measures are needed for different ages, many cited studies provide guidance in the selection of appropriate measures of impairment from preschool through adulthood.

Impairment in social relationships, educational and occupational attainment, and physical safety has been found to be associated with ADHD even after controlling for a range of factors that appear to be associated with ADHD: lower intelligence, lower socioeconomic status of the family, and concurrent mental disorders. There are two implications of this important evidence for clinical practice:

1. *The clinical assessment of individuals who may meet criteria for ADHD should include standardized assessments of intelligence and academic achievement, comorbid mental disorders, and the family circumstances of the child.* The assessment of intelligence provides information that can be used with other

measures of development to determine whether the apparently symptomatic behaviors are more frequent and severe than is typical of individuals at a comparable developmental level. In addition, standardized measures of intelligence and academic achievement can be used together to determine whether the child is achieving at a level that is substantially below the level expected for her or his intelligence and age (Frick et al., 1991).

2. *Because ADHD appears to be associated with significant functional impairment, the discussion of treatment options with patients or their caregivers should carefully weigh the potential risks and benefits of treatment against the potential risks of impairment in social, academic, and occupational domains and the risks of morbidity and mortality from accidents.* Although there are risks inherent in any form of treatment, there also appear to be risks associated with not treating. Future research should focus on the extent to which various treatments for ADHD reduce the most serious aspects of impairment, rather than focusing only on amelioration of symptoms, to assist clinicians in balancing the risks of treating versus not treating. Contrary to earlier understandings of the prognosis of ADHD, substantial evidence suggests that ADHD may not increase the likelihood of antisocial behavior in adolescence and adulthood unless the child also exhibits high numbers of oppositional behaviors or conduct problems during childhood. Although more research is needed on the long-term outcomes of children who meet criteria for ADHD, clinicians should no longer make unqualified statements to the parents of children who meet criteria for ADHD, but who do not exhibit substantial numbers of oppositional behavior or conduct problems, that their children are at risk for later antisocial behavior. Instead, parents should be informed that this is a point that must be resolved through future research. On the other hand, there is substantial evidence that children who meet criteria for ADHD who also exhibit conduct problems during childhood are at very high risk for serious later antisocial behavior and should, in most cases, receive interventions to prevent antisocial behavior as well.

Implications for Public Policy

There is currently strong evidence that ADHD is a prevalent condition that is associated with marked social, educational, and occupational impairment. For this reason, funds invested in research on the causes, prevention, and treatment of ADHD could be expected to produce significant benefits to the nation in terms of improvements in human well-being, reduced need for costly mental health and special education services, and increased productivity of the work force. In addition, there is evidence that children who meet criteria for ADHD are at increased risk for other mental disorders. Therefore, the prevention and early treatment of ADHD may reduce the likelihood of other serious disorders as well.

Areas to Target in Future Research

Future studies must continue to pursue both topics about which much is known and topics about which little is currently known. Although much progress has been made in recent years, it is essential to learn more about the concurrent and predictive validity of ADHD and the discriminant validity of the dimensions and subtypes of ADHD. Currently, there is good evidence that the distinction between the C and I types of ADHD is clinically important, but less is known about the H-I type. An ongoing longitudinal study will test the hypothesis that preschool and primary school children who meet criteria for the H-I type eventually meet criteria for the C type as their attentional capacity is challenged in school (Lahey et al., 1998), but more remains to be learned about this and other key topics.

In addition, new research initiatives are sorely needed on potential gender differences in ADHD. Findings from a meta-analytic review (Gaub & Carlson, 1997b) of the few existing studies that have examined ADHD in girls suggest that the implications of clinically significant elevations of ADHD symptoms may vary by gender. In comparison to boys, girls who met criteria for ADHD exhibited fewer hyperactive behaviors and symptoms of other disruptive disorders but tended to have lower intelligence scores. The authors cautioned, however, that these findings should be viewed as tentative due to the small number of studies that included girls. More information on the validity of the diagnosis of ADHD among girls is urgently needed, therefore. In the same way, research on potential ethnic and cultural differences in ADHD is sorely needed.

Similarly, a priority must be placed on studies of the validity of the diagnosis of ADHD in young children. A recent study (Lahey et al., 1998) indicated that the diagnosis is valid among 4- through 6-year-old children, but this study awaits replication by other researchers. In addition, clinicians often must decide whether or not to treat 2- or 3-year-old children who appear to meet all diagnostic criteria for ADHD. Because ADHD symptoms are common at this age, it is possible that many toddlers who meet criteria for ADHD exhibit transient problems that should not be treated. On the other hand, if enough is learned about assessing ADHD in the context of the child's developmental level to accurately identify 2- to 3-year-olds who are in need of assistance, it may be possible to prevent much of the impairment that is associated with ADHD through early intervention. More research on the longitudinal outcomes of young children who exhibit ADHD will be needed to make progress in the area of early identification and intervention, however.

Barkley (1990) has raised an important question about the validity of the DSM-IV diagnostic criteria across the age span that must be addressed in future studies. He suggested that different diagnostic criteria are needed at different ages. Because the number of symptoms of ADHD declines with increasing age, particularly symptoms of hyperactivity/impulsivity, the number of symptoms that would place an individual at any given percentile in the distribution of numbers of symptoms is lower at older than younger ages. In addition, the importance of different symptoms may be quite different at different ages (e.g., running around and climbing on things may be salient among children, whereas disorganization and forgetfulness may be more important at older ages). Indeed, symptoms of ADHD may appear in adulthood that are not relevant to children at all. Before symptoms and diagnostic thresholds could be modified to be age-specific, however, it would need to be demonstrated that different numbers of symptoms (or different symptoms) at different ages identify equally impaired individuals. That is, data are needed to distinguish between two possibilities: (1) some individuals "outgrow" ADHD, in the sense that both their symptoms and the impairment caused by their symptoms decline, or (2) although the number of symptoms of ADHD declines with age, a smaller number of symptoms is as impairing at older ages as a larger number is at younger ages.

The question of age-specific diagnostic criteria is a complicated one for at least two reasons. First, it will be difficult to compare the amount of impairment related to different numbers and kinds of symptoms at different ages because the nature of functional impairment also changes with age. For example, during late adolescence, impaired operation of motor vehicles is a key facet of impairment that is not an issue during elementary school. Similarly, social relationship problems during the preschool and elementary years relate mostly to friendships, whereas romantic relationships become an issue during adolescence and adulthood. Second, in conducting such studies, it will be essential to distinguish between impairment in adolescence or adulthood that was actually caused during childhood. For example, an adolescent may drop out of high school more because of a cumulative deficit in academic progress that began in kindergarten than because of the interference of symptoms of ADHD that are present during adolescence. Research strategies that thoughtfully address these issues, however, might lead to the development of age-specific diagnostic criteria. The same reasoning and line of research that could lead to age-specific diagnostic criteria could similarly lead to gender-specific diagnostic criteria or even criteria specific to other definable subgroups of individuals. At this point, however, there is not sufficient evidence to support different diagnostic criteria for different groups of individuals.

Ideally, the future also will bring studies that use the methods of population and molecular genetics to address the taxonomy of ADHD. Twin studies offer powerful advantages in assessing the discriminant validity of dimensions of psychopathology, including ADHD. Powerful behavior genetic methods can combine analyses of the internal validity of the dimensions and subtypes of ADHD with analyses of similarities and differences in the contributions of genetic, shared environmental, and unshared environmental factors to the dimensions or subtypes. Such studies can also do much to resolve the debate on categorical versus dimensional views of ADHD. In the future (perhaps the near future), an extraordinary kind of iterative bootstrapping will emerge between taxonomy and genetic research. Taxonomic research had defined (and will refine) phenotypes that can be related to genotypes. In turn, discovery of genotype-phenotype correlations will sometimes lead to revisions in taxonomy, such as by defining subgroups that are, and are not, related to a variant of a given gene. These improvements will facilitate future genetic studies, and so on. For example, there is some evidence that the dimensions of inattention and hyperactivity/impulsivity may each be associated with risk alleles of different genes that control separate aspects of dopaminergic neural transmission (Rowe et al., 1998; Waldman et al., 1998). If replicated, such findings would provide strong support for the divergent validity of the two dimensions. Ideally, the future will bring many such advances.

Footnotes

[1] In new analyses of the DSM-IV field trials data, the hyperactivity/impulsivity dimension was associated with conduct disorder symptoms, $\chi^2 = 14.65$, $p < .0001$, whereas inattention was associated with anxiety symptoms (overanxious disorder, separation anxiety disorder, specific phobia, social phobia, and agoraphobia), $\chi^2 = 63.96$, $p < .0001$, and depression symptoms (major depression and dysthymia), $\chi^2 = 98.76$, $p < .0001$, in joint models. The number of symptoms of oppositional defi-

ant disorder was associated with both inattention, $\chi^2 = 8.80$, $p < .005$, and hyperactivity/impulsivity symptoms, $\chi^2 = 142.66$, $p < .0001$, but the association was stronger for hyperactivity/impulsivity in joint models.

[2] Initial analyses of covariance included the diagnosis of ADHD as the predictor and age, gender, ethnicity, family income, and diagnoses of oppositional defiant disorder, conduct disorder, and any anxiety or depressive disorder as covariates. Covariates that were not significant at $p < .05$ were not included in the final models. In the final models, youths who met criteria for DSM-IV ADHD received lower parent ratings on the Children's Global Assessment Scale, F $(1, 227) = 40.41$, $p < .0001$, controlling for age, F $(1, 227) = 5.06$, $p < .05$. Youths who met criteria for DSM-IV ADHD received lower interviewer ratings on the Children's Global Assessment Scale, F $(1, 220) = 53.89$, $p < .0001$, controlling for the diagnosis of conduct disorder, F $(1, 220) = 19.45$, $p < .0001$, and the diagnosis of any anxiety or depressive disorder, F $(1, 220) = 9.05$, $p < .005$. Youths who met criteria for DSM-IV ADHD received higher parent ratings of homework problems, F $(1, 203) = 78.05$, $p < .0001$, controlling for the diagnosis of conduct disorder, F $(1, 203) = 6.07$, $p < .05$. Youths who met criteria for DSM-IV ADHD received lower teacher ratings of classroom academic performance, F $(1, 116) = 22.66$, $p < .0001$.

[3] To avoid circularity in assessing the impairment associated with ADHD, the requirement of impairment in more than one setting was not required for the diagnosis in this study.

[4] Initial analyses of covariance included age, gender, ethnicity, family income, and diagnoses of oppositional defiant disorder, conduct disorder, and any anxiety or depressive disorder as covariates. Covariates that were not significant at $p < .05$ were not included in the final models. In the final models, the three groups differed on parent ratings on the Children's Global Assessment Scale, F $(2, 265) = 40.02$, $p < .0001$, and the parent's rating of homework problems, F $(2, 174) = 32.14$, $p < .0001$. In addition, the three groups differed on interviewer ratings on the Children's Global Assessment Scale, F $(2, 269) = 15.95$, $p < .0001$, controlling for the diagnosis of conduct disorder, F $(1, 269) = 23.47$, $p < .0001$, and the diagnosis of any anxiety or depressive disorder, F $(1, 269) = 22.70$, $p < .0001$.

[5] In logistic regression, the contrast between the combined and inattentive types was significant for oppositional defiant disorder, Wald $\chi^2 = 11.56$, $p < .001$, and for conduct disorder, Wald $\chi^2 = 5.11$, $p < .05$.

References

American Psychiatric Association. (1968). *Diagnostic and statistical manual of mental disorders* (2nd ed.). Washington, DC: Author.

American Psychiatric Association. (1980). *Diagnostic and statistical manual of mental disorders* (3rd ed.). Washington, DC: Author.

American Psychiatric Association. (1987). *Diagnostic and statistical manual of mental disorders* (3rd ed., rev.). Washington, DC: Author.

American Psychiatric Association. (1994). *Diagnostic and statistical manual of mental disorders* (4th ed.). Washington, DC: Author.

Applegate, B., Lahey, B. B., Hart, E. L., Biederman, J., Hynd, G. W., Barkley, R. A., Ollendick, T., Frick, P. J., Greenhill, L., McBurnett, K., Newcorn, J. H., Kerdyk, L., Garfinkel, B., Waldman, I., & Shaffer, D. (1997). Validity of the age of onset criterion for attention-deficit/hyperactivity disorder: A report from the DSM-IV field trials. *Journal of the American Academy of Child and Adolescent Psychiatry, 36,* 1211–1221.

Bandura, A. (1969). *Principles of behavior modification.* New York: Holt, Rinehart & Winston.

Barkley, R. A. (1990). *Attention-deficit hyperactivity disorder. A handbook for diagnosis and treatment.* New York: Guilford Press.

Barkley, R. A., & Biederman, J. (1997). Toward a broader definition of the age-of-onset criterion for attention-deficit hyperactivity disorder. *Journal of the American Academy of Child and Adolescent Psychiatry, 36,* 1201–1210.

Barkley, R. A., DuPaul, G. J., & McMurray, M. B. (1991). Attention deficit disorder with and without hyperactivity: Clinical response to three dose levels of methylphenidate. *Pediatrics, 87*, 519–531.

Bauermeister, J. (1992). Factor analysis of teacher ratings of attention-deficit hyperactivity and oppositional defiant symptoms in children aged four through thirteen years. *Journal of Clinical Child Psychology, 21*, 27–34.

Bauermeister, J. J., Bird, H. R., Canino, G., Rubio-Stipec, M., Bravo, M., & Alegra, M. (1995). Dimensions of attention deficit hyperactivity disorder: Findings from teacher and parent reports in a community sample. *Journal of Clinical Psychology, 24*, 264–271.

Baumgaertel, A., Wolraich, M. L., & Dietrich, M. (1995). Comparison of diagnostic criteria for attention deficit disorders in a German elementary school sample. *Journal of the American Academy of Child and Adolescent Psychiatry, 34*(5), 629–638.

Biederman, J., Faraone, S., Keenan, K., Benjamin, J., Krifcher, B., Moore, C., Sprich-Buckminster, S., Ugaglia, K., Jellinek, M. S., Steingard, R.,Spencer, T., Norman, D., Kolodny, R., Kraus, I., Perrin, J., Keller, M. B., Tsuang, M. T. (1992). Further evidence for family-genetic risk factors in attention deficit hyperactivity disorder: Patterns of comorbidity in probands and psychiatrically and pediatrically referred samples. *Archives of General Psychiatry, 49*, 728–738.

Biederman, J., Faraone, S. V., Weber, W., Russell, R. L., Rater, M., & Oark, K. S. (1997). Correspondence between DSM-III-R and DSM-IV attention-deficit/hyperactivity disorder. *Journal of the American Academy of Child and Adolescent Psychiatry, 36*, 1682–1687.

British Psychological Society. (1996). *Attention deficit hyperactivity disorder (ADHD): A psychological response to an evolving concept.* Leicester, UK: Author.

Buitelaar, J. K., van der Gagg, R. J., Swaab-Barneveld, H., & Kuiper, M. (1995). Prediction of clinical response to methylphenidate in children with attention-deficit hyperactivity disorder. *Journal of the American Academy of Child and Adolescent Psychiatry, 34*, 1025–1032.

Burns, G. L., Walsh, J. A., Owen, S. M., & Snell, J. (1997). Internal validity of attention deficit hyperactivity disorder, oppositional defiant disorder, and overt conduct disorder symptoms in young children: Implications from teacher ratings for a dimensional approach to symptom validity. *Journal of Clinical Child Psychology, 26*, 266–275.

Burns, G. L., Walsh, J. A., Patterson, D. R., Holte, C. S., Sommers-Flanagan, R., & Parker, C. M. (1997). Internal validity of the disruptive behavior disorder symptoms: Implications from parent ratings for a dimensional approach to symptom validity. *Journal of Abnormal Child Psychology, 25*, 307–320.

Conners, C. K. (1973). Rating scales for use in drug studies of children [Special issue]. *Psychopharmacology Bulletin Pharmacotherapy of Children*, pp. 24–29.

Conners, C. K., Sitarenios, G., Parker, J. D. A., & Epstein, J. N. (1998a). Revision and restandardization of the Conners Parent Rating Scale (CPRS-R): Factor structure, reliability, and criterion validity. *Journal of Abnormal Child Psychology, 26*, 257–268.

Conners, C. K., Sitarenios, G., Parker, J. D. A., & Epstein, J. N. (1998b). Revision and restandardization of the Conners Teacher Rating Scale (CTRS-R): Factor structure, reliability, and criterion validity. *Journal of Abnormal Child Psychology, 26*, 279–291.

Douglas, V., & Peter, K. (1979). Toward a clearer definition of the attentional deficit of hyperactive children. In G. Hale & M. Lewis (Eds.), *Attention and the development of cognitive skills* (pp. 173–248), New York: Plenum Press.

DuPaul, G. J., Anastopoulos, A. D., McGoey, K. E., Power, T. J., Reid, R., & Ikeda, M. J. (1997). Teacher ratings of attention deficit hyperactivity disorder symptoms: Factor structure and normative data. *Psychological Assessment, 9*, 436–444.

DuPaul, G. J., Anastopoulos, A. D., Power, T. J., Reid, R., Ikeda, M. J., & McGoey, K. E. (1998). Parent ratings of attention-deficit/hyperactivity disorder symptoms: Factor structure and normative data. *Journal of Psychopathology and Behavioral Assessment, 20*, 83–102.

Eiraldi, R. B., Power, T. J., & Nezu, C. M. (1997). Patterns of comorbidity association with subtypes of attention-deficit/hyperactivity disorder. *Journal of the American Academy of Child and Adolescent Psychiatry, 36*, 503–514.

Faraone, S. V., Biederman, J., Weber, W., & Russell, R. L. (1998). Psychiatric, neuropsychological, and psychosocial features of DSM-IV subtypes of attention-deficit/hyperactivity disorder: Results from a clinically referred sample. *Journal of the American Academy of Child and Adolescent Psychiatry, 37*, 185–193.

Fergusson, D. M., & Horwood, J. (1995). Predictive validity of categorically and dimensionally scored measures of disruptive childhood behaviors. *Journal of the American Academy of Child and Adolescent Psychiatry, 34*, 477–485.

Frick, P. J., Kamphaus, R. W., Lahey, B. B., Loeber, R., Christ, M. A. G., Hart, E. L., & Tannenbaum, L. E. (1991). Academic underachievement and the disruptive behavior disorders. *Journal of Consulting and Clinical Psychology, 59*, 289–294.

Gaub, M., & Carlson, C. L. (1997a). Behavioral characteristics of DSM-IV ADHD subtypes in a school-based population. *Journal of Abnormal Child Psychology, 25*, 103–111.

Gaub, M., & Carlson, C. L. (1997b). Gender differences in ADHD: A meta-analysis and critical review. *Journal of the American Academy of Child and Adolescent Psychiatry, 36*, 1036–1045.

Goldman, L. S., Genel, M., Bezman, R. J., & Slanetz, P. J. (1998). Diagnosis and treatment of attention-deficit/hyperactivity disorder in children and adolescents. Council on Scientific Affairs, American Medical Association. *Journal of the American Medical Association, 279*, 1100–1107.

Hart, E. L., Lahey, B. B., Loeber, R., Applegate, B., Green, S. M., & Frick, P. J. (1995). Developmental change in attention-deficit hyperactivity disorder in boys: A four-year longitudinal study. *Journal of Abnormal Child Psychology, 23*, 729–749.

Hill, J. C., & Schoener, E. P. (1996). Age-dependent decline of attention deficit hyperactivity disorder. *American Journal of Psychiatry, 153*, 1143–1146.

Hinshaw, S. P. (1994). *Attention deficits and hyperactivity in children.* Thousand Oaks, CA: Sage.

Hinshaw, S. P., & Melnick, S. M. (1995). Peer relationships in boys with attention-deficit hyperactivity disorder with and without comorbid aggression. *Development and Psychopathology, 7*, 627–647.

Hudziak, J. J., Heath, A. C., Madden, P. F., Reich, W., Bucholz, K. K., Slutske, W., Beirut, L. J., Neuman, R. J., & Todd, R. D. (1998). Latent class and factor analysis of DSM-IV ADHD: A twin study of female adolescents. *Journal of the American Academy of Child and Adolescent Psychiatry, 37*, 848–857.

Kanbayashi, Y., Nakata, Y., Fujii, K., Kita, M., & Wada, K. (1994). ADHD-related behavior among non-referred children: Parents' ratings of DSM-III-R symptoms. *Child Psychiatry and Human Development, 25*, 13–29.

Lahey, B. B., Applegate, B., McBurnett, K., Biederman, J., Greenhill, L., Hynd, G. W., Barkley, R. A., Newcorn, J., Jensen, P., Richters, J., Garfinkel, B., Kerdyk, L., Frick, P. J., Ollendick, T., Perez, D., Hart, E. L., Waldman, I., & Shaffer, D. (1994). DSM-IV Field Trials for attention deficit hyperactivity disorder in children and adolescents. *American Journal of Psychiatry, 151*, 1673–1685.

Lahey, B. B., Carlson, C. L., & Frick, P. J. (1997). Attention deficit disorder without hyperactivity: A review of research relevant to DSM-IV. In T. A. Widiger, A. J. Frances, W. Davis, & M. First (Eds.), *DSM-IV sourcebook* (Vol. 1, pp. 163–188). Washington, DC: American Psychiatric Press.

Lahey, B. B., McBurnett, K., & Loeber, R. (2000). Are attention-deficit hyperactivity disorder and oppositional defiant disorder developmental precursors to conduct disorder? In M. Lewis & A. Sameroff (Eds.), *Handbook of developmental psychopathology* (pp. 431–446). New York: Plenum Press.

Lahey, B. B., Miller, T. L., Gordon, R. A., & Riley, A. (1999). Developmental epidemiology of the disruptive behavior disorders. In H. Quay & A. Hogan (Eds.), *Handbook of the disruptive behavior disorders* (pp. 23–48). New York: Kluwers Academic.

Lahey, B. B., Pelham, W. E., Schaughency, E. A., Atkins, M. S., Murphy, H. A., Hynd, G. W., Russo, M., Hartdagen, S., & Lorys-Vernon, A. (1988). Dimensions and types of attention deficit disorder. *Journal of the American Academy of Child and Adolescent Psychiatry, 27*, 330–335.

Lahey, B. B., Pelham, W. E., Stein, M. A., Loney, J., Trapani, C., Nugent, K., Kipp, H., Schmidt, E., Lee, S., Cale, M., Gold, E., Hartung, C. M., Willcutt, E., & Baumann, B. (1998). Validity of DSM-IV attention-deficit/hyperactivity disorder for younger children. *Journal of the American Academy of Child and Adolescent Psychiatry, 37*, 695–702.

Lamminaki, T. A., Narhi, V., Lyytinen, H., & Todd de Barra, H. (1995). Attention deficit hyperactivity disorder subtypes: Are there differences in academic problems? *Developmental Neuropsychology, 11,* 297–310.

Levy, F., Hay, D. A., McStephen, M., Wood, C., & Waldman, I. (1997). Attention-deficit hyperactivity disorder: A category or a continuum? Genetic analysis of a large-scale twin study. *Journal of the American Academy of Child and Adolescent Psychiatry, 36,* 737–744.

Lilienfeld, S. O., & Waldman, I. D. (1990). The relation between childhood attention-deficit hyperactivity disorder and adult antisocial behavior reexamined: The problem of heterogeneity. *Clinical Psychology Review, 10,* 699–725.

Mannuzza, S., Klein, R. G., Bessler, A., Malloy, P., & LaPadula, M. (1993). Adult outcome of hyperactive boys: Educational achievement, occupational rank, and psychiatric status. *Archives of General Psychiatry, 50,* 565–576.

Mariani, M. A., & Barkely, R. A. (1997). Neuropsychological and academic functioning in preschool boys with attention deficit disorder. *Developmental Neuropsychology, 13,* 111–129.

McBurnett, K., Pfiffner, L. J., Wilcutt, E., Tamm, L., Lerner, M., Ottolini, Y. L., & Furman, M. B. (1999). Experimental cross-validation of DSM-IV types of attention-deficit hyperactivity disorder. *Journal of the American Academy of Child and Adolescent Psychiatry, 38*(1), 17–24.

McGee, R., Partridge, F., Williams, S., & Silva, P. A. (1991). A twelve-year follow-up of preschool hyperactive children. *Journal of the American Academy of Child and Adolescent Psychiatry, 30,* 224–232.

Morgan, A. E., Hynd, G. W., Riccio, C. A., & Hall, J. (1996). Validity of DSM-IV ADHD predominantly inattentive and combined type: Relationship to previous DSM diagnoses/subtype differences. *Journal of the American Academy of Child and Adolescent Psychiatry, 35,* 325–333.

Nada-Raja, S., Langley, J. D., McGee, R., Williams, S. M., Begg, D. J., & Reeder, A. I. (1997). Inattentive and hyperactive behaviors and driving offenses in adolescence. *Journal of the American Academy of Child and Adolescent Psychiatry, 36,* 515–522.

Orvaschel, H. (1995). *Schedule for Affective Disorders and Schizophrenia for School-Age Children, Version 5.* Fort Lauderdale, FL: Nova Southeastern University.

Ostrander, R., Weinfurt, K. P., Yarnold, P. R., & August, G. J. (1998). Diagnosing attention deficit disorders with the Behavioral Assessment System for Children and the Child Behavior Checklist: Test and construct validity analyses using optimal discriminant classification trees. *Journal of Consulting and Clinical Psychology, 66,* 600–672.

Paternite, C. E., Loney, J., & Roberts, M. A. (1996). A preliminary validation of subtypes of DSM-IV attention-deficit/hyperactivity disorder. *Journal of Attention Disorders, 1,* 70–86.

Pelham, W. E., Evans, S. W., Gnagy, E. M., & Greenslade, K. E. (1992). Teacher ratings of DSM-III-R symptoms for the disruptive behavior disorders: Prevalence, factor analyses, and conditional probabilities in a special education sample. *School Psychology Review, 21,* 285–299.

Pelham, W. E., Gnagy, E. M., Greenslade, K. E., & Milich, R. (1992). Teacher ratings of DSM-III-R symptoms for the disruptive behavior disorders. *Journal of the American Academy of Child and Adolescent Psychiatry, 31,* 210–218.

Pillow, D. R., Pelham, W. E., Hoza, B., Molina, B. S. G., & Stultz, C. H. (1998). Confirmatory factor analyses examining attention deficit hyperactivity disorder symptoms and other childhood disruptive behavior disorders. *Journal of Abnormal Child Psychology, 26,* 293–309.

Pliszka, S. R. (1989). Effect of anxiety on cognition, behavior, and stimulant response in ADHD. *Journal of the American Academy of Child and Adolescent Psychiatry, 28,* 882–887.

Porrino, L. J., Rapoport, J. L., Behar, D., Sceery, W., Ismond, D. R., & Bunney, W. E. (1983). A naturalistic assessment of the motor activity of hyperactive boys: I. Comparison with normal controls. *Archives of General Psychiatry, 40,* 681–687.

Prior, M., & Sanson, A. (1986). Attention deficit disorder with hyperactivity: A critique. *Journal of Child Psychology and Psychiatry, 27,* 307–319.

Quay, H. C., & Peterson, D. R. (1983). *Interim manual of the revised Behavior Problem Checklist.* Miami, FL: Authors.

Rowe, D. C., Stever, C., Giedinghagen, L. N., Gard, J. M., Cleveland, H. H., Terris, S. T., Mohr, J. H., Sherman, S., Abramowitz, A., & Waldman, I. D. (1998). Dopamine DRD4 receptor polymorphism and attention deficit hyperactivity disorder. *Molecular Psychiatry, 3*, 419–426.

Safer, D. J., & Krager, J. M. (1992). Effect of a media blitz and a threatened lawsuit in stimulant treatment. *Journal of the American Medical Association, 268*, 1004–1007.

Satterfield, J. H., & Schell, A. (1997). A prospective study of hyperactive boys with conduct problems and normal boys: Adolescent and adult criminality. *Journal of the American Academy of Child and Adolescent Psychiatry, 36*, 1726–1735.

Schwab-Stone, M., Shaffer, D., Dulcan, M., Jensen, P., Fisher, P., Bird, H., Goodman, S. H., Lahey, B. B., Lichtman, J. H., Canino, G., Rubio-Stipec, M., & Rae, D. S. (1996). Criterion validity of the NIMH Diagnostic Interview Schedule for Children (DISC 2.3). *Journal of the American Academy of Child and Adolescent Psychiatry, 35*, 878–888.

Setterberg, S., Bird, H., & Gould, M. (1992). *Parent and Interviewer Version of the Children's Global Assessment Scale.* New York: Columbia University.

Shaffer, D., Fisher, P., Dulcan, M. K., Davies, M., Piacentini, J., Schwab-Stone, M. E., Lahey, B. B., Bourdon, K., Jensen, P. S., Bird, H. R., Canino, G., & Regier, D. A. (1996). The NIMH diagnostic interview schedule for children version 2.3 (DISC-2.3): Description, acceptability, prevalence rates, and performance in the MECA study. *Journal of the American Academy of Child and Adolescent Psychiatry, 35*, 865–877.

Sherman, D. K., Iacono, W. G., & McGue, M. K. (1997). Attention-deficit hyperactivity disorder dimensions: A twin study of inattention and impulsivity-hyperactivity. *Journal of the American Academy of Child and Adolescent Psychiatry, 36*, 745–753.

Spencer, T., Biederman, J., Wilens, T., & Faraone, S. V. (1994). Is attention-deficit hyperactivity disorder in adults a valid disorder? *Harvard Review of Psychiatry, 1*, 326–335.

Tannock, R., & Ickowicz, A. (1995). Differential effects of methylphenidate on working memory in ADHD children with and without comorbid anxiety. *Journal of the American Academy of Child and Adolescent Psychiatry, 34*, 886–896.

Taylor, E., Chadwick, O., Heptinstall, E., & Danckaerts, M. (1996). Hyperactivity and conduct problems as risk factors for adolescent development. *Journal of the American Academy of Child and Adolescent Psychiatry, 35*, 1213–1226.

Teicher, M. H., Ito, Y., Glod, C. A., & Barber, N. I. (1996). Objective measurement of hyperactivity and attentional problems in ADHD. *Journal of the American Academy of Child and Adolescent Psychiatry, 35*, 334–342.

Tripp, G., Luk, S. L., Schaughency, E. A., & Singh, R. (1999). DSM-IV and ICD-10: A comparison of the correlates of ADHD to hyperkinetic disorder. *Journal of the American Academy of Child and Adolescent Psychiatry, 38*(2), 156–164.

Urman, R., Ickowicz, A., Fulford, P., & Tannock, R. (1995). An exaggerated cardiovascular response to methylphenidate in ADHD children with anxiety. *Journal of Child and Adolescent Psychopharmacology, 5*, 29–37.

Waldman, I. D., Rowe, D. C., Abramowitz, A., Kozel, S. T., Mohr, J. H., Sherman, S. L., Cleveland, H. H., Sanders, M. L., Gard, J. M., & Stever, C. (1998). Association and linkage of the dopamine transporter gene and attention-deficit hyperactivity disorder in children: Heterogeneity owing to diagnostic subtype and severity. *American Journal of Human Genetics, 63*, 1767–1776.

Willcutt, E. (1998). *A twin study of the validity of attention-deficit/hyperactivity disorder.* Unpublished doctoral dissertation, University of Denver.

Wolraich, M. L., Hannah, J. N., Pinnock, T. Y., Baumgaertel, A., & Brown, J. (1996). Comparison of diagnostic criteria for attention-deficit hyperactivity disorder in a county-wide sample. *Journal of the American Academy of Child and Adolescent Psychiatry, 35*, 319–324.

World Health Organization. (1992). *International statistical classification of diseases and related health problems* (10th rev.). Geneva, Switzerland: Author.

Chapter 2

The Diagnostic Classification, Epidemiology, and Cross-Cultural Validity of ADHD

Hector R. Bird, M.D.

Introduction 2-1
Changes in the Nosology and Effects on Rates 2-2
    Earlier Diagnostic Definitions 2-2
    Current Diagnostic Taxonomies 2-2
    Unresolved Classification Issues 2-3
Prevalence of the Disorder 2-3
Cross-Cultural Validity of the Construct 2-6
Presence of a Syndrome of Hyperkinesis/ADHD in Different Settings 2-8
Analysis of Epidemiological Data 2-9
    Risk Factors and Comorbidities 2-9
    Other Outcomes 2-11
Summary 2-12

INTRODUCTION

Although ideally we should have consensus definitions of disorders that are consistent across different taxonomies and over time, it is not uncommon to have alternative diagnostic criteria for a given diagnosis in different nosological systems, or even within different iterations of the same nosology (American Psychiatric Association, 1980, 1987, 1994; World Health Organization, 1978, 1992). Few psychiatric disorders have been as plagued by difficulties in arriving at a consensus definition as the syndrome of attentional deficits and hyperactivity, or attention deficit hyperactivity disorder (ADHD). A large variation in the prevalence of this syndrome has been observed in epidemiologic surveys carried out in recent years, much of it due to the constantly changing nosology and the ways in which the disorder is operationalized. Generally, rates are found to be higher when we use diagnostic criteria according to the *Diagnostic and Statistical Manual of Mental Disorders* (DSM; American Psychiatric Association, 1980, 1987, 1994) than when we employ the scheme according to the *International Statistical Classification of Diseases and Related Health Problems* (ICD; World Health Organization, 1978, 1992). Several explanations have been provided to explain this difference. One is the fact that ICD requires a single diagnosis in instances that DSM would consider comorbid, such as the ICD requirement that a primary diagnosis be given when conduct and hyperactivity features coexist (Danckaerts & Taylor, 1995). Moreover, the diagnostic criteria for hyperkinetic disorder in ICD-10 (World Health Organization, 1992), the most recent version, are the most restrictive so far due to the cross-situational requirement that full criteria for the disorder must be met in each of two or more settings in which the child is observed.

The changes that have occurred over the past two decades in the DSM system itself have also led to differences in the rates reported across different studies employing the DSM nosology over that span of time. The differences in operationalization seem to be more related to how the syndrome is constructed than to the diagnostic criteria themselves. Fortunately, all the taxonomies, including the different iterations of DSM and ICD, classify the syndrome using similar concepts of behavioral disturbance, with overactivity, inattention, and impulsivity being the hallmark features.

CHANGES IN THE NOSOLOGY AND EFFECTS ON RATES

Earlier Diagnostic Definitions

The evolution of the nosology has undergone seemingly minor, but important, changes over the past two decades that have a bearing on the prevalence rates obtained in different studies. To summarize, DSM-III (American Psychiatric Association, 1980) emphasized attentional deficit and impulsivity, providing two subcategories that depended on whether or not hyperactivity was present, so that the syndrome could be diagnosed even when hyperactivity was not present. DSM-III-R (American Psychiatric Association, 1987) included all three domains of symptomatology (inattention, hyperactivity, and impulsivity) under a single continuum. This was found to result in a widely heterogeneous grouping of children to whom the diagnosis could be applied, which many consider made DSM-III-R overly inclusive. ICD-9 (World Health Organization, 1978) emphasized hyperactivity and inattention, but impulsivity was given a secondary role.

Current Diagnostic Taxonomies

The two diagnostic taxonomies currently employed, ICD-10 (World Health Organization, 1992) and DSM-IV (American Psychiatric Association, 1994), have come close to a convergence in terms of the specific symptoms included, with the requirements for duration and developmental inappropriateness being identical. The two differ in the way the diagnosis is constructed. ICD-10 requires a minimum number of symptoms in each of the three dimensions. DSM-IV has established two, rather than three, sets of symptoms, with the symptoms of inattention and those of hyperactivity/impulsivity grouped separately to determine whether either inattention or hyperactivity/impulsivity predominate. Although the occurrence requirements for inattention are similar in both systems, those for hyperactivity and impulsivity differ. ICD-10 requires three of five hyperactivity and one of four impulsivity symptoms whereas DSM-IV requires a total of six out of nine hyperactivity/impulsivity symptoms. Thus, whereas the total symptom requirements for ICD-10 are lower in these two dimensions than in DSM-IV, even within the same sample, the prevalence of the

DSM-IV diagnosis is likely to be higher for other reasons. With DSM-IV, it is possible for a child to have the disorder when the criteria are met for only one of the two dimensions. This is not the case with ICD-10, which requires that the necessary number of criteria in each of the three dimensions be present for the diagnosis. Furthermore, although both ICD-10 and DSM-IV require that the behaviors produce cross-situational impairment, the ICD-10 pervasiveness requirement is more stringent in that full criteria must be met in at least two different situational contexts. ICD-10 also has depressive episode, manic episode, anxiety disorders and pervasive developmental disorders (PDD) as exclusionary diagnoses; that is, any child meeting diagnostic criteria for these other disorders cannot receive the diagnosis of hyperkinetic disorder.

Unresolved Classification Issues

From an epidemiological perspective, a further complication with evaluating the prevalence of the disorder is the fact that the behaviors under consideration are all variants of normative behaviors. The extent to which the behaviors are pathological depends on the frequency, severity, and degree to which they interfere with the child's functioning. Both ICD-10 and DSM-IV require that the symptom be present to a degree that is developmentally inappropriate, that it be persistent over at least six months, and that the symptoms occur "often." However, neither system operationalizes the frequency of "often," nor can one assume that when questioned about it, informants would be able to present the frequency of occurrence of each symptom with a great deal of precision. Although a clinician may not find it difficult to determine the presence or absence of what could be considered a symptom in terms of its frequency, pervasiveness, severity, and functional interference, it is difficult, if not impossible, to operationalize these factors in structured assessments that are employed for research purposes (Bird, 1996). We therefore have two major unresolved issues within both of the two classification systems that are employed to diagnose the syndrome of attentional deficits and hyperactivity/impulsivity: First is the difficulty in operationalizing both frequency and severity of the symptomatology; second, is the fact that the behaviors that characterize the syndrome tend to be distributed in the population on a continuum.

PREVALENCE OF THE DISORDER

The studies conducted in the United States over the past ten years using clinical diagnostic criteria (Table 2.1) show a prevalence of the disorder as defined by DSM-III (Cohen et al., 1993; Costello et al., 1988; Kashani et al., 1987) hovering around 2 to 3 percent. When DSM-III-R is employed, it ranges from a low of 1.9 percent in the Great Smoky Mountains Study (Costello et al., 1996; Costello, Farmer, Angold, Burns, & Erkanli, 1997) to a high of 15.1 percent in the Jensen et al. (1995) study of children of the U.S. military, with the aggregate of all DSM-III-R studies placing the prevalence in the vicinity of 3–6 percent.

Reports of studies in the international literature that have also used a categorical diagnostic construct of clinical criteria to ascertain the presence of the disorder (Table 2.2) show that DSM-III prevalence rates are somewhat higher in international studies

Table 2.1
Estimated Prevalence of DSM ADD/ADHD in U.S. Community Surveys Over the Past Ten Years

Study Site	Time Frame	Nosology	Ages (in years)	Prevalence of ADHD	
Missouri (Kashani et al., 1987)	current	DSM–III	14–16	2.0	
Pittsburgh (Costello et al., 1988)	past 12 months	DSM–III	7–11	2.2	
New York (Cohen et al., 1993)	past 6 months	DSM–III–R	9–19	4.3	
Oregon (Lewinsohn et al., 1993)	lifetime	DSM–III–R	High school	3.1	
			Boys	4.5	
			Girls	1.8	
U.S. Military in Washington, D.C. (Jensen et al., 1995)	past 6 months	DSM–III–R + impairment	6–17	Parent	11.9
				Child	0.8
				Combined	15.1
Midwest city, USA. (August et al., 1996)	current. (?)	DSM–III–R	Gr. 1–4	not reported est. 2.8	
MECA Study 3 U.S. sites & Puerto Rico (Shaffer et al., 1996)	past 6 months	DSM–III–R	9–17	6.4	
North Carolina (Costello et al., 1996, 1997)	past 3 months	CAPA/DSM–III–R	9–13	1.94	
			Native Amer.	1.2	
			White	1.9	

(Anderson, Williams, McGee, & Silva, 1987; Bird et al., 1988; McGee et al., 1990; Shen, Wang, & Xan, 1985) than those reported in the United States, with prevalences in the vicinity of 6 to 9 percent. DSM-III-R rates are more difficult to compare with

Table 2.2
Estimated Prevalence of ADD/ADHD/Hyperkinesis in Community Surveys Other Than U.S. Over the Past Fifteen Years

Study Site	Time Frame	Nosology	Ages (in years)	Prevalence of ADHD
Beijing, China (Shen, Wang, & Xan, 1985)	past 6 months	DSM-III	7–14	5.8
			Boys	10.0
			Girls	1.5
Dunedin, New Zealand (Anderson et al., 1987; McGee et al., 1990)	past 12 months	DSM-III	11	6.7
	past 12 months	DSM-III	15	2.1
Puerto Rico (Bird et al., 1988)	past 6 months	DSM-III + Impairment	4–16	9.5
Manheim, Germany (Esser, Schmidt & Woerner, 1990)	past 6 months	ICD-9	8	4.
East London, UK (Taylor et al., 1991)	current	ICD-10	7–8	1.7
Christchurch, NZ (Fergusson, Horwood, & Lynskey, 1993)	current	DSM-III-R	15	3.0 (parent) 2.8 (self)
Netherlands (Verhulst et al., 1997)	past 6 months	DSM-III-R	13–18	2.6

U.S. rates because the two reports available that used DSM-III-R (Fergusson, Horwood, & Lynskey, 1993; Verhulst, van der Ende, Ferdinand, & Kasius, 1997) included only adolescents, among whom the rates are expectably low (3 percent) because of the age group involved. The two studies employing the ICD classification (Esser, Schmidt, & Woerner, 1990; Taylor, Sandberg, Thorley, & Giles, 1991) show that ICD-10 yields the lowest rates.

Because the symptomatology of this disorder tends to occur on a continuum, a number of studies, both in the United States and in other countries, have determined prevalence employing rating scales which consist of listings of DSM symptoms (Baumgaertel, Wolraich, & Dietrich, 1995; Bhatia, Nigam, Botua, & Malik, 1991; Gallucci et al., 1993; Kanbayashi, Nakata, Fuji, Kita, & Wada, 1994; Leung et al., 1996; Offord et al., 1987; Pelham, Gnagy, Greenslade, & Milich, 1992; Szatmari, Offord, & Boyle, 1989; Wolraich, Hannah, Pinnock, Baumgaertel, & Brown, 1996; Wolraich, Feurer, Hannah, Baumgaertel, & Pinnock, 1998). Each investigator has established his or her own method to set threshold criteria, some using a strictly statistical definition and others using the thresholds as set forth by DSM. When rating scales are employed as the methodology to ascertain the presence of the disorder, rates appear to be higher than the rates obtained in the diagnosis-based studies (see, e.g., Bhatia et al., 1991; Table 2.3). Somewhat alarmingly high rates of ADHD seem to be evident in the two studies, one in the United States (Wolraich et al., 1996), and one in Germany (Baumgaertel et al., 1995) that have determined the prevalence of the disorder using DSM-IV criteria. Employing similar methods and definitions, both of the latter two studies have elicited all the criteria for DSM-III, DSM-III-R, and DSM-IV on the same subjects, thus enabling an unbiased comparison of the rates when different taxonomies are employed. They show that DSM-IV rates are considerably higher than DSM-III-R or DSM-III rates.

Despite the divergences noted in all these reports, most diagnostic studies using the criteria that are stipulated in the nosology show a prevalence that is under 10 percent and a better approximation would be that the expected prevalence of children suffering from this disorder during middle childhood should lie somewhere around 5 percent. Prevalence fluctuates depending on the gender and the age group studied, with a male and middle childhood predominance. There is no particular reason to anticipate that every cultural setting will necessarily have identical rates, because there might be reasons for the rate to be higher in one setting than another. Nevertheless, the wide discrepancies in prevalence observed in different studies carried out in different settings could well be a function of which diagnostic system is employed to classify the syndrome, the methods of ascertainment, and other methodological artifacts, rather than a reflection of actual cultural or contextual differences. The consensus among investigators seems to be that cross-national differences in rates of diagnosed hyperactivity are likely to reflect these diagnostic and methodological inconsistencies, rather than major differences in children's behavior in different settings (Holborow & Berry, 1986; Taylor & Sandberg, 1984). As has been previously observed (Prendergast et al., 1988), and as can be noted in Tables 2.1, 2.2, and 2.3, the lowest rates are obtained with the use of the ICD diagnostic classification of hyperkinetic syndrome and the highest rates, with the recent studies (Baumgaertel et al., 1995; Wolraich et al., 1996, 1998) that have employed DSM-IV criteria. Studies that used DSM-III and DSM-III-R obtained rates somewhere between these two extremes.

CROSS-CULTURAL VALIDITY OF THE CONSTRUCT

Differences or similarities in prevalence rates do not illuminate the issue of cross-cultural validity because it could be argued that searching in different settings for predetermined behaviors, which in their milder forms are normative behaviors, is bound to produce a certain proportion of individuals in each setting who meet the criteria for the disorder purely by chance. The question has therefore been raised as to whether

Table 2.3
Estimated Prevalence of Using Rating Scales Based on Symptoms in the DSM/ICD, ADD/ADHD/Hyperkinesis Categories

Study Site	Time Frame	Nosology	Ages (in years)	Prevalence of ADHD
Ontario, Canada (Offord et al., 1991; Szatmari, Offord, & Boyle, 1989)	past 6 months	DSM-III Sx	4–16 Boys 4–11 Girls 12–16	6.3 10.1 7.3
New Delhi, India (Bhatia, Nigam, Botua, & Malik, 1991)	current	DSM-III used Connors scale as proxy	Overall 3–4 11–12	11.2 5.2 29.0 (!)
Pittsburgh, PA (Pelham et al., 1992)	? current	DSM-III-R Sx (teachers)	boys in K–8th grade 7–8	7.1
Perugia, Italy (Gallucci et al., 1993)	past 6 months	DSM-III-R Sx (teachers)	8–10 M & F Boys	3.9
Ichikawa, Japan (Kanbayashi et al., 1994)	lifetime	DSM-III-R Sx (parents)	Children 4–12	7.7
Regensburg, Bavaria, Germany (Baumgaertel, Wolraich, & Dietrich, 1995)	past 6 months	DSM-III DSM-III-R DSM-IV	5-12	9.6 10.9 17.8
Hong Kong, China (Leung et al., 1996)	past 6 months	DSM-III DSM-III-R ICD-10	First-grade boys—age 7	6.1 8.9 0.78
Tennessee (Wolraich et al., 1996; Wolraich et al., 1998)	? current	DSM-III-R & DSM-IV Sx (teachers)	children in K–5th grade	7.3 DSM-III-R 11.4 DSM-IV 6.0 DSM-IV H/I & combined

the concept of childhood hyperactivity is a product of Western culture, and whether Western cultures are imposing their own notions of permissible or unacceptable behaviors on others (Anderson, 1996; Barkley, 1998). As noted previously, a similarity in rates, or even the fact that any rate is measurable at all, is not an argument for the disorder's cross-cultural validity.

When assessing a syndrome's validity and its applicability across cultures, a number of factors other than prevalence need to be considered. The first and foremost is whether experienced mental health professionals and clinicians in a given setting describe a condition in terms that are similar to the descriptions of problem children by their counterparts in other settings and whether they see this condition as deviant and producing psychological impairment in those suffering from it. In other words, does the syndrome have face validity as a psychopathological entity in the setting in which it is applied. For this information one must rely not only on the anecdotal reports of mental health professionals and on the collective clinical wisdom of these professionals in a given cultural setting but on the systematic gathering and analysis of epidemiological data derived from both clinical and community samples. Second, one must determine whether there is a coincidence across settings in the risk factors that relate to the syndrome; in other words, a consistency in the factors that might have etiological significance. A third consideration is whether other conditions that tend to co-occur with the syndrome also replicate across cultures. Fourth, one must ascertain whether there is a commonality in the outcomes described for the condition, including laboratory and other biological or neurophysiological data. A commonality of risk factors, comorbidities, and outcomes would provide strong support for the syndrome's validity. Finally, it would be important to investigate whether treatment response and outcome are similar when the condition is treated through similar means in different cultural settings.

PRESENCE OF A SYNDROME OF HYPERKINESIS/ADHD IN DIFFERENT SETTINGS

Evidence exists for the validity of the syndrome in different cultures from both an empirical and a clinical perspective. The investigators involved in the international studies cited in Tables 2.2 and 2.3 recognized the existence of the syndrome that they set out to measure. Some of these studies (Gallucci et al., 1993; Leung et al., 1996) have been prompted by anecdotal and clinical reports that have led the investigators to test whether the syndrome, as defined by the North American and European nosologies, exists in their local settings and if it does, how prevalent it is. The existence of the syndrome in different settings has been substantiated, but variations in the ratings of the behaviors and in the prevalence of ADHD have been documented and have been attributed to cultural differences among raters. For example, a study in Hong Kong (Ho et al., 1996) obtained rates of hyperactivity that were twice as high as those reported in other studies in the literature. The investigators attributed the higher rate to different thresholds of recognition and reporting; that is, a low tolerance by Chinese adults for hyperactive behaviors in children would lead them to set a lower threshold for the behaviors and therefore they would be more likely to report them. This interpretation seems to be confirmed by other reports. For example, in another study (Mann et al., 1992), standardized videotape vignettes of subjects participating in individual and group activities were rated by clinicians proceeding from different cultural backgrounds. Chinese and Indonesian clinicians gave significantly higher scores for hyperactive-disruptive behaviors than did their Japanese and American colleagues.

Such findings suggest that although different cultures conceptualize the ADHD syndrome as having similar characteristics, the threshold for deviance, both among clinicians, as well as among informants, may have strong cultural determinants, thereby producing an informant effect on both reporting and ascertainment that could have a bearing on the prevalence rates that are obtained and reported. Despite the cultural differences in how behaviors may be viewed across different cultures, the syndrome of inattention, overactivity, and impulsivity appears to have face validity and to be consistently described in different cultural settings by clinicians and investigators alike.

ANALYSIS OF EPIDEMIOLOGICAL DATA

Using factor-analytic as well as cluster and latent variable analyses, Western studies have confirmed that the hyperactive, impulsive, and inattentive behaviors characteristic of the disorder tend to co-occur as a coherent syndrome (Bauermeister, Alegria, Bird, Rubio-Stipec, & Canino, 1992; DuPaul, 1991; Fergusson, Harwood, & Lloyd, 1991; Healey et al., 1993; Lahey et al., 1988; Magnusson, Smari, Gretarsdottie, & Prandardottir, 1999; McGee, Williams & Silva, 1985; Yager, Bird, Staghezza-Jaramillo, Gould, & Canino, 1993). Notwithstanding variations in the rates at which specific behaviors are observed in different populations, and the variations in prevalence rates of the disorder across different settings, the syndrome of behaviors repeatedly shows high internal consistency and factor-analytic results across different settings. Results are similar across different cultural settings as disparate from each other as the United States, Italy, New Zealand, China, Japan, Germany, Brazil, and Puerto Rico (Table 2.4). These studies, as well as studies within the United States across different cultural and ethnic settings (Reid et al., 1998; Samuel et al., 1999), repeatedly reveal a syndrome that is internally consistent, breaks down into two main factors of inattention and hyperactivity/impulsivity, and appears to exist independent from other conditions (Trites & Laprade, 1983).

Risk Factors and Comorbidities

Several of the studies cited in Tables 2.1, 2.2, and 2.3, as well as other studies (Li, Su, Townes, & Varley, 1989; Wang, Chong, Chou, & Yang, 1993), show that the demographic risk factors of attention deficit disorders and hyperactive syndrome have a profile that is fairly consistent across different settings. The demographic findings all indicate that the disorder is predominantly a male disorder with male-to-female ratios in the range of 3:1 to 10:1. In epidemiological studies employing a categorical taxonomy, the prevalence of the disorder seems to peak in middle childhood and to occur more frequently in lower socioeconomic groups (Erlenmeyer-Kimling & Cornblatt, 1978). Although the pattern of demographic correlates of the disorder is highly consistent across studies, different epidemiological studies have also revealed associations to other risk factors that tend to repeat themselves across the studies that measure them. The risk factors most commonly associated have been other chronic illnesses, lower academic achievement and school failure, poor peer relations, and low

Table 2.4
Internal Consistency Reliability and Factor Structure in Selected Studies

Study Site	Scale Used	Dimension	Internal Consistency	Eigen Value
Worcester, MA (DuPaul, 1991)	Scale of DSM-III-R current symptoms	Total scale	.96	N.R.
		Inattentive/hyperactive	.95	
		Impulsive/hyperactive	.94	
Cities across U.S. (Pelham et al., 1992)	Scale of DSM-III-R symptoms	Total scale	.96	> 1
		Inattention	.95	> 1
		Overactivity/impulsivity	.95	
Puerto Rico (Bauermeister et al., 1992; Yager et al., 1993)	DSM-III symptoms	Total scale	.89	6.11
		Hyperactivity/impulsivity	.84	> 1
		Inattention	.93	> 1
Perugia, Italy (Gallucci et al., 1993)	Scale of DSM-III-R symptoms	Total score	.92	N.R.
New York (Healey et al., 1993)	DSM-III	Hyperactivity/Impulsivity	> .95	N.R.
		Inattention/Impulsivity	> .95	
	DSM-III-R	Hyperactivity/Impulsivity	> .95	
		Inattention	> .95	
Ichikawa, Japan (Kanbayashi et al., 1994)	Scale of DSM-III-R symptoms	Inattention	N.R.	> 1
		Hyperactivity/Impulsivity		> 1
		Verbosity		> 1
Brazil (Brito, Pinto & Lins, 1995)	Teacher scale based on DSM-III-R	Hyperactivity/Impulsivity	N.R.	6.52
		Inattention		1.35
Hong Kong, China (Ho et al., 1996)	Rutter P/T Q	Hyperactivity	.80 (P)	5.45 (P)
			.88 (T)	2.67 (T)
Tennessee (Wolraich et al., 1998)	Vanderbilt ADTRS (based on DSM-IV symptoms)	Hyperactivity/Impulsivity	.90	4.2
		Inattention	.92	4.9
		ODD/CD	.87	14.5
		Anxiety/Depression	.80	1.9

self-esteem. Strong and consistent patterns of comorbidity with other disruptive disorders have also been observed in different settings. In China (Leung et al., 1996; Ho et al., 1996), as well as in Western countries, the preexistence of the attentional deficit and hyperactive syndromes has been found to be a risk factor associated with the development of antisocial behaviors, conduct disorders, and delinquency in later childhood and adolescence.

Other Outcomes

A number of other outcomes are also similar across settings in studies that have measured them. These include cognitive and neurodevelopmental problems, soft neurological signs, lower scores on IQ testing, a history of motor and language delays, and delayed academic achievement, especially in reading and spelling. Certain neurobiological findings have been repeatedly associated with the attentional deficit syndrome in Western studies. These include inefficiency in the Continuous Performance Test (CPT) (Erlenmeyer-Kimling & Cornblatt, 1978; Halperin, Wolf, Greenblatt, & Young, 1991), significantly higher activity and inattentiveness levels in terms of actometer readings and direct observations of body movements and gaze (Sandberg. Rutter, & Taylor, 1978), more frequently reported histories of motor and language delays, and higher biological risk indices, including lower birthweights and complications during the neonatal and perinatal periods.

Some studies attempt to replicate neurobiological findings across different cultural settings as a way of demonstrating the generalizability of the syndrome. As an example, a major study of more than 3,000 Chinese schoolboys in Hong Kong (Leung et al., 1996) has provided an important contribution to the cross-cultural literature in this respect. In that study, criteria for ICD-10 hyperkinetic disorder, DSM-III attention deficit disorder with hyperactivity (ADDH), and DSM-III-R ADHD were ascertained. Through additional testing, children who met criteria for any or all of these three diagnostic constructs were confirmed to be significantly more active and inattentive by actometer readings and by direct, blind observations of body movement and gaze aversion. All three groups also demonstrated significant inefficiency on the CPT, an indicator of poor attention performance. The ADDH and ADHD diagnosed children in particular displayed significant deficiencies on cognitive measures and scored significantly worse on measures of academic performance and impulsivity. On neurological examination, all three groups had significantly more signs of "soft" neurological abnormalities, and the hyperkinetic and ADDH diagnosed children also had more frequently reported histories of motor and language delays. The hyperkinetic children had significantly greater exposure to biological risks as measured by a risk index that included possible complications of the neonatal period, such as prematurity/postmaturity and low/high birthweight. They differed significantly in this risk index from conduct-disordered and control children. Based on their study, Leung and his colleagues concluded that a disorder of hyperactivity exists in Chinese culture, displaying the same kinds of symptomatology and neurophysiological and other correlates that are described in Western cultures. They also found that the DSM-III and ICD-10 categories of ADDH and hyperkinetic disorder, respectively, were strongest in their association to known correlates and concluded that the DSM-III-R category of ADHD may be overinclusive.

To our knowledge, there are no comparative studies that assess treatment response simultaneously across different cultural groups. But treatment studies as well as anecdotal reports from clinicians in different settings report a favorable response to and a reduction of the target symptomatology through the use of psychostimulants and other psychopharmacological agents. Well-controlled comparative studies of treatment response in different cultural settings would be useful. Although the evidence for the cross-cultural validity of the syndrome is compelling, more studies, similar to the Leung et al. (1996) study in China, that look at other neurophysiological outcomes of the disorder in other cultural settings, would be useful.

SUMMARY

This chapter reviews a number of epidemiological studies carried out in child and adolescent populations in different cultural settings. It provides prevalence findings in different countries and cultural groups as well as information about the cross-cultural generalizability and validity of the syndrome of ADHD based on the results of studies carried out in widely disparate cultural settings.

Two types of studies are highlighted: those that are based on categorical nosological constructs (primarily DSM and ICD) and those that have employed continuous measures (primarily those using behavior items of DSM and ICD ratings). These studies, carried out in different cultural settings throughout the world, including the United States and Canada, Great Britain, several other countries in Western Europe, China, India, Brazil, Japan, Puerto Rico, and New Zealand, have found remarkable similarity in the construct of behaviors characteristic of the syndrome.

There are fluctuations across cultures in the reported rates of the disorder with prevalence rates ranging from less than 1 percent to over 20 percent, although a reasonable estimate of the prevalence of the disorder in the United States is approximately 4–5 percent. Although different rates might be expected in different settings, these wide differences may be more a function of which diagnostic system is employed to classify the syndrome, the methods of ascertainment, and other methodological artifacts than an actual manifestation of cultural differences. Despite what seems to be a convergence in diagnostic criteria, lowest rates are obtained with the ICD-10 diagnostic classification of hyperkinetic syndrome and highest rates with the DSM-IV classification of ADHD, primarily due to the dissimilarities in the way that the criteria are aggregated and to the pervasiveness requirements. Studies that used DSM-III and DSM-III-R obtained rates somewhere between these two extremes. Moreover, important variations have been noted in the ratings of the behaviors and in the prevalence of ADHD due to cultural differences among raters. Such findings suggest that although different cultures conceptualize the ADHD syndrome in similar ways, the threshold for deviance, both among clinicians and among other informants, may have strong cultural determinants, thereby producing an informant effect that could have a strong bearing on differences in rates.

Studies are cited which provide validation of the ADHD syndrome in different cultures from both a statistical and a clinical perspective. Despite variations in the rates at which specific behaviors occur in different populations, the overall syndrome repeatedly shows high internal consistency across different settings. When behavior questionnaires are subjected to factor-analytic procedures, the results are similar across different cultural settings as disparate as the United States, Japan, Italy, China, Germany, and Brazil. These analyses repeatedly show a syndrome that breaks down into two factors of inattention and hyperactivity/impulsivity. Further evidence for the cross-cultural validity of the syndrome is provided by a study of Chinese schoolboys in Hong Kong. The study replicates many of the neurobiological findings that have been associated with the attentional deficit syndrome in Western studies. These include inefficiency in the CPT, significantly higher activity and inattentiveness levels in terms of actometer readings, direct observations of body movements and gaze, more frequent reported histories of motor and language delays, and higher biological risk indices, including lower birth weights and complications during the neonatal period.

The consistency in the findings of multiple studies over the past fifteen years carried out in different cultural settings provides strong support for the cross-cultural validity of the syndrome of attentional deficits and hyperactivity as a clinical entity.

References

American Psychiatric Association. (1980). *Diagnostic and statistical manual of mental disorders* (3rd ed.). Washington, DC, Author.

American Psychiatric Association. (1987). *Diagnostic and statistical manual of mental disorders* (3rd ed., rev.). Washington, DC, Author.

American Psychiatric Association. (1994). *Diagnostic and statistical manual of mental disorders* (4th ed.). Washington, DC, Author.

Anderson J. (1996). Is childhood hyperactivity the product of western culture? *The Lancet, 348,* 73–74.

Anderson, J., Williams, S., McGee, R., & Silva, P. (1987). DSM-III disorders in pre-adolescent children. *Archives of General Psychiatry, 44,* 69–76.

August, G. J., Realmuto, G. M., MacDonald, A. W., Nugent, S. M., & Crosby, R. (1996). Prevalence of ADHD and comorbid disorders among elementary school children screened for disruptive behavior. *Journal of Abnormal Child Psychology, 24,* 571–595.

Barkley, R. A. (1998). The prevalence of ADHD, Is it just a U.S. disorder? *The ADHD Report, 6*(2), 1–6.

Bauermeister, J. J., Alegria, M., Bird, H. R., Rubio-Stipec, M., & Canino, G. (1992). Are attentional-hyperactivity deficits unidimensional or multidimensional syndromes?, Empirical findings from a community survey. *Journal of the American Academy of Child and Adolescent Psychiatry, 31*(3), 423–431.

Baumgaertel, A., Wolraich, M. L., & Dietrich, M. (1995). Comparison of diagnostic criteria for attention deficit disorders in a German elementary school sample. *Journal of the American Academy of Child and Adolescent Psychiatry, 34*(5), 629–638.

Bhatia, M. S., Nigam, V. R., Botua, N., & Malik, S. K. (1991). Attention deficit disorder with hyperactivity among pediatric outpatients. *Journal of Child Psychology and Psychiatry, 32,* 297–306.

Bird, H. (1996). Epidemiology of childhood disorders in a cross-cultural context. *Journal of Child Psychology and Psychiatry, 37*(1), 35–49.

Bird, H. R., Canino, G., Rubio-Stipec, M., Gould, M. S., Ribera, J., Sesman, M., Woodbury, M., Huertas, S., Pagan, A., Sanchez-Lacay, A., & Moscoso, M. (1988). Estimates of the prevalence of childhood maladjustment in a community survey in Puerto Rico. *Archives of General Psychiatry, 45,* 1120–1126.

Brito, G. N. (1987). The Conners' Abbreviated Teacher Rating Scale, a factor analysis study in Brazil. *Brazilian Journal of Medical and Biological Research, 20*(5), 553–556.

Brito, G. N., Pinto, R. C., & Lins, M. F. (1995). A behavioral assessment scale for attention deficit disorder in Brazilian children based on DSM-IIIR criteria. *Journal of Abnormal Child Psychology, 23*(4), 509–520.

Cohen, P., Cohen, J., Kasen, S., Velez, C. N., Hartmark, C., Johnson, J., Rojas, M., Brook, J., & Struening, E. L. (1993). An epidemiological study of disorders in late childhood and adolescence, I. Age and gender-specific prevalence. *Journal of Child Psychology and Psychiatry, 34*(6), 851–867.

Costello, E. J., Angold, A., Burns, B. J., Stangl, D. K., Tweed, D. L., Erkanli, A., & Worthman, C. M. (1996). The Great Smoky Mountains Study of Youth: Goals, design, methods, and the prevalence of DSM-III-R disorders. *Archives of General Psychiatry, 53*(12), 1129–1136.

Costello, E. J., Costello, A. J., Edelbrock, C., Burns, B. J., Dulcan, M. K., Brent, D., & Janiszewski, S. (1988). Psychiatric disorders in pediatric primary care. *Archives of General Psychiatry, 45,* 1107–1116.

Costello, E. J., Farmer, M. Z., Angold, A., Burns, B. J., & Erkanli, A. (1997). Psychiatric disorders among American Indian and white youth in Appalachia: The Great Smoky Mountains study. *American Journal of Public Health, 87*(5), 827–832.

Danckaerts, M., & Taylor, E. J. (1995). The epidemiology of childhood hyperactivity. In F. C. Verhulst & H. M. Koot (Eds.), *The epidemiology of child and adolescent psychopathology*. New York: Oxford University Press.

DuPaul, G. J. (1991). Parent & teacher ratings of ADHD symptoms: Psychometric properties in a community based sample. *Journal of Clinical Child Psychology, 20,* 242–253.

Erlenmeyer-Kimling, N., & Cornblatt, B. (1978). Attentional measures in a study of children at high-risk for schizophrenia. *Journal of Psychiatric Research, 14,* 93–98.

Esser, G., Schmidt, M. H., & Woerner, W. (1990). Epidemiology and course of psychiatric disorders in school age children. Results of a longitudinal study. *Journal of Child Psychology and Psychiatry, 31,* 243–263.

Fergusson, D. M., Harwood, C. J., & Lloyd, M. (1991). Confirmatory factor models of attention deficit and conduct disorder. *Journal of Child Psychology and Psychiatry, 32,* 257–274.

Fergusson, D. M., Horwood, L. J., & Lynskey, M. T. (1993). Prevalence and comorbidity of DSM-III-R diagnoses in a birth cohort of 15 year olds. *Journal of the American Academy of Child and Adolescent Psychiatry, 32,* 1127–1134.

Gallucci, F., Bird, H. R., Berardi, C., Gallai, V., Pfanner, P., & Weinberg, A. (1993). Symptoms of ADHD in an Italian school sample, findings of a pilot study. *Journal of the American Academy of Child and Adolescent Psychiatry, 32*(5), 1051–1058.

Halperin, J. M., Wolf, L. E., Greenblatt, E. R., & Young, J. G. (1991). Subtype analysis of commission errors on the continuous performance test in children. *Developmental Neuropsychology, 7,* 207–217.

Healey, J. M., Newcorn, J. H., Halperin, J. M., Wolf, L. E., Pascualvaca, D. M., Schmeidler, J., & O'Brien, J. D. (1993). The factor structure of ADHD items in DSM-III-R, internal consistency and external validation. *Journal of Abnormal Child Psychology, 21*(4), 441–453.

Ho, T. P., Leung, P. W., Luk, E. S., Taylor, E., Bacon-Shone, J., & Mak, F. L. (1996). Establishing the constructs of childhood behavioral disturbances in a Chinese population: A questionnaire study. *Journal of Abnormal Child Psychology, 24*(4), 417–431.

Holborow, P., & Berry, P. (1986). A multinational, cross-cultural perspective on hyperactivity. *American Journal of Orthopsychiatry, 56*(2), 320–322.

Jensen, P. S., Watanabe, H. K., Richters, J. E., Cortes, R., Roper, M., & Liu, S. (1995). Prevalence of mental disorder in military children and adolescents, Findings from a two-stage community survey. *Journal of the American Academy of Child and Adolescent Psychiatry, 34,* 1514–1524.

Kanbayashi, Y., Nakata, Y., Fujii, K., Kita, M., & Wada, K. (1994). ADHD-related behavior among non-referred children: Parents' ratings of DSM-III-R symptoms. *Child Psychiatry and Human Development, 25,* 13–29.

Kashani, J. H., Beck, N. C., Hoeper, E. W., Fallahi, C., Corcoran, M. A., McAllister, J. A., Rosenberg, T. K., & Reid, J. C. (1987). Psychiatric disorders in a community sample of adolescents. *American Journal of Psychiatry, 144,* 584–589.

Lahey, B. B., Pelham, W. E., Schaughency, E. A., Atkins, M. S., Murphy, H. A., Hynd, G., Russo, M., Hartdagen, S., & Lorys-Vernon, A. (1988). Dimensions and types of attention deficit disorder. *Journal of the American Academy of Child and Adolescent Psychiatry, 27*, 330–335.

Leung, P. W., Luk, S. L., Ho, T. P., Taylor, E., Mak, F. L., & Bacon-Shone, J. (1996). The diagnosis and prevalence of hyperactivity in Chinese schoolboys. *British Journal of Psychiatry, 168*(4), 486–496.

Lewinsohn, P. M., Hops, H., Roberts, R. E., Seeley, J. R., & Andrews, J. A. (1993). Adolescent psychopathology, I. Prevalence and incidence of depression and other DSM-III-R disorders in high school students. *Journal of Abnormal Psychology, 102*, 133–144.

Li, X. R., Su, L. Y., Townes, B. D., & Varley, C. K. (1989). Diagnosis of attention deficit disorder with hyperactivity in Chinese boys. *Journal of the American Academy of Child and Adolescent Psychiatry, 28*(4), 497–500.

Luk, S. L., Leung, P. W., & Lee, P. L. (1988). Conners' Teacher Rating Scale in Chinese children in Hong Kong. *Journal of Child Psychology and Psychiatry, 29*(2), 165–174.

Magnusson, P., Smari, J., Gretarsdottie, H., & Prandardottir, H. (1999). Attention-deficit/hyperactivity symptoms in Icelandic schoolchildren: Assessment with the attention deficit/hyperactivity rating scale IV. *Scandinavian Journal of Psychology, 40*(4), 301–306.

Mann, E. M., Ikeda, Y., Mueller, C. W., Takahashi, A., Tao, K. T., Humris, E., Li, B. L., & Chin, D. (1992). Cross-cultural differences in rating hyperactive-disruptive behaviors in children. *American Journal of Psychiatry, 149*(11), 1539–1542.

McGee, R., Feehan, M., Williams, S. M., Partridge, F., Silva, P. A., & Kelly, J. (1990). DSM-III disorders in a large sample of adolescents. *Journal of the American Academy of Child and Adolescent Psychiatry, 29*, 611–619.

McGee, R., Williams, S., & Silva, P. A. (1985). Factor structure and correlates of ratings of inattention, hyperactivity and antisocial behavior in a large sample of 9 year old children from the general population. *Journal of Consulting Child Psychology, 53*, 480–490.

Offord, D. R., Boyle, M. H., Szatmari, P., Rae-Grant, N. I., Links, P. S., Cadman, D. T., Byles, J. A., Crawford, J. W., Blum, H. M., Byrne, C., Thomas, H., & Woodward, C. A. (1987). Ontario child health study. II. Six-month prevalence of disorder and rates of service utilization. *Archives of General Psychiatry, 44*, 832–836.

Pelham, W. E., Gnagy, E. M., Greenslade, K. E., & Milich, R. (1992). Teacher ratings of DSM-IIIR symptoms for the disruptive behavior disorders. *Journal of the American Academy of Child and Adolescent Psychiatry, 31*, 210–218.

Prendergast, M., Taylor, E., Rapoport, J. L., Bartko, J., Donnelly, M., Zametkin, A., Ahearn, M. B., Dunn, G., & Wieselberg, H. M. (1988). The diagnosis of childhood hyperactivity: A U.S.-U.K. cross-national study of DSM-III and ICD-9. *Journal of Child Psychology and Psychiatry, 29*(3), 289–300.

Reid, R., DuPaul, G. J., Power, T. J., Anastopoulos, A. D., Rogers-Adkinson, D., Noll, M. B., & Riccio, C. (1998). Assessing culturally different students for attention deficit hyperactivity disorder using behavior rating scales. *Journal of Abnormal Child Psychology, 26*(3), 187–198.

Samuel, V. J., George, P., Thornell A., Curtis, S., Taylor, A., Brome, D., Mick, E., Faraone, S. V., & Biederman, J. (1999). A pilot controlled family study of DSM-III-R and DSM-IV ADHD in African-American children. *Journal of the American Academy of Child and Adolescent Psychiatry, 38*, 34–39.

Sandberg, S. T., Rutter, M., & Taylor, E. (1978). Hyperkinetic disorder in psychiatric clinic attenders. *Developmental Medicine and Child Neurology, 20*, 279–299.

Shaffer, D., Fisher, P., Dulcan, M. K., Davies, M., Piacentini, J., Schwab-Stone, M. E., Lahey, B. B., Bourdon, K., Jensen, P. S., Bird, H. R., Canino, G., & Regier, D. A. (1996). The NIMH diagnostic interview schedule for children version 2.3 (DISC-2.3): Description, acceptability, prevalence rates, and performance in the MECA study. *Journal of the American Academy of Child and Adolescent Psychiatry, 35*, 865–877.

Shen, Y. C., Wang, Y. F., & Xan, X. L. (1985). An epidemiological investigation of minimal brain dysfunction in six elementary schools in Beijing. *Journal of Child Psychology and Psychiatry, 26*, 777–788.

Szatmari, P., Offord, D. R., & Boyle, M. H. (1989). Ontario Child Health Study: Prevalence of attention deficit disorder with hyperactivity. *Journal of Child Psychology and Psychiatry, 30*, 219–230.

Taylor, E., & Sandberg, S. (1984). Hyperactive behavior in English schoolchildren: A questionnaire survey. *Journal of Abnormal Child Psychology, 12*(1), 143–155.

Taylor, E., Sandberg, S., Thorley, G., & Giles, S. (1991). The epidemiology of childhood hyperactivity. *Institute of Psychiatry, Maudsley Monographs* (No. 33). London: Oxford University Press.

Trites, R. L., & Laprade, K. (1983). Evidence for an independent syndrome of hyperactivity. *Journal of Child Psychology and Psychiatry, 24*(4), 573–586.

Verhulst, F. C., van der Ende, J., Ferdinand R. F., & Kasius, M. C. (1997). The prevalence of DSM-III-R diagnoses in a national sample of Dutch adolescents. *Archives of General Psychiatry, 54,* 329–336.

Wang, Y. C., Chong, M. Y., Chou, W. J., & Yang, J. L. (1993). Prevalence of attention deficit hyperactivity disorder in primary school children in Taiwan. *Journal Formosan Medical Association, 92*(2), 133–138 .

Wolraich, M. L., Feurer, I. D., Hannah, J. N., Baumgaertel, A., & Pinnock, T. Y. (1998). Obtaining systematic reports of disruptive behavior disorders utilizing DSM-IV. *Journal of Abnormal Child Psychology, 26*(2), 141–152.

Wolraich, M. L., Hannah, J. N., Pinnock, T. Y., Baumgaertel, A., & Brown, J. (1996). Comparison of diagnostic criteria for attention-deficit hyperactivity disorder in a county-wide sample. *Journal of the American Academy of Child and Adolescent Psychiatry, 35*, 319–324.

World Health Organization. (1978). *International classification of diseases* (9th rev.). Geneva, Switzerland: Author.

World Health Organization. (1992). *International statistical classification of diseases and related health problems* (10th rev.). Geneva, Switzerland: Author.

Yager, T., Bird, H. R., Staghezza-Jaramillo, B., Gould, M. S., & Canino, G. (1993). Symptom counts and diagnostic algorithms as measures of five common psychiatric disorders in children. *International Journal of Methods Psychiatric Research, 3*, 177–191.

Yao, K. N., Solanto, M. V., & Wender, E. H. (1988). Prevalence of hyperactivity among newly immigrated Chinese-American children. *Journal Developmental and Behavioral Pediatrics, 9*(6), 367–373.

Chapter 3

Is ADHD a Valid Disorder?

by William B. Carey, M.D.

Overview 3-1
The ADHD Diagnosis 3-2
    Increasingly Frequent Diagnosis 3-2
    Shortcomings of Diagnostic Criteria 3-3
An Area of Consensus 3-3
Major Diagnostic Problems 3-4
    ADHD Behaviors Not Clearly Distinguishable From
        Normal Temperament Variations 3-5
    Absence of Clear Evidence That ADHD Symptoms Are
        Related to Brain Malfunction 3-7
    Neglect of the Role of the Environment and Interactions
        With It as Factors in Etiology 3-8
    Diagnostic Questionnaires Now in Use Are Highly
        Subjective and Impressionistic 3-9
    Most Important Predisposing Factors May Be Low
        Adaptability and Cognitive Problems 3-10
    Lack of Evolutionary Perspective 3-12
    Small Practical Usefulness and Possible Harm From
        Label 3-12
    Widespread Misapplication of the Present ADHD
        Label 3-13
    Nonspecific Effects of Methylphenidate and Other
        Stimulants 3-14
Conclusion 3-14

OVERVIEW

Despite the general agreement on the existence of a small group of "hyperkinetic" children (1–2 percent of the population), there is considerable uncertainty about the diagnostic terminology of attention deficit hyperactivity disorder (ADHD) used to describe another 5–10 percent of children, who are the chief concern of this chapter. The abnormal ADHD behaviors of activity, inattentiveness, and impulsiveness are not clearly distinguishable from normal temperament variations. The assumption that the

ADHD symptoms arise from cerebral malfunction has not been supported even after extensive investigations. The current diagnostic system ignores the probable contributory role of the environment; the problem is supposedly all in the child. The questionnaires most commonly used to diagnose ADHD are highly subjective and impressionistic. The current view of ADHD fails to achieve the evolutionary perspective that the behaviors regarded as troublesome in the modern classroom may have had survival value in primitive times. The ADHD label, which is widely thought of as being beneficial, has little practical specificity and may become harmful. In addition to problems with the diagnosis itself, there are concerns about the loose way it is being applied and the widespread misinformation about the specificity of the effects of methylphenidate.

ADHD fails to meet the criteria for a mental disorder according to the *Diagnostic and Statistical Manual of Mental Disorders* (DSM). What is apparently being described in most cases now is normal behavioral variations of inattention and activity that, accompanied by low adaptability and/or cognitive disabilities, sometimes lead to dysfunction through dissonant environmental interactions. A DSM disorder should be defined in terms of the dysfunction itself, such as problems in social relationships or school achievement, rather than in terms of risk factors like activity. Brain malfunction should be diagnosed only when there is objective evidence of it. Problems in attention deserve a much more sophisticated analysis. This situation calls for a paradigm shift, a different way of looking at this area of children's problems.

THE ADHD DIAGNOSIS

Increasingly Frequent Diagnosis

The diagnosis of ADHD is being made with ever increasing frequency. The label is confidently being attached to children by their parents, their child-care workers, over the telephone by professionals, and in a number of other alarming ways. Methylphenidate prescriptions have increased enormously. Although there is some dispute as to the exact figures (Safer, Zito, & Fine, 1996), there is no question that the usage of the drug in the United States has increased severalfold in the last decade, making this country the world leader in its consumption by a wide margin (United Nations International Narcotics Control Board, 1995).

Medical, psychological, and educational professional organizations have expressed little concern about this epidemic. For example, the Council on Scientific Affairs of the American Medical Association (AMA) concluded recently that "there is little evidence of widespread over-diagnosis or misdiagnosis of ADHD or of widespread over-prescription of methylphenidate by physicians" (Goldman, Genel, Bezman, & Slanetz, 1998, p. 1100) but this opinion was derived from a library review of papers already published without collecting any fresh, impartial, and more competent data.

The reasons for this great increase in diagnosis and treatment are undoubtedly complex and diverse, but a full exploration of these reasons would go beyond the scope of this chapter. The most comprehensive and reliable review of the problem is presented in the recently published book *Running on Ritalin,* by Lawrence Diller (1998). Certainly great social pressures by parents and teachers on physicians and psychologists have been a major factor in finding the fault within the child.

Shortcomings of Diagnostic Criteria

This chapter focuses on the shortcomings in the basic construction of the diagnostic criteria of the disorder of ADHD, which are probably the main source of the current confusion. Although the recently revised fourth edition of *Diagnostic and Statistical Manual of* Mental Disorders (DSM-IV; American Psychiatric Association, 1994) has made the standards a bit clearer, the criteria still allow for the lumping together of a diverse collection of normal variations of temperament, problems in cognition, environmental dissonances, behavioral adjustment issues, and sometimes neurological immaturities under one vague, all-encompassing label. Substantial problems are evident in (1) the pathologization of normal temperament variations; (2) the continuing failure to demonstrate a neurological basis for the diagnosis; (3) the neglect of the participation of the environment in the clinical disorder; (4) the use of highly impressionistic and subjective questionnaires for diagnosis; (5) the likelihood that the most common predisposition in children now receiving this diagnosis is low adaptability, rather than inattention or high activity, and also problems in cognition; (6) the lack of an evolutionary perspective; and (7) the questionable value and possible harm of the label. Two additional troublesome problems are (8) the widespread failure to apply the diagnosis correctly at the practical level and (9) the common misperception of the specificity of methylphenidate for ADHD.

The diagnostic criteria for ADHD are officially set forth in DSM-IV. The child must have six or more of the nine inattention symptoms or six or more of the nine hyperactivity/impulsivity symptoms present "for at least six months to a degree that is maladaptive and inconsistent with developmental level." Some of the symptoms must have been present in the child before the age of 7. Some impairment must be present in two or more settings, in social, academic, or occupational functioning. "The symptoms do not occur exclusively during the course of Pervasive Developmental Disorder, Schizophrenia, or other Psychotic Disorder and are not better accounted for by another mental disorder . . ." (American Psychiatric Association, 1994, p. 78).

DSM-IV presents itself as purely descriptive without attempting to assign causes for the various conditions defined. (This may be regarded by some as a strength of the system, but it is probably also a great weakness.) For that reason, DSM-IV does not offer any explanation of where this set of ADHD behaviors comes from. Nevertheless, articles in journals and textbooks and reviews of the subject (Barkley, 1990; Cantwell, 1996; Tannock, 1998) have not hesitated to enlarge on this basic definition with several additional assumptions. These suppositions include the notions that the ADHD behaviors are abnormal and clearly distinguishable from normal, the condition constitutes a neurodevelopmental disability, it is relatively uninfluenced by the environment, and yet it can be adequately diagnosed by brief questionnaires. All these postulates, and some others, must be challenged because of the weakness of the empirical support and the strength of the contrary evidence, as this chapter will indicate.

AN AREA OF CONSENSUS

There does seem to be a general agreement on the existence of a small group of readily recognizable children with "hyperkinetic disorder," as defined more conservatively and rather briefly by the tenth edition of *International Statistical Classification of Diseases and Related Health Problems* (ICD-10; World Health Organization, 1992):

> A group of disorders characterized by an early onset (usually in the first five years of life), lack of persistence in activities that require cognitive involvement, and a tendency to move from one activity to another without completing one, together with disorganized, ill-regulated, and excessive activity. Several other abnormalities may be associated . . . often reckless and impulsive . . . in disciplinary trouble because of unthinking breaches of rules . . . unpopular with other children. . . . Impairment of cognitive functions is common and specific delays in motor and language development are disproportionately frequent. . . . (p. 378)

Studies in the United Kingdom of children so defined have revealed a prevalence of 1–2 percent of the primary school boys:

> The typical abnormalities found in school-age children are reduced verbal and performance IQ, immature articulation of speech, a history of language delay in earlier development, poor motor coordination in skilled tasks with marked overflow movements from one side of the body to the other, and impersistence in sustained acts. Such abnormalities have not generally been found in studies of children with ADHD. It is not yet possible to go further and assert that neurodevelopmental immaturity is the cause of hyperactive behavior. (Taylor, 1994, p. 294)

In fact, it is not clear whether the symptoms come primarily from abnormal brains or adverse environments. These children have been found to have a relatively high rate of positive response to methylphenidate (Rutter, 1997). For them, the disorganized high activity and broadly pervasive impersistence are clearly problems themselves in virtually all settings whether or not there are secondary dysfunctions in social or academic performance due to unfavorable interactions.

These children would certainly be given a diagnosis of ADHD in North America, but so also would a large number of others for whom the criteria are less well defined, ranging from 3–15 percent or more depending on whose estimate is used. The discussion that follows is concerned with the DSM-IV diagnostic system as presently used to identify these many other children as having ADHD. Nine major problems require consideration.

MAJOR DIAGNOSTIC PROBLEMS

For thirty-three years of my career I was in primary care pediatrics practice, observing the development and behavior of two generations of a great variety of children growing up in diverse circumstances. I have been impressed with the broad range of normal behavior and distressed by the ease with which some mental health professionals have ascribed abnormality to some of it. During the last thirty years, my chief research interest has been in normal temperament differences: how to measure them, how they matter clinically, how they differ from behavioral adjustment problems, and how to manage them better to prevent or treat such secondary behavior problems arising from dissonant child-environment interactions. My concern with the problem of ADHD was sparked by the abundant evidence that behavioral scientists and practitioners have, in distressing numbers, failed to recognize the existence and importance of temperament variations. Common patterns in professional thinking have been to ignore, trivialize, or pathologize temperament. DSM-IV does not even mention it. Thus, I have several concerns with the diagnosis of ADHD.

ADHD Behaviors Not Clearly Distinguishable From Normal Temperament Variations

The DSM-IV criteria for ADHD and the accompanying journal and textbook literature define the inattention and high-activity behaviors as abnormal and easily differentiated from normal, using "cutpoints" in the numbers of symptoms. As mentioned earlier, if the child displays six of the nine inattention or six of the nine hyperactivity/impulsivity behaviors and the other conditions are met, the child earns the diagnosis of ADHD. Typical items in the two categories are "is often forgetful in daily activities" and "often talks excessively." (We are not told what is meant by "often" or who decides what constitutes "excessively.") If only five descriptions apply, the child does not have ADHD; if six apply, the child has the neurodevelopmental disorder. Thus, what makes these behaviors into a disorder is less the intrinsic properties of the items themselves or their interactions with caregivers than the accumulation of them to or beyond the "cutpoint" level of six. Available reports of the establishment of these cutpoints make it clear that it was a decision by a committee, which seems to have determined arbitrarily the levels at which normal amounts of high activity and inattentiveness leave off and abnormal amounts begin. Several observers have questioned the soundness of this subjective approach (Achenbach, Howell, McConaughy, & Stanger, 1995; Levy, Hay, McStephen, Wood, & Waldman, 1997).

The principal problem with this technique is the fact that these behaviors are probably from various sources, in particular normal temperament variations. What makes them clinically important is not necessarily the number of them present but, rather, an abrasive interaction of any number of them with expectations and responses of the environment. The resulting "poor fit" and interactional stress lead to reactive behavioral and functional problems. The large and growing body of research concerning children's temperaments and their clinical significance puts these matters in a perspective that has not been absorbed by the DSM diagnostic system. The pioneering work of Chess and Thomas (1996), as supported by the studies of many others (e.g., Carey & McDevitt, 1995, pp. 117–127), has established the view that although pathology in the environment, the child, or both can be responsible for malfunction in the child, there are many occasions when the pathogenic influence is to be found primarily in a dissonant interaction between a normal child and a normal but incompatible environment.

All humans have a set of largely congenital temperament traits, which have most commonly been defined as activity, regularity, initial approach or withdrawal in novel situations, adaptability, intensity of reactions, prevalent mood, persistence and attention span, distractibility, and sensory threshold. All nine traits vary from high to low in the general population: from high to low activity, from high to low adaptability, from high to low sensory threshold, and so on. All these variations at all levels are considered to be normal in themselves. Therefore, by definition half the population is more active than average and half the population is less attentive than average without any implication of abnormality (Thomas & Chess, 1977).

Certain temperament traits are particularly likely to induce a "poor fit" and interactional stress with the values and expectations of the caretakers. Children with the "difficult" temperament cluster (low adaptability, negative mood, high intensity, etc.) are more likely to develop social behavior problems, as demonstrated initially by Thomas, Chess, and Birch (1968) and by many others since then. Those with the "low task orientation" cluster (high activity, low persistence/attention span, and high distractibility) are more liable to do poorly in academic achievement, as shown by Keogh (1989) and Martin (1989). In fact, any temperament trait, as a risk factor, may set up such a dissonant relationship with a particular environment (e.g., an inactive child in an athletic family that prizes and expects high activity).

These temperamental predispositions to social and academic dysfunction, however, do not, even in their extremes, inevitably result in problems. Children who are highly "difficult" may be well adjusted behaviorally, even though a challenge to manage, if the family and other circumstances are supportive (Maziade, 1989). Those with the "low task orientation" cluster of high activity, low persistence/attention span, and high distractibility may do satisfactorily or even well at school provided there are enough favorable factors, such as a supportive family or high intelligence and absence of learning disabilities in the child (Kanbayashi, Nakata, Fujii, Mita, & Wada, 1994). In fact, one cross-sectional study demonstrated that only half of those with extreme amounts of high activity, low attention span, and high distractibility were having problems in school, whereas the other half were doing acceptably or even well (Carey & McDevitt, 1995, p. 151). What appears to matter for the generation of dysfunction in the child is not the number of normal yet challenging temperament traits but, rather, the "goodness of fit" between any number of potentially aversive traits and the particular requirements of the environment.

One of the problems contributing to the lack of diagnostic clarity in the present DSM formulation has undoubtedly been the study methods used. Investigations based on referred samples suffer from the self-selection of subjects. If one sees the high activity and low attention span only in clinical referrals, one could easily fail to appreciate the frequency with which these traits occur also in normal children. A comparison of fourteen children with pervasive hyperactive behavior who were referred with a comparable group of thirteen who were equally hyperactive but not referred showed that the "best predictors of clinical referral were a parent's ability to cope with child behavior, child emotional disturbance, school relationship problems, and parental disciplinary indulgence" (Woodward, Dowdney, & Taylor, 1997, p. 479). Cross-sectional studies should be able to avoid this selection bias. Yet, they have typically failed to provide clarity for other reasons, such as when they have assumed that normally functioning children with high activity and low attention span are underdiagnosed with ADHD rather than simply normal (Wolraich, Hannah, Baumgaertel, & Feurer, 1998).

To summarize, the current ADHD formulation, which makes the diagnosis when a certain number of troublesome behaviors are present (and other criteria met), overlooks the fact that these behaviors are probably usually normal but potentially aversive temperament traits that lead to dysfunction not by their total numbers but when any number of them generates dissonant interactions between the child and his or her incompatible setting. This use of cutpoints has not been validated.

Absence of Clear Evidence That ADHD Symptoms Are Related to Brain Malfunction

DSM-IV does not say so but virtually all articles in the professional journals and textbooks assume that the ADHD behaviors of high activity and low attention span are largely or entirely due to abnormal brain function. For example, "ADHD is now recognized as the most common neurobehavioral disorder of childhood . . ." (Shaywitz, Fletcher, & Shaywitz, 1995, p. S52). The most plausible explanation of this attribution lies in the ancestral origins of the concept of ADHD in the now discarded terms of minimal brain damage and minimal brain dysfunction. The term now used, "ADHD," no longer explicitly announces a damaged or dysfunctional brain, but the implicit assumption apparently continues in the minds of most of its users. But do the data support this presumption? Some preliminary brain imaging studies have shown inconsistent differences in children with the ADHD diagnosis, but there is no proof that they are deviations. Most recent speculations conclude that "frontal-striatal networks may be involved in ADHD" (Tannock, 1998, p. 83).

Several lines of evidence oppose this supposed neurological link for ADHD:

1. We do know that various brain insults like lead poisoning, fetal alcohol syndrome, low birthweight, and traumatic brain injury may be associated with increased activity and decreased attention span (e.g., Max et al., 1998). However, no consistent pattern of high activity or inattention is seen in children with established brain injury, as demonstrated by Hertzig (1983) and Rutter (1983b).

2. No consistent structural, functional, or chemical neurological marker is found in children with the ADHD diagnosis as currently formulated (see reviews by Peterson, 1995; Zametkin, Ernst, & Silver, 1998). Reports of suspected associations will be obliged to clarify to which aspect of the poorly defined syndrome the findings are related. Also needed are some clear indications as to what is cause, what is consequence, and what is coincidence. Furthermore, distinctions are necessary between what is inborn and what is acquired after birth.

3. Differences in brain function, on the other hand, have been demonstrated in healthy children with normal temperamental variations. For example, in a sample of forty-eight 4-year-old children studied with electroencephalograms, those "who displayed social competence (high degree of social initiations and positive affect) exhibited greater relative left frontal activation, while children who displayed social withdrawal (isolated, onlooking, and unoccupied behavior) during the play session exhibited greater right frontal activation" (Fox et al., 1995, p. 1770). Therefore, in the future when any consistent test differences are demonstrated with children given the ADHD diagnosis, proof will be required that those differences are related to the social or scholastic dysfunction itself and not just to a nonpathological temperamental or other predisposition. Controls must be selected with greater care.

4. Evidence of a genetic basis for the current diagnosis of ADHD (Sherman, Iacono, & McGue, 1997) cannot be taken as providing proof of an underlying brain abnormality. The data of a large twin study suggest that the behavior ascribed to ADHD "varies genetically throughout the entire population rather than as a disorder with discrete determinants" (Levy et al., 1997, p. 737). Furthermore, there is strong evidence of a substantial genetic contribution to variations of temperament (Plomin, Owen, & McGuffin, 1994) and coping strategies (Mellins, Gatz, & Baker, 1996), which occur both with and without accompanying social and scholastic dysfunction.

One wonders why the belief in the solely neurological basis of ADHD is so persistent and strong in the face of such a continuing lack of supportive evidence. Perhaps it truly exists and has simply eluded our present diagnostic techniques. On the other hand, it appears that there may be some powerful social reasons why professional persons and parents, especially in the United States, want to believe that the ADHD behaviors can be attributed to a faulty nervous system in the child—reasons such as parental guilt and avoidance of responsibility, trouble meeting requirements for flexibility by the school system, and simplifying medical theory and practice. Readers are referred elsewhere for more extensive explorations of these factors (see descriptions by Diller, 1998; Reid, Maag, & Vasa, 1993).

To summarize, the behaviors associated with ADHD are almost universally assumed to be the result of some sort of brain malfunction. However, in spite of diligent efforts by many talented researchers, no consistent evidence of pathological brain changes has been uncovered. If these behaviors are usually normal behavioral variations, it seems likely that pathology of the brain will seldom be found.

Neglect of the Role of the Environment and Interactions With It as Factors in Etiology

As psychological theory escaped from the excessive environmentalism that peaked in the 1950s ("It's all mom's fault."), many observers assumed that we were moving into an enlightened period of interactionism in which neither nature nor nurture is dominant but are intertwined from before birth and through life. However, the DSM-IV criteria for ADHD describe only the behaviors in the child and specify that the child be having problems at home, at school, or elsewhere. Nowhere is there any requirement that there be consideration of the quality of the environment and of the child's interaction with it. The assumption that the problem is coming entirely from the child's faulty brain seems to have eliminated or greatly reduced the evaluation of the caregiving the child has been receiving. This biased view has deterred progress toward an improved understanding of children now receiving the ADHD diagnosis and toward evaluating better ways of helping individual children in their particular situations.

The whole body of the temperament research of the last thirty years, however, is in agreement that what matters for clinical outcome is not the sometimes aversive behavioral predispositions alone but, rather, the way in which they do or do not fit with the child's particular setting. Something else is needed in addition to the normal predisposition for the creation of a clinical disorder. The outcome of children with "difficult" temperament depends on whether the parents and other essential elements of the environment provide a harmonious fit or one that generates excessive conflict and stress, as described by Maziade (1994) and Chess and Thomas (1984). For example, a sample of highly active children from the Puerto Rican subculture of New York City were not dysfunctional and were not regarded as such by their parents until they entered the more restrictive milieu of the public school system. What becomes of a school child with the "low task orientation" cluster of high activity, low attention span, and high distractibility will be determined by the qualities of the parents and teachers and other assets or liabilities in the child like adaptability and motivation (Levine, 1994).

Only a small component of the ADHD research has explored the impact of the environment. One line has investigated how the social adversity of institutional upbringing is associated with inattentive and impulsive behavior (Tizard & Hodges, 1978). Also, "adversity in close personal relationships has a robust association with hyperactive behavior" (Taylor, 1994, p. 298). "Chronic conflict, decreased family cohesion, and exposure to family psychopathology, particularly maternal psychopathology, were common in ADHD families compared with control families" (Biederman et al., 1995, p. 1498). More severe forms of ADHD are associated with psychosocial adversity (Scahill et al., 1999, p. 976). Furthermore, as previously noted, whatever may be the origins of the behaviors regarded as ADHD, the nature of the caregiving environment determines which children are more likely to be referred for therapeutic intervention.

In brief, despite the absence of a requirement by DSM-IV to consider the environment in the diagnosis and despite the widespread assumption that ADHD is all in the child's brain, there is strong evidence that the environment matters for the outcome of the children with this label as much as in other areas of behavioral and emotional adjustment.

Diagnostic Questionnaires Now in Use Are Highly Subjective and Impressionistic

It would be difficult to present a detailed and accurate survey of just how physicians, psychologists, and teachers actually arrive at the diagnosis of ADHD in their patients, clients, or students at present. DSM-IV merely describes the condition and its criteria, reports that there are no reliable diagnostic physical or laboratory tests, and leaves the practitioner to his or her own devices to determine the presence or absence of the disorder. Given this latitude, most professional and laypersons have probably chosen the simplest and most readily available methods. Extensive conversations with many fellow pediatricians yield the impression that most primary care physicians either conduct an abbreviated informal interview based loosely on DSM-IV criteria or use one of the questionnaires designed specifically for the purpose of diagnosing ADHD. The best known of these are the Conners Parent Rating Scale—Revised, the Conners Teacher Rating Scale—Revised, the Conners Abbreviated Parent-Teacher Questionnaire, and the ADD-H Comprehensive Teacher's Rating Scale (ACTeRS), all of which can be completed in a few minutes. Apparently in this simple manner the presence of the neurodevelopmental disorder of ADHD is currently being assessed by the majority of primary care and perhaps also consultant professionals (Angold, Erkanli, Egger, & Costello, 2000; Wasserman et al., 1999).

Despite the widespread and uncritical use of these diagnostic scales and their reports of standardization with various populations, they all have major methodological problems. Although there are claims to the contrary (see review by Barkley, 1990), the scales cannot be regarded as having adequately met necessary psychometric criteria. They consist of as few as ten defining items. These items are phrased in highly impressionistic and subjective terms, such as "talks too much," "fidgets," and "messy work." The rater is not advised as to how much is too much, how much motion and how often under what circumstances constitutes fidgetiness, and so on. The rating options are as to frequency of the specific behavior, typically ranging from never to sometimes to often. The decision as to what constitutes "often" or "excessive" is left to the parent or teacher. Thus, these questionnaires place on the parents and teachers much of the responsibility not only for reporting on the behavior itself but also for making clinical judgments as to whether it is normal or excessive. If the parent or teacher believes that the child is overactive or insufficiently attentive, the questionnaire establishes it for certain with the assumption of objectivity. Variations in experience, tolerance, emotional status (e.g., depression), or other qualifications of the parents or teachers are not allowed for in any way. These questionnaires may be more a measure of the discomfort of the parent or teacher than of a disability in the child. Yet, despite this considerable vagueness, proponents claim that the scales make an accurate all-or-nothing diagnosis of the neurodevelopmental disorder of ADHD.

The psychometric problems of the questionnaires have led to several undesirable consequences. In the first place, the convergence between results from the different scales used for the diagnosis is unsatisfactorily low (Bussing, Schuhmann, Belin, Widawski, & Perwien, 1998), leading to the question as to which may be the most accurate method. Other problems include poor interrater reliability, overdiagnosis, misdiagnosis, and inclusion of "comorbid" problems. This lack of precision has encouraged the development of various unvalidated techniques such as the Continuous Performance Test and electroencephalograms (Kuperman, Johnson, Arndt, Lindgren, & Wolraich, 1996), which claim to provide a clearer answer.

As Reid and Maag (1994) put it:

> Because behavior rating scales have a patina of objectivity, practitioners may be misled into accepting the scores they ascertain as being indicative of ADHD. However, as we have noted, a rating scale diagnosis may be no more accurate than a flip of a coin in some instances . . . they are no substitute for informed professional judgment . . . there is simply no unerring standard for diagnosing ADHD. (p. 350)

In summary, several brief questionnaires are currently used clinically to diagnose ADHD, but they are highly subjective and impressionistic and should be regarded as no more than the perceptions and discomforts of parents and teachers, which are not as reliable as clinical interviewing and observations and are insufficient for diagnosis of brain malfunction.

Most Important Predisposing Factors May Be Low Adaptability and Cognitive Problems

The DSM-IV diagnosis states that the defining traits of ADHD are inattention and hyperactivity/impulsivity and that there must be some impairment of function in two or more settings. DSM-IV also lists a broad range of "associated features and disorders." Among them are "low frustration tolerance, temper outbursts, bossiness, stubbornness, excessive and frequent insistence that requests be met, mood lability, demoralization, dysphoria, rejection by peers, and poor self-esteem" (p. 80). The list goes on, but DSM-IV asserts that the inattention and high activity are the disorder itself, not just a predisposition to problems.

Evidence is accumulating about the children currently identified as having behavioral and academic problems attributed to ADHD that factors other than the inattention and activity may be more potent predispositions to their disorders. The data point both to different behavioral traits and to the typical presence of cognitive disabilities.

The more likely behavioral predisposition has been variously described but has generally centered around the dimension of low adaptability or flexibility. In an early study of sixty-one children referred by teachers to a pediatric neurologist for problems in behavior and learning at school, those diagnosed with minimal brain dysfunction (MBD) (this was 1979) were rated by their parents on the Behavioral Style Questionnaire as significantly more active and inattentive than controls, but the trait defining most strongly both the whole referred group of sixty-one and the thirty given the MBD label was low adaptability (Carey, McDevitt, & Baker, 1979). In standardizing a new teacher questionnaire for preschool children, Billman and McDevitt (1998) found a .80 correlation between items defining low adaptability and those fulfilling the criteria for ADHD-primarily hyperactive-impulsive type. Other observers have come to similar conclusions, such as "limited ability to modify their behavior according to the needs and demands of the situation" (Rutter, 1983a, p. 267), "the problem rather is to do with the way that children regulate their responsiveness" (Taylor, 1994, p. 293), and "a failure in self-control" (Barkley, 1998, p. 66).

How did it happen that this more significant behavioral predisposition was not identified correctly at an earlier time? Possibly an element in this delay has been a lack of familiarity among the framers of DSM-IV with the strong evidence of the importance of children's temperament, and in particular with the trait of adaptability, for their social and academic adjustment. Another factor in the confusion may have been that adaptability was actually being indirectly measured when assessing activity and inattention. In a review of the standardization sample of the Behavioral Style Questionnaire (McDevitt & Carey, 1978) for 3–7-year-old children, there is a significant relationship between high activity and low adaptability (chi square = 18.45, $p <$ .001). Similarly low persistence/attention span is correlated significantly with low adaptability (chi square = 10.39; $p < .01$) (Carey, 1998). A direct measurement of the more significant trait of adaptability would seem to be the preferred course.

The other major predisposition to behavioral and scholastic problems that is not recognized in the definition of ADHD is cognitive disabilities. Levine (1999) has described in detail the "heterogeneity of manifestations and associated dysfunctions encountered among children with attentional difficulty . . . that impede organized and goal-directed attention during the school years" (p. 499). Denckla (1996) identifies encoding processes such as working memory as prominent among them. Attempting to make the diagnosis of ADHD without an adequate psychological assessment runs the risk of overlooking these important factors.

Thus, one must question the DSM claim that inattention and high activity are the disorder of ADHD itself or at least the principal risk factors for it. Low adaptability, which is usually a normal variation, and cognitive disabilities, which are a problem for all, are increasingly recognized as the outstanding etiological factors in children presently receiving this diagnosis.

Lack of Evolutionary Perspective

DSM-IV and the current general climate of professional opinion state or imply strongly that children who seem too active or insufficiently attentive in school have something wrong with their brains. Because schools are a traditional and powerful instrument of education and socialization, only abnormal individuals would not fit easily into their requirements for performance, or so the argument goes:

> Would it not be fairer to acknowledge that our bodies and minds, which presumably evolved over many millennia of hunting and gathering on the savannas of Africa, may not yet have evolved beyond the requirements of the Stone Age and become adapted to the highly artificial environment of the modern school? Short attention spans and high activity may have been highly adaptive and served our ancestors well, promoting survival in a world full of predators. (Carey & McDevitt, 1995, p. 152)

Our modern schools are, after all, an innovation of at most the last 400 years and for the general population only about 100 years:

> The "response-ready" individual would likely have been advantaged under the brutal or harsh circumstances of the frozen steppe or humid jungle, whereas the excessively contemplative, more phlegmatic individual would have been "environmentally challenged." . . . As society has become increasingly industrialized and organized, "response-ready" characteristics may have become less adaptive. . . . (Jensen et al., 1997, p. 1674–1675)

Thus, the assumption of brain malfunction in inattentive, active school children suffers from too narrow an evolutionary and anthropological perspective of what is normal in human brain function.

Small Practical Usefulness and Possible Harm From Label

The professional and popular literatures report the gratitude that many people feel about having the ADHD label applied to their children or to themselves. Many believe that it represents a major step forward in mental health practice to relieve these individuals and their caregivers of any feelings of guilt that they may have willfully created their problems in living. Affixing the label to the child validates the parents' reports that the child functions differently and that the aberrant behavior is not due to failures in their parenting. Schools understandably welcome the formal recognition of the child as the source of the behavioral or academic problems. The diagnosis of a neurodevelopmental disorder helps the school to obtain funding for resources for special education. The certification of a medical disorder facilitates the use of medications such as methylphenidate because it would be much harder to justify this treatment merely for a diagnosis of a poor fit between a child and the parents or the school.

The negative aspects of labeling are often overlooked but cannot be ignored:

1. The label has limited practical value for teachers, psychologists, and physicians in that it offers no articulation of the individual's problems and strengths; one diagnosis does not fit everyone. There is no information on the child's specific cognitive assets and weaknesses, and no indication of what areas should receive specific remediation from parents and teachers. The complex phenomenon of attention is analyzed in too simple a way to be of clinical use. Temperament differences are not recognized and not evaluated. Behavioral adjustment and motivations are not considered separately.

2. Management can actually be misled by the automatic exoneration of the parents and the school as participants in the creation of the presenting problem, particularly when accompanied by the notion that medication is the only effective form of treatment. Without considering and dealing with the contributions of the environment and other liabilities in the child, successful handling of the situation will be greatly impaired. No matter what the temperamental predisposition of the child may be, there has been an interaction of the child with the parental and educational caregivers. Parents may be tempted to rely entirely on medication to undo years of stressful interactions. As for teachers, "Because we are part of the environment, we are necessarily part of the problem and, hopefully, a part of the solution" (Reid, 1996, p. 263). Furthermore, supervision of children with equal degrees of educational distress but without the label of ADHD because of a more conservative physician or psychologist may suffer because the available resources are given more generously to those who have received this diagnosis of a neurodevelopmental disorder. The needs of the unlabeled children for accommodations of the educational system are just as great.

3. The label may be stigmatizing and harmful in the long term in ways that are only dimly appreciated today. The diagnosis of brain malfunction, which seems so useful and comforting today, may at a later time come back to plague the person. We have not yet had sufficient time to observe fully the possible consequences it may have for educational opportunities; employment; the military draft and service; security clearance; life insurance policies; licenses to operate machinery such as cars, buses, and airplanes; and so on. Labels stick firmly, especially when they involve neurological disability.

4. "The heterogeneous nature of groups now identified with ADHD significantly impedes the scientific process by leading to inconsistent and confusing results across studies, by not allowing predictions to be made concerning the course or outcome of the disorder, by interfering with the ability to investigate the etiologies and mechanisms underlying the disorder, and by hindering communication among scientists" (Shaywitz et al., 1995, p. S54).

Thus, the application of the label of ADHD has limited value and possible harm.

Widespread Misapplication of the Present ADHD Label

Whether or not one approves of the ADHD criteria as they stand today, there is strong evidence that at the practical level they are not being faithfully applied in most cases. Recently, two comprehensive studies, one of more than 400 pediatricians throughout the country (Wasserman et al., 1999) and one of family physicians and pediatricians in western North Carolina (Angold et al., 2000) demonstrated that the accepted diagnostic criteria were used less than half the time in making the diagnosis and starting administration of stimulants. Another survey found a dramatic increase in the prescription of these drugs to children as young as 2 years of age (Zito et al., 2000). We have no evidence that reports from other sources would be more reassuring.

Nonspecific Effects of Methylphenidate and Other Stimulants

Many professional persons and members of the general public still believe that if stimulant medication leads to improvement in the child's behavior, it is solid proof of the diagnosis of ADHD and good reason to continue the drug. What they evidently do not understand is that, as with other cerebral stimulants such as caffeine, the effect is experienced by almost all who take it, including completely normal children (Bernstein et al., 1994; Rapoport et al., 1978; Rapoport et al., 1980). The popular practice of "a trial of Ritalin" for diagnosis is, therefore, irrational (Diller, 1998). Furthermore, although methylphenidate has proven helpful in many cases, its value in comparison to well-designed psychological management is sometimes overestimated (Carey, 2000).

CONCLUSION

Is ADHD a valid disorder? The assigned title for this chapter might better be rephrased as follows: How should the diagnosis be reformulated in view of these several major problems? The best way to arrive at an answer may be to look at DSM-IV's own definition of a mental disorder. The introduction to that volume indicates the following:

> [It should be] a clinically significant behavioral or psychological syndrome or pattern that occurs in an individual and that is associated with present distress (e.g., a painful symptom) or disability (i.e., impairment in one or more important areas of functioning) or with a significantly increased risk of suffering death, pain, disability or an important loss of freedom. . . . Whatever its original cause, it must currently be considered a manifestation of a behavioral, psychological, or biological dysfunction in the individual. (p. xxi)

In other words, a disorder is a distressing behavior pattern or disability resulting from a dysfunction in the individual. Wakefield (1992) clarifies the definition of a disorder further by calling it "a harmful dysfunction, wherein harmful is a value term based on social norms, and dysfunction is a scientific term referring to the failure of a mental mechanism to perform a natural function for which it was designed by evolution" (p. 373).

Although there is a small "hyperkinetic" group of 1–2 percent of the child population in whom a true dysfunction of the brain may be suspected now and possibly proven later, it seems likely that the great majority of children receiving the ADHD diagnosis today do not have a brain dysfunction or disorder. The behavior of the larger group does indeed produce distress, but evidence is wanting for signs of an underlying dysfunction in the individual or of the "failure of a mental mechanism." What appears to be going on with most children being diagnosed with ADHD today is normal variations, especially of temperament, in neurologically intact individuals, especially low adaptability and low persistence/attention span, which are interacting stressfully with the child's particular environment with the production of reactive behavioral symptoms. The dysfunction appears to be in the interaction between child and environment, both of which may be normal but incompatible with each other, with the resulting disorder in the child's behavior. That does not mean, however, that there is an underlying disorder in the child.

We do not speak of a "difficult child disorder" even when there is a behavior problem associated with the "difficult" temperament, because we recognize that the temperamental adversity is within the range of normal and the behavior problem may or may not arise as a consequences of the interactions of the temperament with the environment. Why should there be an "attention deficit hyperactivity disorder," as presently defined, when children with the characteristics of high activity or low attention span are frequently in no trouble socially or academically?

If one can acknowledge the considerable inadequacies of the current diagnostic system, the highest priority for research should be given to modification of that system. Until this is done, further investigations of etiology, diagnostic techniques, treatment methods, and prognosis will be meaningless. The design of such research would go beyond the expected scope of this chapter, but it is appropriate to mention several main objectives based on the points made previously.

The DSM system should finally acknowledge the existence and importance of temperamental differences in children. The move away from the environmental determinism of fifty years ago has swung so rapidly toward a biological determinism that it has failed to incorporate one of the leading advances in mental health theory and practice. Even the briefest experience in primary pediatric care informs the observer that parental concerns about normal but uncongenial temperamental differences are encountered daily, probably more often than true behavioral dysfunctions.

In keeping with the requirements of DSM-IV, any newly described disorder should be defined in terms of areas of present function and dysfunction (and service needs) rather than in terms of risk factors that only sometimes lead to dysfunction and disorder. Such areas of clinical problems include the following:

- Social relationships—the degree of social competence and skill versus various forms of undersocialization like aggressiveness or opposition;

- The extent of task performance, in particular school achievement versus underachievement;

- The amount of self-assurance or problems in self-care, self-esteem, and self-control;

- The child's internal status—general satisfaction or disturbances in feelings, thinking, and physiological function (such as sleep, eating, and elimination); and

- The success or failure of his or her coping strategies.

A social relations disorder can be described as arising from interactions with the child's aversive temperament or from physical problems or external psychosocial factors. A school performance problem can be diagnosed as involving low intelligence, learning disabilities, or emotional adjustment problems, or it can arise from a poor fit between the child's qualities and the requirements of the school. A revision of the diagnostic terminology along these lines would require a major paradigm shift, a fundamental change in the way professionals, parents, and the general public think about these matters. Criteria for abnormal function can, and should, be more precise.

For the small number of "hyperkinetic" children, whose high activity and inattentiveness are so severe as to present difficulties for even the most resourceful parents and teachers, these behaviors are the clinical problem itself. For them, a revised diagnosis of ADHD might prove valid and useful if it is based on the pervasiveness of the behavior and its qualitative differences from the broad range of normal. Of course, this description does not apply to the majority of children now getting the ADHD diagnosis because they apparently have temperamental variables that require something else in the children or in the caregiving to bring on the adjustment disorder or other dysfunctional behavior.

Any diagnosis that reports or implies malfunction of the nervous system should be based on objective evidence that it is present, not on a guess that it might or ought to be found. Such confirmatory tests do not exist at present. Any new candidates for establishing abnormal brain function must be scrutinized with great care because of the great need felt by many to find such a test. Such tests must not be measures only of temperamental or other predispositions.

In the meanwhile, the overly simple and broad diagnostic process for ADHD should be phased out and replaced by more comprehensive individual assessments of children with behavioral and scholastic problems. Instead of squeezing such children into the convenient ADHD category, we should be performing functional evaluations of them as to their physical and neurological status, developmental and cognitive status, temperament, and behavioral adjustment. Strengths should be noted as well as weaknesses. The quality of significant elements of the environment and the child's interactions with them must be included. Only in this way can the uniqueness of the individual child be appreciated and the treatment or management be matched with his or her special needs.

References

Achenbach, T. M., Howell, C. T., McConaughy, C. H., & Stanger, C. (1995). Six-year predictors of problems in a national sample of children and youth: Cross-informant syndromes. *Journal of the American Academy of Child and Adolescent Psychiatry, 34*, 336–347.

American Psychiatric Association. (1994). *Diagnostic and statistical manual of mental disorders* (4th ed.). Washington, DC: Author.

Angold, A., Erkanli, A., Egger, H. L., & Costello, E. J. (2000). Stimulant treatment for children: A community perspective. *Journal of the American Academy of Child and Adolescent Psychiatry, 39*, 975–984.

Barkley R. A. (1990). *Attention deficit hyperactivity disorder: A handbook for diagnosis and treatment.* New York: Guilford Press.

Barkley, R. A. (1998). Attention deficit hyperactivity disorder. *Scientific American, 279*, 66–71.

Bernstein, G. A., Carroll, M. E., Crosby, R. D., Perwien, A. R., Go, F. S., & Benowitz, N. L. (1994). Caffeine effects on learning, performance, and anxiety in normal school-age children. *Journal of the American Academy of Child and Adolescent Psychiatry, 33*, 407–415.

Biederman, J., Milberger, S., Faraone, S. V., Kiely, K., Guite, J., Mick, E., Ablon, J. S., Warburton, R., Reed, E., & Davis, S. G. (1995). Impact of adversity on functioning and comorbidity in children with attention-deficit hyperactivity disorder. *Journal of the American Academy of Child and Adolescent Psychiatry, 34*, 1495–1503.

Billman, J., & McDevitt, S. C. (1998, October 16). *TACTIC: A measure of temperament, attention, conduct, and emotion for 2–6 year old children in out-of-home settings.* Paper presented at the twelfth Occasional Temperament Conference, Philadelphia.

Bussing, R., Schuhmann, E., Belin, T. R., Widawski, M., & Perwien, A. R. (1998). Diagnostic utility of two commonly used ADHD screening measures among special education students. *Journal of the American Academy of Child and Adolescent Psychiatry, 37*, 74–82.

Cantwell, D. P. (1996). Attention deficit disorder: A review of the past 10 years. *Journal of the American Academy of Child and Adolescent Psychiatry, 35*, 978–987.

Carey, W. B. (1998). *The relationship between low adaptability and inattention.* Unpublished data.

Carey, W. B. (2000). What the multimodal treatment study of children with attention-deficit/hyperactivity disorder did and did not say about the use of methylphenidate for attention deficits. *Pediatrics, 105*, 863–864.

Carey, W. B., & McDevitt, S. C. (1995). *Coping with children's temperament. A guide for professionals.* New York: Basic Books.

Carey, W. B., McDevitt, S. C., & Baker, D. (1979). Differentiating minimal brain dysfunction and temperament. *Developmental Medicine and Child Neurology, 21*, 765–772.

Chess, S., & Thomas, A. (1984). *Origins and evolution of behavior disorders from infancy to early adult life.* New York: Brunner/Mazel.

Chess, S., & Thomas, A. (1996). *Temperament theory and practice.* New York: Brunner/Mazel.

Denckla, M. B. (1996). Biological correlates of learning and attention: What is relevant to learning disability and attention-deficit hyperactivity disorder? *Journal of Developmental and Behavioral Pediatrics, 17*, 114–119.

Diller, L. H. (1998). *Running on Ritalin. A physician reflects on children, society, and performance in a pill.* New York: Bantam Books.

Fox, N. A., Rubin, K. H., Calkins, S. D., Marshall, T. R., Coplan, R. J., Porges, S. W., Long, J. M., & Stewart, S. (1995). Frontal activation asymmetry and social competence at four years of age. *Child Development, 66*, 1770–1784.

Goldman, L. S., Genel, M., Bezman, R. J., & Slanetz, P. J. (1998). Diagnosis and treatment of attention-deficit/hyperactivity disorder in children and adolescents. Council on Scientific Affairs, American Medical Association. *Journal of the American Medical Association, 279*, 1100–1107.

Hertzig, M. E. (1983). Temperament and neurological status. In M. Rutter (Ed.), *Developmental neuropsychiatry* (pp. 164–180). New York: Guilford Press.

Jensen, P. S., Mrazek, D., Knapp, P. K., Steinberg L., Pfeffer, C., Schowalter, J., & Shapiro, T. (1997). Evolution and revolution in child psychiatry: ADHD as a disorder of adaptation. *Journal of the American Academy of Child and Adolescent Psychiatry, 36*, 1672–1679.

Kanbayashi, Y., Nakata, Y., Fujii, K., Kita, M., & Wada, K. (1994). ADHD-related behavior among non-referred children: Parents' ratings of DSM-III-R symptoms. *Child Psychiatry and Human Development, 25*, 13–29.

Keogh, B. K. (1989). Applying temperament research to school. In G. A. Kohnstamm, J. E. Bates, & M. K. Rothbart (Eds.), *Temperament in childhood* (pp. 437–450). New York: Wiley.

Kuperman, S., Johnson, B., Arndt, S., Lindgren S., & Wolraich, M. (1996). Quantitative EEG differences in a nonclinical sample of children with ADHD and undifferentiated ADD. *Journal of the American Academy of Child and Adolescent Psychiatry, 35*, 1009–1017.

Levine, M. D. (1994). *Educational care.* Cambridge MA: Educators Publishing.

Levine, M. D. (1999). Attention and dysfunctions of attention. In M. D. Levine, W. B. Carey, & A. C. Crocker (Eds.), *Developmental-behavioral pediatrics* (3rd ed., pp. 499–519). Philadelphia: Saunders.

Levy, F., Hay, D. A., McStephen, M., Wood, C., & Waldman, I. (1997). Attention-deficit hyperactivity disorder: A category or a continuum? Genetic analysis of a large-scale twin study. *Journal of the American Academy of Child and Adolescent Psychiatry, 36,* 737–744.

Martin, R. P. (1989). Activity level, distractibility and persistence: Critical characteristics in early schooling. In G. A. Kohnstamm, J. E. Bates, & M. K. Rothbart (Eds.), *Temperament in childhood* (pp. 451–462). New York: Wiley.

Max, J. E., Arndt, S., Castillo, C. S., Bokura, H., Robin, D. A., Lindgren, S. D., Smith, W. L. Jr., Sato, Y., & Mattheis, P. J. (1998). Attention-deficit hyperactivity symptomatology after traumatic brain injury: A prospective study. *Journal of the American Academy of Child and Adolescent Psychiatry, 37,* 841–847.

Maziade, M (1989). Should adverse temperament matter to the clinician? An empirically based answer. In G. A. Kohnstamm, J. E. Bates, & M. K. Rothbart (Eds.), *Temperament in childhood* (pp. 421–436). New York: Wiley.

Maziade, M. (1994). Temperament research and practical implications for clinicians. In W. B. Carey & S. C. McDevitt (Eds.), *Prevention and early intervention* (pp. 69–80). New York: Brunner/Mazel.

McDevitt, S. C., & Carey, W. B. (1978). The measurement of temperament in 3–7 year old children. *Journal of Child Psychology and Psychiatry, 19,* 245–253.

Mellins, C. A., Gatz, M., & Baker, L. (1996). Children's methods of coping with stress: A twin study of genetic and environmental influences. *Journal of Child Psychology and Psychiatry, 37,* 721–730.

Peterson, B. S. (1995). Neuroimaging in child and adolescent neuropsychiatric disorders. *Journal of the American Academy of Child and Adolescent Psychiatry, 34,* 1560–1576.

Plomin, R., Owen, M. J., & McGuffin, P. (1994). The genetic basis of complex human behaviors. *Science, 264,* 1733–1739.

Rapoport, J. L., Buchsbaum, M. S., Zahn, T. P., Weingartner, H., Ludlow, C., & Mikkelsen, E. J. (1978). Dextroamphetamine: Cognitive and behavioral effects on normal prepubertal boys. *Journal of the American Academy of Child and Adolescent Psychiatry, 199,* 560–563.

Rapoport, J. L., Buchsbaum, M. S.,Weingartner, H., Zahn, T. P., Ludlow, C., & Mikkelsen, E. J. (1980). Dextroamphetamine. Its cognitive and behavioral effects in normal and hyperactive boys and normal men. *Archives of General Psychiatry, 37,* 933–943.

Reid, R. (1996). Three faces of attention-deficit hyperactivity disorder. *Journal of Child and Family Studies, 5,* 249–265.

Reid, R., & Maag, J. W. (1994). How many fidgets in a pretty much: A critique of behavior rating scales for identifying students with ADHD. *Journal of School Psychology, 32,* 339–354.

Reid, R., Maag, J. W., & Vasa, S. F. (1993). Attention deficit hyperactivity disorder as a disability category: A critique. *Exceptional Children, 60,* 198–214.

Rutter, M. L. (1983a). Behavioral studies: Questions and findings on the concept of a distinctive syndrome. In M. L. Rutter (Ed.), *Developmental neuropsychiatry* (p. 267). New York: Guilford Press.

Rutter, M. L. (1983b). Issues and prospects in developmental neuropsychiatry. In M. L. Rutter (Ed.), *Developmental neuropsychiatry* (pp. 577–593). New York: Guilford Press.

Rutter, M. L. (1997). Motivation and delinquency. In *Nebraska Symposium on Motivation* (Vol. 44, p. 73). Lincoln: University of Nebraska Press.

Safer, D. J., Zito, J. M., & Fine, E. M. (1996). Increased methylphenidate usage for attention deficit disorder in the 1990s. *Pediatrics, 98,* 1084–1088.

Scahill, L., Schwab-Stone, M., Merikangas, K. R., Leckman, J. F., Zhang, H., & Kasl, S. (1999). Psychosocial and clinical correlates of ADHD in a community sample of school-age children. *Journal of the American Academy of Child and Adolescent Psychiatry, 38,* 976–984.

Shaywitz, B. A., Fletcher, J. M., & Shaywitz, S. E. (1995). Defining and classifying learning disabilities and attention-deficit/hyperactivity disorder. *Journal of Child Neurology, 10*, S50–S57.

Sherman, D. K., Iacono, W. G., & McGue, M. K. (1997). Attention-deficit hyperactivity disorder dimensions: A twin study of inattention and impulsivity-hyperactivity. *Journal of the American Academy of Child and Adolescent Psychiatry, 36*, 745–753.

Tannock, R. (1998). Attention deficit hyperactivity disorder: Advances in cognitive, neurobiological, and genetic research. *Journal of Child Psychology and Psychiatry, 39*, 65–99.

Taylor, E. (1994). Syndromes of attention deficit and overactivity. In M. L. Rutter, E. Taylor, & L. Hersov (Eds.), *Child and adolescent psychiatry* (3rd ed., pp. 293–299). Oxford, UK: Blackwell Scientific.

Thomas, A., & Chess, A. (1977). *Temperament and development.* New York: Brunner/Mazel.

Thomas, A., Chess, A., & Birch, H. G. (1968). *Temperament and behavior disorders in children.* New York: New York University Press.

Tizard, B., & Hodges, J. (1978). The effect of early institutional rearing on the development of eight year old children. *Journal of Child Psychology and Psychiatry, 19*, 99–118.

United Nations International Narcotics Control Board. (1995). *Report of the UN International Narcotics Control Board.* New York: UN Publications.

Wakefield, J. C. (1992). The concept of mental disorder. On the boundary between biological facts and social values. *American Psychologist, 47*, 373–388.

Wasserman, R. C., Kelleher, K. J., Bocian, A., Baker, A., Childs, G. E., Indacochea, F., Stulp, C., & Gardner, W. P. (1999). Identification of attentional and hyperactivity problems in primary care: A report from pediatric research in office settings and the ambulatory sentinel practice network. *Pediatrics, 103*, E38.

Wolraich, M. L., Hannah, J. N., Baumgaertel, A., & Feurer, I. D. (1998). Examination of DSM-IV criteria for attention deficit/hyperactivity disorder in a county-wide sample. *Journal of Developmental and Behavioral Pediatrics, 19*, 162–168.

Woodward, L., Dowdney, L., & Taylor, E. (1997). Child and family factors influencing the clinical referral of children with hyperactivity: A research note. *Journal of Child Psychology and Psychiatry, 38*, 479–485.

World Health Organization. (1992). *International statistical classification of diseases and related health problems* (10th rev.). Geneva, Switzerland: Author.

Zametkin, A. J., Ernst, M., & Silver, R. (1998). Laboratory and diagnostic testing in child and adolescent psychiatry: A review of the past 10 years. *Journal of the American Academy of Child and Adolescent Psychiatry, 37*, 464–472.

Zito, J. M., Safer, D. J., dosReis, S., Gardner, J. F., Boles, M., & Lynch, F. (2000). Trends in prescribing of psychotropic medications to preschoolers. *Journal of the American Medical Association, 283*, 1025–1030.

Chapter 4

ADHD—Long-Term Course, Adult Outcome, and Comorbid Disorders

by Russell A. Barkley, Ph.D.

Introduction 4-1
Limitations of Methodology 4-2
    Lack of Consensus on Diagnostic Criteria 4-2
    Use of Different Assessment Instruments 4-2
    Unreliability of Measurement Over Time 4-3
    Developmental Issues 4-3
    Shifting Information Sources 4-4
    Attrition 4-4
Outcome at Adolescence 4-5
    Persistence of ADHD Symptoms 4-5
    Occurrence of Comorbid Disorders 4-6
Outcome at Adulthood 4-7
    Persistence of ADHD Symptoms 4-7
    Risk for Antisocial or Criminal Behavior 4-8
    Risk of Substance Abuse 4-9
    Risk of Mood Disorders 4-10
Conclusion 4-10

INTRODUCTION

This chapter focuses on the long-term course and adult status for the disorder of attention deficit hyperactive disorder (ADHD) specifically and the likely comorbid psychiatric disorders found in association with ADHD across its developmental course into adolescence and adulthood. In regard to these two issues, this chapter emphasizes two separate periods: adolescence (ages 13–19 years) and then young adulthood (ages 20–30 years). To address these issues, the author focuses chiefly on the prospective longitudinal studies that have been conducted on hyperactive or ADHD children. This chapter does not deal with issues related to areas of impairment produced by or often seen in conjunction with the disorder, such as school performance problems, peer relationship difficulties, family interaction problems, or difficulties in occupational settings (in the case of adults with ADHD).

LIMITATIONS OF METHODOLOGY

Before the questions at issue here can be addressed, a number of important methodological caveats must be appreciated that plague any effort to interpret the scientific literature in these areas in a simple and completely straightforward manner. This section discusses these limitations to interpretation of the facts.

Lack of Consensus on Diagnostic Criteria

Many of the longest-running follow-up studies (Barkley, Fischer, Edelbrock, & Smallish, 1990; Mannuzza et al., 1993; Weiss & Hechtman, 1993) did not have available at the time empirically based consensus diagnostic criteria for the disorder according to such classifications as the third, revised edition of *Diagnostic and Statistical Manual of Mental Disorders* (DSM-III-R; American Psychiatric Association, 1987) or the fourth edition (DSM-IV; American Psychiatric Association, 1994), to employ as part of subject selection criteria to identify children as ADHD at entry into the study. They employed either clinical impressions of the children as being "hyperactive" or a mixture of clinical impression and significantly elevated scores on a behavior rating scale, such as the Conners Parent Rating Scale or the Werry-Weiss-Peters Activity Rating Scale. Such scales were not well normed at the time, however, and thus it cannot be stated unequivocally that all subjects in these and other similarly afflicted follow-up studies would have met today's standards for a diagnosis of ADHD.

Use of Different Assessment Instruments

With few exceptions, most follow-up studies did not employ the same assessment instruments across their follow-up points, making direct calculations of the stability, persistence, and desistence of disorder across development highly problematic. For instance, studies may have used a clinical diagnosis of "hyperactivity" and a rating scale in childhood, then a DSM-III- (American Psychiatric Associaiton, 1980) or DSM-III-R-based interview at adolescence, and then a DSM-III-R- or DSM-IV-based interview for evaluating the subjects as young adults. Such measures do not yield identical results for either ADHD or potential comorbid disorders. Therefore, the percentage of subjects having those outcomes at one follow-up phase cannot be directly compared with those same disorders in the same samples at another phase without some qualification on this issue.

The methods used to assess persistence of symptoms and disorder across time as well as comorbid psychiatric disorders are not similar or identical across studies, making straightforward comparisons of the results across those studies difficult. For instance, subjects may have been initially selected as hyperactive using clinical impression in one study but with a rating scale and interview in another. At adolescent follow-up, presence of disorder may then have been determined by a structured psychiatric interview in one study that may have been based on a version of the DSM but using a different interview or a different version of the DSM criteria in another. The symptom items in these instruments would not have been identical to the items used for initial diagnosis or in the initial rating scale—neither in that study nor in the studies to which it is being compared. Then, at adult follow-up, a different structured interview probably relying on a different version of the DSM diagnostic criteria would have been employed in the same study that once again would not be the same as that instrument used at that same follow-up age in a different study.

Unreliability of Measurement Over Time

Related to the foregoing issue of measurement, none of the follow-up studies attempted to correct their figures dealing with persistence of disorder for unreliability of measurement across time. In their defense, this would have been difficult to do, because the same instruments were not employed across follow-up points with the subjects. Even so, anyone wishing to understand this literature needs to appreciate the fact that other studies of related disorders, such as oppositional and conduct disorder or learning disabilities, often find substantially higher rates of persistence of disorder when measurement unreliability is corrected for in the analyses of the results (Fergusson, Horwood, & Lynskey, 1995). The same is likely to apply to follow-up studies of ADHD as well.

Developmental Issues

The method by which ADHD is diagnosed across development fails to take into consideration the strong probability that ADHD is a *developmental disorder* of a cognitive mechanism or set of such mechanisms. ADHD is increasingly being conceptualized as primarily a disorder of response inhibition and executive functioning, or self-regulation. Like mental retardation (MR) or the learning disabilities (LD), ADHD most likely comprises a chronic developmental delay in certain cognitive capacities. Consequently, as with other developmental disorders, its diagnosis at any particular age must include a developmentally referenced comparison to normal children at the same developmental stage. The diagnosis, in other words, is developmentally relative. For instance, children with MR, followed across development, are diagnosed in comparison to developmental attainments in intelligence or general cognitive abilities in normal peers of the same chronological age. This is exactly the purpose of intelligence tests or adaptive behavior inventories.

Such developmentally based comparisons in the definition of disorder take into account two important issues: (1) the diagnosis at any age is based on comparison to age-matched normal individuals and (2) the set of items on which this comparison is being made are not only standardized but are developmentally speeded—that is, the items progress from simple to complex abilities as reflected in the developmental progression of the cognitive mechanism or construct. This is evident in examining the item sets used to construct any intelligence test or adaptive behavior inventory.

Though likely a developmental disorder, ADHD is not diagnosed with consideration given to these important issues. It is diagnosed using a fixed set of items whose wording is based on a relatively narrow age span of children (5 to 12 years) and whose diagnostic cutoff score on this list remains fixed across the lifespan. Moreover, the field trial on which this cutoff score was based employed individuals only in the 4–16-year-old range, without the inclusion of preschoolers or adults. Yet, the diagnostic criteria are said to be applicable across the lifespan with no adjustments being made to the item set or diagnostic thresholds. Just as important, the eighteen-item set now used in DSM-IV to diagnose ADHD does not employ a developmentally speeded item set; that is, one that progresses from more developmentally basic or primitive levels of ability to more developmentally sophisticated and complex levels of that same ability. If such an approach were used to diagnose MR or LD, the result would be the appearance of a decline in the disorder with age as progressively more subjects were able to succeed or pass the items at normal levels of functioning with age even though remaining disordered. That is, subjects would outgrow the item set used for diagnosis but would not be outgrowing their disorder.

Shifting Information Sources

Some studies shifted the source of the information about the subjects and their disorder at different follow-up points. For instance, the New York longitudinal study of hyperactive children (Gittelman, Mannuzza, Shenker, & Bonagura, 1985; Mannuzza, Gittelman-Klein, Bessler, Malloy, & LaPadula, 1993) employed parental reports of the subjects' symptoms through adolescence but then employed the subjects' own self-reports of their symptoms in adulthood. This is problematic because there is reason to believe that subjects with ADHD may have more limited self-awareness of their symptoms and thus may under-report the extent of their disorder and comorbidities (Barkley, 1998). In any case, this type of change in source of information makes comparisons difficult or impossible between one follow-up point that used one source and a later follow-up point using a different source within the same longitudinal study. Though Mannuzza et al. (1993) presented some evidence from a small subset of their subjects to suggest that this may not have posed problems for interpretation of their results for adult outcome, more recent evidence from the author's own longitudinal study in Milwaukee indicates that self-report may differ from prevalence of disorder based on parental reports by as much as seven- to elevenfold (Fischer, 1997), depending on the criteria used for diagnosis. This more recent evidence implies that relying exclusively on self-reports of symptoms in adulthood may vastly underestimate persistence of disorder relative to parental reports that have been employed throughout the follow-up study.

Attrition

The percentage of subjects relocated and reevaluated at follow-up varies markedly across studies, ranging from 51 to 98 percent (see Gittelman et al., 1985, Table 1, for a review). In studies with high attrition rates, it is highly likely that subjects lost to the follow-up evaluation are not similar to those who were able to be reevaluated and may well have been more likely to have had persistent disorder as well as greater comorbidity than those subjects who were evaluated.

Such methodological problems as those outlined previously should give serious pause to anyone who might simply extract figures dealing with persistence from these studies and then combine them into a statistical analysis to calculate average persistence as a function of age, as some have recently done (Hill & Schoener, 1996). Any mathematical function so derived would not be interpretable—it could not accurately reflect a single disorder across development (see Barkley, 1998, for a detailed critique).

For the sake of brevity, the present summary lists its results in table form within the text, recognizing that the aforementioned methodological problems must be kept in mind in any effort to collapse across studies for the sake of interpretation of these results.

OUTCOME AT ADOLESCENCE

Persistence of ADHD Symptoms

Three prospective studies could be located that dealt with the issue of merely the persistence of significant symptoms from childhood to adolescence. These found that 70–80 percent of their subjects continued with significant symptoms into adolescence (Barkley et al., 1990; Mendelson, Johnson, & Stewart, 1971; Lambert, Hartsough, Sassone, & Sandoval, 1987).

Eight studies employed structured psychiatric interviews at adolescence using chiefly parents as informants. They are shown in Table 4.1 along with the results concerning presence of full disorder. Clearly this table indicates that a substantial majority of those diagnosed as hyperactive or ADHD in these studies persisted in having their full disorder at the time of follow-up. But it is also evident that the follow-up period of early to mid adolescence (10 to 15 years old) had rates of disorder (68–85 percent) somewhat higher than did the period of later adolescence to young adulthood (16 to 19 years old) where the persistence of full disorder was 30–50 percent. Although this can be interpreted as evidence for a possible developmental decrease in persistence of disorder over life course (increasing recovery), it may also simply indi-

Table 4.1
Persistence of Full Disorder Into Adolescence

Age	Period (yrs.)	Mean Follow-up ADHD Prevalence	Studies
10	4	80%	Cantwell & Baker, 1989
14	4	85%	Biederman et al., 1996
14	4	84%	August, Stewart, & Holmes, 1983
15	6	68%	Klein & Mannuzza, 1991
15	8–10	72%	Barkley, Fischer, Edelbrock, & Smallish, 1990
18	9	30–43%	Gittelman et al., 1985; Mannuzza, Klein, Bonagura, et al., 1991; Manuzza, Klein, & Addalli, 1991
19	12	71%	Claude & Firestone, 1995 (since age 13)
		50%	Claude & Firestone, 1995 (at follow-up)

cate the point made earlier that individuals are outgrowing the relatively fixed criteria for the diagnosis and not the true disorder.

Occurrence of Comorbid Disorders

Retrospective follow-up studies suggest that several comorbid disorders are more likely to occur in hyperactive or ADHD children if they were followed into adolescence. For instance, Mendelson et al. (1971) reported a rate of 26 percent of hyperactive children having conduct disorder in their retrospective study. Given the strong relationship of oppositional defiant disorder (ODD) to conduct disorder (CD), one should not be surprised to learn that ODD was significantly more prevalent in ADHD children followed across time. Prospective studies indeed indicate a prevalence of 59 percent (Barkley et al., 1990) to 73 percent (Biederman et al., 1996) in clinical samples followed for a period of eight to ten years and four years, respectively.

Five prospective follow-up studies were located that reported rates of CD at adolescence in their samples. These studies are displayed along with their results in Table 4.2. They clearly indicate a significantly elevated risk for CD among hyperactive or ADHD children as teens. It would, therefore, appear that a sizable minority of children with ADHD have a significantly elevated risk for CD of 20–50 percent at adolescent follow-up. It would also seem that the likelihood of comorbid conduct disorder increases with age within the samples.

The relationship of ADHD to risk for mood or anxiety disorders has been controversial. Some follow-up studies (Barkley et al., 1990) simply did not examine their subjects for these comorbid disorders given that others (Gittelman et al., 1985; Mannuzza, Klein, & Addalli, 1991; Weiss & Hechtman, 1993) had not reported higher rates of these disorders in their own samples at adolescent follow-up. But more recent investigations of clinic-referred children suggest that such comorbid disorders may be more common than was once believed. A review of the literature on the

Table 4.2
Persistence of Comorbid Conduct Disorder at Adolescent Follow-up

Age	Period (yrs.)	Mean Follow-up CD Prevalence	Studies
13	4–6	25%	Weiss & Hechtman, 1993
14	4	28%	Biederman et al., 1996
14	4	20%	August, Stewart, & Holmes, 1983
15	8–10	43%	Klein & Mannuzza, 1991
15	9	50%	Barkley, Fischer, Edelbrock, & Smallish, 1990
18		30–43%	Gittelman et al., 1985; Mannuzza, Klein, Bonagura, et al., 1991

comorbidity of major depression or mood disorder (dysthymia) in ADHD children found a range of between 15 and 75 percent but with most studies reporting rates of 9–32 percent having major depression (Biederman, Newcorn, & Sprich, 1991). Similar reviews have found anxiety disorder to occur in about 25 percent of children (Jensen, Martin, & Cantwell, 1997; Tannock, 2000). Some prospective follow-up studies that have examined for rates of these disorders at adolescence reported 44 percent had anxiety disorders (vs. 9 percent in controls) and 45 percent had depression (vs. 6 percent of controls) (Biederman et al., 1996). Cantwell and Baker (1989), however, reported that only 14 percent of their subjects had either type of disorder at follow-up. Until more follow-up studies are done that specifically examine for psychiatric diagnoses of these affective disorders, the issue of comorbidity for these disorders at adolescent follow-up will remain a controversial one.

Biederman et al. (1997) examined the rate of psychoactive substance use disorders (PSUD) among their sample followed up four years later into early adolescence and found a rate of 15 percent. This was not significantly different from the control group at this age. Though Barkley et al. (1990) did not use formal criteria for diagnosing PSUD in their study, they did report a higher rate of alcohol and tobacco use among their subjects, particularly the subjects having comorbid CD, but not for other substances.

OUTCOME AT ADULTHOOD

Persistence of ADHD Symptoms

Three studies reported on only the persistence of significant symptoms into adulthood as opposed to full psychiatric disorder. Weiss and Hechtman (1993) found that 66 percent of their sample continued to report significant levels of hyperactive symptoms in adulthood. In the study by Borland and Heckman (1976), 50 percent were said to have persistent symptoms at the twenty- to twenty-five-year follow-up (this was a retrospective study, however). A single report from China (Wenwei, 1996) found that at a mean age of 25 years, 70 percent of 197 children diagnosed previously with minimal brain dysfunction/hyperactivity continued to have persistent symptoms (a fifteen-year retrospective follow-up study). And so it would seem that some 50–70 percent of formerly hyperactive children continue to manifest some significant symptoms of disorder into young adulthood.

The author's Milwaukee follow-up study (Barkley, Fischer, Fletcher, & Smallish, 1998) has recently reported that 25 percent of subjects have self-reported a significant level of ADHD symptoms sufficient to exceed the ninety-third percentile for a normal control group. In contrast, the parents of these children reported that 68 percent of them continued to exceed this level of severity of symptoms in young adulthood (Fischer, 1997). The persistence of symptoms clearly is partly a function of the source of the information, with those who know the subjects well reporting substantially higher persistence of symptoms than the subjects themselves.

Table 4.3 shows two studies that have examined the percentage of subjects meeting diagnostic criteria for full disorder in young adulthood. In comparison to the rates of disorder reported by these same studies in adolescence (see Table 4.1), the persistence of disorder into adulthood would seem to be markedly lower. This may well represent developmental recovery from disorder, as some have suggested (Hill & Schoener, 1996). But most of the methodological limitations discussed earlier come into play in these long-running studies that would advise caution about rendering such a conclusion too readily. Chief among these would seem to be the fact that the source of information changed from other (parent) reports to self-reports in the Mannuzza et al. (1993) study. As can be seen in the Milwaukee study by Barkley et al. (1998) in Table 4.3, this can result in a substantial underestimate of disorder relative to what parents may have to report about the subjects. Even if parent reports continue to be employed from adolescence to adulthood, however, as was done in the Milwaukee project, there is still a steep decline by more than half in persistence of disorder. Yet if an empirical definition of disorder, such as placement above the ninety-third percentile for age relative to the control group, is substituted for the formal DSM diagnostic criteria, then 68 percent continue to exceed this threshold by parent report. Such a finding of disparity between clinical diagnostic criteria and empirically defined criteria lends some credence to the idea noted earlier that children in these follow-up studies may not be outgrowing the disorder as much as outgrowing the relevance of the diagnostic criteria for disorder when applied to adults. Until better, more developmentally referenced criteria are developed for use in the diagnosis of ADHD in adulthood, the issue will remain an open and undoubtedly controversial one.

Risk for Antisocial or Criminal Behavior

Earlier prospective follow-up studies that did not use full diagnostic criteria for disorders have suggested that hyperactive children have a significantly elevated risk for antisocial and criminal activities. For instance, Satterfield, Hoppe, and Schell (1982) reported that 36–58 percent of their ADHD children, depending on social class, had been arrested at least once by the time they were reevaluated in late adolescence (age 17). This is in contrast to rates of 2–11 percent in the control group. And at least 25–45 percent of ADHD subjects (vs. 0–6 percent of control group) had been arrested multiple times by this follow-up period, again depending on the social class of the ADHD subjects. Arrest rates have been found to be markedly lower in other

Table 4.3
Persistence of Full Disorder Into Adulthood

Age	Period (yrs.)	Mean Follow-up ADHD Prevalence	Studies
26	16	8%	Manuzza et al., 1993 (by self-report)
21	13–15	3%	Barkley, Fischer, Fletcher, & Smallish, 1998 (by self-report)
		27%	Barkley, Fischer, Fletcher, & Smallish, 1998 (by parent report)

prospective follow-up studies (Weiss & Hechtman, 1993) but to still be significantly greater than was evident in control groups.

A number of studies have examined the percentage of their subjects at young adult follow-up who met criteria for antisocial personality disorder (APD). Table 4.4 illustrates these studies. With the exception of the study by Loney, Kramer, and Milich (1981), these results for APD in young adulthood are surprisingly consistent, showing a range of 18–27 percent. Such results may not be subject to the criticism raised previously about ADHD (i.e., that the diagnostic criteria were not as developmentally sensitive nor relevant to adults). In contrast, criteria for APD were developed on adults, are not applied until individuals are at least 18 or older, and rely on items that are highly developmentally relevant to adult functioning but would not be relevant to childhood adaptive functioning. Even so, given that most of these studies relied on the subjects' self-report, it remains possible that these studies would produce underestimates of true disorder if a similar problem with source of reporting is relevant to APD criteria as was found for adult ADHD symptoms. That is, subjects may tend to underreport their symptoms relative to what another adult would have reported about them.

Risk of Substance Abuse

Turning to the related issue of substance use disorders (SUDS), four of the prospective follow-up studies examined this issue at young adulthood. At age 18, the New York study (Gittelman et al., 1985; Mannuzza, Klein, Bonagura, et al., 1991) reported that 10–16 percent of hyperactive subjects now had at least one SUDS. These disorders were primarily associated with those subjects having APD. This rate is lower than the 37 percent prevalence of SUDS reported at age 19 in the Claude and Firestone (1995) study. Subsequently, the rate in the New York study was found to have stayed nearly the same at the later follow-up at 26 years of age, where 16 percent of these subjects had a SUDS (Mannuzza et al., 1993). The Milwaukee follow-up study has

Table 4.4
Prevalence of Antisocial Personality Disorder at Adulthood Follow-up

Age	Period (yrs.)	Mean Follow-up APD Prevalence	Studies
18	9	27–32%	Gittelman et al, 1985; Mannuzza, Klein, Bongura, et al., 1991
26	15	18%	Mannuzza, Klein, Bongura, et al., 1991
21	13–15	22%	Barkley, Fischer, Fletcher, & Smallish, 1998
22	10	23%	Weiss & Hechtman, 1993
30	20–25	25%	Borland & Heckman, 1976
	21–23	45%	Loney, Kramer, & Milich, 1981

recently found that up to 24 percent of its subjects had either alcohol or cannabis dependence disorder, by their own self-report. However, this rate was not significantly different from the rate found in the control group. Few subjects in either group qualified for either form of substance abuse disorder.

Risk of Mood Disorders

The New York study did not report a higher than normal prevalence for any mood or anxiety disorders in their sample at adult follow-up. In contrast, the author's Milwaukee study has recently found a rate of nearly 28 percent for major depression, which is significantly higher than the rate for the control group. Consistent with the New York study, the rates for dysthymia or for anxiety disorders in the Milwaukee study were not significantly different from the control group rates for these same disorders. Again, because self-report serves as the basis for the establishment of comorbid disorders, these rates may be underestimates of true comorbidity.

CONCLUSION

In summary, it appears that a majority of hyperactive children continue to either manifest significant symptoms of disorder (70–80 percent) into adolescence or to qualify for a diagnosis of full disorder. Approximately 65–80 percent will have full disorder in early adolescence while 30–50 percent may continue to have full disorder by late adolescence (16–19 years), assuming that parental report is the source of information. By adulthood, it first appears that only a small percentage of hyperactive or ADHD children retain their disorder if formal diagnostic criteria are used at the adult follow-up point and self-reports serve as the basis for diagnosis (3–8 percent). But there are numerous legitimate reasons for questioning such results. One major reason is the apparent developmental insensitivity of the diagnostic criteria to the disorder in this older age group. Another is the apparent underreporting of symptoms by the subjects relative to reports given by their parents. Anywhere from 3 to 68 percent of hyperactive subjects have ADHD in adulthood depending on these various methodological factors, with rates being higher (25–68 percent) when based on parent reports and/or on empirically based (developmentally referenced) definitions of disorder. The persistence rates are dramatically lower when based on DSM criteria using self-reports (3–8 percent).

Approximately 20–50 percent of hyperactive children are likely to have conduct disorder by adolescence. It is not surprising, then, given the link of CD to APD, that 25 percent of hyperactive subjects will have APD in young adulthood. And because APD is a known risk factor for substance use, dependence, and abuse, the elevated risk of 10–37 percent having a substance dependence or use disorder in adulthood found in several studies is also not unexpected.

Studies differ in finding major depression present in the adolescent or young adulthood years of hyperactive subjects followed prospectively. The New York (Mannuzza et al., 1993) study found no significant elevation of risk at either age period. In contrast, the study by Biederman et al. (1996) found such an elevation in risk at adolescence. The more recent Milwaukee study found a rate of nearly 28 percent in young adulthood. Given the higher than normal rate of conduct disorder and subsequent APD in a substantial minority of hyperactive children and the known association of CD/APD with major depression, it should not be surprising to discover that this subgroup has a higher than normal risk for depression in young adulthood, as the Milwaukee study has recently discovered.

In conclusion, hyperactivity or ADHD is a highly persistent disorder from childhood to adolescence. It also conveys a greater risk for ODD, CD, and APD among a substantial minority of these children as they progress through adolescence and into adulthood. Consequently, there may also be an elevated risk for SUDS among this subset of ADHD children having comorbid CD or APD. Whether or not ADHD conveys a greater risk for mood disorders, such as major depression, remains unsettled at this time. It apparently does not elevate the risk for later anxiety disorders, however. The extent to which ADHD persists into adulthood cannot be easily determined from the existing data. Where fixed (childhood-based) diagnostic criteria such as the DSM are applied to these formerly hyperactive or ADHD children as they become adults and their own self-reports are used, rates of persistence of disorder are low indeed. More than 90 percent of subjects no longer seem to meet criteria for full disorder. However, where developmentally referenced and empirically based definitions are employed (e.g., symptoms > 93rd percentile for age) and others, such as parents, serve as the source of information, persistence of disorder is present in the majority of subjects (68 percent). Which of these approaches to determining persistence of disorder into adulthood yields the more valid picture of the adult outcome for ADHD awaits further study.

References

American Psychiatric Association. (1980). *Diagnostic and statistical manual of mental disorders* (3rd ed.). Washington, DC: Author.

American Psychiatric Association. (1987). *Diagnostic and statistical manual of mental disorders* (3rd ed., rev.). Washington, DC: Author.

American Psychiatric Association. (1994). *Diagnostic and statistical manual of mental disorders* (4th ed.). Washington, DC: Author.

August, G. J., Stewart, M. A., & Holmes, C. S. (1983). A four-year follow-up of hyperactive boys with and without conduct disorder. *British Journal of Psychiatry, 143*, 192–198.

Barkley, R. A. (1998). *Attention deficit hyperactivity disorder: A handbook for diagnosis and treatment* (2nd ed.). New York: Guilford Press.

Barkley, R. A., Fischer, M., Edelbrock, C. S., & Smallish, L. (1990). The adolescent outcome of hyperactive children diagnosed by research criteria. I: An 8 year prospective follow-up study. *Journal of the American Academy of Child and Adolescent Psychiatry, 29*, 546–557.

Barkley, R. A., Fischer, M., Fletcher, K., & Smallish, L. (1998). *Young adult outcome of hyperactive children diagnosed by research criteria* (NIMH Grant #42181). Manuscript in preparation.

Biederman, J., Faraone, S., Milberger, S., Guite, J., Mick, E., Chen, L., Mennin, D., Ouellette, C., Moore, P., Spencer, T., Norman, D., Wilens, T., Kraus, I., & Perrin, J. (1996). A prospective 4-year follow-up study of attention-deficit hyperactivity and related disorders. *Archives of General Psychiatry, 53*, 437–446.

Biederman, J., Newcorn, J., & Sprich, S. (1991). Comorbidity of attention deficit hyperactivity disorder with conduct, depressive, anxiety, and other disorders. *American Journal of Psychiatry, 148*, 564–577.

Biederman, J., Wilens, T., Mick, E., Faraone, S. V., Weber, W., Curtis, S., Thornell, A., Pfister, K.,

Jetton, J. G., & Soriano, J. (1997). Is ADHD a risk factor for psychoactive substance use disorders? Findings from a four-year prospective follow-up. *Journal of the American Academy of Child and Adolescent Psychiatry, 36*, 21–29.

Borland, H. L., & Heckman, H. K. (1976). Hyperactive boys and their brothers: A 25-year follow-up study. *Archives of General Psychiatry, 33*, 669–675.

Cantwell, D. P., & Baker, L. (1989). Stability and natural history of DSM-III childhood diagnoses. *Journal of the American Academy of Child and Adolescent Psychiatry, 28*, 691–700.

Claude, D., & Firestone, P. (1995). The development of ADHD boys: A 12-year follow-up. *Canadian Journal of Behavioral Science, 27*, 226–249.

Fergusson, D. M., Horwood, L. J., & Lynskey, M. T. (1995). The stability of disruptive childhood behaviors. *Journal of Abnormal Child Psychology, 23*, 379–396.

Fischer, M. (1997). The persistence of ADHD into adulthood: It depends on whom you ask. *The ADHD Report, 5*(4), 8–10.

Gittelman, R., Mannuzza, S., Shenker, R., & Bonagura, N. (1985). Hyperactive boys almost grown up: I. Psychiatric status. *Archives of General Psychiatry, 42*, 937–947.

Hill, J. C., & Schoener, E. P. (1996). Age-dependent decline of attention deficit hyperactivity disorder. *American Journal of Psychiatry, 153*, 1143–1146.

Jensen, P. S., Martin, D., & Cantwell, D. P. (1997). Comorbidity in ADHD: Implications for research, practice, and DSM-V. *Journal of the American Academy of Child and Adolescent Psychiatry, 36*, 1065–1079.

Klein, R. G., & Mannuzza, S. (1991). Long-term outcome of hyperactive children: A review. *Journal of the American Academy of Child and Adolescent Psychiatry, 30*, 383–387.

Lambert, N. M., Hartsough, C. S., Sassone, S., & Sandoval, J. (1987). Persistence of hyperactive symptoms from childhood to adolescence and associated outcomes. *American Journal of Orthopsychiatry, 57*, 22–32.

Loney, J., Kramer, J., & Milich, R. (1981). The hyperkinetic child grows up: Predictors of symptoms, delinquency, and achievement at follow-up. In K. Gadow & J. Loney (Eds.), *Psychosocial aspects of drug treatment for hyperactivity* (pp. 381–415). Boulder, CO: Westview Press.

Mannuzza, S., Klein, R. G., & Addalli, K. A. (1991). Young adult mental status of hyperactive boys and their brothers: A prospective follow-up study. *Journal of the American Academy of Child and Adolescent Psychiatry, 30,* 743–751.

Mannuzza, S., Klein, R., Bessler, A., Malloy, P., & LaPadula, M. (1993). Adult outcome of hyperactive boys: Educational achievement, occupational rank, and psychiatric status. *Archives of General Psychiatry, 50*, 565–576.

Mannuzza, S., Klein, R., Bonagura, N., Malloy, P., Giampino, T. L., & Addalli, K. A. (1991). Hyperactive boys almost grown up: V. Replication of psychiatric status. *Archives of General Psychiatry, 48*, 77–83.

Mendelson, W., Johnson, N., & Stewart, M. A. (1971). Hyperactive children as teenagers: A follow-up study. *Journal of Nervous and Mental Disease, 153*, 273–279.

Satterfield, J., Hoppe, C. M., & Schell, A. M. (1982). A prospective study of delinquency in 110 adolescent boys with attention deficit disorder and 88 normal adolescent boys. *American Journal of Psychiatry, 139*, 795–798.

Tannock, R. (2000). Attention deficit disorders with anxiety disorders. In T. E. Brown (Ed.), *Attention deficit disorders and comorvidities in children, adolescents, and adults* (pp. 125–170). Washington, DC: American Psychiatric Press.

Weiss, G., & Hechtman, L. T. (1993). *Hyperactive children grown up* (2nd ed.). New York: Guilford Press.

Wenwei, Y. (1996). An investigation of adult outcome of hyperactive children in Shanghai. *Chinese Medical Journal, 109*, 877–880.

Chapter 5

Is ADHD an Impairing Condition in Childhood and Adolescence?

by Stephen P. Hinshaw, Ph.D.

Introduction 5-2
Methodological and Conceptual Issues 5-3
    Current Definitions of ADHD May Lead to Circular Reasoning
        Regarding Impairment 5-3
    Types of Samples and Kinds of Measures Used to Appraise
        Impairment Crucial to Unbiased Definitions 5-3
    Comorbidities, Rather Than ADHD Per Se, May Explain
        Impairment 5-4
    Which Subtypes of ADHD Show Impairment? 5-5
    Does Impairment Change Across the Developmental Span
        From Preschool to Adolescence? 5-5
    Summary 5-5
ADHD-Related Impairment: Evidence 5-6
    Academic Achievement and School Functioning 5-6
        Academic Achievement 5-6
        School-Related Impairment: Special Education, Suspension,
            Expulsion 5-7
        Summary 5-7
    Family Relationships and Home Life 5-8
        Impaired Family Relationship Patterns 5-8
        Escalating Pattern of Discordant Interchanges 5-8
        Impact of Comorbid Aggression 5-9
        Summary 5-9
    Peer Relationships 5-10
        Peer Rejection 5-10
        Impact of Comorbid Aggression 5-10
        Effect of ADHD Subtype on Likelihood of Rejection 5-11
        ADHD Children's Social Competence 5-11
        Summary 5-12

Self-Esteem and Self-Perception 5-12
    Lower Self-Esteem 5-12
    Overconfidence 5-12
    Summary 5-12
Accidental Injury 5-13
    Personal and Familial Variables 5-13
    Developmental Factors. 5-13
    Summary 5-14
Overall Adaptive Functioning 5-14
Conclusions 5-14
Summary of Findings 5-14
Practical Implications 5-16

INTRODUCTION

The central question addressed in this chapter is whether, during childhood and adolescence, attention deficit hyperactivity disorder (ADHD) is associated with compromised functioning in key domains that are salient for optimal development. In other words, is ADHD an impairing condition? Do its symptom patterns really matter? Does ADHD incorporate behavior patterns that are merely bothersome to adult caregivers? Or, rather, does it place the child's opportunities for attaining competence at risk?

Extrapolating these questions to a broader perspective, one might ask the following: Has the importance of ADHD been exaggerated in the media? Or, has a lack of appropriate focus on the impairment that accompanies ADHD potentially understated the disorder's developmental significance?

Such questions are important for a number of reasons. At a clinical level it is essential to know whether extremes of inattention, impulsivity, and motoric overactivity—the core symptom areas of ADHD—are related to meaningful impairments at home, in school, and in the peer group. Indeed, treatment efforts would be far more strongly justified if ADHD were shown to transcend symptom patterns per se by leading to impaired functioning and development. Thus, impairment is centrally related to the field's rationale for intervention.

In all, documentation and elaboration of impairment, as well as explanation of its processes and mechanisms, is a major agenda item for those who live with, work with, treat, and investigate ADHD. This chapter critically evaluates research findings on the impairment related to ADHD in six crucial domains: (1) academic achievement and school performance, (2) family interactions and home life, (3) peer relationships, (4) self-esteem and self-image, (5) the presence of accidental injuries, and (6) overall adaptive functioning. This survey therefore goes from the "outer world" of school, home, and peer environments to the psychological realm of self-concept; it also includes the child's ability to negotiate the many hazards present in home, school, and neighborhood settings and to master self-care skills independently. Note that the present review spans impairments from preschool age through adolescence (see Chapter 6 for a discussion featuring ADHD-related impairment in adulthood).

At the outset, the main conclusion of this review is headlined: Although ADHD is an extremely heterogeneous disorder, with a diversity of etiological pathways, clinical manifestations, and levels of severity, on the whole it is associated with severe, pervasive, long-lasting, and often debilitating impairments in the very domains of life functioning that are essential for achieving competence. This impairment magnifies the need to develop viable and durable intervention strategies; it provides validation of the disorder from a scientific and nosologic perspective; it illustrates the need for ecological research on the interplay between afflicted individuals and their social contexts; and it underscores the need for coordinated social policy related to preventing and accommodating ADHD. Before providing the specific evidence for these conclusions, the chapter begins with the consideration of several issues related to the conceptualization and assessment of impairment, issues that are essential to consider in interpreting the database related to ADHD as an impairing condition.

METHODOLOGICAL AND CONCEPTUAL ISSUES

Current Definitions of ADHD May Lead to Circular Reasoning Regarding Impairment

The most recent diagnostic guidelines for ADHD explicitly include impairment as a definitional criterion, potentially leading to tautological, circular reasoning. Most notably, the fourth edition of *Diagnostic and Statistical Manual of Mental Disorders* (DSM-IV; American Psychiatric Association, 1994) states explicitly that " impairment from the symptoms is present in two or more settings (e.g., at school (or work) and at home)" (p. 84). The upshot is that if ADHD is defined as incorporating impairment, it is quite obvious that associated impairments will be uncovered.

Many of the key investigations discussed herein were based on earlier diagnostic criteria, which were not as explicit in requiring impairment—and certainly not explicit at all in requiring "pervasive" impairment in at least two domains of functioning, as does DSM-IV. These studies may therefore not be as "circular" as those using later definitions. For investigations using more current diagnostic standards, one solution would be to require symptom counts at or above diagnostic thresholds but to exclude impairment itself as an inclusion criterion. Then, patterns of functional impairment could be noted, unconfounded by a circular definition. Only a handful of high-quality investigations meet this criterion (Lahey et al., 1998), and they are weighted heavily in the discussion that follows.

Types of Samples and Kinds of Measures Used to Appraise Impairment Crucial to Unbiased Definitions

First, it is well-known that clinic-referred samples differ, in important ways, from epidemiological, representative samples. For example, referred samples are more likely to display significant comorbidities, their parents are better educated and more likely to have received clinical services, and they are (almost by definition) more prone to suffer impairments (Goodman et al., 1997). Given that much of the database reviewed herein involves clinical rather than population-based samples, it is conceivable that corresponding estimates of impairment are inflated.

Yet matters are not so clear-cut. Although epidemiological investigations of child psychopathology would presumably yield less biased estimates of impairment, these kinds of studies are not only expensive and relatively rare but are also likely to rely on rather basic indices of impairment, such as parent (or in some cases teacher) endorsement of single items or simple scales during interviews. This method of appraising impairment is potentially problematic: When the same persons who provide information related to the child's diagnostic status also appraise impairment, such biases as "halo effects" (or, more pertinent to psychopathology, "negative halo effects") may spuriously inflate the appraisal of impaired functioning. In other words, shared method variance in epidemiological reports may outweigh the representative nature of the sample investigated.

Thus, impairment should be rated by informants who do not yield the information necessary for diagnosis (e.g., peers who make sociometric assessments of social impairment) or even by objective measures (e.g., achievement tests to appraise academic impairment), to eliminate or at least minimize the influence of method variance. Yet such measures are far more difficult and costly to obtain than are parent or teacher items, usually beyond the scope of epidemiological investigation.

Complicating matters further, "objective" documentation of impairment has its own set of problems. To a large extent, impairment involves some subjective accounting of the impact of symptoms or problem behavior. Thus, objective behavioral counts of, for example, externalizing classroom behavior provide an incomplete index, at best, of classroom impairment. Other objective measures (e.g., suspensions or expulsions from school and special education placement) would be preferable, as they reflect a teacher's or district's judgment as to the nonnormative and impairing nature of the behavior pattern. Finding valid indicators of impairment is a continuing challenge for the field (Goodman et al., 1998).

Comorbidities, Rather Than ADHD Per Se, May Explain Impairment

Comorbidity is an important topic, both conceptually and practically, for child psychopathology (Caron & Rutter, 1991). Furthermore, comorbid psychiatric disorders are the rule rather than the exception for ADHD (Biederman, Newcorn, & Sprich, 1991; Jensen, Martin, & Cantwell, 1997). In addition, it is well-known that such comorbid conditions as aggressive-spectrum disorders (Hinshaw, 1987; Jensen et al, 1997), depression (Capaldi, 1991), and learning disorders (Hinshaw, 1992; Semrud-Clikeman et al., 1992) each carries its own risks for substantial impairment. A central issue, then, is to ascertain whether any impairments relate to the core symptom patterns of ADHD as opposed to comorbid conditions that may accompany ADHD.

Unfortunately, as aptly described by Loney and Milich (1982), all too many studies of ADHD in the literature fail to even consider the potential comorbidities that pertain to the ADHD samples under investigation. In such cases, the specificity of attribution to ADHD is highly suspect. On the other hand, as shown later, some investigations with good controls of comorbidity have documented that serious impairments are indeed specifically related to ADHD. Yet in other domains (e.g., parent-child relationships), the lion's share of the impairments appears to be related to comorbidity (in this case, overlap with aggressive-spectrum disorder). Because of the importance of comorbidity for all investigations of ADHD—particularly those that aim to document impairment—discussion of comorbidity is incorporated into each section of the substantive review of ADHD-related impairments that follows.

Which Subtypes of ADHD Show Impairment?

Demonstrating that impairment pertains to ADHD as broadly construed does not answer the question as to whether it results more from the inattentive-disorganized versus the hyperactive-impulsive symptoms that constitute the two major symptom clusters of this disorder. Several investigations in recent years—including the seminal field trials for DSM-IV (Lahey et al., 1994)—have begun to examine the differential impairments that emanate from the subtypes or subdimensions of ADHD.

Note that the subtype issue is confounded with the point previously made above about comorbidity. It is increasingly appreciated that the ADHD subtypes show substantially different patterns of comorbidity, with the inattentive type more likely to demonstrate association with internalizing features and disorders (particularly anxiety) and the hyperactive-impulsive and combined types more prone to incorporate serious aggression and conduct disturbance (Paternite, Loney, & Roberts, 1996). Thus, controlling for both ADHD subtype and comorbidity would be necessary for full knowledge of the relationship of ADHD to impairment. Yet, as might be surmised, both large samples and careful controls are required to effect such dual control (Lahey et al., 1998).

Does Impairment Change Across the Developmental Span From Preschool to Adolescence?

It would be expectable that the different settings and social worlds in which ADHD preschoolers versus adolescents reside would yield different patterns of impairment across this age span. Throughout this review, such developmental differences are highlighted, but there are almost no prospective longitudinal investigations of individuals across this age range that document differing patterns of impairment as a function of developmental level. Such information would be important in order not only to document the severity of impairment with increasing age but also to begin to explain mechanisms of impairment.

Summary

A host of issues, ranging from methodological (definitions of ADHD, types of sampling, measurement strategies) to those related to comorbidity, subtype, and development are essential to consider in establishing the types of impairment that pertain to children and adolescents with ADHD. Several of these issues are revisited following the substantive review of ADHD-related impairments in childhood and adolescence.

ADHD-RELATED IMPAIRMENT: EVIDENCE

Academic Achievement and School Functioning

The structured, adult-directed, and academically laden nature of school settings places a premium on the attentional capacities of all children and adolescents, particularly those with ADHD. In fact, school settings reveal some of the most significant impairments that pertain to youngsters with attentional deficits and hyperactivity. First, children with ADHD show marked degrees of behavioral disruption in classroom settings (Barkley, 1998). Indeed, almost by definition, the core symptoms of ADHD—dysfunctional levels of sustained attention, difficulties with inhibition and impulse control, motoric overactivity—lead to difficulties in behavioral control in settings that mandate self-regulated behavior. What, then, are the implications for actual measures of impairment at school?

Academic Achievement. One indicator of impairment pertains to the child's actual level of attainment in academic subjects. Not only is this measure a "face valid" indicator of impairment, but it also is a key predictor of success in later life. Clear evidence exists that youth with ADHD suffer from lower grades in school, higher rates of significant academic failure, and worse scores on standardized achievement tests than do comparison samples (Barkley, Dupaul, & McMurray, 1990; Casey, Rourke, & Del Dotto, 1996; Hinshaw, 1992; Semrud-Clikeman et al., 1992). As discussed by Barkley (1998), depending on the particular sample employed, ADHD children score from just under 1 to at least 2 standard deviations below their peers on tests of reading, arithmetic, and spelling. Such indicators of poor academic attainment are related to—but transcend—the tendency for youth with ADHD to score slightly (but significantly) lower than their peers on measures of IQ (Barkley, 1998; Hinshaw, 1992). In all, it is evident that children and adolescents with ADHD suffer from marked academic impairment.

Immediately, however, the issue of comorbidity must be invoked. If ADHD is highly overlapping with learning disabilities, which by definition involve subaverage academic attainment, then any academic impairment related to ADHD may not be specific. Yet, when strict, IQ-achievement discrepancy criteria are used to define learning disabilities (LD), the actual comorbidity between ADHD and LD (particularly reading disability) is approximately 15 percent —that is, no more than 15–20 percent of ADHD children have comorbid learning disabilities (Hinshaw, 1992). Although well above chance levels, this rate is far below the 50–80 percent overlap that is sometimes reported with extremely loose definitions of LD. Furthermore, academic attainment is poor in those children with ADHD who are not disabled in reading or other academic subjects (Barkley, 1998). It thus appears that much of the achievement-related impairment that accrues from ADHD is related to effects of behavioral disruption, poor attentional control, and other aspects of the disorder that prohibit full engagement in academic learning. It is also possible, however, that some forms of ADHD involve subtle but real processing deficits that compromise not only attentional regulation but also academic underachievement. Far more remains to be learned about processes and mechanisms related to such impairment (see Chapter 6 for further discussion of mechanisms and processes related to impairment).

It has also been contended that aggressive children suffer from academic under-achievement. Might the specific linkage, then, involve aggressive-spectrum disorders that are often comorbid with ADHD? It appears not. In a systematic review, Hinshaw (1992) found that although academic underachievement per se is often attributed to aggression and conduct disturbance in youth, the specific relationship (prior to ado-lescence) is between ADHD and underachievement. In fact, any apparent relationship between aggression-spectrum behavior and poor attainment is entirely accounted for by the empirical overlap between ADHD and such aggression (Frick et al., 1991). By adolescence, however, there does appear to be a specific linkage between delinquent behavior patterns and underachievement, not necessarily mediated by ADHD. Thus, the relationships between ADHD, comorbid conditions, and indicators of impairment appear to change with development.

Although data are not plentiful, the academic problems of adolescents with ADHD are instructive to note. With their multiple subjects, multiple teachers, and multiple shifts in classes throughout the day, secondary schools place a premium on organization, self-direction, and independence. Indeed, poor organizational and poor study skills are extremely salient for adolescents with ADHD (Evans, Pelham, & Grudberg, 1994).

School-Related Impairment: Special Education, Suspension, Expulsion. Ad-ditional indicators of academic impairment are that children with ADHD are overrep-resented in special education settings, in the need for supplemental educational inter-vention, and on such academic/behavioral indicators as suspensions and expulsions from school. As reviewed by Barkley (1998), more than half the children with ADHD may require tutoring, nearly a third are retained or "held back" at least a grade level in school, and a similar percentage are formally placed in some form of special edu-cation placement (e.g., resource rooms). Nearly half may receive suspensions from school, and dropout rates are estimated at levels from one in ten to nearly one in three (Faraone et al., 1993). Clearly, ADHD is associated with marked impairment in the ability to benefit from public education (this is the case even among very young chil-dren with ADHD; Lahey et al., 1998).

Comorbidity is, once again, important to consider in this regard. Given the well-documented overlap of ADHD with such disruptive behavior disorders as oppositional-defiant disorder (ODD) and conduct disorder (CD), perhaps such indicators as special education placement, suspension, and expulsion pertain more to such comorbidity than to ADHD itself. Few investigations of such school-related impairment have con-trolled for this overlap. Whereas ADHD is clearly and specifically related to academ-ic underachievement per se (Lahey et al., 1998), some of the more discipline-related impairments (e.g., suspensions and even special education placements) would appear to be particularly salient for those ADHD children with comorbid ODD and/or CD.

Summary. In all, the academic impairments that pertain to ADHD are of marked clin-ical significance. Children and adolescents with this disorder are prone to under-achievement in key academic subjects, regardless of comorbid status. In addition, school-related indicators of impairment such as the need for special education, repeat-ing of grades, suspensions, and early termination are strikingly prevalent for ADHD samples, although the role of comorbidity in shaping such impairment is less clear.

The loss of academic potential, the huge investments in special services, and the compromised vocational opportunities that result from these impairments must be counted heavily in any account of impairment that pertains to ADHD.

Family Relationships and Home Life

Impaired Family Relationship Patterns. On the basis of several important indicators, the negative impact of raising a child with dysregulated attention, behavior, and self-control is noteworthy. Families of children with ADHD have greater levels of marital discord (Befera & Barkley, 1985; Cunningham, Benness, & Siegel, 1988), parenting distress and a lack of feeling of competence as parents (Donenberg & Baker, 1994; Mash & Johnston, 1990), and actual separation and divorce (Befera & Barkley, 1985) than do comparison samples. Furthermore, in terms of parenting practices and beliefs, parents (particularly mothers) of ADHD children display more discordant, negative, and harsh parenting behaviors than do comparison parents during parent-child interactions (Anderson, Hinshaw, & Simmel, 1994; Barkley, Cunningham, & Karlsson, 1983; Buhrmester, Camparo, Christensen, Gonzalez, & Hinshaw, 1992; Tallmadge & Barkley, 1983), and they are less likely than comparison parents to adhere to authoritative (warm, structuring, independence-promoting) parenting beliefs (Hinshaw, Zupan, Simmel, Nigg, & Melnick, 1997). The negative parent-child interactions that ensue from such suboptimal practices and beliefs are predictive of (1) persistence of ADHD-related symptomatology from preschool years through the elementary grades (Campbell, Pierce, Moore, & Marakvitz, 1996), (2) greater levels of noncompliant and covert antisocial behavior in children diagnosed with ADHD (Anderson, Hinshaw, & Simmel, 1994), and (3) peer rejection in ADHD children (Hinshaw et al., 1997).

Thus, ADHD is associated with marked impairments in essential family relationship patterns, including marital dissolution itself. Reciprocally, such maladaptive family relationships and parent-child interactions predict persistence, antisocial comorbidity, and compromised social competence with peers.

Escalating Pattern of Discordant Interchanges. For several decades, debate has centered on the directionality of such negative family effects—from parent to child versus child to parent (Lytton, 1990). Evidence from stimulant medication trials appears to favor the "child effects" model, in that reducing the disruptive symptoms of ADHD with stimulant treatment reduces negative parenting behaviors (Barkley & Cunningham, 1979). Yet, for full explanation of the relationships of families with an ADHD child, bidirectional and transactional models are needed. That is, young children with difficult temperaments and early signs of ADHD tend to elicit frustration and discordant responses to the child, which, in turn, exacerbate the child's behavioral tendencies (Campbell, 1990; Hinshaw, 1999). The impairment is thus not "located" exclusively in the child or exclusively in the parent. Indeed, the difficult "fit" between the child's temperament and the parent's responses is explainable not only by the severity of the child's proclivities but also by the strong likelihood that biological parents of an ADHD child will themselves suffer from attentional deficits and behavioral dysregulation (Barkley, 1998). Thus, from both heritable and psychosocial perspectives, the escalating pattern of discordant interchanges leads to exacerbation of intense and underregulated behavior on the part of the child, which is particularly likely to increase aggressive comorbidity (Patterson, Reid, & Dishion, 1992). The field's research designs and analytic strategies, which are still dominated by linear cause-effect models, do not do justice to the complex patterns of impairment that pertain to the family interactions and relationships related to ADHD.

Impact of Comorbid Aggression. As with school-related impairment, comorbidity is essential to consider in relation to the familial ramifications of ADHD. Particularly salient is the frequent overlap of ADHD with disruptive disorders (ODD and CD). Indeed, a wealth of literature documents the harsh, negativistic parent-child interaction patterns that typify children's (especially boys') antisocial trajectories (Patterson et al., 1992). All too little research in the domain of aggression and conduct disturbance has considered the potential association of disruptive, aggressive patterns with ADHD, and the ADHD literature on familial interactions has too often neglected the parallel comorbidity with disruptive disorders. Noteworthy exceptions to this statement are found in the work of Barkley and colleagues (Barkley, Anastopoulos, Guevremont, & Fletcher, 1992; Fletcher, Fischer, Barkley, & Smallish, 1996), who have shown that the majority of the negativity in the family interactions related to ADHD pertains to comorbid aggression in the child (and particularly in the interactions of such ADHD/ODD or ADHD/CD sons with their mothers). Overall, negative parenting styles, dysfunctional parenting attitudes, and multiple markers of family distress and discord are likely to be magnified in families of those ADHD children with comorbid aggression. Indeed, in such families, parental depression, substance abuse, and antisocial behavior patterns are likely to complement the strong parental tendencies to show ADHD-related symptomatology, compounding mightily the genetic and psychosocial risks for negative cycles of discordant interaction (Barkley, 1998; Hinshaw, 1999). Thus, comorbidity of ADHD with aggressive-spectrum disorders will magnify, to a great degree, the types of family-related impairments addressed in this section.

It is important to note that there are some family-related areas in which ADHD is not associated with impairment. For example, there is no published evidence to the effect that ADHD children have higher rates of insecure attachments with caregivers than do non-ADHD youngsters. Crucially, however, comorbid aggression in the child is strongly associated with marked levels of insecure attachment (Greenberg, Speltz, & DeKlyen, 1993; Hinshaw, 1999). In addition, in impoverished, high-risk samples, there is evidence that insensitive maternal response to their offspring predicts ADHD in later life (Carlson, Jacobvitz, & Sroufe, 1995). For the most part, however, ADHD does not appear to be a disorder marked by a primarily relational etiology, although family relations pertain directly to the maintenance and escalation of ADHD and its linkages with key comorbidities.

Summary. Familial interaction patterns do not appear to be a primary causal factor for ADHD, but having a child with this disorder predisposes families to show a great deal of impairment in parental harmony, parenting distress and perceived incompetence, parent-child interaction patterns, and parental childrearing beliefs, with strong implications for general parental distress and severe marital discord. As emphasized throughout this section, child-effects versus parent-effects models must give way to more complex, transactional models of effect. All the impairments noted herein are magnified in intensity and deleterious consequences when ADHD is comorbid with clinically significant aggression.

Peer Relationships

Perhaps the most devastating impact of ADHD is found in the domain of peer relations. First, the development of social skills and the attainment of peer regard and friendships are crucial developmental milestones during childhood (Hartup, 1996). Second, peer relationships are strongly predictive of functioning in later life. Indeed, as extensively reviewed by Parker and Asher (1987), rejection by age-mates during the elementary grades is strongly related to such long-term negative outcomes as school dropout, delinquency, and adult mental health problems. Such predictions hold when initial level of problem behavior is statistically controlled (Greene, Biederman, Faraone, Sienna, & garcia-Jetton, 1997), meaning that peer rejection is not simply redundant with early signs of problematic behavior—it conveys unique risk for serious maladaptation in adolescence and adulthood. In other words, peer rejection does more than reflect early psychopathology; it reciprocally incurs even further behavioral, emotional, and prognostic problems.

Peer Rejection. Given this strong empirical link between peer rejection and later incompetence, what is known about the peer status of children with ADHD? Simply put, there is a clear and strong tendency for children with this disorder to be rejected sociometrically by their peers (Whalen & Henker, 1992). That is, children with ADHD are highly likely to receive high levels of negative sociometric ratings and nominations from age-mates while earning low numbers of positive endorsements (Hinshaw & Melnick, 1995; Milich & Landau, 1982; Pelham & Bender, 1982). In the peer sociometric literature, "social preference" is typically indicated by the difference between positive and negative nominations from age-mates, meaning that ADHD children have extremely low social preference (and, thus, extremely high peer rejection). Also, in reports using teacher estimates of peer liking and disliking, ADHD children are clearly seen as rejected by classmates (Gaub & Carlson, 1997; Lahey et al., 1994, 1998).

Indeed, although direct comparisons have seldom been made, it appears that children with ADHD are more likely to incur peer rejection than are those in any other diagnostic category in childhood (Asarnow, 1988). In addition, the time it takes an ADHD child to become socially rejected is distressingly short (measurable in minutes or hours; Bickett & Milich, 1990; Erhardt & Hinshaw, 1994; Pelham & Bender, 1982). Thus, given that (1) ADHD children are at extremes in terms of peer rejection and (2) peer rejection is a robust predictor of multiple indices of maladjustment in later life, it is no wonder that ADHD children have been found to be at risk for long-term adjustment difficulties. Peer rejection may well be a key mechanism underlying the ultimate impairments that may accrue to ADHD.

Impact of Comorbid Aggression. Such peer disapproval appears to emanate from the intrusive behavioral styles, lack of reciprocation, and disruptive behavioral tendencies of children with ADHD (Erhardt & Hinshaw, 1994; Whalen & Henker, 1985). With regard to the latter, issues of comorbidity are salient. Because aggressive behavior patterns are also linked to peer rejection, and because peer rejection is predicted by aggressive behavior patterns in ADHD boys (Erhardt & Hinshaw, 1994) as well as girls (Hinshaw, 2001), the specificity of the ADHD/peer rejection association can be questioned. Yet several pieces of information are crucial in this regard. First, aggressive youth without significant attentional problems are likely to be sociometrically controversial (meaning that they receive both positive and negative nominations from classmates) rather than rejected (Milich & Landau, 1989). "Pure" aggression appears to incur respect and admiration as well as fear and disapproval, whereas the intrusive, bothersome nature of the social interactions of ADHD youth more specifically promotes disapprobation and rejection. Second, ADHD children without significant aggression—or without comorbid disruptive behavior disorders—are still rejected far more than their comparison age-mates. Indeed, Hinshaw and Melnick (1995) found that the most peer-rejected subgroup contained ADHD-aggressive boys, who were significantly more rejected than nonaggressive ADHD males, but the latter group, in turn, was significantly more rejected than comparison age-mates. Thus, although the subgroup of ADHD children with comorbid ADHD and aggression incurs particularly severe peer disapproval (Hinshaw & Melnick, 1995; Milich & Landau, 1989), ADHD is more specifically linked to peer rejection than is aggression itself.

Effect of ADHD Subtype on Likelihood of Rejection. In terms of ADHD subtypes, evidence suggests that the inattentive type of ADHD is more likely to receive peer neglect (i.e., they receive few positive or negative nominations from peers), whereas the combined type is highly rejected (Carlson, Lahey, Frame, Walker, & Hynd, 1987; Wheeler & Carlson, 1994). This higher level of rejection for the combined type may well relate to the propensity for this subgroup to display comorbid aggression, yet Lahey et al. (1998) found that the children in the combined type were rated by teachers as socially rejected even when numbers of ODD and CD symptoms were statistically controlled.

ADHD Children's Social Competence. Over and above social rejection per se, recent evidence also points to the specific difficulties experienced by children with ADHD in making and keeping friends (Blachman & Hinshaw, 1998; Lahey et al., 1998). Because friendship is an indicator of social competence that is not redundant with peer rejection (Hartup, 1996), such findings add to the documentation of social impairment for children with ADHD.

With respect to mechanisms, the extreme social difficulties of children with ADHD do not appear to be related specifically to deficits in social knowledge or social skill (Whalen & Henker, 1992). ADHD children appear to know what to do in social and peer-related situations, but they typically fail to do it (Barkley, 1997; Whalen & Henker, 1985). Thus, their deficits are ones of performance rather than knowledge, of implementation of skills rather than skills per se. Social goals (Melnick & Hinshaw, 1996) and emotion regulation (Melnick & Hinshaw, 2000) have been invoked as potential mediators of ADHD children's social competence and incompetence. Furthermore, an important research initiative is the linking of family processes and impairments with the social/peer skills and status of children with ADHD (Hinshaw et al., 1997).

Summary. In terms of conceptual underpinnings, developmental significance, and treatment implications, the peer rejection of children and adolescents with ADHD looms large in terms of its impairing nature. Whereas comorbid aggression leads to the most extreme levels of peer rejection, ADHD children without ODD or CD also show marked social impairments with their age-mates. The tendencies toward peer rejection for children with ADHD are clinically and prognostically meaningful; a major priority for clinical efforts is to attempt to develop social competence in ADHD youngsters sufficient to improve their often-dismal peer standing.

Self-Esteem and Self-Perception

Far fewer investigations have been conducted on the self-esteem of children with ADHD, largely because of (1) the measurement and instrumentation problems that surround assessment of this variable and (2) the questions often raised about the validity of the self-report of youth with ADHD. Nonetheless, intriguing findings on the self-perceptions of children and adolescents with ADHD have emerged, pointing to the potential importance of this domain with respect to a further impairment pertinent to ADHD.

Lower Self-Esteem. As a group, children and adolescents with ADHD appear to have less accurate self-perceptions and lower levels of self-esteem than do comparison children (Ialongo, Lopez, Horn, Pascoe, & Greenberg, 1994; Treuting & Hinshaw, 1998). Findings are not consistent, however (Hoza, Pelham, Milich, Pillow, & McBride, 1993). Importantly, these self-esteem deficits when found predict poorer social and occupational adjustment in adulthood (Slomkowski, Klein, & Mannuzza, 1995). It may be that the accumulated toll of behavioral deficits and excesses; school-, family- and home-related impairment; and resultant demoralization begins to erode the self-worth of youth with this disorder.

Overconfidence. With regard to expectations for subsequent performance, however, children with ADHD may have self-perceptions and expectations that are actually inflated over levels displayed by comparison children (Diener & Milich, 1997). In other words, ADHD youth may approach tasks with exaggerated levels of confidence, perhaps as a compensation for skill deficits. Yet these inflated self-perceptions and expectations appear to be fragile in that they drop quickly once negative feedback is obtained.

Comorbidity with aggressive-spectrum disorders will be important to monitor in future investigations of this domain. That is, in some cases aggressive behavior patterns may well be associated with spuriously high levels of self-worth and self-appraisal. It is conceivable, then, that subgroups of ADHD children may show either (1) the sorts of compromised self-worth noted earlier or (2) overinflated self-perceptions, which maintain maladaptive interpersonal behavioral patterns. In all, the contradictory results in the area of self-perceptions and self-esteem reflect the difficulties in operationalizing and appraising these aspects of the phenomenology of ADHD; this area bears closer scrutiny.

Summary. Despite mixed evidence, it appears that children with ADHD have global self-esteem that is lower than that of their non-ADHD peers. The self-perceptions of youth with this disorder are also fragile: Self-protective mechanisms may inflate initial levels of self-regard. Individual differences in self-esteem should be taken into account in future research investigations.

Accidental Injury

The small amount of relevant research suggests strongly that children with ADHD experience higher rates of accidental injuries than do comparison children (Hartsough & Lambert, 1985; Lahey et al., 1998; Matheny & Fisher, 1984; Stewart, Thach, & Freidin, 1970; Szatmari, Offord, & Boyle, 1989). The definitions of "injury" or "accident" used in these studies include accidental poisonings, broken limbs, head injuries, and hospitalizations, as well as risk factors for accidents (Farmer & Peterson, 1995) and injuries during sports activities (Johnson & Rosen, 2000). Given that such accidental injuries may significantly contribute to time away from school, personal and family distress, and risk for further morbidity (particularly in the case of head injury), this area of impairment is significant. Indeed, if falling from high places, swallowing poisonous materials, running into dangerous places, and the like lead to risk for head injuries and subsequent brain injury, exacerbation of the underlying behavior patterns may well occur. Even without head trauma per se, cuts requiring stitches, broken bones, and other sequelae of poor judgment and impulsivity are costly in their own right.

Personal and Familial Variables. Similar risk has been associated with aggressive behavior patterns in children (Davidson, Hughes, & O'Connor, 1988). Thus, it is unknown whether ADHD-related propensity for accidental injury is specific to ADHD. In a carefully controlled investigation of young children, however (Lahey et al., 1998), it was found that high rates of accidental injury in ADHD youngsters held up when comorbidity with ODD was statistically controlled. As in all other domains of impairment-related research, examination of comorbid subgroups is essential. Furthermore, risk for accidental injury is associated with such family characteristics as poor parental monitoring (Davidson et al., 1988), suggesting that both intraindividual and familial variables are related to this significant domain of impairment.

Developmental Factors. Developmental factors are important to consider regarding impairment in this domain. Preschoolers with clinically significant attentional problems and impulsivity appear to be at high risk for accidental injury (Davidson et al., 1988). Furthermore, by late adolescence, there is documentation of clear risk for increased rates of traffic accidents in individuals with ADHD (Barkley et al., 1993; Nada-Raja et al., 1997). Thus, with development comes the opportunity for risk-taking behavior and poor judgment with increasingly dangerous implements (i.e., cars) that can harm others as well as the self. Yet again, comorbidity with aggressive-spectrum disorders (including increased risk for substance abuse) must be considered in future investigations of the area of driving-related risks.

Barkley (1998) has speculated that the multiple risks of ADHD youth related to impulse control deficits, poor judgment, accidental injury, substance abuse, and antisocial behavior may well lead to a reduced life expectancy for this population. No definitive data are as of yet available in this regard, however.

Summary. Overall, the understudied area of accidental injury appears to be an under-appreciated and potentially severe area of impairment for youth with ADHD. Indeed, when injury involves the region of the head, the resultant brain trauma may well exacerbate the symptoms of ADHD that helped to promote the initial impulsive and poorly regulated tendencies leading to the injury.

Overall Adaptive Functioning

In the past decade, evidence has been presented regarding the adaptive functioning of youth with ADHD, referring to overall levels of independence, abilities to perform self-care skills, and motoric competence. The chief conclusions have been that, in spite of overall intelligence levels that are in the normal range, children and adolescents with ADHD are all too often sorely deficient in adaptive functioning (Greene et al., 1996; Stein, Szumowski, Blondis, & Roizen, 1995). Indeed, many youth with ADHD demonstrate levels of independence and performance of self-care skills that might be expected from individuals with markedly deficient cognitive skills. Adaptive functioning deficits in ADHD youth are predictive of extremely negative outcomes several years later (Greene et al., 1997). Such adaptive behavior deficits bespeak the immaturity, need for close monitoring, and severe performance (as opposed to ability) problems that relate to ADHD. Whereas comorbidity has not always been ruled out as an explanatory factor in such investigations, the disparities between "potential" and actual performance of adaptive life skills in ADHD populations are worthy of clinical as well as theoretical attention.

It must be pointed out that assessments of adaptive functioning typically used involve the same caregivers who provide the diagnostic information. In other words, shared method variance may play a role in the determination of such impairment. On the other hand, parents and caregivers are in a unique position to appraise the independent life skills of their children. More research in this area would be an important addition to understanding the types of impairment that youth with ADHD suffer.

CONCLUSIONS

Summary of Findings

As highlighted at the outset of this chapter, the chief conclusion from this review is that the impairments related to ADHD can be severe, pervasive, long lasting, and often debilitating, reflecting the clinical importance and public health significance of this disorder. Indeed, the most serious impairments relevant to ADHD pertain to just those areas of functioning—academic achievement, family relations and interactions, peer competence, self-perceptions, accidental injuries, and adaptive functioning—that are necessary for optimal development. In short, there can be little doubt that ADHD is indeed an impairing condition.

There are several methodological and conceptual issues that surround the appraisal of impairment. Whereas several of these points were addressed explicitly in the content areas of the review, we now revisit them to ascertain, at a general level, whether attribution of impairment related to ADHD can survive key methodological challenges.

First, there is the important issue of circularity: Do current definitions of ADHD, which require cross-situational impairment, lead tautologically to the conclusion that ADHD is impairing? For one thing, many of the citations herein used definitions of ADHD well before the advent of DSM-IV, definitions that did not explicitly mandate impairment in the diagnostic criteria. More important, the current, careful investigations of Lahey et al. (1994, 1998)—using the DSM-IV criterion set—defined samples on the basis of symptomatology and not impairment per se. The findings were clear: Dimensional and categorical examination of ADHD yielded sound evidence of social, academic, familial, and accident-related impairment. Thus, the circularity argument can be laid to rest.

Second, it is also essential to document impairment with either objective measures or by informants (parents, teachers) who do not supply the symptoms used to make diagnosis. As shown in the foregoing review, ADHD-related impairment has, in fact, been demonstrated by such means the following:

1. *Academic and school.* Objective achievement tests and such school-based indicators as retention and suspension;

2. *Familial.* Video coded parent-child interactions and objective measures such as divorce;

3. *Peer-related.* Sociometric ratings and nominations from age-mates;

4. *Self-perceptions.* The child's self-reported attitudes and beliefs; and

5. *Accidental injury.* Objective indicators of injuries and hospitalizations.

On the other hand, adaptive functioning is typically appraised by the caregivers who yield diagnostic information. On the whole, then, impairment uncontaminated by method variance has clearly been demonstrated.

Third, the issue of comorbidity is essential in any consideration of ADHD-related impairment. As documented throughout this chapter, ADHD frequently co-occurs with externalizing, internalizing, and learning-related disorders, making specific attribution of impairment highly suspect unless careful controls are used. As noted, however, ADHD children without LD show clear academic impairments, and ADHD children without comorbid aggression show evidence of marked peer rejection. Yet in other domains (parent-child interactions and family conflict and accidental injury), the impairments may relate just as much to aggressive-spectrum comorbidities as to ADHD. Furthermore, children with overlapping ADHD and ODD/CD clearly carry the highest risk for peer sociometric rejection. Some have contended, in fact, that impairment thought to pertain to ADHD is actually "contained" in comorbid conditions (Paternite et al., 1996).

Importantly, however, Lahey et al. (1998) demonstrated with young children that social, accident-related, and academic impairment related to ADHD does exist, even when comorbid internalizing and externalizing disorders were rigorously controlled. Thus, whereas ADHD's common comorbidities must be taken into account in any documentation of impairment, ADHD does appear to carry risk for substantial impairment irrespective of such comorbidities.

Fourth, regarding subtypes, all three DSM-IV subtypes (inattentive, hyperactive-impulsive, and combined) have been shown to display clear impairment (Lahey et al., 1994, 1998). Evidence exists that the hyperactive-impulsive and combined types are particularly likely to receive active peer rejection, compared to the inattentive type (Wheeler & Carlson, 1994), but mixed evidence suggests that the latter subtype may have more difficulties in the domain of academic achievement (Lahey et al., 1994). Whereas the subtypes' differential rates of comorbidity complicate specific attribution of impairment to a particular subgroup, Lahey et al. (1998) showed specificity of impairment by subtype, controlling for comorbidity.

Fifth, with respect to development, ADHD carries risk for serious impairment across the span from the preschool years (Lahey et al., 1998) through middle childhood (see the bulk of evidence presented earlier) to adolescence (Barkley et al., 1990). The changing forms of impairment, and the mechanisms and processes responsible for such changes, still require elucidation and elaboration.

In sum, given the weight of evidence presented herein, it would be extremely difficult to contend that ADHD is merely, for example, a nuisance to adults, a diagnosis made for the convenience of overburdened school districts, or a "medicalization" of relatively minor problems of childhood and adolescence. The impairments documented herein are the products of sound research methodology, which hold up with control of circularity, method variance, comorbidity, subtype, and development. Furthermore, they are often of large magnitude. Specifically, in terms of standard deviation units, effect sizes of achievement-related impairment range from 0.3 to over 1.5; sociometric data reveal that children with ADHD are among the most clearly rejected in all child psychopathology; rates of accidental injury are far above comparison levels. Impairment appears to be clinically, and not just statistically, significant.

Practical Implications

What, then, are the implications of the severe impairment related to ADHD? Such implications are discussed in terms of four crucial areas: rationale for treatment, diagnostic validity, investigations of social context, and policy ramifications.

1. *Rationale for treatment.* ADHD is a condition in childhood and adolescence that must receive high priority for state-of-the-art intervention research (Richters et al., 1995). Indeed, the developmental significance of ADHD is such that the field—and society—cannot afford to take a "wait and see" approach. Although short-term benefits for both pharmacological and psychosocial (behavioral) interventions have been well documented, the longer-term benefits of these treatments in real-world settings require elucidation (MTA Cooperative Group, 1999; Richters et al., 1995).

2. *Diagnostic validity.* As carefully documented by Lahey and Willcutt (see Chapter 1), both the dimensions and categorical diagnoses related to ADHD have received extensive internal and external validation in recent years. Clearly, the serious impairments pertinent to ADHD are a major external validating criterion. Thus, the real-world problems that accrue to ADHD, along with their developmental significance, have proven important for the scientific status of ADHD as a construct and diagnostic entity.

3. *Need for examination of the social context of ADHD.* It was noted earlier that

documentation of ADHD-related impairments would place a premium on understanding the contexts in which ADHD exists and on elucidating the reciprocally interacting social processes that maintain and exacerbate ADHD-related problems. Given the evidence presented herein, I believe that research on these social-ecological mechanisms and processes must receive emphasis, supplementing current and important work on genetics and biological risk processes. Indeed, ADHD is likely to be related to susceptibility genes rather than major genetic loci; its genesis appears quite related to the "fit" between temperament and family interaction patterns; its exacerbation and comorbidities are highly embedded in complex family, peer, and school environments (Barkley, 1998; Hinshaw, 1999). Thus, research on interactional processes must receive priority along with research on biological and cognitive mechanisms.

4. *Policy implications for prevention and accommodation.* The levels of impairment related to ADHD first demand greater efforts toward prevention. Indeed, given the spiraling impairments that accrue to ADHD across development, preventive efforts require far more attention than is currently allocated. As just one example, low birthweight is a known and significant predictor of later ADHD (Breslau et al., 1996; Whitaker et al., 1997). Adequate prenatal monitoring of mother and fetus could go a long way toward preventing low birthweight. In addition, ADHD-related impairment requires greater focus on the kinds of accommodations our society is willing to make for such activities as the taking of entrance examinations, the use of higher education facilities, and alterations of workplace environments and expectations. As noted aptly by Murphy and Gordon (1998), qualification of individuals with ADHD under the Americans with Disabilities Act requires impairment with respect to the average American citizen—not, for example, with respect to such highly selected groups as others accepted into a professional school or program. Thus, this salient and current legal definition of impairment is quite stringent. Whereas this chapter has focused on presentation of the impairments of ADHD samples or populations, individual assessment of impairment is an important focus for ascertaining the need for accommodations in society. [*Author's Note:* The entire foregoing discussion is predicated on careful, accurate evaluation of ADHD. If attentional deficits and hyperactivity are inferred simply by high scores on single-informant rating scales—which can lead to over-inflated estimates of "prevalence"—then impairment will often not be found, and society will have justification for downplaying the importance of this condition. On the other hand, with careful assessment, ADHD can and does lead to impairments of major developmental significance. The field must continue to demand care and caution in assessment-related and diagnostic practices and procedures.]

References

American Psychiatric Association. (1994). *Diagnostic and statistical manual of mental disorders* (4th ed.). Washington, DC: Author.

Anderson, C. A., Hinshaw, S. P., & Simmel, C. (1994). Mother-child interactions in ADHD and comparison boys: Relationships to overt and covert externalizing behavior. *Journal of Abnormal Child Psychology, 22*, 247–265.

Asarnow, J. (1988). Peer status and social competence in child psychiatric inpatients: A comparison of children with depressive, externalizing, and depressive and externalizing disorders. *Journal of Abnormal Child Psychology, 16*, 151–162.

Barkley, R. A. (1997). *ADHD and the nature of self-control.* New York: Guilford Press.

Barkley, R. A. (1998). *Attention-deficit hyperactivity disorder: A handbook for diagnosis and treatment* (2nd ed.). New York: Guilford Press.

Barkley, R. A., Anastopoulos, A. D., Guevremont, D. G., & Fletcher, K. F. (1992). Adolescents with attention-deficit hyperactivity disorder: Mother-adolescent interactions, family beliefs and conflicts, and maternal psychopathology. *Journal of Abnormal Child Psychology, 20,* 263–288.

Barkley, R. A., & Cunningham, C. (1979). The effects of methylphenidate on the mother-child interactions of hyperactive children. *Archives of General Psychiatry, 36,* 201–208.

Barkley, R. A., Cunningham, C., & Karlsson, J. (1983). The speech of hyperactive children and their mothers: Comparisons with normal children and stimulant drug effects. *Journal of Learning Disorders, 16,* 105–110.

Barkley, R. A., DuPaul, G. J., & McMurray, M. B. (1990). Comprehensive evaluation of attention deficit disorder with and without hyperactivity as defined by research criteria. *Journal of Consulting and Clinical Psychology, 58,* 775–789.

Befera, M., & Barkley, R. A. (1985). Hyperactive and normal girls and boys: Mother-child interactions, parent psychiatric status, and child psychopathology. *Journal of Child Psychology and Psychiatry, 26,* 439–452.

Bickett, L., & Milich, R. (1990). First impressions formed of boys with attention deficit disorder. *Journal of Learning Disorders, 23,* 253–259.

Biederman, J., Newcorn, J., & Sprich, S. (1991). Comorbidity of attention deficit hyperactivity disorder with conduct, depressive, anxiety, and other disorders. *American Journal of Psychiatry, 148,* 564–577.

Blachman, D., & Hinshaw, S. P. (1998). *Friendship patterns in girls with attention-deficit hyperactivity disorder.* Poster presented at the annual meeting of the American Psychological Society, Washington, DC.

Breslau, N., Brown, G. G., Del Dotto, J. E., Kumar, S., Exhuthachan, S., Andreski, P., & Hufnagle, K. G. (1996). Psychiatric sequelae of low birth weight at 6 years of age. *Journal of Abnormal Child Psychology, 24,* 285–300.

Buhrmester, D., Camparo, L., Christensen, A., Gonzalez, L. S., & Hinshaw, S. P. (1992). Mothers and fathers interacting in dyads and triads with normal and hyperactive sons. *Developmental Psychology, 28,* 500–509.

Campbell, S. B. (1990). *Behavior problems in preschool children.* New York: Guilford Press.

Campbell, S. B., Pierce, E. W., Moore, G., & Marakvitz, S. (1996). Boys' externalizing problems at elementary school age: Pathways from early behavior problems, maternal control, and family status. *Developmental Psychopathology, 8,* 701–719.

Capaldi, D. M. (1991). Co-occurrence of conduct problems and depressive symptoms in adolescent boys: I. Familial factors and general adjustment. *Developmental Psychopathology, 3,* 277–300.

Carlson, C. L., Lahey, B. B., Frame, C. L., Walker, J., & Hynd, G. (1987). Sociometric status of clinic-referred children with attention deficit disorders with and without hyperactivity. *Journal of Abnormal Child Psychology, 15,* 537–547.

Carlson, E. A., Jacobvitz, D., & Sroufe, L. A. (1995). A developmental investigation of inattentiveness and hyperactivity. *Child Development, 66,* 37–54.

Caron, C., & Rutter, M. (1991). Comorbidity in child psychopathology: Concepts, issues, and research strategies. *Journal of Child Psychology and Psychiatry, 32,* 1063–1080.

Casey, J. E., Rourke, B. P., & DelDotto, J. E. (1996). Learning disabilities in children with attention deficit disorder with and without hyperactivity. *Child Neuropsychology, 2,* 83–98.

Cunningham, C. E., Benness, B. B., & Siegel, L. S. (1988). Family functioning, time allocation, and parental depression in the families of normal and ADDH children. *Journal of Clinical Child Psychology, 17,* 169–177.

Davidson, L. L., Hughes, S. J., & O'Connor, P. A. (1988). Preschool behavior problems and subsequent risk of injury. *Pediatrics, 90,* 697–702.

Diener, M. B., & Milich, R. (1997). Effects of positive feedback on the social interactions of boys with attention deficit hyperactivity disorder: A test of the self-protective hypothesis. *Journal of Clinical Child Psychology, 26*, 256–265.

Donenberg, G., & Baker, B. L. (1994). The impact of young children with externalizing behaviors on their families. *Journal of Abnormal Child Psychology, 21*, 179–198.

Erhardt, D., & Hinshaw, S. P. (1994). Initial sociometric impressions of attention deficit hyperactivity disorder and comparison boys: Predictions from social behaviors and from nonbehavioral variables. *Journal of Consulting and Clinical Psychology, 62*(4), 833–842.

Evans, S. W., Pelham, W. E., & Grudberg, M. V. (1994). The efficacy of notetaking to improve behavior and comprehension of adolescents with attention deficit hyperactivity disorder. *Exceptionality, 5*, 1–17.

Faraone, S. V., Biederman, J., Lehman, B., Keenan, K., Norman, D., Seidman, L. J., Kolodny, R., Kraus, I., Perrin, J., & Chen, W. (1993). Evidence for independent familial transmission of attention deficit hyperactivity disorder and learning disabilities: Results from a family genetic study. *American Journal of Psychiatry, 150*, 891–895.

Farmer, J. E., & Peterson, L. (1995). Injury risk factors in children with attention deficit hyperactivity disorder. *Health Psychology, 14*, 325–332.

Fletcher, K., Fischer, M., Barkley, R. A., & Smallish, L. (1996). A sequential analysis of the mother-adolescent interactions of ADHD, ADHD/ODD, and normal teenagers during neutral and conflict discussions. *Journal of Abnormal Child Psychology, 24*, 271–297.

Frick, P. J., Kamphaus, R. W., Lahey, B. B., Loeber, R., Christ, M. A. G., Hart, E. L., & Tannenbaum, L. E. (1991). Academic underachievement and the disruptive behavior disorders. *Journal of Consulting and Clinical Psychology, 59*, 289–294.

Gaub, M., & Carlson, C. L. (1997). Behavioral characteristics of DSM-IV ADHD subtypes in a school-based population. *Journal of Abnormal Child Psychology, 25*, 103–111.

Goodman, S. H., Hoven, C. W., Narrow, W. E., Cohen, P., Fielding, B., Alegria, M., Leaf, P. J., Kandel, D., Horwitz, S. M., Bravo, M., Moore, R., & Dulcan, M. K. (1998). Measurement of risk for mental disorders and competence in a psychiatric epidemiologic community survey: The National Institute of Mental Health Methods for the Epidemiology of Child and Adolescent Mental Disorders (MECA) Study. *Social Psychiatry and Psychiatric Epidemiology, 33*, 162–173.

Goodman, S. H., Lahey, B. B., Fielding, B., Dulcan, M., Narrow, W., & Regier, D. (1997). Representativeness of clinical samples of youths with mental disorders: A preliminary population-based study. *Journal of Abnormal Psychology, 106*, 3–14.

Greenberg, M. T., Speltz, M. L., & DeKlyen, M. (1993). The role of attachment in the early development of disruptive behavior problems. *Developmental Psychopathology, 5*, 191–213.

Greene, R. W., Biederman, J., Faraone, S. V., Ouellette, C. A., Penn, C., & Griffin, S. M. (1996). Toward a new psychometric definition of social disability in children with attention-deficit hyperactivity disorder. *Journal of the American Academy of Child and Adolescent Psychiatry, 35*, 571–578.

Greene, R., Biederman, J., Faraone, S. V., Sienna, M., & Garcia-Jetton, J. (1997). Adolescent outcome of boys with attention-deficit/hyperactivity disorder and social disability: Results from a four-year follow-up study. *Journal of Consulting and Clinical Psychology, 65*, 758–767.

Hartup, W. W. (1996). The company they keep: Friendships and their developmental significance. *Child Development, 67*, 1–13.

Hartsough, C. S., & Lambert N. M. (1985). Medical factors in hyperactive and normal children: Prenatal, developmental, and health history findings. *American Journal of Orthopsychiatry, 55*, 190–210.

Hinshaw, S. P. (1987). On the distinction between attentional deficits/hyperactivity and conduct problems/aggression in child psychopathology. *Psychological Bulletin, 101*, 443–463.

Hinshaw, S. P. (1992). Externalizing behavior problems and academic underachievement in childhood and adolescence: Causal relationships and underlying mechanisms. *Psychological Bulletin, 111*, 127–155.

Hinshaw, S. P. (1999). Psychosocial intervention for childhood ADHD: Etiologic and developmental themes, comorbidity, and integration with pharmacotherapy. In D. Cicchetti & S. L. Toth (Eds.), *Rochester Symposium on Developmental Psychopathology (Vol. 9): Developmental approaches to prevention and intervention* (pp. 221–270). Rochester, NY: University of Rochester Press.

Hinshaw, S. P. (2001). *Preadolescent girls with attention-deficit/hyperactivity disorder: Background characteristics, comorbidity, cognitive and social functioning, and parenting practices.* Unpublished manuscript, University of California, Berkeley.

Hinshaw, S. P., & Melnick, S. M. (1995). Peer relationships in children with attention-deficit hyperactivity disorder with and without comorbid aggression. *Development and Psychopathology, 7,* 627–647.

Hinshaw, S. P., Zupan, B. A., Simmel, C., Nigg, J. T., & Melnick, S. M. (1997). Peer status in boys with and without ADHD: Predictions from overt and covert antisocial behavior, social isolation, and authoritative parenting beliefs. *Child Development, 64,* 880–896.

Hoza, B., Pelham, W. E., Milich, R., Pillow, D., & McBride, K. (1993). The self perceptions and attributions of attention deficit hyperactive disordered and nonreferred boys. *Journal of Abnormal Child Psychology 21*(3), 271–286.

Ialongo, N. S., Lopez, M., Horn, W. F., Pascoe, J. M., & Greenberg, G. (1994). Effects of psychoactive medication on self-perceptions of competence, control, and mood in children with attention deficit hyperactivity disorder. *Journal of Clinical Child Psychology, 23,* 161–173.

Jensen, P. S., Martin, D., & Cantwell, D. P. (1997). Comorbidity in ADHD: Implications for research, practice, and DSM-V. *Journal of the American Academy of Child and Adolescent Psychiatry, 36,* 1065–1079.

Johnson, R. C., & Rosen, L. A. (2000). Sports behavior of ADHD children. *Journal of Attention Disorders, 4,* 150–160.

Lahey, B. B., Applegate, B., McBurnett, K., Biederman, J., Greenhill, L., Hynd, G. W., Barkley, R. A., Newcorn, J., Jensen, P., Richters, J., Garfinkel, B., Kerdyk, L., Frick, P. J., Ollendick, T., Perez, D., Hart, E. L., Waldman, I., & Shaffer, D. (1994). DSM-IV Field Trials for attention deficit hyperactivity disorder in children and adolescents. *American Journal of Psychiatry, 151,* 1673–1685.

Lahey, B. B., Pelham, W. E., Stein, M. A., Loney, J., Trapani, C., Nugent, K., Kipp, H., Schmidt, E., Lee, S., Cale, M., Gold, E., Hartung, C. M., Willcutt, E., & Baumann, B. (1998). Validity of DSM-IV attention-deficit/ hyperactivity disorder for younger children. *Journal of the American Academy of Child and Adolescent Psychiatry, 37*(7), 695–702.

Loney, J., & Milich, R. (1982). Hyperactivity, inattention, and aggression in clinical practice. In M. Wolraich & D. K. Routh (Eds.), *Advances in developmental behavioral pediatrics* (Vol. 2, pp. 113–147), Greenwich, CT: JAI Press.

Lytton, H. (1990). Child and parent effects in boys' conduct disorder: A reinterpretation. *Developmental Psychology, 26,* 683–697.

Mash, E. J., & Johnston, C. (1990). Determinants of parenting stress: Illustrations from families of hyperactive children and families of physically abused children. *Journal of Clinical Child Psychology, 19,* 313–328.

Matheny, A. P., & Fisher, J. E. (1984). Behavioral perspectives on children's accidents. In M. L. Wolraich & D. K. Routh (Eds.), *Advances in developmental and behavioral pediatrics* (Vol. 5, pp. 221–264). Greenwich, CT: JAI Press.

Melnick, S. M., & Hinshaw, S. P. (1996). What they want and what they get: The social goals of boys with ADHD and comparison boys. *Journal of Abnormal Child Psychology, 24,* 169–185.

Melnick, S. M., & Hinshaw, S. P. (2000). Emotion regulation and parenting in ADHD and comparison boys. Linkages with social behaviors and peer preference. *Journal of Abnormal Child Psychology, 28,* 73–86.

Milich, R., & Landau, S. (1982). Socialization and peer relations in hyperactive children. In K. D. Gadow & I. Bialer (Eds.), *Advances in learning and behavioral disabilities* (Vol. 1, pp. 283–339). Greenwich, CT: JAI Press.

Milich, R., & Landau, S. (1989). The role of social status variables in differentiating subgroups of hyperactive children. In L. M. Bloomingdale & J. M. Swanson (Eds.), *Attention deficit disorder* (Vol. 4, pp. 1–16). Oxford: Pergamon Press.

MTA Cooperative Group. (1999). A 14-month randomized clinical trial of treatment strategies for attention-deficit/hyperactivity disorder: Multimodal Treatment Study of Children with ADHD. *Archives of General Psychiatry, 56*(12), 1073–1086.

Murphy, K. R., & Gordon, M. (1998). Assessment of adults with ADHD. In R. A. Barkley (Ed.), *Attention-deficit hyperactivity disorder: A handbook for diagnosis and treatment* (2nd ed., pp. 345–369). New York: Guilford Press.

Nada-Raja, S., Langley, J. D., McGee, R., Williams, S. M., Begg, D. J., & Reeder, A. I. (1997). Inattentive and hyperactive behaviors and driving offenses in adolescence. *Journal of the American Academy of Child and Adolescent Psychiatry, 36*, 515–522.

Parker, J. G., & Asher, S. R. (1987). Peer relations and later personal adjustment: Are low-accepted children at risk? *Psychological Bulletin, 102*, 357–389.

Paternite, C. E., Loney, J., & Roberts, M. A. (1996). A preliminary validation of subtypes of DSM-IV attention-deficit/hyperactivity disorder. *Journal of Attention Disorders, 1*, 70–86.

Patterson, G. R., Reid, J. B., & Dishion, T. J. (1992). *A social interactional approach: Vol. 4: Antisocial boys.* Eugene, OR: Castalia.

Pelham, W. E., & Bender, M. E. (1982). Peer relationships in hyperactive children: Description and treatment. In K. D. Gadow & I. Bialer (Eds.), *Advances in learning and behavioral disabilities* (Vol. 1, pp. 365–436). Greenwich, CT: JAI Press.

Richters, J. E., Arnold, L. E., Jensen, P. S., Abikoff, H., Conners, C. K., Greenhill, L. L., Hechtman, L., Hinshaw, S. P., Pelham, W. E., & Swanson, J. M. (1995). NIMH collaborative multisite multimodal treatment study of children with ADHD: I. Background and rationale. *Journal of the American Academy of Child and Adolescent Psychiatry, 34*, 987–1000.

Semrud-Clikeman, M., Biederman, J., Sprich-Buckminster, S., Lehman, B. K., Faraone, S. V., & Norman, D. (1992). Comorbidity between ADDH and learning disability: A review and report in a clinically referred sample. *Journal of the American Academy of Child and Adolescent Psychiatry, 31*, 439–448.

Slomkowski, C., Klein, R. G., & Mannuzza, S. (1995). Is self-esteem an important outcome in hyperactive children? *Journal of Abnormal Child Psychology, 23*, 303–315.

Stein, M. A., Szumowski, E., Blondis, T. A., & Roizen, N. J. (1995). Adaptive skills dysfunction in ADD and ADHD children. *Journal of Child Psychology and Psychiatry, 36*, 663–670.

Stewart, M. A., Thach, B. T., & Friedin, M. R. (1970). Accidental poisoning and the hyperactive child syndrome. *Diseases of the Nervous System, 31*, 403–407.

Szatmari, P., Offord, D. R., & Boyle, M. H. (1989). Correlates, associated impairments, and patterns of service utilization of children with attention deficit disorders: Findings from the Ontario child health study. *Journal of Child Psychology and Psychiatry, 30*, 205–217.

Tallmadge, J., & Barkley, R. A. (1983). The interactions of hyperactive and normal boys with their mothers and fathers. *Journal of Abnormal Child Psychology, 11*, 565–579.

Treuting, J., & Hinshaw, S. P. (1998). *Depression and self-esteem in boys with ADHD: Relationships with comorbid aggression and explanatory attributional mechanisms.* Berkeley: University of California Press.

Whalen, C. K., & Henker, B. (1985). The social worlds of hyperactive (ADDH) children. *Clinical Psychology Review, 5*, 447–478.

Whalen, C. K., & Henker, B. (1992). The social profiles of attention-deficit hyperactivity disorder: Five fundamental facets. *Child and Adolescent Psychiatric Clinics of North America, 1*, 395–410.

Wheeler, J., & Carlson, C. L. (1994). The social functioning of children with ADD with hyperactivity and ADD without hyperactivity: A comparison of their peer relationships and social deficits. *Journal of Emotional and Behavior Disorders, 2*, 2–12.

Whitaker, A. H., Van Rossem, R., Feldman, J. F., Schonfeld, I. S., Pinto-Martin, J. A., Torre, C., Shaffer, D., & Paneth, N. (1997). Psychiatric outcomes in low-birth-weight children at age 6 years: Relation to neonatal cranial ultrasound abnormalities. *Archives of General Psychiatry, 54*, 847–856.

Chapter 6

The Impact of Attention Deficit Hyperactivity Disorder on Social and Vocational Functioning in Adults

by Charlotte Johnston, Ph.D.

Introduction 6-2
Identification and Study of ADHD in Adults 6-2
    Challenges to Reliability of Diagnosis 6-3
        Lack of Consensus on Diagnostic Criteria 6-3
        Manifestation of ADHD in Adults 6-3
        Reliability of Childhood History 6-4
        Differentiation of ADHD From Other Disorders 6-4
    Prevalence of Adult ADHD 6-4
    Summary 6-5
Evaluating Evidence of the Impact of ADHD on Adult
  Functioning 6-6
Educational and Vocational Functioning in Adults With
  ADHD 6-7
    Montreal Longitudinal Study 6-7
    New York Longitudinal Study 6-8
    Other Findings 6-8
    Lifelong Impact of Childhood Difficulties 6-9
    Employment Discrimination Challenges 6-9
    Summary 6-10
Social Functioning in Adults With ADHD 6-10
    Impairments in Psychological Functioning 6-11
    Social Skills Deficits 6-13
    Family Functioning 6-13

    Marital Ties 6-13

    Parenting 6-14

Conclusions 6-15

Recommendations for Clinical Practice and

    Future Research 6-16

INTRODUCTION

This chapter discusses the impairments associated with attention deficit hyperactivity disorder (ADHD) (Weiss & Hechtman, 1993) in adulthood, with an emphasis on functioning in social and occupational roles. Within the past ten years, the persistence of ADHD into adulthood has been increasingly recognized (Weiss & Hechtman, 1993; Wender, 1997). To date, much of the empirical work in this area has focused on issues related to the identification of the disorder (Ward, Wender, & Reimherr, 1993), its psychiatric comorbidities (Shekim, Asarnow, Hess, Zaucha, & Wheeler, 1990), and the use of medication in its treatment (Wilens, Biederman, Spencer, & Prince, 1995). The impact of ADHD on adult academic and occupational functioning and on interpersonal domains, such as family and marital relationships, has been less studied.

The first section of this chapter briefly considers general issues in the diagnosis and study of ADHD in adulthood. This section notes difficulties in establishing diagnostic criteria and limitations of existing research, such as the confounding of diagnosis with gender and comorbidity and the lack of subtype specificity. Next, this chapter provides a summary of studies of social and vocational functioning in adults with ADHD. These studies fall into two main categories: (1) those where the ADHD is diagnosed in childhood and individuals are followed prospectively into adulthood and (2) those where the diagnosis of ADHD is made during adulthood on the basis of current behavior and/or retrospectively on the basis of childhood behavior. Similarities and differences in results from these two methodologies are noted. Studies of the parents of children with ADHD are also considered, with respect to the likelihood of ADHD in these parents. Case studies are included to supplement areas in which the empirical literature is particularly scarce. Throughout the chapter, studies are included that address issues of adult ADHD if the average age of the sample is 18 years or older. The chapter concludes with recommendations for promoting clinical practice and research in this area.

IDENTIFICATION AND STUDY OF ADHD IN ADULTS

As noted previously, the continuation of ADHD into adulthood is now well documented, although the rate at which this occurs remains contentious (Barkley, 1997; Hill & Schoener, 1996). Several advances have been made in developing measures and criteria that permit reliable and valid diagnosis of the condition in adulthood (American Academy of Child and Adolescent Psychiatry, 1997; Conners et al., 1999; Murphy & Gordon, 1998; Ward et al., 1993). The protocols that have been developed for assessing ADHD in adulthood typically include self-reports of both current and retrospective symptoms as well as collaborative reports of the same symptoms from parents and/or spouses. Checklists, interviews, and archival records have all been used to gather the information.

Challenges to Reliability of Diagnosis

Lack of Consensus on Diagnostic Criteria. Despite this beginning work in assessment, the diagnosis of ADHD in adults remains contentious, at least in part due to a number of challenges to the reliability of the diagnosis (Roy-Byrne et al., 1997; Shaffer, 1994). Not the least of these difficulties is the lack of consensus on the specific diagnostic criteria that should be employed. Each of the existing adult assessment protocols and sets of criteria has advantages and disadvantages, but their differences mean that somewhat different groups of individuals will be identified as having ADHD across studies.

For example, Wender's criteria, one of the first developed for adult diagnoses, focuses on hyperactivity and impulsivity and excludes the inattentive subtype of ADHD. In addition, the presence of other disorders such as depression or antisocial personality serve as exclusion criteria for the ADHD diagnosis, virtually eliminating comorbidity. This is in contrast to the criteria specified for both children and adults in the fourth edition of *Diagnostic and Statistical Manual of Mental Disorders* (DSM-IV; American Psychiatric Association, 1994) and the procedure recommended by the American Academy of Child and Adolescent Psychiatry (1997) practice parameters, which suggest differential diagnoses but do not rule out ADHD on the basis of comorbid conditions.

In addition to the concern of differences across existing diagnostic standards, there is also concern regarding the general lack of attention to subtype diagnoses among adults. Evidence is building in the child literature that there are real and important differences among the inattentive, hyperactive-impulsive, and combined subtypes of the disorder (Barkley, 1998). Whether or not these same subtypes are appropriate and have the same correlates in adult samples is an important question for future research.

Manifestation of ADHD in Adults. The reliability of adult diagnosis of ADHD is also hampered by uncertainty regarding how the disorder is manifest at this point in the lifespan. In particular, the behaviors that indicate the disorder in children may not be appropriate to describing the disorder in adolescence or adulthood and the thresholds that define deviance are likely to differ from children to adults (Murphy & Barkley, 1996b). To enhance their appropriateness for adults, existing adult diagnostic protocols have modified the diagnostic criteria (changing both the description of symptoms and the number required for clinical cutoffs) or offered additional examples of how the symptoms listed in DSM-IV may manifest in adults. Further research is urgently needed to test whether the construct identified by these protocols is comparable to ADHD as assessed in childhood. For example, recent work by Conners et al. (1999) has found that adult self-ratings of symptoms ascribed to adult ADHD load onto four factors—(1) inattention/executive functions/academic problems, (2) hyperactivity/restlessness, (3) impulsivity/emotional lability, and (4) problems with self-concept—and it is argued that these factors coincide closely with those found in studies of children and adolescents. Finally, assessment in adults must be sensitive, not only to differences in how the core symptoms of the disorder may be expressed at this age but to the possibility that, in adults, symptoms or impairment may be masked by the presence of well-developed compensatory mechanisms (Denckla, 1993).

Reliability of Childhood History. The requirement of a childhood history of ADHD also presents a challenge to the reliability and validity of adult diagnoses, Although a childhood history is widely recognized as an essential feature of adult ADHD (Barkley & Biederman, 1997), it is difficult to ascertain reliably. Changes in diagnostic criteria over time and notorious inaccuracies in retrospective recall (Bradburn, Rips, & Shevell, 1987) are two of the difficulties in this area. Mannuzza, Klein, Bessler, Malloy, and LaPadula (1993), in a longitudinal study of individuals diagnosed in childhood as ADHD, found that, at 26 years of age, approximately 20 percent of the participants failed to report their childhood diagnosis in assessment interviews. From a slightly different perspective, Downey, Stelson, Pomerleau, and Giordani (1997), in a sample of adults referred to an ADHD clinic, reported that parents confirmed the adult's reported childhood history of ADHD in only 76 percent of cases. In combination, these findings suggest difficulties in both over- and underreporting of childhood histories of ADHD. Although convergence of adult reports with parent reports or archival records can increase confidence in identification of the historical element of the adult ADHD diagnosis, we need strategies for proceeding in the absence of corroborating evidence or in the face of conflicting information.

Differentiation of ADHD From Other Disorders. Differentiating ADHD from other mental disorders in adults can also be difficult. As in childhood, many of the symptoms of adult ADHD are also characteristic of other disorders. For example, concentration difficulties are also characteristic of mood disorders and impulsivity occurs in borderline personality disorder. The diagnostician must determine whether an adult's presenting problems represent a constellation consistent with ADHD or whether they are better captured by another syndrome. This differentiation is further complicated by the high rates of comorbidity between ADHD and other psychiatric disorders (Biederman et al., 1993). Strategies such as relying on a childhood diagnosis of ADHD or otherwise establishing different onsets for different sets of symptoms, or discounting attentional problems that occurred only in the course of other disorders (e.g., during depressive episodes), offer some potential for avoiding the confounding of ADHD and other adult diagnoses (Alpert et al., 1996).

Prevalence of Adult ADHD

The lack of consensus on the criteria and procedures for the diagnosis of ADHD in adults remains a significant impediment to this area of research. In part because of these difficulties in establishing diagnostic criteria, systematic epidemiological data on the prevalence of ADHD in adulthood have not yet been gathered. Estimates based on existing information vary widely. In longitudinal studies that have followed children diagnosed with ADHD, rates of the adult disorder range from less than 5 percent to over 50 percent. For example, Weiss and Hechtman (1993) reported that, at 24 years of age, 66 percent of the ADHD children in their sample continued to complain of some degree of disability related to at least one criteria of inattention, hyperactivity, or impulsivity. Claude and Firestone (1995) reported that 50 percent of a group of children with ADHD continued to meet diagnostic criteria at 19 years of age. In contrast, Mannuzza et al. (1993, 1998), reporting on two cohorts of ADHD children followed into early adulthood, reported rates of the adult disorder at 4 percent in one sample and 8–11 percent in the second.

There are several differences in the samples and methods employed by Weiss and Hechtman (1993) and Claude and Firestone (1995) versus those employed by Mannuzza et al. (1993) that may account for the discrepant rates. Perhaps most important, Weiss and Hechtman reported on rates of continuation for single symptoms based on interviews conducted by psychiatrists who were not blind to the individual's childhood status. Claude and Firestone did use interviewers blind to diagnostic status but assigned diagnosis based on reports of symptom presence by either the young adult or the parent—a procedure that may have inflated estimates. The adults in this sample were also the youngest of the three longitudinal studies. The Weiss and Hechtman and the Claude and Firestone samples also included more children with aggression than did the Mannuzza samples, a factor known to increase the risk of poor adult outcome (Loney, Whaley-Klahn, Kosier, & Conboy, 1983). Mannuzza et al. (1993) not only used blind interviewers and reported rates of participants meeting full diagnostic criteria in adulthood; they also required that the adult report childhood impairment. As noted earlier, up to 20 percent of the adults in the ADHD group did not recall their childhood diagnoses (Mannuzza et al., 1993); therefore, this methodological decision would have resulted in an underestimate of the number of adults affected.

Fischer (1997) has recently reported data that offer some reconciliation of these differences. In a sample of children with ADHD followed to an average of 21 years, only 3 percent met criteria for ADHD in adulthood according to self-report. However, this figure climbed to 42 percent if parent report of the young adult's behavior was used in making the diagnosis. Thus, in addition to differences in samples and diagnostic criteria, method of assessment and informant are also likely to contribute to discrepancies in rates of adult ADHD across studies.

Other estimates of the prevalence of adult ADHD can be found in studies assessing community samples. Weyandt, Linterman, and Rice (1995) had a group of 770 college students complete a DSM-IV rating scale and Wender's childhood rating scales to assess ADHD symptoms. In this relatively well-functioning sample, 2.5 percent were 1.5 standard deviations above the group mean on both rating scales and .5 percent were 2 standard deviations above this cutoff. In a sample of 720 adults who were seeking a new or renewed driver's license, Murphy and Barkley (1996b) assessed self-report of both current and childhood symptoms of ADHD. They found that 1.3 percent of the adults met DSM-IV criteria for ADHD–inattentive type, 2.5 percent for hyperactive/impulsive type, and 0.9 percent for combined type (for a total of 4.7 percent). If one takes an averaged continuation rate of 10 to 30 percent from longitudinal studies combined with a childhood prevalence of 3 to 11 percent (American Psychiatric Association, 1994; Wolraich, Hannah, Pinnock, Baumgaertel, & Brown, 1996), adult prevalence would be estimated between .3 and 3.3 percent, which is only slightly lower than estimates from community samples of adults (approximately 2 to 5 percent).

Summary

Our knowledge regarding the identification of ADHD in adulthood is in its early stages. There is good evidence that the disorder exists in adults, and progress has been made in establishing assessment methods. Although preliminary work is encouraging, research is still needed to establish adult diagnostic criteria and assessment devices, to demonstrate the convergence of diagnostic criteria across the lifespan, and to clarify the distinctiveness of ADHD from other adult conditions. Similarly, although estimates of prevalence can be generated from existing information, confidence in these awaits the development of standard diagnostic protocols and the completion of careful epidemiological studies.

EVALUATING EVIDENCE OF THE IMPACT OF ADHD ON ADULT FUNCTIONING

Two primary types of studies provide information regarding the impact of ADHD on adult functioning. In the first, longitudinal studies, children are diagnosed with ADHD (or its earlier versions) and followed into adulthood. Information describing this group of individuals speaks to the impact of childhood ADHD, as well as possible continuation of the disorder on adult performance. Sometimes individuals with and without evidence of the adult diagnosis are considered distinct groups in such longitudinal samples, allowing for separation of the effects of a remitted childhood diagnosis versus a childhood diagnosis plus continuing adult problems with ADHD. The second type of study focuses on individuals diagnosed in adulthood, based on current problems with symptomatology and a childhood history of ADHD.

Studies using child-identified and adult-identified samples have a rather complementary pattern of risks and benefits. The longitudinal studies provide a certainty regarding childhood history but do not always report outcomes separately for adults with continuing versus remitted problems. In addition, the childhood diagnosis reflects the diagnostic criteria in vogue at the time of study initiation, which may or may not be comparable to current criteria. Given the dates of initiation of most of these studies, they are also limited to reporting on adults of a relatively young age (mid-20s). In contrast, the adult-identified samples confront the difficulties of reliably establishing a childhood history but provide more homogeneous groups than do the longitudinal samples with respect to adult symptomatology and current diagnostic standards. Adult-identified samples are also typically older (mid-30s) than the longitudinal samples and thus have entered farther into the window of opportunity for various problems. Finally, confidence in the generalizability of the results from longitudinal studies is dependent on low rates of attrition, and both child- and adult-identified samples have various referral biases.

In summarizing studies in this area there is a need to be continually alert to potential differences across studies in sample characteristics such as gender, comorbidities, and subtypes of ADHD. For example, although there are exceptions, it can be generally stated that child-identified samples followed longitudinally consist of males with both inattentive and hyperactive/impulsive symptoms, and, if they have comorbid disorders, these are most likely to be of the externalizing nature. In contrast, adult-identified samples are likely to have greater representations of females, to have more individuals of the inattentive subtype, and to have more internalizing comorbidities. Perhaps of most concern, these differences in gender, subtype, and comorbidity are often inextricably confounded within studies. Thus it is difficult, if not impossible, to tease apart the effects on outcome that are attributable to ADHD versus those attributable to some combination of gender, subtype, and comorbidity.

EDUCATIONAL AND VOCATIONAL FUNCTIONING IN ADULTS WITH ADHD

Montreal Longitudinal Study

Two main groups of investigators have published evidence regarding adult school and job performance from longitudinal studies of children with ADHD. Weiss and Hechtman (1993) in Montreal, Canada, conducted five-, ten-, and fifteen-year follow-ups of children diagnosed as ADHD. One hundred and four children (90 percent males) were initially diagnosed between 1962 and 1965, when they were 6 to 12 years of age. Although diagnoses were made prior to the third edition of DSM-III (American Psychiatric Association, 1980), inclusion criteria focused on pervasive, early-onset problems with restlessness and concentration and the authors indicate that the children would have met criteria for attention deficit hyperactivity disorder (ADDH) in DSM-III. In addition, many of the children had associated conduct problems.

The children participated in medication trials at the time of diagnoses, but ongoing treatment with medication or psychotherapy was variable and not consistently related to outcome. A control group of thirty-five adolescents was recruited from local high schools at the five-year follow-up and an additional nine control subjects were recruited at the ten-year follow-up. At the fifteen-year follow-up, 61 (59 percent) of the original 104 children were compared to 41 of the 45 controls. The high rate of attrition is one of the major limitations of this data set, particularly because, at the ten-year follow-up, a comparison of the ADHD participants who were assessed and those who were lost indicated a trend for lower initial ratings of aggression in the retained participants.

The participants in Weiss and Hechtman's sample averaged 24 years of age at the fifteen-year follow-up. As noted previously, 66 percent of the young adults in the ADHD group continued to report difficulties with at least one symptom of ADHD at that time. Compared to controls, the young adults in the ADHD group had academic histories marred by various difficulties, including lower average marks, more failed grades, more expulsions, and more premature departures from high school. Not surprisingly, at 24 years of age, the ADHD adults had completed less education than had controls (3 percent had a university degree compared to 17 percent of controls). In terms of employment, participants in the ADHD group reported having had more jobs and being laid off more often, and their overall job status was lower than that of controls. However, there was no difference in current rate of employment in the two groups. There was a trend indicating that adults in the ADHD group found more aspects of their jobs difficult and liked jobs because of the social aspects rather than the learning experience. The investigators also asked to send questionnaires to participants' employers; thirty-three of the forty-one controls agreed to this assessment compared to only thirty-seven of the sixty-two ADHD participants. Of these, young adults in the ADHD group were rated by their employers as having more work-related difficulties (e.g., problems working independently, problems completing tasks).

New York Longitudinal Study

In New York, Mannuzza et al. (1993, 1998; Mannuzza, Klein, Bessler, Malloy, & Hynes, 1998) also conducted prospective studies, following two independent cohorts of Caucasian, male children diagnosed as ADHD into young adulthood. Both cohorts were assessed between 1970 and 1977 and were diagnosed by psychiatrists as meeting DSM-II (American Psychiatric Association, 1968) diagnoses for hyperkinetic reaction of childhood, based on the referring problem and teacher and parent ratings. Children received medication treatment and/or behavior therapy at the time of assessment, but information regarding ongoing treatment is not provided. Children were not included if aggression was the presenting problem and, in contrast to the Weiss and Hechtman sample, Mannuzza et al. (1998) reported that only one of the children in their sample would have met criteria for conduct disorder. The first cohort of 103 children was designated as those who were 16 at the time of the first follow-up evaluation and the second cohort of 104 children were those who were younger than 16 at this time. The two cohorts were first reassessed when they averaged 16 years of age and again at approximately 26 years. Control groups were added at the time of the first follow-up and included males recruited from nonpsychiatric outpatient clinics and the community. Data from the fifteen-year, adult follow-up is most relevant to this chapter and included, for the first cohort, 91 of 103 (88 percent) of the ADHD group and 95 of 100 controls and, for the second cohort, 85 of 104 (82 percent) in the ADHD group, and 73 of 78 (94 percent) controls.

As noted previously, only 4 to 11 percent of the young men in the two cohorts from the New York studies continued to meet criteria for ADHD in adulthood. In both cohorts, the young men in the ADHD group had completed less schooling than had controls (an average of 2.2 and 2.5 years less). In the first cohort, the men in the ADHD group had lower occupational rankings than did controls (e.g., carpenters vs. accountants), and there was a trend toward this same difference in the second cohort. There was no indication of greater unemployment in the ADHD group in either cohort. These findings remained even when the adults in the ADHD group who had antisocial personality disorder were removed from the comparison and when IQ differences were controlled.

Other Findings

Other longitudinal studies yield data consistent with the Montreal and New York findings. Earlier studies of adults retrospectively diagnosed with childhood ADHD found that these individuals stayed in jobs for shorter periods and achieved lower socioeconomic status than did their non-ADHD siblings (Borland & Heckman, 1976) and had less schooling and fewer professional careers when compared to adults referred in childhood for other psychiatric disorders (Morrison, 1980). Claude and Firestone (1995) reported follow-up at an average age of 19 for fifty-two males from an initial sample of ninety-seven children (male and female) with ADHD and compared these individuals to a group of controls recruited at follow-up. Young adults in the ADHD group had lower scores on standardized measures of spelling, arithmetic, and reading; had completed less high school; and had failed more courses. Participants in the ADHD group were also less likely to be pursuing postsecondary education. These educational deficits were not attributable to IQ and did not differ across subtypes of inattentive only versus inattentive and aggressive, however the sample sizes for these comparisons were small. Finally, Fergusson, Lynskey, and Horwood (1997) reported associations between attentional difficulties, measured dimensionally, when children were 8 and various outcomes at age 18. Children with more attentional problems were more likely to have left school early, passed fewer grades, and had reading delays. These relationships persisted even when confounds such as family factors and conduct problems were controlled.

Lifelong Impact of Childhood Difficulties

None of the longitudinal studies of ADHD has reported educational and vocational functioning separately for groups of individuals who have continuing problems with ADHD and those who do not. However, given that the studies have varied considerably in the rates of adult ADHD reported and yet remained consistent in their reports of the level and types of educational and job problems, it may be that adult symptoms are less important in this realm than childhood history. Particularly for educational achievement, it is logical that childhood difficulties will continue to exert a lifelong impact, regardless of the degree to which ADHD symptoms remit.

Consistent with the findings from longitudinal studies, individuals diagnosed in adulthood also demonstrated educational and occupational impairment. Murphy and Barkley (1996a) compared two groups of adults in their 30s who were referred to an ADHD clinic: those who met diagnostic criteria and those who did not. Although there was no difference in level of education between the two groups, the adults with ADHD reported histories of more school problems (e.g., suspensions, behavior problems, and underachievement), had been fired from or impulsively left employment more often, had held more jobs, and had more chronic employment difficulties. Barkley, Murphy, and Kwasnik (1996) compared small groups of controls and adults with ADHD on several educational and vocational variables. Perhaps because of low statistical power and the relative young age of the sample (average age was 22 years), many of the variables did not differ between groups. However, adults in college with ADHD reported not only more ADHD symptoms but also more behaviors characteristic of oppositional defiant disorder (ODD) in their college setting than did controls, behaviors which might well pose a significant obstacle to educational achievement. The adults with ADHD had also held jobs for shorter periods of time and reported more ADHD and ODD behaviors in the work place than controls, again likely risk factors for job security and advancement.

Employment Discrimination Challenges

The impact of ADHD on adult occupational functioning has significant ramifications for decisions regarding employers' responsibilities to these employees, the need for job accommodations, and disability compensation. In the United States, between 1993 and 1995 there was a 407 percent increase in calls to the Job Accommodations Network (an international toll-free consulting service provided by the President's Committee on Employment of People with Disabilities) related to the impact of ADHD on adult work performance (Means, Stewart, & Dowler, 1997). A survey of callers indicated that most job accommodations for ADHD were self-designed, primarily environmental changes (e.g., rearranging the work environment to reduce distractions), and were effective in helping to maintain employment. Considering ADHD as one disability that would be incorporated in the broader category of learning problems, other surveys have found that resource services and accommodations for adults with ADHD are often not available in postsecondary educational institutions (Parks, Antonoff, Drake, Skiba, & Soberman, 1987) and only 51 percent of employers would be willing to hire a person with such problems (Minskoff, Sautter, Hoffman, & Hawks, 1987). Given these attitudes regarding the educational and vocational needs of adults with ADHD, it is not surprising that Wyld (1997) has recently argued that ADHD presents a new and significant challenge for employment discrimination law.

Summary

The evidence is convincing that adults with either childhood histories of ADHD and/or a diagnosis made in adulthood, on average, experience educational and occupational impairments. As a group, adults with ADHD are unlikely to pursue education beyond high school and are most likely to be employed in skilled labor positions and to experience various job disruptions. In addition, these educational and vocational impairments do not appear to be entirely attributable to antisocial behavior or deficits in cognitive functioning.

Although troubling, the evidence of comparatively worse educational and occupational functioning between ADHD and control groups should be considered within the context of relatively high levels of employment found among adults with ADHD. In addition, at least two other factors caution against drawing conclusions that focus exclusively on deficits:

1. Studies to date have examined education outcomes only within the confines of relatively traditional institutions. We do not know about other avenues that adults with ADHD may pursue in furthering their education. For example, it is possible that ADHD adults return to education later in life or pursue alternate educational routes (e.g., via the Internet or on-the-job experience). Our knowledge of the impact of ADHD on educational outcomes would be greatly enhanced by a broader consideration of such possibilities.

2. There are aspects of ADHD that may prove to be employment benefits, rather than disadvantages. Particularly in some occupations, characteristics such as risk taking, a fast-paced approach, and an outgoing style may prove to be advantages. This possible matching or congruence of characteristics of ADHD and the demands of some occupations is also worthy of further exploration.

SOCIAL FUNCTIONING IN ADULTS WITH ADHD

As with educational and vocational performance, evidence concerning the social functioning of adults with ADHD also comes from follow-up studies of children with ADHD and from adult-identified samples. However, social functioning is less well defined than educational and occupational functioning, and evidence in this realm must often be gleaned from a variety of indicators of adjustment. This chapter considers psychological functioning as it speaks to interpersonal performance, measures of social role functioning (e.g., social skills), and indicators of family role responsibilities (parenting and marital functioning).

Impairments in Psychological Functioning

In the Weiss and Hechtman (1993) fifteen-year follow-up, the young adults in the ADHD group complained of more sexual, neurotic, and interpersonal problems and reported more suicide attempts than did controls. Data from the Weiss and Hechtman follow-up have also been examined for differences between those individuals who continued to have problems with ADHD compared to those who appeared to have "outgrown" their ADHD. Greenfield, Hechtman, and Weiss (1988) divided the participants into those with mild or no continuing ADHD symptoms versus those with moderate to severe continuing symptoms. It was in the group with continuing symptoms that problems with antisocial behavior, emotional difficulties, and substance use were highest. In many respects the group without continuing ADHD problems did not differ from the controls. Consistent with the findings from the Weiss and Hechtman sample, Mannuzza et al. (1993) also reported that young men who had continuing problems with ADHD were more likely to have drug abuse problems than were those whose ADHD had remitted, and the difference for alcohol problems and antisocial personality disorder were in the same direction, although not significant (perhaps due to small sample sizes).

Studies of individuals diagnosed as ADHD in adulthood have generally reported higher rates and a greater diversity of comorbidities and psychological maladjustment in comparison to the longitudinal studies of child-identified samples. Barkley, Murphy, and Kwasnik (1996) reported that in their sample of twenty-five adults with ADHD, 88 percent had at least one disorder and 56 percent had two other disorders, although the differences in these frequencies between the ADHD and control group were not significant. The ADHD group did report significantly more psychological problems on the Symptom Checklist 90—Revised (SCL-90-R) and more antisocial activities than the control group, but not more alcohol or drug use. Murphy and Barkley (1996a) compared two groups of adults referred to an adult ADHD clinic: those who met criteria for the diagnosis and those who did not. The adults meeting diagnostic criteria had more alcohol problems, more symptoms of oppositional and conduct disorder, and higher SCL-90-R scores than did the control group. There was no difference between groups on anxiety or mood disorders.

Rucklidge and Kaplan (1997) found that adult women with ADHD reported a range of psychological problems compared to controls (both the ADHD and control women were mothers of children with ADHD), including greater anxiety and depression, and more stress coupled with less effective coping strategies. Finally, Biederman et al. (1993) found that, compared to controls, both referred and nonreferred adults with ADHD had higher rates of antisocial personality disorder, conduct and oppositional defiant disorder behaviors, substance use, anxiety disorders, enuresis, and various speech and language disorders. Even the 14 percent of the ADHD adults in this sample who did not have any comorbid disorder had lower global functioning scores and more cognitive difficulties than did the comparison group, suggesting that not all impairments in adults with ADHD can be attributed to co-occurring psychiatric disorders.

Other studies report rates of psychological disturbance in adult ADHD samples but do not provide comparisons with controls. For example, Shekim et al. (1990) found that only 14 percent of their sample of adults with ADHD had no comorbidity and 33 percent met criteria for four other Axis I diagnoses (Axis II disorders, such as personality disorders, were not assessed). Most common of the comorbidities were mood and anxiety disorders and substance abuse problems. Similarly, Millstein, Wilens, Biederman, and Spencer (1997) reported that among adults with ADHD who were referred to a pharmacology clinic, only 3 percent had no comorbidity and 56 percent had four or more lifetime comorbidities. Comorbidities were particularly common in individuals who met criteria for combined or hyperactive-impulsive subtype of ADHD. Males were more likely to be comorbid for conduct and substance abuse problems and females for mood and eating disorders. Downey et al. (1997) reported that almost half of a sample of adults referred to an ADHD clinic had concurrent diagnoses of anxiety or depressive disorders and 13 percent had diagnoses of antisocial personality disorder. Although no control group was available, within the ADHD group, those with childhood oppositional disorder had more comorbidities as adults than did those without.

In summary, there is general agreement across studies that adults with childhood histories of ADHD and/or adult symptoms are affected by a variety of psychological problems. In both child-identified and adult-identified samples, antisocial personality disorder or general problems with antisocial behavior appear as a common comorbidity. Problems with alcohol and drug use and with affective or anxiety disorders are more common in samples of individuals identified as ADHD in adulthood than in longitudinal studies of ADHD, perhaps due to differences in referral patterns for children versus adults. The longitudinal studies indicate that there is good evidence that substance or alcohol abuse and criminality are better predicted by childhood aggression and/or adult antisocial personality disorder, than by ADHD symptoms. (For a more extensive review of antisocial personality disorder and substance use outcomes, see Chapter 4).

The impact of ADHD on adult social functioning can also be discerned from studies showing elevated rates of the disorder among groups of adults with various psychological problems, particularly difficulties of inhibitory control. For example, Carlton et al. (1992) found that, even after matching for characteristics such as age, education, and income, individuals with histories of pathological gambling reported more childhood symptoms of ADHD than did controls. Among adult males with alcoholism, Wood, Wender, and Reimherr (1983) found that 33 percent met the Utah criteria for ADHD, and Horner, Scheibe, and Stine (1996) reported significant relationships between use of cocaine and ADHD symptoms in a sample of male cocaine abusers. Horner et al. (1996) offer the interpretation that at least some cocaine abusers are using the drug to self-medicate for the symptoms of ADHD, an explanation similar to that put forward to explain high rates of smoking in adult ADHD samples (Conners et al., 1996; Pomerleau, Downey, Stelson, & Pomerleau, 1995). Elevated rates of ADHD in other psychiatric groups may also reflect reactions to the lifelong struggles that accompany the diagnosis. For example, Alpert et al. (1996) reported that 16 percent of adults with major depressive disorder also had childhood histories of ADHD. The exclusion of individuals with antisocial personality disorder and/or substance use problems from this study would lead this estimate to be on the low side. In summary, ADHD in adulthood appears to carry risk for a range of associated psychological problems. One implication of this high rate of comorbidity is the need to alert clinicians to the necessity of carefully assessing for ADHD symptomatology among adults who present with a range of mental health problems.

Social Skills Deficits

Although results from studies of psychiatric comorbidities do not speak directly to the social impairment of adults with ADHD, the relatively high degree of comorbidity and psychological distress does suggest a group that is unlikely to be free of impairment in the social realm. For example, social difficulties are well documented in individuals with depressive disorders (Coyne, Burchill, & Stiles, 1991), as well as individuals with substance abuse problems (McCrady & Epstein, 1995). And the diagnostic criteria for antisocial personality disorder are self-evident in indicating a significant degree of dysfunction in interpersonal relationships (e.g., deceitfulness and indifference to having hurt others). Thus, the elevated rates of these psychological problems among adults with ADHD stand as a strong proxy indicator of impairments in social functioning.

A few studies have assessed social behaviors among adults with ADHD in a more specific manner. In their fifteen-year follow-up, Weiss and Hechtman (1993) compared thirty-nine controls and fifty-eight ADHD participants and found that the young adults in the ADHD group were significantly worse at social skills in job interview, heterosocial, and assertion situations, whether measured via oral enactments of responses to the situations or written, multiple-choice questions. Murphy and Barkley (1996a) found that, among adults referred to an ADHD clinic, those who met diagnostic criteria reported significantly more problems making friends than did those who did not meet criteria. Clearly, the symptoms of ADHD, such as inattention and impulsivity, are likely to contribute to many of the social difficulties these individuals experience. However, the existing research does not allow isolation of the effects of ADHD symptomatology versus the effects of co-occurring problems such as aggression or depression on social functioning. Further research is needed to test for these effects, and also to elaborate more specifically on the types of social behavior and the social situations most likely to be problematic for adults with ADHD.

Family Functioning

Marital Ties. One indicator of family functioning is the stability of marital ties. In longitudinal studies, Mannuzza and Klein (1999), Weiss and Hechtman (1993), and Claude and Firestone (1995) all reported no difference in marital status between their ADHD and control groups. Not surprisingly, given the relatively young age of the samples, the majority of participants in both groups were still single. In contrast, among adults referred to ADHD clinics (with average ages in their 30s), Murphy and Barkley (1996a) found that those who met diagnostic criteria had a higher divorce rate and a trend toward lower marital satisfaction than did those who did not meet diagnostic criteria. Similarly, Biederman et al. (1993) found that adults with ADHD had higher rates of divorce and separation than did comparison adults. At least in adult-identified samples, ADHD appears to have a negative impact on marital stability.

Parenting. Related to marital functioning are data concerning the parenting status of adults with ADHD. Despite the relatively young age of their sample at follow-up, Weiss and Hechtman (1993) found that the adults in their ADHD group had significantly more children than did controls (ADHD mean = .76 children vs. control mean = .12 children), although Claude and Firestone (1995) did not replicate this difference. In considering parental status among adults with ADHD, it is important to recognize that parents with ADHD are likely to be faced with the challenge of parenting a child with ADHD, and conversely that many children with ADHD are living in homes with a parent with the same difficulties. Using samples identified through ADHD in the children, Biederman, Munir, Knee, and Habelow (1986) found that 45 percent of fathers of boys with ADHD reported a childhood history of ADHD (compared to 10 percent of the fathers of controls), and Rucklidge and Kaplan (1997) reported that among mothers of ADHD children, those mothers with ADHD themselves had significantly more children with ADHD than did non-ADHD mothers (1.90 vs. 1.35). Conversely, using a sample identified through ADHD in the parents, Biederman et al. (1995) found that 84 percent of adults with ADHD had at least one child with ADHD. Startlingly, 52 percent had at least two children with the disorder.

Looking not at current adult symptoms but at childhood history of ADHD, Loney, Paternite, Schwartz, and Roberts (1997) found significant relationships between reports of both mothers' and fathers' childhood inattention-overactivity and sons' current inattention-overactivity. Frick, Lahey, Christ, Loeber, and Green (1991) found that 40 percent of fathers of boys with ADHD and 48 percent of fathers of boys with both ADHD and conduct disorder reported symptoms of ADHD during childhood. Similarly, Schachar and Wachsmuth (1990) reported that as many as 64 percent of children diagnosed with ADHD had at least one parent with a history of childhood hyperactivity. Thus, ADHD in parents most often occurs in the context of having to face the difficulties of parenting a child with ADHD, placing these families at double risk.

Indeed, in families of children with ADHD, Arnold, O'Leary, and Edwards (1997) found that the father's level of ADHD symptomatology interacted with father involvement in predicting parenting behavior. Father involvement in parenting resulted in more negative and overreactive parenting if the father had more ADHD symptoms, whereas involvement was associated with reduced overreactivity in fathers without ADHD symptoms. The authors speculate that ADHD interferes with fathers' patience and ability to use effective parenting strategies. Presumably, this interference is particularly damaging to the family because of the ADHD child's need for clear and consistent parenting direction. Evans, Vallano, and Pelham (1994) described a case study in which treatment of the mother's ADHD was initiated because her symptoms were judged to be an obstacle to the use of behavioral strategies in the child's treatment. The mother was unable to complete monitoring tasks and was inconsistent in the implementation of management techniques. Due to her difficulties with concentration and organization, the mother was also incapable of reliably dispensing medication to her child. Initiation of psychostimulant treatment for the mother not only decreased her ADHD symptoms but also increased her reported consistency in monitoring and managing her child's behavior. Daly and Fritsch (1995) also described a case study in which the diagnosis and pharmacological treatment of maternal ADHD was crucial in alleviating failure to thrive in the mother's 2-month-old infant. Assessment revealed that the mother's fidgeting and distractibility were significantly impairing her ability to engage the infant in feeding sessions, and these difficulties were relieved through the use of methylphenidate. Clearly, treating parents who have ADHD has positive implications not only for the adults but also for their children.

In addition to this limited direct evidence regarding parenting among individuals diagnosed with ADHD, other information can be drawn from the wider literature describing families of children with ADHD. Given the data cited previously, it is apparent that the prevalence of the disorder is significantly elevated among parents of children with ADHD, and therefore extrapolations from studies of parents of children with ADHD can offer insights into the functioning of adults with ADHD. It is reasonable to expect that ADHD in the parents accounts for some proportion of the increased adaptive and interpersonal problems such as stress, depression, marital distress, and parent-child conflict found among families of children with ADHD (Johnston & Pelham, 1990; Mash & Johnston, 1982, 1983, 1990). However, the extent to which ADHD versus other parent problems (e.g., antisocial personality disorder) contribute to these problems has yet to be investigated. Similarly, the contribution of child versus parent symptoms to the parenting impairments is unknown. Clearly, these parents are responding to a challenging and stressful childrearing situation and their impairments may be a reaction to this challenge. For example, Hechtman (1996) reported that over their ten-year follow-up, when ADHD children left home, the emotional climate of the family home improved. In contrast, Rucklidge and Kaplan (1997) recently published a report comparing mothers with ADHD to mothers without ADHD, but all mothers in the study had children with ADHD. Their result indicate that the mothers diagnosed with ADHD reported more depression and anxiety, lower self-esteem, more stress, more emotion-focused coping, and more external locus of control than did mothers without ADHD. Because all mothers were parenting an ADHD child, the study offers insight into the added risk that comes from the mother carrying the diagnosis herself.

In 1982, noting the need to differentiate ADHD from aggressive or oppositional behavior, Jan Loney remarked that we did not so much have literature on ADHD as literature on comorbid ADHD and aggression (Loney & Milich, 1982). I would now make a similar point concerning our knowledge of the families of children with ADHD. We have a large literature that does not differentiate among parents of ADHD children who themselves do and do not have the disorder. Making this distinction in future research will be important to clarifying the impact of ADHD on parenting. Future research in this area will also need to attend to possible interactions between ADHD symptomatology and parent gender, in that ADHD may have a differential impact on the parenting of mothers versus that of fathers.

CONCLUSIONS

Across studies of both adults who were identified in childhood as having ADHD and those diagnosed in adulthood, there is a convergence of evidence suggesting that the disorder has a negative impact on educational achievement and occupational functioning. In addition, these difficulties cannot be completely accounted for by the individual's concurrent problems with antisocial behavior or intellectual functioning. Similarly, there is agreement across studies that childhood ADHD poses a risk factor for adult antisocial behavior, particularly, but not exclusively, in individuals with a childhood history of aggression. The high level of antisocial behavior characteristic of groups of adults with ADHD is one strong indicator of the social impairments that this group experiences. Within the family domain, adults with ADHD appear less likely to have stable marriages. Finally, ADHD is likely to co-occur in parents and children and its presence in the parent interferes with effective childrearing.

Despite these consistencies, some differences do emerge across studies. First, among the longitudinal studies, there are differences in the rates at which the disorder is found to persist into adulthood. As noted earlier, these differences appear due to variations in strictness of diagnostic criteria, attrition rates, and levels of aggression in the initial samples of children. Small differences also emerge in the types of impairments seen in child- versus adult-identified samples. For example, the longitudinal studies are quite consistent in showing little elevation in mood or anxiety disorders associated with a childhood history of ADHD. In contrast, studies of adults with ADHD typically do find elevated rates of these disorders. Such differences may be due to differences in the gender ratio in the two types of studies. Adult samples tend to have close to balanced number of males and females (Carlton et al., 1992; Shaywitz & Shaywitz, 1987), or at least ratios of males to females that are lower than the 6:1 ratio typically reported in clinic-referred child samples (Biederman et al., 1993; Murphy & Barkley, 1996a). Differences in referral patterns for children versus adults may account for this difference in gender ratios. Perhaps girls with ADHD are less likely than boys to be referred, because of their lower rates of comorbid oppositional or conduct disorders (Shaywitz & Shaywitz, 1987). Conversely, in adulthood, women with ADHD may be more willing than men to self-identify and to seek help. Supporting this argument is a recent study by Arcia and Conners (1998) indicating that, although adult males and females with ADHD were similar in cognitive performance and ratings of behavior by others, females self-reported more problems than did the males. Thus, as noted at the beginning of this chapter, the confounding of gender, comorbidity, and subtypes of ADHD across studies places limits on the conclusions that can be drawn across studies.

RECOMMENDATIONS FOR CLINICAL PRACTICE AND FUTURE RESEARCH

The lack of reliable and valid assessment protocols and diagnostic criteria continues to present a stumbling block to understanding the impact of this disorder in adulthood. The estimated prevalence of ADHD in adulthood ranges widely depending on factors such as diagnostic criteria, demographic composition of the sample, and method of assessment. Differences in diagnostic standards are likely culprits in explaining discrepancies across studies in the characteristics and correlates of the disorder. Scientifically, research that assists in reaching a standard protocol and set of criteria for adult diagnosis is a primary recommendation for the future. Without this we have no consensual basis for what is under investigation, and discrepancies among studies are likely to continue unexplained. For clinicians who face immediate demands for the assessment and diagnosis of adult ADHD, the best advice is to select the strongest of the current assessment tools, to be cognizant of the advantages and disadvantages of different diagnostic criteria, to limit diagnostic statements with appropriate cautions, and to follow the research literature expecting rapid changes in this area.

As this chapter demonstrates, the impact of ADHD on adult functioning is only beginning to be understood. Although the data are quite convincing in demonstrating lower levels of educational and occupational attainment in adults with ADHD, more extensive study is needed concerning the nature and quality of these impairments and the mechanisms through which they appear. Such research will provide important building blocks for interventions designed to prevent or remediate academic and vocational difficulties. Similarly, although many studies have documented high comorbidities between ADHD and other adult psychiatric disorders, less research describes, more directly, the types of interpersonal difficulties these adults face in areas such as friendships, marital relationships, or parenting. Given the core characteristics of the disorder and the high rates of comorbidity, it is obvious that adults with ADHD will struggle to function optimally in these various social domains, but more direct and objective information is needed to suggest the best routes of clinical assistance for these difficulties.

In addition to further investigation of the nature of the impairments associated with adult ADHD, researchers and clinicians must also consider the severity of these impairments and the subjective experience of those affected. In particular, assessment of the subjective quality of life experienced by adults with ADHD would offer an important supplement to more objective measures of impairment. Do these individuals report distress, and if so, what types of assistance are they seeking? Consideration of this perspective may be important in helping professionals avoid any tendency to overpathologize or overtreat.

As noted throughout this chapter, there is a rather desperate need for research differentiating the effects of ADHD from the effects of the various comorbid conditions. As in the child literature, it is important to develop an understanding of the risks and effects that are unique to ADHD and those that arise due to co-occurring disorders. Although research struggles to fill this gap in knowledge, clinicians are well advised to conduct thorough assessments of individuals with ADHD in anticipation of these high rates of comorbidity, to include ADHD as a possible comorbidity in assessment of other adult disorders, and to remain cautious in attributing a client's difficulties solely to ADHD in the face of such comorbidities.

One particular social role that needs further study among adults with ADHD is childrearing. ADHD is perhaps best thought of a family disorder, given the relatively high likelihood that children with ADHD are being reared by parents with ADHD. When one considers the impact of disorganized, inconsistent, or impulsive parenting on the behavior of a child with ADHD, the importance of understanding the disorder among parents is obvious. Family factors such as parent psychopathology (e.g., antisocial personality disorder), social disadvantage, and punitive childrearing are all predictors of poor outcome among children with ADHD (Hechtman, Weiss, Perlman, & Amsel, 1984; Loney et al., 1983), and all occur frequently among parents with ADHD. Offering support to parents with ADHD may be particularly important, not only in assisting the parents in fulfilling their parenting role but also in offsetting longer-term negative outcomes for the child with ADHD. Families with multiple problems are likely to require multiple services and clinicians/researchers will need considerable expertise and creativity in finding the best blend of adult-based, child-based, and family-based interventions to meet the needs of ADHD families.

Finally, although the focus of this chapter is on the impairments in adults with ADHD, it must be recognized that these difficulties occur in the context of many strengths and competencies, both within and across individuals. First, the limitations of group data and averaged reports of functioning must be remembered. Many individuals with ADHD do not have educational, vocational, or social impairments and, in fact, achieve and adapt in life at above-average levels. In addition, many adults with ADHD have developed a wide variety of compensatory strategies that allow them to overcome or circumvent the difficulties of the disorder (Denckla, 1993). Assessment and study of these strengths and competencies will be informative, both at the group and individual level, in developing optimum treatment strategies for this population.

In summary, research regarding the impact of ADHD on adult functioning has been, until now, relatively scarce and predominant ly descriptive. It is time for this area of research to develop more conceptual models that will drive research designed to test the parameters of the condition in adulthood. As well, research that focuses more on questions of the processes or mechanisms of action of adult ADHD impairment, rather than descriptive questions, will be more useful in guiding the development of effective supports and treatments for individuals with the condition.

References

Alpert, J. E., Maddocks, A., Nierenberg, A. A., O'Sullivan, R., Pava, J. A., Worthington III, J. J., Biederman, J., Rosenbaum, M., & Fava, M. (1996). Attention deficit hyperactivity disorder in childhood among adults with major depression. *Psychiatry Research, 62*, 213–219.

American Academy of Child and Adolescent Psychiatry. (1997). Practice parameters for the assessment and treatment of children, adolescents, and adults with attention-deficit/hyperactivity disorder. *Journal of the American Academy of Child and Adolescent Psychiatry, 36*(Suppl.), 85S–121S.

American Psychiatric Association. (1968). *Diagnostic and statistical manual of mental disorders* (2nd ed.). Washington, DC: Author.

American Psychiatric Association. (1980). *Diagnostic and statistical manual of mental disorders* (3rd ed.). Washington, DC: Author.

American Psychiatric Association. (1994). *Diagnostic and statistical manual of mental disorders* (4th ed.). Washington, DC: Author.

Arcia, E., & Conners, C. K. (1998). Gender differences in ADHD? *Journal of Developmental and Behavioral Pediatrics, 19*, 77–83.

Arnold, E. H., O'Leary, S. G., & Edwards, G. H. (1997). Father involvement and self-reported parenting of children with attention deficit-hyperactivity disorder. *Journal of Consulting and Clinical Psychology, 65*, 337–342.

Barkley, R. A. (1997). Advancing age, declining ADHD. *American Journal of Psychiatry, 154*, 1323–1324.

Barkley, R. A. (1998). *Attention-deficit hyperactivity disorder: A handbook for diagnosis and treatment* (2nd ed.). New York: Guilford Press.

Barkley, R. A., & Biederman, J. (1997). Toward a broader definition of the age-of-onset criterion for attention-deficit hyperactivity disorder. *Journal of the American Academy of Child and Adolescent Psychiatry, 36*, 1201–1210.

Barkley, R. A., Murphy, K. R., & Kwasnik, D. (1996). Psychological adjustment and adaptive impairments in young adults with ADHD. *Journal of Attention Disorders, 1*, 41–54.

Biederman, J., Faraone, S. V., Mick, E., Spencer, T., Wilens, T., Kiely, K., Guite, J., Ablon, J. S., Reed, E., & Warburton, R. (1995). High risk for attention deficit hyperactivity disorder among children of parents with childhood onset of the disorder: A pilot study. *American Journal of Psychiatry, 152*, 431–435.

Biederman, J., Faraone, S. V., Spencer, T., Wilens, T., Norman, D., Lapey, K. A., Mick, E., Lehman, B. K., & Doyle, A. (1993). Patterns of psychiatric comorbidity, cognition, and psychosocial functioning in adults with attention deficit hyperactivity disorder. *American Journal of Psychiatry, 150*, 1792–1798.

Biederman, J., Munir, K., Knee, D., & Habelow, W. (1986). A family study of patients with Attention Deficit Disorder and normal controls. *Journal of Psychiatric Research, 20*, 263–274.

Borland, H., & Heckman, H. (1976). Hyperactive boys and their brothers: A 25-year follow-up study. *Archives of General Psychiatry, 33*, 669–675.

Bradburn, N. M., Rips, L. J., & Shevell, S. K. (1987). Answering autobiographical questions: The impact of memory and inference on surveys. *Science, 236*, 157–161.

Carlton, P. L., Manowitz, P., McBride, H., Nora, R., Swartzburg, M., & Goldstein, L. (1992). Attention deficit disorder and pathological gambling. *Journal of Clinical Psychiatry, 48*, 487–488.

Claude, D., & Firestone, P. (1995). The development of ADHD boys: A 12-year follow-up. *Canadian Journal of Behavioral Science, 27*, 226–249.

Conners, C. K., Erhardt, D., Epstein, J. N., Parker, J. D. A., Sitarenios, G., & Sparrow, E. (1999). Self-ratings of ADHD symptoms in adults: I. Factor structure and normative data. *Journal of Attention Disorders, 3*, 141–151.

Conners, C. K., Levin, E. D., Sparrow, E., Hinton, S. C., Erhardt, D., Meck, W. H., Rose, J. E., & March, J. (1996). Nicotine and attention in adult attention deficit hyperactivity disorder (ADHD). *Psychopharmacological Bulletin, 32*, 67–73.

Coyne, J. C., Burchill, S. L., & Stiles, W. B. (1991). Handbook of social and clinical psychology: The health perspective. In C. R. Snyder & D. R. Forsyth (Eds.), *An interactional perspective on depression* (pp. 327–349.) New York: Pergamon Press.

Daly, J. M., & Fritsch, S. L. (1995). Case study: Maternal residual attention deficit disorder associated with failure to thrive in a two-month-old infant. *Journal of the American Academy of Child and Adolescent Psychiatry, 31*, 55–57.

Denckla, M. B. (1993). The child with developmental disabilities grown up: Adult residua of childhood disorders. *Neurological Clinics, 11*, 105–125.

Downey, K. K., Stelson, F. W., Pomerleau, O. F., & Giordani, B. (1997). Adult attention deficit hyperactivity disorder: Psychological test profiles in a clinical population. *Journal of Nervous and Mental Disease, 185*, 32–38.

Evans, S. W., Vallano, G., & Pelham, W. (1994). Treatment of parenting behavior with a psychostimulant: A case study of an adult with attention-deficit hyperactivity disorder. *Journal of Child and Adolescent Psychopharmacology, 4*, 64–69.

Fergusson, D. M., Lynskey, M. T., & Horwood, L. J. (1997). Attentional difficulties in middle childhood and psychosocial outcomes in young adulthood. *Journal of Child Psychology and Psychiatry, 38*, 633–644.

Fischer, M. (1997).The persistence of ADHD into adulthood: It depends on whom you ask. *ADHD Report, 5*(4), 8–10.

Frick, P. J., Lahey, B. B., Christ, M. G., Loeber, R., & Green, S. (1991). History of childhood behavior problems in biological relatives of boys with attention-deficit hyperactivity disorders and conduct disorder. *Journal of Clinical Child Psychology, 20*, 445–451.

Greenfield, B., Hechtman, L., & Weiss, G. (1988). Two subgroups of hyperactives as adults: Correlations of outcome. *Canadian Journal of Psychiatry, 33*, 505–508.

Hechtman, L. (1996). Families of children with attention deficit hyperactivity disorder: A review. *Canadian Journal of Psychiatry, 41*, 350–360.

Hechtman, L., Weiss, G., Perlman, T., & Amsel, R. (1984). Hyperactives as young adults: Initial predictors of adult outcome. *Journal of the American Academy of Child Psychiatry, 23*, 250–260.

Hill, J. C., & Schoener, E. P. (1996). Age-dependent decline of attention deficit hyperactivity disorder. *American Journal of Psychiatry, 153*, 1143–1146.

Horner, B., Scheibe, K., & Stine, S. (1996). Cocaine abuse and attention-deficit hyperactivity disorder: Implications of adult symptomatology. *Psychology of Addictive Behaviors, 10*, 55–60.

Johnston, C., & Pelham, W. E. (1990). Maternal characteristics, ratings of child behavior, and mother-child interactions in families of children with externalizing disorders. *Journal of Abnormal Child Psychology, 18*, 407–417.

Loney, J., & Milich, R. (1982). Hyperactivity, inattention, and aggression in clinical practice. In M. Wolraich & D. K. Routh (Eds.), *Advances in developmental behavioral pediatrics* (Vol. 2, pp. 113–147), Greenwich, CT: JAI Press.

Loney, J., Paternite, C. E., Schwartz, J. E., & Roberts, M. A. (1997). Associations between clinic-referred boys and their fathers on childhood inattention-overactivity and aggression dimensions. *Journal of Abnormal Child Psychology, 25*, 499–510.

Loney, J., Whaley-Klahn, M. A., Kosier, T., & Conboy, J. (1983). Prospective studies of crime and delinquency In K. T. Van Dusen & S. A. Mednick (Eds.), *Hyperactive boys and their brothers at 21: Predictors of aggressive and antisocial outcome* (pp. 181–207). Boston: Kluwer-Nijhoff.

Mannuzza, S., & Klein, R. G. (1999). Adolescent and adult outcomes in attention-deficit/hyperactivity disorder. In H. L. Quay (Ed.), *Handbook of disruptive behavior disorders* (pp. 279–294). New York: Kluwer Academic/Plenum Press.

Mannuzza, S., Klein, R. G., Bessler, A., Malloy, P., & Hynes, M. E. (1997). Educational and occupational outcome of hyperactive boys grown up. *Journal of the American Academy of Child and Adolescent Psychiatry, 36*, 1222–1227.

Mannuzza, S., Klein, R. G., Bessler, A., Malloy, P., & LaPadula, M. (1993). Adult outcome of hyperactive boys: Educational achievement, occupational rank, and psychiatric status. *Archives of General Psychiatry, 50*, 565–576.

Mannuzza, S., Klein, R. G., Bessler, A., Malloy, P., & LaPadula, M. (1998). Adult psychiatric status of hyperactive boys grown up. *American Journal of Psychiatry, 155*, 493–498.

Mash, E. J., & Johnston, C. (1982). A comparison of the mother-child interactions of younger and older hyperactive and normal children. *Child Development, 52*, 1371–1381.

Mash, E. J., & Johnston, C. (1983). Parental perceptions of child behavior problems, parenting self-esteem, and mothers' reported stress in younger and older hyperactive and normal children. *Journal of Consulting and Clinical Psychology, 51*, 86–99.

Mash, E. J., & Johnston, C. (1990). Determinants of parenting stress: Illustrations from families of hyperactive children and families of physically abused children. *Journal of Clinical Child Psychology, 19*, 313–328.

McCrady, B. S., & Epstein, E. E. (1995). Directions for research on alcoholic relationships: Marital- and individual-based models of heterogeneity. *Psychology of Addictive Behaviors, 9*, 157–166.

Means, C. D., Stewart, S. L., & Dowler, D. L. (1997). Job accommodations that work: A follow-up study of adults with attention deficit disorder. *Journal of Applied Rehabilitation Counseling, 28*, 13–17.

Millstein, R. B., Wilens, T. E., Biederman, J., & Spencer, T. J. (1997). Presenting ADHD symptoms and subtypes in clinically referred adults with ADHD. *Journal of Attention Disorders, 2*, 159–166.

Minskoff, E., Sautter, S., Hoffmann, F. J., & Hawks, R. (1987). Employer attitudes toward hiring the learning disabled. *Journal of Learning Disorders, 20*, 53–57.

Morrison, J. R. (1980). Childhood hyperactivity in an adult psychiatric population: Social factors. *Journal of Clinical Psychiatry, 41*, 40–43.

Murphy, K., & Barkley, R. A. (1996a). Attention deficit hyperactivity disorder adults: Comorbidities and adaptive impairments. *Comprehensive Psychiatry, 37*, 393–401.

Murphy, K., & Barkley R. A. (1996b). Prevalence of DSM-IV symptoms of ADHD in adult licensed drivers: Implications for clinical diagnosis. *Journal of Attention Disorders, 1*, 147–161.

Murphy, K. R., & Gordon, M. (1998). Assessment of adults with ADHD. In R. A. Barkley (Ed.), *Attention-deficit hyperactivity disorder: A handbook for diagnosis and treatment* (2nd ed., pp. 345–369). New York: Guilford Press.

Parks, A., Antonoff, S., Drake, C., Skiba, W., & Soberman, J. (1987). A survey of programs and services for learning disabled students in graduate and professional schools. *Journal of Learning Disorders, 20*, 181–187.

Pomerleau, O. F., Downey, K. K., Stelson, F. W., & Pomerleau, C. S. (1995). Cigarette smoking in adult patients diagnosed with attention deficit hyperactivity disorder. *Journal of Substance Abuse, 7*, 373–378.

Roy-Byrne, P., Scheele, L., Brinkley, J., Ward, N., Wiatrack, C., Russo, J., Townes, B., & Varley, C. (1997). Adult attention-deficit hyperactivity disorder: Assessment guidelines based on clinical presentation to a specialty clinic. *Comprehensive Psychiatry, 38*, 133–140.

Rucklidge, J. J., & Kaplan, B. J. (1997). Psychological functioning of women identified in adulthood with attention-deficit/hyperactivity disorder. *Journal of Attention Disorders, 2*, 167–176.

Schachar, R., & Wachsmuth, R. (1990). Hyperactivity and parental psychopathology. *Journal of Child Psychology and Psychiatry, 31*, 381–392.

Shaffer, D. (1994). Attention deficit hyperactivity disorder in adults. *American Journal of Psychiatry, 151*, 633–638.

Shaywitz, S. E., & Shaywitz, B. A. (1987). Attention deficit disorder: Current perspectives. *Pediatric Neurology, 3*, 129–135.

Shekim, W. O., Asarnow, R. F., Hess, E., Zaucha, K., & Wheeler, N. (1990). A clinical and demographic profile of a sample of adults with attention deficit hyperactivity disorder, residual state. *Comprehensive Psychiatry, 31*, 416–425.

Ward, M. F., Wender, P. H., & Reimherr, F. W. (1993). The Wender Utah Rating Scale: an aid in the retrospective diagnosis of childhood attention deficit hyperactivity disorder. *American Journal of Psychiatry, 150*, 885–890.

Weiss, G., & Hechtman, L. T. (1993). *Hyperactive children grown up* (2nd ed.). New York: Guilford Press.

Wender, P. (1997). Attention deficit hyperactivity disorder in adults: A wide view of a widespread condition. *Psychiatric Annals, 27*, 556–562.

Weyandt, L. L., Linterman, I., & Rice, J. A. (1995). Reported prevalence of attentional difficulties in a general sample of college students. *Journal of Psychopathology and Behavior Assessment, 17*, 293–364.

Wilens, T. E., Biederman, J., Spencer, R. J., & Prince, J. (1995). Pharmacotherapy of adult attention deficit/hyperactivity disorder: A review. *Journal of Clinical Psychopharmacology, 5*, 270–279.

Wolraich, M. L., Hannah, J. N., Pinnock, T. Y., Baumgaertel, A., & Brown, J. (1996). Comparison of diagnostic criteria for attention-deficit hyperactivity disorder in a county-wide sample. *Journal of the American Academy of Child and Adolescent Psychiatry, 35*, 319–324.

Wood, D., Wender, P. H., & Reimherr, F. W. (1983). The prevalence of attention deficit disorder, residual type, or minimal brain dysfunction, in a population of male alcoholic patients. *American Journal of Psychiatry, 140*, 95–98.

Wyld, D. C. (1997). Attention deficit/hyperactivity disorder in adults: Will this be the greatest challenge for employment discrimination law? *Employee Responsibilities and Rights Journal, 10*, 103–125.

Part 2

What Causes ADHD?

It is generally acknowledged that British pediatrician George Still set the stage for the concept of attention deficit hyperactivity disorder (ADHD) by identifying children with an impulsive pattern, motivated by need for immediate gratification without regard to consequences, often accompanied by learning deficits, mostly apparent in boys, and sometimes associated with retardation or known organic insults to the brain. This volitional impairment was, in turn, due to an inability to focus attention on alternative paths of action. Still's description included the full range of externalizing behavior disorders, which might now be used to subclassify ADHD individuals as aggressive, delinquent, oppositional-defiant, and attention-deficit disordered. However, all the key features of ADHD were observed, and the syndrome was clearly distinguished from retardation or organic syndromes. The notion of an impulsive syndrome in children, who are not simply brain-injured or retarded, was an original idea in the medical literature.

Since Still's time, there have been many theories, some supported by research, but no single cause of ADHD has yet been identified, and its exact etiology and pathophysiology remain obscure. As recently as the 1998 National Institutes of Health Consensus Development Conference on the Diagnosis and Treatment of ADHD (see Appendix A), consensus panelists concluded that the etiology of ADHD is unknown. As the chapters in this section make clear, that situation has not changed; however, that is not a cause for dismay. We must remember that ADHD is a heterogeneous condition and it likely has many causes, with the final ADHD symptoms and syndrome best viewed as a final common pathway for a variety of complex brain processes.

This section presents substantial evidence that ADHD symptomatology has a central nervous system basis (as do all normal and abnormal behaviors, thoughts, and emotions). By way of caution, such brain-behavior correlations do not constitute proof that ADHD reflects a disordered physiological or anatomic state. For example, variations in biological processes such as height and pulse rate do not necessarily reflect disturbed biological processes, even at the tail ends of their natural distributions. Two preeminent scholars, who themselves have made some of the most important contributions to addressing these questions, present excellent, in-depth overviews of current research on the topic. As they show, factors implicated in the etiology of ADHD generally fall into a small handful of categories: (1) family and genetic factors, (2) prenatal/perinatal factors, (3) chemical toxins, (4) exacerbating psychosocial stressors and combined factors, and (5) brain structure/function abnormalities (which could themselves result from factors 1–4).

In Chapter 7, Swanson provides an excellent summary of how the new tools of neuroimaging and genetics have been used to investigate the biologic basis of ADHD. In terms of brain structure and function, the first generation of these studies relied on electroencephalography (EEG), followed more recently by positron emission tomography (PET), magnetic resonance imaging (MRI), and functional MRI (fMRI). In addition, a range of candidate gene and whole-genome scanning approaches have been and are now being applied to ADHD. Swanson and his collaborators have contributed (and continue to contribute) to many of the most important findings in this area. In this chapter he also discusses the role of pre- and perinatal factors as possible etiological explanations for ADHD, other variables such as environmental toxins, and traumatic brain injury (leading to "secondary" ADHD).

Given that we in truth know little concerning the etiology of ADHD, we therefore know little about its prevention. We must ask ourselves why essentially no research has been done in the ADHD *prevention* area, and whether the field has unwittingly excluded this area of research from consciousness—perhaps because of taken-for-granted assumptions that because ADHD symptoms have a biological basis they must also be *immutable*? Such an assumption, if in fact predominant, cannot be correct, however, given the number of children who show significant remission (20–40%) over the course of development. How and why do such significant improvements in symptoms take place? What developmental processes are at work? Could similar factors come into play and be used to clinical advantage early in the course of the disorder, perhaps before full expression of symptoms, via some targeted prevention strategies?

As the cognitive and developmental neurosciences rapidly advance, it is important that the latest theories and findings are integrated into meaningful overall conceptual frameworks, in order to guide subsequent clinical and research activities (including prevention studies). In Chapter 8, Tannock provides an elegant overview of the current conceptual approaches to understanding cognitive functioning in ADHD, including theories related to arousal, motor preparation and control, and response inhibition, and she links these theories to specific findings on neuropsychological and cognitive functioning tests. A full understanding of the core deficits in ADHD and their implicated brain regions is still in flux, but her overview provides a thoughtful conceptual framework for negotiating this complex territory.

—**P.S. Jensen**
—**C.K. Conners**

Chapter 7

Biological Bases of ADHD— Neuroanatomy, Genetics, and Pathophysiology

by James M. Swanson, Ph.D. and F. Xavier Castellanos, M.D.

Introduction 7-1
    DSM-IV/ICD-10 Overlap 7-2
    Dopamine Theory of ADHD 7-4
Research on Neuroanatomical Abnormalities 7-4
    Differences in Neuroanatomic Structures in Children
       With ADHD 7-5
           Basal Ganglia and Cerebellum 7-5
           Frontal Regions 7-6
    Areas of Difference Among the Findings 7-6
    Overall Consistency of Findings 7-7
Research on Functional Brain Imaging and ADHD 7-7
Genetic Investigations 7-9
    Twin Studies 7-9
    Genes Associated With ADHD/HKD 7-9
    Populations and Family Studies of Candidate Genes 7-10
        DRD4 Gene 7-11
        DAT1 Gene 7-11
    Study Replications 7-12
Investigations of Nongenetic Etiologies 7-12
Neurobiological Bases for Pharmacological Treatment 7-13
    Methylphenidate as a Dopamine Blocker 7-13
    Debate Regarding Net Effect of Dopamine Blockade 7-14
Alternative Site-of-Action Hypotheses 7-14
Summary 7-15

INTRODUCTION

Robins and Guze (1970) have recommended a multistage process for validation of a psychiatric disorder. For the purposes of this chapter, Table 7.1 has adapted and reordered these five stages.

Table 7.1
Stages for Validation of Psychiatric Disorders

Stage 1: Description of Clinical Phenotype (Symptom Domains in DSM-IV)

Stage 2: Differentiation from other syndromes (Comorbid Status in ICD-10)

Stage 3: Delineation of Clinical Course (Long-term Outcome Investigations)

Stage 4: Definition of Biological Characteristics (Regional Abnormalities in MRI)

Stage 5: Specification of Genetic Basis (Association with Dopamine Genes)

Chapters 1 and 3 and Sections III and V of this book address the first three stages, but this chapter focuses principally on Stages 4 and 5. In this introduction, however, we briefly address Stages 1 and 2 in the service of defining a refined phenotype of research diagnostic criteria for investigations of biological bases of ADHD.

DSM-IV/ICD-10 Overlap

As a part of an international group, Swanson, Sergeant, et al. (1998) described the way in which the fourth edition of *Diagnostic and Statistical Manual of Mental Disorders* (DSM-IV; American Psychiatric Association, 1994) addresses Stages 1 and 2. DSM-IV provides the criteria for attention deficit hyperactivity disorder (ADHD) and the tenth edition of *International Classification of Diseases* (ICD-10; World Health Organization, 1992) provides the criteria for hyperkinetic disorder (HKD). After decades of differences, the DSM-IV and ICD-10 manuals now list the same eighteen symptoms for ADHD and HKD; thus there is a consensus about Stage 1 in terms of the underlying behaviors used to specify the clinical phenotype. However, the decision rules (inclusion and exclusion criteria) still differ for making categorical diagnoses, so in terms of Stage 2 there is no consensus about how to differentiate ADHD and HKD from other syndromes. In the symptom domain, ICD-10 restricts the phenotype by requiring the full syndrome (manifestation of some symptoms from all three subsets of inattention, hyperactivity, and impulsivity). In contrast, DSM-IV allows diagnosis of subtypes defined by the partial syndromes (i.e., manifestation of symptoms from just one of the subset groups as either inattention or hyperactivity/impulsivity symptoms). Furthermore, in the comorbidity domain, ICD-10 restricts the phenotype by usually excluding cases with concurrent diagnoses of internalizing disorders (anxiety or mood disorders) whereas DSM-IV usually does not. Based on these symptom and comorbidity domains, the international team from Europe and the United States (Swanson, Sergeant, et al., 1998) proposed twelve possible (logical) subgroups of ADHD as defined in DSM-IV, which overlap with just two subgroups defined in ICD-10 (see Table 7.2).

The two overlapping DSM-IV/ICD-10 consensus subgroups shown in Table 7.2 specify a restricted phenotype—ADHD combined type without comorbidity other than conduct (CD) or oppositional defiant disorder (ODD)—that is similar to the

Table 7.2
ADHD Subgroups Based on DSM-IV and ICD-10 Criteria

	Symptom Subtype[1]	Comorbidity Ext.[2,6]	Int.[3,4,5]	DSM-IV Label	Codes[8,9]	ICD-10 Label[7]	Code[10]
Consensus Subgroups	Combined	-C/OD	-A/M	ADHDc	314.1/F90.0	HKDaa	F90.0
	"	+C/OD	-A/M	"	"	HKDco	F90.1
Nonconsensus Subgroups	"	-C/OD	+A/M	"	"	A or M	F3 or F4
	"	+C/OD	+A/M	"	"	Mixed	F92.-
	Hyper/Imp	-C/OD	-A/M	ADHDh	314.1/F90.0	Other	F98.8
	"	+C/OD	-A/M	"	"	C/OD	F91.-
	"	-C/OD	+A/M	"	"	A or M	F3 or F4
	"	+C/OD	+A/M	"	"	Mix C/E	F92.-
	Inattentive	-C/OD	-A/M	ADHDi	314.0/F98.8	Other	F98.8
	"	+C/OD	-A/M	"	"	C/OD	F91.-
	"	-C/OD	+A/M	"	"	A/M	F3 or F4
	"	+C/OD	+A/M	"	"	Mix C/E	F92.-

1. Minor difference in criteria for total and diversity of symptoms from hyperactive and impulsive subdomains. 2. Conduct or Oppositional Defiant (C/OD) disorders. 3. Anxiety, mood, or pervasive developmental (A/M) disorders. 4. DSM-IV guidelines recommend exclusion if ADHD symptoms are present "only at home" or have "late onset." 5. Unanticipated in the clinical criteria (1992) and excluded in the research criteria (1993) of ICD-10. 6. If criteria for both C/OD and HKD are met in ICD-10, the HKD diagnosis takes precedence. 7. "aa" refers to disorder of attention and activity; "co" refers to conduct or oppositional defiant disorder. 8. In the DSM-IV manual, ICD-9 codes are used in the body. 9. ICD-10 codes are listed in an appendix of DSM-IV, but not all listed codes are consistent with the ICD-10 manuals. 10. By international treaty, by the year 2000, ICD-10 codes should be implemented in the United States.

"refined phenotype" used in most investigations of biological bases of ADHD that are reviewed in this chapter. It is estimated that this phenotype characterizes about 3 percent of the school-age populations in countries around the world (Swanson, Sergeant, et al., 1998).

This refined phenotype certainly does not represent a majority of the ADHD cases recognized and treated in clinical practice in the United States. For example, only 179 of the 579 ADHD children who were subjects in the Multimodal Treatment of ADHD (MTA) study (all of whom were diagnosed with ADHD—combined type) meet the ICD-10 criteria for HKDaa (ADHD with no comorbidity with internalizing or other externalizing disorders; see Table 7.2), and only 169 of the 579 meet the ICD-10 criteria for HKDco (see Table 7.2). Thus, in the seven-site U.S./Canadian clinical sample of the MTA study (MTA Cooperative Group, 1999), a total of 348 of the 579 cases (60 percent) meet the proposed criteria for a refined phenotype defined by the ICD-10-DSM-IV overlap. Because most of the studies reviewed here have used a similarly restricted phenotype of ADHD to define research cases, readers must be cautioned that the conclusions drawn from this literature may not hold for the broader clinical syndrome of ADHD as defined by DSM-IV.

Dopamine Theory of ADHD

Much of the research on brain anatomy and molecular genetics was partially inspired by the "dopamine hypothesis" of ADHD (Castellanos et al., 1996; Levy, 1991; Wender, 1971). This hypothesis is a site-of-action theory (Swanson, Castellanos, Murias, LaHoste, & Kennedy, 1998), which assumes that the primary sites of action of the stimulants are in the dopamine pathways (mesocortical and nigrostriatal). Recent research at Brookhaven National Laboratories using positron emission tomography (PET) scans to visualize methylphenidate binding (Volkow et al., 1995; Volkow et al., 1997) has confirmed the hypothesis that the primary site of action of methylphenidate is in these dopamine pathways.

The dopamine theory of ADHD is used here to guide and organize this selective review of literature. The focus is on investigations of the neuroanatomy of ADHD based on MRI and investigations of the association of dopamine genes with ADHD based on the analysis of DNA.

RESEARCH ON NEUROANATOMICAL ABNORMALITIES

One of the most important current developments has been the convergence of findings from magnetic resonance imaging (MRI) studies of brain anatomy. These images can be used to estimate the size of structures in the brain by outlining each slice of the MRI.

Four of the MRI studies that have been conducted by teams are:

- University of Georgia: Hynd, Semrud-Clikeman, Lorys, and Novey (1990, 1991) and Hynd, Hern, Novey, and Eliopulos (1993) investigated a small group of ADHD children ($n = 11$) and contrasted them with a group of children with learning disabilities.

- Harvard University: Semrud-Clikeman, Filipek, Biederman, and Steingard (1994) and Filipek et al. (1997) investigated a small group of ADHD children ($n = 15$) referred to a child psychiatry clinic. These children were selected on the basis of ADHD without comorbid conditions, though the sample did include children with the inattentive as well as combined types of ADHD).

- National Institute of Mental Health (NIMH): Giedd et al. (1994), Castellanos et al. (1994 and 1996), Casey et al. (1997), and Berquin et al. (1998) accumulated a large sample of ADHD boys ($n = 57$) and control boys ($n = 55$); the NIMH team is now accumulating a large sample of ADHD girls ($n = 53$) and control girls ($n = 42$).

- Johns Hopkins University: Singer, Reiss, Brown, and Aylward (1993), Aylward et al. (1996), and Mostofsky, Reiss, Lockhart, and Denckla (1998) investigated a small group of ADHD children ($n = 13$), contrasting them with groups with Tourette's syndrome and healthy controls (some of whom were siblings of children with defined genetic conditions).

Because not all the publications of these four teams appear to describe independent samples, the multiple articles from each team are considered together (i.e., as one

Table 7.3
Summary of MRI Studies by Four Teams

		Estimate of Effect Size[5] and % Reduction[6] by Brain Region			
Team and Diagnosis	Sample Size, Age, and Clinical Contrast Group	Corpus Callosum	Basal Ganglia	Frontal Lobes	Cerebellar Vermis
University of Georgia[1] DSM-III ADDH, all but 2 HKD	n = 7 to 11 11.1 yrs., learning disabilities	.51[5] 10.9%[6]	.88 19.0%	.69 3.6%	- -
Harvard University[2] DSM-III-R ADHD, all HKD	n = 15 12.4 yrs. response to stimulants	.80 12.2%	.72 11.4%	.82 12.7%	- -
Johns Hopkins[3] DSM-III-R ADHD, all HKD	n = 10 to 13 11.3 yrs., Tourette's syndrome	.44 5.7%	.7 11.8%	- -	.79 12.3%
NIMH[4] DSM-III-R ADHD, all but 2 HKD	n = 18 to 57 12.0 yrs. none	.53 11.2%	.40 5.4%	.64 9.6%	.80 11.1%

1. Hynd et al., 1990 (anterior width of frontal lobes on single slice; es = .69); Hynd et al., 1991 (5 areas of cc; es = .51); Hynd et al., 1993 (left caudate head; es = .88). 2. Semrud-Clikeman et al., 1994 (7 areas of cc; overall es = .80); Filipek et al., 1997 (volumetric MRI; 1 caudate es = .81; r caudate es = .63; ant.sup. es = .74;. ant.-sup. wm es = .81; ant.-inf. es = .89). 3. Aylward et al., 1996 (volume of basal ganglia; 1 caudate es = .56; r caudate es = .34; 1 globus pallidus es = 1.1; r globus pallidus es = .80); Mostofsky et al., 1998 (area of cerebellar vermis lobules VIII-X es = .79). 4. Giedd et al., 1994 (7 areas of cc; rostrum es = .62; rostral body es = .81; total es = .15); Castellanos et al., 1994 (volume of basal ganglia; 1 caudate es = .29; r caudate es = .54); Castellanos et al.,, 1996 (volumetric MRI; total area cc es = .06; 1 caudate es = .20; r caudate es = .52; 1 globus pallidus es = .25; r globus pallidus es = .60; ant. frontal es = .64); Berquin et al., 1998 (volume of cerebellar vermis lobules VIII-X es = .80). 5. effect size = (ADHD mean–Control mean)/(standard deviation of control group). 6. % reduction = (Control mean–ADHD mean)/Control mean.

study) for the purposes of this review. Table 7.3. summarizes the findings reported in these twelve MRI studies. In these studies, similar research diagnostic criteria were used by the teams to select cases based on the same inclusion criteria (mostly DSM-III-R ADHD, the precursor to DSM-IV combined type) and exclusion criteria (usually without comorbidities other than ODD), and the ages of the subjects were about the same across the teams (average age about 12 years). Using MRI, these teams have documented anatomical differences between groups of ADHD and control subjects (with some understandable variation in the specific patterns) in four brain regions: the corpus callosum, basal ganglia, frontal lobes, and cerebellar vermis.

Differences in Neuroanatomic Structures in Children With ADHD

Basal Ganglia and Cerebellum. What do these twelve studies indicate about potential differences in neuroanatomic structures in children with ADHD? First, given that one of the core symptom domains of ADHD is overactivity, those brain structures that play a key role in the control of movement—the basal ganglia and cerebellum—are considered. One variant of the dopamine hypothesis of ADHD is based on assumed dopamine deficits, suggesting that brain regions that are rich in dopamine receptors may be smaller in ADHD children than in control children. The studies reviewed here are consistent with this hypothesis: All four teams reported that dopamine-rich basal ganglia regions (e.g., caudate and globus pallidus) were smaller in ADHD groups than in the control groups. Furthermore, there is substantial consistency across teams in both the direction of these differences (all found that these regions were smaller in the ADHD group) as well as the size of the differences (an effect size of about .75, or about a 12 percent decrease relative to the control groups).

Second, another brain structure that is involved in the control of movement (the cerebellum) demonstrates some noteworthy findings in these studies. Thus, both of the two teams that investigated the cerebellar regions reported that the same region (inferior posterior lobe, lobules VIII-X of the vermis) was smaller in the ADHD groups than in the normal groups. This brain structure may thus be implicated in the expression of one type of symptom (hyperactivity) that defines the clinical syndrome of ADHD.

Frontal Regions. The frontal regions that have been related to processes of attention also demonstrate an important pattern of findings. These brain regions include the anterior cingulate gyrus region (linked to executive control functions), the right frontal region (linked to alerting functions), and the left dorsolateral region (linked to the cognitive process of verbal working memory). All three teams that investigated the frontal lobes, key areas related to attention, reported that this region was smaller in the ADHD groups than in the control groups. Here, too, there is consistency in the direction (smaller) and size (effect size about .7, or about a 10 percent decrease relative to the controls groups) of brain regions linked to the attentional symptom of ADHD. These regions are also rich in dopamine receptors.

Other findings from these teams are of further interest. Two teams reported that some regions of the corpus callosum (e.g., anterior and posterior) were smaller in ADHD groups than in control groups. Also, in several studies, comparisons with clinical controls were done. Smaller than normal frontal regions are associated with ADHD but not with learning disability, which was instead associated with smaller than normal posterior brain regions (Hynd et al., 1990, 1991; Hynd et al., 1993). In addition, smaller than normal size of the corpus callosum and caudate is associated with ADHD but not Tourette's syndrome (Aylward et al., 1996). Also, the loss of asymmetry of the caudate (reported to be characteristic of a group of ADHD children compared to a normal control group; see Castellanos et al., 1994; Castellanos et al., 1996) was not characteristic of a clinical contrast group with Tourette's syndrome (Castellanos et al., 1996).

Areas of Difference Among the Findings

Despite the convergence across these teams, there are differences that complicate the interpretation of these findings. First, the initial reports of differences in two subregions (genu and splenium) of the corpus callosum (Hynd et al., 1990) have been questioned. Subsequent studies have reported significant differences between ADHD and control groups but not for the same subregions (e.g., Giedd et al., 1994, implicated the rostrum and rostral body but not the splenium, and Semrud-Clikeman et al., 1994, implicated only the splenium). Most problematic is that the initial finding by one team (Giedd et al., 1994) was not replicated in the largest sample yet studied (Castellanos et al., 1996). In addition, the consistent reports of smaller caudate nuclei have differed in terms of the side that may be smaller in the ADHD group compared to the control group. For example, Filipek et al. (1997) suggest that the left caudate is smaller than normal, but Castellanos et al. (1996) suggest that the right caudate is smaller than normal. Also, cross-sectional analyses of age groups suggest that the normal developmental course of decreasing caudate size may not occur in ADHD children, so that by late adolescence the size difference between ADHD and control groups may not be maintained (Castellanos et al., 1996). This possibility of developmental and age-related changes in caudate size defines an extremely important area of research and requires the use of prospective follow-up (longitudinal) designs in which the same children are rescanned at different ages as they develop, reach puberty, and become adults.

Overall Consistency of Findings

Despite the limitations of this pioneering work, overall consistency has been found across four research teams in terms of the following:

- Location in the brain (all investigated brain regions hypothesized to be associated with symptoms of ADHD);

- Direction of effects (all found the ADHD groups to have smaller than normal brain regions); and

- Size (all reported about a 10 percent reduction in size, which corresponds to modest effect sizes of about .5).

Perhaps most important, because a wealth of other investigations have linked these same regions to functions related to the core symptoms of ADHD, some moderate degree of confidence in the overall findings appears warranted.

RESEARCH ON FUNCTIONAL BRAIN IMAGING AND ADHD

In addition to the investigations in anatomical imaging using MRI, considerable work has been done with a variety of techniques for functional imaging of the brain. Four methods for functional brain imaging have been used in many studies to investigate ADHD. Thus, some of the findings reviewed here are based on single photon emission tomography (SPECT) (Lou, Henriksen, & Bruhn, 1984, 1990; Lou, Henriksen, Bruhn, Borner, & Nielsen, 1989), functional magnetic resonance imaging (fMRI; Vaidya et al., 1998), electroencephalogram (EEG; Oades, Dittmann-Balcar, Schepker, & Eggers, 1996; Satterfield, Swanson, Schell, & Lee, 1994), and PET (Ernst, Cohen, Liebenauer, Jons, & Zametkin, 1997; Ernst et al., 1999; Zametkin et al., 1990 and 1993).

The initial reports of functional imaging studies of ADHD were based on SPECT, which provides estimates of regional blood flow. Three SPECT studies based on the Xenon inhalation method (Lou et al., 1984, 1990; Lou et al., 1989) used strict DSM-III-R (American Psychiatric Association, 1987) criteria to identify subjects. The subjects were scanned during rest, without the use of an activation task. These three studies represent serial publications as the team accumulated cases over a period of years, so they are not independent, and the last study (Lou et al., 1990) in this series provides the best description of the results. The pure ADHD group ($n = 9$) had lower than normal perfusion in striatum (and posterior periventricular) brain regions and increased perfusion in occipital regions, but the previously reported hypoperfusion of prefrontal brain regions was not significant in this accumulated group of subjects.

fMRI also provides a measure of regional blood flow. In a recent fMRI study (Vaidya et al., 1998), small groups of ADHD ($n = 10$) and normal ($n = 6$) subjects were scanned on and off methylphenidate during performance of a response inhibition (go/no go) task that varied in difficulty. In an unmedicated state and for a task with stimulus presentation every two seconds, the ADHD group had lower striatal perfusion related to task activation than did the control group. Although the conditions and methods differed, this finding supports the perfusion results from SPECT by Lou et al. (1990).

In these two functional imaging studies, measures of regional cerebral blood flow were used to localize the neural response to a stimulant medication (i.e., methylphenidate). In the Lou et al. (1984, 1989, and 1990) studies, treatment with methylphenidate increased perfusion of the striatum. This pattern held for the Vaidya et al. (1998) study: for the condition described previously, administration of a clinical dose of methylphenidate increased striatal perfusion substantially in the children with ADHD. Interestingly, the control group of normal children in the Vaidya et al. (1998) study showed the opposite change in striatal perfusion when evaluated on medication.

The convergence of findings within and across investigations has not emerged for functional imaging studies using PET (Ernst & Zametkin, 1995). Thus, initial reports of global reduction in metabolism in ADHD adults relative to age-matched controls (Zametkin et al., 1990) were not replicated by the same team in a study of ADHD and control adolescents (Ernst & Zametkin, 1995; Zametkin et al., 1993). However, when normalized regional areas were evaluated, these two studies did show similar differences between the ADHD and control groups: In both age groups, lower than normal metabolism in the frontal lobes (i.e., left anterior frontal region) was observed in the ADHD groups, but this consistent difference was embedded in the context of differences in other regions that were not consistent across studies. Also, age-related changes in glucose metabolism may be different for males and females, which may explain some of the inconsistent findings across studies that do not control for age and gender (Ernst et al., 1997).

The same team conducted studies based on PET imaging to investigate the effects of stimulant medication on adults with ADHD. In several studies, a computerized performance task (CPT) was used during PET scans performed in off-medication or on-medication states, with acute (Matochik et al., 1993) and chronic (Matochik et al., 1994) administration of d-amphetamine and methylphenidate and intraveneous (IV) administration of d-amphetamine (Ernst & Zametkin, 1995). Overall, this research program suggested that the stimulants produce no consistent change in glucose metabolism.

Recently, this team used fluoro-dopa PET scans to evaluate adults and adolescents with ADHD. Using this promising method, abnormally low dopaminergic activity was documented in the frontal lobes of adults, but this was not observed in adolescents (Ernst et al., 1999).

An extensive literature exists on the use of EEG measures to study brain function of children with ADHD, but this literature will not be reviewed in this chapter. It is important to note that some of the best and most recent work (Oades, et al., 1996; Satterfield et al., 1994) emphasizes the need for prospective studies that track changes over development. These studies suggest that differences between groups of ADHD and control children at a young age (e.g., 6 years) may disappear or even reverse at an older age (e.g., 12 years). This is a common theme that emerges in the literature of all the functional and anatomical brain imaging methods and highlights the need for caution in the interpretation of single studies as well as the need for both longitudinal and prospective investigations.

GENETIC INVESTIGATIONS

Twin Studies

Family (Faraone et al., 1992) and adoption (Deutsch, Matthysse, Swanson, & Farkas, 1990) studies suggest a strong genetic basis for ADHD/HKD (Swanson et al., 2000). The twin study methods offer ways to test this hypothesis and to estimate heritability of ADHD, which Goodman and Stevenson (1989) estimated to be about .75. Over the past decade, more than a dozen research teams have confirmed the initial finding in large twin studies that provided estimates of the heritability of ADHD-like symptoms. Table 7.4 lists some of these studies. All estimated heritability of ADHD, but the measures used to assess the symptoms differed questionnaires of general behavior problems that can provide an estimate of attention problems, DSM-symptom rating scales, structured interviews about DSM symptoms, etc.). In all cases, about 75 percent of the variance in phenotype can be attributed to genetic rather than environmental factors. It is interesting that geographical location of the sample did not alter this estimate.

Genes Associated With ADHD/HKD

The twin studies support the hypothesis of a major genetic basis for ADHD, with a heritability of about .75. However, these studies do not identify specific genes linked to the disorder. Molecular genetic studies are necessary to identify allelic variations of specific genes that are functionally associated with ADHD/HKD. As indicated earlier dopamine genes have been the initial candidates for application of advances in molecular biology based on the site of action of the stimulant drugs (Volkow et al., 1995), which are the primary pharmacological treatment for ADHD/HKD (Greenhill, Halperin, & Abikoff 1999).

Two candidate dopamine genes (DAT1 and DRD4) have been investigated and reported to be associated with ADHD/HKD (Table 7.5 lists the teams and actual studies of these two genes).

The different forms of these genes are defined by variable numbers of tandem

Table 7.4
Genetics of ADHD: Twin Studies

Study	Estimated Heritability
Goodman & Stevenson (1989)	.50
Gjone, Stevenson, & Sundet (1996)	.75
Levy, Hay, McStephen, Wood, & Waldman (1997)	.91
Silberg et al. (1996)	.57
Sherman, Iacono, & McGue (1997)	.60
Hudziak et al. (1998)	.75
Willcutt, Pennington, & DeFries (2000)	.94

repeats (VNTR), which for the DAT1 gene is a 40-bp repeat sequence on chromosome 5p15.3 and for the DRD4 gene is a 48-bp repeat sequence on chromosome 11p15.5. Variation in the human population is created by different alleles of these genes. For example, the most common variants of the DAT1 gene are specified by 9 or 10 repeats (copies) of the 40-bp sequence, and the most common variants of the DRD4 gene are specified by 2, 4, or 7 repeats (copies) of the 48-bp sequence.

Because each individual has two alleles (one contributed by the father and one by the mother), a genotype can be specified. Often in studies of a disorder such as ADHD, one, sometimes both, of the alleles may be suspected to be associated with the disorder. Genotypes are specified that compare the frequency of individuals with either one or both alleles of the suspected variant. For example, for the DRD4 gene, the 7+ genotype is defined by individuals who have either 1 or 2 7-repeat alleles, and the 7- genotype is used to classify the others with both alleles that are not 7-repeat variants.

Population and Family Studies of Candidate Genes

The literature on these candidate genes and ADHD is increasing, with population-based and family-based association studies providing the primary designs so far. In population-based association studies, the allele frequency in the ADHD group (based on the two alleles from each ADHD proband) is compared to the allele frequency in a control group. However, because these groups may differ on other factors that affect allele frequency (e.g., ethnicity), careful matching is required. Thus, results from population-based association designs should be considered with caution, as significant differences between the groups may be due to population stratification rather than the condition being investigated.

An alternative design is the family-based study, in which the DNA from parents of the ADHD proband is investigated. In this design, the sources of the two alleles of the ADHD proband are traced by deducing which allele from each parent was transmitted to the ADHD child (proband). This also specifies which allele was not transmitted at conception of the proband. This information from each family is used to con-

Table 7.5
Research Teams Investigating Dopamine Genes and ADHD

Emory	Rowe et al., 1998; Waldman et al., 1998
Ireland	Gill, Daly, Heron, Hawl, & Fitzgerald, 1997
National Institute of Mental Health	Castellanos et al., 1998
University of California—Irvine	LaHoste et al., 1996; Swanson, Sunohara, et al., 1998
UCLA	Smalley et al., 1998
University of Chicago	Cook et al., 1995
University of Toronto	Sunohara & Kennedy, 1998; Barr et al., 2000

struct a "theoretical" control child specified by the alleles of the parents that were not transmitted to the ADHD proband. This allows for perfect matching on factors such as ethnicity which are known to affect allele frequency and genotype frequency in the human population.

DRD4 Gene. To illustrate these methods, in one study, LaHoste et al. (1996) used the population-based association design to compare allele frequency for the variants defined by the short (2-repeat), middle (4-repeat), and long (7-repeat) variants of the DRD4 gene. For this small sample (n = thirty-nine ADHD probands), the 7-repeat allele was overrepresented in the ADHD sample (29 percent of the alleles were 7-repeats) compared to the ethnically-matched control group (12 percent of the alleles were 7-repeats). In this study, the frequency of the 7+ genotype was higher in the ADHD group than in the control group (49 percent vs. 20 percent). Although the 7-repeat allele appeared to be associated with increased likelihood of ADHD, it was not a necessary or sufficient condition for the disorder.

In a more methodologically sound study with larger sample size (n = 220) and a family-based association design (Smalley et al., 1998), a comparison was made of transmitted and nontransmitted alleles from the 129 parents who were heterozygous for the 7-repeat allele. This design allows the use of a Transmission Disequilibrium Test (TDT) for association that is not affected by population stratification. The results confirmed the earlier population-based study of LaHoste et al. (1996): the TDT test was significant, and the relative risk of 1.5 suggests a modest genetic association of ADHD with the DRD4 gene. Most recently, Barr et al. (2000) extended the studies of the dopamine receptor gene (D4), providing further support its role in ADHD.

DAT1 Gene. Four studies have investigated the association of the DAT1 gene and ADHD. In three of these, evidence of a significant association was obtained (Cook et al., 1995; Gill et al., 1997; Waldman et al., 1998). For example, Waldman et al. (1998) studied 122 children, as well as their parents and siblings. TDT analyses showed that the 10-repeat allele of the DAT1 gene was related to children's levels of hyperactive/ impulsive symptoms. Siblings with the higher number of high-risk alleles had much higher symptom levels. Their findings indicated that the DAT1 10-repeat allele association was especially strong with the combined but not the inattentive subtype.

Study Replications

Thus, in the investigations of the DRD4 gene and the DAT1 gene, we see a pattern of replication by most, but not all, research teams. This pattern of replication and nonreplication is expected for susceptibility genes with a relative risk of 1.5 to 2.0 for a disorder with a polygenic basis; thus, these results do not discount either of the candidate genes. It is likely that multiple genes will be identified that contribute to ADHD, and that each may confer only a slight increase in risk for the disorder. For example, some hypotheses have raised the possibility that specific alleles of these dopamine genes may alter dopamine transmission in various points in the neural networks implicated in ADHD/HKD. For example, the 10-repeat allele of the DAT1 gene may be associated with hyperactive reuptake of dopamine, or the 7-repeat allele of the DRD4 gene could be associated with a subsensitive postsynaptic receptor.

Despite the convergence of results described foregoing, there are many limitations to these initial studies of dopamine genes and ADHD. First, the effects are relatively small, so this does not offer a full account of the etiology of ADHD. Thus, this may identify just one of several etiologies of this disorder. Other genetic factors, as well as nongenetic factors, must operate. Also, because the DRD4 gene is in the coding region, the alleles do result in a different structure of the D4 receptor. However, the DAT1 gene is not in the coding region, so it does not produce structural differences in the dopamine transporter, but it may be linked to another gene that does. The next step in this research is to investigate the functional significance of the alleles of these dopamine genes that are associated with ADHD.

INVESTIGATIONS OF NONGENETIC ETIOLOGIES

Specific genetic models have incorporated a high phenocopy rate to account for a sporadic as well as a genetic form of the disorder (Deutsch et al., 1990; Faraone et al., 1992). In addition to rare genetic mutations, sporadic cases may be due to nongenetic etiologies such as acquired brain damage. For decades, theories of minimal brain damage and minimal brain dysfunction (MBD) have been proposed and rejected (Brown, Chadwick, Shaffer, Rutter, & Traub, 1981), due to the lack of empirical evidence of suspected brain damage in children manifesting behavioral soft signs and the lack of specificity of the behavioral consequences of traumatic brain injury. However, recent theories based on animal models and brain damage have revived this approach. For example, Lou (1996) proposed that during fetal development, bouts of hypoxia and hypotension could selectively damage neurons located in some of the critical regions of the anatomical networks implicated in ADHD/HKD (i.e., the striatum). Fetal exposure to alcohol, lead, nicotine, and other substances may produce similar neurotoxic effects.

Recently, several investigators have investigated secondary ADHD (S-ADHD) that may emerge after traumatic brain injury (Gerring et al., 1998). Max et al. (1998) has documented that about 20 percent of children with severe (but not mild or moderate) traumatic brain injury have new-onset and lasting manifestation of symptoms of inattention and impulsivity, though often not hyperactivity (Brown et al., 1981). Some brain regions are selectively damaged by traumatic injury due to proximity to the skull (frontal), some due to shearing (long white matter tracts), and others due to swelling and hypoperfusion (striatum). These are areas implicated in ADHD, but the measurement of specific lesions in these areas has been difficult. New methods for this are being developed, but results based on these new methods have not yet been published.

An association of psychosocial adversity with S-ADHD (Gerring et al., 1998) complicates investigations of brain damage. Also, ADHD may be a risk factor for traumatic brain injury, so genetic and brain injury etiologies may not be independent. Despite these difficult problems, a resurgence of investigations in this area may provide confirming sources of data for the imaging data on primary ADHD. This would be of historical significance, because it may link modern nosology with the outdated concepts of minimal brain damage (Clements, Peters, & John, 1962).

NEUROBIOLOGICAL BASES FOR PHARMACOLOGICAL TREATMENT

Methylphenidate as a Dopamine Blocker

The abnormalities in neuroanatomical networks associated with ADHD/HKD (smaller frontal and basal ganglia regions) and the biochemical pathways (specific alleles of dopamine genes) support a theory of ADHD (e.g., a dopamine deficit) proposedmore than twenty-five years ago (Wender, 1971). This biochemical theory provides the basis for the standard pharmacological treatments of ADHD/HKD with stimulant drugs, which are considered to be dopamine agonists (Greenhill et al., 1999). The primary treatment with the stimulant medication methylphenidate has stood the test of time and the scrutiny of controlled research (MTA Cooperative Group, 1999; Swanson et al., 1993; Wilens & Biederman, 1992).

The site-of-action of methylphenidate has been documented in a series of investigations at Brookhaven National Laboratory. Using PET to measure the temporal and spatial distribution of 11C-labeled methylphenidate after IV administration, this team (Ding et al., 1997; Volkow et al., 1995; Wang et al., 1995) demonstrated that d-threo-methylphenidate accumulated in the striatum, which is consistent with the binding of methylphenidate to the dopamine transporter (Volkow et al., 1997). Using this method, the pharmacokinetic properties of this accumulation have been defined (Volkow et al., 1995): After IV administration, the peak concentration occurs rapidly (within ten minutes) and is maintained for about twenty minutes, and the half-life of binding in striatum (and presumably the blockade of dopamine transporters) is about one and a half hours. After IV administration of a dose that produces occupancy of over 50 percent of dopamine transporters (e.g., .5 mg./kg.), methylphenidate produces euphoria for a short time (twenty minutes). However, euphoria does not emerge after oral administration, even when over 50 percent of dopamine transporters are occupied by the methylphenidate that reaches the brain after the delay imposed by the pharmacokinetic properties of oral administration. Based on an impressive research program, this team concluded that not only the site-of-action but also the time course of effect on the dopamine transporter is crucial for eliciting specific behavioral and subjective effects of methylphenidate.

Debate Regarding Net Effect of Dopamine Blockade

The net effect of methylphenidate's blockade of the dopamine transporter has been debated. Some (Solanto, 2000) suggest that the presynaptic effects are most important, and that the therapeutic effects are due to an autoreceptor mediated reduction in synthesis and release of dopamine that results in a net decrease in extracellular dopamine at the synapse. Others suggest the opposite (Levy, 1991; Volkow et al., 1995). Castellanos (1997) proposed that presynaptic effects may predominate in D2-rich subcortical regions where presynaptic receptors are abundant, producing decreased synaptic dopamine, and postsynaptic effects may predominate in D4-rich cortical regions which lack presynaptic receptors, producing increased synaptic dopamine. Also, Seeman and Madras (1998) have proposed that clinically relevant doses of stimulants may increase the resting level of extracellular level far more than they increase the action-potential-associated release of dopamine, which may account for why these dopamine agonist drugs result in a reduction in psychomotor activity.

Microdialysis studies of synaptic dopamine in rats (Ding et al., 1997) have defined the effects of acute administration of methylphenidate on extracellular levels of dopamine, which rise in parallel with serum levels of d-threo-methylphenidate but fall more rapidly. These recent studies support the notion that methylphenidate is a dopamine agonist, but that clockwise hystersis occurs that produces acute tolerance (tachyphalaxis). Acute tolerance after oral administration of clinical doses of methylphenidate has been observed in the treatment of ADHD children (Swanson et al., 1999). Possibly, long-term tolerance may be avoided by the dissipation of tolerance in the evening and night after clearance of the daytime doses.

ALTERNATIVE SITE-OF-ACTION HYPOTHESES

Over the past decade, the dopamine hypothesis of ADHD and the site of action of stimulant drugs have influenced both the investigations of neuroanatomical correlates of ADHD, which have focused on the basal ganglia and cortical-striatal networks, and the recent investigations of molecular genetic associations with ADHD, which have focused on the DAT1 and DRD4 genes. The evidence in favor of this theory produced by these focused investigations (which were reviewed earlier) does not discount other neuroanatomical or genetic mechanisms. A competing theory is based on a norepinephrine hypothesis of ADHD (e.g., see Pliszka, McCracken, & Maas, 1996) and the site of action of antihypertensive drugs (clonidine and guanfacine), which have been second-line pharmacological treatments for ADHD (Riddle et al., 1999).

The neuroanatomical basis for this theory is derived from the work of Goldman-Rakic (1987), Foote, Aston-Jones, and Bloom (1980), and Posner and Raichle (1996), who all propose prefrontal-posterior parietal-locus coeruleus networks that are involved in attention. These networks operate by selectively inhibiting the processing of irrelevant sensory stimuli and prime the prefrontal cortex for processing task-relevant stimuli.

In comparison to the investigations of the cortical-striatal network, MRI studies have not focused on the prefrontal-posterior parietal network, but some evidence has emerged from the literature. For example, Filipek et al. (1997) documented that the posterior parietal regions were smaller than normal in a subset of ADHD children (those who were nonfavorable responders to stimulant medications). Also, in investigations of neurotransmitter metabolites, a consistent finding (e.g., Elia, Stoff, & Coccaro, 1992) has been that groups of ADHD children have lower than normal levels of urinary MHPG, a metabolite of norepinephrine.

The investigations of the nonstimulant drugs that target the alpha-2 noradrenergic receptors (the antihypertensive drugs clonidine and guanfacine) have also been limited (Riddle et al., 1999). Despite a large and increasing clinical use of these drugs, few controlled studies have been performed. Even though the theoretical basis for effects of these drugs suggests an effect on attention (Arnsten, Steere, & Hunt, 1996), clinical experience suggests that they are most useful on hyperactive/impulsive behavior and associated features such as agitations, tics, and stress-induced behavior (Greenhill et al., 1999).

SUMMARY

Recent investigations provide converging evidence that a refined phenotype of ADHD/HKD is characterized by reduced size in specific neuroanatomical regions of the corpus callosum, frontal lobes, basal ganglia, and cerebellum. These specific deficits suggest abnormalities in neural networks that affect input-output processing and attention (alerting and executive function), including the brain areas in the basal ganglia and cerebellum that play an important role in the control of responding (movement).

These neural networks are modulated by catecholamines, which are affected by stimulant drugs. The site of action of methylphenidate (the primary stimulant now used to treat ADHD/HKD) suggests that dopamine is the principal neurotransmitter involved, although norepinephrine has also been implicated. Recent molecular genetic studies have documented significant association of a refined phenotype of ADHD/HKD with polymorphisms in dopamine genes, which may alter the functions of the implicated neural networks. Recent investigations of brain development and brain injury also suggest that damage to these specific neural networks may produce symptoms of ADHD/HKD.

The reported findings from multiple methods of brain imaging suggest that specific abnormalities may be associated with ADHD. Taken together, the anatomical and functional imaging studies suggest that these abnormalities may be localized in theoretical frameworks of neural networks related to attention, information processing, alerting, orienting, and working memory. Thus, in terms of the neuroanatomical networks of attention proposed by Posner and Raichle (1996), the altering (right frontal) and executive function (anterior cingulate) networks include the brain regions shown to be abnormal in size or function in groups of ADHD subjects. Similar accounts have been offered by several investigators in the ADHD area (Castellanos, 1997; Swanson, Castellanos, et al., 1998), as well as others. These common theoretical approaches have been useful for the organization of the empirical findings from brain imaging studies and their relationship to executive function deficits of ADHD/HKD children that have been documented by neuropsychological tests (Tannock, 1998).

References

American Psychiatric Association. (1987). *Diagnostic and statistical manual of mental disorders* (3rd. ed., rev.). Washington, DC: Author.

American Psychiatric Association. (1994). *Diagnostic and statistical manual of mental disorders* (4th ed.). Washington, DC: Author.

Arnsten, A. F., Steere, J. C., & Hunt, R. D. (1996). The contribution of alpha 2-noradrenergic mechanisms to prefrontal cortical cognitive function. *Archives of General Psychiatry, 53*, 448–455.

Aylward, E. H., Reiss, A. L., Reader, M. J., Singer, H. S., Brown, J. E., & Denckla, M. B. (1996). Basal ganglia volumes in children with attention-deficit hyperactivity disorder. *Journal of Child Neurology, 11*, 112–115.

Barr, C. L., Wigg, K. G., Bloom, S., Schachar, R., Tannock, R., Roberts, W., Malone, M., & Kennedy, J. L. (2000). Further evidence from haplotype analysis for linkage of the dopamine D4 receptor gene and attention-deficit hyperactivity disorder. *American Journal of Medical Genetics, 96*(3), 262–267.

Berquin, P. C., Giedd, J. N., Jacobsen, L. K., Hamburger, S. D., Krain, A. L., Rapoport, J. L., & Castellanos, F. X. (1998). Cerebellum in attention-deficit hyperactivity disorder: A morphometric MRI study. *Neurology, 50*, 1087–93

Brown, G., Chadwick, O., Shaffer, D., Rutter, M., & Traub, M. (1981). A prospective study of children with head injuries: III. Psychiatric sequelae. *Psychological Medicine, 11*, 63–78.

Casey, B. J., Castellanos, F. X., Giedd, J. N., Marsh, W. L., Hamburger, S. D., Schubert, A. B., Vauss, Y. C., Vaituzis, A. C., Dickstein, D. P., Sarfatti, S. E., & Rapoport, J. L. (1997). Implication of right frontostriatal circuitry in response inhibition and attention-deficit/hyperactivity disorder. *Journal of the American Academy of Child and Adolescent Psychiatry, 36*, 374–383.

Castellanos, F. X. (1997). Toward a pathophysiology of attention-deficit/hyperactivity disorder. *Clinical Pediatrics, 36*, 381–393.

Castellanos, F. X., Giedd, J. N., Eckburg, P., Marsh, W. L., Vaituzis, A. C., Kaysen, D., Hamburger, S. D., & Rapoport, J. L. (1994). Quantitative morphology of the caudate nucleus in attention deficit hyperactivity disorder. *American Journal of Psychiatry, 151*, 1791–1796.

Castellanos, F. X., Giedd, J. N., Marsh, W. L., Hamburger, S. D., Vaituzis, A. C., Dickstein, D. P., Sarfatti, S. E., Vauss, Y. C., Snell, J. W., Lange, N., Kaysen, D., Krain, A. L., Ritchie, G. F., Rajapakse, J. C., & Rapoport, J. L. (1996). Quantitative brain magnetic resonance imaging in attention-deficit hyperactivity disorder. *Archives of General Psychiatry, 53*, 607–616.

Castellanos, F. X., Lau, E., Tayebi, N., Lee, P., Long, B. E., Giedd, J. N., Sharp, W., Marsh, W. L., Walker, J. M., Hamburger, S. D., Ginns, E. I., Rapoport, J. L., & Sidransky, E. (1998). Lack of an association between a dopamine-4 receptor polymorphism and attention-deficit/hyperactivity disorder: Genetic and brain morphometric analyses. *Molecular Psychiatry, 3*(5), 431–434.

Clements, S., Peters, D., & John, E. (1962). Minimal brain dysfunction in the school-age child: Diagnosis and treatment. *Archives of General Psychiatry, 6*(3), 185–197.

Cook, E. H., Stein, M. A., Krasowski, M. D., Cox, N. J., Olkon, D. M., Kieffer, J. E., & Leventhal, B. L. (1995). Association of attention deficit disorder and the dopamine transporter gene. *American Journal of Human Genetics, 56*, 993–998.

Deutsch, C. K., Matthysse, S., Swanson, J. M., & Farkas, L. G. (1990). Genetic latent structure analysis of dysmorphology in attention deficit disorder. *Journal of the American Academy of Child and Adolescent Psychiatry, 29*, 189–194.

Ding, Y. S., Fowler, J., Volkow, N., Dewey, S., Wang, G. J., Logan, J., Gatley, S. J., & Pappas, N. (1997). Clinical drugs: Comparison of the pharmacokinetics of [11C]d-threo and 1-threo-methylphenidate in the human and baboon brain. *Psychopharmacology, 131*, 71–78.

Elia, J., Stoff, D. M., & Coccaro, E. F. (1992). Biological correlates of impulsive disruptive behavior disorders: Attention deficit hyperactivity disorder, conduct disorder, and borderline personality disorder. In E. Peschel & R. Peschel (Eds.), *Neurobiological disorders in children and adolescents.*

New directions for mental health services [No. 54, Social and Behavioral Sciences Series] (pp. 51–57). San Francisco: Jossey-Bass.

Ernst, M., Cohen, R. M., Liebenauer, L. L., Jons, P. H., & Zametkin, A. J. (1997). Cerebral glucose metabolism in adolescent girls with attention-deficit/hyperactivity disorder. *Journal of the American Academy of Child and Adolescent Psychiatry, 36*, 1399–1406.

Ernst, M., & Zametkin, A. (1995). The interface of genetics, neuroimaging, and neurochemistry in attention-deficit hyperactivity disorder. In F. Bloom & D. Kupfer (Eds.), *Psychopharmacology: The fourth generation of progress* (pp. 1643–1652). New York: Raven Press.

Ernst, M., Zametkin, A. J., Matochik, J. A., Pascualvaca, D., Jons, P. H., & Cohen, R. M. (1999). High midbrain [18F]DOPA accumulation in children with attention-deficit hyperactivity disorder. *American Journal of Psychiatry, 156*, 1209–1215.

Faraone, S. V., Biederman, J., Chen, W. J., Krifcher, B., Keenan, K., Moore, C., Sprich, S., & Tsuang, M. T. (1992). Segregation analysis of attention deficit hyperactivity disorder. *Psychiatric Genetics, 2*, 257–275.

Filipek, P. A., Semrud-Clikeman, M., Steingard, R. J., Renshaw, P. F., Kennedy, D. N., & Biederman, J. (1997). Volumetric MRI analysis comparing subjects having attention-deficit hyperactivity disorder with normal controls. *Neurology, 48*, 589–601.

Foote, S. L., Aston-Jones, G., & Bloom, F. E. (1980), Impulse activity of locus coeruleus neurons in awake rats and monkeys is a function of sensory stimulation and arousal. *Proceedings of the National Academy of Science USA, 77*, 3033–3037.

Gerring, J. P., Brady, K. D., Chen, A., Vasa, R., Grados, M., Bandeen-Roche, K. J., Bryan, R. N., & Denckla, M. B. (1998). Premorbid prevalence of ADHD and development of secondary ADHD after closed head injury. *Journal of the American Academy of Child and Adolescent Psychiatry, 37*, 647–654.

Giedd, J. N., Castellanos, F. X., Casey, B. J., Kozuch, P., King, A. C., Hamburger, S. D., & Rapoport, J. L. (1994). Quantitative morphology of the corpus callosum in attention deficit hyperactivity disorder. *American Journal of Psychiatry, 151*, 665–669.

Gill, M., Daly, G., Heron, S., Hawl, Z., & Fitzgerald, M. (1997). Confirmation of association between attention deficit hyperactivity disorder and a dopamine transporter polymorphism. *Molecular Psychiatry, 2*, 311–313.

Gjone, H., Stevenson, J., & Sundet, J. M. (1996). Genetic influence on parent-reported attention-related problems in a Norwegian general population twin sample. *Journal of the American Academy of Child and Adolescent Psychiatry, 35*, 588–596.

Goldman-Rakic, P. S. (1987). Development of cortical circuitry and cognitive function. *Child Development, 58*, 601–622.

Goodman, R., & Stevenson, J. (1989). A twin study of hyperactivity: II. The aetiological role of genes, family relationships, and perinatal adversity. *Journal of Child Psychology and Psychiatry, 30*, 691–709.

Greenhill, L. L., Halperin, J. M., & Abikoff, H. (1999). Stimulant medications. *Journal of the American Academy of Child and Adolescent Psychiatry, 38*, 503–512.

Hudziak, J. J., Heath, A. C., Madden, P. F., Reich, W., Bucholz, K. K., Slutske, W., Bierut, L. J., Neuman, R. J., & Todd, R. D. (1998). Latent class and factor analysis of DSM-IV ADHD: A twin study of female adolescents. *Journal of the American Academy of Child and Adolescent Psychiatry. 37*, 848–857.

Hynd, G. W., Hern, K. L., Novey, E. S., & Eliopulos, D. (1993). Attention deficit-hyperactivity disorder and asymmetry of the caudate nucleus. *Journal of Child Neurology, 8*, 339–343.

Hynd, G. W., Semrud-Clikeman, M., Lorys, A. R., & Novey, E. S. (1990). Brain morphology in developmental dyslexia and attention deficit disorder/hyperactivity. *Archives of Neurology, 47*, 919–926.

Hynd, G. W, Semrud-Clikeman, M., Lorys, A. R., & Novey, E. S. (1991). Corpus callosum morphology in attention deficit-hyperactivity disorder: Morphometric analysis of MRI. *Journal of Learning Disabilities, 24*, 141–146.

LaHoste, G. J., Swanson, J. M., Wigal, S. B., Glabe, C., Wigal, T., King, N., & Kennedy, J. L. (1996). Dopamine D4 receptor gene polymorphism is associated with attention deficit hyperactivity disorder. *Molecular Psychiatry, 1*, 121–124.

Levy, F. (1991). The dopamine theory of attention deficit hyperactivity disorder (ADHD). *The Australian and New Zealand Journal of Psychiatry, 25*, 277–283.

Levy, F., Hay, D. A., McStephen, M., Wood, C., & Waldman, I. (1997), Attention-deficit hyperactivity disorder: A category or a continuum? Genetic analysis of a large-scale twin study. *Journal of the American Academy of Child and Adolescent Psychiatry, 36*, 737–744.

Lou, H. C. (1996). Etiology and pathogenesis of attention-deficit hyperactivity disorder (ADHD): Significance of prematurity and perinatal hypoxic-haemodynamic encephalopathy. *Acta Paediatrica, 85*, 1266–1271.

Lou, H. C., Henriksen, L., & Bruhn, P. (1984). Focal cerebral hypoperfusion in children with dysphasia and/or attention deficit disorder. *Archives of Neurology, 41*(8), 825–829.

Lou, H. C., Henriksen, L., & Bruhn, P. (1990). Focal cerebral dysfunction in developmental learning disabilities. *Lancet, 335*(8680), 8–11.

Lou, H. C., Henriksen, L., Bruhn, P., Borner, H., & Nielsen, J. B. (1989), Striatal dysfunction in attention deficit and hyperkinetic disorder. *Archives of Neurology, 46*, 48–52.

Matochik, J. A., Liebenauer, L. L., King, A. C., Szymanski, H. V., Cohen, R. M., & Zametkin, A. J. (1994). Cerebral glucose metabolism in adults with attention deficit hyperactivity disorder after chronic stimulant treatment. *American Journal of Psychiatry, 151*, 658–664.

Matochik, J. A., Nordahl, T. E., Gross, M., Semple, W. E., King, A. C., Cohen, R. M., & Zametkin, A. J. (1993). Effects of acute stimulant medication on cerebral metabolism in adults with hyperactivity. *Neuropsychopharmacology, 8*, 377–386.

Max, J. E., Arndt, S., Castillo, C., Bokura, H., Robin, D. A., Lindgren, S. D., Smith, W. L., Sato, Y., & Mattheis, P. J. (1998). Attention-deficit hyperactivity symptomatology after traumatic brain injury: A prospective study. *Journal of the American Academy of Child and Adolescent Psychiatry, 37*, 841–847.

Mostofsky, S. H., Reiss, A. L., Lockhart, P., & Denckla, M. B. (1998). Evaluation of cerebellar size in attention-deficit hyperactivity disorder. *Journal of Child Neurology, 13*, 434–439.

MTA Cooperative Group. (1999). A 14-month randomized clinical trial of treatment strategies for attention-deficit/hyperactivity disorder: Multimodal Treatment Study of Children with ADHD. *Archives of General Psychiatry, 56*(12), 1073–1086.

Oades, R. D., Dittmann-Balcar, A., Schepker, R., & Eggers, C. (1996). Auditory event-related potentials (ERPs) and mismatch negativity (MMN) in healthy children and those with attention-deficit or Tourette/tic symptoms. *Biological Psychology, 43*, 163–185.

Pliszka, S. R., McCracken, J. T., & Maas, J. W. (1996), Catecholamines in attention-deficit hyperactivity disorder: Current perspectives. *Journal of the American Academy of Child and Adolescent Psychiatry, 35*, 264–272.

Posner, M. I., & Raichle, M. (1996). *Images of mind* (rev.). Washington, DC: Scientific American Books.

Riddle, M. A., Bernstein, G. A., Cook, E. H., Leonard, H. L., March, J. S., & Swanson, J. M. (1999). Anxiolytics, adrenergic agents, and naltrexone. *Journal of the American Academy of Child and Adolescent Psychiatry, 38*, 546–556.

Robins, E., & Guze, S. B. (1970). Establishment of diagnostic validity in psychiatric illness: Its application to schizophrenia. *American Journal of Psychiatry, 126*, 983–987.

Rowe, D. C., Stever, C., Giedinghagen, L. N., Gard, M. J., Cleveland, H. H., Terris, S. T., Mohr, J. H., Sherman, S., Abramowitz, A., & Waldman, I. D. (1998), Dopamine DRD4 receptor polymorphism and attention deficit hyperactivity disorder. *Molecular Psychiatry, 3*, 419–426.

Satterfield, J., Swanson, J. M., Schell, A., & Lee, F. (1994). Prediction of antisocial behavior in attention-deficit hyperactivity disorder boys from aggression/defiance scores. *Journal of the American Academy of Child and Adolescent Psychiatry, 33*, 185–190.

Seeman, P., & Madras, B. K. (1998). Anti-hyperactivity medication: Methylphenidate and amphetamine. *Molecular Psychiatry, 3*, 386–396.

Semrud-Clikeman, M., Filipek, P. A., Biederman, J., & Steingard, R. (1994). Attention-deficit hyperactivity disorder: Magnetic resonance imaging morphometric analysis of the corpus callosum. *Journal of the American Academy of Child and Adolescent Psychiatry, 33*, 875–881.

Sherman, D. K., Iacono, W. G., & McGue, M. K. (1997). Attention-deficit hyperactivity disorder dimensions: A twin study of inattention and impulsivity-hyperactivity. *Journal of the American Academy of Child and Adolescent Psychiatry, 36*, 745–753.

Silberg, J., Rutter, M., Meyer, J., Maes, H., Hewitt, J., Simonoff, E., Pickles, A., & Loeber, R. (1996). Genetic and environmental influences on the covariation between hyperactivity and conduct disturbance in juvenile twins. *Journal of Child Psychology and Psychiatry and Allied Disciplines, 37*, 803–816.

Singer, H. S., Reiss, A. L., Brown, J. E., & Aylward, E. H. (1993). Volumetric MRI changes in basal ganglia of children with Tourette's syndrome. *Neurology, 43*, 950–956.

Smalley, S. L., Bailey, J. N., Palmer, C. G., Cantwell, D. P., McGough, J. J., Del-Homme, M. A., Asarnow, J. R., Woodward, J. A., Ramsey, C., & Nelson, S. F. (1998). Evidence that the dopamine D4 receptor is a susceptibility gene in attention deficit hyperactivity disorder. *Molecular Psychiatry, 3*, 427–430.

Solanto, M. V. (2000), Neuropharmacological mechanisms of stimulant drug action in attention-deficit hyperactivity disorder: A review and integration. *Behavior and Brain Research, 94*, 127–152.

Sunohara, G. A., & Kennedy, J. L. (1998). *The dopamine D4 receptor gene and neuropsychiatric disorders: Dopaminergic disorders.* New York: IBC Press.

Swanson, J., Castellanos, F. X., Murias, M., LaHoste, G., & Kennedy, J. (1998). Cognitive neuroscience of attention deficit hyperactivity disorder and hyperkinetic disorder. *Current Opinion in Neurobiology, 8*, 263–271.

Swanson, J. M., Flodman, P., Kennedy, J., Spence, M. A., Moyzis, R., Schuck, S., Murias, M., Moriarity, J., Barr, C., Smith, M., & Posner, M. (2000). Dopamine genes and ADHD. *Neuroscience and Biobehavioral Reviews, 24*(1), 21–25.

Swanson, J. M., Gupta, S., Guinta, D., Flynn, D., Agler, D., Lerner, M., Williams, L., Shoulson, I., & Wigal, S. (1999). Acute tolerance to methylphenidate in the treatment of attention deficit hyperactivity disorder in children. *Clinical Pharmacology and Therapeutics, 66*, 295–305.

Swanson, J. M., McBurnett, K., Wigal, T., Pfiffner, L. J., Lerner, M. A., Williams, L., Christian, D. L., Tamm, L., Willcutt, E., Crowley, K., Clevenger, W., Khouzam, N., Woo, C., Crinella, F., & Fisher, T. D. (1993). Effect of stimulant medication on children with attention deficit disorder: A "review of reviews." *Exceptional Children, 60*, 154–162.

Swanson, J. M., Sergeant, J. A., Taylor, E., Sonuga-Barke, E. J., Jensen, P. S., & Cantwell, D. P. (1998). Attention-deficit hyperactivity disorder and hyperkinetic disorder. *Lancet, 351*, 429–433.

Swanson, J. M., Sunohara, G. A., Kennedy, J. L., Regino, R., Fineberg, E., Wigal, T., Lerner, M., Williams, L., LaHoste, G. J., & Wigal, S. (1998). Association of the dopamine receptor D4 (DRD4) gene with a refined phenotype of attention deficit hyperactivity disorder (ADHD): A family-based approach. *Molecular Psychiatry, 3*, 38–41.

Tannock, R. (1998). *ADHD as a disorder in children, adolescents, and adults—etiology/risk factors: Genetics and pathophysiology.* Paper presented at the National Institutes of Health Consensus Development Conference on Diagnosis and Treatment of Attention Deficit Hyperactivity Disorder (ADHD), Washington, DC.

Vaidya, C. J., Austin, G., Kirkorian, G., Ridlehuber, H. W., Desmond, J. E., Glover, G. H., & Gabrieli, J. D. (1998). Selective effects of methylphenidate in attention deficit hyperactivity disorder: a functional magnetic resonance study. *Proceedings of the National Academy of Sciences of the United States of America, 95*, 14494–14499.

Volkow, N. D., Ding, Y-S., Fowler, J. S., Wang, G-J., Logan, J., Gatley, J. S., Dewey, S., Ashby, C., Lieberman, J., Hitzemann, R., et al. (1995). Is methylphenidate like cocaine? Studies on their pharmacokinetics and distribution in the human brain. *Archives of General Psychiatry, 52*, 456–463.

Volkow, N. D., Wang, G. J., Fowler, J. S., Logan, J., Angrist, B., Hitzemann, R., Lieberman, J., &

Pappas, N. (1997). Effects of methylphenidate on regional brain glucose metabolism in humans: Relationship to dopamine D2 receptors. *American Journal of Psychiatry, 154*, 50–55.

Wang, G. J., Volkow, N., Fowler, J. S., Ding, Y. S., Logan, J., Gatley, J. S., MacGregor, R., & Wolf, A. (1995). Comparison of two PET radiologands for imaging extrastriatal dopamine transporters in human brain. *Life Science, 57*, 185–191.

Waldman, I. D., Rowe, D. C., Abramowitz, A., Kozel, S. T., Mohr, J. H., Sherman, S. L., Cleveland, H. H., Sanders, M. L., Gard, J. M., & Stever, C. (1998). Association and linkage of the dopamine transporter gene and attention-deficit hyperactivity disorder in children: Heterogeneity owing to diagnostic subtype and severity. *American Journal of Human Genetics, 63*, 1767–1776.

Wender, P. (1971). *Minimal brain dysfunction in children.* New York: Wiley-Liss.

Wilens, T., & Biederman, J. (1992). The stimulants. *Psychiatric Clinics of North America, 15*, 191–222.

Willcut, E. G., Pennington, B. F., DeFries, J. C. (2000). Twin study of the etiology of comorbidity between reading disability and attention-deficit/hyperactivity disorder. *American Journal of Medical Genetics, 96*, 293–301.

World Health Organization. (1992). *International statistical classification of diseases and related health problems* (10th rev.). Geneva, Switzerland: Author.

Zametkin, A. J., Liebenauer, L. L., Fitzgerald, G. A., King, A. C., Minkunas, D. V., Herscovitch, P., Yamada, E. M., & Cohen, R. M. (1993). Brain metabolism in teenagers with attention-deficit hyperactivity disorder. *Archives of General Psychiatry, 50*, 333–340.

Zametkin, A. J., Nordahl, T. E., Gross, M., King, A. C., Semple, W. E., Rumsey, J., Hamburger, S., & Cohen, R. M. (1990). Cerebral glucose metabolism in adults with hyperactivity of childhood onset. *New England Journal of Medicine, 323*, 1361–1366.

Chapter 8

Cognitive Correlates of ADHD

by Rosemary Tannock, Ph.D.

Introduction 8-2
Conceptual and Methodological Challenges 8-3
     Diverse and Shifting Definitions of ADHD 8-3
     Effect of Co-Occurring Disorders, Age, and Gender 8-3
     State of the Science 8-4
     Impact on Current Study 8-4
General Intellectual Function 8-4
Academic Achievement 8-6
     Low Productivity 8-6
     Underachievement 8-6
     Academic Outcomes 8-7
Neuropsychological Function 8-8
     Impairments in Executive Functioning 8-8
     Other Neuropsychological Impairments 8-9
     Cognitive Functions Not Directly Affected by ADHD 8-10
     Summary 8-10
Impact of Comorbidity on Neuropsychological Profile 8-10
     Reading Disorder 8-10
     Anxiety Disorder 8-11
     Conduct Disorder 8-11
Specificity of Cognitive Correlates to Neuropsychological
   Functioning 8-12
Information Processing 8-13
     Impairments in Sustained Attention 8-13
     Response Inhibition Deficits 8-14
     Spatial Allocation of Attention 8-15
Implications for Neural Substrate and Pathophysiology of ADHD 8-15
Clinical Implications 8-16
     Diagnosis 8-16
     Assessment and Treatment 8-17
Implications for Future Research 8-18

INTRODUCTION

The validity of a diagnostic construct may be evaluated by systematic investigation of the clinical phenomenology, demographic factors, biological (including cognitive) factors, and family genetic and family environmental factors, as well as the natural history, outcome, and treatment response (Cantwell, 1995). This chapter focuses on cognitive factors.

Cognitive correlates provide one useful set of criteria for examining the validity of attention deficit hyperactivity disorder (ADHD), because they do not share method variance with clinical measures used to assess psychiatric symptomatology (e.g., reports of parents and teachers). Standardized tests of intellectual, academic, and neuropsychological function, as well as experimental cognitive paradigms, provide direct and objective measures of an individual's current cognitive status, thinking processes, and prior learning. Thus, performance is not subject to confounding factors such as recall bias or halo effects These data are useful for clarifying etiological and risk factors, gaining insights into the neural substrates of the disorder, and developing a comprehensive treatment plan to address the cognitive and emotional needs of the individual or group of individuals (Halperin & McKay, 1998; Lezak, 1995). On the other hand, these measures do not assess functioning in the natural environment and rarely provide direct evidence about the presence or absence of psychiatric symptoms. As with any test in medicine, data from neuropsychological and cognitive tests in isolation cannot provide a diagnosis: They must be interpreted in the context of a comprehensive clinical evaluation.

A systematic review of the literature was undertaken using Medline and Psychlit bibliography databases, covering the following correlates: (1) general intellectual function, (2) academic achievement, (3) neuropsychological function (motor function, perception, visual-motor integration, language, memory, executive functions), and (4) cognitive processes (alerting, orienting, executive control). This review addressed four questions:

- *What are the impairments/strengths associated with ADHD?* Evidence was sought for a specific profile of impairments in one or more of the four aforementioned areas.

- *Are these impairments/strengths moderated by age, gender, subtype, or coexisting disorders?* Evidence was sought to confirm that the impairments are not an artifact of confounding factors and to determine whether the impairments are restricted to a subgroup of individuals with ADHD (e.g., in one of the subtypes according to the fourth edition of *Diagnostic and Statistical Manual of Mental Disorders* [DSM-IV; American Psychiatric Associaiton, 1994], or a specific comorbidity) or evident universally in this population. In this review, specific emphasis was given to the common comorbidity with learning disorders (particularly reading disorder), anxiety disorders, and conduct disorder.

- *Are the impairments uniquely associated with ADHD?* The critical evidence required is that at least some of the impairments occur only in ADHD (or subgroups of ADHD) and not in other clinical populations.

- *What neural networks are implicated?* Evidence was sought not only for the underlying neural substrate of the identified impairments but also that these brain regions or neural networks are implicated in ADHD, based on neuroimaging studies.

Prior to presenting a synthesis of this literature, an essential detour is warranted to comment on the conceptual and methodological challenges encountered in this endeavor.

CONCEPTUAL AND METHODOLOGICAL CHALLENGES

Diverse and Shifting Definitions of ADHD

A critical analysis of existing research on the cognitive correlates of ADHD is challenged by the diverse conceptualizations and methodologies of the studies, which often preclude direct comparisons among studies. One set of challenges concerns the differences in the North American and European conceptualization of ADHD and the shifts in these conceptualizations over the past two decades. Specifically, clinicians and researchers on either side of the Atlantic differ in the emphasis they place on the three core clusters of symptoms (inattention, impulsiveness, and hyperactivity), the requirement for pervasiveness of symptomatology, the relative weight given to other concurrent problems and psychopathology, and their conceptualization of the developmental significance of the symptom clusters and the disorder (Reason, 1999; Sergeant & Steinhausen, 1992; Tannock, 1998; Taylor et al., 1998; Tripp, Luk, Schaughency, & Singh, 1999). Thus, ADHD/hyperkinetic samples in North American and European studies may represent overlapping but not identical populations. Also, given the recent changes to the diagnostic classification of ADHD in DSM-IV (particularly, the conceptualization of impulsivity and hyperactivity symptoms as a single cluster), the subtypes of ADHD delineated by DSM-IV may not be comparable to those subtypes differentiated in previous versions of DSM. For example, the DSM-IV predominantly inattentive subtype may not be comparable to the DSM-III (American Psychiatric Association, 1980) subtype of attention deficit disorder without hyperactivity or to the DSM-III-R (American Psychiatric Association, 1987) undifferentiated type. Likewise, the DSM-IV combined type may not be comparable with either the DSM-III attention deficit disorder with hyperactivity or the DSM-III-R category of ADHD.

Effect of Co-Occurring Disorders, Age, and Gender

A second, but related challenge concerns sample heterogeneity in terms of comorbidity and demographics. The majority of individuals in clinic-referred samples present with one or more additional disorders (e.g., oppositional, conduct, anxiety, or learning disorders), although comorbidity rates are likely to differ in North America and Europe because the two classification systems differ in how they handle co-occurring disorders (Biederman, Newcorn, & Sprich, 1991; Jensen, Martin, & Cantwell, 1997; Reason, 1999; Sergeant & Steinhausen, 1992; Taylor et al., 1998). Many studies have failed to control for comorbidity, so that differences observed between ADHD and comparison groups could be attributable to the coexisting disorder rather than ADHD per se.

Also, from the perspective of demographics, most of the research is based on cross-sectional studies of school-age boys with ADHD (7 to 11 years old). Typically, data are aggregated from subjects at different developmental stages, from differing environments, and across gender. This methodological approach seemingly ignores the broader evidence for age-related and gender-related differences in cognitive functioning, and the likely impact of multiple interacting influences (genetic, biological, developmental, systemic processes of family, school, and community) in shaping both adaptive and maladaptive adjustment over time. These problems are exacerbated by the use of small sample sizes in most studies conducted over the past two decades. Because the effect sizes (magnitude of group differences) that may exist in cognitive abilities are likely to be in the small to medium range, many studies may not have had the statistical power to detect group differences.

State of the Science

The third challenge reflects the scientific maturity of this field of investigation. Most of the available research on cognitive correlates (and the study of ADHD, in general) is exploratory and descriptive rather than theoretically motivated and designed to test hypothesized deficits or contrasting hypotheses for a pattern of deficits. Thus a broad battery of neuropsychological measures have been administered, often without statistical adjustments to control for the risk of spurious results associated with the conduct of multiple comparisons. Moreover, many of the measures do not have adequate norms and may lack adequate assessment of reliability and validity for the age range under investigation. Finally, investigators have often used a classical approach to the design and interpretation of neuropyschological studies, which constructs models of brain-behavior relationships (often static models) on the basis of disorders seen following known brain lesions sustained in adults with previously established skills (i.e., in a mature and previously intact brain system). By contrast, a more recent application of cognitive neuropsychology to children (particularly in Europe) constructs models on the basis of functional lesions manifest within developing systems with no known neurological injury (Temple, 1998).

Impact on Current Study

Given the preceding conceptual and methodological challenges, the goal of this review was to seek evidence of consistent and systematic findings across studies using different methodologies and levels of analysis. Greater weight was given to those studies with large, rigorously diagnosed and defined samples that gave adequate consideration to moderating variables (age, comorbidity, context) and included measures from contrasting cognitive domains or types of processing (e.g., controlled vs. automatic; slow and careful vs. fast and accurate instructional sets).

GENERAL INTELLECTUAL FUNCTION

Intelligence tests provide a broad index of higher cortical functioning that can be used to generate hypotheses for further investigation using neuropsychological and experimental cognitive techniques. Their psychometric properties remain robust for the clinical group of ADHD, and, in general, the mean levels of intellectual functioning are well within the normal range (Schwean & Saklofske, 1998). However, ADHD is associated with somewhat lower full-scale scores and relatively lower scores on the Freedom from Distractibility (FFD) and Processing Speed (PS) indices compared to normative data (Anastopoulos, Spisto, & Maher, 1994; Mayes, Calhoun, & Crowell, 1998; Mealer, Morgan, & Luscomb, 1998; Reinecke, Beebe, & Stein, 1999; Schwean & Saklofske, 1998). These findings hold across various versions of intelligence tests (Saklofske, Schwean, Yackalic, & Quinn, 1994; Schwean & Saklofske, 1998). They hold for both epidemiological and clinic samples, across the lifespan (preschool through adulthood) in both cross-sectional and longitudinal studies, and for both girls and boys, although in clinic-referred samples girls may exhibit greater intellectual impairment than do boys (Barkley, DuPaul, & McMurray, 1990; Biederman et al., 1998; Gaub & Carlson, 1997b; Mariani & Barkley, 1997; McGee, Williams, Moffit, & Anderson, 1989; Saklofske et al., 1994; Seidman, Biederman, Faraone, Weber, & Oullette, 1997; Seidman, Biederman, Faraone, Weber, Mennin, & Jones, 1997; Sharp et al., 1999; Sonuga-Barke, Lamparelli, Stevenson, Thompson, & Henry, 1994). Also, the findings generally hold for studies that have controlled the presence of comorbid disorders (Faraone et al., 1993; Faraone, Biederman, Weber, & Russell, 1998; Newby, Recht, Caldwell, & Schaefer, 1993).

In contrast, recent evidence suggests that the findings may not hold across the three DSM-IV subtypes. Specifically, recent studies, involving fairly large samples of clinic-referred children with ADHD, indicate that the predominantly hyperactive subtype of ADHD does not exhibit the same attenuation of test scores as do the predominantly inattentive and combined types (who do not differ) (Faraone et al., 1998; Lahey et al., 1998; McBurnett et al., 1993; Tannock, Schachar, & Ickowicz, 1997). The IQ differences among the subtypes are not large, ranging from 4 to 8 standard score points (i.e., a difference of 0.25 to 0.5 standard deviations). However, the findings of relatively lower scores for the inattentive and combined subtypes compared to the hyperactive/impulsive subtype are consistent across the studies, despite methodological differences in the age range of the children and in the diagnostic protocols. On the one hand, these data suggest that the intellectual profile of low FFD and PS relative to other factors according to the Wechsler Intelligence Scale for Children—Third Edition (WISC-III; Wechsler, 1991) may be a correlate of the dimension of inattention rather than that of hyperactivity/impulsiveness. On the other hand, the pattern of low FFD is not specific to ADHD; it is also associated with learning disabilities and other disruptive behavior disorders (Newby et al., 1993; Reinecke et al., 1999). Moreover, it is important to keep in mind the fact that the findings refer to *group* data and do not necessarily hold for individual children. According to one study, less than one-third of the children with ADHD had FFD scores that were significantly lower than either the Verbal Comprehension Index or the Perceptual Organization Index—a rate no greater than in the standardization sample for the WISC-III (Prifitera, Weiss, & Saklofske, 1998; Reinecke et al., 1999).

Although the WISC-III profile has no utility in the differential diagnosis of ADHD, it may have conceptual significance. The FFD Index is best conceptualized as an index of working memory, rather than distractibility (Prifitera et al., 1998). Working memory is defined as the ability to hold information in mind temporarily while performing some operation or manipulation with that information, or to engage in an interfering task and still be able to retrieve and use that information accurately. Thus, evidence of relative impairments on subtests comprising the FFD Index (Digit Span, Arithmetic) suggests impairments in working memory (particularly if Digit Span Backwards is weak).

Also, evidence of relative weakness in the Processing Speed Index (reflected by lower-scaled scores in Coding and Symbol Search subtests) is indicative of impairments in psychomotor speed, or visual scanning and tracking speed, or generalized slow speed of information processing.

ACADEMIC ACHIEVEMENT

Academic achievement tests provide a more detailed profile of strengths and weaknesses in underlying component skills that contribute to academic competency and may indicate the presence of a learning disability. One of the most robust findings is a higher rate of school failure, even in the absence of developmental learning disorders (Barkley, Anastopoulos, Guevremont, & Fletcher, 1991; Hinshaw, 1992; Semrud-Clikeman et al., 1992). This is evidenced most clearly by low productivity but also by academic underachievement, elevated rates of grade repetition, learning disabilities, remedial tutoring, and special class placement, despite average levels of intellectual functioning.

Low Productivity

Low productivity refers to the quantity of work completed in a specified time, regardless of accuracy. This limited output most likely gives rise to the ubiquitous high severity rating given by parents and teachers for the DSM symptom of inattention (diagnostic symptom 1(d)) "often does not follow through on instructions and fails to finish schoolwork, chores, or duties in the work place" (American Psychiatric Association, 1994, p. 84).

Underachievement

Underachievement is reflected by lower scores (on average, 0.5 standard deviations lower) on standardized tests of arithmetic, reading, and spelling. There is converging evidence that basic skills in arithmetic are impaired in ADHD per se. The impairments are not attributable to either deficient knowledge of arithmetic facts or IQ differences but, rather, to impairments in rapid retrieval of facts (i.e., slower computational performance), which in turn predict impairments in higher-level problem solving that involves multiple steps or multiple procedures (Ackerman, Anhalt, Holcomb, & Dykman, 1986; Zentall, 1990).

Preliminary evidence also indicates that reading comprehension is impaired in ADHD per se, even after controlling for other reading abilities that might contribute to reading comprehension difficulties (e.g., word identification, word attack, reading speed, and vocabulary) (Brock, & Knapp, 1996; Javorsky, 1996). Comprehension problems increase as passage length is increased, indicating that even when children with ADHD do not have a comorbid reading disorder, they have difficulty constructing meaning from texts. The documented association between listening/reading comprehension and working memory is relevant here (Daneman & Merikle, 1996). However, we need confirmation of reading comprehension impairments along with working memory impairments in a larger sample before firm conclusions can be drawn. By contrast, decoding of single words is not impaired in ADHD per se, but rather in those with comorbid developmental reading disorder (dyslexia).

Academic Outcomes

The academic outcome in adolescence is unexpectedly poor given the average or above-average level of intellectual functioning. Adolescents with ADHD are three times as likely as their normal peers to have failed a grade, more likely to score in the lower end of the normal range on standardized tests of academic achievement (particularly arithmetic), and more likely to have dropped out of school, despite various interventions, such as extra help, special class placement and pharmacological and/or psychosocial therapy (Barkley, Murphy, & Kwasnik, 1996; Fischer, Barkley, Edelbrock, & Smallish, 1990). However, as noted later, some aspects of the poor academic outcome may be attributable to comorbid disorders rather than ADHD per se.

Academic underachievement is evident in girls and boys as well as siblings, occurring in preschool years and enduring through adolescence (Ackerman et al., 1986; Barkley et al., 1990; Faraone, 1998; Faraone et al., 1993). It is a correlate of ADHD per se and cannot be accounted for by comorbid learning disabilities or by psychiatric comorbidity, which tends to influence school placement rather than school failure or intellectual ability (Faraone et al., 1993; Faraone et al., 1998; Taylor, Chadwick, Hepinstall, & Danckaerts, 1996). However, the findings do not hold across the three DSM-IV subtypes:

- Academic problems, particularly in arithmetic, are more common among predominantly inattentive and combined subtypes of ADHD (Baumgaertel, Wolraich, & Dietrich, 1995; Gaub and Carlson, 1997a, 1997b; Hynd et al., 1991; Lahey et al., 1994; Lamminmaki et al., 1995; Marshall, Hynd, Handwerk, & Hal, 1997).

- The inattentive and combined subtypes show more academic problems and fewer behavioral problems, as reported by teachers (Gaub & Carlson, 1997a; Lahey et al., 1994; Lamminmäki, Ahonen, Närhi, Lyytinen, & Todd de Barra, 1995; McBurnett et al., 1993; Wolraich, Hannah, Baumgaertel, & Fuerer, 1998).

- The hyperactive/impulsive subtypes show the reverse pattern of more frequent behavioral and fewer academic problems.

The differential pattern of impairments across the subtypes suggests that academic problems are related to inattention rather than hyperactivity/impulsivity. Moreover, the nature of the academic impairments (particularly in individuals *without* comorbid learning disabilities) suggests problems in working memory, processing speed, and effortful processing. However, there is no evidence that this profile is uniquely associated with ADHD.

NEUROPSYCHOLOGICAL FUNCTION

Neuropsychological tests provide a detailed assessment of a wide array of cognitive functions that afford insights into brain-behavior relationships; they are sensitive to subtle deficits that interfere with learning and achievement. Three different approaches are discernible in the neuropsychological studies. Most attempt an exploratory approach that uses a broad battery of neuropsychological measures +to determine whether ADHD has associated neuropsychological impairments. These studies have generated hypotheses about how and why ADHD is associated with some deficits and not others, which have been tested subsequently in more recent theoretically motivated studies (Carte, Nigg, & Hinshaw, 1996; Nigg, Hinshaw, Carte, & Treuting, 1998; Pennington & Ozonoff, 1991; Reader, Harris, Schuerholz, & Denckla, 1994; Shue & Douglas, 1992). The implicit aim of the second approach is to determine which of the candidate deficits are primary and how the primary deficits explain both other cognitive impairments and symptoms of the disorder. Primary deficits are specific to the disorder, universal (occur in virtually all individuals with the disorder), are persistent across the lifespan, and exhibit causal precedence (precede and predict the disorder) (Pennington & Ozonoff, 1996). The third and related approach aims to identify cognitive-behavioral marker(s) or latent traits for the disorder, which refer to a marker that may be found in all or many affected individuals and a substantial number of relatives but may not necessarily be the primary underlying deficit. This latter approach is important for molecular genetics, because latent traits rather than the disorder per se may be transmitted genetically.

Impairments in Executive Functioning

The most consistent (albeit not invariable) finding is of mild impairments in "executive functioning," which is an umbrella term denoting a range of higher-order, effortful, self-regulatory functions whose formal definition and measurement (particularly in children) remain elusive and under debate (Eslinger, 1996; Pennington, 1997; Pennington & Ozonoff, 1991; Tannock, 1998). For example, a recent and comprehensive review reported that fifteen of the eighteen studies of ADHD reviewed (i.e., 83 percent) found significant differences between ADHD and normal controls on at least one measure of executive function (Pennington & Ozonoff, 1991). Important executive functions include inhibition, working memory, planning, self-monitoring, verbal self-regulation, motor control, maintaining and changing mental set, and emotional regulation (Eslinger, 1996; Fuster, 1989; Meyer & Keiras, 1997; Stuss & Benson, 1984). Executive functions have been associated with the frontal cortex, but they are also implicated with subcortical neuronal circuits and thus should not be conceptualized as anatomically localized functions (Stuss, 1992). Neuroanatomical and behavioral research distinguishes at least two executive functions: inhibition (associated with the orbitofrontal regions of the frontal cortex with reciprocal connections with the ventromedial region of the striatum) and working memory (associated with the dorsolateral frontal cortex and central regions of the striatum) (Barkley, 1997; Iversen & Dunnett, 1990; Petrides, Aliviasatos, Meyer, & Evans, 1993). However, recent evidence of disturbances of executive function in patients with pathology restricted to the cerebellum highlights the role of cerebellar modulation of neural circuits that link prefrontal, posterior parietal, superior temporal, and limbic cortices with the cerebellum and which are implicated in response preparation (Dolan, 1998; Schmahmann & Sherman, 1998).

According to a current model of ADHD, deficient response inhibition is the core deficit in ADHD, which in turn has cascaded effects on other executive functions, including working memory and verbal self-regulation (Barkley, 1997). Certainly, there is growing evidence for mild impairments in component functions, particularly those associated with *control* of motor responses (planning, inhibition) and *working* memory. Motor planning deficits are indicated by the fairly consistent evidence of poor performance on such tests as the Tower of Hanoi/London, Porteus Mazes or WISC-Mazes, and Rey-Osterreith Complex Figure Drawing Test—Copy condition (Aman, Roberts, & Pennington, 1998; Nigg et al., 1998; Pennington & Ozonoff, 1991; Seidman, Biederman, Faraone, Weber, Mennin, & Jones, 1997). Motor inhibition deficits in ADHD, which are typically defined as the ability to inhibit a prepotent response, are indicated by more errors of commission on tests such as the go/no-go and continuous performance tasks (CPTs), decreased accuracy and/or shorter latency to first response on the Matching Familiar Figures, and greater interference effects of conflicting stimuli on tasks such as the Stroop Word-Color Association (Corkum & Seigel, 1993; Iaboni, Douglas, & Baker, 1995; Losier, McGrath, & Klein, 1996; Milich, Hartung, Martin, & Haigler, 1994; Pennington & Ozonoff, 1991; Shue & Douglas, 1992; Trommer, Hoeppner, Lorber, & Armstrong, 1988; Voeller & Heilman, 1988). Difficulties in shifting response sets (set switching) are indicated by more perseverative errors on the Wisconsin Card Sort Test and fewer items completed on the Trails-B, although findings are inconsistent (McBurnett et al., 1993; Pennington & Ozonoff, 1991; Reader, Harris, Schuerholz, & Denckla, 1994; Seidman, Biederman, Faraone, Weber, Mennin, & Jones, 1997). Deficits in verbal and visual-spatial working memory in ADHD are reflected by poor performance on Digit Span Backwards, Self-Ordered Pointing, and such tasks as the Paced Auditory Serial Addition Test, Simon Tone/Color Game, and Dot Test of Visuospatial Working Memory (Barkley et al., 1996; Karetekin & Asarnow, 1998; Pennington & Ozonoff, 1991; Wiers, Gunning, & Sergeant, 1998).

Other Neuropsychological Impairments

Neuropsychological impairments in ADHD are not restricted to executive functions. Rather, impairments are also evident on tasks that have been thought traditionally to be sensitive to functioning in nonfrontal brain regions (e.g., posterior regions, temporal lobe, right parietal lobe, and cerebellum), although recent evidence suggests a large distributed network that would include frontal lobe circuitry (Mesulam, 1990; Posner & Raichle, 1994). Impairments are found on tasks that measure neuromotor function, such as timed motor movements, but which are free of planning or problem-solving requirements (e.g., Physical and Neurological Evaluation of Subtle Signs; Developmental Test of Visual-Motor Integration) (Beery, 1982; Carte et al., 1996; Denckla, 1985; Nigg et al., 1998; Robins, 1992). Impairments have also been found on verbal tasks, such as rapid automatized naming and narratives, as well as on vigilance tasks (indexed by omission errors on CPTs) and time estimation (Barkley, Koplowicz, Anderson, & McMurray, 1998; Brock & Knapp, 1996; Carte et al., 1996; Corkum & Seigel, 1993; Iaboni et al., 1995; Losier et al., 1996; Nigg et al., 1998; Sonuga-Barke, Saxton, & Hall, 1998; Tannock, Martinussen, & Frijters, 2000).

However, it is important to note that the impairments tend to occur on tasks that require effortful and controlled processing (e.g., timed and sequenced movements, object naming, color naming, and story retelling) rather than on those that can be accomplished with automatic processing (simple isolated movements, letter naming, digit naming, and word meaning) (Carte et al., 1996; Nigg et al., 1998; Tannock et al., 2000; Zentall, 1988).

Cognitive Functions Not Directly Affected by ADHD

Importantly, it is not the case that ADHD is associated with deficits in *all* aspects of cognitive function. Specifically, ADHD is not associated with deficits in basic sensory, perceptual, and short- or long-term memory abilities per se (Douglas & Benezra, 1990; Kaplan, Dewey, Crawford, & Fischer, 1998; Mealer et al., 1998; Shue & Douglas, 1992). Rather, deficits in these basic processes only emerge as the demand for attention, working memory, and sustained, strategic effort increases (Benezra & Douglas, 1988; Douglas & Benezra, 1990; Kaplan et al., 1998;). For example, individuals with ADHD perform more poorly on memory tasks that involve longer lists, repeated learning trials, the need to organize items into categories, and deliberate rehearsal strategies (August, 1987; Borcherding, Thompson, Kruesi, & Bartko, 1988; Douglas & Benezra, 1990). Further evidence that memory per se is intact in ADHD is provided by an intervention study, which demonstrated that the provision of support in terms of metacognitive strategy (rather than just information) eliminated performance differences between children with ADHD and normal peers on strategic memory tasks (Cornoldi, BArbieri, Gainani, & Zocchi, 1999).

Summary

To summarize, ADHD is associated with a range of impairments in executive function and non-executive function. Impairments are evident on tasks that require seemingly different types of processing: those that require *fast* and accurate processing of information and those that require *slow* and careful processing. These findings generally hold for preschoolers, children, adolescents, and adults with ADHD, and for girls as well as boys, although evidence for girls is less strong (Arcia & Conners, 1998; Katz, Goldstein, & Geckle, 1998; Mariani & Barkley, 1997; Nigg et al., 1998; Pennington & Ozonoff, 1991; Seidman, Biederman, Faraone, Weber, Mennin, & Jones, 1997; Seidman, Biederman, Faraone, Weber, & Ouellette, 1997; Seidman et al., 1995). The next section considers whether some of these impairments are specific to ADHD, attributable to co-occurring disorders (rather than ADHD), or are evident in other disorders as well as ADHD and thus not a unique correlate of ADHD (Jensen et al., 1997; Nigg et al., 1998; Seidman et al., 1995).

IMPACT OF COMORBIDITY ON NEUROPSYCHOLOGICAL PROFILE

Reading Disorder

Most studies indicate that comorbidity with reading disorder (RD) *adds* to rather than alters the neuropsychological profile associated with ADHD. For example, children with ADHD + RD are typically found to exhibit the deficits associated with ADHD (i.e., deficits in sustained attention, response inhibition and other executive functions) *and* those associated with RD (i.e., in phonological processing, naming speed, and verbal memory deficits), suggesting that ADHD + RD is a hybrid condition (Douglas & Benezra, 1990; Felton & Wood, 1989; Korkman & Pesonen, 1994; Narhi & Ahonen, 1995; Nigg et al., 1998; Tannock et al., 2000). By contrast, a few studies indicate that the comorbid group exhibits the cognitive deficits of RD but not of ADHD (e.g., exhibit an impairment in phonological processing but not in executive functions), suggesting that RD leads to secondary symptoms but not the full syndrome of ADHD (i.e., a phenocopy) (Pennington, Groisser, & Welsh, 1993). Alternatively, others have found that the comorbid condition may exhibit a different pattern or more marked impairments than either of the single disorders, suggesting that it may reflect an etiologically distinct subtype (Narhi & Ahonen, 1995; Purvis & Tannock, 2000). In weighing the evidence, the most parsimonious interpretation is that the neuropsychological impairments discussed in the previous section are associated with ADHD and are not an artifact of comorbidity with RD.

Anxiety Disorder

The impact of comorbid anxiety (ANX) on the cognitive profile of ADHD has been subjected to far less scrutiny (Tannock, 2000). In general, the findings suggest that children with ADHD + ANX are more impaired on some measures of executive function (e.g., the serial addition task, Trailmaking Test-B, complex display of memory scanning task) but less impaired on others (e.g., CPT) compared to the nonanxious ADHD children (Tannock, 2000). Notably, the tasks on which the ADHD + ANX children are found to be more impaired are cognitively complex and place high demands on short-term or working memory. By contrast, tasks on which children with ADHD + ANX do not show impairments are generally those that require speeded responses or response inhibition but do not require any appreciable retention of information. Thus, these few studies yield a remarkably consistent pattern of findings and suggest that one effect of comorbid anxiety is to increase (but does not account for) the association between ADHD and problems with working memory and effortful processing. It is unclear whether comorbid anxiety serves to enhance performance on speeded performance in general, to counteract the inhibitory control deficits associated with ADHD or to produce both effects (Barkley, 1997). Nor is it known whether the impact on cognitive function is attributable primarily to a specific cluster or type of anxiety symptoms (i.e., generalized vs. specific anxiety) or to heightened levels of anxiety in general.

Conduct Disorder

According to most population-based studies, the greatest neuropsychological deficits, as well as the poorest long-term outcome, are associated with the comorbid condition of ADHD with conduct disorder (ADHD + CD) (Moffitt, 1990; Moffitt & Henry, 1988; Moffitt & Silva, 1988). Given the high rates of comorbidity between ADHD and comorbid CD or oppositional defiant disorder (ODD), particularly in clinical samples, and the fact that few clinical studies have controlled for these comorbidities, it is particularly important to determine whether the neuropsychological impairments ascribed to ADHD are in fact confined to the comorbid condition of ADHD + CD or are a feature of ODD/CD rather than ADHD (Biederman et al., 1991; Moffitt, 1990; Nigg et al., 1998). The findings are mixed and the inconsistent findings are likely attributable in part to the small samples as well as to differences in diagnosis and the particular measures used. Briefly, children with ADHD + CD have been found to perform like those with ADHD alone, or like those with CD, to differ from either ADHD or CD, or to exhibit the deficits of both single disorders (Koriath, Gulatieri, van Bourgondien, Quade, & Werry, 1985; Nigg et al., 1998; Schachar & Tannock, 1995; Seidman, Biederman, Faraone, Weber, & Ouellette, 1997). Most of the findings indicate that the neuropsychological profile of ADHD + CD more closely resembles that of ADHD than of CD, indicating that the impairments are a correlate of ADHD rather than CD.

SPECIFICITY OF COGNITIVE CORRELATES TO NEUROPSYCHOLOGICAL FUNCTIONING

A recent and comprehensive review concluded that deficits in executive function appear to be correlates of ADHD and autism but not of CD or Tourette's syndrome (Pennington & Ozonoff, 1991). Moreover, both the profile and severity of deficits were found to differ across ADHD and autism. Specifically, impairments in motor response inhibition appeared to be more strongly associated with ADHD than with autism, whereas impairments in working memory appeared to be associated with autism rather than with ADHD (Pennington & Ozonoff, 1991). That presumptive dissociation has yet to be confirmed empirically. Also, because most of the studies reviewed restricted the comparisons to ADHD versus normal controls, they cannot address the issue of specificity of deficits to ADHD.

Impairments in executive function (including motor inhibition, planning, set-shifting, verbal fluency, and working memory) are evident in other clinical populations, including schizophrenia, obsessive-compulsive disorder, and cerebellar cognitive affective syndrome (Dolan, 1998; Gold, Carpenter, Randolph, Goldberg, & Weinberger, 1997; Matier-Sharma, Perachio, & Newcorn, 1995; Purcell, Maruff, Hyrios, & Pantelis, 1998). However, these studies did not include a sample of individuals with ADHD. Evidence of specificity requires *direct* comparisons between ADHD and at least one other clinical group (ideally controlling for comorbidity) tested under the same conditions and with the same measures. For example, one study using this design found that both schizophrenic and ADHD children exhibited deficits in verbal and spatial working memory (Karetekin & Asarnow, 1998). By contrast, mild impairments in executive function have been found in boys with childhood ADHD but not in boys of multigenerational alcoholics—a population thought to be at high risk for executive function deficits (Wiers et al., 1998). These findings suggest that at least some impairments in executive function are not specific to any of the disorders.

Similarly, deficits in non-executive functions do not appear to be specific to ADHD. For example, most of the language-based impairments found in ADHD even in the absence of learning disabilities (e.g., rapid automatized naming of common visual stimuli, comprehension, and difficulties in *use* of language for organization of information and self-regulation), have been traditionally associated with RD (Brock

& Knapp, 1996; Carte et al., 1996; Tannock et al., 2000; Tannock & Schachar, 1996). Notably, these types of tasks frequently require controlled, effortful processing and/or place heavy demands on working memory (Tannock et al., 2000). Also, a persistent pattern of impairments in attention, perception, motor control, language and reading is evident in a substantial subset of children meeting diagnostic criteria for ADHD (Gillberg, Rasmussen, Carlstrom, Svenson, & Waldenstrom, 1982; Hellgren, Gillberg, Bagenholm, & Gillberg, 1994). These findings suggest that ADHD, RD, and perhaps developmental coordination disorder may share at least some common underlying factors.

INFORMATION PROCESSING

The neuropsychological evidence supports a current tenet that response inhibition is associated with ADHD but also suggests that it may not be uniquely related to ADHD. However, the construct validity of many of the measures is questionable (Halperin, McKay, Matier, & Sharma, 1994). Moreover, these measures tap a complex web of processes, so that poor performance may arise from any one or more of the component processes. By contrast, methods derived from information-processing theory are particularly valuable in determining mechanisms underlying poor task performance because they afford more precise measurement (i.e., latency, variability, and accuracy) of component processes (Cohen, 1993).

The most robust finding from studies of information processing, is of slow, variable, and inaccurate response latencies across a range of different measures, which does not support the notion of an impulsive response style (Reason, 1999; Swanson, Castellanos, Murias, LaHoste, & Kennedy, 1998; Tannock, 1998). Rather, this pattern of findings may implicate impairments in several component processing systems, including: sustained attention or vigilance that refers to a state of readiness to respond; response inhibition that is defined variously as the ability to inhibit a prepotent response, stopping an ongoing response; selective attention or spatial allocation of attention; and suppression of reflexive saccades and generation of voluntary saccades.

Impairments in Sustained Attention

Sustained attention has been measured with a variety of CPT methods that yield measures of response times as well as "hits" and "false alarms" (Corkum & Seigel, 1993; Losier et al., 1996; Sergeant & Van der Meere, 1990; Van der Meere, 1996). In general, ADHD is associated with inefficient performance (slow, inaccurate) and vigilance decrements (faster than normal decline in performance) that occur with increased demand for effortful processing (Sergeant & Van der Meere, 1990; Van der Meere, 1996). These impairments in sustained attention are evident across the lifespan (preschool through adulthood) regardless of comorbidity, but findings are influenced strongly by temporal parameters (interstimulus interval, trial length, etc.), stimulus modality, memory load, and context (presence/absence of experimenter, rewards) (Chee, Logan, Schachar, Lindsay, & Wachsmuth, 1989; Corkum & Seigel, 1993; Halperin, Wolf, Greenblatt, & Young, 1991; Losier et al.; Sergeant & Van der Meere, 1990; Van der Meere, 1996).

Performance impairments on vigilance tasks are exhibited by a wide range of clinical populations, however, once again challenging the notion of specificity for ADHD per se (Corkum & Seigel, 1993; Purcell, Maruff, Hyrios, & Pantelis, 1998). Moreover, according to one recent investigation, performance impairments on an inhibition version of the CPT were associated with RD and not with ADHD (McGee, Clark & Symons 2000). Furthermore, findings from a recent study that incorporated measures of event-related brain potentials (ERPs) of the electroencephalogram to reveal neurophysiological correlates of poor performance, suggested that the poor performance of children with ADHD (i.e., detection of fewer signals, more false alarms) may be attributable to impairments in preparatory processing of the stimuli (i.e., in orienting to the stimuli) rather than to impairments in later stages of executive-level processing of the stimuli (van Leeuwen et al., 1998).

Response Inhibition Deficits

Response inhibition deficits in ADHD have been demonstrated using theoretically distinct methods (Casey et al., 1997; Daugherty, Quay, & Ramos, 1993; Leung & Connolly, 1997; Logan, 1994; Oosterlaan, Logan, & Sergeant, 1998; Schachar & Logan, 1990; Schachar, Tannock, Marriott, & Logan, 1995; Tannock & Marriott, 1992). One approach used widely throughout North America and Europe is the stop signal paradigm that is based on a well-established theory of response inhibition and purports to measure the ability to stop a planned or ongoing thought and action (Logan, 1994; Logan & Cowan, 1984). A recent meta-analysis of eight studies using this method to investigate response inhibition in ADHD, CD, ADHD + CD, and ANX found robust evidence for response inhibition deficits in ADHD (Oosterlaan, et al., 1998). Response inhibition deficits were not found to be associated with anxiety disorder, but they were with CD, ODD, and aggression, indicating that these deficits are not a unique correlate of ADHD. Moreover, findings regarding the impact of comorbid RD and the association of response inhibition deficits with RD per se remain equivocal (Nigg, 1999; Purvis & Tannock, 2000; Schachar & Logan, 1990; Tannock & Marriott, 1992; Willcutt et al., 2001). Also, it is not known whether these response inhibition deficits continue into adulthood and there is little evidence that this central inhibitory control impairment relates to behavioral self-regulation (impulsivity, overactivity, inattention). Furthermore, findings from one study that incorporated ERP measures with the stop signal paradigm suggested that slow inhibitory processes associated with ADHD could be determined by impairments in the initial orienting of attention, rather than reflecting poor response inhibition per se (Brandeis et al., 1998).

An alternate conceptualization of response inhibition characterizes the impairment as delay avoidance, defined as a response style aimed at minimizing total time on task rather than an underlying cognitive deficit (Sonuga-Barke, Taylor, & Hepenstall, 1992; Sonuga-Barke, Williams, Hall, & Saxton, 1996). However, findings from a more recent study using a variation of a delay-avoidance paradigm indicated that hyperactive children exhibited a systematic tendency to respond before the response window was presented but had no difficulty inhibiting responses when required. This pattern of findings was interpreted as indicative of impairments in time perception, such as interval discrimination and estimation (Sonuga-Barke et al., 1998). Notably, deficits in interval discrimination and estimation have been reported in ADHD (Barkley et al., 1998; Tannock, Schachar, Logan, & Hetherington, 1999). The continuity of this response style (or potential time perception problem) into adulthood, or its variation with gender or comorbidity is unknown.

Spatial Allocation of Attention

Dysfunction of the visuospatial orienting system (particularly in the right hemisphere) is suggested by a few studies of covert orienting that investigate shifts in allocation of visual attention in the absence of saccadic eye movements (Nigg, Swanson, & Hinshaw, 1997; Pearson, Yaffee, Loveland, & Norton, 1995; Swanson et al., 1991; Tannock, Schachar, & Logan, 1993). The finding of similar impairments in one study of biological parents is of particular interest, suggesting the influence of genetic factors (Sonuga-Barke et al., 1996). Also, evidence of orienting deficits using these paradigms is consistent with the evidence of orienting deficits during performance on the stop-signal and CPT paradigms that are purported measures of response inhibition and sustained attention, respectively (Brandeis et al., 1998; van Leeuwen et al., 1998). However, inconsistencies of findings across studies and across child and parent samples do not allow firm conclusions.

Recently, the control of saccadic eye movements (inhibition of reflexive eye movements and generation of voluntary eye movements) has been investigated as a potential diagnostic marker for various disorders that have been linked with the frontal cortex and basal ganglia, including ADHD (Everling & Fischer, 1998; Munoz, Hampton, Moore, & Goldring, 1999; Ross, Hommer, Breiger, Varley, & Radant, 1994; Rothlind, Posner, & Schaughency, 1991). The limited data available from studies that used different versions of the anti-saccade task suggest that children with ADHD have more difficulty in accurately controlling visual fixation and in suppressing unwanted saccades compared to controls (Munoz et al., 1999; Ross et al., 1994; Rothlind et al., 1991). However, numerous clinical populations exhibit difficulties inhibiting reflexive saccades, including schizophrenia, Alzheimer's disease, amyotrophic lateral sclerosis, Huntington's, dyslexia, but not affective disorders, although poor performance may be due to deficits in different underlying subprocesses (Tannock et al., 1993).

IMPLICATIONS FOR NEURAL SUBSTRATE AND PATHOPHYSIOLOGY OF ADHD

The pattern of cognitive impairments associated with ADHD shows correspondence with findings of subtle anomalies in brain anatomy and neurochemistry in individuals with ADHD (Tannock, 1998). There is preliminary evidence of a link between performance decrements on a variety of response inhibition tasks and subtle anatomical anomalies in the frontal-striatal circuitry (prefrontal cortex, caudate, and globus pallidus) in children and adolescents with ADHD (Casey et al., 1997). Also, vigilance deficits implicate neural networks in the right frontal lobe and locus ceruleus; impairments in response control and cognitively demanding information processing implicate the dopaminergically mediated anterior attentional system associated with anterior cingulate and frontostriatal circuitry; and the potential deficits in visuospatial orienting implicate posterior attentional systems comprising superior parietal cortex, pulvinar, and superior colliculus (Posner & Raichle, 1994). Moreover, the overall difficulties in dynamic, on-line adjustment and adaptation to changes in the immediate environment, which are evident in both clinical and cognitive studies of ADHD, implicate cerebellar networks that play a major integrative role in prediction and preparation of neural conditions needed for a particular motor or nonmotor operation (Courchesne & Allen, 1997). Reduced cerebellar volumes in individuals with ADHD are one of the most robust findings among the neuroimaging studies of ADHD (Castellanos, 2001; Tannock, 1998).

CLINICAL IMPLICATIONS

Diagnosis

There is converging evidence that the North American construct of ADHD and the European construct of hyperkinetic disorder (HD) are both associated with mild impairments in a diverse array of cognitive abilities. The impairments are not attributable to a more fundamental and global type of problem such as low IQ or general disadvantage, nor can they be ascribed completely to coexisting disorders. There is no evidence to date for a specific cognitive marker for ADHD, its presumptive subtypes, or component symptoms, although a few cognitive correlates (e.g., response inhibition, planning) appear to differentiate ADHD from some of the disorders that frequently co-occur with ADHD (e.g., anxiety disorder and specific learning disorder). As such, the cognitive correlates provide only minimal evidence for the validity of ADHD (or HD) as a distinct clinical entity. On the other hand, the association of cognitive impairments with ADHD has important clinical implications.

Currently, the diagnosis of ADHD is based solely on clinical evaluation, but there is ongoing concern with the lack of operational definition of the behavioral symptoms or the critical descriptors (e.g., "often") in DSM-IV (Reason, 1999). Thus, the evidence of group differences on various psychological measures of attention, impulsivity, executive function, and activity has motivated recommendations for the inclusion of these objective tests in the clinical evaluation (Goldstein & Goldstein, 1990; Gordon, 1983; Grodinsky & Diamond, 1992). The problem is that much of the "evidence" reflects differences between children with ADHD and normal controls rather than between ADHD and other psychiatric or developmental disorders. Moreover, differences demonstrated at the group level have not translated into differences at the level of the individual, which is essential for diagnosis. This is because the tests suffer from low specificity and sensitivity and, more important, have poor positive and negative predictive value for ADHD (Barkley & Grodinsky, 1994; Matiah-Sharma, Perachio, Newcorn, Sharma, & Halperin, 1995). (It should be noted that many of the limited number of studies available are subject to biases of sampling [study not representative of target population; higher prevalence of disease among subjects than the prior probability of disease in clinical practice], measurement [nonindependent or blinded determinations of the results of the diagnostic tests and disorder status], and reporting [publication bias of reporting positive results rather than negative results].) Thus, the present review argues strongly that an individual's intellectual profile (e.g., the WISC-III Third Factor—FFD), academic achievement scores, or performance on neuropsychological tests or measures of information processing cannot be used either to rule in or to rule out the diagnosis of ADHD.

Assessment and Treatment

If measures of intellectual function, academic achievement, or neuropsychological function do not have utility in the *diagnosis* of ADHD, the next question from a clinical perspective is, Do they have any relevance for the *assessment* of ADHD? Here, the answer is a resounding "yes" (American Academy of Child and Adolescent Psychiatry, 1997; Reason, 1999; Taylor et al., 1998). "Good measures of current intellectual functioning and current academic achievement are useful for every child" (Cantwell, 1996, p. 982). Testing is always indicated in the presence of problems related to classroom adjustment, lack of or limited progress in academic or social functioning, or current problems or history of communication difficulties. Systematic and comprehensive assessment of intellectual function, academic achievement, and neuropsychological function plays a useful role in understanding the cognitive strengths and difficulties of an individual with ADHD. This information is particularly important in treatment planning, given the limited evidence that standard pharmacotherapy or psychosocial interventions for ADHD have any substantial impact on academic *achievement* (as opposed to academic productivity) or on the cognitive processing deficits underlying comorbid learning disabilities (Abikoff, 1985; Schachar, Tannock, & Cunningham, 1996; Spencer et al., 1996; Tannock & Brown, 2000). For example, the identification of additional impairments in receptive language, phonological processing, and working memory in a child with ADHD would indicate the need for modifications to a typical treatment plan for ADHD. Modifications might include the following:

- Establishing a collaborative alliance between the family, educational, and mental health systems;

- Education of parents, child, and teacher about the nature of these additional difficulties, their implications in terms of everyday life at home and school, and the potential risk of misinterpreting failure to comply as "oppositional behavior" rather than "noncomprehension" or "failure to process";

- Guidelines to parents and teachers for modifying the rate, length, and complexity of their utterances when talking with the child;

- Recommendations for individual or small-group instruction for language and/or specific reading remediation, cues, and strategies to help with the language and working memory problems;

- Modifications of the "language of instruction" of any psychosocial interventions for the child, to recognize and accommodate the child's special needs; and

- Ongoing monitoring of appropriateness of school interventions, in collaboration with parents, child, and school personnel (American Academy of Child and Adolescent Psychiatry, 1998; Tannock & Brown, 2000).

Given the high rates of comorbidity with learning disorders, the ubiquitous problems of underachievement in academic and social domains, and the high risk for poor outcome, a comprehensive and systematic assessment of intellectual function, academic achievement and neuropsychological function should be a routine component of an assessment for ADHD (American Academy of Child and Adolescent Psychiatry,

1997, 1998; Taylor et al., 1998). This conclusion is made even with the knowledge of limited resources and a period of fiscal restraint and cutbacks, because failure to identify and address these additional deficits may result in the use of costly but ineffective treatment approaches.

IMPLICATIONS FOR FUTURE RESEARCH

To date, there is no known cognitive correlate that is uniquely associated with ADHD. Rather, the cognitive profile of ADHD may be best characterized as one that is particularly sensitive to the rate at which information is presented and to contextual factors such as the provision of external regulation through social or motivational variables. There is converging evidence that ADHD is associated with problems in motor preparation and control (planning, execution, inhibition) and/or with dynamic adjustment of state or energetic mechanisms (effort, activation) that modulate elemental operations of the cognitive system. These problems are not readily explainable by comorbidity but are not necessarily specific to ADHD. Although it is possible that there is no single underlying psychological mechanism that accounts for the behavioral manifestations currently classified as ADHD, this review should not be interpreted as indicating that this is indeed the case.

First, despite the plethora of data, interpretation of this body of research is challenged by the heterogeneity of this symptom complex, the study of small samples, and measurement problems of both the "independent" and "dependent' variables (i.e., case identification/group assignment and reliability, validity and developmental sensitivity of the cognitive measures, respectively). Thus, direct comparisons across studies are often not possible. Second, many studies have restricted their investigation to a comparison between ADHD and normally developing, age-matched peers. Yet, evidence of specificity of impairment requires comparisons with other clinical groups. Third, there has been an excessive reliance on poor performance on individual neuropsychological or cognitive tests as a global index of deficits in "attention" or "impulsivity." Most tests inevitably tap several aspects of cognitive function, and even the most "elemental" cognitive function is likely to implicate a complex web of cognitive processes. Thus, it is unlikely that any single test could accurately separate and measure specific processes or a specific dimension of the multidimensional constructs of attention and impulsiveness. Cognitive markers are likely to be subtle, distributed in multiple brain systems, and hence difficult to measure. Fourth, neuropsychological and cognitive measures that provide indirect measures of brain function and information about the current state of function (i.e., at the time of measurement) are typically based on models of adult psychology and assume linear growth patterns of development. By contrast, current developmental models and recent applications of neuroimaging methods indicate dynamic and on-line interactions between brain function and the immediate environment, wide variation in development in different domains of function both within and across individuals, and nonlinear growth patterns (Fischer & Rose, 1996; Giedd et al., 1996; Mash & Dozois, 1996; Thatcher, 1996).

The challenges for future research are numerous but not insurmountable. First, a more precise characterization of the ADHD phenotype is required. The focus to date has been at the level of the disorder, using boundaries for case identification that lack details for operational definition of thresholds for onset, duration, severity, and impairment. Future studies may be more informative if ADHD is conceptualized as a composite of two quantitative, continuously distributed dimensions of inattention and hyperactivity/impulsivity, rather than as three categorical subtypes. Alternatively, the examination of symptom clusters or theory-based phenotypes may be more informative than the current constructs of ADHD or HD. Also, large samples are required to afford adequate statistical power for multivariate techniques to examine the impact of gender, age, symptom dimensions, and comorbidity. Comparisons with multiple clinical/medical groups are required to examine the issue of specificity of neuropsychological impairment. Measurement approaches are required that select measures of contrasting constructs (automatic vs. controlled processing, linguistic vs. non-linguistic, fast vs. slow pace, motoric vs. non-motoric, high vs. low working memory load, etc.), require different levels of processing, or are based on latent abilities derived from multidimensional models of cognitive function. The incorporation of recent advances in psychophysiological and brain-imaging techniques may provide further insight into the nature of the cognitive deficits by linking them to the temporal stages of information processing, and regions of over- or underactivation involved in the specific cognitive activity or type of information processing. Delineation of the neuropsychological and neural mechanisms of ADHD must be an iterative process in which clinical subtypes are defined, tested and redefined, using more precisely controlled and validated measures.

Acknowledgments

Preparation of this review chapter was supported in part by an MRC Scientist Award and NIH Project Grant # RO1HD31714.

References

Abikoff, H. (1985). Efficacy of cognitive training interventions in hyperactive children: A critical review. *Clinical Psychology Review, 5*, 479–512.

Ackerman, P. T., Anhalt, J. M., Holcomb, P. J., & Dykman, R. A. (1986). Presumably innate and acquired automatic processes in children with attention and/or reading disorders. *Journal of Child Psychology and Psychiatry, 27*, 513–529.

Aman, C. J., Roberts, R. J., & Pennington, B. F. (1998). A neuropsychological examination of the underlying deficit in attention deficit hyperactivity disorder: Frontal lobe versus right parietal lobe theories. *Developmental Psychology, 34*, 956–969.

American Academy of Child and Adolescent Psychiatry. (1997). Practice parameters for the assessment and treatment of children, adolescents, and adults with attention-deficit/hyperactivity disorder. *Journal of the American Academy of Child and Adolescent Psychiatry, 36*(Suppl.), 85S–121S.

American Academy of Child and Adolescent Psychiatry. (1998). Practice parameters for the assessment and treatment of children and adolescents with language and learning disorders. *Journal of the American Academy of Child and Adolescent Psychiatry, 37*(Suppl.), 46S–62S.

American Psychiatric Association. (1980). *Diagnostic and statistical manual of mental disorders* (3rd ed.). Washington, DC: Author.

American Psychiatric Association. (1987). *Diagnostic and statistical manual of mental disorders* (3rd ed., rev.). Washington, DC: Author.

American Psychiatric Association. (1994). *Diagnostic and statistical manual of mental disorders* (4th ed.). Washington, DC: Author.

Anastopoulos, A. D., Spisto, M. A., & Maher, M. (1994). The WISC-III Freedom From

Distractibility factor: Its utility in identifying children with attention deficit hyperactivity disorder. *Psychological Assessment, 6,* 368–371.

Arcia, E., & Conners, C. K. (1998). Gender differences in ADHD? *Journal of Developmental and Behavioral Pediatrics, 19,* 77–83.

August, G. J. (1987). Production deficiencies in free recall: A comparison of hyperactive, learning disabled, and normal children. *Journal of Abnormal Child Psychology, 15,* 429–440.

Barkley, R. A. (1997). Behavioral inhibition, sustained attention, and executive functions: Constructing a unifying theory of ADHD. *Psychological Bulletin, 121,* 65–94.

Barkley, R. A., Anastopoulos, A. D., Guevremont, D. C., & Fletcher, K. E. (1991). Adolescents with ADHD: Patterns of behavioral adjustment, academic functioning, and treatment utilization. *Journal of the American Academy of Child and Adolescent Psychiatry, 30,* 752–761.

Barkley, R. A., DuPaul, G. J., & McMurray, M. B. (1990). Comprehensive evaluation of attention deficit disorder with and without hyperactivity as defined by research criteria. *Journal of Consulting and Clinical Psychology, 58,* 775–789.

Barkley, R. A., & Grodinsky, G. M. (1994). Are tests of frontal lobe functions useful in the diagnosis of attention deficit disorders? *The Clinical Neuropsychologist, 8,* 121–139.

Barkley, R. A., Koplowicz, S., Anderson, T., & McMurray, M. B. (1998). Sense of time in children with ADHD: Effects of duration, distraction, and stimulant medication. *Journal of the International Neurological Society, 3,* 359–369.

Barkley, R. A., Murphy, K. R., & Kwasnik, D. (1996). Psychological adjustment and adaptive impairments in young adults with ADHD. *Journal of Attention Disorders, 1,* 41–54.

Baumgaertel, A., Wolraich, M. L., & Dietrich, M. (1995). Comparison of diagnostic criteria for attention deficit disorders in a German elementary school sample. *Journal of the American Academy of Child and Adolescent Psychiatry, 34*(5), 629–638.

Beery, K. (1982). *Revised administration, scoring, and teaching manual for the developmental test of visual-motor integration.* Cleveland, OH: Modern Curriculum Press.

Benezra, E., & Douglas, V. I. (1988). Short-term serial recall in ADD-H, normal and reading-disabled boys. *Journal of Abnormal Child Psychology, 16,* 511–525.

Biederman, J., Faraone, S. V., Taylor, A., Sienna, M., Williamson, S., & Fine, C. (1998). Diagnostic continuity between child and adolescent ADHD: Findings from a longitudinal clinical sample. *Journal of the American Academy of Child and Adolescent Psychiatry, 37,* 305–313.

Biederman, J., Newcorn, J., & Sprich, S. (1991). Comorbidity of attention deficit hyperactivity disorder with conduct, depressive, anxiety and other disorders. *American Journal of Psychiatry, 148,* 564–577.

Borcherding, B., Thompson, K., Kruesi, M., & Bartko, J. J. (1988). Automatic and effortful processing in attention deficit/hyperactivity disorder. *Journal of Abnormal Child Psychology, 16,* 333–345.

Brandeis, D., van Leeuwen, T. H., Rubia, K., Vitacco, D., Steger, J., Pascual-Marqui, R. D., & Steinhausen, H-Ch. (1998). Neuroelectric mapping reveals precursor of stop failures in children with attention deficits. *Behavioural Brain Research, 94,* 111–123.

Brock, S. W., & Knapp, P. K. (1996). Reading comprehension abilities of children with attention-deficit/hyperactivity disorder. *Journal of Learning Disabilities, 1,* 173–186.

Cantwell, D. P. (1995). Child psychiatry: Introduction and overview. In H. I. Kaplan & B. J. Saddock (Eds.), *Comprehensive textbook of psychiatry-IV* (pp. 2151–2154). Baltimore: Williams & Wilkins.

Cantwell, D. (1996). Attention deficit disorder: A review of the past 10 years. *Journal of the American Academy of Child and Adolescent Psychiatry, 35,* 978–987.

Carte, E. T., Nigg, J. T., & Hinshaw, S. P. (1996). Neuropsychological functioning, motor speed, and language processing in boys with and without ADHD. *Journal of Abnormal Child Psychology, 24,* 481–498.

Castellanos, F. X. (2001). Neuroimaging studies of ADHD. In M. V. Solanto, A. F. T. Arnsten, & F. X. Castellanos (Eds.), *Stimulant drugs and ADHD: Basic and clinical neurosciences* (pp. 243–258). New York: Oxford University Press.

Casey, B. J., Castellanos, F. X., Giedd, J. N., Marsh, W. L., Hamburger, S. D., Schubert, A. B., Vauss, Y. C., Vaituzis, C., Dickstein, D. P., Sarfetti, S. E., & Rapoport, J. L. (1997). Implication of right frontostriatal circuitry in response inhibition and attention-deficit/hyperactivity disorder. *American Journal of Child and Adolescent Psychiatry, 36*, 374–383.

Chee, P., Logan, G., Schachar, R., Lindsay, P., & Wachsmuth, R. (1989). Effects of event rate and display time on sustained attention in hyperactive, normal and control children. *Journal of Abnormal Child Psychology, 17*, 371–391.

Cohen, R. A. (1993). *The neuropsychology of attention.* New York: Plenum Press.

Corkum, P., & Siegel, L. S. (1993). Is the Continuous Performance Task a valuable research tool for use with children with attention-deficit-hyperactivity disorder? *Journal of Child Psychology and Psychiatry, 34*, 1217–1239.

Cornoldi, C., Barbieri, A., Gaiani, C., & Zocchi, S. (1999). Strategic memory deficits in attention deficit disorder with hyperactivity participants: the role of executive processes. *Developmental Neuropsychology, 15*, 53–71.

Courchesne, E., & Allen, G. (1997). Prediction and preparation, fundamental functions of the cerebellum. *Learning and Memory, 4*, 1–35.

Daneman, M., & Merikle, P. M. (1996). Working memory and language comprehension: A meta-analysis. *Psychonomic Bulletin and Review, 3*, 422–433.

Daugherty, T. K., Quay, H. C., & Ramos, L. (1993). Response perseveration, inhibitory control, and central dopaminergic activity in childhood behavior disorders. *Journal of Genetic Psychology, 154*, 177–188.

Denckla, M. B. (1985). Revised neurological examination for subtle signs. *Psychopharmacological Bulletin, 21*, 773–800.

Dolan, R. J. (1998). Editorial: A cognitive affective role for the cerebellum. *Brain, 121*, 545–546.

Douglas, V. I., & Benezra, E. (1990). Supraspan verbal memory in attention deficit disorder with hyperactivity, normal and reading disabled boys. *Journal of Abnormal Child Psychology, 18*, 617–638.

Eslinger, P. J. (1996). Conceptualizing, describing, and measuring components of executive function, a summary. In G. R. Lyon & N. A. Krasnegor (Eds.), *Attention, memory, and executive function* (pp. 367–396) London: Paul H. Brookes.

Everling, S., & Fischer, B. (1998). The antisaccade: A review of basic research and clinical studies. *Neuropsychologia, 36*, 885–899.

Faraone, S. V., Biederman, J., Lehman, B. K., Spencer, T., Norman, D., Seidman, L. J., Kraus, I., Perrin, J., Chen, W. J., & Tsuang, M. T. (1993). Intellectual performance and school failure in children with attention deficit hyperactivity disorder and in their siblings. *Journal of Abnormal Psychology, 102*, 616–623.

Faraone, S. V., Biederman, J., Weber, W., & Russell, R. (1998). Psychiatric, neuropsychological, and psychosocial features of DSM-IV subtypes of attention-deficit/hyperactivity disorder: Results from a clinically referred sample. *Journal of the American Academy of Child and Adolescent Psychiatry, 37*, 185–193.

Felton, R. H., & Wood, F. B. (1989). Cognitive deficits in reading disability and attention deficit disorder. *Journal of Learning Disabilities, 22*, 3–13.

Fischer, K. W., & Rose, S. P. (1996). Dynamic growth cycles of brain and cognitive development. In R. W. Thatcher, G. R. Lyon, J. Rumsey, & N. Krasnegor (Eds.), *Developmental neuroimaging: Mapping the development of brain and behavior* (pp. 263–279). San Diego: Academic Press.

Fischer, M., Barkley, R. A., Edelbrock, C. S., & Smallish, L. (1990). The adolescent outcome of hyperactive children diagnosed by research criteria: II. Academic, attentional, and neuropsychological status. *Journal of Consulting and Clinical Psychology, 58*, 580–588.

Fuster, J. M. (1989). *The prefrontal cortex: Anatomy, physiology, and neuropsychology of the frontal lobe* (2nd ed.). New York: Raven Press.

Gaub, M., & Carlson, C. L. (1997a). Behavioral characteristics of DSM-IV ADHD subtypes in a school-based population. *Journal of Abnormal Child Psychology, 25*, 103–111.

Gaub, M., & Carlson, C. L. (1997b). Gender differences in ADHD: A meta-analysis and critical review. *Journal of the American Academy of Child and Adolescent Psychiatry, 36*, 1036–1045.

Giedd, J. N., Snell, J. W., Lange, N., Rajapakse, J. C., Casey, B. J., Kozuch, P. L., Vaituzis, A. C., Vauss, Y. C., Hamburger, S. D., Kaysen, D., & Rapoport, J. L. (1996). Quantitative magnetic resonance imaging of human brain development: Ages 4–18. *Cerebral Cortex, 6*, 551–560.

Gillberg, C., Rasmussen, P., Carlstrom, G., Svenson, B., & Waldenstrom, E. (1982). Perceptual, motor and attentional deficits in six-year-old children. Epidemiological aspects. *Journal of Child Psychology and Psychiatry, 23,* 131–144.

Gold, J. M., Carpenter, C., Randolph, C., Goldberg, T. E., & Weinberger, D. R. (1997). Auditory working memory and Wisconsin Card Sorting Test Performance in Schizophrenia. *Archives of General Psychiatry, 54*, 159–165.

Goldstein, S., & Goldstein, M. (1990). *Managing attention disorders in children.* New York: Wiley.

Gordon, N. G. (1983). *The Gordon diagnostic system.* DeWitt, NY: Gordon Systems.

Grodinsky, G. M., & Diamond, J. (1992). Frontal lobe functioning in boys with attention deficit hyperactivity disorder. *Developmental Neuropsychology, 8*, 427–446.

Halperin, J. M., & McKay, K. E. (1998). Psychological testing for child and adolescent psychiatrists: A review of the past 10 years. *Journal of the American Academy of Child and Adolescent Psychiatry, 37*, 575–584.

Halperin, J. M., McKay, K. E., Matier, K., & Sharma, V. (1994). Attention, response inhibition and activity level in children: Developmental neuropsychological perspectives. In M. G. Tramontana & S. R. Hooper (Eds.), *Advances in child neuropsychology* (Vol. 2, pp. 1–54). New York: Springer-Verlag.

Halperin, J. M., Wolf, L. E., Greenblatt, E. R., & Young, J. G. (1991). Subtype analysis of commission errors on the continuous performance test in children. *Developmental Neuropsychology, 7*, 207–217.

Hellgren, L., Gillberg, I. C., Bagenholm, A., & Gillberg, C. (1994). Children with deficits in attention, motor control and perception (DAMP) almost grown up: Psychiatric and personality disorders at age 16 years. *Journal of Child Psychology and Psychiatry, 35*, 1255–1271.

Hinshaw, S. P. (1992). Externalizing behavior problems and academic underachievement in childhood and adolescence: Causal relationships and underlying mechanisms. *Psychological Bulletin 111*, 127–155.

Hynd, G. W., Lorys, A. R., Semrud-Clikeman, M., Nieves, N., Huettner, M. I. S., & Lahey, B. B. (1991). Attention deficit disorder without hyperactivity: A distinct behavioral and neurocognitive syndrome. *Journal of Child Neurology, 6*(Suppl.), S37–S41.

Iaboni, F., Douglas, V. I., & Baker, A. G. (1995). Effects of reward and response costs on inhibition in ADHD children. *Journal of Abnormal Psychology, 104*, 232–240.

Iversen, S. D., & Dunnett, S. B. (1990). Functional organization of striatum as studied with neural graphs. *Neuropsychologia, 28*, 601–626.

Javorsky, J. (1996). An examination of youth with attention-deficit/hyperactivity disorder and language learning disabilities: A clinical study. *Journal of Learning Disabilities, 29*, 247–258.

Jensen, P. S., Martin, B. A., & Cantwell, D. P. (1997). Comorbidity in ADHD: Implications for research, practice, and DSM-IV. *Journal of the American Academy of Child and Adolescent Psychiatry, 36*, 1065–1079.

Kaplan, B. J., Dewey, D., Crawford, S. G., & Fischer, G. C. (1998). Deficits in long-term memory are not characteristic of ADHD. Attention Deficit Hyperactivity Disorder. *Journal of Clinical and Experimental Neuropsychology, 20*, 518–528.

Karetekin, C., & Asarnow, R. F. (1998). Working memory deficits in childhood-onset schizophrenia and attention-deficit/hyperactivity disorder. *Psychiatry Research, 80*, 165–176.

Katz, L. J., Goldstein, G., & Geckle, M. (1998). Neuropsychological and personality differences between men and women with ADHD. *Journal of Attention Disorders, 2,* 239–247.

Koriath, U., Gualtieri, C. T., van Bourgondien, M. E., Quade, D., & Werry, J. S. (1985). Construct validity of clinical diagnosis in pediatric psychiatry: Relationship among measures. *Journal of the American Academy of Child Psychiatry, 24*(4), 429–436.

Korkman, M., & Pesonen, A. E. (1994). A comparison of neuropsychological test profiles of children with attention deficit-hyperactivity disorder and/or learning disabilities. *Journal of Learning Disabilities, 27*, 383–392.

Lahey, B. B., Applegate, B., McBurnett, K., Biederman, J., Greenhill, L., Hynd, G. W., Barkley, R. A., Newcorn, J., Jensen, P., Richters, J., Garfinkel, B., Kerdyk, L., Frick, P. J., Ollendick, T., Perez, D., Hart, E. L., Waldman, I., & Shaffer, D. (1994). DSM-IV Field Trials for attention deficit hyperactivity disorder in children and adolescents. *American Journal of Psychiatry, 151*, 1673–1685.

Lahey, B. B., Pelham, W. E., Stein, M. A., Loney, J., Trapani, C., Nugent, K., Kipp, H., Schmidt, E., Lee, S., Cale, M., Gold, E., Hartung, C. M., Willcutt, E., & Baumann, B. (1998). Validity of DSM-IV Attention-Deficit/Hyperactivity Disorder for younger children. *Journal of the American Academy of Child and Adolescent Psychiatry, 37*(7), 695–702.

Lamminmäki, T. A., Ahonen, T., Närhi, V., Lyytinen, H., & Todd de Barra, H. (1995). Attention deficit hyperactivity disorder subtypes: Are there differences in academic problems? *Developmental Neuropsychology, 11*, 297–310.

Leung, P. W. L., & Connolly, K. J. (1997). Test of two views of impulsivity in hyperactive and conduct-disordered children. *Developmental Medicine and Child Neurology, 39*, 574–582.

Lezak, M. D. (1995). *Neuropsychological assessment* (3rd ed.). New York: Oxford University Press.

Logan, G. D. (1994). On the ability to inhibit thought and action: A user's guide to the stop signal paradigm. In D. Dagenbach & T. H. Carr (Eds.), *Inhibitory processes in attention, memory, and language* (pp. 189–239). San Diego: Academic Press.

Logan, G. D., & Cowan, W. B. (1984). On the ability to inhibit thought and action: A theory of an act of control. *Psychological Review, 91*, 295–327.

Losier, B. J., McGrath, P. J., & Klein, R. M. (1996). Error patterns on the Continuous Performance Test in non-medicated and medicated samples of children with and without ADHD: A meta-analytic review. *Journal of Child Psychology and Psychiatry, 37*, 971–987.

Mariani, M. A., & Barkley, R. A. (1997). Neuropsychological and academic functioning in preschool boys with attention deficit hyperactivity disorder. *Developmental Neuropsychology, 13*, 111–129.

Marshall, R. M., Hynd, G. W., Handwerk, M. J., & Hal, J. (1997). Academic underachievement in ADHD subtypes. *Journal of Learning Disabilities, 30*, 635–642.

Mash, E. J., & Dozois, D. J. A. (1996). Child psychopathology: A developmental systems perspective. In E. J. Mash & R. A. Barkley (Eds.), *Child psychopathology* (pp. 3–60). New York: Guilford Press.

Matier-Sharma, K., Perachio, N., Newcorn, J. H., Sharma, V., & Halperin, J. M. (1995). Differential diagnosis of ADHD: Are objective measures of attention, impulsivity, and activity level helpful? *Child Neuropsychology, 1*, 118–127.

Mayes, S. D., Calhoun, S. T., & Crowell, E. W. (1998). WISC-III Freedom From Distractibility as a measure of attention in children with and without attention deficit hyperactivity disorder. *Journal of Attention Disorders, 2*, 217–227.

McBurnett, K., Harris S. M., Swanson, J. M., Pfiffner, L. J., Tamm, L., & Freeland, D. (1993). Neuropsychological and psychophysiological differentiation of inattention/overactivity and aggression/defiance symptom groups. *Journal of Clinical Child Psychology, 22*, 165–171.

McGee, R. A., Clark, S. E., & Symons, D. K. (2000). Does the Conners' continuous performance test aid in ADHD diagnosis? *Journal of Abnormal Child Psychology, 28*, 415–424.

McGee, R., Williams, S., Moffit, T., & Anderson, J. (1989). A comparison of 13-year-old boys with Attention Deficit and/or reading disorder on neuropsychological measures. *Journal of Abnormal Child Psychology, 17*, 37–53.

Mealer, C., Morgan, S., & Luscomb, R. (1998). Cognitive functioning of ADHD and non-ADHD boys on the WISC-III and WRAML: An analysis within a memory model. *Journal of Attention Disorder, 3*, 133–145.

Mesulam, M. M. (1990). Large-scale neural networks and distributed processing for attention, language, and memory. *Annals of Neurology, 19*, 320–325.

Meyer, D. E., & Keiras, D. E. (1997). A computational theory of executive cognitive processes and multiple-task performance: Part 1. Basic processes. *Psychological Review, 104*, 3–65.

Milich, R., Hartung C. M., Martin C. A., & Haigler, E. D. (1994). Behavioral disinhibition and underlying processes in adolescents with disruptive behavior disorders. In D. K. Routhm (Ed.), *Disruptive behavior disorders in childhood* (pp. 109–138). New York: Plenum Press.

Moffitt, T. E. (1990). Juvenile delinquency and attention-deficit disorder: Developmental trajectories from age 3 to 15. *Child Development, 61,* 893–910.

Moffitt, T. E., & Henry, B. (1988). Neuropsychological assessment of executive functions in self-reported delinquents. *Development and Psychopathology, 1,* 105–118.

Moffitt, T. E., & Silva, P. (1988). Self-reported delinquency, neuropsychological deficit, and history of attention deficit disorder. *Journal of Abnormal Child Psychology, 16,* 553–569.

Munoz, D. P., Hampton, K. A., Moore, K. D., & Goldring, J. E. (1999). Control of purposive saccadic eye movements and visual fixation in children with attention deficit hyperactivity disorder. In W. Becker, H. Deubel, & T. Mergner (Eds.), *Current occulomotor research: Physiological and psychological aspects* (pp. 415–423). New York: Plenum Press.

Narhi, V., & Ahonen, T. (1995). Reading disability with and without attention deficit hyperactivity disorder: Do attentional problems make a difference? *Developmental Neuropsychology, 11,* 337–350.

Newby, R. F., Recht, D. R., Caldwell, J., & Schaefer, J. (1993). Comparison of WISC-III and WISC-R IQ changes over a 2-year time span in a sample of children with dyslexia. In B. A. Bracken & R. S. McCalum (Eds.), *Journal of Psychoeducational Assessment WISC-III Monograph.*

Nigg, J. T. (1999). The ADHD response-inhibition deficit as measured by the stop task: Replication with DSM-IV combined type, extension, and qualification. *Journal of Abnormal Child Psychology, 27,* 393–402.

Nigg, J. T., Hinshaw, S. P., Carte, E. T., & Treuting, J. J. (1998). Neuropsychological correlates of childhood attention deficit hyperactivity disorder: Explainable by comorbid disruptive behavior or reading problems? *Journal of Abnormal Psychology, 107,* 468–480.

Nigg, J. T., Swanson, J. M., & Hinshaw, S. P. (1997). Covert visual spatial attention in boys with attention deficit hyperactivity disorder: lateral effects, methylphenidate response and results for parents. *Neuropsychologia, 35,* 165–176.

Oosterlaan, J., Logan, G. D., & Sergeant, J. A. (1998). Response inhibition in AD/HD, CD, comorbid AD/HD+CD, anxious and control children: A meta-analysis of studies with the stop task. *Journal of Child Psychology and Psychiatry, 39,* 411–426.

Pearson, D. A., Yaffee, L. S., Loveland, K. A., & Norton, A. M. (1995). Covert visual attention in children with attention deficit hyperactivity disorder: Evidence for developmental immaturity? *Development and Psychopathology, 7,* 351–167.

Pennington, B. F. (1997). Dimensions of executive functions in normal and abnormal development. In N. Krasnegor, R. Lyon, & P. Goldman-Rakic (Eds.), *Development of the prefrontal cortex: Evolution, neurobiology, and behavior* (pp. 265–291). Baltimore: Paul H. Brookes.

Pennington, B. F., Groisser, D., & Welsh, M. C. (1993). Contrasting cognitive deficits in attention deficit hyperactivity disorder versus reading disability. *Developmental Psychology, 29,* 511–523.

Pennington, B. F., & Ozonoff, S. (1991). A neuroscientific perspective on continuity and discontinuity in developmental psychopathology. In D. Cicchetti (Ed.), *Rochester Symposium on developmental psychopathology* (Vol. III, pp. 117–159). Rochester, NY: University of Rochester Press.

Pennington, B. F., & Ozonoff, S. (1996). Executive functions and developmental psychopathology. *Journal of Child Psychology and Psychiatry, 37,* 51–87.

Petrides, M., Aliviasatos, B., Meyer, E., & Evans, A. C. (1993). Functional activation of the human frontal cortex during performance of verbal working memory tasks. *Proceedings of the National Academy of Science, 90,* 878–882.

Posner, M. I., & Raichle, M. E. (1994). *Images of mind.* New York: Freeman.

Prifitera A., Weiss L. G., & Saklofske D. H. (1998). The WISC-III in Context. In A. Prifitera & D. H. Saklofske (Eds.), *WISC-III Clinical use and interpretation: Scientist-practitioner perspectives* (pp. 1–38). New York: Academic Press.

Purcell, R., Maruff, P., Hyrios, M., & Pantelis, C. (1998). Neuropsychological deficits in obsessive-compulsive disorder: A comparison with unipolar depression, panic disorder, and normal controls. *Archives of General Psychiatry, 55*, 415–423.

Purvis, K., & Tannock, R. (2000). Phonological processing, not inhibitory control differentiates ADHD and reading disability. *Journal of the American Academy of Child and Adolescent Psychiatry, 39*, 485–494.

Reader, M. J., Harris, E. L., Schuerholz, L. J., & Denckla, M. B. (1994). Attention deficit hyperactivity disorder and executive dysfunction. *Developmental Neuropsychology, 11*, 493–512.

Reason, R. (1999). ADHD: A psychological response to an evolving concept. Report of a Working Party of the British Psychological Society. *Journal of Learning Disabilities, 32*, 85–91.

Reinecke, M. A., Beebe, D. W., & Stein, M. A. (1999). The third factor of the WISC-III: It's (probably) not freedom from distractibility. *Journal of the American Academy of Child and Adolescent Psychiatry, 38*, 322–328.

Robins, P. M. (1992). A comparison of behavioral and attentional functioning in children diagnosed as hyperactive or learning-disabled. *Journal of Abnormal Child Psychology, 20*, 65–82.

Ross, R. G., Hommer, D., Breiger, D., Varley, C., & Radant, A. C. (1994). Eye movement task related to frontal lobe functioning in children with attention deficit disorder. *Journal of the American Academy of Child and Adolescent Psychiatry, 33*, 869–874.

Rothlind, J. C., Posner, M. I., & Schaughency, E. A. (1991). Lateralized control of eye movements in attention deficit hyperactivity disorder. *Journal of Cognitive Neuroscience, 3*, 377–381.

Saklofske, D. H., Schwean, V. L., Yackalic, R. A., & Quinn, D. (1994). WISC-III and SB:FE performance of children with Attention Deficit Disorder. *Canadian Journal of School Psychology, 10*, 167–171.

Schachar, R., & Logan, G. D. (1990). Impulsivity and inhibitory control in normal development and childhood psychopathology. *Developmental Psychology, 26*, 710–720.

Schachar, R., & Tannock, R. (1995). A test of four hypotheses for the comorbidity of attention deficit hyperactivity disorder and conduct disorder. *Journal of the American Academy of Child and Adolescent Psychiatry, 34*, 639–648.

Schachar, R., Tannock, R., & Cunningham, C. (1996). Treatment. In S. Sandberg (Ed.), *Hyperactivity disorders of childhood* (pp. 433–476). Cambridge: Cambridge University Press.

Schachar, R., Tannock, R., Marriott, M., & Logan, G. (1995). Deficient inhibitory control in attention deficit hyperactivity disorder. *Journal of Abnormal Child Psychology, 23*, 411–437.

Schmahmann, J. D., & Sherman, J. C. (1998). The cerebellar cognitive affective syndrome. *Brain, 121*, 561–579.

Schwean, V. L., & Saklofske, D. H. (1998). WISC-III assessment of children with Attention Deficit/Hyperactivity Disorder. In A. Prifitera & D. Saklofske (Eds.), *WISC-III clinical use and interpretation* (pp. 91–118). San Diego: Academic Press.

Seidman, L. J., Biederman, J., Faraone, S. V., Millberger, S., Norman, D., Sieverd, K., Benedict, K., Guite, J., Mick, E., & Kiely, K. (1995). Effects of family history and comorbidity on the neuropsychological performance of children with ADHD: Preliminary findings. *Journal of the American Academy of Child and Adolescent Psychiatry, 34*, 1015–1024.

Seidman, L. J., Biederman, J., Faraone, S. V., Weber W., Mennin, D., & Jones, J. (1997). A pilot study of neuropsychological function in girls with ADHD. *Journal of the American Academy of Child and Adolescent Psychiatry, 36*, 366–373.

Seidman, L. J., Biederman, J., Faraone, S. V., Weber, W., & Ouellette, C. (1997). Toward defining a neuropsychology of attention deficit-hyperactivity disorder: Performance of children and adolescents from a large clinically referred sample. *Journal of Consulting and Clinical Psychology, 65*, 150–160.

Semrud-Clikeman, M., Biederman, J., Sprich-Buckminster, S., Lehman, B. K., Faraone, S. V., & Norman, D. (1992). Comorbidity between ADDH and learning disability: A review and report in a clinically referred sample. *Journal of the American Academy of Child and Adolescent Psychiatry, 31*, 439–448.

Sergeant, J. A., & Steinhausen H. C. (1992). European perspectives on hyperkinetic disorder. *European Journal of Child Psychiatry, 1*, 34–41.

Sergeant, J. A., & Van der Meere, J. J. (1990). Convergence of approaches in localizing the hyperactivity deficit. In B. B. Lahey & A. E. Kazdin (Eds.), *Advances in clinical psychology* (pp. 207–246). New York: Plenum Press.

Sharp, W. S., Walter, J. M., Marsh, W. L., Ritchie, G. F., Hamburger, S. D., & Castellanos, F. X. (1999). ADHD in girls: Clinical comparability of a research sample. *Journal of the American Academy of Child and Adolescent Psychiatry, 38*, 40–47.

Shue, K. L., & Douglas, V. I. (1992). Attention deficit hyperactivity disorder and the frontal lobe syndrome. *Brain and Cognition, 20*, 104–124.

Sonuga-Barke, E. J. S., Lamparelli, M., Stevenson, J., Thompson, M., & Henry, A. (1994). Behaviour problems and preschool intellectual attainment: The associations of hyperactivity and conduct problems. *Journal of Child Psychology and Psychiatry, 35*, 949–960.

Sonuga-Barke, E. J., Saxton, T., & Hall, M. (1998). The role of interval underestimation in hyperactive children's failure to suppress responses over time. *Behavioral Brain Research, 94*, 45–50.

Sonuga-Barke, E. J. S., Taylor, E., & Hepenstall, E. (1992). Hyperactivity and delay aversion-II: The effects of self versus externally imposed stimulus presentation periods on memory. *Journal of Child Psychology and Psychiatry, 33*, 399–409.

Sonuga-Barke, E. J. S., Williams, E., Hall, M., & Saxton, T. (1996). Hyperactivity and delay aversion III: the effects on cognitive style of imposing delay after errors. *Journal of Child Psychology and Psychiatry, 37*, 189–194.

Spencer, T., Biederman, J., Wilens, T., Harding, M., O'Donnell, D., & Griffin, S. (1996). Pharmacotherapy of attention-deficit hyperactivity disorder across the life cycle. *Journal of the American Academy of Child and Adolescent Psychiatry, 35*, 409–432.

Stuss, D. T. (1992). Biological and psychological development of executive functions. *Brain and Cognition, 20*, 3–28.

Stuss, D. T., & Benson, D. F. (1984). Neuropsychological functions of the frontal lobes. *Psychological Bulletin, 95*, 3–28.

Swanson, J., Castellanos, F. X., Murias, M., LaHoste, G., & Kennedy, J. (1998). Cognitive neuroscience of attention deficit hyperactivity disorder and hyperkinetic disorder. *Current Opinion in Neurobiology, 8*, 263–271.

Swanson, J. M., Posner, M. I., Potkin, S., Bonforte, S., Youpa, D., Cantwell, D., & Crinella, F. (1991). Activating tasks for the study of visal-spatial attention in ADHD children: A cognitive anatomical approach. *Journal of Child Neurology, 6*(Suppl.), S119–S127.

Tannock, R. (1998). Attention deficit hyperactivity disorder: Advances in cognitive, neurobiological, and genetic research. *Journal of Child Psychology and Psychiatry, 39*, 65–99.

Tannock, R. (2000). Attention deficit disorders with anxiety disorders. In T. E. Brown (Ed.), *Attention deficit disorders and comorbidities in children, adolescents and adults* (pp. 125–170). Washington, DC: American Psychiatric Press.

Tannock, R., & Brown, T. E. (2000). Attention deficit disorders with learning disorders in children and adolescents. In T. E. Brown (Ed.), *Attention deficit disorders and comorbidities in children, adolescents and adults* (pp. 231–295). Washington, DC: American Psychiatric Press.

Tannock, R., & Marriott, M. (1992). Learning disabilities: Converging evidence of deficits in inhibitory processes [abstract]. *Proceedings of the 39th annual meeting of the American Academy of Child and Adolescent Psychiatry, 8*, 89.

Tannock, R., Martinussen, R., & Frijters, I. (2000). Naming speed performance and stimulant effects Indicate controlled processing deficits in attention-deficit hyperactivity disorder. *Journal of Abnormal Child Psychology, 28*, 237–252.

Tannock, R., & Schachar, R. (1996). Executive dysfunction as an underlying mechanism of behavior and language problems in attention deficit hyperactivity disorder. In J. H. Beitchman, N. Cohen, M. M. Konstantareas, & R. Tannock (Eds.), *Language, learning, and behavior disorders: Developmental, biological, and clinical perspectives* (pp. 128–155). New York: Cambridge University Press.

Tannock, R., Schachar, R., & Ickowicz, A. (1997). *Disentangling the DSM-IV ADHD subtypes.* Paper presented at the annual meeting of the American Psychological Association, Toronto, Canada.

Tannock, R., Schachar, R. J., & Logan, G. (1993). Does methylphenidate induce overfocusing in hyperactive children? *Journal of Clinical Child Psychology, 22,* 28–41.

Tannock, R., Schachar, R., Logan, G., & Hetherington, R. (1999, June 16–20). *Do deficits in inhibitory control or time perception best characterize ADHD?* Paper presented at the International Society for Research in Child and Adolescent Psychopathology, Barcelona, Spain.

Taylor, E., Chadwick, O., Hepinstall, E., & Danckaerts, M. (1996). Hyperactivity and conduct problems as risk factors for adolescent development. *Journal of the American Academy of Child and Adolescent Psychiatry, 35,* 1213–1226.

Taylor, E., Sergeant, J., Doepfner, M., Gunning, B., Overmeyer, S., Mobius, H. J., & Eisert, H. G. (1998). Clinical guidelines for hyperkinetic disorder. *European Child and Adolescent Psychiatry, 7*(4), 184–200.

Temple, C. M. (1998). Cognitive neuropsychology and its application to children. *Journal of Child Psychology and Psychiatry, 38,* 27–52.

Thatcher, R. W. (1996). Neuroimaging of cyclical cortical reorganization during human development. In R. W. Thatcher, G. R. Lyon, J. Rumsey, & N. Krasnegor (Eds.), *Developmental neuroimaging: Mapping the development of brain and behavior* (pp. 91–106). San Diego: Academic Press.

Tripp, G., Luk, S. L., Schaughency, E. A., & Singh, R. (1999). DSM-IV and ICD-10: A comparison of the correlates of ADHD and hyperkinetic disorder. *Journal of the American Academy of Child and Adolescent Psychiatry, 38*(2), 156–164.

Trommer, B. L., Hoeppner, J. B., Lorber, R., & Armstrong, K. J. (1988). The go-no-go paradigm in attention deficit disorder. *Annals of Neurology, 2,* 610–614.

Van der Meere, J. J. (1996). The role of attention. In S. T. Sandberg (Ed.), *Monographs in child and adolescent psychiatry. Hyperactivity disorders of childhood* (pp. 109–146). Cambridge: Cambridge University Press.

van Leeuwen, T. H., Steinhausen, H-Ch., Overtoom, C. C. E., Pascual-Marqui, R. D., van't Klooster, B., Tothenberger, A., Sergeant, J. A., & Brandeis, D. (1998). The continuous performance test revisited with neuroelectric mapping: Impaired orienting in children with attention deficits. *Behavioural Brain Research, 94,* 97–110.

Voeller, K. K. S., & Heilman, K. M. (1988). Motor impersistence in children with attention deficit disorder: Evidence for right hemisphere dysfunction [abstract]. *Annals of Neurology, 24,* 323.

Wechsler, D. (1991). *Wechsler Intelligence Scale for Children* (3rd ed.). San Antonio, TX: Psychology Corporation.

Wiers, R. W., Gunning, B., & Sergeant, J. A. (1998). Is a mild deficit in executive functions in boys related to childhood ADHD or to parental multigenerational alcoholism? *Journal of Abnormal Child Psychology, 26,* 415–430.

Willcutt, E. G., Pennington, B. F., Boada, R., Ogline, J. S., Tunick, R. A., Chhabildas, N. A., & Olson, R. K. (2001). A comparison of cognitive deficits in reading disability and attention-deficit/hyperactivity disorder. *Journal of Abnormal Psychology, 110,* 157–172.

Wolraich, M. L., Hannah, J. N., Baumgaertel, A., & Fuerer, I. D. (1998). Examination of DSM-IV criteria for attention-deficit/hyperactivity disorder in a county-wide sample. *Journal of Developmental and Behavioral Pediatrics, 19,* 162–168.

Zentall, S. S. (1990). Fact-retrieval automatization and math problem solving by learning disabled, attention-disordered, and normal adolescents. *Journal of Educational Psychology, 82,* 856–865.

Zentall, S. S. (1988). Production deficiencies in elicited language but not in spontaneous verbalizations of hyperactive children. *Journal of Abnormal Child Psychology, 16,* 657–673.

Part 3

Are ADHD Treatments Safe and Effective?

What is the best line of treatment for attention deficit hyperactivity disorder (ADHD): medication, psychosocial interventions, or alternative treatments such as diet or vitamin supplementation, etc.? Various explanations for ADHD have been put forth involving diet, allergic food sensitivity, vitamin and mineral deficiencies, environmental pollutants, or all these at once. These theories usually carry with them their own untested prescriptions for remedy in the form of special diets, supplementation, environmental engineering, and so forth. Special diets and dietary supplements have many adherents. Costly laboratories are often consulted for complex biochemical profiles, followed by tricky patterns of supplementation.

ADHD has always had a number of "alternative" speculations and treatments. As noted by Arnold (in this section), two unscientific pitfalls must be avoided: embracing new treatments uncritically and rejecting them without fair examination. That job is complicated by proposals mixing real science with untested assumptions. For example, a frightening list of food additives known to create allergic reactions became the basis of a new food additive-free diet and etiological theory of ADHD, which turned out to be largely unsupported by the evidence. Enzymatic reactions governed by essential fatty acids suggested a new treatment involving evening primrose oil, but double-blind trials failed to show any efficacy with ADHD In another example, the powerful tools of quantitative EEG were used to capture the differences in patterns of brain electrical activity between ADHD children and their normal peers. ADHD patients learned to use feedback from their own brain rhythms to increase the production of more physiologically mature rhythms at will. Over months of training (which might also include Ritalin and tutoring), symptoms are said to diminish in proportion to this increased control. But whether this is a fact or merely a potent but highly expensive placebo effect augmented by the trappings of science remains a matter to be decided by clinical trials with adequate placebo controls. The advocates of these new theories seem too often willing to skip the last, laborious (but necessary) step in the argument: clinical trials with adequate placebo controls.

Some of these controversies appear to reflect fundamental attitudes and beliefs regarding the use of behavior-altering drugs with children. Psychostimulants and other drugs turn out to be powerful and undeniably effective ways of removing ADHD and related symptoms. Despite this overwhelming evidence for efficacy, concerns are raised about what else the drugs might do. Perhaps they teach children to attribute success to the pills, not to their own skills, thus harming their self-esteem. Perhaps the pills quash the free-spirited and creative impulses that lead to divergent thinking and creative problem solving. The charge is made that ADHD is a myth, created as a means of validating widespread use of performance enhancement in the fierce competition faced by children for academic and social success. Often linked with the antipathy to stimulants is a preference for nondrug therapies. These include classical psychodynamic psychotherapy and cognitive-behavioral therapies based on social learning theory.

In this section we present the sizable body of evidence concerning the efficacy of medications (principally the stimulants and tricyclics), behavioral therapies, and combined (multimodal) treatments. In addition, the evidence (pro and con) for the various "alternative" treatments is provided (see Arnold, Chapter 13). As seen throughout this section, medications (see Greenhill, Chapter 9, and Biederman & Spencer, Chapter 11), behavioral therapies (see Pelham, Chapter 12), and their combination (see Ambroggio & Jensen, Chapter 14) are all quite effective. The preponderance of evidence indicates that medications are somewhat more effective than behavioral therapy in head-to-head comparisons, a conclusion reached by the National Institute of Health Consensus Conference panelists (see Appendix A) after an extensive review of the evidence. In Chapter 15, Abikoff offers important insights into the clinical application of the information previously set forth in this section, namely, the matching a given treatment to a given patient's needs

This section also highlights the potential risks of ADHD treatments, specifically the stimulant medications. In Chapter 9, Greenhill presents a hard-hitting but factual summary of the available data concerning the short- and long-term consequences of stimulant medication treatments. In Chapter 10, Rowland and colleagues sound a note of caution about the possible overuse of these treatments and the continuing need for long-term studies. Yet, as will be seen by reviewing the data from this chapter, the risks of these treatments are often vastly overstated.

—**P.S. Jensen**
—**J.R. Cooper**
—**C.K. Conners**

Chapter 9

Stimulant Medication Treatment of Children With Attention Deficit Hyperactivity Disorder

by Laurence L. Greenhill, M.D.

Introduction 9-2
Pharmacology 9-3
Absorption and Metabolism 9-4
Toxicology 9-6
Stimulant Adverse Events 9-6
Are There Long-Term Risks of Stimulant Use? 9-6
Short-Term Efficacy Shown in Randomized Controlled
   Trials of Stimulants 9-7
Benefits of Stimulant Medications 9-9
      Amelioration of Disruptive Behaviors 9-9
      Improvement of Cognitive Functioning 9-9
      Placebo vs. Medication Response 9-9
Efficacy of Long-Duration Stimulant Preparations 9-12
Limitations of Short-Term Stimulant Trials 9-13
Long-Term Randomized Controlled Trials of Stimulant
   Medications 9-14
      The MTA Study 9-14
         MTA Study Design 9-14
         Study Outcome 9-18
         MTA Study's Answers to Treatment Questions 9-18
      Other Long-Term Studies 9-19
Issues for Practitioners 9-19
      Do the Research Findings Inform Practice? 9-19
      Limitations of Available Stimulants 9-20
         Response/Dosing Issues 9-20
         Side Effects 9-21
Recommendations 9-21

INTRODUCTION

Psychostimulants are the most commonly prescribed medication treatments for attention deficit hyperactivity disorder (ADHD). This group of medications includes methylphenidate (Ritalin®), amphetamine (Dexedrine® and Adderall®), and pemoline (Cylert®). Prescribing patterns suggest that stimulants are a mainstay of treatment for ADHD children, and methylphenidate (MPH) is the most-often prescribed psychostimulant. Outpatient visits devoted to ADHD have increased from 1.6 to 4.2 million per year during the years 1990–1993 (Swanson, Lerner, & Williams, 1995); by 1995, these figures had climbed to 2 million visits and 6 million stimulant drug mentions (Jensen et al., 1999). During those visits, 90 percent of the children were given prescriptions, 71 percent of which were for MPH. MPH production in the United States increased from 1,784 kg to 5,110 kg during the same period, so that over 10 million prescriptions for MPH were written in 1996 (Vitiello & Burke, 1998). It has been estimated that 2.8 percent of U.S. youth, ages 5 to 18 years were prescribed stimulants in 1995 (Goldman, Genei, Bazman, & Stanetz, 1998), but epidemiological surveys suggest that twelve-month prescription rates for the school-age group—ages 6 to 12 years—may be higher, ranging between 6 percent urban (Safer, Zito, & Fine, 1996) and 7 percent rural (Angold, Erkanli, Costello, & Egger, 2000).

Psychostimulant use has increased fivefold over the past twelve years, and this has raised concerns at the U.S. Drug Enforcement Administration (DEA), which regulates their production, about the risk of abuse and diversion. Production of MPH has tripled over a ten-year period, and 90 percent of U.S.-produced MPH is used in the United States. Increased MPH use could mean increases in ADHD prevalence; a change in the ADHD diagnosis; improved recognition of ADHD by physicians; broadened indications for use; or an increase in drug diversion, prescription for profit, or abuse (Goldman et al., 1998). Analyses of managed care datasets reveal a two and half-fold increase in prescribing in the 1990–1995 period, accounted for by longer durations of treatment, inclusion of girls and those with predominately inattention, and treatment of high school students (Safer et al., 1996). Although the abuse liability of MPH and other stimulants has been established in animal research, the evidence that MPH's ability to generate euphoria and to lead to abuse is less clear. National surveys indicate that snorting ground-up MPH tablets does occur among high school seniors, although this occurs far less frequently than marijuana or cocaine use (Loney & Milich, 1982); however, the lifetime nonmedical use has remained constant at 1 percent for years (Goldman et al., 1998). Analyses of annual school surveys of drug use and the Drug Abuse Warning network data on emergency room visit monitoring have not suggested growing abuse of MPH (Goldman et al., 1998).

The increase in stimulant prescribing in the United States led to shortages in 1993, as a result of a delay in setting quotas, which resulted in an effort by parent support groups to declassify MPH (Horn, Parker, Evans, & Portnoy, 1994). Although this petition failed, procedures for final quota notice approval were improved (Goldman et al., 1998).

Epidemiologically based surveys that include child diagnoses and treatment services have addressed the question whether stimulant drugs are overused or misused in the United States. One survey in four different communities found that only one-eighth of diagnosed ADHD children received adequate stimulant treatment (Jensen et al., 1999), while another survey in rural North Carolina found that many school-age children on stimulants did not meet criteria for a diagnosis of ADHD (Angold et al., 2000).

PHARMACOLOGY

The psychostimulants in clinical use for treatment of children with ADHD have putative effects on central catecholamine pathways (Pliszka, McCracken, & Maas, 1996). Psychostimulants are amines and are occasionally described as the "noncatecholamine sympathomimetics," due to their close chemical resemblance to those neurotransmitters. Sympathomimetics have potent agonist effects at alpha-adrenergic and beta-adrenergic receptors, where they serve as both direct and indirect agonists. Presynaptically, the stimulants cause a stoichiometric displacement of norepinephrine from storage sites in the presynaptic terminal (Weiner, 1991). Postsynaptically, they function as direct agonists at the adrenergic receptor.

Neurophysiological, neurochemical, and neuroimaging studies in animals reveal that the facilitative effects of stimulants on locomotor activity, reinforcement processes, and rate dependency are mediated by the dopaminergic effects at nucleus accumbens, where effects on delayed responding and working memory are mediated by noradrenergic afferents from the locus coeruleus to prefrontal cortex (Solanto, 1998). Stimulants block the reuptake of dopamine (DA) and norepinephrine (NE) into the presynaptic neuron. One model of action posits a stimulant-related frontal cortex inhibitory action, which in turn acts on dopamine-rich striatal structures (Zametkin & Rapoport, 1987). Dextroamphetamine's release of dopamine can be blocked by alpha-methyl-tyrosine, but not reserpine, suggesting the monoamine originates from a cytoplasmic pool of newly synthesized dopamine (Scheel-Kruger, 1971). The release of DA by MPH, on the other hand, can be blocked by reserpine pretreatment, and has therefore been thought to involve vesicular storage. MPH and cocaine both have affinity for the dopamine transporter. Although the mechanism for psychostimulant enhancement of attention is unknown, positron emission tomography (PET) scan data show that [11C] MPH concentration in the brain is maximal in striatum (Volkow et al., 1995). The structure of the psychostimulants has been related to their central nervous system (CNS) activity. Early studies (Arnold, Wender, McCloskey, & Snyder, 1972) postulated that d-isomers of amphetamine were selectively more effective for norepinephrine release, but both d- and l- amphetamine had equal effects on dopamine. A double-blind crossover study (Arnold et al., 1972) comparing the two isomers did not support this, for l-amphetamine was found to take longer to act and was not as effective on measures of attention as the d-isomer. Similarly, it appears that the d-isomer of MPH may have a greater effect on locomotor activity and reuptake inhibition of labeled dopamine than does the l-isomer (Patrick, Mueller, Gualtieri, & Breese, 1987).

The MPH molecule has two asymmetric carbon atoms, resulting in four optical isomers: both d- and l- forms of the threo and erythro racemates. The threo isomer appears to have more potency than the erythro, perhaps due to the sixty-degree skew relationship between the tertiary amine and the carbomethoxy groups, as they are in cocaine (Buckner, Patil, Tye, & Malspeis, 1969). This key relationship may increase these compounds' ability to block cellular membrane reuptake processes. In the erythro form, these groups are transstaggered, and therefore no weak bond is formed between the nitrogen and carbonyl atoms (Buckner et al., 1969; Patrick et al., 1987). The commercial manufacturing process produces the dl-threo-methylphenidate racemate exclusively.

Their action enhances the functioning of executive control processes, overcoming the deficits in inhibitory control and working memory reported in children with ADHD (Douglas, Barr, Amin, O'Neill, & Britton, 1988). These effects are brief because of the rapid absorption and metabolism of these drugs (Patrick et al., 1987). The pharmacodynamic (PD) effects of the immediate-release (IR) formulations of MPH, Dexedrine (DEX) and Adderall appear within thirty minutes, reach a peak within one to three hours, and are gone by five hours (Swanson et al., 1998), making in-school dosing a necessity, despite the resulting problems of peer ridicule and added adult supervision requirements. Sustained-release formations of MPH and DEX, as well as pemoline, have been shown to have effects on attention up to nine hours after dosing (Pelham et al., 1990). However, clinicians have not found that these drugs successfully cover the entire schoolday with only one morning administration. In addition, hepatoxicity has been reported for children chronically treated with pemoline (Berkovitch, Pope, Phillips, & Koren, 1995; Wroblewski, Leary, Phelan, Whyte, & Manning, 1992).

The putative action of psychostimulants in ADHD has been attributed directly to their ability to release dopamine and to block its reuptake at the presynaptic terminal. For example, the most potent inhibitors of MPH uptake are also the most specific inhibitors of DA uptake. Radioligand binding studies have demonstrated the direct action of psychostimulants, particularly MPH, at the dopamine transporter located on the presynaptic terminal (Scheel-Kruger, 1971). The dopaminergic action of psychostimulants also explains the appearance of behavioral stereotypies, seen at high doses. Tritiated-MPH binding in the rat brain is highest in striatum and is highly dependent on sodium concentration, suggesting that the receptors for MPH are associated with a neurotransmitter uptake or transport system (Hauger, Angel, Janowsky, Berger, Hulihan-Gibin, 1990).

Solanto's (1998) authoritative review of neuropsychological research found that MPH significantly improved sustained attention and attentional allocation, as well as the organization and speed of motor response processes and motor inhibitory control. Because these effects are observed in both ADHD and non-ADHD children, she concluded that stimulant effects do not target a specific neurobiological deficit in ADHD but, rather, exert compensatory effects.

ABSORPTION AND METABOLISM

Psychostimulants are rapidly absorbed from the gut—often within the first thirty minutes following ingestion—with food-enhancing absorption (Chan, Swanson, Soldin, Thiessen, & MacLeod, 1983). Early pharmacokinetic data reported that MPH bioavailabilities reached the 80 percent range, but more recent studies (Chan et al., 1983) place the actual figure closer to 30 percent. Dextroamphetamine concentrations in plasma range between 40 to 120 ng/ml in treated ADHD children (Borcherding, Keysor, Cooper, & Rapoport, 1989; Brown, Hunt, Ebert, Bunney, & Kopin, 1979). MPH produces lower plasma concentrations—as low as 7 to 10 ng/ml—suggesting a large first-pass effect. Yet relatively low concentrations of MPH are surprisingly effective. This is due, in part, to MPH's low plasma binding (15 percent), which makes it highly available to cross the blood-brain barrier (Perel & Dayton, 1976). This situation creates a favorable brain-plasma partition, with higher concentration in CNS than in plasma (Patrick et al., 1987).

Effects on behavior appear during absorption, beginning thirty minutes after ingestion and lasting three to four hours. Half-lives range between three hours for MPH and eleven hours for d-amphetamine. The concentration-enhancing and activity-reducing effects of MPH can disappear well before the medication leaves the plasma, a phenomenon termed "clockwise hysteresis" (Cox, 1990).

Methylphenidate's metabolism is especially rapid and complete (Faraj et al., 1974). MPH is metabolized rapidly because it is not highly bound to plasma protein, nor does it disappear into fat stores. MPH peaks in plasma two to two and a half hours (Tmax) and later falling to half the peak (half-life) after three hours. The parent compound is metabolized by hydrolysis of the ester group to give the equivalent carboxylic acid, ritalinic acid. Approximately 20 percent is oxidized (to p-hydroxy- and oxo-methylphenidate) as well as conjugated derivatives by the liver (Perel & Dayton, 1976).

MPH's short half-life prevents steady state plasma concentrations to be achieved; thus the standard tablet must be given several times a day for sustained benefit throughout the school schedule. Standard administration times are after breakfast, and before school (8 A.M.); just after lunch (12 noon); and just before homework (about 3:30 P.M.). Standard doses and available preparations of the psychostimulants are shown in Table 9.1.

Pemoline effects on cognitive processing begin within the first two hours after administration. Unlike MPH, the effects last up to six hours. While the therapeutic effects of MPH and dextro-amphetamine are confined to the absorption phase, pemoline has significant postabsorptive effect lasting into the postdistribution phase (Sallee, Stiller, & Perel, 1992). Unlike previous clinical suggestions that pemoline requires three to six weeks to work (Page, Bernstein, Janicki, & Michelli, 1974),

Table 9.1
Stimulant Drugs, Doses, and Pharmacodynamics

Medication	D-amphetamine (doses per day)	Methylphenidate (doses per day)	Pemoline (doses per day)
Tablets and dosages available in brand medications	5 mg tablets 5,10, 15 mg spansule	5, 10, 20 mg tablets 20 mg SR	18.75, 37.5, 75 mg tablet; 37.5 chewable
Package insert dose range	10–40 mg/day in split doses (3)	10–60 mg/day in split doses (3)	37.75–112.5 mg/day (2)
Administration	BID or TID	BID or TID	qAM or BID
Maximum effect	1–3 hours	1–3 hours	2–4 hours
Length of effect	3–5 hours	2–4 hours	7 hours

pemoline has been shown to be effective after the first dose (Collier et al., 1985; Pelham, Swanson, Furman, & Schwint, 1995).

Group studies have consistently shown linear dose-response curves for the psychostimulants for their peak effects, although individual's dose-response curves may differ across domains, exhibiting curvilinear or quadratic effects. Although a 1977 study suggested that optimal effects on cognitive functioning may be predictable using a weight-adjusted dose of 0.3 mg/kg (Sprague & Sleator, 1977), more recent work shows no consistent relationships between weight-adjusted doses and most response domains (Rapport, DuPaul, & Kelly, 1989).

TOXICOLOGY

Animal studies have shown a wide therapeutic to toxic ratio for MPH. A 100:1 margin of safety exists between a single dose approximating a human clinical dose and one that produces lethality in two other animal species (Diener, 1991). As a result, MPH is one of the safest medications used in the treatment of children, when given in the standard 0.3–1.2 mg/kg/day oral dose range. In the animal lab, the median lethal dose (LD50) is 48.3 mg/kg by intravenous route and 367 mg/kg by oral route. In comparison, the LD50 for amphetamine in rats is 55 mg/kg. Ninety-day subchronic toxicity studies of MPH in rats (with doses up to 120 mg/kg/day) showed decreases in body weight but no signs of growth inhibition, reproductive problems, or carcinogenicity; a 120-day study of beagles treated with 10 mg/kg/day (ten times human dose) of MPH produced hyperactivity and hyperexcitability in the dogs, but there was no appetite suppression, growth suppression, convulsions, or changes in liver tissue.

STIMULANT ADVERSE EVENTS

Adverse events in short-duration controlled stimulant studies of children with ADHD—most often insomnia, reduced appetite, stomachache, headache, and dizziness—average 4 percent of those treated (Barkley, McMurray, Edelbroch, & Robbins, 1990). A third, mid-afternoon dose of MPH added to the usual twice-daily regimen does not lead to additional sleep problems, although it may affect appetite (Meltzer & Arora, 1991). Staring, daydreaming, and irritability decrease with increasing stimulant dose. Fewer children will demonstrate motor tics while on stimulants. No consistent relationship has been found in short-term controlled studies between stimulant dose and the less frequently reported adverse events—behavioral rebound, motor tics, compulsive picking of nose or skin, emotional or cognitive constriction, and growth delays (Spencer, Biederman, Harding, et al., 1996). One twelve-month study reported a 15 percent incidence of persistent and worsening of side effects—overfocusing and affective symptoms—that eventually led to drug discontinuation (Schachar, 1998), going against the popular notion that children adjust to the adverse events of stimulant medications.

ARE THERE LONG-TERM RISKS OF STIMULANT USE?

Growth delays, particularly failure to attain weight at an expected rate during development (Gillberg et al., 1997), have been cited as a possible long-term risk of stimulant treatment. These effects were thought to respond to short periods off drugs ("drug holidays") (Gittelman-Klein, Landa, Mattes, & Klein, 1988). However, prospective follow-up into adult life (Mannuzza et al., 1991) has revealed no significant impairment of height attained. A later single-observation, cross-sectional study of adolescents with ADHD suggested that growth curves of untreated ADHD children may show significantly slowed growth in early years, and late catch-up, compared to nonaffected children (Spencer, Biederman, Harding, et al., 1996). Other long-term studies which incorporate pretreatment and multiple measures do not agree, showing a decrement in weight gain during treatment when MPH-treated children are compared to those on nondrug treatments (Schachar, 1998).

Hepatic tumors in rodents treated with high oral doses of 4–47 mg/kg of MPH (Dunnick & Hailey, 1995) have been reported. However, hepatic tumors are species specific and the MPH doses are far higher than ever used in treatment. Furthermore, hepatic tumors have not been reported in children with ADHD who have been treated with MPH and are exceedingly rare in preschool and school age children. Other studies show the same species-specific hepatic vulnerability to high MPH doses, particularly when given with beta-adrenergic agonist drugs (Roberts, Harbison, Roth, & James. 1994). However, altered liver function tests and fulminant hepatoxicity were reported in forty-four children treated with pemoline (PEM; Berkovitch et al., 1995), which is four to seventeen times the expected rate, leading to a warning inserted in the drug's package insert.

Methylphenidate has some abuse potential, but the actual addiction liability of these medications is unclear. Klein (1980) finds that the psychostimulants differ in their ability to induce euphoria, with "dextroamphetamine the most euphorigenic, methylphenidate, less so, and magnesium pemoline, hardly at all." Adolescents and young adults with ADHD do not list the psychostimulants among medications used recreationally, whether or not they had received treatment with psychostimulants (Gittelman & Mannuzza, 1988). Adolescents previously diagnosed as having ADHD during their school-age years are at greater risk for substance abuse than are controls, but those who do abuse medications do not pick stimulants. Reports of MPH abuse are limited to poly-substance-abusing adults who use intravenous methods. Because injectable MPH is not available, some addicts have attempted to solubilize the tablets before injecting them. Talc granulomatosis results, with severe pulmonary hypertension or ocular lesions developing in some patients. (For more on the potential addiction liability, see Part 4 of this book.)

SHORT-TERM EFFICACY SHOWN IN RANDOMIZED CONTROLLED TRIALS OF STIMULANTS

Psychostimulants have consistently shown robust behavioral efficacy in randomized controlled trials (RCTs). This began in the early 1960s, with small-numbered, single-site, short-duration trials. By 1993, Swanson's "Review of reviews" reported on the voluminous stimulant treatment literature, with over 3,000 citations and 250 reviews. Searching this field, Spencer, Biederman, Wilens, et al. (1996) reported robust short-term stimulant-related improvements in ADHD symptoms in 161 RCTs encompassing 5 preschool, 140 school-age, 7 adolescent, and 9 adult RCTs. Although early articles suggested that stimulant medications uniquely and paradoxically calmed school-age children with ADHD, these drugs have proven effective for diverse age groups.

Improvement was noted for 65–75 percent of the 5,899 patients assigned to stimulant treatment versus only 4–30 percent of those assigned to placebo for MPH ($n = 133$ trials), DEX ($n = 22$ trials), and PEM ($n = 6$ trials). Compared to placebo in short-term, double-blind trials, the stimulants demonstrate robust efficacy in improving the two prominent symptom clusters found in ADHD—inattentiveness and hyperactivity-impulsivity assessed on the basis of parent and teacher rating scales, direct observations in natural settings, and laboratory tests (Greenhill, 1998; Jacobvitz, Srouge, Stewart, & Leffert, 1990; Spencer, Biederman, Wilens, et al., 1996; Swanson, 1993). Three meta-analyses, conducted in the early 1980s, separately concluded that the efficacy for stimulants—in placebo-controlled, double-blind trials—was strong, with effect sizes on behavior 0.8–1.0 standard deviations (Kavale, 1982; Ottenbacher & Cooper, 1983; Thurber & Walker, 1983). Less powerful effects are found for laboratory measures for cognitive changes, in particular on the continuous performance task (CPT), where effect sizes of these medications range between 0.6 and 0.5 for omissions and commissions, respectively, in a within-subject design (Milich, Licht, & Murphy, 1989) and 0.6 and 1.8 in a between-subject study (Schechter & Keuezer, 1985).

Greatly improved methodology can be found in RCTs published within the past fifteen years, as shown by their use of multiple-dose conditions with multiple stimulants (Elia, Borcherding, Rapoport, & Keysor, 1991), parallel designs (Spencer et al., 1995), use of a common definition of response as normalization (Abikoff & Gittelman, 1985; Rapport, Denney, DuPaul, & Gardner, 1994). These trials now address psychostimulant responses in adolescents (Klorman, Brumagham, Fitzpatrick, & Burgstedt, 1990), adults (Spencer et al., 1995), mentally challenged (Horn et al., 1991) ADHD subjects with anxiety disorders and internalizing disorders, and ADHD subjects with tic disorders (Gadow et al., 1995). As shown in Table 9.2 (on pages 9-10 and 9-11), 70 percent of ADHD subjects in these more recent RCTs respond to stimulants and less than 10 percent to placebo.

Data on RCTs on the treatment of ADHD involving stimulants compared to treatments other than placebo can be found in a 1997 report prepared by McMaster Evidence-based Practice Center, which was supported by the Agency for Health Care Policy (Jadad & Atkins, 2000). Beginning with a search yield of 2,402 citations, the review selected seventy-six RCTs of treatments other than stimulant versus placebo for analysis. Twenty-two studies were identified comparing the stimulants—DEX, MPH, and PEM—and found no significant overall differences. Five studies compared stimulants to nondrug interventions, suggesting that MPH may be more effective. An additional eighteen studies evaluated combination therapies—adding another therapy to stimulants—and found no advantage for the combination. This review did not include the most recent large studies cited in this report. Thirteen studies examined treatment of ADHD that lasted longer than three months—not including the four studies in this chapter (see later)—and found advantages for improving behavior as long as a stimulant is taken but no improvement in academics. Thirty-two reports from twenty-nine studies focused on the adverse effects of stimulant treatments and suggested that side effects from stimulants are mild, of short duration, and respond to dosing or timing adjustments. However, the majority of these side effect reports are from short-term trials and are subject to self-selection biases—patients with severe side effects may drop out.

Studies also have attempted to study stimulant nonresponders. A study conducted at the National Institute of Mental Health in a day hospital found that the 32 percent nonresponse rate to a single psychostimulant dropped to less than 4 percent when two stimulants, DEX and MPH, were titrated sequentially in the same subject (Elia et al., 1991).

BENEFITS OF STIMULANT MEDICATIONS

Amelioration of Disruptive Behaviors

Stimulants have been shown in controlled studies to ameliorate disruptive ADHD behaviors cross-situationally (classroom, playground, and home) when repeatedly administered throughout the day:

- *In the classroom*, stimulants decrease interrupting, fidgetiness, and finger tapping and increase on-task behavior (Abikoff & Hechtman, 1998).

- *On the playground*, stimulants reduce overt (Gadow, Nolan, Sverd, Sprafkin, & Paolicelli, 1990) aggression, covert (Hinshaw, Heller, & McHale, 1992) aggression, and signs of conduct disorder (Klein et al., 1997) and increase attention during baseball (Richters et al., 1995).

- *At home,* stimulants improve parent-child interactions, on-task behaviors, and compliance.

- *In social settings*, stimulants ameliorate peer nomination rankings of social standing.

Improvement of Cognitive Functioning

Stimulants decrease response variability and impulsive responding on cognitive tasks (Tannock, Schachar, & Logan, 1995b), increase the accuracy of performance, and improve short-term memory, reaction time, seatwork computation, problem-solving games with peers (Whalen et al., 1989), and sustained attention. Studies of time-action stimulant effects show a different pattern of improvement for behavioral and for attentional symptoms, with behavior affected more than attention (Swanson et al., 1998). For example, a controlled, analog classroom trial ($n = 30$) of Adderall (Swanson et al., 1998) revealed rapid improvements on teacher ratings and math performance one and a half hours after administration, with time of peak effects and duration of action dependent on dose. While stimulant drugs show a large 0.8–1.0 effect size for behavioral measures, smaller effect sizes (0.6–0.8) are reported on cognitive measures (Spencer, Biederman, Wilens, et al., 1996).

Placebo vs. Medication Response

Children with ADHD demonstrate low placebo response rate during clinical drug trials, ranging between 3 percent and 30 percent (Gillberg et al., 1997), with a mode of 10 percent. This leads to large placebo-active drug differences, enabling small-N, single-site controlled trial designs to identify significant drug effects. The drugs' very short elimination half-lives make stimulants highly eligible for crossover designs

Table 9.2
Controlled Stimulant Studies (*N* = 1702) Showing Efficacy for ADHD Symptoms

Study (Year)	*N*	Age Range	Design	Drug(Dose)	Duration	Response	Comment
Abikoff & Gittelman (1985)	28	6–12	ADHDx	MPH Controls (PB, 41 mg)	8 weeks	80.9%	ADHD kids normalized
Abikoff & Hechtman (1998)	103	6–12	ADHD	MPH (33.7 mg) tid	2 years	100% 2.7 SD	Multisite, multimodal study. All children on MPH.
Barkley et al. (1989)	74	6–13	Xover	MPH 37 agg (PB, 0.3) 37 non-agg (PB, 0.5)	4 weeks	80%	Agg = nonaggressive ADHD response
Barkley et al. (1991)	40	6–12	Xover	MPH BID 23 ADHD (5, 10, 15 BID) 17 ADHD-W PB BID	6 weeks	ADHD 95% ADHD-W 76%	Fewer ADHD-W respond, need low dose
Castellanos et al. (1997)	20b	6–13	Xover	MPH 45mgbid DEX 22.5 mg bid	9 weeks	ADHD + TS	Tics dose-related
Douglas et al. (1988)	19	7–13	Xover	MPH (PB, 0.15, 0.3, 0.6)	2 weeks	100%*	Linear D/R relationships
Douglas et al. (1995)	17	6–11	Xover	MPH (0.3, 0.6, 0.9) PB	4 weeks	behavior 70%	No cognitive toxicity at high doses, Linear D/R curves
DuPaul & Rapoport (1993)	31	6–12	Xover	MPH 31 ADHD (20 mg) 25 normals PB BID	6 weeks	behavior 78% attention 61% Efficient 75%	MPH can normalize classroom behavior 25% of ADHD Ss didn't normalize academics
DuPaul (1994)	40	6–12	Xover	MPH 12 high internal (5, 10, 15 mg) 17 mid internal PB 11 low	6 weeks	High 68% nor Mid 70% nor Low 82% nor	25% in internalizing group deteriorated on meds ADHD Ss with comorbid int disorders less to be normalized or to respond to MPH
Elia et. al. (1991)	48	6–12	Xover	MPH (0.5; 0.8, 1.5) PB BID DEX (0.25, 0.5, 0.75)	6 weeks	MPH 79% DEX 86%	Response rate for two stim = 96%
Gadow et al. (1995)	34	6–12	Xover ADHD + tic Disorder	MPH (0.1,0.3,0.5) PB BID	8 weeks	100% behavior	No nonresponders to behavior; MD's Increases 2 min MD rating of motor tics. Only shows effects of 8 wks treatment.
Gillberg et al. (1997)	62	6–12	Parallel	Amp (17mg) PB BID	60 weeks	70% respond 27–40% impr	No dropouts but only 25% placebo grp at 15-month assessment.

Doses listed as mg/kg/dose, and medication is given twice daily unless otherwise stated. * = MPH responders selected. Abbreviations: PB = placebo; Xover = crossover design; Anx = child has comorbid anxiety disorder; ADHD = attention deficit/ hyperactivity disorder; MPH = Methylphenidate; DEX = dextroamphetamine; PEM = pemoline; AMP = d,l-amphetamine; mg/kg/d = dosage in milligram/kilogram/day.

**Table 9.2
(Continued)**

Study (Year)	N	Age Range	Design	Drug(Dose)	Duration	Response	Comment
Klorman et al. (1990)	48	12–18	Xover	MPH TID (0.26) PB BID	6 weeks	MPH 60%	Less med benefits for adolescents
Klein et al. (1997)	84	6–15	Parallel	MPH BID (1.0)	5 weeks	MPH 59–78%	MPH reduced ratings of anti-social behaviors Pb 9–29%
MTA Group (1999)	579	7–9	Parallel	MPH TID (< 0.8)	4 weeks (14mo)	MPH 77% DEX 10% None 13%	Titration Trial for multisite multimodal study. Full study data for 288 on 38.7 mg MPH
Musten et al. (1997)	31	4–6	Xover	MPH BID (0.3, 0.5)	3 weeks	MPH > NA	MPH improves attention, not compliance
Pelham et al. (1990)	22	8–13	Xover	MPH 10 BID; PB BID; DEX span 10 mg PEM 56.25 daily	24 days	stim 68%	DEX span, PEM best for behavior. 27% did best on DEX; 18% on SR; 18% on PEM; 5% on MPH BID
Pelham et al. (1995)	28	5–12	Xover	PEM (18.75,37.5, 75, 112.5 mg) PB, once daily dosing	7 weeks	PEM resp 89% PB resp 0%	PEM dose > 37.5 mg/day act 2–7 hr. period. Efficacy and time course = MPH
Rapport et al. (1988)	22	6–10	Xover	MPH (PB, 5, 10, 15 mg)	5 weeks	72%	MPH response same in 2 settings.
Rapport et al. (1994)	76	6–12	Xover	MPH (5, 10, 15, 20 mg) PB BID	5 weeks	94% beh 53% att	MPH normalizes behavior > academics. Higher doses better, linear D/R curve
Schachar (1998)	91	6–12	Parallel	MPH (33.5 mg) PB BID	52 weeks	0.7 SD	15% side effects: affective, overfocusing. Led to dropouts
Spencer et al. (1995)	23	18–60	Xover	MPH (1 mg/kg/d)	7weeks	78% PB 4%	MPH at 1 mg/kg/d produces improvement equivalent to that seen from MPH in kids
Swanson et al. (1998)	29	7–14	Xover	Adderall (5, 10, 15, 20, Pb, MPH)	7 weeks	100%*	Adderall peaks at 3 hrs, MPH at 1.5 hrs
Tannock (1995)	40	6–12	Xover	MPH (0.3, 0.6, 0–9) 22 ADHD 17 ADHD-Anx	2 weeks	70%activ	Activity level better in both groups; 80% working memory not better in anxious
Tannock et al. (1995)	28	6–12	Xover	MPH (0.3, 0.6, 0.9) PB	2 weeks	70%	Effects on behavior D/R curve linear, but effects on resp inhibition U-shaped suggest adjust dose on obj measures
Taylor et al. (1987)	38	6–10	Xover	MPH (PB, 0.2–1.4)	6 weeks	58%	Severe ADHD sx, better response
Whalen et al. (1989)	25	6.3–12	Xover	MPH(PB, 0.3,0.5)	5 weeks	48–72%	MPH helps, not normalizes, peer status

Doses listed as mg/kg/dose, and medication is given twice daily unless otherwise stated. * = MPH responders selected. Abbreviations: PB = placebo; Xover = crossover design; Anx = child has comorbid anxiety disorder; ADHD = attention deficit/ hyperactivity disorder; MPH = Methylphenidate; DEX = dextroamphetamine; PEM = pemoline; AMP = d,l-amphetamine; mg/kg/d = dosage in milligram/kilogram/day.

(Swanson et al., 1998), because pharmacokinetic carryover of active drug into placebo periods is unlikely.

The beneficial effects of stimulants on behavior and attention have also been shown in children with no mental disorder (Rapoport et al., 1980); thus the response to stimulants is not diagnostically specific for ADHD. Stimulant medications continue to play a therapeutic role in other medical conditions, such as narcolepsy and depression (Goldman et al., 1998).

EFFICACY OF LONG-DURATION STIMULANT PREPARATIONS

The main limitation of stimulant medications—the short duration of action of the immediate release preparations—has spurred the development of sustained-release preparations.

Sustained-release preparations have been marketed for DEX and for MPH (Whitehouse, Shah, & Palmer, 1980). MPH's sustained-release preparation is available only at 20 mg strength, and DEX spansules in 5, 10, and 15 mg strengths. Ritalin-SR uses a wax-matrix vehicle for slow release, while dextroamphetamine "spansule" is a capsule containing small medication particles.

The efficacy of the long-acting preparations is controversial. A controlled study of nine children with ADHD reported that DEX spansules and tablets produced identical duration of behavioral effects over twelve hours, despite the spansule's high plasma levels (Brown et al., 1980). One center published an initial report that MPH-SR20 was judged to be less effective than MPH-IR 10 mg BID (twice a day) for the treatment of ADHD children ($N = 13$) in a summer program (Pelham et al., 1987). In a later study (Page et al., 1974), the same investigators reported that MPH-SR20, PEM, and DEX spansules were equally effective on a laboratory task of attention over a nine-hour period. In a six-week, double-blind, crossover study of thirty-four children with ADDH, no differences in teacher's ratings or on performance on a CPT were detected six hours after ingestion of a single SR20 tablet or 10 mg of standard MPH, 8 A.M. and noon, yet all the children stopped responding to the MPH-SR within six months (Fried, Greenhill, Torres, Martin, & Solomon, 1987).

Clinicians in office practice find MPH-SR less effective, and combine it with MPH-IR, even though this combination was not found to be more effective than MPH-SR alone (Fitzpatrick, Klorman, Brumaghim, & Borgstedt, 1992). The reports from the Summer Treatment Program (STP) may have benefited the MPH-SR reports because it is far more structured than a standard schoolday (8 A.M. to 3 P.M.). Yet the second STP study results agree with the results reported by others (Fried et al., 1987; Safer, 1994), which found the two types of preparations equally effective. A group of forty-two children with ADHD were studied in a parallel-design, double-blind eight-week study comparing MPH 10 mg BID, MPH SR-20, and placebo (Aman & Turbott, 1991). Despite the differences in CMAX (maximum blood level concentration) between MPH SR-20 and MPH 10 mg BID, no differences were seen in CPT performance, motor activity levels, or teacher's reports for the two groups. Thus, even though the controlled studies as a whole show that MPH-SR is equally effective as MPH-IR, clinicians find the long-duration MPH less effective, and it shows only a 14 percent market share of all stimulants sold. Table 9.3 summarizes these reports.

Table 9.3
Sustained Release Stimulant Preparations: Efficacy

Study (Year)	N	Age (yrs)	Long-Acting Drug	Study Design	Daily Dose	Efficacy
Brown et al. (1980)	9	5–12	Dex SPANXPb	Crossover	0.5 mg/kg	Effect < 3hrs
Whitehouse (1980)	30	5–12	MPH-SR	Parallel MPHSR20 x MPH	MPH10mg BID MPH-SR 20q A.M.	Equivalent
Pelham et al. (1987)	13	7–11	MPH-SR	Crossover MPHSR20 x MPH X Placebo	MPH10mg BID MPH-SR 20q A.M.	MPH-SR late onset MPH > MPH-SR20
Greenhill et al. (1996)	38	7–12	MPH-SR	Crossover MPHSR20 x MPH X Placebo	MPH10 mg BID MPH-SR 20q A.M.	MPH = MPH-SR20
Birmaher et al. (1989)	17	8–12	MPH-SR	Open Study	MPH-SR20 MPH 1 mg/kg	MPH higher concentr > MPH-SR20
Pelham et al. (1990)	22	8–13	MPH-SR, DEX Pemoline	Crossover Dex x MPH-SR x PEM x MPH x Placebo	MPH-SR20 MPH 10 mg BID DEX span 10 Pemoline 56.5	All Drugs > PB
Greenhill (2002)	42	8–12	MPH-SR20	Parallel MPH-SR20 x X MPH 10 mg BID x Placebo	MPH-SR20, 40 MPH 10 mg BID	MPHSR = MPH > PB
Fitzpatrick et al. (1992)	19	6.8–11.5	MPH-SR20	Crossover MPH-SR20 x X MPH10 BID x Combination Combined SR + Regular	MPH-SR20 MPH 10 mg BID	All drugs = All > PB
TOTAL	190				MPH-SR20 = MPH	

LIMITATIONS OF SHORT-TERM STIMULANT TRIALS

When the four marketed stimulants were developed—more than twenty years ago—most Phase I (safety) and Phase II (dosing and early efficacy) data were collected in animals and adults. As a result, modern New Drug Application (NDA) Phase I studies (e.g., effect of fatty diet on absorption and basic pharmacokinetics in children), Phase II studies (e.g., combined pharmacokinetic/pharmacodynamic), or Phase III studies (e.g., population pharmacokinetics) were not carried out for those stimulants now in use for children with ADHD.

Without the demands of the NDA approval process, the stimulant trials published in the last decade did not consistently use design features or analytic approaches employed in multisite RCTs submitted to the Food and Drug Administration (FDA) for drug approval. For example, the ethnicity of the sample was not mentioned, nor were representative child patient samples included that would allow the findings to be generalizable. Most studies lasted less than twelve weeks (Schachar & Tannock, 1993) and thus could not inform maintenance treatment of children with ADHD. Most used relatively small sample sizes and lacked controls treated intensively with a nonmedication therapy. Most did not individually titrate medication doses to optimize each child's response. Many studies did not report comorbid disorders, which can alter the response to medication.

Other studies did not report the fidelity with which the treatments were administered by staff, nor did they always list results of the compliance measures used (Richters et al., 1995). Other details were not listed by most studies, such as the exact method of randomization (including a central randomization group apart from the site) and details of dropouts. Few, if any, of the current RCTs are parallel designs, which can really test to see whether placebo response emerges at some point over the entire drug trial. Few treatment studies prescreen for placebo responders; thus the numbers of actual medication responders in any sample of ADHD children might be closer to 55 percent, not the 75–96 percent often quoted. Furthermore, these estimates apply to group effects, and do not inform the clinician about the individual patient. Table 9.4 (on pages 9-16 and 9-17) details the methodological strengths and limitations of the twenty-four most recent stimulant RCTs.

LONG-TERM RANDOMIZED CONTROLLED TRIALS OF STIMULANT MEDICATIONS

Although short-duration stimulant studies have shown robust efficacy, their effects last only as long as the patient continues medication. ADHD is a chronic disorder lasting many years; thus maintenance treatment constitutes the main component of care. Unfortunately, most stimulant RCTs last less than three months, with only twenty-two published studies lasting longer (Schachar & Tannock, 1993). Until recently, most of these long-duration studies were severely constrained by their retrospective methods, lack of nonstandard outcome measures, irregular prescribing patterns (Sherman, 1991), and lack of compliance measures. More recently, long-duration trials have been conducted to show maintenance of stimulant medication effects over periods ranging from twelve months (Gillberg et al., 1997) to twenty-four months (Abikoff & Hechtman, 1998).

The MTA Study

MTA Study Design. The National Institute of Mental Health (NIMH) Multimodal Treatment Study of Children with Attention Deficit Hyperactivity Disorder (MTA Study) was established to compare the effects of four randomly assigned, fourteen-month treatments of children with ADHD:

- Stimulants alone (Med Mgt);
- Behavioral interventions (Beh);

- Stimulants in combination with behavioral interventions (Comb); or

- Assessment and referral to routine community care (CC).

The study addressed the following questions, among others: (1) Do psychosocial and medication treatments result in comparable levels of improvement at study end? (2) Do participants assigned to Comb show higher levels of improvement at study end than those assigned to either Med Mgt or Beh alone? (3) Do participants assigned to any of the three MTA intensive treatments (Med Mgt, Beh, Comb) show greater improvement at study end than those assigned to CC? The moderating effect of baseline patient characteristics on treatment response was also evaluated. To have sufficient power to address these questions, it used a large sample size of 576 children with ADHD gathered at multiple performance sites (Arnold et al., 1997; Richters et al., 1995).

The MTA Study's design addresses design and implementation limitations of the small-numbered, single-site, crossover design, short-duration trials now in the pediatric psychopharmacology stimulant literature. The MTA Study has a rigorous, controlled methodology enhanced by its NIMH-based study management, randomization procedure, data cleaning, and analysis, all conducted away from the performance sites. Unlike any ADHD treatment study that precedes it, the randomization is run offsite, allowing concealment of allocation—hiding of randomization choice until the very last minute. Other methodological refinements include implementation of manuals to guide each treatment, cross-site weekly teleconference panels, audiotaped monitoring of treatment fidelity, and the multiple compliance check of each treatment. This adds an unusual amount of quality control to this child psychiatry trial, elevating it above the standards imposed by the FDA for new drug development. The medication treatment arm, which proved to be effective, built on the field's best methodology—optimization of each child's dose, three-times daily dosing, using multiple informants to guide individual treatment decisions over the one year of maintenance, manualized support, the use of algorithms, a prominent aspect of adult psychopharmacology.

Stimulant medication management in the MTA Study involved five elements:

1. Treatment began with a careful initial titration with MPH (Greenhill et al., 1996), followed by thirteen months of maintenance office management.

2. The MPH was prescribed on a three-times daily schedule, so that benefits would be seen both at school and at home, potentially enhancing parental compliance for medication administration.

3. MTA pharmacotherapists performed monthly clinical assessments, based on ratings from the child's parent and teacher, and discussed their findings in weekly national teleconferences—the MTA Cross-Site Psychopharmacology Panel (CSPP)—with all the other MTA sites.

4. Manualized algorithms guided dosage adjustments and the systematic testing of other drugs—if needed to achieve an adequate response. The order in which medications were tried was methylphenidate, dextroamphetamine, pemoline, imipramine, then other drugs as determined by the CSPP. Deviations from the foregoing order required prior CSPP approval.

Table 9.4
Design Features of Randomized Controlled Trials of Stimulants in Children

Study	Design	New?	Duration	Dosing	Ethnic?	Comorbid?	Impairment?	Multiple Domains	Compliance?	ITT	History?	Setting
Abikoff et al. (1985)	Xover	No	8 weeks	Opt/BID	N/A	N/A	N/A	School only	N/A	N/A	N/A	School
Abikoff et al. (1998)	Parallel	Yes	104 wks	Opt/TID	Yes	Yes	Yes, C-GAS	Yes	Saliva Levels	Yes	Respon	Clinic
Barkley et al. (1989)	Xover	No	4 wks	Fix/OD	N/A	N/A	N/A	Yes	Pill counts	No	No	Clinic
Barkley et al. (1991)	Xover	No	6 wks	Fix/BID	N/A	N/A	N/A	Yes	Pill counts	N/A	N/A	Clinic
Castellanos et al. (1997)	Xover	Yes	9 wks	Fix/BID	Boys	Yes; TS	Yes, C-GAS	Yes	Staff Adm	N/A	Yes	Lab
Douglas et al. (1988)	Xover	No	2 wks	Fix/OD	N/A	Yes	N/A	Yes	Staff Adm	N/A	Respon	Lab
Douglas et al. (1995)	Xover	No	4 wks	Fix/OD	N/A	N/A	N/A	Yes	Staff Adm	N/A	N/A	Clinic
DuPaul & Rapoport (1993)	Xover	No	6 wks	Fix/BID	N/A	N/A	N/A	No, School	Staff Adm	N/A	N/A	Clinic
DuPaul et al. (1994)	Xover	No	6 wks	Fix/OD	N/A	N/A	N/A	No, School	Parent report	N/A	N/A	Clinic
Elia et al. (1991)	Xover	No	9 wks	Fix/BID	boys;n/a	Yes	CGAS	Yes	Staff Administer	N/A	Yes	Lab
Gadow et al. (1995)	Xover	No	8 wks	Fix/BID	Yes	Yes	N/A	ADHD,	Pill counts	N/A	Yes	Clinic
Gillberg et al. (1997)	Parallel	Yes	60 wks	Opt/OD	Yes	Yes	N/A	Yes	Pill counts	Yes	Yes	Clinic
Klein et al. (1997)	Parallel	Yes	5 wks	Opt/BID	N/A	Yes	N/A	Yes	N/A	No	N/A	Clinic
Klorman et al. (1990)	Xover	No	3 wks	Fix/TID	Yes	Yes	N/A	Yes	Staff Administer	N/A	Yes	Clinic

Study	Design	New?	Duration	Dosing	Ethnic?	Comorbid?	Impairment?	Multiple Domains	Compliance?	ITT	History?	Setting
MTA Group (1999)	Parallel	Yes	56 wks	Opt/TID*	Yes	Yes	Yes	Yes	Saliva levels	Yes	Yes	Clinic
Musten et al. (1997)	Xover	No	3 wks	Fix/BID	No	Yes	N/A	Yes	Pill counts	n-a	N/A	Clinic
Pelham et al. (1990)	Xover	No	4 wks	Fix/OD	N/A	Yes	N/A	Yes	Staff administer	n-a	Yes	STP
Pelham et al. (1995)	Xover	No	7 wks	Fix/OD	N/A	N/A	N/A	Yes	Staff administer	n-a	N/A	"Lab"
Rapport et al. (1988)	Xover	No	5 wks	Fix/OD	N/A	N/A	N/A	School, Lab	Staff administer	n-a	Respon	Lab
Rapport et al. (1994)	Xover	No	6 wks	Fix/OD	Yes	N/A	N/A	School	Envelope counts	n-a	Yes	Clinic
Schachar (1998)	Parallel	Yes	52 wks	Opt	N/A	N/A	N/A	School/Home	Pill counts	N/A	Yes	Clinic
Spencer et al. (1995)	Xover	No	7wks	Fix/TID	N/A	N/A	N/A	ADHD, Dep, Anx	Serum samples	n-a	N/A	Clinic
Swanson et al. (1998)	Xover	Yes	7 wks	Fix/OD	N/A	N/A	N/A	N/A	Staff administer	n-a	Yes	Lab
Tannock et al. (1995a)	Xover	No	4 days	Fix/OD	N/A	Yes	N/A	Cognitive	Staff administer	n-a	Yes	Lab
Tannock al. (1995b)	Xover	No	5 days	Fix/OD	N/A	Yes (Anx)	N/A	Cognitive	Staff administer	n-a	Yes	Lab
Taylor et al. (1987)	Xover	No	6 wks	Opt/Flex	boys;n/a	No	N/A	Yes	N/A	n-a	N/A	Clinic
Whalen et al. (1989)	Xover	No	5 wks	Fix/BID	boys;n/a	Yes	N/A	Peer judgment	Staff administer	n-a	N/A	STP

Legend. Design = type of design (i.e., did study use a parallel design?); New? = did study include a new method for handling placebo?; Duration = length of study (e.g., did study exceed the 3 months in duration?); dosing = type of dosing (fixed, did study optimize child's dose?); ethnic = did study indicate whether it used representative samples (mention ethnicity)?; comorbid = did study evaluate comorbidity?; impairment = did study use measure of impairment? Multiple domains = did study use multi-informant, multidomain outcome measures?; compliance = did study measure fidelity or compliance?; ITT = did study use intent-to-treat measures; History = does study include a measure of previous stimulant treatment history?; setting = study in clinic, laboratory, or STP; N/A = not addressed in the journal article. * = daily switching of stimulant dose; Abbreviations: Xover = crossover design; wks = weeks; fix = fixed dose; Opt = each child on his/her optimal dose; OD = once a day; BID = twice daily; TID = three times daily; n-a = Not applicable; CGAS = Children's Global Assessment Scale; Anx = children had a comorbid diagnosis of anxiety.

5. Each pharmacotherapist provided encouragement or brief advice to parents—but not behavior therapy—and reading material from an approved list.

These MTA medication treatments could be readily delivered in a pediatric or psychiatric setting without extensive behavior therapy expertise.

Study Outcome. The MTA study outcome showed that carefully managed stimulant medication was highly effective. Robust differences between stimulants alone and behavioral intervention were seen from two different informants—parents and teachers. Parents' and teachers' ratings of inattention and hyperactivity-impulsivity showed superiority for children on medication. Stimulants in combination with behavioral interventions and stimulants-alone treatment conditions were superior to behavioral intervention alone for improvements in ADHD symptoms, social skills, and oppositional-aggressive behaviors. Stimulants in combination with behavioral interventions tended to be superior to stimulants alone in lowering children's anxiety symptoms, but for parents' ratings only. For parent and teacher ratings of children's ADHD symptoms, subjects who received stimulants in combination with behavioral interventions and those who received stimulants alone had baseline scores that improved during treatment by 1.5 to 1.8 standard deviations (SD), compared to 0.9 to 1.2 SD changes in subjects who received behavioral interventions alone or who were assessed and referred to routine community care.

Overall MTA results indicate that long-term combined and medication-only treatments reduce ADHD, oppositional-aggressive, and internalizing symptoms, while enhancing children's social skills. Medication management reduces not just classic ADHD symptoms but also problems due to poor social skills or anxiety—areas less well established as medication treatment targets.

MTA Study's Answers to Treatment Questions. The MTA stands as the landmark study in the half-century history of randomized clinical trials of stimulant treatments for children with ADHD. It is the largest and most methodologically sophisticated randomized multisite trial in a mature treatment field, comparing therapeutic strategies that have been shown previously to be effective in simpler two arm (active vs. placebo) controlled studies (Pelham, 1989; Pelham & Murphy, 1986). Because of its size, the MTA is able to address key treatment questions that could not be answered by the many previous small-numbered, less-than-three-month, single-site, controlled two-arm crossover studies:

1. It shows that the robust efficacy from stimulant medication can be realized across diverse settings and patient groups, and can be maintained during chronic therapy lasting more than a year. These findings replicate those reported by the other long-duration stimulant trials: the New York/Montreal (Abikoff & Hechtman, 1998), Schachar (1998), and Gillberg et al. (1997) studies. In addition, the MTA is the first large-scale, parallel design, multisite, large-numbered trial of stimulants that meets all the rigorous criteria for a pivotal efficacy trial required by the FDA for approval of new drug.

2. Adding psychosocial interventions to stimulant treatments—creating a multimodal intervention, the current "gold standard" for ADHD treatment—yielded few benefits. This replicates the findings from the New York/Montreal study.

3. Third, despite the prediction that extending multidomain, intensive psychosocial interventions over a long duration would increase their efficacy (Hinshaw, Abikoff, & Klein, 1998), the MTA's purely behavioral treatment for ADHD did not equal the effects of stimulants, and did no better than community standard care. The MTA was not able to replicate the findings of Klein et al. (1997) that intensive classroom behavioral modification treatments of ADHD using token economies matched MPH in efficacy (Gittleman, 1987). This may have been due to the measurement of treatment effects of psychosocial intervention when it was being faded, whereas the measurement of medication effects were done while the child with ADHD was still taking medication.

Taken together, these MTA Study findings will have direct relevance for clinicians and policymakers. For the future, the MTA's multisite, parallel design RCT using manualized treatments will set a high standard for trials of new treatments for childhood ADHD.

Other Long-Term Studies

In addition to the MTA Study, there have been three stimulant medication RCTs completed that have lasted twelve months or longer (Abikoff & Hechtman, 1998; Arnold et al., 1997; Schachar, 1998). As shown in Table 9.5, these have been large studies (numbering 62–579 patients) of parallel designs and long duration and have each shown robust treatment effects for stimulants.

Collectively, these studies show a persistence of medication effects over time, in contrast to earlier reports. Within-subject effect sizes reported after twelve to twenty-four months of MPH treatment resembled those previously reported in short-duration studies (Elia et al., 1991; Thurber & Walker, 1983). Domain of greatest improvement differs among studies, with some (Gillberg et al., 1997) showing greater effects at home and others (Schachar, 1998) showing greater effects at school. The total mean MPH daily doses reported by three long duration studies ranged between 33 and 37.5 mg. Family-initiated treatment discontinuation was associated with persistent stimulant drug side effects or assignment to placebo treatment. Surprisingly, attrition from placebo assignment is slow, allowing ample time for standard eight-week efficacy trials to be conducted.

ISSUES FOR PRACTITIONERS

Do the Research Findings Inform Practice?

Although there is a large database of controlled stimulant medication studies attesting to the overall efficacy and safety of these medications in children with ADHD, most data are group based and do not inform the clinician about fine points of management for the individual patient (Greenhill et al., 1996). Practical issues of managing the individual patient—such as the best dose to initiate treatment for young children, identifying the optimal stimulant drug for preschoolers, determining whether twice-daily or three-times daily dosing is best, choosing to increase, decrease, or keep the stimulant dose the same across the day, and whether to stop stimulants at the first sign of a motor tic—remain unanswered in current research designs.

The individual practitioner must make key decisions when treating an individual

Table 9.5
Long Duration Stimulant Clinical Trials in Medication-Only Treatment Arm: Within-Subjects Effects

Study (Year)	Med. Only Number (Study Total)	Design (Drug)	Duration (Months)	Compliance	Total mg Daily Dose (schedule)	Measure	Effect Size at Study End in SD
Abikoff et al. (1998)	33 (103)	Parallel RCT (MPH)	24	Saliva levels	33.7 (TID)	Teacher CTRS	2.7
Gilberg et al. (1997)	56 (62)	Double-blind Discont-inuation RCT (DEX)	15	N/A	17 (BID) Amphetamine	Teacher CTRS Hyper-activity	27–40%*
Schachar (1998)	24 (91)	Parallel RCT (MPH)	12	Pill counts	33.5 (BID)	Telephone interview probe	0.7
MTA Group (1998)	133 (576)	Parallel RCT (MPH)	14	Saliva levels Pill counts	38.7 mg (TID)	SNAP Teacher Hyperactivity	1.5–1.8

* Effect size presented as percentage.

patient, often without an authoritative answer or direction from the research literature. Selection of the proper stimulant for a particular patient is hampered by the inability to predict response from patient characteristics (Buitelaar, Gary, Swaab-Barneveld, & Kuiper, 1995); domain-dependent dose response characteristics (Pelham & Milich, 1991); lack of consistent therapeutic effects across the IQ range (Aman, Marks, Turbott, Wilsher, & Merry, 1991); the effects of other comorbid Axis I disorders on stimulant response (Pliszka, 1992); the short, time-action effects of stimulants with rapid changes during schoolday (Swanson, Kinsbourne, Roberts, & Zucker, 1978); the hepatoxicity of pemoline (Berkovitch et al., 1995); and the potential abuse liability of psychostimulants. Similarly, they rely on averaged group data to evaluate medication effects, possibly missing important subgroup differences in treatment response.

Limitations of Available Stimulants

Response/Dosing Issues. Even with their robust efficacy and strong safety records, stimulant medication treatments may not be ideal for every child with ADHD. Not all children respond to the first stimulant given. Twenty-three percent of the 288 children titrated with MPH in the MTA Study showed no response to methylphenidate over placebo (13 percent with powerful responses to placebo, and 10 percent with no response to either methylphenidate or to placebo). Immediate-release (IR) MPH tablets have a four-hour duration of action, requiring dosing during school, by school personnel (Swanson et al., 1998). This in turn leads to peer ridicule and irregular supervision by busy school personnel.

Time-action effects can produce drug wear-off during the late morning, mid-afternoon, or evening with return of the ADHD symptoms. Given too late in the day, stimulants suppress appetite at dinner and delay sleep onset. As a result, parents are reluctant to use stimulants late in the day to help with evening homework inattention and noncompliance. Longer-acting pemoline treatment is hampered by concerns about hepatotoxicity appearing late during chronic treatment. The efficacy of combination IR and sustained-release stimulant preparations, though popular in practice, has been tested in only one controlled study and found no different than monotherapy (Fitzpatrick et al., 1992). Further, these drugs show differential responses across settings and domains in the same child (Pelham & Milich, 1991), made all the more problematic because reliable predictors of drug response are not available (Jacobvitz et al., 1990).

Side Effects. The most troublesome stimulant side effects, including anorexia, weight loss, headaches, insomnia, and tics, do affect many children and do not improve over time (Schachar, 1998). Also, MPH and DEX are classified as schedule II medications with presumed high abuse potential with severe psychic or physical dependence liability.

RECOMMENDATIONS

The percentage of U.S. youth being treated with psychostimulants still remains within the estimates of the prevalence of ADHD. However, this does not ensure that the children with ADHD are the only ones receiving MPH treatment. A recent American Medical Asscociation Council report concluded that more cases are being recognized and treated, and the duration of treatment with stimulants is increasing (Goldman et al., 1998). Other surveys suggest that ADHD is being misdiagnosed at times, perhaps because the evaluation is not long or thorough enough, or does not follow recently published guidelines (Dulcan, 1997).

Within the caveats of careful diagnostic evaluations, rigorous titration, and systematic maintenance, the stimulant medications can be strongly recommended. Their safety, dosing and efficacy are the best studied of all psychopharmacological treatments across the lifespan (Spencer, Biederman, Wilens, et al., 1996). Stimulant medication provides short-term behavioral and academic improvement, but children must remain on stimulants long term to maintain the benefits found in the latest controlled studies lasting up to two years. The risk-benefit of stimulant treatment in ADHD has been determined to be highly favorable (Goldman et al., 1998) but must be monitored on a continuous basis over time.

References

Abikoff, H., Ganeles, D., Reiter, G., Blum, C., Foley, C., & Klein, R. (1988). Cognitive training in academically deficient ADDH boys receiving stimulant medication. *Journal of Abnormal Child Psychology, 16*(4), 411–432.

Abikoff, H., & Gittelman, R. (1985). Hyperactive children treated with stimulants: Is cognitive training a useful adjunct? *Archives of General Psychiatry, 42*, 953–961.

Abikoff, H., & Hechtman, L. (1998). *Multimodal treatment for children with ADHD: Effects on ADHD and social behavior and diagnostic status.* Unpublished manuscript.

Aman, M., Marks, R., Turbott S., Wilsher, C., & Merry, S. (1991). Methylphenidate and thioridazine in intellectually subaverage children. Effects on cognitive-motor performance. *Journal of the American Academy of Child and Adolescent Psychiatry, 30*, 816—824.

Aman, M., & Turbott, S. (1991). Prediction of clinical response in children taking methylphenidate. *Journal of Autism and Developmental Disorders, 21*, 211–228.

Angold, A., Erkanli, A., Egger, H. L., & Costello, E. J. (2000). Stimulant treatment for children: A community perspective. *Journal of the American Academy of Child and Adolescent Psychiatry, 39*, 975–984.

Arnold, L. E., Abikoff, H. B., Cantwell, D. P., Conners, C. K., Elliott, G., Greenhill, L. L., Hechtman, L., Hinshaw, S. P., Hoza, B., Jensen, P. S., Kraemer, H., March, J., Newcorn, J., Pelham, W. E., Richters, J., Severe, J. B., Schiller, E., Swanson, J. M., Vereen, D., & Wells, K. (1997). National Institute of Mental Health Collaborative Multimodal Treatment Study of Children with ADHD (MTA): Design challenges and choices. *Archives of General Psychiatry, 54*, 865–870.

Arnold, L. E., Wender, P. W., McCloskey, K., & Snyder, S. H. (1972). Levoamphetamine and dextroamphetamine: Comparative efficacy in the hyperkinetic syndrome. *Archives of General Psychiatry, 27*(6), 816–824.

Barkley, R., DuPaul, G., & McMurray, M. (1991). Attention deficit disorder with and without hyperactivity: Clinical response to three dose levels of methylphenidate. *Pediatrics, 87*, 519–531.

Barkley, R., McMurray, M., Edelbrock, C., & Robbins, K. (1989). The response of aggressive and nonaggressive children to two doses of methylphenidate. *Journal of the American Academy of Child and Adolescent Psychiatry, 28*, 873–881.

Barkley, R., McMurray, M., Edelbrock, C., & Robbins, K. (1990). Side effects of MPH in children with attention deficit hyperactivity disorder: A systematic placebo-controlled evaluation. *Pediatrics, 86*, 184–192.

Berkovitch, M., Pope, E., Phillips, J., & Koren, G. (1995). Pemoline-associated fulminant liver failure: Testing the evidence for causation. *Clinical Pharmacology and Therapeutics, 57*, 696–698.

Birmaher, B. B., Greenhill, L., Cooper, T., Fried, J., & Maminski, B. (1989). Sustained release methylphenidate: Pharmacokinetic studies in ADDH males. *Journal of the American Academy of Child and Adolescent Psychiatry, 28*(5), 768–772.

Borcherding, B. G., Keysor, C. S., Cooper, T. B., & Rapoport, J. L. (1989). Differential effects of methylphenidate and dextroamphetamine on the motor activity level of hyperactive children. *Neuropsychopharmacology, 2*, 255–263.

Brown, G. L., Ebert, M. H., Mikkelsen, E. J., & Hunt, R. D. (1980). Behavior and motor activity response in hyperactive children and plasmas amphetamine levels following a sustained release preparation. *Journal of the American Academy of Child Psychiatry, 19*, 225–239.

Brown, G. L., Hunt, R. D., Ebert, M. H., Bunney, W. E., & Kopin, I. J. (1979). Plasma levels of d-amphetamine in hyperactive children: Serial behavior and motor responses. *Psychopharmacology, 62*, 133–140.

Buckner, C. K., Patil, P. N., Tye, A., & Malspeis, L. (1969). Steric aspects of adrenergic drugs. XII. Some peripheral effects of (+/-)-Erythyo-and (+/-)-threo-methylphenidate. *Journal of Pharmacology and Experimental Therapeutics, 166*, 308–319.

Buitelaar, J., Gary, R., Swaab-Barneveld, H., & Kuiper, M. (1995). Prediction of clinical response to methylphenidate in children with attention deficit hyperactivity disorder. *Journal of the American Academy of Child and Adolescent Psychiatry, 34*, 1025–1032.

Castellanos, X., Giedd, J., Elia, J., Marsh, W. L., Ritchie, G. F., Hamburger, S. D., & Rapoport, J. L. (1997). Controlled stimulant treatment of ADHD and comorbid Tourette's syndrome: Effects of stimulant and dose. *Journal of the American Academy of Child and Adolescent Psychiatry, 36*, 589–596.

Chan, Y. P., Swanson, J. M., Soldin, S. S., Thiessen, J. J., & Macleod, S. M. (1983). Methylphenidate hydrochloride given with or before breakfast: II. Effects on plasma concentration of methylphenidate and ritalinic acid. *Pediatrics, 72*(1), 56–59.

Collier, C., Soldin, S., Swanson, J., MacLeod, S., Weinberg, F., & Rochefort, J. (1985). Pemoline pharmacokinetics and long term therapy in children with attention deficit disorder and hyperactivity. *Clinical Pharamcokinetics, 10*, 269–277.

Cox, B. M. (1990). Drug tolerance and physical dependence. In W. B. Pratt & P. Taylor (Eds.), *Principles of drug action: The basis of pharmacology* (pp. 639–690). New York: Churchill Livingstone.

Diener, R. (1991). Toxicology of methylphenidate. In B. Osman & L. L. Greenhill (Eds.), *Ritalin: Theory and patient management* (pp. 435–455). New York: Mary Ann Liebert.

Douglas, V. I., Barr, R. G., Amin, K., O'Neill, M. E., & Britton, B. G. (1988). Dose effects and individual responsivity to methylphenidate in attention deficit disorder. *Journal of Child Psychology and Psychiatry, 29*, 453–475.

Douglas, V., Barr, R. G., Desilets, J., & Sherman, E. (1995). Do high doses of stimulants impair flexible thinking in ADHD? *Journal of the American Academy of Child and Adolescent Psychiatry, 34*, 877–885.

Dulcan, M. (1997). Practice parameters for the assessment and treatment of attention-deficit / hyperactivity disorder. *Journal of the Academy of Child and Adolescent Psychiatry, 36*, 85s–121s.

Dunnick, J., & Hailey, J. (1995). Experimental studies on the long-term effects of methylphenidate hydrochloride. *Toxicology, 103*, 77–84.

DuPaul, G., Barkley, R., & McMurray, M. (1994). Response of children with ADHD to methylphenidate: Interaction with internalizing symptoms. *Journal of the American Academy of Child and Adolescent Psychiatry, 33*(6), 894–903.

DuPaul, G., & Rapport, M. (1993). Does MPH normalize the classroom performance of children with attention deficit disorder? *Journal of the American Academy of Child and Adolescent Psychiatry, 32*, 190–198.

Elia, J., Borcherding, B., Rapoport, J., & Keysor, C. (1991). Methylphenidate and dextroamphetamine treatments of hyperactivity: Are there true non-responders? *Psychiatry Research, 36*, 141–155.

Faraj, B. A., Israili, Z. H., Perel, J. M., Jenkins, M. L., Holtzman, S. G., Cucinell, S. A., & Dayton, P. G. (1974). Metabolism and disposition of methylphenidate-14C: Studies in man and animals. *Journal of Pharmacology and Experimental Therapeutics, 210*, 422–428.

Fitzpatrick, P., Klorman, R., Brumaghim, J., & Borgstedt, A. (1992). Effects of sustained-release and standard preparations of methylphenidate on attention deficit disorder. *American Academy of Child and Adolescent Psychiatry, Scientific Proceedings of the Annual Meeting, 31*(2), 226–234.

Fried, J., Greenhill, LL., Torres, D., Martin, J., & Solomon, M. (1987). Sustained-release methylphenidate: Long-term clinical efficacy in ADDH males. *American Academy of Child and Adolescent Psychiatry, Scientific Proceedings of the Annual Meeting, 3*, 47.

Gadow, K. D., Nolan, E. E., Sverd, J., Sprafkin, J., & Paolicelli, L. (1990). Methylphenidate in aggressive-hyperactive boys: I. Effects on peer aggression in public school settings. *Journal of the American Academy of Child and Adolescent Psychiatry, 29*(5), 710–718.

Gadow, K., Sverd, J., Sprafkin, J., Nolan, E., & Ezor, S. (1995). Efficacy of methylphenidate for attention deficit hyperactivityin children with tic disorder. *Archives of General Psychiatry, 52*, 444–455.

Gillberg, C., Melander, H., von Knorring, A., Janols, L. O., Thernlund, G., Hagglof, B., Eidevall-Wallin, L., Gustafsson, K., & Kopp, S. (1997). Long-term central stimulant treatment of children with attention-deficit hyperactivity disorder. A randomized double-blind placebo-controlled trial. *Archives of General Psychiatry, 54*, 857–864.

Gittelman, K. (1987). Pharmacotherapy of childhood hyperactivity: An update. In H. Y. Meltzer (Ed.), *Psychopharmacology: The third generation of progress* (pp. 1215–1224). New York: Raven Press.

Gittelman, R., & Mannuzza, S. (1988). Hyperactive boys almost grown up: III. Methylphenidate effects on ultimate height. *Archives of General Psychiatry, 45*, 1131–1134.

Gittelman-Klein, R., Landa, B., Mattes, J. A., & Klein, D. F. (1988). Methylphenidate and growth in hyperactive children. *Archives of General Psychiatry, 45*, 1127–1130.

Goldman, L. S., Genei, M., Bazman, R., & Stanetz, P. (1998). Diagnosis and treatment of attention-deficit/hyperactivity disorder. *Journal of the American Medical Association, 279*, 1100–1107.

Greenhill, L. (2002). Childhood attention deficit hyperactivity disorder: Pharmacological treatments. In P. E. Nathan & J. Gorman (Eds.), *Treatments that work* (pp. 25–55). Philadephia: Saunders.

Greenhill, L. L., Abikoff, H. B., Arnold, L. E., Cantwell, D. P., Conners, C. K., Elliott, G., Hechtman, L., Hinshaw, S. P., Hoza, B., Jensen, P. S., March, J. S., Newcorn, J., Pelham, W. E., Severe, J. B., Swanson, J. M., Vitiello, B., & Wells, K. (1996). Medication treatment strategies in the MTA study: Relevance to clinicians and researchers. *Journal of the American Academy of Child and Adolescent Psychiatry, 35*, 1304–1313.

Hauger, R. L., Angel, L., Janowsky, A., Berger, P., & Hulihan-Gibin, B. (1990). Brain recognition sites for methylphenidate and amphetamines. In S. Deutsch, A. Weizman, & R. Weizman (Eds.), *Application of basic neuroscience to child psychiatry* (pp. 77–100). New York: Plenum Press.

Hinshaw, S., Abikoff, H., & Klein, R. (1998). Psychosocial treatments for attention-deficit hyperactivity disorder. In P. E. Nathan & J. Gorman (Eds.), *Treatments that work* (pp. 21–40). Philadelphia: Saunders.

Hinshaw, S., Heller, T., & McHale, J. (1992). Covert antisocial behavior in boys with attention-deficit hyperactivity disorder: External validation and effects of methylphendiate. *Journal of Consulting and Clinical Psychology, 60*, 274–281.

Horn, W. F., Ialongo, N. S., Pascoe, J. M., Greenberg, G., Packard, T., Lopez, M., Wagner, A., & Puttler, L. (1991). Additive effects of psychostimulants, parent training, and self-control therapy with ADHD children. *Journal of the American Academy of Child and Adolescent Psychiatry, 30*(2), 233–240.

Horn, W., Parker, H., Evans, J., & Portnoy, E. (1994). *Petition for rulemaking to reclassify methylphenidate from Schedule II to Schedule III controlled substance and alternatively to eliminate all likely future methylphenidate shortages.* Unpublished manuscript.

Jacobvitz, D., Sroufe, L. A., Stewart, M., & Leffert, N. (1990). Treatment of attentional and hyperactivity problems in children with sympathomimetic drugs: A comprehensive review. *Journal of the American Academy of Child and Adolescent Psychiatry, 29*(5), 677–688.

Jadad, A., & Atkins, D. (2000). *The treatment of attention-deficit/hyperactivity disorder: An evidence report* (Technology Assessment No. 11). Prepared by McMaster University under contract 290–97–007.

Jensen, P. S., Kettle, L., Roper, M., Sloan, M. T., Dulcan, M. K., Hoven, C., Bird, H. R., Bauermeister, J. J., & Payne, J. D. (1999). Are stimulants overprescribed? Treatment of ADHD in 4 U.S. Communities *Journal of the American Academy of Child and Adolescent Psychiatry, 38*, 797–804.

Kavale, K. (1982). The efficacy of stimulant drug treatment for hyperactivity: A meta-analysis. *Journal of Learning Disabilities, 15*, 280–289.

Klein, D. (1980). Treatment of anxiety, personality, somatoform and factitious disorders. In D. Klein, R. Gittelman, F. Quitkin, & A. Rifkin (Eds.), *Diagnosis and drug treatment of psychiatric disorders: Adults and children* (pp. 539–573). Baltimore: Williams & Wilkins.

Klein, R., Abikoff, H., Klass, E., Ganales, D., Seese, L., & Pollack, S. (1997). Clinical efficacy of methylphenidate in conduct disorder with and without attention deficit hyperactivity disorder. *Archives of General Psychiatry, 54*, 1073–1080.

Klorman, R., Brumagham, J., Fitzpatrick, P., & Burgstedt, A. (1990). Clinical effects of a controlled trial of methylphenidate on adolescents with Attention Deficit Disorder. *Journal of the American Academy of Child and Adolescent Psychiatry, 29*, 702–709.

Loney, J., & Milich, R. (1982). Hyperactivity, inattention, and aggression in clinical practice. In M. Wolraich & D. K. Routh (Eds.), *Advances in developmental behavioral pediatrics* (Vol. 2, pp. 113–147), Greenwich, CT: JAI Press.

Mannuzza, S., Klein, R., Bonagura, N., Malloy, P., Giampino, T. L., & Addalli, K. A. (1991). Hyperactive boys almost grown up: V. Replication of psychiatric status. *Archives of General Psychiatry, 48*, 77–83.

Meltzer, H., & Arora, R. (1991). Platelet serotonin studies in affective disorders: evidence for a serotonergic abnormality? In M. Sandler., A. Coppen., & S. Harnett (Eds.), *5-Hydroxytryptamine in Psychiatry: A spectrum of ideas* (pp. 23–55). New York: Oxford University Press.

Milich, R., Licht, B., & Murphy, D. (1989). Attention-deficit hyperactivity disordered boys evaluations of and attributions for task performance on medication versus placebo. *Journal of Abnormal Psychology, 98,* 280–284.

MTA Cooperative Group. (1999). 14-month randomized clinical trial of treatment strategies for attention deficit hyperactivity disorder. *Archives of General Psychiatry, 56*(12), 1073–1086.

Musten, L., Firestone, P., Pisterman, S., Bennett, S., & Mercer, J. (1997). Effects of methylphenidate on preschool children with ADHD: Cognitive and behavioral functions. *Journal of the American Academy of Child and Adolescent Psychiatry, 36,* 1407–1415.

Ottenbacher, J., & Cooper, H. (1983). Drug treatment of hyperactivity in children. *Developmental Medicine and Child Neurology, 25,* 358–366.

Page, J. G., Bernstein, J. E., Janicki, R. S., & Michelli, F. A. (1974). A multicenter trial of pemoline (cylert) in childhood hyperkinesis. In C. K. Conners (Ed.), *Clinical use of stimulant drugs in children* (p. 98). The Hague, Netherlands: Excerpta Medica.

Patrick, K. S., Mueller, R. A., Gualtieri, C. T., & Breese, G. R. (1987). Pharmocokinetics and actions of methyphenidate. In H. Y. Meltzer (Ed.), *Psychopharmacology: A third generation of progress* (pp. 1387–1395). New York: Raven Press.

Pelham, W. E. (1989). Behavior therapy, behavioral assessment and psychostimulant medication in the treatment of attention deficit disorders: An interactive approach. In J. Swanson & L. Bloomingdale (Eds.), *Attention deficit disorder: 4. Emerging trends in the treatment of attention and behavioral problems in children* (pp. 169–195). London: Pergamon.

Pelham, W. E., Greenslade, K. E., Vodde-Hamilton, M. A., Murphy, D. A., Greenstein, J. J., Gnagy, E. M., Guthrie, K. J., Hoover, M. D., & Dahl, R. E. (1990). Relative efficacy of long-acting stimulants on ADHD children: A comparison of standard methylphenidate, Ritalin-SR, Dexedrine spansule, and pemoline. *Pediatrics, 86,* 226–237.

Pelham, W., Hoza, B., Sturges, J., Schmidt, C., Bijlsma, J., & Moorer, S. (1987). Sustained release and standard methylphenidate effects on cognitive and social behavior in children with attention deficit disorder. *Pediatrics, 80,* 491–501.

Pelham, W. E., & Milich, R. (1991). Individual differences in response to Ritalin in classwork and social behavior. In L. L. Greenhill & B. Osman (Eds.), *Ritalin: Theory and patient management* (pp. 203–222). New York City: Mary Ann Liebert.

Pelham, W., & Murphy, H. (1986). Behavioral and pharmacological treatment of hyperactivity and attention deficit disorders. In M. Hersen & J. Breuning (Eds.), *Pharmacological and behavioral treatment: An integrative approach* (pp. 108–147). New York: Wiley.

Pelham, W. E., Sturges, J., Hoza, J., Schmidt, C., Biilsma, J. J., Milich, R., & Moorer, S. (1989). The effects of sustained release 20 and 10 mg Ritalin bid on cognitive and social behavior in children with attention deficit disorder. *Pediatrics, 80,* 491–501.

Pelham, W., Swanson, J., Furman, M., & Schwint, H. (1995). Pemoline effects on children with ADHD: A time response by dose-response analysis on classroom measures. *Journal of the American Academy of Child and Adolescent Psychiatry, 34,* 1504–1514.

Perel, J. W., & Dayton, P. (1976). Methylphenidate. In E. Usdin & I. Forrest (Eds.), *Psychotherapeutic drugs. Part II* (p. 1287). New York: Marcel Dekker.

Pliszka, S. R. (1992). Comorbidity of attention-deficit hyperactivity disorder and overanxious disorder. *Journal of the American Academy of Child and Adolescent Psychiatry, 31*(2), 197–203.

Pliszka, S., McCracken, J., & Maas, J. (1996). Catecholamines in attention-deficit hyperactivity disorder: Current perspectives. *Journal of the American Academy of Child and Adolescent Psychiatry, 35,* 264–272.

Rapoport, J. L., Buchsbaum, M. S., Weingartner, H., Zahn, P., Ludlow, C., & Mikkelsen, E. J. (1980). Dextroamphetamine: Cognitive and behavioral effects in normal and hyperactive boys and normal men. *Archives of General Psychiatry, 37,* 933–943.

Rapport, M., Denney, C., DuPaul G., & Gardner, M. (1994). Attention deficit disorder and methylphenidate: Normalization rates, clinical effectiveness and response prediction in 76 children. *Journal of the American Academy of Child and Adolescent Psychiatry, 33*(6), 882–893.

Rapport, M. D., DuPaul, G. J., & Kelly, K. L. (1989). Attention deficit hyperactivity disorder and methylphenidate: The relationship between gross body weight and drug response in children. *Psychopharmacology Bulletin, 25*(2), 285–290.

Rapport, M., Stoner, G., DuPaul, G., Kelly, K., Tucker, S., & Schoder, T. (1988). Attention deficit disorder and methylphenidate: A multi-step analysis of dose-response effects on children's impulsivity across settings. *Journal of the American Academy of Child and Adolescent Psychiatry, 27*, 60–69.

Richters, J. E., Arnold, L. E., Jensen, P. S., Abikoff, H., Conners, C. K., Greenhill, L. L., Hechtman, L., Hinshaw, S. P., Pelham, W. E., & Swanson, J. M. (1995). NIMH collaborative multisite multimodal treatment study of children with ADHD: I. Background and rationale. *Journal of the American Academy of Child and Adolescent Psychiatry, 34*, 987–1000.

Roberts, S., Harbison, R., Roth, L., & James, R. (1994). Methylphenidate-induced hepatoxicity in mice and its potentiation by beta-adrenergic agonist drugs. *Life Sciences, 55*, 269–281.

Safer, D. (1994). The impact of eight law suits on methylphenidate sales. *American Academy of Child and Adolescent Psychiatry, Scientific Proceedings of the Annual Meeting, 9*, 46.

Safer, D. J., Zito, J. M., & Fine, E. M. (1996). Increased methylphenidate usage for attention deficit disorder in the 1990's. *Pediatrics, 98*, 1084–1088.

Sallee, F., Stiller, R., & Perel, J. (1992). Pharmacodynamics of pemoline in attention deficit disorder with hyperactivity. *Journal of the American Academy of Child and Adolescent Psychiatry, 31*(2), 244–251.

Schachar, R. (1998). *Treatment of ADHD with methylphenidate and parent programs.* Unpublished manuscript.

Schachar, R., & Tannock, R. (1993). Childhood hyperactivity and psychostimulants: A review of extended treatment studies. *Journal of Child and Adolescent Psychopharmacology, 3*, 81–97.

Schechter, M., & Keuezer, E. (1985). Learning in hyperactive children: Are there stimulant-related and state-dependent effects? *Journal of Clinical Pharmacology, 25*, 276–280.

Scheel-Kruger, J. (1971). Comparative studies of various amphetamine analogues demonstrating different interactions with the metabolism of catecholamines in the brain. *European Journal of Pharmacology, 14*, 47–59.

Sherman, M. (1991). Prescribing Practice of methylphenidate: The Suffolk County Study. In B. Osman & L. L. Greenhill (Eds.), *Ritalin: Theory and patient management* (pp. 401–420). New York: Mary Ann Liebert.

Solanto, M. (1998). Neuropsychopharmacological mechanisms of stimulant drug action in attention-deficit hyperactivity disorder: A review and integration. *Behavioral Brain Research, 94*, 127–152.

Spencer, T. J., Biederman, J., Harding, M., O'Donnell, D., Faraone, S. V., & Wilens, T. (1996). Growth deficits in ADHD children revisited: Evidence for disorder-associated growth delays? *Journal of the American Academy of Child and Adolescent Psychiatry, 35*, 1460–1469.

Spencer, T., Biederman, J., Wilens, T., Harding, M., O'Donnell, D., & Griffin, S. (1996). Pharmacotherapy of attention-deficit hyperactivity disorder across the life cycle. *Journal of the American Academy of Child and Adolescent Psychiatry, 35*, 409–432.

Spencer, T., Wilens, T., Biederman, J., Farone, S., Ablen, S., & Lapey, K. (1995). A double-blind., crossover comparison of methylphenidate and placebo in adults with childhood onset ADHD. *Archives of General Psychiatry, 52*, 434–443.

Sprague, R. L., & Sleator, E. K. (1977). Methylphenidate in hyperkinetic children: Differences in dose effects on learning and social behavior. *Science, 198*, 1274–1276.

Swanson, J. (1993). Effect of stimulant medication on hyperactive children: A review of reviews. *Exceptional Child, 60*, 154–162.

Swanson, J., Kinsbourne, M., Roberts, W., & Zucker, K. (1978). Time-response analysis of the effect of stimulant medication on the learning ability of children referred for hyperactivity. *Pediatrics, 61*, 21–29.

Swanson, J., Lerner, M., & Williams, L. (1995). More frequent diagnosis of attention deficit-hyperactivity disorder. *New England Journal of Medicine, 333*, 944.

Swanson, J., Wigal, S., Greenhill, L., Browne, R., Waslik, B., Lerner, M., Williams, L., Flynn, D., Agler, D., Crowley, K., Fineberg, E., Baren, M., & Cantwell, D. P. (1998). Analog classroom assessment of Adderall in children with ADHD. *Journal of the American Academy of Child and Adolescent Psychiatry, 37*, 1–8.

Tannock, R., Ickowicz, A., & Schachar, R. (1995a). Differential effects of MPH on working memory in ADHD children with and without comorbid anxiety. *Journal of the American Academy of Child and Adolescent Psychiatry, 34*, 886–896.

Tannock, R., Schachar, R., & Logan, G. D. (1995b). Methylphenidate and cognitive flexibility: Dissociated dose effects in hyperactive children. *Journal of Abnormal Child Psychology, 23*, 235–267.

Taylor, E., Schachar, R., Thorley, G., Wieselberg, H. M., Everitt, B., & Rutter, M. (1987). Which boys respond to stimulant medication? A controlled trial of methyphenidate in boys with disruptive behavior. *Psychological Medicine, 17*, 121–143.

Thurber, S., & Walker, C. (1983). Medication and hyperactivity: A meta-analysis. *Journal of General Psychiatry, 108*, 79–86.

Vitiello, B., & Burke, L. (1998). Generic methylphenidate versus brand Ritalin: Which should be used. In L. Greenhill & B. Osman (Eds.), *Ritalin: Theory and practice* (pp. 221–226). Larchmont, NY: Mary Ann Liebert.

Volkow, N. D., Ding, Y-S., Fowler, J. S., Wang, G-J., Logan, J., Gatley, J. S., Dewey, S., Ashby, C., Lieberman, J., Hitzemann, R., et al. (1995). Is methylphenidate like cocaine? Studies on their pharmacokinetics and distribution in the human brain. *Archives of General Psychiatry, 52*, 456–463.

Weiner, N. (1991). Drugs that inhibit adrenergic nerves and block adrenergic receptors. In A. Gilman & L. Goodman (Eds.), *Norepinephrine., epinephrine and the sympathomimetic amines* (pp. 145–180). New York: Pharmacological Basis of Therapeutics.

Whalen, C., Henker, B., Buhrmester, D., Hinshaw, S., Huber, A., & Laski, K. (1989). Does stimulant medication improve the peer status of hyperactive children? *Journal of Consulting and Clinical Psychology, 57*, 545–549.

Whitehouse, D., Shah, U., & Palmer, F. B. (1980). Comparison of sustained-release and standard methylphenidate in the treatment of minimal brain dysfunction. *Journal of Clinical Psychiatry, 41*(8), 282–285.

Wroblewski, B., Leary, J., Phelan, A., Whyte, J., & Manning, K. (1992). Methylphenidate and seizure frequency in brain injured patients with seizure disorders. *Journal of Clinical Psychiatry, 53*, 86–89.

Zametkin, A. J., & Rapoport, J. L. (1987). Neurobiology of attention deficit disorder with hyperactivity: Where have we come in 50 years? *Journal of the American Academy of Child and Adolescent Psychiatry, 26*, 676–686.

Chapter 10

Public Health and Toxicological Issues Concerning Stimulant Treatment for ADHD

by Andrew S. Rowland, Ph.D., David M. Umbach, Ph.D.,
James P. O'Callaghan, Ph.D., Diane B. Miller, Ph.D.,
and June K. Dunnick, Ph.D.

Introduction 10-2
Prevalence 10-2
Toxicology 10-3
    Methylphenidate 10-3
    Amphetamines 10-4
    Pemoline (Cylert) 10-5
Efficacy of Stimulant Treatment 10-5
    Short-Term Efficacy 10-5
    Long-Term Effcctiveness 10-6
Safety 10-7
    Short-Term Safety 10-7
        Methylphenidate and Amphetamines 10-7
        Pemoline (Cylert) 10-7
    Long-Term Safety 10-8
        Limits of Adverse Drug-Reporting Systems 10-8
        Need for Large-Scale Cohort and Drug Surveillance
           Studies 10-9
        Phenobarbital as Analogy 10-10
Future Research Needs 10-11
    Toxicology 10-11
    Efficacy/Effectiveness 10-11
    Safety 10-12
An Opportunity and a Responsibility 10-12

INTRODUCTION

Attention deficit hyperactivity disorder (ADHD) was once considered a child-hood disorder, but recent research suggests that ADHD is usually chronic and may last into adulthood (Barkley, 1990; Mannuzza, Klein, Bessler, Malloy, & La Padula, 1993; Shaffer, 1994). This new perspective has important implications for treatment. No longer restricted to elementary school children, the population being treated with stimulant medication now includes preschoolers, adolescents, and adults. Their number is large and growing.

The purpose of this chapter is to summarize the existing information about the prevalence, toxicology, efficacy, and safety of stimulant medication treatment for ADHD and to point out the most pressing data gaps and their implications for public health. We end the chapter with a set of research recommendations to address some of these data gaps.

PREVALENCE

Existing data on the prevalence of stimulant medication treatment for ADHD are incomplete; no official estimates of the number of people treated for ADHD with stimulants in the United States exist. Prevalence can only be inferred by combining data from several national databases that are based on prescription sales, drug mentions from surveys of physician visits, or more detailed data from regional epidemiological studies in community settings (Zito et al., 1998) Nevertheless, the following important points can be inferred.

The rate of stimulant prescribing for ADHD has been rising rapidly since 1985 (Greenhill, Halperin, & Abikoff, 1999; Safer, Zito, & Fine, 1996). Overall physician visits that included a prescription for stimulant medication increased from 0.57 million in 1985 to 2.86 million in 1994, (Pincus et al., 1998), and stimulants have become the most frequently prescribed psychotropic medicines for children (Jensen et al., 1999). Between 1990 and 1995, the rate of stimulant medication use almost tripled among school-age children (Robison, Sclar, Skaer, & Galin, 1999). Methylphenidate is, by far, the most widely used drug for treating ADHD; roughly 80 percent of all children treated for ADHD with medication are taking methylphenidate (the generic name for Ritalin) (Bussing, Zima, & Belin, 1998; Greenhill et al., 1999; Wolraich et al., 1990). More than 10 million prescriptions for methylphenidate were written in 1996 (Greenhill et al., 1999). Almost all these prescriptions were for treating ADHD.

Estimating the number of people treated with stimulants each year is difficult because most of the national datasets are based on health care visits or amount of stimulants prescribed but not the number of people being treated. Using interpolation methods, two sets of authors estimated that, in 1995, about 1.5 million people in the United States were treated with methylphenidate (Robison et al., 1999; Safeet al., 1996). This number represented about 2.8 percent of all American children ages 5–18 (Robison et al., 1999). Because stimulant prescription rates are rising and methylphenidate prescriptions are only a subset of all stimulant prescriptions, the number of children being treated with stimulant medication is higher. One review estimates that between 2 and 2.5 million children are receiving psychotropic medications to treat ADHD (Safer & Zito, 1999).

Stimulant treatment varies widely in different locales, however. A Michigan-based study reported up to tenfold differences in prescribing rates in different counties across the state (Rappley, Gardiner, Jetton, & Houang, 1995). One study in Baltimore and another in rural North Carolina reported that between 6 percent and 7 percent of the school-age population was being treated for ADHD with stimulants (Greenhill et al., 1999). Another study estimated that the prevalence of school-based treatment of ADHD among second- to fifth-grade students in two cities in Virginia was between 8 and 10 percent (Lefever, Dawson, & Morrow, 1999). Whether the proportion of school-age children taking stimulants is closer to 3 percent, as the limited national data suggest, or 6 percent or higher, as the latter three regional studies suggest, remains unclear. To date, researchers have not identified the main determinants of differences in the prevalence of treatment within, and between, regions.

In the past, drug treatment for ADHD often lasted only a few years; now, the length of treatment is increasing as the number of teenagers and adults treated grows. Nationally, between 1990 and 1995 the mean patient age for children being treated with stimulants for ADHD increased by more than a year, from age 9.7 to age 10.8 (Robison et al., 1999). The Baltimore study reported that in 1975, only about 11 percent of the population being treated with methylphenidate were in middle school or high school; in 1993, 30 percent were (Safer & Krager, 1994). Many children in this study had been on medication for a long time; for high school students it averaged seven to eight years and for junior high students, four to five years.

TOXICOLOGY

The toxicology of stimulant medications has been extensively studied in animal models, but research has mostly focused on brief, high doses that mimic human exposure patterns among drug abusers. Here, interest is primarily in animal data that address effects at low doses or from chronic dosing that is more comparable to humans undergoing treatment for ADHD.

Methylphenidate

Few chronic toxicity data on methylphenidate exist. In one of the few long-term animal studies, the National Toxicology Program (NTP) at the National Institute of Environmental Health Sciences (NIEHS) examined the carcinogenic effects of methylphenidate in rodents exposed most of their lifetime (Dunnick & Hailey, 1995). The low dose of methylphenidate used was approximately comparable to an average human dose on a milligram per body surface basis, and the high dose was within a ten- to twentyfold safety factor range. Rats treated with methylphenidate showed a decreased incidence of tumors. Among both male and female mice, however, non-malignant liver tumors (hepatocellular adenomas) increased in a dose-dependent fashion. In male mice, a dose-dependent increase in a rare type of malignant liver tumor (hepatoblastoma) was also seen. Methylphenidate was not mutagenic in the Salmonella assay, which suggests the mechanism may not be genotoxic. In addition, the mouse strain used (B6C3F1) is susceptible to developing liver tumors. The NTP concluded that there was "some" evidence of carcinogenicity for methylphenidate based on the mouse liver tumor data. The relevance of this finding for humans is unclear.

Carcinogenesis is one of the few long-term end points of methylphenidate use that has been studied in animals. Data on other end points (e.g., the effect of prenatal exposure on developmental outcome in the offspring) are lacking.

Amphetamines

Behavioral changes including social withdrawal and stereotyped self-grooming have been seen in groups of adult vervet monkeys given low, nonchronic doses of d-amphetamine (0.1–0.7 mg/kg body weight) (Schiorring, 1979).

The NTP ran a similar set of long-term carcinogenicity studies on mice and rats treated with dl-amphetamine sulfate (a mixture of the isomers of amphetamine and one of the ingredients of Adderall®) (Dunnick & Eustis, 1991). As with methylphenidate, body weight and tumor incidence in rats decreased. In contrast to methylphenidate, long-term treatment with amphetamine was also associated with a reduction in spontaneous tumors in mice. Decreases in tumors have previously been seen in two-year rodent studies in groups of animals that have reduced body weight in comparison to controls, but the spectrum of reduction in spontaneous neoplasms after treatment with amphetamine was broader than previously observed. Again the relevance of these data for humans is unclear.

Many studies have examined the potential neurotoxic effects of amphetamine and its congeners in animals (Bowyer & Holson, 1995; O'Callaghan & Miller, in press). These studies employed a variety of experimental models, including subhuman primates, and were designed to assess adverse effects on the central nervous system associated with recreational use of these drugs. Unlike methylphenidate, high dosage regimens of amphetamine and its substituted analogues produce long-term (days to months) decrements in the brain neurotransmitters, dopamine and serotonin (Bowyer & Holson, 1995; Miller & O'Callaghan, 1994, 1996; Zaczek, Battaglia, Contrera, Culp, & DeSouza, 1989) (including in man; Wilson et al., 1996). Although these changes are not necessarily indicative of neuronal damage (O'Callaghan & Miller, 1994), they are indicative of a persistent action of the compound in the absence of continued drug exposure. Although slowly reversible, the persistence of these drug-induced neurotransmitter depletions have been viewed by some as an adverse neurotoxic effect (Tilson, MacPhail, & Crofton, 1995). Elevated ambient temperature contributes to the propensity of amphetamines to deplete brain neurotransmitters (Miller & O'Callaghan, 1994), a finding of potential relevance to humans working or playing in a warm environment. In comparison to the adult nervous system, the developing nervous system is somewhat resistant to the neurotransmitter depleting actions of amphetamine and its analogues (Broening, Bacon, & Slikker, 1994). Nevertheless, protracted decrements in brain neurotransmitter levels have been observed after administration of acute high dosages of the neonate as well as the adult (Broening et al., 1994; Pu & Vorhees, 1993). Neurotransmitter depletion, whether a reflection of "neurotoxicity" or not, is not a desirable action for drugs given on a chronic basis to children. Neurotransmitters, including dopamine and serotonin, serve as endogenous growth factors essential for normal brain development of the mammalian brain (Lauder, 1983). This finding suggests that administration of amphetamines to humans throughout postnatal development (through the late teens) at dosages that decrease neurotransmitter levels might interfere with normal brain development. Because transmitter depletion in adults or neonates (experimental animals and humans) has only been demonstrated following the administration of acute high-dose regimens of amphetamine, the relevance of existing data to people being chronically treated with stimulants is unclear.

Pemoline (Cylert)

Little research has been conducted with chronic doses of pemoline in animals. In one study, even high doses (150 mg/kg/day for eighteen months) did not increase the incidence of any neoplasm among treated animals compared to controls ("Pemoline," 1999). Side effects associated with human use are reported later in this chapter.

EFFICACY OF STIMULANT TREATMENT

Short-Term Efficacy

Short-term clinical trials have reported robust and similar efficacy of methylphenidate, d-amphetamine, and pemoline in children with ADHD (Greenhill et al., 1999). Several reviews of the clinical trial data suggest that these medications are effective in about 70 to 75 percent of ADHD subjects (Spencer, Biederman, Wilens, et al., 1996; Swanson et al., 1993). Another review estimated that by substituting other stimulants when response is initially poor, a positive response can eventually be found about 85 to 90 percent of the time (Cantwell, 1996). In general, the improvements in behavior are more dramatic than those in seen in academic achievement (Swanson et al., 1993).

Pemoline is no longer used as a first-line treatment for ADHD because of its potential liver toxicity (see later), but it is less clear why such a high proportion of the children with ADHD are treated with methylphenidate rather than amphetamines. Both the efficacy data and the side effect profiles of the two drugs are similar (Elia, Ambrosini, & Rapoport, 1999). Both compounds have similar abuse potential (Martin, Sloan, Sapira, & Jasinski, 1971). Recent reports have compared the efficacy of Adderall, a mixture of amphetamine salts, with methylphenidate, and concluded that because of a slightly longer half-life in the body, one dose of Adderall was about as effective as a two daily doses of methylphenidate (Manos, Short, & Findling, 1999; Pelham et al., 1999). One of these papers pointed out, however, that it would be worthwhile to go back and compare the efficacy and side effect profiles of d-amphetamine and methylphenidate because relatively little work had been done comparing the two (even though both had been available for more than forty years). One review commented: "Methylphenidate is much more widely prescribed than dextroamphetamine because it has been studied more often and has been prescribed more extensively by the drug industry. It was also suggested, without evidence, that it was more effective and had fewer adverse effects than dextroamphetamine" (Elia et al., 1999).

When Ritalin (methlyphenidate) was first produced, it quickly replaced d-amphetamine as the treatment of choice, with little evidence of it superior safety or efficacy. In the last few years, Adderall has been heavily promoted and is gaining market share now that Ritalin® is available in generic form (methylphenidate), again with few data to suggest that Adderall is a better drug. We find this pattern troubling; pharmaceutical marketing strategies, not children's health or even cost-effectiveness, appear to be the most important factors influencing which medications are being used to treat ADHD.

Long-Term Effectiveness

The randomized controlled trial data on efficacy may be somewhat misleading about the effectiveness of stimulant medication treatment in actual clinical practice. NIEHS is conducting an epidemiological study among elementary school children in a diverse county in North Carolina (Paule et al., 2000). Preliminary data from this study suggest that nine of thirty-four children (26 percent) being treated for ADHD with medication met full epidemiological case criteria, despite treatment. This is consistent with reports of suboptimal management of ADHD medication treatment in at least 30 percent of children receiving treatment (Miller, 1999). The recently completed Multimodal Treatment (MTA) study conducted by the National Institute of Mental Health (NIMH) also found that a substantial proportion of the "usual care group," including many on medication, still met symptom criteria for ADHD after the study (MTA Cooperative Group, 1999). The MTA study data suggest that careful and regular follow-up with parents and with schools is critical for the successful treatment of ADHD with medication. Without systematic follow-up, the clinician may miss problems with the initial diagnosis, including other comorbidity, with patient compliance, or with patient response to the medication. Yet few data about the quality of follow-up in community settings are available (Jacobvitz, Sroufe, Stewart, & Leffert, 1990; Schachar & Tannock, 1993). More data are needed on whether regular follow-up with parents and schools is occurring after stimulant medication is prescribed, and if not, why. The concern is that children who receive medication without careful follow-up do not gain the full benefits of treatment, but they do incur any associated risks.

The few available data on treatment problems in community settings suggest that problems with follow-up, effectiveness, side effects, comorbidity, and compliance might increase over time, limiting the benefits of stimulant drug therapy. Clinicians certainly appreciate the difficulty of maintaining effective compliance to psychoactive drug treatment among teenagers (Zametkin & Ernst, 1999), yet clinicians are prescribing stimulant medication to increasing numbers of adolescents.

Much of what we know about the natural history of ADHD comes from a few, longitudinal follow-up studies of hyperactive children (Barkley, Fischer, Edelbrock, & Smallish, 1990; Hechtman, Weiss, Perlman, Hopkins, & Wener, 1981; Mannuzza et al., 1993). Yet, most of these studies followed 100 or fewer subjects, only included children with the combined or hyperactive subtype, and relied on clinic-based samples. Large cohort studies of children recruited from population-based samples simultaneously could provide data about the natural history of ADHD, patterns of treatment and diagnosis of ADHD across communities, and the long-term effectiveness of stimulant treatment.

Data on the long-term effectiveness of stimulant medication are badly needed. In 1973, Sroufe and Stewart wrote that "more than 150,000 children with behavior or learning problems are now being treated with stimulant drugs" and "we believe that the use of stimulant drugs should be critically appraised before society moves farther in this direction" (p. 412). They underscore the lack of long-term effictiveness data on stimulant medication. More than twenty-five years later that data gap is more apparent and the need to address it, more pressing.

SAFETY

Short-Term Safety

Methylphenidate and Amphetamines. The short-term safety data are summarized elsewhere in this volume (see Chapter 9). Briefly, for stimulants other than pemoline, the most common side effects are insomnia, decreased appetite, stomachache, headache, and jitteriness (Goldman, Genel, Bezman, & Sianetz, 1998). Concerns that stimulants may increase motor tics, growth delays, and overfocusing among children being treated remain controversial because some of the available evidence suggests that these side effects may be related to the underlying disorder and not to drug effects themselves (Elia, Ambrosini, & Rapoport, 1999; Greenhill et al., 1999; Spencer, Biederman, Harding, et al., 1996; Spencer, Biederman, Wilens, et al., 1996; Tannock, Schachar, & Logan, 1993) Nevertheless, in clinical practice, published estimates suggest that as many as 30 percent of affected individuals do not respond or may not tolerate stimulant treatment. (Spencer, Biederman, Wilens, et al., 1996) This observation suggests that nonpharmaceutical treatments still have an important role, and additional research is needed to find behavioral approaches that are both practical and effective.

Even though methylphenidate is one of the most studied pediatric drug treatments (Greenhill et al., 1999), there may be susceptible subgroups in which the side effects have been underestimated. For example, most of the clinical trials have focused on elementary school boys with the hyperactive or combined subtype. Few studies have focused on girls, ethnic minorities, preschoolers, adolescents, children with the predominately inattentive subtype, or children with comorbid conditions that might affect outcome, for example, depression, anxiety, or aggression (Spencer, Biederman, Wilens, et al., 1996). Methylphenidate is one of the top ten drugs being prescribed off label to children (Riddle, Labellarte, & Walkup, 1998). (At the present time, all methylphenidate prescriptions for children under age 6 are off label.) Few studies have evaluated whether the side effect profile differs between toddlers and older children using methylphenidate, but two recent studies suggest that it may (Firestone, Musten, Pisterman, Mercer, & Bennett, 1998; Handen, Feldman, Lurier, & Murray, 1999). In these studies, side effects in preschoolers (nightmares, decreased appetite, sadness, drowsiness, and lack of interest in others) were more frequent and more variable than those generally observed in school-age children. Combined pharmacotherapy is becoming more common among children with ADHD, yet few trials have specifically monitored side effects or safety in children being treated with stimulants in combination with other drugs (Spencer, Biederman, Wilens, et al., 1996; Wilens, Spencer, Biederman, Woziak, & Connor, 1995). More research along these lines is warranted.

Pemoline (Cylert). Pemoline was first introduced in Europe in the 1960s and in the United States in the 1970s for the treatment of memory defects in the elderly and for treating ADHD. In 1973, a report of two cases of reversible hepatotoxicity in two patients who had taken pemoline was published (Tolman, Freston, Berenson, & Sannella, 1973). Since then, numerous reports of liver toxicity, including a number of deaths due to fulminate liver failure, have been reported (Marotta & Roberts, 1998; Nehra, Mullick, Ishak, & Zimmerman, 1990; Rosh, Dellert, Narkewicz, Birnbaum, & Whitington, 1998; Shevell & Schreiber, 1997; Tolman, Freston, Berenson, & Sannella, 1973). Although it is still being used in clinical practice, the Food and Drug Administration (FDA) has issued a warning label stating that "because of its association with life threatening hepatic failure, pemoline should not ordinarily be considered as first line drug therapy for ADHD."

Long-Term Safety

Despite hundreds of shorter clinical trials, only four randomized clinical trials of stimulant medication treatment have lasted twelve months or longer (Greenhill et al., 1999). Many logistic constraints make long-term randomized clinical trials of stimulant treatment difficult; the longest of these trials was twenty-four months (Greenhillet al., 1999). Neither the long-term effectiveness nor the long-term safety of stimulant medications has ever been demonstrated (Gillberg et al., 1997; Jacobvitz et al. 1990; Klein, 1993; Spencer, Biederman, Wilens, et al., 1996). Yet, precisely this information is needed to effectively weigh the risks and benefits of treatment and to provide or receive truly informed consent.

Limits of Adverse Drug-Reporting Systems. Adverse drug-reporting systems are the main tool for monitoring the toxic effects of stimulant medication or other drugs after they are placed on the market, yet this type of surveillance has important limitations (Wood, Stein, & Woosley, 1998). Adverse drug-reporting systems are most likely to catch acute severe illness like sudden death or liver failure related to drug treatment. They are most likely to miss subtle or chronic effects. For example, studies suggest that only 1 to 2 percent of clinical events related to drug treatment are reported and only about 10 percent of the most serious adverse drug events are detected (Center for Drug Evaluation and Research, 1996; Fletcher, 1991; Sachs & Bortnichak, 1986). In addition, adverse drug-reporting systems typically do not define the size of the population at risk. Without knowing the size of the denominator (or in most cases, even the number of adverse events in the numerator), determining whether the rate of an adverse event differs from background levels is difficult. A recent policy paper suggested that an independent drug safety board is needed and that formal prospective postmarketing surveillance should be routine and mandatory because the current voluntary reporting system used by the FDA is inadequate (Wood et al., 1998). Other investigators, considering this problem have proposed that adverse drug- reporting systems must be supplemented with ongoing systems that match medical records and computerized databases of medication users and nonusers (Brewer & Colditz, 1999). These authors also note that "large cohorts, not established solely for adverse drug report detection, offer a rich data source of disease risk factors and can add surveillance . . . at low marginal cost" (Brewer & Colditz, 1999). The conventional wisdom has been that long-term postmarketing surveillance was particularly problematic because the only design that would provide convincing data was the randomized clinical trial, and conducting these types of studies over long periods was prohibitively expensive. However, cohort designs provide a possible alternative. Two recent meta-analyses compared the findings of observational cohort studies to data generated by randomized, controlled trials on the same intervention; both concluded that well-designed observational studies produce similar estimates of the effect of treatment when compared to randomized controlled trials on the same topic (Benson & Hartz, 2000; Concato, Shah, & Horwitz, 2000).

Need for Large-Scale Cohort and Drug Surveillance Studies. To date, the main tools that have been used to monitor the safety of stimulant medications, adverse drug-reporting systems, and extended clinical trials have important limitations that constrain their effectiveness. Because of the large proportion of children who are being treated, new tools are needed to monitor the long-term safety of stimulant medications. These include both large cohort studies that employ ongoing active, not passive, follow-up and large drug surveillance systems that link the records of treated patients with medical outcome data routinely being collected in large databases. Large samples are needed to monitor safety because the treated population is so large that even if adverse effects were rare they potentially could have a large public health impact. For example, if one assumes that 2 million children take stimulant medication and drug-related long-term adverse effects only occur at an annual rate of one per 1,000, about 2,000 children would be affected each year. Unless the health effect was specifically associated only with that drug treatment, it might be missed.

What outcomes should be monitored in studies of possible long-term adverse effects? The answer to this question is not entirely clear. Nevertheless, possible outcomes might include effects on child and adolescent development, blood pressure and cardiovascular function, liver function (particularly to catch other drug interactions), reproductive function, central nervous system function, and cancer risk. Despite the controversy about stimulants and growth, few studies have followed development in teenagers across puberty. Most clinical trials have reported small increases in blood pressure among those treated with stimulants. In elementary school children under a relatively short course of medication, these changes may seem unimportant. With longer periods of treatment extending through adolescence into adulthood, however, these small increases could accumulate and constitute a health risk. Susceptible subpopulations may exist. For example, one study reported an exaggerated cardiovascular response to methylphenidate in ADHD children with anxiety (Urman, Ickowicz, Fulford, & Tannock, 1995) and another suggested exaggerated effects on blood pressure among African-American adolescents (Brown & Sexon, 1989). To address the concern that stimulants might increase the risk of hypertension among certain subgroups of patients, large diverse groups of children receiving treatment would need to be followed for an extended period of time.

In 1980, Satterfield, Schell, and Barb published one of the few studies on the long-term health effects of stimulant treatment in children. These authors followed seventy children for one year and thirty-six children for three years. After three years of follow-up, they found statistically significant increases in both systolic blood pressure (8 mm Hg) and diastolic blood pressure (5 mm Hg) among children with ADHD being treated with methylphenidate. The authors concluded that "prolonged administration of methylphenidate hydrochloride was not associated with disturbances in the hematopoietic, endocrine, hepatic, or cardiovascular functions analyzed." What is interesting about this report is that the authors chose to dismiss consistent, statistically significant increases in blood pressure as unimportant. Even if one accepts this choice about the blood pressure findings, the study provides little reassurance about the long-term safety of stimulants because it had limited statistical power to detect even very large changes in adverse event rates.

In Table 10.1, simple sample size calculations are presented to find a doubling or a tripling of risk of an adverse outcome in a cohort of treated and untreated children. To be able to detect a threefold increase for a common side effect that occurred in 10 percent of untreated children, one would have to follow 142 children for one year, or about 50 children for three years. To be able to detect a threefold increase in risk of a rare condition that incurred in only 1 out of 1,000 children, for example, a childhood cancer, one would need to include more than 17,000 children.

Table 10.1
Sample Sizes Needed to Detect Adverse Outcomes Caused by Stimulant Medication

Rate of Adverse Outcome Among Untreated	Minimal Detectable Relative Risk	Sample Size Required
0.001	2	50,942
0.01	2	5,028
0.1	2	438
0.001	3	17,608
0.01	3	1,730
0.1	3	142

Note. Sample sizes depend on rate of adverse outcomes among untreated individuals and on the desired minimum detectable relative risk. Calculations assume that the study has equal numbers of treated and untreated individuals, a type 1 error rate of 0.05, and power of 0.80.

Phenobarbital as Analogy. How likely is it that a widely used drug marketed for decades could cause long-term adverse effects that previously have gone undetected? Here, the analogy of phenobarbital may be instructive. Phenobarbital was first used to treat epilepsy in 1912 (Painter & Gaus, 1995). It quickly gained the reputation as a safe drug and became the drug of choice for treating children with seizures. Children who had experienced a febrile seizure were often prescribed phenobarbital when they next developed a febrile illness. Efficacy tended to be poor, however. During the 1960s, some physicians advocated administering chronic daily doses of phenobarbital to prevent febrile seizures from reoccurring (Carter, 1964) This practice became common during the 1970s. In 1980, a National Institutes of Health (NIH, 1981) consensus conference concluded that treatment risks outweighed benefits because the medicine caused behavioral side effects in about a third of the treated children and some treated children showed evidence of developmental delays (Freeman, 1980). However, the practice did not end until an NIH clinical trial published in 1990 found additional evidence of developmental delays and decrements in IQs among treated children (Farwell et al., 1990). The additional research on subtle long-term health effects substantially changed the risk-benefit equation for the treatment of febrile seizures (even though phenobarbital is still used to treat children with epilepsy because the risk-benefit picture is different). Febrile seizures are common; between 2 and 5 percent of all children experience a febrile seizure before age 5 and about a third have a second febrile convulsion (Hauser, 1991). Over the years that phenobarbital was used as a chronic, daily preventive treatment for febrile seizures, potentially hundreds of thousands of children were exposed. The use of stimulants to treat ADHD may or may not be analogous, but collecting long-term data is warranted.

FUTURE RESEARCH NEEDS

Toxicology

Two areas need study:

1. Additional toxicology studies are needed that use young animals (equivalent to the ages at which humans begin to receive medication), in case toxicity is related to developmental stage. Chronic low-dose studies should examine other end points besides carcinogenesis. Studies should explore the mechanisms underlying any adverse effects. For example, research on the mechanism underlying the increased rate of liver tumors observed in mice exposed to methylphenidate might help clarify whether this finding is relevant for humans.

2. With respect to amphetamine, studies using chronic low-level dosing are needed to determine whether the doses used in clinical practice might result in depletion of brain transmitters. As neurotransmitter depletion during childhood may serve as a risk factor for altered neuroanatomical measures of brain development (Lauder, 1988), such studies could be used to establish margins of safety for human dosage. Long-term studies should include elevated ambient temperatures as a variable, because heat increases the depleting action of amphetamine.

Efficacy/Effectiveness

Three areas of research are indicated:

1. More data are needed about the effectiveness of stimulant therapy as it is being delivered in clinical practice. If, as it appears, important gaps in efficacy are occurring, we need to understand how widespread they are and what is causing them. For example, if patient follow-up after the initial prescription is written tends to be erratic, the barriers to more effective follow-up need to be identified and addressed. Learning how to effectively treat teenagers with ADHD is particularly important.

2. Stimulant medication is not efficacious in a small proportion of children and not an acceptable option for others. For this reason, more research is needed on psychosocial approaches to managing ADHD that are practical and effective.

3. Epidemiological studies on the long-term effectiveness of stimulant medication are needed. The most practical design may be to follow sufficiently large cohorts of children from population-based samples longitudinally. Both behavioral and academic measures of performance should be included as end points. However, the most important end point should be how well treatment is able to help children minimize impairment and maximize their potential and happiness as adults. Studies should consider whether effectiveness varies among children with different ADHD subtypes and among those who have ADHD with various types of comorbidity, particularly conduct disorder/aggression, anxiety, or learning disabilities.

Safety

Two areas require further study:

1. Long-term studies on the safety of stimulant treatment are needed. Two possible designs should be considered. First, surveillance of large cohorts of children should be conducted by linking treatment files with health databases such Medicaid or large health maintenance organizations. Second, safety should be included as an end point in cohort studies monitoring long-term effectiveness. Surveillance should be based on active follow-up (e.g., with annual questionnaires and monitoring of outcomes). As with efficacy, safety studies should look for unusually susceptible subpopulations.

2. Additional research is needed on the long-term safety of the alternative pharmacological treatments for ADHD so that the risks and benefits of stimulant treatment can be put into proper perspective. For example, existing research does not adequately define the possible risks associated with taking Clonidine (Elia et al., 1999; Cantwell, Swanson, & Connor, 1997) or tricyclic antidepressants (Committee on Children With Disabilities and Committee on Drugs, 1996; Elia et al., 1999).

AN OPPORTUNITY AND A RESPONSIBILITY

The public health community now has an opportunity to address two of the most pressing concerns of parents. Will this medication help my child? Will it be safe? In the short run, for many children, stimulant medication is both helpful and safe. But, because so many children are being medicated for many years, an additional responsibility arises—to monitor long-term treatment risks and benefits more effectively. This research is the responsibility of both the government and the pharmaceutical industry. Additional epidemiological research may yield important information that will improve service delivery and help quantify long-term risks and benefits of existing treatments. As scientists, as health care providers, and as health care consumers, we need to ask ourselves, "Can we afford to neglect these questions?" It is time to answer them.

References

Barkley, R. A. (1990). *Attention-deficit hyperactivity disorder: A handbook for diagnosis and treatment.* New York: Guilford Press.

Barkley, R. A., Fischer, M., Edelbrock, C. S., & Smallish, L. (1990). The adolescent outcome of hyperactive children diagnosed by research criteria. I: An 8 year prospective follow-up study. *Journal of the American Academy of Child and Adolescent Psychiatry, 29*, 546–557.

Benson, K., & Hartz, A. J. (2000). A comparison of observational studies and randomized controlled trials. *New England Journal of Medicine, 342*, 1878–1886.

Bowyer, J. F., Davies, D. L., Schmued, L., Broening, H. W., Newport, G. D., Slikker, W., Jr., & Holson, R. R. (1994). Further studies of the role of hyperthermia in methamphetamine neurotoxicity. *Journal of Pharmacology and Experimental Therapeutics, 268*, 1571–1580.

Bowyer, J. F., & Holson, R. R. (1995). Methamphetamine and amphetamine neurotoxicity: characteristics, interactions with body temperature and possible mechanisms. In L. W. Chang & R. S. Dyer (Eds.), *Handbook of neurotoxicology* (Vol. II, pp. 845–870). New York: Marcel Dekker.

Brewer, T., & Colditz, G. A. (1999). Postmarketing surveillance and adverse drug reactions: Current perspectives and future needs. *Journal of the American Medical Association, 281*, 824–829.

Broening, H. W., Bacon, L., & Slikker, W. Jr. (1994). Age modulates the long-term but not the acute effects of the serotonergic neurotoxicant, 3,4-methylenedioxymethampheatmine. *Journal of Pharmacology and Experimental Therapeutics, 271*, 285–293.

Brown, R. T., & Sexon, S. B. (1989). Effects of methylphenidate on cardiovascular responses in attention deficit hyperactivity disordered adolescents. *Journal of Adolescent Health Care, 10*, 179–183.

Bussing, R. A., Zima, B. T., & Belin, T. R. (1998). Variations in ADHD treatment among special education students. *Journal of the American Academy of Child and Adolescent Psychiatry, 37*, 968–976.

Cantwell, D. P. (1996). Attention deficit disorder: A review of the past 10 years. *Journal of the American Academy of Child and Adolescent Psychiatry, 35*, 978–987.

Cantwell, D. P., Swanson, J. M., & Connor, D. F. (1997). Case study: Adverse response to Clonidine. *Journal of the American Academy Child and Adolescent Psychiatry, 36*, 539–544.

Carter, S. (1964). Diagnosis and treatment: management of the child who has had one convulsion. *Pediatrics, 33*, 431–434.

Center for Drug Evaluation and Research, U.S. Food and Drug Administration. (1996). The clinical impact of adverse event reporting (*Medwatch* continuing education article, pp. 1–9). Available on-line: http://www.fda.gov/medwatch/articles/med.pdf.

Committee on Children With Disabilities and Committee on Drugs. (1996). Medication for children with attentional disorders. *Pediatrics, 98*, 301–304.

Concato, J., Shah, N., & Horwitz, R. I. (2000). Randomized, controlled trials, observational studies, and the hierarchy of research designs. *New England Journal of Medicine, 342*, 1887–1892.

Dunnick, J. K., & Eustis, S. L. (1991). Decreases in spontaneous tumors in rats and mice after treatment with amphetamine. *Toxicology, 67*, 325–332.

Dunnick, J. K., & Hailey, J. R. (1995). Experimental studies on the long-term effects of methylphenidate hydrochloride. *Toxicology, 103*, 77–84.

Elia, J., Ambrosini, P. J., & Rapoport, J. L. (1999). Treatment of attention-deficit-hyperactivity disorder. *New England Journal of Medicine, 340*, 780–788.

Emerit, M. B., Riad, M., & Hamon, M. (1992). Trophic effects of neurotransmitters during brain maturation. *Biology of the Neonate, 62*, 193–201.

Farwell, J. R., Lee, Y. J., Hirtz, D. G., Sulzbacher, S. I., Ellenberg, J. H., & Nelson, K. B. (1990). Phenobarbital for febrile seizures—Effects on intelligence and on seizure recurrence. *New England Journal of Medicine, 322*, 364–369.

Firestone, P., Musten, L. M., Pisterman, S., Mercer, J., & Bennett, S. (1998). Short-term side effects of stimulant medication are increased in preschool children with attention-deficit/hyperactivity disorder: A double-blind placebo-controlled study. *Journal of Child and Adolescent Psychopharmacology, 8*, 13–25.

Fletcher, A. P. (1991). Spontaneous adverse drug reporting vs. event monitoring: A comparison. *Journal of the Royal Society of Medicine, 84*, 341–346.

Freeman, J. M. (1980). Febrile seizures: A consensus of their significance, evaluation, and treatment. *Pediatrics, 66*, 1009–1012.

Gillberg, C., Melander, H., von Knorring, A., Janols, L. O., Thernlund, G., Hagglof, B., Eidevall-Wallin, L., Gustafsson, P., & Kopp, S. (1997). Long-term stimulant treatment of children with attention-deficit hyperactivity disorder symptoms: A randomized, double-blind, placebo-controlled trial. *Archives of General Psychiatry, 54*, 857–864.

Goldman, L. S., Genel, M., Bezman, R. J., & Slanetz, P. J. (1998). Diagnosis and treatment of attention-deficit/hyperactivity disorder in children and adolescents. Council on Scientific Affairs, American Medical Association. *Journal of the American Medical Association, 279*, 1100–1107.

Greenhill, L., Halperin, J. M., & Abikoff, H. (1999). Stimulant medications. *Journal of the American Academy of Child and Adolescent Psychiatry, 38*, 503–512.

Handen, B. L., Feldman, H. M., Lurier, A., & Murray, P. J. (1999). Efficacy of methylphenidate among preschool children with developmental disabilities and ADHD. *Journal of the American Academy of Child and Adolescent Psychiatry, 38*, 805–812.

Hauser, W. A. (1991). The natural history of febrile seizures. In K. B. Nelson & J. H. Ellenberg (Eds.), *Febrile seizures* (pp. 5–17). New York: Raven Press.

Hechtman, L., Weiss, G., Perlman, T., Hopkins, J., & Wener, A. (1981). Hyperactive children in young adulthood: A controlled, prospective, ten-year follow-up. In M. Gittleman (Ed.), *Strategic interventions for hyperactive children* (pp. 186–201), Armonk, NY: M.E. Sharpe.

Jacobvitz, D., Sroufe, L. A., Stewart, M., & Leffert, N. (1990). Treatment of attentional and hyperactivity problems in children with sympathomimetic drugs: A comprehensive review. *Journal of the American Academy of Child and Adolescent Psychiatry, 29*, 677–688.

Jensen, P. S., Bhatara, V. S., Vitiello, B., Hoagwood, K., Feil, M., & Burke, L. B. (1999). Psychoactive medication prescribing practices for U.S. children: Gaps between research and clinical practice. *Journal American Academy of Child and Adolescent Psychiatry, 38*, 557–565.

Klein, R. G. (1993). Clinical efficacy of methylphenidate in children and adolescents. *Encephale, 19*, 89–93.

Lauder, J. M. (1983). Hormonal and humoral influences on brain development. *Psychoneuroendocrinology, 8*, 121–155.

Lauder, J. M. (1988). Neurotransmitters as morphogens. *Progress in Brain Research, 73*, 365–387.

LeFever, G. B., Dawson, K. V., & Morrow, A. L. (1999). The extent of drug therapy for attention deficit-hyperactivity disorder among children in public schools. *American Journal of Public Health, 89*, 1359–1364.

Mannuzza, S., Klein, R. G., Bessler, A., Malloy, P., & LaPadula, M. (1993). Adult outcome of hyperactive boys: Educational achievement, occupational rank, and psychiatric status. *Archives of General Psychiatry, 50*, 565–576.

Manos, M. J., Short, E. J., & Findling, R. L. (1999). Differential effectiveness of methylphenidate and adderall in school-age youths with attention-deficit hyperactivity disorder. *Journal of the American Academy of Child and Adolescent Psychiatry, 38*, 813–819.

Marotta, P. J., & Roberts, E. A. (1998). Pemoline hepatotoxicity in children. *Journal of Pediatrics 132*, 894–897.

Martin, W. R., Sloan, J. W., Sapira, B. D., & Jasinski, D. R. (1971). Physiologic, subjective, and behavioral effects of amphetamine, methamphetamine, ephedrine, phenmetrazine, and methylphenidate in man. *Clinical Pharmacology and Therapeutics, 12*, 245–258.

Miller, A. (1999). Appropriateness of psychostimulant prescription to children: theoretical and empirical perspectives. *Canadian Journal of Psychiatry, 44*, 1017–1024.

Miller, D. B., & O'Callaghan, J. P. (1994). Environment-, drug- and stress-induced alterations in body temperature affect the neurotoxicity of substituted amphetamines in the C57BL/6J mouse. *Journal of Pharmacology and Experimental Therapeutics, 270*, 752–760.

Miller, D. B., & O'Callaghan, J. P. (1996). Neurotoxicity of d-amphetamine in the C57BL/6J and CD-1 mouse; interactions with stress and the adrenal system. *Annals of the New York Academy of Sciences, 801*, 148–167.

MTA Cooperative Group. (1999). 14-month randomized clinical trial of treatment strategies for attention-deficit/hyperactivity disorder. *Archives of General Psychiatry, 56*(12), 1073–1086.

National Institutes of Health. (1981). Consensus development conference on febrile seizures, National Institutes of Health, May 19–21, 1980. *Epilepsia, 22*, 377–381.

Nehra, A., Mullick, F., Ishak, K. G., & Zimmerman, H. J. (1990). Pemoline-associated hepatic injury. *Gastroenterology, 99*, 1517–1519.

O'Callaghan, J. P., & Miller, D. B. (1994). Neurotoxicity profiles of substituted amphetamines in the C57BL/6J mouse. *Journal of Pharmacology and Experimental Therapeutics, 270*, 741–751.

O'Callaghan, J. P., & Miller, D. B. (in press). Neurotoxic effects of substituted amphetamines in rats and mice: Challenges to current dogma. In E. Massaro & P. A. Broderick (Eds.), *Handbook of neurotoxicity* (Vol. 2). New York: Humana Press.

Painter, M. J., & Gaus, L. M. (1995). Phenobarbital: Clinical use. In R. H. Levy, R. H. Mattson, & B. S. Meldrum (Eds.), *Anti-epileptic drugs* (pp. 401–407). New York: Raven Press.

Paule, M. G., Rowland, A. S., Ferguson, S. A., Chelonis, J. J., Tannock, R., Swanson, J. M., & Castellanos, F. X. (2000) Attention deficit/hyperactivity disorder: Characteristics, interventions, and models. *Neurotoxicology and Teratology, 22* , 631–651.

Pelham, W. E., Aronoff, H. R., Midlam, J. K., Shapiro, C. J., Gnagy, E. M., Chronis, A. M., Onyango, A. N., Forehand, G., Nguyen, A., & Waxmonsky, J. (1999). A comparison of Ritalin and Adderall: Efficacy and time-course in children with attention-deficit hyperactivity/disorder. *Pediatrics, 103*, e43.

Pemoline. (1999). *Physician's desk reference* (pp. 416–417). Montvale, NJ: Medical Economics.

Pincus, H. A., Taneilian, T. L., Marcus, S. C., Olfson, M., Zarin, D. A., Thompson, J., & Zito, J. M. (1998). Prescribing trends in psychotropic medications: primary care, psychiatry, and other medical specialties. *Journal of the American Medical Association, 279*, 526–531.

Pu, C., & Vorhees, C. V. (1993). Developmental dissociation of methamphetamine-induced depletion of dopaminergic terminals and astrocyte reaction in rat striatum. *Brain Research: Developmental Brain Research, 72*, 325–328.

Rappley, M. D., Gardiner, J. C., Jetton, J. R., & Houang, R. T. (1995). The use of methylphenidate in Michigan. *Archives of Pediatrics and Adolescent Medicine, 149*, 675–679.

Riddle, M. A., Labellarte, M. J., & Walkup, J. T. (1998). Pediatric psychopharmacology: problems and prospects. *Journal of Child and Adolescent Psychopharmacology, 8*, 87–97.

Robison, L. M., Sclar, D. A., Skaer, T. L., & Galin, R. S. (1999). National trends in the prevalence of attention-deficit/hyperactivity disorder and the prescribing of methylphenidate among school-age children 1990–1995. *Clinical Pediatrics, 38*, 209–217.

Rosh, J. R., Dellert, S. F., Narkewicz, M., Birnbaum, A., & Whitington, G. (1998). Four cases of severe hepatotoxicity associated with pemoline; possible autoimmune pathogenesis. *Pediatrics, 101*, 921–923.

Sachs, R. M., & Bortnichak, E. A. (1986). An evaluation of spontaneous adverse drug reaction monitoring systems. *American Journal of Medicine, 81*, 49–55.

Safer, D. J., & Krager, J. M. (1994). The increased rate of stimulant treatment for hyperactive/inattentive students in secondary schools. *Pediatrics, 94*, 462–464.

Safer, D. J., & Zito, J. M. (1999). Psychotropic medication for ADHD. *Mental Retardation and Developmental Disabilities: Research Reviews, 5*, 237–242.

Safer, D. J., Zito, J. M., & Fine, E. M. (1996). Increased methylphenidate usage for attention deficit disorder in the 1990s. *Pediatrics, 98*, 1084–1088.

Satterfield, J. H., Schell, A. M., & Barb, S. D. (1980). Potential risk of prolonged administration of stimulant medication for hyperactivity. *Journal of Developmental and Behavioral Pediatrics, 1*, 102–107.

Schachar, R. J., & Tannock, R. (1993). Childhood hyperactivity and psychostimulants: A review of extended treatment studies. *Journal of Child and Adolescent Psychopharmacology, 3*, 81–97.

Schiorring, E. (1979). Social isolation and other behavioral changes in groups of adult vervet monkeys produced by low, nonchronic doses of d-amphetamine. *Psychopharmacology, 64*, 297–304.

Shaffer, D. (1994). Attention deficit hyperactivity disorder in adults. *American Journal of Psychiatry, 151*, 633–638.

Shevell, M., & Schreiber, R. (1997). Pemoline-associated hepatic failure; a critical analysis of the literature. *Pediatric Neurology, 16*, 14–16.

Spencer, T. J., Biederman, J., Harding, M., O'Donnell, D., Faraone, S. V., & Wilens, T. (1996). Growth deficits in ADHD children revisited: Evidence for disorder-associated growth delays? *Journal of the American Academy of Child and Adolescent Psychiatry, 35*, 1460–1469.

Spencer, T. J., Biederman, J., Wilens, T., Harding, M., O'Donnell, D., & Griffin, S. (1996). Pharmacology of attention-deficit hyperactivity disorder across the life cycle. *Journal of the American Academy of Child and Adolescent Psychiatry, 35*, 409–432.

Sroufe, L. A., & Stewart, M. (1999). Treating problem children with stimulant drugs. *New England Journal Medicine, 289*, 407–413.

Swanson, J. M., McBurnett, K., Wigal, T., Pfiffner, L. J., Lerner, M. A., Williams, L., Christian, D. L., Tamm, L., Willcutt, E., Crowley, K., Clevenger, W., Khouzam, N., Woo, C., Crinella, F., & Fisher, T. D. (1993). Effect of stimulant medication on children with attention deficit disorder: A "review of reviews." *Exceptional Children, 60*, 154–162.

Tannock, R., Schachar, R. J., & Logan, G. D. (1993). Does methylphenidate induce overfocusing in hyperactive children? *Journal of Clinical Child Psychology, 22*, 28–41.

Tilson, H. A., MacPhail, R. C., & Crofton, K. M. (1995). Defining neurotoxicity in a decision-making context. *Neurotoxicology, 16*, 363–375.

Tolman, K. G., Freston, J. W., Berenson, M. M., & Sannella, J. J. (1973). Hepatoxicity due to pemoline. Report of two cases. *Digestion, 9*, 532–539.

Urman, R., Ickowicz, A., Fulford, P., & Tannock, R. (1995). An exaggerated cardiovascular response to methylphenidate in ADHD children with anxiety. *Journal of Child and Adolescent Psychopharmacology, 5*, 29–37.

Wilens, T. E., Spencer, T., Biederman, J., Wozniak, J., & Connor, D. (1995). Combined pharmacotherapy: An emerging trend in pediatric psychopharmacology. *Journal of the American Academy of Child and Adolescent Psychiatry, 34*, 110–112.

Wilson, J. M., Kalasinsky, K. S., Levey, A. I., Bergeron, C., Reiber, G., Anthony, R. M., Schmunk, G. A., Shannak, K., Haycock, J. W., & Kish, S. J. (1996). Striatal dopamine nerve terminal markers in human, chronic methamphetamine users. *Nature Medicine, 2*, 699–703.

Wolraich, M. L., Lindgren, S. D., Stromquist, A., Milich, R., Davis, C., & Watson, D. (1990). Stimulant medication use by primary care physicians in the treatment of attention deficit hyperactivity disorder. *Pediatrics, 86*, 95–101.

Wood, A. J., Stein, C. M., & Woosley, R. (1998). Making medicines safer—The need for an independent drug safety board. *New England Journal of Medicine, 339*, 1851–1854.

Zaczek, R., Battaglia, G., Contrera, J. F., Culp, S., & DeSouza, E. B. (1989). Methylphenidate and pemoline do not cause depletion or rat brain monamine markers similar to that observed with methamphetamine. *Toxicology and Applied Pharmacology, 100*, 227–233.

Zametkin, A., & Ernst, M. (1999). Problems in the management of attention-deficit-hyperactivity disorder. *New England Journal of Medicine, 340*, 40–46.

Zito, J. M., Safer, D. J., Riddle, M. A., Johnson, R. E., Speedie, S. M., & Fox, M. (1998). Prevalence variations in psychotropic treatment of children. *Journal of Child and Adolescent Psychopharmacology, 8*, 99–105.

Chapter 11

Nonstimulant Treatments for ADHD

by Joseph Biederman, M.D. and Thomas J. Spencer, M.D.

Introduction 11-1
    Evolving Nosology of ADHD 11-2
    Drawbacks of Using Stimulants to Treat ADHD 11-2
Alternative Treatments for ADHD: Tricyclic Antidepressants 11-4
    Advantages of TCAs 11-4
    Favorable Results With Desipramine 11-4
        DMI in Treating Children 11-4
        DMI in Treating Adults 11-5
    Efficacy of Nortriptyline 11-5
    Comparison of TCAs to Stimulants 11-5
    Safety of TCAs 11-6
Non-TCA Antidepressants 11-6
    Bupropion 11-6
    MAOIs and SSRIs 11-6
    Tomoxetine 11-7
Alpha-2 Noradrenergic Agonists 11-7
    Other Drugs 11-7
    New Directions: Cholinergic Drugs 11-8
Summary and Discussion 11-9
    Viability of Nonstimulant Treatments 11-9
    Need for Further Research 11-10

INTRODUCTION

Attention deficit hyperactivity disorder (ADHD) is a heterogeneous disorder of unknown etiology. It is one of the major clinical and public health problems in the United States because of its associated morbidity and disability in children, adolescents, and perhaps adults. Its impact on society is enormous in terms of the financial cost, the stress to families, the impact on academic and vocational activities, as well as the negative effects on self-esteem. Data from cross-sectional, retrospective, and follow-up studies indicate that children with ADHD are at risk for developing other psychiatric disorders in childhood, adolescence, and adulthood such as antisocial behaviors, alcoholism, and substance abuse, as well as depressive and anxiety symptoms and disorders.

Although its etiology remains unknown, data from family-genetic, twin, and adoption studies as well as segregation analysis suggest a genetic origin for some forms of this disorder (Abramowitz, 1990; Adler, Resnick. Kunz, & Devinsky, 1995; Bailey et al., 1997; Barkley, 1990, Barrickman et al., 1995, Biederman et al., 1995; Biederman, Baldessarini, Goldblatt, et al., 1993; Biederman, Baldessarini, Wright, Keenan, & Faraone, 1993). However, other etiologies are also likely, such as psychological adversity, perinatal insults, and perhaps other yet unknown biological causes (Biederman, Baldessarini, Wright, Knee, & Harmatz, 1989; Biederman et al., 1992).

Even though follow-up studies show that ADHD persists into adulthood in 10 percent to 60 percent of childhood-onset cases (Biederman, Faraone, Keenan, Knee, & Tsuang, 1990; Biederman, Gastfriend, & Jellinek, 1986; Biederman et al., 1999; Biederman, Thisted, Greenhill, & Ryan, 1995; Buitelaar, van de Gaag, Swaab-Barneveld, & Kuiper, 1996), little attention has been paid to the adult form of this disorder. Its high prevalence in childhood, combined with the follow-up results, suggests that approximately 2 percent of adults may suffer from ADHD. If so, this would make ADHD a relatively common adult disorder that may be underidentified in adult psychiatry clinics.

Evolving Nosology of ADHD

The nosology of ADHD has undergone a number of changes. The disorder was known as hyperkinetic reaction of childhood in the second edition of *Diagnostic and Statistical Manual of Mental Disorders* (DSM-II; American Psychiatric Association, 1962), and attention deficit disorder in DSM-III (American Psychiatric Association, 1980). It recently underwent yet another change with the introduction of DSM-IV (American Psychiatric Association, 1994). The disorder will continue to be known as attention deficit hyperactivity disorder. However, it is now possible for an individual to meet criteria for the disorder if he or she has symptoms of inattention and/or hyperactivity/impulsivity. A subtype is assigned depending on the symptoms endorsed (combined, predominantly hyperactive/impulsive, or predominantly inattentive). Additional criteria have been added requiring the presence of symptoms in two or more situations (e.g., at school and at home) to reduce the number of false-positive diagnoses.

Drawbacks of Using Stimulants to Treat ADHD

While there is no doubt that the stimulants are effective in the treatment of ADHD, it is estimated that at least 30 percent of affected individuals do not adequately respond or cannot tolerate stimulant treatment (Casat, Pleasants, Schroeder, & Parler, 1989; Casat, Pleasants, & van Wyck Fleet, 1987; Castellanos et al., 1997). In addition, stimulants are short-acting drugs that require multiple administrations during the day with their attendant impact on compliance and need to take treatment during school or work hours. While this problem may be offset by the development of an effective long-acting stimulant, this class of drugs often has an adverse impact on sleep, making their use in the evening hours difficult when children and adults need the ability to concentrate to help them deal with daily demands and when they interact with family members and friends.

In addition to these problems, the fact that stimulants are controlled substances, continues to fuel worries in children, families, and the treating community that further inhibit their use. These fears are based on lingering concerns about the abuse potential of stimulant drugs by the child, family member or his or her associates, the possibility of diversion, and safety concerns regarding the use of a controlled substance by patients who are impulsive and frequently have antisocial tendencies (Chappell et al., 1995). Similarly, the controlled nature of stimulant drugs poses important medicolegal concerns to the treating community that further increase the barriers to treatment.

Although recent work suggests that ADHD may be associated with a delay in the tempo of growth and that this effect appears to be independent of stimulant treatment, lingering concerns remain regarding the potential detrimental impact of stimulant drugs on growth and development. Similarly mixed is the existing literature on the use of stimulants in children with ADHD plus tic disorders. Recent studies of stimulants in children with ADHD and Tourette's syndrome have reported frequencies of tic exacerbation in both short-term (controlled) and medium-term follow-up studies ranging from 0 percent to 36 percent (Conners et al., 1996; Connor, Ozbayrak, Benjamin, Ma, & Fletcher, 1997; Cox, 1982; Deutsch, Matthysse, Swanson, & Farkas, 1990; Dillon, Salzman, & Schulsinger, 1985; DuPaul, Barkley, & McMurray, 1994).

In addition to these unresolved problems, it is increasingly evident that ADHD is frequently comorbid with mood and anxiety disorders, conditions that may have an adverse impact on responsivity to stimulant drugs. For example, of pediatric studies that examined ADHD children with depression and anxiety, 75 percent (six of eight) reported a lesser response to stimulants in improving ADHD symptoms in children with comorbid mood and anxiety disorders (Faraone & Biederman, 1994; Faraone et al., 1992; Faraone et al., 1999; Findling, Schwartz, Flannery, & Manos, 1996; Frazier et al., 1999; Fung, 1988). Moreover, a recent report indicates that stimulants are poorly effective in the treatment of ADHD in the context of coexisting manic symptomatology, and that their use in such patients may result in worsening of mood instability (Fung & Lau, 1989). These shortcomings and problems associated with the stimulants support the need for alternative treatments.

The search for alternative therapeutic approaches to improve disease management has been the rule rather than the exception in the medical sciences. Not only have such efforts generated improved versions of old therapeutic agents, but they have also led to the development of novel drugs with new mechanisms of action offering patients true alternatives to standard treatments. This has certainly been the case with the advent of serotonergic specific drugs in the treatment of depression that revolutionized the pharmacotherapy of mood and anxiety disorders. Although not all efforts at drug development led to superior compounds, they did lead to the development of alternative agents critical for the management of patients who do not respond or cannot tolerate other treatments. However, in contrast to these trends, the field of ADHD has not enjoyed similar advances. For example, the last medicine approved for the treatment of ADHD is the stimulant drug pemoline, more than two decades ago.

ALTERNATIVE TREATMENTS FOR ADHD: TRICYCLIC ANTIDEPRESSANTS

Advantages of TCAs

Although tricyclic antidepressants (TCAs) have a wide range of neurochemical effects on neurotransmitters, it is assumed that their activity in ADHD stems from their actions on catecholamine (norepinephrine and dopamine) reuptake. Advantages of this class of drugs include their relative long half life (approximately twelve hours), obviating the need to administer medication during school hours, absence of abuse potential, and putative positive effects on mood and anxiety, sleep, and tics. Of thirty-three studies (twenty-one controlled; twelve open) evaluating TCAs in children, adolescents (N =1,139), and adults (N = 78), 91 percent reported positive effects on ADHD symptoms. Imipramine and desipramine are the most studied TCAs, followed by a handful of studies on other TCAs. Although most TCA studies (73 percent) were relatively brief, lasting a few weeks to several months, nine studies (27 percent) reported enduring effects for up to two years. Outcomes in both short- and long-term studies were equally positive. Although one study (Gadow, Nolan, & Sverd, 1992) reported a 50 percent dropout rate after one year, it is noteworthy that improvement was sustained for those who remained on imipramine. More recent studies using aggressive doses of TCAs reported sustained improvement for up to one year with desipramine (> 4 mg/kg) (Gadow, Sverd, Sprafkin, Nolan, & Ezor; Gadow, Sverd, Sprafkin, Nolan, & Grossman, 1999) and nortriptyline (2.0 mg/kg) (Garfinkel, Wender, Sloman, & O'Neill, 1983). Although response was equally positive in all dose ranges, it was more sustained in those studies that used higher doses. A high interindividual variability in TCA serum levels has been consistently reported for imipramine and desipramine with little relationship between serum level to daily dose, response, or side effects. In contrast, nortriptyline appears to have a positive association between dose and serum level (Garfinkel et al., 1983).

Favorable Results With Desipramine

DMI in Treating Children. In the largest controlled study of a TCA in children, our group reported favorable results with desipramine (DMI) in sixty-two clinically referred ADHD children, most of whom had previously failed to respond to psychostimulant treatment (Gasfriend, Biederman, & Jellinek, 1985). The study was a randomized, placebo-controlled, parallel-design, six-week clinical trial. Clinically and statistically significant differences in behavioral improvement were found for DMI over placebo, at an average daily dose of 5 mg/kg. Specifically, 68 percent of DMI-treated patients were considered very much or much improved, compared with only 10 percent of placebo patients ($p < 0.001$). In a further analysis we examined whether comorbidity of ADHD with conduct disorder, major depression, or an anxiety disorder or a family history of ADHD predicted response to DMI treatment (Gittelman, 1980). Although the presence of comorbidity increased the likelihood of a placebo response, neither comorbidity with conduct disorder, depression, or anxiety nor a family history of ADHD yielded differential responses to DMI treatment. In addition, DMI-treated ADHD patients showed a substantial reduction in depressive symptoms compared with placebo-treated patients.

DMI in Treating Adults. Our group obtained similar results in a similarly designed controlled clinical trial of DMI in forty-one adults with ADHD (Gittelman, Mannuzza, Shenker, & Bonagura, 1985). DMI, at an average daily dose of 150 mg (average serum level of 113 ng/ml), was statistically and clinically more effective than placebo. Sixty-eight percent of DMI treated patients responded compare with none of the placebo-treated patients ($p < 0.0001$). Moreover, at the end of the study, the average severity of ADHD symptoms was reduced to below the level required to meet diagnostic criteria in patients receiving DMI. Importantly, while the full DMI dose was achieved at week 2, clinical response improved further over the following four weeks, indicating a latency of response. Response was independent of dose, serum DMI level, gender, or lifetime psychiatric comorbidity with anxiety or depressive disorders.

Efficacy of Nortriptyline

In a prospective placebo-controlled discontinuation trial, we recently demonstrated the efficacy of nortriptyline in doses of up to 2 mg/kg daily in thirty-five school-age youth with ADHD (Gittelman-Klein, 1974). In that study, 80 percent of youth responded by week 6 in the open phase. During the discontinuation phase, subjects randomized to placebo lost the anti-ADHD effect compared to those receiving nortriptyline who maintained a robust anti-ADHD effect. Again there was a lag in response and loss of response to medication administration and discontinuation. While the full dose was achieved by week 2, the full effect evolved slowly over the ensuing four weeks. ADHD youth receiving nortriptyline also were found to have more modest but statistically significant reductions in oppositionality and anxiety. Nortriptyline was well tolerated with some weight gain. Weight gain is frequently considered to be a desirable side effect in this population. In contrast, a systematic study in fourteen treatment-refractory ADHD youth receiving protriptyline (mean dose of 30 mg) reported less favorable results. We found that only 45 percent of ADHD youth responded or could tolerate protriptyline secondary to adverse effects (Goldman, Genel, Bezman, & Slanetz, 1998).

Comparison of TCAs to Stimulants

Thirteen of the thirty-three TCA studies (40 percent) compared TCAs to stimulants. Five studies each reported that stimulants were superior to TCAs (Goodman, 1989; Goodman & Stevenson, 1989a, 1989b; Greenberg, Yellin, Spring, & Metcalf, 1975) or equal to TCAs (Gross, 1973; Gualtieri & Evans, 1988; Gunning, 1992; Hechtman, 1992; Hoge & Biederman, 1986), and three studies reported that TCAs were superior to stimulants (Hornig-Rohan & Amsterdam, 1995; Horrigan & Barnhill, 1995; Huessy & Wright, 1970). Analysis of response profiles indicate that TCAs more consistently improve behavioral symptoms, as rated by clinicians, teachers, and parents, than they impact cognitive function, as measured in neuropsychological testing (Gadow et al., 1992; Gunning, 1992; Hornig-Rohan & Amsterdam, 1995; Hunt, 1987). As noted previously, studies of TCAs have uniformly reported a robust rate of response of ADHD symptoms in ADHD subjects with comorbid depression or anxiety (Garfinkel et al., 1983; Gittelman, 1980; Hunt, Arnsten, & Asbell, 1995; Hunt, Minderaa, & Cohen, 1985). In addition, studies of TCAs have consistently reported a robust rate of response in ADHD subjects with comorbid tic disorders (Johns, Louis, Becker, & Means, 1982; Jones, Sahakian, Levy, Warburton, & Gray, 1992; Kennedy et al., 1997; Konkol, Fischer, & Newby, 1990; Kupietz & Balka, 1976; LaHoste et al., 1996). For example, in a recent controlled study, Spencer, Biederman, Kerman, Steingard, and Wilens (1993) replicated data from a retrospective chart review indicating that desipramine had a robust beneficial effect on ADHD and tic symptoms (Lanau, Zenner, Civelli, & Hartman, 1997).

Safety of TCAs

The potential benefits of TCAs in the treatment of ADHD have been clouded by concerns about their safety stemming from reports of sudden unexplained death in four ADHD children treated with DMI (Law & Schachar, 1999), although the causal link between DMI and these deaths remain uncertain. A rather extensive literature evaluating cardiovascular parameters in TCA exposed youth consistently identified mostly minor, asymptomatic, but statistically significant increases in heart rate and ECG measures of cardiac conduction times associated with TCA treatment (Levin et al., 1996). A recent report estimated that the magnitude of DMI-associated risk of sudden death in children may not be much larger than the baseline risk of sudden death in this age group (Luh, Pliszka, Olvers, & Tatum, 1996). However, because of this uncertainty, prudence mandates that until more is known, TCAs should be used as a second-line treatment for ADHD and only after carefully weighing the risks and benefits of treating or not treating an affected child.

NON-TCA ANTIDEPRESSANTS

Bupropion

Bupropion hydrochloride is a novel-structured antidepressant of the aminoketone class related to the phenylisopropylamines but pharmacologically distinct from known antidepressants (Malhotra & Santosh, 1998). Bupropion appears to posses both indirect dopamine agonist and noradrenergic effects. Bupropion has been shown to be effective for ADHD in children, in a controlled multisite study ($N = 72$) (Malhotra & Santosh, 1998; Mannuzza et al., 1991; Mannuzza, Klein, Bessler, Malloy, & Padula, 1993) and in a comparison with methylphenidate ($N = 15$) (Manshadi, Lippman, O'Daniel, & Blackman, 1983). In an open study of ADHD adults, sustained improvement was documented at one year at an average of 360 mg for six to eight weeks (Mattes, 1986). While bupropion has been associated a slightly increased risk (0.4 percent) for drug-induced seizures relative to other antidepressants, this risk has been linked to high doses, a previous history of seizures and eating disorders.

MAOIs and SSRIs

Although a small number of studies suggested that monoamine oxidase inhibitors (MAOIs) may be effective in juvenile and adult ADHD, their potential for hypertensive crisis associated with the irreversible MAOIs (e.g. phenelzine and tranylcypromine), with dietetic transgressions (tyramine-containing foods, i.e., most cheeses) and drug interactions (pressor amines, most cold medicines, amphetamines) seriously limits their use. Although not available in the United States, this "cheese effect" may be obviated with the reversible MAOIs (e.g., moclobemide) that have shown promise in one open trial (Meck & Church, 1987). While a single small open study (Mereu, Yoon, Gessa, Naes, & Westfall, 1987) suggested that fluoxetine may be beneficial in the treatment of ADHD children, the usefulness of selective serotonin reuptake inhibitors (SSRIs) in the treatment of core ADHD symptoms is not supported by clinical experience (Milberger, Biederman, Faraone, Guite, et al., 1997). Similarly uncertain is the usefulness of mixed serotonergic/noradrenergic atypical antidepressant venlafaxine in the treatment of ADHD. While a 77 percent response rate was reported in completers in open studies of ADHD adults, 21 percent dropped out due to side effects ($n = 4$ open studies; $N = 61$ adults) (Milberger, Biederman, Faraone, Chen, & Jones, 1996, 1997; National Institutes of Mental Health, 1996; Parrott & Winder, 1989). Similarly, a single, open study of venlafaxine in sixteen ADHD children reported a 50 percent response rate in completers with a 25 percent rate of dropout due to side effects, most prominently increased hyperactivity (Peeke & Peeke, 1984).

Tomoxetine

More promising results have been associated with the experimental noradrenergic specific compound tomoxetine. One initial controlled clinical trial in adults documented efficacy and good tolerability (Pliszka, 1989). These initial encouraging results coupled with extensive safety data in adults, fueled efforts at developing this compound in the treatment of pediatric ADHD and an initial open study of this compound in pediatric ADHD documented strong clinical benefits with excellent tolerability, including a safe cardiovascular profile (Pomerlau, Downey, Stelson, & Pomerlau, 1996).

ALPHA-2 NORADRENERGIC AGONISTS

Despite its wide use in ADHD children, there have been very few studies ($n = 4$ studies [2 controlled], $N = 122$ children) (Prince, et al., 2000; Quinn & Rapoport, 1975; Rapoport, Quinn, Bradbard, Riddle, & Brooks, 1974; Rapport, Carlson, Kelly, & Pataki, 1993) supporting the efficacy of clonidine. Treatment with clonidine appears to have mostly a behavioral effect in disinhibited and agitated youth, with limited impact on cognition. Even more limited is the literature on guanfacine. There are only three small open studies of guanfacine in children and adolescents with ADHD. In these studies, beneficial effects on hyperactive behaviors and attentional abilities were reported (Ratey, Greenberg, & Lindem, 1986; Reimherr, Hedges, Strong, & Wender, 1995). Several cases of sudden death have been reported in children treated with clonidine plus methylphenidate, raising concerns about the safety of this combination (Silva, Munoz, & Alpert, 1996).

Other Drugs

Beta, noradrenergic blockers also have been studied for use in ADHD. An open study of propranolol for ADHD adults with temper outbursts reported improvement at daily doses of up to 640 mg/day (Singer et al., 1994). Another report indicated that beta blockers may be helpful in combination with the stimulants (Spencer, 1997). In a controlled study of pindolol in fifty-two ADHD children, symptoms of behavioral dyscontrol and hyperactivity were improved with less apparent cognitive benefit (Spencer, Biederman, Kerman, et al., 1993). However, prominent adverse effects such as nightmares and paraesthesias led to discontinuation of the drug in all test subjects. An open study of nadolol in aggressive, developmentally delayed children with ADHD symptoms reported effective diminution of aggression with little apparent effect on ADHD symptoms (Spencer et al., 1996).

A recent open study of twelve ADHD children, reported that the non-benzodi-azepine anxiolytic buspirone at 0.5 mg/kg/day improved both ADHD symptoms and psychosocial function in ADHD youth (Spencer, Biederman, Wilens, Prince, & Rea, 1999). Buspirone has a high affinity to 5-HT 1-A receptors, both pre- and postsynap-tic, as well as a modest effect on the dopaminergic system and alpha-adrenergic activity. However, results from a recent multisite controlled clinical trial of transdermal buspirone failed to separate it form placebo in a large sample of children with ADHD. (Bristol Myers Squib, 2000). While an old literature suggested that typical antipsy-chotics were effective in the treatment of children with ADHD (Castellanos et al., 1997), their spectrum of both short- (extrapyramidal reactions) and long-term (tardive dyskinesia) adverse effects greatly limits their usefulness. A recent study of an atypi-cal antipsychotic reported no anti-ADHD effect in manic children (Spencer, Biederman, Wilens, Steingard, & Geist, 1993). Thus, neuroleptics, either typical or atypical, have limited use in the treatment of ADHD and should not be used in routine treatment. A recent meta-analysis pooling data from ten studies provided preliminary evidence that carbemazepine may have activity in ADHD (Spencer, Wilens, & Biederman, 1995).

New Directions: Cholinergic Drugs

In recent years, evidence has emerged that nicotinic dysregulation may contribute to the pathophysiology of ADHD. This is not surprising considering that nicotinic acti-vation enhances dopaminergic neurotransmission (Steingard, Biederman, Spencer, Wilens, & Gonzalez, 1993; Sunohara et al., 1997). Independent lines of investigation have documented that ADHD is associated with an increased risk and earlier age of onset of cigarette smoking (Swanson, Kinsbourne, Roberts, & Zucker, 1978; Tannock, Ickowicz, & Schachar, 1995), that maternal smoking during pregnancy increases the risk for ADHD in the offspring and that *in utero* exposure to nicotine in animals con-fers a heightened risk for an ADHD-like syndrome in the newborn (Taylor et al., 1987; Trott, Friese, Menzel, & Nissen, 1991; Voelker, Lachar, & Gdowski, 1983; Watter & Dreyfuss, 1973). In non-ADHD subjects, central nicotinic activation has been shown to improve temporal memory (Weiss, Hechtman, Milroy, & Perlman, 1985), attention (Wender & Reimherr, 1990; Werry, 1980; Wesnes & Warburton, 1984), cognitive vig-ilance (Werry, 1980; Wesnes & Warburton, 1984; Westfall, Grant, & Perry, 1983), and executive function (Wesnes & Warburton, 1984).

Support for a "nicotinic hypothesis" of ADHD can be derived from a recent study that evaluated the therapeutic effects of nicotine in the treatment of adult with ADHD (Wilens, Biederman, Abrantes, & Spencer, 1996). Although this controlled clinical trial in adults with ADHD documented that commercially available transdermal nicotine patch resulted in significant improvement of ADHD symptoms, working memory, and neuropsychological functioning (Wilens et al., 1996), the trial was short (two-day) and included only a handful of patients. More promising results supporting the usefulness of nicotinic drugs in ADHD derives from a recent controlled clinical trial of ABT-418 in adults with ADHD (Wilens, Biederman, Geist, Steingard, & Spencer, 1993). ABT-418 is a central nervous system cholinergic nicotinic activating agent with structural similarities to nicotine. Phase one studies of this compound in humans indicated its low abuse liability, as well as adequate safety and tolerability in elderly adults (Abbott Laboratories, 2000). A double-blind, placebo-controlled, randomized crossover trial, comparing a transdermal patch of ABT-418 (75 mg daily) to placebo in adults with DSM-IV ADHD showed a significantly higher proportion of ADHD adults to be very much improved while receiving ABT-418 than when receiving placebo (40 percent vs. 13 percent; $c2 = 5.3$, $p = .021$). Although preliminary, these results suggest that nicotinic analogs may have activity in ADHD.

SUMMARY AND DISCUSSION

Viability of Nonstimulant Treatments

A substantial literature supports the viability of nonstimulant treatments for ADHD. Despite their chemical differences, the various compounds with documented anti-ADHD activity share a common noradrenergic/dopaminergic (NE/DA) activity. The most established of the alternative treatments for ADHD are the tricyclic antidepressants, particularly the more noradrenergic, secondary amines TCAs desipramine and nortriptyline. Despite lingering concerns regarding their cardiovascular safety, TCAs have been documented to be effective and well tolerated in controlling symptoms of ADHD in studies with over 1,000 children. In addition, to the TCAs, the atypical mixed noradrenergic/dopaminergic antidepressant bupropion and the novel noradrenergic specific antidepressant tomoxetine have also been documented to be effective in the treatment of ADHD in controlled clinical trials. In contrast, the scientific base supporting the efficacy of alpha-2, noradrenergic agonists continues to be extremely limited.

In addition to drugs with NE/DA activity, several lines of evidence provide preliminary support for the potential benefits of cholinergic drugs in the treatment of ADHD. A nicotinic analog demonstrated efficacy in a controlled clinical trial of adults with ADHD and a trial of the cholinergic cognitive enhancing drug donepezil in adults with ADHD is ongoing. Whether their mechanism of action is through cholinergic modulation of dopaminergic systems or an independent effect remains unknown. In addition to their anti-ADHD activity, this class of medications may also prove helpful in improving executive functions deficits that have heretofore been intractable to existing treatments. In light of replicated findings linking the D4 receptor gene to juvenile (Wilens, Biederman, Mick, & Spencer, 1995; Wilens, Biederman, Prince, et al., 1996; Wilens et al., 1999) and adult (Wilens & Spencer, 1999; Winsberg, Bialer, Kupietz, & Tobias, 1972) ADHD, drugs with activity on this receptor may warrant further investigation in this disorder. In this regard it is notable that both noradrenaline as well as dopamine are potent agonists at the D4 receptor (Yepes, Balka, Winsberg, & Bialer, 1977).

Need for Further Research

The congruence of adult and juvenile ADHD in clinical features, neurobiology (familiality, neuropsychology, imaging, and associations to candidate genes [D4 receptor]), as well as similar drug responsivity to well documented anti-ADHD treatments (i.e., stimulants, TCAs, bupropion), affords the testing of promising experimental products first in adults with this disorder before testing in children. Examples of such an approach have been the initial trials with the novel compounds tomoxetine and ABT-418 that separated from placebo under double-blind conditions in ADHD adults as a viable test of their applicability in juveniles.

Despite a promising literature supporting the efficacy of nonstimulant treatments for ADHD, more efforts are needed to further develop safe and effective alternative treatments for ADHD. Strong impetus for such efforts derives from the well-documented evidence that a substantial minority of stimulant-treated patients cannot tolerate or do not adequately respond to stimulant drugs, as well as their short duration of action and their controlled status, that seriously limit their usefulness. Other similarly important factors include the heterogeneity of the disorder and its patterns of comorbidity that further argue for the need to develop viable, safe, and effective alternatives for the treatment of ADHD. It is hoped that advances in the understanding of the underlying neurobiology of ADHD will lead to the development of a new generation of safe and effective treatments for this disorder. Such developments have the promise of revolutionizing the field and improving the quality of life of the millions of affected patients and their families worldwide.

References

Abbott Laboratories. (2000). Unpublished data.

Abramowicz, M. (1990). Sudden death in children treated with tricyclic antidepressant. *The Medical Letter on Drugs and Therapeutics, The Medical Letter, 32*, 37–40.

Adler, L., Resnick, S., Kunz, M., Devinsky, O. (1995). *Open-label trial of venlafaxine in attention deficit disorder*. Orlando, FL: New Clinical Drug Evaluation Unit Program.

American Psychiatric Association. (1968). *Diagnostic and statistical manual of mental disorders* (2nd ed.). Washington, DC: Author.

American Psychiatric Association. (1980). *Diagnostic and statistical manual of mental disorders* (3rd ed.). Washington, DC: Author.

American Psychiatric Association. (1994). *Diagnostic and statistical manual of mental disorders* (4th ed.). Washington, DC: Author.

Bailey, J. N., Palmer, C. G. S., Ramsey, C., Cantwell, D., Kim, K., Woodward, J. A., McGough, J., Asarnow, R. F., Nelson, S., Smalley, S. L.. (1997). DRD4 gene and susceptibility to attention deficit hyperactivity disorder: Differences in familial and sporadic cases. *American Journal of Medical Genetics, Neuropsychiatric Genetics, 74*, 623.

Barkley, R. A. (1977). A review of stimulant drug research with hyperactive children. *Journal of Child Psychology and Psychiatry, 18*, 137–165.

Barrickman, L., Noyes, R., Kuperman, S., Schumacher, E., & Verda, M. (1991). Treatment of ADHD with fluoxetine: A preliminary trial. *Journal of the American Academy of Child and Adolescent Psychiatry, 30*, 762–767.

Barrickman, L., Perry, P., Allen, A., Kuperman, S., Arndt, S., Herrmann, K., & Schumacher, E. (1995). Bupropion versus methylphenidate in the treatment of attention-deficit hyperactivity disorder. *Journal of the American Academy of Child and Adolescent Psychiatry, 34*, 649–657.

Biederman, J., Baldessarini, R., Goldblatt, A., Lapey, K., Doyle, A., & Hesslein P. (1993). A naturalistic study of 24-hour electrocardiographic recordings and echocardiographic finding in children and adolescents treated with desipramine. *Journal of the American Academy of Child and Adolescent Psychiatry*, *32*, 805–813.

Biederman, J., Baldessarini, R., Wright, V., Keenan, K., & Faraone, S. (1993). A double-blind placebo controlled study of desipramine in the treatment of attention deficit disorder: III. Lack of impact of comorbidity and family history factors on clinical response. *Journal of the American Academy of Child and Adolescent Psychiatry*, *32*, 199–204.

Biederman, J., Baldessarini, R., Wright, V., Knee, D., & Harmatz, J. (1989). A double-blind placebo controlled study of desipramine in the treatment of attention deficit disorder: I. Efficacy. *Journal of the American Academy of Child and Adolescent Psychiatry*, *28*, 777–784.

Biederman, J., Faraone, S. V., Keenan, K., Benjamin, J., Krifcher, B., Moore, C., Sprich-Buckminster, S., Ugaglia, K., Jellinek, M. S., & Steingard, R. (1992). Further evidence for family-genetic risk factors in attention deficit hyperactivity disorder. Patterns of comorbidity in probands and relatives psychiatrically and pediatrically referred samples. *Archives of General Psychiatry*, *49*, 728–738.

Biederman, J., Faraone, S. V., Keenan, K., Knee, D., & Tsuang, M. T. (1990). Family-genetic and psychosocial risk factors in DSM-III attention deficit disorder. *Journal of the American Academy of Child and Adolescent Psychiatry*, *29*, 526–533.

Biederman, J., Gastfriend, D. R., & Jellinek, M. S. (1986). Desipramine in the treatment of children with attention deficit disorder. *Journal of Clinical Psychopharmacology*, *6*, 359–363.

Biederman, J., Mick, E., Prince, J., Bostic, J. Q., Wilens, T. E., Spencer, T., Wozniak, J., & Faraone, S. V. (1999). Systematic chart review of the pharmacologic treatment of comorbid attention deficit hyperactivity disorder in youth with mania disorder. *Journal of Child and Adolescent Psychopharmacology*, *9*, 247–256.

Biederman, J., Milberger, S., Faraone, S., Kiely, K., Guite, J., Mick, E., Ablon, S., Warburton, R., & Reed, E. (1995). Family environmental risk factors for attention deficit hyperactivity disorder: A test of Rutter's indicators of adversity. *Archives of General Psychiatry*, *52*, 464–470.

Biederman, J., Thisted, R., Greenhill, L., & Ryan, N. (1995). Estimation of the association between desipramine and the risk for sudden death in 5- to 14-year-old children. *Journal of Clinical Psychiatry*, *56*, 87–93.

Bristol Myers Squibb. (2000). Unpublished data.

Buitelaar, J., van der Gaag, R., Swaab-Barneveld, H., & Kuiper, M. (1996). Pindolol and methylphenidate in children with attention deficit hyperactivity disorder. *Journal of Child and Adolescent Psychiatry*, *36*, 587–595.

Casat, C. D., Pleasants, D. Z., Schroeder, D. H., & Parler, D. W. (1989). Bupropion in children with attention deficit disorder. *Psychopharmacology*, *25*, 198–201.

Casat, C. D., Pleasants, D. Z., & Van Wyck Fleet, J. (1987). A double-blind trial of bupropion in children with attention deficit disorder. *Psychopharmacology*, *23*, 120–122.

Castellanos, F. X., Giedd, J. N., Elia, J., Marsh, W. L., Ritchie, G. F., Hamburger, S. D., & Rapoport, J. L. (1997). Controlled stimulant treatment of ADHD and comorbid Tourette's syndrome: Effects of stimulant and dose. *Journal of the American Academy of Child and Adolescent Psychiatry*, *36*, 589–596.

Chappell, P., Riddle, M., Scahill, L., Lynch, K., Schultz, R., Arnsten, A., Leckman, J., & Cohen, D. (1995). Guanfacine treatment of comorbid attention-deficit hyperactivity disorder and Tourette's syndrome. *Journal of the American Academy of Child and Adolescent Psychiatry*, *34*, 1140–1146.

Conners, C., Casat, C., Gualtieri, C., Weller, E., Reader, M., Reiss, A., Weller, R., Khayrallah, M., & Ascher, J. (1996). Bupropion hydrochloride in attention deficit disorder with hyperactivity. *Journal of the American Academy of Child and Adolescent Psychiatry*, *35*, 1314–1321.

Connor, D., Ozbayrak, K., Benjamin, S., Ma, Y., & Fletcher, K. (1997). A pilot study of nadolol for overt aggression in developmentally delayed individuals. *Journal of the American Academy of Child and Adolescent Psychiatry*, *36*, 826–834.

Cox, W. (1982). An indication for the use of imipramine in attention deficit disorder. *American Journal of Psychiatry*, *139*, 1059–1060.

Deutsch, C. K., Matthysse, S., Swanson, J. M., & Farkas, L. G. (1990). Genetic latent structure analysis of dysmorphology in attention deficit disorder. *Journal of the American Academy of Child and Adolescent Psychiatry*, *29*, 189–194.

Dillon, D. C., Salzman, I. J., & Schulsinger, D. A. (1985). The use of imipramine in Tourette's syndrome and attention deficit disorder: Case report. *Journal of Clinical Psychiatry*, *46*, 348–349.

DuPaul, G., Barkley, R., & McMurray, M. (1994). Response of children with ADHD to methylphenidate: Interaction with internalizing symptoms. *Journal of the American Academy of Child and Adolescent Psychiatry*, *33*, 894–903.

Faraone, S., & Biederman, J. (1994). Is attention deficit hyperactivity disorder familial? *Harvard Review of Psychiatry*, *1*, 271–287.

Faraone, S., Biederman, J., Krifcher, B., Keenan, K., Moore, C., Sprich, S., & Tsuang, M. (1992). Segregation analysis of attention deficit hyperactivity disorder: Evidence for single gene transmission. *Psychiatric Genetics*, *2*, 257–275.

Faraone, S., Biederman, J., Weiffenbach, B., Keith, T., Chu, M. P., Weaver, A., Spencer, T. J., Wilens, T. E., Frazier, J., Cleves, M., & Sakai, J. (1999). Dopamine D4 gene 7-repeat allele and attention deficit hyperactivity disorder. *American Journal of Psychiatry*, *156*, 768–770.

Findling, R., Schwartz, M., Flannery, D., & Manos, M. (1996). Venlafaxine in adults with ADHD: An open trial. *Journal of Clinical Psychiatry*, *57*, 184–189.

Frazier, J., Meyer, M., Biederman, J., Wozniak, J., Wilens, T., Spencer, T., & Shapiro, S. (1999). Risperidone treatment for juvenile bipolar disorder: A case series. *Journal of the American Academy of Child and Adolescent Psychiatry*, *38*, 960–965.

Fung, Y. K. (1988). Postnatal behavioural effects of maternal nicotine exposure in rats. *Journal of Pharmacy and Pharmacology*, *40*, 870–872.

Fung, Y. K., & Lau, Y. S. (1989). Effects of prenatal nicotine exposure on rat striatal dopaminergic and nicotinic systems. *Pharmacology, Biochemistry and Behavior*, *33*, 1–6.

Gadow, K. D., Nolan, E. E., & Sverd, J. (1992). Methylphenidate in hyperactive boys with comorbid tic disorder: II. Short-term behavioral effects in school settings. *Journal of the American Academy of Child and Adolescent Psychiatry*, *31*, 462–471.

Gadow, K., Sverd, J., Sprafkin, J., Nolan, E., & Ezor, S. (1995). Efficacy of methylphenidate for attention-deficit hyperactivity disorder in children with tic disorder [published erratum appears in *Archives of General Psychiatry*, *52*(10), 836 (1995, October)]. *Archives of General Psychiatry*, *52*, 444–455.

Gadow, K. D., Sverd, J., Sprafkin, J., Nolan, E., & Grossman, S. (1999). Long-term methylphenidate therapy in children with comorbid attention-deficit hyperactivity disorder and chronic multiple tic disorder. *Archives of General Psychiatry*, *56*, 330–336.

Garfinkel, B. D., Wender, P. H., Sloman, L., & O'Neill, I. (1983). Tricyclic antidepressant and methylphenidate treatment of attention deficit disorder in children. *Journal of the American Academy of Child and Adolescent Psychiatry*, *22*, 343–348.

Gastfriend, D. R., Biederman, J., & Jellinek M. S. (1985). Desipramine in the treatment of attention deficit disorder in adolescents. *Psychopharmacology*, *21*, 144–145.

Gittelman, R. (1980). Childhood disorders. In D. Klein, F. Quitkin, A. Rifkin, & R. Gittelman (Eds.), *Drug treatment of adult and child psychiatric disorders* (pp. 576–756.) Baltimore: Williams & Wilkins.

Gittelman, R., Mannuzza, S., Shenker, R., & Bonagura, N. (1985). Hyperactive boys almost grown up: I. Psychiatric status. *Archives of General Psychiatry*, *42*, 937–947.

Gittelman-Klein, R. (1974). Pilot clinical trial of imipramine in hyperkinetic children. In C. Conners (Ed.), *Clinical use of stimulant drugs in children* (pp. 192–201). The Hague, Netherlands: Excerpta Medica.

Goldman, L. S., Genel, M., Bezman, R. J., & Slanetz, P. J. (1998). Diagnosis and treatment of attention-deficit/hyperactivity disorder in children and adolescents. Council on Scientific Affairs, American Medical Association. *Journal of the American Medical Association*, *279*, 1100–1107.

Goodman, R. (1989). Genetic factors in hyperactivity: Account for about half of the explainable variance. *British Medical Journal, 298*, 1407–1408.

Goodman, R., & Stevenson, J. (1989a). A twin study of hyperactivity: I. An examination of hyperactivity scores and categories derived from Rutter teacher and parent questionnaires. *Journal of Child Psychology and Psychiatry, 30*, 671–689.

Goodman, R., & Stevenson, J. (1989b). A twin study of hyperactivity: II. The aetiological role of genes, family relationships and perinatal adversity. *Journal of Child Psychology and Psychiatry, 30*, 691–709.

Greenberg, L., Yellin, A., Spring, C., & Metcalf, M. (1975). Clinical effects of imipramine and methylphenidate in hyperactive children. *International Journal of Mental Health, 4*, 144–156.

Gross, M. (1973). Imipramine in the treatment of minimal brain dysfunction in children. *Psychosomatics, 14*, 283–285.

Gualtieri, C. T., & Evans, R. W. (1988). Motor performance in hyperactive children treated with imipramine. *Perceptual Motion, 66*, 763–769.

Gunning, B. (1992). *A controlled trial of clonidine in hyperkinetic children.* Doctoral thesis, Department of Child and Adolescent Psychiatry, Academic Hospital Rotterdam-Sophia Children's Hospital Rotterdam, The Netherlands.

Hechtman, L. (1992). Long-term outcome in attention-deficit hyperactivity disorder. *Psychiatric Clinics of North America, 1*, 553–565.

Hoge, S. K., & Biederman, J. (1986). A case of Tourette's syndrome with symptoms of attention deficit disorder treated with desipramine. *Journal of Clinical Psychiatry, 47*, 478–479.

Hornig-Rohan, M., & Amsterdam, J. (1995). *Venlafaxine vs. stimulant therapy in patients with dual diagnoses of ADHD and depression.* Orlando, FL: New Clinical Drug Evaluation Unit Program.

Horrigan, J. P., & Barnhill, L. J. (1995). Guanfacine for treatment of attention-deficit hyperactivity disorder in boys. *Journal of Child and Adolescent Psychophamacology, 5*, 215–223.

Huessy, H., & Wright, A. (1970). The use of imipramine in children's behavior disorders. *Acta Paedopsychiatrie, 37*, 194–199.

Hunt, R. D. (1987). Treatment effects of oral and transdermal clonidine in relation to methylphenidate: An open pilot study in ADD-H. *Psychopharmacology, 23*, 111–114.

Hunt, R., Arnsten, A., & Asbell, M. (1995). An open trial of guanfacine in the treatment of attention-deficit hyperactivity disorder. *Journal of the American Academy of Child and Adolescent Psychiatry, 34*, 50–54.

Hunt, R. D., Minderaa, R. B., & Cohen, D. J. (1985). Clonidine benefits children with attention deficit disorder and hyperactivity: Report of a double-blind placebo-crossover therapeutic trial. *Journal of the American Academy of Child Psychiatry, 24*, 617–629.

Johns, J. M., Louis, T. M., Becker, R. F., & Means, L. W. (1982). Behavioral effects of prenatal exposure to nicotine in guinea pigs. *Neurobehavioral Toxicology and Teratology, 4*, 365–369.

Jones, G., Sahakian, B., Levy, R., Warburton, D., & Gray, J. (1992). Effects of acute subcutaneous nicotine on attention, information and short-term memory in Alzheimer's disease. *Psychopharmacology, 108*, 485–494.

Kennedy, J. L., Richter, P., Swanson, J. M., Wigal, S. B., LaHoste, G. J., & Sunohara, G. (1997). *Association of dopamine D4 receptor gene and ADHD.* Paper presented at the annual meeting of the American Psychiatric Association, San Diego, CA.

Konkol, R., Fischer, M., & Newby, R. (1990). Double-blind, placebo-controlled stimulant trial in children with Tourette's syndrome and ADHD: Abstract. *Annals of Neurology, 28*, 424.

Kupietz, S. S., & Balka, E. B. (1976). Alterations in the vigilance performance of children receiving amitriptyline and methylphenidate pharmacotherapy. *Psychopharmacology, 50*, 29–33.

LaHoste, G. J., Swanson, J. M., Wigal, S. B., Glabe, C., Wigal, T., King, N., & Kennedy, J. L. (1996). Dopamine D4 receptor gene polymorphism is associated with attention deficit hyperactivity disorder. *Molecular Psychiatry, 1*, 121–124.

Lanau, F., Zenner, M., Civelli, O., & Hartman, D. (1997). Epinephrine and norepinephrine act as potent agonists at the recombinant human dopamine D4 receptor. *Journal of Neurochemistry, 68,* 804–812.

Law, S., & Schachar, R. (1999). Do typical clinical doses of methylphenidate cause tics in children treated for ADHD? *Journal of the American Academy of Child and Adolescent Psychiatry, 38,* 944–951.

Levin, E., Conners, C., Sparrow, E., Hinton, S., Erhardt, D., Meck, W., Rose, J., & March, J. (1996). Nicotine effects on adults with attention-deficit/hyperactivity disorder. *Psychopharmacology, 123,* 55–63.

Luh, J., Pliszka., S., Olvers, R., & Tatum, R. (1996). *An open trial of venlafaxine in the treatment of attention deficit hyperactivity disorder: A pilot study.* San Antonio: University of Texas Health Science Center.

Malhotra, S., & Santosh, P. J. (1998). An open clinical trial of buspirone in children with attention deficit/hyperactivity disorder. *Journal of the American Academy of Child and Adolescent Psychiatry, 37,* 364–371.

Mannuzza, S., Klein, R., Bonagura, N., Malloy, P., Giampino, T. L., & Addalli, K. A. (1991). Hyperactive boys almost grown up: V. Replication of psychiatric status. *Archives of General Psychiatry, 48,* 77–83.

Mannuzza, S., Klein, R. G., Bessler, A., Malloy, P., & LaPadula, M. (1993). Adult outcome of hyperactive boys: Educational achievement, occupational rank and psychiatric status. *Archives of General Psychiatry, 50,* 565–576.

Manshadi, M., Lippmann, S., O'Daniel, R. G., & Blackman, A. (1983). Alcohol abuse and attention deficit disorder. *Journal of Clinical Psychiatry, 44,* 379–380.

Mattes, J. A. (1986). Propranolol for adults with temper outbursts and residual attention deficit disorder. *Journal of Clinical Psychopharmacology, 6,* 299–302.

Meck, W., & Church, R. (1987). Cholinergic modulation of the content of temporal memory. *Behavioral Neuroscience, 101,* 457–464.

Mereu, G., Yoon, K., Gessa, G., Naes, L., & Westfall, T. (1987). Preferential stimulation of ventral tegmental area dopaminergic neurons by nicotine. *European Journal of Pharmacology, 141,* 395–399.

Milberger, S., Biederman, J., Faraone, S. V., Chen, L., & Jones, J. (1996). Is maternal smoking during pregnancy a risk factor for attention deficit hyperactivity disorder in children? *American Journal of Psychiatry, 153,* 1138–1142.

Milberger, S., Biederman, J., Faraone, S. V., Chen, L., & Jones, J. (1997a). ADHD is associated with early initiation of cigarette smoking in children and adolescents. *Journal of the American Academy of Child and Adolescent Psychiatry, 36,* 37–44.

Milberger, S., Biederman, J., Faraone, S. V., Guite, J., & Tsuang, M. T. (1997). Pregnancy delivery and infancy complications and ADHD: Issues of gene-environment interactions. *Biological Psychiatry, 41,* 65–75.

National Institute of Mental Health. (1996). *Alternative pharmacology of ADHD.* Washington, DC: Author.

Parrott, A. C., & Winder, G. (1989). Nicotine chewing gum (2 mg, 4 mg) and cigarette smoking: Comparative effects upon vigilance and heart rate. *Psychopharmacology, 97,* 257–261.

Peeke, S., & Peeke, H. (1984). Attention, memory, and cigarette smoking. *Psychopharmacology, 84,* 205–216.

Pliszka, S. R. (1989). Effect of anxiety on cognition, behavior, and stimulant response in ADHD. *Journal of the American Academy of Child and Adolescent Psychiatry, 28,* 882–887.

Pomerleau, O. F., Downey, K. K., Stelson, F. W., & Pomerleau, C. S. (1995). Cigarette smoking in adult patients diagnosed with attention deficit hyperactivity disorder. *Journal of Substance Abuse, 7,* 373–378.

Prince, J., Wilens, T., Biederman, J., Spencer, T., Millstein, R., Polisner, D., & Bostic, J. *A controlled study of nortriptyline in children and adolescents with attention deficit hyperactivity disorder.* Manuscript submitted for publication.

Quinn, P. O., & Rapoport, J. L. (1975). One-year follow-up of hyperactive boys treated with imipramine or methylphenidate. *American Journal of Psychiatry, 132,* 241–245.

Rapoport, J. L., Quinn, P., Bradbard, G., Riddle, D., & Brooks, E. (1974). Imipramine and methylphenidate treatment of hyperactive boys: A double-blind comparison. *Archives of General Psychiatry, 30,* 789–793.

Rapport, M., Carlson, G., Kelly, K., & Pataki, C. (1993). Methylphenidate and desipramine in hospitalized children: I. Separate and combined effects on cognitive function. *Journal of the American Academy of Child and Adolescent Psychiatry, 32,* 333–342.

Ratey, J., Greenberg, M., & Lindem, K. (1991). Combination of treatments for attention deficit disorders in adults. *Journal of Nervous and Mental Disorders, 176,* 699–701.

Reimherr, F., Hedges, D., Strong, R., & Wender, P. (1995). *An open-trial of venlaxine in adult patients with attention deficit hyperactivity disorder.* Orlando, FL: New Clinical Drug Evaluation Unit Program.

Riddle, M. A., Hardin, M. T., Cho, S. C., Woolston, J. L., & Leckman, J. F. (1988). Desipramine treatment of boys with attention-deficit hyperactivity disorder and tics: Preliminary clinical experience. *Journal of the American Academy of Child and Adolescent Psychiatry, 27,* 811–814.

Silva, R., Munoz, D., & Alpert, M. (1996). Carbamazepine use in children and adolescents with features of attention-deficit hyperactivity disorder: A meta-analysis. *Journal of the American Academy of Child and Adolescent Psychiatry, 35,* 352–358.

Singer, S., Brown, J., Quaskey, S., Rosenberg, L., Mellits, E., & Denckla, M. (1994). The treatment of attention-deficit hyperactivity disorder in Tourette's syndrome: A double-blind placebo-controlled study with clonidine and desipramine. *Pediatrics, 95,* 74–81.

Spencer, T. (1997, October). *A double-blind, controlled study of desipramine in children with ADHD and tic disorders.* Paper presented at the annual meeting of the American Academy of Child and Adolescent Psychiatry, Toronto.

Spencer, T., Biederman, J., Kerman, K., Steingard, R., & Wilens, T. E. (1993). Desipramine in the treatment of children with Tic disorder or Tourette's Syndrome and attention deficit hyperactivity disorder. *Journal of the American Academy of Child and Adolescent Psychiatry, 32,* 354–360.

Spencer, T., Biederman, J., Wilens, T., Harding, M., O'Donnell, D., & Griffin, S. (1996). Pharmacotherapy of attention-deficit hyperactivity disorder across the life cycle. *Journal of the American Academy of Child and Adolescent Psychiatry, 35,* 409–432.

Spencer, T., Biederman, J., Wilens, T. E., Prince, J., & Rea, J. (1999, June). *An open, dose ranging study of tomoxetine in children with ADHD.* Paper presented at the scientific proceedings of International Society for Research in Child and Adolescent Psychopathology, Barcelona, Spain.

Spencer, T., Biederman, J., Wilens, T. E., Steingard, R., & Geist, D. (1993). Nortriptyline in the treatment of children with attention deficit hyperactivity disorder and tic disorder or Tourette's syndrome. *Journal of the American Academy of Child and Adolescent Psychiatry, 32,* 205–210.

Spencer, T., Wilens, T. E., & Biederman, J. (1995). *A double-blind, crossover comparison of tomoxetine and placebo in adults with ADHD.* Paper presented at the 12th scientific proceedings of the American Academy of Child and Adolescent Psychiatrists, New Orleans, LA.

Steingard, R., Biederman, J., Spencer, T., Wilens, T., & Gonzalez, A. (1993). Comparison of clonidine response in the treatment of attention deficit hyperactivity disorder with and without comorbid tic disorders. *Journal of the American Academy of Child and Adolescent Psychiatry, 32,* 350–353.

Sunohara, G., Barr, C., Jain, U., Schachar, R., Roberts, W., Tannock, R., Malone, M., & Kennedy, J. L. (1997). *Association of the D4 receptor gene in individuals with ADHD.* Baltimore: American Society of Human Genetics.

Swanson, J., Kinsbourne, M., Roberts, W., & Zucker, K. (1978). Time-response analysis of the effect of stimulant medication on the learning ability of children referred for hyperactivity. *Pediatrics, 61,* 21–29.

Tannock, R., Ickowicz, A., & Schachar, R. (1995). Differential effects of MPH on working memory in ADHD children with and without comorbid anxiety. *Journal of the American Academy of Child and Adolescent Psychiatry, 34,* 886–896.

Taylor, E., Schachar, R., Thorley, G., Wieselberg, H. M., Everitt, B., & Rutter, M. (1987). Which boys respond to stimulant medication? A controlled trial of methylphenidate in boys with disruptive behaviour. *Psychology and Medicine, 17,* 121–143.

Trott, G. E., Friese, H. J., Menzel, M., & Nissen, G. (1991). Wirksamkeit und vertraglichkeit des selektiven MAO-A-Inhibitors moclobemid bei kindern mit hyperkinetischem syndrom [Use of moclobemide in children with attention deficit hyperactivity disorder] (both English and German versions). *Jugendpsychiatrica, 19,* 248–253.

Voelker, S. L., Lachar, D., & Gdowski, L. L. (1983). The personality inventory for children and response to methylphenidate: Preliminary evidence for predictive validity. *Journal of Pediatric Psychology,* 8, 161–169.

Watter, N., & Dreyfuss, F. E. (1973). Modifications of hyperkinetic behavior by nortriptyline. *Virginia Medical Monthly, 100,* 123–126.

Weiss, G., Hechtman, L., Milroy, T., & Perlman, T. (1985). Psychiatric status of hyperactives as adults: A controlled prospective 15-year follow-up of 63 hyperactive children. *Journal of the American Academy of Child Psychiatry, 24,* 211–220.

Wender, P. H., & Reimherr, F. W. (1990). Bupropion treatment of attention-deficit hyperactivity disorder in adults. *American Journal of Psychiatry, 147,* 1018–1020.

Werry, J. (1980). Imipramine and methylphenidate in hyperactive children. *Journal of Child Psychology and Psychiatry, 21,* 27–35.

Wesnes, K., & Warburton, D. (1984). The effects of cigarettes of varying yield on rapid information processing performance. *Psychopharmacology, 82,* 338–342.

Westfall, T., Grant, H., & Perry, H. (1983). Release of dopamine and 5-hydroxytryptamine from rat striatal slices following activation of nicotinic cholinergic receptors. *Genetic Pharmacology, 14,* 321–325.

Wilens, T. E., Biederman, J., Abrantes, A. M., Spencer, T. J. (1996). A naturalistic assessment of protriptyline for attention-deficit hyperactivity disorder. *Journal of the American Academy of Child and Adolescent Psychiatry, 35,* 1485–1490.

Wilens, T. E., Biederman, J., Geist, D. E., Steingard, R., & Spencer, T. (1993). Nortriptyline in the treatment of attention deficit hyperactivity disorder: A chart review of 58 cases. *Journal of the American Academy of Child and Adolescent Psychiatry, 32,* 343–349.

Wilens, T. E., Biederman, J., Mick, E., & Spencer, T. (1995). A systematic assessment of tricyclic antidepressants in the treatment of adult attention-deficit hyperactivity disorder. *Journal of Nervous and Mental Disorders, 183,* 48–50.

Wilens, T. E., Biederman, J., Prince, J., Spencer, T. J., Faraone, S. V., Warburton, R., Schleifer, D., Harding, M., Linehan, C., & Geller, D. (1996). Six-week, double-blind, placebo-controlled study of desipramine for adult attention deficit hyperactivity disorder. *American Journal of Psychiatry, 153,* 1147–1153.

Wilens, T. E., Biederman, J., Spencer, T., Bostic, J., Prince, J., Monteaux, M., Soriano, J., Fine, C., Abrams, A., Rater, M., & Polisner, D. (1999, December). A pilot controlled clinical trial of ABT-418, a cholinergic agonist, in the treatment of adults with attention deficit hyperactivity disorder. *American Journal of Psychiatry, 156,* 1931–1937.

Wilens, T. E., & Spencer, T. J. (1999). Combining methylphenidate and clonidine: A clinically sound medication option. *Journal of American Child and Adolescent Psychiatry, 38,* 614–622.

Winsberg, B. G., Bialer, I., Kupietz, S., & Tobias, J. (1972). Effects of imipramine and dextroamphetamine on behavior of neuropsychiatrically impaired children. *American Journal of Psychiatry, 128,* 1425–1431.

Yepes, L. E., Balka, E. B., Winsberg, B. G., & Bialer, I. (1977). Amitriptyline and methylphenidate treatment of behaviorally disordered children. *Journal of Child Psychology and Psychiatry, 18,* 39–52.

Chapter 12

Psychosocial Interventions for ADHD

by William E. Pelham, Ph.D.

Introduction 12-2
Limitations of Pharmacological Interventions 12-3
    Little Effect on Interpersonal Relationships or Family
        Functioning 12-3
    Individual Differences in Response 12-3
    Long-Term Prognosis Discouraging 12-4
Psychosocial Interventions 12-4
    Cognitive-Behavioral Treatment 12-5
    Clinical Behavior Therapy 12-6
        Improved Behavior 12-8
        Impact on School Functioning. 12-9
        Effect of Concurrent Medication Therapy 12-10
    Contingency Management 12-10
        Use of Negative Consequences 12-11
        Treatment Effects 12-11
    Intensive Treatments 12-12
        The Children's Summer Treatment Program 12-12
        Treatment Response. 12-13
        Need for Comprehensive Long-Term
           Intervention 12-14
Shortcomings of Behavioral Interventions 12-14
Combined Pharmacological and Behavioral
    Interventions 12-15
    Advantages of Combining Behavioral and
        Pharmacological Treatments 12-15
    Long-Term Impact 12-16
    Research Findings Show Positive Results 12-16
    Long-Term Efficacy 12-18
Summary and Future Directions 12-18
    Efficacy of Behavioral Treatment Is Clear 12-18

Open Questions 12-19
    Does Child's Age Affect Treatment Choice? 12-19
    How Should Comorbidities Affect Treatment Choice? 12-21
    How Do Family Factors Affect Treatment Choice? 12-21
    Can Medication Dosage or Parent Training Mitigate
       Treatment Intensity? 12-21
    What Is Optimum Treatment Sequence? 12-22
    How Long Must Treatment Continue? 12-22
Cost-Effectiveness 12-23
Exportability of Programs to Real-World Settings 12-24
Long-Term Effectiveness 12-24

INTRODUCTION

A variety of psychosocial and other treatments have been tried and are widely used for attention deficit hyperactivity disorder (ADHD), including traditional one-on-one therapy, play therapy, restrictive or supplemental diets, allergy treatments, chiropractics, biofeedback, perceptual-motor training, treatment for inner ear problems, and pet therapy. However, none of these interventions has shown evidence of effectiveness in treating ADHD. Only three treatments have been validated as effective for ADHD: (1) behavior modification, (2) psychostimulants and other related medications, and (3) the combination of (1) and (2). Each of these three interventions has been shown to be effective in the short term; no treatments have yet been shown to influence adolescent or adult outcome. This chapter discusses two of these validated treatments (behavioral and combined interventions) (see Chapters 9 and 10 of this volume for a discussion of pharmacotherapy) and focuses on the evidence for the effectiveness of psychosocial and combined treatments unto themselves (Chapters 14 and 15 discuss comparisons among psychosocial, pharmacological, and combined treatments). Treatment comparisons are mentioned on occasion to provide a context for psychosocial or combined treatment effects (e.g., the meaning of the magnitude of a treatment effect).

It should be emphasized at the outset that the only form of psychosocial treatment that discuss in this chapter is behavioral interventions, because they are the only treatments with demonstrated efficacy. Behavioral treatments have been used for more than twenty years with children specifically diagnosed as having ADHD (O'Leary, Pelham, Rosenbaum, & Price, 1976), and they have been used for more than thirty years to treat children variously described as disruptive, aggressive, or conduct disordered at home or school (O'Leary & Becker, 1967). Based on current epidemiological studies and clinical studies of comorbidity, it would be expected that the majority of children treated in studies of disruptive/aggressive children have been ADHD and would have been diagnosed as ADHD—with or without comorbid aggression, conduct disorder (CD), or oppositional defiant disorder (ODD)—had criteria according to the *Diagnostic and Statistical Manual of Mental Disorders* (DSM) been employed (O'Leary & Becker, 1967; Patterson, 1974). Thus, there is an extensive literature on behavioral treatments for ADHD, covering hundreds of studies and thousands of children over several decades (Brestan & Eyberg, 1998; Pelham, Wheeler, & Chronis, 1998).

LIMITATIONS OF PHARMACOLOGICAL INTERVENTIONS

Any discussion of psychosocial treatments for ADHD must begin with a brief review of pharmacological treatments, which are ubiquitously employed and therefore provide the contrast and often the background for behavioral treatment of ADHD. Pharmacological interventions for ADHD are reviewed elsewhere in this chapter, and the efficacy for stimulants therefore are not discussed herein. However, the limitations of pharmacotherapy are central to the question of the utility of psychosocial treatments with ADHD.

Little Effect on Interpersonal Relationships or Family Functioning

First, despite their clear beneficial effects on daily classroom performance (e.g., on-task behavior and academic productivity), stimulants have not been shown to cause changes in academic achievement (Swanson, McBurnett, Christian, & Wigal, 1995). Similarly, although stimulants clearly improve disruptive social behavior and peer interactions in acute studies (Hinshaw, 1991), there is no evidence that stimulants effect long-term changes in interpersonal relationships—relationships that are disturbed in ADHD adolescents and adults.

Although stimulants positively affect ADHD children's behavior during structured parent-child interactions in analog settings (Barkley, Karlsson, Pollard & Murphy, 1985), families of ADHD children are often dysfunctional in multiple domains, including maternal stress and depression, paternal alcohol abuse, and inappropriate parental discipline (Fischer, 1990; Mash & Johnston, 1990). Even though some of these parental problems are a response to the difficulties inherent in dealing with the child (Pelham, Lang, et al., 1998), there is little reason to believe that providing a medication to the ADHD child will resolve such family problems. Even if medication had a beneficial effect on family functioning, in order to avoid growth suppressant effects that may accompany three-times-daily (TID), seven-days-a week dosing, psychostimulants are now most often administered only during school hours, and their effects do not last into the evening. Parents are thus often left to their own means to control their children's behavior during nonschool hours.

Individual Differences in Response

Further, even in studies in which large beneficial drug effects on academic and social domains are found, only approximately 70 to 80 percent of ADHD children respond positively to the stimulant regimen, and the remaining quarter show either an adverse response or no response (Swanson et al., 1995). Of those children who do respond, only a minority show sufficient improvement for their behavior to fall entirely within the normal range; the rest are improved but their behavior is not normalized—often remaining a standard deviation above the norm (Pelham & Murphy, 1986). Further, there are large individual differences in the size and topography of the drug response among the three-fourths of ADHD children who respond to stimulants (Pelham & Smith, 2000), with the medication benefiting some domains of functioning but not others. Thus, other interventions are needed for nonresponders or incomplete responders to medication.

Long-Term Prognosis Discouraging

In addition to the limitations noted previously, the major limitation of stimulant therapy is that studies that have followed children treated with psychostimulant medication for periods up to ten years have failed to provide any evidence that the drugs improve ADHD children's long-term prognosis (Charles & Schain, 1981; Satterfield, Hoppe, & Schell, 1982; Weiss & Hechtman, 1993). Although their methodological inadequacies require that these studies be interpreted cautiously, beneficial treatment effects do not appear to be maintained when psychostimulant medication, as typically administered, is used as a long-term treatment for the average ADHD child. The explanation for this failure is not clear and may simply reflect difficulties in long-term compliance or long-term prescription. A survey of all prescriptions in one county for a year (Sherman & Hertzig, 1991) revealed that the majority of ADHD children for whom physicians prescribed stimulants received only one or two prescriptions. Given that ADHD is a chronic condition often requiring ongoing pharmacological treatment, these data suggest that most physicians and/or parents in this survey were terminating medication prematurely. Beyond childhood, it appears likely that many adolescents with ADHD—particularly those who are also antisocial—will stop taking their medications, after which point there will be no residual benefit from medication. Thus, long-term compliance with medication may be a problem.

A final limitation regarding medication is that when a child is a positive responder to medication, both parents and teachers (but particularly teachers) may be inclined to rely on medication as the sole form of treatment. That is, when medication works and is used at doses that virtually eliminate acute problems, as is the case with high doses in classroom settings (Klein & Abikoff, 1997), the psychosocial and psychoeducational treatments to which the medication is supposed to be an adjunct may be less likely to be employed, compared to unmedicated children. Given that medication used as the sole treatment does not affect children's adolescent or adult prognosis, using medication at high doses or to initiate treatment may actually undermine the child's long-term treatment and outcome.

Thus, despite the overwhelming evidence for their safety and efficacy in short-term studies, shortcomings such as these of central nervous system (CNS) stimulants have given rise to the investigation of psychosocial treatment for ADHD—primarily behavioral interventions—for the home and school. Because of these limitations, it is our contention that psychosocial treatments should always be employed with ADHD children and that they should be employed as first-line treatments, with medication added when necessary as adjunctive therapy.

PSYCHOSOCIAL INTERVENTIONS

This chapter examines behavioral treatments by separating them into five categories (Pelham & Murphy, 1986; Pelham & Wachsbusch, 1999): (1) cognitive-behavioral interventions; (2) clinical behavior therapy (ClBT); (3) direct contingency management (CM); (4) intensive, packaged behavioral treatments; and (5) combined behavioral and pharmacological treatments (CT). These categories are discussed separately because they differ in the nature and efficacy of their effects. The chapter concludes with a brief discussion of future directions for research on the psychosocial treatment of ADHD.

Exhibit 12.1 (beginning on page 12-25) lists sixty studies that have used behavioral treatments of ADHD and is referred to throughout this chapter. Exhibit 12.1 includes descriptions of the subjects, design, type and length of treatment, control conditions, and dependent measures. The exhibit does not list outcomes because the studies generally included a large number of dependent measures and, in many cases, a large number of treatment conditions, and results typically differed as a function of dependent measure and treatment condition, with the consequence that a table of results would have been unwieldy. However, all these studies showed evidence of efficacy of psychosocial treatment for ADHD on at least one key dependent measure. The text discusses general trends in the results, as well as the results of exemplar studies. Exhibit 12.1 does not include studies of cognitive therapy for ADHD because cognitive therapy does not show efficacy for ADHD, as numerous recent studies have demonstrated (Bloomquist, August, & Ostrander, 1991) and reviews have concluded (Pelham, Wheeler, & Chronis, 1998).

Cognitive-Behavioral Treatment

Many different types of cognitive-behavioral treatments have been applied to children with ADHD, including verbal self-instructions, problem-solving strategies, cognitive modeling, self-monitoring, self-evaluation, self-reinforcement, and others (Abikoff, 1987, 1991). The underlying theme of these types of treatments is the development of self-controlled behavior through the enhancement of self-mediated strategies (Hinshaw & Erhardt, 1991). Beginning with a seminal article by Meichenbaum and Goodman (1971), a great deal of attention has been directed toward the development of cognitive-behavioral therapy for treatment of ADHD. Typical intervention involves a series of sessions, usually once or twice weekly, in which a therapist or paraprofessional works with an individual child and attempts to teach the child, through modeling, role play, and practice, cognitive techniques (e.g., saying "stop, look, and listen" to him- or herself at the onset of a problem) that the child can use to control his or her inattention and impulsive behavior problems in other settings. Cognitive therapy was designed in part to provide internal mediators that would serve to facilitate generalization and maintenance of effects of behavioral treatment. Because the absence of such internal mediators appears to characterize ADHD, cognitive-behavioral treatments have appeared to be a natural match for the disorder.

There have been many investigations examining the effectiveness of cognitive-behavioral treatments for ADHD. The results of many studies conducted in both the clinic and school settings (Abikoff et al., 1988; Bloomquist et al., 1991; Brown, Borden, Wynne, Spunt, & Clingerman, 1987) are remarkably consistent in showing that cognitive-behavioral treatment of ADHD generally does not provide clinically important changes in the behavior and academic performance of children with ADHD. Thus, in spite of the high face validity of cognitive treatments for ADHD, and in spite of the fact that there is some demonstrated efficacy of cognitive treatments for other childhood disorders (Kendall & Gosch, 1994; Lochman, 1992), there is no demonstrated efficacy for cognitive treatment of ADHD.

There may be exceptions to this conclusion in which cognitive training may have some clinical efficacy for ADHD, especially when combined with intensive, multicomponent treatment packages. Social skills training (Pelham, Lang, et al., 1988;

Pelham & Hoza, 1996; Pfiffner & McBurnett, 1997) provided as adjunctive treatments to operant behavioral or clinical behavioral interventions may be beneficial. Teaching anger control (Hinshaw & Erhardt, 1991) and social problem-solving training (Kazdin, 1996; Lochman & Lenhart, 1993; Pelham & Hoza, 1996) may also be beneficial as adjunctive treatments. Finally, although the hypothesis has not been tested, it might reasonably be argued that cognitive interventions could have enhanced adjunctive value in maintenance and generalization in the context of a lengthy and intensive behavioral and pharmacological treatment intervention (although there are noncognitive ways to fade and facilitate maintenance of behavioral treatments) (Sullivan & O'Leary, 1990; Turkewitz, O'Leary, & Ironsmith, 1975). Although cognitive-behavioral interventions were originally developed to facilitate maintenance of operant interventions, not as treatments sufficient unto themselves, no studies have addressed that issue. Given that they are not effective treatments, it would appear that cognitive interventions for ADHD should be used and studied only as adjunctive components in the context of clinical behavior therapy or contingency management and then only with the goal of facilitating maintenance of treatment effects if a goal of treatment is to withdraw more intensive behavioral components.

Clinical Behavior Therapy

Applications of traditional, outpatient-based ClBT have typically involved training either parents or teachers or both to implement CM programs with their children (Anastopoulos, Shelton, DuPaul, & Guevremont, 1993; Horn, Ialongo, Popovich, & Peradotto, 1987; O'Leary & Pelham, 1978; Pelham, Lang, et al., 1988; Pisterman et al., 1989). In typical clinical parent training programs, parents are given assigned readings and in a series of eight to sixteen weekly group or individual sessions are taught standard behavioral techniques such as those shown in Table 12.1 (Barkley, 1987, 1995; Cunningham, Bremner, & Secord-Gilbert, 1994; Forehand & Long, 1996; Forehand & McMahon, 1981; Forgatch, & Patterson, 1989; Patterson, 1975). These programs typically employ well-manualized approaches and teach the fundamentals of social learning theory, as well as basic information about ADHD. Parent training is usually accomplished in group sessions, with homework assignments made for parents to track behavior and practice techniques with their children and bring results back to the subsequent group session for review and discussion.

Similarly, therapists in ClBT often work simultaneously with teachers in a consultation model to teach the same kinds of behavioral strategies that are taught to parents (see also Table 12.1), including the following:

- Daily report cards (DRCs) that target individualized problems for children, establish procedures for teacher to monitor and give feedback to the child for those problems, and provide feedback to parents on the children's school performance, for which parents provide a positive consequence at home (Kelley & McCain, 1995; O'Leary et al., 1976); and

- Other classroom management strategies that can be implemented by the teacher with the target children.

Figure 12.1 (on page 12-8) depicts a typical DRC for an ADHD child.

Table 12.1
Typical Sequence of Sessions for Parent Training and Teacher Consultation in a Clinical Behavioral Intervention

PARENT TRAINING

1. Review of ADHD and its Treatment

2. Overview of Social Learning and Behavior Management Principles

3. Home/School Daily Report Card

4. Giving Effective Commands and Reprimands

5. Time Out

6. Attending, Rewarding and Ignoring Skills

7. Establishing and Enforcing Rules/When...Then Contingencies

8. Home Point System-Reward and Response-cost

9. Home Reward and Response-cost

10. Planned Activities and Setting Generalization Outside of the Home

11. Homework Problems

12. Facilitating Peer Relationships

13. Level Systems

14. Interacting with the School

15. Parental Stress, Anger, and Mood Management

TEACHER CONSULTATION

1. Introduction to ADHD, rationale for and overview of treatment; obtain teacher/school commitment to implement intervention, assess teacher knowledge and use of behavioral procedures, and design content of subsequent sessions accordingly

2. Home/School Daily report card

3. Classroom rules and structure/instructional modifications for an individual child

4. Ignoring mild inappropriate behaviors that are not reinforced by peer attention and praising appropriate behaviors

5. Giving effective commands and reprimands

6. When...then contingencies

7. Class-wide interventions

8. Group contingencies

9. Response-cost/reward point or token system for the target child

10. Time out (classroom, office, systematic exclusion)

11. Discussion of special services or special class placement

In contrast to parent training interventions, which are quite standardized and do not vary much in the number of sessions provided, there is considerably more variability in the nature of classroom interventions. The number of contacts between

Figure 12.1
Sample Daily Report Card

Child's Name: _____	Date: _____

Special LA Math Reading SS/Science

Follows class rules with no more than 3 rule violations per period.   Y N

Completes assignments within the designated time.   Y N

Completes assignments at 80% accuracy.   Y N

Complies with teacher requests.
 (no more than 3 instances of noncompliance per period)   Y N

No more than 3 instances of teasing per period.   Y N

OTHER

Follows lunch rules.   Y N

Follows recess rules.   Y N

Total Number of Yeses _____

Teacher's Initials

Comments: _____

_____

_____

therapist/consultant and teacher varies widely across these studies, ranging from one to three phone or face-to-face contacts over the course of a study (Horn, Ialongo, Greenberg, Packard, & Smith-Winberry, 1990; Horn et al., 1991) to ten weekly sessions over the course of treatment (O'Leary & Pelham, 1978; Pelham, Schnedler, Bologna, & Contreras, 1980; Pelham et al., 1988). The primary differences between studies appears to be that the former group of studies has one or two teacher contacts as part of assessment and to establish a daily home-school note but no ongoing teacher contact. The latter group combines (1) initial assessment and establishment of a formalized DRC with (2) ongoing consultation to monitor and modify the DRC and development of other classroom management strategies, as necessary.

Improved Behavior. The efficacy of clinical behavior therapy approaches has been evaluated in a number of studies. Typically, these outcome studies last eight to twenty weeks and many can be traced to the O'Learys' laboratory at the State University of New York at Stony Brook (Klein & Abikoff, 1997; O'Leary et al., 1976; O'Leary

& Pelham, 1978; Pelham et al., 1980; Pelham, et al., 1988). The format of therapy in these studies generally consisted of weekly sessions with parents in the clinic, and weekly (except for the Klein study) visits to teachers, during which basic behavior management skills were taught by therapists. As Exhibit 12.1 illustrates, impact in these studies was typically measured from pre- to posttreatment with parent/teacher ratings of symptoms, impairment of various types, measures of severity, and direct observations (often in classroom settings and occasionally of parent-child interactions). In general, the clinical behavior therapy examined in these studies consistently revealed considerable improvement relative to control conditions on the measures examined, and this was true in both classroom and home settings. These results are generally similar to those reported in numerous studies of behavioral treatments of aggressive (e.g., CD and ODD) children (Brestan & Eyberg, 1998), many of whom also had comorbid ADHD. In addition, some studies examined a broad array of measures of parental functioning (e.g., measures of stress and parenting sense of competence) and found that behavioral parent training improved such measures (Anastopoulos et al., 1993; Pisterman et al., 1992b).

For example, Anastopoulos et al. (1993) reported a 22 percent reduction in parent ratings on the ADHD rating scale, a pre-post change equivalent to an effect size of 1.2 for the ClBT parent training. Assessing this change for clinical significance using the methods developed by, Jacobson and Truax (1991), they reported that 21 percent, 32 percent, and 32 percent of their sample, respectively, showed minimal, reliable or recovery changes, compared to 13 percent, 27 percent, and zero percent for the wait-list group. Comparable results were obtained for the measure of parenting stress. The same effect size, 1.2, for parent training on parent behavior ratings for parent training was reported by Horn et al. (1990), and comparable changes were reported by Pelham et al. (1988) and Klein and Abikoff (1997). Pisterman et al. (1989) reported comparable effect sizes on direct observations of child behavior, as well as parenting behaviors, in parent-child interactions. Klein and Abikoff, for example, reported improvement rates on the National Institute of Mental Health's Clinical Global Improvement Scale (CGI) of 64 percent for their ClBT group as rated by mothers, a percentage not significantly different from their medication treated group. Pisterman et al. (1989) reported comparable levels of clinical improvement with behavioral parent training.

Impact on School Functioning. Reliable improvements have also been obtained in the studies that evaluated school functioning when there was a school intervention component to the ClBT. However, the degree of improvement appears to be related to the amount of teacher consultation, with the studies with ongoing teacher contact yielding more change than those that involve only a contact or two. For example, Pelham et al. (1988) showed a reduction on the Abbreviated Conners Teacher's Rating Scale (ACTRS) from 18.9 (4.0) to 12.1 (5.6), a change that reflects an effect size of almost 3.0. Klein and Abikoff reported baseline-to-end-of-treatment reductions on the CTRS that ranged from 25 percent to 44 percent on relevant factors, with teachers rating 57 percent of the subjects as improved on the CGIs, an effect not significantly different from their medication-treated group.

In contrast to these effects, obtained in studies with weekly teacher contact, Horn et al. (1987) included no school intervention with their parent training program and found no change in teacher ratings. Further, Horn et al. (1990) included only three teacher contacts over the assessment and three-month-long study, and they reported a reduction of only 3.1 points on the ACTRS. Given that the behavioral teacher consultation literature casts doubt on the effectiveness of one or two teacher contacts without follow-up (Fuchs & Fuchs, 1989), this pattern is not surprising. To have a clinically important impact on school functioning for an ADHD child, the school component of the ClBT must include not only the initial development of an intervention but also ongoing contact with the teacher to monitor and modify the intervention.

Effect of Concurrent Medication Therapy. Thus, clinical behavior therapy of the sort that can easily be implemented by therapists and counselors and in community mental health, primary care, private practice, and school settings (e.g., eight to twelve weekly sessions with parents and teachers conducted over periods of two to five months) results in reliable, substantial, and clinically important improvement on multiple measures in home and school settings for many if not most children with ADHD who receive treatment. It should be noted that these ClBT studies often include groups in which medication is combined with behavioral interventions (Abikoff & Hechtman, 1996; Horn et al., 1991; Pelham et al., 1988). In these studies, outcomes are typically more positive in the combined treatment groups than in the groups treated with ClBT alone, and we discuss this further later in the chapter.

At the same time, it is important to note that the improvements obtained with clinical behavioral interventions are typically not as strong as those obtained with medication while medication is being administered. For example, Klein and Abikoff (1997) showed that clinical behavior therapy alone, although effective, was inferior to methylphenidate (MPH) alone on five of fourteen categories of direct observations of disruptive behavior in the classroom for ADHD children treated over eight weeks, as well as on teacher ratings on the CTRS; however, ClBT in their study was equivalent to MPH when Conners parent ratings and parent and teacher global improvement ratings were examined. In head-to-head comparison studies, subjects in medication groups are typically still medicated, whereas those receiving psychosocial treatment are not, perhaps setting up unfair comparisons. It might be argued that the most important issue is how psychosocial treatment stacks up to medication when medication is withdrawn. Consider, for example, O'Leary and Pelham (1978), who showed that a group of ADHD children who had been successfully medicated could be withdrawn from medication and treated for four months with clinical behavior therapy, showing levels of functioning on both observational and rating measures after behavior therapy that were equivalent to those they had shown while medicated before behavioral intervention. This point is discussed in more detail later.

Contingency Management

In contrast to clinical behavior therapy, CM approaches are characterized by relatively more intensive behavioral interventions. Although the treatment components may be the same as or similar to those implemented in clinical behavior therapy, CM approaches are implemented directly in the setting of interest and typically by a paraprofessional, consulting professional, or specially trained teacher rather the child's parent or regular teacher. Instead of being conducted in outpatient settings, CM programs usually take place in specialized treatment facilities or in demonstration classroom settings where greater control can be gained over treatment implementation. The techniques employed in CM programs range from relatively more potent components such as point/token economy reward systems, time out, and response-cost (RC) to relatively less potent components such as manipulations of teacher attention, reprimands, and removal of privileges. Some studies cannot clearly be categorized as CM versus ClBT because they contain components of each. For example, Atkins, Pelham, and White (1989) and Rapport, Murphy, and Bailey (1982) used RC programs—typically employed in CM programs—but the programs were implemented by the children's regular classroom teachers with the assistance of and observed by the study investigators.

Rapport, Murphy, and Bailey (1980) implemented a RC program with two children in regular classroom settings. They employed a flip-card system in which the child and teacher had cards with numbers in descending order from 20 to 0. The child was told the he could earn up to twenty minutes of free time by staying on task. If the teacher noticed that the child was not working, she flipped a card down, and the child lost one minute of free time. The child monitored the teacher's number on the flip card and matched it on his flip card. This RC system showed clearly beneficial effects on both classroom work and classroom behavior (see discussion later). Group studies (Carlson, Pelham, Milich, & Dixon, 1992; Pelham et al., 1993), as well as other case studies (Abramowitz, Eckstrand, O'Leary, & Dulcan, 1992; Atkins et al., 1989; DuPaul, Guevremont, & Barkley, 1992; Hoza, Pelham, Sams, & Carlson, 1992; Kelley & McCain, 1995; Rapport et al., 1982) have shown similar results with CM programs.

Use of Negative Consequences. A major question of interest has been whether negative procedures such as punishment are necessary components of CM programs. Behavioral clinicians who have worked with conduct-disordered (CD) children have long argued that the effective use of punishment is the key to parent management of CD children (Patterson, 1982). The same conclusion appears to apply to ADHD children. O'Leary and colleagues (Abramowitz, O'Leary, & Futtersak, 1988; Abramowitz, O'Leary, & Rosen, 1987; Acker & O'Leary, 1987; Pfiffner & O'Leary, 1987; Pfiffner, O'Leary, Rosen, & Sanderson, 1985; Pfiffner, Rosen, & O'Leary, 1985; Rosen, O'Leary, Joyce, Conway, & Pfiffner, 1984) have found that prudent negative consequences (verbal reprimands, given consistently and immediately, and backed up with time out and loss of privileges) are an effective and necessary component of classroom behavioral interventions, whereas positive consequences are not. Interestingly, this appears to be particularly true for the maintenance of treatment effects after behavioral interventions are withdrawn (Sullivan & O'Leary, 1990). The implication of these studies is that ClBT studies that have employed only DRCs with positive consequences for appropriate behavior are employing techniques that are at the less potent end of the CM continuum.

Treatment Effects. Efficacy studies of contingency management have typically been conducted using within-subject or single-case designs rather than the between group studies that are more common in ClBT. As might be expected given that CM approaches are often implemented in controlled settings by trained individuals and employ more potent behavioral components, treatment effects are typically larger than those obtained in clinical behavior therapy studies (DuPaul & Eckert, 1997). For example, Klein and Abikoff (1997) reported few effects of ClBT on directly observed classroom behavior. In contrast, three single-subject design studies of RC in school settings revealed large effects of an RC procedure as implemented by the children's regular teachers in their regular classrooms (Atkins, Pelham, & White, 1989; Kelley & McCain, 1995; Rapport et al., 1982). For example, on-task behavior and seatwork completion went from rates of 30 percent to 50 percent in Rapport et al. to rates of 80 percent to 100 percent (essentially normal rates) with the RC program; these effects were larger than those produced by low doses and comparable to those produced by moderate doses of methylphenidate. Atkins et al. (1989) reported comparable results comparing RC with pemoline. Both Atkins et al. (1989) and Kelley and McCain (1995) demonstrated that RC procedures were far more effective than DRCs with their subjects, indicating that more intensive CM procedures are more effective than the DRCs typically employed in ClBT studies even when the CM procedures are implemented by the child's regular classroom teacher (DuPaul & Eckert, 1997). In two within-subject studies with larger samples, Carlson et al. (1992) and Pelham et al. (1993) showed large effects of CM programs (reward, RC, time out, DRC) with ADHD children, with individually weighted effect sizes for children averaging 1.24 for the CM behavioral classroom in the latter study.

It should be clear from this discussion that strict CM approaches such as teacher- or paraprofessional-implemented RC programs produce large effects in ADHD children, primarily in the classroom settings in which these studies have been conducted. There have been no comparable studies of CM approaches conducted with parents, but there is no reason to expect results to be any different. Notably, while the CM procedures are in effect, their impact is as great as that produced by stimulant medication while it is in effect. As has been the case with stimulant medication, the major question regarding CM studies has long been how to facilitate maintenance of treatment effects when the initial treatment structures are withdrawn (see later discussion of limitations).

Intensive Treatments

The Children's Summer Treatment Program. Given the shortcomings of medication, the effective but often insufficient results of ClBT, the powerful effects of CM, and the severity and chronicity of ADHD, it is perhaps not surprising that some interventions attempt to combine ClBT and CM in intensive psychosocial treatment programs. The Children's Summer Treatment Program (STP; Pelham et al., 1996) is one such intensive treatment program. The STP is based on the premise that combining an intensive summer day treatment program with a school-year, outpatient follow-up program will provide a maximally effective psychosocial intervention for ADHD (Pelham et al., 1996). The STP runs for nine hours on weekdays for eight weeks. In the context of a summer-camp/summer-school-like program with a broad treatment focus, children are placed in groups of twelve that stay together throughout the day, so that children receive intensive experience in functioning as a group and in making friends. Each group spends two hours daily in classrooms in which behavioral interventions and appropriately individualized paper-and-pencil, peer tutoring, and computer-assisted instruction is provided. The remainder of each day consists of recreationally based group activities.

The behavioral intervention in the STP is a collection of empirically supported techniques interwoven into an intensive treatment package. Components include a point system with both reward and RC components that is implemented in every setting throughout the day, time out, and DRCs. Points are exchanged for privileges (e.g., weekly field trips), public recognition, and home-based rewards. The STP has a major focus on treating difficulties in peer relationships, given (1) the disturbances that ADHD children show in this domain, arguably their most salient and severe domain of impairment (Pelham & Bender, 1982); (2) the domain's importance in development and prognosis (Milich & Landau, 1982; Parker & Asher, 1987); and (3) the failure of clinic-based cognitive-behavioral social skills training to effect changes in peer relationships. Peer programming in the STP includes daily training in social skills; cooperative group tasks designed to foster friendship reciprocity, anger management, group problem-solving, and intensive coaching; and supervised practice in sports and game skills. Through DRCs, the children's progress in individualized target behaviors is tracked and rewarded at home by parents, who are attending ClBT parent training in the evenings. If these standard interventions do not produce the desired behavior change for a child, a functional analysis of the problematic behavior is conducted and an individualized program is developed. Detailed descriptions of the program components and procedure, as well procedures for ensuring and evaluating treatment adherence and fidelity, are comprehensively manualized (Pelham, Greiner, & Gnagy, 1997).

Treatment Response. Pelham and Hoza (1996) reported pre-post measures of functioning for a sample of 258 ADHD boys of normal intelligence between the ages of 5 and 12 who attended STPs conducted at the University of Pittsburgh from 1987 through 1992. The sample was ethnically and socioeconomically diverse, and 58 percent were comorbid for aggressive disorders. Treatment response was measured in numerous ways, including parent, teacher, and staff ratings of improvement, standardized parent ratings of disruptive behavior, direct observations of social and academic behaviors, self-esteem, parental satisfaction, and measures of social validity. Large effects of treatment were obtained on all these measures. For example, 96 percent of the parents rated the children as improved and 93 percent said that they would recommend the program to other parents. Comparisons of the effect sizes of pre-post treatment gains with other studies in the literature revealed that changes in self concept and disruptive behavior yielded effect sizes that were twice the size of those reported in studies employing ClBT. Notably, these positive treatment effects were equivalent for ADHD children with and without comorbid aggression, for ADHD children from single-parent and two-parent households, and for ADHD children from low- versus middle-/upper-income families. These three characteristics routinely predict poor response to treatment in the extant literature (see later discussion), suggesting that the STP effects are sufficiently potent to overcome variables that interfere with treatment in other contexts.

A major difference between this intensive packaged summer program and most other treatment programs for children with externalizing disorders is that the STP dropout rate is extremely low, 3 percent over the years in which these data were gathered, compared to rates up to 50 percent that characterize other treatment approaches such as clinical behavioral parent training (Miller & Prinz, 1990). Because attendance at therapy is a prerequisite to changing, the STP would appear to offer a unique advantage to other forms of behavioral intervention.

Need for Comprehensive Long-Term Intervention. In summary, these data suggest that intensive treatment packages that combine ClBT and CM, such as the STP, may be a powerful treatment for ADHD. The low dropout rate, excellent parent satisfaction ratings, and children's overall improvement are all superior to those generally reported for ClBT treatment programs for ADHD boys. At the same time, no eight-week treatment will be sufficient for a chronic disorder. The STP must be combined with ongoing parent training and school-based follow-up. One study has employed such an intensive intervention—an STP combined with ClBT involving parent and teacher training—the Multimodal Treatment Study for ADHD (Arnold et al., 1997; MTA Cooperative Group, 1999a, 1999b; Richters et al., 1995). That study employed the behavioral treatment package for twelve to fourteen months, including more than thirty parent training sessions (group and individual), up to ten teacher visits per school year, and an STP in the summer. This behavioral treatment package was crossed with stimulant medication to yield four groups (N of 144 per cell across 6 sites) in a large, controlled clinical trial: (1) psychosocial treatment alone, (2) pharmacological treatment alone, (3) combined psychosocial and pharmacological treatment, and (4) community comparison (control) treatment (these children were not treated in the study but referred back to their community providers for whatever services they chose to obtain). Children in the psychosocial-only group had reductions in parent and teacher ratings of ADHD symptoms of 34 percent and 46 percent, respectively, and of oppositional defiant symptoms of 23 percent and 32 percent, respectively. These reductions were comparable to those that occurred in the community comparison group. When the community comparison group was split into those subgroups that were medicated or not by their community provider, results revealed that the psychosocial group showed greater change than did the community group that was unmedicated and was comparable to the community group that were medicated.

As an index of clinical significance, it is noteworthy that 66 percent of the ADHD children treated with this behavioral intervention package no longer met diagnostic criteria for ADHD posttreatment. These results are especially noteworthy in two respects. First, they show that a comprehensive psychosocial treatment package is as effective as stimulant medication administered by a community physician. Second, the active components of the psychosocial treatment had been faded three to six months prior to the posttreatment measures; thus the posttreatment measures reflected the maintenance of psychosocial treatment effects after active contact with the therapists had ended. Thus, these results demonstrate that a psychosocial treatment package consisting of ClBT and a CM STP affords parents who desire it an alternative to medication for their ADHD child.

SHORTCOMINGS OF BEHAVIORAL INTERVENTIONS

Despite the clear evidence for their efficacy, behavioral interventions, particularly ClBT, have shortcomings, and these are in many ways similar to those of psychostimulant medication (Pelham & Murphy, 1986; Pelham & Wachsbusch, 1999). First, although ClBT interventions improve children greatly, they are less likely than medication (while active) to normalize children on parent and teacher rating scales (Abikoff & Gittelman, 1984; Pelham et al., 1988; Pelham et al., 1993). Second, as the results we noted earlier suggest, a substantial minority of children (comparable to the proportion cited for stimulant medication) fail to show improvement with ClBT. Although moving to a CM behavioral intervention would in many cases dramatically increase improvement, some parents and teachers are unable or unwilling to implement a complicated behavioral intervention. Even when parents and teachers are willing to start more complex interventions, they typically do not continue them after initiation without ongoing consultation. For example, single mothers with relatively lower levels of education, income, and contact with other adults have great difficulty implementing and maintaining behavioral treatments, often with poor treatment outcomes including high rates of dropout (Miller & Prinz, 1990; Wahler, 1980).

A final possible limitation of behavior therapy with ADHD children—again similar to a limitation of stimulant effects—is the lack of evidence for long-term effects. No studies have been conducted that examine the long-term impact—that is, into adolescence and adulthood—of behavioral interventions with ADHD children. Demonstration of the continuation and/or maintenance of treatment effects over time is one of the major concerns of those employing behavioral interventions with children, and research regarding how to maintain effects in the long run has not been conducted. These limitations have led to the growing practice of combining behavioral treatments with pharmacological interventions for ADHD.

COMBINED PHARMACOLOGICAL AND BEHAVIORAL INTERVENTIONS

Advantages of Combining Behavioral and Pharmacological Treatments

Theoretically, the effects of combined treatments, such as combined pharmacological and behavioral treatments, can differ from the effects of the component treatments in several different ways: potentiation, inhibition, reciprocation, addition, or complementarity (Pelham & Murphy, 1986). There are a number of advantages to combining behavioral and pharmacological treatments of ADHD (Pelham & Murphy, 1986). First, the behavioral component of treatment may be able to be reduced in scope and complexity if combined with low dosages of medication (Atkins et al., 1989). Because less complex behavioral treatments require less personnel time and are therefore less expensive, the cost-effectiveness of treatment may be improved with a combined intervention.

Second, the dose of medication for most children can be reduced by 50 percent to 75 percent when medication is combined with a behavioral intervention (Carlson et al., 1992; Pelham et al., 1980). Third, these treatments often have complementary effects. For example, parent training is a standard component of a behavioral intervention for ADHD, thus ensuring that a treatment is available for the times of the day that are typically not addressed by medication for a child on a twice-a-day (BID) schedule. Similarly, psychostimulant medication can reduce problematic behaviors that are difficult to treat with practical behavioral programs, such as the low-rate, peer-directed aggression and stealing that occur in the absence of adult authority (Hinshaw,

Heller, & McHale, 1992). In several ways, then, a combined intervention appears to be more comprehensive in coverage than either treatment alone.

Long-Term Impact

Finally, there are several reasons to speculate that long-term maintenance of treatment effects might be improved with a combined intervention. First, it is clear that ADHD children suffer from a lack of cognitive and behavioral skills that are necessary for academic and social adjustment. To the extent that these skills must be acquired for successful long-term outcome, medication alone, which does not teach a child alternative behaviors for coping with problematic situations, would not be expected to be a sufficient treatment. The addition of a behavioral intervention that focused in part on teaching such skills should improve the long-term outcome that would be achieved with medication alone. Similarly, to facilitate maintenance of behavioral treatment effects, the intervention should be able to be continued by the child's parents or teachers for a protracted time and/or maintained by naturally occurring contingencies following therapy termination. Because the addition of a low dose of psychostimulant medication enables relatively greater effects to be achieved with less restrictive and more natural behavioral programs, a combined intervention may be more likely to be maintained by parents and teachers following termination of therapeutic contact.

Research Findings Show Positive Results

In 1986, the nineteen studies that existed at that time in which a combination of behavioral and stimulant treatments had been used with ADHD children were reviewed and several conclusions were drawn (Pelham & Murphy, 1986). First, thirteen of the nineteen independent studies (68 percent) showed superiority for CT on at least one key classroom-based task, motor, or social measure. For those studies in which a behavioral or pharmacological effect was found, only rarely was either of these treatments alone superior to their combination. If order of condition means, rather than statistical significance, was used to interpret results, CT was superior to component treatments in virtually every study reviewed. Although there were clearly individual differences and variability in effects, for the average ADHD child treated in these studies, a combined intervention resulted in greater improvement than did either treatment alone.

Consider, for example, the Klein and Abikoff (1997) ClBT study discussed earlier. They reported global improvement rates for children in the CT of 93 percent, 93 percent, and 97 percent for teachers, mothers, and psychiatrists, respectively, considerably higher than the 50 percent to 79 percent rates that were obtained for ClBT and medication. Children who received CT were more likely to be normalized than those in the ClBT- and medication-alone groups. Several single-subject and within subject studies have shown that low (e.g., 0.3 mg/kg) doses of MPH and behavioral treatments have roughly additive effects (Atkins et al., 1989; Carlson et al., 1992; Pelham et al., 1980), yielding a larger treatment effect than either medication or behavioral intervention alone. One study conducted in the State University of New York's Buffalo (SUNY-Buffalo) laboratory (Pelham et al., 1988) was designed to determine whether these enhancing effects of a low dose of MPH would be obtained if combined with a ClBT over a longer period than the brief probes of the previous studies. The low dose of medication had a clearly beneficial ongoing additive effect. While medication was active, the Conners teacher ratings obtained by children in the combined treatment group were equivalent to those obtained by Klein and Abikoff's CT group even though the dose of MPH employed was only 40 percent of that used in the Klein and Abikoff study.

The MTA study discussed previously also employed a CT group that was treated over fourteen months (medication for twelve to fourteen months, including at post-treatment and psychosocial treatment actively for six to nine months and faded for three to six months). The CT treatment was effective, producing substantial change from pretreatment to posttreatment—more so than psychosocial and community comparison groups but generally statistically equivalent to (although usually slightly better than) the medication-alone condition, albeit with a lower dose of medication and generally larger effects on measures of impaired functioning than the medication-alone group.

Pelham et al. (1993) asked a question about combined treatments that was somewhat different from that asked in other studies. That is, what percentage of children show enhanced functioning with combined treatment when the baseline for comparison is (1) psychosocial treatment or (2) medication. In addition to standard dependent measures, individual effect sizes (each child's treatment mean minus his or her no treatment mean, divided by his standard deviation over no-treatment days) were computed that were weighted according to children's baseline symptom severity. Thus, we asked how many children showed incremental benefit from combined treatment on their individual target behaviors; it was found that 41 percent of the boys showed incremental improvement to combined treatment over their MPH-alone response, while 78 percent showed incremental improvement to combined treatment over their behavior-modification-alone response. Thus, a substantial proportion of individuals clearly benefited from combined treatments, although more children derived benefit from adding medication to behavioral treatment than vice versa. This is the only study that has examined the percentage of individuals who respond to combined versus sole treatments in ADHD. It suggests that there are substantial individual differences in the form of combined treatment response among ADHD children, which should not be a surprising outcome given the importance of individual differences in response to medication and behavioral treatments in this population.

In summary, extant studies provide strong evidence for the efficacy of combining psychostimulant medication and behavioral therapy in treating children with ADHD. At the same time, several qualifications are in order. One of them is that compared to the large numbers of subjects who have been studied over considerably longer periods with pharmacological interventions, behavioral parent training, and classroom contingency management, CT is relatively unstudied. Only 167 children were treated in the nineteen studies reviewed by Pelham and Murphy (1986), and the median duration of treatment was less than three weeks. Only approximately 100 additional ADHD children have been treated with combined treatments in published studies in the decade since our original review (other than the 144 MTA CT children), and most of the studies have been acute, single-subject, crossover designs. Much more evidence is required before we have adequate knowledge about the effects of combined treatments and the procedures that will ensure maximal responsiveness in treated children. It is our firm belief that the research to date suggests that the combined approach shows more promise of producing long-term positive effects than any other form of intervention with ADHD children.

Long-Term Efficacy

One key question regarding CT merits discussion: Do the effects of CT remain when either or both treatments are withdrawn. This question is clearly a critical one regarding long-term outcome for treated ADHD individuals. Only four studies have addressed this issue (Abikoff & Hechtman, 1996; Ialongo et al., 1993; MTA Cooperative Group, 1999a; Pelham et al., 1988). Horn et al. (1991) reported that CT subjects who had received parent training maintained treatment gains on parent ratings of ADHD symptoms on the Conners hyperkinesis index and the SNAP (an acronym for the names of the instrument's developers—Swanson, Nolan, and Pelham) rating scale nine months after medication withdrawal (as did parents who received parent training without medication), whereas those in the medication groups did not. Klein and Abikoff (1997) and Pelham et al. (1988) both reported the same result—CT subjects maintained the gains they had made from the ClBT while losing the acute effects of medication when medication was withdrawn. The MTA study withdrew psychosocial treatment but not medication and found at posttreatment that CT was generally not significantly better than medication alone. However, medication was not withdrawn in that study, with posttreatment measures being taken while children were actively medicated. Therefore, maintenance of psychosocial treatment effects in the CT group could not be evaluated.

Thus after medication withdrawal, only the effects of behavioral treatment remain. Although such a result could be viewed as a glass half empty, the fact that the behavioral treatment effects remained following medication is quite important. If medication is discontinued—and this appears not only quite likely for most ADHD children at some point in time (Sherman & Hertzig, 1991) but indeed may be a goal of treatment for most parents—then a combination regimen of behavioral and low-dose pharmacological treatments will yield better long-term functioning than a medication-only regimen. Studies that evaluate CT effects without withdrawing medication to assess treatment maintenance and therefore consideration of this obvious methodological issue are missing one of the major points of the potential of combined treatment. Somewhat surprisingly, all other existing studies of combined treatment regimens have focused on acute effects rather than maintenance. Whether a systematic medication withdrawal and maintenance program could effectively maintain all the beneficial effects of CT (as opposed to just the behavioral treatment effects) over the long term has yet to be investigated.

SUMMARY AND FUTURE DIRECTIONS

Efficacy of Behavioral Treatment Is Clear

This chapter has described and reviewed evidence for the efficacy of different types of behavioral treatment for ADHD, including cognitive-behavioral treatment, clinical behavior therapy, contingency management, intensive treatments, and combined pharmacological and behavioral treatment. It is clear from a number of studies that ClBT, CM, intensive, and combined behavioral/pharmacological treatments for ADHD have established effectiveness with ADHD children. However, cognitive-behavioral treatments do not. With respect to ClBT and CM treatments, this review reaches a conclusion similar to that of other recent reviews of treatment for children with externalizing problems/ADHD. For example, Weisz, Weiss, Han, Granger, and Morton (1995) conducted a meta-analysis of the effects of child treatment in which they concluded that behavioral treatments (typically the ClBT group-based studies conducted in controlled settings) were effective for children with externalizing disorders, whereas clinic-based, typically nonbehavioral treatments were not. Similarly, Kazdin and Weisz (1998) identified behavioral parent training as the most researched and efficacious treatment for aggressive children (as we have noted previously, epidemiological and clinic-based studies show that the majority of children recruited for studies of aggression are comorbid ADHD). Recently, a task force of Division 12 of the American Psychological Association addressed the empirical support for currently used treatment for childhood mental health disorders (Lonigan et al., 1998). With respect to ADHD, both behavioral parent training and classroom interventions met task force criteria for the "empirically supported treatment" category (the "best" category) (Pelham, Wheeler, & Chronis, 1998). Behavioral parent training was similarly categorized for aggressive behaviors/conduct/oppositional problems by the same task force (Brestan & Eyberg, 1998). The evidence for the efficacy of behavioral interventions in classroom settings, conducted over the past thirty years (O'Leary & Becker, 1967) in hundreds of studies is so clear that classroom behavioral interventions are virtually required components of school-based interventions for children with ADHD and other disruptive behavior disorders under the 1997 reauthorization of the Individuals With Disabilities Education Act, the federal law that governs education for handicapped individuals. DuPaul and Eckert (1997) recently reviewed sixty-three classroom intervention studies for ADHD with more than 600 participants and concluded, as did we, that classroom behavioral interventions have well-documented effects and substantial effect sizes with ADHD children.

Based on our review, it is clear that psychosocial treatments for ADHD are effective. We believe a comprehensive treatment for ADHD is a multicomponent intervention that includes three psychosocial facets—parent training, school intervention, and child intervention—and, often, concurrent medication. Table 12.2 (on page 12-20) summarizes key points about this comprehensive approach.

Open Questions

Despite the evidence for their effectiveness in home and classroom settings, a number of issues remain to be resolved regarding comprehensive, psychosocial/behavioral treatments for ADHD (Pelham, Lang, et al., 1998; Pelham & Wachsbusch, 1999), and this chapter concludes with a discussion of several of these issues.

Does Child's Age Affect Treatment Choice? One important question that remains to be answered is whether the different types of behavioral treatments have differing efficacy for different types of children. One of the most important individual difference

Table 12.2
Components of Effective, Comprehensive Treatment for ADHD

PARENT TRAINING

Behavioral approach

Focus on behavior and family relationships

Parent implemented

Group-based, weekly sessions with therapist initially, then contact faded

Continued support and contact as long as necessary (e.g., 2 or 3 years)

Program for maintenance and relapse prevention (e.g., develop plans for dealing with concurrent cyclic parental problems, such as maternal depression, parental substance abuse, and divorce)

Reestablish contact for major developmental transitions (e.g., adolescence)

SCHOOL INTERVENTION

Behavioral approach

Focus on classroom behavior, academic performance, and peer relationships

Teacher implemented

Consultant work with teacher—initial weekly sessions, then contact faded

Continued support and contact for multiple years

Program for maintenance and relapse prevention (e.g., school-wide programs, train all school staff, including administrators; eventually train parent to implement and monitor)

Reestablish contact for major developmental transitions (e.g., adolescence)

CHILD INTERVENTION

Behavioral and developmental approach

Focus on teaching academic, recreational, and social/behavioral competencies, decreasing aggression, developing close friendships, and building self-efficacy

Paraprofessional implemented

Intensive treatments such as summer treatment programs (9 hours daily for 8 weeks), and/or school-year, after-school, and Saturday (6 hours) sessions

Provided as long as necessary (e.g., 2 or 3 years)

Program for generalization and relapse prevention (e.g., integrate with school and parent treatments)

CONCURRENT PSYCHOSTIMULANT MEDICATION

Only rarely use as first line treatment

Need determined following initiation of behavioral treatments; timing depends on severity and responsiveness

Individualized, randomized, school-based medication trial conducted to determine need and minimal dose to complement the behavioral intervention

Need for TID or long-acting medication also determined during initial assessment based on child's impairment across settings

Repeated annual trials to adjust dosages and justify continued need variables to be examined is age. Given that younger and older ADHD children have been shown to differ on at least some studies of cognitive and social functioning, it may be that younger and older ADHD children differ in response to behavioral treatments. For example, perhaps older (i.e., young adolescents) ADHD children are more responsive to adjunct treatments (e.g., problem solving and self-monitoring) than are younger ADHD children (Kazdin & Weisz, 1998) and therefore will show greater maintenance of treatment effects. On the other hand, it is usually more feasible for a parent and teacher to implement CM procedures such as time out with a young child rather than an older one. No studies of which we are aware have evaluated the relationship between age and responsivity to behavioral treatments. Indeed, only one study in Exhibit 12.1 deals with ADHD adolescents. Given that these children's problems often worsen as they move into the difficult transitions of adolescence, more research on psychosocial and combined treatments of adolescents is absolutely critical.

How Should Comorbidities Affect Treatment Choice? A similar argument can be made for the evaluation of differential treatment response for ADHD children with comorbidities such as aggression/defiance, internalizing disorders, and learning disabilities. We are aware of only three studies that have examined the response of children comorbid for aggression to behavioral treatments, and both showed that comorbid aggressive ADHD boys responded as well as nonaggressive boys to behavioral treatments (MTA Cooperative Group, 1999a; Pelham et al., 1993; Pelham & Hoza, 1996). Given that comorbid aggression greatly increases the severity of impairment and the risk for poor prognosis, this result is a welcome one. Only one study has examined comorbid anxiety and that reported that effects of psychosocial treatment appeared to be more positive with comorbidly anxious ADHD children (MTA Cooperative Group, 1999b). We are not aware of studies examining the impact of comorbid learning disorders on response to psychosocial treatment, but the MTA will shed light on this question in future analyses.

How Do Family Factors Affect Treatment Choice? As noted previously, family factors such as single parenthood predict dropout and poor response to behavioral parent training (Miller & Prinz, 1990). Although this fact has long been known (Wahler, 1980), what has not been studied is the kinds of modifications to be made to behavioral interventions for ADHD families to minimize dropout (Miller & Prinz, 1990). For example, the fact that single-parent status and low socioeconomic status did not affect treatment response or completion rate in the STP (Pelham & Hoza, 1996) suggests that providing intensive CM, child-based treatment for children in at-risk families may enhance treatment responsiveness beyond that of typical ClBT interventions.

Can Medication Dosage or Parent Training Mitigate Treatment Intensity? A virtually unstudied aspect, in both behavioral interventions and CT, concerns dosage effects and which components of treatment are necessary. Although Table 12.2 describes our view of comprehensive treatment , there has been little or no research directed toward which of the three psychosocial components is necessary and whether concurrent medication would reduce the need for the more intensive components. For example, it is widely viewed that school intervention is a necessary component of treatment for ADHD, and the literature documents that CM interventions in the classroom are more potent than ClBT interventions. However, could a low dose of medication be added to an ongoing ClBT in the school setting and therefore avoid the need for a more intensive CM (or other intensive treatment component) without a loss in effectiveness? With one single case exception (Atkins et al., 1989), none of the combined treatment studies have systematically manipulated the strength of the psychosocial treatments employed (e.g., CM vs. ClBT) and examined interactions with medication dose. If the addition of a low dose of stimulant medication could substantially reduce the $5,000 annual cost for the SUNY-Buffalo clinic's comprehensive intervention, for example, by reducing the intensity of the classroom intervention required or eliminating the need for the STP or Saturday follow-up programs, without a loss of effectiveness, then that combination would quickly become the preferred mode of comprehensive treatment. It is becoming increasingly important to answer such cost-benefit questions in the current era of managed care and health care reform.

Can parents be taught to develop and implement a school intervention, thus eliminating the need for therapist contact with the teacher and therefore reducing the cost of treatment and providing for built-in maintenance of the program over school years? Do such modifications interact with family or child characteristics? For example, could the most intensive components of intensive treatment packages, such as the STP, be eliminated for all but the most severely aggressive ADHD children, thereby reducing the complexity and cost of treatment for the majority of cases? If higher (vs. lower) doses of medication result in normalization of functioning for many children (as long as medication is continued), then do such doses interfere with concurrent psychosocial treatment implementation (Klein & Abikoff, 1997), as we have suggested elsewhere?

What Is Optimum Treatment Sequence? Another question relates to the optimal way to sequence components of comprehensive treatments. Should intensive psychosocial components be provided first in order to bring children under control prior to ClBT approaches such as outpatient parent training? Or might that approach reduce parents' motivation for parent training. For example, should behavioral and pharmacological treatments be begun simultaneously in a combined treatment regimen, as every previous ClBT study has done, or, as has long been argued, should medication lag the behavioral treatment? If medication undercuts the parents' and teacher's motivation to learn and implement psychosocial treatments, then it clearly should be implemented as suggested in Table 12.3. It is noteworthy that subjects were three times more likely to cross over from psychosocial to combined treatment in the MTA study (MTA Cooperative Group, 1999a) if they had been previously medicated, meaning that parents, teachers, and therapists, who had not seen the child medicated were more willing to stick out psychosocial treatments than were parents, teachers, and therapists who had not been exposed to the medicated child. How would different sequencing arrangements affect maintenance of treatment effects?

How Long Must Treatment Continue? Finally, an important question concerns whether/how to fade psychosocial and combined treatments for ADHD. Some authors have argued that the fact that the effects of behavioral treatments dissipate when contingencies are removed means that the treatments have limited effectiveness (Hinshaw, Klein, & Abikoff, 1998). Interestingly, those same authors do not consider the fact that medication has the same limitation to be a drawback for medication. Indeed, it is often argued that because ADHD is a chronic disorder, medication needs to be a lifetime proposition for an ADHD child. The same may be true for psychosocial treatments for ADHD. These children's parents and teachers may well need to learn behavioral procedures and implement them for as long as is needed—just as is the case with medication. Given that the disorder is chronic, it appears likely that treatments will need to be chronic whatever the modality. Psychosocial treatments may change form over different developmental stages in the individual's life, but they may never be able to be completely eliminated. The relevant question is not how behavioral treatments should be faded but rather how do therapists, parents, and educators best cooperate to coordinate the resources and programs needed to institutionalize and maintain over the long haul behavioral interventions in the child's environment at home, in school, and with peers (see Table 12.2). There are simply no studies addressing such questions regarding the parameters of psychosocial and combined treatments for ADHD, and they are badly needed.

Cost-Effectiveness

Another central issue that remains to be addressed concerning behavioral treatment of ADHD is cost-effectiveness relative to other types of treatments. Behavioral treatments are much less cost-effective than administering stimulant medication, given that medications are administered only once or twice a day at a cost measured in cents, whereas behavioral treatments need to be constantly administered by professionals, teachers, and parents at considerably greater cost in effort and money. Long-term impacts—positive or negative—of the types and combinations of treatments need also be considered when assessing cost-benefit ratios. In terms of short-run costs, New York State currently funds community mental health centers in Buffalo that provide only nonbehavioral, ineffective, office-based treatments for ADHD (e.g., play therapy and individual therapy). It would cost no more for these centers to provide effective behavioral treatments to ADHD children than they currently spend to provide ineffective treatments—the staff simply need to change the therapeutic practices in which they currently engage. In fact, the eventual short-term costs per patient should be reduced because the number of therapeutic contacts per case should decrease as more efficacious treatments are provided. A resulting benefit would be that the community mental health system could provide treatment to an increased number of patients at the same current staffing levels.

Although comprehensive treatment as outlined may have relatively high initial costs, these costs may be far offset by long-term savings. Consider, for example, the SUNY-Buffalo clinic. We can provide a year of intensive ClBT/CM treatment for ADHD (a summer program, a school-year Saturday program, parent training with booster sessions, school consultation/intervention, and a double-blind, placebo controlled medication assessment) at a break-even cost of $5,000. The current cost for the New York State's State Division of Youth to maintain a young adolescent in residential treatment for a single year is $70,000, with a recidivism rate of 70 percent. Notably, a large proportion of the adolescents currently in residence are ADHD, typically with comorbid aggression (Williams, Levine, & Pelham, 2001). For each adolescent residential treatment year avoided, New York State could provide fourteen comprehensive treatment years for severely disturbed, comorbid, aggressive ADHD children. There are no data on long-term impact of comprehensive psychosocial treatments, but it is not unreasonable to speculate that providing some number of years of comprehensive treatment in childhood would be cost-effective in the long run for the state.

Exportability of Programs to Real-World Settings

An important but unstudied aspect of behavioral treatments for ADHD is their exportability to clinic settings—the issue of efficacy versus effectiveness (Hoagwood, Hibbs, Brent, & Jensen, 1995; Weisz, Donenberg, Han, & Weisz, 1995). With few exceptions (Pelham & Hoza, 1996), most studies of behavioral and combined treatments for ADHD have been conducted in controlled university settings using highly homogeneous samples rather than in settings that are part of the mental health system and with samples that are more representative of those seen in "real world" settings. As Weisz, Donenberg, et al. (1995) have noted, that fact likely overestimates the effectiveness of behavioral treatments for ADHD as they are likely to be conducted in the mental health system. Research on the exportability of behavioral treatment needs to be conducted and excellent suggestions are available (Weisz, Donenberg, et al., 1995).

One area in which behavioral treatments for ADHD are far superior to other forms of treatment for childhood disorders is the relatively long history of reliance on treatment manuals. Most forms of behavioral parent training, for example, have long been well manualized, as have teacher interventions and intensive treatment programs. The use of manualized treatments has many advantages that should serve behavioral treatments well as they are exported into community settings (Wilson, 1996).

Long-Term Effectiveness

Finally, and perhaps most important, the long-term effects of different types of behavioral and combinations of behavioral/pharmacological therapy need to be studied. The short-term efficacy of most types of behavior therapy is well documented. However, virtually no studies have yet examined whether these short-term improvements have any substantial impact, either alone or in combination with medication, on the adolescent and adult outcome of children with ADHD. Given the chronicity and poor outcome of ADHD, and given the absence of medication effects on long-term outcome, the answer to this question is critical. As we have discussed, it may well differ depending on the intensity of the behavioral treatment, the consistency and duration in which it was administered, and whether appropriate pharmacological treatments were adjunctively applied.

[Chapter references begin on page 12-30.]

Exhibit 12.1
Studies of Behavioral Treatments for ADHD

Study	Subject	Design	Type of Tx/ Setting	Length/ Amount of Tx	Control Conditions	Measures
Abramowitz & O'Leary, 1990	4 (100% male), grades 1&2, 100% hyperactive (CTRS)	Within subject ABCBA	CM-laboratory classroom immediate vs. delayed reprimands	27 days	Delayed reprimands; reversal	5
Abramowitz et al., 1987	16 (75% male) 7.9 (7–9), 100% hyperactive (CTRS)	Within subject ABA and crossover	CM; special summer classroom Manipulated teacher feedback	5 weeks, 2.5 hours per day	Encouragement vs.reprimands vs. no feedback	5,7
Abramowitz et al., 1988	7 (100% male), grades 2&3, 100% "hyperactive"	Within subject alternating treatments	CM-laboratory classroom Manipulated teacher reprimands	13 days	Short vs. long reprimands	5,7
Abramowitz et al., 1992	3 (100% male), 10.47 (10.1–11), 100% ADHD, 67% CD	Within subject alternating treatments	CM-intensive summer treatment program classroom with reward and response-cost system; manipulated teacher reprimands and medication	18 days	MPH; delayed vs. immediate reprimands	5
Acker & O'Leary, 1987	9 (89% male), 1st to 4th grade, 100% behavior, impulsivity & attention problems	Within subject reversal	CM-special summer classroom; manipulated teacher reprimands and praise	23 days	No treatment reversal	8,5
Acker & O'Leary, 1988	4 (100% male), 2nd to 3rd grade, 100% behavior, impulsivity & attention problems	Within subject ABABAB	CM-laboratory classroom; consistent vs. inconsistent teacher reprimands	24 days	Inconsistent reprimands	5
Anastopoulos et al., 1993	34 (74% male), 8.14 (6.25–10.25), 100% ADHD, 41.2% ODD	Between group	CIBT-group parent training	9 weekly sessions	Wait-list control group	2,3,4
Atkins et al., 1989	1 (male), 9, ADHD, CD	Single subject	CIBT-parent training; Teacher consultation; DRC; response-cost	9 months	No-treatment reversal; multiple baseline; pemoline	5,7,10
Ayllon et al., 1975	3 (67% male), 9 (8–10), 100% hyperactive	Within subject	CIBT-special education classroom; token system	32 days	MPH; multiple baseline	5,7
Barkley et al., 1980	7 (100% male), (7-10), 100% hyperactive (CTRS)	Within subject reversal	CM-laboratory classroom; Self instruction and self monitoring training with rewards	8 weeks, 2 hours/day	No-treatment reversal	5,15
Barkley et al., 1992	64 (92% male), 14 (12–17) 100% ADHD	Between group	(1) CIBT-family training (2) Problem solving and communication training (3) Structural family therapy	8–10 weekly sessions in each condition	Structural family therapy, communication training	1, 2, 3, 4, 11, 12, 13

**Exhibit 12.1
(Continued)**

Study	Subject	Design	Type of Tx/ Setting	Length/ Amount of Tx	Control Conditions	Measures
Barkley et al., 1996	158 (66% boys), (4.5–6) 100% aggressive-hyperactive (parent rating); 67% ADHD, 64% ODD, 18% CD	Between group	(1) CIBT-parent training, (2) CM-special treatment classrooms (response-cost, time out, self-control training, SST, school-home report), (3) Combination of (1) and (2)	(1) 10 weekly sessions + monthly booster sessions group (2) 1 academic year (3) 1 academic year with concurrent PT	No-treatment control group	1, 2, 5, 6, 8
Carlson et alm, 1992	24 (100% male), 9.2 (6–12), 100% ADHD, 29% CD, 50% ODD	Within subject crossover; order counter-balanced	CM-intensive summer treatment program (STP) classroom with reward/response-cost; time out	6 days	MPH; "regular classroom"	5, 7, 11
Dubey et alm, 1983	37 (87% male), 8.4 (6–10), 100% hyperactive (WWP)	Between group	(1) CIBT- group parent training (2) Parent communi-cation training	9 weeks; weekly 2-hr. sessions	Parent effectiveness training,wait-list control group	1, 2, 3, 13
DuPaul et al., 1992	2 (100% male), 6.5 (6-7), 100% ADHD, 50% ODD	Within subject ABABCB reversal	CIBT-special education classroom (attention training, response-cost)	40 days	No-treatment reversal	5, 6, 7
DuPaul & Henningson, 1993	1 (male), 7, ADHD	Single subject ABAB reversal	CIBT-school intervention (peer tutoring) with points, rewards	28 days	No-treatment reversal	5, 7
Erhardt & Baker, 1990	2 (100% male), 5.5 (5.2–5.8), 100% ADHD	Within subject Pre-post	CIBT-parent training	10 weeks: 6, 120-min. group sessions, 4, 60-min. individual sessions	Uncontrolled	2, 3, 14
Evans et al., 1995	1 (male), 11, ADHD	Single subject ABAB reversal	CIBT- Special education classroom (attention training, response-cost)	12 weeks	No-treatment reversal	5
Firestone et al., 1981, with Firestone et al., 1986	1981: 43; 1986: 52 1st, 30 2nd, 7.32 (5-9), 100% ADHD	Between group	(1) CIBT-group parent training, school consultation (2) CIBT + medication (3) Medication only	12 weeks: 9 PT sessions 2 school sessions	Medication; Medication + CIBT	2, 3, 6, 8, 9
Gittelman et al., 1980 (partial *N* in1976; expanded *N* in 1984, 1985, 1997)	89 (95% male), 8.25 (6–12), 100% hyperactive (CTRS)	Between group	(1) CIBT-parent training; school intervention (2) CIBT + MPH (3) MPH only	8 weeks: 8 PT sessions 8 school sessions	MPH; MPH + CIBT	2, 5, 6, 8, 12
Hops et al., 1978	54 (95% male), K–2nd grade, behavior problems	Between group	CIBT-Teacher-consultant mediated intervention program	15 days	No-treatment control group	5, 12, 13

**Exhibit 12.1
(Continued)**

Study	Subject	Design	Type of Tx/ Setting	Length/ Amount of Tx	Control Conditions	Measures
Horn et al., 1987	24, 9.59 (7–11.5), 100% ADHD	Between group	(1) CIBT-parent training (2) Cognitive-self-control training (SCT; child) (3) Combination of (1) and (2)	8 weeks weekly 90-min. sessions for parent and for child	SCT; CIBT + SCT	2, 3, 4, 5, 6, 8, 9
Horn et al., 1990	42 (81% male), 8.76 (7–11), 100% ADHD, 52.4% CD, 43% ODD	Between group	(1) CIBT-parent training (2) Cognitive-SCT (child) (3) Combination of (1) and (2)	12 weeks weekly 90-min. sessions for parent and for child 3 teacher sessions	SCT; CIBT + SCT	2, 6, 8, 9, 11
Horn et al., 1991 with Ialongo et al., 1993 (follow-up)	96 (77% male), (7–11), 100% ADHD, 7.4% CD, 43% ODD	Between group	(1) CIBT-parent training, school consultation (DRC) + SCT; (2) No treatment, crossed with (1) placebo; (2) low dose MPH; (3) high dose MPH	12 weeks PT/SCT 3 teacher sessions	MPH; CIBT + SCT + MPH	2, 3, 5, 6, 8, 9, 11
Hoza et al., 1992	2 (100% male), 10.96 (10.9–11), 100% ADHD, 50% ODD	Within subject	CM- intensive STP classroom; added contingencies	8 weeks	MPH, increased potency	5, 7
Kelley & McCain, 1995	5 (40% male), 7 (6–9), 40% ADHD, 60% inattentive or hyperactive (CTRS, CPRS)	Within subject ABAB reversal	CIBT-DRC with response-cost	30 days	DRC without response-cost	5, 7, 13
Kent & O'Leary, 1976	16, 10, behavior problems (referred by teachers)	Between group	CIBT- parent training, school intervention (praise, private reprimands, DRC)	4 months (3-4 hr assessment, 8 hr school, 7 hr. parent/ child, 2 hr. fading)	No-treatment control group	5, 6, 9
Kent & O'Leary, 1977	23, 7–9, conduct problems	Between group	CIBT- parent training, school intervention; treatment delivered by (1) PhDs, (2) BA level paraprofessionals, (3) PhD/BA teams.	20 hours 14 hr. school; 3 hr. parent, 3 hr. child contact	Ph.D. vs. B.A. implemented tx; no-treatment control group	5, 6, 9
Loney et al., 1979	12 (100% male), 6–12, 100% hyperkinesis (CTRS)	Between group	(1) CIBT-teacher interventions based on positive rewards (2) MPH	8–12 weeks teacher sessions as needed	MPH; classroom control group	5
McCain & Kelley, 1993	1 (male), 5, ADHD, conduct problems (CTRS)	Within subject ABAB	CIBT-preschool class; DRC	24 days	No-treatment reversal	5

**Exhibit 12.1
(Continued)**

Study	Subject	Design	Type of Tx/ Setting	Length/ Amount of Tx	Control Conditions	Measures
MTA Cooperative Group, 1998	579 (82% male), 7–9, 100% ADHD, 40% ODD, 14% CD	Between group	(1) CIBT-parent training, school consultation, with CM-intensive STP and paraprofessional-implemented classroom intervention (2) Medication only (3) Combination of (1) and (2)	14 months P.T.: 26 group sessions + 8 individual sessions + 22 phone conferences Teacher: 16 sessions + 20 phone meetings 40-day STP 4-month school parapro-fessional	Medication; BT + Medication Community-treated comparison group	1, 2, 3, 5, 6, 8, 10, 11, 12 (7, 13, 14 in STP)
O'Leary & Pelham, 1978	7, 8.33 (7.25–10.25),100% hyperactive	Pre-post	CIBT-parent training DRC	18 sessions over 4 mos.; half with school and parent	Pretreatment MPH; normal comparison group	2, 5, 6
O'Leary et al, 1970	10, 2nd-3rd grade, behavior problems	Within subject ABAB	CIBT-teacher intervention (loud and soft reprimands)	4 months	Loud vs. soft reprimands	5
O'Leary et al, 1976	17, 10 (8.9-10.9), 100% hyperkinesis	Between group	CIBT-home-based rewards, DRC	10 weeks; weekly teacher meetings	Wait list control group	6
Pelham & Hoza, 1996	258 (100% male), 9.1 (5–12), 100% ADHD, 58% aggressive	Pre-post	CM-Intensive multi-component summer treatment program; parent training	8 weeks Daily STP, weekly parent sessions	Pre-post	2, 3, 6, 11, 13
Pelham et al, 1980	8 (88% male), 8.3 (6.5–11.5), 100% hyperkinesis	Pre-post	CIBT-parent training, teacher consultation, self-control training (child)	5 months; 12 parent and 12 teacher sessions; 22 self-control sessions	Pretreatment MPH and base line	1, 2, 5, 6
Pelham et al, 1988	32 (88% male), 7 (5–10), 100% ADHD	Between group	Clinical- parent training, teacher consultation (DRC) combined with (1) medication or placebo and (2) Social Skills Training (SST) or no SST	5 months; P.T. M 9.7 sessions Teacher M 10.3 sessions SST 8 sessions	MPH + CIBT; SST + CIBT; contrast control (SST only)	2, 5, 6, 8, 10
Pelham et al, 1993	31 (100% male), 8.23 (5.42–9.92), 100% ADHD, 32.3% ODD, 48.4% CD	Within subject crossover; order counter-balanced	CM-intensive summer reatment program (STP) tclassroom with reward/ response-cost; time out	8 weeks	MPH; MPH + CM; "regular classroom"	5,6,7
Pelham, 1977	1 (male), 9, hyperkinesis	Uncontrolled case study	CIBT-parent training School intervention (DRC)	7 months; 14 P.T. sessions, 8 teacher sessions	Uncontrolled	2,6,

Exhibit 12.1
(Continued)

Study	Subject	Design	Type of Tx/ Setting	Length/ Amount of Tx	Control Conditions	Measures
Pfiffner & McBurnett, 1997	27 (70% male), 8–10, 93% ADHD, 1% UADD, 70% ODD, 1% CD	Between group	(1) CIBT-SST with parent-mediated generalization (2) Child-only SST	8 weeks 8 SST sessions, 8 parent sessions	Wait-list control group; child-only SST	2, 6, 8, 13
Pfiffner, O'Leary et al., 1985	7 (63% male), 2nd–3rd grade, behavior and attention problems	Within subject crossover; order counter-balanced	CM-laboratory classroom; manipulated consistency of reprimands and response-cost	4 weeks	Baseline, inconsistent reprimands, inconsistent response-cost	5
Pfiffner & O'Leary, 1987	8 (63% male), 2nd–3rd grade, behavior and attention problems	Within subject ABCBD	CM-summer laboratory classroom; manipulated positive (e.g., praise, reward system) and negative (e.g., reprimands, loss of recess) consequences	5 weeks	"Regular" positive consequences baseline and reversal	5, 8
Pfiffner, Rosen et al., 1985	8 (63% male), 2nd–3rd grade, behavior problems	Within subject ABCBACA	CM-laboratory classroom; positive (praise) and negative (loss of recess) consequences	46 days	Baseline and reversal	5, 8
Pisterman et al., 1989	46 (80% male), 4.15 (3–6) 100% ADHD	Between group	CIBT- parent training	12 weeks: 10 group sessions, 2 indiv. sessions	Delayed treatment control group	1
Pisterman et al., 1992a	91 (86% male), 4.37, 100% ADHD	Between group	CIBT-parent group compliance and attention training	12 weekly sessions	Delayed treatment control group	1, 2, 3
Pisterman ct al., 1992b	45 (93% male), 4.13 100% ADHD	Between group	CIBT-parent group compliance and attention training	12 weekly sessions	Delayed treatment control group	1, 2, 3
Pollard et al., 1983	3 (100% male), 100% ADHD	Within CIBT-subject additivedesign	Parent training	4 weeks; twice-weekly sessions	MPH; MPH + parent training; no-treatment baseline	2, 4, 5
Rapport et al., 1980	2 (50% male), 7.5 (7–8), 100% hyperkinesis	Within subject (a) reversal; (b) additive design	CIBT-school intervention; response-cost	(a) 14 days (b) MPH 6 days,MPH + BT 6 days; BT 4 days	(a) No-treatment reversal; (b) MPH; MPH + response-cost	5, 7
Rapport et al, 1982	2 (100% male), 7.5 (7–8), 100% ADHD	Within subject ABACBC	CIBT-school intervention; response-cost	82 days	MPH; no-treatment baseline and reversal	5, 6, 7
Robinson et al, 1981	18 (100% male), 3rd grade, behavior problems	Within subject BAB	CIBT-school intervention; token system	4 weeks	No treatment reversal	8
Rosen et al., 1984	23 (over 4 studies) 2nd–3rd grade, 100% hyperactive (CTRS)	Within subject crossover with reversal	CM-laboratory classroom; negative and positive consequences	20 days	No-treatment reversal	5, 7

**Exhibit 12.1
(Continued)**

Study	Subject	Design	Type of Tx/ Setting	Length/ Amount of Tx	Control Conditions	Measures
Rosenbaum et al., 1975	10, 10.3 (8.9–12.1), 100% hyperactive	Between group	CIBT-school intervention; group reward vs. individual reward	4 weeks	Group vs. individual reward	6, 13
Stableford et al., 1976	2 (100% male), 9.5 (8-11), hyperactive behavior	Within subject	CIBT-home point system; school intervention (behavior tracking card, group rewards)	7 weeks	MPH, gradually reducing dosage to none	6, 14
Sullivan & O'Leary, 1990	10 (50% male), 8.58 (6.92–9.83), behavior/academic problems, inattention, hyperactivity	Within subject ABABA; setting counter- balanced	CM-special summer classroom; positive vs. negative consequences and fading	6 weeks	Baseline; reward vs. response-cost with fading	5
Thurston, 1979	18, 6–9, 100% hyperactive	Between group	(1) CIBT-parent training (2) MPH	4–6 weeks twice-weekly PT sessions	MPH; wait-list control group	2, 9, 15
Umbreit, 1995	1 (male), 8, ADHD	Within subject multiple baseline	CIBT-school intervention (self-monitoring, token system)	7 weeks	No-treatment baseline	5
Walker et al., 1975	8 (90% male), 6–9, behavior problems	Between group	CM-experimental classroom; token economy, reinforcement/ response-cost; manipulatedmaintenance procedures	4 months	Baseline, maintenance vs. no maintenance	5
Wolraich et al., 1978	20, 7.58 (6–9), 100% hyperactive (TRS)	Within subjects ABA with between- group test of MPH	CM-laboratory classroom; token economy system	6 weeks	MPH; regular classroom reversal	5, 6, 7

References

Abikoff, H. (1987). An evaluation of cognitive behavior therapy for hyperactive children. In B. B. Lahey & A. E. Kazdin (Eds.), *Advances in clinical child psychology* (pp. 171–216). New York: Plenum Press.

Abikoff, H. (1991). Cognitive training in ADHD children: Less to it than meets the eye. *Journal of Learning Disabilities, 24*, 205–209.

Abikoff H., Ganeles D., Reiter G., Blum C., Foley C., & Klein, R. (1988). Cognitive training in academically deficient ADDH boys receiving stimulant medication. *Journal of Abnormal Child Psychology, 16*(4), 411–432.

Abikoff, H., & Gittelman, R. (1984). Does behavior therapy normalize the classroom behavior of hyperactive children? *Archives of General Psychiatry, 41*, 449–454.

Abikoff, H., & Hechtman, L. (1996). Multimodal therapy and stimulants in the treatment of children with attention deficit hyperactivity disorder. In E. D. Hibbs & P. S. Jensen (Eds.), *Psychosocial treatments for child and adolescent disorders: Empirically based strategies for clinical practice* (pp. 341–369). Washington, DC: American Psychological Association.

Abramowitz, A. J., Eckstrand, D., O'Leary, S. G., & Dulcan, M. K. (1992). ADHD children's responses to stimulant medication and two intensities of a behavioral intervention. *Behavior Modification, 16*, 193–203.

Abramowitz, A. J., & O'Leary, S. G. (1990). Effectiveness of delayed punishment in an applied setting. *Behavior Therapy, 21*, 231–239.

Abramowitz, A. J., O'Leary, S. G., & Futtersak, M. W. (1988). The relative impact of long and short reprimands on children's off-task behavior in the classroom. *Behavior Therapy, 19*, 243–247.

Abramowitz, A. J., O'Leary, S. G., & Rosen, L. A. (1987). Reducing off-task behavior in the classroom: A comparison of encouragement and reprimands. *Journal of Abnormal Child Psychology, 15*, 153–163.

Acker, M. M., & O'Leary, S. G. (1987). Effects of reprimands and praise on appropriate social behavior in the classroom. *Journal of Abnormal Child Psychology, 5*, 549–557.

Acker, M. M., & O'Leary, S. G. (1988). Effects of consistent and inconsistent feedback on inappropriate child behavior. *Behavior Therapy, 19*, 619–624.

American Psychiatric Association. (1994). *Diagnostic and statistical manual of mental disorders* (4th ed.). Washington, DC: Author.

Anastopoulos, A. D., Shelton, T. L., DuPaul, G. J., & Guevremont, D. C. (1993). Parent training for attention-deficit hyperactivity disorder: Its impact on parent functioning. *Journal of Abnormal Child Psychology, 21*, 581–596.

Arnold, L. E., Abikoff, H. B., Cantwell, D. P., Conners, C. K., Elliott, G., Greenhill, L. L., Hechtman, L., Hinshaw, S. P., Hoza, B., Jensen, P. S., Kraemer, H., March, J., Newcorn, J., Pelham, W. E., Richters, J., Severe, J. B., Schiller, E., Swanson, J. M., Vereen, D., & Wells, K. (1997). National Institute of Mental Health Collaborative Multimodal Treatment Study of Children with ADHD (MTA): Design challenges and choices. *Archives of General Psychiatry, 54*, 865–870.

Atkins, M. S., Pelham, W. E., & White, K. J. (1989). Hyperactivity and attention deficit disorders. In M. Hersen (Ed.), *Psychological aspects of developmental and physical disabilities: A casebook* (pp. 137–156). Thousand Oaks, CA: Sage.

Ayllon, T., Layman, D., & Kandel, H. J. (1975). A behavioral-educational alternative to drug control of hyperactive children. *Journal of Applied Behavior Analysis, 8*, 137–146.

Barkley, R. A. (1987). *Defiant children: Parent-teacher assignments.* New York: Guilford Press.

Barkley, R. A. (1995). *Taking charge of ADHD: The complete, authoritative guide for parents.* New York: Guilford Press.

Barkley, R. A., Copeland, A. P., & Sivage, C. (1980). A self-control classroom for hyperactive children. *Journal of Autism and Developmental Disorders, 10*, 75–89.

Barkley, R. A., Guevremont, D. C., Anastopoulos, A. D., & Fletcher, K. E. (1992). A comparison of three family therapy programs for treating family conflicts in adolescents with attention-deficit hyperactivity disorder. *Journal of Consulting and Clinical Psychology, 60*(3), 450–462.

Barkley, R. A., Karlsson, J., Pollard, S., & Murphy, J. V. (1985). Developmental changes in the mother-child interactions of hyperactive boys: Effects of two dose levels of Ritalin. *Journal of Child Psychiatry and Allied Disciplines, 26*, 705–715.

Barkley, R. A., Karlsson, J., Strzelecki, E., & Murphy, J. V. (1984). Effects of age and ritalin dosage on the mother-child interactions of hyperactive children. *Journal of Consulting and Clinical Psychology, 52*, 739–749.

Barkley, R. A., Shelton, T. L., Crosswait, C., Moorehouse, M., Fletcher, K., Barrett, S., Jenkins, L., & Metevia, L. (1996). Preliminary findings of an early intervention program with aggressive hyperactive children. *Annals of the New York Academy of Sciences, 794*, 277–289.

Bloomquist, M. L., August, G. J., & Ostrander, R. (1991). Effects of a school-based cognitive-behavioral intervention for ADHD children. *Journal of Abnormal Child Psychology, 19*, 591–605.

Brestan, E. V., & Eyberg, S. M. (1998). Effective psychosocial treatments of conduct-disordered children and adolescents: 29 years, 82 studies, and 5,272 kids. *Journal of Clinical Child Psychology, 27*, 180–189.

Brown, R. T., Borden, K. A., Wynne, M. E., Spunt, A. L., & Clingerman, S. R. (1987). Compliance with pharmacological and cognitive treatment for attention deficit disorder. *Journal of the American Academy of Child and Adolescent Psychiatry, 26*, 521–526.

Carlson, C. L., Pelham, W. E., Milich, R., & Dixon, J. (1992). Single and combined effects of methylphenidate and behavior therapy on the classroom performance of children with attention-deficit hyperactivity disorder. *Journal of Abnormal Child Psychology, 20*, 213–232.

Charles, L., & Schain, R. (1981). A four-year follow-up study of the effects of methylphenidate on the behavior and academic achievement of hyperactive children. *Journal of Abnormal Child Psychology, 9*, 495–505.

Cunningham, C. E., Bremner, R., & Secord-Gilbert, M. (1994). *The community parent education (COPE) program: A school based family systems oriented course for parents of children with disruptive behavior disorders.* Unpublished manuscript, McMaster University and Chedoke-McMaster Hospitals.

Dubey, D. R., O'Leary, S. G., & Kaufman, K. F. (1983). Training parents of hyperactive children in child management: A comparative outcome study. *Journal of Abnormal Child Psychology, 11*, 229–246.

DuPaul, G. J., & Eckert, T. L. (1997). The effects of school-based interventions for attention deficit hyperactivity disorder: A meta-analysis. *School Psychology Review, 26*, 5–27.

DuPaul, G. J., Guevremont, D. C., & Barkley, R. A. (1992). Behavioral treatment of attention-deficit hyperactivity disorder in the classroom: The use of the attention training system. *Behavior Modification, 16*, 204–225.

DuPaul, G. J., & Henningson, P. N. (1993). Peer tutoring effects on the classroom performance of children with ADHD. *School Psychology Review, 22*, 134–143.

Erhardt, D., & Baker, B. L. (1990). The effects of behavioral parent training on families with young hyperactive children. *Journal of Behavior Therapy and Experimental Psychiatry, 21*, 121–132.

Evans, J. H., Ferre, L., Ford, L. A., & Green, J. L. (1995). Decreasing ADHD symptoms utilizing an automated classroom reinforcement device. *Psychology in the Schools, 32*, 210–219.

Firestone, P., Crowe, D., Goodman, J. T., & McGrath, P. (1986). Vicissitudes of follow-up studies: Differential effects of parent training and stimulant medication with hyperactives. *American Journal of Orthopsychiatry, 56*, 184–194.

Firestone, P., Kelly, M. J., Goodman, J. T., & Davey, J. (1981). Differential effects of parent training and stimulant medication with hyperactives. *Journal of the American Academy of Child Psychiatry, 20*, 135–147.

Fischer, M. (1990). Parenting stress and the child with attention deficit hyperactivity disorder. *Journal of Clinical Child Psychology, 19*, 337–346.

Forehand, R., & Long, N. (1996). *Parenting the strong-willed child.* Chicago: Contemporary Books.

Forehand, R. E., & McMahon, R. J. (1981). *Helping the noncompliant child. A clinician's guide to parent training.* New York: Guilford Press.

Forgatch, M., & Patterson, G. R. (1989). *Parents and adolescents living together: Part 2: Family problem solving.* Eugene, OR: Castalia.

Fuchs, D., & Fuchs, L. S. (1989). Exploring effective and efficient prereferral interventions: A component analysis of behavioral consultation. *School Psychology Review, 18*, 260–283.

Gittelman, R., Abikoff, H., Pollack, E., Klein, D. F., Katz, S., & Mattes, J. (1980). A controlled trial of behavior modification and methylphenidate in hyperactive children. In C. K. Whalen & B. Henker (Eds.), *Hyperactive children: The social ecology of identification and treatment* (pp. 221–243). New York: Academic Press.

Hinshaw, S. P. (1991). Stimulant medication and the treatment of aggression in children with attentional deficits. *Journal of Clinical Child Psychology, 20*, 301–312.

Hinshaw, S. P., & Erhardt, D. (1991). Attention-deficit hyperactivity disorder. In P. Kendall (Ed.), *Child and adolescent therapy: Cognitive-behavioral procedures* (pp. 98–128). New York: Guilford Press.

Hinshaw, S. P., Heller, T., & McHale, J. P. (1992). Covert antisocial behavior in boys with attention deficit hyperactivity disorder: External validation and effects of methylphenidate. *Journal of Consulting and Clinical Psychology, 60*, 274- 281.

Hinshaw, S. P., Klein, R. G., & Abikoff, H. (1998). Childhood attention deficit hyperactivity disorder: Nonpharmacological and combination treatments. In P. E. Nathan & J. M. Gorman (Eds.), *A guide to treatments that work* (pp. 26–41). New York: Oxford University Press.

Hoagwood, K., Hibbs, E., Brent, D., & Jensen, P. (1995). Introduction to the special section: Efficacy and effectiveness in studies of child and adolescent psychotherapy. *Journal of Consulting and Clinical Psychology, 63*, 683–687.

Hops, H., Walker, H. M., Fleischman, D. H., Nagoshi, J. T., Omura, R. T., Skindrud, K., & Taylor, J. (1978). CLASS: A standardized in-class program for acting-out children: II. Field test evaluations. *Journal of Educational Psychology, 70*, 636–644.

Horn, W. F., Ialongo, N. S, Greenberg, G., Packard, T., & Smith-Winberry, C. (1990). Additive effects of behavioral parent training and self-control therapy with ADHD children. *Journal of Clinical Child Psychology, 19*, 98–110.

Horn, W. F., Ialongo, N. S, Pascoe, J. M., Greenberg, G., Packard, T., Lopez, M., Wagner, A., & Puttler, L. (1991). Additive effects of psychostimulants, parent training, and self-control therapy with ADHD children. *Journal of the American Academy of Child and Adolescent Psychiatry, 30(2)*, 233–240.

Horn, W. F., Ialongo, N. S, Popovich, S., & Peradotto, D. (1987). Behavioral parent training and cognitive-behavioral self-control therapy with ADD-H children: Comparative and combined effects. *Journal of Clinical Child Psychology, 16*, 57–68.

Hoza, B., Pelham, W. E., Sams, S. E., & Carlson, C. (1992). An examination of the dosage effects of both behavior therapy and methylphenidate on the classroom performance of two ADHD children. *Behavior Modification, 16*, 164–192.

Ialongo, N. S., Horn, W. F., Pascoe, J. M., Greenberg, G., Packard, T., Lopez, M., Wagner, A., & Puttler, L. (1993). The effects of a multimodal intervention with attention-deficit hyperactivity disorder children: A 9-month follow up. *Journal of the American Academy of Child and Adolescent Psychiatry, 32*, 182–189.

Jacobson, N. S., & Truax, P. (1991). Clinical significance: A statistical approach to defining meaningful change in psychotherapy research. *Journal of Consulting and Clinical Psychology, 59*, 12–19.

Kazdin, A. E. (1996). Problem solving and parent management in treating aggressive and antisocial behavior. In E. D. Hibbs & P. S. Jensen (Eds.), *Psychosocial treatments for child and adolescent disorders: Empirically based strategies for clinical practice* (pp. 377–408), Washington, DC: American Psychological Association.

Kazdin, A. E., & Weisz, J. R. (1998). Identifying and developing empirically supported child and adolescent treatments. *Journal of Consulting and Clinical Psychology, 66*, 19–36.

Kelley, M. L., & McCain, A. P. (1995). Promoting academic performance in inattentive children: The relative efficacy of school-home notes with and without response-cost. *Behavior Modification, 19*, 357–375.

Kendall, P. C., & Gosch, E. A. (1994). Cognitive-behavioral interventions. In T. H. Ollendick, N. J. King, & W. Yule (Eds.), *International handbook of phobic and anxiety disorders in children and adolescents* (pp. 415–438). New York: Plenum Press.

Kent, R. N., & O'Leary, K. D. (1976). A controlled evaluation of behavior modification with conduct problem children. *Journal of Consulting and Clinical Psychology, 44*, 586–596.

Kent, R. N., & O'Leary, K. D. (1977). Treatment of conduct problem children: BA and/or PhD therapists. *Behavior Therapy, 8*, 653–658.

Klein, R. G., & Abikoff, H. (1997). Behavior therapy and methylphenidate in the treatment of children with ADHD. *Journal of Attention Disorders, 2*, 89–114.

Lochman, J. E. (1992). Cognitive-behavioral intervention with aggressive boys: Three-year follow up and preventive effects. *Journal of Consulting and Clinical Psychology, 60*, 426–432.

Lochman, J. E., & Lenhart, L. A. (1993). Anger coping intervention for aggressive children: Conceptual models and outcome effects. *Clinical Psychology Review, 13*, 785–805.

Loney, J., Weissenberger, F. E., Woolson, R. F., & Lichty, E. C. (1979). Comparing psychological and pharmacological treatments for hyperkinetic boys and their classmates. *Journal of Abnormal Child Psychology, 7*, 133–143.

Lonigan, C. J., Elbert, J. C., & Johnson, S. B. (1998). Empirically supported psychosocial interventions for children: An overview. *Journal of Clinical Child Psychology, 27*, 138–145.

Mash, E. J., & Johnston, C. (1990). Determinants of parenting stress: Illustrations from families of hyperactive children and families of physically abused children. *Journal of Clinical Child Psychology, 19*, 313–328.

McCain, A. P., & Kelley, M. L. (1993). Managing the classroom behavior of an ADHD preschooler: The efficacy of a school-home note intervention. *Child and Family Behavior Therapy, 15*, 33–44.

Meichenbaum, D., & Goodman, J. (1971). Training impulsive children to talk to themselves: A means of developing self-control. *Journal of Abnormal Psychology, 77*, 115–126.

Milich, R., & Landau, S. (1982). Socialization and peer relations in the hyperactive child. In K. Gadow & I. Bialer (Eds.), *Advances in learning and behavioral disabilities* (Vol. 1, pp. 283–339), Greenwich, CT: JAI Press.

Miller, G. E., & Prinz, R. J. (1990). Enhancement of social learning family interventions for childhood conduct disorder. *Psychological Bulletin, 108*, 291–307.

MTA Cooperative Group. (1999). A 14-month randomized clinical trial of treatment strategies for attention-deficit/hyperactivity disorder: Multimodal Treatment Study of Children with ADHD. *Archives of General Psychiatry, 56*(12), 1073–1086.

MTA Cooperative Group. (1999b). Moderators and mediators of treatment response for children with attention-deficit/hyperactivity disorder. *Archives of General Psychiatry, 56*, 1088–1096.

O'Leary, S. G., & Pelham, W. E. (1978). Behavior therapy and withdrawal of stimulant medication with hyperactive children. *Pediatrics, 61*, 211–217.

O'Leary, K. D., & Becker, W. C. (1967). Behavior modification of an adjustment class: A token reinforcement program. *Exceptional Children, 33*, 637–642.

O'Leary, K. D., Kaufmann, K. F., Kass, R. E., & Drabman, R. S. (1970). The effects of loud and soft reprimands on the behavior of disruptive students. *Exceptional Children, 37*, 145–155.

O'Leary, K. D., Pelham, W. E., Rosenbaum, A., & Price, G. (1976). Behavioral treatment of hyperkinetic children: An experimental evaluation of its usefulness. *Clinical Pediatrics, 15*, 510–515.

Parker, J. G., & Asher, S. R. (1987). Peer relations and later personal adjustment: Are low-accepted children at risk? *Psychological Bulletin, 102*, 357–389.

Patterson, G. R. (1974). Intervention for boys with conduct problems: Multiple settings, treatment, and criteria. *Journal of Consulting and Clinical Psychology, 42*, 471–481.

Patterson, G. R. (1982). *Coercive family process.* Eugene, OR: Castalia.

Patterson, G. R. (1975). *Families: Application of social learning to family life.* Champaign, IL: Research Press.

Pelham, W. E. (1977). Withdrawal of a stimulant drug and concurrent behavioral intervention in the treatment of a hyperactive child. *Behavior Therapy, 8*, 473–479.

Pelham, W. E., & Bender, M. E. (1982). Peer relationships in hyperactive children: Description and treatment. In K. Gadow & I. Bialer (Eds.), *Advances in learning and behavior disabilities* (Vol. 1, pp. 365–436). Greenwich, CT: JAI Press.

Pelham, W. E., Carlson, C., Sams, S. E., Vallano, G., Dixon, M. J., & Hoza, B. (1993). Separate and combined effects of methylphenidate and behavior modification on boys with ADHD in the classroom. *Journal of Consulting and Clinical Psychology, 61*(3), 506–515.

Pelham, W. E., Greiner, A. R., & Gnagy, E. M. (1997). *Children's summer treatment program manual.* Buffalo, NY: Comprehensive Treatment for Attention Deficit Disorder.

Pelham, W. E., Greiner, A. R., Gnagy, E. M., Hoza, B., Martin, L., Sams, S. E., & Wilson, T. (1996). A summer treatment program for children with ADHD. In M. Roberts & A. LaGreca (Eds.), *Model programs for service delivery for child and family mental health* (pp. 193–212). Hillsdale, NJ: Erlbaum.

Pelham, W. E., & Hoza, B. (1996). Intensive treatment: A summer treatment program for children with ADHD. In E. Hibbs & P. Jensen (Eds.), *Psychosocial treatments for child and adolescent disorders: Empirically based strategies for clinical practice* (pp. 311–340). New York: American Psychological Association Press.

Pelham, W. E., Lang, A. R., Atkeson, B., Murphy, D. A., Gnagy, E. M., Greiner, A. R., Vodde-Hamilton, M., & Greenslade, K. E. (1998). Effects of deviant child behavior on parental alcohol consumption: Stress-induced drinking in parents of ADHD children. *American Journal of Addictions, 7*, 103–114.

Pelham, W. E., & Murphy, H. A. (1986). Attention deficit and conduct disorder. In M. Hersen (Ed.), *Pharmacological and behavioral treatment: An integrative approach* (pp. 108–148). New York: Wiley.

Pelham, W. E., Schnedler, R. W., Bender, M. E., Miller, J., Nilsson, D., Budrow, M., Ronnei, M., Paluchowski, C., & Marks, D. (1988). The combination of behavior therapy and methylphenidate in the treatment of hyperactivity: A therapy outcome study. In L. Bloomingdale (Ed.), *Attention deficit disorders* (Vol. 3, pp. 29–48). London: Pergamon Press.

Pelham, W. E., Schnedler, R. W., Bologna, N., & Contreras, A. (1980). Behavioral and stimulant treatment of hyperactive children: A therapy study with methylphenidate probes in a within-study design. *Journal of Applied Behavioral Analysis, 13*, 221–236.

Pelham, W. E., Jr., & Smith, B. H. (2000). Prediction and measurement of individual responses to Ritalin by children and adolescents with ADHD. In L. Greenhill & B. Osman (Eds.), *Ritalin: Theory and patient management* (2nd ed.). New York: Mary Ann Liebert.

Pelham, W. E., & Waschbusch, D. A. (1999). Behavioral intervention in ADHD. In H. C. Quay & A. E. Hogan (Eds.), *Handbook of disruptive behavior disorders* (pp. 255–278), New York: Plenum Press.

Pelham, W. E., Wheeler, T., & Chronis, A. (1998). Empirically supported psychosocial treatments for ADHD. *Journal of Clinical Child Psychology, 27*, 190–205.

Pfiffner, L. J., & McBurnett, K. (1997). Social skills training with parent generalization: Treatment effects for children with ADD/ADHD. *Journal of Consulting and Clinical Psychology, 65*, 749–757.

Pfiffner, L. J., & O'Leary, S. G. (1987). The efficacy of all-positive management as a function of the prior use of negative consequences. *Journal of Applied Behavior Analysis, 20*, 265–271.

Pfiffner, L. J., O'Leary, S. G., Rosen, L. A., & Sanderson, W. C., Jr. (1985). A comparison of the effects of continuous and intermittent response-cost and reprimands in the classroom. *Journal of Clinical Child Psychology, 14*, 348–352.

Pfiffner, L. J., Rosen, L. A., & O'Leary, S. G. (1985). The efficacy of an all-positive approach to classroom management. *Journal of Applied Behavior Analysis, 18*, 257–261.

Pisterman, S., Firestone, P., McGrath, P., Goodman, J. T., Webster, I., Mallory, R., & Goffin, B. (1992a). The role of parent training in treatment of preschoolers with ADD-H. *American Journal of Orthopsychiatry, 62*, 397–408.

Pisterman, S., Firestone, P., McGrath, P., Goodman, J. T., Webster, I., Mallory, R., & Goffin, B. (1992b). The effects of parent training on parenting stress and sense of competence. *Canadian Journal of Behavioural Science, 24*, 41–58.

Pisterman, S., McGrath, P., Firestone, P., Goodman, J. T., Webster, I., & Mallory, R. (1989). Outcome of parent-mediated treatment of preschoolers with attention deficit disorder with hyperactivity. *Journal of Consulting and Clinical Psychology, 57*, 628–635.

Pollard, S., Ward, E. M., & Barkley, R. A. (1983). The effects of parent training and Ritalin on the parent-child interactions of hyperactive boys. *Child and Family Behavior Therapy, 5*, 51–69.

Rapport, M. D., Murphy, A., & Bailey, J. S. (1980). The effects of a response-cost treatment tactic on hyperactive children. *Journal of School Psychology, 18*, 98–111.

Rapport, M. D., Murphy, H. A., & Bailey, J. S. (1982). Ritalin vs. response-cost in the control of hyperactive children: A within-subjects comparison. *Journal of Applied Behavior Analysis, 15*, 205–216.

Richters, J. E., Arnold, L. E., Jensen, P. S., Abikoff, H., Conners, C. K., Greenhill, L. L., Hechtman, L., Hinshaw, S. P., Pelham, W. E., & Swanson, J. M. (1995). NIMH collaborative multisite multimodal treatment study of children with ADHD: I. Background and rationale. *Journal of the American Academy of Child and Adolescent Psychiatry, 34*, 987–1000.

Robinson, P. W., Newby, T. J., & Ganzell, S. L. (1981). A token system for a class of underachieving hyperactive children. *Journal of Applied Behavior Analysis, 14*, 307–315.

Rosen, L. A., O'Leary, S. G., Joyce, S. A., Conway, G., & Pfiffner, L. J. (1984). The importance of prudent negative consequences for maintaining the appropriate behavior of hyperactive students. *Journal of Abnormal Child Psychology, 12*, 581–604.

Rosenbaum, A., O'Leary, S. G., & Jacob, R. G. (1975). Behavioral intervention with hyperactive children: Group consequences as a supplement to individual contingencies. *Behavior Therapy, 6*, 315–323.

Satterfield, J. H., Hoppe, C. M., & Schell, A. M. (1982). A prospective study of delinquency in 110 adolescent boys with attention deficit disorder and 88 normal adolescents. *American Journal of Psychiatry, 139*, 795–798.

Sherman, M., & Hertzig, M. E. (1991). Prescribing practices of Ritalin: The Suffolk County, New York study. In L. L. Greenhill & B. B. Osman (Eds.), *Ritalin: Theory and patient management* (pp. 187–193). New York: Mary Ann Liebert.

Stableford, W., Butz, R., Hasazi, J., Leitenberg, H., & Peyser, J. (1976). Sequential withdrawal of stimulant drugs and use of behavior therapy with two hyperactive boys. *American Journal of Orthopsychiatry, 46*, 302–312.

Sullivan, M. A., & O'Leary, S. G. (1990). Maintenance following reward and cost token programs. *Behavior Therapy, 21*, 139–149.

Swanson, J. M., McBurnett, K., Christian, D. L., & Wigal, T. (1995). Stimulant medication and treatment of children with ADHD. In T. H. Ollendick & R. J. Prinz (Eds.), *Advances in clinical child psychology* (Vol. 17, pp. 265–322).s New York: Plenum Press.

Thurston, L. P. (1979). Comparison of the effects of parent training and of Ritalin in treating hyperactive children. *International Journal of Mental Health, 8*, 121–128.

Turkewitz, H., O'Leary, K. D., & Ironsmith, M. (1975). Generalization and maintenance of appropriate behavior through self-control. *Journal of Consulting and Clinical Psychology, 43*, 577–583.

Umbreit, J. (1995). Functional assessment and intervention in a regular classroom setting for the disruptive behavior of a student with ADHD. *Behavior Disorders, 20*, 267–278.

Wahler, R. G. (1980). The insular mother: Her problems in parent-child treatment. *Journal of Applied Behavior Analysis, 13*, 207–219.

Walker, H. M., Hops, H., & Johnson, S. M. (1975). Generalization and maintenance of classroom treatment effects. *Behavior Therapy, 6*, 188–200.

Weiss, G., & Hechtman, L. (1993). *Hyperactive children grown up* (2nd ed.). New York: Guilford Press.

Weisz, J. R., Donenberg, G. R., Han, S. S., & Weisz, B. (1995). Bridging the gap between laboratory and clinic in child and adolescent psychotherapy. *Journal of Consulting and Clinical Psychology, 63*, 688–701.

Weisz, J. R., Weiss, B., Han, S. S., Granger, D. A., & Morton, T. (1995). Effects of psychotherapy with children and adolescents revisited: A meta-analysis of treatment outcome studies. *Psychological Bulletin, 117*, 450–468.

Williams, A., Levine, M., & Pelham, W. E. (2001). *Prevalence of attention-deficit hyperactivity disorder and related disruptive behavior disorders in non-detainees in the juvenile justice system: A pilot study.* Manuscript in preparation.

Wilson, G. T. (1996). Manual-based treatments: The clinical application of research findings. *Behaviour Research and Therapy, 34*, 295–314.

Wolraich, M., Drummond, T., Solomon, M. K., O'Brien, M. L., & Sivage, C. (1978). Effects of methylphenidate alone and in combination with behavior modification procedures on the behavior and academic performance of hyperactive children. *Journal of Abnormal Child Psychology, 6*, 149–161.

Chapter 13

Treatment Alternatives for Attention Deficit Hyperactivity Disorder

by L. Eugene Arnold, M.Ed., M.D.

Introduction 13-2
Eliminaton Diets (Few-Foods Diets/Oligoantigenic) 13-2
    Recent Research Documents Efficacy 13-2
    Probable Responders to Elimination Diets 13-3
    Sugar Elimination Alone Unlikely to Work 13-4
    Possible Risks 13-7
Immune Therapy 13-7
Nutritional Supplements 13-7
    Amino Acid Supplementation 13-7
    Essential Fatty Acid Supplementation 13-8
    Possible L-Carnitine Effect 13-9
    Glyconutritional Supplements 13-9
    Dimethylaminoethanol 13-9
    Vitamin Supplementation 13-10
    Mineral Supplements 13-11
        Iron Supplementation. 13-11
        Zinc Supplementation 13-11
        Magnesium Supplementation 13-12
Herbal and Homeopathic Treatments 13-12
Acupuncture 13-13
EEG Biofeedback 13-13
EMG Biofeedback, Relaxation Training, and Hypnosis 13-14
Meditation 13-15
Mirror Feedback 13-15
Perceptual Stimulation/Training 13-15
    Massage 13-15
    Vestibular Stimulation 13-16
    Channel-Specific Perceptual Training 13-17
Antifungal Treatment 13-17

Thyroid Treatment 13-17
Deleading 13-18
Recommendations for Clinical Practice 13-18
    Weighing Alternatives 13-18
        Category 1: Unproven 13-18
        Category 2: Ineffective/Unsafe. 13-19
        Category 3: Indicated Only for Selected Etiologies 13-19
        Category 4: Proven Efficacy 13-19
        Category 5: Worth Trying Despite Limited Evidence
          of Efficacy 13-20
    Approach to Selecting Treatment 13-20
Recommendations for Future Research 13-20

INTRODUCTION

Attention deficit hyperactivity disorder (ADHD) has attracted many kinds of proposed treatments. The National Institute of Health (NIH) Consensus Development Conference on Diagnosis and Treatment of ADHD, held November 16–18, 1998, in Bethesda, Maryland, required a comprehensive review of possible treatments. Alternative treatments, or treatment alternatives, were defined for this purpose as any treatment other than prescription psychoactive drugs or standard behavioral/ psychosocial treatments, both of which have already been extensively and well reviewed in the extant literature, with undoubted efficacy. In contrast to those two more general, established treatments, many alternative treatments are etiologically targeted (Table 13.1, on pages 13-4 and 13-5) and consequently applicable to a smaller subpopulation of patients with ADHD. Therefore, scientific evaluation and clinical use of such treatments requires more etiological depth of diagnosis than the phenomenological criteria according to the fourth edition of *Diagnostic and Statistical Manual of Mental Disorders* (DSM-IV; American Psychiatric Association, 1994).

The treatments summarized here do not exhaust all the alternatives tried or advocated but are those for which either published reports or unpublished data could be found through two strategies: (1) search on numerous keywords in Medline and PsychInfo from the beginning through 2000 and (2) informal contacts with dozens of people—both professional and nonprofessional—-knowledgeable about or active in various alternative treatments.

ELIMINATION DIETS (FEW-FOODS DIETS/OLIGOANTIGENIC)

Recent Research Documents Efficacy

At the time of the 1982 Consensus Development Conference on Defined Diets and Hyperactivity (National Institutes of Health, 1982), most elimination diets (defined diets) were popularly known as Feingold diets. The Feingold (1975) hypothesis had stated that many children are sensitive to dietary salicylates and artificially added colors, flavors, and preservatives, and that learning and behavior problems, including ADHD, could be ameliorated by eliminating the offending substances from the diet. Despite a few positive studies (Swanson & Kinsbourne, 1980; Williams & Cram, 1978), most controlled studies were interpreted by the investigators and reviewers as nonsupportive of the hypothesis (Conners, 1980; Kavale & Forness, 1983; Mattes, 1983). These interpretations were challenged by Feingold (1981) and his advocates (Rimland, 1983; Rippere, 1983) on several grounds, including the following: (1) narrow restriction of tests to food dyes—Feingold (1981) actually anticipated within different children hypersensitivity to thousands of different substances, and had merely suggested food colorings as a good place to begin controlled studies because of their ubiquity and ease of control; he had not meant to equate his diet with elimination of dyes; (2) too low dosage levels of dyes used in challenges; (3) arbitrary ignoring of positive findings in certain subgroups; and (4) ignoring of animal studies. In such equivocal circumstances, the 1982 consensus panel called for more controlled research.

Since then, at least eight controlled studies (see Table 13.2 on page 13-6; Breakey, 1997) have demonstrated either significant improvement compared to a placebo condition (disguised full diet) (Kaplan, McNicol, Conte, & Moghadam, 1989a; Schmidt et al., 1997) or deterioration on a placebo-controlled challenge of offending substances after an open diet trial and open challenge to identify the substance (Boris & Mandel, 1994; Carter et al., 1993; Egger, Carter, Graham, Gumley, & Soothill, 1985; Egger, Stolla, & McEwen, 1992; Pollock & Warner, 1990; Rowe & Rowe, 1994). One report (Rowe, 1988) suggested that those who reliably respond to dye challenges constitute a small proportion and are more likely the hyperactive-impulsive subtype. On the other hand, Stevenson et al. (2001) recently reported unpublished data on an epidemiologically drawn nonclinical sample of 3-year-olds, 30 percent of whom showed significant improvements in behavior and attention with a more comprehensive diet.

The finding of scientifically acceptable documentation of efficacy since 1982 appears associated with broadening the range of suspected food items, selecting subjects more carefully (e.g., for allergic diathesis), and allowing for the timing peculiarities of food sensitivities. A typical oligoantigenic or few-foods diet might exclude everything except the following: lamb, chicken, potatoes, rice, banana, apple, brassica (cabbage, cauliflower, broccoli, brussel sprouts), cucumber, celery, carrots, parsnip, salt, pepper, calcium, and vitamins. A related treatment possibility arises from the documentation of successful desensitization to the offending food by enzyme-potentiated desensitization (Egger et al., 1992).

Probable Responders to Elimination Diets

The main scientific task remaining is to refine the diagnostic characteristics of diet responders and delineate what percentage of the ADHD population they constitute. Though half or more of enriched samples selected for suspicion of food sensitivity seem to respond well under controlled conditions, it is not clear what proportion this represents of the whole ADHD population. Preliminary evidence suggests that the profile of a probable responder is a middle- or upper-class preschooler with atopy and prominent irritability and sleep disturbance, with physical as well as behavioral symptoms, and possibly high copper levels (Brenner, 1979), but the definition needs more work.

Table 13.1
Scientific Status of Alternative Treatments for ADHD

Treatment	Etiology or Mechanism	Type of Data	ES or p	Rating* (0–6); Recommendation	Risks
Few-foods diet (oligoantigenic)	Food/additive sensitivity	Controlled trial; placebo challenges	ES 0.5–1.5 p .05–.001	5; define subgroup (profile; % ADHD)	Nuisance, expense, nutrition
Enzyme-potentiated desensitization	Food/additive sensitivity	Controlled comparison to placebo injections	p .001	4; replication Define subgroup	Injection
Elimination of sugar alone	Sugar malaise	Placebo-controlled challenges; PI diet	p > .1	0; take FH of DM	Delay std. Tx
Amino acid supplementation	Precursors of catecholamines	Placebo-controlled comparisons	ES up to 0.6, p .01	0; despite short-lived effect of little utility	Eosinophilia, Neurotoxicity
Essential fatty acid (EFA) supplement	Prostaglandins neur.membrane	Serum level of cntrl. plac-contr. trials	ES 0.5 1 > p > .05	3; trials of n = 3	Upsetting balance
L-carnitine	Promotes EFA anabolism	Placebo trial other disorder, no ADHD	ES > 2, p < 0.05	2; Placebo trial in ADHD	Upsetting balance
Glyconutritional supplementation	Need for glycoconjugates	Open trials, SNAP-IV ratings	p .05–.002; 1 neg. trial	1; Placebo trial	Upsetting balance, Expense
Dimethylamino-ethanol (DMAE)	Acetylcholine precursor	Many open & DB trials, most poor	ES 0.1–0.6; 0.1 > p > 0.05	3; rigorous placebo trial in ADHD	Modest effect, SE Expense
Vitamins	Deficiency vs. idiopathic need for higher dose	Placebo-controlled trials megavitamin combo, not RDA	Megadose combo no benefit	0 for mega-combo; 1 for RDA, specific megavit; Pilot trials	Hepatotoxicity, neuropathy in megadose
Iron supplementation	Co-factor make catecholamines	Open trial supplementation	ES 1.0 p < .05	3**; controlled trials	Hemochromatosis from excess
Zinc supplementation	Co-factor for many enzymes	Comparison zinc lvl. of ADHD to contrl.	ES 2.4 p < .001	2**; controlled trials	WBC aplasia from excess

* Ratings: 0 = not worth considering further (despite, in the case of amino acids, some evidence of short-lived effect); 1 = credible hypothesis or collateral support or wide clinical experience, needs pilot data; 2 = promising systematic data, but not prospective trial; 3 = promising prospective data (perhaps with random assignment to control or objective/blind measures) lacking some important control, or controlled trial(s) with trends suggesting further exploration; 4 = one significant double-blind controlled trial needing replication, or multiple positive controlled trials in a treatment not easily blinded; 5 = convincing double-blind controlled evidence but needs further refinement (e.g., define target subgroup) for clinical application; 6 = should be considered established Tx for the appropriate subgroup.

** The rating would be 6 for patients showing frank deficiency of vitamins, iron, zinc, or other nutrients.

ES = effect size, Cohen's d; p = probability; AD = attention deficit hyperactivity disorder; DB = double-blind; DM = diabetes mellitus; FH = family history; Grth = growth; MPH = ethylphenidate; N.A. = not applicable; n.s. = nonsignificant; PI = placebo; Psy = Psychological; SE = side effects; Ss = subjects; Sx = symptoms; Tx = treatments; WBC = white blood count; Xover = crossover.

Sugar Elimination Alone Unlikely to Work

A related dietary strategy, simple elimination of sugar or candy, has not garnered convincing scientific support from repeated placebo-controlled acute challenge stud-

Table 13.1
(Continued)

Treatment	Etiology or Mechanism	Type of Data	ES or p	Rating* (0–6); Recommendation	Risks
Magnesium supplementation	Deficiency cf. to controls	Open trial with control group	ES 1.2–1.4 $p < .05$	3**; placebo trials	Aggression from excess
Chinese herbals	Clinical exper.	Open trials, one with MPH control	$p < .05$; no diff. MPH	3; placebo trials	Interstitial renal fibrosis
Other herbals	Clinical exper.	No data	N.A.	1; pilot trials	Delay Tx
Homeopathic prep.	Clinical exper.	No data	N.A.	1; pilot trials	Delay Tx
Laser Acupuncture	Stimulate foci for calming	Open trial	ES 1.0	2; controlled trial	Delay other Tx, burn
EEG biofeedback	Suppress theta, increase beta	Open & randomized wait-list ctrl. trials	$p < 0.05$	3; Sham-controlled trial	Expense, time
EMG biofeedback, relaxtn., hypnosis	Lower arousal, muscle tone	Randomized trials with controls	ES 1.0–1.3 $p < 0.01$	0; for hypnosis; 4; for EMG/relaxation; cf. med	Delay other Tx
Meditation	Autonomic effect focused attn.	Cf. relaxation, wait-list ctrl., med	$p < .05$	3; Rigorous replication, sham ctrl.	Delay other Tx
Mirror feedback	Improve defic. self-focus	Randmzd Xover w/ & w/o, cf. controls	ES 0.5 $p < .05$	3; Replication, instr. look	May impair non-ADHD children
Massage	Vagal tone, 5HT, soothing	Single–blind comp. to relaxation	ES med–lg $p < 0.05$	3; Replication, better assessments	Negligible. possible bruise?
Vestibular stimulation	Modulate behav attn, perception	Open and single-blind trials	ES 0.4–1.2 p n.s.–0.001	3; Randomized sham-controlled trials	Nausea, accident
Channel-specific perceptual training	Basic readiness skills, focus	Randmzd prev. trial with 2 control grps.	ES 0.9 $p < 0.01$	3; Controlled Tx trials	Delay other Tx
Antifungal Tx	GI yeast toxin; breach mucosa	No data in ADHD; other placebo trial	ES 1.1–3; $p < 0.003$	1; Trials in ADHD	Med risk
Thyroid Tx	Thyroid Fx affects AD Sx	Placebo trial: 5/8 Grth, 1/9 other	n.s. if thyr. not abnrml.	0 if thyroid nrml.; 6 if thyroid abnrml.	Thyroid toxicity
Deleading	Lead toxicity causes AD Sx	Placebo-ctrl. trial of chelation (= MPH)	ES 0.7–1.6 p .05–.001	4 if blood Pb > 20; 2 if Pb < 20; ctrl trial	Toxicity of chelator

* Ratings: 0 = not worth considering further (despite, in the case of amino acids, some evidence of short-lived effect); 1 = credible hypothesis or collateral support or wide clinical experience, needs pilot data; 2 = promising systematic data, but not prospective trial; 3 = promising prospective data (perhaps with random assignment to control or objective/blind measures) lacking some important control, or controlled trial(s) with trends suggesting further exploration; 4 = one significant double-blind controlled trial needing replication, or multiple positive controlled trials in a treatment not easily blinded; 5 = convincing double-blind controlled evidence but needs further refinement (e.g., define target subgroup) for clinical application; 6 = should be considered established Tx for the appropriate subgroup.

** The rating would be 6 for patients showing frank deficiency of vitamins, iron, zinc, or other nutrients.

ES = effect size, Cohen's d; p = probability; AD = attention deficit hyperactivity disorder; DB = double-blind; DM = diabetes mellitus; FH = family history; Grth = growth; MPH = ethylphenidate; N.A. = not applicable; n.s. = nonsignificant; Pl = placebo; Psy = Psychological; SE = side effects; Ss = subjects; Sx = symptoms; Tx = treatments; WBC = white blood count; Xover = crossover.

ies (Krummel, Seligson, & Guthrie, 1996; Wolraich, Wilson, & White, 1995) despite a few encouraging reports (Goldman, Lerman, Contois, & Udall, 1986). Even a well-controlled three-week trial of a sugar-restricted diet found no effect (Wolraich et al.,

Table 13.2
Controlled Studies of Few-Foods (Oligoantigenic) Diets

Reference	Subjects	Design	Results	ES, *p*
Egger et al., 1985	Special diet clinic, HK, Conners > 14	76 Ss open trial few foods; 28 Ss placebo Xover challenge	62/76 improved in trial 23/28 better on placebo, worse on challenge.	*p* .001
Kaplan et al., 1989	ADs, DSM-III, Conners 1sd, physical Sx	24 preschoolers placebo diet Xover (3 + 4 wk.) with all food provided; multiple elimination	Over half had reliable behavior improvement, no placebo effect	ES 0.5 *p* .01
Pollock & Warner, 1990	Ped. allergy clinic, survey; selected by parent observ. behvr.	39 Ss placebo-controlled dye challenge while on elimination diet; only 19 completed	Food colors small adverse eff. on Conners rating, not globally detected by parent	ES small *p* < .01
Egger et al, 1992	Special diet clinic, HK criteria, Conners Index > 15	185 Ss 4-wk. open few foods; 40 Ss parallel random assignm to Plac or EPD	116/185 responded openly with reintroduction 16/20 with EPD, only 4 with PI became tolerant	*p* .001
Carter et al., 1993	Special diet clinic, HK criteria, Conners Index > 15	78 Ss open trial few foods; 23 placebo Xover challenge with provoking foods; 19 compl.	59/78 improved openly 14/19 placebo better behavior and Psy test	*p* .05–.01 ES 0.6
Rowe & Rowe, 1994	Hyperactivity referrals hospital ped. clinic	200 Ss 6-wk open dye-free diet 34 Ss (23 reactors, 11 uncertain) & 20 controls 3-wk. daily repeat Plac cf. to 6 doses tartrazine	150/200 improved, relapsed on open chall. 19/23, 3/11, and 2/20 clear reactors: irritable restless, sleep disturb.	ES 0.8 *p* .05
Boris & Mandel, 1994	DSM-III-R criteria for ADHD	26 Ss open multiple elimination 19 responders placebo-controlled DB challenge; 16 completed	19/26 openly responded Placebo days significant better than challenged.	*p* .001 *p* .003 ES 1.5
Schmidt et al., 1997	Hyperactive, disruptive inpatients	49 Ss in DB placebo Xover of oligoantigenic & control diet; 36 also compared to MPH	12/49 signif. behavioral improvement cf. control diet. 16/36 resp. MPH	

ADs = attention deficit disorder subjects; ES = effect size, Cohen's d; DB = double-blind; EPD = emzyme-potentiated desensitization; HK = hyperkinesis index; MPH = methylphenidate; PI, plac = placebo; Psy = Psych; Ss = subjects; Xover = crossover; 1sd = 1 standard deviation.

1994). Further, most cross-sectional comparisons have not shown excess consumption of sugar by children with ADHD compared to controls (Kaplan, McNicol, Conte, & Moghadam, 1989b; Kruesi, Rapoport, Berg, Stables, & Bou, 1987; Wolraich, Stumbo, Milch, Chenard, & Schultz, 1986), though some have found correlations between dietary sugar or refined carbohydrate intake and measures of hyperactivity, aggression, or inattention/cognition in children either with ADHD (Prinz, Roberts, & Hantman, 1980; Wolraich et al., 1986) or unselected for ADHD (Lester, Thatcher, & Monroe-Lord, 1982). It does not appear that sugar or candy restriction alone is a widely applicable treatment for ADHD, though it is conceivable that continued sugar/candy elimination partially contributes to the documented benefit of the few-foods diet for some children with ADHD.

Possible Risks

The side effects, risks, and ripple effects of dietary eliminations remain as controversial as the diets themselves. For example, Krummel et al. (1996) warn that coercively enforced parental restrictions on the child's diet (or putting the rest of the family unnecessarily on the same diet) could worsen family dynamics, whereas Lipton and Mayo (1983) say the nonspecific placebo effects are beneficial to families. There is some concern about breadth of nutrient intake on the one hand, and, on the other hand, the comment that eliminating junk foods improves essential nutrient intake (Rimland, 1983). On balance, it seems the main risk associated with dietary elimination is the delay of more effective treatment if the child is a nonresponder.

IMMUNE THERAPY

Food-borne allergy may not be the only immunological consideration for etiological subgroups of ADHD. In fifty children (mean age 9) with pediatric autoimmune neuropsychiatric disorders associated with streptococcal group A beta-hemolytic infection (PANDAS), Swedo et al. (1998) found a 40 percent rate of ADHD. It is not clear what proportion of an unselected ADHD sample would have PANDAS. However, Hagerman and Falkenstein (1987) reported twice the rate of otitis media in hyperactive children compared to controls, suggesting either immune problems or greater exposure to infectious agents. Perlmutter et al. (1999) tried two kinds of immune therapy in thirty children with PANDAS in a placebo-controlled parallel design, with ten children randomly assigned to each condition. Obsessive-compulsive symptoms improved impressively with either plasma exchange or intravenous immunoglobulin; tics also improved with plasma exchange. Unfortunately, Perlmutter et al. (1999) did not report the effect on ADHD symptoms. Immunological therapy targeting Candida (Palacios, 1976, 1977) might be a logical alternative to the antifungal therapy discussed later but apparently has not been proposed for ADHD. For food sensitivities, Egger et al. (1992) have reported significant ($p < 0.001$) benefit from enzyme-potentiated desensitization in a double-blind placebo-controlled trial.

NUTRITIONAL SUPPLEMENTS

In a sense, nutritional supplementation is the opposite of elimination or few-foods diets, which are based on the assumption that something in the diet is noxious and should be removed. Supplementation is based on the assumption that something is lacking in the diet in optimal amount and should be added. Both macronutrients (amino acids, lipids, carbohydrates) and micronutrients (vitamins and minerals) have been proposed as treatments for ADHD.

Amino Acid Supplementation

Amino acid supplementation is theoretically supported by report of low levels of amino acids in ADHD, including the precursors of catecholamines and serotonin (Baker, Bornstein, Rouget, Therrien, & van Muyden, 1991; Bornstein et al., 1990). Stein and Sammaritano (1984) reported that compared to matched normals with similar dietary intake, 8- to 10-year-old hyperkinetic boys excreted more nitrogen (ES = 5, $p < 0.01$) and showed different distribution patterns of excretion, flux, and protein synthesis. Several open and controlled studies have reported a short-term benefit from tryptophan, tyrosine, phenylalanine, or S-adenosyl-l-methionine supplementation (Nemzer, Arnold, Votolato, & McConnell, 1986; Reimherr, Wender, Wood, & Ward, 1987; Shekim, Antun, Hanna, & McCracken, 1990; Wood, Reimherr, & Wender, 1985a). However, no lasting benefit beyond two to three months has been demonstrated; tolerance usually develops (Wood, Reimherr, & Wender, 1985b). Even short-term benefit was not found in some studies (Eisenberg, Asnis, van Praag, & Vela, 1988; Ghose, 1983; Zametkin, Karoum, & Rapoport, 1987).

Further, such supplementation, although originally considered benign, may carry some risk (Pakes, 1978; Sidransky, 1997; Sternberg, 1996). The best-publicized risk was the 1989 epidemic of eosinophilia-myalgia linked to tryptophan use. However, this association was more likely due to impurities rather than to the tryptophan itself (Sidransky, 1997; Williamson, Tomlinson, Mishra, Gleich, & Naylor, 1998), and it may have partly resulted from circular diagnostic practice (Blackburn, 1997; Wagner, Elmore, & Horwitz, 1996). In sum, amino acid supplementation does not appear a promising area to explore further, though protein-rich diets might be explored as a specific correction of the reported nitrogen-wasting metabolic aberrations.

Essential Fatty Acid Supplementation

Neuronal membranes are composed of phospholipids containing large amounts of polyunsaturated fatty acids, especially the n-3 and n-6 (or omega-3 and omega-6) acids (with the first unsaturated bond 3 or 6 carbons, respectively, from the noncarboxyl "tail" of the molecule), which humans cannot manufacture de novo and hence are "essential" in the diet. Essential fatty acids (EFAs) are also metabolized to prostaglandins and other eicosanoids, which modify many metabolic processes. Lab animal behavior can be manipulated by varying the quantity and quality of essential fatty acids (Arnold, Kleykamp, Votolato, Gibson, & Horrocks, 1994). Juvenile and young adult monkeys with long-term n-3 fatty acid deficiency show increased activity, and both human and monkey infants show changes in visual attention with n-3 deficiency (Neuringer, 1998). In adult humans, n-6 EFAs correlated positively and n-3 EFAs correlated negatively with cerebral-spinal-fluid 5-HIAA and HVA, the metabolites, respectively, of serotonin and dopamine (Hibbeln et al., 1998). Both the n-3 series (progenitor alpha-linolenic acid) and the n-6 series (progenitor linoleic acid) have been reported to be significantly lower in children with ADHD than in comparison controls (Mitchell, Aman, Turbott, & Manku, 1987; Mitchell, Lewis, & Cutler, 1983; Stevens et al., 1995). Even total serum-free fatty acids were lower in ADHD, with ES = 2.4, $p < .001$ (Bekaroglu et al., 1996). Aggression has been significantly inhibited in young adults by docosohexaenoic acid of the n-3 series (Hamazaki et al., 1996).

Two double-blind placebo-controlled trials of gamma-linolenic acid (n-6 series, evening primrose oil) supplementation yielded equivocal results from ADHD subjects not selected for low n-6 acids (Aman, Mitchell, & Turbott, 1987; Arnold et al., 1989); in one trial, the serum triglyceride gamma-linolenic acid correlated inversely with Conners Rating Scale scores (Arnold et al., 1994). A controlled pilot trial of n-3 supplementation in ADHD subjects selected for symptoms of EFA deficiency (but not for specific n-3 deficiency in plasma) showed a trend of advantage for the supplement despite a huge placebo effect (pre-post ES 1.8 vs. 1.4), and changes in serum phospholipid n-3 acids correlated negatively with changes in Conners Rating Scale scores (J. R. Burgess & L. Stevens, personal communication, 1998). In preliminary data on 70 subjects not selected for deficiency, Voigt et al. (2001) found no effect of docosohexaenoic acid (n-3) compared to placebo.

In sum, the data suggest the need for further controlled trials in patients selected for low serum levels of the specific EFA supplemented.

Possible L-Carnitine Effect

A possible explanation for the failure of EFA trials to show dramatic effects despite demonstrated low levels of EFAs in ADHD may lie in the interaction of EFA with l-carnitine. Carnitine is essential for fatty acid metabolism, transporting lipids across the microsomal inner membrane as acylcarnitine (Arduini et al., 1994) and supporting elongation of EFAs (Ricciolini et al., 1998). Humans synthesize only one-fourth of their needed supply of carnitine, making it a partially essential nutrient. In dialysis and parenteral nutrition, which typically cause low levels of EFA, supplementation with l-carnitine improved the EFA level (Ahmad, Dasgupta, & Kenny, 1989). Acetyl-l-carnitine is suspected of cholinergic activity similar to acetylcholine. A trial in fragile X showed significant improvement in hyperactive behavior on the parent, but not teacher, Conners ten-item scale compared to placebo controls; the effect was clinically modest despite an ES > 4.0 (Torrioli et al., 1999). Trials in ADHD are indicated.

Glyconutritional Supplements

Glyconutritional supplement contains basic saccharides necessary for cell communication and formation of glycoproteins and glycolipids: glucose, galactose, mannose, N-acetylneuraminic acid, fucose, N-acetylgalactosamine, and xylose. Only the first two are abundant in the ordinary diet. In an open trial of glyconutritional and phytonutritional (flash freeze-dried fruits and vegetables) supplementation with seventeen ADHD subjects, Dykman and Dykman (1998) found significant ($p < .05 - p < .001$) reductions in parent SNAP-IV ratings of inattention, hyperactivity/impulsivity, and oppositional symptoms, with similar trends on teacher ratings (the SNAP-IV, an acronym for the instrument's developers, Swanson, Nolan, and Pelham, is a behavior checklist based on DSM-IV symptoms of ADHD; Swanson, 1992). In a second open trial of the same supplements in eighteen children, Dykman and McKinley (1997) found reductions in parent inattention ratings from 2.47 to 2.05 ($p < .06$) and hyperactivity/impulsivity ratings from 2.23 to 1.54 ($p < .003$), sustained for six weeks. However, a third open trial reportedly failed to duplicate such results.

Dimethylaminoethanol

Dimethylaminoethanol (DMAE) has several accepted names in the literature, including deanol and dimethylethanolamine, and sometimes is preceded by an unnecessary "2-". It is the immediate precursor of choline (trimethylaminoethanol) and is claimed to increase production of acetylcholine. Interestingly, it is part of the same metabolic cycle as dimethylglycine (DMG), a popular unproven nutrient treatment for autism; DMG comes three steps after choline and considerably before DMAE in the cycle.

DMAE was originally marketed as a drug (Deaner®) for hyperactivity/minimal brain dysfunction, but was withdrawn as less than effective in the 1980s, after the Food and Drug Administration began requiring efficacy evidence as well as safety evidence. It is now marketed as a nutrient for attention deficit disorder (ADD) and learning problems. It has more placebo-controlled studies (and open trials) than most nutrient treatments (e.g., Coleman, Dexheimer, DiMascio, Redman, & Finnerty, 1976; Geller, 1960; Kugel & Alexander, 1963; Lewis & Young, 1975; Millichap, 1973; Saccer, 1978). Unfortunately, most studies were flawed by the dated (1960–1975) clinical trials methodology, questionable sample selection (e.g., mental retardation and endocrine dyscrasia), poor choice of assessment instruments, inconsistent dosing, possible leaks in the blinding, unclear analytic method (sometimes lacking statistical test), insufficient detail to judge validity, and/or equivocal results. Some studies showed no effect, or even placebo superiority. However, a few showed encouraging enough results to be considered promising pilot data. Probably the best study was Lewis and Young's (1975) three-group parallel study, which showed placebo-controlled ESs of 0.1 to 0.6 on--1.3 in the same study. A global estimate of ES considering all the positive studies (disregarding the negative) would be 0.2 to 0.5 if the dose is 500 mg a day or more.

Although it appears that this ex-drug will likely not yield anywhere near the effect seen with prescription medication, it could be worth a well-designed trial with sensitive instruments to document a mild to moderate effect for patients with mild problems or those who do not wish prescription medication.

Vitamin Supplementation

Three strategies for vitamin supplementation are (1) recommended daily allowances (RDA) multivitamin preparations, (2) megavitamin multiple combinations, and (3) megadoses of specific vitamins.

The first strategy is noncontroversial, but there is no research on effects in diagnosed ADHD even though some reports suggest mild deficiencies in diet and blood levels that might be addressed. However, in a randomly assigned double-blind placebo-controlled trial of RDA vitamin and mineral supplementation in forty-seven 6-year-old children not selected for ADHD, Benton and Cook (1991) found an 8.3-point IQ advantage ($p < .001$), represented mainly in nonverbal ability. They also found increased concentration and decreased fidgeting on a frustrating task ($p < .05$), and advantage on a reaction time task reflecting sustained attention (ES = 1.3, $p < .05$). These data warrant a controlled trial in ADHD, although the benefit may be confined to a subgroup with poor diets (Benton & Buts, 1990).

The second strategy, megavitamin multiple combinations, has not been found effective in double-blind placebo-controlled short (two-week) and longer (up to six-month) trials examining ADHD and the related comorbidity of learning disorder (Arnold, Christopher, Huestis, & Smeltzer, 1978; Haslam, Dalby, & Rademaker, 1984; Kershner & Hawke, 1979). The researchers who conducted those trials have been challenged on the basis of not using the correct mix of vitamins and minerals.

Also, Kershner and Hawke's (1979) study used a preliminary elimination diet that removed so much deviance that the vitamin trial suffered from a ceiling effect. On balance, megavitamin multiple combinations do not seem worth pursuing.

The third strategy, judicious use of single vitamins in megadosage to alter neural metabolism in specific ways, is actually more like psychopharmacology and has not been adequately explored despite some encouraging early reports (Brenner, 1982; Coleman et al., 1979).

Though megavitamins, like any pharmacological intervention, pose some risk, the hepatotoxic (Haslam et al., 1984; Shaywitz, Siegel, & Pearson, 1977), neuropathic (Bernstein, 1990; Schaumburg et al., 1983; Snodgrass, 1992), and other (Anonymous, 1984; Sato, Taguchi, Maeda, & Yoshikawa, 1993; Snodgrass, 1992) dangers may be overstated in some quarters: the hepatotoxicity reported by Shaywitz et al. (1977) resulted from accidental overdosage of vitamin A, not from megavitamin therapy, and the doses of pyridoxine (B6) reported to cause neuropathy (generally 2 grams or more a day) are higher than the doses usually recommended in most megavitamin regimens; and pyridoxine toxicity seems largely reversible on cessation of supplementation. In intermediate doses (e.g., 100–150 mg/day), pyridoxine is more likely to counteract toxicity of other ingestants, including drugs, food colors, and excess other nutrients than to be toxic itself (Bernstein, 1990; Brown, Mallett, Fiser, & Arnold, 1984; Durlach, Durlach, Bac, Bara, & Guiet-Bara, 1994; Houben & Penninks, 1994). Except for rare genetic disorders, RDA multivitamins do not appear to pose any risk other than sensitivity to added coloring or flavors.

Mineral Supplements

The main mineral candidates for supplementation are iron, zinc, magnesium, and calcium, all of which have been reported deficient in subjects with ADHD compared to matched controls (Kozielec, Starobrat-Hermelin, & Kotokowiak, 1994).

Iron Supplementation. Iron is a co-enzyme in anabolism of catecholamines. In an open thirty–day supplementation trial with seventeen nonanemic ADHD boys age 7–11, Sever, Ashkenazi, Tyano, and Weizman (1997) found improvement in Conners Rating Scale parents' scores from 17.6 to 12.7 (ES = 1.0), but not in teacher ratings. In a double-blind placebo-controlled trial in seventy-three teenage nonanemic but iron-deficient girls, Bruner, Joffe, Duggan, Casella, & Brandt (1996) found improvements in verbal learning and memory. In a trial of gastroprotected ferritin in thirty-three iron-deficient children, Burattini et al. (1990) found a decrease of hyperactivity.

Iron supplementation merits further study, with focus on whether any benefit found is confined to those with laboratory evidence of iron deficiency, and with due concern for possible toxicity of excess iron.

Zinc Supplementation. Zinc is a cofactor for 100 enzymes, many involved in neural metabolism, and is necessary for fatty acid absorption and for production of melatonin, which helps regulate dopamine function (Sandyk, 1990). Animal data suggest involvement of zinc deficiency in hyperactivity (Halas & Sandstead, 1975; Sandstead et al., 1977), and human deficiency syndrome includes concentration impairment and jitters (Aggett & Harries, 1979). Zinc has been reported deficient in ADHD compared to controls, with ES up to 2.4 ($p < .001$) (Bekaroglu et al., 1996; Toren et al., 1996). However, McGee, Williams, Anderson, McKenzie-Parnell, and Silva (1990) did not find a significant correlation of parent and teacher hyperactivity ratings with hair or serum zinc in the epidemiological Dunedin sample. Arnold, Volotano, Kleykamp, Baker, and Bornstein (1990) reported data suggesting that stimulant response may depend on adequate zinc nutrition. Sandyk (1990) speculated that stimulants might work via their reported propensity for increasing melatonin production, a process dependent on zinc.

Despite clinical advocacy of zinc supplementation, no systematic prospective trials could be found. The obvious need is a placebo-controlled double-blind trial of RDA zinc supplementation with pretreatment assessment of zinc status to determine whether zinc deficiency is a prerequisite for any benefit found. Though excess zinc can cause white cell aplasia (Forsyth & Davies, 1995), it does not appear to be a risk for RDA doses.

Magnesium Supplementation. Magnesium deficiency can cause a wide spectrum of neurological and psychiatric disturbance and can result from a wide variety of causes, including increased requirement during childhood (Flink, 1981). Kozielec and Starobrat-Hermelin (1997) examined hair, red cell, and serum magnesium of 116 children ages 9–12 with ADHD and found 95 percent (34 percent by serum alone) deficient in magnesium; there was no control group other than lab norms. They assigned fifty children age 7–12 with ADHD according to DSM-IV and magnesium deficiency to six months of open supplementation with about 200 mg/day (in addition to usual treatment), and thirty similar controls were assigned to usual treatment without magnesium. It was not clear whether assignment was random; the supplemented group significantly decreased their Conners' Rating Scales parent and teacher ratings (ES = 1.2-1.4) compared to the control group (Starobrat-Hermelin & Kozielec, 1997). Thus, magnesium supplementation merits a randomized placebo-controlled double-blind trial and replication by other investigators. Dosage of supplementation may be important, because animal work suggests a U-shaped behavioral dose-response curve (Izenwasser, Garcia-Valdez, & Kantak, 1986). Therefore, it is possible that children not deficient in magnesium could be made worse by supplementation. Further, doses > 10 mg/kg/day can cause toxic symptoms (Durlach et al., 1994).

HERBAL AND HOMEOPATHIC TREATMENTS

Many herbal and homeopathic remedies have been proposed for use in ADHD. No systematic data regarding ADHD efficacy could be found for hypericum, Gingko biloba, Calmplex, Defendol, or pycnogenol. Although a case report of successful pycnogenol treatment was found (Heimann, 1999), a representative of one of the companies selling pycnogenol said that the company had dropped ADHD as an indication because pycnogenol does not appear to work on ADHD. The first few remedies listed may be worth pilot trials based on clinical experience. For example, hypericum is reportedly used for ADHD in Europe without controlled trials.

There are more data for traditional Chinese herbals. In a randomly assigned open trial, Zhang and Huang (1990) compared a Chinese herbal cocktail (80 subjexts) to methylphenidate 5–15 mg twice a day (20 Ss) for one to three months; 23/80 herbal cocktail cases were "cured" (disappearance of all clinical symptoms and no recurrence for six months) compared to 6/20 taking methylphenidate. Including improved cases, the effectiveness rates were 86 percent versus 90 percent; the groups did not differ except for lower side effects and greater IQ rises in the herbal group. In an open trial of Tiaoshen Liquor with 100 hyperkinetic children, Wang, Li, and Li (1995) found an effectiveness rate of 94 percent, including reduction of hyperactivity, improved attention, and improved academics. In another open trial with sixty-six hyperkinetic children, Sun et al. (1994) found an effectiveness rate of 85 percent with Yizhi wit-increasing syrup, including significant improvement in behavior, school records, and soft neurological signs. Shen and Wang (1984) reported that eight children with minimal brain dysfunction showed the same decrease in urinary 3-methoxy-4-hydroxyphenylglycol from Chinese herbal treatment as did thirty-eight similar children from methylphenidate. Thus, the open pilot data warrant placebo-cotrolled double-blind trials of Chinese herbals, keeping in mind the risk of interstitial renal fibrosis reported for some Chinese herbals (Chang, Wang, Yang, & Chiang, 2001).

ACUPUNCTURE

Despite the popularity of acupuncture, no published systematic data on its efficacy with ADHD could be found. M. Loo (personal communication, 1998), in unpublished, preliminary, pre-post, single-blind data from students in grades K–3, found improvements in Conners' Rating Scale ten-item scores by teachers ($n = 7$) from 17.0 to 12.0, and in analogous parent scores ($n = 6$) from 23.1 to 15.5. She noted that children with the most severe ADHD could not cooperate with the treatment.

EEG BIOFEEDBACK

Electroencephalographic (EEG) biofeedback induces beta-band EEG rhythms, either sensorimotor (12–15 Hertz) or higher (15–18 Hertz) and suppresses theta rhythms, by visual and auditory feedback. Research into EEG biofeedback for ADHD arose from (1) the observation that some ADHD children have more theta and less beta rhythm than controls and (2) animal work that demonstrated reduced motor activity associated with sensorimotor rhythm (Mann, Lubar, Zimmerman, Miller, & Muenchen, 1992; Shouse & Lubar, 1978). There are several promising pilot trials. Lubar (1991) and Lubar and Shouse (1977) reported that in a single-subject ABA design (on-off-on crossover), four hyperactive children selected for low arousal showed better behavior and work habits without stimulant at the end of all treatment (ABA) than at the beginning with or without stimulant and their unmedicated level of undesirable behaviors dropped by over half to the level of the normal controls; three of them showed synchrony of behavior changes with the ABA cossovers. An uncontrolled open trial with thirty-seven hyperactive children yielded significant grade-point and achievement score improvements (Lubar, 1991). In an intensive summer treatment regimen, twelve children who showed EEG changes also improved on significantly more TOVA (Tests of Variables of Attention) than did seven who failed to show EEG changes (Lubar, Swartwood, Swartwood, & O'Donnell, 1995). Linden, Habib, and Radojevic (1996) randomly assigned eighteen children with ADD/ADHD according to the revised third edition of *Diagnostic and Statistical Manual of Mental Disorders* (DSM-III-R; American Psychiatric Association, 1987) to either a waiting list ($n = 9$) or to forty EEG biofeedback sessions over a forty-week period. The treated group showed a 9-point IQ rise compared to the waiting list rise of < 1 point ($p < 0.05$) and a 28 percent reduction on the inattention score of the SNAP scale with DSM ADHD symptoms on Conners metric) compared to a 4 percent increase for the waiting list group ($p < .05$). Thus, this treatment merits a sham-controlled randomized trial (Arnold, 1995).

EMG BIOFEEDBACK, RELAXATION TRAINING, AND HYPNOSIS

These three related treatment modalities are typically used in some combination. The few published data on hypnotherapy alone for treatment of ADHD are discouraging: Calhoun and Bolton (1986) were unsuccessful in three attempts each to hypnotize ten of the eleven hyperactive children with whom they tried it. Breathing control alone, used not only in hypnosis but also in meditation and relaxation, showed no difference from sham training in six hyperactive intelligent 6–8-year-olds (Simpson & Nelson, 1974). However, the hypnotic techniques of imagery and progressive relaxation have often been incorporated into successful electromyography (EMG) biofeedback protocols.

There are more literature citations for EMG than for EEG biofeedback (Lee, 1991), but they are generally older, suggesting a recent waning of interest. Denkowski, Denkowski, and Omizo (1983) randomly assigned hyperactive junior high school boys to six twenty-five–minute EMG-assisted relaxation training sessions ($n = 24$) or to a control condition ($n = 24$); the treated group attained significantly higher reading and language performance and made a significant internal shift in locus of control. In ten hyperactive boys ages 6–12, Dunn and Howell (1982) found significant improvement in behavior observations, parent ratings, and psychological tests after ten relaxation training sessions but none after ten neutral sessions. Omizo and Michael (1982) randomly assigned hyperactive boys ages 10–12 to either four sessions of EMG biofeedback-induced relaxation ($n = 16$) or sham treatment ($n = 16$) of equal length; compared to the sham, the relaxation induced significant improvements in attention and impulsivity as indicated from results on the Matching Familiar Figures test (ES = 1.0 to 1.3, $p < .01$). In twenty-seven children ages 7–11 with attention deficit disorder-hyperactivity (ADD-H) according to DSM-III (American Psychiatric Association, 1980), Krieger (1985) found significant improvement on Conners' parent and teacher rating scales compared to an equal-n matched wait-list control group. Success is largely moderated by baseline locus of control (Denkowski, Denkowski, & Omizo, 1984). However, the reports were not uniformly positive; Irving (1987) found in twenty-four boys ages 6–12 that EMG biofeedback/relaxation added nothing to stimulant benefit, but stimulant added to biofeedback benefit. Denkowski and Denkowski (1984) assigned forty-five hyperactive elementary school children to eight sessions of group progressive relaxation training, relaxation training with frontalis biofeedback, or placebo (listening to taped children's stories); the trend of advantage for the two active treatments was not significant at the group size of 15. Cobb and Evans (1981) reviewed the then extant literature and concluded that there was no evidence that biofeedback was superior to "more conventional treatments" for learning or behavior disorders. Nevertheless, the data on balance suggest that despite recent neglect, EMG biofeedback-facilitated relaxation training merits further study for children with ADHD who do not benefit from stimulants or whose parents object to stimulants.

MEDITATION

Meditation, though resulting in relaxation, is different from the preceding treatments in not directly targeting relaxation but achieving it indirectly. Kratter (1983) randomly assigned twenty-four children ages 7–12 with DSM-III ADD-H to either meditation training, progressive relaxation, or wait-list control, with four weeks of twice-weekly sessions; both active treatments but not wait list reduced impulsivity and improved scores on parent behavior scales but not teacher scales; only meditation training showed significant improvement on a test assessing selective attention. Moretti-Altuna (1987) randomly assigned twenty-three boys ages 6–12 with ADD-H to meditation training, medication, or standard therapy; meditation showed significant advantage in classroom behavior but not in parent ratings or psychological tests. Thus, meditation warrants further study.

MIRROR FEEDBACK

Mirrors have been proposed as a way of increasing self-control and attentional focus by increasing self-focus in children with ADHD (Zentall, Hall, & Lee, 1998). In a single-blind randomized trial on sixteen hyperactive-inattentive (HI) and twenty-seven normal middle-school students, a word puzzle that differentiated the HI from the control subjects with an effect size of 0.75 ($p < .05$) in the no-mirror condition showed a between-groups ES of only 0.2 (n.s.) with a mirror in front of the child as he or she worked. The mirror condition improved the performance of the HIs by half the no-mirror difference between groups. With no instruction about the mirror, the HIs who actually looked in the mirror scored equal to the no-mirror scores of the controls. This intervention carries a risk associated with diagnostic validity: The normal controls showed a trend of performance decrement with the mirror, especially if they looked in it (Zentall et al., 1998). Though probably not applicable to a regular classroom, mirror feedback may be useful in learning carrels specifically used by ADHD students and for homework and deserves further trials.

PERCEPTUAL STIMULATION/TRAINING

Perceptual and sensory stimulation and training include a wide variety of modalities, some with few or no data. The literature search found no systematic data on sensorimotor integration or optometric training for ADHD despite their widespread use. The "Interactive Metronome" (1998) provides perceptual-motor concentration training with biofeedback about accuracy from motion sensors as the child taps to the beat provided by the program; open trials show improvements in timing that correlate at 0.2–0.4 with teacher ratings of attention, but there are no controlled data ("Interactive metronome," 1998).

Massage

The tactile and deep pressure stimulation of massage has been reported to have a number of effects. In an uncontrolled study, Imamura, Weiss, and Parham (1990) reported that Grandin's (1992) "squeeze machine" reduced hyperactivity in four of nine autistic children ages 3–7. Similar calming was obtained by one child with a tight blanket roll. In better-controlled studies, massage reduced the anxiety and activity levels of inpatient adolescents (Field et al., 1992) and increased the attentiveness/ responsivity of autistic children (Field et al., 1997). It also increased serotonin levels (Field et al., 1997; Ironson et al., 1996), enhanced cytotoxic immune function (Ironson et al., 1996), and increased vagal activity, reported to be associated with increased attention span (Field et al., 1997). In adults, it improved math performance (Field et al., 1996), which is sometimes used as an objective outcome measure in pharmacological treatment of ADHD.

In a massage trial directly targeting ADHD, Field, Quintino, Hernandez-Reif, and Koslovsky (1998) randomly assigned twenty-eight adolescent boys with DSM-III-R ADHD to ten fifteen-minute sessions of either massage or relaxation therapy (on consecutive school days). Massage consisted of thirty ten-second moderate-pressure back-and-forth strokes in each of three body regions: neck, from neck to shoulders and back, and thoracolumbar vertebral column. The control relaxation training condition targeted the same three body regions. At the end, teachers rated the massaged group as showing less hyperactivity and spending more time on task than the relaxation group (77 percent vs. 51 percent, compared to 43 percent and 40 percent at baseline). On the Conners ten-item scale, the massaged boys improved from 28 at baseline to 11.3 while the controls deteriorated from 19.6 to 28.5. The massaged adolescents also rated themselves happier after than before the sessions (Field et al., 1998). This treatment deserves replication studies, but the effect size could not be evaluated because standard deviations (and p values) were not supplied.

Vestibular Stimulation

Mulligan (1996) reported significant impairment of vestibular processing in 309 children with ADHD compared to 309 matched children without ADHD ($p < 0.01$). Both the semicircular canals and the otolithic utricles/saccules of the vestibular system activate the autonomic nervous system (Yates, 1992). Previc (1993) suggests that the utricles/otoliths produce noradrenergic sympathetic brain stimulation while the semicircular canals produce cholinergic parasympathetic brain stimulation. In a single-blind crossover in eighteen children with DSM-II hyperkinetic reaction, Bhatara, Clark, Arnold, and Gonsett (1981) found improvement in Conners teacher ratings from rotational vestibular stimulation of the semicircular canals compared to a sham condition ($p < .05$), mainly confined to the fourteen children below age 10 and those without comorbid conduct disorder. In another single-blind crossover with twelve children identified through teacher scale screening, Arnold, Clark, Sachs, Jakim, and Smithies (1985) found an ES of 0.5 between vestibular rotational stimulation alone and two control conditions (missing significance at the sample size), compared to an ES of 0.2 between visual rotational stimulation alone and the same control conditions in a similar group of eighteen children. The Comprehensive Motion Apparatus provides vestibular stimulation in all vectors through complex motion, stimulating both semicircular canals and otoliths; an open trial in fourteen dyslexic children (mean age 12 + 2.6 yrs.) showed pre-post improvement in parent rating of attention (ES = 1.5, $p < .003$) and objective cognitive/achievement tests (ES 0.4–1.2, p 0.05-0.001) (M. Stillman, personal communication, 1998).

Channel-Specific Perceptual Training

In a single-blind prevention paradigm, Arnold et al. (1977) randomly assigned matched trios and quads of first-graders selected for vulnerability on a perceptual screening battery to either six months of channel-specific perceptual training ($n = 23$), the same length of regular academic tutoring ($n = 23$), or no-contact control ($n = 40$); at one-year follow-up, the trained group surpassed both control groups in blinded teacher Conners ratings (ES = 1.0, $p < .01$), Wide Range Achievement Test reading achievement (12.6 standard points difference, $p < 0.01$), and Wechsler IQ (8 points difference, $p < 0.05$), though baseline measures were not different.

ANTIFUNGAL TREATMENT

Treatment with antifungal agents such as nystatin (in combination with sugar restriction and other measures) is advocated by Crook (1985, 1989, 1991) and others on the hypothesis that repeated antibiotic use for otitis media changes intestinal flora, allowing yeast overgrowth, which compromises immune function and changes the gut mucosal barrier to allow absorption of food antigens. Several components of this hypothesis are supported by collateral documentation from other fields (Hagerman & Falkenstein, 1987; Nsouli et al., 1994; Vargas, Patrick, Ayers, & Hughes, 1993), and the hypothesis would make sense of the reported association of chronic sugar intake with ADHD symptoms (Prinz et al., 1980) without acute effects, in that sugar could promote yeast overgrowth chronically without showing acute effects on behavior. However, this hypothesis is not supported by any systematic prospective trial data in ADHD. A trial of nystatin alone for fatigue, premenstrual tension, gastrointestinal symptoms, and depression associated with candida vaginitis was reported negative (Dismukes, Wade, Lee, Dockery, & Hain, 1990), but Crandall (1991) challenged this conclusion on methodological grounds (loss of power by inclusion of subjects receiving only local treatment), and Truss (1991), reanalyzing the published crossover data, found an advantage for double nystatin (oral and vaginal) over double placebo significant at $p < 0.01$ (two-tailed). A systematic randomly assigned trial in ADHD should be carried out, preferably double-blind placebo-controlled and accompanied by the sugar restriction and other supportive measures recommended by the advocates of this treatment.

THYROID TREATMENT

Despite initial enthusiasm about resistance to thyroid hormone being a key to a large proportion of ADHD, this genetic syndrome appears extremely rare in ADHD samples. The same studies, however, reveal a rate of other thyroid dysfunction ranging from 2 percent to 5 percent (Valentine et al., 1997; Weiss, Stein, Trommer, & Refetoff, 1993), and the rate may be higher in those with comorbid mood disorder (West et al., 1996). In children with thyroid dysfunction, the thyroid status seems related to attentional and hyperactive-impulsive symptoms (Hauser, Soler, Brucker-Davis, & Weintraub, 1997; Rovet & Alvarez, 1996). In a double-blind placebo crossover trial of thyroid supplementation, only one of nine children with ADHD and normal thyroid function improved compared to five of eight with ADHD and resistance to thyroid hormone (Weiss, Stein, & Refetoff, 1997). Thus, thyroid treatment does not seem promising in ADHD children with normal thyroid function but would seem the treatment of choice for those with thyroid dysfunction. Therefore, all children with ADHD should be screened for historical and physical exam signs of possible thyroid dysfunction (Weiss & Stein, 1999).

DELEADING

Animal data (Silbergeld & Goldberg, 1975) document hyperactivity as one symptom of chronic lead poisoning, and suggest that lead-induced hyperactivity depends on lead levels and can be reversed by chelation (Gong & Evans, 1997). In humans (David, Hoffman, Sverd, & Clark, 1977), the blood level considered toxic for subtle neuropsychiatric symptoms has declined with increasing knowledge: in 1991 the Centers for Disease Control adopted 10 mcg/dL for developing children, and some authors place it as low as single digits (Kahn, Kelly, & Walker, 1995). Whether or not tissue lead levels correlate with behavioral and cognitive measures is the subject of some controversy, partly depending on the sample size, consequent power, and range of lead burden in the population studied (Gittleman & Eskanazi, 1983; Needleman et al., 1979).

David, Hoffman, Sverd, Clark, and Voeller (1976) openly treated thirteen children who had hyperkinetic reaction and blood lead levels > 25mcg/dL with penicillamine (CaEDTA if allergic to penicillin); the seven with no other probable medical cause of their hyperkinesis improved in teacher hyperactivity rating (ES = 1.4, $p < 0.01$) and parent hyperactive-impulsive rating (ES = 2.2, $p < 0.05$) but not significantly in teacher inattention rating (ES = 0.6), while the six with another probable medical cause did not improve. In a double-blind placebo-controlled twelve-week trial, David, Hoffman, Clark, Grad, and Sverd (1983) randomly assigned hyperactive children with "minimally elevated lead levels" (mean 28 + 6 mcg/dL) to either penicillamine plus methylphenidate placebo ($n = 22$), methylphenidate (5–40 mg/day) plus penicillamine placebo ($n = 11$), or double placebo ($n = 11$): compared to placebo, penicillamine improved Conners' teacher hyperactivity scores (ES = 1.6, $p < 0.001$), parent Werry-Weiss-Peters hyperactivity scores (ES = 0.7, $p < 0.05$), and Clinical Global Impression (ES = 1.4, $p < 0.01$); across measures the penicillamine group did nonsignificantly better than the methylphenidate group.

Thus, it appears that deleading would be the treatment of choice for children with ADHD who have blood lead elevations in the range treated by David and associates. How low a blood lead level this treatment should extend to is a research question of high priority.

RECOMMENDATIONS FOR CLINICAL PRACTICE

Weighing Alternatives

There seem to be five categories of alternatives in treating ADHD (alternatives being defined as treatments other than psychoactive medication and psychosocial/behavioral treatments).

Category 1: Unproven. Many of the treatment alternatives for ADHD are in various stages of scientific exploration, ranging from hypothesis through pilot data, and therefore do not enjoy the database necessary for making definite clinical practice recommendations. These treatments are neither proven nor found lacking in definitive controlled trials. Included in this category are essential fatty acid supplementation, l-carnitine, glyconutritional supplementation, dimethylaminoethanol, RDA vitamins, single-vitamin megadosage, herbals, homeopathic remedies, Laser acupuncture, EEG biofeedback, mirror feedback, channel-specific perceptual training, vestibular stimulation, antifungal therapy, and some types of immune therapy.

Category 2: Ineffective/Unsafe. A few of the alternatives proposed have been demonstrated to be probably ineffective or possibly dangerous. Prominent among these are the various forms of megadose multivitamins (as opposed to RDA multivitamins) which have not only failed to show benefit in controlled studies but also carry a mild risk of hepatotoxicity and peripheral neuropathy. Thus, megavitamin multiple combinations have enough evidence to warn physicians and the public away from their indiscriminate use. Megadosage of one or two specific vitamins may be more effective but has not been adequately explored for ADHD. Amino acid supplementation (except for remedy of specific deficits), though possibly effective in the short term, does not seem to be a practical long-term treatment; there may also be some risk. Simple sugar restriction has not been found effective in most controlled studies but does not appear to pose any risk.

Category 3: Indicated Only for Selected Etiologies. Some of the alternatives are ineffective or dangerous for the majority of children with ADHD but clearly indicated by clinical common sense for those with the etiology targeted. For example, chelation ("deleading") would be the preferred treatment for patients with demonstrated blood elevations of lead (or other heavy metals) but would be irrelevant (at our current state of knowledge) and pose some risk for a child with blood lead below 10 mcg/dL. For the 2–5 percent of children with ADHD who have thyroid abnormality, correction of the thyroid problem should logically be the first line of treatment but is not indicated for the majority with normal thyroid function.

For children with demonstrated deficiencies of any nutrient (e.g., zinc, iron, magnesium, and vitamins), correction of that deficiency is the logical first-line treatment. It is not clear what proportion of children have such a nutritional deficiency, but it may be higher than generally suspected because of the confluence of two factors: (1) Many children have a preference for highly processed sugary foods lacking in nutritional balance and succeed in subsisting on these despite parents' intentions to the contrary, and (2) many pediatricians and parents subscribe to the axiom that if one eats a balanced diet, vitamin supplementation is not necessary; because they intend for their children to eat a balanced diet, they overlook the first factor and conclude that vitamin pills are not necessary.

Category 4: Proven Efficacy. A few of the alternatives have rather convincing scientific evidence or other features suggesting that they should be implemented when appropriate and practical. Chief among these is the few-foods (oligoantigenic) diet, for which there is good evidence of efficacy in the subgroup with sensitivity to foods. Note that the proportion of diagnosed ADHD children who have food sensitivities has not been empirically established; however, it is certainly a minority, perhaps as low as

5 percent, but more likely double digits. The diet can be rather onerous, and the desensitization procedure may be more practical in many cases. A more generally applicable treatment with reasonable evidence of efficacy is the combination of relaxation training and EMG biofeedback, which is relatively inexpensive (some studies reporting results with only four to eight sessions), and group administration is feasible.

Category 5: Worth Trying Despite Limited Evidence of Efficacy. Some treatments, though not yet supported with convincing evidence, seem sufficiently safe, cheap, easy, and reasonable that they could be empirically tried as adjuncts to established treatments while awaiting better data:

- Meditation, though not definitively proven in ADHD, has been reported beneficial in two small comparison trials and is accepted for other areas of health. It seems to carry no risk.

- Massage has controlled pilot data and can be implemented by parents with minimal training.

- RDA multivitamins for children with junky diets seem a conservative intervention.

- Mirror feedback, with controlled pilot data, is cheap and easily implemented by parents for homework time and seems safe if the diagnosis is assured.

- Vestibular stimulation, with controlled pilot data, can be implemented by parents with swings, hammocks, swivel chairs, scooter boards, and so on, with risk not beyond routine daily child activities.

Approach to Selecting Treatment

Because many of the alternative treatments target specific etiologies, they should paradoxically be considered (not necessarily implemented) first during the diagnostic evaluation, which should consider etiologies for the symptoms. Only after etiologies amenable to specific treatment are ruled out should the standard, generic treatments (psychotropic medication and behavioral treatment) be implemented as the main therapeutic thrust. Therefore, a good history and physical exam will check for signs of thyroid dysfunction, allergic history, food intolerance, dietary balance/deficiency, and general medical problems. As individually indicated, a complete blood count and electrolytes/minerals are desirable as a general screen and to pick up mineral deficiencies. In areas with high rates of subclinical lead poisoning, a serum lead should be done. More complete screening for all minerals (e.g., iron and zinc) could be justified, especially if there is any question from the dietary history. In questionable cases, a therapeutic trial may be indicated.

RECOMMENDATIONS FOR FUTURE RESEARCH

Future research efforts should (1) mount definitive trials and replications of promising treatments that may have some advantage over the standard treatments if proven effective, (2) mount controlled clinical trials of treatments for which a controlled trial is easy and cheap (Arnold, 1995), (3) mount open pilot trials of well-considered hypotheses for which there are no pilot data and for which a controlled trial would be expensive or difficult, and (4) define subgroups (characteristics and proportion of diagnosed ADHD children) appropriate for treatments for which efficacy has been demonstrated. We recommend the following:

- *Replications and definitive trials.* The following treatments have either enough promising pilot data to warrant a definitive clinical trial or a controlled study deserving replication by other investigators: Chinese herbals, EEG biofeedback, mirror feedback, massage, channel-specific perceptual training, vestibular stimulation (e.g., comprehensive motion apparatus), magnesium supplementation, enzyme-potentiated desensitization for food allergies, meditation, n-3 essential fatty acid supplementation in patients with low plasma levels, and possibly dimethylaminoethanol.

- *Controlled trials that are cheap/easy.* It would be easy enough and cheap enough to do a controlled trial of the following that it makes sense to take this step directly to settle the issue: RDA multivitamins, zinc RDA supplementation, antifungal therapy (with sugar restriction).

- *Pilot and open trials.* The following need some pilot data to tell whether a controlled clinical trial is indicated: homeopathic remedies, non-Chinese herbals, acupuncture, l-carnitine, and other mineral supplementation.

- *Definition of applicable subgroups of ADHD.* The following treatments, with either convincing controlled-trial evidence of efficacy or else commonsense clinical justification for appropriate patients need better definition of the appropriate subgroups of ADHD patients: few-foods (oligoantigenic) diets, chelation (what is the critical blood level of lead responsive to chelation?), iron supplementation (how iron-deficient, or is deficiency even needed?), and EMG biofeedback/relaxation.

The most basic recommendation for future research on treatment alternatives for ADHD is that there should be more. Most of the alternatives have been relatively neglected by most mainstream investigators and by peer-reviewed funding, despite the fact that some of them could be relatively cheaply tested. This neglect has three unfortunate consequences: (1) dogma—both establishment and antiestablishment) fills the void left by absence of data, (2) potentially useful treatments are rejected or neglected without a fair trial by clinicians who demand scientific validation, and (3) possibly ineffective or even dangerous treatments can be advocated without the data necessary to debunk them. This area needs more scientific attention.

References

Agget, P. J., & Harries, J. T. (1979). Current status of zinc in health and disease states. *Archives of Disease in Childhood, 54*, 909–917.

Ahmad, S., Dasgupta, A., & Kenny, M. A. (1989). Fatty acid abnormalities in hemodialysis patients: Effect of l-carnitine administration. *Kidney International, 36*(Suppl. 27), S-243–S-246.

Aman, M. G., Mitchell, E. A., & Turbott, S. H. (1987). The effects of essential fatty acid supplementation by Efamol in hyperactive children. *Journal of Abnormal Child Psychology, 15*, 75–90.

American Psychiatric Association. (1980). *Diagnostic and statistical manual of mental disorders* (3rd ed.). Washington, DC: Author.

American Psychiatric Association. (1987). *Diagnostic and statistical manual of mental disorders* (3rd ed., rev.). Washington, DC: Author.

American Psychiatric Association. (1994). *Diagnostic and statistical manual of mental disorders* (4th ed.). Washington, DC: Author.

Anonymous. (1984). Vitamin B6 toxicity: A new megavitamin syndrome. *Nutrition Reviews, 42*, 44–46.

Arduini, A., Denisova N., Virmani A., Avrova, N., Federici, G., & Arrigoni-Martelli, E. (1994). Evidence for the involvement of carnitine-dependent long-chain acyltransferases in neuronal triglyceride and phospholipid fatty acid turnover. *Journal of Neurochemistry, 62*, 1530–1538.

Arnold, L. E. (1995). Some nontraditional (unconventional and/or innovative) psychosocial treatments for children and adolescents: Critique and proposed screening principles. *Journal of Abnormal Child Psychology, 23*(1), 125–140.

Arnold, L. E., Barnebey, N., McManus, J., Smeltzer, D., Conrad, A., Winer, G., & Desgranges, L. (1977). Prevention by specific perceptual remediation for vulnerable first-graders: Controlled study and follow-up of lasting effects. *Archives of General Psychiatry, 34*, 1279–1294.

Arnold, L. E., Christopher, J., Huestis, R. D., & Smeltzer, D. J. (1978). Megavitamins for minimal brain dysfunction: A placebo-controlled study. *Journal of the American Medical Association, 240*(24), 2642–2643.

Arnold, L. E., Clark, D. L., Sachs, L. A., Jakim, S., & Smithies, C. (1985). Vestibular and visual rotational stimulation as treatment for attention deficit and hyperactivity. *American Journal of Occupational Therapy, 39*(2), 84–91.

Arnold, L. E., Kleykamp, D., Votolato, N., Gibson, R. A., & Horrocks, L. (1994). Potential link between dietary intake of fatty acids and behavior: Pilot Exploration of Serum lipids in ADHD. *Journal of Child and Adolescent Psychopharmacology, 4*(3), 171–180.

Arnold, L. E., Kleykamp, D., Votolato, N. A., Taylor, W. A., Kontras, S. B., & Tobin, K. (1989). Gamma-linolenic acid for attention-deficit hyperactivity disorder: Placebo controlled comparison to d-amphetamine. *Biological Psychiatry, 25*, 222–228.

Arnold, L. E., Votolato, N. A., Kleykamp, D., Baker, G. B., & Bornstein, R. A. (1990). Does hair zinc predict amphetamine improvement of ADHD/Hyperactivity? *International Journal of Neuroscience, 50*, 103–107.

Baker, G. B., Bornstein, R. A., Rouget, A. C., Therrien, S., & van Muyden, J. (1991). Phenylethylaminergic mechanisms in attention-deficit disorder. *Biological Psychiatry, 29*, 15–22.

Bekaroglu, M., Yakup, A., Yusof, G., Orhan, D., Hilal, M., Erol, E., & Caner, K. (1996). Relationships between serum free fatty acids and zinc and ADHD. *Journal of Child Psychology and Psychiatry, 37*, 225–227.

Benton, D., & Buts, J. P. (1990). Vitamin/mineral supplementation and intelligence. *Lancet, 335*, 1158–1160.

Benton, D., & Cook, R. (1991). Vitamin and mineral supplements improve the intelligence scores and concentration of six-year-old children. *Personality and Individual Differences, 12*, 1151–1158.

Bernstein, A. L. (1990). Vitamin B6 in clinical neurology. *Annals of the New York Academy of Sciences, 585*, 250–260.

Bhatara, V., Clark, D. L., Arnold, L. E., Gonsett, R., & Smeltzer, D. J. (1981). Hyperkinesis treated by vestibular stimulation: An exploratory study. *Biological Psychiatry, 16*(3), 269–279.

Blackburn, W. D., Jr. (1997). Eosinophilia myalgia syndrome. *Seminars in Arthritis and Rheumatism, 26*, 788–793.

Boris, M., & Mandel, F. S. (1994). Foods and additives are common causes of the attention deficit hyperactive disorder in children. *Annals of Allergy, 72*, 462–468.

Bornstein, R. A., Baker, G. B., Carroll, A., King, G., Wong, J. T., & Douglass, A. B. (1990). Plasma amino acids in attention deficit disorder. *Psychiatry Research, 33*, 301–306.

Breakey, J. (1997). The role of diet and behavior in childhood. *Journal of Pediatrics and Child Health, 33*, 190–194.

Brenner, A. (1979). Trace mineral levels in hyperactive children responding to the Feingold diet. *Journal of Pediatrics, 94*, 44.

Brenner, A. (1982). The effects of megadoses of selected B complex vitamins on children with hyperkinesis; controlled studies with long-term follow-up. *Journal of Learning Disabilities, 15*, 258–264.

Brown, A., Mallett, M., Fiser, D., & Arnold, W. C. (1984). Acute isoniazid intoxication: Reversal of CNS symptoms with large doses of pyridoxine. *Pediatric Pharmacology, 4*, 199–202.

Bruner, A. B., Joffe, A., Duggan, A. K., Casella, F., & Brandt, J. (1996). Randomized study of cognitive effects of iron supplementation in non-anemic iron-deficient girls. *Lancet, 348*(9033), 992–996.

Burattini, M. G., Amendola, F., Aufierio, T., Spano, M., Di Bitonto, G., Del Vecchio, G. C., & De Mattia, D. (1990). Evaluation of the effectiveness of gastro-protected proteoferrin in the therapy of sideropenic anemia in childhood. *Minerva Pediatrica, 42*, 343–347.

Calhoun, G. Jr., & Bolton, J. A. (1986). Hypnotherapy: A possible alternative for treating pupils affected with attention deficit disorder. *Perceptual and Motor Skills, 63*, 1191–1195.

Carter, C. M., Urbanowicz, M., Hemsley, R., Mantilla, L., Strobel, S., Graham, P. J., & Taylor, E. (1993). Effects of a few food diets in attention deficit disorder. *Archives of Disease in Childhood, 69*, 564–568.

Chang, C. H., Wang, Y. M., Yang, A. H., & Chiang, S. S. (2001). Rapidly progressive interstitial renal fibrosis associated with Chinese herbal medications. *American Journal of Nephrology, 21*(6), 441–448.

Cobb, D. E., & Evans, J. R. (1981). The use of biofeedback techniques with school-aged children exhibiting behavioral and/or learning problems. *Journal of Abnormal Child Psychology, 9*, 251–281.

Coleman, M., Steinberg, G., Tippett, J., Bhagavan, H. N., Coursin, D. B., Gross, M., Lewis, C., & DeVeau, L. (1979). A preliminary study of the effect of pyridoxine administration in a subgroup of hyperkinetic children: A double-blind crossover comparison with methylphenidate. *Biological Psychiatry, 14*, 741–751.

Coleman, N., Dexheimer, P., DiMascio, A., Redman, W., & Finnerty, R. (1976). Deanol in the treatment of hyperkinetic children. *Psychosomatics, 17*, 68-72.

Conners, C. K. (1980). *Food additives and hyperactive children.* London: Plenum Press.

Crandall, M. (1991). A controlled trial of nystatin for the candidiasis hypersensitivity syndrome [Letter to editor]. *New England Journal of Medicine, 323*, 1717–1723.

Crook, W. G. (1985). Pediatricians, antibiotics, and office practice. *Pediatrics, 76*(1), 139-140.

Crook, W. G. (1989). *The yeast connection* (3rd ed.). Jackson, TN: Professional Books.

Crook, W. G. (1991). A controlled trial of nystatin for the candidiasis hypersensitivity syndrome [Letter to editor]. *New England Journal of Medicine, 323*, 1766–1767.

David, O. J., Hoffman, S. P., Clark, J., Grad, G., & Sverd, J. (1983). The relationship of hyperactivity to moderately elevated lead levels. *Archives of Environmental Health, 38*, 341–346.

David, O. J., Hoffman, S. P., Sverd, J., & Clark, J. (1977). Lead and hyperactivity: Lead levels among hyperactive children. *Journal of Abnormal Child Psychology, 5*, 405–416.

David, O. J., Hoffman, S. P., Sverd, J., Clark, J., & Voeller, K. (1976). Lead and hyperactivity. Behavioral response to chelation: A pilot study. *American Journal of Psychiatry, 133*, 1155–1158.

Denkowski, K. M., & Denkowski, G. C. (1984). Is group progressive relaxation training as effective with hyperactive children as individual EMG biofeedback? *Biofeedback and Self-Regulation, 9*, 353–364.

Denkowski, K. M., Denkowski, G. C., & Omizo, M. M. (1983). The effects of EMG-assisted relaxation training on the academic performance, locus of control, and self-esteem of hyperactive boys. *Biofeedback and Self-Regulation, 8*, 363–375.

Denkowski, K. M., Denkowski, G. C., & Omizo, M. M. (1984). Predictors of success in the EMG biofeedback training of hyperactive male children. *Biofeedback and Self-Regulation, 9*, 253–264.

Dismukes, W. E., Wade, J. S., Lee, J. Y., Dockery, B. K., & Hain, J. D. (1990). A randomized double-blind trial of nystatin therapy for the candidiasis hypersensitivity syndrome. *New England Journal of Medicine, 323*, 1717–1723.

Dunn, F. M., & Howell, R. J. (1982). Relaxation training and its relationship to hyperactivity in boys. *Journal of Clinical Psychology, 38*, 92–100.

Durlach, J., Durlach, V., Bac, P., Bara, M., & Guiet-Bara, A. (1994). Magnesium and therapeutics. *Magnesium Research, 7*, 313–328.

Dykman, K. D., & Dykman, R. A. (1998). Effect of nutritional supplements on attentional-deficit hyperactivity disorder. *Integrative Physiological and Behavioral Science, 33*, 49–60.

Dykman, K. D., & McKinley, R. (1997). Effect of glyconutritionals on the severity of ADHD. *Proceedings of the Fisher Institute for Medical Research, 1*(1), 24–25.

Egger, J., Carter, C. M., Graham, P. J., Gumley, D., & Soothill, J. F. (1985). Controlled trial of oligoantigenic treatment in the hyperkinetic syndrome. *Lancet, 1*(8428), 540–545.

Egger, J., Stolla, A., & McEwen, L. M. (1992). Controlled trial of hyposensitization in children with food-induced hyperkinetic syndrome. *Lancet, 339*(8802), 1150–1153.

Eisenberg, J., Asnis, G. M., van Praag, H. M., & Vela, R. M. (1988). Effect of tyrosine on attention deficit disorder with hyperactivity. *Journal of Clinical Psychiatry, 49*, 193–195.

Feingold, B. F. (1975). *Why your child is hyperactive.* New York: Random House.

Feingold, B. F. (1981). Refutes criticism of diet (Reply to nutrition foundation report). *Clinical Psychiatry News, pp.* 2–3.

Field, T., Morrow, C., Valdeon, C., Larson, S., Kuhn, C., & Schanberg, S. (1992). Massage reduces anxiety in child and adolescent psychiatric patients. *Journal of the American Academy of Child and Adolescent Psychiatry, 31*(1), 125–131.

Field, T., Ironson, G., Pickens, J., Nawrocki, T., Fox, N., Scafidi, F., Burman, I., & Schanberg, S. (1996). Massage therapy reduces anxiety and enhances EEG pattern of alertness and math computations. *International Journal of Neuroscience, 86*, 197–205.

Field, T. M., Lasko, D., Mundy, P., Henteleff, T., Kabat, S., Talpins, S., & Dowling, M. (1997). Autistic children's attentiveness and responsivity improve after touch therapy. *Journal of Autism., & Developmental Disorders 27*, 333–338.

Field, T. M., Quintino, O., Hernandez-Reif, M., & Koslovsky, G. (1998). Adolescents with attention-deficit hyperactivity disorder benefit from massage therapy. *Adolescence 33*(129), 103–108.

Flink, E. B. (1981). Magnesium deficiency. Etiology and clinical spectrum. *Acta Medica Scandinavica, 647*(Suppl.), 125–137.

Forsyth, P. D., & Davies, J. M. (1995). Pure white cell aplasia and health food products. *Postgraduate Medical Journal, 71*, 557–558.

Geller, S. J. (1960). Comparison of a tranquillizer and psychic energizer used in treatment of children with behavior disorders. *Journal of the American Medical Association, 174*, 481–484.

Ghose, K. (1983). L-tryptophan in hyperactive child syndrome associated with epilepsy: A controlled study. *Neuropsychobiology, 10*, 111–114.

Gittelman, R., & Eskanazi, B. (1983). Lead and hyperactivity revisited: An investigation of nondisadvantaged children. *Archives of General Psychiatry, 40*, 827–833.

Goldman, J. A., Lerman, R. H., Contois, J. H., & Udall, J. N., Jr. (1986). Behavioral effects of sucrose on preschool children. *Journal of Abnormal Child Psychology, 14*, 565–577.

Gong, Z., & Evans, H. L. (1997). Effect of chelation with meso-dimercaptosuccinic acid (DMSA) before and after the appearance of lead-induced neurotoxicity in the rat. *Toxicology and Applied Pharmacology, 144*, 205–214.

Grandin, T. (1992). Calming effects of deep touch pressure in patients with autistic disorder, college students, and animals. *Journal of Child and Adolescent Psychopharmacology, 2*(1), 63–72.

Hagerman, R. J., & Falkenstein, A. R. (1987). An association between recurrent otitis media in infancy and hyperactivity. *Clinical Pediatrics, 26*, 253–257.

Halas, E. S., & Sandstead, H. H. (1975). Some effects of prenatal zinc deficiency on behavior of the adult rat. *Pediatric Research, 9*, 94–97.

Hamazaki, T., Sawazaki, S., Itomura, M., Asaoka, E., Nagao, Y., Nishimura, N., Yazawa, K., Kuwamori, T., & Kobayashi, M. (1996). The effect of docosohexaenoic acid on aggression in young adults. A placebo-controlled double-blind study. *Journal of Clinical Investigation, 97*, 1129–1133.

Haslam, R. H. A., Dalby, J. T., & Rademaker, A. W. (1984). Effects of Megavitamin therapy on children with attention deficit disorders. *Pediatrics, 74*, 103–111.

Hauser, P., Soler, R., Brucker-Davis, F., & Weintraub, B. D. (1997). Thyroid hormones correlate with symptoms of hyperactivity but not inattention in ADHD. *Psychoneuroendocrinology, 22*, 107–114.

Heimann, S. W. (1999). Pycnogenol for ADHD? *Journal of the American Academy of Child and Adolescent Psychiatry, 38*, 357-358.

Hibbeln, J. R., Umhau, J. C., Linnoila, M., George, D. T., Ragan, P. W., Shoaf, S. E., Vaughan, M. R., Rawlings, R., & Salem, N. Jr. (1998). Essential fatty acids predict metabolistes of serotonin and dopamine in cerebrospinal fluid among healthy control subjects, and early-and late-onset alcoholics. *Biological Psychiatry, 44*(4), 243–349.

Houben, G. F., & Penninks, A. H. (1994). Immunotoxicity of the colour additive caramel colour III: A review on complicated issues in the safety evaluation of a food additive. *Toxicology, 91*, 289–302.

Imamura, K. N., Weiss, P., & Parham, D. (1990). The effects of hug machine usage on behavioral organization of children with autism and autism-like characteristics. *Sensory Integration Quarterly, 27*, 1–5.

Interactive metronome [On-line]. (1998). Available: http://www.interactivemetronome.com/adhd.htm.

Ironson, G., Field, T. M., Scafidi, F., Kumar, M., Patarca, R., Price, A., Goncalves, A., Hashimoto, M., Kumar, A., Burman, I., Tetenman, C., & Fletcher, M. A. (1996). Massage therapy is associated with enhancement of the immune system's cytotoxic capacity. *International Journal of Neuroscience, 84*, 205-218.

Irving, W. C. III (1987). A comparison of biofeedback-assisted relaxation and psychostimulants in treating children with attention deficit disorder with hyperactivity. *Dissertation Abstracts International, 48*(04), 0876A.

Izenwasser, S. E., Garcia-Valdez, K., & Kantak, K. M. (1986). Stimulant-like effects of magnesium on aggression in mice. *Pharmacology, Biochemistry, and Behavior, 25*, 1195–1199.

Kahn, C. A., Kelly, P. C., & Walker, W. O. Jr. (1995). Lead screening in children with ADHD and developmental delay. *Clinical Pediatrics, 34*, 498–501.

Kaplan, B. J., McNicol, J., Conte, R. A., & Moghadam, H. K. (1989a). Dietary replacement in preschool-aged hyperactive boys. *Pediatrics, 83*, 7–17.

Kaplan, B. J., McNicol, J., Conte, R. A., & Moghadam, H. K. (1989b). Overall nutrient intake of preschool hyperactive and normal boys. *Journal of Abnormal Child Psychology, 17*, 127.

Kavale, K. A., & Forness, S. R. (1983). Hyperactivity and diet treatment: A meta-analysis of the Feingold hypothesis. *Journal of Learning Disabilities, 16*, 324–330.

Kershner, J., & Hawke, W. (1979). Megavitamins and learning disorders: A controlled double-blind experiment. *Journal of Nutrition, 159*, 819–826.

Kozielec, T., & Starobrat-Hermelin, B. (1997). Assessment of magnesium levels in children with ADHD. *Magnesium Research, 10*, 143–148.

Kozielec, T., Starobrat-Hermelin, B., & Kotkowiak, L. (1994). Deficiency of certain trace elements in children with hyperactivity. *Psychiatria Polska, 28*, 345–53.

Kratter, J. (1983). The use of meditation in the treatment of attention deficit disorder with hyperactivity. *Dissertation Abstracts International, 44*, 1965.

Krieger, G. D. R. (1985). Reduction of hyperactivity using progressive muscle relaxation imagery and autogenic exercises with electromyographic biofeedback. *Dissertation Abstracts International, 46*(10), 3617B.

Kruesi, M. J., Rapoport, J. L., Berg, C., Stables, G., & Bou, E. (1987). Seven-day carbohydrate and other nutrient intakes of preschool boys alleged to be behavior-responsive to sugar and their peers. In W. B. Essman (Ed.), *Nutrients and brain function* (pp. 133–137). Basel, Switzerland: Karger.

Krummel, D. A., Seligson, F. H., & Guthrie, H. A. (1996). Hyperactivity: Is candy causal? *Critical Reviews in Food Science and Nutrition, 36*, 31–47.

Kugel, R. B., & Alexander, T. (1963, April). The effect of a central nervous system stimulant (deanol) on behavior. *Pediatrics,* 651-655.

Lee, S. W. (1991). Biofeedback as a treatment for childhood hyperactivity: A critical review of the literature. *Psychological Reports*, pp. 163–192.

Lester, M. L., Thatcher, R. W., & Monroe-Lord, L. (1982). Refined carbohydrate intake, hair cadmium levels, and cognitive functioning in children. *Nutrition and Behavior, 1*, 3–13.

Lewis, J. A., & Young, R. (1975). Deanol and methylphenidate in minimal brain dysfunction. *Clinical Pharmacology and Therapeutics, 17*, 534-540.

Linden, M., Habib, T., & Radojevic, V. (1996). A controlled study of the effects of EEG biofeedback on cognition and behavior of children with attention deficit disorder and learning disabilities. *Biofeedback and Self-Regulation, 21*, 35–49.

Lipton, M. A., & Mayo, J. P. (1983). Diet and hyperkinesis—An update. *Journal of the American Dietetic Association, 83*, 132–134.

Lubar, J. F. (1991). Discourse on the development of EEG diagnostics and biofeedback for attention-deficit/hyperactivity disorders. *Biofeedback and Self-Regulation, 16*, 201–225.

Lubar, J. F., & Shouse, M. N. (1977). Use of biofeedback in the treatment of seizure disorders and hyperactivity. In B. B. Lahey & A. E. Kazdin (Eds.), *Advances in clinical child psychology* (Vol. 1, pp. 203–265). New York: Plenum Press.

Lubar, J. F., Swartwood, M. O., Swartwood, J. N., & O'Donnell, P. H. (1995). Evaluation of the Effectiveness of EEG Neurofeedback training for ADHD in a clinical setting as measured by changes in TOVA scores, behavior ratings, and WISC-R performance. *Biofeedback and Self-Regulation 20*, 83–99.

Mann, C. A., Lubar, J. F., Zimmerman, A. W., Miller, C. A., & Muenchen, R. A. (1992). Quantitative analysis of EEG in boys with attention-deficit-hyperactivity disorder: Controlled study with clinical implications. *Pediatric Neurology, 8*(1), 30–36.

Mattes, J. A. (1983). The Feingold diet: A current reappraisal. *Journal of Learning Disabilities, 16*, 319–323.

McGee, R., Williams, S., Anderson, J., McKenzie-Parnell, J. M., & Silva, P. A. (1990). Hyperactivity and serum and hair zinc levels in 11-year-old children from the general population. *Biological Psychiatry, 28*, 165–168.

Millichap, J. G. (1973). Drugs in the management of minimal brain dysfunction. *Annals of New York Academy of Sciences, 205*, 321-334.

Mitchell, E. A., Aman, M. G., Turbott, S. H., & Manku, M. (1987). Clinical characteristics and serum essential fatty acid levels in hyperactive children. *Clinical Pediatrics, 26*, 406–411.

Mitchell, E. A., Lewis, S., & Cutler, D. R. (1983). Essential fatty acids and maladjusted behavior in children. *Prostaglandins Leukotrienes & Medicine, 12*, 281–287.

Moretti-Altuna, G. (1987). The effects of meditation versus medication in the treatment of attention deficit disorder with hyperactivity. *Dissertation Abstracts International, 47*, 46–58.

Mulligan, S. (1996). An analysis of score patterns of children with attention disorders on the sensory integration and praxis tests. *American Journal of Occupational Therapy, 50*, 647–654.

National Institutes of Health. (1982). NIH consensus development conference: Defined diets and childhood hyperactivity. *Clinical Pediatrics, 21*, 627–630.

Needleman, H. L., Gunnoe, C., Leviton, A., Reed, R., Peresie, H., Maher, C., & Barrett, P. (1979). Deficits in psychologic and classroom performance of children with elevated dentine lead levels. *New England Journal of Medicine, 300*, 689–695.

Nemzer, E., Arnold, L. E., Votolato, N. A., & McConnell, H. (1986). Amino acid supplementation as therapy for attention deficit disorder (ADD), *Journal of the American Academy of Child and Adolescent Psychiatry, 25*(4), 509–513.

Neuringer, M. (1998, September 2–3). *Overview of omega-3 fatty acids in infant development: Visual, cognitive, and behavioral outcomes.* Paper presented at NIH Workshop on Omega-3 Essential Fatty Acids and Psychiatric Disorders, Bethesda, MD.

Nsouli, T. M., Nsouli, S. M., Linde, R. E., O'Mara, F., Scanlon, R. T., & Bellanti, J. A. (1994). Role of food allergy in serous otitis media. *Annals of Allergy, 73*, 215–219.

Omizo, M. M., & Michael, W. B. (1982) Biofeedback-induced relaxation training and impulsivity, attention to task, and locus of control among hyperactive boys. *Journal of Learning Disabilities, 15*, 414–416.

Pakes, G. E. (1978). Death and liquid protein. *American Pharmacy, 18*, 4–5.

Palacios, H. J. (1976). Hypersensitivity as a cause of dermatologic and vaginal moniliasis resistant to topical therapy. *Annals of Allergy, 37*, 110–113.

Palacios, H. J. (1977). Desensitization for monilial hypersensitivity. *Virginia Medical Journal, 104*, 393–395.

Perlmutter, S. J., Leitman, S. F., Garvey, M. A., Hamburger, S., Feldman, E., Leonard, H. L., & Swedo, S. E. (1999). Therapeutic plasma exchange and intravenous immunoglobulin for obsessive-compulsive and tic disorders in childhood. *Lancet, 354*(9185), 1153–1158.

Pollock, I., & Warner, J. O. (1990). Effect of artificial food colors on childhood behavior. *Archives of Disease in Childhood, 65*, 74–77.

Previc, F. H. (1993). Do the organs of the labyrinth differentially influence the sympathetic and parasympathetic systems? *Neuroscience and Biobehavioral Reviews, 17*, 397–404.

Prinz, R. J., Roberts, W. A., & Hantman, E. (1980). Dietary correlates of hyperactive behavior in children. *Journal of Consulting and Clinical Psychology, 6*, 760–769.

Reimherr, F. W., Wender, P. H., Wood, D. R., & Ward, M. (1987). An open trial of l-tyrosine in the treatment of attention deficit disorder, residual type. *American Journal of Psychiatry, 144*, 1071–1073.

Ricciolini, R., Scalibastri, M., Kelleher, J. K., Carminati, P., Calvani, M., & Arduini, A. (1998). Role of acetyl-l-carnitine in rat brain lipogenesis: Implications for polyunsaturated fatty acid synthesis. *Journal of Neurochemistry, 71*, 2510-2517.

Rimland, B. (1983). The Feingold diet: An assessment of the reviews by Mattes, by Kavale, & Forness, and others. *Journal of Learning Disabilities, 16*, 45–49.

Rippere, V. (1983). Food additives and hyperactive children: A critique of Conners. *British Journal of Clinical Psychology, 22*(pt. 1), 19–32.

Rovet, J., & Alvarez, M. (1996). Thyroid hormone and attention in school-age children with congenital hypothyroidism. *Journal of Child Psychology and Psychiatry, 37*, 579–585

Rowe, K. S. (1988). Synthetic food colorings and hyperactivity: A double-blind crossover study. *Australian Pediatric Journal, 24*, 143–147.

Rowe, K. S., & Rowe, K. J. (1994). Synthetic food coloring and behavior: A dose-response effect in a double-blind, placebo-controlled, repeated-measures study. *Journal of Pediatrics 125*, 691-698.

Saccar, C. L. (1978). Drug therapy in the treatment of minimal brain dysfunction. *American Journal of Hospital Pharmacy, 35*, 554-552.

Sandstead, H. H., Fosmire, G. J., Halas, E. S., Jacob, R. A., Strobel, D. A., & Marks, E. O. (1977). Zinc deficiency: Effects on brain and behavior of rats and Rhesus monkeys. *Teratology, 16*, 229–234.

Sandyk, R. (1990). Zinc deficiency in attention-deficit/hyperactivity disorder. *International Journal of Neuroscience, 52*, 239–241.

Sato, K., Taguchi, H., Maeda, T., & Yoshikawa, K. (1993). Pyridoxine toxicity to cultured fibroblasts cause by near-ultraviolet light. *Journal of Investigative Dermatology, 100*, 266–270.

Schaumburg, H., Kaplan, J., Windebank, A., Vick, N., Rasmus, S., Pleasure, D., & Brown, M. J. (1983). Sensory neuropathy from pyridoxine abuse: A new megavitamin syndrome. *New England Journal of Medicine, 309*, 445–448.

Schmidt, M. H., Mocks, P., Lay, B., Eisert, H. G., Fojkar, R., Fritz-Sigmund, D., Marcus, A., & Musaeus, B. (1997). Does oligoantigenic diet influence hyperactive/conduct-disordered children—A controlled trial. *European Child and Adolescent Psychiatry, 6*, 88–95.

Sever, Y., Ashkenazi, A., Tyano, S., & Weizman, A. (1997). Iron treatment in children with ADHD: A preliminary report. *Neuropsychobiology 35*, 178–180.

Shaywitz, B. A., Siegel, N. J., & Pearson, H. A. (1977). Megavitamins for minimal brain dysfunction: A potentially dangerous therapy. *Journal of the American Medical Association, 238*, 1749–1750.

Shekim, W. O., Antun, F., Hanna, G. L., & McCracken, J. T. (1990). S-adenosyl-L-methionine (SAM) in adults with ADHD, RS: Preliminary results from an open trial. *Psychopharmacology Bulletin, 26*, 249-253.

Shen, Y. C., & Wang, Y. F. (1984). Urinary 3-methoxy-4-hydroxyphenylglycol sulfate excretion in seventy-three schoolchildren with minimal brain dysfunction. *Biological Psychiatry, 19*, 861–870.

Shouse, M. N., & Lubar, J. F. (1978). Physiological basis of hyperkinesis treated with methylphenidate. *Pediatrics, 62*, 343–351.

Sidransky, H. (1997). Tryptophan and carcinogenesis: Review and update on how tryptophan may act. *Nutrition and Cancer, 29*, 181–194.

Silbergeld, E. K., & Goldberg, A. M. (1975). Pharmacological and neurochemical investigations of lead-induced hyperactivity. *Neuropharmacology, 14*, 431–444.

Simpson, D. D., & Nelson, A. L. (1974). Attention training through breathing control to modify hyperactivity. *Journal of Learning Disabilities, 7*, 15–23.

Snodgrass, S. R. (1992). Vitamin neurotoxicity. *Molecular Neurobiology, 6*, 41–73.

Starobrat-Hermelin, B., & Kozielec, T. (1997). The effects of magnesium physiological supplementation on hyperactivity in children with ADHD: Positive response to magnesium oral loading test. *Magnesium Research, 10*, 149–156.

Stein, T. P., & Sammaritano, A. M. (1984). Nitrogen metabolism in normal and hyperkinetic boys. *American Journal of Clinical Nutrition, 39*, 520–524.

Sternberg, E. M. (1996). Pathogenesis of L-tryptophan eosinophilia-myalgia syndrome. *Advances in Experimental Medicine and Biology, 398*, 325–330.

Stevens, L. J., Zentall, S. S., Deck, J. L., Abate, M. L., Watkins, B. A., Lipp, S. R., & Burgess, J. R. (1995). Essential fatty acid metabolism in boys with attention-deficit hyperactivity disorder. *American Journal of Clinical Nutrition, 62*, 761–768.

Stevenson, J., Bateman, B., Hutchinson, E., Warner, J., Dean, T., Rowlandson, P., Grant, C., Grundy, J., & Fitzgerald, C. (2001, June 30). *The effects of a double-blind placebo-controlled artificial food colourings and benzoate preservatives challenge on hyperactivity in a general population sample of preschool children.* Poster presented at 10th scientific meeting of the International Society for Research in Child and Adolescent Psychopathology, Vancouver, British Columbia.

Sun, Y., Wang, Y., Qu, X., Wang, J., Fang, J., & Zhang, L. (1994). Clinical observations and treatment of hyperkinesia in children by traditional Chinese medicine. *Journalof Traditional Chinese Medicine, 14*(2), 105-109.

Swanson, J. (1992). *School-based assessments and interventions for ADD students.* Irvine, CA: K.C. Publishing. (SNAP-IV also available online: www.ADHD.net)

Swanson, J., & Kinsbourne, M. (1980, March 28). Food dyes impair performance of hyperactive children on a laboratory learning test. *Science, 207*(4438), 1485–1487.

Swedo, S. E., Leonard, H. L., Garvey, M., Mittleman, B., Allen, A. J., Perlmutter, S., Dow, S., Zamkoff, J., Dubbert, B. K., & Lougee, L. (1998). Pediatric autoimmune neuropsychiatric disorders associated with streptococcal infections: Clinical description of the first 50 cases. *American Journal of Psychiatry, 155*, 264–271.

Toren, P., Sofia, E., Sela, B. A., Wolmer, L., Weitz, R., Dov, I., Koren, S., Reiss, A., Weizman, R., & Laor, N. (1996). Zinc deficiency in ADHD. *Biological Psychiatry, 40*, 1308–1310.

Torrioli, M. G., Vernacotola, S., Mariotti, P., Bianchi, E., Calvani, M., DeGaetano, A., Chiurazzi, P., & Neri, G. (1999). Double-blind, placebo-controlled study of l-acetylcarnitine for the treatment of hyperactive behavior in fragile X syndrome. *American Journal of Medical Genetics, 87*, 366-368.

Truss, C. O. (1991). A controlled trial of nystatin for the candidiasis hypersensitivity syndrome [Letter to editor]. *New England Journal of Medicine, 324*(22), 1592.

Valentine, J., Rossi, E., O'Leary, P., Parry, T. S., Kurinczuk, J. J., & Sly, P. (1997). Thyroid function in a population of children with ADHD. *Journal of Pediatrics and Child Health, 33*, 117–120.

Vargas, S. L., Patrick, C. C., Ayers, G. D., & Hughes, W. T. (1993). Modulating effect of dietary carbohydrate supplementation on Candida albicans colonization and invasion in a neutropenic mouse model. *Infection and Immunity, 61*, 619-626.

Voight, R. G., Liarente, A. M., Jenden, C. L., Fraley, J. K., Berretta, M. C., & Heird, W. C. (2001). A randomized double-blind placebo-controlled trial of docosahexaenoic acid supplementation in children with attention-deficit/hyperactivity disorder. *Journal of Pediatrics, 139*, 189–196.

Wagner, K. R., Elmore, J. G., & Horwitz, R. I. (1996). Diagnostic bias in clinical decision-making: An example of L-tryptophan and the diagnosis of eosinophilia-myalgia syndrome. *Journal of Rheumatology, 23*, 2079–2085.

Wang, L. H., Li, C. S., & Li, G. Z. (1995). Clinical and experimental studies on tiaoshen liquor for infantile hyperkinetic syndrome. *Chung-Kuo Chung Hsi i Chieh Ho Tsa Chih, 15*, 337-340.

Weiss, R. E., & Stein, M. A. (1999). Thyroid function and attention deficit hyperactivity disorder. In P. Accardo, B. Whitman, T. Blondis, & M. A. Stein (Eds.), *Attention deficits and hyperactivity in children and adults* (2nd ed., pp. 419–430). New York: Marcel Dekker.

Weiss, R. E., Stein, M. A., & Refetoff, S. (1997). Behavioral effects of liothyronine (L-T3) in children with ADHD in the presence and absence of resistance to thyroid hormone *Thyroid, 7*, 389–393.

Weiss, R. E., Stein, M. A., Trommer, B., & Refetoff, S. (1993). Attention-deficit hyperactivity disorder and thyroid function. *Journal of Pediatrics, 123*, 539–545.

West, S. A., Sax, K. W., Stanton, S. P., Keck, P. E. Jr., McElroy, S. L., & Strakowski, S. M. (1996). Differences in thyroid function studies in acutely manic adolescents with and without ADHD. *Psychopharmacology Bulletin, 32*, 63–66.

Williams, J. I., & Cram, M. C. (1978). Diet in the management of hyperkinesis. *Canadian Psychiatric Association Journal, 23*, 241–248.

Williamson, B. L., Tomlinson, A. J., Mishra, P. K., Gleich, G. J., & Naylor, S. (1998). Structural characterization of contaminants found in commercial preparations of melatonin: Similarities to case-related compounds from L-tryptophan associated with eosinophilia-myalgia syndrome. *Chemical Research in Toxicology, 11*, 234–240.

Wolraich, M. L., Lindgren, S. D., Stumbo, P. J., Stegink, L. D., Appelbaum, M. I., & Kiritsy, M. C. (1994). Effects of diets high in sucrose or aspartame on the behavior and cognitive performance of children. *New England Journal of Medicine, 330*, 301–307.

Wolraich, M. L., Stumbo, P. J., Milch, R., Chenard, C., & Schultz, F. (1986). Dietary characteristics of hyperactive and control boys. *Journal of the American Dietetic Association, 86*(4), 500-504.

Wolraich, M. L., Wilson, D. B., & White, J. W. (1995). The effect of sugar on behavior or cognition in children. *Journal of the American Medical Association, 274*, 1617–1621.

Wood, D. R., Reimherr, F. W., & Wender, P. H. (1985a). Treatment of attention-deficit disorder with dl-phenylalanine. *Psychiatry Research, 16*, 21–26.

Wood, D. R., Reimherr, F. W., & Wender, P. H. (1985b). Amino acid precursors for the treatment of attention-deficit disorder, residual type. *Psychopharmacology Bulletin, 21*, 146–149.

Yates, B. J. (1992). Vestibular influences on the sympathetic nervous system. *Brain Research Reviews, 17*, 51–59.

Zametkin, A. J., Karoum, F., & Rapoport, J. (1987). Treatment of hyperactive children with d-phenylalanine. *American Journal of Psychiatry, 144*, 792–794.

Zentall, S. S., Hall, A. M., & Lee, D. L. (1998). Attentional focus of students with hyperactivity during a word-search task. *Journal of Abnormal Child Psychology, 26*, 335–343.

Zhang, H., & Huang, J. (1990). Preliminary study of traditional Chinese medicine treatment of minimal brain dysfunction: Analysis of 100 cases. *Chung Hsi i Chieh Ho Tsa Chih Chinese Journal of Modern Developments in Traditional Medicine, 10*, 278–279.

Chapter 14

Behavioral and Medication Treatments for ADHD— Comparisons and Combinations

by Jennifer D. Ambroggio, M.S. and Peter S. Jensen, M.D.

Background 14-2
Short-Term Treatment Studies 14-4
    Medication vs. Behavior Therapy vs. Combined Treatment 14-4
    Medication/Psychosocial Treatment 2 x 3 Study 14-4
    Small-Sample Studies 14-4
        Cognitive Treatment Plus Medication vs. Medication
          Alone 14-4
        Behavior Treatment With and Without Medication 14-5
        Dose-Reduction Study 14-5
        Medication With and Without Auditory Feedback or
          Contingency Management 14-6
    Durability of Treatment 14-6
    Studies Favoring Combined Treatment Over Medication
      Alone in the Minority 14-7
Long-Term Treatment Studies 14-8
    The MTA Study 14-9
        Intensive Psychosocial/Behavioral Treatment vs.
          Medication Management 14-9
        Combined Treatment vs. Unimodal Treatments 14-9
        MTA-Delivered Treatments vs. Community Standard
          Care 14-10
        Summary of MTA Findings 14-10
Research Limitations 14-10
    Small Samples 14-10
    Short Duration of Most Studies 14-11
    Insufficiently Intensive Psychosocial Treatment 14-11
    Treatments Not Adjusted to Subject-Specific Needs 14-11

Summary and Conclusion 14-12
Future Research Needs 14-12

BACKGROUND

Abundant evidence has accumulated over the last three decades indicating that both medication and behavioral treatments are efficacious in improving the symptoms of attention deficit hyperactivity disorder (ADHD) (Richters et al., 1995). Given both the well-established benefits of these two major forms of treatment and the lack of total "normalization" of symptoms and behavior with any single form of treatment for most children with ADHD, since the late 1970s investigators have compared these two forms of treatment, alone and in combination. In particular, researchers have sought to determine whether the combination of these two approaches yields any advantages over unimodal (i.e., only medication or only psychotherapeutic approaches) treatments. Although early investigators (Satterfield, Cantwell, Satterfield, 1979; Satterfield, Satterfield, & Cantwell, 1981; Satterfield, Satterfield, & Schell, 1981; 1987) reported reduced antisocial behavior among ADHD youngsters receiving intensive, long-term combined (multimodal) treatment, these early studies did not use random assignment or employ appropriate control groups, and follow-up assessments were hampered by attrition.

Since Satterfield et al.'s (1979) first report, a total of fifteen well-controlled studies have compared psychostimulant medication, alone and in combination with various psychotherapeutic approaches, including parent training in behavioral modification approaches, child-focused cognitive treatments, social skills training, other forms of behavioral therapy or contingency management, and combinations of these psychotherapeutic approaches (see Table14.1). These fifteen studies were identified through two major sources: The Agency for Health Care Policy Research commissioned a systematic review of seven main areas concerning the relative efficacy and safety of various ADHD treatments. This review, completed by the McMaster University Evidence-Based Practice Center (1998), constitutes the most rigorous review of ADHD treatment efficacy to date. The review identified a total of thirteen studies conducted since 1971 that tested various psychosocial and medication treatments alone and in combination. Of these, four studies did not focus on change in ADHD symptoms as a primary outcome and were therefore excluded from further consideration. Furthermore, two additional studies from this group provided so little methodological detail concerning the nature of the medication and/or psychosocial treatment conditions as to render their findings uninterpretable, leaving only seven studies for review. Beyond this small group of studies, however, an additional eight studies of significant interest were identified, some ongoing and in prepublication status, others completed that were not included in the McMaster review. Thus, in total there were fifteen studies available for review in this chapter. Fourteen of these fifteen studies employed complete random assignment across all treatment arms, while one contrasted two different classroom based treatments, within which subjects were randomly assigned to different medication doses.

Despite the limitations of these fifteen studies, a review of their major findings is illustrative, in a number of instances providing evidence of the relative benefit of various unimodal and combined treatment approaches.

Table 14.1
Behavioral and Medication Treatments: Comparisons

Authors, Year	Design	Results
MTA Coop. Group, 1999	MedMgt; MedMgt + Beh (Comb); Beh; community providers' care	Comb = MedMgt > Beh only = community treatments for ADHD symptom domains, parents and teachers Comb > MedMgt for selected non-ADHD domains, e.g., parent-child relations, child anxiety, social skills MedMgtand Beh only equivalent for most non-ADHD symptom domains.
Hechtman & Abikoff, 1995	MPH; MPH + PS "placebo"; MPH + MMT (multimodal treatment)	CT = MPH alone = MPH + PS placebo for all comparisons.
Horn et al., 1991; Ialongo et al., 1993	Low-dose MPH; high-dose MPH; PBO; PT/SC + low MPH; PT/SC + high MPH; PT/SC + PBO	Low dose + PT/SC = high dose alone = high dose + PT/SC > PBO = Low dose = PBO + PT/SC PT/SC led to increased knowledge of behav. principles. 9-month follow-up: PT/SC = continued parent-reported benefits after the end of treatment, Med only = no further gains or modest deterioration.
Schachar et al., 1997	MPH + PT; PBO + PT; MPH + self-help; PBO + SH	Substantial attrition in PBO group (only 29 of 45 adhering after 4 months; of these only 18 taking PBO meds regularly); substantial "crossovers" preclude comparisons
Klein & Abikoff, 1997	MPH; BT + PBO; BT+ MPH	MPH + BT > MPH for Tchr. cooperation, attention seeking, impulse control, and trend for aggressive behavior; tchr. & psychiatrist CGI ratings; classroom observation ratings of minor and gross motor, attention-seeking & impulse control. MPH + BT = MPH > BT + PBO for almost all other comparisons
Firestone, et al., 1986	MPH; BT + PBO; BT + MPH	BT + MPH = MPH > PBO for decreasing hyperactivity and reaction time; no academic effect; no residual effects found at 2-year follow-up
Abikoff & Gittelman, 1985	MPH; attn. control + MPH; CogT + MPH	MPH = attention control + MPH = CogT + MPH on all outcomes
Brown, et al., 1985	CogT; MPH; CogT + MPH; untreated	CogT + MPH = MPH > CogT > control for attention; only MPH improved behavior. No differences in academic measures; MPH continued through post-testing.
Brown, et al., 1986	CogT + PBO; CogT + MPH; MPH + attn. cntrl.; attn. cntrl. + PBO	CogT + MPH = MPH + attention control = CogT + PBO > attention control + PBO. MPH discontinued prior to post-testing. Med effects dissipate rapidly.
Gittelman-Klein, et al., 1976	MPH; BT + MPH; BT + PBO	BT + MPH = MPH > PBO + BT on all outcomes
Long et al., 1993	MPH; MPH + bibliotherapy	MPH + bibliotherapy > MPH for parent/teacher ratings of behav. probs. Trend ($p < .06$) for improvement in parents' knowledge in MPH + bibliotherapy
Carlsonet al., 1992	Crossover: low-, high-dose MPH; PBO; x regular class; BM classroom	BM + low-dose MPH = high-dose MPH > low-dose MPH = BM + PBO for behavioral effects; only MPH improved academics
Hinshaw, et al., 1984	Crossover: MPH; PBO; x CBT; extrinsic reinforcement.	MPH + CBT > MPH = CBT > PBO = extrinsic reinforcement = PBO + extrinsic reinforcement
Solanto et al, 1997	Crossover: MPH + feedback; MPH + contingencies; PBO + feedback; PBO + contingencies	MPH + feedback = MPH + contingencies > contingencies + PBO > feedback + PBO
Thurston, 1979	Wait-list control; MPH; PT + MPH	No significant differences in impulsivity for any groups; PT + MPH > MPH > control for decreased activity level

Beh = behavioral therapy; BM = behavioral modification; CBT = cognitive-behavioral therapy; CGI = clinical global improvement; CogT = cognitive training; Comb = combined treatment; MedMgt = medication management; MPH = methylphenidate; PBO = placebo; PS = psychosocial treatment; PT = parent training; SC = child self-control training; SH = parent self-help and advocacy.

SHORT-TERM TREATMENT STUDIES

Medication vs. Behavior Therapy vs. Combined Treatment

Klein and Abikoff (1997) performed an eight-week experimental clinical trial comparing the effects of twice-daily stimulant medication, behavior therapy plus placebo medication, and the combination of behavior therapy plus active medication on eighty-nine children. These investigators found that the medication-only and combination groups outperformed the behavior therapy-only group, despite the considerable improvements that accrued to the behavior-treatment-only condition. The two medication groups were statistically indistinguishable on most, but not all, measures. Specifically, the combined group showed significantly more improvement than did the medication-only group in teacher ratings of cooperation and impulse control. However, modest sample sizes precluded determination of which subgroups of children (e.g., by comorbidity or parental psychopathology status) benefited most from combined treatment.

Medication/Psychosocial Treatment 2 x 3 Study

In a 2 x 3 factorial design study with ninety-six ADHD children, Horn and colleagues (1991) examined the additive and interactive effects of methylphenidate (placebo, low-, and high-dose) and two psychosocial treatment groups (none vs. parent behavioral training and child self-control training [PT/SC]). Results showed significant main effects for medication and PT/SC status, and a significant interaction of medication status x PT/SC for teacher (but not parent) behavior ratings. Moreover, teacher Hyperkinesis Index ratings showed significant interactions with medication x PT/SC status over time. These findings were most consistent with the interpretation that placebo, low dose, and placebo plus PT/SC did not yield meaningful pre-post improvements. In addition, findings suggest that low dose + PT/SC condition was equivalent to the high dose alone and high dose with PT/SC conditions. In addition, in post hoc analyses, PT/SC + low dose proved significantly superior to low dose only. In contrast to these promising findings, direct child measures showed significant main effects for medication status only, including academic measures, children's self-concept, continuous performance task measures, and observational ratings.

Interestingly, at nine months posttreatment, Ialongo et al. (1993) assessed seventy-one of their original ninety-six subjects. Their follow-up findings indicated that children receiving the behavioral PT/SC treatment showed continued accumulation of parent-reported benefits after the end of treatment, compared to medication-only subjects who showed either no further gains or even modest deterioration.

Small-Sample Studies

Cognitive Treatment Plus Medication vs. Medication Alone. The attempts of these largest and most rigorous short-term studies have been mirrored by a number of other studies of comparable length, but smaller sample size. Abikoff and Gittelman-Klein (1985) developed a sixteen-week cognitive training program for ADHD children in which they compared the effectiveness of three methods of treatment. All fifty subjects received a stimulant medication twice daily, none exceeding 80 mg/day of methylphenidate (MPH), 50 mg/day of dextroamphetamine, or 150 mg/day of pemoline. In addition to medication alone as a randomly assigned treatment, children were also either given cognitive training or treatment of similar intensity but with no presumed active therapeutic components ("attentional control therapy"). Outcome measures included teacher and parent reports and achievement and cognitive tests. No differential effects were noted by any of these standards; neither attention control nor cognitive training provided any benefits over medication alone. Moreover, during a four-week follow-up it was noted that cognitive training did not facilitate discontinuation of active medication. This study lacked a treatment arm testing the psychosocial treatments with pill placebo, which would have elucidated any potential benefits over no treatment at all.

Behavior Treatment With and Without Medication. In an earlier study, Gittelman-Klein et al. (1976) did compare behavior therapy (BT) with and without medication to stimulant treatment alone. This previous study was only half the duration, and had just thirty-six ADHD children. Subjects were randomly assigned to a treatment group, and those scheduled for medication received 10 mg/day MPH for the first week, after which their doses were individually titrated. In the tradition of operant conditioning, BT implemented positive reinforcement at home and in school. Results indicate no significant differences between medication alone versus in combination with BT, even though teachers rated the former group as more inattentive and observers found them to be more disruptive. Regardless, both these treatments proved superior to BT with placebo.

The authors noted that behavior therapy might have proven more potent given more time, thereby underscoring one of the advantages of long-term treatment studies. Another question that remains unanswered by this study is whether the dosage of medication can be lowered due to supplementation with psychosocial treatment. The plausibility of this interactive enhancement was suggested by the findings of Horn and colleagues in 1991, described previously.

Dose-Reduction Study. To further examine this "dose-reduction" hypothesis, Carlson, Pelham, Milich, and Dixon (1992) designed a 2 x 3 factorial medication crossover study capable of testing the usefulness of behavioral modification (BM) therapy in reducing stimulant dosage required to obtain clinical benefit. For each child they tested the effects of placebo (PBO), low (0.3 mg/kg), and high (0.6 mg/kg) doses of MPH (presented in a randomized order on separate days), in combination with either a regular classroom setting or a token economy classroom with daily home report cards. As twenty-four boys went through an eight-week summer treatment program, their progress was evaluated according to behavior ratings, academic measures, and self-reports of performance. Overall, MPH improved the greatest number of outcome measures, regardless of classroom setting. However, the MPH low dose was equivalent to BM + PBO for behavioral effects. When combined with BM, the low and high doses affected on-task and disruptive behavior equally well, suggesting that in some instances BM may reduce the amount of stimulant required to achieve maximum benefit. Lack of statistical power precludes definitive conclusions in this regard, however.

Medication With and Without Auditory Feedback or Contingency Management. Solanto, Wender, and Bartell (1997) designed a study combining a medication condition of either MPH or placebo with a behavioral intervention of either auditory feedback or contingencies. A modified continuous performance test (CPT) measured sustained attention, and also provided feedback dependent on each child's responses. With the reward of earning a toy in mind, children received pennies for right answers and lost them for wrong answers. Of the twenty-two children who participated in the four test sessions, more than half had various comorbidities. MPH improved attention span by reducing disinhibited and off-task behaviors but combining medication with contingencies provided no additional benefit. Contingency treatment enabled subjects to discriminate between target and false targets better than feedback plus placebo; however, attention span showed no enhancement due to treatment with either of these conditions. The results of this study support the general consensus that stimulant medication is generally more effective than behavioral strategies for the treatment of ADHD, and that combined approaches offer few if any advantages over medication alone.

Durability of Treatment

Although these findings are encouraging, are they durable? After only several months of investigation, any conclusions drawn about the malleability of ADHD behaviors are precarious at best. This was evinced by a duet of studies conducted by Brown and colleagues in 1985 and 1986. In the original experiment, thirty ADHD children were randomly assigned to either cognitive training (CT in combination with 0.3 mg/kg MPH, or stimulant medication alone. A group of ten children who had been on a wait list at the clinic comprised the nontreatment group. After three months, CT + MPH and MPH alone equally improved ratings of attention, whereas CT alone achieved only slightly better results than did the control group. Only treatment with MPH improved behavior, although none of the treatments made a difference in academic measures. Subjects continued on medication through posttest assessment in this study, which limited the interpretation of findings. The study was repeated the following year with a slightly different twist in order to remedy this limitation; medication was discontinued before posttesting. This time, Brown and colleagues found that medication effects dissipated rapidly. Unhappily, in their 1993 follow-up, Ialongo and colleagues found similarly discouraging results.

The only other study that was reviewed with a comparable follow-up period was conducted by Firestone, Crowe, Goodman, and McGrath (1986). By random assignment, seventy-three children were placed in a group receiving either parent training (PT) with medication, PT with placebo, or medication only. MPH doses were titrated to the optimal dose, which ranged between 10 and 30 mg/day. Parents participating in PT read a book on child management and then joined a group that discussed childrearing behavior management principles. The outcome measures applied during these three months included mean reaction time, impulsivity, academics, and behavior ratings. No advantage was found for PT with medication over medication alone, but both treatments proved more effective for decreasing hyperactivity and reaction time than PT with placebo. In concurrence with the findings of Brown, Wynne, and Medenis (1985), none of the treatments significantly affected academic performance.

For the one-year follow-up, the rate of attrition averaged 40 percent. The following year only 22 percent of the initial subjects remained; no significant difference was found between the three groups. Firestone et al. (1986) suggested that the high dropout rate could have been responsible for the discrepancy between primary and subsequent results, but another explanation consistent with the other studies noted earlier is that behavioral gains are apparent only as long as the child is maintained on medication.

Studies Favoring Combined Treatment Over Medication Alone in the Minority

Discrepancy is, however, inherent to the process of scientific investigation. The studies in our review generally favor medication over any other combination or permutation of treatments, but a subset of the fifteen is not in accordance with this trend. The leading alternative trend is that a combined therapy of medication and psychosocial treatment is superior to either option alone.

In a crossover factorial design, Hinshaw, Henker, and Whalen (1984) tested medication or placebo versus cognitive-behavioral self-evaluation (CBT) or extrinsic reinforcement. As part of a five-week summer program, twenty-four boys were tested twice during one of the weeks and rated by direct observers on measures of appropriate and negative social interactions. Results indicated that CBT with medication was the optimal treatment, yet only the condition of extrinsic reinforcement plus placebo fared significantly worse than all the others. Only groups receiving medication reported enhanced accuracy of self-evaluation. The critically weakening element of the design of this study is its extremely short duration. Results from two days of investigation cannot reasonably be generalized to longer periods.

In a more recent study, Long, Rickert, and Ashcraft (1993) reported data that support the conclusions of Hinshaw and colleagues. Thirty-two families took part in this two-month study, in which all ADHD children were receiving MPH. The experimental group consisted of parents reading a written protocol, which outlined behavioral techniques for managing children's disruptive behavior. This additional "bibliotherapy" led to significant differences in the amount of difficult behavior reported at home as well as at school. A four- to six-week study of eighteen children by Thurston (1979) reached similar conclusions. As compared to a medication-only group and a wait-list group, PT plus medication resulted in greater decreases in activity level. No treatment groups showed any significant differences in ratings of impulsivity.

Despite their relatively modest sample sizes and brief treatment periods, these three studies collectively suggest that under some conditions, combined treatments may offer advantages over medication-only treatments for some outcomes of interest. In addition, these studies suggest that medication treatments alone are generally superior to psychosocial-only treatment over a range of short-term outcomes, when tested in head-to-head comparisons. These conclusions are consistent with the recently completed McMaster University Evidence-Based Practive Center (1998) report.

Though evidence for additive effects of medication and behavioral procedures has not always resulted from extant investigations, complementary benefits have been reported. Thus, medication may provide benefits in domains such as impulsivity or hyperactive behavior, whereas psychosocial interventions may improve behavior at home during unmedicated periods (Horn et al., 1991). As noted earlier, combined treatments have enabled a reduction in stimulant medication dosage needed for optimal behavior control in other studies (Horn et al., 1991; Pelham et al., 1988).

Although most studies to date suggest clear superiority of medication over behavioral treatments in the short term, as well as the possible incremental benefit of combination treatments over medication-only treatments under some conditions, it is not clear from these findings whether a treatment that is most effective in the short term offers similar advantages in the long term. Some clues to this possibility are found in the report by Ialongo et al. (1993), as they noted that children initially receiving the PT/SC treatments (with or without medication) during the four-month treatment period showed evidence of continuing gains at nine months posttreatment, compared to subjects receiving only medication, where no further gains or even modest deterioration was noted. Short-term studies suggest patterns that necessitate further testing to establish solid points of reference for actual application. Thus, examination of studies that have employed longer-term treatments is essential, both to examine the extent to which these longer-term treatments bode potentially different outcomes as a function of treatment duration as well as to take more fully into account the impact of various forms of treatment on ADHD children's development over time.

LONG-TERM TREATMENT STUDIES

A recent study by Schachar, Tannock, Cunningham, and Corkum (1997) is one of the few randomized treatment studies of relatively long duration. In a study of ninety-one children and their families, the authors compared the effectiveness of yearlong treatment with MPH plus PT, MPH plus parent self-help and advocacy (SH), placebo plus PT, and placebo plus SH. Although no evidence was found for the efficacy of the PT interventions, either alone or in combination with MPH, the study was hampered by a 50 percent crossover rate to active medication in the placebo groups, in part because parents had the latitude to request reassignment to the alternative treatment during the course of the study. In addition, the study suffered from difficulties with compliance (e.g., 25 percent of parents never attended any parenting sessions, and those attending averaged only 40 percent across all sessions). Other limitations included the twice-daily (morning and lunchtime), five-days-a-week MPH dosing regimen, perhaps accounting for the fact that few behavioral improvements were reported at home.

Hechtman and Abikoff (1995) conducted a twelve-month treatment study comparing stimulant alone, stimulant plus psychosocial placebo treatment, and stimulant plus active multimodal psychosocial treatment (PT/counseling, social skills training, academic skills assistance, and individual psychotherapy). Some 103 children participated in a twelve-month active treatment period. This treatment period was augmented by a twelve-month follow-up period during which subjects received monthly "booster sessions" to sustain the potential benefits of treatment.

Of note, this study failed to demonstrate any evidence of superiority of combined treatments over stimulant alone, whether at the twelve-, eighteen-, or twenty-four-month assessment points. Moreover, rechallenging children with placebo at eighteen and twenty-four months resulted almost universally in significant symptom relapse, regardless of which of the three groups to which the children had been assigned. However, definitive interpretation of the findings from this study may not be possible, given power limitations resulting from the small number of subjects per treatment group (thirty-three to thirty-four). In addition, there is some evidence that the two combined treatment groups had fewer children meeting ADHD criteria by the end of the study (10 percent for both, vs. 20 percent for the medication-only group). Also, inclusion in this study was limited to youngsters who had already demonstrated short-term benefit with MPH, precluding any head-to-head comparison of the two unimodal treatments. Consequently, the medication condition held a slight edge in subsequent comparisons. Furthermore, this study did not include intensive direct contingency management or a psychosocial-only treatment group, and children who met full criteria for conduct disorder were not eligible for inclusion in the study. Nonetheless, prior to the Multimodal Treatment of Children with ADHD study (the "MTA"; MTA Cooperative Group, 1999), the multimodal treatment study by Hechtman and Abikoff (1995) was the most intensive and well-designed investigation to date.

The MTA Study

Although the studies cited earlier were by and large grounded in sound method, they have provided somewhat inconsistent results. Design limitations in previous studies include short duration; small sample sizes; failure to include the most severely impaired, comorbid ADHD children; restriction of samples to stimulant responders; failure to include the most intensive behavioral therapy; and failure to compare alternative yet credible treatments. Thus, more definitive research information is needed to guide clinical practice and policy. The MTA, which included an intensive, integrated psychosocial treatment (alone and in combination with medication), was developed to (1) clarify the discrepant reports concerning relative merits of medication and psychosocial treatments, (2) test possible benefits of combined treatments over short- and long-term durations, and (3) compare these more intensive state-of-the-art treatments to the less intensive treatments generally available in the community. Five hundred seventy-nine ADHD children, ages 7 to 9, were treated at six different performance sites (ninety-six to ninety-eight per site). Subjects were randomly assigned to one of three manualized, intensive, fourteen-month treatments (medication plus brief supportive care, intensive behavioral treatment alone, or both) or to community standard care. Assessments included repeated measures (up to fourteen months) of core ADHD symptoms, aggression and oppositional-defiant symptoms, anxiety/depression, social skills, academic achievement, parenting measures, objective classroom observations and peer ratings, and videotaped, blindly scored ratings of parent-child interactions (Arnold et al., 1997; Greenhill et al., 1996).

Intensive Psychosocial/Behavioral Treatment vs. Medication Management. Random regression analyses yielded robust differences according to both parents and teachers, indicating the superiority of the medication management (MedMgt) versus behavioral treatment (Beh) for the inattention, hyperactivity-impulsivity, and oppositional/aggressive domains. However, for other domains (including parent- and teacher-reported social skills, as well as all children's reports), few to no significant differences were found between the medication management and behavior groups.

Combined Treatment vs. Unimodal Treatments. Random regression analyses indicated that combined treatment (Comb) is superior to Beh treatment for the inattentive, hyperactive-impulsive, and oppositional/aggressive symptom domains, according to both parent and teacher informants. In contrast, combined and medical management treatments differed on none of the ADHD symptom domains, according to both informants. Further, combined treatment was superior to behavioral treatment for parent-reported internalizing symptoms and social skills (in contrast to the medication management/behavioral comparison, which indicated no differences). However, combined treatment did not differ from either medication management or behavioral treatment for parenting problems from either parents' or children's perspectives.

MTA-Delivered Treatments vs. Community Standard Care. These analyses generally reveal that both combined and medication management treatments were superior to community standard care for inattentive, hyperactive-impulsive, oppositional/ aggressive, internalizing symptoms, and social skills, whereas behavioral treatment was not. The exceptions to this general rule were found with teachers' reports, which suggest superiority of behavioral treatment over community treatment for parent-child relations. Of note, 65 percent of community standard care subjects reported some medication use during the fourteen-month initial treatment period.

Summary of Findings. Overall MTA results indicate that sustained, combined, and medication-only treatments reduce symptoms of ADHD while enhancing social skills. In a few (but not most) areas of functioning (specifically, in non-ADHD symptom domains), combined approaches appear to be modestly superior to medication-only approaches. Likewise, medication management and behavioral treatments alone appear equivalent for most non-ADHD areas of functioning. Notably, this overall pattern of findings is also seen in the examination of objective (blinded) observers' ratings of children's classroom-based inattention, off-task, gross-motor, and aggressive behaviors, as well as nominations and ratings of peers of MTA children concerning their likability and friendship status. In these domains, combined and medication management treatment approaches appear comparable for most outcomes, and generally superior to behavioral and standard community treatments. Concerning academic achievement, however, only combined treatment proved superior to community standard treatments in achieving reading achievement gains on the Wechsler Individual Achievement Test (WIAT) over the fourteen-month course of treatment.

RESEARCH LIMITATIONS

Small Samples

Excluding the one exception noted previously (MTA), sample sizes of these studies were relatively modest, ranging from 18 to 103 subjects. Given the fact that most of these studies used at least three or four treatment groups, fourteen of fifteen have been underpowered to establish the presence of any incremental benefits of combination over unimodal treatments, unless such effects were moderate to large. For example, based on a review of established literature (Richter et al., 1995), the likely advantage of combined treatments (medication plus psychotherapy) over unimodal treatment has been estimated to have an effect size d = ~ 0.4, over and above the already substantial and well-established effect size d = 1.0 of stimulant medication versus placebo. With alpha set at .05, beta = .20, power = .80, with an assumed effect size d = .40 for any two-group contrast (i.e., unimodal vs. combined treatment, one-tailed comparison), seventy-five or more subjects would be needed per treatment arm. Even this small to moderate estimated effect size may be generous, given the probability that only a subgroup of children would show a substantial incremental benefit from the combined versus unimodal treatments. Of note, the only study to date that has had sufficient power to examine unimodal versus additive effects, as well as to explore which subgroups might require combined treatments, is the recently completed MTA study (Arnold et al., 1997; Greenhill et al., 1996; Jensen et al., 2001; MTA Cooperative Group, 1999).

Short Duration of Most Studies

A second major difficulty with treatment studies to date has been the fact that most have been relatively short term, with treatments lasting generally no more than three months. Only two studies have spanned a longer active treatment period—the Multimodal Treatment (MMT) study by Hechtman and Abikoff (1995) (twelve months active treatment), and the MTA (fourteen months active treatment). The longer time to assess treatment outcomes is of great interest, because among the critical outcomes of ADHD and its treatments one must include the onset and maintenance of comorbidities, such as oppositional and conduct problems, school failure, decreased self-esteem, and substance use. An exclusive focus on ADHD symptoms alone is insufficient to examine the more wide-ranging and far-reaching outcomes of clinical interest.

Insufficiently Intensive Psychosocial Treatment

A third difficulty with comparative treatment studies to date consists of the fact that most psychosocial treatments have not been sufficiently intensive. Given the well-known difficulties with generalization and maintenance of psychosocial treatment effects (Richters et al., 1995), the likelihood that any relatively modest, single-setting, short-term psychosocial treatment would be sufficiently robust to secure longer-term benefits is highly questionable. Of note, only the MMT and MTA studies have been of sufficient intensity to offer some promise of maintenance of treatment gains after the immediate treatment period.

Treatments Not Adjusted to Subject-Specific Needs

A fourth difficulty with studies to date is that most have not optimally adjusted the treatment, whether medication or behavioral, to the child's specific level and type of symptoms. In the case of medication, this would require some form of individual titration to achieve optimal symptom control, versus standard dosing procedures (mg/kg, fixed dose, etc.). With psychosocial/behavioral treatments, this would require the careful selection of target symptoms and behaviors, toward which the psychosocial treatments should be directed. Only five of the fifteen studies noted earlier conducted individual titration of medication to achieve an optimal response for each child, and only the MTA and Hechtman and Abikoff (1995) studies conducted this titration under double-blind conditions.

SUMMARY AND CONCLUSION

Generally speaking, careful medication management alone appears consistently superior to psychosocial-only behavioral treatments across all studies that have conducted rigorous head-to-head comparisons of ADHD symptoms. However, the superiority of medication management over behavioral treatments for other areas of functioning (i.e., non-ADHD symptoms) is not well established. Across studies, combined and medication management approaches usually appear comparable in achieving short- and long-term treatment gains, although there is evidence in three of the four most rigorous studies conducted to date (Horn et al., 1991; Klein & Abikoff, 1997; MTA Study, 1999) that for some outcomes, combined treatments may offer modest advantages over medication strategies alone.

FUTURE RESEARCH NEEDS

Further follow-up analyses of the long-term outcomes of the MTA subjects will be needed to determine whether behavioral or combined treatments offer increasing advantages over medication management strategies as subjects mature. If this proves to be the case, which types of outcomes will be affected? It would be interesting to note how one therapy might be better than another for one outcome while the opposite effect holds for another outcome. Understanding the basis for differential effects will invariably enlighten our comprehension of the myriad facets of ADHD. Consequently, depending on which aspects of ADHD each subject manifests, the most beneficial form of treatment could then be implemented. This could be ascertained by careful exploration of which subjects benefit most from which forms of treatment. For example, if a subset of subjects with certain characteristics (e.g., comorbidity) can be shown to specifically require and benefit from the combined and behavioral treatments, substantial benefits to these patients may accrue by targeting such treatments to their specific needs. Research along these lines could help determine the importance of fitting a specific treatment to each child and family, versus a "one-size-fits-all" approach.

In addition, other forms of psychotherapy should be considered and tested as alternatives to strictly behavioral programs. Our clinical experience suggests that under some circumstances, behavioral therapies can provoke irritation or other untoward effects in a subset of children. For example, if a child is resistant to a form of psychosocial treatment, such an impasse might be comparable to the negative side effects some children experience on medication. Further studies are needed that explore other psychotherapeutic approaches, again with the goal of finding the best form of therapy based on a particular family's needs, attitudes, and values.

Although most studies suggest that careful medication management should be a core component of an effective ADHD treatment strategy, it is unclear whether its benefits derive solely from the properties of the drug itself or to the combination of medication, parent guidance, encouragement to maintain compliance, and ongoing medication adjustments when required. For the sake of simplicity and cost-effectiveness, a simple refill might seem preferable to a more intensive and attentive ongoing relationship with the care provider. However, the latter treatment may offer advantages which cannot be compromised.

The question of effectiveness is equally significant in the course of any treatment program. For some families, intensive behavioral treatments may be difficult to implement, even when such treatments are efficacious. The ultimate test of research findings is feasibility, palatability, and applicability in the real world. Thus, effective treatment strategies must be made available to care providers in such a way that they can be properly implemented. Further, they must be affordable, which necessitates a thorough cost-benefit analysis of less versus more intensive treatments. Similarly, explicit and "doable" guidelines and policies need to be established to guide the practices of physicians, other health care providers, and third-party payers.

References

Abikoff, H., & Gittelman-Klein, R. (1985). The normalizing effects of methylphenidate on the classroom behavior of hyperactive children. *Journal of Abnormal Child Psychology, 13*, 33–44.

Arnold, L. E., Abikoff, H. B., Cantwell, D. P., Conners, C. K., Elliott, G., Greenhill, L. L., Hechtman, L., Hinshaw, S. P., Hoza, B., Jensen, P. S., Kraemer, H., March, J., Newcorn, J., Pelham, W. E., Richters, J., Severe, J. B., Schiller, E., Swanson, J. M., Vereen, D., & Wells, K. (1997). National Institute of Mental Health Collaborative Multimodal Treatment Study of Children with ADHD (MTA): Design challenges and choices. *Archives of General Psychiatry, 54*, 865–870.

Brown, R. T., Borden, K. A., Wynne, M. E., Schleser, R., & Clingerman, S. R. (1986). Methylphenidate and cognitive therapy with ADD children: A methodologic reconsideration. *Journal of Abnormal Child Psychology, 14*, 481–497.

Brown, R. T., Wynne, M. E., & Medenis, R. (1985). Methylphenidate and cognitive therapy: A comparison of treatment approaches with hyperactive boys. *Journal of Abnormal Child Psychology, 13*, 69–87.

Carlson, C. L., Pelham, W. E., Milich, R., & Dixon, J. (1992). Single and combined effects of methylphenidate and behavior therapy on the classroom performance of children with attention-deficit hyperactivity disorder. *Journal of Abnormal Child Psychology, 20*, 213–232.

Firestone, P., Crowe, D., Goodman, J. T., & McGrath, P. (1986). Vicissitudes of follow-up studies: Differential effects of parent training and stimulant medication with hyperactives. *American Journal of Orthopsychiatry, 56*, 184–194.

Gittelman-Klein, R., Klein, D. F., Abikoff, H., Katz, S., Gloisten, A. C., & Kates, W. (1976). Relative efficacy of methylphenidate and behavior modification in hyperkinetic children: An interim report. *Journal of Abnormal Child Psychology, 4*, 361–379.

Greenhill, L. L., Abikoff, H. B., Arnold, L. E., Cantwell, D. P., Conners, C. K., Elliott, G., Hechtman, L., Hinshaw, S. P., Hoza, B., Jensen, P. S., March, J. S., Newcorn, J., Pelham, W. E., Severe, J. B., Swanson, J. M., Vitiello, B., & Wells, K. (1996). Medication treatment strategies in the MTA study: Relevance to clinicians and researchers. *Journal of the American Academy of Child and Adolescent Psychiatry, 35*, 1304–1313.

Hechtman, L., & Abikoff, H. (1995, October). *Multimodal treatment plus stimulants vs. stimulant treatment in ADHD children: Results from a two-year comparative treatment study.* Paper presented at the annual meeting of the American Academy of Child and Adolescent Psychiatry. New Orleans, LA.

Hinshaw, S. P., Henker, B., & Whalen, C. K. (1984). Self-control in hyperactive boys in anger-inducing situations: Effects of cognitive-behavioral training and of methylphenidate. *Journal of Abnormal Child Psychology, 12*, 55–77.

Horn, W. F., Ialongo, N. S., Pascoe, J. M., Greenberg, G., Packard, T., Lopez, M., Wagner, A., &

Puttler, L. (1991). Additive effects of psychostimulants, parent training, and self-control therapy with ADHD children. *Journal of the American Academy of Child and Adolescent Psychiatry, 30*(2), 233–240.

Ialongo, N. S., Horn, W. F., Pascoe, J. M., Greenberg, G., Packard, T., Lopez, M., Wagner, A., & Puttler, L. (1993). The effects of a multimodal intervention with attention-deficit hyperactivity disorder children: A 9-month follow-up. *Journal of the American Academy of Child and Adolescent Psychiatry, 32*, 182–189.

Jensen, P. S., Hinshaw, S. P., Swanson, J. M., Greenhill, L. L., Conners, C. K., Arnold, L. E., Abikoff, H. B., Elliott, G., Hechtman, L., Hoza, B., March, J. S., Newcorn, J. H., Pelham, W. E., Severe, J. B., Vitiello, B., Wells, K., & Wigal, T. (2001). Findings from the NIMH multimodal treatment study of ADHD (MTA). *Journal of Developmental and Behavioral Pediatrics, 22*, 1–14.

Klein, R. G., & Abikoff, H. (1997). Behavior therapy and methylphenidate in the treatment of children with ADHD. *Journal of Attention Disorders, 2*, 89–114.

Long, N., Rickert, V. I., & Ashcraft, E. W. (1993). Bibliotherapy as an adjunct to stimulant medication in the treatment of attention-deficit hyperactivity disorder. *Journal of Pediatric Health Care, 7*, 82–88.

McMaster University Evidence-Based Practice Center. (1998). *The treatment of attention-deficit/hyperactivity disorder: An evidence report* (Contract No. 290–97–0017). Rockville, MD: Agency for Health Care Policy and Research.

MTA Cooperative Group. (1999). A 14-month randomized clinical trial of treatment strategies for attention-deficit/hyperactivity disorder: Multimodal Treatment Study of Children with ADHD. *Archives of General Psychiatry, 56*(12), 1073–1086.

Pelham, W. E., Carlson, C. L., Sams, S. E., Vallano, G., Dixon, M. J., & Hoza, B. (1993). Separate and combined effects of methylphenidate and behavior modification on boys with ADHD in the classroom. *Journal of Consulting and Clinical Psychology, 61*(3), 506–515.

Pelham, W. E., Schnedler, R. W., Bender, M. E., Miller, J., Nilsson, D., Budrow, M., Ronnei, M., Paluchowski, C., & Marks, D. (1988). The combination of behavior therapy and methylphenidate in the treatment of hyperactivity: A therapy outcome study. In L. Bloomingdale (Ed.), *Attention deficit disorders* (Vol. 3, pp. 29–48). London: Pergamon Press.

Richters, J. E., Arnold, L. E., Jensen, P. S., Abikoff, H., Conners, C. K., Greenhill, L. L., Hechtman, L., Hinshaw, S. P., Pelham, W. E., & Swanson, J. M. (1995). NIMH collaborative multisite multimodal treatment study of children with ADHD: I. Background and rationale. *Journal of the American Academy of Child and Adolescent Psychiatry, 34*, 987–1000.

Satterfield, J. H., Cantwell, D. P., & Satterfield, B. T. (1979). Multimodality treatment: A one-year follow-up of 84 hyperactive boys. *Archives of General Psychiatry, 36*, 965–974.

Satterfield, J. H., Satterfield, B. T., & Cantwell, D. P. (1981). Three-year multimodality treatment study of 100 hyperactive boys. *Journal of Pediatrics, 98*, 650–655.

Satterfield, J. H., Satterfield, B. T., & Schell, A. M. (1987). Therapeutic interventions to prevent delinquency in hyperactive boys. *Journal of the American Academy of Child and Adolescent Psychiatry, 26*, 56–64.

Schachar, R. J., Tannock, R., Cunningham, C., & Corkum, P. V. (1997). Behavioral, situational, and temporal effects of treatment of ADHD with methylphenidate. *Journal of the American Academy of Child and Adolescent Psychiatry, 36*, 754–763.

Solanto, M. V., Wender, E. H., & Bartell, S. S. (1997). Effects of methylphenidate and behavioral contingencies on sustained attention in attention-deficit hyperactivity disorder: A test of the reward dysfunction hypothesis. *Journal of Child and Adolescent Psychopharmacology, 7*, 123–136.

Thurston, L. P. (1979). Comparison of the effects of parent training and of Ritalin in treating hyperactive children. *International Journal of Mental Health, 8*, 121–128.

Chapter 15

Matching Patients to Treatments

by Howard Abikoff, Ph.D.

Introduction 15-1
ADHD and Disruptive Behaviors 15-2
    Response to MPH Treatment 15-2
    Stimulant vs. Psychosocial Treatment 15-3
ADHD and Anxiety Disorders 15-4
    Response to Medication 15-4
    Stimulant vs. Psychosocial Treatment 15-5
ADHD and Comorbidity Patterns 15-7
ADHD and Mood Disorders 15-7
ADHD and Mental Retardation 15-8
ADHD Subtypes 15-9
Recommendations for Clinical Practice 15-9
    Children Who Clearly Benefit From Stimulant Treatment 15-10
    Treatment of Children With Internalizing Problems 15-10
    When Psychosocial Treatment Is Indicated 15-10
    Gray Areas 15-11
Recommendations for Future Research 15-11

INTRODUCTION

A primary goal in working with individuals with attention deficit hyperactivity disorder (ADHD) is to optimize the match between patients and treatments. This is a fundamental clinical issue for a number of reasons. First, as attested to in the voluminous treatment literature (see Chapter 13, this volume; Hinshaw, Klein, & Abikoff, 1998; Spencer et al., 1996) there are a host of treatment strategies available in the ADHD clinical armamentarium. By far, the best studied of these approaches are pharmacotherapy (especially stimulant treatment), psychosocial treatment (particularly behavioral interventions), and multimodal interventions, which combine pharmacological and behavioral treatment. Second, for many individuals with ADHD, no one treatment, including stimulant medication, results consistently in improvement across all key functional domains. Third, ADHD is associated with a wide range of comorbid conditions (Biederman, Newcorn, & Sprich, 1991; Jensen, Martin, & Cantwell, 1997). The high rate of comorbidities, coupled with individual differences in other salient child and family characteristics, increases the need for guidelines regarding matching individual patients with the most appropriate treatment regimen.

Knowledge about matching patients to treatments is gleaned most directly from three classes of studies in the ADHD treatment literature. In the first, specific types of patients are treated to test theoretical and/or clinical hypotheses. Patients who differ on the characteristic of interest (e.g., comorbid diagnosis and diagnostic subtype) are randomized to the study treatment arms. Treatment by subject interaction effects is paramount and denotes whether there are differential treatment effects as a function of patient type.

A second class of studies consists of controlled trials that report on differential treatment effects on specific aspects of functioning (e.g., aggression). These studies provide heuristic information regarding matching patients to treatments.

The third class of studies, relatively rare in the treatment literature across all childhood psychiatric disorders, is potentially more far-reaching in its detection of treatment by patient interactions. Noteworthy features of these studies include treatment randomization, large sample sizes, narrow exclusion criteria which facilitate sample heterogeneity, broad-based recruitment strategies, a comprehensive, multimethod, multi-informant assessment battery, and several treatment arms. When sufficiently powered, such studies can evaluate the effects of several moderators, separately and combined, on treatment response, and can be especially informative regarding which types of patients respond optimally, in which domains, to which kind of treatment. Illustrative examples are found in the depression treatment literature, where patient-by-treatment interactions have been reported for patient factors such as initial symptom severity (Elkin et al., 1995), and referral source (Brent et al., 1998). The National Institute of Health (NIMH) Multimodal Treatment Study of Children with ADHD (Arnold et al., 1997; MTA Cooperative Group, 1998), in which 579 7–9-year-old children with ADHD were randomized to pharmacotherapy alone, psychosocial treatment alone, the treatment combination, or community treatment, is the only ADHD clinical trial with all of these study design features. MTA results that have relevance regarding matching patients to treatments are included in the literature review which follows.

ADHD AND DISRUPTIVE BEHAVIORS

Overt and covert conduct problems, as well as oppositional behavior, are common in ADHD, and the disorder is associated with high rates of comorbid conduct disorder (CD) and oppositional defiant disorder (ODD). In light of the increased dysfunction associated with these comorbid conditions (Kuhne, Schachar, & Tannock, 1997), and the fact that the continued co-occurrence of conduct problems is associated with higher rates of negative outcomes (Barkley, Fischer, Edelbrook, & Smallish, 1990; Herrero, Hechtman, & Weiss, 1994), there is clinical import in identifying effective treatments for disruptive ADHD youngsters.

Response to MPH Treatment

Several studies have evaluated whether youngsters defined as aggressive or nonaggressive on the basis of teacher or parent ratings respond differentially to methylphenidate (MPH). A double-blind, placebo-controlled crossover study found that children with ADHD with high or low teacher ratings on the IOWA (inattention, overactivity, with or without aggression) Conners Aggression Scale, an index of oppositional behavior, demonstrated similar improvements in behavioral measures of clinical functioning, in their performance on a laboratory vigilance task, and in ERP cognitive processing measures (Klorman et al., 1988). Decreases in IOWA Aggression ratings were found in the "aggressive" but not in the "not aggressive" subgroup. As noted by the authors, floor effects on the IOWA Aggression scale prevented the detection of change in the nonaggressive youngsters.

Similar MPH response profiles in aggressive and nonaggressive youngsters have also been reported by Barkley, McMurray, Edelbrook, and Robbins (1989) using a double-blind, placebo-controlled crossover design employing two doses of MPH (0.3 mg/kg and 0.5 mg/kg). Aggressive and nonaggressive youngsters, defined by parent ratings on the Aggressive scale of the Child Behavior Checklist (CBCL), demonstrated significant improvements on a host of behavioral and laboratory measures with both doses of MPH. Reductions in aggressive behavior with MPH have been reported in a number of studies (Hinshaw, 1991), and appear to be a robust finding.

Stimulant treatment has been evaluated not only in ADHD youngsters with elevated rates of aggressive/oppositional behavior, but in children with a comorbid disruptive behavior disorder as well. A recent parallel group placebo-controlled study evaluated the efficacy of short-term treatment (five weeks) with MPH in youngsters comorbid for ADHD and CD (Klein et al., 1997). Clear benefits were found for stimulant treatment. There were significant reductions in multiple aspects of CD, including overt and covert antisocial behavior. These findings have also been demonstrated with longer-term MPH treatment (one year) (Klein & Abikoff, 1994), and denote that stimulant medication holds promise as an important treatment component in patients with comorbid CD.

Stimulant vs. Psychosocial Treatment

The findings from two randomized clinical trials that evaluated medication and behavioral interventions are informative regarding the treatment of associated disruptive behaviors in ADHD. The first compared the efficacy of 12 months of treatment with MPH alone vs. MPH combined with either intensive multimodal or placebo (attention control) psychosocial treatment (Hechtman & Abikoff, 1995). The participants were 103 7-9 year old children with ADHD, all of whom demonstrated short-term benefit with MPH prior to study initiation. All children were on a three-times-a-day MPH dosing regimen throughout the yearlong course of the study. Psychosocial treatment targeted the children and parents. Children received social skills training, individual psychotherapy, and academic organizational skills training followed by remedial tutoring. Parents participated in behavior management training and parent counseling and implemented a home-based reinforcement program for school and home behavior. Despite the breadth of psychosocial treatment, MPH alone was found to be as effective as combined treatment in decreasing observed classroom aggressive behavior, oppositional behaviors, and decreased the percentage of children who met diagnostic criteria for ODD.

The second trial compared the efficacy of eight weeks of MPH, clinical behavior therapy (which included parent management training, a home token economy, teacher training and consultation in contingency management techniques) or the treatment combination in eighty-nine 6–12-year-old youngsters with ADHD (Klein & Abikoff, 1997). Here too, there were significant and equivalent reductions in the rate of observed aggressive classroom behavior, not only with MPH alone and combined treatment, but also with clinical behavior therapy alone. Teacher ratings of children's aggressive behavior initiated toward peers also indicated significant and similar reductions in the MPH and behavior therapy alone groups. Notably, there was some support for the relative superiority of combined treatment in curtailing aggressiveness. The treatment combination resulted in significantly greater reductions in teachers' ratings of the initiation of aggressive behavior compared to behavior therapy alone, with the reduction in the combined group approaching significance in comparison with MPH alone.

ADHD AND ANXIETY DISORDERS

Anxiety disorders co-occur in approximately 25 percent of clinic-referred children with ADHD (Biederman et al., 1991). There are conflicting reports as to whether the comorbid condition occurs more often in youngsters with the inattentive subtype of ADHD. As noted by Tannock (2000), the anxiety profile in youngsters with ADHD and an anxiety disorder is quite similar to the profile of youngsters with a diagnosis of anxiety alone. Similarly, there appears to be little difference in the presentation of ADHD symptomatology in comorbid children compared to those with ADHD alone. When such differences are reported, they are likely a reflection of sampling issues, including the presence or absence of other comorbid conditions, such as conduct disorder or learning diabilities.

Response to Medication

Notwithstanding the similarities in symptom profiles, some reports indicate that anxious and nonanxious children with ADHD have a somewhat different stimulant response profile. Compared to nonanxious ADHD youngsters, children with a diagnosed comorbid anxiety disorder (or with high levels of self-reported anxiety), demonstrate less improvement in working memory (Tannock, Ickowitz, & Schachar, 1995), and show alterations in diastolic blood pressure with stimulant medication (Urman, Ickowitz, Fulford, & Tannock, 1995).

The findings regarding the behavioral response of "anxious" ADHD children to stimulants are less clear-cut. It is conceivable that the inconsistencies across studies result, in part, from the use of different diagnostic and dosing procedures, and the length of time on stimulant treatment. Taylor et al. (1987) evaluated the response to MPH in a double-blind placebo-controlled crossover study with thirty-eight boys with serious behavior problems, twenty-four of whom met criteria for ADDH (attention deficit disorder with hyperactivity according to the third edition of Diagnostic and Statistical Manual of Mental Disorders (DSM-III; American Psychiatric Association, 1980). Each treatment condition lasted for three weeks, with a flexible dosing schedule, to a maximum of 30 mg/d. Severity of the children's "emotional symptoms," based on parent interview, was found to be a predictor of treatment response. Youngsters with higher levels of anxiety and depression showed less benefit with stimulant treatment than those without internalizing problems. Notably, only three youngsters met diagnostic criteria for "disturbance of emotions specific to childhood" according to the ninth edition of *International Statistical Classification of Diseases and Related Health Problems* (ICD-9; World Health Organization, 1978); it is unknown how many met DSM criteria for an anxiety disorder.

Others have also reported an attenuated stimulant response in children with ADHD with high levels of parent rated internalizing problems (DuPaul, Barkley, & McMurray, 1994). Forty youngsters with ADHD with varying levels of internalizing problems were exposed to three doses of MPH in a double-blind, placebo-controlled study, with one week at each condition. The large majority of children with low or borderline levels of internalizing problems showed a positive response to MPH. In contrast, 25 percent of those high in internalizing problems were deemed to be nonresponders, and another 25 percent had an adverse response to MPH, as indicated by deterioration in their classroom functioning with active medication.

In contrast to studies that entered children on the basis of ratings or reports of internalizing or emotional problems, three studies included youngsters with diagnosed anxiety disorders. Diamond, Tannock, and Schachar (1999) compared the response of thirty-four nonanxious ADHD children after one year of MPH treatment to the response of twenty children, ten of whom had self-rated anxiety scores above the clinical cutoff on the Revised Children's Manifest Anxiety Scale (RCMAS; $N = 10$), and ten of whom met DSM-III-R (American Psychiatric Association, 1987) criteria for overanxious, separation anxiety or avoidant disorder, based on a parent interview schedule developed by the authors. Children in all three subgroups improved equivalently in measures of aggression, attention, hyperactivity, oppositionality, and academic achievement. The only exceptions were that parent-reported anxious children showed significantly less improvement than did the other subgroups in teacher ratings of hyperactivity on the IOWA Conners scale (the groups did not differ on other teacher measures of hyperactivity). In addition, there were differential changes on some but not all measures of anxiety. Specifically, whereas none of the subgroups improved in parent ratings of anxiety, and all three subgroups showed similar decreases in teacher ratings of anxiety, only the self-reported anxious children showed a substantial decrease in their levels of self-reported anxiety on the RCMAS. A regression to the mean effect is a possible explanation for the latter finding.

A double-blind, placebo-controlled study evaluated the response to MPH in forty-three elementary school children with ADHD, thirteen of whom met DSM-III-R criteria for overanxious disorder, based on interviews with the children (Pliszka, 1989). The children remained on each condition (placebo, low and high dose MPH) for a week. Teacher ratings, as well as laboratory observations of ADHD related behaviors while the children worked on arithmetic problems, suggested a less robust response to stimulants in the comorbid compared to the non-comorbid group. The results need to be tempered, however, because of a relatively high placebo response rate in the overanxious subgroup, which appears to have contributed considerably to the reported subgroup differences.

Stimulant vs. Psychosocial Treatment

As noted previously, the recently completed MTA study, which included fourteen months of treatment, randomized children to four study arms: medication management, behavioral treatment, the combination of medication management and behavioral treatment, or community treatment. Medication management consisted of a number of features, beginning with careful titration with MPH for each child (Greenhill et al., 1996). Algorithms were then used to select each child's optimal dosage regimen, or to systematically test other drugs, if needed, to achieve an adequate response (The order in which medications were tried was methylphenidate, dextroamphetamine, pemoline, imipramine). This was followed by monthly maintenance visits, in which assessments of clinical functioning (including side effects, and teacher and parent reports) guided any necessary dosage adjustments. Brief parent education and support was also provided during each monthly visit.

The MTA behavioral treatment arm, a treatment regimen that bridged two school years, included three integrated treatment components:

1. Parent behavior management training;

2. A school-based intervention consisting of a paraprofessional behavioral aide, teacher consultation in classroom behavior management techniques, and a Daily Report Card (DRC), individualized for each child, and completed by the teacher. (children were rewarded at home by their parents for meeting DRC goals); and

3. An eight-week intensive summer treatment program for the children.

Complete details of the MTA psychosocial treatment interventions are detailed elsewhere (Wells et al., 2000).

The MTA study design, coupled with the large sample size ($N = 579$) and rate of comorbid anxiety (34 percent, excluding specific phobia and obsessive-compulsive disorder), enabled a test of the hypothesis, heretofore unexamined, that comorbid anxiety predicts worse response to treatment with medication alone, and a better response to psychosocial treatment. The first part of this hypothesis was not supported by the study findings (MTA Cooperative Group, 1999). Within the medication management arm (in which the large majority of children were treated with MPH), youngsters with and without a comorbid anxiety disorder improved similarly with pharmacological treatment. For all study outcome domains, including core ADHD symptoms, conduct problems, anxiety, social skills, and academic achievement, the presence of an anxiety disorder did not moderate the children's response to medication.

The results regarding a hypothesized differential response to behavioral treatment in anxious children were less straightforward. Although the children's anxiety status did not differentially affect treatment outcome for most domains, parents' ratings of children's internalizing problems, and of ADHD symptomatology, were moderated by the presence of an anxiety disorder, as were children's self-ratings of anxiety. For all three parent measures, contrasts between the medication management and behavioral treatment arms were significant. Although the level of improvement was greater overall in the medication compared to psychosocial arms, inspection of the triple interactions indicated differences in the rate of improvement in the two treatment groups as a function of children's anxiety status. Specifically, in nonanxious children, there was a relatively shallow rate of change with behavioral treatment, whereas the rate of change was considerably steeper in behaviorally treated anxious youngsters. In contrast, among youngsters in the medication management group, the relative rate of change was similarly steep in those with and without an anxiety disorder. Thus, at least in some aspects of functioning, the relative advantage of medication management versus behavioral treatment appears to be moderated somewhat in children with an anxiety disorder. Clearly, replication of these MTA study findings is needed. Additional comments about this issue are included in the section below on clinical recommendations.

ADHD AND COMORBIDITY PATTERNS

Most recently, within the MTA study, Jensen et al. (2001) explored the impact of comorbidity patterns (i.e., the impact of various forms of comorbidity when they do or do not overlap with each other). Thus, grouping children into ADHD-only, ADHD with anxiety-only (anxiety or depressive disorders, but no disruptive behavior disorders such as CD or ODD), children with CD/ODD-only (children with CD or ODD but no anxiety or depressive disorders) and children with both forms of comorbidity (ADHD + Anxiety + CD/ODD), results indicated that various subgroups of children do in fact show a preferential benefit to specific treatments, in a pattern different from the overall pattern of the MTA's findings. Thus, the impact of parent-reported anxiety disorder with ADHD affects children's treatment responses, depending on whether the anxiety occurs with or without a disruptive disorder such as ODD or CD.

A simple rule of thumb that summarizes these findings suggests the following:

- If a child presents with an ADHD/anxiety-only profile, all interventions (other than routine community care) are likely to be effective.

- If a child presents with ADHD-only or ADHD/CD-ODD, treatments with medication appear especially indicated, and behavioral treatment-alone strategies may be contraindicated.

- Finally, if a child presents with ADHD+anxiety+CD-ODD, the combined medication management and behavioral interventions appear to offer substantial advantages over other treatments, particularly in overall impairment and functioning outcomes.

By way of caution, however, additional research is needed to further examine the validity of parent-reported anxiety disorders in children, since these conditions were usually not similarly reported by the children.

ADHD AND MOOD DISORDERS

Youngsters with ADHD often experience low self-esteem, demoralization, and dysphoria. For some, the duration, nature, and associated impairment of their affective symptomatology is severe enough to meet criteria for a mood disorder. There is little literature which has evaluated the impact of pharmacotherapy on depressive symptomatology. Unfortunately, many of the early studies were plagued by diagnostic and measurement problems which limit conclusions regarding treatment efficacy (Pliszka, 1987). The results of two controlled studies are more informative, however.

A double-blind, placebo controlled Latin Square crossover study compared the differential efficacy of MPH, and two tricyclic antidepressants—clomipramine (CMI) and desipramine (DMI)—in twelve psychiatrically hospitalized elementary school-age boys who met DSM-III criteria for attention deficit disorder, and no other diagnosis (Garfinkel, Wender, Sloman, & O'Neill, 1983). There was some evidence of differential drug efficacy across domains of functioning. Compared to the other treatment conditions, CMI resulted in significantly greater improvement on the "depressive/affective" factor on the Conners' Teacher Rating Scale (CTRS) whereas DMI produced more improvement in childcare workers' ratings on the CTRS "self-esteem" factor. In contrast, for CTRS scores of ADHD symptomatology, MPH was superior to both tricyclics.

Further evidence of DMI's impact on affective symptomatology is found in a placebo-controlled trial which included youngsters with ADHD comorbid for other conditions, including major depressive disorder (MDD) (Biederman, Baldessarini, Wright, Keenan, & Faraone, 1993). Regardless of diagnostic status—ADHD alone, comorbid CD, anxiety disorder, or major depression—all subgroups had lower scores on the parent and child completed Children's Depression Inventory with DMI compared to placebo. Moreover, this difference was statistically significant in the ADHD + MDD subgroup. Further, all subgroups showed significant improvement in ADHD behaviors with DMI. Notably, the use of DMI in children with ADHD and comorbid depression has diminished considerably in light of subsequent reports of cardiac complications, leading to sudden death of 3 children.

The findings from a recent open-label series of case reports are heuristic regarding a treatment strategy for individuals with co-occurring ADHD and major depression (Findling, 1996). Eleven comorbid patients (seven children, four adults), whose affective, but not ADHD, symptoms improved with selective serotonin reuptake inhibitor(SSRI) (fluoxetine or sertraline) monotherapy, demonstrated substantial clinical improvement in both symptom domains with combined stimulant and SSRI treatment. Interpretation of the study results must, of necessity, be tempered in light of the absence of appropriate controls, standardized diagnostic procedures and outcome assessments.

ADHD AND MENTAL RETARDATION

Relatively few studies have evaluated treatment response in children with comorbid ADHD and mental retardation, and these have all been evaluations of pharmacotherapy. The efforts of Aman and colleagues to develop and test a theoretical model of medication response in this population are especially noteworthy. The authors hypothesized an attenuated response to MPH in individuals with co-occurring ADHD and mental retardation, and that the degree of response would be moderated by one's level of "cognitive maturity." Several studies provide some support for these hypotheses (Aman, Turbot, Wilsher, & Merry, 1991; Aman, Kern, McGhee, & Arnold, 1993). Compared to youngsters with IQs below 45, who showed a poor response to MPH, those with mild mental retardation demonstrated benefit from stimulant treatment. However, the percentage of children who improved tended to be slightly lower, 62–68 percent (Aman et al., 1993; Mayes, Crites, Bixler, Humphrey, & Mattison, 1994) than the 80 percent rate typical in nonhandicapped children with ADHD. In contrast, Handen, Janofsky, McAuliffe, Breaux, and Feldman (1994) did not find a differential drug response in youngsters with IQs ranging from 48 to 77. However, the clinical utility of these findings is tempered somewhat because the diagnosis of ADHD was based solely on scale ratings, and was not established via clinical diagnostic procedures.

ADHD SUBTYPES

The ADHD treatment literature is characterized almost exclusively by studies of youngsters with a diagnosis of either attention deficit disorder with hyperactivity (i.e., ADDH, as per DSM-III) or ADHD combined type (as per DSM-IV). There is little information regarding the treatment of children with attention deficit disorder without hyperactivity, or those who meet DSM-IV criteria for ADHD, predominantly inattentive type. A notable exception is a study by Barkley, DuPaul, and McMurray (1991) in which children who met study criteria for ADD with (ADDH) or without hyperactivity (ADD) were evaluated on three doses of MPH in a triple-blind, placebo-controlled crossover design. Both groups improved significantly with MPH on a host of behavioral and laboratory measures, with no significant group differences on these measures. However, the groups differed in the benefits associated with the different dose levels. Specifically, whereas the ADD youngsters did best at the lowest dose, without accrued benefits at higher doses, the ADDH youngsters showed a more linear dose response, with improvements tending to occur with increasing doses. Moreover, clinical judgments and recommendations based on the children's pattern of medication response indicated a higher rate of "no response" (24 percent) in the ADD - H group compared to 5 percent in the ADDH group. Additionally, there were more recommendations for either no medication or low dose for ADD children than for ADDH youngsters.

In contrast to the findings of Barkley et al. (1991), a recent study found no difference in the stimulant response of youngsters with the inattentive ($N = 37$) or combined type ($N = 46$) of ADHD (Manos, Short, & Findling, 1999). In a double-blind, placebo-controlled crossover design, both subgroups responded equally well to MPH or Adderall. Moreover, χ^2 analysis of the "best dose response" findings reported by the authors indicate no significant differences in the rate of nonresponders, or in the distribution of dose levels (5, 10, or 15 mg twice a day of MPH) associated with best response in the inattentive and combined types.

RECOMMENDATIONS FOR CLINICAL PRACTICE

The empirical database that can inform on clinical decision making regarding matching patients to treatments remains relatively small. With a few notable exceptions, the relevant literature consists of studies of the effects of pharmacotherapy, either in specific subgroups of youngsters with ADHD, or on certain aspects of functioning. The dearth of systematic information regarding matching patients to treatments should serve as a beacon for research in this area. Several suggested research efforts are noted in the following section. In the interim, the available findings offer some clinical guidelines.

Children Who Clearly Benefit From Stimulant Treatment

Stimulant medication, especially methylphenidate, remains the most widely investigated treatment modality, and its clinical efficacy in ameliorating the primary symptoms of the disorder is one of the best-established findings in pediatric psychiatry. The studies reviewed above suggest that MPH can also serve an important role in the treatment of children with ADHD who present with other dysfunctions. There is strong evidence that youngsters with either ODD or CD, which together comprise the largest comorbid subgroup, benefit substantially with stimulant treatment. These children experience reductions in key ADHD symptoms, as well as decreases in behaviors symptomatic of the disruptive behavior disorders. Moreover, in youngsters for whom aggression is part of the symptom picture, the results from a number of studies indicate that reductions in aggression can occur using either MPH or behavioral treatment, and that additional benefit might accrue with the treatment combination, especially when the latter includes a classroom-based behavioral intervention.

Treatment of Children With Internalizing Problems

Guidelines for the treatment of youngsters with internalizing problems are less clear-cut. There is some evidence from short-term studies that these children are less responsive to stimulant treatment, with one report indicating adverse affects of MPH on school functioning. However, the indeterminate diagnostic status of the children in these studies obfuscates treatment recommendations. Recommendations are further tempered in light of the MTA study, which found that youngsters with and without anxiety disorders responded equally well to fourteen months of treatment with medication (almost always stimulants). It is possible that the study's comprehensive, individualized medication management strategy contributed to the positive outcomes of pharmacotherapy, regardless of the youngsters' comorbid status. The long-term study by Diamond et al. (1999), which included an individualized flexible dosing strategy, lends further support to this notion. Moreover, both studies reported decreased ratings with medication not only in ADHD but in internalizing symptomatology as well, suggesting that improvements in ADHD and associated problem areas can result in decreases in children's anxiety. Further clinical trials in ADHD children with comorbid anxiety disorders are needed to place pharmacotherapy recommendations on firm grounds.

When Psychosocial Treatment Is Indicated

For anxious ADHD children who do not benefit from medication, or whose parents refuse medication, psychosocial treatment of the sort provided in the MTA could prove beneficial in the treatment of core ADHD symptoms, as well as in reducing anxiety symptoms. Notably, the MTA psychosocial treatment regimen targeted difficulties characteristic of ADHD, as well as problem areas often associated with the disorder, such as oppositionality and other conduct problems, academic productivity, poor social skills, and so on. Significant problems associated with comorbid internalizing disorders per se were not targeted for treatment in the study. (Outside referral for treatment of these difficulties could occur if they became especially problematic and clinical intervention was deemed necessary). It is unknown whether the provision of psychosocial interventions which are specific for the treatment of anxiety disorders (Kendall, 1994; Kendall et al., 1997) would result in similar, if not greater benefits in anxious ADHD children.

Gray Areas

There is little empirical information to guide treatment decisions for children with comorbid ADHD and affective disorders. Reductions in ADHD symptoms can be expected with MPH; however, there is no evidence of improvement in mood disturbance with stimulants. Although there is some suggestion that tricyclics can improve both ADHD and affective symptomatology, concerns about side effects limit this treatment option. Notwithstanding their methodological limitations, case report findings are heuristic and suggest that the combination of stimulants and SSRIs might have clinical utility in youngsters with ADHD and comorbid depression.

Youngsters with ADHD and mild retardation can be expected to benefit from stimulant treatment, although the percentage of responders is likely to be somewhat smaller than the responder rate in ADHD children of average intelligence. In contrast, a positive response to MPH treatment is relatively unlikely in children with ADHD with more severe mental retardation.

Finally, little is known about the treatment of youngsters with the inattentive subtype of the disorder. An initial report that a quarter of these children are nonresponders to MPH, and that responders benefit most from low dose MPH and do not show the linear dose response common in children with the full disorder, was not corroborated in a subsequent study. Further trials with inattentive-only children are obviously needed to clarify whether their response profile differs from youngsters with the combined type. In the meantime, the available evidence indicates that these youngsters benefit from MPH, and that stimulant medication is an effective intervention that should be considered as part of their treatment regimen.

RECOMMENDATIONS FOR FUTURE RESEARCH

Numerous issues regarding matching patients to treatments strategies in ADHD remain unaddressed to date. Before discussing some of these concerns, two important points need to be noted. First, school-aged children continue to be, by far, the most widely studied age group. There is a dearth of controlled clinical trials in adolescents or adults that can inform on optimizing treatment selection for these individuals. Treatment research with these age groups is sorely needed. Second, at the risk of stating the obvious, improvements in clinical decision-making regarding matching patients to treatments are more likely as the number of efficacious treatment options increases. The current selection list remains quite limited. More theoretically driven treatment research is needed to test and develop novel pharmacological and nonpharmacological interventions.

In addition, several issues relevant to the process of matching patients to treatments have gone almost entirely unexplored (Jensen & Abikoff, 2000). For example, clinical wisdom suggests that parental ADHD or depression can compromise the implementation of behavioral treatments. These observations require empirical confirmation. Information is needed about how parental psychopathology, as well as family factors such as marital discord, influences the effectiveness and ordering of treatment strategies. Ongoing analyses from the MTA study should yield information about the moderating effects of these parental characteristics on treatment outcome.

Also unknown is whether differential outcomes occur in families that are provided their preferred treatment(s) (e.g., medication and/or psychosocial treatment) versus. those who are randomized to treatment. Finally, the ideal procedure for matching patients to treatments involves the application of validated tailored treatment strategies. To this end, research designs are needed which compare standard treatments versus tailored approaches which are based on patients' needs, impairments, and goals. Coincidentally, parallel research efforts are called for in two areas: (1) the development of measures to assess these patient characteristics and (2) the development of clinical treatment algorithms which facilitate the formulation of tailored treatment strategies (Jensen & Abikoff, 2000).

References

Aman, M. G., Kern, R. A., McGhee, D. E., & Arnold, L. E. (1993). Fenfluramine and methylphenidate in children with mental retardation and ADHD: Clinical and side effects. *Journal of the American Academy of Child and Adolescent Psychiatry, 32*, 851–859.

Aman, M. G., Turbott, S. H., Wilsher, C. P., & Merry, S. N. (1991). The clinical effects of methylphenidate and thioridazine in intellectually subaverage children. *Journal of the American Academy of Child and Adolescent Psychiatry, 30*, 246–256.

American Psychiatric Association. (1980). *Diagnostic and statistical manual of mental disorders* (3rd ed.). Washington, DC: Author.

American Psychiatric Association. (1987). *Diagnostic and statistical manual of mental disorders* (3rd ed., rev.). Washington, DC: Author.

American Psychiatric Association. (1994). *Diagnostic and statistical manual of mental disorders* (4th ed.). Washington, DC: Author.

Arnold, L. E., Abikoff, H. B., Cantwell, D. P., Conners, C. K., Elliott, G., Greenhill, L. L., Hechtman, L., Hinshaw, S. P., Hoza, B., Jensen, P. S., Kraemer, H., March, J., Newcorn, J., Pelham, W. E., Richters, J., Severe, J. B., Schiller, E., Swanson, J. M., Vereen, D., & Wells, K. (1997). National Institute of Mental Health Collaborative Multimodal Treatment Study of Children with ADHD (MTA): Design challenges and choices. *Archives of General Psychiatry, 54*, 865–870.

Barkley, R. A., DuPaul, G. J., & McMurray, M. B. (1991). Attention deficit disorder with and without hyperactivity: Clinical response to three dose levels of methylphenidate. *Pediatrics, 87*, 519–531.

Barkley, R. A., Fischer, M., Edelbrock, C. S., & Smallish, L. (1990). The adolescent outcome of hyperactive children diagnosed by research criteria. I: An 8-year prospective follow-up study. *Journal of the American Academy of Child and Adolescent Psychiatry, 29*, 546–557.

Barkley, R. A., McMurray, M. B., Edelbrock, C. S., & Robbins, K. (1989). The response of aggressive and nonaggressive ADHD children to two doses of methylphenidate. *Journal of the American Academy of Child and Adolescent Psychiatry, 28*, 873–881.

Biederman, J., Baldessarini, R. J., Wright, V., Keenan, K., & Faraone, S. (1993). A double-blind placebo controlled study of desipramine in the treatment of attention deficit disorder, III: Lack of impact of comorbidity and family history factors on clinical response. *Journal of the American Academy of Child and Adolescent Psychiatry, 32*, 199–204.

Biederman, J., Newcorn, J., & Sprich, S. E. (1991). Comorbidity of attention deficit hyperactivity disorder with conduct, depressive, anxiety and other disorders. *American Journal of Psychiatry, 148*(5), 564–577.

Brent, D. A., Kolko, D. J., Birmaher, B., Baugher, M., Bridge, J., Roth, C., & Holder, D. (1998). Predictors of treatment efficacy in a clinical trial of three psychosocial treatments for adolescent depression. *Journal of the American Academy of Child and Adolescent Psychiatry, 37*, 906–914.

Diamond, I. R., Tannock, R., & Schachar, R. (1999). Response to methylphenidate in children with ADHD and comorbid anxiety. *Journal of the American Academy of Child and Adolescent Psychiatry*, 38(4), 402–409.

DuPaul, G. J., Barkley, R. A., & McMurray, M. B. (1994). Response of children with ADHD to methylphenidate: Interaction with internalizing symptoms. *Journal of the American Academy of Child and Adolescent Psychiatry, 33*(6), 894–903.

Elkin, I., Gibbons, R. D., Shea, M. T., Sotsky, S. M., Watkins, J. T., Pilkonis, P. A., & Hedeker, D. (1995). Initial severity and differential treatment outcome in the National Institute of Mental Health Treatment of Depression Collaborative Research Program. *Journal of Consulting and Clinical Psychology, 63*, 841–847.

Findling, R. L. (1996). Open-label treatment of comorbid depression and attentional disorders of co-administration of serotonin reuptake inhibitors and psychostimulants in children, adolescents, and adults: A case series. *Journal of Child and Adolescent Psychopharmology, 6*, 165–175.

Garfinkel, B. D., Wender, P. H., Sloman, L., & O'Neill, R. N. (1983). Tricyclic antidepressant and methylphenidate treatment of attention deficit disorder in children. *Journal of the American Academy of Child and Adolescent Psychiatry, 22*, 343–348.

Greenhill, L. L., Abikoff, H. B., Arnold, L. E., Cantwell, D. P., Conners, C. K., Elliott, G., Hechtman, L., Hinshaw, S. P., Hoza, B., Jensen, P. S., March, J. S., Newcorn, J., Pelham, W. E., Severe, J. B., Swanson, J. M., Vitiello, B., & Wells, K. (1996). Medication treatment strategies in the MTA study: Relevance to clinicians and researchers. *Journal of the American Academy of Child and Adolescent Psychiatry, 35*, 1304–1313.

Handen, B. J., Janosky, K., McAuliffe, S., Breaux, A. M., & Feldman, H. (1994). Prediction of response to methylphenidate among children with ADHD and mental retardation. *Journal of the American Academy of Child and Adolescent Psychiatry, 33*, 1185–1193.

Hechtman, L., & Abikoff, H. (1995, October). *Multimodal treatment plus stimulants vs. stimulant treatment in ADHD children: Results from a two-year comparative treatment study.* Paper presented at the annual meeting of the American Academy of Child and Adolescent Psychiatry. New Orleans, LA.

Herrero, M. E., Hechtman, L., & Weiss, G. (1994). Antisocial disorders in hyperactive subjects from childhood to adulthood: predictive factors and characterization of subgroups. *American Journal of Orthopsychiatry, 64*, 510–521.

Hinshaw, S. P. (1991). Stimulant medication and the treatment of aggression in children with attentional deficits. *Journal of Clinical Child Psychology, 20*, 301–312.

Hinshaw, S. P., Klein, R. G., & Abikoff, H. (1998). Childhood attention deficit hyperactivity disorder: Nonpharmacological and combination treatments. In P. E. Nathan & J. M. Gorman (Eds.), *A guide to treatments that work* (pp. 26–41). New York: Oxford University Press.

Jensen, P. S., & Abikoff, H. (2000). Tailoring treatment interventions for individuals with ADD. In T. Brown (Ed.), *Attention deficit disorders and comorbidities in children, adolescents, and adults* (pp. 637–652). Washington, DC: American Psychiatric Press.

Jensen, P. S., Hinshaw, S. P., Kraemer, H. C., Lenora, N., Newcorn, J. H., Abikoff, H. B., March, J. S., Arnold, L. E., Cantwell, D. P., Conners, C. K., Elliott, G. R., Greenhill, L. L., Hechtman, L., Hoza, B., Pelham, W. E., Severe, J. B., Swanson, J. M., Wells, K. C., Vitiello, B., & Wigal, T. (2001). ADHD comorbidity findings from the MTA study: Comparing comorbid subgroups. *Journal of the American Academy of Child and Adolescent Psychiatry, 40*, 147–158.

Jensen, P. S., Martin, D., & Cantwell, D. P. (1997). Comorbidity in ADHD; Implications for research, practice, and DSM-V. *Journal of the American Academy of Child and Adolescent Psychiatry, 36*, 1065–1079.

Kendall, P. C. (1994). Treating anxiety disorders in children: Results of a randomized clinical trial. *Journal of Consulting and Clinical Psychology, 62*, 100–110.

Kendall, P. C., Flannery-Schroeder, E., Panichelli-Mindel, S. M., Southam-Gerow, M., Henin, A., &

Warman, M. (1997). Therapy for youths with anxiety disorders: A second randomized clinical trial. *Journal of Consulting and Clinical Psychology, 65*, 366–380.

Klein, R. G., & Abikoff, H. (1997). Behavior therapy and methylphenidate in the treatment of children with ADHD. *Journal of Attention Disorders, 2*, 89–114.

Klein, R., Abikoff, H., Klass, E., Ganales, D., Seese, L., & Pollack, S. (1997). Clinical efficacy of methylphenidate in conduct disorder with and without attention deficit hyperactivity disorder. *Archives of General Psychiatry, 54*, 1073–1080.

Klein, R., Klass, E., & Abikoff, H. (1994). Controlled trial of methylphenidate, lithium, and placebo in children and adolescents with conduct disorders. *Proceedings of the annual meeting of the Society for Research in Child and Adolescent Psychopathology* (Vol. 3). London, UK.

Klorman, R., Brumaghim, J. T., Salzman, L. F., Strauss, J., Borgstedt, A. D., McBride, M. C., & Loeb, S. (1988). Effects of methylphenidate on Attention-Deficit Hyperactivity Disorder with and without aggressive/noncompliant features. *Journal of Abnormal Psychology, 97*, 413–422.

Kuhne, M., Schachar, R., & Tannock, R. (1997). Impact of comorbid oppositional or conduct problems on attention-deficit hyperactivity disorder. *Journal of the American Academy of Child and Adolescent Psychiatry, 36*, 1715–1725.

Manos, M. J., Short, E. J., & Findling, R. L. (1999). Differential effectiveness of methylphenidate and adderall in school-age youth with attention deficit/ hyperactivity disorder. *Journal of the American Academy of Child and Adolescent Psychiatry, 38*(7), 813–819.

Mayes, S. D., Crites, D. L., Bixler, E. O., Humphrey, F. J., & Mattison, R. E. (1994). Methylphenidate and ADHD: Influence of age, IQ and neurodevelopmental status. *Developmental Medicine and Child Neurology, 36*, 1099–1107.

MTA Cooperative Group. (1999). A 14-month randomized clinical trial of treatment strategies for attention-deficit/hyperactivity disorder: Multimodal Treatment Study of Children with ADHD. *Archives of General Psychiatry, 56*(12), 1073–1086.

Pliszka, S. R. (1987). Tricyclic antidepressants in the treatment of children with Attention Deficit Disorder. *Journal of the American Academy of Child and Adolescent Psychiatry, 26*, 127–132.

Pliszka, S. (1989). Effect of anxiety on cognition, behavior, and stimulant response in ADHD. *Journal of the American Academy of Child and Adolescent Psychiatry, 28*, 882–887.

Spencer, T., Biederman, J., Wilens, T., Harding, M., O'Donnell, D., & Griffin, S. (1996). Pharmacotherapy of attention-deficit hyperactivity disorder across the life cycle. *Journal of the American Academy of Child and Adolescent Psychiatry, 35*, 409–432.

Tannock, R. (2000). Attention deficit disorders with anxiety disorders. In T. E. Brown (Ed.), *Attention deficit disorders and comorbidities in children, adolescents, and adults* (pp. 125–170). Washington, DC: American Psychiatric Press.

Tannock, R., Ickowicz, A., & Schachar, R. (1995). Differential effects of methylphenidate on working memory in ADHD children with and without comorbid anxiety. *Journal of the American Academy of Child and Adolescent Psychiatry, 34*, 886–896.

Taylor, E., Schachar, R., Thorley, H. M., Wieselberg, H. M., Everitt, B., & Rutter, M. (1987). Which boys respond to stimulant medication? A controlled trial of methylphenidate in boys with disruptive behavior. *Psychological Medicine, 17*, 121–143.

Urman, R., Ickowicz, A., Fulford, P., & Tannock, R. (1995). An exaggerated cardiovascular response to methylphenidate in ADHD children with anxiety. *Journal of Child and Adolescent Psychopharmacology, 5*, 29–37.

Wells, K. C., Pelham, W. E., Swanson, J. M., Kotkin, R. A., Hoza, B., Abikoff, H. B., Abramowitz, A., Arnold, L. E., Cantwell, D. P., Conners, C. K., Elliott, G., Greenhill, L. L., Hechtman, L., Hibbs, E., Hinshaw, S. P., Jensen, P. S., March, J. S., Swanson, J. M., & Schiller, E. (2000). Psychosocial treatment strategies in the MTA study: rationale, methods, and critical issues in design and implementation. *Journal of Abnormal Child Psychology, 28*(6), 483–505.

World Health Organization. (1978). *International classification of diseases* (9th rev.). Geneva, Switzerland: Author.

Part 4

Does Stimulant Use for ADHD Lead to Substance Abuse?

Perhaps one of the most controversial subjects in the field of attention deficit hyperactivity disorder (ADHD) is the use of stimulants for treatment. The topic of greatest concern is whether the use of stimulants in the treatment of ADHD could lead to future substance abuse (see, e.g., Lambert, Chapter 18), or whether the increased availability of stimulant treatments portends an increased level of drug diversion among non-ADHD youth (for contrasting views, see Feussner, Chapter 20, and Cooper, Chapter 21). Although there is a good deal of research on the abuse potential of stimulants, including some evidence concerning abuse among individuals with ADHD, few data are available that conclusively address whether the use of stimulants in the medically supervised treatment settings (vs. self-medication) predisposes to the subsequent abuse of a variety of substances, including stimulants, cocaine, tobacco, and alcohol. This section outlines available research on this topic, as well as the general correlation of ADHD with substance abuse.

Does treatment with stimulants predispose to later substance use? Most studies *have not* suggested that such is the case (just the opposite, in fact), but no fully experimental studies (parallel groups with random assignment, etc.) have been done to date. Given ethical concerns, such studies may never be done, in fact, though epidemiological data sometimes suggest an association (see, e.g., Lambert, Chapter 18). Animal data are interesting but generally inconclusive or not altogether applicable. In the absence of definitive evidence, however, we must be careful to disentangle the propensity for substance abuse among youth with ADHD (a real risk, as noted in Klein, Chapter 16, and Wilens, Chapter 19) with the disorder's treatment with stimulants. Perhaps the best study to date on the long-term impact of treatment with stimulants on substance use outcomes is provided by Loney, Chapter 17, who concluded that careful treatment may be associated with *decreased* substance abuse, compared to untreated children with ADHD. Despite much misinformation and overstatements about the dangers of stimulants in the press, concerning the question of the risks of stimulant use, there is no evidence that careful therapeutic use is harmful (see Appendix for the National Institutes of Health Consensus statement). This thoughtful conclusion should assist those spokespersons who are asked to respond to the frequent misrepresentations of the abundant safety evidence, as well as aid physicians who seek to alleviate parental concerns.

—J.R. Cooper
—P.S. Jensen

Chapter 16

Alcohol, Stimulants, Nicotine, and Other Drugs in ADHD

by Rachel G. Klein, Ph.D.

Introduction 16-1
Rationale for Hypothesis That Individuals With ADHD Are Likely to
    Abuse Drugs 16-2
Retrospective Surveys of ADHD in Substance Use Disorders
    (Adults and Adolescents) 16-3
        ADHD and Alcohol-Related Disorders 16-3
        ADHD and Cocaine Use 16-5
        ADHD and Use of Opiates 16-6
        ADHD and Mixed Substance Use Disorders 16-6
Retrospective Reports of Drug Use and Abuse in Adults
    With ADHD 16-7
Retrospective Report in Adolescents in the General Population 16-8
Current ADHD and Patterns of SUD 16-8
Longitudinal Studies of Children With ADHD 16-9
        Clinical Studies 16-9
        Community Studies 16-11
Public Health and Clinical Implications 16-12
        Problems in Drawing Inferences From Multiple Studies 16-13
        The Conduct Disorder Link 16-14
Conclusions 16-15

INTRODUCTION

The trajectory of drug use to abuse and dependence has been conceptualized in a developmental framework within which specific features of the individual and his or her environment are viewed as interactive causal influences on the initiation of drug abuse (Hawkins, Catalano, & Miller, 1992). Among the individual's influential characteristics, psychiatric diagnosis has played a large role. Recently, there has been increasing interest in a possible link between childhood hyperactivity and subsequent drug history. Other chapters in this volume address the issue whether children with attention deficit hyperactivity disorder (ADHD) are at an elevated risk for subsequent substance use disorders (SUD). This chapter has the narrower purpose of examining whether individuals with SUD and had ADHD in childhood prefer stimulants to other drugs of abuse. The question reflects a specific subset of the overall relationship between childhood ADHD and later SUD.

RATIONALE FOR HYPOTHESIS THAT INDIVIDUALS WITH ADHD ARE LIKELY TO ABUSE DRUGS

Several observations have fostered concerns regarding illicit stimulant use by individuals with a history of ADHD. First, when studies of the effectiveness of psychostimulants appeared in the 1960s, concern was expressed that treated children would become psychologically, if not physically, dependent on these drugs and would develop a drug-taking attitude that would foster their reliance on drugs to resolve future life stresses, which would thus lead to drug abuse and dependence. In the absence of informative longitudinal data, it is understandable that this social-learning model of drug abuse was highly influential, and that it greatly limited parental willingness to expose their children to stimulant treatment.

Second, the more cogent argument raises the possibility that adolescents and adults with symptoms of ADHD would use stimulants, including cocaine and nicotine, to treat themselves (Kaminer, 1992; Khantzian, 1985; Levin et al., 1996; Levin & Kleber, 1995; Pomerleau, Downey, Stelson, & Pomerleau, 1995). The self-medicating model predicts that substance abusers with ADHD will make greater use of nicotine, cocaine, and other stimulants than will their non-ADHD counterparts. Furthermore, in certain individuals with ADHD, self-medicating attempts might evolve into abuse and dependence, so that ADHD could be overrepresented among persons who abuse or are dependent on stimulants.

Third, rat pups who are exposed to psychostimulants early in their development may become especially sensitive to the reinforcing properties of stimulants as mature animals (Schenk & Partridge, 1997). If brain mechanisms that regulate animals' predilection for stimulants can be altered permanently, it is conceivable that a similar process might occur in humans as well. If such were the case, individuals who were exposed to stimulants in childhood would have greater affinity for stimulants than for other compounds. Therefore, compared to controls, stimulant treated children with ADHD should display preferential use of nicotine, cocaine, and other stimulants, in later life.

In sum, several postulated developmental pathways predict a specific pattern of stimulant use and abuse in persons with a current or past history of ADHD. They foster the hypothesis that individuals with an early or current history of ADHD are more likely to abuse stimulants than other drugs, compared to peers who never had ADHD.

It is now well established that ADHD is a major risk factor for the development of conduct disorder (CD). Because there is a strong association between CD and drug use, one cannot ignore the possible influence of CD on the relationship between ADHD and drug use or abuse.

RETROSPECTIVE SURVEYS OF ADHD IN SUBSTANCE USE DISORDERS (ADULTS AND ADOLESCENTS)

Much of the relevant evidence derives from retrospective reports of childhood ADHD from adolescents and adults with substance use disorders and retrospective reports of earlier drug use and abuse from adults with ADHD. Retrospective reports have limited validity insofar as they are influenced by current function and lifelong experiences that may shape recall of earlier events. Another source of bias stems from the fact that, in most cases, assessment of early function cannot be conducted without knowledge of adult diagnosis. As a result, inferences about the childhood psychiatric status of individuals assessed retrospectively is problematic, and it is generally acknowledged that prospective, longitudinal investigations are necessary for establishing the role of earlier function in later outcome. In spite of their limitations, observations from retrospective studies have been seminal by stimulating clinical hypotheses regarding the impact of childhood ADHD on substance use. Therefore, they are included in this review.

Because current standards for diagnosing ADHD are relatively recent, any study anteceding the mid-1980s refers to "hyperactivity" rather than ADHD. However, from the reports' clinical descriptions, the terms appear to reflect similar clinical constructs; consequently, no distinction is made between early and late studies in this review.

A link between ADHD and SUD originated from clinical observations in drug-abusing adults. Although any compound could conceivably be used for treatment purposes by individuals with ADHD, the self-medication model would clearly be supported if a relative excess of ADHD were found among those who abuse primarily stimulants. Table 16.1 summarizes the pertinent retrospective studies of ADHD in adults and adolescents with SUD.

ADHD and Alcohol-Related Disorders

In the first investigation to examine childhood ADHD and alcoholism, Goodwin Schulsinger, Hermansen, Guze, and Winokur (1975) studied an unselected group of 133 Danish adult male adoptees in whom ADHD diagnoses were based on clinical judgments derived from a psychiatric evaluation whose coverage of ADHD symptoms has high face validity. The men with a history of alcoholism reported a markedly elevated rate of childhood ADHD compared to those without a similar drug history (50 percent vs. 15 percent, $p < .01$). The study had the major desideratum of identifying alcoholics from a nonreferred population, thereby avoiding the potential bias for disproportionate rates of childhood dysfunction due to the self-selection process inherent in treatment seeking. However, as a result, it incurs the disadvantage of having a small cohort of alcoholics ($N = 14$). All other studies of alcohol disorders have dealt with clinical samples.

Tarter, McBride, Buonpane, and Schneider (1977) reported that self-ratings of childhood symptoms of ADHD were significantly more prevalent among severe alcoholics, compared to mild alcoholics, psychiatric comparisons, and normals. No attempt was made to classify patients into diagnosed and undiagnosed ADHD cases,

Table 16.1
Rates of ADHD in Individuals With Substance Abuse Disorder

	N	% of ADHD	ADHD Definition
Alcohol			
Goodwin et al., 1975 (133 Danish male adoptees)	14	50% (vs. 15% in non-ADHD, $p < .01$)	Clinical interview about childhood
Tarter et al., 1977 (inpatients and outpatients)	66	Significant*	Self-rating scale of symptoms
De Obaldia et al., 1983 (inpatients)	55	Significant[†]	Tarter's self-rating scale
Wood et al., 1983 (inpatients)	27	33% residual type	Clinical interview, parent rating scale
Milin et al., 1997 (inpatients)	15	13% childhood only, 27%; childhhod and adulthood	2 Self-rating scales (child and adult symptoms)
Cocaine			
Weiss et al., 1988 (inpatients)	149	8%	Clinical interview
Rounsaville et al., 1991 Carroll & Rounsaville, 1998			Clinical interview
(inpatient applicants and outpatients)	298	35%	
(Community Ss)	101	24%	
DeMilio, 1989 (inpatient adolescents)	56	21%	Clinical interviews and rating
Opiates			
Weiss et al., 1988	298	1%	Clinical interview
Eyre et al., 1982 (treatment applicants)	157	22%	Interview
Mixed SUD			
Milin et al., 1997	21	57%	Self-rating scales
Horner & Scheibe, 1997 (adolescents: 4 outpatients, 26 inpatients)	30	50%	Diagnosed ADHD in childhood or 3 self-rating scales
Whitmore et al., 1997 (adolescents)			
(inpatient males)	285	11%	
(outpatient females)	82	11%	DISC-C diagnosis
(inpatient males)	285	22%	
(outpatient females)	82	25%	DISC-C: 8 ADHD Sx

Note. Ss = subjects; Sx = symptoms.

*Significantly elevated in severe (primary) alcoholics ($N = 38$) compared with milder (secondary) cases ($N = 28$), psychiatric controls ($N = 49$), or normals ($N = 27$). [†] Significantly elevated in severe (primary) alcoholics ($N = 22$) compared with milder (secondary) cases ($N = 33$), (19.00% vs. 10.67% Hk/MBD).

but the items that distinguish the groups are clearly congruent with the diagnosis (overactive, cannot sit still, short attention span, does not complete projects, impulsive, cannot tolerate delay, gets into things, etc.). However, there is no way of determining the coaggregation of items within individuals and, therefore, the frequency of the syndrome. A study designed to replicate the findings of Tarter et al. (1977) used a median split to define cases as high or low ADHD (median split: thirteen symptoms). Findings replicated that severe alcoholics had relatively higher endorsement of ADHD symptoms than did mild alcoholics (77 percent vs. 27 percent, $p < .001$). Non-alcohol-abusing comparisons were not included in the replication study.

The diagnosis of ADHD requires detailed information about childhood comportment. Invariably, this information is obtained from adults whose recollections often may be hazy. Ideally, parent reports should contribute to the determination of childhood status (although it is possible that we err if we assume that parents are more accurate retrospective informants of their children's early behavior than are the grown children themselves). Wood, Wender, and Reimherr (1983) are unique in having obtained parent ratings of childhood ADHD in a group of young adult males with alcohol dependence. In addition, the determination of adult ADHD was made independently of the information provided by parents. A third of the sample (9/27) was judged to have current ADHD. Unfortunately, the authors do not indicate the rate of ADHD in childhood which is bound to exceed the adult rate as a current diagnosis required a positive childhood history.

Relying on self-rating scales, a recent report notes a 40 percent rate of ADHD in a small group of adults (6/15) with alcohol-related disorders; 27 percent (4/15) judged themselves as still symptomatic as adults (Milin, Loh, Chow, & Wilson, 1997).

ADHD and Cocaine Use

Findings in individuals who use, abuse, or are dependent on cocaine are critical to the question of preferential stimulant use and abuse in those with a history of ADHD. Weiss, Mirin, Griffin, and Michael (1988) in Boston reported a low frequency of residual ADHD in a sizable group of hospitalized cocaine abusers (4.7 percent, 7/149). However, the main thrust of the study was the evaluation of affective disorders in SUD, and it is not clear that ADHD was assessed systematically.

The New Haven group has conducted the only other investigation in cocaine abusers (Carroll & Rounsaville, 1993; Rounsaville et al., 1991). Of a large group of cocaine abusers, refined to exclude those with an antecedent history of heroin dependence, 34.6 percent (103/298) were diagnosed with childhood ADHD, based on systematic clinical interviews. Because of potential biases for psychiatric morbidity in clinical samples of drug abusers, the investigators conducted similar examinations in a cohort of community cocaine abusers. ADHD was diagnosed in 23.8 percent (24/101)—a rate which is significantly lower than the one obtained in the clinical cases ($P < .001$). The test-retest reliability for ADHD (at about three-week intervals) was moderate (Kappa = .47), but consistent with the reliabilities of other psychiatric diagnoses in the same population. Importantly, those with ADHD had younger onsets and more severe and chronic cocaine use, regardless of the occurrence of antisocial personality disorder in adulthood. However, interpretation of this finding is complicated by the fact that 93 percent of the patients with ADHD also had a childhood history of conduct disorder (as compared to 71 percent of those without ADHD). It is difficult, if not impossible, to disentangle the respective contribution of each disorder to other clinical phenomena. However, because ADHD was associated with worse cocaine abuse even in the absence of a history of current antisocial personality disorder (Carroll & Rounsaville, 1993), the study supports the influence of ADHD on aspects of cocaine abuse independent of antisocial disorder in adulthood, but not in childhood.

DeMilio (1989) found a current diagnosis of ADHD in 18 percent (2/11) of a small cohort of hospitalized adolescents with exclusive current and past cocaine abuse. This frequency does not appear to exceed that found in other types of abusers (e.g., 13 percent (2/15) in exclusive alcoholics). The rate of ADHD reaches 22 percent (8/36) if one includes cocaine abusers who, in the past, had abused other drugs. DeMilio (1989), as well as Horner and Scheibe (1997), asked the adolescent drug abusers to identify their preferred substance. In the first report, adolescents with and without ADHD indicated that cocaine was the preferred drug 17 percent versus 21 percent of the time (DeMilio, 1989); in the second report, respective rates are 47 percent and 40 percent (Horner & Scheibe, 1997). Neither study found that the patients with SUD and ADHD selected cocaine more frequently than did their counterparts free of ADHD.

ADHD and Use of Opiates

The Boston group of Weiss et al (1988) found minimal rates of residual ADHD among opioid and depressant abusers combined (0.7 percent, 2/293). As noted previously, the thrust of the study, which relied on thorough clinical evaluations aimed at assessing mood disorders, may not have inquired systematically about ADHD.

In a large clinical sample of opiate addicts, Eyre, Rounsaville, and Kleber (1982), in New Haven, reported a rate of 22 percent (35/157) of childhood ADHD, based on structured clinical interviews. The definition of ADHD followed early criteria put forth by Cantwell (1972), which required at least one antisocial symptom. This diagnostic convention is likely to have reduced the frequency of ADHD because it excluded those without conduct disorder.

ADHD and Mixed Substance Use Disorders

The mixed SUD studies include individuals who abuse a variety of substances, without any single substance predominating, and also combines individuals with different SUDs whether single or multiple. For the sake of providing a comprehensive overview, studies on groups of mixed SUD are summarized, although they are less pointedly relevant to the issue at hand than are studies on specific SUDs. A small clinical study of inpatient adults reports a 57 percent rate of ADHD (12/21) based on self-ratings of past and current symptoms (Milin et al., 1997).

One small study of inpatient adolescents (Horner & Scheibe, 1997) identified 50 percent (15/30) as having ADHD. The diagnosis was established based on chart entries that indicated that the child was diagnosed in childhood. In addition, those without a chart-documented diagnosis were considered to have ADHD if they obtained elevated scores on three self-rating scales.

A second large study examined ADHD in adolescents with SUD, who also had conduct disorder. Because it relied on the DISC 2.1, an interview that does not generate lifetime diagnoses (Fisher et al., 1993), only current status is reported. (An exception was made for conduct disorder which was assessed for lifetime occurrence.) Relatively low rates of ADHD were found, with equivalent frequencies in girls and boys (10 percent and 11 percent, respectively). The rates double to 22 percent and 25 percent in each group when less stringent criteria for ADHD are applied, in that the diagnosis required eight or more ADHD symptoms, without regard to age of onset and impairment criteria.

RETROSPECTIVE REPORTS OF DRUG USE AND ABUSE IN ADULTS WITH ADHD

The assessment of patterns of drug abuse in adults with ADHD is a complementary strategy to the study of ADHD in drug abusers. Do adults with ADHD have a specific history of stimulant use or abuse? Table 16.2 presents results of the two studies that have addressed the question. Both used systematic interviews to diagnose ADHD. In the study by Biederman et al. (1995), the adults with ADHD had a sixfold increase in the relative risk (RR) of abusing cocaine compared to non-ADHD adults (RR = 6.1). This ratio is larger than for alcohol, or marijuana, but it is similar to the ratio for other drugs (i.e., RR for sedatives, 5.3; for hallucinogens, 9.5; for opiates, 16.7). If the contrast between adults with and without ADHD is restricted to the individuals with substance use disorders, there is no relative increase in cocaine or stimulant use in the ADHD patients (see Table 16.2). In contrast, Murphy and Barkley (1996) found a tenfold excess of stimulant use in adults with ADHD relative to non-ADHD comparisons (RR = 9.56) (see Table 16.2). Yet, the largest group difference is not for stimulant use but for opiates (RR = 16.7), although the latter is a function of having no opiate users in the comparison group. This report offers some support to the expectation that a history of cocaine use may be associated with ADHD.

An uncontrolled study of cigarette smoking reports a lifetime prevalence of 55

Table 16.2
Relative Risk for Substance Abuse Reported by Adults With ADHD

Substance	Biederman et al., 1995[a]	Murphy & Barkley, 1996[b]
Alcohol	1.8	3.4
Marijuana	3.2	1.8
Cocaine	3.2	9.6
Stimulants	6.1	Not reported
Hallucinogens	9.5	4.9
Sedatives	5.3	1.5
Opiates	16.7	1.7

[a] Among those with SUD ADHD, $N = 62/120$; comparisons, $N = 73/268$; nominator = Ss with a SUD; denominator = Total N.
[b] ADHD, $N = 172$; comparisons, $N = 30$.

percent in males and 68 percent in females with ADHD (Pomerleau et al., 1995). These smoking frequencies are viewed as high relative to the general population. However, the lack of appropriately matched controls limits interpretation of the high frequencies reported.

RETROSPECTIVE REPORT IN ADOLESCENTS IN THE GENERAL POPULATION

All the studies discussed previously have targeted clinical samples of convenience. Only one study has reported childhood attention deficit and current drug and cigarette use in a population sample of adolescents (Windle, 1993). Sophomore and junior year high school students completed questionnaires about ADHD and antisocial behaviors that had occurred prior to age 12. A thirty-day time frame was used for substance use and smoking. In addition, parents provided ratings of their children's childhood comportment. Table 16.3 summarizes the relationships of attention deficit ratings and substance use. The self and parent ratings of attention deficit did not predict cigarette smoking to a greater degree than alcohol or marijuana use. In fact, on parent ratings, the results were in the opposite direction, that is, greater association of attention deficit with alcohol use ($r = .23$) than with cigarettes ($r = .09$). The measure of conduct disorder was relatively more predictive of substance use than was attention deficit. However, ADHD conduct problems were highly correlated ($r = .80$ in boys, .71 in girls), and it is not clear that the predictive relationships for attention deficit are independent of the contribution of conduct disorder. This lone retrospective population study does not support a link between attention deficit and later preferential use of nicotine.

Table 16.3
Relationships of Adolescent and Parent Ratings of Childhood Attention Deficit with Adolescents' Ratings of Substance Use

	Self-Ratings of Attention Deficit		Parent Ratings of Attention Deficit (N = 479)*	
Substance	Boys (N = 520)	Girls (N = 564)	Boys	Girls
Alcohol	0.19[†]	0.31[†]	0.23[†]	0.16[‡]
Cigarettes	0.14[†]	0.29[†]	0.09	0.17
Marijuana	0.14[†]	0.16[†]	0.13[†]	0.14[‡]

*N of girls and boys not specified. [†]$p < .01$. [‡]$p < .05$

CURRENT ADHD AND PATTERNS OF SUD

Some cross-sectional studies of the relationship between current SUD and ADHD have targeted adolescents treated for SUD, whereas others have assessed SUD in adolescents with ADHD. Table 16.4 presents the pattern of drug use in adolescents with SUD with and without ADHD, all of whom also had a lifetime history of conduct disorders. Thompson, Riggs, Mikulich, and Crowley (1996) systematically evaluated 171 adolescent boys in residential treatment for drug abuse. Based on a direct structured interview (DISC 2.1), adolescents were classified as (1) meeting criteria for ADHD, (2) meeting the symptom count criterion for ADHD (at least eight symptoms) without qualifying for the age of onset and impairment criteria, and (3) without current ADHD (i.e., less than eight symptoms). As may be noted in Table 16.4, the relative risks for smoking (1.3) and stimulants (2.5) among the adolescents with ADHD are not especially elevated relative to the risks for other drugs (RRs, 1.0–4.0). The findings do not differ when a symptomatic definition of ADHD is applied. As shown in Table 16.4, similar findings were reported by Horner and Scheibe (1997) in a small group ($N = 30$) who were judged to have ADHD, provided they had been diagnosed as such in childhood (as indicated in Table 16.4) or had high scores on both self- and clinician- rated scales.

Table 16.4
Relative Risk of Substance Used/Abused in Conduct Disordered Adolescents With SUD and ADHD vs. Controls

Substance	Thompson et al., 1996a ADHD ($N = 64$); Not ADHD ($N = 79$)	Horner & Shiebe, 1997b ADHD ($N = 15$); Not ADHD ($N = 15$)
Alcohol	1.1	1.0
Cigarettes	1.3	NI
Marijuana	1.0	1.1
Cocaine	1.6	0.9
Stimulants	2.5	1.3
Sedatives	4.0	2.9
Hallucinogens	1.9	1.7
Inhalants	2.2	2.0
Opiates	2.3	1.9

LONGITUDINAL STUDIES OF CHILDREN WITH ADHD

It is generally acknowledged that longitudinal, prospective studies are the most valid, informative approach to discerning the predictive contribution of ADHD to substance use. They eschew problems of distorted recall that compromise the ability to detect associations between the two domains. The field is in the advantageous position of having prospective studies of children in the general population, in addition to studies conducted in clinical settings in which bias may result from a preponderance of severe clinical forms of the disorder.

Clinical Studies

Four longitudinal studies of clinical cases have been reported, with intervals ranging from four to fifteen years, between initial diagnosis and follow-up, and subjects' ages ranging from 9 to 33 years at follow-up. The first study, by Hechtman and Weiss (1986) in Canada, does not reveal any preferential use of stimulants (RR for cocaine,

0.7, and other stimulants, 0.7) in ADHD children evaluated at the average age of 25 (Table 16.5). If anything, the ADHD subjects had relatively lower rates of stimulant use. However, the time frame was for the past three months, and illicit substance use was rare in the area in which the study was conducted at the time, thereby limiting the opportunity to detect relationships between ADHD and drug abuse.

A different pattern emerges from results reported by Barkley and colleagues in Milwaukee (Barkley, Fischer, Edelbrock, & Smallish, 1990; R. A. Barkley, personal communication, November 15, 1998), and by Klein and Mannuzza (1999; Mannuzza & Klein, 2000) in New York. Although absolute frequencies cannot be compared directly as different definitions of drug use were applied in the two studies, the relative risks may be contrasted. At eight-year follow-up (mean ages = 15), Barkley et al. (1990) found relatively high risk for any cocaine and stimulant use in 123 subjects with ADHD compared to 66 comparisons (RRs, 8.0 and 12.0, respectively) (Table 16.5). Relative risks for other drugs range from 1 to 4. The follow-ups by Klein and Mannuzza (1999; Mannuzza & Klein, 2000) combine data obtained from two cohorts of boys with ADHD and matched comparisons (Gittelman, Mannuzza, Shenker, &

Table 16.5
Relative Risk for Substance Use or Abuse in ADHD Children Followed Longitudinally

Substance	Hetchman/ Weiss, 1986; 15 yrs.[a] [Mean age 25], N = 61 & 41[b]	Barkley, 1990 (1) 8 yrs.[a] [Mean age 15], N = 123 & 66[b] (2) [c]14 yrs.[a]; [Mean age 21], N = 148 & 76[b]			Klein/Mannuzza, 1999; (1) 8yrs.[a] [Mean age 18], N = 194 & N = 194 & 178[b]; (2) [c]15 yrs.[a] [Mean age 25], N = 176 & 168[b]		Milburger/ Biederman 1997, 4 yrs.[a] [Mean age 14], [N = 128 & 109-17b]	Hartsough/ Lambert, 1987e, 7 yrs.[a] [Mean age 15], N = 54 & 47[b]	Lynskey/ Ferguson, 1995[e], 7 yrs.[a] [Age 15], N = 168 & 778[b]
Alcohol	0.8	1.8	1.09[d]	1.5[d]	0.5	1.2[d]	—	0.9	1.6
Cigarettes	—	1.8	—	—	—	1.8	1.9	1.6	1.1
Marijuana	0.7	3.4	1.0	1.4	1.0	1.1	1.0	0.9	—
Cocaine	0.7	8.0	2.0	1.3	12.0	1.1	2.0	0.8	—
Stimulants	0.7	12.0	3.5	3.7	3.0	0.7	0.0	1.3	—
Sedatives	—	1.6	1.0	4.0	2.0	1.3	—	—	—
Psychedelic	6.6	1.2	1.1	2.6	3.0	1.2	0.6	0.7	—
Opiates	—	—	—	1.0	2.0	1.4	—	2.0	—
Barbiturates	—	2.0	4.2	—	2.0	1.0	—	—	—

[a]Length of follow-up. [b]Number of children with ADHD and number of controls as follow-up. [c]Unpublished. [d]Relative risk values for follow-up 2; relative risk values for substance abuse or disorder are bolded, other values reflect substance use. [e]Community sample.

Bonagura, 1985; Mannuzza, Klein, Bessler, Malloy, & LaPaduls, 1993, 1998; Mannuzza, Klein, Bonagura, Faraone, Chen, & Jones, 1991). As may be noted in Table 16.5, at eight-year follow-up (mean age = 18), relative risks for cocaine and stimulants were higher than for other drugs—including smoking, which was not particularly elevated. Results in the eight-year follow-up from the Milwaukee and New York groups support the notion that there is preferential use of stimulants in adolescence among those who had ADHD in childhood. However, in both studies, use of cocaine and stimulants was uncommon in the ADHD cases, and the high relative risk ratios often are due to the fact that no individual in the comparison groups had used these drugs. A slight increase among comparisons would deflate the apparent elevated risk in probands. The confidence limits of these high relative risk ratios are large, and lack of power due to low frequencies precludes an estimate of their true value.

The subsequent follow-ups report on the adult status of children with ADHD. Barkley finds a two- and threefold increase in cocaine and stimulant use in the ADHD group compared to controls, a rate which exceeds the risks for other drugs but not the risk for barbiturates (RR = 4) (see Table 16.5). As indicated in Table 16.5, relative risk for abuse and dependence of stimulants was also elevated (3.7), and higher than any other relative risk at the fourteen-year follow-up (Barkley, personal communication, November 15, 1998). In contrast, the Klein and Mannuzza New York study finds no evidence of preferential cocaine or stimulant use in adulthood (Table 16.5).

The most recent longitudinal study by Biederman and his group, in Boston, followed ADHD cases, their siblings, and matched comparisons over four years (Biederman et al., 1997; Milberger et al., 1997a, 1997b, 1997c). Siblings present advantages as controls because they share virtually the same familial context and many economic and social influences with the index cases. It is difficult, if not impossible, to control satisfactorily for these factors through matching of unrelated subjects. Among the ADHD children, the pattern of relative risk does not indicate a specific preference for smoking (Milberger et al., 1997a), for cocaine, or for stimulants (Biederman et al., 1997). For purposes of examining patterns of drug use, the distinction made by the authors between siblings with ADHD and without ADHD is informative (Milberger, Biederman, Faraone, Chen, & Jones, 1997a, 1997b; Milberger, Biederman, Faraone, Wilens, & Chu, 1997). Compared to siblings without ADHD, those with ADHD do not use cigarettes preferentially to alcohol (RR, cigarettes = 1.6, alcohol = 2.7), and risk for "other drugs" in siblings with ADHD is higher than for cigarettes (RR = 3.6); however, it is unclear whether cocaine and stimulants abuse contribute to this relative rate. Contrary to expectations, the non-ADHD siblings show preferential use for smoking over alcohol and "other drugs," compared to unrelated comparisons. The study followed up children who were 9 through 17 years of age at the time they were referred to the clinic. Information regarding the course of ADHD, regardless of age at referral, is of great value. However, for the specific purpose of determining risk for illicit substance use, which is typically initiated in adolescence, we need to focus on the longitudinal course of preadolescents with ADHD.

Community Studies

Three population-based studies, from California (Hartsough & Lambert, 1987), Canada (Boyle et al., 1993), and New Zealand (Lynskey & Fergusson, 1995), have reported on the pattern of drug use in children with ADHD followed prospectively. In the seven-year follow-up study by Hartsough and Lambert (1987), the highest relative risk is for tranquilizers (RR = 18). Opiates are next, but with a much lower ratio (RR = 2.0). Thus, cigarettes and stimulants (1.58 and 1.31, respectively) were not found to be used preferentially, and cocaine was used relatively less by the children with ADHD than their non-ADHD peers (see Table 16.5). A Canadian study by Boyle et al. (1993) reports on tobacco and nicotine use in 12- to 16-year-olds who had been classified as having ADHD four years earlier, based on parent and teacher ratings. Tobacco was not used preferentially relative to alcohol by adolescents with earlier ADHD; if anything, the opposite was found. (The paper reports prevalence ratios, and rates of use cannot be inferred.) The New Zealand population study by Lynskey and Fergusson (1995) provides information on abuse of alcohol and nicotine. Children diagnosed at age 8 were reevaluated at age 15. As indicated in Table 16.5, there was no increase in the relative risk of smoking compared to that of alcohol among children with ADHD.

The population studies fall short of providing evidence documenting self-selection of stimulants among individuals with a history of ADHD. The epidemiological studies are important in permitting a determination of the effect of treatment on subsequent drug abuse because, unlike cases in clinical populations, a large proportion is likely to have been untreated with stimulants in childhood. Especially informative in this regard is the study from New Zealand where there has been little use of pharmacotherapy for the management of children with ADHD. In the only systematic attempt to address this issue, Chilcoat and Breslau's (1999) five-year prospective population study did not find that stimulant treatment had a significant influence on the self-initiation of drug use of ADHD children. However, the children were only 11 years of age at follow-up; more extended observations are required for definitive answers.

PUBLIC HEALTH AND CLINICAL IMPLICATIONS

The identification of precursors of substance abuse has important public health implications; these precursors allow the identification of individuals at risk and may enable the development of preventive interventions. Consequently, the mechanisms that account for specific drug abuse are potentially important to these goals. There is sound reason to conjecture that individuals with ADHD are at risk for what has been referred to as the drug-of-choice phenomenon (Khantzian, 1985) with regard to stimulants.

No investigation provides a direct, rigorous test of the hypothesis. However, a fairly large body of empirical data bears on the issue. High rates of ADHD, far exceeding those to be expected in the general population, have been reported in every study of alcohol abusers (see Table 16.1). The rate is remarkably consistent given the multiple sources of method variance that include sampling differences and disparate standards for identifying ADHD.

On the whole, results do not conform to the expectation that ADHD is relatively more prevalent in cocaine abusers than in alcohol or mixed-drug disorders. The findings by Weiss et al. (1988) are the exception. They report a sixfold difference between inpatient cocaine abusers and opiate/depressant abusers (4.7 percent vs. .7 percent; relative risk = 6.7), but the absolute level of ADHD among the cocaine abusers is low.

Nevertheless, they raise the possibility of differential selection of cocaine versus opiates in abusers with ADHD. This report has the main advantage of permitting direct comparisons by having applied identical diagnostic procedures to the two groups of SUD.

Problems in Drawing Inferences From Multiple Studies

Drawing inferences from comparisons across multiple studies is problematic. We are hampered by greatly variable means of diagnosing ADHD that are bound to generate divergent rates. For example, because the studies on opiate and cocaine abusers were conducted by the same investigative team in New Haven, results have been compared directly and the conclusion drawn that the rate of ADHD in cocaine abusers is higher than in opiate addicts (35 percent vs. 22 percent) (Carroll & Rounsaville, 1993). Problematically, the studies' definitional standards for establishing ADHD may have biased the group difference in the direction of finding a greater frequency of ADHD among cocaine addicts who, unlike the opiate addicts, were not required to have antisocial behavior to meet criteria for ADHD.

Retrospective studies in substance disorders may be hindered by several methodological features. Poor reliability of ADHD diagnoses is likely to attenuate group differences. That this is a probable limitation in these clinical groups is suggested by the finding that the test-retest reliability of psychiatric diagnosis is poorer in current versus past drug abusers (Bryant, Rounsaville, Spitzer, & Williams, 1992). The New Haven group is unique in providing reliability estimates of ADHD. Others have ignored the issue. Diagnostic validity is more difficult to extricate. There appears to be poor agreement between parental and self-reports among persons with SUD (Rounsaville, Kleber, Wilber, Rosenbergere, & Rosenberger, 1981). Certain features that regularly have been found to distinguish individuals with ADHD from their peers do not differ between cocaine abusers with and without ADHD—for example, sex ratio in disfavor of males and lower educational attainment. However, diagnostic validity of retrospectively diagnosed ADHD is supported by the finding in some studies that the diagnosis is associated with earlier onsets and more chronic and intense use of cocaine independently of the presence of an adult antisocial personality disorder but, problematically, not a childhood conduct disorder (Carroll & Rounsaville, 1993). The hope of correlating childhood or current ADHD with a specific drug of abuse, such as stimulants, may be illusory in retrospective studies, as abuse of a single nonalcoholic substance is almost never the rule. All these issues minimize detection of relationships between ADHD and stimulant abuse from retrospective studies, should these truly exist.

The evidence from current diagnostic studies is conflicting, but some support for the preferential use of stimulant drugs has been found. It may be that the phenomenon is stronger than it appears from retrospective and current diagnostic studies that rely on self-reports of ADHD, because the presence of ADHD symptoms has been found to be markedly underestimated by adolescents' self-reports (Mannuzza & Gittelman, 1986). (We do not know if the same is true of adults' self-reports.) If the diagnosis is underestimated, differences between self-identified ADHD and non-ADHD groups may be blurred by a high rate of false-negative diagnoses. Therefore, much of the research is likely to underestimate a relationship between stimulant treatment and

ADHD. The question that arises is whether there is a direct path between ADHD and stimulant use or abuse.

The Conduct Disorder Link

As noted earlier, a link between ADHD and conduct disorder is now well established. Does CD play a mediating role in the drug-of-choice phenomenon? The literature does not address the issue directly, but four longitudinal studies that have reported on the independent influence of ADHD and CD on substance use provide relevant evidence. In their eight-year longitudinal study, Barkley et al. (1990) report on rates of nicotine, cocaine, and stimulants in ADHD subjects—with and without CD—and comparisons. It is evident from a perusal of Table 16.6, that the group with ADHD and CD accounts entirely for stimulant use among ADHD subjects relative to comparisons, and that ADHD itself is noncontributory. Relevant data on smoking are available from the Boston four-year longitudinal study (Milberger et al., 1997a, 1997b). As shown in Table 16.6, an excess of smoking is restricted to the ADHD subjects with CD. Finally, the large New Zealand epidemiological study also found that after controlling for CD, the presence of ADHD symptoms eight years earlier had no predictive relationship with either alcohol or nicotine abuse.

If indeed it is the individuals with conduct disorder who account for elevations in stimulant use relative to other drugs, are they medicating themselves? The fact that stimulants have been reported to ameliorate symptoms of conduct disorder (Klein et al., 1997) may suggest this possibility. However, it will not be a simple matter to implement studies that disentangle pleasure seeking from self-medicating mechanisms of stimulant use in those with conduct or antisocial personality disorders with a childhood diagnosis of ADHD.

Table 16.6
Relative Risk for Substance Use in ADHD as a Function of Conduct Disorder

Substance Used	Barkley et al., 1990			Milberger et al., 1997a, 1997b		
	ADHD with CD vs. no CD (N = 53 & 10)	ADHD with CD vs Comparisons (N = 10 & 66)	ADHD without CD vs. Comparisons (N = 53 & 66)	ADHD with CD vs no CD (N = 28 & 100)	ADHD with CD vs. Comparisons (N = 28 & 109)	ADHD without CD vs. Comparisons (N = 100 & 109)
Cigarettes	2.0	2.2	1.1	3.0	3.9	1.3
Cocaine	4.0	4.0	X[a]	—	B	—
Stimulants	8.0	80	X[a]	—	—	—

[a]Zero frequencies in both groups.

What about the issue of priming children for stimulant abuse if they are exposed to these compounds in childhood? All prospective follow-up studies have included a large proportion of stimulant-treated cases, but relationships between early stimulant treatment and subsequent abuse have not been reported. Unfortunately, such examinations must perforce rely on experiments of nature and are likely to be misleading. Thus, it is likely that many aspects of stimulant treatment, such as the decision to implement it and its duration, are related to clinical severity. In turn, chronic cases of ADHD are overrepresented among those who develop CD, which, in turn, is inescapably associated with SUD, including nicotine dependence. However, stimulant treatment does not cause the development of CD, and because its occurrence appears to mediate entirely the association between ADHD and SUD, it seems reasonable to conclude that priming for stimulant or other drug abuse does not occur as a function of exposure to stimulants in childhood.

CONCLUSIONS

We can draw two conclusions from the literature on the relationship among ADHD, CD, and stimulant use. First, although results are inconsistent, some report that ADHD children are more prone to use nicotine, cocaine, and stimulants. However, it is unlikely that ADHD has a direct influence on stimulant use, and conduct disorder appears to be a powerful mediating factor. Second, studies that relate ADHD to substance use without taking into account the prior or current presence of symptoms of conduct disorder or antisocial personality disorder fall short of providing interpretable information about the contribution of ADHD to patterns of drug use and abuse.

References

Barkley, R. A., Fischer, M., Edelbrock, C. S., & Smallish, L. (1990). The adolescent outcome of hyperactive children diagnosed by research criteria. I: An 8 year prospective follow-up study. *Journal of the American Academy of Child and Adolescent Psychiatry, 29*, 546–557.

Biederman, J., Wilens, T., Mick, E., Faraone, S. V., Weber, W., Curtis, S., Thornell, A., Pfister, K., Jetton, J. G., & Soriano, J. (1997). Is ADHD a risk factor for psychoactive substance use disorders? Findings from a four-year prospective follow-up study. *Journal of the American Academy of Child and Adolescent Psychiatry, 36*, 21–29.

Biederman, J., Wilens, T., Mick, E., Milberger, S., Spencer, T. J., & Faraone, S. V. (1995). Psychoactive substance use disorders in adults with attention deficit hyperactivity disorder (ADHD): Effects of ADHD and psychiatric comorbidity. *American Journal of Psychiatry, 152*, 1652–1658.

Boyle, M. H., Offord, D. R., Racine, Y. A., Fleming, J. E., Szatmari, P., & Links, P. S. (1993). Predicting substance use in early adolescence based on parent and teacher assessments of childhood psychiatric disorder: Results from the Ontario child health study follow-up. *Journal of Child Psychology and Psychiatry, 34*, 535–544.

Bryant, K. J., Rounsaville, B., Spitzer, R. L., & Williams, J. B. W. (1992). Reliability of dual diagnosis substance dependence and psychiatric disorders. *Journal of Nervous Mental Disorders, 180*, 251–257.

Cantwell, D. P. (1972). Psychiatric illness in the families of hyperactive children. *Archives of General Psychiatry, 27*, 414–417.

Carroll, K. M., & Rounsaville, B. J. (1993). History and significance of childhood attention deficit disorder in treatment-seeking cocaine abusers. *Comprehensive Psychiatry, 34*, 75–82.

Chilcoat, H. D., & Breslau, N. (1999). Pathways from ADHD to early drug use. *Journal of the American Academy of Child and Adolescent Psychiatry, 38*(11), 1347–1354.

DeMilio, L. (1989). Psychiatric syndromes in adolescent substance abusers. *American Journal of Psychiatry, 146*, 1212–1214.

De Obaldia, R., Parsons, O. A., & Yohman, R. (1983). Minimal brain dysfunction symptoms claimed by primary and secondary alcoholics: Relation to cognitive functioning. *International Journal of Neuroscience, 20*, 173–182.

Eyre, S. L., Rounsaville, B. J., & Kleber, H. D. (1982). History of childhood hyperactivity in a clinic population of opiate addicts. *Journal of Nervous and Mental Disease, 170*, 522–529.

Fisher, P. W., Shaffer, D., Piacentini, J. C., Lapkin, J., Kafantaris, V., Leonard, H., & Herzog, D. B. (1993). Sensitivity of the Diagnostic Interview Schedule for Children, 2nd Edition (DISC 2.1) for specific diagnoses of children and adolescents. *Journal of the American Academy of Child and Adolescent Psychiatry, 32*, 666–673.

Gittelman, R., Mannuzza, S., Shenker, R., & Bonagura, N. (1985). Hyperactive boys almost grown up: I. Psychiatric status. *Archives of General Psychiatry, 42*, 937–947.

Goodwin, D. W., Schulsinger, F., Hermansen, L., Guze, S., & Winokur, G. (1975). Alcoholism and the hyperactive child syndrome. *Journal of Nervous and Mental Disease, 160*, 349–353.

Hartsough, C. S., & Lambert, N. M. (1987). Pattern and progression of drug use among hyperactives and controls: A prospective short-term longitudinal study. *Journal of Child Psychology and Psychiatry, 28*, 543–553.

Hawkins, J. D., Catalano, R. F., & Miller, J. Y. (1982). Risk and protective factors for alcohol and other drug problems in adolescence and early adulthood: Implications for substance abuse prevention. *Psychological Bulletin, 112*, 64–105.

Hechtman, L., & Weiss, G. (1986). Controlled prospective fifteen year follow-up of hyperactives as adults: Non-medical drug and alcohol use and anti-social behaviour. *Canadian Journal of Psychiatry, 31*, 557–567.

Horner, B. R., & Scheibe, K. E. (1997). Prevalence and implications of attention-deficit hyperactivity disorder among adolescents in treatment for substance abuse. *Journal of the American Academy of Child and Adolescent Psychiatry, 36*, 30–36.

Kaminer, Y. (1992). Clinical implications of the relationship between attention-deficit hyperactivity disorder and psychoactive substance use disorders. *American Journal on Addictions, 1*, 257–264.

Khantzian, E. J. (1985). The self-medication hypothesis of addictive disorders: Focus on heroin and cocaine dependence. *American Journal of Psychiatry, 142*, 1259–1264.

Klein, R., Abikoff, H., Klass, E., Ganales, D., Seese, L., & Pollack, S. (1997). Clinical efficacy of methylphenidate in conduct disorder with and without attention deficit hyperactivity disorder. *Archives of General Psychiatry, 54*, 1073–1080.

Klein, R. G., & Mannuzza, S. (1999). The importance of childhood hyperactivity in the development of substance use disorders. In D. Bailly & J. Venisse (Eds.), *Addictions et psychiatrie* (pp. 107–122). Paris, France: Editions Masson.

Levin, E. D., Conners, C. K., Sparrow, E., Hinton, S. C., Erhardt, D., Meck, W. H., Rose, J. E., & March, J. (1996). Nicotine effects on adults with attention deficit/hyperactivity disorder. *Psychopharmacology, 123*, 55–63.

Levin, F. R., & Kleber, H. D. (1995). Attention-deficit hyperactivity disorder and substance abuse: Relationships and implications for treatment. *Harvard Review of Psychiatry, 2*, 246–258.

Lynskey, M. T., & Fergusson, D. M. (1995). Childhood conduct problems, attention deficit behaviors, and adolescent alcohol, tobacco, and illicit drug use. *Journal of Abnormal Child Psychology, 23*, 281–302.

Mannuzza, S., & Gittelman, R. (1986). Informant variance in the diagnostic assessment of hyperactive children as young adults. In J. E. Barrett & R. M. Rose (Ed.), *Mental disorders in the community* (pp. 243–254), New York: Guilford Press.

Mannuzza, S., & Klein, R. G. (2000). Long-term prognosis in attention-deficit/hyperactivity disorder. *Child and Adolescent Psychiatric Clinics of North America, 9*, 711–726.

Mannuzza, S., Klein, R. G., Bessler, A., Malloy, P., & LaPadula, M. (1993). Adult outcome of hyperactive boys: Educational achievement, occupational rank, and psychiatric status. *Archives of General Psychiatry, 50,* 565–576.

Mannuzza, S., Klein, R. G., Bessler, A., Malloy, P., & LaPadula, M. (1998). Adult psychiatric status of hyperactive boys grown up. *American Journal of Psychiatry, 155,* 493–498.

Mannuzza, S., Klein, R., Bonagura, N., Malloy, P., Giampino, T. L., & Addalli, K. A. (1991). Hyperactive boys almost grown up: V. Replication of psychiatric status. *Archives of General Psychiatry, 48,* 77–83.

Milberger, S., Biederman, J., Faraone, S. V., Chen, L., & Jones, J. (1997a). ADHD is associated with early initiation of cigarette smoking in children and adolescents. *Journal of the American Academy of Child and Adolescent Psychiatry, 36,* 37–44.

Milberger, S., Biederman, J., Faraone, S. V., Chen, L., & Jones, J. (1997b). Further evidence of an association between attention-deficit/hyperactivity disorder and cigarette smoking. *American Journal of Addiction, 6,* 205–217.

Milberger, S., Biederman, J., Faraone, S. V., Wilens, T., & Chu, M. P. (1997c). Associations between ADHD and psychoactive substance use disorders. *American Journal of Addiction, 6,* 318–329.

Milin, R., Loh, E., Chow, J., & Wilson, A. (1997). Assessment of symptoms of attention-deficit hyperactivity disorder in adults with substance use disorders. *Psychiatric Services, 48,* 1378–1380.

Murphy, K., & Barkley, R. A. (1996). Attention deficit hyperactivity disorder adults: Comorbidities and adaptive impairments. *Comprehensive Psychiatry, 37,* 393–401.

Pomerleau, O. F., Downey, K. K., Stelson, F. W., & Pomerleau, C. S. (1995). Cigarette smoking in adult patients diagnosed with attention deficit hyperactivity disorder. *Journal of Substance Abuse, 7,* 373–378.

Rounsaville, B. J., Anton, S. F., Carroll, K., Budde, D., Prusoff, B. A., & Gawin, F. (1991). Psychiatric diagnoses of treatment-seeking cocaine abusers. *Archives of General Psychiatry, 48,* 43–51.

Rounsaville, B. J., Kleber, H. D., Wilber, C., Rosenberger, D., & Rosenberger, P. (1981). Comparison of opiate addicts' reports of psychiatric history with reports of significant-other informants. *American Journal of Drug and Alcohol Abuse, 8,* 51–69.

Schenk, S., & Partridge, B. (1997). Sensitization and tolerance in psychostimulant self-administration. *Pharmacology, Biochemistry, and Behavior, 57,* 543–550.

Tarter, R. E., McBride, H., Buonpane, N., & Schneider, D. U. (1977). Differentiation of alcoholics. *Archives of General Psychiatry, 34,* 761–768.

Thompson, L. L., Riggs, P. D., Mikulich, S. K., & Crowley, T. J. (1996). Contribution of ADHD symptoms to substance problems and delinquency in conduct-disordered adolescents. *Journal of Abnormal Child Psychology, 24,* 325–347.

Weiss, R. D., Mirin, S. M., Griffin, M. L., & Michael, J. L. (1988). Psychopathology in cocaine abusers. *Journal of Nervous and Mental Disease, 176,* 719–725.

Whitmore, E. A., Mikulich, S. K., Thompson, L. L., Riggs, P. D., Aarons, G. A., Crowley, T. J. (1997). Influences on adolescent substance dependence: conduct disorder, depression, attention deficit hyperactivity disorder, and gender. *Drug and Alcohol Dependence, 47,* 87–97.

Windle, M. (1993). A retrospective measure of childhood behavior problems and its use in predicting adolescent problem behaviors. *Journal of Studies on Alcohol, 54,* 422–431.

Wood, D., Wender, P. H., & Reimherr, F. W. (1983). The prevalence of attention deficit disorder, residual type, or minimal brain dysfunction, in a population of male alcoholic patients. *American Journal of Psychiatry, 140,* 95–98.

Chapter 17

Medicated vs. Unmedicated ADHD Children—Adult Involvement With Legal and Illegal Drugs

by Jan Loney, Ph.D., John R. Kramer, Ph.D. and Helen Salisbury, Ph.D.

Introduction 17-2
Implicit Theories About Medication and Drug Abuse 17-3
   Theories That Medication Causes or Predisposes to Drug Abuse 17-3
      Pharmacological Predisposition 17-3
      Psychological Predisposition 17-3
   Theories That Medication Prevents or Protects Against Drug Abuse . . . 17-3
      Pharmacological Protection. 17-4
      Psychological Protection 17-4
Findings From Early Investigations 17-4
Recent California Study 17-5
New Iowa Study 17-5
   Who Was Chosen to Receive Medication, and Why 17-5
   Follow-up Review of Patients' Attitudes Toward and
     Experience With ADHD Medication 17-6
      Central Questions About Childhood Medication and
        Drug Abuse 17-7
      Adult Attitudes About Medication Prescribed in
        Childhood 17-7
      Relationships Between Childhood Medication Status
        and Adult Attitudes About Drugs 17-8
      Relationships Between Childhood Medication Status
        and Later Involvement With Drugs 17-8
      Relationships Between Childhood Medication Status and
        Adult Psychiatric Diagnoses 17-11

Implications of Newer Studies 17-11
Future Directions 17-13

INTRODUCTION

A substantial proportion of children with attention deficit hyperactivity disorder (ADHD*) develop substance use disorders, and a substantial proportion of children with ADHD are treated with central nervous system (CNS) stimulants. It is therefore inevitable that some substance use disorders will develop in ADHD children who have been treated with CNS stimulants. This does not logically mean that treatment with CNS stimulants leads to later drug use or causes substance abuse or related psychiatric disorders. To determine the effects of CNS stimulants on later drug use, the real question is: Do ADHD children who are treated with stimulant medication become more involved with drugs than comparable ADHD children who are not treated with stimulant medication?

It is hard to draw conclusions from the existing literature concerning childhood stimulant medication and later drug involvement. First, completely adequate prospective studies of the long-term effects of treatment with stimulant medication are rare, because completely random and fully informed assignment to long-term medicated and unmedicated groups is ethically and pragmatically difficult. For that reason, most studies of the impact of CNS stimulant treatment on the subsequent use of illegal drugs have had to rely on naturally occurring groups of medicated and unmedicated ADHD children. However, many naturally occurring unmedicated ADHD children remained untreated because they were less severely or pervasively hyperactive, less socially or academically impaired, and/or had fewer comorbid aggressive disorders. In other words, the naturally occurring unmedicated groups in these studies had lower initial risks for later drug abuse than did the naturally occurring medicated groups. Thus, any differences in subsequent drug use between groups that are medicated or unmedicated by choice, rather than by chance, cannot be attributed to medication status.

Because unmedicated ADHD children are rare in many clinical settings, some studies have divided medicated ADHD children into (1) "responders" (those who improved) versus "nonresponders" (those who did not improve), (2) those treated for a long versus a short time, or (3) those treated with stimulant medications versus those treated with nonstimulant medications. These studies leave unanswered central questions about drug outcomes in medicated versus unmedicated ADHD individuals. Many other studies have compared medicated ADHD children with normal control groups (neither ADHD nor medicated), thereby confounding the probably negative effects of the disorder with the possibly positive effects of its treatment.

Further, many early investigators studied initial experimentation with alcohol and marijuana in small numbers of young adolescent subjects who had barely entered the risk period for many illegal drugs. Few of these adolescent subjects had escalated their

---

* For convenience, in this chapter the term ADHD includes largely overlapping populations of children who in earlier studies were said to have childhood hyperactivity, minimal brain dysfunction (MBD), the hyperkinetic reaction of childhood, and attention deficit disorder with and without hyperactivity. However, the generic use of the term "ADHD" in this context does not imply that all members of an ADHD group had the disorder we now call ADHD. Nor does it imply that all group members had ADHD only, because many children with ADHD have additional complicating disorders.

use of the "gateway" drug marijuana, and few had even experimented with additional illegal drugs.

Finally, early studies of ADHD and drug use did not control for co-occurring oppositional defiant disorder (ODD) and conduct disorder (CD), which later proved to be more important predictors of drug involvement than ADHD as such (Barkley, Fischer, Edelbrock, & Smallish, 1990; Biederman et al., 1997; Halikas, Meller, Morse, & Lyttle, 1990; Mannuzza et al., 1991). One of the most important questions in interpreting both past and current studies of ADHD and drug use is whether the medicated and unmedicated ADHD groups differ in the proportion who have ODD or CD.

All the foregoing factors have combined to reduce the number of adequate and relevant studies of adult drug involvement in medicated and unmedicated ADHD children. Into this knowledge vacuum, a great deal of speculation and misinformation has flowed, particularly to tabloid newspapers, popular magazines, and sites along the information superhighway where personal agendas abound. Assertions that ADHD does not exist, accusations that Ritalin is being pushed on children by physicians who know that it is dangerous, and claims that ADHD children will be cured if only they are given more adult attention, less boring school assignments, fewer candy bars, expensive biofeedback training, or grape seed extract seem to have been disseminated more widely than actual research findings on diagnosis and treatment.

IMPLICIT THEORIES ABOUT MEDICATION AND DRUG ABUSE

There have long been concerns that stimulant treatment might predispose children to experiment with and abuse illegal drugs (Jacobvitz, Sroufe, Stewart, & Leffert, 1990; Topaz, 1971). Most of these concerns can be viewed as implicit theories that attempt to explain how early treatment could lead to later drug abuse.

Theories That Medication Causes or Predisposes to Drug Abuse

Pharmacological Predisposition. Medication could predispose children to drug abuse by means of an iatrogenic process in which children become addicted to their medication. Among the signs of this iatrogenic process would be early indicators of dependence (e.g., taking more pills than prescribed, reluctance to discontinue treatment, and experiencing a "high" from taking the medication).

Psychological Predisposition. Medication could predispose children to drug abuse by means of an initiation process in which children's attitudes about legal and illegal substances become more positive. This is often referred to as sending a message that "Using drugs is O.K." Among the signs of this initiation process would be positive attitudes toward drugs.

Theories That Medication Prevents or Protects Against Drug Abuse

Less widely proposed, but also plausible, are implicit theories that stimulant treatment could protect children from subsequent drug abuse.

Pharmacological Protection. Medication could protect children from later drug abuse by means of an improvement process in which symptoms that place children at risk for drug abuse are ameliorated by treatment. Among the signs of this improvement process would be the reduction of symptoms that are risk factors for drug abuse, such as impulsiveness and low self-esteem (Cohen & Thompson, 1982).

Psychological Protection. Medication could protect children from later drug abuse by means of a psychological immunization process in which negative experiences (e.g., feelings of external control, embarrassment, and unpleasant side effects) are associated with taking medication and then generalize to related illegal drugs. Among the signs of this immunization process would be reports of negative experiences with stimulant medication.

FINDINGS FROM EARLY INVESTIGATIONS

Kramer and Loney (1982) reviewed much of the early literature on hyperactivity (ADHD) and drug use. Most studies from that period reported no effects of stimulant treatment on later drug use. However, Blouin, Bornstein, and Trites (1978) found that clinically medicated children tended to use more beer and wine than did clinically unmedicated children but that good responders to stimulants used less alcohol than poorer responders did.

In one of the earliest and most thorough longitudinal studies of adolescent and adult ADHD, Weiss, Hechtman, and colleagues (Weiss, Kruger, Danielson, & Elman, 1975; Hechtman, Weiss, & Perlman, 1984) failed to find increased drug involvement in medicated hyperactive individuals from Canada, although both the Canadian and subsequent American (Kramer, Loney, & Whaley-Klahn, 1981) studies found that fewer medicated ADHD children than normal ones later tried hallucinogens.

In the five-year follow-up phase of the Iowa study (Kramer et al., 1981; Loney, Kramer, & Milich, 1981), adolescents who had been medicated were rated by their mothers as being more coordinated and having higher self-esteem than adolescents who had not been medicated, suggesting some medication-related symptom improvement. There were relatively few medication-related differences in drug experiences, but adolescents who had been medicated had less experience with marijuana and binge drinking, as well as fewer drunk driving and alcohol-related police contacts, than did their unmedicated counterparts. Medicated boys whose early progress notes showed a positive response to medication were rated by their mothers as less irritable at adolescent follow-up than were the boys who showed negative or no response to medication, and the positive responders were also less involved with illegal drugs at adolescence by self and parent report.

Goyer, Davis, and Rapoport (1979) described a hyperactive (and antisocial) teenager who took more medication than prescribed and said it made him feel "high," and a similar case was later reported by Jaffe (1991). While important and sobering, these appear to be isolated instances, and their relevance is mainly cautionary (Goldman, Genel, Bezman, & Slanetz, 1998). Subsequent accounts (Levin & Kleber, 1995; Schubiner et al., 1995) have suggested that, with appropriate care, drug-abusing adolescents and adults can be treated with methylphenidate (MPH).

RECENT CALIFORNIA STUDY

The most widely cited recent information about stimulant medication and drug abuse comes from the California community study. This large study followed 77 percent of 282 community-ascertained ADHD boys and girls into young adulthood. Twenty-three percent were African-American, Asian, or Hispanic. In the adult phase of the study, Lambert and Hartsough (1998) reported that adults who were medicated as children for ADHD were more likely to be dependent on tobacco and cocaine than were adults who were not medicated. However, these differences did not reach conventional levels of statistical significance (tobacco $p < .08$; cocaine $p < .13$), and the difference between medicated and unmedicated individuals in adult dependence on stimulants was reported as not significant. Although provocative, the conclusions by Lambert and Hartsough (1998) concerning cocaine do not correspond to the findings of the sparse literature on the long-term effects of stimulant medication on drug abuse. Modern brain imaging studies (Volkow et al., 1995) suggest that orally administered MPH does not produce euphoria at doses in the ordinary treatment range, but there is speculation that MPH may sensitize medicated individuals to drugs such as cocaine. The opportunity to use cocaine usually does not occur until early adolescence, when most ADHD children are no longer receiving stimulant medication. If the results of Lambert and Hartsough could be obtained in randomly assigned groups, it would suggest that orally administered MPH can create a lasting sensitivity to other stimulants, even after MPH treatment has been terminated.

NEW IOWA STUDY

Another comprehensive data archive on drug use in medicated and unmedicated ADHD children has been compiled by Loney and her colleagues (see Paternite, Loney, Salisbury, & Whaley, 1999). They have studied 295 ADHD boys born between 1954 and 1968, referred between ages 4 and 12 to the University of Iowa child psychiatry clinic for outpatient evaluation and treatment, and followed up as young adults between ages 21 and 23. At referral, the boys' average age was 8 years, their average full scale IQ was 100, their socioeconomic class (parents' education and occupation) varied widely, and 98 percent were white (like the Iowa population at the time). Of those eligible for the young adult follow-up, 74 percent were seen in person and completed a battery of tests and interviews. There were no differences between those who were seen as adults and those who were not across a range of initial symptom, intellectual, socioeconomic, and familial variables.

Who Was Chosen to Receive Medication, and Why

During this early period, parents who called the University of Iowa clinic to schedule an outpatient psychiatric evaluation for their son were assigned by an intake worker to an available diagnostic day and thus to one of three supervising child psychiatrists. Two of these faculty child psychiatrists recommended stimulant medication for 63 percent of their young male patients. The third supervising child psychiatrist recommended stimulant medication for 3 percent of his. Because of this "random" assignment to faculty physicians with different treatment preferences, 182 of the boys in the Iowa sample received stimulant medication, and 37 did not (instead, their parents and teachers were given short-term behaviorally oriented counseling). Senior members of the research team reviewed the pretreatment charts of all unmedicated subjects, retaining for follow-up only those who had ADHD and would therefore have been medicated had they been assigned to one of the medication-preferring psychiatrists. These reviewers were blind to adult outcomes.

The medicated and unmedicated Iowa ADHD boys did not differ in initial age, IQ, or socioeconomic status. However, trained judges who examined the psychiatric charts of all subjects rated the medicated boys as more inattentive-overactive before treatment than the unmedicated boys, who tended to be rated as more aggressive-defiant. However, neither parent nor teacher rating scales confirmed these differences. It is probable that the medicated and unmedicated groups did not actually differ in their childhood behavioral symptoms but that the supervising physicians described the boys differently because of differences in their psychiatric training, diagnostic beliefs, and treatment philosophies. Thus, the American-trained medication-preferring psychiatrists emphasized attention deficit disorder (i.e., inattention-hyperactivity) in the charts of their patients, while the British-trained medication-avoiding psychiatrist emphasized conduct disorder (i.e., aggression-defiance). This kind of difference between American and British experts in the diagnosis of attention deficit and conduct disorder is well documented (Prendergast et al., 1988). To be conservative, however, scores on both the inattention-overactivity and aggression-defiance behavioral dimensions were held constant in all analyses before testing for medication-related differences.

The medicated and unmedicated groups in the Iowa study did not differ on a long list of subsequent family-selected psychoeducational treatments (e.g., parent groups, family therapy, child psychotherapy, child groups, educational tutoring, and special classes). Eight percent of the medicated boys discontinued stimulant medication within the first month, but 84 percent took medication for at least a year (average duration of treatment was thirty-six months), and some continued on medication as long as seven years. The average daily maintenance dosage of MPH was 32 mg. Physicians and/or parents terminated medication when individual boys were between 6 and 17 years old (average termination age was 12). By the time of the young adult follow-up evaluation, all medicated individuals had discontinued CNS stimulant treatment for at least four years.

Follow-up Review of Patients' Attitudes Toward and Experience With ADHD Medication

At young adult follow-up, a forty-nine-question structured Medication Attitude Interview was administered. This instrument asked a variety of questions about the respondent's experience with and attitudes about treatment with medication (e.g., "Did taking the medication ever seem like a nuisance?"). A second instrument, the Medication Experience Questionnaire, contained twenty-four pairs of true-false statements about medication (e.g., "Medication made it easier to concentrate" and "Medication made it harder to concentrate") and four true-false statements about side effects (e.g., "Medication made my stomach hurt"). The twenty-five-item Licit-Illicit

Drug Scale (LIDS) surveyed attitudes about use of over-the-counter preparations, alcohol, marijuana, and hard drugs (e.g., "It is okay to use alcohol to cope with stress or to get over difficult times"). A federal epidemiological instrument, the National Survey on Drug Abuse (NSDA), included details of the respondents' experiences with eleven drugs: alcohol, tobacco, nonmedical barbiturates, nonmedical tranquilizers, nonmedical stimulants, marijuana, glue, cocaine, LSD, heroin, and other opiates. A standard structured interview, the 1979 lifetime version of the Schedule for Affective Disorders and Schizophrenia (SADS-L; Andreasen et al., 1981), was used to obtain adult psychiatric diagnoses according to the third edition of *Diagnostic and Statistical Manual of Mental Disorders* (DSM-III; American Psychiatric Association, 1980).

Central Questions About Childhood Medication and Drug Abuse. For this chapter, analyses designed to answer the following questions were carried out in the Iowa data archives.

1. What attitudes do adults who were treated with stimulant medication in childhood have about their treatment?

2. What relationship does childhood medication status (medicated versus unmedicated) have to adult attitudes about drug use and users?

3. What relationship does childhood medication status have to adult involvement with legal and illegal drugs?

4. What relationship does childhood medication status have to drug-related adult psychiatric diagnoses?

Adult Attitudes About Medication Prescribed in Childhood. There appear to have been few systematic surveys about the attitudes of medicated children or adults toward their treatment. In 1978, 81 percent of twenty-six medicated boys studied by Baxley and Turner (1978) said they would continue taking their medication if given the choice (because it helped them behave better), although 77 percent said they did not like taking it. In 1998, none of 161 children treated with Ritalin® (MPH) and surveyed five years later by Musser et al. (1998) believed that prescribed stimulants could lead to abuse.

The young Iowa men who were medicated in childhood had generally negative recollections of many aspects of their treatment. Many said they had disliked taking their medication (62 percent), avoided taking it (49 percent), or considered it a nuisance (49 percent). Some (26 percent) reported having been embarrassed about taking medication, and some (21 percent) said peers had teased them about it. Forty-two percent believed that medication had helped people control them, while 53 percent believed that medication had helped them control themselves. Between 6 percent and 18 percent had experienced unpleasant initial side effects (throwing up, stomach pains, and headaches).

Despite these negative associations, most of the previously medicated young adults described presumably positive effects of medication on the behaviors and feelings that treatment is typically intended to improve. Sixty-three percent reported that medication had made them more calm, 59 percent believed that medication made it easier to concentrate, and 60 percent said that medication made it easier for them to control their temper. Consistent with these reports, about two-thirds of the medicated young men thought medication had been a good or partly good idea for them.

With respect to possible dependence on their medication, 15 percent of the previously medicated adults reported that medication had made them feel "high," compared to 29 percent who said it had made them feel "dopey." Thirteen percent reported ever having taken more than their prescribed amount of MPH, 7 percent before a test or a game. Fewer than 2 percent reported ever taking their pills to feel good or get "high." Eight percent knew someone who had used medical or nonmedical pills to get "high," and 7 percent had worried about getting "hooked" on their medication. Twelve percent said that someone had wanted pills from them at least once, compared to 16 percent in a recent study by Musser et al. (1998). In addition, 8 to 10 percent believed that medication made them more likely to try other medications or drugs. Another 28 to 31 percent said that medication made them less likely to try other medications or drugs. The majority of the sample (another 59 to 64 percent) saw no relationship between their medication and subsequent use of medication or drugs.

Relationships Between Childhood Medication Status and Adult Attitudes About Drugs. Hierarchical and logistic regression analyses were carried out in the Iowa data to determine the relationship between childhood medication status (medicated or unmedicated) and a set of dependent variables measuring subsequent drug attitudes. For all analyses, the era in which each boy grew up (year of birth) and his scores on central behavioral symptom dimensions (inattention-overactivity and aggression-defiance) were held constant statistically before the effects of medication status were tested.

For all eleven drugs (tobacco, alcohol, nonmedical prescription drugs [barbiturates, tranquilizers, and stimulants], marijuana, glue, cocaine, LSD, heroin, and other opiates), there were no discernible differences between medicated and unmedicated individuals in their attitudes about use or users. There were no significant differences between medicated and unmedicated individuals in their opinions about whether specific drugs were addictive, with one exception: fewer medicated than unmedicated individuals considered nonmedical stimulants to be addictive (68 percent medicated versus 96 percent unmedicated; $p < .02$). Similarly, medicated individuals did not differ significantly from unmedicated ones in their stated intentions to use any of the illegal drugs in the future, even if they were legal.

Relationships Between Childhood Medication Status and Later Involvement With Drugs. Drug involvement was the sum of responses to three NSDA questions about (1) whether the adult respondent had ever tried the drug (experimentation), (2) whether he had used it at least once in the past month (continuation), and (3) whether his frequency of use during that month placed him in the top one-third of those who had ever tried the drug (escalation). Year of birth, inattention-overactivity, and aggression-defiance were again statistically controlled before the effects of medication status were tested.

Figures 17.1 and 17.2 summarize the differences between medicated and unmedicated ADHD groups on drug involvement. Significant differences between medicated and unmedicated ADHD individuals are indicated with a * symbol

Figure 17.1
Adult Involvement With Legal Substances and Nonmedical Pills in Medicated and Unmedicated ADHD Groups

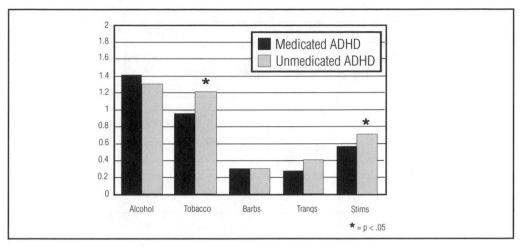

Figure 17.2
Adult Involvement With Illegal Drugs in Medicated and Unmedicated ADHD Groups

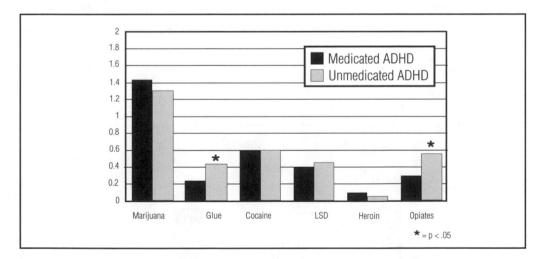

(all *p*'s < .05, two-tailed). For four of eleven surveyed drugs—tobacco, nonmedical stimulants, glue, and opiates other than heroin—medicated subjects were significantly less involved than comparable unmedicated subjects. Thus, for each of these drugs, medicated subjects had not progressed as far as unmedicated ones along the path from experimentation, through any continuing use at the time of the young adult follow-up, to more frequent current use than two-thirds of those who had tried the drug. For seven remaining drugs (alcohol, nonmedical barbiturates and tranquilizers, marijuana, cocaine, LSD, and heroin), childhood medication status was not associated with extent of involvement.

Figure 17.3
Adult Experimentation With Substances (Percent Who Ever Tried Them)
in Medicated and Unmedicated ADHD Groups

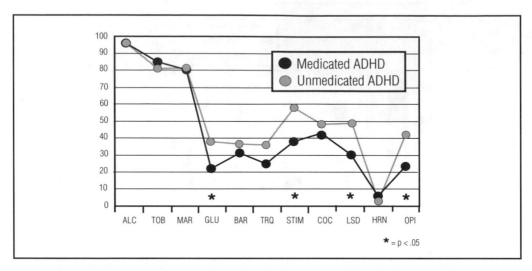

Figure 17.4
Adult Psychiatric Diagnoses in Medicated and Unmedicated ADHD Groups

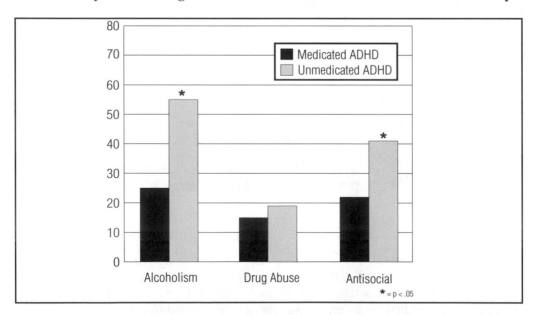

For easier comparison between drugs, and with other investigations, Figure 17.3 presents similar data on the common "ever tried" or experimentation measure. For four of eleven surveyed drugs—nonmedical stimulants, glue, LSD, and opiates—significantly fewer medicated subjects had ever tried the drug. This section of the NSDA also asked a question about experimentation with the drug PCP, which significantly fewer medicated subjects had ever tried. For seven remaining drugs (alcohol, tobacco, marijuana, nonmedical barbiturates and tranquilizers, cocaine and heroin), medication status was not associated with experimentation.

Relationships Between Childhood Medication Status and Adult Psychiatric Diagnoses. Three adult psychiatric diagnoses were selected from the SADS-L to measure progression of drug-related and norm-violating problems to the point of severe impairment: alcoholism, drug abuse disorder, and antisocial personality disorder (Figure 17.4). Year of birth, inattention-overactivity, and aggression-defiance were again held constant before the effects of medication status were tested. Significant differences between medicated and unmedicated subjects were obtained for two of those diagnoses: fewer medicated boys than unmedicated boys had adult diagnoses of alcoholism (27 percent of medicated ADHD versus 56 percent of unmedicated ADHD; $p = .002$) and antisocial personality disorder (24 percent of medicated ADHD versus 44 percent of unmedicated ADHD; $p = .004$). For the important diagnosis of drug abuse disorder (i.e., use of any nonprescribed drug except alcohol is excessive or compulsive, causes physical symptoms or alterations in mood or behavior, or interferes with expected daily routines or duties), medicated subjects did not differ from unmedicated ones (17 percent of medicated ADHD versus 19 percent of unmedicated ADHD).

IMPLICATIONS OF NEWER STUDIES

At ages 21 to 23, medicated ADHD boys in the Iowa study were significantly less involved than unmedicated ones with tobacco, nonmedical stimulants, glue, and opiates. Fewer medicated ADHD boys had even tried nonmedical stimulants, glue, LSD, or opiates. It is especially notable that ADHD boys who were medicated in childhood were significantly less likely as young adults to have experimented with nonmedical stimulants than comparable ADHD individuals who were not medicated—38 percent of medicated subjects had tried nonmedical stimulants, compared to 58 percent of unmedicated subjects (and 35 percent of normal classmates). Medicated ADHD boys were significantly less likely to have adult psychiatric diagnoses of alcoholism and antisocial personality disorder. Also of note, there were no significant differences between medicated and unmedicated ADHD boys in adult involvement with cocaine, or in subsequent diagnoses of drug abuse disorder.

For all significant differences between the Iowa medicated and unmedicated groups, it was the unmedicated individuals who were more involved with drugs and more likely to have developed drug-related adult psychiatric disorders. Contrary to popular opinion, these findings indicate that the risk of adult drug involvement and related psychiatric disorders is greater for children who are not medicated than for children who are. This may reflect the attempts of the unmedicated individuals to "self-medicate" their continuing problems, or it may represent the effects in unmedicated individuals of continuing behavioral and emotional risk factors, such as impulsiveness, irritability, and low self-esteem. Because childhood hyperactivity and aggressiveness were statistically controlled, however, the differences in drug involvement cannot be attributed to any differences between medicated and unmedicated boys in those symptom dimensions.

In contrast to the Iowa findings, the California medicated ADHD group is said to have used tobacco more heavily than the California unmedicated ADHD group and to have been more dependent on tobacco and cocaine (Lambert & Hartsough, 1998). The obvious problem is explaining why the two studies obtained different answers to what seems to be the same question. There are certain similarities between the two studies. For example, both sustained considerable attrition, probably because both initially had to solicit participation from entire clinic or school rosters, and not from a sample that had already been enrolled as children in a research investigation.

However, there are important differences between the two studies. To begin with, all Iowa subjects were referred to a university hospital clinic that was a tertiary care center for the state of Iowa. California subjects were identified from private, parochial, and public school classrooms; from letters sent to parents; or from contact with physicians in the community, and subjects were identified as ADHD by one, two, or three sources (school, home, physician). Thus, the clinic-referred ADHD subjects in the Iowa study were presumably more severely symptomatic, impaired, and comorbid before treatment than many of the community-identified ADHD subjects in the California study, and more representative of other clinical-referred ADHD boys. In addition, the California sample included girls and ethnic minorities. These differences should have made the California study more representative of its community than the Iowa study, and less subject to the referral biases that make children seen in clinics different from children not seen in clinics. However, the central question here is less epidemiological (e.g., "How many ADHD children are medicated?") than it is clinical (e.g., "How many medicated ADHD children abuse drugs compared to unmedicated ADHD children?"). The most important prerequisite for validly answering that question is not whether the ADHD children are representative of the community but whether the medicated and unmedicated groups were equivalent prior to treatment.

In the California community sample, ADHD children received medication or not based on family and physician choices rather than by random assignment. The California study has answered important questions about the natural prevalence of ADHD as defined by different segments of the community (Lambert, Sandoval, & Sassone, 1981), but it is not ideally designed for comparing the outcomes of medicated and unmedicated ADHD subjects. Because parents and practitioners in the California study decided who did or did not receive stimulant treatment, the medicated group contained more severely and pervasively hyperactive, impulsive, oppositional, and aggressive individuals, who would be expected to have worse adult outcomes, including more drug dependence. For example, only 8 percent of the California medicated group had mild ADHD, compared to 30 percent of the unmedicated group (Lambert, 1998). Similarly, almost all (92 percent) of the medicated individuals in the California study were pervasively ADHD—identified by all three informants (parent, school, and physician) instead of by one or two, as was the case for many of the unmedicated ADHD individuals. Some of the unmedicated ADHD children were not referred to physicians at all for diagnosis or treatment, creating another potentially confounding difference between the California medicated and unmedicated ADHD children.

In the Iowa clinical sample, referred boys were assigned independently of family or symptom factors to diagnostic appointment times supervised by faculty child psychiatrists with different treatment preferences. This semirandom procedure is believed to have created medicated and unmedicated groups with comparable symptom pro-files—but if it did not, scores on hyperactivity and aggression dimensions were sta-tistically controlled. Therefore, it is believed that the Iowa study had the advantage of a better design because its medicated and unmedicated groups had equivalent initial risks for later drug problems.

Taken alone, the Iowa findings would alleviate the general concern that treatment with CNS stimulants such as MPH has significant negative effects on children's sub-sequent attitudes about or use of a wide range of legal or illegal drugs, including tobacco, nonmedical stimulants, and cocaine. The implications of these findings, and those of the adolescent investigations with which they essentially agree (Kramer et al., 1981; Loney et al., 1981), should be carefully considered by those who advocate ignoring ADHD or replacing medication with no treatment, or with treatments of unknown effectiveness. However, taken alone, the California findings have been inter-preted to suggest that CNS medication in childhood increases the risks for subsequent dependency on tobacco and cocaine (but apparently not nonmedical stimulants). Although the Iowa study appears to be better controlled than the California study, it is important that more research be carried out to resolve the underlying questions.

FUTURE DIRECTIONS

The short-term effectiveness of treatment with CNS stimulant medication is unde-niable, and most studies comparing pharmacological and psychological treatments have found stimulant medication to be more effective. However, until recently (MTA Cooperative Group, 1999a, 1999b) there has been little convincing evidence for the continuing effectiveness of either short- or long-term medication after the treatment is terminated, leaving open the concern about long-term risks of medication treatments. Concerning the putative long-term risks of psychostimulant treatment, several other studies have recently attempted to shed some light on this problem. For example, Biederman, Wilens, Mick, Spencer, and Faraone (1999) prospectively examined the incidence of substance use in a sample of treated and untreated ADHD youth and found that untreated ADHD was a significant risk factor for substance use disorder in later adolescence. In contrast, pharmacotherapy treatment for ADHD was associated with an 85 percent reduction in overall likelihood of subsequent substance use disor-der. Similarly, other investigators have recently reported that the increased risk for substance use among youth with ADHD is borne largely by the comorbidity of CD with ADHD: thus, ADHD youth are at greater for the development of CD, which accounts for their increased risk for substance use—not the ADHD condition alone or its treatment with psychostimlants (Chilcoat & Breslau, 1999; Disney et al., 1999). Although these studies rely largely on case-control methods and/or retrospective reports, they do call into further question the presumed association between stimulant treatment and longer-term risks for substance use disorder.

Because both the California and Iowa studies of community and clinic ADHD samples as adults have reported effects of stimulant treatment on drug involvement years after medication was discontinued (although, importantly, in opposite direc-tions), it is essential that additional ethically designed longitudinal studies of ran-domly assigned medicated and unmedicated samples be attempted. In the National Institute of Mental Health (NIMH) Multimodal Treatment Study of ADHD (MTA),

(MTA Cooperative Group, 1999a, 1999b), for example, investigators plan eventually to compare longer-term drug attitudes and experimentation in ADHD children who were randomly assigned to medication or nonmedication (psychosocial treatment)—and, ultimately, to help resolve the debate about whether CNS stimulants increase or decrease later drug involvement. It should also be possible to test implicit theories concerning the associations among treatment with stimulant medication, attitudes about medication and illegal drugs, and involvement with legal and illegal drugs, especially within groups of young ADHD children who are being treated early in the risk period for drug experimentation. Longitudinal research of this type could study the development of attitudes about medication and drugs before, during, and after treatment, rather than measuring attitudes and drug use only later in life. In addition, the associations between aspects of childhood treatment with CNS stimulants (e.g., dosage, symptom reduction, and treatment duration) and later drug use and abuse must be further examined in medicated ADHD children from existing longitudinal studies (Paternite et al., 1999).

References

American Psychiatric Association. (1980). *Diagnostic and statistical manual of mental disorders* (3rd ed.). Washington, DC: Author.

Andreasen, N. C., Grove, W. M., Shapiro, K. W., Keller, M. B., Hirschfeld, R. M., & McDonald Scott, P. (1981). Reliability of lifetime diagnosis. A multicenter collaborative perspective. *Archives of General Psychiatry, 38*, 400–405.

Barkley, R. A., Fischer, M., Edelbrock, C. S., & Smallish, L. (1990). The adolescent outcome of hyperactive children diagnosed by research criteria. I: An 8-year prospective follow-up study. *Journal of the American Academy of Child and Adolescent Psychiatry, 29*, 546–557.

Baxley, G. B., & Turner, P. F. (1978). Hyperactive children's knowledge and attitudes concerning drug treatment. *Journal of Pediatric Psychology, 3*, 172–176.

Biederman, J., Wilens, T., Mick, B. A., Faraone, S. V., Weber, W., Curtis, S., Thornell, A., Pfister, K., Jetton, J. G., & Soriano, J. (1997). Is ADHD a risk factor for psychoactive substance use disorders? Findings from a four-year prospective follow-up study. *Journal of the American Academy of Child and Adolescent Psychiatry, 36*, 21–29.

Biederman, J., Wilens, T., Mick, E., Spencer, T., & Faraone, S. V. (1999, August). Pharmacotherapy of attention-deficit/hyperactivity disorder reduces risk for substance use disorder. *Pediatrics, 104*(2), e20.

Blouin, A. G., Bornstein, R. A., & Trites, R. L. (1978). Teenage alcohol use among hyperactive children: A five year follow-up study. *Journal of Pediatric Psychology, 3*, 188–194.

Chilcoat, H. D., & Breslau, N. (1999). Pathways from ADHD to early drug use. *Journal of the American Academy of Child and Adolescent Psychiatry, 38*(11), 1347–1354.

Cohen, N. J., & Thompson, L. (1982). Perceptions and attitudes of hyperactive children and their mothers regarding treatment with methylphenidate. *Canadian Journal of Psychiatry, 27*, 40–42.

Disney, E. R., Elkins, I. J., McGue, M., & Iacono, W. G. (1999). Effects of ADHD, conduct disorder, and gender on substance use and abuse in adolescence. *American Journal of Psychiatry, 156*, 1515–1521.

Goldman, L. S., Genel, M., Bezman, R. J., & Slanetz, P. J. (1998). Diagnosis and treatment of attention-deficit/hyperactivity disorder in children and adolescents. Council on Scientific Affairs, American Medical Association. *Journal of the American Medical Association, 279*, 1100–1107.

Goyer, P. F., Davis, G. C., & Rapoport, J. L. (1979). Abuse of prescribed stimulant medication by a 13-year-old hyperactive boy. *Journal of the American Academy of Child Psychiatry, 18*, 170–175.

Halikas, J. A., Meller, J., Morse, C., & Lyttle, M. D. (1990). Predicting substance abuse in juvenile offenders: Attention deficit disorder versus aggressivity. *Child Psychiatry and Human Development, 21*, 49–55.

Hechtman, L., Weiss, G., & Perlman, T. (1984). Hyperactives as young adults: Past and current substance abuse and antisocial behavior. *American Journal of Orthopsychiatry, 54*, 415–425.

Jacobvitz, D., Sroufe, L. A., Stewart, M., & Leffert, N. (1990). Treatment of attentional and hyperactivity problems in children with sympathomimetic drugs: A comprehensive review. *Journal of the American Academy of Child and Adolescent Psychiatry, 29*(5), 677–688.

Jaffe, S. L. (1991). Intranasal abuse of prescribed methylphenidate by an alcohol and drug abusing adolescent with ADHD. *Journal of the American Academy of Child and Adolescent Psychiatry, 30*, 773–775.

Kramer, J., & Loney, J. (1982). Childhood hyperactivity and substance abuse: A review of the literature. *Advances in Learning and Behavioral Disabilities, 1*, 225–259.

Kramer, J., Loney, J., & Whaley-Klahn, M. A. (1981). *The role of prescribed medication in hyperactive youths' substance use.* Paper presented at the 1981 annual meeting of the American Psychological Association, Los Angeles.

Lambert, N. M. (1998). *Stimulant treatment as a risk factor for nicotine use and stimulant abuse* [abstract]. Paper presented at NIH Consensus Development Conference on Diagnosis and Treatment of Attention Deficit Hyperactivity Disorder, Bethesda, MD.

Lambert, N. M., & Hartsough, C. S. (1998). Prospective study of tobacco smoking and substance dependencies among samples of ADHD and non-ADHD subjects. *Journal of Learning Disabilities, 31*, 533–544.

Lambert, N. M., Sandoval, J., & Sassone, D. M. (1981). Prevalence of hyperactivity and related treatments among elementary school children. In K. D. Gadow & J. Loney (Eds.), *Psychosocial aspects of drug treatment for hyperactivity* [AAAS Selected Symposium Series] (pp. 249–294)., Boulder, CO: Westview Press.

Levin, F. R., & Kleber, H. D. (1995). Attention-deficit hyperactivity disorder and substance abuse: Relationships and implications for treatment. *Harvard Review of Psychiatry, 2*, 246–258.

Loney, J., Kramer, J., & Milich, R. (1981). The hyperkinetic child grows up: Predictors of symptoms, delinquency, and achievement at follow-up. In K. Gadow & J. Loney (Eds.), *Psychosocial aspects of drug treatment for hyperactivity* (pp. 381–415). Boulder, CO: Westview Press.

Mannuzza, S., Klein, R. G., Bonagura, N., Malloy, P., Giampino, P. L., & Addalli, K. A. (1991). Hyperactive boys almost grown up: V. Replication of psychiatric status. *Archives of General Psychiatry, 48*, 77–83.

MTA Cooperative Group. (1999). A 14-month randomized clinical trial of treatment strategies for attention-deficit/hyperactivity disorder: Multimodal Treatment Study of Children with ADHD. *Archives of General Psychiatry, 56*(12), 1073–1086.

MTA Cooperative Group. (1999b). Moderators and mediators of treatment response for children with attention-deficit/hyperactivity disorder. *Archives of General Psychiatry, 56*, 1088–1096.

Musser, C. J., Ahmann, P. A., Theye, F. W., Mundt, P., Broste, S. K., & Mueller-Rizner, N. (1998). Stimulant use and the potential for abuse in Wisconsin as reported by school administrators and longitudinally followed children. *Journal of Developmental and Behavioral Pediatrics, 19*, 187–192.

Paternite, C. E., Jr., Loney, J., Salisbury, H., & Whaley, M. A. (1999). Childhood inattention-overactivity, aggression, and medication history as predictors of young adult outcomes. *Journal of Child and Adolescent Psychopharmacology, 9*(3), 169–184.

Prendergast, M., Taylor, E., Rapoport, J. L., Bartko, J., Donnelly, M., Zametkin, A., Ahearn, M. B., Dunn, G., & Wieselberg, H. M. (1988). The diagnosis of childhood hyperactivity: A U.S.-U.K. cross-national study of DSM-III and ICD-9. *Journal of Child Psychology and Psychiatry, 29*(3), 289–300.

Schubiner, H., Tzelepis, A., Isaacson, H., Warbasse, L. H., Sacharek, M., & Musial, J. (1995). The dual diagnosis of attention-deficit/hyperactivity disorder and substance abuse: Case reports and literature review. *Journal of Clinical Psychiatry, 56*, 146–150.

Topaz, P. M. (1971). Preliminary study of drug abuse and minimal brain dysfunction. *Journal of Learning Disabilities, 4*, 503–505.

Volkow, N. D., Ding, Y-S., Fowler, J. S., Wang, G-J., Logan, J., Gatley, J. S., Dewey, S., Ashby, C., Lieberman, J., Hitzemann, R., et al. (1995). Is methylphenidate like cocaine? Studies on their pharmacokinetics and distribution in the human brain. *Archives of General Psychiatry, 52,* 456–463.

Weiss, G., Kruger, E., Danielson, U., & Elman, M. (1975). Effect of long-term treatment of hyperactive children with methylphenidate. *Canadian Medical Association Journal, 112,* 159–165.

Chapter 18

Stimulant Treatment as a Risk Factor for Nicotine Use and Substance Abuse

by Nadine M. Lambert, Ph.D.

Introduction 18-2
Perspectives on ADHD as a Risk Factor for Tobacco Smoking
　and Substance Use 18-3
Hypotheses Pertaining to Higher Rates of Smoking and Substance
　Use by ADHD Individuals 18-3
　　Self-Medication Hypothesis 18-3
　　Stimulant Treatment Sensitization Hypothesis 18-4
Other Risk Factors for Substance Use 18-5
　　Tobacco as the Gateway to Substance Use 18-5
　　Problem Behavior as a Risk Factor for Substance Use 18-6
Research Objectives and Methods 18-6
　　Hypotheses Explored 18-6
　　Study Participants 18-7
　　Development of Research Diagnostic Proxies for ADHD 18-7
　　DSM-IV Criteria of Onset of Symptoms 18-8
　　Criteria for Severity of ADHD 18-8
　　DSM-IV ADHD Classification Compared With Original
　　　Classification of Subjects 18-9
Procedures for Collecting Tobacco and Substance Use Data 18-9
　　Variables in the Statistical Analyses 18-10
　　　Dependent Variables 18-10
　　　Independent Variables 18-11
　　　Statistical Analysis 18-12
Study Results 18-12
　　Survival Analyses 18-12
　　　Survival Analysis of Delay in Onset of Regular
　　　　Smoking by Severity of ADHD 18-12

Survival Analysis of Delay in Onset of Regular
Smoking by Use of CNS Stimulant
Treatment in Childhood 18-13
Relationship of Severity of ADHD and Childhood Stimulant
Treatment to Adult Smoking 18-15
Multivariate Prediction of Adult Daily Smoking and DSM-III-R
Psychoactive Substance Use Disorders 18-15
Support for the Self-Medicating Hypothesis 18-17
Support for the Sensitization Hypothesis 18-18
Partial Support for Tobacco Gateway Hypothesis 18-19
Childhood Problem Behavior Not Supported as a Factor in
PSUD 18-19
Conclusion 18-20

INTRODUCTION

Longitudinal research with attention deficit hyperactivity disorder (ADHD) participants and agemate controls has shown that those individuals with ADHD smoke at an earlier age (Hartsough & Lambert, 1987) and in early adulthood have higher rates of daily smoking, nicotine dependence, and cocaine and stimulant dependence (Lambert & Hartsough, 1998) but not marijuana and alcohol dependence. A significant relationship between stimulant treatment in childhood and daily smoking in adulthood and between tobacco and cocaine dependence also has been reported (Lambert & Hartsough, 1998).

This chapter explores the role of severity of ADHD according to the fourth edition of *Diagnostic and Statistical Manual of Mental Disorders* (DSM-IV; American Psychiatric Association, 1994) and the length of childhood stimulant medication treatment as risk factors for tobacco smoking and DSM-III-R (American Psychiatric Association, 1987) substance dependency and heavy use (abuse). The chapter reports on an investigation that explored the roles of ADHD and histories of childhood central nervous system (CNS) stimulant treatment as risk factors for adult tobacco and substance use for 399 of 492 participants in a prospective longitudinal investigation begun in childhood. The participants and their CNS stimulant treatment status were as follows: 104 severe ADHD (42 percent treated with stimulants), 72 moderate ADHD (57 percent treated), 51 mild ADHD (12 percent treated), and 192 participants (5 percent treated) who did not satisfy DSM-IV ADHD research criteria. Other independent variables included severity (pervasiveness) of ratings of conduct problems in childhood, age of initiation into tobacco, gender, and birth-year cohort groups.

The dependent variables in the analyses were the uptake of regular smoking during the developmental period, daily smoking in adulthood, and adult DSM-III-R psychoactive substance use disorders. Lifetime use was not reported.

Severity of ADHD was significantly related to the age of becoming a regular smoker, daily smoking in adulthood, and DSM-III-R diagnoses of tobacco, cocaine, and stimulant dependence but not to marijuana and alcohol dependence. Stimulant treatment in childhood was significantly related to the age regular smoking began, adult daily smoking, and DSM-III-R substance dependence diagnoses of tobacco and cocaine.

The results are anylyzed in terms of support for both a self-medicating process for those with severe ADHD symptoms and a sensitization hypothesis for those who were treated with CNS stimulants. This chapter also explores evidence for the tobacco gateway theory and problem behavior theory as competing explanations for adult involvement with tobacco and substances.

PERSPECTIVES ON ADHD AS A RISK FACTOR FOR TOBACCO SMOKING AND SUBSTANCE USE

Longitudinal studies have reported a pattern of excessive tobacco use among ADHD individuals (Milberger, Biederman, Faraone, Chen, & Jones, 1997), with higher rates of cigarette smoking at mid-adolescence and an earlier onset of smoking compared with agemate controls (Barkley, Fischer, Edelbrock, & Smallish, 1990; Lynskey & Ferguson, 1995). Conduct disorders have also been implicated in these studies and raise questions about the relative strength of ADHD as the primary risk factor. One recent study (Milberger et al., 1997) reported that even with controls for adolescent conduct disorders, ADHD was still a significant predictor. A four-year follow-up study of children ages 6–17 (Biederman et al., 1997) showed no differences between ADHD subjects and normal controls for psychoactive substance use disorder (PSUD), but these participants were not at the age at which one could expect maximum use of substances.

Several longitudinal studies have reported elevated rates of illegal drug use by ADHD subjects as adults (Gittelman, Mannuzza, Shenker, & Bonagura, 1985; Mannuzza, Gittelman-Klein, & Addalli, 1991; Mannuzza, Klein, Bessler, Malloy, & LaPadula, 1993), but these studies did not differentiate among types of psychoactive substances used and provided no information about adult smoking status. Higher rates of drug abuse and dependency among adults with ADHD (Biederman et al., 1993) were reported when comorbid DSM-III-R diagnoses of psychiatric disorders were accounted for. Conduct disorder was also an independent predictor of substance use disorders, and there were different patterns of comorbidity among ADHD subjects and controls related to substance use outcomes (Biederman et al., 1995).

Persistent ADHD, with and without psychiatric disorders, was associated with age of onset of PSUD (Wilens, Biederman, Mick, Faraone, & Spencer, 1997; Wilens, Biederman & Spencer, 1996). Further exploration of ADHD and PSUD by these authors (Wilens, Biederman, & Mick, 1998) concluded that the duration of PSUD was longer (twelve years vs. five years) and the rates of remission were lower for ADHD subjects.

HYPOTHESES PERTAINING TO HIGHER RATES OF SMOKING AND SUBSTANCE USE BY ADHD INDIVIDUALS

Self-Medication Hypothesis

Self-medication is often cited as the most reasonable hypothesis to explain the higher rates of substance use among individuals with ADHD. Particular drugs are selected because of the interplay between the psychopharmacological action of the drug and the dominant emotional feeling of the individual (Brook, Whiteman, Gordon, & Cohen, 1986; Cocores, Davies, Mueller, & Gold, 1987; Khantzian, 1985). A survey of adult patients seeking treatment for cocaine abuse reported that 35 percent of them had been diagnosed with ADHD (Rounsaville et al., 1991). Cocaine abusers have been reported (Cocores et al., 1987) to include those who were depressed, those with bipolar disorders who used cocaine for its self-medicating effects, and adults with ADHD who used cocaine to increase attention span and reduce motor restlessness. It has also been suggested (Cocores et al., 1987) that ADHD has an etiological and self-mediating role in cocaine abuse. Treatment of adult cocaine abusers (with and without an ADHD diagnosis) with methylphenidate treatment (Gawin & Kleber, 1986; Kleber & Gawin, 1986) showed that the methylphenidate treatment effected reduced cocaine use in the ADHD subjects.

The anecdotal reports and small sample sizes of some of the studies on which the self-medication proposition is based and the lack of control over the contributions of other competing factors (Kaminer, 1992) weaken the proposition that individuals with ADHD may be self-medicating with cocaine or stimulants. On the other hand, clinical reports suggest that substance-dependent persons self-medicate because they cannot regulate their self-esteem, relationships, or self-care. Their addictive vulnerability results from exposure to drugs combined with the inability to tolerate or to know their feelings and their deficits in self-care. Such conditions derive from developmental deficiencies in the individual's failure to consider, at the cognitive level, cause-consequence relationships involving harmful or dangerous conditions and the inability to anticipate harm and danger (Barkley, 1997). The self-medicating hypothesis for ADHD individuals, therefore, can be considered a cognitively compromised capacity to control or self-regulate the impulse to use substances and to become dependent on them.

The self-medicating hypothesis in this chapter predicts that the more severe the ADHD symptoms, the greater the use of stimulants because stimulants work to reduce the distress and compromising conditions presented by the ADHD symptoms.

Stimulant Treatment Sensitization Hypothesis

Behavioral sensitization is a process whereby intermittent stimulant exposure produces a time-dependent, enduring, and progressively greater or more rapid behavioral response. It has been demonstrated in every mammalian species in which it has been examined, but it has been little studied in humans (Strakowski & Sax, 1998). The results of a carefully controlled, randomized, double-blind study of increased doses of d-Amphetamine, administered alternately with matched placebo, supported a sensitization effect for some amphetamine-induced behaviors, such as faster rates of eye blinks and increased motor activity/energy (Strakowski & Sax, 1998). Sensitization may underlie the development of drug craving in humans, thereby contributing to substance dependence (Robinson & Berridge, 1993).

Animal models of sensitization are well established. Methylphenidate, the most commonly used CNS stimulant treatment has pharmacological properties that closely resemble other stimulant drugs, including cocaine and amphetamine (Volkow et al., 1996); therefore, repeated exposure to methylphenidate may be expected to produce effects similar to repeated exposure to other psychostimulants. Rats that are pre-exposed with amphetamine or cocaine learn to self-administer amphetamines and cocaine more rapidly than do rats that are not exposed. (Horger, Giles, & Schenk, 1992; Lett, 1989; Piazza, Deminiere, Lemma, & Simon, 1989; Piazza, Deminiere, LeMoal, & Simon, 1990; Schenk & Partridge, 1997; Shippenberg & Heidbreder, 1995; Vezina, 1996). Schenk and Partridge (1999) have shown in a recent study that rats pretreated with methylphenidate more rapidly reacquired cocaine self-adminis-tration. The motor-activating effects of cocaine were more evident in rats that were exposed to methamphetamine (Kaneto & Hori, 1988) and amphetamine (Schuster, Grace, & Bates, 1977). Similarly, exposure to amphetamine (Schenk et al., 1993) or nicotine (Horger et al., 1992) sensitized rats to the reinforcing effects of cocaine. The sensitizing effects of the preexposure regimen are persistent and have been demon-strated to effect stimulant responsiveness for months following the last exposure (Kolta, Shreve, De Souza, & Uretsky, 1985; Valadez & Schenk, 1994). These studies suggest that a similar form of sensitization may be occurring in humans who are exposed to methylphenidate and other CNS stimulants, and that the propensity to self-administer cocaine and other stimulants may be, at least in part, determined by the individual's pharmacological history.

Longitudinal studies of individuals with ADHD (Hechtman, Weiss, & Perlman, 1984) have reported that stimulant treatment in childhood is associated with elevated levels of substance use in childhood, age of initiation into cocaine use, and age of maximum use of cocaine. The age of first CNS treatment and the number of years of stimulant treatment was significantly related to tobacco smoking from ages 16–18 (Lambert, 1988).

The sensitization hypothesis predicts that CNS stimulant treatment is a risk factor for subsequent use of stimulants such as tobacco and cocaine but not for marijuana and alcohol. The prospective longitudinal research with community samples of both ADHD and agemate controls with different psychostimulant treatment histories and different presenting problems in childhood provides a natural laboratory for investigating this hypothesis. Documented histories of stimulant exposure are available in order to avoid problems associated with inaccurate adult reports of prescription drugs used in child-hood. It should be noted at the outset, however, that the rationale for the investigation does not argue for a decisive role for either an ADHD self-medicating hypothesis or a CNS stimulant sensitization hypothesis as these two risk factors appear to be jointly involved in the dynamics of substance abuse among individuals with ADHD.

OTHER RISK FACTORS FOR SUBSTANCE USE

Tobacco as the Gateway to Substance Use

Studies of the initiation into substance use consistently show that most people who had ever used illegal drugs had earlier used cigarettes or alcohol whereas those who had never smoked only infrequently abused illicit substances (Kandel, Kessler, & Margulies, 1978; Kandell, Yamaguchi, & Chen, 1992). Not only is tobacco depen-dence an important addiction on its own merits (Henningfield, Clayton, & Pollin, 1990), but the incidence and severity of various drug dependencies are related to tobacco use, and tobacco use, in turn, may be increased by dependence-producing drugs (Fleming, Leventhal, Glynn, & Ershler, 1989; Henningfield, Cohen, & Slade, 1991; Torabi, Bailey, & Madj-Jabbari, 1993).

Problem Behavior as a Risk Factor for Substance Use

Several investigators (Jessor & Jessor, 1980; Robins, 1990) have suggested initiation to tobacco as well as other illicit drugs may have common determinants in psychosocial unconventionality. General behavior dysfunction in childhood and adolescence, characterized by problem behavior in childhood and the presence of conduct disorders in adolescence—both of which are also prevalent among ADHD groups—leads to both more intensive substance use and use of a variety of different substances.

ADHD symptoms can be considered a subset of behaviors within the domain of behavior problems and psychosocial unconventionality. Hinshaw (1987) noted that there is sufficient evidence for considering the domains of hyperactivity/attention deficits and conduct problems/aggression as partially independent, and urged investigators to use measures of conduct problems/aggression as well as attention/hyperactivity-impulsivity in order to clarify the relationships of these problem behaviors to outcomes.

RESEARCH OBJECTIVES AND METHODS

Hypotheses Explored

This chapter explores the roles of ADHD and CNS stimulant treatment in the age at which one becomes a regular smoker; daily smoking in adulthood; and DSM-III-R PSUD of tobacco, cocaine, stimulant, marijuana, and alcohol dependence.

These hypotheses are as follows:

1. Severity of ADHD symptoms will be reflected in (a) earlier regular smoking and adult smoking status and (b) significantly higher rates of dependence and lifetime use of substances with stimulating properties—tobacco, cocaine, and stimulants—but not with substances acting as depressants, such as marijuana and alcohol. If tenable, this hypothesis would support the self-medicating needs of individuals with ADHD because it could be argued that aspects of behavioral inhibition reflected in the symptomatology of ADHD are risk factors for seeking out these substances.

2. The CNS stimulant treatment sensitization hypothesis proposes that early exposure to either methylphenidate or amphetamines predisposes individuals to adult tobacco, stimulant, and cocaine use, because the increased neurochemical sensitization enhances responsiveness to cocaine's reinforcing properties. The sensitization hypothesis predicts that participants treated with CNS stimulants in childhood will become regular smokers earlier, have higher rates of adult smoking, and be significantly related to dependence on tobacco, cocaine, and stimulants but not to marijuana and alcohol.

3. In multivariate analysis both severity of ADHD and childhood CNS stimulant treatment will jointly affect the dependent variables of adult daily smoking and DSM-III-R dependence on substances with stimulating properties, namely,

tobacco, cocaine, and stimulants, but not on substances that act as depressants, such as marijuana or alcohol.

Study Participants

The participants in this investigation were 399 adults who have been subjects since childhood in a prospective longitudinal investigation of the life histories of 492 subjects, approximately one-third of whom were diagnosed and treated for ADHD symptoms. The ADHD subjects and agemate controls, born 1962 to 1968, were selected from a sample of 5,212 kindergarten through fifth-grade children attending the public, parochial, and private schools in the East Bay Region of the San Francisco Bay Area in the 1973–1974 school year. These participants were evaluated prospectively through the end of high school and later as young adults. Of the initial 492 subjects, 22 percent were female and 23 percent were members of minority ethnic groups. The procedures for identifying the subjects have been explicated elsewhere (Lambert, Sandoval, & Sassone, 1978, 1979), but are summarized herein.

The diagnostic criteria for "hyperactivity" (ADHD) required agreement among the three social systems involved in the identification and treatment of the child: the physician, the parent, and the teacher. Parents and school teachers of all 5,212 children in 191 K–5 classrooms were asked to inform investigators if the child was being treated for hyperactivity or if they were planning to request a medical evaluation. Every physician in the area who treated children was contacted and asked to notify the investigators, after receiving parental permission, with the names of children they were treating for hyperactivity or those for whom they were prescribing stimulant treatment. A standard medical evaluation and diagnostic system was developed based on surveys of physicians (pediatricians, pediatric neurologists, child psychiatrists, and family practice physicians) who were treating children referred for evaluation (Sandoval, Lambert, & Yandell, 1979) of "overactivity, restlessness, distractibility, and short attention span" (American Psychiatric Association, 1968, p. 50), the cardinal symptoms used for the diagnosis of hyperkinetic disorder of childhood. Of the 5,212 children, 175 were classified as "primary hyperactive," 39 were "secondary hyperactive" (possible competing medical problems), 68 were untreated hyperactives (evidence from two, but not three of the diagnostic sources, or the parents did not seek medical assistance with the child's problem), 51 were behavior controls (children who had behavior problems, but did not meet the diagnostic criteria), and 159 were agemate controls attending the same classrooms with the hyperactive subjects.

Development of Research Diagnostic Proxies for ADHD

Concomitant with the identification of all the children in the representative sample who met the social system definition for hyperactivity, parent and teacher rating scales were prepared, composed of items from the research literature that had been shown to be sensitive to CNS treatment effects or that differentiated between hyperactive and normal children. The results of these ratings were not used to identify participants for the prevalence phase.

Four subscales on the Children's Attention and Adjustment Survey (CAAS) (Lambert & Hartsough, 1987; Lambert, Hartsough, & Sandoval, 1990), reflecting "inattention," "hyperactivity," "impulsivity," and "conduct problems" were defined by factor-analytic studies. The items composing each scale were consistent with the DSM criteria for these symptoms permitting the development of research diagnostic criteria for DSM-III attention deficit disorder with and without hyperactivity (American Psychiatric Association, 1980; Lambert, 1988), DSM-III-R attention deficit hyperactivity disorder (American Psychiatric Association, 1987; Lambert & Hartsough, 1998), and DSM-IV ADHD (American Psychiatric Association, 1994). The alphas for the school and home form scales were respectively: 0.89 and 0.85 (inattention), 0.85 and 0.89 (hyperactivity), 0.78 and .78 (impulsivity), and 0.92 and 0.91 (conduct problems).

The research diagnostic criteria for DSM-IV ADHD include pervasive (both home and school) and situational (either home or school) ratings on the CAAS on inattention and hyperactivity-impulsivity, and evidence for early onset of symptoms. The alpha reliabilities for the scale combining hyperactivity and impulsivity were 0.89 for the school form and 0.83 for the home form.

Reclassifications of the participants according to DSM-IV research diagnostic criteria are not retrospective; they are based on parent and teacher ratings on the CAAS at the time a subject entered the study. An average rating of 2.5 (on a scale from 1 to 4) identified subjects who would have met the DSM-IV symptom criteria.

DSM-IV Criteria of Onset of Symptoms

Our proxy for onset of symptoms was the presence of one of the following:

- A parent report that the symptoms first were noted before age 8;

- Medical assistance was sought before the age of 8; or

- Parent rating of the child's temperament during infancy and early childhood of high "activity level" (hyperactivity) or low "attention span and persistence" (inattention) based on analysis of temperament questions from the Berkeley parent interview (Lambert, 1982).

Criteria for Severity of ADHD

We followed the lead of other investigators (Beck, Young, & Tarnowski, 1990; Boudreault et al., 1988; Goodman & Stevenson, 1989; Schachar, Rutter, & Smith, 1981) who have shown the importance of distinguishing between subjects whose symptoms are situational or characteristic of behavior in one setting and those whose symptoms are pervasive or characteristic of behavior in more than one setting as necessary prerequisites to clarifying the behavioral antecedents of cognitive and social outcomes.

We established four levels of severity of ADHD:

- *CAAS DSM-IV ADHD—Severe.* A subject was classified as pervasive and severe ADHD if one of the following research criteria was met on both the home and school forms of the CAAS: (1) combined type—both inattentive and hyperactive/impulsive; (2) primarily inattentive; and (3) primarily hyperactive-impulsive.

- *CAAS DSM-IV ADHD—Moderate.* These participants were situationally ADHD with ratings on either the home form or the school form that met the research criteria for inattention and hyperactive/impulsive or showed a mixed patterns of symptoms: inattention on one form and hyperactive/impulsive on another.

- *CAAS DSM-IV ADHD—Mild.* Only one of the symptoms in one setting was present.

- *CAAS DSM-IV ADHD—No symptoms present.* None of the research diagnostic criteria was met.

Note: An average rating of 2.5 or higher on the conduct problem scales of either the home or school form of the CAAS was used to classify a participant as "severe" (pervasive) if both parent and teacher ratings were in the criterion range and "moderate" (situational) if only one rating was in the criterion range.

DSM-IV ADHD Classification Compared With Original Classification of Subjects

Evaluation of the diagnostic efficiency of these criteria (Kessel & Zimmerman, 1993) comparing the social system criteria with the DSM-IV ADHD research criteria for the total original sample of 492 produced sensitivity and specificity estimates of 93 percent and 86 percent with a 90 percent positive predictive power. The false-negative rate was 7 percent and the false-positive rate was 14 percent with a kappa of 0.79.[1]

Table 18.1 presents the distribution of the 399 participants in this investigation by DSM-IV ADHD by the original classification. Table 18.2 provides data on the numbers of participants who were treated with CNS stimulants by the original classification and the DSM-IV research diagnostic criteria.

PROCEDURES FOR COLLECTING TOBACCO AND SUBSTANCE USE DATA

The tobacco and substance use data for this research were obtained as part of an adult interview containing eight major sections, portions of which were selected for this study. The first section provided information on ADHD symptoms and treatment history. A second section replicated the child and adolescent interview questions of life history reports of tobacco use and current smoking status and use of cocaine, stimulants, marijuana, beer and wine, alcohol, heroin/opiates, glue/inhalants, and psychedelics. The Quick Diagnostic Interview Schedule III-R or QDIS III-R (Marcus, Robins, & Bucholz, 1990) was administered to provide DSM-III-R diagnoses of psychoactive substance use disorders and diagnoses of the major psychiatric disorders.

Interview protocols were obtained for 399 (81 percent) of the original 492 subjects (77 percent of the ADHD and 86 percent of the controls), and analyses of differential loss (Hartsough, Babinski, & Lambert, 1996) showed no significant differences in the interviewed group compared to rates in the total sample for ADHD, gen-

Table 18.1
Number and Percent of Adult Participants Initially Identified by Social System Definers Reclassified With DSM-IV ADHD Research Diagnostic Proxies ($N = 399$)

DSM-IV ADHD	Original Classification Groups—N & % Satisfying DSM-IV ADHD Research Diagnostic Criteria				
Patterns & Severity	Primary $N = 136$	Hyperactives Secondary $N = 31$	Untreated $N = 50$	Controls Behavior $N = 41$	Agemates $N = 141$
Severe Pervasive Combined	37 (27%)	5 (16%)	5 (10%)	0	0
Pervasive Inattentive	21 (16%)	9 (29%)	11 (22%)	2 (5%)	3 (2%)
Pervasive Hyper-Impulsive	7 (5%)	1 (3%)	3 (6%)	0	0
Total Severe	**65 (48)%**	**15 (48%)**	**19 (38%)**	**2 (5%)**	**3 (2%)**
Moderate SituationalMixed	3 (2%)	0	3 (6%)	0	0
Situational Combined	41 (30)%	9 (29%)	8 (16%)	3 (7%)	5 (4%)
Total Moderate	**44 (32%)**	**9 (29%)**	**11 (22%)**	**3 (7%)**	**5 (4%)**
Mild Situational Inattentive	12 (9%)	3 (10%)	12 (24%)	3 (7%)	7 (5%)
Situational Hyper-Impulsive	7 (5%)	0	4 (18%)	0	3 (2%)
Total Mild	**19 (14%)**	**3 (10%)**	**16 (32%)**	**3 (7%)**	**10 (7%)**
Symptom Criteria Not Met	**8 (6%)**	**4 (13%)**	**4 (8%)**	**33 (81%)**	**123 (87%)**
Symptom Criteria Met	**128 (94%)**	**27 (87%)**	**46 (92%)**	**8 (19%)**	**18 (13%)**

der, family configuration, social class, and ethnic status and indicated that there was no appreciable impact on reported rates of tobacco and substance use that could be attributed to attrition at follow-up.

Variables in the Statistical Analyses

Dependent Variables. There were three dependent variables:

- *Age of regular smoking.* Our life history records compared with the adult interview provided a record of the age when regular smoking began for all of those who had tried a cigarette.

Table 18.2
Rates of Treatment With CNS Stimulants for Participants Grouped by Initial Classification and Research Diagnostic Criteria for Severity of DSM-IV ADHD

| Severity of DSM-IV ADHD | N Prescribed Stimulant Treatment and Total N in Each Group | | | | | Total by Severity of ADHD |
| | Primary | Hyperactives Secondary | Untreated | Controls Behavior | Agemates | |
	N = 136	N = 31	N = 50	N = 41	N = 141	
Severe	51 of 64	11 of 15	0 of 19	0 of 2	0 of 3	62 of 103 (60%)
Moderate	40 of 44	7 of 10	0 of 11	1 of 3	0 of 5	48 of 73 (66%)
Mild	10 of 19	1 of 3	0 of 16	0 of 3	0 of 10	11 of 51 (22%)
Not ADHD	7 of 8	2 of 4	0 of 4	0 of 33	1 of 123	10 of 172 (6%)
Total by Original Classification	108 of 135 (80%)	21 of 32 (66%)	0 of 50	1 of 41 (2%)	1 of 141 (< 1%)	131 of 399 (33%)

- *Adult smoking status.* An adult smoker was defined as having smoked 100 cigarettes lifetime and being a current smoker (Pierce & Burns, 1990). Participants were grouped as a daily smoker, smoker—but not a daily smoker, not a smoker, and initiated or never smoked.

- *DSM-III-R diagnoses of PSUD.* The QDISIIIR provided dependency diagnoses of nicotine, cocaine, stimulants, marijuana, and alcohol.

Independent Variables. There were five independent variables:

- *Severity of ADHD.* Levels of severity: severe, moderate, mild, and not ADHD.

- *Severity of Conduct Problems.* Levels of severity: severe or pervasive, moderate or situational, or no conduct problems

- *Childhood CNS Stimulant Treatment.* Prospective histories of treatment interventions for ADHD participants included age at which CNS stimulants were first prescribed, the number of years the stimulant treatment was used, and the age at which treatment stopped. Among those subjects who used CNS stimulants, 69 percent used only methylphenidate, 16 percent used combinations of methylphenidate with other CNS stimulants and 15 percent used other CNS stimulants (Dexedrine, Benzedrine, Cylert, or Deaner). CNS stimulants were used by 46 percent of the severe DSM-IV ADHD, 57 percent of the moderate DSM-IV ADHD, 12 percent of the mild DSM-IV ADHD, and 5 percent who were not classified as DSM-IV ADHD. Subjects were categorized for the analysis as no CNS stimulant treatment; treatment up to one year (32 percent of those treated), and treatment up two or more years (68 percent of those treated).

- *Age of initiation into smoking.* This variable was categorized as initiated before age 11, initiated between ages 11 and 15, initiated after age 15, or not yet initiated.

- *Gender and birth-year cohort.* Other independent variables included gender and birth year cohort groups. Birth-year cohorts were grouped into three categories: participants born before 1964, those born in 1964 through 1966, and those born in 1967 or later.

Statistical Analysis. *Effects of ADHD and Childhood CNS Stimulant Treatment with Age of Regular Smoking and Adult Smoking Status.* Survival analyses (Cox & Oakes, 1984) were used to ascertain the nature of the relationships of ADHD and CNS stimulant treatment with age on becoming a regular smoker. Subjects who at the time of the adult interview had not become regular smokers were assigned an age of regular smoking that occurred after the interview; a status variable was computed that indicated that this age was "censored" or had not yet occurred and those cases were censored in the survival analysis. The method produces a survival function displaying the cumulative proportions of subjects in each group who have not yet become regular smokers at each age.

Chi-square statistics provided evidence of the association of ADHD and CNS stimulant treatment with adult smoking status.

Effects of Independent Variables in Prediction of DSM-III-R Substance Dependence Diagnoses. Logistic regressions were conducted to provide evidence for the effects of the independent variables on adult daily smoking and the DSM-III-R diagnoses of tobacco, cocaine, stimulants, marijuana, and alcohol dependence for all subjects classified as dependent or not dependent. The DSM-III-R dependency criteria do not require a high lifetime use rate or current rate of use. If a participant reported using the substance five or more times "to get high," the follow-up questions focused on use of more than intended, difficulty in cutting down despite problems, and development of a tolerance to the drug. Of these participants, the proportion of heavy users who were also dependent were 77 percent (80 of 104) of the daily smokers, 51 percent (47 out of 93) of heavy users of cocaine (20+ times), 60 percent (55 out of 91) of heavy users of stimulants (20+ times), 55 percent (94 out of 170) of heavy users of marijuana (40+ times), and 51 percent (56 of 98) of heavy users of alcohol (40+ times).

STUDY RESULTS

Survival Analyses

Survival Analysis of Delay in Onset of Regular Smoking by Severity of ADHD. The survival analysis for severity of ADHD (Figure 18.1) was significant ($p \leq .01$). Pairwise comparisons showed that the survival curves for severe ADHD subjects ($p \leq .001$) and moderate ADHD subjects ($p \leq .05$) were significantly different from the curve for the non-ADHD subjects. The survival curves for the mild ADHD subjects

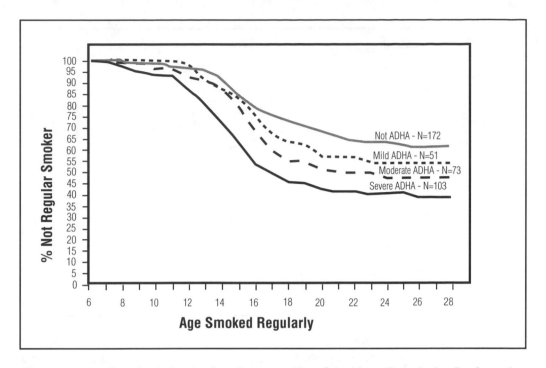

Figure 18.1. Survival Analysis—Percent Not Smoking Regularly During the Developmental Period by ADHD Classification. Overall Comparison: Lee Desu Statistic 15.166, df = 3, $p \leq .01$; Pairwise Comparisons: Severe vs. Never, $p \leq .000$; Severe vs. Mild $p \leq .05$; Severe vs Moderate, $p \leq .10$; Moderate vs. Never, $p \leq .10$

compared with the non-ADHD subjects and for the severe ADHD subjects compared with the moderate ADHDs were marginally significant ($p \leq .10$).

Survival Analysis of Delay in Onset of Regular Smoking by Use of CNS Stimulant Treatment in Childhood. Figure 18.2 shows that the percentage of participants who have not yet become regular smokers is significantly different ($p \leq .05$) for those who used CNS stimulant treatment versus those who were not treated.

To examine a possible protective effect where using stimulant treatment might delay onset of regular smoking, subjects were grouped by the age at which stimulant treatment ended and these groups were studied in a survival analysis (Figure 18.3). The result was significant ($p \leq .01$). Pairwise comparisons showed that the proportion of participants who stopped taking CNS stimulants by age 10 were more likely to become regular smokers at an earlier age than either those who never used stimulant treatment ($p \leq .001$) or those ($p \leq .10$) who stopped treatment after age 14. Stimulant treatment appears to "protect" against becoming a young regular smoker in childhood. The three groups also differed with respect to the number of years they had been treated (1.72 years for the terminated treatment by age 10 group, 3.79 years for the terminated treatment between 11 and 13, and 6.66 for the terminated treatment after age 14).

This "protective" effect is short-lived, however. When the data for daily smoking in adulthood were examined, there was no significant difference by length of treat-

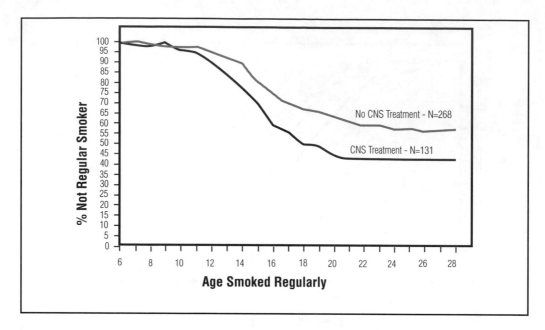

Figure 18.2. Survival Analysis—Percent Not Smoking Regularly During Developmental Period for Subjects Who Used CNS Stimulant Treatment Before They Became Regular Smokers. Overall Comparison: Lee Desu Statistic 5.825 df =1, $p \le .05$.

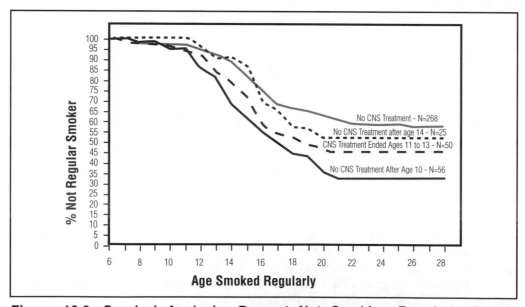

Figure 18.3. Survival Analysis—Percent Not Smoking Regularly During Developmental Period for Subjects With Different CNS Stimulant Treatment Histories. Overall Comparison: Lee Desu Statistic 15.280, df = 3, $p \le .01$; pairwise comparisons: no CNS after age 10 vs. no CNS, $p \le .001$; no CNS after age 10 vs. off CNS after age 14 $p \le .10$

ment in rates of daily smoking—46 percent for the terminated treatment by age 10 group, 40 percent for the group that terminated between ages 11 and 13, 44 percent for the participants who terminated after age 14, compared with 19 percent for those who were never received stimulant treatment. Among the participants, 57 percent who reported that they had been regular smokers in childhood smoked daily in adulthood.

Relationship of Severity of ADHD and Childhood Stimulant Treatment to Adult Smoking

Next, the relationship of ADHD and childhood CNS stimulant treatment to rates of smoking in adulthood was examined. The participants were grouped as ADHD (severe or moderate DSM-IV ADHD) versus non-ADHD (mild and non-ADHD) (Figure 18.4). The chi-square for this comparison was significant ($p \leq .001$); childhood ADHD is significantly associated with adult daily smoking.

The chi-square analysis of rates of adult smoking for groups defined by CNS stimulant treatment of six months or more versus never using CNS stimulants in childhood (Figure 18.5) was also significant ($p \leq .001$). The relative effects of ADHD and CNS stimulant treatment are explored in the multivariate analysis below.

Multivariate Prediction of Adult Daily Smoking and DSM-III-R Psychoactive Substance Use Disorders

There were significant differences between the ADHD (severe and moderate) and non-ADHD (mild and not) groups on adult daily smoking (38 percent vs. 18 percent) and the DSM-III-R dependency diagnoses of tobacco (45 percent vs. 22 percent), cocaine (23 percent vs. 11 percent), and stimulant dependence (25 percent vs. 13 per-

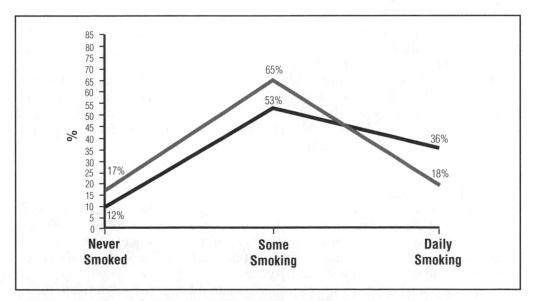

Figure 18.4. Adult Smoking Status for ADHDs (Severe and Moderate) and Not ADHDs (Mild and Not ADHD). Chi-square df = 2 = 16.835, $p \leq .001$.

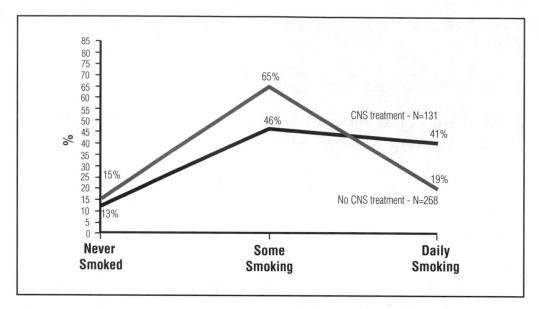

Figure 18.5. Adult Smoking Status of Subjects Treated With CNS Stimulants in Childhood Compared With Those Who Were Not Treated With CNS Stimulants. Chi-square df = 2 = 23.156, $p \leq .000$.

cent), but not marijuana (29 percent vs. 28 percent) and alcohol dependence (40 percent vs. 31 percent.). There were significant differences in use of stimulant treatment for six months or more and adult daily smoking (43 percent vs. 19 percent), tobacco dependence (48 percent vs. 26 percent), and cocaine dependence (24 percent vs. 13 percent).

Logistic regressions were used to estimate the joint effects of the independent variables. Other potentially relevant independent variables, such as socioeconomic status, cognitive ability, and ethnic status, were examined in preliminary analyses but were not were found to be associated with these dependent variables.

Table 18.3 displays the adjusted odds ratios for adult daily smoking and for each of the DSM-III-R dependence diagnoses. Childhood conduct problems were not included in the summary table because they did not contribute significantly to any of the dependent variables. Although ADHD subjects smoked (daily) significantly more than did non-ADHD subjects, the adjusted odds ratio for ADHD in the prediction of daily smoking was not significant; however, the adjusted odds ratios for any use of CNS stimulants in childhood was significant.

The adjusted odds ratio for severe ADHD was significantly associated with dependence on all of the substances with stimulating properties—tobacco, cocaine, stimulants, and either cocaine or stimulant dependence—but not for marijuana and alcohol. There was a significant adjusted odds ratio for CNS stimulant treatment for cocaine dependence and marginally significant odds ratios for predictions of tobacco dependence and stimulant or cocaine dependence.

The adjusted odds ratios for early initiation into tobacco were significant for all substances. The adjusted odds ratio for gender was significant for tobacco dependence, marijuana dependence, and alcohol dependence, indicating that more males were tobacco, marijuana, and alcohol dependent.

Table 18.3
Adjusted Odds Ratios in Logistic Regressions Predicting Adult Daily Smoking and DSM-III-R Psychoactive Substance Use Disorders ($N = 360$)

| Variables in the analysis | Adult Daily Smoking | DSM-III-R Psychoactive Substance Use Dependence | | | | | |
| | | Tobacco | Cocaine | Stimulant | Cocaine or Stimulant | Marijuana | Alcohol |
Odds Ratio	Adjusted Odds Ratio	Adjusted Odds Ratio	Adjusted Odds Ratio	Adjusted Odds Ratio	Adjusted Odds Ratio	Adjusted Odds Ratio	Adjusted Odds Ratio
DSM-IV ADHD							
Severe	1.600	2.465*	3.778**	2.965*	2.695*	.859	1.475
Moderate	1.516	1.671	1.763	2.560*	1.417	.660	.789
Gender	1.329	2.212*	1.806	1.619	1.378	2.499***	3.677***
Smoking Status							
Initiated before age 11	2.144+	4.818***	5.253**	3.751**	3.748**	4.550***	2.170*
Initiated by age 11–13	3.128**	4.862***	4.666**	4.281**	4.117**	4.835***	2.294**
CNS Stimulant Treatment							
More than 1 yr.	2.817**	1.900+	2.251*	1.194	1.893+	1.280	1.520
Less than 1 yr.	3.951**	1.239	1.963	.767	.999	1.072	1.184
Age Group at Entry							
Oldest	1.098	1.095	2.436*	1.075	1.496	1.063	.806
Middle	.930	.887	1.794	1.093	1.401	1.038	.932

Note. Logistic regressions also controlled for childhood conduct problems. None of the interactions between independent variables and the dependent variables was significant.

*$p \leq .05$. **$p \leq .01$. ***$p \leq .001$. +$p \leq .10$.

Support for the Self-Medicating Hypothesis

The severity of ADHD symptoms was shown to be significantly related to the age of onset of regular smoking during the developmental period; the more severe the ADHD symptoms, the earlier the onset of regular smoking. Rates of adult smoking were significantly different for ADHD (severe and moderate) versus non-ADHD (mild and not) participants, indicating that a greater number of ADHD adolescents who were regular smokers become daily smokers in adulthood. The results of the survival analysis and the chi-square analysis of adult smoking support a self-medicating hypothesis. Support for a self-medicating process is reflected as well in significant differences between severe and moderate ADHD subjects and mild and non-ADHD subjects on rates of DSM-III-R dependence diagnoses of tobacco, cocaine, and stimulants.

The more severe the DSM-IV ADHD symptoms, the more likely individuals were to become dependent on tobacco, cocaine, stimulants, and either cocaine or stimulants but not marijuana or alcohol. A self-medicating hypothesis predicts the use of particular substances, not any substance. And the substances of interest for ADHD individuals are those that would be most likely to affect the ADHD symptoms, namely, stimulants.

When the severity of ADHD was entered into a logistic equation (with age of initiation into tobacco, gender, stimulant treatment, conduct problems, and birth-year cohort group) predicting adult daily smoking and DSM-III-R substance dependence diagnoses, severe ADHD subjects were 2.5 times more likely than those who were not ADHD to become tobacco dependent, 3.8 times more likely to become cocaine dependent, and 3.0 times more likely to become stimulant dependent. Such findings suggest that aspects of ADHD symptomatology cognitively compromise the capacity to control or self-regulate the impulse to use substances with stimulating properties and to become dependent on them.

The fact that severity of ADHD was not a significant predictor of adult daily smoking but was a significant predictor for tobacco dependence suggests that ADHD may be more implicated in dependence on substances with stimulating properties (self-medication) and stimulant treatment more implicated in heavy use of tobacco (sensitization). Further exploration of such differential effects for substance dependence versus substance abuse of stimulants is warranted.

To explore further the self-regulating processes involved in dependence on tobacco, cocaine, and stimulants, subsequent investigation should align itself with recent proposals (Barkley, 1997) to distinguish between those individuals whose problems reside in the behavioral inhibition domain (hyperactive-impulsive) in contrast to those with primarily inattentive symptoms. The cognitive processes on which behavioral inhibition rely affect ability to anticipate outcomes and to regulate behavior to avoid harmful conditions such as involvement with substances.

Support for the Sensitization Hypothesis

The survival analysis comparing age at which regular smoking began for those who received stimulant treatment to that of those not receiving stimulant treatment provided support for a sensitization hypothesis in humans because stimulant treatment predisposed to regular smoking at an earlier age. Although there seemed to be a "protective effect" for the length of time stimulant treatment was used, and those being treated longer smoked regularly at a later age, this protective effect was short-lived because the rates of adult daily smoking did not differ by length of stimulant treatment.

Significant differences in rates of adult daily smoking for those using stimulant treatment and those not treated also supported the sensitization hypothesis.

The logistic regression of the childhood variables with adult daily smoking also supported a sensitization effect in that the odds ratio for severity of ADHD was not significant when the effects of CNS stimulant treatment and age of initiation into tobacco were accounted for. Children who used stimulant treatment for less than one year were four times more likely than those who did not use stimulant treatment to become daily smokers in adulthood, and those who used stimulant treatment for more than a year were 2.8 times more likely to become daily smokers.

The logistic regressions of childhood variables with DSM-III-R substance dependence diagnoses showed that children who used CNS stimulants for more than one year were 2.3 times more likely than those who did not use stimulants or those who had only a trial of stimulant treatment to become cocaine dependent. The odds ratios were marginally significant for tobacco and stimulant dependence. But there was no relationship between use of stimulant treatment and dependence on marijuana or alcohol.

The pattern of sensitization appears to follow the path of CNS stimulant treatment to early onset of regular smoking to adult daily smoking to adult tobacco, cocaine, and stimulant dependence. The investigation did not permit definitive conclusions, however, regarding the relative strength of either a sensitization or a self-medicating explanation.

Partial Support for Tobacco Gateway Hypothesis

There is increasing evidence that "tobacco use is involved, possibly more than by simple association, in the use of other substances containing psychoactive chemicals" (Fleming et al., 1989, p. 279). In the study under discussion in this chapter, there were earlier and higher rates of regular tobacco use among ADHD participants and those treated with stimulants. The inferences follow that in childhood, individuals with ADHD are more likely to self-medicate with nicotine and that stimulant treatment may sensitize to early tobacco use (Horger et al., 1992). Early involvement with nicotine, in turn, predisposes these individuals to higher rates of dependence on cocaine and stimulants in adulthood. The significant role of tobacco in marijuana and alcohol dependence is not answered in this investigation.

Childhood Problem Behavior Not Supported as a Factor in PSUD

The study under discussion in this chapter provided no support for the childhood problem behavior hypothesis predicting higher rates of smoking and substance abuse. It is important to distinguish childhood evidence for conduct problems based on parent and teacher ratings as used in this study from subsequent adolescent diagnoses of conduct disorders and oppositional defiant disorders (Hinshaw, 1987; Loeber & Stouthamer-Loeber, 1998; Loney, 1980; Robins, 1980). Some investigators (Loeber & Stouthamer-Loeber, 1998) have provided evidence to refute the commonly held belief that individuals who have a history of early childhood problem behavior always persist in their aggressive behavior through adolescence. A developmental model of aggression is the more reasonable approach. Ratings of participants' behavior in this study occurred when they were at an average age of 9. There was a significant linear relationship between severity of childhood conduct problems and severity of ADHD, but among those rated as having childhood conduct problems are those who develop both conduct disorders and/or oppositional defiant disorder in adolescence as well as those with transitory problem behavior in childhood whose problems will not persist past adolescence. Methods that group subjects into the life-course, transitional, and late-onset types of aggressive behavior will be necessary to explain the relationship between types of childhood conduct problems, adolescent conduct disorders and oppositional defiant disorders, and adult substance use for these participants.

CONCLUSION

This prospective longitudinal study of ADHD and agemate control subjects, reconfigured according to research diagnostic proxies for severity of DSM-IV ADHD, has provided evidence that childhood use of CNS stimulant treatment is significantly and pervasively implicated in the uptake of regular smoking, in daily smoking in adulthood, and in DSM-III-R diagnoses of tobacco and cocaine dependence. The severity of ADHD was a significant risk factor in adult dependence on substances with stimulating properties, namely, tobacco, cocaine, and stimulants. The use of stimulant treatment in childhood was significantly related to the age of onset of regular smoking, daily smoking in adulthood, and cocaine dependence. Early initiation into tobacco was generally related to predictions of PSUD. Further research to clarify the differential role of nicotine as a sensitizing agent in heavy lifetime use of substances with stimulating properties in contrast to its role in dependence on marijuana and alcohol would be desirable.

Acknowledgment

This study was supported by Tobacco-Related Disease Research Program #IRT251, University of California July 1990 through June 1994 and by NIDA DA 08624 October 1994 through September 1997.

Footnote

[1] Ten of the seventeen false negatives were receiving stimulant medication at the time they were rated. Three others were later classified as learning disabled and one had moderate conduct problems, leaving only three of seventeen who did not meet any diagnostic criteira. There were twenty-nine false positives in the analysis of the diagnostic efficiency of the DSM-IV ADHD research diagnostic criteria for the entire sample. Fifteen of these were learning disabled, eight satisfied the criteria for conduct problems, five met the ADHD diagnostic criteria for inattentive, and one received stimulant medication later on.

References

American Psychiatric Association. (1968). *Diagnostic and statistical manual of mental disorders* (2nd ed.). Washington, DC: Author.

American Psychiatric Association. (1980). *Diagnostic and statistical manual of mental disorders* (3rd ed.). Washington, DC: Author.

American Psychiatric Association. (1987). *Diagnostic and statistical manual of mental disorders* (3rd ed., rev.). Washington, DC: Author.

American Psychiatric Association. (1994). *Diagnostic and statistical manual of mental disorders* (4th ed.). Washington, DC: Author.

Barkley, R. A. (1997). Behavioral inhibition, sustained attention and executive functions: Constructing a unifying theory of ADHD. *Psychological Bulletin, 121*, 65–94.

Barkley, R. A., Fischer, M., Edelbrock, C. S., & Smallish, L. (1990). The adolescent outcome of hyperactive children diagnosed by research criteria. I: An 8-year prospective follow-up study. *Journal of the American Academy of Child and Adolescent Psychiatry, 29*, 546-557.

Beck, S. J., Young, G. H., & Tarnowski, K. J. (1990). Maternal characteristics and perceptions of pervasive and situational hyperactives and normal controls. *Journal of the American Academy of Child and Adolescent Psychiatry, 29*, 558–565.

Biederman, J., Faraone, S. V., Spencer, R., Wilens, T., Norman, D., Lapey, K. A., Mick, E., Lehman, B. K., & Doyle, A. (1993). Patterns of psychiatric comorbidity, cognition, and psychosocial functioning in adults with attention deficit hyperactivity disorder. *American Journal of Psychiatry, 150*,1792–1798.

Biederman, J., Wilens, R., Mick, E., Faraone, S. F., Weber, W., Curtis, S., Thornell, A., Pfister, K., Jetton, J. G., & Soriano, J. (1997). Is ADHD a risk factor for psychoactive substance use disorders? Findings from a four-year prospective follow-up study. *Journal of the American Academy of Child and Adolescent Psychiatry, 36*, 21–29.

Biederman, J., Wilens, R., Mick, E., Milberger, S., Spencer, T. J., & Faraone, S. V. (1995). Psychoactive substance use disorders in adults with attention deficit hyperactivity disorder (ADHD): Effects of ADHD and psychiatric comorbidity. *American Journal of Psychiatry, 152*, 1652–1658.

Boudreault, M., Thivierge, J., Cote, R., Boutin, P., Julien, Y., & Bergeron, S. (1988). Cognitive development and reading achievement in pervasive-ADD, situational-ADD and control children. *Journal of Child Psychology and Psychiatry, 29*, 611-619.

Brook, J. S., Whiteman, M., Gordon, A. S., & Cohen, P. (1986). Dynamics of childhood and adolescent personality traits and adolescent drug use. *Developmental Psychology, 22*, 403–414.

Cocores, J. A., Davies, R. K., Mueller, P. S., & Gold, M. S. (1987). Cocaine abuse and adult attention deficit disorder. *Journal of Clinical Psychiatry, 48*, 376–377.

Cox, D. R., & Oakes, D. (1984). *Analysis of survival data.* London: Chapman & Hall.

Fleming, R., Leventhal, H., Glynn, K., & Ershler, J. (1989). The role of cigarettes in the initiation and progression of early substance use. *Addictive Behaviors, 14*, 261-272.

Gawin, F. H., & Kleber, H. (1986). Pharmacologic treatments of cocaine abuse. *Psychiatric Clinics of North America, 9*, 573–583.

Gittelman, R., Mannuzza, S., Shenker, R., & Bonagura, N. (1985). Hyperactive boys almost grown up: I. Psychiatric status. *Archives of General Psychiatry, 42*, 937–947.

Goodman, R., & Stevenson, J. (1989). A twin study of hyperactivity: I. An examination of hyperactivity scores and categories derived from Rutter teacher and parent questionnaires. *Journal of Child Psychology and Psychiatry, 30*, 671–689.

Hartsough, C. S., Babinski, L. M., & Lambert, N. M. (1996). Tracking procedures and attrition containment in a long-term follow-up of a community-based ADHD sample. *Journal of Child Psychology and Psychiatry, 37*, 705–713.

Hartsough, C. S., & Lambert, N. M. (1987). Pattern and progression of drug use among hyperactives and controls: A prospective short-term longitudinal study. *Journal of Child Psychology and Psychiatry, 28*, 543–553.

Hechtman, L., Weiss, G., & Perlman, T. (1984). Young adult outcomes of hyperactive children who received long-term stimulant treatment. *Journal of the American Academic of Child Psychiatry, 23*(3), 261–269.

Henningfield, J. E., Clayton, R., & Pollin, W. (1990). Involvement of tobacco in alcoholism and illicit drug use. *British Journal of Addiction, 85*, 279–291.

Henningfield, J. E., Cohen, C., & Slade, J. D. (1991). Is nicotine more addictive than cocaine? Special Issue: Future directions in tobacco research. *British Journal of Addiction, 86*, 565–569.

Hinshaw, S. P. (1987). On the distinction between attentional deficits/hyperactivity and conduct problems/aggression in child psychopathology. *Psychological Bulletin, 101*, 443–463.

Horger, B. A., Giles, M. K., & Schenk, S. (1992). Preexposure to amphetamine and nicotine predisposes rats to self-administer a low dose of cocaine. *Psychopharmacology, 107*, 271–276.

Jessor, R., & Jessor, S. (1980). A social-psychological framework for studying drug use. In D. J. Letteri, M. Sayers, & H. W. Pearson (Eds.), *Theories on drug abuse: Selected contemporary perspectives* (pp. 95–101), Rockville, MD: National Institute on Drug Abuse.

Kaminer, Y. (1992). Clinical implications of the relationship between attention-deficit hyperactivity disorder and psychoactive substance use disorders. *American Journal on Addictions, 1*, 257–264.

Kandel, D. B., Kessler, R. C., & Margulies, R. A. (1978). Antecedents of adolescent initiation into stages of drug use: A developmental analysis. *Journal of Youth and Adolescence, 7*, 13–40.

Kandel, D. B., Yamaguchi, K., & Chen, K. (1992). Steps in the progression in drug involvement from adolescence to adulthood: Further evidence for the gateway theory. *Journal of Studies in Alcohol, 53*, 447–457.

Kaneto, H., & Hori, A. (1988). Pharmacological interactions between dependence-liable drugs. *Japan Journal of Psychophamacology, 8*, 405–415.

Kessel, J. B., & Zimmerman, M. (1993). Reporting errors in studies of the diagnostic performance of self-administered questionnaires: Extent of the problem, recommendations for standardized presentation of results, and implications for the peer review process. *Psychological Assessment, 5*, 395–399.

Khantzian, E. J. (1985). The self-medication hypothesis of addictive disorders: Focus on heroin and cocaine dependence. *American Journal of Psychiatry, 142*, 1259–1264.

Khantzian, E. J. (1997). The self-medication hypothesis of substance use disorders: A reconsideration and recent applications. *Harvard Review of Psychiatry, 4*, 231–244.

Kleber, H., & Gawin, F. H. (1986). Psychopharmacological trials in cocaine abuse treatment. Annual meeting of the American Psychiatric Association (1985, Dallas, TX). *American Journal of Drug and Alcohol Abuse, 12*, 235–246.

Kolta, M. G., Shreve, P., De Souza, V., & Uretsky, N. J. (1985). Time course of the development of the enhanced behavioral and biochemical responses to amphetamine after pretreatment with amphetamine. *Neuropharmacology, 24*, 823–829.

Lambert, N. M. (1982). Temperament profiles of hyperactive children. *American Journal of Orthopsychiatry, 52*, 458–467.

Lambert, N. M. (1988). Adolescent outcomes for hyperactive children: Perspectives on general and specific patterns of childhood risk for adolescent educational, social, and mental health problems. *American Psychologist, 43*, 786–799.

Lambert, N. M., & Hartsough, C. S. (1987). The measurement of attention deficit disorder with behavior ratings of parents. *American Journal of Orthopsychiatry, 57*, 361–370.

Lambert, N. M., & Hartsough, C. S. (1998). Prospective study of tobacco smoking and substance dependence among samples of ADHD and non-ADHD subjects. *Journal of Learning Disabilities, 31*, 533–544.

Lambert, N. M., Hartsough, C. S., & Sandoval, J. (1990). *Children's Attention and Adjustment Survey home and school versions.* Circle Pines, MN: American Guidance Service.

Lambert, N. M., Sandoval, J., & Sassone, D. (1978). Prevalence of hyperactivity in elementary school children as a function of social system definers. *American Journal of Orthopsychiatry, 48*, 446–463.

Lambert, N. M., Sandoval, J., & Sassone D. (1979). Prevalence of treatment regimens of children considered to be hyperactive. *American Journal of Orthopsychiatry, 49*, 482–490.

Lett, B. W. (1989). Repeated exposures intensify rather than diminish the rewarding effects of amphetamine, morphine and cocaine. *Psychopharmacology, 98*, 357–362.

Loeber, R., & Stouthamer-Loeber, M. (1998). Development of juvenile aggression and violence: Some common misconceptions and controversies. *American Psychologist, 53*, 242–259.

Loney, J. (1980). The Iowa theory of substance abuse among hyperactive adolescents. In D. J. Letteri, M. Sayers, & H. W. Pearson (Eds.), *Theories on drug abuse: Selected contemporary perspectives* (pp. 131–136), Rockville, MD: National Institute on Drug Abuse.

Lynskey, M. T., & Ferguson, D. H. (1995). Childhood conduct problems, attention deficit behaviors and adolescent alcohol, tobacco, and illicit drug use. *Journal of Abnormal Child Psychology, 23*, 281–302.

Mannuzza, S., Klein, R., & Addalli, K. A. (1991). Young adult mental status of hyperactive boys and their brothers: A prospective follow-up study. *Journal of the American Academic of Child and Adolescent Psychiatry, 30*, 743–751.

Mannuzza, S., Klein, R. G., Bessler, A., Malloy, P., & LaPadula, M. (1993). Adult outcome of hyperactive boys. *Archives of General Psychiatry, 50*, 565–576.

Marcus, S. C., Robins, L. N., & Bucholz, K. K. (1990). *Quick Diagnostic Interview Schedule, III-R* [computer program]. Department of Psychiatry, Washington University School of Medicine. St. Louis, MO.

Milberger, S., Biederman, J., Faraone, S. V., Chen, L., & Jones, J. (1997a). ADHD is associated with early initiation of cigarette smoking in children and adolescents. *Journal of the American Academy of Child and Adolescent Psychiatry, 36*, 37–44.

Piazza, P. V., Deminiere, J. M., Lemma, M., & Simon, H. (1989). Factors that predict individual vulnerability to amphetamine self-administration. *Science, 245*, 1511–1513.

Piazza, P. V., Deminiere, J. M., LeMoal, M., & Simon, H. (1990). Stress and pharmocologically-induced behavioral sensitization increases vulnerability to aquisition of amphetamine self-administration. *Brain Research, 514*, 22–26.

Pierce, J., & Burns, D. (1990). *California Smoking Baseline Survey: Adult attitudes and practices*. Unpublished survey, University of California, San Diego, CA.

Robins, L. N. (1990).The natural history of drug abuse. In D. J. Letteri, M. Sayers, & H. W. Pearson (Eds.), *Theories on drug abuse: Selected contemporary perspectives* (pp. 215–224), Rockville, MD: National Institute on Drug Abuse.

Robinson, T. E., & Berridge, K. C. (1993). The neural basis of drug craving: An incentive-sensitization theory of addiction. *Brain Research Review, 18*, 247–291.s

Rounsaville, B. J., Anton, S. F., Carroll, K., Budde, D., Prusoff, B. A., & Gawin, F. (1991). Psychiatric diagnoses of treatment seeking cocaine abusers. *Archives of General Psychiatry, 48*, 43–51.

Sandoval, J., Lambert, N. M., & Yandell, W. (1979). Current medical practice and hyperactive children. *American Journal of Orthopsychiatry, 46*, 323–324.

Schachar, R., Rutter, M., & Smith, A. (1981). The characteristics of situationally and pervasively hyperactive children: Implications for syndrome definition. *Journal of Child Psychology and Psychiatry, 22*, 375–392.

Schenk, S., & Partridge, B. (1997). Sensitization and tolerance in psycohstimulant self-administration. *Pharmacology, Biochemistry and Behavior, 57*, 543–550.

Schenk, S., & Partridge, B. (1999). Cocaine-seking produced by experimenter-administered drug injections: Dose-effect relationships in rats. *Psychopharmacology, 147*, 285–290.

Schenk, S., Valadez, A., McNamara, C., House, D., Higely, D., Bankson, M. T., Gibbs, S., & Horger, B. A. (1993). Development and expression of sensitization to cocaine's reinforcing properties: Role of NMDA receptors. *Psychopharmacology, 111*, 332–338.

Schuster, L., Grace, Y., & Bates, A. (1977) Sensitization to cocaine stimulation in mice. *Psychopharmacology, 52*, 185–190.

Shippenberg, T. S., & Heidbreder, C. A. (1995). Sensitization to the conditioned rewarding effects of cocaine: Pharmacological and temporal characteristics. *Journal of Pharmocology and Experimental Therapeutics, 273*, 808–815.

Strakowski, S. M., & Sax, K. W. (1998). Progressive behavioral response to repeated d-Amphetamine challenge: Further evidence for sensitization in humans. *Biological Psychiatry, 44*, 1171–1177.

Torabi, M. R., Bailey, W. J., & Madj-Jabbari, M. (1993). Cigarette smoking as a predictor of alcohol and other drug use by children and adolescents: Evidence of the gateway drug effect. *Journal of School Health, 63*, 302–305.

Valadez, A., & Schenk, S. (1994). Persistence of the ability of amphetamine preexposure to facilitate acquisition of cocaine self-administration. *Pharmacology, Biochemistry and Behavior, 47*, 203–205.

Vezina, P. (1996). DI dopamine receptor activation is necessary for the induction of sensitization by amphetamine in the ventral tegmental area. *Journal of Neuroscience, 16*(7), 2411–2420.

Volkow, N. D., Wang, G. J., Gatley, S. J., Fowler, J. S., Ding, Y. S., Logan, J., Hitzeman, R., Angrist, B., & Lieberman, J. (1996). Temporal relationships between the pharmacokinetics of methylphenidate in the human brain and its behavioral and cardiovascular effects. *Psychopharmacology, 123*, 26–33.

Wilens, T., Biederman, J., & Mick, E. (1998). Does ADHD Affect the course of substance abuse? Findings from a sample of adults with and without ADHD. *American Journal on Addictions, 7*, 156–163.

Wilens, T. E., Biederman, J., Mick, E., Faraone, S. V., & Spencer, T. (1997). Attention deficit hyperactivity disorder (ADHD) is associated with early onset substance use disorders. *Journal of Nervous and Mental Disease, 185*(8), 475–482.

Wilens, T. E., Biederman, J., & Spencer, T. J. (1996). Attention-deficit hyperactivity disorder and the psychoactive substance use disorders. *Child and Adolescent Clinics of North America, 5*, 73–91.

Chapter 19

Attention Deficit Hyperactivity Disorder and Substance Use Disorders— The Nature of the Relationship, Subtypes at Risk, and Treatment Issues

by Timothy E. Wilens, M.D.

Introduction 19-1
Overlap Between ADHD and SUD 19-2
ADHD as a Risk Factor for SUD 19-3
     Longitudinal Studies: ADHD 19-3
     ADHD Treatment and SUD 19-3
     Longitudinal Studies of SUD 19-5
SUD Pathways Associated With ADHD 19-5
Familial Relationships Between ADHD and SUD 19-6
Implications of Current Research 19-7
     Increased Risk of SUD for ADHD Youth 19-8
     Parental SUD a Risk Factor for Juvenile ADHD/Conduct Disorder . . . 19-8
     Self-Medication a Likely Factor 19-8
     Impact of Psychosocial Risk Factors 19-9
Diagnosis and Treatment Guidelines 19-10
     Evaluation 19-10
     Stabilization of the Addiction 19-10
     Psychotherapeutic Interventions 19-11
     Pharmacotherapy 19-11
Summary 19-12

INTRODUCTION

The overlap between attention deficit hyperactivity disorder (ADHD) and alcohol or drug abuse or dependence (referred to here as substance use disorders, or SUDs) in adolescents and adults has been an area of increasing clinical, research, and public health interest (Kaminer, 1992; Wilens, Biederman, Spencer, & Frances, 1994). ADHD (the term ADHD used here also refers to previous definitions of the disorder) onsets in early childhood and affects from 6 to 9 percent of juveniles (Anderson, Williams, McGee, & Silva, 1987) and up to 5 percent of adults (Murphy & Barkley, 1996). Longitudinal data suggest that childhood ADHD persists in 75 percent of cases into adolescence and in approximately one-half of cases into adulthood (Weiss, 1992). SUDs usually onset in adolescence or early adulthood and affect between 10 to 30 percent of U.S. adults and a less defined but sizable number of juveniles (Ross, Glaser, & Germanson, 1988; Kessler et al., 1994; Mathias, 1997). As reviewed, recent work demonstrates a bidirectional overlap between ADHD and SUDs (Kaminer, 1992; Levin & Kleber, 1995; Schubiner et al., 1995; Wilens, Spencer, & Biederman, 2000).

The study of comorbidity between SUD and ADHD is relevant to both research and clinical practice in developmental pediatrics, psychology, and psychiatry with implications for diagnosis, prognosis, treatment, and health care delivery. The identification of specific risk factors of SUD within ADHD may permit more targeted treatments for both disorders at earlier stages of their expression potentially dampening the morbidity, disability, and poor long-term prognosis in adolescents and adults with this comorbidity (Mannuzza, Klein, Bessler, Malloy, & LaPadula, 1993; Weiss, 1992). This chapter reviews data relevant to understanding the overlap between ADHD and SUD with an emphasis on tangible factors mediating this association.

OVERLAP BETWEEN ADHD AND SUD

Three recent studies have incorporated structured psychiatric diagnostic interviews assessing ADHD and other disorders in substance-abusing groups of adolescents. DeMilio and associates (DeMilio, 1989), applying criteria according to the third edition of *Diagnostic and Statistical Manual of Mental Disorders* (DSM-III; American Psychiatric Association, 1980), reported that one-quarter of fifty-seven inpatient adolescents with SUD had current ADHD with conduct and mood disorders also present. Similarly, there were significantly higher rates of ADHD in juvenile offenders with SUD (23 percent) than in non-SUD juveniles (0 percent) (Milin, Halikas, Meller, & Morse, 1991). In addition, higher rates of ADHD were reported in this study in juveniles with drug abuse compared to alcohol abuse. In another study of psychiatric comorbidity in fifty-two inpatient adolescents with SUD, 31 percent of these adolescents had ADHD with no differences among the various substances of abuse reported (Hovens, Cantwell, & Kiriakos, 1994). In these studies, there was an overrepresentation of both mood and conduct disorders with from 60 percent to 90 percent of SUD adolescents with conduct disorder.

The findings of studies in SUD adults are similar to those in adolescents. For example, studies of alcohol abusers yielded rates of between 35 percent to 71 percent of adult alcoholics with childhood-onset and persistent ADHD (Goodwin, Schulsinger, Hermansen, Guze, & Winokur, 1975; Wilens, Spencer, & Biederman, 1995). Including both alcohol and drug addiction, from 15 percent to 25 percent of adult addicts and alcoholics have current ADHD (Wilens et al., 1995). Furthermore, adults with ADHD and SUD have been reported to have earlier onset and more severe

SUD than SUD adults without ADHD (Carroll & Rounsaville, 1993; Levin, Evans, Rosenthal, & Kleber, 1997; Wilens, Biederman, Mick, Faraone, & Spencer, 1997).

An overrepresentation of SUD has also been consistently observed in studies of ADHD adults. All the eight investigations of adults with ADHD reported higher rates of SUD in ADHD adults than in the general population: 17 percent to 45 percent of ADHD adults have alcohol abuse or dependence and 9 percent to 30 percent drug abuse or dependence (Wilens et al., 1995). The risk of SUD developing over the lifespan in an ADHD individual is twofold compared to non-ADHD adults (52 percent vs. 27 percent, respectively) (Biederman et al., 1995). Hence, the literature strongly indicates a bidirectional overrepresentation of SUD and ADHD among subjects with these disorders.

ADHD AS A RISK FACTOR FOR SUD

The association of ADHD and SUD is particularly compelling from a developmental perspective as ADHD manifests itself earlier than SUD; therefore, SUD as a risk factor for ADHD is unlikely. Thus, it is important to evaluate to what extent ADHD is a precursor of SUD. Longitudinal studies of children with ADHD, or children who develop SUD, provide the most compelling data on this developmental hypothesis.

Longitudinal Studies: ADHD

Prospective studies of ADHD children have provided evidence that the group with conduct or bipolar disorders co-occurring with ADHD have the poorest outcome with respect to developing SUD and major morbidity (Biederman et al., 1997; Lambert, Hartsough, Sassone, & Sandoval, 1987; Lynskey & Fergusson, 1995; Mannuzza et al., 1993; Weiss, Hechtman, Milroy, & Perlman, 1985). For example, in five- and eight-year follow-up studies, more alcohol use was shown among hyperactive and largely conduct-disordered ADHD adolescents compared to non-ADHD controls (Blouin, Bornstein, & Trites, 1978; Satterfield, Hoppe, & Schell, 1982). Moreover, as part of an ongoing prospective study of ADHD, differences in the risk for SUD in ADHD adolescents (mean age 15 years) compared to non-ADHD controls (which were accounted for by comorbid conduct or bipolar disorders) were found (Biederman et al., 1997). It is of interest, however, that in the older siblings of these probands we were able to show that ADHD is an independent risk factor for the development of SUD (Milberger, Biederman, Faraone, Wilens, & Chu, 1997). These data support retrospectively derived data from ADHD adults, indicating an earlier age of SUD onset in ADHD adults (mean age of full SUD at 19 years) compared to non-ADHD controls (mean age 22 years, $p < 0.01$), which is notable in the presence of comorbid conduct or bipolar disorder (Wilens, Biederman, Mick, et al., 1997).

ADHD Treatment and SUD

Clarification of the critical influence of ADHD treatment in youth on later SUD remains hampered by methodological issues. Because prospective studies in ADHD youth are naturalistic, and hence not randomized for treatment, attempts to disentangle positive or deleterious effects of treatment from the severity of the underlying condition(s) are hampered by serious confounds. Whereas concerns of the abuse liability and potential kindling of specific types of abuse (i.e., cocaine) secondary to early stimulant exposure in ADHD children have been raised (Drug Enforcement Administration, 1995), the preponderance of clinical data (Biederman et al., 1999; Hechtman, 1985) and consensus in the field do not appear to support such a contention.

A paucity of data exists addressing the important question of the effects of long-term treatment on outcome (including SUD) in ADHD youth. Two such nonrandomized investigations were follow-ups of ADHD adolescents and young adults naturalistically treated with stimulants (Loney, Kramer, & Milich, 1981). In the first, older adolescents whose symptoms responded best to medication were less likely to demonstrate subsequent irritable behavior and illegal drug use (Loney et al., 1981). In another sample of medicated ADHD youth compared to an unmatched ADHD group, stimulant medication decreased the risk of subsequent use of illegal drugs (Kramer, Loney, & Whaley-Klahn, 1981). These results mirror naturalistic observations of thirty ADHD adolescents treated, as children, with methylphenidate compared to thirty ADHD adolescents not treated as children, demonstrating trends to higher drug use and abuse in the untreated youth (Beck, Langford, Mackay, & Sum, 1975).

It has recently been found that medicated youth with ADHD were at lower risk for subsequent SUD than were their unmedicated ADHD peers (see Figure 19.1; Biederman et al., 1999). In this family genetic-based, four-year follow-up study of ADHD in which medicated ADHD ($N = 117$), unmedicated ADHD ($N = 45$), and

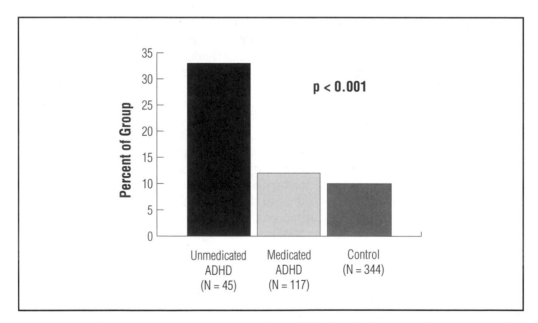

Figure 19.1. Substance Use Disorders in ADHD Youth Growing Up. As part of a longitudinal study of ADHD, medicated ADHD (N=117), unmedicated ADHD (N = 45), and unmedicated non-ADHD controls (N = 344) were evaluated in midadolescence (mean age of 15 years). ADHD children treated with pharmacotherapy at baseline four years earlier for their ADHD were found to manifest significantly lower rates of SUD including alcohol, cocaine, stimulants, and other illicit drugs compared to unmedicated ADHD youth ($p < 0.001$).

unmedicated non-ADHD controls ($N = 344$) were compared in midadolescence, baseline ADHD pharmacotherapy was strongly associated with lower rates of SUD in midadolescence including alcohol, cocaine, stimulant, and other illicit drugs compared to unmedicated ADHD youth. Moreover, rates of SUD were similar between the medicated ADHD and non-ADHD control groups. Clearly, more work evaluating these important issues for longer durations are necessary (see also Chapter 17, in this volume, for further discussion of these issues).

Longitudinal Studies of SUD

If ADHD is a risk for SUD, then ADHD should be overrepresented in those children and adolescents who develop a SUD. Similar to data from studies of ADHD children, longitudinal research of children who later develop SUD also indicates that ADHD (plus conduct disorder) may be an important antecedent in some individuals who develop SUD (Wilens & Biederman, 1993). For instance, in the Chicago-based "Woodlawn Study" (Kellam, Ensminger, & Simon, 1980), children who were rated aggressive, impulsive, and inattentive as first-graders had higher rates of substance use ten years later as adolescents. Although not clearly articulated in these studies, the patterns of behavior described are consistent with ADHD and other comorbidity commonly associated with ADHD.

SUD PATHWAYS ASSOCIATED WITH ADHD

Cigarette smoking in youth is often thought to be a gateway to more severe alcohol and drug use disorders (Kandel & Faust, 1975; Kandel & Logan, 1984). In this context, an increasing body of literature shows an intriguing association between ADHD and cigarette smoking. In a recent report, Milberger, Biederman, Faraone, Chen, and Jones (1997) found that, for boys, ADHD was a significant predictor for early initiation of cigarette smoking (before age 15) and higher risk for cigarette use, after adjusting for potential confounding variables (e.g., socioeconomic status, IQ, and psychiatric comorbidity). In addition, ADHD probands with comorbid conduct, mood, and anxiety disorders had especially high rates of cigarette smoking.

Interesting associations also were found between ADHD and cigarette smoking in families. A strong and significant association between cigarette smoking in mothers during pregnancy and ADHD in their children has been shown (Milberger, Biederman, Faraone, Chen, & Jones, 1996). In addition, cigarette smoking appeared to be familial among the ADHD families but not the control families. ADHD in probands increased the risk for cigarette smoking in siblings regardless of the sibling's own ADHD status; however, the presence of ADHD and/or other psychiatric comorbidity in the high-risk siblings was associated with higher rates of cigarette smoking along with a significantly younger age at onset.

The presence of ADHD also appears to influence the transition into and out of SUD. Recent work indicates that ADHD and related comorbidities accelerate the transition from less severe drug or alcohol abuse to more severe dependence (Figure 19.2A) (Wilens, Biederman, & Mick, 1998). Furthermore, ADHD may heighten the risk for a drug use disorder, particularly in individuals with an alcohol use disorder (Biederman, Wilens, Mick, Faraone, & Spencer, 1998). Conduct or bipolar disorder

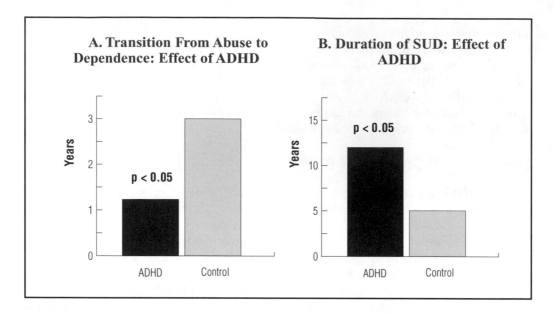

Figure 19.2. Effect of ADHD on the Transition From Substance Abuse to Dependence (A) and the Duration of SUD (B). Compared to their non-ADHD peers, ADHD individuals had a more rapid transition from less severe abuse to more severe dependence of substances (1.2 years vs. 3 years, $p < 0.05$). Moreover, ADHD was associated with a longer duration of SUD (133.1 ± 99.8 vs. 95.9 ± 97, $p < 0.05$).

co-occurring with ADHD tends to markedly heighten the risk for SUD and accelerate the process.

Moreover, ADHD may affect remission from SUD. Whereas early investigations suggested that adolescents and young adults with ADHD were more likely to have a briefer course of SUD than matched controls (Hechtman & Weiss, 1986), contrary findings have been reported recently. In a study of 130 referred adults with ADHD + SUD and 71 SUD adults without ADHD, the rate of remission and duration of SUD differed between ADHD subjects and controls (Wilens et al., 1998). The median time to SUD remission was more than twice as long in ADHD than in control subjects (Figure 19.2B) with SUD lasting over three years longer in the ADHD adults compared to their non-ADHD peers. Hence, the aggregate data indicate that ADHD and associated conditions developmentally influence the initiation, transitions, and recovery from SUD.

FAMILIAL RELATIONSHIPS BETWEEN ADHD AND SUD

Family studies are highly informative to help examine the nature of the association between two co-occurring disorders. For instance, if ADHD and SUD are related in a familial/genetic nature, then family members of individuals (probands) with SUD or ADHD should be at elevated risk for the other disorder. The available literature shows that adolescent and adult offspring of SUD parents are at increased risk not only for SUD but also for aggressive and antisocial behaviors (Chassin, Rogosch, &

Barrera, 1991; Mathew, Wilson, Blazer, & George, 1993; Sher, Walitzer, Wood, & Brent, 1991; Tarter & Edwards, 1988). Child and adolescent children of alcoholics (COAs) have also been reported in controlled studies to have abnormal cognitive and behavioral traits including lower attention spans, as well as higher impulsivity, aggressiveness, hyperactivity, and elevated rates of ADHD compared to non-COAs (Aronson & Gilbert, 1963; Fine, Yudin, Holmes, & Heinemann, 1976; Steinhausen, Gobel, & Nestler, 1984; Wilens, 1994). For example, Earls, Reich, Jung, and Cloninger (1988) found elevated rates of ADHD in COAs compared to children of controls which were more robust in families when both parents were affected by SUD.

The link between ADHD children and SUD has been noted for many years to aggregate in families. Independent studies by Morrison and Stewart (1971) and Cantwell (1972) found elevated rates of alcoholism in the parents of youth with ADHD. The transmission of SUD in ADHD families remains under study with family-genetic studies showing a preferentially elevated risk for SUD in relatives of ADHD children with conduct disorder (Biederman, Faraone, Keenan, Knee, & Tsuang, 1990; Milberger, Biederman, Faraone, Wilens, & Chu, 1997), and independent transmission of ADHD and SUD in families (Milberger, Faraone, Biederman, Chu, & Wilens, 1998).

Although the influence of prenatal substance exposure is confounded by many factors (Griffith, Azuma, & Chasnoff, 1994; Richardson & Day, 1994), several reports have documented increased risk of postnatal complications, including neuropsychiatric abnormalities, in the offspring of alcohol- and cocaine-dependent mothers (Abel & Sokol, 1987; Finnegan, 1976; Volpe, 1992). For example, in one of the few follow-up studies of children diagnosed with fetal alcohol syndrome, high rates of psychiatric disturbance including ADHD were found in over two-thirds of the thirty-three adolescents (Steinhausen, Willms, & Spohr, 1993). Data in cocaine-exposed youth are complex, with data suggesting that confounding variables, and not cocaine exposure per se, may be the major factor leading to ADHD-like symptoms (Griffith et al., 1994; Richardson & Day, 1994). In addition, because family-genetic data are generally lacking, it is unknown to what extent reported outcomes are due to exposure to substances versus the contribution of parental psychopathology.

IMPLICATIONS OF CURRENT RESEARCH

A review of the literature indicates important associations between ADHD and SUD, namely:

- There is a clinical and statistical bidirectional overlap of ADHD and SUD;

- ADHD is a risk factor for SUD; however, co-occurring conduct and bipolar disorders confer a much greater risk independently and when comorbid with ADHD;

- ADHD is associated with earlier onset of alcohol and drug use disorders as well as particular pathways of their development;

- High rates of ADHD-like symptoms are consistently reported in children who develop SUD in later years; and

- The familial risks for ADHD and SUD have been found to be increased in studies of both ADHD and SUD individuals.

Thus, although a robust relationship between ADHD and SUD is supported in the literature, the nature of this association remains unclear.

Increased Risk of SUD for ADHD Youth

Combined data from retrospective accounts of adults and prospective observations of youth would suggest that juveniles with ADHD are at increased risk for cigarette smoking and SUD during adolescence. ADHD youth with bipolar or conduct disorder are at risk for very early cigarette use and SUD (i.e., < 16 years of age), whereas the typical age of risk for the onset of SUD accounted for by ADHD itself is probably between 17 and 22 years of age. Recent work suggests that ADHD youth disproportionately become involved with cigarettes, alcohol, and then drugs (Biederman et al., 1998; Milberger, Biederman, Faraone, Chen, & Jones, 1997). ADHD accelerates the transition from less severe alcohol or drug abuse to more severe dependence (Wilens et al., 1998). Conduct or bipolar disorder co-occurring with ADHD tends to further heighten the risk for SUD and accelerate the process. Individuals with ADHD, independent of comorbidity, tend to maintain their addiction longer compared to their non-ADHD peers (Wilens et al., 1998).

Parental SUD a Risk Factor for Juvenile ADHD/Conduct Disorder

There is also substantial evidence that parental SUD especially with antisocial disorder is associated with elevated rates of ADHD and conduct disorder (Biederman et al., 1990; Biederman, Faraone, Keenan, Benjamin, & Krifcher, 1992; Cantwell, 1972; Earls et al., 1988; Stewart, DeBlois, & Cummings, 1980) and early-onset SUD in their offspring (Milberger et al., 1998). Moreover, specificity of familiality of cigarette smoking in families of ADHD youth exists in that ADHD in youth bestows additional risk for smoking in their siblings independent of ADHD status. Hence, familial relationships between SUD and ADHD, especially early-onset SUD, appear to be most significant in the presence of conduct and antisocial disorders.

Self-Medication a Likely Factor

The precise mechanism(s) mediating the expression of SUD in ADHD remains to be seen. In studies of drug- and alcohol-dependent populations, the self-medication of anxiety, depressive, and aggressive symptoms has been forwarded as a plausible explanation for SUD (Khantzian, 1997). However, similar efforts have not been systematically undertaken for ADHD (Bukstein, Brent, & Kaminer, 1989; Kaminer, 1992). This self-medication hypothesis is compelling in ADHD considering that the disorder is chronic and often associated with demoralization and failure (Biederman et al., 1993; Mannuzza et al., 1993; Weiss, 1992), factors frequently associated with SUD in adolescents (Kandel & Logan, 1984; Yamaguchi & Kandel, 1984). Along these lines, it was previously speculated that the development of SUD in youth with

ADHD plus conduct or bipolar disorder (BPD), the accompanying poor judgment, aggressivity, and impulsivity may be particularly noxious for development of SUD during adolescence (Wilens, Biederman, et al., 1999) considering that adolescence is a time of high risk for the development of SUD.

Despite a paucity of systematically derived data, evidence exists for a subgroup of ADHD individuals to be self-medicating. For example, one study has suggested a developmental progression from ADHD to conduct disorder and eventual SUD which is speculated to be related to demoralization and failure (Mannuzza, Gittelman-Klein, Konig, & Giampino, 1989). Other evidence of self-medication includes data indicating preference of drugs over alcohol in both ADHD adolescents (Gittelman, Mannuzza, Shenker, & Bonagura, 1985; Hartsough & Lambert, 1987) and adults (Biederman et al., 1995). Along these lines, a recent small study in inpatient, substance abusing adolescents found that ADHD adolescents continued substances to alter their mood compared to nonADHD adolescents who reported continuing drugs for their euphorogenic properties (Horner & Scheibe, 1997).

The potential importance of self-medication needs to be tempered against more systematic data showing the strongest relationship between ADHD and SUD being mediated by the presence of conduct, bipolar, and antisocial disorders in addition to familial contributions. In addition, among drug-abusing individuals, ADHD adults and youth were indistinguishable from their non-ADHD peers in the type of substance abused, generally marijuana (Biederman et al., 1995). Moreover, ADHD substance abusers tend to prefer the class of drugs over alcohol with no evidence of a preference for specific types of drugs (Biederman et al., 1995). Contrary to anecdotal reports (Khantzian, 1983), systematic data indicate that cocaine and stimulant abuse is not overrepresented in ADHD; in fact, as is the case in non-ADHD abusers, marijuana continues to be the most commonly abused agent (Biederman et al., 1995). Furthermore, SUD in ADHD youth may be accounted for largely by family history of SUD (Milberger et al., 1998). The robust findings of a family-genetic nature coupled with recent findings of postsynaptic dopamine D4 receptor polymorophisms in association with ADHD (LaHoste et al., 1996) suggest that a polygenic mechanism may be operant. It may also be that ADHD and early-onset SUD represent variable expressivity of a shared risk factor (Comings et al., 1991; Ebstein et al., 1996). Clearly, more work needs to be done examining the contribution of psychiatric symptoms and deficits to explain the relationship of SUD and ADHD.

Impact of Psychosocial Risk Factors

It is unknown to what extent putative psychosocial risk factors, alone or in conjunction with ADHD, influence the emergence or course of SUD. In addition to putative family-genetic risk factors, environmental factors such as psychosocial adversity may also play a role in mediating the overlap between ADHD and SUD. Some biological vulnerabilities may be expressed when the individual is challenged by psychosocial risk factors. Having a parent with ADHD or SUD provides at least two sets of risk factors: genetic and environmental (i.e., exposure to an ill parent) (Mrazek & Haggerty, 1994). This may be especially applicable as up to one-third of ADHD children may be living with a parent(s) with antisocial disorder or SUD (Morrison, 1980). The high-risk children of parents with SUD also are at risk for additional factors such as teratogenic effects of substances. It remains to be determined whether the risk for SUD in ADHD subjects is due to biological, psychosocial, or combined influences.

The combination of ADHD and SUD is of high clinical and public health concern. Clinically, the symptoms of one disorder may exacerbate the other. For instance, impulsivity may impair a patient's quality of life while adversely affecting substance moderation or abstinence and treatment retention. SUD plus ADHD have been associated consistently with SUD chronicity, treatment difficulties, and poor outcomes (Carroll & Rounsaville, 1993; Levin et al., 1996; Schubiner et al., 1997; Tarter, McBride, Buonpane, & Schneider, 1977). The identification and treatment of ADHD-related symptoms may improve SUD treatment and reduce associated morbidity (Khantzian, 1983; Levin et al., 1998; Wender, Reimherr, & Wood, 1981). From the public health perspective, the identification of subtypes of individuals with ADHD plus SUD may be helpful for prevention, early intervention, and treatment for those affected as well as high risk children (Mrazek & Haggerty, 1994; Tarter & Edwards, 1988; Wilens & Biederman, 1993).

DIAGNOSIS AND TREATMENT GUIDELINES

Evaluation

Evaluation and treatment of comorbid ADHD and SUD should be part of a plan in which consideration is given to all aspects of the adolescent or adult's life. Any intervention in this group should follow a careful evaluation of the patient, including psychiatric, addiction, social, cognitive, educational, and family evaluations. A thorough history of substance use should be obtained, including past and current usage and treatments. Careful attention should be paid to the differential diagnosis(es), including medical and neurological conditions whose symptoms may overlap with ADHD (hyperthyroidism) or be a result of SUD (i.e., withdrawal, intoxication, and hyperactivity). Current psychosocial factors contributing to the clinical presentation need to be explored thoroughly. Although no specific guidelines exist for evaluating the patient with active SUD, generally, at least one month of abstinence is useful in accurately and reliably assessing for ADHD symptoms. Semistructured psychiatric interviews such as the structured clinical interview for DSM-IV and the Kiddie-Schedule for Affective Disorders and Schizophrenia (KSADS) module for childhood ADHD (Orvaschel, 1985) are invaluable aids for the systematic diagnostic assessments of this group.

ADHD symptoms in SUD adolescents and adults appear to be developmentally related to those in children, namely, inattention, impulsivity, and hyperactivity (Millstein, Wilens, Biederman, & Spencer, 1997). In addition, patients may have associated stubbornness, low frustration tolerance, and chronic conflicts in social relations with peers and authorities. ADHD-related impulsivity appears to be especially problematic in SUD adolescents and adults as impulsivity may be a major obstacle in addiction treatment (Tarter & Edwards, 1988).

Stabilization of the Addiction

The treatment needs of individuals with SUD and ADHD should be considered simultaneously; however, the SUD needs to be addressed initially (Riggs, 1998). If the SUD is active, immediate attention needs to be paid to *stabilization of the addic-*

tion(s). Depending on the severity and duration of the SUD, adolescents or adults may require inpatient treatment. Self-help groups offer a helpful treatment modality for many with SUD. In tandem with addiction treatment, SUD patients with ADHD require intervention(s) for the ADHD (and if applicable, comorbid psychiatric disorders). Education of the individual, family members, and other caregivers is a useful initial step to improve the recognition of the ADHD.

Psychotherapeutic Interventions

Although the efficacy of various psychotherapeutic interventions for ADHD or SUD remain to be established, pilot data suggest efficacy of behavioral and cognitive therapies for adults with ADHD (Wilens, McDermott, et al., 1999). It appears that effective psychotherapy for this comorbid group combine the following elements: structured and goal-directed sessions, proactive therapist involvement, and knowledge of SUD and ADHD (McDermott, 2000). Often, SUD and ADHD therapeutics are completed in tandem with other addiction modalities (e.g., Alcoholics Anonymous, Narcotics Anonymous, and Rational Recovery), including pharmacotherapy

Pharmacotherapy

Medication serves an important role in reducing the symptoms of ADHD and other concurrent psychiatric disorders. Effective agents for ADHD include the psychostimulants, antidepressants, and antihypertensives (Spencer et al., 1996). Findings from open trials suggest that medications used in SUD patients with ADHD may reduce, and not exacerbate, substance misuse or cravings (Levin, Evans, McDowell, & Kleber, 1997; Riggs, Thompson, Mikulich, Whitmore, & Crowley, 1996). For example, Levin, Evans, McDowell, and Kleber (1997) showed that in cocaine-addicted adults with ADHD, methylphenidate administration reduced ADHD symptoms without exacerbating cocaine craving, but another study showed that bupropion reduced ADHD and substance misuse concurrently (Levin et al., 1998). Similarly, open trials have demonstrated reductions in ADHD in delinquent adolescent substance abusers with ADHD receiving pemoline (Riggs et al., 1996) and bupropion (Riggs, Leon, Mikulich, & Pottle, 1998). Short-term controlled clinical trials of pemoline and bupropion in adolescents and adults with ADHD plus SUD are currently under way. Current evidence suggests a beneficial effect of long-term ADHD treatment on reducing SUD (Loney, 1988).

In ADHD adolescents and adults with SUD, the antidepressants (bupropion, tricyclics, venlafaxine) and longer-acting stimulants such as magnesium pemoline (Drug Enforcement Administration, 1995; Langer, Sweeney, Bartenbach, DAvis, & Menander,, 1986) with lower abuse liability are preferable (Riggs, 1998). Preclinical and human studies suggest variable profiles of stimulants with methylphenidate having less abuse liability than amphetamine or methamphetamine (Drug Enforcement Administration, 1995). When choosing antidepressants, one should be mindful of potential drug interactions with substances of abuse such as those reported between tricyclic antidepressants and marijuana (Wilens, Biederman, & Spencer, 1997). Families and patients should be educated as to the concern of diversion of medications such as stimulants to others. In individuals with SUD and ADHD, frequent monitoring of pharmacotherapy should be undertaken, including evaluation of compliance with treatment, random toxicology screens as indicated, and coordination of care with addiction counselors and other caregivers.

SUMMARY

There is a robust literature supporting a relationship between ADHD and SUD. Noncomorbid ADHD appears to confer an intermediate risk factor for SUD, although conduct and bipolar disorder appear to heighten the risk for the early onset of SUD. Both family-genetic and self-medication influences appear to be operational in the development and continuation of SUD in ADHD subjects. Patients with ADHD and SUD require multimodal intervention incorporating addiction and mental health treatment. Pharmacotherapy in ADHD and SUD individuals needs to take into consideration abuse liability, potential drug interactions, and compliance concerns.

The existing literature has provided important information on the relationship of ADHD and SUD, but it also points to a number of areas in need of further study. The long-term effects of specific pharmacotherapy with stimulant and nonstimulants as well as overall treatment of ADHD on ultimate SUD need to be better understood. Given the prevalence and major morbidity and impairment caused by SUD and ADHD, prevention and treatment strategies for these patients need be further developed and evaluated.

Acknowledgment

This research was supported by NIMH K20MHO1175, DA11929, and DA 11315, awarded to T. Wilens, MD.

References

Abel, E. L., & Sokol, R. J. (1987). Incidence of fetal alcohol syndrome and economic impacy of FAS-related anomalies. *Drug and Alcohol Dependence, 19*, 51–79.

American Psychiatric Association. (1980). *Diagnostic and statistical manual of mental disorders* (3rd ed.). Washington., DC: Author.

Anderson, J., Williams, S., McGee, R., & Silva, P. A. (1987). DSM III disorders in preadolescent children. *Archives of General Psychiatry, 44*, 69–76.

Aronson, H., & Gilbert, A. (1963). Preadolescent sons of male alcoholics. *Archives of General Psychiatry, 8*, 235–241.

Beck, L., Langford, W., Mackay, M., & Sum, G. (1975). Childhood chemotherapy and later drug abuse and growth curve: A follow-up study of 30 adolescents. *American Journal of Psychiatry, 132*(4), 436–438.

Biederman, J., Faraone, S., Keenan, K., Benjamin, J., Krifcher, B., Moore, C., Sprich-Buckminster, S., Ugaglia, K., Jellinek, M. S., Steingard, R.,Spencer, T., Norman, D., Kolodny, R., Kraus, I., Perrin, J., Keller, M. B., Tsuang, M. T. (1992). Further evidence for family-genetic risk factors in attention deficit hyperactivity disorder: Patterns of comorbidity in probands and psychiatrically and pediatrically referred samples. *Archives of General Psychiatry, 49*, 728–738.

Biederman, J., Faraone S. V., Keenan, K., Knee, D., & Tsuang, M. T. (1990). Family-genetic and psychosocial risk factors in DSM-III attention deficit disorder. *Journal of the American Academy of Child and Adolescent Psychiatry, 29*, 526–533.

Biederman, J., Faraone S. V., Spencer, T., Wilens, T. E., Norman, D., Lapey, K. A., Mick. E., Lehman, B., & Doyle, A. (1993). Patterns of psychiatric comorbidity, cognition, and psychosocial functioning in adults with attention deficit hyperactivity disorder. *American Journal of Psychiatry, 150,* 1792–1798.

Biederman, J., Wilens, T., Mick, E., Faraone, S. V., & Spencer, T. (1998). Does attention deficit hyperactivity disorder impact the developmental course of drug and alcohol abuse and dependence? *Biological Psychiatry, 44,* 269–273.

Biederman, J., Wilens. T., Mick, E., Faraone, S., & Spencer, T. (1999). Pharmacotherapy of ADHD reduces substance abuse in midadolescence: A longitudinal study. *Pediatrics, 104*(2), e20.

Biederman, J., Wilens, T., Mick, E., Faraone, S., Weber, W., Curtis, S., Thornell, A., Pfister, K., Jetton, J., & Soriano, J. (1997). Is ADHD a risk for psychoactive substance use disorder? Findings from a four year follow-up study. *Journal of the American Academy of Child and Adolescent Psychiatry, 36,* 21–29.

Biederman, J., Wilens, T., Mick, E., Milberger, S., Spencer, T. J., & Faraone, S. V. (1995). Psychoactive substance use disorders in adults with attention deficit hyperactivity disorder (ADHD): Effects of ADHD and psychiatric comorbidity. *American Journal of Psychiatry, 152,* 1652–1658.

Blouin, A., Bornstein, R., & Trites, R (1978). Teenage alcohol use among hyperactive children: A five year follow-up study. *Journal of Pediatric Psychology, 3,* 188–194.

Bukstein, O. G., Brent, D. A., & Kaminer, Y. (1989). Comorbidity of substance abuse and other psychiatric disorders in adolescents. *American Journal of Psychiatry, 146,* 1131–1141.

Cantwell, D. (1972). Psychiatric illness in the families of hyperactive children. *Archives of General Psychiatry, 27,* 414–417.

Carroll, K. M., & Rounsaville, B. J. (1993). History and significance of childhood attention deficit disorder in treatment-seeking cocaine abusers. *Comprehensive Psychiatry, 34,* 75–82.

Chassin, L., Rogosch, F., & Barrera, M. (1991). Substance use and symptomatology among adolescent children of alcoholics. *Journal of Abnormal Psychology, 100*(4), 449–463.

Comings, D., Comings, B., Muhleman, D., Dietz, G., Shahbahrami, B., Tast, D., Knell, E., Kocsis, P., Baumgarten, R., Kovacs, B., Levy, D., Smith, M., Borison, R., Evans, D., Klein, D., MacMurray, J., Tosk, J., Sverd, J., Gysin, R., & Flanagan, S. (1991). The dopamine D2 receptor locus as a modifying gene in neuropsychiatric disorders. *Journal of the American Medical Association, 266,* 1793–1800.

DeMilio, L. (1989). Psychiatric syndromes in adolescent substance abusers. *American Journal of Psychiatry, 146,* 1212–1214.

Drug Enforcement Administration. (1995). *Methylphenidate review document.* Washington, DC: Author.

Earls, F., Reich, W., Jung, K. G., & Cloninger, C. R. (1988). Psychopathology in children of alcoholic and antisocial parents. *Alcoholism: Clinical and Experimental Research, 12,* 481–487.

Ebstein, R., Novick, O., Umansky, R., Priel, B., Osher, Y., Blaine, D., Bennett, E., Nemanov, L., Katz, M., & Belmaker, R. (1996). Dopamine D4 receptor exon III polymorphism associated with the human personality trait of novelty seeking. *Nature Genetics, 12,* 78–80.

Fine, E. W., Yudin, L. W., Holmes, J., & Heinemann, S. (1976). Behavioral disorders in children with parental alcoholism. *Annals of the New York Academy of Science, 273,* 507–517.

Finnegan, L. P. (1976). Clinical effects of pharmacologic agents on pregnancy, the fetus and the neonate. *Annals of the New York Academy of Sciences, 281,* 74–89.

Gittelman, R., Mannuzza, S., Shenker, R., & Bonagura, N. (1985). Hyperactive boys almost grown up: I. Psychiatric status. *Archives of General Psychiatry, 42,* 937–947.

Goodwin, D. W., Schulsinger, F., Hermansen, L., Guze, S. B., & Winokur, G. (1975). Alcoholism and the hyperactive child syndrome. *Journal of Nervous and Mental Disorders, 160,* 349–353.

Griffith, D. R., Azuma, S. D., & Chasnoff, I. J. (1994). Three-year outcome of children exposed prenatally to drugs. *Journal of the American Academy of Child and Adolescent Psychiatry, 33,* 20–27.

Hartsough, C. S., & Lambert, N. M. (1987). Pattern and progression of drug use among hyperactives and controls: A prospective short-term longitudinal study. *Journal of Child Psychology and Psychiatry, 28,* 543–553.

Hechtman, L. (1985). Adolescent outcome of hyperactive children treated with stimulants in childhood: A review. *Psychopharmacology Bulletin, 21*(2), 178–191.

Hechtman, L., & Weiss, G. (1986). Controlled prospective fifteen year follow-up of hyperactives as adults: Non-medical drug and alcohol use and anti-social behaviour. *Canadian Journal of Psychiatry, 31*, 557–567.

Horner, B., & Scheibe, K. (1997). Prevalance and implications of ADHD among adolescents in treatment for substance abuse. *Journal of the American Academy of Child and Adolescent Psychiatry, 36*, 30–36.

Hovens, J. G., Cantwell, D. P., & Kiriakos, R. (1994). Psychiatric comorbidity in hospitalized adolescent substance abusers. *Journal of the American Academy of Child and Adolescent Psychiatry, 33*(4), 476–483.

Kaminer, Y. (1992). Clinical implications of the relationship between attention-deficit hyperactivity disorder and psychoactive substance use disorders. *American Journal on Addictions, 1*, 257–264.

Kandel, D., & Faust, R. (1975). Sequence and stages in patterns of adolescent drug use. *Archives of General Psychiatry, 32*, 923–932.

Kandel, D. B., & Logan, J. A. (1984). Patterns of drug use from adolescence to young adulthood: I. Periods of risk for initiation, continued use, and discontinuation. *American Journal of Public Health, 74*, 660–666.

Kellam, S. G., Ensminger, M. E., & Simon, M. B. (1980). Mental health in first grade and teenage drug, alcohol, and cigarette use. *Drug and Alcohol Dependence, 5*, 273–304.

Kessler, R. C., McGonagle, K. A., Zhao, S., Nelson, C. B., Hughes, M., Eshleman, S., Wittchen, H., & Kendler, K. S. (1994). Lifetime and 12-month prevalence of DSM-III-R psychiatric disorders in the United States. *Archives of General Psychiatry, 51*, 8–19.

Khantzian, E. J. (1983). An extreme case of cocaine dependence and marked improvement with methylphenidate treatment. *American Journal of Psychiatry, 140*, 784–785.

Khantzian, E. J. (1997). The self-medication hypothesis of substance use disorders: A reconsideration and recent applications. *Harvard Review of Psychiatry, 4*, 231–244.

Kramer, J., Loney, J., & Whaley-Klahn, M. A. (1981). *The role of prescribed medication in hyperactive youths' substance use.* Paper presented at the 1981 annual meeting of the American Psychological Association, Los Angeles.

LaHoste, G. J., Swanson, J. M., Wigal, S. B., Glabe, C., Wigal, T., King, N., & Kennedy, J. L. (1996). Dopamine D4 receptor gene polymorphism is associated with attention deficit hyperactivity disorder. *Molecular Psychiatry, 1*, 121–124.

Lambert, N., Hartsough, C., Sassone, D., & Sandoval, J. (1987). Persistence of hyperactivity symptoms from childhood to adolescence and associated outcomes. *American Journal of Orthopsychiatry, 57*(1), 22–32.

Langer, D. H., Sweeney, K. P., Bartenbach, D. E., Davis, P. M., & Menander, K. B. (1986). Evidence of lack of abuse or dependence following pemoline treatment: results of a retrospective survey. *Drug and Alcohol Dependency, 17*, 213–227.

Levin, F., Evans, S. M., Lugo, L., Seham, J., Baird, D., & Kleber, H. (1996). *ADHD in cocaine abusers: Psychiatric comorbidity and pattern of drug use.* Paper presented at the annual meeting of College on Problems of Drug Dependence, San Juan, Puerto Rico.

Levin, F., Evans, S., McDowell, D., Brooks, D., Rhum, M., & Kleber, H. (1998). *Bupropion treatment for adult ADHD and cocaine abuse.* Paper presented at the annual meeting of College on Problems of Drug Dependence, Scottsdale, AZ.

Levin, F. R., Evans, S. M., McDowell, D., & Kleber, H. D. (1997). Methylphenidate treatment for cocaine abusers with adult attention-deficit/hyperactivity disorder: A pilot study. *Journal of Clinical Psychiatry, 58*, 1–21.

Levin, F. R., Evans, S. M., Rosenthal, M., & Kleber, H. D. (1997). *Psychiatric comorbidity in cocaine abusers in outpatient settings or a therapeutic community.* Paper presented at the annual meeting of College on Problems of Drug Dependence, Nashville, TN.

Levin, F. R., & Kleber, H. D. (1995). Attention-deficit hyperactivity disorder and substance abuse: Relationships and implications for treatment. *Harvard Review of Psychiatry, 2*, 246–258.

Loney, J. (1988). Substance abuse in adolescents: Diagnostic issues derived from studies of attention deficit disorder with hyperactivity. *NIDA Research Monograph, 77*, 19–26.

Loney, J., Kramer, J., & Milich, R. S. (1981). The hyperactive child grows up: Predictors of symptoms, delinquency and achievement at follow-up. In K. Gadow & J. Loney (Eds.), *Psychosocial aspects of drug treatment for hyperactivity* (pp. 381–415). Boulder., CO: Westview Press.

Lynskey, M., & Fergusson, D. (1995). Childhood conduct problems, attention deficit behaviors and adolescent alcohol, tobacco, and illicit drug use. *Journal of Abnormal Child Psychology, 23*, 281–302.

Mannuzza, S., Gittelman-Klein, R., Konig, P. H., & Giampino, T. L. (1989). Hyperactive boys almost grown up: IV. Criminality and its relationship to psychiatric status. *Archives of General Psychiatry, 46*, 1073–1079.

Mannuzza, S., Klein, R. G., Bessler, A., Malloy, P., & LaPadula, M. (1993). Adult outcome of hyperactive boys: Educational achievement., occupational rank., and psychiatric status. *Archives of General Psychiatry, 50*, 565–576.

Mathew, R. J., Wilson, W. H., Blazer, D. G., & George, L. K, (1993). Psychiatric disorders in adult children of alcoholics: Data from the epidemiologic catchment area project. *American Journal of Psychiatry, 150*(5), 793–800.

Mathias, R. (1997). Marijuana and tobacco use up again among 8th and 10th graders. *NIDA Notes, 12*(2), 12–19.

McDermott, S. P. (2000). Cognitive and emotional impediments to treating the adult with ADHD: A cognitive therapy perspective. In T. Brown (Eds.), *Subtypes of attention deficit disorders in children, adolescents, and adults* (pp. 569–606). Washington, DC: American Psychiatric Press.

Milberger, S., Biederman, J., Faraone, S., Chen, L., & Jones, J. (1996). Is maternal smoking during pregnancy a risk factor for attention deficit hyperactivity disorder in children? *American Journal of Psychiatry, 153*, 1138–1142.

Milberger, S., Biederman, J., Faraone, S. V., Chen, L., & Jones, J. (1997a). ADHD is associated with early initiation of cigarette smoking in children and adolescents. *Journal of the American Academy of Child and Adolescent Psychiatry, 36*, 37–44.

Milberger, S., Biederman, J., Faraone, S., Wilens, T., & Chu, M. (1997). Associations between ADHD and psychoactive substance use disorders: Findings from a longitudinal study of high-risk siblings of ADHD children. *American Journal on Addictions, 6*, 318–329.

Milberger, S., Faraone, S., Biederman J., Chu, M., & Wilens, T. (1998). Familial risk analysis of the association between ADHD and psychoactive substance use disorders. *Archives of Pediatric and Adolescent Medicine, 152*, 945–951.

Milin, R., Halikas, J. A., Meller, J. E., & Morse, C. (1991). Psychopathology among substance abusing juvenile offenders. *Journal of the American Academy of Child and Adolescent Psychiatry, 30*(4), 569–574.

Millstein, R. B., Wilens, T. E., Biederman, J., & Spencer, T. J. (1997). Presenting ADHD symptoms and subtypes in clinically referred adults with ADHD. *Journal of Attention Disorders, 2*, 159–166.

Morrison, J. (1980). Adult psychiatric disorders in parents of hyperactive children. *American Journal of Psychiatry, 137*, 825–827.

Morrison, J. R., & Stewart, M. A. (1971). A family study of the hyperactive child syndrome. *Biological Psychiatry, 3*, 189–195.

Mrazek, P. J., & Haggerty, R. J. (Ed.). (1994). *Reducing risks for mental disorders: Institute of Medicine.* Washington, DC: National Academy Press.

Murphy, K., & Barkley, R. A. (1996). Prevalence of DSM-IV symptoms of ADHD in adult licensed drivers: Implications for clinical diagnosis. *Journal of Attention Disorders, 1*, 147–161.

Orvaschel, H. (1985). Psychiatric interviews suitable for use in research with children and adolescents. *Psychopharmacology Bulletin, 21*, 737–748.

Richardson, G. A., & Day, N. L. (1994). Detrimental effects of prenatal cocaine exposure: Illusion or reality? *Journal of the American Academy of Child and Adolescent Psychiatry, 33,* 28–34.

Riggs, P. (1998). Clinical approach to treatment of ADHD in adolescents with substance use disorders and conduct disorder. *Journal of the American Academy of Child and Adolescent Psychiatry, 37*(3), 331–332.

Riggs, P., Leon, S. L., Mikulich, S. K., & Pottle, L. C. (1998). An open trial of bupropion for ADHD in adolescents with SUDs and conduct disorder. *Journal of the American Academy of Child and Adolescent Psychiatry, 37*, 1271–1278.

Riggs, P. D., Thompson, L. L., Mikulich, S. K., Whitmore, E. A., & Crowley, T. J. (1996). An open trial of pemoline in drug dependent delinquents with attention deficit hyperactivity disorder. *Journal of the American Academy of Child and Adolescent Psychiatry, 35*, 1018–1024.

Ross, H. E., Glaser, F. B., & Germanson, T. (1988). The prevalence of psychiatric disorders in patients with alcohol and other drug problems. *Archives of General Psychiatry, 45*, 1023–1031.

Satterfield, J. H., Hoppe, C. M., & Schell, A. M. (1982). A prospective study of delinquency in 110 adolescent boys with attention deficit disorder and 88 normal adolescent boys. *American Journal of Psychiatry, 139*, 795–798.

Schubiner, H., Tzelepis, A., Isaacson, J. H., Warbasse, L. H., Zacharek, M., & Musial, J. (1995). The dual diagnosis of attention-deficit/hyperactivity disorder and substance abuse: Case reports and literature review. *Journal of Clinical Psychiatry, 56*, 146–150.

Schubiner, H., Tzelepis, A., Schoener, E., Lockhart, N., Kruger, M., & Kelley, B. (1997). *Prevalence of ADHD among substance abusers.* Paper presented at the annual meeting of College on Problems of Drug Dependence, Nashville, TN.

Sher, K. J., Walitzer, K. S., Wood, P. K., & Brent, E. E. (1991). Characteristics of children of alcoholics: Putative risk factors., substance use and abuse, and psychopathology. *Journal of Abnormal Psychology, 100*, 427–448.

Spencer, T., Biederman, J., Wilens, T., Harding, M., O'Donnell, D., & Griffin, S. (1996). Pharmacotherapy of attention-deficit hyperactivity disorder across the life cycle. *Journal of the American Academy of Child and Adolescent Psychiatry, 35*, 409–432.

Steinhausen, H., Gobel, D., & Nestler, V. (1984). Psychopathology in the offspring of alcoholic parents. *Journal of the American Academy of Child and Adolescent Psychiatry, 23*, 465–471.

Steinhausen, H. C., Willms, J., & Spohr, H. L. (1993). Long-term psychopathological and cognitive outcome of children with fetal alcohol syndrome. *Journal of the American Academy of Child and Adolescent Psychiatry, 32*, 990–994.

Stewart, M. A., DeBlois, C. S., & Cummings, C. (1980). Psychiatric disorder in the parents of hyperactive boys and those with conduct disorder. *Journal of Child Psychology and Psychiatry, 21*, 283–292.

Tarter, R. E., & Edwards, K. (1988). Psychological factors associated with the risk for alcoholism. *Alcoholism: Clinical and Experimental Research, 12*, 471–480.

Tarter, R. E., McBride, H., Buonpane, N., & Schneider, D. U. (1977). Differentiation of alcoholics. *Archives of General Psychiatry, 34*, 761–768.

Volpe, J. J. (1992). Effect of cocaine use on the fetus. *New England Journal of Medicine, 327*, 399–406.

Weiss, G. (1992). *Attention-deficit hyperactivity disorder.* Philadelphia: Saunders.

Weiss, G., Hechtman, L., Milroy, T., & Perlman, T. (1985). Psychiatric status of hyperactives as adults: A controlled prospective 15-year follow-up of 63 hyperactive children. *Journal of the American Academy of Child and Adolescent Psychiatry, 24*, 211–220.

Wender, P. H., Reimherr, F. W., & Wood, D. R. (1981). Attention deficit disorder ("minimal brain dysfunction") in adults: A replication study of diagnosis and drug treatment. *Archives of General Psychiatry, 38*, 449–456.

Wilens, T. E. (1994). The children and adolescent offspring of alcoholic parents. *Current Opinions in Psychiatry, 7*, 319–323.

Wilens, T., & Biederman, J. (1993). Psychopathology in preadolescent children at high risk for substance abuse: A review of the literature. *Harvard Review of Psychiatry, 1*, 207–218.

Wilens, T., Biederman, J., & Mick, E. (1998). Does ADHD Affect the course of substance abuse? Findings from a sample of adults with and without ADHD. *American Journal on Addictions, 7*, 156–163.

Wilens, T. E., Biederman, J., Mick, E., Faraone, S. V., & Spencer, T. (1997). Attention deficit hyperactivity disorder (ADHD) is associated with early onset substance use disorders. *Journal of Nervous and Mental Disease, 185*(8), 475–482.

Wilens, T., Biederman, J., Millstein, R., Wozniak, J., Hahesy, A., & Spencer, T. (1999). Risk for substance use disorders in youth with child- and adolescent-onset bipolar disorder. *Journal of the American Academy of Child and Adolescent Psychiatry, 38*, 680–685.

Wilens, T. E., Biederman J., & Spencer, T. J. (1997). Case study: Adverse effects of smoking marijuana while receiving tricyclic antidepressants. *Journal of the American Academy of Child and Adolescent Psychiatry, 36*, 45–48.

Wilens, T. E., Biederman, J., Spencer, T. J., & Frances, R. J. (1994). Comorbidity of attention deficit hyperactivity disorder and the psychoactive substance use disorders. *Hospital and Community Psychiatry, 45*, 421–435.

Wilens, T., McDermott, S., Biederman, J., Abrantes, A., Hahesy, A., & Spencer, T. (1999). Cognitive therapy for adults with ADHD: A systematic chart review of 26 cases. *Journal of Cognitive Psychotherapy, 13*, 215–226.

Wilens, T., Spencer, T., & Biederman, J. (1995). Are attention-deficit hyperactivity disorder and the psychoactive substance use disorders really related? *Harvard Review of Psychiatry, 3*, 260–262.

Wilens, T. E., Spencer, T., & Biederman, J. (2000). Attention deficit disorder with substance abuse. In T. Brown (Ed.), *Subtypes of attention deficit disorders in children, adolescents, and adults* (pp. 319–340). Washington, DC: American Psychiatric Press.

Yamaguchi, K., & Kandel, D. B. (1984). Patterns of drug use from adolescence to young adulthood: III. Predictors of progression. *American Journal of Public Health, 74*, 673–681.

Chapter 20

Diversion, Trafficking, and Abuse of Methylphenidate

by Gretchen Feussner

Introduction 20-1
Abuse Liability Studies 20-2
    Amphetamine- and Cocaine-Like Effects 20-2
    Dose-Reinforcing Effects 20-2
    Disruptive and Stimulus Effects 20-5
    Summary 20-6
MPH Manufacture, Distribution, and Use 20-7
    Increased Production and Sale 20-7
    Disparities in Usage 20-8
Diversion and Trafficking 20-9
Issues Related to MPH Medication for ADHD 20-12
    Growing Problem of Abuse by Schoolchildren 20-12
    Increased Abuse Among Adolescents 20-12
    Diversion of Children's Prescribed Medication 20-14
    Three-State Diversion Survey Findings 20-15
        Why and How Survey Was Conducted 20-15
        MPH Diversion Not Rare 20-15
        Factors Contributing to Diversion of MPH
           Intended for ADHD Treatment 20-16
Conclusion 20-17

INTRODUCTION

Ritalin® (methylphenidate, or MPH) is classified as a Schedule II stimulant under the federal Controlled Substances Act (CSA). The Drug Enforcement Administration (DEA) is the primary agency involved in enforcing the CSA and is, therefore, responsible for establishing manufacturing quotas for Schedule I and II substances, registering handlers of controlled substances, and monitoring the distribution and use of these substances. The Schedule II classification requires that a drug or other substance (1) have a high potential for abuse, (2) have a currently accepted medical use in treatment in the United States, and (3) show that abuse may lead to severe psychological or physical dependence. Studies that address the abuse liability of a drug and data relating to the diversion of a drug from legitimate handlers, combined with clinical experience of actual abuse, provide critical information about the abuse potential and dependence profile for a drug. This chapter reviews the data that explain why MPH has been placed in this classification and provides data concerning the manufacture, distribution, diversion, trafficking, and abuse of MPH.

ABUSE LIABILITY STUDIES

Abuse liability studies provide information relating to the probability that a drug or other substance will be abused by humans; these studies are used to assess the abuse potential and dependence profile of a substance. Various behavioral paradigms including drug discrimination and self-administration analyses are sensitive models of human subjective and reinforcing effects. Although a comprehensive review of these studies has been published elsewhere (Sannerud & Feussner, 1999), a brief summary of these data is provided here.

Amphetamine- and Cocaine-Like Effects

Preclinical research shows that MPH produces strong discriminative stimulus effects and will substitute for cocaine, d-amphetamine, cathinone, GBR12909 (a dopamine uptake inhibitor), and cocaine analogues across several training doses, species, and training conditions (Table 20.1). Animals trained to discriminate d-amphetamine from saline show generalization to MPH (De la Garza & Johanson, 1987; Evans & Johanson, 1987; Huang & Ho, 1974; Porsolt, Pawelec, & Jalfre, 1982; Rosen, Young, Beuthin, & Louis-Ferdinand, 1986), animals trained to discriminate cocaine from saline show generalization to amphetamine and MPH (Colpaert, Nimegeers, & Janssen, 1979; Emmett-Oglesby, Wurst, & Lal, 1983; McKenna & Ho, 1980; Silverman & Schultz, 1989; Wood & Emmett-Oglesby, 1988), and animals trained to discriminate MPH from saline show generalization to amphetamine and cocaine (Overton, 1982; Perkins, Eckerman, & McPhail, 1991). These data suggest that MPH produces psychomotor stimulant effects in animal models that are amphetamine or cocaine-like in character.

In human drug discrimination studies, MPH substitutes for d-amphetamine and cocaine and produces similar patterns of subjective effects, including increased ratings of euphoria and drug liking and decreased sedation (Table 20.2). The physiological, subjective, and behavioral effects of MPH have been studied in narcotic abusers (Martin, Sloan, Sapira, & Jasinski, 1971), psychiatric patients (Huey et al., 1980), and normal subjects (Brown, 1977; Brown, Corriveau, & Ebert, 1978; Chait, 1994; Smith & Davis, 1977). MPH administration produces increases in "positive" mood scores, and dose-dependently increases measures of "drug liking." Low and intermediate doses of MPH produce feelings of relaxation, well-being, and contentment, whereas higher doses intensify these feelings and produce dysphoria, nervousness, and anxiety. MPH also, dose-dependently, reduces appetite and decreases caloric intake. Similar subjective effects are seen with d-amphetamine and d-methamphetamine, suggesting that these drugs have similar mechanisms of action underlying their abuse potential.

Dose-Reinforcing Effects

Table 20.3 summarizes studies using self-administration paradigms to evaluate the reinforcing effects of MPH in animals. MPH maintains self-administration behav-

Table 20.1
Discriminative Stimulus Effects of Methylphenidate in Animals

Training/Species	MPH Doses Tested (mg/kg/inj)	Like Training Drug?	Other Effects	Reference
Amphetamine Trained				
Rats	2.5	Yes	MPH = Methamphetamine = Cocaine = Ephedrine	Huang & Ho, 1974
Rats	0.5–2.0	Yes	MPH = Cocaine	Porsolt et al., 1982
Rats	0.1–10	Yes		Rosen et al., 1986
Rhesus monkeys	1.0–30.0	Yes	No changes in activity	Dela Garza & Johanson, 1987
Pigeons	0.1–3.0	Yes		Evans & Johanson, 1987
Cocaine Trained				
Rats	2.5	Partial		McKenna & Ho, 1980
Rats	4.5 and 6.0	Yes	MPH = Amphetamine	Silverman & Schultz, 1989
Rats	0.31–1.25	Yes	MPH = Methamphetamine = Cocaine	Colpaert et al., 1979
Rats	10	Yes	MPH = d-Amphetamine = Cocaine	Emmett-Oglesby et al., 1984; Wood & Emmett-Oglesby, 1988
Cathinone-Trained				
Rats	0.5–4.0	Yes	MPH = Cathinone = Cocaine = Amphetamine	Goudie et al., 1986
GBR12909-Trained				
Rats	0.1–0.3	Yes	MPH = GBR = Cocaine = Cocaine Analogues = Amphetamine	Melia & Spealman, 1981
DOM-Trained				
Rats	2.5 and 5.0	Partial	MPH = Amphetamine	Silverman & Ho, 1980
MPH-Trained				
Rats	0.5-8.0	Yes	Dose-related increases	Perkins et al., 1981
Rats	15 and 40	Yes	Trained within 7–14 days	Overton, 1982

ior in monkeys trained to self-administer intravenous cocaine (Aigner & Balster, 1979; Spealman, Madras, & Bergman, 1989; Wilson, Hitomi, & Schuster, 1971; Wilson & Schuster, 1972) and in rats trained to self-administer intravenous d-amphetamine (Nielson, Duda, Mokler, & Moore, 1984). In these studies, MPH substituted for the cocaine or d-amphetamine training dose and continued to maintain self-administration behavior. The reinforcing effects of MPH are potent. Drug-naive animals readily acquire self-injection of MPH (Downs, Harrigan, Wiley, Robinson, & Labay, 1979; Dworkin, Vrana, Broadbent, & Robinson, 1993; Collins, Weeks, Cooper, Good, & Russell, 1984; Risner & Jones, 1975, 1976). In rats, the rates of acquisition of MPH are faster than those of d-amphetamine, nicotine, or caffeine. In monkeys, unlimited access to MPH produces a higher rate of mortality than the other drugs; 75 percent of

Table 20.2
Reinforcing Effects of Methylphenidate in Animals

Training/Species	MPH Doses Tested (mg/kg/inj)	Maintained Behavior	Other Effects	Reference
Substitution: Cocaine trained				
Squirrel monkeys	0.01–0.3 mg/kg	Yes	Psychomotor stimulant effects	Spealman et al., 1989
Rhesus monkeys	0.025–0.4 mg/kg	Yes	8 MPH intake, 9food intake	Wilson et al., 1971
Rhesus monkeys	0.05 mg/kg	Yes	Blocked by chlorpromazine	Wilson & Schuster, 1972
Rhesus monkeys	0.01 and 0.1 mg/kg	Yes	8 MPH intake, 9 food intake	Aigner & Balster, 1979
Substitution: Amphetamine trained				
Rats	4 and 8 mg/kg	Yes	MPH blocked amphetamine	Nielsen et al., 1984
Progressive ratio:				
Baboons	0.1–0.8 mg/kg	Yes	Increasing responses for MPH MPH. Amphetamine	Griffiths et al., 1975
Choice paradigm: MPH vs. cocaine				
Rhesus monkeys	0.1–0.8 mg/k		MPH > Saline	Johanson & Schuster, 1975
	0.075 vs. 0.7 mg/kg	Yes	High MPH >> Low MPH doses	Schuster, 1975
	0.075–0.7 mg/kg MPH vs.	Yes	High MPH >> Cocaine	
	0.05 mg/kg Cocaine	Yes	0.5 MPH = 0.5 Cocaine	
Acquisition paradigm:				
Rhesus monkeys	0.1 mg/kg	Yes, MPH = Cocaine = Amphetamine	Cyclicity, 8 stereotypies, 9 weight, Death	Downs et al., 1979
Dogs	0.025–0.4 mg/kg	Yes MPH = Amphetamine	Cyclicity, 8 stereotypies, and locomotor activity	Risner & Jones, 1975
Dogs	0.025–0.4 mg/kg	Yes MPH > Amphetamine	Cyclicity, 8 stereotypies, locomotor activity and toxicity	Risner & Jones, 1976
Rats	1.0 and 0.32 mg/kg	Yes, MPH = Cocaine = Amphetamine		Collins et al., 1984
Rats	0.33 mg/kg	Yes MPH > Cocaine		Dworkin et al., 1993

the monkeys self-injecting MPH died, compared to 66 percent and 25 percent of the monkeys self-injecting cocaine and d-amphetamine, respectively. In dogs and monkeys, MPH, cocaine, d-amphetamine and phenmetrazine produces a cyclic pattern of self-administration, as well as weight loss, stereotypy, and death; this pattern of behav-

Table 20.3
Discriminative, Reinforcing, and Subjective Effects in Humans

MPH Dose (mg)	Results	Other Effects	Reference
7.5–60 mg, po Stimulant abusers	↑ "Positive" mood scores & drug liking ↑ Stimulant subjective effects Identified as amphetamine (44%) or cocaine (81%)	↑ Talkativeness, ↑ drive ↑ Blood pressure, ↑ Heart rate ↑ Temperature	Heischman & Henningfield 1991
15–60 mg, sc Narcotic abusers	↑ "Positive" mood scores, ↑ Drug liking MPH = d-Amphetamine = Methamphetamine (7.5–30 mg) (15–30 mg)	Low: ↑ Relaxation, well-being ↓ Appetite High: Nervousness, anxiety & dysphoria	Martin et al., 1971
20–40 mg po (mean = 31 mg) Normal volunteers	MPH chosen on 28% of sessions Placebo chosen on 9% of sessions MPH = Amphetamine No increase on drug liking	↑ Activity level ↑ "Positive" mood scales ↑ Euphoria ↑ Toxicity, dysphoria	Chait, 1994
10 & 20 mg, po Psychiatrists and psychologists	↑ Positive mood and subjective effects ↑ Talkative and friendly ↑ Euphoria	↑ Activity and ↓ Anxiety	Smith & Davis, 1977
10 & 20 mg po Normal volunteers	↑ Elation and ↑ euphoria	MPH = Amphetamine	Brown, 1977, 1978
35 mg, iv Psychiatric patients	↑ "High" and ↑ Euphoria	MPH = Amphetamine	Huey et al., 1980
45–60 mg, sc Cocaine abusers	MPH: ↓ Craving for cocaine	Self-administered MPH	Khantzian et al., 1984
60 mg MPH-dependent patients	Disruptions in behavior Affective and thought disorders	Maintained on MPH dose	Keeley & Light, 1985

po = by mouth; sc = subcutaneous; iv = intravenous

ior and profile of effects is characteristic of psychomotor stimulant abuse. In a choice procedure paradigm using rhesus monkeys, MPH and cocaine were chosen over saline in over 75 percent of the monkeys (Johanson & Schuster, 1975); higher doses of each drug were chosen over lower doses and the preference for cocaine decreased as the dose of MPH increased. At the highest dose of MPH versus cocaine, MPH was chosen by individual monkeys in 85–94 percent of the trials.

Disruptive and Stimulus Effects

Preclinical studies have also shown that chronic administration of MPH produces tolerance to its disruptive and stimulus effects and shows cross-tolerance with d-amphetamine and cocaine (Emmett-Oglesby & Brewin, 1978; Emmett-Oglesby & Taylor, 1981; Kolta, Shreve, & Uretsky, 1985; Leith & Barrett, 1981; McNamara, Davidson, & Shenk, 1993; Wood & Emmett-Oglesby, 1988; Wood, Lal, & Emmett-Oglesby, 1984). Like d-amphetamine and cocaine, chronic administration of MPH produces psychomotor stimulant toxicity, including aggression, agitation, disruption in food intake, weight loss, stereotypic movements, and death (Downs et al., 1979;

Wesson & Smith, 1978). These same effects have been well documented in humans (Brooks, O"Donoghue, Rissing, Soapes, & Smith, 1974; Goyer, Davis, & Rapoport, 1979; Jaffe, 1991; Jaffe & Koschmann, 1970; Keeley & Light, 1985; McCormick & McNeel, 1963; Rioux, 1960; Spensley & Rockwell, 1973). These case reports demonstrate that high doses of MPH often produce euphoria as well as agitation, tremors, tachycardia, palpitations, and hypertension. Psychotic episodes and paranoid delusions characteristic of amphetamine-like toxicity are associated with chronic MPH abuse. The pattern of abuse is characterized by escalation in dose, binge use followed by severe depression, and an overpowering desire to continue the use of this drug despite negative medical and social consequences. In addition, the Food and Drug Administration (FDA) Spontaneous Reporting System (SRS) shows that the administration of MPH can be associated with a number of central nervous system (CNS) effects, including twitching, personality disorder, hyperkinesia, hostility, insomnia, nervousness, hallucination and psychosis. Other serious adverse drug effects reported to the FDA include drug abuse, dependence, addiction and death.

Medical consequences associated with parenteral abuse of MPH is well documented. Pulmonary hypertension brought on by repeated intravenous injections of MPH was strongly implicated in the deaths of numerous individuals in Oregon and Washington (Lewman, 1972). Other fatalities associated with intravenous MPH abuse have been reported (Levine, Caplan, & Kauffman, 1986; Lundquest, Young, & Edland, 1986). Brooks et al. (1974) provided case reports of MPH abusers who presented on the medical-surgical services for eikenella abscesses at injection sites. Lindell, Porter, and Langstron (1972) discussed problems created by intra-arterial injection of MPH. Chillar, Jackson, and Alaan (1982) presented two cases of hemiplegia brought on by intracarotid injection of MPH. Arnett, Battle, Russo, and Roberts (1976) presented a case of a patient with staphylococcal tricuspid valve endocarditis with septic embolic pneumonia resulting from intravenous MPH abuse. Elenbaas, Waeckerle, and McNabney (1976) and Zemplenji and Colman (1984) reported abscess formation as a complication of parenteral MPH abuse. Other serious complications of intravenous MPH abuse have included osteomyelitis (Abino & Pandarinath, 1977), precocious emphysema (Sherman, Hudson, & Pierson, 1987), severe eosinophilia (Wolf, Fein, & Fehrenbacher, 1978), multiple organ failure (Stecyk, LoIudice, Demeter, & Jacobs, 1985), retinopathy (Gunby, 1979), and hepatic injury (Mehta, Murray, & LoIudice, 1984).

Summary

MPH produces d-amphetamine and cocaine-like reinforcing effects in both humans and nonhuman animals. Preclinical self-administration studies show that MPH is self-administered by animals under a variety of conditions, including when substituted for cocaine or d-amphetamine in drug-experienced animals or when initiated in drug-naive animals. MPH has reinforcing efficacy similar to cocaine and d-amphetamine. In nonhuman primates, MPH can maintain high rates of self-injection in progressive ratio studies and is chosen over cocaine in preference studies. MPH is self-administered by humans and the pattern of abuse is similar to the abuse pattern of other potent psychostimulants, including amphetamine, methamphetamine, and cocaine. Clinical data demonstrate that MPH abuse is associated with a number of CNS effects and may result in dependence and addiction.

MPH MANUFACTURE, DISTRIBUTION, AND USE

Increased Production and Sale

Each year, the DEA establishes an aggregate production quota (APQ) for MPH to meet the legitimate medical, scientific, and industrial needs for the United States. Since 1990, there has been a dramatic increase in the APQ for MPH: from 1,768 kg in 1990 to 14, 442 kg in 1998. Domestic sales reported by the manufacturers increased nearly fivefold during this same time period (Figure 20.1). Prior to 1991, domestic sales of MPH reported by the manufacturers remained stable at approximately 2,000 kg per year. In 1997, domestic sales reached nearly 10,000 kg.

This increase can be attributed to the increased use of MPH in the treatment of ADHD. According to IMS Health, National Disease and Therapeutic Index™, about 90 percent of all MPH prescriptions are for children diagnosed with ADHD although the use of MPH for adults with attentional problems has been escalating. IMS Health, National Prescription Audit Plus™ data suggest that prescriptions for MPH have leveled off in the past two years after significant increases earlier this decade

Figure 20.1
Methylphenidate: Annual Production Quota vs. Sales

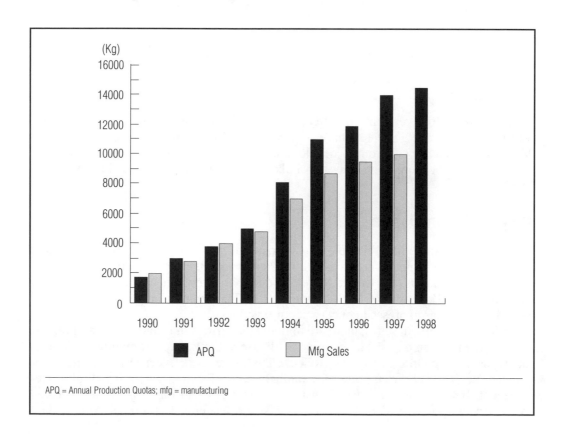

APQ = Annual Production Quotas; mfg = manufacturing

Figure 20.2
Methylphenidate and Amphetamine Prescriptions

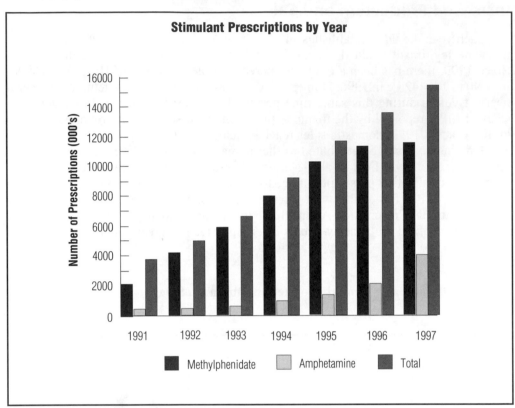

(Figure 20.2). However, stimulant treatment for ADHD continues to rise as amphetamine products take a greater share of the market. Recent increases in the APQ for MPH reflect increased product development and new manufacturers entering the market. In 1990, there were only two bulk manufacturers for MPH; in 1998 there were seven.

Disparities in Usage

It should be noted that the use of psychostimulants in the treatment of ADHD in the United States is not in keeping with medical trends in other countries. According to the United Nations, the United States produces and consumes about 90 percent of the entire world's supply of MPH (Figure 20.3). The International Narcotic Control Board (INCB) has expressed concern about this disparity.

Within the United States, there are regional disparities in usage. For example, one data source that can be used to examine MPH use is the DEA Automation of Reports and Consolidated Orders System (ARCOS). This system tracks certain controlled substances such as MPH from point of manufacture to a location where it will ultimately be distributed to the consumer. Consumption is defined as those quantities received by pharmacies, hospitals/clinics, practitioners, and teaching institutions. Assessed on

Figure 20.3
Methylphenidate Consumption

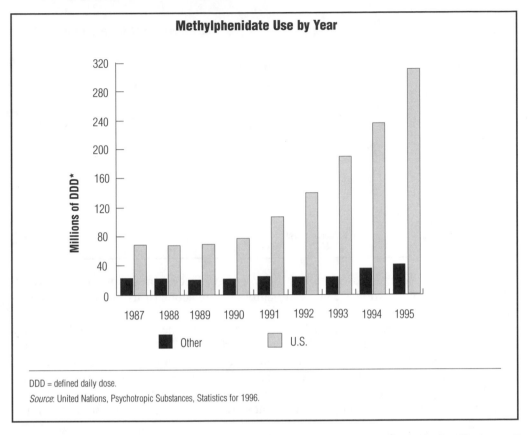

DDD = defined daily dose.

Source: United Nations, Psychotropic Substances, Statistics for 1996.

a per capita basis, ARCOS data indicate that there is wide variability in the use of MPH from one state to another and one community to another within the states. For example, in 1997, Michigan used more than twice as much MPH than either New York or California. Within all three of these states there was more than a fivefold difference between the highest-prescribing three-digit ZIP code region and the lowest. These data are consistent with epidemiological studies using actual prescription data (Kaufman, 1996; Rappley, 1995) that show areas of very low and very high prescribing of MPH. Table 20.4 includes those states with the highest levels of MPH use in 1997.

DIVERSION AND TRAFFICKING

All Schedule II stimulants, including cocaine and methamphetamine, have medical utility in the United States, and pharmaceutical products containing these substances are available for medical use. Unlike cocaine and methamphetamine where illicit manufacturing and illegal smuggling into the United States account for the vast majority of drugs available for abuse, pharmaceutical products diverted from legitimate channels are the only sources of MPH available (DEA is not aware of any clandestine production of MPH). Diversion of MPH has been identified by drug

Table 20.4
1997 ARCOS

Rank	State	MPH Grams per 10,000 Population
1	Delaware	515
2	New Hampshire	485
3	Virginia	481
4	Iowa	455
5	Wisconsin	429
6	Michigan	427
7	Vermont	427
8	South Dakota	426
9	Montana	425
10	Ohio	416

Note. 1997 U.S. average = 311 grams per 10K population; Hawaii and California have the lowest (153 and 177, respectively).

thefts, illegal sales, and prescription forgery. Law enforcement encounters involving illegal activities with MPH are good indicators of the scope of its diversion and trafficking.

From January 1990 to May 1995, MPH ranked in the top ten most frequently reported controlled pharmaceuticals diverted from licensed handlers, with nearly 2,000 incidents of drug theft. Most reports were generated by pharmacies and most thefts occurred during night break-ins. From January 1996 to December 1997, about 700,000 dosage units were reported missing or stolen from licensed handlers. Night break-in, armed robbery, and employee theft were the three major sources of the diverted MPH.

The DEA does not routinely receive data from state law enforcement agencies or their forensic laboratories concerning drug-related cases. However, the MPH data that have been shared with DEA by state officials (primarily as a result of DEA's request for information when conducting a review in 1995), combined with data from DEA's own case files and forensic laboratories, indicate that MPH is diverted in a number of ways by a wide range of individuals and organized groups, from health care professionals to organized drug trafficking rings. DEA case files show that MPH is associated with criminal drug-trafficking activities, including street sales, multistate distribution rings, multidrug distribution rings, smuggling from Mexico, and distribution and use by narcotic addicts. The extent and severity of these activities is similar to other nonclandestinely produced Schedule II substances of comparable availability (i.e., morphine sulfate, meperidine, and pentobarbital).

Law enforcement data indicate that a number of states have experienced significant problems with MPH diversion and abuse. In the 1970s and 1980s, MPH was extensively abused among street addicts and methadone clinic clients in Missouri, Oregon, and Washington. Studies conducted in Washington (Haglund & Howerton, 1982) and Oregon (Lewman, 1972) evaluated the extent and severity of this abuse. Intravenous abuse of MPH alone or in combination with narcotics was most commonly found. Talwin NX and Ritalin combination (referred to by addicts as "T&R") was trafficked in a number of states including Ohio, Kansas, Illinois, and Missouri as well as major western Canadian cities. Abuse of this drug combination was also documented in the medical literature (Bryan, Franks, & Torres, 1973; Carter & Watson, 1994; Kishorekumer, Yagnik, & Dhopesh, 1985; Lundquist et al., 1987). For example, Carter and Watson (1994) identified twenty-nine emergency room patients who presented at the Truman Medical Center in Kansas City, Missouri, from August 1987 to November 1992 with complications associated with abuse of this combination.

In light of recent diversion trends related to the treatment of ADHD, it is interesting to note that one of the first "attention deficit scams" occurred in Missouri in the early 1980s and was associated with obtaining Ritalin for T&R traffickers. In this scam, Medicaid patients took their children who allegedly had attention deficit disorder to several doctors to obtain Ritalin prescriptions. The prescriptions were filled in numerous pharmacies to avoid detection and both the office visit and the medication were paid by Medicaid. The parents then sold the Ritalin ($500/1,000 tablets) to drug traffickers who combined a Ritalin tablet with a Talwin NX tablet and sold the set for anywhere from $8 to $50. Various permutations of this doctor-shopping scam have been reported in Iowa, Ohio, New York, Wisconsin, Colorado, and Illinois.

Various states have documented the diversion and trafficking of MPH in recent years. Nebraska investigative services for the state reported that MPH ranked among the top three pharmaceutical drugs most frequently submitted to crime laboratories for analysis from 1991 through 1993 and MPH ranked sixth among drugs involved in incidents of forged or altered prescriptions from April 1992 through January 1995. In Ohio, from March 1979 to January 1994, MPH ranked second among pharmaceutical drugs reported for false or forged prescriptions and the Ohio Board of Pharmacy reported eighteen separate cases involving pharmacists who were diverting this drug. Except for one case of insurance fraud, all other cases involved Ohio pharmacists who were drug trafficking and diverting MPH for self-abuse. One pharmacist was even videotaped crushing MPH and snorting the powder. From 1992 to 1995, the Washington State Board of Pharmacy identified ten pharmacy technicians and pharmacists who were diverting MPH for their own use. A number of other medical professionals have diverted MPH for profit or personal use. For example, a physician in Ohio was writing fraudulent prescriptions to enable him to bill welfare for office visits. In another case in Illinois, a physician was supplying multiple prescriptions to a group of individuals involved in a multistate drug trafficking ring. In total, from January 1990 through May 1995, the DEA initiated nearly 200 cases involving physicians and pharmacists. Cases ranged in severity from relatively minor infractions of the CSA to diverting large quantities of MPH to known drug abusers and drug traffickers.

Although diversion, trafficking, and abuse of methylphenidate have been documented throughout the United States, with some instances of a severe nature, the incidence of these activities in the adult population has remained relatively stable. This is consistent with what the DEA would expect of a substance with a high abuse potential but no clandestine production, little prescriptions written for adults, and stringent regulatory controls applied to its production, distribution, and prescription. However, diversion and misuse/abuse of MPH medication intended for the treatment of ADHD is escalating and of particular concern to the DEA. The next section reviews data relating to this issue.

ISSUES RELATED TO MPH MEDICATION FOR ADHD

Growing Problem of Abuse by Schoolchildren

Few articles in the ADHD treatment literature address the abuse potential of MPH, and only a limited number of case reports have documented MPH abuse within the context of ADHD treatment (Fulton & Yates, 1988; Goyer et al., 1979; Jaffe, 1991). The vast majority of articles in these professional journals fail to address this issue—or often comment that MPH is a mild psychostimulant that is not associated with drug abuse. However, a significant amount of data from school surveys, emergency room reports, poison control centers, adolescent drug treatment centers, and law enforcement encounters all indicate a growing problem with the abuse of MPH among schoolchildren.

Since 1990, there has been a sixfold increase in the number of estimated drug abuse emergency room (ER) visits associated with the use of MPH in the Department of Health and Human Services Substance Abuse and Mental Health Services Administration (DHHS-SAMHSA) Drug Abuse Warning Network (DAWN). The design and methodology of DAWN are described elsewhere (http://www.samhsa.gov/OAS/dawn/dawnfile.htm). In 1990 it was estimated that there were 271 ER visits while in 1996 the estimated number was 1,725. When these DAWN mentions are compared to other potent psychostimulants such as methamphetamine (MAMP) and cocaine (COC), the total number of mentions for MPH pales in comparison (Figure 20.4). To a large extent, this disparity reflects the much greater availability of MAMP and COC. However, if DAWN data are examined for children ages 10–14, a group that has much easier access to MPH as a result of the expanded use of MPH for ADHD treatment, an entirely different profile emerges for these drugs (Figure 20.5). In 1995 and 1996, 10–14-year-old patients were just as likely to mention MPH use as cocaine in a drug abuse DAWN ER episode. Eighty-five percent of the MPH cohort reported no other drug used in combination with MPH and in nearly 75 percent of the episodes patients reported drug use for psychic effects (44 percent) or recreational use (30 percent).

Increased Abuse Among Adolescents

Survey data also indicate that a growing number of adolescents are misusing/abusing MPH. Monitoring the Future, a national school survey conducted by the Institute of Social Research at the University of Michigan, indicates that about 1 percent of all 1994 and 1995 high school seniors used Ritalin without a doctor's order during the previous year. In 1997, that percentage increased to 2.8. Whereas 1997 statistics show a significant increase in illicit use, the percentages of high school seniors that have used Ritalin/MPH illicitly may be much higher. As explained by the authors (Johnston, O'Malley, & Bachman, 1998), twelfth-graders were asked about their use of Ritalin only if they answer that they used "amphetamines" nonmedically in the prior twelve months. Failure to recognize that Ritalin is an amphetamine would mean that they would not respond to a question about Ritalin use and therefore not be counted. Indiana's drug use survey may reflect a more accurate prevalence. In 1997, Indiana University Prevention Resource Center Survey, representing a sampling of 44,232 students in 137 different schools, added questions relating to nonmedical use of Ritalin in the general drug use section (internal source documents, Drug Enforcement Agency). Nearly 7 percent of all high school students reported using

Figure 20.4
DAWN Estimated Emergency Room Mentions: Methamphetamine and Cocaine

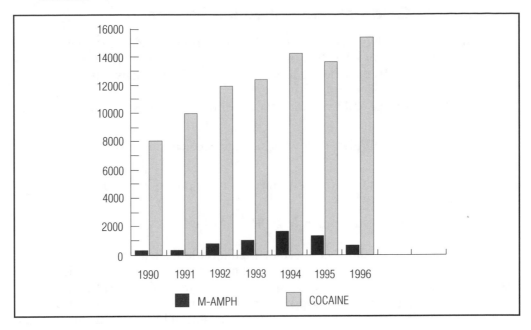

Figure 20.5
DAWN Estimated Emergency Room Mentions: Methylphenidate, Methamphetamine, and Cocaine

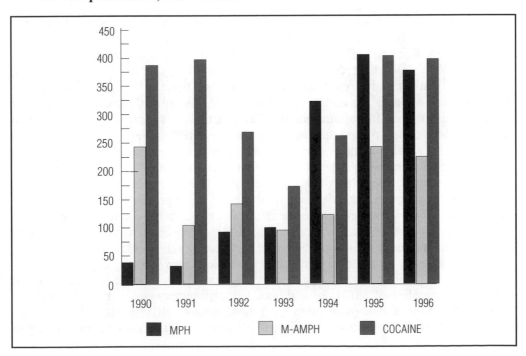

Ritalin nonmedically at least once in the previous year, and 2.5 percent reported using it on a monthly or more frequent basis.

Diversion of Children's Prescribed Medication

Incidents that involve diversion of MPH medication intended for ADHD treatment have been reported to the DEA by a wide variety of sources. State and local law enforcement cases have identified four different types of illicit activities:

1. Adults who divert children's medication for their own personal use or to sell or trade it for other drugs;

2. Children who sell/give their own/siblings medication to friends and classmates;

3. Adolescents who abuse their own medication or obtain it from friends or classmates; and

4. Theft of school-held supplies of MPH.

Parents who "doctor shop" or abuse their children's medication are not engaging in a particularly new type of diversion, as documented in the earlier discussion on the "attention deficit disorder scam" in Missouri. Recent law enforcement cases involving doctor shopping for MPH have been reported in Ohio, New York, Kentucky, Louisiana, and Virginia. Although Missouri has considerably less documented abuse of methylphenidate than in the 1980s, seven drug treatment centers reported that they had clients who were using their children's MPH prescriptions (documented in a 1995 survey on Ritalin conducted by the Missouri Department of Health (internal source documents, Drug Enforcement Agency).

As a result of DEA inquiries about adolescent misuse/abuse of MPH during the 1995 review, the DEA received numerous reports of students who gave, sold, traded, and/or abused their own MPH medication or that of a sibling, friend, or classmate. State and local law enforcement cases involving high school students in Iowa, Missouri, Michigan, and Virginia were reported to the DEA. In 1995, MPH was a contributing cause of death of a college freshman in Mississippi and the cause of death of a teenager in Virginia. In both instances MPH tablets were supplied by someone who had a legitimate prescription for the drug and the MPH tablets were crushed and snorted. Police reports of interviews with teenagers who were snorting MPH indicated that these youngsters did not view this activity as dangerous. Adolescent drug treatment centers in Michigan and Missouri reported having several clients who were abusing MPH but few clients who identified MPH as their primary drug of abuse. The vast majority of incidents brought to the DEA's attention involving students who were using MPH illicitly (selling, giving, trading, abusing) at school were not reported to law enforcement authorities at all but were handled by school officials and parents. Penalties frequently involved suspension or expulsion from school.

Schools in Connecticut, Michigan, and Virginia reported break-ins and thefts of school-held supplies of MPH. In addition, law enforcement case files have documented the theft of this medication by school personnel. For example, a highly respected teacher was videotaped stealing MPH from the nurse's office the evening of an awards ceremony that was honoring him as "teacher of the year." In another incident, a school nurse who was responsible for safeguarding school supplies of medication stole the children's MPH medication. In a school that required a student to provide proof of medication need (i.e., a doctor's prescription), the principal was discovered taking the MPH prescriptions and having them filled by pharmacies throughout the state for his own personal use. It is important to note that many schools have as much, if not more, MPH stored on a daily basis than many pharmacies—but without the safeguards and accountability required of registered handlers.

Three-State Diversion Survey Findings

Why and How Survey Was Conducted. At the conclusion of the DEA's review in 1995, there was little doubt that children were diverting and using MPH illicitly. However, due to a number of factors including privacy issues relating to children and the lack of a formalized method to obtain state or local law enforcement data, it was difficult to determine how widespread this problem actually was. In other words, was this a random problem in certain areas or was it a more pervasive problem that was not being reported/captured by traditional sources of information? To address these questions, the DEA conducted a survey in three states: Indiana, South Carolina, and Wisconsin. These states shared two characteristics: ARCOS data indicated that all three states were considered high users of MPH, and the DEA had not received a single anecdotal or law enforcement case involving illicit use of MPH by adolescents from these states. The high-use criteria was made to eliminate any doubt about not finding cases because too few children were being treated with MPH. The second criteria was selected because it was felt that a fair assessment required not knowing whether any ADHD-related MPH diversion or abuse would be found. Because it was postulated that traditional data sources such as law enforcement case files, forensic laboratory reports, and state-controlled substances authorities could not provide the information sought, a number of nontraditional sources of information were explored. Interviews were conducted with physicians, adolescent treatment center personnel, school officials, nurses, and teachers. When available, poison control data and MPH prescription data were obtained. No effort was made to do a randomized sampling of the various sources of information. However, an effort was made to obtain information from communities of varying populations and locations within each state and the physicians who were interviewed were pediatric specialists for ADHD and child psychiatrists. Data were collected over a one-week period in each state by this author and a trained DEA diversion investigator from each state. No attempt was made to do an exhaustive search of all possible cases related to MPH diversion as resources and time did not permit that type of investigation. The results were reported at a 1996 DEA conference on Stimulant Use in the Treatment of ADHD (Feussner, 1996) and are summarized here.

MPH Diversion Not Rare. All three states had incidents within the previous year that fit the profile of the types of diversion and misuse/abuse previously outlined. Although there were not an overwhelming number of incidents in each state, there was a sufficient number of events "unmasked" by this cursory examination to suggest that these activities are far from rare. Some examples of these incidents include the following:

- Indiana:

  — A 14-year-old sold his girlfriend's MPH medication to an undercover agent.

  — A 16-year-old crushed his MPH tablets and brought the powder to school.

  — An 18-year-old female student was encountered with crushed MPH powder at school and admitted to abusing it for longer than a year.

  — A school nurse reported missing/stolen MPH from supplies held at school.

  — Twelve high school students were trafficking MPH at school.

  — A student was stealing MPH medication from another student's medication bottle. Although prescribed MPH, he said he needed more.

- South Carolina:

  — A father brought a MPH tablet to the police for identification: His son later admitted he was snorting Ritalin

  — A 16-year-old was arrested for marijuana possession and was found to be carrying sixty-five MPH tablets. He admitted to crushing the tablets and snorting the powder. He did not have a prescription for MPH.

  — School officials reported MPH theft from the nurse's office.

  — Several students were suspended from school for distributing MPH on the school bus.

  — Four male Citadel students were expelled for nonmedical use of MPH.

- Wisconsin:

  — Twelve students were suspended/expelled for selling MPH on the school bus.

  — A 13-year-old boy was selling his brother's medication at school.

  — A 16-year-old male was found to be trading his MPH medication for marijuana.

  — A female student distributed her MPH medication on the school bus. She had left home with sixty tablets and arrived at school with four.

  — Three schools were broken into and MPH medication was taken

Factors Contributing to Diversion of MPH Intended for ADHD Treatment. Information gathered from interviews combined with poison control data suggest that a number of factors may be contributing to the diversion and misuse/abuse of medication intended for ADHD treatment. For example:

- *Medications are kept in relatively unsecured areas at home and at school.* Keeping medication on the kitchen counter or table makes it accessible to other siblings and children who visit. Many schools reported keeping medication in unlocked drawers or teacher's desks, making theft at school relatively easy.

- *Physicians rarely address drug abuse issues with parents or children.* If parents are unaware of the abuse potential associated with a medication, they are unlikely to take any special precautions.

- *School procedures are inadequate.* Although many schools have rules against children carrying medication at school, those rules are variably applied especially for older students. In addition, few schools have a nurse on duty to dispense medication, and frequently untrained personnel are given this task. Some schools that reported missing/stolen medication could not identify the amounts missing, or even which children were affected by the loss, as no records or log books were maintained.

Adolescent drug treatment centers reaffirmed what had previously been reported to the DEA: There is a high incidence of illicit use of MPH among adolescents who are already abusing other drugs. In South Carolina, one treatment center started requiring routine urine checks for MPH because the incidence of MPH abuse was so high. However, illicit use of MPH is not the exclusive domain of "bad kids." School officials seemed genuinely surprised by the actions of some of their better students who were identified as using MPH illicitly. In general, adolescents who want to use MPH for any reason (to get high, to lose weight, to stay up late and study) have little difficulty obtaining it. They do not need to rob a drugstore, forge a prescription, or make a visit to the local drug dealer.

CONCLUSION

The DEA recognizes that psychostimulants such as MPH and amphetamine are effective in treating the symptoms associated with ADHD. The present data indicate that chronic, oral, low-dose stimulant medication in the treatment of properly diagnosed ADHD is generally not associated with children abusing their own medication. However, given the high abuse potential of these drugs and significant data that show that they are being used illicitly by a growing number of children, the DEA remains concerned about the ease in which these drugs are available to individuals who choose to use them illicitly. The DEA concurs with other medical professionals who have urged the proactive efforts of many groups including physicians, parents, school personnel, and law enforcement to curb the continued diversion, misuse, and abuse of these medications. Failure to ensure medication compliance and continued lax handling of medication coupled with persisting efforts to have more children recognized and treated with stimulants is a formula for increased stimulant drug abuse among U.S. children.

References

Abino, P. D., & Pandarinath, S. (1977). Methylphenidate (Ritalin) abuse. *Journal of the Medical Society of New Jersey, 74*, 1061–1062.

Aigner, T. G., & Balster, R. L. (1979). Rapid substitution procedure for intravenous drug self-administration studies in rhesus monkeys. *Pharmacology, Biochemistry, and Behavior, 10*, 105–112.

Arnett, E. N., Battle, W. E., Russo, J. V., & Roberts, W. C. (1976). Intravenous injection of talc-containing drugs intended for oral use. *American Journal of Medicine, 60*, 711–718.

Brooks, G. F., O'Donoghue, J. M., Rissing, J. P., Soapes, K., & Smith, J. W. (1974). Eikenella corrodens, a recently recognized pathogen: Infections in medical-surgical patients and in association with methylphenidate abuse. *Medicine, 53*, 325–342.

Brown, W. A. (1977). Psychologic and neuroendocrine response to methylphenidate. *Archives of General Psychiatry, 34*, 1103–1108.

Brown, W. A., Corriveau, D. P., & Ebert, M. H. (1978). Acute psychologic and neuroendocrine effects of dextroamphetamine and methylphenidate. *Psychopharmacology, 58*, 189–195.

Bryan, V., Franks, L., & Torres, H. (1973) Pseudomonas Aeeruginosa cervical diskis with chondro-osteomyelitis in an intravenous drug abuser. *Surgical Neurology, 1*, 142–144.

Carter, H. S., & Watson, W. A. (1994). IV pentazocine/methylphenidate abuse—The clinical toxicology of another Ts and blues combination. *Clinical Toxicology, 32*(5), 541–547.

Chait, L. D. (1994). Reinforcing and subjective effects of methylphenidate in humans. *Behavioral Pharmacology, 5*, 281–288.

Chillar, R. K., Jackson, A. L., & Alaan, L. (1982). Hemiplegia after intracarotid injection of methylphenidate. *Archives of Neurology, 39*, 598–599.

Collins, R. J., Weeks, J. R., Cooper, M. M., Good, P. I., & Russell, R. R. (1984). Prediction of abuse liability of drugs using IV self-administration by rats. *Psychopharmacology, 82*, 6–13.

Colpaert, F. C., Niemegeers, C. J. E., & Janssen, P. A. J. (1979). Discriminative stimulus properties of cocaine: Neuropharmacological characteristics as derived from stimulus generalization experiments. *Pharmacology, Biochemistry, and Behavior, 10*, 535–546.

De la Garza, R., & Johanson, C. E. (1987). Discriminative stimulus properties of intragastrically administered d-amphetamine and pentobarbital in rhesus monkeys. *Journal of Pharmacology and Experimental Therapeutics, 243*, 955–962.

Downs, D. A., Harrigan, S. E., & Wiley, J. N., Robinson, T. E., & Labay, R. J. (1979). Research communications in psychology. *Psychology and Behavior, 4*, 39–49.

Dworkin, S. I., Vrana, S. L., Broadbent, J., & Robinson, J. H. (1993). Comparing the reinforcing effects of nicotine, caffeine, methylphenidate, and cocaine. *Medicine and Chemical Research, 2*, 593–602.

Elenbaas, R. M., Waeckerle, J. F., & McNabney, W. K. (1976). Abscess formation as a complication of parenteral methylphenidate abuse. *Journal of ACEP, 5*, 977–980.

Emmett-Oglesby, M. W., & Brewin, A. (1978). Tolerance to the behavioral effects of methylphenidate after daily and intermittent administration. *Journal of the American Osteopathic Association, 78*, 143–144.

Emmett-Oglesby, M. W., & Taylor, K. E. (1981). Role of dose interval in the acquisition of tolerance to methylphenidate. *Neuropharmacology, 20*, 995–1002.

Emmett-Oglesby, M. W., Wurst, M., & Lal, H. (1983). Discriminative stimulus properties of a small dose of cocaine. *Neuropharmacology, 22*, 97–101.

Evans, S. E., & Johanson, C. E. (1987). Amphetamine-like effects of anorectic and related compounds in pigeons. *Journal of Pharmacology and Experimental Therapeutics, 241*, 817–825.

Feussner, G. (1996). Actual abuse data: State surveys. In *Conference report: Stimulant use in the treatment of ADHD* (pp. 1–48). Washington, DC: Drug Enforcement Administration, Office of Diversion Control.

Fulton, A., & Yates, W. R. (1988). Family abuse of methylphenidate. *American Family Physician, 38*, 143–145.

Goyer, P. F., Davis, G. C., & Rapoport, J. L. (1979). Abuse of prescribed stimulant medication by a 13-year-old hyperactive boy. *Journal of the American Academy of Child Psychiatry, 18*, 170–175.

Gunby, P. (1979). Methylphenidate abuse produces retinopathy. *Journal of the American Medical Association, 241*, 546.

Haglund, R. M., & Howerton, L. L. (1982). Ritalin: Consequences of abuse in a clinical population. *International Journal of Addiction, 17*, 349–356.

Huang, J. T., & Ho, B. T. (1974). Discriminative stimulus properties of d-amphetamine and related compounds in rat. *Pharmacology, Biochemistry and Behavior, 2*, 669–673.

Huey, L. Y., Janowsky, D. S., Judd, L. L., Roitman, N. A., Clopton, P. L., Segal, D., Hall, L., & Parker, D. (1980). The effects of naloxone on methylphenidate-induced mood and behavioral changes: A negative study. *Psychopharmacology, 67*, 125–130.

Jaffe, R. B., & Koschmann, E. B. (1970). Intravenous drug abuse: Pulmonary, cardiac, and vascularcomplications. *American Journal of Roentgenology, 109*, 107–120.

Jaffe, S. L. (1991). Intranasal abuse of prescribed methylphenidate by alcohol and drug abusing adolescent with ADHD. *Journal of the American Academy of Child and Adolescent Psychiatry, 30*, 773–775.

Johanson, C. E., & Schuster, C. R. (1975). A choice procedure for drug reinforcers: Cocaine and methylphenidate in the rhesus monkey. *Journal of Pharmacology and Experimental Therapeutics, 193*, 676–688.

Johnston, L. D., O'Malley, P. M., & Bachman, J. G. (1998). Trends in prevalence rates for specific drugs within general classes. In *National survey results on drug use from Monitoring the Future Study, 1975–1997. Volume I, Secondary school students*. Washington, DC: U.S. Government Printing Office.

Kaufman, G. (1996). Epidemiology of methylphenidate in the U.S. In *Conference report: Stimulant use in the treatment of ADHD* (pp. 19–20). Washington, DC: U.S. Department of Justice, Drug Enforcement Administration.

Keeley, K. A., & Light, A. L. (1985). Gradual vs. abrupt withdrawal of methylphenidate in two older dependent males. *Journal of Substance Abuse Treatment, 2*, 123–123.

Kishorekumar, R., Yagnik, P., & Dhopesh, V. (1985). Acute myopathy in a drug abuser following an attempted neck vein injection. *Journal of Neurological and Neurosurgical Psychiatry, 48*, 843–844.

Kolta, M., Shreve, P., & Uretsky, N. J. (1985). Effects of methylphenidate pretreatment on the behavioral and biochemical response to amphetamine. *European Journal of Pharmacology, 117*, 279–282.

Leith, N. J., & Barrett, R. J. (1981). Self-stimulation and amphetamine: Tolerance to d and l isomers and cross tolerance to cocaine and methylphenidate. *Psychopharmacology, 74*, 23–28.

Levine, B., Caplan, Y. H., & Kauffman, G. (1986) Fatality resulting from methylphenidate overdose. *Journal of Analytical Toxicology, 10*, 209–210.

Lewman, L. V. (1972). Fatal pulmonary hypertension from intravenous injection of methylphenidate (Ritalin) tablets. *Human Pathology, 3*, 67–70.

Lindell, T. D., Porter, J. M., & Langstron, C. (1972). Intra-arterial injections of oral medications: Complications of drug addition. *New England Journal of Medicine, 287*, 1132–1133.

Lundquest, D. E., Young, W. K., & Edland, J. F. (1987). Maternal death associated with intravenous methylphenidate (Ritalin) and pentazocine (Talwin) abuse. *Journal of Forensic Science, 32*, 798–801.

Martin, W. R., Sloan, J. W., Sapira, J. D., & Jasinski, D. R. (1971). Physiological, subjective, and behavioral effect of amphetamine, methamphetamine, ephedrine, phenmetrazine, and methylphenidate in man. *Clinical Pharmacology and Therapeutics, 12*, 245–258.

McCormick, T. C., & McNeel, T. W. (1963). Case report: Acute psychosis and Ritalin abuse. *Texas Journal of Medicine, 59*, 99–100.

McKenna, M. L., & Ho, B. T. (1980). The role of dopamine in the discriminative stimulus properties of cocaine. *Neuropharmacology, 19*, 297–303.

McNamara, C. G., Davidson, E. S., & Shenk, S. A. (1993). Comparison of the motor-activating effects of acute and chronic exposure to amphetamine and methylphenidate. *Pharmacology, Biochemistry, and Behavior, 45*, 729–732.

Mehta, H., Murray, B., & LoIudice, T. A. (1984). Hepatic dysfunction due to intravenous abuse of methylphenidate hydrochloride. *Journal of Clinical Gastroenterology, 6*, 149–151.

Nielsen, J. A., Duda, N. J., Mokler, D. J., & Moore, K. E. (1984). Self-administration of central stimulants by rats: A comparison of the effects of d-amphetamine, methylphenidate and McNeil 4612. *Pharmacology, Biochemistry, and Behavior, 20*, 227–232.

Overton, D. A. (1982) Comparison of the degree of discriminability of various drugs using a T-maze drug discrimination paradigm. *Psychopharmacology, 76*, 385–395.

Perkins, A. N., Eckerman, D. A., & McPhail, R. C. (1991). Discriminative stimulus properties of tri-adimefon: Comparison with methylphenidate. *Pharmacology, Biochemistry, and Behavior, 40*, 757–761.

Porsolt, R. D., Pawelec, C., & Jalfre, M. (1982) Use of drug discrimination procedures to detect amphetamine-like effects of antidepressants. In F. C. Colpaert & J. L. Slangen (Eds.), *Drug discrimination: Applications in CNS pharmacology* (pp. 193–202). Amsterdam: Elsevier Biomedical Press.

Rappley, M. D. (1995). The descriptive epidemiology of methylphenidate in Michigan. *Archives of Pediatric and Adolescent Medicine, 149*, 675–679.

Rioux, B. (1960). Is Ritalin an addiction-producing drug? *Diseases of the Nervous System, 21*, 346–349.

Risner, M. E., & Jones, B. E. (1975). Self-administration of CNS stimulants by dogs. *Psychopharmacology, 43*, 207–213.

Risner, M. E., & Jones, B. E. (1976). Characteristics of unlimited access to self-administered stimulant infusion in dogs. *Biological Psychiatry, 11*, 625–634.

Rosen, J. R., Young, A. M., Beuthin, F. C., & Louis-Ferdinand, R. T. (1986). Discriminative stimulus properties of amphetamine and other stimulants in lead-exposed and normal rats. *Pharmacology, Biochemistry, and Behavior, 24*, 211–215.

Sannerud, C., & Feussner, G. (1999). Is methylphenidate a Schedule II stimulant? In B. Osman & L. Greenhill (Eds.), *Ritalin: Theory and practice* (2nd ed., pp. 27–42). New York: Mary Ann Liebert.

Sherman, C. B., Hudson, L. D., & Pierson, D. J. (1987). Severe precocious emphysema in intravenous methylphenidate (Ritalin) abusers. *Chest, 92*, 1085–1087.

Silverman, P. B., & Schultz, K. A. (1989). Comparison of cocaine and procaine discriminative stimuli. *Drug Development and Research, 16*, 427–433.

Smith, R. C., & Davis, J. M. (1977). Comparative effects of d-amphetamine, l-amphetamine, and methylphenidate on mood in man. *Psychopharmacology, 53*, 1–12.

Spealman, R. D., Madras, B. K., & Bergman, J. (1989). Effects of cocaine and related drugs in non-human primates. II. Stimulant effects on schedule controlled behavior. *Journal of Pharmacology and Experimental Therapeutics, 251*, 142–149.

Spensley, J., & Rockwell, D. A. (1972). Psychosis during methylphenidate abuse. *New England Journal of Medicine, 286*, 880–881.

Stecyk, O., Loludice, T. A., Demeter, S., & Jacobs, J. (1985). Multiple organ failure resulting from intravenous abuse of methylphenidate hydrochloride. *Annals of Emergency Medicine, 14*, 597/113.

Wesson, D. R., & Smith, D. E. (1978). A clinical approach to diagnosis and treatment of amphetamine abuse. *Journal of Psychedelic Drugs, 10*, 343–349.

Wilson, M. C., Hitomi, M., & Schuster, C. R. (1971). Psychomotor stimulant self-administration as a function of dosage per injection in the rhesus monkey. *Psychopharmacology, 22*, 271–281.

Wilson, M. C., & Schuster, C. R. (1972). The effects of chlorpromazine on psychomotor stimulant self-administration in the rhesus monkey. *Psychopharmacology. (Berl.) , 26*, 115–126.

Wolf, J., Fein, A., & Fehrenbacher, L. (1978). Eosinophilic syndrome with methylphenidate abuse. *Annals of International Medicine, 89*, 224–225.

Wood, D. M., & Emmett-Oglesby, M. W. (1988). Substitution and cross-tolerance profiles of anorectic drugs in rats trained to detect the discriminative stimulus properties of cocaine. *Psychopharmacology, 95*, 364–368.

Wood, D. M., Lal, H., & Emmett-Oglesby, M. (1984). Acquisition and recovery of tolerance to the discriminative stimulus properties of cocaine. *Neuropharmacology, 23*, 1419–1423.

Zemplenyi, J., & Colman, M. F. (1984). Deep neck abscesses secondary to methylphenidate (Ritalin) abuse. *Head and Neck Surgery, 6*, 858–860.

Chapter 21

Availability of Stimulant Medications—Nature and Extent of Abuse and Associated Harm

by James R. Cooper, M.D.

Introduction 21-1
Monitoring the Future 21-4
    Design and Methodology 21-4
    Sampling Procedures 21-5
    Questions Pertaining to the Medical and Nonmedical Use of
        Amphetamines 21-5
The Drug Abuse Warning Network 21-6
    Design and Methodology 21-6
    DAWN Sample 21-7
Community Epidemiology Work Group 21-8
What the Ongoing Studies Reveal About Drug Abuse 21-8
    MTF Results 21-8
    DAWN Results 21-10
    CEWG Results 21-13
Discussion 21-13

INTRODUCTION

The abuse potential of the stimulants commonly used in the treatment of attention deficit disorder with hyperactivity (ADHD) is well documented. Amphetamines and methylphenidate produce reinforcing effects both in poly-drug-abusing populations and among stimulant trained laboratory animals in a variety of behavioral paradigms (Ellinwood & Cohen, 1971; Martin, Sloan, Sapira, & Jasinski, 1971). Both drugs produce dose-dependent liking scores (i.e., self-reports of "liking" the effects of the drug after administration) among polydrug abusers. Although pemoline is reported not to induce self-administering behavior (i.e., drug-seeking behavior) in cocaine-dependent rhesus monkeys (Schuster & Thompson, 1969), it shares common relevant biochemical and behavioral effects with amphetamine (Fuller, Perry, Bymaster, & Wong, 1978;

Mueller & Hsiao, 1980). Moreover, a number of marketed prescription and over-the-counter phenylethylamines and cocaine possess qualitatively similar clinical and pre-clinical properties, albeit varying quantitative differences among individual drugs (Chait, Uhlenhuth, & Johanson, 1986a, 1986b; Gawin & Ellinwood, 1988; Woolverton & English, 1997). Reports of actual abuse and illicit diversion of amphet-amines and related phenylethylamines, methylphenidate and pemoline in both the United States and internationally further document the abuse liability of these med-ications (Cohen, 1975; Connell, 1968; Parran & Jasinski, 1991; Willey, 1971; World Health Organization, 1988).

Notwithstanding the preclinical abuse potential and the actual abuse of stimulants among the poly-drug-abusing population, the nature and extent to which exposure to stimulant medications in children and adolescents with ADHD predicts subsequent stimulant abuse is less well understood and remains controversial. The preclinical and clinical abuse liability studies demonstrate clear individual differences in the reinforc-ing properties in animals and humans exposed to stimulants (Davidson, Finch, & Schenk, 1993; Piazza, Deroche, Rouge-Pont & Le Moal, 1993). Preclinical stimulant abuse liability studies alone do not predict risk of abuse in the general population or within sub-populations of those with medical illnesses, irrespective of reinforcing effi-cacy data (De Wit, Uhlenhuth, & Johanson, 1987). Many patients exposed to stimulant medications never misuse or abuse their medication (Hechtman, Weiss, & Perlman, 1984; Lambert, Hartsough, Sassone, & Sandoval, 1987; Masand & Tesar, 1996; Spier, 1995). However, subpopulations of ADHD patients have been identified who are at risk to abuse nicotine (Hartsough & Lambert, 1987; Hughes, 1997), other stimulants (Schenk & Davidson, 1993), and sedatives, including alcohol (Carroll, Rounsaville, & Bryant, 1993). Furthermore, ADHD is over represented in adult substance use disorder (SUD) populations; comorbid conduct disorder, antisocial personality, and bipolar dis-order have been identified as mediating factors for SUD (Ball, Carroll, & Rounsaville, 1994; Biederman et al, 1995; Biederman et al, 1997; Carroll & Rounsaville, 1993; Gittelman, Mannuzza, Shenker, & Bonagura, 1985; Hechtman & Weiss, 1986; Herrero, Hechtman, & Weiss, 1994; Mannuzza, Klein, Bessler, Malloy, & LaPadula, 1998; Milberger, Biederman, Faraone, Wilens, & Chu, 1997; Wilens, Biederman, Mick, Faraone, & Spencer, 1997; Wilens, Prince, Biederman, Spencer, & Frances, 1995; Zeidonis, Rayford, Bryant, & Rounsaville, 1994). The limitations of this association between ADHD and SUD have been review elsewhere (Levin & Kleber, 1995; Wilens, Spencer, & Biederman, 1995). Over the last ten years, there has been a significant increase in the annual production quotas and prescriptions for methylphenidate and amphetamine as reflected in Figures 21.1 and 21.2. (See also discussion in Chapter 21, in this volume.) The amphetamine quota has increased 663 percent since 1986. Methylphenidate has increased by 577 percent. According to the IMS America (Figure 21.1), annual prescriptions for methylphenidate, amphetamine, and pemoline increased since 1986 by 513 percent, 124 percent and 195 percent respectively. Unlike methylphenidate, amphetamine prescriptions were in steady decline until 1993 and have since increased by 150 fold. Pemoline prescriptions have recently decreased.

Various media and law enforcement reports (Drug Enforcement Administration, 1995a, 1995b) suggest a proportional increase in morbidity and mortality associated with the increased availability of methylphenidate based primarily on its intrinsic abuse potential and anecdotal reports of methylphenidate abuse, diversion, and public

Figure 21.1
Projected Retail Pharmacy Rx's

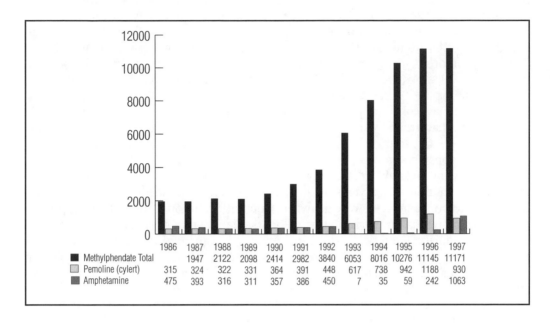

	1986	1987	1988	1989	1990	1991	1992	1993	1994	1995	1996	1997
■ Methylphendate Total		1947	2122	2098	2414	2982	3840	6053	8016	10276	11145	11171
☐ Pemoline (cylert)	315	324	322	331	364	391	448	617	738	942	1188	930
■ Amphetamine	475	393	316	311	357	386	450	7	35	59	242	1063

Figure 21.2
DEA Quota (in kgs)

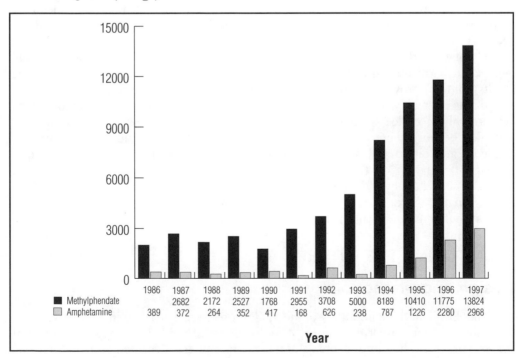

	1986	1987	1988	1989	1990	1991	1992	1993	1994	1995	1996	1997
■ Methylphendate		2682	2172	2527	1768	2955	3708	5000	8189	10410	11775	13824
☐ Amphetamine	389	372	264	352	417	168	626	238	787	1226	2280	2968

Year

health consequences. However, a causal relationship has never been clearly established. An increase in availability alone does not necessarily predict an increase in abuse and consequences given the existing preclinical and clinical abuse liability research. The public health risks associated with stimulant abuse are documented, but most reports of abuse and associated consequences occur among the poly-drug-abusing population (Abiuso, 1977; Chillar, Jackson, & Alaan, 1982; Gunby, 1979; "Increasing morbidity and mortality," 1995; Spensley & Rockwell, 1972; Zemplenyi & Colman, 1984). Reports in the literature of abuse, diversion, and consequences among ADHD patients are anecdotal and uncommon (Fulton & Yates, 1988; Garland, 1998; Goyer, Davis, & Rapoport, 1979; Jaffe, 1991). No analysis currently exists with regard to the nature and extent of the abuse and associated consequences of these medications relative to their increased availability or to other licit and illicit stimulants with known abuse potential.

In reviewing available data, only large national databases which collect yearly information, for at least ten years, on the nature and extent of specific stimulant abuse or associated consequences were analyzed. Such information affords the opportunity to compare individual trends in abuse and/or associated harm of specific licit and illicit stimulants during the time at which there was a documented increase in availability resulting from both licit and illicit production. Moreover, such data provides a clearer perspective on the representativeness of the anecdotal reports concerning increased amphetamine and methylphenidate abuse and their associated consequences.

The data bases analyzed include the Monitoring the Future (MTF) and the Drug Abuse Warning Network (DAWN). These are the only large databases which annually collect, for many years, information on the nature and extent of stimulant abuse and its consequences. Moreover, data from these two sources are often quoted in previous analyses of abuse and harm associated with stimulants in general and methylphenidate in particular. Also included are findings from the National Institute on Drug Abuse (NIDA) Community Epidemiology Work Group (CEWG) as the descriptive and analytical data reported (1) capture, from MTF, emerging trends of stimulant abuse and associated harm on a different population at risk (e.g., school dropouts and young adults) and (2) provide an impression of the relative extent of the abuse of various stimulants in twenty-one U.S. cities. Parenthetically, the DAWN Medical Examiner's Report, which collects annual information on stimulant associated deaths, is not included because there are consistently few (< 10) methylphenidate- or pemoline-related deaths reported. Likewise, the National Household Survey (NHS) stopped collecting information on the nonmedical use of Ritalin® (methylpheidate) in 1994, because the frequency of Ritalin abuse mentions had been consistently small for many years. Finally, the only national data on drug abuse treatment admissions resulting from stimulant abuse do not permit data to be disaggregated.

MONITORING THE FUTURE

Design and Methodology

The design and methodology of the MTF project are described in detail elsewhere (National Institute on Drug Abuse, 1998). In general, the MTF is a repeated series of surveys in which the same segments of the population are presented with the same set of questions over a number of years to see how answers change over time. The project has been conducted since 1975 under a series of research grants from the National Institute on Drug Abuse by the University of Michigan Survey Research Center. Currently, MTF respondents are eighth-, tenth-, and twelfth-grade students who initially participate in school by completing self-administered, machine-readable questionnaires in their normal classrooms.

The survey began with senior classes in 1975, and each year about 16,000 students in approximately 133 public and private high schools nationwide participate. Beginning in 1991, similar surveys of nationally representative samples of eighth- and tenth-graders have been conducted annually. In all, approximately 50,000 students in about 420 public and private secondary schools are surveyed annually.

Sampling Procedures

The data from students are collected during the spring of each year. Each year's data collection takes place in approximately 420 public and private high schools and middle schools selected to provide an accurate representative cross-section of students throughout the coterminous United States at each grade level. A multistage random sampling procedure is used for securing the nationwide sample of students each year at each grade level.

Within each school up to 350 students may be included. In schools with fewer students, the usual procedure is to include all of them in the data collection. In larger schools, a subset of students is selected either by randomly sampling entire classrooms or by some other random method that is judged to be unbiased. Sampling weights are used when the data are analyzed to correct for unequal probabilities of selection which occurred at any stage of sampling.

Questions Pertaining to the Medical and Nonmedical Use of Amphetamines

All high school seniors in the study are asked a limited number of questions about their nonmedical use of amphetamines. Most of the students are asked the following question:

> Amphetamines have been prescribed by doctors to help people lose weight or to give people more energy. They are sometimes called uppers, ups, speed, bennies, dexies, pep pills and diet pills. Drugstores are not supposed to sell them without a prescription from a doctor. Amphetamines do NOT include any non-prescription drugs, such as over-the-counter diet pills (like Dexatrim) or stay-awake pills (like No-Doz), or any mail-order drugs. On how many occasions (if any), have you taken amphetamines on your own—that is, without a doctor telling you to take them?

One sixth of the students are asked more specific questions about their medical and nonmedical use of amphetamines. The amphetamine definition is again broad but includes a list of illicit stimulants as well as some licit stimulants, some of which are not pharmacologically amphetamines. Street names listed within the definition include uppers, ups, speed, bennies, dexies, pep and diet pills, Meth or Crystal Meth.

The following prescription medications are included: Benzedrine, Dexedrine, methedrine, Ritalin, Preludin, Dexamyl, and methamphetamine. Students are specifically asked:

Have you ever taken amphetamines because a doctor told you to use them?

The respondent is given three options:

a. No.

b. Yes, but I had already tried them on my own.

c. Yes, and it was the first time I took any.

On how many occasions (if any), have you taken amphetamines on your own—that is, without a doctor telling you to take them?

Those seniors who acknowledge nonmedical amphetamine use in the past year (taking amphetamines on your own without a doctor telling you to take them), are asked additional questions to determine (1) the frequency of nonmedical amphetamine use during the last year either alone or in combination with either alcohol, marijuana, LSD, or psychedelics other than LSD; (2) the specific prescription medication(s) used; (3) the route of administration; and (4) the most important reason(s) for taking amphetamines without a doctor's orders (identified from a list of possible reasons provided).

THE DRUG ABUSE WARNING NETWORK

Design and Methodology

The design and methodology of DAWN are described in detail elsewhere (http://www.samsha.gov/OAS/dawn/dwnfiles.htm). In general, DAWN is an ongoing national survey of hospital emergency departments and medical examiner facilities. Since the early 1970s, DAWN has collected information on patients seeking hospital emergency department treatment for reasons related to their use of an illegal drug or the nonmedical use of an illegal drug. Data are collected by a trained member of the emergency department or medical records staff who review all emergency department records on admitted patients 6 years and older who meet the following criteria:

- The presenting problem(s) was induced or related to drug use, regardless of when the drug ingestion occurred;

- The case involved the nonmedical use of a legal drug or any use of an illegal drug;

- Patient's reason for taking the substance(s) included one of the following:

  1. Dependence,

  2. Suicide attempt or gesture, or

  3. Psychic effects.

Each report of a drug-related emergency department episode includes demographic information about the patient (age, gender, race) and the circumstances surrounding the episode. Up to four different substances, in addition to alcohol in combination, can be specified for each episode. Several terms used in this presentation need definition:

1. Nonmedical use is defined as follows:

   • The use of prescription drugs in a manner inconsistent with accepted medical practice.

   • The use of over-the-counter (OTC) drugs contrary to approved labeling

   • The use of any substance for psychic effects, dependence, or suicide.

2. Psychic effects include:

   • Recreational Use (to get high, for kicks)

   • Other psychic effects (to improve or enhance any mental, emotional, or physical state)

3. Physical dependence is defined as follows:

   • A psychic and/or physical state characterized by behavior that always includes a compulsion to take the drug on a continuous or periodic basis in order to experience its effects or to avoid the discomfort of its absence (e.g., have to take, had to have, needed a fix)

4. A drug mention refers to a substance that was mentioned during a drug-related emergency department episode. In addition to alcohol in combination, up to four substances may be reported for each drug-related episode; thus, the total number of mentions exceeds the number of total episodes. However, hospital emergency department cases involving single mentions do constitute an episode. It should be noted that a particular drug mention may or may not be the confirmed "cause" of the episode when multiple drugs have been mentioned.

5. A drug episode is defined as an emergency department visit that was involved in the use of an illegal drug or the nonmedical use of a legal drug for persons aged 6 years and older. The number of emergency department episodes reported in DAWN is not synonymous with the number of individuals involved. One person may make repeated visits to an emergency department or to several emergency departments, thus producing a number of episodes. As no patient identifiers are collected, it is impossible to determine the number of individuals involved in the reported episodes.

DAWN Sample

DAWN-eligible hospitals are nonfederal, short-stay general hospitals with a twenty-four-hour emergency department. The DAWN emergency department data are collected from a representative sample of these hospitals located throughout the coterminous United States. Twenty-one metropolitan statistical areas (MSAs) were designated for sampling. Hospitals outside these twenty-one areas were assigned to a national panel and sampled. A total of 612 hospitals were selected for the sample and 452 hospitals (74 percent) participated in the survey in 1996 (Substance Abuse and Mental Health Services Administration, 1998). The data from this sample are then weighted to produce national and MSA estimates of emergency department drug-related episodes and drug mentions in all such hospitals.

The data presented are derived from the current sample selected in 1998 and, for the earlier years, from a fixed panel of hospitals many of which have been reporting since the late 1970s. The panel is designed and weighted to account for atypical reporting, nonresponse, and so on. and is described in detail elsewhere (Substance Abuse and Mental Health Services Administration, 1997).

COMMUNITY EPIDEMIOLOGY WORK GROUP

The CEWG provides an ongoing community level public health surveillance of drug abuse from twenty-one U.S. cities. Established by NIDA in 1976, the CEWG meets semiannually to present and discuss quantitative and qualitative community-level epidemiological and ethnographical drug use and abuse data. The CEWG provides current descriptive and analytical information regarding the nature and patterns of drug abuse, emerging trends, risk factors associated with drug abuse, characteristics of vulnerable populations, and consequences of abuse in the United States.

WHAT THE ONGOING STUDIES REVEAL ABOUT DRUG ABUSE

MTF Results

The MTF reveals that the current annual prevalence of the nonmedical use of these "other licit and illicit stimulants" among high school seniors is actually less (-35 percent) than it was thirteen years ago (Figure 21.3). However, the nonmedical use of this drug class by this group has increased 44 percent since 1992. Likewise, since 1992 there has been a statistically significant increase (56 percent) in the abuse of many types of illicit drugs among seniors including marijuana/hashish (76 percent), heroin (100 percent), cocaine (77 percent) and several hallucinogens (PCP, LSD, and MDMA) (Figure 21.4). The rates of increase for these other types of drugs is greater and statistically more significant than for "other licit and illicit stimulants."

The annual prevalence among high school seniors who reported nonmedical use of "other licit and illicit stimulants" was 10 percent in 1997. Most who used any of these "other licit and illicit stimulants" in 1997 did so less than ten times in that year (Figure 21.5). A relatively small number of seniors (1–2 percent) did so ten or more times; this percentage has remained relatively constant over the past thirteen years. About one-half of the seniors used alcohol and/or marijuana along with these "other licit and illicit stimulants."

The annual prevalence of nonmedical use of these "other licit and illicit stimulants" among females was 10.2 percent; nonmedical use among males was 10.1 percent. Among the most prevalent reasons for using were (1) euphoric effects (get high, escape problems or boredom, good time), (2) lose weight, (3) stay awake, and (4)

Figure 21.3
Stimulant Abuse 1985–1987

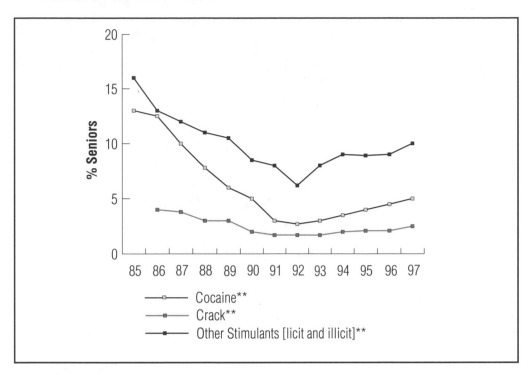

Figure 21.4
Annual Prevalence 1992–1997

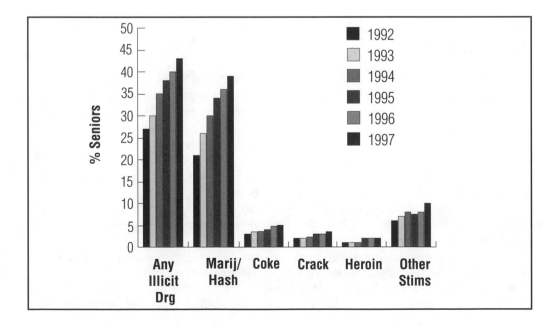

Figure 21.5
Frequency of Abuse Last 12 Months

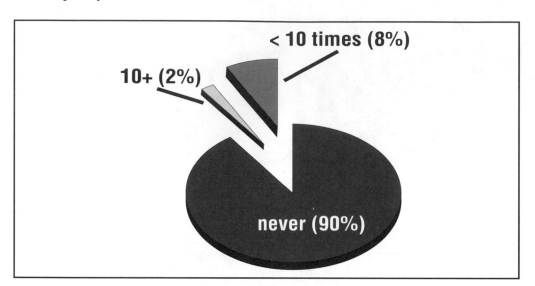

increase energy. Female students were much more likely to use these "other licit and illicit stimulants" for weight control. The route of administration is predominantly oral; however, some reported smoking (16 percent) and/or injecting (3 percent) at least once. Few students considered themselves "hooked" or unable to quit.

Among those prescription stimulants listed, Ritalin mentions have tripled in the last three years among the 10 percent of seniors who report nonmedical use of "other licit and illicit stimulants." Forty percent of those users of "other licit and illicit stimulants," or 3 percent of the high school seniors, acknowledged using Ritalin non-medically at least once in the last year.

DAWN Results

There has been an increase since 1985 in total DAWN hospital emergency department mentions for all licit/illicit stimulants. Cocaine total mentions dwarf all other stimulant mentions (Figure 21.6). Excluding cocaine (Figure 21.7), methamphetamine and amphetamine comprise more mentions than all other drugs combined. Cocaine, methamphetamines, and amphetamine have consistently accounted for over 90 percent of all stimulant emergency department mentions for many years. The largest increase in stimulant mentions between 1985 and 1996 were for cocaine (429 percent) and ephedrine (1297 percent). Pemoline has consistently accounted for the fewest mentions annually. Although methylphenidate mentions have increased since 1985, the rate of increase is the smallest (58 percent) among stimulant mentions with the exception of pseudo-ephedrine.

Notwithstanding the relatively small number and rate increases in mentions, the Drug Enforcement Administration (DEA) and the International Narcotics Control Board (INCB) noted the significant number of methylphenidate mentions among 10- to 17-year-olds. Specifically, the DEA notes that the DAWN shows a fivefold increase

Figure 21.6
Stimulants

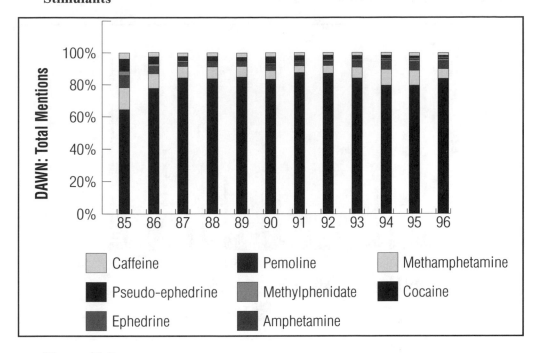

Figure 21.7
Stimulants Without Cocaine

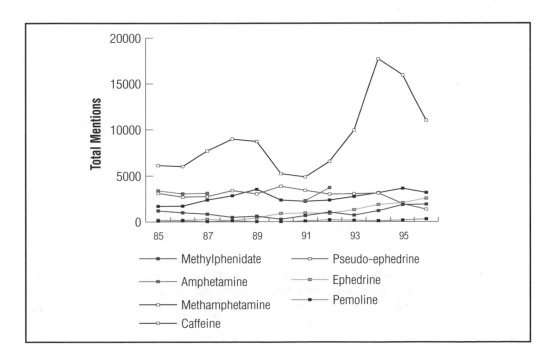

Figure 21.8
Methylphenidate ED Total Mentions

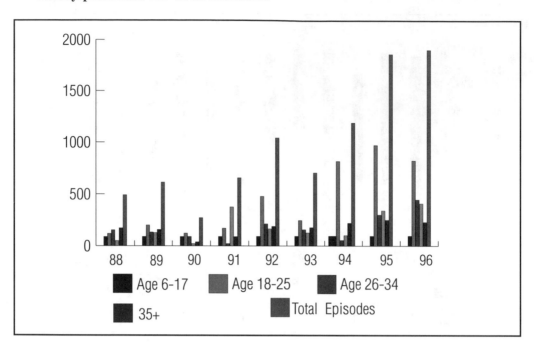

in emergency room mentions for methylphenidate since 1990, suggesting that this increase indicates a growing methylphenidate abuse problem among younger populations despite the tight controls of Schedule II. A closer analysis of the DAWN emergency room methylphenidate mentions since 1988 reveals the following (Figure 21.8):

- An increase in methylphenidate mentions among all age groups.

- The largest rate increase (731 percent) since 1988 has been among the 26–34-year-old age group.

- Ages 6–17 do comprise the largest absolute increase in numbers of methylphenidate mentions (118–823).

- When motive for taking methylphenidate is disaggregated (Figure 21.9), suicide attempt comprises the largest proportion of known mentions irrespective of whether methylphenidate was taken alone or in combination. The number of known emergency room "episodes" resulting from methylphenidate dependence has been less than ten per year since 1992.

Thus methylphenidate accounts for the smallest increase in mentions for prescription stimulants for ADHD. Within this context, ages 6–17 account for the largest increase in absolute numbers of emergency room mentions; however, of those episodes directly attributable to methylphenidate, few are known to be associated with dependence/abuse. Many more known emergency room episodes are a result of suicide attempts.

Figure 21.9
Drug Use Motive—Methylphenidate

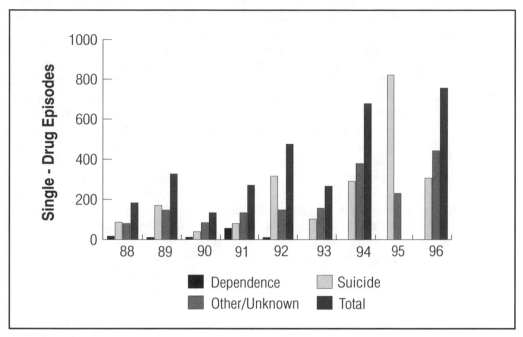

CEWG Results

With regard to CEWG reporting, the vast majority of reports of stimulant abuse and its consequences are for cocaine and methamphetamine (National Institute on Drug Abuse, 1998). Over the last ten years, reports of methylphenidate abuse have been infrequent except for two areas of the country. In Chicago, methylphenidate remains readily available (estimated at $3–$4 per pill). Unlike most of the CEWG cities, methamphetamine abuse is not prevalent. Parenthetically, treatment admissions for primary stimulant dependence have most often been abusers of "lookalike" stimulants containing caffeine, ephedrine or phenylpropanolamine. Geographic and ethnic differences exist in stimulant abuse patterns. For example, white intravenous drug users on the Chicago north side reportedly inject phenmetrazine, whereas black stimulant users on the south side prefer methylphenidate (commonly referred to as West Coast). The stimulants are often mixed with heroin, instead of cocaine, in an effort to enhance euphoria. Michigan has had one of the highest per capita levels among states in methylphenidate distribution. In the Detroit area, reports of sales from schools and sales by adolescents who receive this drug for ADHD have continued, along with reports of adolescents inhaling crushed tablets.

DISCUSSION

The abuse potential and the anecdotal reports of abuse, diversion, and its consequences of methylphenidate and amphetamines, and to a lesser extent pemoline, are well documented. Furthermore, significant increases in the licit production of methylphenidate, amphetamine, and pemoline are evident. Less clear is the relationship between the increases in stimulant production for medical use and the anecdotal accounts of abuse, diversion, and consequences among both the ADHD patients who are prescribed stimulants and the polysubstance abusers without ADHD.

With regard to pemoline, there is no data in the CEWG Reports or the DAWN emergency department or medical examiner reports to suggest that significant increases in availability have led to any significant increase in abuse or associated harm. Likewise, there are no data to suggest that significant increases in licit amphetamine production is associated with significant increases in abuse or associated harm. It is not possible to determine with any confidence the source of DAWN amphetamine/meth-amphetamine mentions. Most of the stimulants, confirmed by analysis in the DEA labs, are methamphetamine and amphetamine produced clandestinely.

In contrast to amphetamine, there are no reports of illicit methylphenidate production. Thus, any increase in methylphenidate abuse or associated morbidity is presumed obtained or diverted from licit production. Nonetheless, such a presumption sheds no light on the relative contribution each potential diversion source makes (patient prescription, forged prescriptions, thefts, etc.). There is no adequate database to clearly determine with any real precision the nature and extent to which patient prescriptions contribute to the diversion pool (Cooper, Czechowicz, Peterson, & Molinari, 1992). Clearly, some ADHD patients divert or abuse their medication. As reported in Chapter 19 (in this volume), there are ADHD subpopulations more at risk for abuse and diversion. However, suggestions in the media and elsewhere that reports of abuse and diversion of prescribed stimulant medication among ADHD patients are representative of ADHD patients, or are the primary source of diversion, are without scientific evidence.

The existing data do suggest that there is a significant increase in a nonmedical use of methylphenidate among seniors who also report a significant recent increase in a variety of other stimulants (including cocaine) along with an even more significant increase in abuse of other types of illicit drugs. Although the annual prevalence of nonmedical stimulant use has increased since 1992, current prevalence is 35 percent below 1985 levels despite the manyfold increases in prescriptions and DEA production quotas of amphetamine and methylphenidate during this time. Furthermore, among those seniors who do use these stimulants nonmedically, most abuse them infrequently (less than ten times per year) do not smoke, snort, or use them intravenously, and report no problems in quitting.

The morbidity associated with methylphenidate is dwarfed in comparison to other Schedule II stimulants such as methamphetamine and cocaine which are predominately produced clandestinely. These findings are further supported by reports from the Office of National Drug Control Policy (1998) and most of the reports from the twenty-one CEWG cities suggesting that illicit amphetamines are a much greater problem with respect to prevalence of abuse, treatment admissions, and other associated consequences of abuse. Reports inferring increased prevalence of DAWN mentions among the 6–17-year-old population as an indication of growing abuse problem within this cohort are misleading. Although prevalence has increased dramatically in absolute numbers, the total number of mentions is small compared to cocaine, methamphetamine, and amphetamine, and most of the episodes, where the intended use is known, are for suicide. Few known episodes are related to drug dependence. This information does suggest, however, a subpopulation of patients with serious comorbid disorder. In addition, media reports of Ritalin-associated deaths of adolescents, although tragic, are uncommon and in stark contrast to illicit methamphetamine and cocaine (DAWN, 2000).

It is reasonable to assume that an increase in the availability of a medicine with an abuse liability may result in an increase in the prevalence of its abuse among the poly-substance-abusing population. However, the extent of the abuse will depend in part on the availability of equally or more desirable drugs with similar pharmacology. The recent increase in the popularity of Ritalin among high school seniors who abuse stimulants may well be in part a reflection of its increased availability. One would also anticipate increased methylphenidate availability resulting in stimulant abuse and diversion among some ADHD patients given the prevalence of comorbid SUD and conduct disorder; however, no available database exists to determine such ratios. Limitations in the MTF survey preclude determining the proportion of abusers who have ADHD, the source of the abused stimulant, or the presence of comorbid disorders. Nonetheless, current prevalence of abuse of stimulant drugs within this class is significantly lower than in 1985 despite the significant increases in availability. Furthermore, the primary stimulants currently abused and associated with harm among non-high school drug abusers are clandestinely produced cocaine and methamphetamine.

There is little public health data to suggest that anecdotal reports in the media of amphetamine and methylphenidate abuse and harm are representative of, or proportional to, the increased availability from licit production and prescription. Perhaps most surprisingly, significant increases in the availability of pemoline, amphetamine, and methylphenidate have not resulted in more reports of abuse and harm given their known abuse potential.

References

Abiuso, P. D. (1977). Methylphenidate (Ritalin) abuse. *Journal of the Medical Society of New Jersey, 74*, 1061–1062.

Ball, S. A., Carroll, K. M., , & Rounsaville, B. J. (1994). Sensation seeking, substance abuse, and psychopathology in treatment-seeking and community cocaine abusers. *Journal of Consulting and Clinical Psychology, 62*, 1053–1057.

Biederman, J., Wilens, T., Mick, E., Faraone, S. V., Weber, W., Curtis, S., Thornell, A., Pfister, K., Jetton, J. G., & Soriano, J . (1997). Is ADHD a risk factor for psychoactive substance use disorders? Findings from a four year prospective follow-up study. *Journal of the American Academy of Child and Adolescent Psychiatry, 36*, 21–29.

Biederman, J., Wilens, T., Mick, E., Milberger, S., Spencer, T. J., & Faraone, S. V. (1995). Psychoactive substance use disorders in adults with attention deficit hyperactivity disorder (ADHD): Effects of ADHD and psychiatric comorbidity. *American Journal of Psychiatry, 152*, 1652–1658.

Carroll, K. M., & Rounsaville, B. J. (1993). History and significance of childhood attention deficit disorder in treatment-seeking cocaine abusers. *Comprehensive Psychiatry, 34*, 75–82.

Carroll, K. M., Rounsaville, B. J., & Bryant, K. J. (1993). Alcoholism in treatment-seeking cocaine abusers: clinical and prognostic significance. *Journal of Studies on Alcohol, 54*, 199–208.

Chait, L. D., Uhlenhuth, E. H., & Johanson, C. E. (1986a). The discriminative stimulus and subjective effects of d-amphetamine, phenmetrazine and fenfluramine in humans. *Psychopharmacology, 89*, 301–306.

Chait, L. D., Uhlenhuth, E. H., & Johanson, C. E. (1986b). The discriminative stimulus and subjective effects of phenylpropanolamine, mazindol and d-amphetamine in humans. *Psychopharmacology and Biochemical Behavior, 24*(6), 1665–1672.

Chillar, R. K., Jackson, A. L., & Alaan, L. (1982). Hemiplegia after intracarotid injection of methylphenidate. *Archives of Neurology, 39*, 598–599.

Cohen, S. (1975). Amphetamine abuse. *Journal of the American Medical Association, 231*, 414–415.

Connell, P. H. (1968). The use and abuse of amphetamines. *Practitioner, 200*, 234–243.

Cooper, J. R., Czechowicz, D. J., Peterson, R. C., Molinari, S. M. (1992). Prescription drug diversion control and medical practice. *Journal of the American Medical Association, 268*, 1306–1310.

Davidson, E. S., Finch, J. F., & Schenk, S. (1993). Variability in subjective responses to cocaine: Initial experiences of college students. *Addictive Behavior, 18*, 445–453.

De Wit, H., Uhlenhuth, M. D., & Johanson, C. E. (1987). The reinforcing properties of amphetamine in overweight subjects and subjects with depression. *Clinical Pharmacology and Therapeutics, 42*, 127–136.

Drug Abuse Warning Network. (2000). Detailed emergency department tables [On-line]. Available: http://www.samhsa.gov/oas/DAWN/DetEDT61/2000/text/00DetTbl.pdf.

Drug Enforcement Administration. (1995a, October). *Methylphenidate (a background paper)*. Washington, DC: Author.

Drug Enforcement Administration. (1995b). *Response to petition to transfer methylphenidate from Schedule II to Schedule III*. Washington, DC: Author.

Ellinwood, E. H., & Cohen, S. (1971). Amphetamine abuse. *Science, 171*, 420–421.

Fuller, R. W., Perry, K. W., Bymaster, F. P., & Wong, D. T. (1978). Comparative effects of pemoline, amfonelic acid and amphetamine on dopamine uptake and release in vitro and on brain 3,4-dihydroxyphenylacetic acid concentration in spiperone-treated rats. *Journal of Pharmacy and Pharmacology, 30*(3), 197–198.

Fulton, A., & Yates, W. R. (1988). Family abuse of methylphenidate. *American Family Physician, 38*, 143–145.

Garland, E. J. (1998). Intranasal abuse of prescribed methylphenidate. *Journal of the American Academy of Child and Adolescent Psychiatry, 37*, 573–574.

Gawin, F. H., & Ellinwood, E. H. (1988). Cocaine and other stimulants. *New England Journal of Medicine, 318*, 1173–1182.

Gittelman, R., Mannuzza, S., Shenker, R., & Bonagura, N. (1985). Hyperactive boys almost grown up: I. Psychiatric status. *Archives of General Psychiatry, 42*, 937–947.

Goyer, P. F., Davis, G. C., & Rapoport, J. L. (1979). Abuse of prescribed stimulant medication by a 13-year-old hyperactive boy. *Journal of the American Academy of Child Psychiatry, 18*, 170–175.

Gunby, P. (1979). Methylphenidate abuse produces retinopathy. *Journal of the American Medical Association, 241*, 546.

Hartsough, C. S., & Lambert, N. M. (1987). Pattern and progression of drug use among hyperactives and controls: A prospective short-term longitudinal study. *Journal of Child Psychology and Psychiatry, 28*, 543–553.

Hechtman, L., & Weiss, G. (1986). Controlled prospective 15-year follow-up of hyperactives as adults: Non-medical drug and alcohol use and anti-social behavior. *Canadian Journal of Psychiatry, 31*, 557–567.

Hechtman, L., Weiss, G., & Perlman, T. (1984). Young adult outcomes of hyperactive children who received long-term stimulant treatment. *Journal of the American Academy of Child Psychiatry, 23*, 261–269.

Herrero, M. E., Hechtman, L., & Weiss, G. (1994). Antisocial disorders in hyperactive subjects from childhood to adulthood: predictive factors and characterization of subgroups. *American Journal of Orthopsychiatry, 64*, 510–521.

Hughes, J. R. (1997). Substance abuse and ADHD. *American Journal of Psychiatry, 154*, 132.

Increasing morbidity and mortality associated with abuse of methamphetamine—United States, 1991–1994. (1995). *Morbidity and Mortality Weekly Report, 1, 44*(47), 882–886.

Jaffe, S. L. (1991). Intranasal abuse of prescribed methylphenidate by an alcohol and drug abusing adolescent with ADHD. *Journal of the American Academy of Child and Adolescent Psychiatry, 30,* 773–775.

Lambert, N. M., Hartsough, C. S., Sassone, D., & Sandoval, J. (1987). Persistence of hyperactivity symptoms from childhood to adolescence and associated outcomes. *American Journal of Orthopsychiatry, 57,* 22–32.

Levin, F. R., & Kleber, H. D. (1995). Attention-deficit hyperactivity disorder and substance abuse: relationships and implications for treatment. *Harvard Review of Psychiatry, 2,* 246–258.

Mannuzza, S., Klein, R. G., Bessler, A., Malloy, P., & LaPadula, M. (1998). Adult psychiatric status of hyperactive boys grown up. *American Journal of Psychiatry, 155,* 493–498.

Martin, W. R., Sloan, J. W., Sapira, J. D., & Jasinski, D. R. (1971). Physiologic, subjective and behavioral effects of amphetamine, methamphetamine, ephedrine, phenmetrazine and methylphenidate in man. *Clinical Pharmacology Therapeutics, 12,* 245–258.

Masand, P. S., & Tesar, G. E. (1996). Use of stimulants in the medically ill. *Psychiatric Clinics of North America, 19,* 515–547.

Milberger, S., Biederman, J., Faraone, S. V., Wilens, T., & Chu, M. P. (1997). Longitudinal study of high-risk siblings of ADHD children. *American Journal of Addiction, 6,* 318–329.

Mueller, K., & Hsiao, S. (1980). Pemoline-induced self-biting in rats and self-mutilation in the deLange syndrome. *Pharmacology and Biochemical Behavior, 13*(5), 627–631.

National Institute on Drug Abuse. (1998). *Epidemiologic trends in drug abuse, Community Epidemiology Work Group; Vol II: Proceedings, June 1997* (NIH Publication No. 98-4208A). Washington, DC: Author.

National Institute on Drug Abuse. (1998). *National survey results on drug use from the Monitoring the Future Study, 1975–1997* (NIH Publication No. 98-4345). Washington, DC: Author.

Office of National Drug Control Policy. (1998). *Pulse check: National trends in drug abuse, summer 1998* (NCJ-171664). Washington, DC: Office of Programs, Budget, Research and Evaluation.

Parran, T. V. Jr., & Jasinski, D. R. (1991). Intravenous methylphenidate abuse. Prototype for prescription drug abuse. *Archives of Internal Medicine, 151,* 781–783.

Piazza, P. V., Deroche, V., Rouge-Pont, F., & Le Moal, M. (1993). Behavioral and biological factors associated with individual vulnerability to psychostimulant abuse. In *Laboratory behavioral studies of vulnerability to drug abuse* (NIDA Monograph No. 169) (pp. 105–133). Rockville, MD: U.S. Government Printing Office.

Schenk, S., & Davidson, E. S. (1993). Stimulant preexposure sensitizes rats and humans to the rewarding effects of cocaine. In *Laboratory behavioral studies of vulnerability to drug abuse* (NIDA Monograph No. 169) (pp. 56–82). Rockville, MD: U.S. Government Printing Office.

Schuster, C. R., & Thompson, M. H. (1969). Self-administration and behavioral dependence on drugs. *Annual Review of Pharmacology, 9,* 483–502.

Spensley, J., & Rockwell, D. A. (1972). Psychosis during methylphenidate abuse. *New England Journal of Medicine, 286,* 880–881.

Spier, S. A. (1995). Toxicity and abuse of prescribed stimulants. *International Journal of Psychiatry and Medicine, 25,* 69–79.

Substance Abuse and Mental Health Services Administration. (1997). *Year-end preliminary estimates for the 1996 DAWN* (DHHS Publication No. SMA 98-3175). Washington, DC: Office of Applied Studies.

Substance Abuse and Mental Health Services Administration. (1998). *Methodology series: M-2, DAWN sample design and estimation procedures; technical report* (DHHS Publication No. SMA 98-3178). Washington, DC: Office of Applied Studies.

Wilens, T. E., Biederman, J., Mick, E., Faraone, S. V., & Spencer, T. (1997). Attention deficit hyperactivity disorder (ADHD) is associated with early onset substance use disorders. *Journal of Nervous and Mental Disease, 185*(8), 475–482.

Wilens, T. E., Prince, J. B., Biederman, J., Spencer, T. J., & Frances, R. J. (1995). Attention-deficit hyperactivity disorder and comorbid substance use disorders in adults. *Psychiatric Services, 46*, 761–765.

Wilens, T. E., Spencer, T. J., & Biederman, J. (1995). Are attention-deficit hyperactivity disorder and the psychoactive substance use disorders really related? *Harvard Review of Psychiatry, 3*, 160–162.

Willey, R. F. (1971). Abuse of methylphenidate. *New England Journal of Medicine, 285*, 464.

Woolverton, W. L., & English, J. A. (1997). Effects of some phenylethylamines in rhesus monkeys trained to discriminate (+)-amphetamine from saline. *Drug and Alcohol Dependence, 14*, 79–85.

World Health Organization. (1988). *Pemoline. 25th Expert Committee on Drug Dependence report.* Geneva, Switzerland: Author.

Zemplenyi, J., Colman, M. F. (1984). Deep neck abscesses secondary to methylphenidate (Ritalin) abuse. *Head and Neck Surgery, 6*, 858–860.

Ziedonis, D. M., Rayford, B. S., Bryant, K. J., & Rounsaville, B. J. (1994). Psychiatric comorbidity in white and African-American cocaine addicts seeking substance abuse treatment. *Hospital and Community Psychiatry, 45*, 43–49.

Chapter 22

Treatment Services for Children With ADHD— A National Perspective

by Kimberly Hoagwood, Ph.D., Kelly J. Kelleher, M.D., M.P.H., Michael Feil, M.B.A., M.S. and Diane Comer, B.A.

Introduction 22-2
Prevalence of Attentional Problems and Available Services 22-3
Review of Treatment Services 22-4
    Trends in Prescription Practices 22-4
        Increasing Levels of Prescribing 22-4
        Prevalence of Medication Treatments 22-5
    Rates of Specialty Mental Health and School Services
      Received 22-5
    Variations in Treatments or Use of Services 22-6
        Gender Variations 22-6
        Racial Variations 22-6
        Geographical Variations 22-6
    Barriers to Care 22-6
    Conclusions From the Review 22-7
The National Ambulatory Medical Care Survey 22-8
    Survey Methods 22-8
        Data Set 22-8
        Data Assessment 22-8
    Increased Identification of ADHD 22-9
    Trends in Types of Treatments and Services 22-9
        Medication Management 22-10
        Diagnostic Services 22-10
        Counseling Services 22-10
        Follow-up Services 22-11
    Types of Services by Provider Type 22-11
        Medication Management 22-11
        Diagnostic Services 22-11

   Mental Health Counseling 22-11
   Other Counseling 22-11
   Psychotherapy 22-11
   Specific Follow-up 22-12
The Child Behavior Study 22-12
   Survey Methods 22-12
   Receipt of Specialty Mental Health Services and
    Stimulant Treatments 22-13
   Service Mix 22-13
   Identified Barriers to Care 22-13
Conclusions and Recommendations 22-13
   Service Patterns and Continuing Problems 22-13
   Continuing Barriers to Care 22-15
   Recommendations for Clinical Practice and Policy 22-15
   Recommendations for Future Research 22-16

INTRODUCTION

This chapter summarizes the state of knowledge on treatment services for children and adolescents with attention deficit hyperactivity disorder (ADHD), trends in services from 1989 to 1996, types of services provided, service mix, and barriers to care. We present a review of the literature and analyses from two national surveys to describe the status of mental health care for children and adolescents with ADHD. Major shifts have occurred in stimulant prescriptions since 1989, with prescriptions now comprising three-fourths of all visits to physicians by children with ADHD. Related services, such as health counseling, increased tenfold between 1989 and 1996. Diagnostic services have increased threefold since 1989, while provision of psychotherapy and follow-up care were less likely to be provided in 1996 than in 1989. Treatment service mix interacts with physician type: Family practitioners are more likely than either pediatricians or psychiatrists to prescribe stimulants and less likely to use diagnostic services, provide mental health counseling, or provide follow-up care. Levels of unmet need depend on the length of time children are followed, demographic variables, and the service setting in which they are studied.

In general, three-fourths of children with ADHD symptoms receive mental health services over at least a three-year period; however, these rates appear to be much lower among girls, minorities, and children receiving care through public service systems. Almost all caregivers and children report at least one and usually multiple significant barrier(s) to care, the primary barriers being lack of information and cost concerns. Physicians also report significant barriers, including lack of pediatric specialists and cumbersome authorization procedures. Recommendations are made for focusing future research on studies that assess service delivery in typical clinical practice, examine the match or mismatch between treatment needs and appropriate care, engage caregivers in treatment planning, examine gender and ethnic disparities in help seeking, and investigate promising models for consolidating treatment services in schools.

PREVALENCE OF ATTENTIONAL PROBLEMS AND AVAILABLE SERVICES

Prevalence estimates derived from population-based studies suggest that from 3 percent to 6 percent of children display serious problems in attentional regulation (Angold, Erkanli, Egger, & Costello, 2000; Jensen, Kettle, et al., 1999; Offord et al., 1987; Szatmari, Offord, & Boyle, 1989). Studies of children who present for care in service settings have found much higher rates. Severe attentional problems are reported to be as high as 9 percent in studies of children seen by primary care physicians (Wasserman et al., 1999), 17 percent among children seen in public mental health clinics (Garland et al., 2001), 20 percent among children referred for crisis psychiatric hospitalization (Henggeler et al., 1999), and 44 percent among children receiving special education services (Bussing, Zima, Perwien, Belin, & Widawski, 1998). Different methods of diagnosing attentional disorders among these studies make comparability difficult. However, these estimates do suggest that attentional problems in children may trigger care seeking and service provision.

Until recently, the types of mental health or other health care services available to and used by children with mental health problems and their families were not typically assessed (Leaf et al., 1996; Stiffman et al., 2000), making it impossible to determine the extent to which need for care was or was not being met. In addition, because treatment planning by states and local agencies depends on having reliable estimates of the need for and use of mental health services, the absence of this information has made it difficult to systematically match treatment needs with mental health problems or to characterize patterns of care for children with specific psychiatric problems, such as ADHD.

Since 1990, however, there has been a shift in emphasis. The majority of population-based studies of children's psychiatric needs now include assessments of the types, intensities, and duration of mental health and other health services (Burns et al., 1995; Costello, Angold, Burns, Erkanli, et al., 1996; Costello, Angold, Burns, Stangl, et al., 1996; Stiffman et al., 2000; Jensen, Kettle, et al., 1999; Kessler et al., 1994; Leaf et al., 1996; Zahner, Pawel-Kiewicz, DeFrancesco, & Adnopoz, 1992). The complex relationships among children's clinical symptoms, functional impairments, and use of services are beginning to be examined (Costello, Angold, Burns, Erkanli, et al., 1996; Stiffman, Chen, Elze, Dore, & Cheng, 1997). Furthermore, methodological development has yielded several reliable and valid measures of services by both caregiver and youth reports (Ascher, Farmer, Burns, & Angold, 1998; Farmer, Angold, Burns, & Costello, 1994; Stiffman et al., 1997; Stiffman et al., 2000).

Despite these advances, however, constructing a national picture of the provision of care for children with ADHD is difficult for three reasons. First, most recent studies of children with ADHD have been studies of treatment efficacy or of concomitant risks rather than studies characterizing usual practices for children with this disorder. Hundreds of treatment studies, especially stimulant treatments, have been conducted, and more than a dozen have met rigorous evidence-based review criteria (see Chapter 14; McMaster, 1998), but these studies do not provide a picture of usual care. Second, of those studies that have examined the relationship between mental health need and service use under natural conditions, the majority have used local, community-based convenience samples, not nationally representative samples, thus providing limited information about gender, ethnic, or geographic variation Third, of those few national surveys that exist, only two included both sufficient samples of physicians in real-world practices and sufficient samples of children with ADHD to enable any conclusions to be drawn about the use of treatment services under usual practice conditions. Even these surveys, however, provide only a picture of physician practices; they do not include the broader group of mental health clinicians who provide care to these children in schools, clinics, or at home through home-based services.

This chapter reviews the status of knowledge about treatment services for children with ADHD. It first summarizes the extant literature drawn largely from local samples; it then presents analyses from a nationally representative survey of practice-based physicians (The National Ambulatory Medical Care Survey, or NAMCS, 1994) and two national networks of primary care physicians (the Pediatric Research in Office Settings, or PROS, and the Ambulatory Sentinel Practice Network, or ASPN). Throughout this review, treatment services are defined broadly to include the following: prescription of psychotropic medications (usually stimulants), outpatient mental health counseling, psychotherapy, health counseling, diagnostic services, referrals, follow-up visits, and school services (usually counseling or special classes). Although we recognize that there are many other kinds of treatment services provided in communities, such as respite care, day treatment or partial care, therapeutic foster care, specialized day care, and parent management training, no data on these services for children with ADHD were located.

In addition to a review of the literature, recent analyses of treatment services for children with diagnosable ADHD were obtained from three community studies: the Great Smoky Mountain Study (GSMS; Costello, Angold, Burns, Erkanli, et al., 1996; Costello, Angold, Burns, Stangl, et al., 1996), a longitudinal study of psychiatric disorders and service need in rural North Carolina; the Caring for Children in the Community Study (CCCS; Angold et al., 2000), a longitudinal study of young children's psychiatric disorders and service use in urban and rural North Carolina; and the Methods for the Epidemiology of Child and Adolescent Mental Disorders (MECA), a four-site study, completed in 1994, in largely urban settings using epidemiological household sampling procedures (Lahey et al., 1996).

REVIEW OF TREATMENT SERVICES

Trends in Prescription Practices

Increasing Levels of Prescribing. Safer and colleagues (Safer & Krager, 1985, 1988, 1994; Safer, Zito, & Fine, 1996) studied levels of methylphenidate use over time and found increased levels of prescribing for all ages of children. The rate of medication treatment for elementary school students increased from 1.07 percent in 1971 to 5.96 percent in 1987; for middle school students, it increased from .59 percent in 1975 to 2.98 percent in 1993; and for high school students, it increased from .22 percent in 1983 to .70 percent in 1993. Methylphenidate use for adolescents increased 2.5 fold from 1990 to 1995, perhaps due to increases in diagnoses of ADHD among girls, increased duration of medication treatment, and increased public acceptance of stimulants.

Similar trends have been found among Medicaid populations and young children. Among Medicaid youth service users, Zito, dosReis, Safer, and Bardner (1998) report that from 1987 to 1995, psychotropic prescriptions for youths increased an average of 4.3 percent per year. Polypharmacy (i.e., multiple psychotropic prescriptions) increased an average of 7.5 percent per year. The classes of psychotropic medications with the greatest increase were stimulants, clonidine, antidepressants, and lithium. Few data are available on stimulant prescriptions for young children, but preliminary reports indicate that they also are on the rise. Zito has found a 180 percent increase between 1991 and 1995 in the number of prescriptions of stimulant drugs for children 5 years old or younger (Zito et al., 2000).

Prevalence of Medication Treatments. Although psychostimulants are the treatment of choice by most physicians (Greenhill, 1998; Spencer et al., 1996), rates of stimulant treatments prescribed for children with ADHD differ considerably. In a survey of all elementary school-age children in one county in Tennessee, Wolraich, Hannah, Pinnock, Baumgartel, & Brosn (1996) found that only one-fourth of children who met criteria for ADHD had received medication. Jensen and colleagues (Jensen, Kettle, et al., 1999) found that over a one-year period only 12 percent of children ages 9 to 17 meeting diagnostic criteria had been treated with stimulants. In an eleven-county community sample of children ages 9 to 13 followed longitudinally, 52.6 percent of children with ADHD had received stimulants over a three-month period; however, when stimulant use was accessed over a three-year period, 72 percent had received them (Angold et al., 2000). These disparities in rates appear to result from the time frame in which this treatment service is assessed, with shorter periods yielding lower prevalence rates.

In an analysis of national pediatric prescribing practices in 1995, levels of psychotropic prescribing in children and adolescents were greatest for stimulants, resulting in almost 2 million office visits and 6 million drug "mentions" (Jensen, Bhatara, et al., 1999). These numbers represent an increase over previous reports. The number of prescriptions per child can only be estimated, however. One study conducted in the mid-1980s by Sherman and Hertzig (1991) found that over half of medicated children in Suffolk County, New York received only one prescription for stimulants during a one-year period and 13.7 percent of medicated children received more than four prescriptions. Zito, dosReis, et al. (1998) report average claims to person ratios of 5:1 and recommend using counts of persons with medication rather than prescription counts to provide best estimates of medication prevalence.

Few studies have assessed use of pediatric health services by children with ADHD. One study has found that over a three-year period, approximately 50 percent of children with diagnosable ADHD received medical services (Angold et al., 2000), usually involving visits to pediatricians.

Rates of Specialty Mental Health and School Services Received

When service use is assessed over at least a three-year period, between 40 percent and 63 percent of children with attentional problems are found to have received specialty mental health services (Angold et al., 2000; Kelleher et al., 2000). Over a one-year period, the rates are lower, generally hovering around 30 percent (Jensen, Kettle, et al., 1999; see also Kelleher, Chapter 27, in this volume).

Rates of school mental health services for children with ADHD vary greatly, depending on whether one uses a one-year or three-year time frame. When service use is assessed over a one-year period, only 24 percent of children with diagnosable ADHD have received school services (Jensen, Kettle, et al., 1999), whereas up to 80 percent of such children receive school services when services are assessed over a three-year period (Angold et al., 2000). School services in these studies were parent-reported services that generally included seeing a school counselor or receiving special instructional help.

Variations in Treatments or Use of Services

Gender Variations. Prevalence estimates converge to indicate a 3:1 ratio of boys to girls in the assignment of ADHD diagnoses (Angold et al., 2000; Wasserman et al., 1999; Zito, Safer, dosReis, Magder, & Riddle, 1997), but it is interesting that a similar ratio of 2:1 or 3:1 (boys to girls) has also been reported for prescription of psychotropic medications (Gardner et al., 2000) and methylphenidate (Zito, Safer, Riddle, Speedie, & Fox, 1996; Safer et al., 1997). However, in use of specialty mental health services, the opposite finding has been reported: Girls who are diagnosed with ADHD are twice as likely to use specialty mental health services as boys with this diagnosis, whereas boys are three times as likely to use pediatric services as girls (Angold et al., 2000). This may suggest differences in the interface between service systems and the service-triggering problems of girls versus boys.

Racial Variations. Some racial differences have also been noted, although few studies have had sufficient sample sizes to adequately analyze these differences. In a population-based study of rural service use (the GSMS), Caucasian youths meeting diagnostic criteria for ADHD were significantly more likely to use general medical services and twice as likely to use specialty mental health services than African-American youths (Angold & Costello, 2000). Two studies have found that minority youths, primarily African American, are less than half as likely as Caucasian youths to have been prescribed psychotropic medications (Bussing, Zima, & Belin, 1998; Zito et al., 1996; Zito et al., 1997; Zito, Safer, dosReis, & Riddle, 1998).

Racial differences have also been reported in prescriptions of psychotropic medications among Medicaid patients, with African-American youths less than half as likely as Caucasian youths to have been prescribed psychotropic medications (Zito et al., 1996; Zito et al., 1997).

Geographical Variations. Finally, geographical region has been associated with differences in prescription rates of methylphenidate. Rappley found a tenfold difference in prescription rates between counties in Michigan (Rappley, Gardiner, Jetton, & Houang, 1995), and Zito et al. (1997) found fivefold rate differences in Maryland.

Barriers to Care

Few studies have investigated reasons why families and children seek care, why they terminate services, and what obstacles they encounter in seeking help for mental health problems. Barriers to services or treatment among children with ADHD have

Table 22.1
Barriers to Care for ADHD

Barriers Reported by Children (GSMS)		Barriers Reported by Children (CCCS):	
Lack of information	30%	Fear/dislike/distrust of professionals	18%
Anticipation of out-of-home placement	29%	Self-consciousness	15%
Anticipation of loss of parental rights	27%	Anticipation of negative reaction	10%
Anticipation of negative reaction	24%		
Fear/dislike/distrust of professionals	23%	**Barriers Reported by Caregiver (CCCS):**	
		Lack of information	38%
Barriers Reported by Parents (GSMS)		Concern about cost	37%
Concern about cost	74%	Child or parent refused services	31%
Lack of information	73%	Lack of time	26%
Lack of time	51%		
Negative experience with professionals	42%		
Services withheld	38%		
Unavailability	32%		

Note. 94% of parents reported at least one barrier at some point during the 3 years.

Note. 73% of parents reported at least one barrier at the first assessment and most reported multiple barriers.

Barriers Reported by Primary Care Physicians (CBS):	
Lack of pediatric specialists	64.4%
Difficulty/delay in getting appointment	64.1%
Specialists won't accept Medicaid	61.6%
Physician panel restrictions	48.3%
Complex appeals process for utilization of out-of-plan specialists	42.9%
Authorization procedures	39.0%
Financial disincentives	34.9%
Burdensome paperwork	29.2%

*Barriers reported by all clinicians in the practice network.

been identified in two population-based studies (GSMS and the CCCS; see Table 22.1; Angold et al., 2000). In these cases, barriers are defined as events, actions, or inactions that delayed or prevented the use of mental health services. The major barriers reported by children with ADHD and by their primary caregivers differed. Children reported barriers that involved anticipatory loss (e.g., fear of being placed out of the home or losing contact with one's parent), previous negative experiences with professionals, and lack of information. Caregivers reported more pragmatic barriers, such as costs of care, time involved in getting help, and (similarly to children) lack of information. Angold et al. (2000) found that 94 percent of caregivers reported at least one barrier at some point during the three years of the study.

Conclusions From the Review

Data from the studies reviewed previously offer an uneven picture of the patterns of treatment services used by children with ADHD. Stimulant treatments are prescribed with greater frequency than they were ten years ago and are obtained by about three-fourths of children with ADHD at some point in their childhood; however, the availability and use of stimulants varies substantially by geographic region and also seems to be influenced by gender and race. Although the longer children are identified as "having" ADHD, the more likely they are to receive specialty mental health services and school-related help, here again, there are large variations in receipt of such care by gender, race, and geography. No studies were identified that examined the prevalence or distribution of services for caregivers to help them manage their children's behavior, even though behavior management and parent training have been recommended in professional association practice parameters (Dulcan et al., 1997). Finally, the studies reviewed earlier represented local samples only, and by definition the findings cannot necessarily be extrapolated to other locales. To understand treatment variations, data from nationally representative samples of practice-based care must be examined, with inclusion of sufficient samples of children with ADHD. Only two such surveys could be identified, and these investigated only physician-delivered care: the NAMCS and the Child Behavior Study (CBS) from the PROS and ASPN Networks. Trends in identification of ADHD and in types of treatments and services from 1989 to 1996 were analyzed and are described in the following sections, as well as physician differences in care provision, service mix, and clinician-identified barriers to care.

THE NATIONAL AMBULATORY MEDICAL CARE SURVEY

Survey Methods

Data Set. NAMCS, a survey conducted by the National Center for Health Statistics, uses a multistage probability design of samples of medical practices within primary sampling units and patient visits within practices. The basic sampling unit is the visit to medical practices engaged in office-based patient care. For these analyses, a sample was constructed of all children ages 0–17 seen by either a pediatrician, family practice physician, or psychiatrist, and coded with an diagnosis of ADHD according to the ninth edition of *International Classification of Diseases* (ICD-9; World Health Organization, 1978). All analyses of NAMCS data refer to this sample.

Data were obtained for the years 1989, 1991, 1993, 1995, and 1996. A total of 38,389 patient record forms were obtained for 1989, 33,795 for 1991, 35,978 for 1993, 36,875 for 1995, and 29,805 in 1996. These were obtained from a sample of 2,535 office-based physicians who participated in the survey in 1989; 2,540 in 1991, 3,400 in 1993, 3,724 in 1995, and 3,173 in 1996. The basic sampling unit was the visit to the medical practices. The sampling frame consisted of all nonfederally employed and office-based physicians listed in the master files maintained by the American Medical Association (AMA) and the American Osteopathic Association (AOA) who were primarily involved in patient care. The physician universe, so defined, was composed of 317,512 physicians in 1989, 333,023 in 1991, 359,598 in 1993, 375,467 in 1995, and 385,155 in 1996. See Exhibit 22.1 at end of this chapter for specific sample sizes, point estimates, and confidence intervals.

Data Assessment. The survey does not include independent assessments. Data on patient variables, including ICD-9 diagnoses and services, were obtained during each visit and collected by physicians, aided by their office staff. For the purposes of these analyses, all children ages 0–17 with an ICD-9 code of either 314.00 or 314.01 (attention deficit disorder with or without hyperactivity) were selected, and this comprised the study sample. Service variables included diagnostic services, defined by NAMCS

Table 22.2
Trends in Percent of Mental Health Problem Visits and All Visits Where ADHD Was Identified (NAMCS)

Trends in % of Mental Health Problem Visits Where ADHD Was Identified		Trends in % of All Visits Where ADHD Was Identified	
1989	40.91%	1989	0.74%
1991	35.98%	1991	0.84%
1993	54.80%	1993	2.0%
1995	55.23%	1995	1.6%
1996	59.73%	1996	1.9%

as "services that were ordered or provided during this visit for the purpose of screening or diagnosis"; mental health counseling, defined as counseling about mental health issues, including referrals to other mental health professionals for counseling; psychotherapy, defined as "all treatments involving the intentional use of verbal techniques to explore or alter the patient's emotional life in order to effect symptom reduction or behavior change"; and other counseling, defined as advice provided during the visit, including guidance about diet, exercise, use of tobacco, injury prevention, growth or development, and so on.

Because the NAMCS is a complex multistage sample survey and is characterized by unequal probability of selection at three stages of sampling, the SUDAAN statistical software (La Vange, Stearns, Lafata, Koch, & Shah, 1996) was employed to account for the sample design effects in the analyses. The National Center for Health Statistics (NCHS) provides formulas for the calculation of standard errors of point estimates, and these were used to compute 95 percent confidence intervals around those estimates.

Increased Identification of ADHD

Analyses from NAMCS indicate that the percentage of visits to physicians where ADHD was identified has risen from less than 1 percent in 1989 (0.74 percent) to almost 2 percent (1.9 percent) in 1996. The percentage of mental health problem visits where ADHD was specifically identified has risen as well. In 1989, 40.91 percent of all visits to physicians by children where a mental health problem was identified as the primary reason for visit included attentional problems. In 1996, the percentage of mental health problem visits involving attentional problems had risen to 59.73 percent (see Table 22.2).

Trends in Types of Treatments and Services

Types of services provided to children identified as having ADHD were analyzed in the NAMCS from 1989 to 1996. These included the following: medication management, diagnostic services (i.e., screening or assessment services to establish a diagnosis), mental health counseling, other counseling (i.e., health-related advice), psychotherapy, and follow-up visits (see Table 22.3).

Table 22.3
Trends in Types of Services for Children With ADHD (NAMCS, 1989–1996)

Types of Services	Year				
	1989	1991	1993	1995	1996
Med. management					
stimulants	54.8%	77.8%	76.3%	74.8%	75.4%
Other psychotropics	15.3%	3.5%	5.6%	4.0%	7.5%
Other drugs	6.5%	2.5%	2.6%	6.3%	4.3%
No drugs	23.4%	16.2%	15.5%	14.9%	12.8%
Dx services	22.3%	76.6%	43.1%	60.6%	62.1%
Mh counseling	24.3%	59.4%	34.3%	44.2%	39.3%
Other counseling	3.5%	29.7%	45.3%	29.9%	35.2%
Psychotherapy	40.1%	38.3%	5.6%	21.3%	25.2%
Specific follow-up	91.0%	84.5%	75.5%	83.4%	75.1%

Medication Management. A larger percentage of visits now include prescription of some kind of drug. The most often prescribed drugs are now stimulants.

- *Stimulants.* Prescriptions of stimulants increased from 54.8 percent of visits in 1989 to 75.4 percent in 1996. The largest increase was between 1989 and 1991, but has remained relatively constant since 1991.

- *Other psychotropics.* There was a 50 percent decrease from 15.3 percent in 1989 to 7.5 percent in 1996. The biggest drop occurred between 1989 and 1991, but there has been a slight trend upwards since 1991.

- *Other drugs.* Prescriptions of other drugs dropped from 6.5 percent in 1989 to 4.3 percent in 1996.

- *No drugs.* There has been a 45 percent decrease in visits where no drugs are prescribed, from 23.4 percent in 1989 to 12.8 percent in 1996.

Diagnostic services. There was a threefold increase in diagnostic or screening services for children with attentional problems, from 22.3 percent in 1989 to 62.1 percent in 1996. The largest increase occurred between 1989 and 1991.

Counseling Services. Following are types of counseling services that often are available to clients:

- *Mental health counseling.* This service increased from 24.3 percent of visits in 1989 to 39.3 percent in 1996.

- *Other counseling.* This service had the largest change over time, increasing 10 fold from 3.5 percent in 1989 to 35.2 percent in 1996.

- *Psychotherapy.* There was a sizable decrease in the percentage of visits where children received psychotherapy, falling from 40.1 percent of visits in 1989 to 25.2 percent in 1996.

Follow-up Services. There was a decrease in number of visits when follow-up services were recommended, dropping from 91 percent in 1989 to 75.1 percent in 1996.

Types of Services by Provider Type

The three major medical providers for children with attentional problems are pediatricians, family practice physicians, and psychiatrists. Analyses of NAMCS data from 1996 revealed pronounced differences in types of services provided by these different physician specialties (see Table 22.4).

Medication Management. Approximately three-fourths of both psychiatrists and pediatricians (74.2 percent and 75.4 percent, respectively) prescribed stimulants to children identified with ADHD, whereas 94.9 percent of family practitioners did so. Prescription of other psychotropics had an opposite pattern: Most such prescriptions were given by psychiatrists (14.8 percent), whereas pediatricians and family practitioners prescribed far less often (4.3 percent and 1.9 percent). The category of "no drugs prescribed" occurred most often among psychiatrists (11 percent) and pediatricians (9.4 percent) and least often among family practice physicians, where this occurred on only 3.2 percent of the visits.

Diagnostic Services. There were large differences between providers in use of diagnostic services: 80.6 percent of visits to psychiatrists included these, whereas only 32.6 percent of visits to family practice physicians did. Pediatricians used these services on 64 percent of the visits.

Mental Health Counseling. This service followed a similar pattern to diagnostic services, with 67.3 percent of visits to psychiatrists including this service and only 7.3 percent of family practitioners doing so. Pediatricians again fell in the middle, using these services on 44.2 percent of the visits.

Other Counseling. Pediatricians were more likely to provide general health-related counseling than were the other physician specialists. It was provided on 54.1 percent of visits to pediatricians, 42.4 percent of visits to family practitioners, and only 15.6 percent of visits to psychiatrists.

Psychotherapy. This service followed a similar pattern to mental health counseling and diagnostic services, with psychiatrists using psychotherapy more often than did the other specialists. Forty-four percent of visits to psychiatrists included psychother-

Table 23.45
Types of Services by Physician (NAMCS 1996)

Type of Service	Psychiatry	Pediatrics	Family Practice	Other
Med. management				
Stimulants	74.2%	75.4%	94.9%	43.9%
Other psychotropics	14.8%	4.3%	1.9%	9.2%
Other drugs	—	10.9%	—	—
No drugs	11.0%	9.4%	3.2%	46.9%
Dx services	80.6%	64.0%	32.6%	55.6%
Mh counseling	67.3%	44.2%	7.3%	—
Other counseling	15.6%	54.1%	42.4%	7.7%
Psychotherapy	44.3%	29.7%	—	—
Specific follow-up	88.5%	79.0%	45.7%	75.9%

apy and 29.7 percent of visits to pediatricians, whereas family practitioners did not use it at all (0 percent).

Specific Follow-up. This was most likely to be provided by psychiatrists (88.5 percent) and pediatricians (79 percent) but likely to be recommended in less than half of the visits to family practitioners (45.7 percent).

THE CHILD BEHAVIOR STUDY

Survey Methods

The CBS is a representative sample from two national practice-based primary care research networks, the PROS (Wasserman, Slora, Bocian, Fleming, & Kessel, 1998) and the ASPN (Green et al., 1984). PROS is a pediatric network established in 1986 which currently comprises more than 1,300 clinicians from more than 475 practices in all fifty states and the Commonwealth of Puerto Rico who provide care for approximately 1.75 million children in the United States. ASPN is a family medicine network established in 1978 which currently consists of 125 practices and approximately 750 clinicians from thirty-eight states and six Canadian provinces who provide care for about a half million patients. Eighty-nine percent of PROS clinicians are pediatricians, 10 percent are nurse practitioners, and 1 percent are physician assistants. Eighty-five percent of ASPN clinicians are family physicians, 7 percent are nurse practitioners, and 8 percent are physician assistants. Recruitment of PROS and ASPN clinicians into the study has been described fully elsewhere (Kelleher et al., 1997). This study included 401 pediatric and family practice clinicians in forty-four states, Puerto Rico, and four Canadian provinces.

Participating clinicians were asked to enroll seventy consecutive children ages 4–15 who presented for nonemergency care (acute or well-child-only visits excluded), accompanied by a parent or primary caregiver who spoke English or Spanish. Ninety-one percent of eligible children across all sites participated. No differences in age or gender were detected in a comparison of participating and nonparticipating children. Children in the western United States were slightly more likely to participate. Results on 22,059 visits are reported. Among those visits, 909 (4 percent) had inadequate or missing data sufficient to preclude further analyses, resulting in a total sample of 21,150 visits with adequate data. Of these subjects, 4,012 (19 percent) were identified by the clinician as having a psychosocial problem, and 2,007 (9 percent) were identified by the clinician as having "attention deficit/hyperactivity problems," and these comprise the study sample.

Receipt of Specialty Mental Health Services and Stimulant Treatments

Of the sample of children with attentional problems identified in the CBS, 63.3 percent had received specialty mental health services and 72 percent had received psychotropic medication at some point in their lives.

Service Mix

Service mix was assessed in the CBS and defined to include counseling, medication prescribing, and referrals to other specialists. On any given day, 27.5 percent of children being seen by primary care physicians for attentional problems receive no counseling, no medications, and no referrals—simply monitoring or follow-up; another 27 percent receive counseling and medications; 17 percent receive no counseling but do receive medications; and 11.5 percent receive counseling only and no medications. Thus on any given day, over 50 percent of children with attentional problems being seen by primary care clinicians receive either counseling, medications, or both.

Identified Barriers to Care

The CBS study of primary care physicians measured barriers from the physicians' perspective. All clinicians completed a questionnaire which asked them to list the factors which limited the number of referrals they made for mental health problems in children. Almost two-thirds reported that the major barriers to care were lack of pediatric specialists, difficulty or delay in getting appointments, and nonacceptance of Medicaid patients. Close to half reported that physician panel restrictions and complex appeals processes were major barriers (see Table 22.1).

CONCLUSIONS AND RECOMMENDATIONS

Service Patterns and Continuing Problems

Patterns of services for children with ADHD are changing. Since 1989, prescriptions of stimulants have risen from about half of all visits to three-fourths of all visits. During the same period, prescriptions of other medications have dropped. Children with ADHD who are seen by physicians are more likely now to receive diagnostic services, mental health counseling, and general health counseling than they were in 1989. The largest increases in services have occurred in health-related counseling, prescribing of stimulants, and provision of diagnostic services. Decreases were found in the provision of psychotherapy, and in recommendations for follow-up services. It is interesting to note that in the only study to examine psychotropic medication prescription practices for children seen in office-based care from NAMCS (Kelleher, Hohmann, & Larson, 1989), the authors reported that over 26 percent of children with any kind of psychosocial problem were not scheduled for follow-up visits. Ten years later, 25 percent of children identified with ADHD are not scheduled for follow-up care. This does not suggest improvement.

Preliminary reports from two ongoing studies indicate that children under the age of 5 are more likely to be prescribed stimulant drugs than in the past, despite the lack of evidence for its safety in this age group. Fewer visits of children now include recommendations for follow-up than in 1989, psychotherapy is provided less often, and the likelihood of a child with ADHD having a visit without a psychotropic prescription being made has diminished. Further, the mix of services children receive depends to a large extent pon the type of physician they see. Family practitioners are more likely than pediatricians or psychiatrists to prescribe stimulants and less likely to prescribe anything else. Family practitioners use diagnostic services and provide mental health counseling less often than do other physician types. They are also about half as likely to follow up with these children than are psychiatrists. Children with ADHD are more likely to receive general health counseling if they are seen by pediatricians or family practitioners than psychiatrists.

Although pronounced differences occurred in the types of services provided to children with ADHD based on physician type (i.e., whether the physician was a family practitioner, pediatrician, or psychiatrist), some clinical variables may influence these differences, and these variables could not be controlled for in the analyses. These include whether the physician was in solo practice, the age of the children seen, and the age of the physicians. Other factors that could account for differences in practice patterns include severity or comorbidity of case mix and training or level of expertise with which service decisions are made.

With respect to the question of service need versus service use, it appears that the majority of children with attentional problems are likely to receive either specialty mental health services, medical services, or school services at some point in their childhood. Almost three-fourths of children with ADHD symptoms received mental health services over at least a three-year period in the GSMS Study (Angold et al., 2000), and this was corroborated by the CBS national study.

The picture on whether all children in need of stimulant treatment are receiving this care is uneven. It appears that there may be a time lag as to when stimulants are received versus when they may be needed: Approximately three-fourths of children with diagnosable ADHD are likely to receive stimulants at some point in their childhood, but over a twelve-month period, only one in eight will have received this treatment. Further, there are significant variations in prescriptions of stimulants by race and by sex, with African-American youths and girls being less likely to receive these treatments than Caucasians and boys, respectively. Further, findings from studies of children with ADHD who are receiving publicly funded services, including special education, suggest that levels of unmet need are as high as 50 percent (Bussing, Zima,

Perwien, et al., 1998), and, once again, highest among girls and minorities. Concern about unmet need is also justified on the basis of the high levels of identified attentional problems found among children referred for crisis psychiatric hospitalization (20 percent) (Henggeler et al., 1999) and children in care at public mental health clinics (17 percent) (Garland et al., 2001). These levels of need represent a three-fold increase over community prevalence estimates of 3–6 percent.

The finding about service mix differs from previous assumptions about usual practice, in that on any given day, more than 50 percent of children with attentional problems being seen by primary care clinicians receive either counseling, medications, or both. This finding suggests that guidelines for care, as recommended by Dulcan et al. (1997) for treating children with ADHD perhaps are being met in about 50 percent of the cases seen in typical practice settings. There is no clear picture about what is happening to the other 50 percent. For example, it is not known whether they have already received appropriate diagnostic, assessment, and supportive services or whether they are falling between the cracks.

Continuing Barriers to Care

Significant barriers to services and treatments are reported by families, children, and clinicians. Ninety-four percent of caregivers report at least one and usually multiple significant barriers to care for their children with ADHD. These barriers include lack of information, concerns about costs, and time constraints. Between one-fourth and one-third of children with ADHD identify lack of information, fear of out-of-home placement or loss of parental rights, and distrust of professionals as major impediments to services. Physician-reported barriers, on the other hand, focus on structural and bureaucratic impediments. Approximately two-thirds of physicians cite unavailability of pediatric specialists, long waiting lists for services, and specialists not accepting Medicaid as major barriers to their referrals of children for mental health services. About 45 percent cite complex appeals processes and physician panel restrictions as major barriers. While the clinician-reported barriers were from a different study than the child- and parent-reported barriers, they point to a convergence of identified and, in large measure, correctable obstacles: lack of information, previous negative experiences, cost concerns, absence of appropriate specialists, unavailability of an adequate labor force to reduce waiting lists, and bureaucratic impediments.

Recommendations for Clinical Practice and Policy

This review has uncovered several areas in which clinical practice or policy could be improved:

- *Location of treatment services.* The unevenness of treatment service delivery to children, especially girls and minorities, suggests that delivery of these treatment services should become less stigmatized and more easily accessed. The spreading popularity of school-based health clinics, for example, provides a potentially powerful vehicle for information dissemination and care provision in a neutral setting. In some locations, schools have become the hub of the service network community, connecting caregivers and children to services in ways that promote accessibility. Approaches such as this may be necessary to break down the barriers to care for girls and minorities.

- *Physician training.* Unevenness in types of treatments provided to children with presumably similar treatment needs suggests a lack of uniformity in knowledge about this condition. Residency programs and continuing education training for general practice physicians who are likely to see increasing number of children with this condition are necessary to ensure that knowledge about best practices and the limits of expertise (i.e., when referral is appropriate) is disseminated widely.

- *Specialty training for clinicians.* The lack of availability of specialty trained clinicians was one of the most frequently cited barriers to care. Developmental pediatricians constitute a small fraction of pediatric practices, yet their expertise may be called on with greater frequency as the number of children with attentional problems continues to rise. Incentives to expand the pool of such specialists are needed, and this may require that federal efforts be joined with medical training programs to provide incentives for such specialized training.

- *Information dissemination.* Lack of information for caregivers and children with ADHD was cited as a common barrier. Although at least two professional associations have written guidelines or parameters for practice with these children (AACAP and AAP), and family associations (such as Children and Adults with Attention Deficit/Hyperactivity Disorder, or CHADD, Federation of Families, and NAMI) should be supported in their efforts to disseminate these practice parameters, as well as evidence-based findings, such as the results from the McMaster reviews (McMaster University Evidence-Based Practice Center, 1998). In addition, community-centered information about treatment services should be made routinely available to families and children through schools, pediatric practice offices, and community clinics. However, to be maximally useful, this information will need to be localized to reflect the availability of services within particular locales and should include reference to federally guaranteed education rights and special education-related services.

Recommendations for Future Research

Several major gaps in knowledge about treatments and services can be identified from this review. First, there are no national data and few local studies that examine the usual practices of mental health clinicians other than physicians. Given that mental health services, when they are available, are provided primarily in schools (Burns et al., 1995), and given that new, popular vehicles of service delivery now include home-based services, improvements in matching treatment needs of children to appropriate care will depend, in part, on knowledge of the nature, type, and quality of typical clinical practice. Such studies will provide a baseline against which improvements in care can be gauged.

Second, although it appears that most children with ADHD do receive some form of service at some point, it is not clear whether these services are appropriate or not, or whether they are meeting even minimal standards of quality. One study (Angold et al., 2000) has found that more than twice as many children received stimulants as received a full diagnosis of ADHD. The issue of the appropriate use of stimulants and, even beyond this, the appropriate match between services and specific treatment needs has not been adequately studied in community settings. The movement of treatment efficacy studies into service delivery settings where issues of effectiveness can be investigated is one effort to address this research gap.

Third, the question of identifying and removing barriers to care for families and children warrants study. Lack of information was listed as a major barrier by both caregivers and children, and other identified barriers were either attitudinal (fear, distrust, or negative anticipations) or pragmatic (costs and time-related). However, most of the studies reviewed for this chapter did not even ask about barriers to care, much less attend to their removal. As it is now known that the major predictor of entry into mental health care for children with psychiatric disorders is family burden or impact (Angold et al., 1998), it would follow that studies should target optimal ways of engaging families in the treatment process as a means of identifying and removing barriers. Studies that investigate the effects of cultural mistrust on either access or barriers to care for this population are nonexistent, although mistrust is associated with failure to seek psychological help among black college students (Nickerson, Helms, & Terrell, 1994). Much more research is needed in this area if elimination of barriers is to occur equitably. In addition, it is not known how racial identity or acculturation affect attitudes toward mental health services or influence help-seeking patterns, but this kind of knowledge is essential to improving service delivery.

Finally, unevenness in the kinds of services received by children who are seen by different providers leads to a series of policy-relevant research questions. Why are children receiving a different mix of services? What factors predict variation in quality of services provided to children and families? How can service organizations be structured to promote an optimal match between treatment needs and appropriate care? Are reported differences in service mix a result of differences in severity of attentional disorders, in their comorbidity with other disorders, in training of the providers, or in less innocent factors, such as race, sex, or geographic variations? How can better links be made between major providers of services, especially the schools and primary care physicians? Research on issues of service quality and appropriateness will be a high priority for the next generation of studies on treatment services for children with ADHD.

References

Angold, A., Erkanli, A., Egger, H. L., & Costello, E. J. (2000). Stimulant treatment for children: A community perspective. *Journal of the American Academy of Child and Adolescent Psychiatry, 39*(8), 975–984.

Angold, A., Messer, S. C., Stangl, D., Farmer, E. M. Z., Costello, E. J., & Burns, B. J. (1998). Perceived parental burden and service use for child and adolescent psychiatric disorders. *American Journal of Public Health, 88*, 75–80.

Ascher, B. A., Farmer, E. M. Z., Burns, B. J., & Angold, A. (1998). The Child and Adolescent Services Assessment (CASA): Description and psychometric. *Journal of Emotional and Behavioral Disorders, 4*, 12–20.

Burns, B. J., Costello, E. J., Angold, A., Tweed, D., Stangle, D., & Farmer, E. M. Z. (1995). Children's mental health service use across service sectors. *Health Affairs, 124*, 147–159.

Bussing, R., Zima, B. T., & Belin, T. R. (1998). Differential access to care for children with ADHD in special education programs. *Psychiatric Services, 49*(9), 1226–1229.

Bussing, R., Zima, B. T., Perwien, A. R., Belin, T. R., & Widawski, M. (1998). Children in special education programs: Attention deficit hyperactivity disorder, use of services, and unmet needs. *American Journal of Public Health, 88*, 880–886.

Costello, E. J., Angold, A., Burns, B. J., Erkanli, A., Stangl, D. K., & Tweed, D. L. (1996). The Great Smoky Mountains Study of Youth: Functional impairment and serious emotional disturbance. *Archives of General Psychiatry, 53*, 1137–1143.

Costello, E. J., Angold, A., Burns, B. J., Stangl, D. K., Tweed, D. L., Erkanli, A., & Worthman, C. M. (1996). The Great Smoky Mountains Study of Youth: Goals, design, methods, and the prevalence of DSM-III-R disorders. *Archives of General Psychiatry, 53*(12), 1129–1136.

Dulcan, M., Dunne, J. E., Ayres, W., Arnold, V., Benson, R. S., Bernet, W., Bukstein, O., Kinlan, J., Leonard, H., Licamele, W., & McClellan, J. (1997). Practice parameters for the assessment and treatment of children, adolescents, and adults with attention-deficit hyperactivity disorder. *Journal of the American Academy of Child and Adolescent Psychiatry, 36*, 85S–121S.

Farmer, E. M. Z., Angold, A., Burns, B. J., & Costello, E. J. (1994). Reliability of self-reported service use: Test-retest consistency of children's responses to the Child and Adolescent Services Assessment (CASA). *Journal of Child and Family Studies, 3*, 307–325.

Garland, A. F., Hough, R. L., McCabe, K. M., Yeh, M., Wood, P. A., & Aarons, G. A. (2001). Prevalences of psychiatric disorders in youths across five sectors of care. *Journal of the American Academy of Child and Adolescent Psychiatry, 40*, 409–418.

Gardner, W., Kelleher, K. J., Wasserman, R., Childs, G., Nutting, P., Lillienfield, H., & Pajer, K. (2000). Primary care treatment of pediatric psychosocial problems: A study from pediatric research in office settings and ambulatory sentinel practice network. *Pediatrics, 106*(4), E44.

Green, L. A., Wood, M., Becker, L., Farley, E. S., Freeman, W. L., Froom, J., Hames, C., Niebauer, L. J., Rosser, W. W., & Seifert, M. (1984). The Ambulatory Sentinel Practice Network: Purpose, methods, and policies. *Journal of Family Practice, 18*, 275–280.

Greenhill, L. (1998). Childhood attention deficit hyperactivity disorder: Pharmacological treatments. In P. E. Nathan & J. M. Gorman (Eds.), *A guide to treatments that work* (pp. 42–64). New York: Oxford University Press.

Henggeler, S. W., Rowland, M. D., Randall, J., Ward, D. M., Pickerel, S., Cunningham, P. B., Miller, S. L., Edwards, J., Zealberg, J. J., Hand, L. D., & Santos, A. B. (1999). Home-based multisystemic therapy as an alternative to the hospitalization of youths in psychiatric crisis: Clinical outcomes. *Journal of the American Academy of Child and Adolescent Psychiatry, 38*(11), 1331–1339.

Jensen, P. S., Bhatara, V. S., Vitiello, B., Hoagwood, K., Feil, M., & Burke, L. B. (1999). Psychoactive medication prescribing practices for US children: Gaps between research and clinical practice. *Journal of the American Academy of Child and Adolescent Psychiatry, 38*, 557–565.

Jensen, P. S., Kettle, L., Roper, M., Sloan, M., Dulcan, M., Hoven, C., & Bauermeister, J. (1999). Are stimulants overprescribed? Treatment of ADHD in 4 US communities. *Journal of the American Academy of Child and Adolescent Psychiatry, 38*(7), 797–804.

Kelleher, K. J., Childs, G. E., Wasserman, R. C., McInerny, T. K., Nutting, P. A., & Gardner, W. P. (1997). Insurance status and recognition of psychosocial problems: A report from the Pediatric Research in Office Settings and the Ambulatory Sentinel Practice Networks. *Archives of Pediatrics and Adolescent Medicine, 151*, 1109–1115.

Kelleher, K. J., McInerny, T., Gardner, W., Childs, G., Wasserman, R., & Nutting, P. (2000). Increasing identification of psychosocial problems: 1979–1997. *Pediatrics, 105*, 1313–1321.

Kelleher, K. J., Hohmann, A. A., & Larson, D. B. (1989). Prescription of psychotropics to children in office-based practice. *American Journal of Diseases of Children, 143*, 855–859.

Kessler, R. C., McGonagle, K. A., Zhao, S., Nelson, C. B., Hughes, M., Eshleman, S., Wittchen, H. U., & Kendler, K. S. (1994). Lifetime and 12-month prevalence of DSM-III-R psychiatric disorders in the United States: Results from the National Comorbidity Study. *Archives of General Psychiatry, 51*, 8–19.

Lahey, B. B., Flagg, E. W., Bird, H. R., Schwab-Stone, M. E., Canino, G., Dulcan, M. K., Leaf, P. J., Davies, M., Brogan, D., Bourdon, K., Horwitz, S. M., Rubio-Stipec, M., Freeman, D. H., Lichtman, J. H., Shaffer, D., Goodman, S. H., Narrow, W. E., Weissman, M. M., Kandel, D. B., Jensen, P. S., Richters, J. E., & Regier, D. A. (1996). The NIMH methods for the epidemiology of child and adolescent mental disorders (MECA) study: Background and methodology. *Journal of the American Academy of Child and Adolescent Psychiatry, 35*, 855–864.

Lavange, L. M., Stearns, S. C., Lafata, J. E., Koch, G. G., & Shah, B. V. (1996). Innovative strategies using SUDAAN for analysis of health surveys with complex samples. *Statistical Methods in Medical Research, 5*, 311–329.

Leaf, P. J., Alegria, M., Cohen, P., Goodman, S. H., Horwitz, S. M., Hoven, C. W., Narrow, W. E., Vaden-Kiernan, M., & Regier, D. A. (1996). Mental health service use in the community and schools: Results from the four-community MECA study. *Journal of the American Academy of Child and Adolescent Psychiatry, 35*, 889–897.

McMaster University Evidence-Based Practice Center. (1998). *The treatment of attention-deficit/hyperactivity disorder: An evidence report* (Contract No. 290–97–0017). Rockville, MD: Agency for Health Care Policy and Research.

National Ambulatory Medical Care Survey. (1994). Summary. National Center for Health Statistics. *Vital Health Statistics 13*, 116.

Nickerson, K. J., Helms, J. E., & Terrell, F. (1994). Cultural mistrust and black students' attitudes toward seeking psychological help from white counselors. *Journal of Counseling Psychology, 41*, 378–385.

Offord, D. R., Boyle, M. H., Szatmari, P., Rae-Grant, N. I., Links, P. S., Cadman, D. T., Byles, J. A., Crawford, J. W., Blum, H. M., Byrne, C., Thomas, H,, & Woodward, C. A. (1987). Ontario child health study. II: Six-month prevalence of disorders and rates of service utilization. *Archives of General Psychiatry, 44*, 832–836.

Rappley, M. D., Gardiner, J. C., Jetton, J. R., & Houang, R. T. (1995). The use of methylphenidate in Michigan. *Archives of Pediatric and Adolescent Medicine, 149*, 675–679.

Safer, D. J. (1997). Changing patterns of psychotropic medication prescribed by child psychiatrists in the 1990's. *Journal of Child and Adolescent Psychopharmacology, 7*, 267–274.

Safer, D. J., & Krager, J. M. (1985). Prevalence of medication treatment for hyperactive adolescents. *Psychopharmacology Bulletin, 21*, 212–215.

Safer, D. J., & Krager, J. M. (1988). A survey of medication treatment for hyperactive/inattentive students. *Journal of the American Medical Association, 260*, 2256–2258.

Safer, D. J., & Krager, J. M. (1994). The increased rate of stimulant treatment for hyperactive/inattentive students in secondary schools. *Pediatrics, 94*, 462–464.

Safer, D. J., Zito, J. M., & Fine, E. M. (1996). Increased methylphenidate usage for attention deficit disorder in the 1990's. *Pediatrics, 98*, 1084–1088.

Sherman, M., & Hertzig, M. E. (1991). Prescribing practices of Ritalin: The Suffolk County, New York study. In L. L. Greenhill & B. B. Osman (Eds.), *Ritalin: Theory and patient management* (pp. 187–193). New York: Mary Ann Liebert.

Sloan, M. T., Jensen, P. S., Hoagwood, K., & Kettle, L. (1999). Assessing the services for children with ADHD: Gaps and opportunities. *Journal of Attention Disorders, 3*, 13–29.

Spencer, T., Biederman, J., Wilens. T., Harding, M., O'Donnell, D., & Griffin, S. (1996). Pharmacotherapy of attention-deficit hyperactivity disorder across the life cycle. *Journal of the American Academy of Child and Adolescent Psychiatry, 35*, 409–432.

Stiffman, A. R., Horwitz, S. M., Hoagwood, K., Compton, W., Cottler, L., Bean, D. L., Narrow, W. E., & Weisz, J. R. (2000). The service assessment for children and adolescents (SACA): Child and adult reports. *Journal of the American Academy of Child and Adolescent Psychiatry, 39*(8), 1032–1039.

Stiffman, A. R., Chen, Y. W., Elze, D., Dore, P., & Cheng, L. C. (1997). Adolescents' and providers' perspectives on the need for and use of mental health services. *Journal of Adolescent Health, 21*, 335–342.

Szatmari, P., Offord, D. R., & Boyle, M. H .(1989). Correlates, associated impairments, and patterns of services utilization of children with attention deficit disorder: Findings from the Ontario Child Health Study. *Journal of Child Psychology and Psychiatry, 30*, 205–217.

Wasserman, R. C., Kelleher, K. J., Bocian, A., Baker, A., Childs, G. E., Indacochea, F., Stulp, C., & Gardner, W. P. (1999). Identification of attentional and hyperactivity problems in primary care: A report from pediatric research in office settings and the ambulatory sentinel practice network. *Pediatrics, 103*, E38.

Wasserman, R., Slora, E. J., Bocian, A. B., Fleming, G. V., & Kessel, W. (1998). Pediatric research in office settings (PROS): I. A national practice-based research network to improve children's health care. *Pediatrics, 102*(6), 1350–1357.

Wolraich, M. L., Hannah, J. N., Pinnock, T. Y., Baumgaertel, A., & Brosn, J. (1996). Comparison of diagnostic criteria for attention-deficit Hyperactivity Disorder in a county-wide sample. *Journal of the American Academy of Child and Adolescent Psychiatry, 35*, 319–324.

World Health Organization. (1978). *International classification of diseases* (9th rev.). Geneva, Switzerland: Author.

Zahner, G. E. P., Pawel-Kiewicz, W., DeFrancesco, J., & Adnopoz, J. (1992). Children's mental health service needs and utilization patterns in an urban community: An epidemiological assessment. *Journal of the American Academy of Child and Adolescent Psychiatry, 31*, 951–960.

Zito, J. M., dosReis, S., Safer, D. J., & Bardner, J. (1998, June 11). *Trends in psychotropic prescriptions for youths with Medicaid insurance from a Midwestern state: 1987–1995.* Paper presented at the NIMH New Clinical Drug Evaluation Unit Meeting, Boca Raton, FL.

Zito, J. M., Safer, D. J., dosReis, S., & Riddle, M. A. (1998). Racial disparity in psychotropic medications prescribed for youths with Medicaid insurance in Maryland. *Journal of the American Academy of Child and Adolescent Psychiatry, 37*, 179–184.

Zito, J. M., Safer, D. J., dosReis, S., Magder, L. S., & Riddle, M. A. (1997). Methylphenidate patterns among Medicaid youths. *Psychopharmacology Bulletin, 30*, 143–147.

Zito, J. M., Safer, D. J., dosReis, S., Gardner, J. F., Boles, M., & Lynch, F. (2000). Trends in the prescribing of psychotropic medications to preschoolers. *Journal of the American Medical Association, 283*, 1025–1030.

Zito, J. M., Safer, D. J., Riddle M, Speedie, S., dosReis, S. (1996). Racial, geographic and gender differences in methylphenidate use among Medicaid youths. *Pharmacoepidemiology and Drug Safety, 5*, S1–S119.

Exhibit 22.1
Sample Size, Point Estimate, and Confidence Intervals for Trends, 1989–1996 NAMCS

Year/Type of Service	Sample Size	%	Point Estimate*	Confidence Interval*
1989				
Med. management				
Stimulant	44	54.8	628	495–762
Other psychotropic drugs	10	15.3	176	53–298
Other drugs	4	6.5	75	3–148
No drugs	16	23.4	268	123–414
Diagnostic services	19	22.3	256	140–370
Mental health counseling	19	24.3	279	165–392
Other counseling	1	3.5	40	—
Psychotherapy	36	40.1	460	348–572
Spec. follow-up	65	91.0	1044	835–1252
1991				
Med. management				
Stimulant	53	77.8	889	720–1057
Other psychotropic drugs	2	3.5	40	0–100
Other ther drugs	2	2.5	29	0–72
No drugs	17	16.2	184	82–287
Diagnostic services	51	76.6	906	
Mental health counseling	39	59.4	702	
Other counseling	30	29.7	351	
Psychotherapy	23	38.3	452	372–532
Spec. follow-up	62	84.5	999	857–1142

Year/Type of Service	Sample Size	%	Point Estimate*	Confidence Interval*
1993				
Med. management				
Stimulant	128	76.3	2249	1918–2579
Other psychotropic drugs	10	5.6	166	0–346
Other drugs	6	2.6	76	19–133
No drugs	41	15.5	457	263–651
Diagnostic services	106	43.1	1294	1027–1561
Mental health counseling	68	34.3	1029	721–1337
Other counseling	77	45.3	1361	1242–1480
Psychotherapy	16	5.6	169	100–237
Spec. follow-up	137	75.5	2266	1932–2599
1995				
Med. management				
Stimulant	114	74.8	1795	1474–2117
Other psychotropic drugs	13	4.0	96	33–160
Other drugs	14	6.3	150	38–262
No drugs	20	14.9	357	172–543
Diagnostic services	85	60.6	1455	1153–1757
Mental health counseling	63	44.2	1059	737–1382
Other counseling	27	29.9	716	451–981
Psychotherapy	49	21.3	511	343–678
Spec. follow-up	144	83.4	2001	1668–2335
1996				
Med.management				
Stimulant	91	75.4	2240	1929–2551
Other psychotropic drugs	15	7.5	224	92–355
Other drugs	2	4.3	128	0–309
No drugs	23	12.8	380	196–565
Diagnostic services	94	62.1	1844	1566–2133
Mental health counseling	61	39.3	1117	848–1485
Other counseling	32	35.2	1045	675–1415
Psychotherapy	42	25.2	747	557–937
Spec. follow-up	109	75.1	2232	1918–2546

*in thousands.

Part 5

Existing Practices and Policies Regarding Assessment and Treatment of ADHD

All the research outlined in the previous sections would have little value unless these findings were applied in "real world" settings. So, what treatments are actually being provided to children with attention deficit hyperactivity disorder (ADHD)? What services are available to them, and what factors might prevent their obtaining an accurate assessment and the best possible treatment? Are current practices in primary and specialty care settings the best that can be offered? How are our schools dealing with the increasing demands for assessment and treatment of ADHD?

This section takes on several thorny issues. The chapters in this section address issues related to possible over- and underdiagnosis of ADHD, as well as the widely varying, inconsistent, and sometimes poor-quality assessment, treatment, and follow-up practices in the real world (see Hoagwood, Chapter 22, and Wolraich, Chapter 23). Available services vary widely from community to community, and access to care differs not just by geographic region but also by socioeconomic and ethnic parameters. The impact of ADHD on schools and other settings (i.e., juvenile justice) is irrefutable and profound, as discussed in Chapters 24, 25, and 26 by Forness, Chemers, and Danielson, respectively. The further fragmentation and lack of care, and almost total absence of *coordination of care* among the various systems (e.g., educational and medical) for ADHD children, are not just astonishing but devastating, in terms of their impact on children's and families' lives. And if these problems were not enough, as described in Chapter 27 by Kelleher, families experience great difficulties obtaining reimbursement and insurance support for ADHD treatments and services, and available financial resources are not commensurate with other common pediatric illnesses.

—P.S. Jensen
—J.R. Cooper

Chapter 23

Current Assessment and Treatment Practices in ADHD

by Mark L. Wolraich, M.D.

Introduction 23-1
History of ADHD 23-2
    Evolving Medical Interest 23-2
    Educational Interest 23-2
    Treatment Diversity and Controversy 23-3
Role of Primary Care Physicians vs. Mental Health Clinicians 23-3
Diagnosis 23-4
    Importance of Multidisciplinary Communication 23-4
    Spectrum of Behavioral Symptoms 23-4
    School and Primary Care Process in Terms of Diagnosis
       and Treatment 23-5
    Presence and Diagnosis of Comorbidity With Other Cognitive
       and Behavioral Disorders 23-6
Treatment 23-7
    Use of Stimulants and Other Psychotropic Medications 23-7
    School System Concerns Regarding Treatment 23-7
    School's Role in Use of Nondrug Therapies 23-8
    Physician Follow-up and Assessment of Treatment 23-8
    Need for Systematic Methods to Provide Comprehensive Services 23-9
Summary 23-10

INTRODUCTION

Although the diagnosis of attention deficit hyperactivity disorder (ADHD) seems to be a new condition, particularly because of its recent identification as a disorder affecting adults, ADHD actually has a long history and has been of interest to a number of professional groups. Despite more extensive research than any other mental disorder in children, the diversity of interest has contributed to the continued controversy, especially over diagnosis and appropriate treatment. Services for children with ADHD span the general medical, mental health, and educational sectors of a community and include both constitutional and environmental issues. This chapter traces the history of the condition, the aspects of its diagnosis and treatment that are some of the sources of its controversy, the important role played by primary care physicians and their ability to play that role, and the importance of communication in the provision of services.

HISTORY OF ADHD

Evolving Medical Interest

The history of ADHD helps to explain the interest in the disorder of a number of medical and behavioral disciplines and the controversy among them. In the mid-nineteenth century, Heinrich Hoffman (1848), a German physician, in his children's book, described the characteristics of ADHD, which were represented by two of his characters—Fidgety Phil and Harry Who Looks in the Air. In 1902, at a meeting of the Royal College of Physicians, George Still (1902) described a disease he characterized as resulting from a defect in moral character. He noted that the problem resulted in a child's inability to internalize rules and limits and, additionally, manifested itself in patterns of restless, inattentive, and overaroused behaviors. He suggested that the children had likely experienced brain damage but that the behavior could also arise from hereditary and environmental factors.

The connection to brain damage increased the interest of both neurology and pediatrics especially in 1917–1918 following a worldwide epidemic of influenza with encephalitis that in some recovering children resulted in symptoms of restlessness, inattention, impulsivity, easy arousability, and hyperactivity (Hochman, 1922). When many cases were seen with similar behavioral manifestations but no clear evidence of brain damage, the name of the disorder was changed to minimal cerebral/brain dysfunction/damage (Clements, 1966).

Psychiatry and psychology also became involved with ADHD. Their interest focused on the behavioral manifestations, and because it was frequently difficult to demonstrate clear evidence of brain damage, the name of the disorder as listed in the psychiatric classification system, *Diagnostic and Statistical Manual of Mental Disorders* (DSM), was again changed to be more behaviorally descriptive, switching from hyperkinetic impulse disorder in DSM-II (American Psychiatric Association, 1967) to attention deficit disorder in DSM-III (American Psychiatric Association, 1980) and, more recently, to attention deficit hyperactivity disorder in DSM-IIIR (American Psychiatric Association, 1987) and DSM-IV (American Psychiatric Association, 1994). In addition to shifting the focus to inattention as the primary deficit, psychiatry, in 1937, also brought attention to the benefits of stimulant medication (Bradley, 1937).

Educational Interest

Educational interest began in the 1940s and 1950s, when some educators focused on the cognitive and academic components of the disorder, and developed and studied educational interventions in children. Many of the children they considered brain-injured (Strauss & Lethinen, 1947) had the characteristics of ADHD or learning disabilities.

Treatment Diversity and Controversy

The broad range of professional interest in this condition has brought a wealth of research published in a great number of journals so that it is impossible for any one clinician to remain current on all its aspects. The varied interest also resulted in disagreements and controversy over concerns such as the appropriate use of stimulant medication (Diller, 1996). With such a broad array of professionals involved in the diagnosis and treatment of this condition, it could be contended that communication among professionals across disciplines is a critical and yet inadequately addressed part of the process of diagnosing and treating children.

Currently in the health care system, three medical disciplines continue to have a primary interest in ADHD: pediatrics, psychiatry, and neurology. Which clinicians treat these children depends on parental preference, the severity and nature of the disorder (in part as reflected by the extent of comorbid conditions), and a community's practices and referral patterns. Historically, pediatricians have played a significant role in the condition since the time the condition was called minimal cerebral/brain dysfunction/damage or hyperactive child syndrome (Laufer & Denhoff, 1957). In recent years, studies of stimulant medication prescriptions substantiate that the majority of treatment with stimulant medication still takes place in primary care with primary care pediatricians in particular providing the majority of the prescriptions (Rappley, Gardiner, Jetton, & Houang, 1995; Ruel & Hickey, 1992; Sherman & Hertzig, 1991).

ROLE OF PRIMARY CARE PHYSICIANS VS. MENTAL HEALTH CLINICIANS

Pediatric participation in the care of children with this disorder stems, in part, from the historical perception of ADHD as a "biological" rather than "emotional" condition, but more probably because of the high prevalence rates of this condition ranging from 1 percent to 14 percent (Szatmari, Offord, & Boyle, 1989), although usually quoted as 3–5 percent (American Psychiatric Association, 1994). There are simply not a sufficient number of mental health clinicians to provide the necessary care. This is not likely to change in the future, and, in fact, the prevalence of children with ADHD may even increase further with the recent changes in diagnostic criteria. Within the same samples, the prevalence rates of ADHD increased from 2.6 percent for DSM-III to 6.1 percent for DSM-III-R (Lindgren et al., 1990), and from 9.6 percent to 17.8 percent (Baumgaertel, Wolraich, & Dietrich, 1995) and 7.2 percent to 11.4 percent (Wolraich et al., 1996) from DSM-III-R to DSM-IV (caution must be exercised regarding the last two studies because the new criteria require a degree of pervasiveness and impairment not determined in those studies). With such high prevalence rates, limited numbers of child psychiatrists, and more restrictions placed on mental health services in managed care, the treatment of children with ADHD will continue to require significant participation by primary care physicians. The children seen in primary care compared to psychiatry appear to be younger, to be more learning disabled, and to have fewer other comorbidities (Wolraich et al., 1990; Zarin, Suarez, Pincus, Kupersanin, & Zito, 1998).

Another reason that a pediatrician will likely be the initial contact made by a family is the negative societal attitude toward mental illness. Society continues to perceive a mind-body duality even though scientific evidence has significantly blurred the distinction. The managed care system continues to perpetuate this distinction through the development of behavioral health carve-outs, pushing more children into the management of primary care physicians by limiting access to mental health services. Further, for some parents, seeking psychiatric help for their children is equivalent to an admission of poor parenting. These parents may find it easier to consider ADHD as a neurological condition—and therefore not caused by their inadequate abilities—and on this basis, usually seek help from their pediatrician or a child neurologist.

As the most frequent initial medical contact for families of children with ADHD, it is important to consider the abilities and training of primary care physicians in their diagnosis and treatment of these children. It is also important to view their activities in the overall context, particularly the communication between physicians and educators.

DIAGNOSIS

Importance of Multidisciplinary Communication

The diagnostic process highlights the importance of multidisciplinary communication. Despite its characterization as a neurological condition, and despite the clear familial pattern found in many of the families of children with this condition, the diagnosis remains dependent on the observation of abnormal behaviors (Baumgaertel & Wolraich, 1998). There are no pathognomonic measures to diagnose children with this disorder despite attempts such as continuous performance tests (Corkum & Siegel, 1993) or neuroimaging (Zametkin et al., 1990) to objectively measure parameters of central nervous system functioning. The diagnosis remains dependent on the observations of those adults most familiar with the children because, as an externalizing condition, their observations are more valid than the reports of the children themselves (Jensen et al., 1999, Lahey et al., 1987). The behaviors observed are also contextually dependent. The greater the need for concentration and the less interesting the stimulus, the harder it is to concentrate. As such, many of the behaviors manifest themselves more readily in the concentration-demanding situation of school, making teacher observation a major consideration in the diagnosis. This makes the communication between physicians and teachers, although difficult, vital to the diagnosis and treatment of children with ADHD.

Spectrum of Behavioral Symptoms

An added consideration in the diagnostic process is that the behaviors rated by parents or teachers appear to follow a normal distribution pattern rather than a distinct bimodal pattern. Behavior rating scales have addressed this issue by defining psychometric criteria, 1.5 or 2 standard deviations (Achenbach & Edelbrock, 1983; Ullman, Sleator, & Sprague, 1984). The children who display marked behavioral symptoms are easily diagnosed without difficulty, but it becomes more difficult to define clear boundaries for where normality ends and disorder begins. This has been more problematic to primary care clinicians and teachers than to psychiatrists and neurologists, who, as specialists, see referral patients who, by the nature of the referral process are already screened toward the more severe end of the spectrum.

There has been an attempt to better characterize the spectrum by the development of the DSM-Primary Care Child and Adolescent Version where categories of normal developmental variations and problems have been defined in addition to the mental disorders (Wolraich, 1996). However, more research is required to better define and determine the significance of problem-level inattention or hyperactivity-impulsivity symptoms.

School and Primary Care Process in Terms of Diagnosis and Treatment

Because, as stated earlier, the majority of children with ADHD are diagnosed and treated by their primary care clinicians, and the children's behaviors and the impact of their treatments are best observed in the school setting, it is important to examine the school and primary care process in terms of both diagnosis and treatment.

As stated previously, the diagnosis of ADHD currently requires reports of specific behaviors by those individuals who have the most contact with the children—most often their parents and teachers. Although direct observation, particularly in the child's natural setting, can provide additional objective information, it is costly and limited to a small sample of time. In the case of physician observation, observations usually occur in settings that do not necessarily correlate with home or school behaviors (Sleator & Ullman, 1981).

Although school is the most likely setting for ADHD symptoms to manifest themselves, information from parents rather than teachers remains the most commonly used source of information for both primary care physicians and psychiatrists. Teachers report that they have little contact with physicians. One past study reported that teacher-physician contact only occurred in 18 percent of the cases (Weithorn & Ross, 1975), and a more recent study reported that only 14 percent of the teachers had been consulted in the diagnosis and ongoing monitoring of medication by outside professionals (Jerome, Gordon, & Hustler, 1994). By physician report, teacher or school reports are used by almost all primary care physicians and three-quarters of psychiatrists (Kwasman, Tinsley, & Lepper, 1995; Wolraich et al., 1990; Zarin et al., 1998); standardized teacher rating scales are used by 53 percent of family practitioners, 64 percent of psychiatrists, and 74 percent of pediatricians (Wolraich et al., 1990; Zarin et al., 1998); and reports of psychoeducational testing are obtained by half to more than three quarters of the physicians. Another survey exclusively of family practitioners found only 29 percent reporting that they used teacher questionnaires (Moser & Kallail, 1995). A study using parent reports (Hazall, McDowell, & Walton, 1996) revealed similar results with 70 percent reporting that their physicians requested information from school, but only 47 percent reporting that teacher questionnaires were utilized. However, a recent audit of two general military hospital clinics found that only 23.5 percent had school reports of the children's behaviors documented in their charts (Jensen, Xenakis, Shervette, Bain, & Davis, 1989).

Obtaining information from teachers is further complicated by the fact that frequently there are discrepancies between parent and teacher reports (Fergusson & Horwood, 1993; Sandberg, Weiselberg, & Shaffer, 1980). Teacher observations however, demonstrate both reasonable interrater reliability (Danforth & DuPaul, 1996) and agreement with direct observations. Employing previous DSM diagnostic criteria (American Psychiatric Association, 1980 & 1987), their observations could be used as a single source in making the diagnosis, because the diagnostic criteria only required the presence of symptoms in one setting. With the most recent revision in DSM-IV (American Psychiatric Association, 1994), the behaviors must be present in more than one setting. Therefore further clarification is required to help clinicians decide how to appropriately consider discrepant reports between parents and teachers.

Currently clinicians appear to be more influenced by parent reports of behavior. One study (Wolraich et al., 1990) found physician agreement to be 70 percent with parents but no more than 50 percent with teachers. A second study found agreement to be 65 percent for inattention and 79 percent for hyperactivity/impulsivity with parents and 60 percent and 70 percent, respectively, with teachers. This translated into a kappa for parents of 0.26 for inattention and 0.58 for hyperactivity-impulsivity and for teachers of 0.16 and 0.38, respectively (Donnelly, Wolraich, Feurer, & Baumgaertel, 1998).

Presence and Diagnosis of Comorbidity With Other Cognitive and Behavioral Disorders

A second important issue in the diagnosis of ADHD is that the majority of the children with this condition will have significant comorbidity with other cognitive and behavioral disorders. These disorders include the externalizing conditions of oppositional defiant disorder (ODD) and conduct disorder (CD), the internalizing conditions of anxiety and depressive disorders, the cognitive deficits of language and learning disabilities, and other less common disorders such as Tourette's syndrome. The appropriate evaluation needs to consider these conditions. Thus, it is important to examine how well primary care physicians identify comorbidity. Previous studies (Costello et al., 1988; Lindgren et al., 1989) have found that primary care physicians underdiagnose conditions such as CD or ODD which are frequently comorbid with ADHD (Biederman, Newcorn, & Sprich, 1991). Using rigorous identification methods, Costello et al. (1988) found that primary care physicians were reasonably specific (0.84) but not very sensitive (0.17) to mental disorders in children.

A number of factors contribute to these findings. Primary care physicians receive relatively little training about mental disorders in children. A review of the pediatric curriculum in 1978 (American Academy of Pediatrics Task Force on Pediatric Education, 1978) reported that many residency training programs offered minimal or no training in the psychosocial aspects of pediatrics. Since then most programs have increased developmental/behavioral pediatric content in their curricula, but in most, it is limited to one month unless the residents themselves elect to pursue the area further training during their elective time. The more recent requirements now include the equivalent of two months. However, mental disorders are not necessarily a focus of the developmental-behavioral training that has a preventive prospective.

In addition to inadequate training, primary care clinicians rarely have sufficient practice time to address psychosocial problems. The average primary care visit is thirteen minutes (Bryant & Shimizu, 1988). In that time, it is difficult, if not impossible, to adequately explore the issues pertinent to psychosocial concerns.

Consequently, primary care clinicians must deal in too short a time with issues with which they have relatively little training. Methods to improve efficiency also have limitations. An analysis of the studies examining the ability of broad-band rating scales such as the Child Behavior Checklist to identify children with mental disorders found their ability to discriminate limited (McMaster University Evidence-Based Practice Center, 1999). There is a need for primary care clinicians to have more time and better training in identifying comorbidity as part of the evaluation of children for ADHD.

TREATMENT

Use of Stimulants and Other Psychotropic Medications

The major role that primary care physicians play in the treatment of children with ADHD has been in prescribing stimulant medications (Kwasman et al., 1995; Wolraich et al., 1990). Stimulant medication, and methylphenidate in particular, remains the most frequently prescribed and most efficacious treatment for children with ADHD ((Greenhill, 1995; Swanson, 1993). Primary care physicians rarely prescribe other psychotropic medications, although, with the pressures from managed care to have more limited access to child psychiatrists, primary care pediatricians report anecdotally of beginning to use a broader array of psychotropic medications. Psychiatrists also report using primarily stimulant medications, although they frequently use other psychotropic medications, particularly antidepressant and alpha-adrenergic agonists (Zarin et al., 1998).

Despite the known efficacy of stimulant medications, their use remains controversial (Diller, 1996). Because the main concern is that too many children are being medicated, the real issue relates back to the previous discussion of diagnostic practices, namely, who gets treated. This is more of an issue in primary care because, as stated previously, children evaluated in psychiatry have already been somewhat selected by the referral process and, therefore, are likely to be significantly impaired. Although all clinicians need to take into consideration the impact of the child's school and home environment, primary care physicians, caring for the less severe end of the spectrum, have a greater need to determine whether a child's environment has caused his or her dysfunction. Particularly with children who are academically impaired, it is important to determine to what extent inadequate school programming, teacher-student mismatch, or learning/language impairments may be the cause of the behaviors.

School System Concerns Regarding Treatment

Because the major effect of stimulant medication is to improve the behavior and function of children in school, the decisions about the diagnosis and the determination of the effects of stimulant medications for a given child, again, depend on physician-teacher communication. Unless there is direct communication between teachers and physicians, the clinician must depend on secondhand and, therefore, less accurate information when deciding about the effects of treatment. As with the diagnostic process, the situation is particularly difficult when there are discrepancies between parents' and teachers' assessments of the effect of medication.

School systems also have their own concerns and procedures regarding the treatment of children with ADHD. Under the Individuals with Disabilities Education Act (IDEA, 1990) and Section 504 of the Rehabilitation Act of 1973, school systems must provide adaptations in the classroom and special education services if needed for children with ADHD. This means that they also must determine a child's diagnosis, make modifications in the classroom, and, often, develop individual education plans after psychoeducational assessments. If a physician prescribes medication, the schools need to monitor the effects and frequently are required to administer daytime doses. The full extent of services a child receives from both the health and educational community is not always clear because most studies do not include the detailed contributions from both systems. This is particularly true for the majority of the children who are managed by primary care clinicians. Little is known about the extent of the treatments and outcomes for these children.

School's Role in Use of Nondrug Therapies

Although other therapies for treating ADHD exist, primary care physicians use few of them. Even though primary care physicians reported using behavior modification, parents from a sample of their patient lists of children with ADHD did not report receiving the intervention (Wolraich et al., 1990). In addition, two clinics found school intervention plans documented in only 16 percent of the records they audited (Hazall et al., 1996). This does not mean that school interventions were not provided, however, as the audit findings could reflect a lack of communication instead of the absence of interventions.

Schools play an important role in providing interventions other than medications. School systems must provide services that frequently include classroom adaptations and classroom behavioral programs. Social skills training, a frequent deficit in children with ADHD, lends itself best to school-based intervention because it is most effectively provided in group settings where children will better generalize the training. The lack of communication between physicians and teachers limits the coordination of interventions and the determination that the interventions are meeting the comprehensive needs of children with ADHD and their families.

Much of the treatment and the observations of the children's behaviors take place in their regular class. Of significance is the concern that regular teachers have negative attitudes toward children with behavioral problems (Algozzine, 1980; Coleman & Gilliam, 1983). A recent survey (Jerome et al., 1994) of teachers found that they had little in-service training about ADHD, but did consider it a valid diagnosis and were knowledgeable about its etiology and its educational implications. However, they were less accurate in their understanding of treatment.

Physician Follow-up and Assessment of Treatment

Relatively few primary care physicians use any systematic method to obtain information about the effect of the stimulant medications that they prescribe. Given the fact that less than half of the primary care physicians use teacher behavior rating scales (Wolraich et al., 1990), it is reasonable to assume that most do not use the scales to receive feedback about medication effects. Also of concern is the frequency with which primary care physicians monitor children. One audit (Jensen et al., 1989) of two military service clinics found follow-up visits at least every four months in 70 percent of the charts they audited. A second study in Southwestern Pennsylvania found only 40 percent who had follow-up visits in at least six months (William Gardner personal communication).

Despite the problem with communication and follow-up, preliminary data so far suggest that although there may be inappropriate use of stimulant medication, there is not necessarily overuse. In surveying all the elementary school-age children in a suburban Tennessee county, it was found that among those meeting the criteria for ADHD combined type, only about one-third were reported by teachers to have been diagnosed, and only one-quarter had been treated with medication (Wolraich, Hannah, Pinnock, Baumgartel, & Brown, 1996; Wolraich, Hannah, Baumgartel, Pinnock, & Feurer, 1998). An analysis of Tenncare data for 1996–1997 found a stimulant medication use rate of 2.4 percent (Phillippi, 1998) and a study of a group of Iowa primary care physicians found a rate of 5 percent (Wolraich et al., 1990). These prevalence rates of stimulant medication use are all in line with, or lower than the expected prevalence rate for ADHD. Data presented by Safer, Zito, and Fine (1996) suggest that the increase in overall use is due to the extension of treatments to older children and in the treatment of adults.

Need for Systematic Methods to Provide Comprehensive Services

As a final concern, no systematic methods provide comprehensive services to the spectrum of children with ADHD of varying severity. This creates both referral and reimbursement problems. In terms of referrals, there are no clear guidelines indicating to whom children should be referred for mental health services. In the past, pediatricians tended to refer children with ADHD to child psychiatrists infrequently (Fritz & Bergman, 1985; Wolraich et al., 1990) and psychiatrists report that only 14 percent of their referrals are from nonpsychiatric physicians (Zarin et al., 1998). Among physicians, family physicians appear to most frequently refer to child and adolescent psychiatrists, but this is only for 27 percent of the practitioners (Moser & Kallail, 1995). Referrals are now further complicated by the use of behavioral health carve-outs; many health care plans now use central screening programs to restrict the type of service approved for treatment. This makes it more difficult for primary care physicians to refer children for mental health services.

The sharing of diagnosis and treatment between the health and educational sectors creates an additional difficulty. Both systems, in attempting to reduce costs, try to shift the burden of cost to the other system. Because there is no mechanism to allocate those responsibilities, families are frequently caught between health maintenance organizations identifying services as "developmental or educational" and, therefore, not their responsibility, and school systems identifying services as "health related" and not their responsibility. Communities have no organized structure to rationally apportion expenses so as not to unduly burden any one sector while attempting to provide adequate comprehensive services.

SUMMARY

Of the many disciplines involved in the diagnosis and treatment of children with ADHD, primary care physicians play a significant role, but problems remain with their ability to diagnose the disorder and common comorbid conditions as well as to monitor treatment. Communication between schools and health care providers is an important link in this process that needs further study and intervention—requiring a system conceptualization of the process in addition to examining individual physician's practices. Further, a more systematic method to organize the broad array of services available is necessary to develop a seamless system of care.

References

Achenbach, T., & Edelbrock, L. (1983). *Manual for the Child Behavior Checklist and Revised Child Behavior Profile.* Burlington, VT: University of Vermont.

Algozzine, R. (1980). The disturbing child: A matter of opinion. *Behavioral Disorders, 5,* 112–115.

American Academy of Pediatrics Task Force on Pediatric Education. (1978). *The future of pediatrics.* Evanston, IL: American Academy of Pediatrics.

American Psychiatric Association. (1968). *Diagnostic and statistical manual of mental disorders* (2nd ed.). Washington, DC: Author.

American Psychiatric Association. (1980). *Diagnostic and statistical manual of mental disorders* (3rd ed.). Washington, DC: Author.

American Psychiatric Association. (1987). *Diagnostic and statistical manual of mental disorders* (3rd ed., rev.). Washington, DC: Author.

American Psychiatric Association. (1994). *Diagnostic and statistical manual of mental disorders* (4th ed.). Washington, DC: Author.

Baumgaertel, A., & Wolraich, M. L. (1998). Practice guideline for the diagnosis and management of attention deficit hyperactivity disorder. *Ambulatory Child Health, 4,* 45–58.

Baumgaertel, A., Wolraich, M. L., & Dietrich, M. (1995). Comparison of diagnostic criteria for attention deficit disorders in a German elementary school. *Journal of the American Academy of Child and Adolescent Psychiatry, 34,* 629–638.

Biederman, J., Newcorn, J., & Sprich, S. (1991). Comorbidity of attention deficit hyperactivity disorder with conduct, depressive, anxiety, and other disorders. *American Journal of Psychiatry, 148,* 564–577.

Bradley, C. (1937). The behavior of children receiving Benzedrine. *American Journal of Psychiatry, 94,* 577–585.

Bryant, E., & Shimizu, I. (1988). *Sample design, sampling variance, and estimation procedures for the National Ambulatory Medical Care Survey.* Bethesda, MD: Vital and Health Statistics, Public Health Service.

Clements, S. D. (1966). *Minimal brain dysfunction in children: Terminology and identification.* Washington, DC: U.S. Department of Health, Education, and Welfare.

Coleman, M., & Gilliam, J. (1983). Disturbing behaviors in the classroom: A survey of teacher attitudes. *Journal of Special Education, 17,* 121–129.

Corkum, P., & Siegel, L. S. (1993). Is the Continuous Performance Task a valuable research tool for use with children with attention-deficit-hyperactivity disorder? *Journal of Child Psychology and Psychiatry, 34,* 1217–1239.

Costello, E. J., Edelbrock, C., Costello, A. J., Dulcan, M. K., Barne, B. J, & Brent, D. (1988). Psychopathology in pediatric primary care: The new hidden morbidity. *Pediatrics, 81,* 415–424.

Danforth, J., & DuPaul, G. J. (1996). Interrater reliability of teacher rating scales for children with attention deficit hyperactivity disorder. *Journal of Psychopathology and Behavioral Assessment, 18,* 227–237.

Diller, L. H. (1996). The run on Ritalin: Attention deficit disorder and stimulant treatment in the 1990's. *Hastings Center Report, 26*, 12–18.

Donnelly, J., Wolraich, M. L., Feurer, I., & Baumgaertel, A. (1998). Evaluating the diagnostic process in determining the presence of attention deficit hyperactivity disorder. Annual meeting of the Society for Developmental and Behavioral Pediatrics, Cleveland, Ohio. *Journal of Developmental and Behavioral Pediatrics, 19*, 383.

Fergusson, D. M., & Horwood, L. J. (1993). The structure, stability, and correlations of the trait components of conduct disorder, attention deficit and anxiety/withdrawal reports. *Journal of Child Psychology and Psychiatry, 34*, 749–766.

Fritz, G. K., & Bergman, A. S. (1985). Child psychiatrists seen through pediatrician's eyes: Results of a national study. *Journal of Child Psychiatry, 24*, 81–86.

Greenhill LL (1995). Attention-deficit hyperactivity disorder: The stimulants. *Child and Adolescent Psychiatry Clinics of North America, 4*, 123–168.

Hazall, P., McDowell, M. J., & Walton, J. M. (1996). Management of children prescribed psychostimulant medication for attention deficit hyperactivity disorder in the Hunter region of NSW. *Medical Journal of Australia, 165*, 477–480.

Hochman, L. B. (1922). Post-encephalitic behavior disorder in children. *Johns Hopkins Hospital Bulletin, 33*, 372–375.

Hoffman, H. (1848). *Der Struwwelpeter*. Germany.

Individuals with Disabilities Education Act of 1990, 20 U.S.C. §§1400 et seq.

Jensen, P., Rubio-Stipec, M., Canino, G., Bird, H., Dulcan, M., Schwab-Stone, M., & Lahey, B. (1999). Parent and child contributions to child psychiatric diagnosis: Are both informants always needed? *Journal of the American Academy of Child and Adolescent Psychiatry, 38*, 1569–1579.

Jensen, P., Xenakis, S. N., Shervette, R. E., Bain, M. W., & Davis, H. (1989). Diagnosis and treatment of attention deficit disorder in two general hospital clinics. *Hospital and Community Psychiatry, 40*, 708–712.

Jerome, L., Gordon, M., & Hustler, P. (1994). A comparison of American and Canadian teachers' knowledge and attitudes towards attention deficit hyperactivity disorder (ADHD). *Canadian Journal of Psychiatry, 39*, 563–567.

Kwasman, A., Tinsley, B. J., & Lepper, H. S. (1995). Pediatrician's knowledge and attitudes concerning the diagnosis and treatment of attention deficit and hyperactivity disorders. A national survey approach. *Archives of Pediatrics and Adolescent Medicine, 149*, 1211–1216.

Lahey, B., McBurnett, K., Piacentinit, J., Hartdagen, S., Walker, J., Frick, P., & Hynd, G. (1987). Agreement of parent and teacher rating scales with comprehensive clinical assessments of attention deficit disorder with hyperactivity. *Journal of Psychological Behavioral Assessment, 9*, 429–439.

Laufer, M., & Denhoff, E. (1957). Hyperkinetic behavior syndrome in children. *Journal of Pediatrics, 50*, 463–474.

Lindgren, S., Wolraich, M. L., Stromquist, A., Davis, C., Milich, R., & Watson, D. (1989). *Diagnosis of attention deficit hyperactivity disorder by primary care physicians.* Paper presented at a research conference for Mental Health Services for Children and Adolescents in Primary Care Settings, New Haven, CT.

Lindgren, S., Wolraich, M. L., Stromquist, A., Davis, C., Milich, R., & Watson, D. (1990). *Diagnostic heterogeneity in attention deficit hyperactivity disorder.* Paper presented at the fourth annual NIMH International Research Conference on the Classification and Treatment of Mental Disorders in General Medical Settings, Bethesda, MD.

McMaster University Evidence-Based Practice Center. (1998). *The treatment of attention-deficit/hyperactivity disorder: An evidence report* (Contract No. 290–97–0017). Rockville, MD: Agency for Health Care Policy and Research.

Moser, S., & Kallail, K. J. (1995). Attention-deficit hyperactivity disorder: Management by family physicians. *Archives of Family Medicine, 4*, 241–244.

Phillippi, R. (1998). *Attention deficit disorder among Tenncare enrollees: A report of prevalence and medication.* Nashville, TN: Bureau of TennCare–Department of Health.

Rappley, M. D., Gardiner, J. C., Jetton, J. R., & Houang, R. T. (1995). The use of methylphenidate in Michigan. *Archives of Pediatric and Adolescent Medicine, 149,* 675–679.

Rehabilitation Act of 1973, 29 U.S.C. §§ 701 et seq.

Ruel, J. M., & Hickey, P. (1992). Are too many children being treated with methylphenidate? *Canadian Journal of Psychiatry, 37,* 570–572.

Safer, D. J., Zito, J. M., & Fine, E. M. (1996). Increased methylphenidate usage for attention deficit disorder in the 1990's. *Pediatrics, 98,* 1084–1088.

Sandberg, S., Weiselberg, M., & Shaffer, D. (1980). Hyperkinetic and conduct problem children in a primary school population: Some epidemiological considerations. *Journal of Child Psychology and Psychiatry, 21,* 293–311.

Sherman, M., & Hertzig, M. E. (1991). Prescribing practices of Ritalin: The Suffolk County, New York study. In L. L. Greenhill & B. B. Osman (Eds.), *Ritalin: Theory and patient management* (pp. 187–193). New York: Mary Ann Liebert.

Sleator, E., & Ullman, R. K. (1981). Can the physician diagnose hyperactivity in the office? *Pediatrics, 67,* 13–17.

Still, G. (1902). The Coulstonian lectures on some abnormal physical conditions in children. *Lancet, 1,* 1008–1012.

Strauss, A. A., & Lethinen, L. E. (1947). *Psychopathology and education of the brain-injured child.* New York: Grune & Stratton.

Swanson, J. M., McBurnett, K., Wigal, T., Pfiffner, L. J., Lerner, M. A., Williams, L., Christian, D. L., Tamm, L., Willcutt, E., Crowley, K., Clevenger, W., Khouzam, N., Woo, C., Crinella, F., & Fisher, T. D. (1993). Effect of stimulant medication on children with attention deficit disorder: A "review of reviews." *Exceptional Children, 60,* 154–162.

Szatmari, P., Offord, D. R., & Boyle, M. H. (1989). Ontario Child Health Study: Prevalence of attention deficit disorder with hyperactivity. *Journal of Child Psychology and Psychiatry, 30,* 219–230.

Ullman, R., Sleator, E., & Sprague, R. (1984). ADD-H Comprehensive Teacher Rating Scale. Champaign, IL: Metntech.

Weithorn, C., & Ross, R. (1975). Who monitors medication? *Journal of Learning Disabilities, 3,* 59–62.

Wolraich, M. L, Hannah, J. N., Baumgaertel, A., Pinnock, TY., & Feurer, I. (1998). Examination of DSM-IV criteria for ADHD in a county-wide sample. *Journal of Developmental and Behavioral Pediatrics, 19,* 162–168.

Wolraich, M. L. (1996). *The classification of child and adolescent mental conditions in primary care: Diagnostic and statistical manual for primary care (DSM-PC), child and adolescent version.* Elk Grove, IL: American Academy of Pediatrics.

Wolraich, M. L, Hannah, J. N., Pinnock, T. Y., Baumgaertel, A., & Brown, J. (1996). Comparison of diagnositic criteria for attention deficit disorder in a county-wide sample. *Journal of American Academy of Child and Adolescent Psychiatry, 35,* 319–323.

Wolraich, M. L., Lindgren, S. D., Stromquist, A., Milich, R., Davis, C., & Watson, D. (1990). Stimulant medication use by primary care physicians in the treatment of attention deficit hyperactivity disorder. *Pediatrics, 86,* 95–101.

Zametkin, A., Nordahl, T. E., Gross, M., King, A. C., Semple, W. E., Rumsey, J., Hamburger, S., & Cohen, R. M. (1990). Cerebral glucose metabolism in adults with hyperactivity of childhood onset. *New England Journal of Medicine, 323,* 1361–1366.

Zarin, D., Suarez, A. P., Pincus, H. A., Kupersanin, E., & Zito, J. M. (1998). Clinical and treatment characteristics of children with attention-deficit/hyperactivity disorder (ADHD) in psychiatric practice. *Journal of the American Academy of Child and Adolescent Psychiatry, 37,* 1262–1270.

Chapter 24

Impact of ADHD on School Systems

by Steven R. Forness, Ed.D. and Kenneth A. Kavale, Ph.D.

Introduction 24-1
Children With ADHD in Special Education 24-3
    Learning Disabilities 24-3
    Emotional Disturbance 24-4
    Other Health Impaired 24-5
    Estimates of ADHD Eligibility in Special Education 24-7
Cost Estimates 24-8
Impact of ADHD on Schools 24-9
    Impact on Segregated Classroom 24-10
    Impact on Inclusive or Mainstream Classrooms 24-12
Conclusions and Recommendations 24-14
    Research 24-15
    Training 24-15
    School Practice and Policy 24-16

INTRODUCTION

The core symptoms of attention deficit hyperactivity disorder (ADHD)—inattention, hyperactivity and impulsivity—seem often to be at the center of what school requires of a child. Paying attention to teachers, to classroom rules, or to details of lessons is the exact starting point for effective learning to begin. Sitting still and focusing on one thing at a time is vital to completing school work and to participating in class discussions. Being able to pause and reflect carefully before responding is absolutely essential to identifying correct answers and to learning accurate information. Inattention, hyperactivity and impulsivity not only interfere with these activities but also impair a child's ability to join in group activities, to play effectively in games or sports, and ultimately to develop meaningful friendships with other children.

Schools often have a limited range of tolerance for individual differences of any child with problems, especially with the recent emphasis on school reform that focuses on strict standards for academic achievement and intolerance of antisocial behavior (Sage & Burrello, 1994). Schools also tend to put limitations on the eligibility of certain children for special education services and do not currently have a special education category specifically for ADHD. Schools are thus left to use available special education categories such as learning disabilities (LD), emotional disturbance (ED), and other health impairments (OHI) or to accommodate a child's disability in the regular classroom under provisions of Section 504 of the 1973 Rehabilitation Act (Davila, Williams, & MacDonald, 1991).

In special education, the LD category is generally reserved for a child who has intelligence in the normal range, no primary emotional disorder or visual or hearing impairments, and at least a reasonable period of instruction in the regular grades but who still remains unable to read, write, do math, or use language at an acceptable level. What constitutes an acceptable level of academic performance, however, depends on whether or not the child has a significant discrepancy between his or her intelligence (as measured by an individually administered IQ test) and his or her academic skill level (as measured by a standardized, individually administered test of achievement in reading, math, or other academic area). In almost every state or school district, this discrepancy is determined to be significant primarily by means of a mathematical discrepancy formula (Mercer, Jordan, Allsopp, & Mercer, 1996). A child with ADHD may do poorly only on certain IQ subtests because he or she has difficulty paying attention, which artificially lowers the entire IQ score. When this happens, the child may not show a significant discrepancy between IQ and achievement test scores and may therefore not qualify for special education services for learning disabilities (Fornes, Youpa, Hanna, Cantwell, & Swanson, 1992).

The current special education criteria for ED contains five different areas, including inability to learn, which cannot be explained by intellectual, sensory, or health factors; inability to build or maintain satisfactory interpersonal relationships with peers and teachers; inappropriate types of behavior or feelings under normal circumstance; general mood of unhappiness or depression; and tendency to develop physical symptoms or fears associated with personal or school problems (Forness & Kavale, 1997). To be eligible for the ED category, a child must have a problem in at least one of these areas and exhibit this problem over a long period, to a marked degree, and to the point that it adversely affects educational performance. A child is further excluded from eligibility in this category if his or her problems are considered to be merely "social maladjustment." The problem with these criteria is that none of the five areas specifically refers to ADHD symptoms. The social maladjustment exclusion, furthermore, often precludes eligibility of many children with ADHD (Forness, Kavale, King, & Kasari, 1993).

The OHI category is generally reserved for a child with chronic or acute medical conditions such as heart disease, asthma, diabetes, or other illness that may affect his or her educational performance. There is, however, a phrase in the federal definition of this category regarding "limited alertness that adversely affects educational performance" (Davila et al., 1991). Because the list of disorders in this category is not exhaustive and ADHD can be considered a "medical condition" if diagnosed by a physician, some children with ADHD can be considered eligible for this category and thus receive special education services. School professionals have not, however, had a great deal of experience in using this category for eligibility for children with ADHD, and clear guidelines for this purpose are not readily available.

This chapter (1) develops estimates from the limited available evidence on numbers of children with ADHD currently served in the LD, ED, or OHI categories, (2) analyzes the approximate school costs of educating these children, and (3) summarizes the impact of children with ADHD on both segregated and inclusive school settings.

CHILDREN WITH ADHD IN SPECIAL EDUCATION

Learning Disabilities

Estimated prevalence of LD in the general population is approximately 5 percent (Lyon, 1994). Studies of children with ADHD suggest a prevalence of comorbid learning disabilities ranging from 10 to 92 percent (DuPaul & Stoner, 1996; Semrud-Clikeman et al., 1992), but, when appropriate diagnostic criteria for LD are applied, the prevalence of comorbid LD appears to be in the range of 10 to 25 percent (Richters et al., 1995). In the collaborative multisite multimodal treatment study of children with ADHD (MTA Cooperative Group, 1999), children have been diagnosed with LD according to two criteria involving discrepancy between measured intelligence and academic achievement (J. M. Swanson, personal communication, May 8, 1998): The simple-difference method produced a rate of comorbid LD of approximately 35 percent, and the predicted-achievement method produced a rate of approximately 18 percent. The latter method is probably more appropriate in that it accounts more fully for overlap between the particular combination of IQ and achievement tests used. There is controversy, however, around use of the LD discrepancy criterion, and possible alternative methods of assessing children by deficits in specific domains of reading or math performance have been suggested but not yet examined in relation to ADHD (Aaron, 1997; Lyon, 1994; Shaw, Cullen, McGuire, & Brickerhoff, 1995).

Estimates of LD in children with ADHD, however, are not the same as estimates of children with ADHD who actually meet LD criteria in the schools. Few studies have specifically examined the latter issue as special education research traditionally focuses on existing categories of disability as defined in the Individuals with Disabilities Education Act (IDEA) (Forness & Kavale, 1994). Only studies from 1990 to the present were selected because changes in reauthorization of IDEA and in public awareness of ADHD issues in school render previous studies less relevant to present policy and practice (Parker, 1989). Table 24.1 presents percentages of children with ADHD in LD and related categories from the three available studies in which such estimates could be derived in a valid manner. MacMillan and colleagues studied children in grades 2 to 4 across several school districts who were currently being referred for special education (Lopez, Forness, MacMillan, Bocian, & Gresham, 1996; MacMillan, Gresham, & Bocian, 1998). They found that of sixty-one children classified as LD by the schools during that period, nineteen (31.1 percent) had been diagnosed by research diagnostic criteria as having ADHD. Although these diagnoses were not confirmed by structured interview, extensive behavioral and social skill ratings were used to establish diagnoses. Bussing, Zima, Belin, and Forness (1998) screened for ADHD in 499 children in both LD and ED classrooms, also in grades 2 to 4 and found that ninety who screened positive for ADHD were in LD and fifty-eight in ED programs. However, only fifty-nine of those in LD programs were subsequently confirmed as ADHD on structured interview. Extrapolating from the total number of children with LD in the school district involved, these fifty-nine children with ADHD accounted for 16.2 percent of children in LD classrooms. McConaughy, Mattison, and Peterson (1994) used the borderline clinical cutoff point for attention problems on the teacher version of the Child Behavior Checklist (CBCL) with 366 children in LD programs and 366 children in ED programs across samples in three different states. They found 28.1 percent of children with presumed ADHD in LD programs.

Table 24.1
Estimates of ADHD Prevalence With LD, EDH, and OHI Categories

Source	LD	ED	OHI
Bussing et al. (1998)	16.2%	31.1%	
Cullwood-Brathwaite & McKinney (1988)		68.3%	
Duncan et al. (1995)		24.7%	
MacMillan et al. (1996, 1998)	33.1%		
Mattison et al. (1993, 1993, 1997)	44.4%		
McConaughy et al (1994)	28.1%	44.8%	
U.S. Department of Education (1990–1997)		39.7%	
Reasonable estimate	26.0%	43.0%	40.0%

Note. See text for method of establishing reasonable estimate.

Although the MTA study has examined special education placements of children with ADHD, data on children with ADHD with respect to what proportion they represent in special education programs is not available (Casey, Rourke, & Del Dotto, 1996; Holborow & Berry, 1986; Levine, Busch, & Aufseeser, 1982; Pisecco, Baker, Silva, & Brooke, 1996; Semrud-Clikeman et al., 1992; Vatz, 1997). Although several studies on comorbidity of ADHD in LD samples are available, only the three studies reviewed previously contain data on specific special education eligibility for our purposes here. Although the Bussing et al. (1998) study is probably the most definitive in terms of ADHD ascertainment, the MacMillan et al. (1998) and McConaughy et al. (1994) studies have somewhat more representative samples and cannot be discounted, so no particular rationale for weighing among these three studies presents itself. The average percentage of children across these three studies is approximately 26 percent of children in LD programs who have ADHD, and this figure is used here to estimate the number of children currently served in the LD category. This estimate also compares favorably with estimates of subtypes of LD children with inattention and impulse-control problems across several subtyping studies which range from 22 to 30 percent (Forness, 1990).

Emotional Disturbance

Epidemiology of emotional or behavioral problems in children suggests that at least 10 to 12 percent may have a diagnosable mental disorder (Brandenberg, Friedman, & Silver, 1990; Friedman, Katz-Leavy, Mandershead, & Sondheimer, 1996). Children with ADHD have other psychiatric disorders at much higher rates, including conduct or oppositional defiant disorders at a rate of 43 percent to 93 percent and anxiety or mood disorders at a rate of 13 percent to 51 percent (Biederman, Newcorn, & Sprich, 1991; Bird, Gould, & Steghezza-Jaramillo, 1994; Jensen, Martin, & Cantwell, 1997).

As with LD, there are very few studies on the proportion of children with ADHD who are in the special education eligibility category of ED. These are also presented in Table 24.1. The study by Bussing et al. (1998) showed that fifty-eight children with possible ADHD were in the special education category of ED, but only forty-two had a confirmed diagnosis of ADHD using structured interview. As a proportion of total children in ED programs in the school district involved, these children with ADHD represented 31.1 percent. The study by McConaughy et al. (1994) indicated that of 366 children in ED programs, 44.8 percent had a clinical cutoff score on the inattention scale of the CBCL. Mattison and his colleagues have completed a series of studies in which they obtained comprehensive psychiatric diagnoses of children and adolescents during the special education eligibility process for ED in one semirural school district (Mattison & Felix, 1997; Mattison, Lynch, Kales, & Gamble, 1993; Mattison, Morales, & Bauer, 1993). Their findings suggest that children with ADHD across these studies averaged 44.4 percent in the ED category. Duncan, Forness and Hartsough (1995) found that 24.7 percent of children from ages 6 to 19 in ED classrooms, across two different county school districts, had a primary diagnosis of ADHD using results of diagnostic workups by local mental health agencies. Finally, Cullwood-Brathwaite and McKinney (1988) used an instrument based on specific symptoms of ADHD according to the fourth edition of *Diagnostic and Statistical Manual of Mental Disorders* (DSM-IV; American Psychiatric Association, 1994) to diagnose ADHD in 120 children in grades 6 through 8 who were in two different public special schools for children with ED within one school district. They found 68.3 percent of children with ADHD.

The range of diagnostic methods, estimates of ADHD as a primary versus a secondary disorder, wide variety of school district eligibility policies, and other research artifacts preclude use of a systematic weighing procedure in obtaining an overall estimate, as was the case in the LD category. The Mattison studies were slightly more definitive in terms of diagnostic ascertainment, but at least some subjects from the Mattison study were also included in the McConaughy, Mattison, and Peterson sample in which overall diagnostic ascertainment was less certain because only checklist scores were reported. The Bussing and Cullwood-Brathwaite studies were relatively definitive in terms of ADHD diagnosis, but only one school district was involved. Although two different school districts were used in the Duncan study, mental health diagnoses were derived from secondary sources in the community. The range of these five studies is approximately 43 percent of children in ED classes with a diagnosis of ADHD. This estimate is close to the percentage from the Mattison and McConaughy studies that together probably have the most representative samples and thus seems a reasonable estimate based on the limited available evidence.

Other Health Impaired

Because OHI currently functions in this context as a category of convenience for special education, the only possible way to ascertain the possible proportion of children with ADHD in this category is to examine increases in numbers of children since this category began to function as a proxy for ADHD. The first significant advocacy for ADHD as a separate category can be traced back to approximately the 1988–1989 school year (Parker, 1989). The first official acknowledgement of ADHD by the U.S. Department of Education in relation to the OHI category under IDEA occurred during the 1991–1992 school year (Davila et al., 1991). For our purposes here, these four years (1988–1992) are considered the baseline years for the OHI category. As of this writing, annual reports to Congress on the child count for each of these categories by the U.S. Department of Education currently only extend to the four subsequent school years, 1992–1996 (U.S. Department of Education, 1990–1997).

Table 24.2 provides data for each of these eight years on the percentage of children enrolled in school who were in the OHI category and on the increase from each prior year in eligibility for that category. The table also presents comparisons for the LD and ED categories. The average yearly increase for the first four years prior to official recognition of ADHD are 3.8 percent for LD, 2.6 percent for ED, and 7.3 percent for OHI. Corresponding increases for the subsequent four years are 4.0 percent, 2.7 percent, and 23.3 percent. Thus, rather consistent average gains occur during the first four years and the last four years in the LD and ED categories but not for the OHI category. No other programmatic factors appear to explain the more than threefold increase in the OHI category in the four years after official school recognition of ADHD. Thus, the excess gain (increase beyond the 7.3 percent average expected gain based on the previous four years) can probably most parsimoniously be accounted for by ADHD eligibility in this category. This suggests that 68.7 percent of new children entering the OHI category in the past four years are children with ADHD. Because the category essentially more than doubled in size during that time from 56,335 to

Table 24.2

Percentages of School Enrollment and of Annual Increase in Children by Year for LD, ED, and OHI Categories

School Year	LD Enrollment	LD Increase	ED Enrollment	ED Increase	OHI Enrollment	OHI Increase
1988–1989	4.71	3.0	0.89	0.7	0.12	7.8
1989–1990	4.79	3.3	0.89	2.2	0.12	5.7
1990–1991	4.88	4.0	0.89	5.0	0.13	8.5
1991–1992	5.02	4.9	0.89	2.6	0.13	7.1
1992–1993	5.25	5.3	0.89	1.0	0.14	13.4
1993–1994	5.27	3.4	0.89	4.1	0.18	26.7
1994–1995	5.34	3.5	0.91	3.2	0.23	28.2
1995–1996	5.44	3.6	0.91	2.5	0.28	24.7

Source: *Annual Report to Congress on IDEA*, Volumes 12–19 (1990–1997).

133,354, an increase of 77,019, then 68.7 percent of that increase represents approximately 40 percent of the total currently in the OHI category. This represents the most reasonable estimate of children in the OHI category who have ADHD.

Estimates of ADHD Eligibility in Special Education

Table 24.3 provides the current available numbers of children in each of these categories of special education and best available estimates as defined previously. As Table 24.3 indicates, as many as 916,447 children with ADHD may be receiving special education services as a total of these three categories.

Available estimates of ADHD in children are in the 3 to 5 percent range, but rates in some epidemiological studies have been closer to 10 percent or above (American Academy of Child and Adolescent Psychiatry, 1997). A recent well-regarded epidemiological study established diagnoses of ADHD using presence of symptoms reported by both parents and children along with a measure of various levels of functional impairment (Shaffer et al., 1996). The findings in this study suggest a prevalence of 1.9 to 4.9 percent. Use of combined symptom agreement from both parent and child and at least a mild level of impairment produced a prevalence rate of approximately 4.1 to 4.9 percent. Thus, a median estimate would be approximately 4.5 percent prevalence. Applying this median estimate to the total school enrollment figure of 45,109,401 (U.S. Department of Education, 1990–1997) provides an estimate of the number of schoolchildren with ADHD of 2,029,923. Using the available total of 916,447 from all three special education categories in Table 24.3 suggests that approximately 45 percent of ADHD children may currently be receiving special education services. This same estimating procedure using a moderate level of impairment from the Shaffer study would produce a 3 percent median estimate and suggest that approximately 68 percent of such children are currently being served.

These estimates, as noted previously, are fraught with potential error in that the current research base for estimating number of ADHD children in the three special education programs dedicated to ADHD is sparse at best.

Table 24.3
Current Available Numbers of Children in LD, ED, and OHI Categories and Best Estimate of Children With ADHD in Each

Category	Children in 1995–1996	Best Estimate	Number With ADHD
LD	2,595,004	26%	674,701
ED	438,150	43%	188,404
OHI	133,354	40%	53,342
Totals	3,166,508		916,447

Note. See text and Table 25.2 for source of estimates; numbers are from *Annual Report to Congress on IDEA*, Volume 19 (1997).

COST ESTIMATES

Although the foregoing estimate of 916,447 children with ADHD in special education is tentative, it is the only reasonable figure available on which to base possible cost estimates. The current costs of special education were the topic of a special study reported in Section 2 of the nineteenth *Annual Report to Congress on IDEA* (U.S. Department of Education, 1997). As reported in this document, cost estimates for special education are relatively complex and are based on spending that is approximately 7 percent federal dollars, 44 percent state dollars, and 49 percent local dollars. These costs are further affected by changes in school enrollment, sociodemographic factors, changes in eligibility categories or type of regular versus segregated classroom settings used, and related services provided by other public or private agencies. Only twenty-four states were able to present cost estimates per pupil, and only nineteen were confident in their data. For these latter states, average estimate of excess costs of special education was $5,435 per pupil. This report did not, however, provide breakout costs for the various categories of disability.

Costs per disability are, however, contained in a related report in which average excess costs for special education expressed in 1989–1990 dollars was $4,153 per pupil across all programs (Chalkind, Danielson, & Brauen, 1993). Expressed as a proportion of this per-pupil expenditure, costs for LD were approximately 46.2 percent for resource or general education placements and 86.7 percent for special classes. For ED, the proportions were 73.7 percent for resource or general education and 1.37 percent for special classes. Data did not permit separate estimates for special schools or facilities, and data for OHI were not used because children with ADHD had not yet become eligible for this category as of that year.

Using the most recent per pupil estimate of $5,435 from the U.S. Department of Education, the per-pupil costs would therefore be as follows: $2,511 for LD in resource or regular classrooms, $4,712 for LD in segregated settings, $4,006 for ED in resource or regular classrooms, and $7,446 for ED in segregated settings.

For purposes of estimating costs for children with ADHD, the percentages of children in various educational environments will be used as obtained from the 1997 *Annual Report to Congress* (U.S. Department of Education, 1997). Table 24.4 depicts these data. Because usable cost estimates, derived previously, were only available for resource or general education placements and for special classes, data from this table are collapsed into two categories with regular class and resource rooms comprising the first and special classes and schools comprising the second. The reader is cautioned that this collapse may serve to underestimate costs, especially in the ED category, where 18.7 percent of children are in more expensive settings such as private schools or residential facilities.

An assumption will also be made that the numbers of children in the OHI category should be folded into the LD category. This assumption rests on the fact that OHI functions as a category of convenience and is therefore used only after a child does not qualify in LD or ED categories; thus intensity or level of special education for children in this category may not be as great and more likely merits levels of service more reflective of children in LD rather than ED programs. The reader is cautioned that this too may serve to underestimate costs in the ED category or overestimate costs in the LD category.

Table 24.4
Percentage of Children in LD, ED, or OHI Categories in Various Special Education Environments

Category	Regular Classrooms With Special Education Support	Resource Rooms	Special Classes	Special Schools
LD	41.1	39.6	18.4	0.9
ED	22.0	24.0	35.2	18.7
OHI	42.6	28.9	18.5	10.0

Source: *Annual Report to Congress on IDEA*, Volume 19 (1997).

Table 24.5
Costs for Children With ADHD in Categories by Setting

Category	Estimated Number	Estimated Per-Pupil Costs	Total Costs
LD-OHI (Combined)			
Regular/resource	587,531	$2,511	$1,475,290,341
Segregated	140,512	$4,712	$ 662,092,544
ED			
Regular/resource	86,666	$4,006	$ 347,183,996
Segregated	101,738	$7,446	$ 757,541,148
Totals	916,447		$3,242,108,029

From Table 24.4, the proportion of children in the LD category is 80.7 percent in resource or regular classrooms (combined) and 19.3 percent in segregated classrooms (combined). These same figures for ED are 46 percent and 54 percent, respectively. Combining these proportions with data on children with ADHD in Table 24.3, children in the collapsed LD-OHI categories total 728,043 with 587,531 in resource or regular and 140,512 in segregated settings. The same proportions for ED are 86,666 and 101,738 respectively.

Table 24.5 depicts the number of children in each of these categories, by setting, along with the per-pupil costs and total dollars for each category. Note that approximately $3.2 billion in annual dollars was spent on children with ADHD in special education. This estimate may be somewhat low in that ED costs may have been underestimated, and no costs are available for children currently served under Section 504 of the 1973 Rehabilitation Act. These costs are also in 1995 dollars.

IMPACT OF ADHD ON SCHOOLS

As noted in the introduction, core symptoms of ADHD are generally incompatible with paying attention, listening carefully, sitting still, thinking before acting, or other skills necessary for school success. Recognition of ADHD as a potential source of these problems is often delayed in school because a child's misbehavior may be seen primarily as volitional. Even special education may be delayed because antisocial behavior is mistakenly viewed as incompatible with eligibility for existing eligibility criteria (Forness, Kavale, King, & Kasari, 1994).

Schools have nonetheless begun to recognize educational significance of this diagnosis. Special issues of major education journals have been devoted to ADHD (Blankstein, Bullock, & Copans, 1998; Hocutt, McKinney, & Montague, 1993; Shaywitz & Shaywitz, 1991), and professional education associations and both federal and state governments have developed resources on ADHD for school professionals (Council for Exceptional Children, 1992; Colorado Department of Education, 1994; U.S. Department of Education, 1994). Because ADHD is not a traditional special education category, educators have had to adopt diagnostic procedures developed in mental health or adapt them for use in school settings (Atkins & Pelham, 1991; Maag & Reid, 1994; McKinney, Montague, & Hocutt, 1993).

Classroom interventions likely to be successful for children with ADHD have also been developed, many having been adapted from clinical settings for school use (Burcham, Carlson, & Milich, 1993; DuPaul & Eckert, 1997; Fiore, Becker, & Nero, 1993; Forness, Sweeney, & Wagner, 1998; Forness & Walker, 1994; Gardill, DuPaul, & Kyle, 1996; Montague & Warger, 1997; Rooney, 1993). These include the following:

- Strategic seating of children with ADHD to reduce distraction or enhance teacher availability;

- Providing additional structure through shortening or changing the format of lessons, careful scheduling of tasks, use of prompts or visual cues, and more frequent breaks during lessons or activities;

- Individualizing instruction through one-to-one teaching, assistant teachers, or after-school tutors;

- Cognitive approaches such as self-monitoring, self-evaluation, and self-reinforcement;

- Cooperative learning through peer tutoring or shared assignments;

- Social skills training and monitoring of problematic social interactions;

- Behavior modification approaches such as judicious use of teacher praise or ignoring, token economies, time out, response cost, and home-school reinforcement systems; and

- Specialized teacher consultation from school psychologists, special education resource teachers, behavioral analysts, or other specialists.

It is noteworthy, however, that these school interventions are not markedly different from those already developed and found to be effective for a wide variety of children with learning or behavioral disorders other than ADHD (Forness, Kavale, Blum, & Lloyd, 1997; Lloyd, Forness, & Kavale, 1998).

Impact on Segregated Classroom

As noted previously, children with ADHD who receive special education are likely to do so through eligibility in one of three different special education categories.

Table 24.4 has depicted the percentage of children in each of these categories who are either in regular or general education classrooms with special education support, partially segregated settings such as resource rooms, or segregated settings such as special classrooms or separate schools. These were the most recent available data from the U.S. Department of Education (1990–1997). Children in resource room placements, by definition, spend less than half their entire school day in the resource room, and their primary classroom is considered to be the general education or regular classroom setting. Note that only about 19 percent of children identified in the LD category (and, by inference, of those in the OHI category) spend more than half their day in segregated school settings. More than half (54 percent) of children identified in the ED categories, on the other hand, are in segregated settings in which they spend more than half their school day. It is not possible to determine from available data the exact school placements of children with ADHD within these categories.

Eligibility category cannot, according to IDEA, be linked to classroom placement. One might nonetheless predict that children with ADHD who have higher rates of psychiatric comorbidity would be placed in the ED category and thus be more frequently found in segregated settings based on their level of need. Such is not necessarily the case. No significant differences were found in levels of comorbid conduct or oppositional disorders, depression, or anxiety disorders between two groups of children with ADHD who were in LD versus ED programs, although presence of comorbid LD in either group was not available (Bussing et al., 1998). In another study, no IQ or achievement differences were found between two groups of children within LD programs; one group had ADHD and the other were presumably free of emotional or behavioral disorders (Lopez et al., 1996). Measured social skills were significantly lower, however, in the ADHD group. These data reflect the complexity of issues regarding academic versus behavioral problems of children with ADHD (Hinshaw, 1992).

Presence of comorbid psychiatric disorders may nonetheless distinguish between children with ADHD who are eligible for special education and those who are not. Comorbid conduct or oppositional disorders appear to distinguish elementary schoolboys with ADHD or related disorders who were found eligible for the ED category from those who were not (Mattison & Forness, 1995). In another study, children with ADHD + CD were generally lower across several areas of academic achievement than those with "pure" ADHD, although both groups were quite similar on measures of intelligence (Forness et al., 1992). Schoolchildren with ADHD + CD have likewise been found not only to be significantly lower on a variety of academic and social interaction measures than nondisabled children, but, on most of these measures, they were also significantly lower than children with other emotional or behavioral disorders (Gresham, MacMillan, Bocian, Ward, & Forness, 1998).

The point here is that impact on segregated classrooms from children with ADHD who are eligible for special education is likely to be significant. Such children may be more likely to have comorbid academic or behavioral problems that distinguish them even from non-ADHD children in the same special education classrooms. Such children also seem equally likely to appear in either LD or ED programs. Teachers in LD classrooms may be less prepared to deal with their emotional or behavioral problems, and teachers in ED classrooms may be less prepared to deal with their academic deficiencies. The nature of children with ADHD who find themselves in segregated special education classrooms may thus push the outer limits of such classrooms as effective special education resources.

Impact on Inclusive or Mainstream Classrooms

The term "mainstreaming" in special education previously referred to children with disabilities spending at least part of their school day in general education classrooms, but the term has largely now been replaced by the term "full inclusion," which denotes full-time assignment to general education classrooms (Fuchs & Fuchs, 1991). Full inclusion has been touted by its proponents as morally correct, more likely to prepare children with disabilities to function in the real world, more apt to expose these children to social role models and appropriate curricula, and more apt to help typical children be more accepting of disability (Lipsky & Gartner, 1996; Stainback & Stainback, 1996). Opponents of full inclusion claim that it denies children with disabilities the right to effective intervention or treatment, exposes them to rejection and isolation in the regular classroom, requires them to meet academic demands they are not always capable of, and does not provide the truly individualized education that was originally guaranteed by IDEA (Kauffman & Hallahan, 1995; MacMillan, Gresham, & Forness, 1996).

The most radical of the full-inclusion advocates consider effective teaching to be all that general education teachers will need in order to maintain children with learning or behavior disorders in the regular classroom. If good teaching were in place in every classroom, they reason that we could, and even should, do away with special education. Full inclusionists who are less extreme in their views see more of a role for special education. They advocate having a special education teacher co-teach certain lessons in the classroom with the general education teacher and/or consult with the teacher on learning and behavioral strategies to use with certain children. Full inclusionists who are more extreme believe that such assistance from special educators will only delay general education teachers from acquiring the skills they need to teach all children, even those with disabilities, in the regular classroom.

Despite the recent proliferation of inclusive teaching practices (King-Sears, 1997) the research literature on these inclusive approaches is mixed at best, with no clear advantage to inclusive over more traditional special education practices (Fisher, Schumaker, & Deshler, 1995; Hunt & Goetz, 1997; Sobsey & Dreimanus, 1993). There is, in fact, a good deal of evidence that although most teachers in general education think full inclusion is a good idea in theory, only about one in four feel either well enough prepared or even willing to accept a child with disabilities in their classrooms (Scruggs & Mastropieri, 1996). General education teachers seem to become even more concerned when it comes to full inclusion of children with emotional or behavioral disorders (MacMillan & Gresham, 1996). Thus, although there are several reasons to be concerned about inclusive practices, new IDEA reauthorization amendments appear to drive the field even closer toward a full-inclusion model (Yell & Shriver, 1997).

Data in Table 24.4 suggest that significant percentages of children with ADHD who receive special education are likely to spend their entire day fully included in general education classrooms (approximately 22 to 42 percent depending on the eligibility category) or mainstreamed into general education classrooms for most of their school day (approximately 24 to 40 percent, depending on the category). From the overall estimate of children with ADHD in special education, discussed earlier in relation to Table 24.3, approximately 32 to 55 percent of children with ADHD may be mainstreamed in general education in the worst possible sense. They are neither recognized nor identified, nor do they receive any special education services at all.

As noted in the introduction, Section 504 of 1973 Rehabilitation Act requires schools to make accommodations for children with ADHD, and most school districts have procedures for meeting with parents or guardians and planning instructional modifications or adaptations for their behavioral or academic needs (Council of Administrators of Special Education, 1992). This law was originally dedicated to providing access to the workplace for adults with disabilities but has been applied to children and schools as well. Because ADHD can be considered a disability under Section 504, this law is available to provide access for children with ADHD to school instruction. Data from the U.S. Office of Civil Rights on specific use of this law are not adequate to track the numbers of children with disruptive behavioral disorders who are currently served under Section 504 or to characterize the specific accommodations they receive in school (Cohen, 1994). The types of accommodations typically suggested, however, are not likely to be as substantial as those provided through special education, and most parents or guardians usually apply for services under Section 504 only after eligibility for special education is denied (Zirkel, 1995). Because there are no federal or local funds attached to Section 504, most classroom adaptations are apt to be very minimal, such as changing seating or reducing length of assignments.

As noted previously, there are a variety of potentially effective school interventions for ADHD. Many of these are being used either in special education or in Section 504 accommodations. Many are also being used during prereferral interventions in which school professionals work with problem children to either prevent or forestall the need for referral to special education (Del'Homme, Kasari, Forness, & Bagley, 1996). Table 24.6 provides a summary of the types of special interventions that teachers report using with children with ADHD (Reid, Maag, & Vasa, 1993). Note that teachers in general education rank one-to-one instruction and consultation with colleagues much lower than teachers in special education. In fact, only one intervention, changing seating, was reportedly used by more than 40 percent of teachers in general

Table 24.6
Rank Order of Reported Use of Selected Interventions for ADHD
by Teachers in General vs. Special Education Settings

Intervention	General Education	Special Education
Changing seating	1	5
Behavior modification	2	1
Time out	3	4
Shortened assignments	4	7
One-to-one instruction	5	3
Special consultation	6	2
Peer tutoring	7	9
Frequent breaks	8	8
Assignment format	9	6

Note. Developed from data reported in Reid, Maag, and Vasa (1993).

education settings. Teachers in special education, on the other hand, reported much higher rates of use in that the first seven interventions were reportedly used by 44 to 72 percent of these teachers. Meta-analysis of interventions for ADHD reveal only sixty-three studies of which all but twenty-five were single-subject research (DuPaul & Eckert, 1997). Only eight studies in this meta-analysis employed a control group, and seventeen studies were pre-post designs. Effect sizes were .45 and .64, respectively, for effectiveness of ADHD interventions from these two groups of studies. Note that effect size (ES) is similar to a standard deviation unit, usually ranging from 0 to 1 or greater and that an ES of .40 indicates only moderate effectiveness while ESs above .50 are considered to be much more substantial (Kavale & Forness, 2000). Comparisons between those interventions done in special education settings versus those used in general education classes suggested a clear advantage for interventions done in special (ES = 1.24) over general education (ES = .49) settings.

The impact of a child with ADHD on general education settings is probably much more significant than it is in segregated special education classrooms. A variety of classroom methods for children with ADHD are available as prereferral interventions, Section 504 accommodations, or inclusive special education practices in general education classrooms. It is not at all clear, however, to what degree they are being used or whether they are effective in such settings.

CONCLUSIONS AND RECOMMENDATIONS

Research in both special education and school psychology does not have a significant tradition of addressing specific disorders such as ADHD. Instead, research emphasis is on assessment and intervention within broad categorical areas such as learning disabilities or emotional disturbance. Education based on disorders or etiology is relatively rare, primarily because of a strong behavioral orientation in special education (Hodapp & Dykens, 1992). Such a tradition extends both to professional training and special education practice. That the research base reported herein on ADHD in schools is sparse is thus not surprising. It is probably more surprising that any research on schooling of children with ADHD exists at all, as special education and school psychology professionals remain skeptical that its diagnostic implications are significantly different from those of other competing disorders (Forness & Kavale, 1994; Reid, Maag, & Vasa, 1993). That a broad range of comorbid disorders and learning problems characterizes ADHD has done little to ease this skepticism. On the other hand, recent synthesis of research on effects of stimulant medication may enhance interest in ADHD, because effects tend to rival those of school-based psychosocial interventions (Crenshaw, Kavale, Forness, & Reeve, 1999; Forness, Kavale, & Crenshaw, 1999). The sheer numbers of children with ADHD and increasing recognition of their impact on both general and special education may also heighten professional interest and attract additional researchers from special education and school psychology (Barkley, 1998).

There are enormous opportunities for research in school-based treatment of children with ADHD as well as for improvement in teacher preparation and educational practice. A number of recommendations for research, training, and practice seem rather obvious given the foregoing review of the impact of ADHD on schools, and these are detailed in the following paragraphs.

Research

The first recommendation in the area of research is to expand the research base on numbers and types of children with ADHD served in various educational settings and in different categories of special education. As noted earlier, there does not seem to be a systematic process whereby certain types of children with ADHD are determined to be eligible in the OHI category only after they are considered ineligible for the LD or ED categories, as one might predict given different types of ADHD or comorbid conditions. Such data may, in turn, bear significantly on the preparation foro teachers in the different categories of special education.

A second recommendation is to develop more efficient and effective assessment procedures for ADHD that can be used in school settings. Many of the current diagnostic or evaluation procedures used by school professionals for children with ADHD are borrowed or adapted from clinical or hospital settings, in which the purpose of treatment may be less focused on cognitive or academic progress and/or the type of treatment may be less able to be individualized in ongoing classroom situations.

A third recommendation is to examine effects of various special education placements on the outcomes of children with ADHD. Outcome research on children in special education, with or without ADHD, is desperately needed given the current trends toward full inclusion, and careful longitudinal research in this area is nearly nonexistent, especially in the area of children with emotional or behavioral disorders.

A fourth recommendation, perhaps the most important, is to conduct systematic inquiry into effects of specific classroom interventions for ADHD. Even the most frequently used strategies, such as changing seating location or shortening assignments, have not been systematically studied as to long-term outcome, nor have they been directly compared with other strategies such as cognitive behavior modification. Even the MTA study was not designed to disentangle the differential effects of social skill, computer assisted, or paraprofessional instruction within the overall psychosocial intervention carried on in school (Richters et al., 1995).

Training

The first recommendation in the area of professional training and teacher preparation is to develop skills in both general and special education teachers in early detection of ADHD. It seems clear that in many children who initially present with school discipline or adjustment problems, premorbid or comorbid ADHD may not be consistently recognized as such, and considerable time passes before appropriate treatment is delivered (Duncan et al., 1995; Forness et al., 1994).

A second recommendation is to incorporate instructional or behavioral interventions that have proven successful with children with ADHD into existing courses in curriculum and teaching methods. Many of the interventions used for schoolchildren with ADHD are also apt to be effective for children with other learning or behavioral disorders (Forness et al., 1997; Lloyd et al., 1998). A corollary to this recommendation is that many of the techniques used in classrooms for children with various disorders other than ADHD, such as learning disabilities, autism, or mental retardation, should be explored for their possible adaptation for children with ADHD. It is not at all clear at this point that medical or psychiatric diagnoses such as ADHD predict a specific aptitude-by-treatment interaction in which only certain designated interventions will be effective (Forness & Kavale, 1994; Reid et al., 1993).

Although not strictly within the scope of this chapter, a third recommendation might nonetheless address the content of both the foregoing recommendations within the context of postsecondary education in college or vocational training settings. That ADHD is a developmental disorder and, like a learning disability, will not necessarily disappear at high school graduation means that professors or instructors in various educational settings into which the individual with ADHD will graduate likewise need to be aware of the diagnostic and instructional implications of ADHD (Kavale & Forness, 1996).

School Practice and Policy

In addition to the implications for school practice also inherent in each of the foregoing recommendations for training, the first recommendation for school practice or educational policy is to develop more readily available consultation and support for both general and special education teachers who have children with ADHD in their classrooms. Teachers often fail to recognize the implications of ADHD in terms of both understanding its clinical presentation and its impact on classroom performance and failing to consider possible multimodality treatments that can markedly enhance their own interventions. Staff development, direct consultation, paraprofessional aides, interagency referral, and other services not only can assist teachers to better understand and deal with the implications of ADHD but can also extend these benefits over time as new children with ADHD enter these classrooms in subsequent years.

A second recommendation is to develop an awareness in school professionals of the particular burden that ADHD places on families and their special need for advocacy. Difficulties in attending school conferences, assisting in homework, managing household routines, obtaining respite care, and the like are all magnified by having a child or possibly even another affected family member with ADHD. School professionals need to recognize that children with ADHD present challenges to families that, although not immediately obvious, may nonetheless call for particular modification of the usual school expectations for parent involvement.

These recommendations regarding ADHD are clearly not exhaustive but are nonetheless among the most pressing in terms of their potential impact on school. ADHD should probably enjoy no more claim to such efforts than other widespread clinical entities, such as childhood depression or conduct disorders. Recognition of clinical and educational significance of such disorders, including ADHD, nonetheless seems a more prudent course than existing research and practice in schools to date.

References

Aaron, P. G. (1997). The impending demise of the discrepancy formula. *Review of Educational Research, 67*, 461–502.

American Academy of Child and Adolescent Psychiatry. (1997). Practice parameters for the assessment and treatment of children, adolescents, and adults with attention-deficit/hyperactivity disorder. *Journal of the American Academy of Child and Adolescent Psychiatry, 36*(Suppl.), 85S–121S.

American Psychiatric Association. (1994). *Diagnostic and statistical manual of mental disorders* (4th ed.). Washington, DC: Author.

Atkins, M. S., & Pelham, W. E. (1991). School-based assessment of attention deficit-hyperactivity disorder. *Journal of Learning Disabilities, 24*, 197–204.

Barkley, R. A. (1998). *Attention deficit hyperactivity disorder: A handbook for diagnosis and treatment* (2nd ed.). New York: Guilford Press.

Biederman, J., Newcorn, J., & Sprich, S. (1991). Comorbidity of attention deficit hyperactivity disorder with conduct, depressive, anxiety, and other disorders. *American Journal of Psychiatry, 148*, 564–577.

Bird, H. R., Gould, M. S., & Staghezza-Jaramillo, B. M. (1994). The comorbidity of ADHD in a community sample of children aged 6 through 16 years. *Journal of Child and Family Studies, 3*, 365–378.

Blankstein, A. M., Bullock, L. M., & Copans, S. A. (1998). Special issue: Improving longterm outcomes for children with ADHD. *Journal of Emotional and Behavioral Problems, 2*(2), 2–3.

Brandenberg, N. A., Friedman, R. M., & Silver, S. E. (1990). The epidemiology of childhood psychiatric disorders: Prevalence findings from recent studies. *Journal of the American Academy of Child and Adolescent Psychiatry, 29*, 76–83

Burcham, B., Carlson, L., & Milich, R. (1993). Promising school-based practices for students with attenton deficit disorder. *Exceptional Children, 60*, 174–180.

Bussing, R., Zima, B. T., Belin, T. R., & Forness, S. R. (1998). Children who qualify for LD and SED programs: Do they differ in level of ADHD symptoms and comorbid psychiatric conditions? *Journal of Emotional Disorders, 22*, 85–97.

Casey, J. E., Rourke, B. P., & Del Dotto, J. E. (1996). Learning disabilities in children with attention deficit disorder with and without hyperactivity. *Child Neuropsychology, 2*, 83–98.

Chalkind, S., Danielson, L. C., & Brauen, M. L. (1993). What do we know about the costs of special education? A selected review. *Journal of Special Education, 26*, 344–370.

Cohen, M. D. (1994). *Children on the boundaries: Challenges posed by children with conduct disorders.* Alexandria, VA: National Association of State Directors of Special Education.

Colorado Department of Education. (1994). *Attention deficit disorders: A handbook for Colorado educators.* Denver: Colorado Department of Education.

Council for Exceptional Children. (1992). *Children with ADD: A shared responsibility.* Reston, VA: Author.

Council of Administrators of Special Education. (1992). *Student access: A response guide for educators on Section 504 of the Rehabilitation Act of 1973.* Albuquerque NM: Author.

Crenshaw, T. M., Kavale, K. A., Forness, S. R., & Reeve, R. E. (1999). Attention deficit hyperactivity disorder and the efficacy of stimulation medication: A meta-analysis. In T. Scruggs & M. Mastropieri (Eds.), *Advances in learning and behavioral disabilities* (Vol. 13, pp. 135–165). Greenwich, CT: JAI Press.

Cullwood-Brathwaite, D., & McKinney, J. D. (1988, May 9). *Co-occurrence of attention deficit hyperactivity disorder in a school identified sample of students with emotional or behavioral disorders: Implications for educational programming.* Paper presented at the Southwest Regional Conference of the Council for Children with Behavioral Disorders, Gulf Shores, FL.

Davila, R. R., Williams, M. L., & MacDonald, J. T. (1991, September 16). *Clarification of policy to address the needs of children with attention deficit disorders within general and/or special education.* Washington, DC: U.S. Department of Education, Office of Special Education and Rehabilitation.

Del'Homme, M., Kasari, C., Forness, S. R., & Bagley, R. (1996). Prereferral intervention and students at risk for emotional or behavioral disorders. *Education and Treatment of Children, 19*, 272–285.

Duncan, B., Forness, S. R., & Hartsough, C. (1995). Students identified as seriously emotionally disturbed in day treatment classrooms: Cognitive, psychiatric, and special education characteristics. *Behavioral Disorders, 20*, 238–252.

DuPaul, G. J., & Eckert, T. L. (1997). The effects of school-based interventions for attention deficit hyperactivity disorder: A meta analysis. *School Psychology Review, 26*, 5–27.

DuPaul, G. J., & Stoner, G. (1996). *ADHD in the schools: Assessment and intervention strategies.* New York: Guilford Press.

Fiore, T. A., Becker, E. A., & Nero, R. C. (1993). Educational interventions for students with attention deficit disorder. *Focus on Exceptional Children, 60,* 163–173.

Fisher, J. B., Schumaker, J. B., & Deshler, D. D. (1995). Seaching for validated inclusive practices: A review of the literature. *Focus on Exceptional Children, 28,* 1–20.

Forness, S. (1990). Subtyping in learning disabilities: Introduction to the issues. In H. L. Swanson & B. Keogh (Eds.), *Learning disabilities: Theoretical and research issues* (pp. 195–200). Hillsdale, NJ: Erlbaum.

Forness, S. R., & Kavale, K. A. (1994). The Balkanization of special education: Proliferation of categories for new behavioral disorders. *Education and Treatment of Children, 17,* 215–227.

Forness, S. R., & Kavale, K. A. (1997). Defining emotional and behavioral disorders in school and related services. In J. W. Lloyd, E. J. Kameenui, & D. Chard (Eds.), *Issues in educating students with disabilities* (pp. 45–61). Hillsdale, NJ: Erlbaum.

Forness, S. R., Kavale, K. A., Blum, I., & Lloyd, J. W. (1997). Mega-analysis of meta-analyses: What works in special education and related services. *Teaching Exceptional Children, 29*(6), 4–9.

Forness, S. R., Kavale, K. A., & Crenshaw, T. M. (1999). Stimulant medication revisited: Effective treatment of children with ADHD. *Journal of Emotional and Behavioral Problems, 7,* 230–235.

Forness, S. R., Kavale, K. A., King, B. H., & Kasari, C. (1993). Conduct disorders in school: Special education eligibility and co-morbidity. *Journal of Emotional and Behavioral Disorders, 1,* 101–108.

Forness, S. R., Kavale, K. A., King, B. H., & Kasari, C. (1994). Simple versus complex conduct disorders: Identification and phenomenology. *Behavioral Disorders, 19,* 306–312.

Forness, S. R., Sweeney, D. P., & Wagner, S. R. (1998). Learning strategies and social skills training for students with ADHD. *Journal of Emotional and Behavioral Problems, 2*(2), 41–44.

Forness, S. R., & Walker, H. M. (1994). *Special education and children with ADD/ADHD.* Mentor, OH: National Attention Deficit Disorder Association.

Forness, S. R., Youpa, D., Hanna, G. L., Cantwell, D. P., & Swanson, J. M. (1992). Classroom instructional characteristics in attention deficit hyperactivity disorder: Comparison of pure and mixed subgroups. *Behavioral Disorders, 17,* 115–125.

Friedman, R. M., Katz-Leavy, J., Mandersheid, R., & Sondheimer, D. L. (1996). *Prevalence of serious emotional and developmental challenges.* New York: McGraw-Hill.

Fuchs, D., & Fuchs, L. S. (1994). Inclusive schools movement and the radicalization of special education reform. *Exceptional Children, 60,* 294–309.

Gardill, M. C., DuPaul, G. J., & Kyle, K. E. (1996). Classroom strategies for managing students with attention-deficit/hyperactivity disorder. *Intervention in School and Clinic, 32*(2), 89–94.

Gresham, F. M., MacMillan, D. L., Bocian, K., Ward, S. L., & Forness, S. R. (1998). Comorbidity of hyperactivity-impulsivity-inattention + conduct problems: Risk factors in social, affecrtive, and academic domains. *Journal of Abnormal Child Psychology, 26,* 393–406.

Hinshaw, S. (1992). Externalizing behavior problems and academic underachievement in childhood and adolescence: Causal relationships and underlying mechanisms. *Journal of Attention Disorders, 111,* 127–155.

Hocutt, A. M., McKinney, J. D., & Montague, M. (1993). Issues in the education of students with attention deficit disorder: Introduction to the special issue. *Exceptional Children, 60,* 103–108.

Hodapp, R. M., & Dykens, E. M. (1992). The role of etiology in education of children with mental retardation. *McGill Journal of Education, 27,* 165–173.

Holborow, P. L., & Berry, P. S. (1986). Hyperactivity and learning difficulties. *Journal of Learning Disabilities, 19,* 426–431.

Hunt, P., & Goetz, L. (1997). Research on inclusive educational programs, practices, and outcomes for students with severe disabilities. *Journal of Special Education, 31,* 329.

Jensen, P. S., Martin, D., & Cantwell, D. P. (1997). Comorbidity in ADHD: Implications for research, practice, and DSM-V. *Journal of the American Academy of Child and Adolescent Psychiatry, 36*, 1065–1079.

Kauffman, J. M., & Hallahan, D. P. (Eds.). (1995). *The illusion of full inclusion: A comprehensive critique of a current special education bandwagon.* Austin, TX: Pro-Ed.

Kavale, K. A., & Forness, S. R. (1996). Learning disabilities grows up: Rehabilitation issues for individuals with learning disabilities. *Journal of Rehabilitation, 62*, 34–41.

Kavale, K. A., & Forness, S. R. (2000). Policy decisions in special education. The role of meta-analysis. In R. M. Gersten & E. P. Schiller (Eds.), *Contemporary special education research: Synthesis of knowledge in critical interactional issues* (pp. 281–326). Mahwah, NJ: Erlbaum.

King-Sears, M. E. (1997). Best academic practices for inclusive classrooms. *Focus on Exceptional Children, 29*(7), 1–22.

Levine, M. D., Busch, B., & Aufseeser, C. (1982). The dimension of inattention among children with school problems. *Pediatrics, 29*(7), 387–395.

Lipsky, D. K., & Gartner, A. (1996). Inclusion, school restructuring, and the remaking of the American society. *Harvard Education Review, 66*, 762–796.

Lloyd, J. W., Forness, S. R., & Kavale, K. A. (1998). Some methods are more effective than others. *Intervention in School and Clinic, 33*, 195–200.

Lopez, M., Forness, S. R., MacMillan, D. L., Bocian, K., & Gresham, F. M. (1996). Children with attention deficit hyperactivity disorder and emotional and behavioral disorders in the primary grades: inappropriate placement in the LD category. *Education and Treatment of Children, 19*, 286–299.

Lyon, G. (1994). Learning disabilities. In K. L. Freiberg (Ed.), *Educating exceptional children* (10th ed.). Guilford, CT: Dushkin-McGraw-Hill.

Maag, J. W., & Reid, R. (1994). Attention-deficit hyperactivity disorder: A functional approach to assessment and treatment. *Behavioral Disorders, 35*, 1237–1246.

MacMillan, D. L., Gresham, F. M., & Bocian, K. (1998). Discrepancy between definition of learning disabilities and school practices: An empirical investigation. *Journal of Learning Disabilities, 31*(4), 314–326.

MacMillan, D. L., Gresham, F. M., & Forness, S. R. (1996). Full inclusion: An empirical perspective. *Behavioral Disorders, 21*, 146–160.

Mattison, R. E., & Felix, B. C. (1997). The course of elementary and secondary school students with SED through their special education experience. *Journal of Emotional and Behavioral Disorders, 5*, 107–117.

Mattison, R. E., & Forness, S. R. (1995). Mental health system involvement in special education placement decisions. In J. M. Kauffman, J. W. Lloyd, D. Hallahan, & T. A. Astuto (Eds.), *Issues in educational placement of children with emotional or behavioral disorders* (pp. 197–211). Hillsdale, NJ: Erlbaum.

Mattison, R. E., Lynch, J. C., Kales, H., & Gamble, A. D. (1993). Checklist identification of elementary schoolboys for clinical referral or evaluation of eligibility for special education. *Behavioral Disorders, 18*, 218–227.

Mattison, R. E., Morales, J., & Bauer, M. A. (1993). Adolescent scholboys in SED classes: Implications for child psychiatry. *Journal of the American Academy of Child and Adolescent Psychiatry, 32*, 1223–1228.

McConaughy, S. H., Mattison, R. E., & Peterson, R. (1994). Behavioral/emotional problems of children with serious emotional disturbance and learning disabilities. *School Psychology Review, 23*, 81–98.

McKinney, J. D., Montague, M., & Hocutt, A. M. (1993). Educational assessment of students with attention deficit disorder. *Exceptional Children, 60*, 125–131.

Mercer, C. D., Jordan, L., Allsopp, D. H., & Mercer, A. R. (1996). Learning disabilities definitions and criteria used by state eduction departments. *Learning Disabilities Quarterly, 19*, 217–232.

Montague, M., & Warger, C. (1997). Helping students with attention deficit hyperactivity disorder succeed in the classroom. *Focus on Exceptional Children, 30*(4), 1–16.

MTA Cooperative Group. (1999). A 14-month randomized clinical trial of treatment strategies for attention-deficit/hyperactivity disorder: Multimodal Treatment Study of Children with ADHD. *Archives of General Psychiatry, 56*(12), 1073–1086.

Parker, H. C. (1989). *Education position paper: Children with attention deficit disorder.* Plantation, FL: Ch.A.D.D. (Children with Attention Deficit Disorder).

Pisecco, S., Baker, D. B., Silva, P. A., & Brooke, M. (1996). Behavioral distinctions in children with reading disabilities and/or ADHD. *Journal of the American Academy of Child and Adolescent Psychiatry, 35*, 1477–1484.

Reid, R., Maag, J. W., & Vasa, S. F. (1993). Attention deficit hyperactivity disorder as a disability category: A critique. *Exceptional Children, 60*, 198–214.

Richters, J. E., Arnold, L. E., Jensen, P. S., Abikoff, H., Conners, C. K., Greenhill, L. L., Hechtman, L., Hinshaw, S. P., Pelham, W. E., & Swanson, J. M. (1995). NIMH collaborative multisite multi-modal treatment study of children with ADHD: I. Background and rationale. *Journal of the American Academy of Child and Adolescent Psychiatry, 34*, 987–1000.

Rooney, K. J. (1993). Classroom interventions for students with attention deficit disorders. *Focus Exceptional Children, 26*(4), 1–16.

Sage, D. D., & Burrello, L. C. (1994). *Leadership in educational reform: An administrators guide to changes in special education.* Baltimore: Paul H. Brookes.

Scruggs, T. E., & Mastropieri, M. A. (1996). Teacher perceptions of mainstreaming/inclusion, 1958–1995: A research synthesis. *Exceptional Children, 63*, 59–74.

Semrud-Clikeman, M., Biederman, J., Sprich-Buckminster, S., Lehman, B. K., Faraone, S. V., & Norman, D. (1992). Comorbidity between ADDH and learning disability: A review and report in a clinically referred sample. *Journal of the American Academy of Child and Adolescent Psychiatry, 31*, 439–448.

Shaffer, D., Fisher, P., Dulcan, M. K., Davies, M., Piacentini, J., Schwab-Stone, M. E., Lahey, B. B., Bourdon, K., Jensen, P. S., Bird, H. R., Canino, G., & Regier, D. A. (1996). The NIMH diagnostic interview schedule for children version 2.3 (DISC-2.3): Description, acceptability, prevalence rates, and performance in the MECA study. *Journal of the American Academy of Child and Adolescent Psychiatry, 35*, 865–877.

Shaw, S. T., Cullen, J. P., McGuire, J. M., & Brickerhoff, L. C. (1995). Operationalizing a definition of learning disabilities. *Journal of Learning Disabilities, 28*, 586–597.

Shaywitz, S. E., & Shaywitz, B. A. (1991). Introduction to the special series on attention deficit disorder. *Journal of Learn Disabilities, 24*, 68–72.

Sobsey, D., & Dreimanis, M. (1993). Integration outcomes: Theoretical models and empirical investigations. *Developmental Disabilities Bulletin, 21*(1), 1–14.

Stainback, W., & Stainback, S. (Eds.) (1996). *Inclusion: A guide for educators.* Baltimore: Paul H. Brookes.

U.S. Department of Education. (1994). *Attention deficit disorders: Adding up the facts.* Washington, DC: U.S. Government Printing Office.

U.S. Department of Education. (1990–1997). *Twelfth through nineteenth annual reports to Congress on the implementation of the Individuals with Disabilities Education Act.* Washington, DC: U.S. Government Printing Office.

Vatz, B. C. (1997, March 16). *Behavioral subtypes of learning disabled children.* Paper presented at the annual convention of the National Association of School Psychologists, San Francisco.

Yell, M. L., & Shriver, J. G. (1997). The IDEA amendments of 1997: Implications for special and general teachers, administrators, and teacher trainers. *Focus on Exceptional Children, 30*(1), 1–19.

Zirkel, P. A. (1995). *Section 504 and the schools.* Horsham, PA: LRP.

Chapter 25

The Impact of Attention Deficit Hyperactivity Disorder on the Juvenile Justice System

by Betty Chemers, M.A.

Introduction 25-1
Trends in Juvenile Offending 25-1
    Growth in Number of Detained Juveniles 25-1
    Prevalence of Mental Health Disorders, ADHD, and
        Conduct Disorders Among Youth in the Juvenile
        Justice System 25-2
    Relationship of ADHD and CD to Antisocial and Violent
        Behavior 25-3
Juvenile Justice System Response 25-3
Research Needs 25-4

INTRODUCTION

Since 1995 the Office of Juvenile Justice and Delinquency Prevention (OJJDP) has identified juvenile mental health issues as a priority for both research and program support. With increasing numbers of juveniles entering the juvenile justice system, there is great interest not only in expanding what is known about the specific behaviors or circumstances that bring youth to the attention of the juvenile justice system but also in understanding the underlying problems, including mental health disorders and substance abuse.

TRENDS IN JUVENILE OFFENDING

Growth in Number of Detained Juveniles

To assess the impact of ADHD on the juvenile justice system, it is useful to look at an updated picture of juvenile crime trends and their impact on juvenile justice agencies. For many Americans, juvenile crime and violence are the most important issues facing our nation today. From 1986 until 1994, crimes by juveniles increased at an alarming rate. In 1995, this trend stopped, and in 1996, for the second consecutive year, the number of juvenile arrests for violent crime index offenses—murder, forcible rape, robbery, and aggravated assault—declined (Snyder, 1997). This increase is reflected in the workload of the juvenile courts, which experienced an increase of 48 percent in the number of delinquency cases between 1988 and 1997 (Sickmund, 2000). The increase in juvenile offending was also reflected in the increased number of juveniles held in detention, correctional, or shelter facilities. On October 29, 1997, the most recent date for which a count is available, more than 105,790 juveniles were in detention. For public facilities, this figure represents almost a doubling of the number of juveniles held from the period (1983) predating the great increase in juvenile arrests (Snyder, Sickmund, Poe-Yamagata, 1997).

Prevalence of Mental Health Disorders, ADHD, and Conduct Disorders Among Youth in the Juvenile Justice System

In his landmark report, Cocozza (1992) concluded from a review of prevalence studies that although it was not possible to offer an exact prevalence rate of mental health disorders for youth in the juvenile justice system, it was clear that the prevalence rate was substantially higher than in the general population. Although the estimates ranged as high as 22 percent, it was likely that the prevalence rate for youth in the juvenile justice system was higher. Although information on the specific types of conduct disorder was lacking, Cocozza offered a safe estimate that at least 20 percent and perhaps as many as 60 percent of the youth in the juvenile justice system had conduct disorders.

Because conduct disorder is currently considered one of a trio of related diagnoses that also includes attention deficit hyperactivity disorder (ADHD) and oppositional defiance disorder (ODD), known collectively as disruptive behavior disorders, many studies do not identify the specific prevalence of ADHD. For those that do, the rates vary widely. In a recent literature review of eleven studies conducted from 1980 to 1997, Teplin (1998) looked at the prevalence of alcohol, drug, and mental health (ADM) disorders in nonreferred juvenile detainees. Prevalence rates of ADHD ranged from a low of 2 percent to a high of 76 percent.

Virginia and Ohio have conducted recent statewide assessments of the mental health needs of juvenile detainees. Virginia authorities identified 8 percent to 10 percent of their youth in secure detention homes as having serious mental problems requiring immediate attention and an additional 39 percent of youth as having mental health problems requiring mental health services but not requiring immediate intervention. Attention problems, possibly ADHD as tested by youth behavior checklist ratings, were found in 6.9 percent of the youth detention population (Virginia Policy Design Team, 1994). In a series of recent studies from 1994 to 1996 conducted in Ohio by the Department of Psychiatry at Case Western Reserve University School of Medicine, mental health needs of incarcerated male and female juveniles were assessed and compared with a 1988 study. In the earlier study (Davis, Bean, Schumacher, & Stronger, 1991), 29 percent of the males exhibited serious mental disorders. In the later study (Timmons-Mitchell et al., 1997), males continued to exhibit high rates of mental illness (27 percent), whereas females exhibited an overwhelming presence of mental illness estimated to be about 84 percent. Conduct disorder was the mental health diagnosis for 100 percent of the males and 96 percent of the females.

Attention deficit was identified as present in 76 percent of the males and 68 percent of the females (Underwood, 1997).

Relationship of ADHD and CD to Antisocial And Violent Behavior

Although exact prevalence rates may vary, analyses show a consistently elevated rate of criminal behavior among children with hyperactivity/inattention (particularly if aggression is present) and other disruptive disorders. And this relationship appears to be consistent with later violent behavior. Unfortunately, the relationship is not well understood. Evidence from a wide range of studies consistently reveals a positive relationship between hyperactivity, concentration or attention problems, impulsivity and risk taking, and later violent behavior (Loeber & Farrington, 1998).

Clearly, the juvenile justice system has a great interest in ADHD and conduct disorders, taken both individually and together. Both are significant risk factors for the development of less serious antisocial behavior as well as more violent behavior. Furthermore, there is evidence that the comorbidity is associated with more arrests and more antisocial behaviors, which start at a younger age, than with conduct disorder alone. The comorbidity of the two disorders seems to combine the worst features of both (Foley, Carlton, & Howell, 1996).

JUVENILE JUSTICE SYSTEM RESPONSE

In the same way that we are beginning to get a sense of the magnitude of the problem, we are at the threshold of understanding what is required to address the needs of youth with ADHD and conduct disorder. We do know that these youth exert great stress on the system. Some of the stress is caused by the sheer numbers and the fact that early onset of ADHD and conduct disorders seems particularly resistant to treatment (Foley et al., 1996). The most promising approaches incorporate multiple components with documented efficacy at the individual, family, and peer levels (Wasserman & Miller, 1998), but unfortunately the restrictive nature of the juvenile justice system, detention in particular, may not lend itself to a multisystemic approach to treatment. Although these youth and their families may have had multiple contacts with the juvenile justice, child welfare, and mental health service systems, these systems are just beginning to form networks of care, to share information, and to employ treatments established in one discipline for use in others. Reactive approaches rather than proactive approaches are the norm. Sanctions are more dominant than either treatment or prevention efforts.

Some important strides have been made to improve the delivery of mental health services to youth in the juvenile justice system. Notable is the Cook County Clinical Evaluation and Services Initiative (CESI), a joint project of Northwestern University School of Law, the University of Chicago, and the Juvenile Court of Cook County in Illinois, which is aimed at a comprehensive redesign of the Department of Clinical Services and a correlating reform of the use and acquisition of information obtained from the provision of clinical services by the juvenile court judges (Dohrn & Leventhal, 1997). As described earlier, Virginia and Ohio are among several states seriously committed to the expansion of mental health services.

Increasing attention has also been focused on new organizational structures (community assessment centers) to better assess the needs of juveniles and on new assessment instruments (Massachusetts youth screening instrument).

An important strategy employed by the juvenile justice field focuses on youth at highest risk. One group at highest risk comprises young juvenile offenders. Efforts are under way to use current knowledge about risk factors and the developmental course of young, serious, violent juvenile offenders to identify appropriate intervention strategies. Early diagnosis and treatment of ADHD and conduct disorders are an important key to preventing future delinquency.

RESEARCH NEEDS

There are numerous significant gaps in our knowledge about youth with ADHD and conduct disorders in the general population and in the juvenile justice system in particular. First, there is a need to identify youth with mental illness and to identify appropriate treatment. As indicated, the juvenile justice system is not well equipped to handle juveniles with mental health disorders. Effective models for screening, diverting, and treating offenders and establishing comprehensive community-based systems of care are needed. Many disorders, including the less severe or pervasive ones, have the potential to be linked with a particular youth's involvement with the juvenile justice system. Ways must be found to treat youth whose mental disorders may not be linked to their delinquent behavior while in the juvenile justice system (Cocozza, 1992).

Second, research is needed on prevalence of ADHD and conduct disorders in females. Increasingly, more girls are coming into the juvenile justice system charged with more serious crimes. There is preliminary evidence in at least three studies that we are seeing a higher incidence of ADHD and conduct disorders among female youth detainees. A majority of girls in the juvenile justice system have been physically abused and/or sexually assaulted, and this needs to be considered in the assessment and screening process as well as in programming and protocols.

Third, increased research on predictors of adolescent antisocial behavior is needed. Most serious violent offenders have a history of earlier childhood misbehavior. Research on the specific risk factors for these behaviors may yield important knowledge that can be used to prevent violent offending. Wasserman and Miller (1998) suggest that if a diagnosis of ADHD is a risk factor for a later conduct disorder, then ameliorating the symptoms of ADHD may decrease the chances of subsequent conduct disorder and violent offending.

Fourth, research is needed on mental disorders among youth of color and their representation in services. Little has been written or researched on this subject since the Cocozza report (1992), which summarizes previous studies' analyses of the mental health needs of children and adolescents of color. Her observation that few researchers have explored systematically the reasons for or consequences of youth of color being over represented in the U.S. juvenile justice system while also being underserved and inappropriately served by the child mental health system appears to still hold true almost ten years later.

Finally, valid estimated costs to society of conduct problems and services to ADHD children in the juvenile justice system have not been done up to this point. This topic is assuredly worthy of future attention by researchers, not just to argue in favor of other research endeavors in the area of ADHD but also to better understand and administer to these children's service needs.

References

Cocozza, J. J. (Ed.). (1992). *Responding to the mental health needs of youth in the juvenile justice system.* Seattle: National Coalition for the Mentally Ill in the Criminal Justice System.

Davis, D. L., Bean, G., Schumacher, J., & Stronger, T. (1991). Prevalence of emotional disorders in a juvenile justice institutional population. *American Journal of Forensic Psychology, 9*, 1–13.

Dohrn, B., & Leventhal, B. (1997). *Clinical evaluation and services initiative.* Cook County, IL: Juvenile Justice and Child Protection Department.

Foley, H., Carlton, C., & Howell, R. (1996). The relationship of attention deficit hyperactivity disorder and conduct disorder to juvenile delinquency: Legal implications. *Bulletin of American Academy of Psychiatry Law, 243*, 333–345.

Loeber, R., & Farrington, D. (Eds.). (1998). *Serious and violent juvenile offenders: risk factors and successful interventions.* Thousand Oaks, CA: Sage.

Sickmund, M. (2000, October). Offenders in juvenile court, 1997. *OJJDP Juvenile Justice Bulletin,* pp. 1–3.

Snyder, H. N. (1997). *Juvenile arrests 1996.* Unpublished internal document, U.S. Department of Justice, Office of Juvenile Justice and Delinquency Prevention, Washington, DC.

Snyder, H. N., Sickmund, M., & Poe-Yamagata, E. (1997). *Juvenile offenders and victims: 1997 update on violence.* Unpublished internal document, U.S. Department of Justice, Office of Juvenile Justice and Delinquency Prevention, Washington, DC.

Teplin, L. (1998). *Assessing the alcohol, drug and mental health service needs in juvenile detainees.* Grant application submitted to National Institute of Mental Health.

Timmons-Mitchell, J., Brown, C., Schulz, S. C., Webster, S. E., Underwood, L. A., & Semple, W. E. (1997). Comparing the mental health needs of female and male incarcerated juvenile delinquents. *Behavioral Sciences and the Law, 15*, 195–202.

Underwood, L. A. (1997). *Ohio's systems approach to dealing with its incarcerated mentally ill juvenile offenders.* Unpublished manuscript.

Virginia Policy Design Team. (1994). *Mental health needs of youth in Virginia's juvenile detention centers*, Richmond, VA.

Wasserman, G. A., & Miller, L. S. (1998). The prevention of serious and violent juvenile offending. In R. Loeber & D. Farrington (Eds.), *Serious and violent juvenile offenders* (pp. 197–247). Thousand Oaks, CA: Sage.

Chapter 26

Educational Policy— Educating Children With Attention Deficit Hyperactivity Disorder

by Louis Danielson, Ph.D., Kelly Henderson, Ph.D., and Ellen Schiller, Ph.D.

Introduction 26-1
Federal Policy History 26-2
    Background 26-2
    Joint Federal Policy Memorandum 26-2
        IDEA Eligibility 26-2
        Rehabilitation Act Section 504 Eligibility 26-3
    Federal Support for ADHD Research and Technical
      Assistance 26-3
U.S. Department of Education Activities Since 1991 26-4
Revised IDEA Regulations 26-5
    State Education Agency Policies 26-6
        Background 26-6
        Adoption of Written Policies 26-6
    ADHD as Part of a Disability Category 26-7
    Policies Specific to Identification and Assessment
      of ADHD 26-7
    Policies Regarding Medication of Students
      With ADHD 26-8
Prevalence of ADHD in States 26-8
Technical Assistance Needs of State and Local Educators 26-8
    ADHD as an "Other Health Impairment" 26-9
    Discussion and Implications 26-10

INTRODUCTION

The U.S. Department of Education has, since 1991, taken several major steps toward improving education for children and youth with attention deficit hyperactivity disorder (ADHD). This chapter summarizes several significant federal education policy initiatives designed to improve identification, assessment, and delivery of appropriate and effective interventions to children and youth with ADHD.[1] Results of a survey of state departments of education are described which evaluate the impact of these recent federal policy efforts.

FEDERAL POLICY HISTORY

Background

The appropriate role of federal policy in the education of children with ADHD has been the subject of much debate over the last decade. Eligibility for students with ADHD was raised by the 101st Congress during consideration of the Education of the Handicapped Act Amendments of 1990 (since renamed the Individuals with Disabilities Education Act, Public Law 101-476) (Aleman, 1991). Advocates proposed that the Act's list of qualifying disability categories be amended to include ADHD. During the markup of the reauthorization bills, both the Senate and House of Representatives authorizing committees included either a bill or accompanying report language that included ADHD as part of the existing disabilities law. The Senate committee report included minimal brain dysfunction under the definition of specific learning disability, whereas the House bill included ADHD in the definition of other health impairment. In the face of strong opposition from large national education organizations, however, the conference bill ultimately dropped the House ADHD language and added two new provisions regarding ADHD (Aleman, 1991). First, the Department of Education was required to collect public comments on several questions about children with ADHD and report findings to the Congress; second, the Department was to establish information centers to disseminate current knowledge about ADHD to parents, principals, and teachers.

A Notice of Inquiry was published in November 1990 and responses to twelve questions on special education for children with ADHD were solicited. The comment period closed in late March 1991 and in May 1991, the Education Department provided to Congress a summary of 2,068 comments received; parents of children with ADHD and school administrators were the two groups most represented in the comments.

Joint Federal Policy Memorandum

IDEA Eligibility. In September 1991, the U.S. Department of Education clarified the provisions under which children with ADHD could be educated in the public schools. On September 16, 1991, three principal offices of the Department—the Office of Special Education and Rehabilitative Services, the Office of Civil Rights, and the Office of Elementary and Secondary Education—issued a memorandum to clarify policy to address the needs of children with ADHD within general and/or special education (Davila, Williams, & MacDonald, 1991). In brief, a child with ADHD may be eligible for special education and related services under the Individuals with Disabilities Education Act (IDEA) if he or she meets the criteria for one of the thirteen recognized categories including other health impairments (OHI), the definition of which includes chronic or acute impairments that result in limited alertness which adversely affects educational performance, specific learning disabilities, or serious emotional disturbance. All IDEA requirements regarding evaluation and procedural safeguards apply to any child suspected of having a disability and who may be in need of special education and related services. Regardless of the condition or disability category, to be eligible for special education and related services under IDEA, the child's educational performance must be adversely affected by the disability.

Part B of IDEA makes the following requirements:

- State and local districts make a free appropriate public education available to all eligible children with disabilities.

- The rights and protections of Part B of IDEA are extended to children with ADD and their parents.

- An evaluation by a multidisciplinary team must be done, without undue delay, to determine if the child has at least one of the thirteen specified disabling conditions (including ADD/ADHD) and requires special education and related services.

- Children with ADD must be classified as eligible for services under the "other health impaired" (OHI) category in instances where ADD is a chronic or acute health problem that results in limited alertness that adversely affects a child's educational performance.

- Local districts may not refuse to evaluate the possible need for special education and related services of a child with a prior medical diagnosis of ADD solely by reason of that medical diagnosis (which does not automatically make a child eligible for services).

- A due process hearing must take place, at the request of the parents, if there is disagreement between the local district and the parent over the request for evaluation, the evaluation, or the determinations for services.

Rehabilitation Act Section 504 Eligibility. Alternatively, the memo clarifies, though a child with ADHD may not be found to be eligible for services under Part B of IDEA, the requirements of Section 504 of the Rehabilitation Act of 1973 may be applicable. Section 504 requires recipients that operate a public education program to address the needs of children who are handicapped as adequately as the program addresses the needs of nonhandicapped children. Section 504 applies to those persons who have a physical or mental impairment which substantially limits a major life activity (i.e., learning). Under Section 504, school districts are obligated to provide regular or special education programs, including necessary modifications and supplementary aids and services to qualified children with ADHD based on their individual needs.

Federal Support for ADHD Research and Technical Assistance

In addition to the joint memorandum, the Department supported several major efforts to synthesize research on ADHD, conduct research to fill knowledge gaps, and link with professional and advocacy organizations to communicate findings. The

Office of Special Education Programs (OSEP) supported centers that initially helped to identify the most critical questions from the field and subsequently collected, synthesized, and analyzed the existing research and practice knowledge. Resulting syntheses examined the effects of medication, assessment, and identification of ADHD, and effects of educational interventions. In fiscal year (FY) 1992 and FY 1995, OSEP funded researchers to conduct additional studies on effective educational practices and the context that supports those practices for children and youth with ADHD. OSEP also supported research to understand the school, child, family, and sociodemographic variables to predict a child's responsiveness to drug treatment.

To enhance the quality, use, and impact of the research syntheses and studies, OSEP facilitated meaningful and lasting exchanges of information across agencies, centers, associations, and other entities representing stakeholders in the education of children and youth with ADHD. These efforts included convening a national forum on the educational needs of children with ADHD, linking with national education and parent associations and teacher unions to communicate consumer-oriented research-based information products through their ongoing publication and professional development activities, releasing a highly accessible information kit for educators and parents on the education of children with ADHD, supporting a leadership training initiative at the University of Oregon to train doctoral-level students to conduct research on the education of children with ADHD, and supporting thirteen personnel preparation projects that focused on ADHD. A topical 1997 issue on ADHD in the journal *Teacher Education in Special Education* summarizes findings from these personnel preparation and professional development projects

More recently, OSEP has supported research projects to examine the effects of school child and family variables on drug responsiveness and to examine the developmental impact of maternal cocaine exposure on attention. In addition, OSEP currently supports three projects to train preservice and inservice teachers, school psychologists, and other school personnel on assessment, intervention, and progress monitoring

U.S. DEPARTMENT OF EDUCATION ACTIVITIES SINCE 1991

Since the issuance of the 1991 joint memorandum, both the Office of Civil Rights (OCR) and the Office of Special Education and Rehabilitative Services (OSERS) have continued to clarify federal education policy for children who have ADHD. For example, in response to misinterpretation of one statement in the 1991 joint memorandum regarding parental requests for evaluation, OCR clarified, in an April 29, 1993, memorandum, that under Section 504, if parents believe their child has a disability, whether ADHD or any other impairment, and the local educational authority (LEA) has reason to believe the child needs special education or related services, the LEA must evaluate the child to determine eligibility. If the LEA does not believe the child needs such services and refuses to evaluate the child, it must notify parents of their due process rights.

Since 1991, OSEP has responded to more than twenty inquiries through written policy letters. OCR has issued findings in nearly ninety complaints relative to alleged discrimination against children with ADHD. The majority of these are decisions and policy clarifications regarding appropriate evaluation and provision of subsequent services to children and youth with ADHD; many restate the policies formalized in the 1991 memo.

REVISED IDEA REGULATIONS

The IDEA Amendments of 1997 (Public Law 105–17) were signed by President Clinton on June 4, 1997. The 1997 reauthorization of the IDEA did not directly address issues of ADHD in legislative language. Throughout its history, IDEA authorizing legislation has placed in statute the categories under which eligibility as a "child with a disability" can be determined but has not defined such categories. Instead, implementing regulations provide definitions for the specific category terms. The regulations for the 1997 reauthorization were proposed and provided for public comment in October 1997. The notice of proposed rulemaking did, however, include some reference to ADHD. The note that accompanies Section 300.7 of the proposed regulations, which defines "child with a disability," addresses circumstances under which a child with ADHD is eligible under part B of the Act. The note restates much of the policy outlined in the 1991 joint memorandum, including the circumstances under which OHI could be used to classify children with ADHD and who need special education and related services. The note also confirms that if a child with ADHD is not eligible for services under Part B, Section 504 may still be applicable.

The final IDEA 1997 regulations were released on Friday, March 12, 1999, and a revised version of the "Regulations Index" was published in the *Federal Register* on June 24, 1999. The major, general issues of the final regulations are:

- Improving teaching and learning, with a specific focus on the individualized education program (IEP) as the primary tool for enhancing the child's involvement and progress in the general curriculum;

- Ensuring that the IEP for each child with a disability includes a statement of the child's present levels of educational performance; measurable annual goals related to meeting the child's needs that result from the child's disability; a statement of the special education and related services, supplementary aids, and services; and the program modifications or supports for school personnel;

- Mandating that, as a condition of state eligibility for funding under Part B of IDEA, children with disabilities are included in general state- and district-wide assessment programs;

- Ensuring that the IEP team for each child with a disability now includes at least one of the child's regular education teachers if the child is, or may be, participating in the regular education environment;

- Addressing discipline limits for children with disabilities;

- Allowing for states to define developmental delay for children ages 3 through 9 and authorizing LEAs to choose to use the category and, if they do, requiring them to use the state's definition;

- Defining the terms "day" and "schoolday";

- Two specific provisions on charter schools:

— In situations in which charter schools are public schools of the LEA, mandating that the LEA must serve children with disabilities in those schools in the same manner that it serves children with disabilities in its other schools, and provide Part B funds to those schools in the same manner as it provides Part B funds to its other schools; and

— Not allowing a state education agency (SEA) to require a charter school that is an LEA to jointly establish its eligibility with another LEA unless it is explicitly permitted to so do under the state's charter school statute; and

• Addressing the issue of parentally placed children with disabilities in private schools.

With regard to children with disabilities who are eligible under Part B, ADD and ADHD remained a part of the OHI category, but, as has been the long-standing policy, the regulations clarify that ADHD has been listed as a condition that could render a child eligible under the oHI category of Part B, and the term "limited strength, vitality, or alertness" in the definition of "OHI," when applied to children with ADHD, includes a child's heightened alertness to environmental stimuli that results in limited alertness with respect to the educational environment.

State Education Agency Policies

Background. To evaluate the impact of the 1991 joint federal policy memorandum on the efforts of SEAs and others to clarify education policy for serving children and youth with ADHD, states were surveyed regarding their own policies and procedures for identifying and serving children with ADHD. This survey was administered in the fall of 1998 and included several questions that were posed in a similar survey issued in the fall of 1993 by the OSEP and supported by the University of Miami Center on Research on ADHD. Findings from the 1998 survey are reported first, followed (where applicable) by comparisons with those from the 1993 administration (U.S. Department of Education, 1998).

Adoption of Written Policies. Table 26.1 summarizes the responses, which were received from forty-two states.[2] Nineteen states (45 percent of respondents) indicated having some type of written policy regarding education of students with attention deficit hyperactivity disorder. Five SEA policies (12 percent) are part of the IDEA special education rules, regulations, or procedures, all of which were adopted or amended since January 1993. One state law (2 percent) includes reference to ADHD policy in its special education statute. Six states (14 percent) report that ADHD is included as part of their Section 504 rules, regulations, or guidelines, including one state that also has IDEA special education rules or regulations which reference ADHD. Six more SEAs (14 percent) provide guidelines consistent with, or summaries of, the 1991 federal joint memorandum to local education agencies, and one state's legislature also passed a resolution in May 1992 requiring all local superintendents to provide all teachers with information on characteristics, assessment, identification, interventions, and service delivery options for students with ADHD. Three additional states (7 percent) reported that they provide LEAs copies of the 1991 federal joint memorandum. Twenty-three states (55 percent) provide no written formal or informal policies or guidelines regarding education of students with ADHD.

Table 26.1
Written State Policies Relating to ADHD

Some Type of Written Policy	19 (45%) of 42 respondents state
As a component of:	
IDEA special education rules, regulations, or procedures	12%
State special education statute	2%
Rules, regulations, or guidelines to implement Section 504 of Rehabilitation Act or Americans with Disabilities Act	14%
Other guidelines consistent with 1991 federal memorandum 14%	

Results reported from the 1993 survey combined all types of written policies or guidance. Eleven states (26 percent of respondents) reported having some type of written guidance or policy regarding ADHD under IDEA in 1993.

ADHD as Part of a Disability Category

Twenty-six states (62 percent) reported that ADHD is not included in the definitions of any specific category of disability, though one of these states' education code does reference ADHD separately and reiterates the 1991 memorandum that students with ADHD may be eligible for special education and related services under the OHI, ED (emotional disturbance), or SLD (specific learning disability) categories. Seven states (17 percent) include ADD/ADHD as part of a definition of specific learning disabilities, or the state's substitute term. Five states (12 percent) include the term within their definition of emotional disturbance, and eleven states (26 percent) specifically reference ADHD in their OHI or substitute category. Of these respondents, five states report that ADHD is included as part of the definitions for all three of these categories. One additional state reported that it is noncategorical and could not respond within the survey options.

The 1993 survey did not collect data regarding ADHD within the definitions of specific disability categories.

Policies Specific to Identification and Assessment of ADHD

Thirteen states (31 percent) reported some type of written policy regarding individual identification or assessment of ADHD. Evaluation procedures and qualifications for assessment specialists specific to identification of children in this category are specified in the IDEA administrative procedures or regulations of two states; both require an appropriate medical evaluation/statement from a licensed physician. One state also required measures of social and physical adaptive behaviors for an ADHD evaluation and the other state specifies use of a norm-referenced rating scale designed to identify students with ADHD.

The remaining eleven states with written identification and assessment policies do not specify such in their statute or regulations. Rather, memoranda of clarification were issued in two states and nine states have adopted guidelines or produced task force reports on the issue. For example, in January 1998, the Vermont Department of Education Family and Educational Support Team published *Vermont Guidelines for Identifying Students with ADD and ADHD* (1998), which summarizes the 1991 federal memo, details definitions of ADHD, and describes the diagnosis of ADHD using DSM-IV. The guidelines further recommend methods of evaluation and list a number of instruments for the assessment of ADHD. Principles outlined in the 1991 federal memo, including determination of the adverse effects of ADHD on performance and the determination of the child's need for special education, are also specified in the Vermont guidelines. Similarly, the Utah State Office of Education, Students at Risk Section issued a 1996 *Utah Attention Deficit Disorder Guide* that does not alter state rules or regulations but serves as a "resource" designed to provide up-to-date and accurate information about students with ADHD. Education diagnosis and assessment is based on DSM-IV definition and criteria and includes a variety of resources for assessing, evaluating, and serving students with ADHD.

Policies Regarding Medication of Students With ADHD

No states maintain written policies which specifically address the medication of students with ADHD. Nine states referenced their general policies for administration of medication to any student, and two states noted that the aforementioned guidelines or task force reports include guidance about the role of medication in serving students with ADHD.

PREVALENCE OF ADHD IN STATES

Under IDEA, state education agencies are required to report annually a child count, by each disability category, as of December 1. Students with ADHD who are also identified with an emotional disturbance, specific learning disability, or other health impairment are included in those categories for child count purposes. No state reported a capacity to disaggregate the number of students in those categories due to their ADHD from the rest of those in the reported categories. Three states, however, did attribute increases in some categories, namely OHI, since 1991, to those students with ADHD.

TECHNICAL ASSISTANCE NEEDS OF STATE AND LOCAL EDUCATORS

The survey of state education agencies included a speculative question about the greatest challenges faced by local school districts regarding educational services for students with ADHD (see Table 26.2). The largest number of respondents ($N = 22$; 52 percent) cited issues around provision of educational services in general education as the greatest challenge. Twenty states (48 percent) rated the determination of eligibility for services under IDEA as a significant challenge, whereas seventeen states (40 percent) identified the same for determination of eligibility under Section 504 or the Americans with Disabilities Act (ADA). Fourteen states (33 percent) identified a particular challenge in the process of how to assess ADHD under Section 504 or ADA.

Findings from the 1993 University of Miami survey found similar priorities reported from SEAs. Table 26.2 compares prevalence of issues reported in the two survey administrations. Issues around provision of educational services in general education was named most often by respondents (71 percent) as a source of frustration for local school systems. Determining eligibility for services under Section 504 was the second most often cited (67 percent of respondents), and how to assess under Section 504 and ADA was cited by 57 percent. Determining eligibility under IDEA was also a concern of the majority of respondents (52 percent).

Table 26.2
Greatest Challenges for Local School Districts

Issue	Percent of States Reporting This Issue as a Source of Challenge for Local Districts	
	1993	1998
Provision of services in general education	71	52
Determination of eligibility for services under IDEA	52	48
Determination of eligibility for services under Section 504 or ADA	67	40
How to assess under Section 504 or Americans with Disabilities Act	57	33

Issues related to providing services in general education, assessment, and determining eligibility were identified as major concerns in both the 1998 and the 1993 surveys. The percentage of SEAs reporting these issues as major concerns for LEAs, however, decreased between the two survey administrations.

These findings are consistent with what we know about the needs of practitioners and school administrators, who are often unsure about the best instructional and administrative procedures to use in serving students with ADHD. Two OSEP-supported centers (the ERIC Clearinghouse on Disabilities and Gifted Education and the National Information Center on Children and Youth with Disabilities) responsible for technical assistance and dissemination of special education information report that petitions for materials and information on addressing ADHD in schools and classrooms average more than 5,400 per year and represent one of the most often requested topics.

ADHD as an "Other Health Impairment"

Survey findings confirm, consistent with the clarifications in the 1991 joint memorandum, that the largest number of states that include ADHD as part of an IDEA disability category do so within the OHI definition ($N = 11$). Three states attributed the increase in use of the OHI within the state to students with ADHD.

The most recent data submitted by SEAs to OSEP, under requirements in Section 618 of IDEA, provide a count of all children and youth served under Part B, grants to states program. Of the 5,388,483 children age 6–21 served in the fifty states, the District of Columbia, and Puerto Rico in 1997–1998, 190,935 (3.5 percent) were reported as having OHI as their primary disabling condition: 97,680 (51 percent of those with OHI) were children 6 through 11 years of age, 86,655 (45 percent) were 12 through 17 years of age, and 6,600 (4 percent) were 18 through 21 years of age.

Data from the 1997–1998 year can be compared with those from past years to gain a better picture of the trends in use of the OHI category for children and youth 6 through 21 years. Between 1996 and 1997 and 1997 and 1998, the number served under OHI increased 18.48 percent, the largest one year increase of all categories, save autism (autism and traumatic brain injury were added as separate categories under IDEA in 1990). An increase of 314.96 percent in the number of children and youth with OHI served over ten years (1987–1988 to 1997–1998) represents the largest increase of any of the twelve categories reported. Ten-year increases in all other categories, with the exception of autism and traumatic brain injury, were less than 50 percent; a ten-year increase of 31.08 percent was reported across all children and youth with disabilities.

Discussion and Implications

The 1991 joint federal policy memorandum on serving students with ADHD within general and/or special education appears to have had a significant impact on state education efforts to identify and serve these children and youth. All written state education agency policies currently in place were adopted or revised since 1991. The percentage of states with written policies increased from 26 percent of respondents to 48 percent between 1993 and 1998. These types of state policies vary; a relatively small number of states (five) reported addressing ADHD directly in the special education/IDEA rules, regulations or procedures. More states, however, issued some type of policy or guidelines under Section 504 or in through memoranda or other clarifying guidelines. All restate, in part or full, the clarifications of the 1991 letter.

Beyond the direct impact of the changes and additions to written state policies, several states have convened task forces and/or developed technical assistance efforts to assist local school personnel to better identify and serve children and youth with ADHD. Memoranda of understanding or clarification were also used to guide individual student assessment and identification.

Two states' rules specified the role of the physician or pediatrician in diagnosing ADHD, but no states reported adoption of medication policies specific to children and youth with ADHD. Nine states do maintain general policies for medication administration by school personnel and two states reported that their guidelines or task force report explore the issue of medication for ADHD.

State education agencies and the local education agencies which they serve still report many technical assistance needs, especially in the areas of provision of services to students with ADHD in general education and eligibility for specialized services under IDEA or Section 504. Although the type of technical assistance needs appears to be consistent with those reported five years earlier, the severity of the needs appear to be less significant.

Finally, the dramatic increases in the number of students with other health impairments being served under Part B of IDEA may reflect the impact of the 1991 policy clarification, though the extent of the increase attributable to students with ADHD is difficult to determine.

These results reveal several areas of need in which the federal government might play a substantial clarifying role. First, the prevalence of ADHD in the population of children and youth is unable to be clearly discerned from current U.S. Department of Education data collection requirements. The number of students identified as having OHI alone is insufficient to accurately estimate the subpopulation of those with ADHD. Similarly, co-occurrence of ADHD with learning disabilities and/or emotional disturbance further complicates efforts to distinguish the ADHD population from that in other IDEA disability categories. In addition, the number of students with ADHD who are receiving services under Section 504 of the Rehabilitation Act, or even the Americans with Disabilities Act, is indistinguishable, under current U.S. Department of Education data collection requirements.

Second, although the increase in the number of states with formal policies and procedures regarding ADHD may indicate a greater awareness of specific individuals' needs and may result in delivery of enhanced special education and other services to students with ADHD, many questions remain about the quality of the education and services, as well as about the outcomes for these students. OSEP supports a large array of longitudinal studies and evaluations of special education. Several of these studies are being designed to address, in part, the educational experiences and outcomes of children and youth with disabilities, as well as the school, district, and state policies that support such experiences.

The state policies reported here reflect a growing awareness of and concern with the provision of special education and related services to children and youth with ADHD. Many of these policies are reflections of U.S. Department of Education policy clarifications initially provided in 1991. State and local education agencies also report frustration with several issues of assessment, eligibility, and provision of services to children and youth with ADHD. Although the last five years have witnessed a greater number of states with formal ADHD policies, accompanied by possibly decreased levels of unmet need and fewer sources of frustration, further education and support to LEAs and SEAs continues to be necessary.

Footnotes

[1] Although most mental health settings use the term "ADHD" to refer to the entire range of attention deficit disorders, an analogous term, "ADD," is also commonly used in Department of Education publications and communications. For simplicity, ADHD is used throughout this chapter and is meant to denote the entire range of disorders of attention as defined within the fourth edition of *Diagnostic and Statistical Manual of Mental Disorders* (DSM-IV; American Psychiatric Association, 1994).

[2] Fifty states, the District of Columbia and Puerto Rico were surveyed. Forty-two states responded; percentages reported are based on the number of states with a given policy divided by 42.

References

ADHD [Special issue]. (1997). *Teacher Education in Special Education, 20*(2), 87–188.

Aleman, S. R. (1991, December 5). *Special education for children with attention deficit disorder: Current issues* (Report No. 91–862 EPW). Washington, DC: Congressional Research Service.

American Psychiatric Association. (1994). *Diagnostic and statistical manual of mental disorders* (4th ed.). Washington, DC: Author.

Davila, R. R., Williams, M. L., & MacDonald, J. T. (1991, September 16). *Clarification of policy to address the needs of children with attention deficit disorders within general and/or special education.* Washington, DC: U.S. Department of Education, Office of Special Education and Rehabilitation.

Rehabilitation Act of 1973, 29 U.S.C. §§ 701 et seq.

U.S. Department of Education. (1998). *20th annual report to Congress on the implementation of the Individuals with Disabilities Education Act.* Washington, DC: Author.

Utah State Office of Education Students at Risk Section. (1996). *Utah attention deficit disorder guide.* Salt Lake City: Author.

Vermont Department of Education Family and Educational Support Team. (1998, January). *Vermont guidelines for identifying students with ADD and ADHD.* Montpelier, VT: Author.

Chapter 27

Use of Services and Costs for Youth With ADHD and Related Conditions

by Kelly J. Kelleher, M.D., M.P.H.

Introduction 27-2
Prevalence of ADHD in Primary Care Settings 27-2
    ADHD Increasingly Diagnosed 27-2
    Demographic Factors 27-3
    Frequency of Comorbidity 27-3
    Summary 27-4
Use of Services 27-4
The Child Behavior Study 27-5
    Setting 27-5
    Sample 27-5
    Procedures 27-6
    Measures 27-6
        Clinician-Reported Items (Clinician Identification) 27-6
        Parent- or Guardian-Reported Items (Services Use) 27-6
    Analysis 27-6
    Results 27-7
        Increased Use of Many Types of Health Services 27-7
        Predictors of Receipt of Specific Treatment
        Services 27-7
Costs of Care—ADHD Cost of Services in Medicaid Study for
  Southwestern Pennsylvania 27-8
    Setting 27-9
    Sample 27-9
    Procedures 27-9
    Measures 27-10
    Analysis 27-10
Need for Cost-Benefit Analysis 27-11
Conclusion 27-12

INTRODUCTION

Attention deficit hyperactivity disorder (ADHD) is the most commonly diagnosed behavioral and emotional disorder of childhood. In primary care settings, it is diagnosed as often as any other chronic condition of childhood, and some evidence suggests that ADHD evaluations and treatment are increasing rapidly. Although frequently diagnosed, information on the use of services and costs of care for ADHD is lacking. To provide some insight into these questions, this chapter (1) reviews the prevalence of ADHD in primary care settings, (2) examines the use of health and mental health services by youth with diagnosed ADHD, (3) compares direct treatment costs between ADHD and asthma, another common illness of childhood, and (4) identifies areas for further research on the impact of ADHD on the health care system. ADHD profoundly affects many areas of a child's life, including his or her interactions with family, school, and society. This chapter focuses on the impact of ADHD in the general medical and specialty mental health settings. Services and cost issues for families, communities, and schools are discussed elsewhere in this volume (see Chapters 25 and 27).

PREVALENCE OF ADHD IN PRIMARY CARE SETTINGS

ADHD Increasingly Diagnosed

Only a handful of studies report the proportion of pediatric visits with recognized psychosocial problems generally, and even fewer report on ADHD specifically. These studies use two methods of identification: (1) structured clinician interview and (2) clinician diagnosis (see Table 27.1). The studies using structured clinical instruments were conducted by Costello et al. (1988), who studied health maintenance organization (HMO) participants in Pittsburgh in 1984–1985, and by Horwitz, Leaf, Leventhal, Forsyth, and Speechley (1992), who screened children in pediatric offices and clinics in New Haven during 1988–1989. The prevalence of children meeting diagnostic criteria for ADHD was nearly six times higher in the New Haven study. Sample differences may account for some of this disparity, but definitional issues and secular trends likely account for some of the increase.

Costello et al. (1988) conducted additional analyses and noted that prevalence rates of ADHD and other disorders in primary care settings were extremely sensitive to symptom thresholds for various disorders. Although she found low rates of ADHD in her study, when altering the threshold to include those without disorder but with ADHD symptoms and significant impairment, she found much higher rates of "threshold" ADHD. Those with this threshold condition were dysfunctional in some areas of their lives.

Despite these methodological issues, prevalence rates based on clinical diagnosis support the notion that ADHD is becoming more common or at least is recognized more often. Three studies provide information on clinical diagnosis of ADHD.

Goldberg, Roughmann, McInerny, and Burke (1984) described more than 19,000 visits by school-age children to pediatricians in Rochester, New York. Primary care clinicians reported on whether or not consecutive children seen by one of the thirty-one pediatricians had a psychosocial problem and what type of problem was present. "Hyperkinesis/inattentiveness" was the most common condition so noted for children 4-15 years old, with 1.4 percent of all visits identified as such by the pediatricians.

Table 27.1
Rates of ADHD[a] by Structured Diagnostic Interview and Clinician Diagnosis in Primary Care Samples

	Years of Study	N	Diagnosed	Age Range
Structured diagnostic interview				
Costello (1988)	1984–1985 789	12 (1.5%)	7–11	
Horwitz (1992)	1988–1989	1,540	135 (8.8%)	5–9
Clinician diagnosis				
Goldberg (1984)	1979	9,612	136 (1.4%)	4–15
Horwitz[b] (1992)	1987–1988	1,886	175 (9.3%)	4–8
Kelleher (2001)	1994–1997	21,151	2,007 (9.5%)	4–15

[a] ADHD and related conditions. [b] Includes mentally retarded, learning disabilities, language delay, speech problems, overactivity, gross motor delay, fine motor delay.

In Horwitz et al.'s (1992) New Haven study, 9.3 percent were noted to have ADHD or related conditions based on diagnoses given by pediatricians. However, the structured diagnostic interviews and clinician diagnoses showed poor agreement, as has been noted in studies of adults.

In the Child Behavior Study, Kelleher (1994–1998) studied more than 20,000 visits to pediatricians and family practitioners from two national primary care research networks. Clinicians identified 9.5 percent of children in primary care visits as having ADHD (Wasserman et al., 1999).

Demographic Factors

Thus, independent of method, newer studies report higher rates of ADHD (Kelleher et al., 2000). This cohort effect may be related to changing demographics in the population of children seen by primary care clinicians (Kelleher et al., 2000). For example, the number of children from single-parent homes seen by primary care physicians in office-based practice increased concurrently with the rise in recognized psychosocial problems among primary care clinicians from 1979 to 1996. Similarly, the proportion of children on Medicaid seen in office-based practices increased by more than 50 percent during the same time. Although demographic changes may account for some of the changes in recognition of psychosocial problems, clinician factors do not appear to account for much of the change.

Frequency of Comorbidity

Primary care clinicians recognize substantial comorbidity among their patients with ADHD. Nearly half of youth with ADHD are thought to have comorbid behavioral or emotional disorders and mood disorders, with behavioral problems most frequently identified. Controlling for the level of parent-reported attentional and hyperactivity symptoms, boys, older youth, and those without emotional symptoms are more likely to be diagnosed with ADHD. However, insurance status and presence of managed care do not alter recognition of psychosocial problems, or ADHD specifically, in primary care (Kelleher et al., 1997). More important for recognition was clinician familiarity with the patient, or continuity of care. Doctors who reported seeing their own patients are much more likely to recognize psychosocial problems. To the extent that certain benefit packages, exclusion clauses, or managed care restrictions facilitate continuity, identification of psychosocial problems will be encouraged.

Summary

In summary, primary care clinicians report that nearly one in ten children seen for nonemergency care in office-based settings suffer from attentional problems of sufficient intensity or duration to warrant intervention or monitoring. Although diagnostic rates among child medical visits vary by the study considered, newer studies report higher rates of ADHD among children seen in primary care settings.

USE OF SERVICES

One measure of the impact of ADHD on families and the health care system is the extent to which ADHD increases service use. Adults with mental disorders use more health and mental health services in general. Although some component of the increased use is related to the receipt of mental health services, additional primary care and non-mental health specialty services are also consumed by persons with mental disorders.

Although this pattern is well established for adults with mental disorders, only a few studies have examined the use of services solely among youth with ADHD. Most primary care based studies find increased use of ambulatory services by youth with psychosocial problems (Kelleher & Starfield, 1990). However, Offord et al. (1987) reported on use of services in the Ontario Child Health Survey, a population-based assessment conducted in Canada during the early 1980s. Parents reported on use of specialty mental health services (including social services) and general medical care, regardless of the reason for consultation in this study. Children with any disorder (including ADHD) were three times as likely as other youth to use specialty mental health or social services but were no more likely to use general medical services. However, they noted that even though those with disorder were much more likely to use specialty services, services were still received by only a minority with disorder. Szatmari, Offord, and Boyle (1989), in the same research team, conducted additional analyses comparing use of services by children with ADHD to those with other conditions and those without any diagnoses. They noted that those children with ADHD and other comorbid conditions were the most likely to use specialty services. However, children with other disorders were as likely as the ADHD children to use mental health and social services. Both were more likely than those without psychosocial disorders to use mental health and social services. Use of general medical services was no different across the three groups.

To determine whether or not youth with ADHD use more mental health or medical services, data from the Child Behavior Study, discussed in the following section, was used to compare the parent-reported use of services in the prior six months of those children seen for ADHD, those seen for non-ADHD psychosocial problems, and those without psychosocial problems. The expectation, in view of the Ontario Child Health Study (Offord et al., 1987), was that mental health visits would be higher for both the ADHD groups and those with other psychosocial problems, compared to those without psychosocial problems. It was also hypothesized that both groups with psychosocial problems would have more medical use than those without problems.

THE CHILD BEHAVIOR STUDY

Setting

The Child Behavior Study (CBS) was conducted in Pediatric Research in Office Settings (PROS) and the Ambulatory Sentinel Practice Network (ASPN), two large practice-based primary care research networks. PROS, a pediatric network established by the American Academy of Pediatrics in 1986, currently comprises over 1,400 clinicians from more than 475 practices in all fifty states and the Commonwealth of Puerto Rico who provide care for approximately 1.75 million children in the United States. ASPN is a family medicine network that was established in 1978 and currently consists of 125 practices, comprising approximately 750 clinicians from thirty-eight states and six Canadian provinces who provide care for about a half million patients. Eighty-nine percent of PROS clinicians are pediatricians, 10 percent are nurse practitioners, and 1 percent are physician assistants. Eighty-five percent of ASPN clinicians are family physicians, 7 percent are nurse practitioners, and 8 percent are physician assistants. ASPN also collaborated with two regional networks to expand the number of participating family physicians. The characteristics of the Wisconsin Research Network (WReN) and the Minnesota Academy of Family Physicians Research Network (MAFPRN) are similar to those of ASPN and contributed thirty-eight and twenty-four participating clinicians, respectively. Recruitment of PROS and ASPN clinicians into the study has been described fully elsewhere (Kelleher et al., 1997). This study included 401 pediatric and family practice clinicians in forty-four states, Puerto Rico, and four Canadian provinces.

Sample

Participating clinicians in the CBS were asked to enroll seventy consecutive children ages 4–15 years who presented for nonemergency care (procedures-only visits excluded) accompanied by a parent or primary care giver who spoke English or Spanish. More than 82 percent of eligible children across all sites participated. No differences in age or gender were detected in a comparison of participating with nonparticipating children. Children in the western United States were slightly more likely to participate. Results on 22,059 visits were reported. Among those visits, 994 (4.5 percent) had inadequate or missing data sufficient to preclude further analyses resulting in a total sample of 21,065 visits with adequate data. Of these subjects, 3,934 (18.7 percent) were identified by the clinician as having a psychosocial problem, and 1,947 (9.2 percent) were identified by the clinician as having "attention deficit/hyperactivity problems," and these comprised the study sample.

Procedures

Procedures and consent forms were approved by institutional review boards affiliated with PROS, ASPN, and the University of Pittsburgh. Study procedures have been described in detail elsewhere (Kelleher et al., 1997). Parents (including primary caregivers) of eligible patients were approached in the practice waiting room for informed consent. Consenting parents completed a brief questionnaire before the visit, assessing demographics, child and family functioning, and use of services in the previous six months. After the visit, the clinician completed a questionnaire describing patient insurance and reason for visit, as well as identification and management of psychosocial problems.

Measures

Clinician-Reported Items (Clinician Identification). Clinician identification of a psychosocial problem was noted as a positive response to the following question: "Is there a new, ongoing or recurrent psychosocial problem present?" Psychosocial problems were defined as any mental disorders, psychological symptoms, or social situations warranting clinical attention or intervention in the opinion of the primary care clinician.

Eleven psychosocial problem categories were developed through focus group discussions and pilot testing for clinician categorization of identified psychosocial problems. The ADHD response category was worded as "attention deficit/hyperactivity problems." Focus group interviews of clinicians indicated that the ADHD response category would include all children thought to carry the diagnosis of ADHD, plus additional children with attentional and hyperactivity symptoms who might not have undergone diagnostic evaluation and/or who might not meet the formal diagnostic criteria for ADHD.

Parent- or Guardian-Reported Items (Services Use). Parents or guardians were asked how many visits their child had made to the following categories of providers during the six months prior to the index primary care visit: mental health professional, emergency room, and his or her own or another doctor or clinician (see Table 27.2). They were also asked, "How many times has this child been admitted to the hospital overnight in the last six months (prior to today)?"

Analysis

The children identified as having ADHD were compared to children with non-ADHD psychosocial problems nd those without an identified psychosocial problem for each of the service use categories. An F-test indicated that the means were different from each other in a general linear model. Because the distributions of services tend to be nonnormal (especially for smaller categories of services), nonparametric rank tests (Wilcoxon) were performed to determine whether the differences are statistically significant when the distributions are not assumed to be normal. Finally, a multiple regression technique using a Poisson distribution was employed to account for demographic differences and possible confounding between the two groups.

Table 27.2
Use of Services in Prior Six Months by Parent Report*

	N	Mental Health	Primary Care	Emergency Room	Total Outpatient	Hospital
ADHD visits	2,007	1.47	2.37	0.19	4.02	0.05
Non-ADHD psychosocial problem visits	2,005	1.25	2.39	0.22	3.87	0.07
Non-psychosocial problem visits	17,139	0.13	1.90	0.15	2.17	0.03

*Mean number of visits are reported in each category.
Source: Child Behavior Study (Kelleher, 1994–1998).

Results

Increased Use of Many Types of Health Services. In the CBS, children with ADHD averaged 0.15 more outpatient visits compared to children with other psychosocial problems and 1.85 more visits than youth without any identified psychosocial problems over a six-month period. Most of the increase in use was related to mental health services, although primary care visits were also increased among those with ADHD. How psychosocial conditions induced or were associated with increased use is not clear. However, family distress, teacher frustration, or the discovery of unmet medical needs during behavioral care ("onset" effect) may all play a role.

Regardless of the mechanism, it appears that youth with ADHD are comparable to youth with other psychosocial problems in their increased use of many types of health services. The fact that there appears to be little difference in utilization between children and adolescents with ADHD and those with other psychosocial problems suggests that the specific aspects of ADHD symptoms (hyperactivity) or treatment (stimulant prescriptions and behavior modification) do not account for the increased use of services but that other family, patient, or community characteristics explain why children with psychosocial problems generally use more services.

Predictors of Receipt of Specific Treatment Services. The specific treatments provided for ADHD in primary care settings include counseling, psychotropic drug prescriptions (see Figure 27.1), and referral to specialty services. Their use in primary care was described further in Chapter 23. Gardner et al. (2000) note that insurance status and managed care are not related to treatment selection by primary care providers. Instead, family concurrence with problem assessment and continuity of care are much better predictors of the receipt of treatment services. Continuity and treatment were less common among uninsured youth, but payor and insurance status were otherwise unrelated to treatment status.

Use of primary care and specialty mental health services of youth recognized with

Figure 27.1
Children Ever on Medications: ADHD vs. Non-ADHD

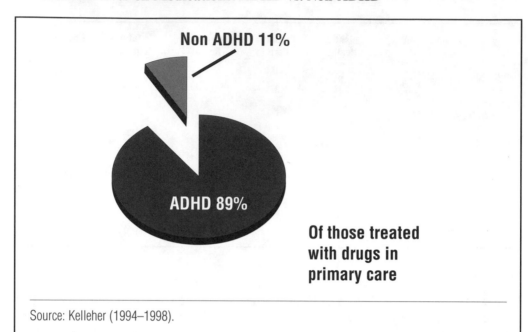

Non ADHD 11%

ADHD 89%

Of those treated
with drugs in
primary care

Source: Kelleher (1994–1998).

ADHD were also analyzed for the six months after the first study-related visit. Regardless of whether children had been referred to specialists or not, use of mental health services was infrequent in the subsequent six months. Insurance status or enrollment in managed care did not predict subsequent use.

Although the existing research on ADHD are thin, CBS data suggest that youth with ADHD have increased use of services compared to those without any mental disorders but similar to those with other psychosocial problems. Whether or not the increased use of care by youth with ADHD is related to family or child help seeking and dissatisfaction with care or to routine visits for a chronic problem is not clear.

COSTS OF CARE—ADHD COST OF SERVICES IN MEDICAID STUDY FOR SOUTHWESTERN PENNSYLVANIA

Studies of the costs of ADHD services in the health care system are another measure of the impact of this condition. As noted by others, the child psychiatric literature is bereft of economic studies on mental health services, particularly for specific disorders. These deficiencies have precluded careful comparative analyses of the benefits of different treatment strategies, providers, settings, or financing systems.

To initiate some discussion on the costs of treatment for ADHD, this chapter compares direct treatment costs for ADHD with another common childhood condition, asthma. A payor perspective focusing on children publicly insured through Medicaid in Southwestern Pennsylvania was employed.

Setting

The ADHD Cost of Services in Medicaid Study (ACSMS) for Southwestern Pennsylvania was conducted using all the eligibility and claims payment records from the Pennsylvania State Department of Public Welfare (DPW) for the seven counties of Allegheny, Armstrong, Beaver, Butler, Greene, Washington, and Westmoreland during the fiscal years 1992–1993, 1993–1994, and 1994–1995.

Sample

Only continuously enrolled children and adolescents ages 7 to 20 at the start of each of the three fiscal years were included in the study sample. Continuous eligibility for the fiscal year was established based on enrollment in the traditional Medicaid fee-for-service (FFS) plan on the fifteenth of each month during the fiscal year (July through June). Those enrolled in available for-profit managed care plans during a given fiscal year were excluded because their full claims were not reported to DPW.

Procedures

During fiscal year 1994–1995, 1,602 children and adolescents were identified as having ADHD and 1,411 as having asthma. Total payments (including federal, state, and private insurance payors) did not exceed $10,000 in order to reduce the impact of outliers on the calculation of the means. Those children and adolescents with ADHD either were identified by using both the primary and secondary diagnoses (i.e., had at least one medical claim with code 314 according to the ninth edition of *International Classification of Diseases* [ICD-9; World Health Organization, 1978]) or had had at least three filled prescriptions for stimulant medications. Classification criteria for both groups were met by seventy-six children and adolescents who were placed in the ADHD group. The stimulant medication prescriptions were identified from the pharmaceutical claims using the Food and Drug Administration's (FDA) national drug codes (NDC) for amphetamine sulfate, dextroamphetamine sulfate (Dexedrine®), methamphetamine HCL (Desoxyn®), amphetamine mixtures (Adderall®), methylphenidate (Ritalin®), and pemoline (Cylert®).

Those children and adolescents with asthma were also identified using primary and secondary diagnoses from the medical claims (claim with ICD-9 code 493), or at least three filled prescriptions for asthma medications. Asthma medications were defined again using the FDA's NDC under the 1940 classification. Certain medications in this classification were excluded because they can also be prescribed primarily to treat other illnesses: Atrovent® Inhalation Aerosol, Carbodec® Syrup, Cardec Syrup, Elixophyllin® Elixir, epinephrine injection, Epipen® auto-injector, Epipen Jr®Auto-injector, Nasalcrom® Nasal Solution, pseudoephedrine HCL, Quad_tuss® tannate pediatric suspension, Quibron T® Sr tablets, Sus Phrine® Suspension for Injection, theo organidin, Tri Tannate Plus®, and Vancenase® Pockethaler.

For the years 1993–1994, 1,909 children and adolescents with ADHD and 1,499 with asthma were identified who met the criteria, with 70 dually classified. We did not make any adjustment for inflation among the three different years. The period represented by the fiscal years 1993–1994 and 1994–1995 in Southwestern Pennsylvania coincided with the introduction of voluntary managed care enrollment among the Medicaid population and the introduction of managed care among private insurers as well. It is unlikely that any inflation adjustment for this period of time would adequately capture the effects of such an introduction.

Measures

For each condition, payments for all services were summed and averaged over pharmacy and nonpharmacy claims to calculate total costs for all of a patient's services during the 1994–1995 fiscal year. In addition, a separate measure for the costs of all mental health services (including both pharmacy and nonpharmacy reimbursements) was calculated to compare differences across health care sectors.

Outpatient visits and inpatient days were also examined between the two groups. Inpatient days were summed over all the hospitalizations for each individual during the given fiscal year based on the number of days reported on the claims using the type and place of service listed. Outpatient visits were summed over all visits to physician offices, emergency and special treatment rooms (when the visit did not result in an inpatient admission), outpatient hospitals, and independent clinics. Multiple outpatient visits occurring on the same day were treated as single visits to avoid double counting due to consultations and multiple procedures. These visits were not separated by health care sector.

Analysis

T-tests were performed to determine whether or not the mean costs were different between the two groups, as well as nonparametric tests to relax the assumption of a normal distribution. In addition, a multiple regression was used to account for other factors such as disability status and other demographics which could confound the differences. For the distributions of outpatient and inpatient services, nonparametric rank tests were performed, along with a multiple regression using a Poisson distribution similar to those listed previously for the CBS.

As noted in Table 27.3, ADHD and asthma bear remarkable similarities to each other, with regard to both their frequency in the eligible population and their cost structure. Children with ADHD and asthma have similar distributions of pharmacy and nonpharmacy services, although children with ADHD receive most services in the mental health arena whereas those with asthma receive them almost exclusively in the general health arena. Outpatient visits and inpatient days were also examined between the two groups. Children with ADHD had nine more total outpatient visits on average than those with asthma, but 0.4 fewer inpatient days. These were not separated by type of service. Any comparison between these utilization figures for a Medicaid population and those from the earlier national primary care population (CBS) using parental six-month recall should note that these claims figures use twelve months of administrative data.

A small percentage of children with ADHD services also received asthma services and were classified as having ADHD. One difference in sample selection, which is probably partly the result of Medicaid reimbursement rules, is the percentage of chil-

Table 27.3
**Comparison of Reimbursements and Services for Children and Adolescents
With ADHD or Asthma in Southwestern Pennsylvania: FY 1994–1995**

	Mean	Standard Deviation	Median	99th Percentile
ADHD ** *N* = 1,602				
All services—payments	$1,795	$2,069	$1,041	$9,442
Pharmaceuticals	$ 508	$ 554	$ 375	$2,352
All other services	$1,287	$1,956	$ 553	$8,788
All psychiatric services	$1,135	$1,857	$ 484	$8,955
Outpatient visits***	28.8	21.7	23	107
Inpatient days	0.1	1.3	0	5
Asthma *N* = 1,411				
All services—payments	$1,666	$1,863	$ 942	$8,858
Pharmaceuticals	$ 413	$ 566	$ 243	$2,676
Other services	$1,252	$1,681	$ 586	$7,844
All psychiatric services	$ 112	$ 681	$ 0	$3,154
Outpatient visits	19.6	15.7	15	74
Inpatient days	0.5	1.8	0	8

*The sample is limited to those ages 7 to 20 years whose total reimbursements did not exceed $10,000 and who were continuously enrolled in Medicaid FFS during the fiscal year in Allegheny, Armstrong, Beaver, Butler, Greene, Washington, and Westmoreland counties. **The seventy-six children who received both types of services during the fiscal year were placed in the ADHD group. ***Outpatient visits include visits to hospital clinics and emergency room visits which did not lead to a hospitalization. Multiple visits on the same day were counted as one visit.

dren identified as having ADHD or asthma through pharmacy claims alone. Few of the children (10 percent) identified with asthma had only pharmacy services, whereas the majority of children with ADHD were identified through filled stimulant prescriptions.

NEED FOR COST-BENEFIT ANALYSES

Although a number of limitations exist in this data, cost-of-illness or burden studies are important first steps in the recognition of a condition's relevance to different settings and payors, and to establish methods for conducting later comparative analyses. In particular, cost-of-illness studies that examine the impact of ADHD to particular groups in the health care arena, such as insurance companies and state

Medicaid agencies, are likely to raise the profile of ADHD and to identify deficiencies in current cost measurements related to this unique condition. Such comparisons are essential decision-making tools, especially for payor perspectives in providing benefits.

Further studies including cost-benefit analyses are necessary to compare costs and benefits in the same units. A complete cost-effectiveness analysis would allow comparative decisions to be made among two or more alternative courses of treatment in order to optimally use limited resources. Such an analysis typically requires an evaluation of both the improvements in outcomes and complete societal costs of the different treatment strategies or interventions being implemented. In most cases a prospective study is conducted to compare a specific intervention against the current standard of care, ideally measuring outcomes in quality adjusted life years to allow for universal comparisons with other studies.

Unfortunately, even basic cost-benefit studies of mental health services for youth with ADHD are lacking. In conducting these analyses, a central goal should be to obtain different perspectives on costs. Although societal costs for ADHD and its treatment are important in the context of taxpayer-funded schools and health care, payor and family/community costs are also critical to provide the fullest picture of how ADHD affects the health care system.

CONCLUSION

ADHD is commonly recognized in primary care settings, and diagnosis and treatment rates appear to be on the rise. Some of this increase may be attributable to the changing demographics of patients seen in primary care offices. Recognition and treatment of ADHD in primary care settings is related to both patient factors and the relationship between patient and clinician. Insurance status and health plan enrollment play an indirect role, if any, in the management of psychosocial problems for primary care.

Although children with ADHD use more specialty mental health and primary care services than do youth without psychosocial problems, their rates of service use are similar to those of children with other psychosocial problems. Moreover, they generally receive few services after an index visit to their primary care clinician.

The costs of ADHD treatment are similar to the treatment costs associated with asthma, the most chronic illness of childhood, and are distributed among pharmacy and clinical services in a similar fashion. Unfortunately, little else is known about the burden of illness for children with ADHD and their families or the cost-effectiveness of interventions.

ADHD is an important condition not only because of its impact on families and children but also because youth with ADHD are major consumers of primary care services, mental health care, and psychotropic drugs. Although the diagnosis is common, little is known about the use of services by children and adolescents with ADHD, patterns of use over time, or any type of cost analyses. Specific questions to be prioritized include the following:

- *How is use of services for ADHD initiated?* What factors predict help seeking for ADHD specifically and are these different than those for other psychosocial problems in childhood? Are some systems more accessible for ADHD care?

- *What burden or costs for ADHD and related treatment are borne by families and communities?* How much out-of-pocket costs are incurred by families whose children have ADHD? What are the costs to communities in loss of productivity and diverted resources?

- *How effective are alternative modes of treatment in community and school settings?* Do services provided in the school or home provide better outcomes at lower costs than medical services? What combinations work best?

- *How do families, employers and communities value various outcomes?* Is better control in the classroom an acceptable outcome for communities with high rates of ADHD treatment? What benefit limits are reasonable for employers and payers faced with increased costs?

Acknowledgments

The authors thank Dr. Sarah Hudson Scholle, and Ms. Diane Comer for their assistance. This work was supported by National Institute of Mental Health Grant No. MH50629 (Kelleher, Principal Investigator), SAMHSA Grant No. SM51911 (Kelleher, Principal Investigator), and the Staunton Farm Foundation of Pittsburgh.

References

Barkley, R. A., Anastopoulos, A. D., Guevremont, D. C., & Fletcher, K. E. (1991). Adolescents with ADHD: Patterns of behavioral adjustment, academic functioning, and treatment utilization. *Journal of the American Academy of Child and Adolescent Psychiatry, 30*, 752–761.

Costello, E. J., Costello, A. J., Edelbrock, C., Burns, B. J., Dulcan, M. K., Brent, D., & Janiszewski, S. (1988). Psychiatric disorders in pediatric primary care. *Archives of General Psychiatry, 45*, 1107–1116.

Gardner, W., Kelleher, K. J., Wasserman, R., Childs, G., Nutting, P., Lillienfield, H., & Pajer, K. (2000). Primary care treatment of pediatric psychosocial problems: A study from pediatric research in office settings and ambulatory sentinel practice network. *Pediatrics, 106*(4), E44.

Goldberg, I. D., Roughmann, K. J., McInerny, T. K., & Burke, J. D., Jr. (1984). Mental health problems among children seen in pediatric practice: Prevalence and management. *Pediatrics, 73*, 278–293.

Horwitz, S. M., Leaf, P. J., Leventhal, J. M., Forsyth, B., & Speechley, K. N. (1992). Identification and management of psychosocial and developmental problems in community-based, primary care pediatric practices. *Pediatrics, 89*, 480–485.

Kelleher, K. J. (Principal Investigator). (1994, June 1–1998, April 30). *Management of psychosocial problems in primary care* (Grant No. MH 50629). Rockville, MD: National Institute of Mental Health.

Kelleher, K. J., Childs, G. E., Wasserman, R. C., McInerny, T. K., Nutting, P. A., & Gardner, W. P. (1997). Insurance status and recognition of psychosocial problems: A report from the Pediatric Research in Office Settings and the Ambulatory Sentinel Practice Networks. *Archives of Pediatrics and Adolescent Medicine, 151*, 1109–1115.

Kelleher, K. J., McInerny, T., Gardner, W., Childs, G., Wasserman, R., & Nutting, P. (2000). Increasing identification of psychosocial problems: 1979–1997. *Pediatrics, 105*, 1313–1321.

Kelleher, K. J., & Starfield, B. (1990). Use of health care by children receiving mental health treatment. *Pediatrics, 185*(1), 114–118.

Offord, D. R., Boyle, M. H., Szatmari, P., Rae-Grant, N. I., Links, P. S., Cadman, D. T., Byles, J. A.,

Crawford, J. W., Blum, H. M., & Byrne, C. (1987). Ontario child health study. II. Six-month prevalence of disorder and rates of service utilization. *Archives of General Psychiatry, 44*, 832–836.

Szatmari, P., Offord, D. R., & Boyle, M. H. (1989). Correlates, associated impairments and patterns of service utilization of children with attention deficit disorder: Findings from the Ontario child health study. *Journal of Child Psychology and Psychiatry, 30*, 205–217.

Wasserman, R. C., Kelleher, K. J., Bocian, A., Baker, A., Childs, G. E., Indacochea, F., Stulp, C., & Gardner, W. P. (1999). Identification of attentional and hyperactivity problems in primary care: A report from pediatric research in office settings and the ambulatory sentinel practice network. *Pediatrics, 103*, E38.

World Health Organization. (1978). *International classification of diseases* (9th rev.). Geneva, Switzerland: Author.

Afterword: ADHD, Past, Present, and Future

by Peter S. Jensen, M.D. and James R. Cooper, M.D.

In this volume, many of the leading experts around the world have summarized the available evidence concerning the diagnosis, epidemiology, pathophysiology and etiology, clinical course, treatment, services, and outcomes related to attention deficit hyperactivity disorder (ADHD). This remarkable compilation of evidence is a testament to the dedication and work of many scientists over the last thirty years as well as substantial investments by the National Institute of Mental Health, other research agencies, private foundations, and industry, all directed toward understanding ADHD. In this Afterword, we summarize some of the major issues that have been consolidated within the pages of this volume in terms of major research advances, and we outline those areas in which future research is most needed.

DIAGNOSTIC ISSUES

We have progressed substantially from initial early considerations of ADHD as due to a general or specific form of brain damage to concepts of hyperactivity, delineation of the important construct of inattention, and more recent notions of disturbances in executive functioning and deficits in impulse inhibition deficits. Increasing diagnostic refinements and research evidence have marched hand in hand to identify core aspects of the syndrome. As noted in Chapter 1 (Lahey & Willcutt), we have increasing knowledge of different subtypes of the disorder, validated through many different epidemiologic and clinical studies using a variety of techniques, including newer statistical approaches (Hudziak, Wadsworth, Heath, & Achenbach, 1999). The accumulated evidence provides substantial support for the validity of the ADHD construct as a disorder every bit as deserving of consideration and intervention as medical conditions such as hypertension. The syndrome can be reliably identified and measured, it is characterized by psychological features that are relatively specific to the syndrome itself, and it is differentiable from other states, as Lahey and Willcutt note. It has a predictable clinical course, characterized by substantial problematic outcomes in adolescence (Hinshaw, Chapter 5), adulthood (Johnston, Chapter 6), and over the life course (Barkley, Chapter 4). As much as, and frequently more than, many other medical conditions, ADHD has a characteristic family history and response to treatment, as well as identifiable biological characteristics that differentiate children with the syndrome from healthy children (Silberstein et al., 1998; Tannock, Chapter 8). As the authors of this text have noted, ADHD is not a U.S.-only or an upper-middle-class Caucasian-only phenomenon (Bird, Chapter 2; Samuel et al., 1999).

Given this weight of evidence concerning ADHD-related impairments in functioning, genetic and pathophysiological characteristics, clinical course, and problematic longer-term outcomes (see Chapters 4, 5, and 6; also Rasmussen & Gillberg,

2000), what are the remaining arguments and controversies concerning the diagnosis? In fact, the most significant argument among scientists and respected thinkers is not whether ADHD "exists." Rather, it is where to draw the line between normal variations of temperament, activity, and attention and significant psychopathology (Lahey & Willcutt, Chapter 1; Carey, Chapter 3). As Carey notes, at times the disorder and its diagnosis are conceptualized in a seemingly simplistic fashion, and a stable, easily measured internal biological characteristic cannot be identified in any specific case of ADHD such that this internal dysfunction can be used to make the diagnosis (Carey, Chapter 3). This state of affairs is not much different than hypertension, however. An elevated blood pressure, with a diastolic pressure above 90, is also not an indicator of dysfunction per se. It is only in the context of its statistical association with longer-term cerebrovascular and cardiovascular disease that we have "medicalized" benign essential hypertension. To the extent that we treat hypertension, increased longevity for groups of people with elevated blood pressures can be achieved, although we cannot determine which people, in fact, actually need the treatment, nor whose lives are lengthened by the treatment. Quite possibly, some people with elevated blood pressure might show no decrement in longevity and merely some of the negative side effects as a function of the treatment. Yet, because of the general group statistical association between elevated blood pressures and adverse outcomes, we choose to treat groups of persons with this easily measured characteristic, even when nothing else is "wrong." At the level of individual patients, we hope that the odds work in their favor, that this indeed serves their best interests, even though that cannot necessarily be known. This state of affairs is very much akin to ADHD, except that in the case of ADHD, there must be *current* evidence of impairment to make the diagnosis and to treat.

Other controversies concerning the diagnosis remain but are approaching resolution, such as from whom information should be obtained to make the diagnosis (Jensen, Rubio-Stipec, et al., 1999; Lahey & Willcutt, Chapter 1). Evolving research suggests that the syndrome, regardless of the presence or absence of comorbidities, in and of itself conveys significant risk for problematic long-term outcomes. Yet, as several contributors to this volume note (Hinshaw, Chapter 5; Johnston, Chapter 6; Loney, Kramer, & Salisbury, Chapter 17), a substantial proportion of the disorder's adverse long-term outcomes might be due not to ADHD alone but to its risk for other consequences, including significant comorbidities of anxiety, depression, substance use, and delinquent and antisocial behavior. Increasing evidence suggests that ADHD as a disorder itself lies on a continuum, however, that children with what Swanson and Castellanos (Chapter 7) call the "refined phenotype," with symptoms across multiple settings, while not qualitatively different from children with less severe forms of ADHD, are nonetheless most easily identified and characterized by their severe impairments and likely life-course persistence.

These questions—from whom to obtain the diagnostic information, the relative impact of comorbidities, and the difficulties distinguishing normal variations from mild ADHD and mild ADHD from severe ADHD also characterize the difficulties in the diagnosis in adults. Should adult ADHD be defined with the same threshold for symptoms as in children (Johnston, Chapter 6)? Also, there is a suspicion by many that the disorder as currently defined is still too heterogeneous. Some better method of subtyping must be found than reliance on one behavioral and one cognitive dimension, leading to an enormous number of "comorbidities."

More use must be made of normative and developmental information. As presently defined, ADHD symptom criteria are the same across the entire age span, despite evidence that there are significant developmental changes for inattention and hyperactivity symptoms. How these symptoms evolve and change in relation to one another is an important unsolved problem. Understanding which aspects of symptom change represent consequences of earlier adaptive failure and which represent emergent new features of the underlying disorder requires a longitudinal and developmental perspective. Relatedly, there is ample evidence that the age of onset criterion for ADHD needs reexamination. Laboratory science for defining behavioral dimensions has developed to a point at which we should consider identifying samples by such measures and then refining the clinical criteria based on the results, rather than going from less well defined clinical concepts to more precise laboratory measures. For example, precise laboratory measures of selective attention could be used to find inattentive individuals, who could then be characterized by clinical, rating, or direct observational measures. Current diagnostic practices tend to rely almost exclusively on the clinical interview or information from a single domain, despite evidence that reliability is poor. More standardized interviewing techniques, as well as training in the combining of information across informant domains, is sorely needed to enhance reliability of clinical assessment.

All these questions will remain the focus of research for the next decade and are likely to be informed by studies of etiology and pathophysiology, the subject to which we next turn.

ETIOLOGY AND PATHOPHYSIOLOGY

As noted in Chapter 7 (Swanson & Castellanos), children with ADHD differ from children without ADHD by group differences observed in neuroimaging studies of brain structure and brain functioning and electrophysiology, as well as studies relying on neuropsychological testing (Tannock, Chapter 8). While important advances continue to be made in identifying physical and pathophysiological differences in children with ADHD (Castellanos et al., 2001; Pliszka, Liotti, & Woldorff, 2000; Silberstein et al., 1998; Spencer, Biederman, & Wilens, 1998), caution is needed in interpreting these findings. Differences in function are not, in and of themselves, disturbances in function or evidence of internal dysfunction. Thus, some children can be shorter than others without necessarily having a "height disorder," whereas other children might be quite tall, also again without any evidence of an internal dysfunction. In some instances, however (e.g., congenital dwarfism and acromegaly), differences in height do, in fact, connote disturbances in bodily systems that can be identified by pathophysiological markers in the instance of a given child. We have not achieved this same level of understanding for ADHD.

Consider, for example, the findings documented by Swanson and Castellanos (Chapter 7) concerning the consistent differences in brain volumes affecting the basal ganglia, prefrontal cortex, and cerebellum. Overmeyer et al. (2000) have noted that siblings of children with ADHD also have smaller cerebral volumes in these same areas similar to their siblings who have ADHD. These differences are found, even though the children themselves do not have the condition. Thus, such differences in brain structure and size might reflect the activity of susceptibility genes or other correlates of the disorder but may not necessarily denote the disorder or a disordered brain state in and of itself.

Although these cautions are appropriate, as Swanson and Castellanos (Chapter 7) and other authors have noted (Mehta et al., 2000; Pliszka et al., 2000; Volkow et al., 1998), a range of studies are providing fairly consistent evidence of the systems involved in the syndrome of ADHD, the mechanisms of action of effective treatments, and the site of action of particular treatments that are consistent with current theories of ADHD that are related to the deficits (differences?) in internal brain structures' function and size. These lines of evidence, though not proof of an internal dysfunction per se, are providing an increasingly compelling story that helps us understand ADHD and the likely mechanisms and processes that are related to the specific symptoms of the syndrome.

One important area of research in terms of etiology and pathophysiology has been the study of genes. Importantly, genetic studies, as noted in Chapter 7 and in many places throughout the literature (Waldman et al., 1998; Winsburg & Comings, 1999), continue to document evidence and implicate specific genes in terms of their increased frequency in the presence of the ADHD syndrome. Thus, findings concerning specific forms of the dopamine transporter (DAT1) and the dopamine four (DRD4) genes have been replicated now in multiple laboratories across the world. In fact, these genes, particularly the DRD4, now constitute the most-replicated genetic finding in all of psychiatry, surpassing by far schizophrenia, manic depressive disease, autism, bipolar disorder, and all other syndromes. Thus, these genes, though not fully explanatory by any means, do indicate that this line of research is quite promising and needs to be further pursued. A more complete understanding of how these genes work, how they are turned on and off, how they affect children differently in terms of the expression of the ADHD syndrome, is an area much in need of further research.

Over the next decade, we will need more sophisticated genetic models, including those that consider the roles of different genes at different points in development, their variable function in the presence or absence of comorbidity (Willcutt & Pennington 2000), their action as a function of genetically mediated environmental factors (see, e.g., Wade & Kendler, 2000), and even interactions of genetic factors by birth cohorts over successive generations (e.g., Kendler, Thornton, & Pedersen, 2000), such that some genes are more important in the etiology of the syndrome during one period of societal development with a certain set of environmental risk factors, versus other periods of development when different sets of risk and protective factors hold sway.

The complexity of such necessary studies is daunting. But better models, newer mathematic approaches, and more precise determination and pinning down of specific genes likely to be involved should continue to yield understanding how environmental and biological factors interact and co-contribute to ADHD and its eventual outcomes (Laucht et al., 2000).

Quite possibly, some genes associated with ADHD might, in fact, predispose to traits that might be adaptive under some circumstances or conditions, whereas, under other conditions, the same genetic factors might be maladaptive (Ding et al., 2002; Jensen et al., 1997). ADHD, of course, is not adaptive per se, by definition, because it is defined by impairment and the constellation of multiple symptoms. However, specific genes associated with ADHD, and which might predispose to its likelihood, in the context of other genes and specific environments, might in fact convey some adaptive functioning and might have resulted as a function of positive selection factors; that is, their continued presence and prevalence in the human species can only be explained by the fact that they enhanced adaptation (Ding et al., 2002).

Unless we appreciate the complexity of these factors and understand that genes might work quite differently in different kinds of environments, we run the risk of underestimating the role of environmental factors that turn genes on and off, inadvertently cutting off opportunities to understand how some ADHD traits might, in fact, emerge as a function of environmental contexts, whether as a function of chemical environmental agents or of psychosocial factors (Overmeyer, Taylor, Blanz, & Schmidt, 1999; Roy, Rutter, & Pickles, 2000; Scahill et al., 1999). With these points in mind, much needed in future studies of gene-environment interactions are more studies of the environment, from food additives to chemical toxins (Arnold, Chapter 13), to the impact of the mass media (Robinson, Wilde, Navracruz, Haydel, & Varady, 2001), as well as how these factors might be manipulated to affect preventive or early-intervention approaches (Sanders, Montgomery, & Brechman-Toussaint, 2000).

Unfortunately, when people excessively reify the diagnosis of ADHD and fail to consider these complexities, a fuller understanding of the emergence of the disorder is not possible. It is ironic that the fields of oppositional-defiant and conduct disorder, depression, and anxiety have spent several decades pursuing studies of early intervention and prevention of these disorders, yet these approaches have not been applied to our understanding of ADHD, how early dysregulation of attention and impulse control might emerge, what factors are related to the expression of these traits, and what early approaches might be tried to intervene before the full-blown expression of the disorder. As Fox has noted (Fox, Henderson, Rubin, Calkins, & Schmidt, 2001), behavioral disinhibition arises early in development. Early diagnosis and intervention might be possible (Hadders-Algra & Groothuis, 1999), not just with methylphenidate (Handen, Feldman, Lurier, & Huszar-Murray, 1999) but also with behavioral interventions (Sonuga-Barke, Daley, Thompson, Laver-Bradbury, & Weeks, 2001). In fact, other models in other disorder areas do suggest that such approaches, delivered early, can lead to behavioral and biological differences in children's outcomes, given young children's malleability in the early years (Fisher, Gunnar, Chamberlain, & Reid, 2000).

Marakovitz and Campbell (1998) provide a note of caution in their report that children with ADHD at age 9, compared to those with other behavioral disorders, could not be differentiated on laboratory and psychological measures at age 4, and they point to the variability and possible malleability in these children's course and outcomes. Certainly, more studies of early diagnosis, outcomes, and the plasticity of these behaviors in young children are urgently needed (Rappley et al., 1999).

So, what is the future likely to hold? As we better understand the role of genes, environmental factors, including psychosocial and biological factors, their variable expression, and their impact as a function of the timing in which they turn genes on and off during the course of development, are likely to lead to an increased understanding that ADHD is a heterogeneous syndrome, most likely with many different kinds of ADHD. Just as the behavioral manifestations of the cough have many causes and constitute a final common pathway for disorders as varied as lung cancer, sarcoidosis, allergies, and upper respiratory infections, so too we are likely to eventually understand that ADHD has many different etiological pathways. Clues to the different types of ADHD might well be found in factors such as family history, particular genetic allelic variations, and even the presence of comorbidities (Hinshaw, Chapter 5; Jensen et al., 2001).

TREATMENTS FOR ADHD

As discussed in Chapters 9 through 15, we have substantial evidence for the safety and efficacy of a range of treatments, from medications to psychological therapies. Our understanding of these treatments and how they work on both brain processes (Ernst et al., 1999; Mehta et al., 2000; Swanson et al., 1999; Volkow et al., 1998; Swanson & Castellanos, Chapter 7) and psychological factors (Hinshaw et al., 2000; Wells et al., 2000) has progressed remarkably in the last decade. Unequivocally, this array of behavioral and pharmacological tools works and works effectively, possibly more for some subgroups of children than for others (Jensen et al., 2001; MTA Cooperative Group, 1999a, 1999b). Nonetheless, these treatments are not perfect, and many children who benefit somewhat from the treatments are not fully "normalized," even with the very best of treatments (Swanson et al., 2001)—hence, the need for the ongoing study and development of other treatments (Connor, Barkley, & Davis, 2000; Connor, Fletcher, & Swanson, 1999; Biederman & Spencer, Chapter 11).

The last few years have witnessed the development of newer medication preparations, those with both longer duration of action and release, to obtain full-day coverage for the treatment of ADHD symptoms (e.g., Swanson et al., 1999), and newer agents such as atomoxetine (Biederman & Spencer, Chapter 11). While all these agents new and old will continue to prove invaluable, they are likely to be insufficient without additional therapies. The behavioral therapies in and of themselves are not likely to be the answer, because even when combined with optimal medication they still leave a third of children not "normalized" (Swanson et al., 2001; Ambroggio & Jensen, Chapter 14). Like medicine, they also do not seem to "stick" for most children over a long period or across settings (Pelham, Chapter 12). As a result, psychosocial and biological treatments that target the remaining social, academic, and behavioral problems that many of these children experience, even after the very best of treatments (MTA Cooperative Group, 1999a), are urgently needed. Unfortunately, studies of alternative treatments have been few and far between, and, as Arnold (Chapter 13) notes, a number of these treatments likely warrant further exploration, as do studies of how to best match patients to specific treatments (Abikoff, Chapter 15; Jensen et al., 2001).

RISKS OF TREATMENT

Despite the misinformation that is so readily disseminated in the mass media, the best available evidence suggests that methylphenidate can be used for a substantial period of time with few meaningful or measurable side effects apart from short-term effects on weight (Greenhill, Chapter 9). Extant evidence also suggests that tics, once thought to contraindicate the use of stimulants, now do not necessitate a change of medication or the exclusion of stimulants as a potential line of treatment (Law & Schachar, 1999). Contributors to this volume have also tackled the thorny problem of whether stimulants predispose to substance abuse (Loney, Kramer, & Salisbury, Chapter 17; Lambert, Chapter 18). Additional evidence in the last several years continues to accumulate and suggests that ADHD treatments are associated with better outcomes and less substance use (Chilcoat & Breslaw, 1999; Disney, Elkins, McGue, & Iacono, 1999). In fact, whereas children with ADHD are at increased risk for substance use, the weight of evidence suggests that this risk is not due to the treatment of the disorder per se, but rather the association of ADHD with conduct disorder, a point emphasized by Klein (Chapter 16) and Loney et al. (Chapter 17). Thus, children with ADHD without conduct disorder are highly unlikely to abuse substances. Given the fact that optimal, well-delivered ADHD treatments appear to reduce conduct, oppositional, and learning disorders at fourteen months (MTA Cooperative Group, 1999a), even longer-term treatment for ADHD is likely to reduce risk for later conduct problems (as well as school dropout, failure, problems with the police, etc.) and thereby decrease these children's risk for substance use.

SERVICES FOR CHILDREN WITH ADHD

Many concerns have been raised about the possible overdiagnosis of children with ADHD. Whereas instances of overdiagnosis certainly exist (LeFever, Dawson, & Morrow, 1999), many children with ADHD, even inside service systems, are often not being treated. Such findings have been shown repeatedly in epidemiological studies (Jensen, Kettle, et al., 1999), health care databases (Olfson, Marcus, Weissman, &Jensen, 2000), and high-risk, high-need, service-sector settings (Bussing, Perwien, Belin, &Widawski, 1998). Although overdiagnosis, misdiagnosis, and inappropriate prescribing certainly do happen, extant evidence implies that approximately 1.5 million children with ADHD in any given year are not being treated with medications, suggesting that underdiagnosis, at least for half of the children with ADHD, is a bigger and more important public health problem than difficulties with overdiagnosis.

Other practical problems in area of diagnosis concern the discrimination of ADHD from other syndromes, such as bipolar disorder. This issue has been marked by significant controversy in the last several years, and concerns have been raised about the extent to which bipolar disorder is being misdiagnosed as ADHD and whether a substantial portion of children diagnosed with ADHD have in fact bipolar disorder (Biederman et al., 1999; Carlson & Kelly, 1998; Geller, Warner, Williams, & Zimmerman, 1998). However, studies of children in well-described family samples with true mania suggested that ADHD and bipolar symptoms might not overlap as much as is sometimes suggested (Egeland, Hostetter, Pauls, & Sussex, 1999). In addition, recent evidence from the MTA study suggests that children with many bipolar-like symptoms (e.g., irritability, excitability, mood swings, depression, and grandiosity) but who do not meet full criteria for mania are no less likely to respond to stimulants, nor are they more likely to have side effects, than ADHD children who do not have these manic-like symptoms. Thus, the assumption that children with ADHD who have any symptoms out of the ordinary might, in fact, be bipolar instead might be unwarranted, and caution is needed not to make inappropriate diagnoses of bipolar disorder in children with more complicated instances of ADHD (Galanter et al., 2002). This issue will require further exploration in future years.

At the practical level, there are substantial difficulties in communication between parents and physicians that might contribute to difficulties of missed diagnoses and misdiagnosis. Studies suggest that physicians and parents might not communicate adequately around the presence of children's symptoms. Frequently, physicians might think that they are inquiring appropriately about the presence of symptoms, yet families might misunderstand these questions (Jensen, 2002). Likewise, families might assume that the disorder is fully biomedical, while primary care physicians might assume that the disorder has principally family causes (family stresses, marital difficulties, etc.) (Klasen & Goodman 2000). Such factors, whether they be the difficulty in communicating or the differing assumptions about the nature and causes of the symptoms, are likely to lead to misdiagnosis and treatment dissatisfaction.

Unfortunately, current services are fragmented, and there are wide variations in the quality of care. The likelihood of follow-up visits, the possibility of referral for additional evaluation, and the likelihood of receiving psychological behavioral treatments in addition to medication vary greatly as a function of the discipline of the provider. Such factors cannot be explained by differences in the nature of children's presentation, and such wide variations reflect difficulties in training and skill level of physicians (Bussing et al., 1998; Hoagwood, Jensen, Feil, Vitiello, & Bhatara, 2000; Klasen & Goodman 2000; Rappley et al., 1999; Sloan, Jensen, Kettle, & Hoagwood, 1999; Zima, Bussing, Crecelius, Kaufman, & Belin, 1999). Likewise, differences have been noted among the various disciplines in the likelihood of follow-up appointments and other aspects of care. Such findings suggest the need for further training of physicians and reorganization of how services are provided, such that better connections and partnerships can be formed between parents, providers, and teachers (Wildman, Kizilbash, & Smucker, 1999).

Finally, in addition to the fragmentation of the service system, studies of the costs of care, as noted by Kelleher (Chapter 27), are very much needed. Some studies have begun in this regard (e.g., Marchetti et al., 2001), and attempts have been made to determine the exact total cost of ADHD treatment, as well as associated medical costs to the child and family (Fischer, Barkley, Fletcher, & Patel, 2001; Guevara, Lozano, Wickizer, Mell, & Gephart, 2001; Leibson, Katusic, Barbaresi, Ransom, & O'Brien, 2001; Swensen, 2001). While the costs of ADHD might be analogous to other pediatric conditions (e.g., asthma), medical care expenses for ADHD are not reimbursed at comparable levels (Kelleher, Chapter 27).

SUMMARY

This volume is a testament made on many fronts, from diagnosis and assessment to pathophysiology to treatment to an understanding of how services can be most effectively delivered in real-world settings. Initially inspired by the prepared scientific testimony of an outstanding group of scientists at the National Institutes of Health Consensus Development Conference on ADHD (National Institutes of Health Consensus Development Conference Statement, 1999), the volume has since been augmented and expanded with new research findings completed in the interim. We can and should take heart that progress has been measurable in the last decade, and significant advances on each of these fronts have been noted. Yet much remains to be done . The current obstacles to the public's (and parts of the health care system's) recognition of ADHD as a medical condition worthy of treatment should give us pause. Likewise, the lingering gaps in the effectiveness of our treatments, the excessive proportion of children who are not normalized even with the best of treatments, the lack of access to treatments for children desperately in need, and the lack of development of early intervention and prevention research programs suggest that we still have much work to do.

References

Biederman, J., Mick, E., Prince, J., Bostic, J. Q., Wilens, T. E., Spencer, T., Wozniak, J., & Faraone, S. V. (1999). Systematic chart review of the pharmacologic treatment of comorbid attention deficit hyperactivity disorder in youth with mania disorder. *Journal of Child and Adolescent Psychopharmacology, 9,* 247–256.

Bussing, R., Zima, B. T., Perwien, A. R., Belin, T. R., & Widawski, M. (1998). Children in special education programs: Attention deficit hyperactivity disorder, use of services, and unmet needs. *American Journal of Public Health, 88,* 880–886.

Carlson, G. A., & Kelly, K. L. (1998). Manic symptoms in psychiatrically hospitalized children— What do they mean? *Journal of Affective Disorders, 51,* 123–135.

Castellanos, F. X., Giedd, J. N., Berquin, P. C., Walter, J. M., Sharp, W., Tran, T., Vaituzis, A. C., Blumenthal, J. D., Nelson, J., Bastain, T. M., Zijdenbos, A., Evans, A. C., & Rapoport, J. L. (2001). A quantitative brain magnetic resonance imaging in girls with attention-deficit/hyperactivity disorder. *Archives of General Psychiatry, 58,* 289–295.

Chilcoat, H. D., & Breslau, N. (1999). Pathways from ADHD to early drug use. *Journal of the American Academy of Child and Adolescent Psychiatry, 38*(11), 1347–1354.

Connor, D. F., Barkley, R. A., & Davis, H. T. (2000). A pilot study of methylphenidate, clonodine, or the combination in ADHD comorbid with aggressive oppositional-defiant or conduct disorder. *Clinical Pediatrics, 39,* 15–25.

Connor, D. F., Fletcher, K. E., & Swanson, J. M. (1999). A meta-analysis of clonidine for symptoms of attention-deficit/hyperactivity disorder. *Journal of the American Academy of Child and Adolescent Psychiatry, 38,* 1551–1559.

Ding, V. C., Chi, H. C., Grady, D. L., Morishima, A., Kidd, J. R., Kidd, K. K., Flodman, P., Spence, M. A., Schuck, S., Swanson, J. M., Zhang, Y. P., & Moyzis, R. K. (2002). Evidence of positive selection acting at the human dopamine receptor D4 gene locus. *Proceedings of the National Academy of Science USA, 99,* 10–12.

Disney, E. R., Elkins, I. J., McGue, M., & Iacono, W. G. (1999). Effects of ADHD, conduct disorder, and gender on substance use and abuse in adolescence. *American Journal of Psychiatry, 156,* 1515–1521.

Egeland, J. A., Hostetter, A. M., Pauls, D. L., & Sussex, J. N. (2000). Prodromal symptoms before onset of manic depressive disorder suggested by first hospital admission histories. *Journal of the American Academy of Child and Adolescent Psychiatry, 39,* 1245–1252.

Ernst, M., Zametkin, A. J., Matochik, J. A., Pascualvaca, D., Jons, P. H., & Cohen, R. M. (1999). High mid-brain [18F] DOPA accumulation in children of attention deficit hyperactivity disorder. *American Journal of Psychiatry, 156,* 1209–1215.

Fischer, M., Barkley, R., Fletcher, K., & Patel, L. (2001, October). Young adult outcomes of childhood ADHD: Costs to society. *Scientific Proceedings of the American Academy of Child and Adolescent Psychiatry,* 75.

Fisher, P. A., Gunnar, M. R., Chamberlain, P., & Reid, J. B. (2000). Preventive intervention for maltreated preschool children: Impact on children's behavior, neuroendocrine activity, and foster-parent functioning. *Journal of the American Academy of Child and Adolescent Psychiatry, 39,* 1356–1364.

Fox, N. A., Henderson, H. A., Rubin, K. H., Calkins, S. D., & Schmidt, L. A. (2001). Continuity and discontinuity of behavioral inhibition and exuberance: Psychophysiological and behavioral influences across the first four years of life. *Child Development, 72,* 1–21.

Galanter, C. A., Carlson, G. A., Jensen, P. S., Greenhill, L. L., Elliott, G. R., Chuang, S. Z., Davies, M., Li, W., & MTA Cooperative Group. (2002). *Response to methylphenidate in children with attention deficit hyperactivity disorder and manic symptoms: Results from the MTA titration trial.* Manuscript submitted for review.

Geller, B., Warner, K., Williams, M., & Zimmerman, B. (1998). Prepubertal and young adolescent bipolarity versus ADHD. Assessment and validity using the Wash-U-KSADS, CBCL, and TRF. *Journal of Affective Disorders, 51*, 93–100.

Guevara, J., Lozano, P., Wickizer, T., Mell, L., & Gephart, H. (2001). Utilization and cost of health care services for children with attention-deficit/hyperactivity disorder. *Pediatrics, 108*, 71–78.

Hadders-Algra, M., & Groothuis, A. M. (1999). Quality of general movements in infancy as related to neurological dysfunction, ADHD, and aggressive behaviour. *Developmental Medicine and Child Neurology, 41*, 381–391.

Handen, B. L., Feldman, H. M., Lurier, A., & Murray, P. J. (1999). Efficacy of methylphenidate among preschool children with developmental disabilities and ADHD. *Journal of the American Academy of Child and Adolescent Psychiatry, 38*, 805–812.

Hinshaw, S. P., Owens, E. B., Wells, K. C., Kraemer, H. C., Abikoff, H. B., Arnold, L. E., Conners, C. K., Elliott, G., Greenhill, L. L., Hechtman, L., Hoza, B., Jensen, P. S., March, J. S., Newcorn, J. H., Pelham, W. E., Swanson, J. M., Vitiello, B., & Wigal, T. (2000). Family processes and treatment outcome in the MTA: Negative/ineffective parenting practices in relation to multimodal treatment. *Journal of Abnormal Child Psychology, 28*, 555–568.

Hoagwood, K., Jensen, P. S., Feil, M., Vitiello, B., & Bhatara, V. S. (2000). Medication management of stimulants in pediatric-practice settings: A national perspective. *Developmental and Behavioral Pediatrics, 21*, 322–331.

Hudziak, J. J., Wadsworth, M. E., Heath, A. C., & Achenbach, T. M. (1999). Latent class analysis of child behavior checklist attention problems. *Journal of the American Academy of Child and Adolescent Psychiatry, 38*, 985–991.

Jensen, P. S. (2002). From ivory towers to earthen trenches: Issues and obstacles in effectiveness studies. *Report on Emotional and Behavioral Disorders in Youth, 2*, 25–26, 47.

Jensen, P. S., Hinshaw, S. P., Kraemer, H. C., Lenora, N., Newcorn, J. H., Abikoff, H. B., March, J. S., Arnold, L. E., Cantwell, D. P., Conners, C. K., Elliott, G. R., Greenhill, L. L., Hechtman, L., Hoza, B., Pelham, W. E., Severe, J. B., Swanson, J. M., Wells, K. C., Wigal, T., Vitiello, B. (2001). ADHD comorbidity findings from the MTA study: Comparing comorbid subgroups. *Journal of the American Academy of Child and Adolescent Psychiatry, 40*, 147–158.

Jensen, P. S., Mrazek, D., Knapp, P. K., Steinberg L., Pfeffer, C., Schowalter, J., & Shapiro, T. (1997). Evolution and revolution in child psychiatry: ADHD as a disorder of adaptation. *Journal of the American Academy of Child and Adolescent Psychiatry, 36*, 1672–1679.

Jensen, P. S., Kettle, L., Roper, M. T., Sloan, M. T., Dulcan, M. K., Hoven, C., Bird, H. R., Bauermeister, J. J., & Paine, J. D. (1999). Are stimulants overprescribed? Treatment of ADHD in four U.S. communities. *Journal of the American Academy of Child and Adolescent Psychiatry, 38*, 797–804.

Jensen, P., Rubio-Stipec, M., Canino, G., Bird, H., Dulcan, M., Schwab-Stone, M., & Lahey, B. (1999). Parent and child contributions to child psychiatric diagnosis: Are both informants always needed? *Journal of the American Academy of Child and Adolescent Psychiatry, 38*, 1569–1579.

Kendler, K. S., Thornton, L. M., & Pedersen, N. L. (2000). Tobacco consumption in Swedish twins reared apart and reared together. *Archives of General Psychiatry, 57*, 886–892.

Klasen, H., & Goodman, R. (2000). Parents and GPs at cross purposes over hyperactivity: A qualitative study of possible barriers to treatment. *British Journal of General Practice, 50*, 199–202.

Laucht, M., Esser, G., Baving, L., Gerhold, M., Hoesch, I., Ihle, W., Steigleider, P., Stock, B., Stoehr, R. M., Weindrich, D., & Schmidt, M. H. (2000). Behavioral sequelae of perinatal insults and early family adversity at eight years of age. *Journal of the American Academy of Child and Adolescent Psychiatry, 39*, 1229–1237.

Law, S. F., & Schachar, R. J. (1999). Do typical clinical doses of methylphenidate cause tics in children treated for attention deficit hyperactive disorder? *Journal of the American Academy of Child and Adolescent Psychiatry, 38*, 944–951.

LeFever, G. B., Dawson, K. V., & Morrow, A. L. (1999). The extent of drug therapy for attention-deficit/hyperactivity among children in public schools. *American Journal of Public Health, 89*, 1359–1364.

Leibson, C., Katusic, S., Barbaresi, W., Ransom, J., & O'Brien, P. (2001). Use and costs of medical care for children and adolescents with and without attention-deficit/hyperactivity disorder. *Journal of the American Medical Association, 285*, 60–66.

Marakovitz, S. E., & Campbell, S. B. (1998). Inattention, impulsivity, and hyperactivity from pre-school to school age: Performance of hard-to-manage boys on laboratory measures. *Journal of Child Psychology and Psychiatry, 39*, 841–851.

Marchetti, A., Magar, R., Lau, H., Murphy, E. L., Jensen, P. S., Conners, C. K., Findling, R., Wineburg, E., Carotenuto, I., Einarson, T. R., & Iskedjian, M. (2001). Pharmacotherapies for atten-tion-deficit/hyperactivity disorder: Expected cost analysis. *Clinical Therapeutics, 23*, 1–18.

Mehta, M. A., Owen, A. M., Sahakian, B. J., Mavaddat, N., Pikard, J. D., & Robbins, G. W. (2000). Methylphenidate enhances working memory by modulating discrete frontal and parietal lobe regions in the human brain. *Journal of Neuroscience, 20*, 1–6.

MTA Cooperative Group. (1999). A 14-month randomized clinical trial of treatment strategies for attention-deficit/hyperactivity disorder: Multimodal Treatment Study of Children with ADHD. *Archives of General Psychiatry, 56*(12), 1073–1086.

MTA Cooperative Group. (1999b). Moderators and mediators of treatment response for children with attention-deficit/hyperactivity disorder. *Archives of General Psychiatry, 56*, 1088–1096.

National Institutes of Health Consensus Development Conference Statement. (1999). Diagnosis and treatment of attention-deficit/hyperactivity disorder (ADHD). *Journal of the American Academy of Child and Adolescent Psychiatry, 39*, 182–188.

Olfson, M., Marcus, S. C., Weissman, M. M., & Jensen, P. S. (2002). National trends in the use of psychotropic medications by children. *Journal of the American Academy of Child and Adolescent Psychiatry*.

Overmeyer, S., Simmons, A., Santosh, J., Andrew, C., Williams, S. C. R., Taylor, A., Chen, W., & Taylor, E. (2000). Corpus colossum may be similar in children with ADHD and siblings of chil-dren with ADHD. *Developmental Medicine and Child Neurology, 42*, 8–13.

Overmeyer, S., Taylor, E., Blanz, B., & Schmidt, M. H. (1999). Psychosocial adversities underesti-mated in hyperkinetic children. *Journal of Child Psychology and Psychiatry, 40*, 259–263.

Pliszka, S. R., Liotti, M., & Woldorff, M. G. (2000). Inhibitory control in children with attention-deficit/hyperactivity disorder: Event-related potentials identify the processing component and tim-ing of an impaired right frontal response-inhibition mechanism. *Biologic Psychiatry, 48*, 238–246.

Rappley, M. D., Mullan, P. B., Alvarez, F. J., Ihouma, U. E., Wang, J., & Gardiner, J. C. (1999). Diagnosis of attention-deficit/hyperactivity disorder and the use of psychotropic medication in very young children. *Archives of Pediatrics and Adolescent Medicine, 153*, 1039–1045.

Rasmussen, P., & Gillberg, C. (2000). Natural outcome of ADHD with developmental coordination disorder at age twenty-two years: A controlled, longitudinal, community-based study. *Journal of the American Academy of Child and Adolescent Psychiatry, 39*, 1424–1431.

Robinson, T. N., Wilde, M. L., Navracruz, L. C., Haydel, K. F., & Varady, A. (2001). Effects of reducing children's television and video-game use on aggressive behavior. *Archives of Pediatrics and Adolescent Medicine, 155*, 17–23.

Roy, P., Rutter, M., & Pickles, A. (2000). Institutional care: Risk from family background or pattern of rearing? *Journal of Child Psychology and Psychiatry, 41*, 139–149.

Samuel, V. J., George, P., Thornell, A., Curtis, S., Taylor, A., Brome, D., Mick, E., Faraone, S. V., & Biederman, J. (1999). A pilot controlled family study of DSM-III-R and DSM-IV ADHD in African-American children. *Journal of the American Academy of Child and Adolescent Psychiatry, 38*, 34–39.

Sanders, M. R., Montgomery, D. T., & Brechman-Toussaint, M. L. (2000). The mass media and the prevention of childhood behavior problems: The evaluation of a television series to promote posi-tive outcomes for parents and their children. *Journal of Child Psychology and Psychiatry and Allied Disciplines, 41*, 939–948.

Scahill, L., Schwab-Stone, M., Merikangas, K. R., Leckman, J. F., Zhang, H., & Kasl, S. (1999). Psychosocial and clinical correlates of ADHD in a community sample of school-age children. *Journal of the American Academy of Child and Adolescent Psychiatry, 38*, 976–984.

Silberstein, R. B., Farrow, M., Levy, F., Pipingas, A., Hay, D. A., & Jarman, F. C. (1998). Functional brain electrical activity mapping in boys with attention-deficit/hyperactivity disorder. *Archives of General Psychiatry, 55*, 1105-1112.

Sloan, M., Jensen, P. S., Kettle, L., & Hoagwood, K. (1999). Assessing services for children with ADHD: Gaps and opportunities. *Journal of Attention Disorders, 3*, 13–29.

Sonuga-Barke, E. J. S., Daley, D., Thompson, M., Laver-Bradbury, C., & Weeks, A. (2001). Parent-based therapies for preschool attention-deficity/hyperactivity disorder: A randomized, controlled trial with a community sample. *Journal of the American Academy of Child and Adolescent Psychiatry, 40*, 402–408.

Spencer, T., Biederman, J., & Wilens, T. (1998). Growth deficits in children with attention deficit hyperactivity disorder. *Pediatrics, 102*, 501–506.

Swanson, J., Gupta, S., Guinta, D., Flynn, D., Agler, D., Lerner, M., Williams, L., Shoulson, I., & Wigal, S. (1999). Acute tolerance to methylphenidate in the treatment of attention deficit hyperactivity disorder in children. *Clinical Pharmacology and Therapeutics, 66*, 295–305.

Swanson, J. M., Kraemer, H. C., Hinshaw, S. P., Arnold, L. E., Conners, C. K., Abikoff, H. B., Clevenger, W., Davies, M., Elliott, G. R., Greenhill, L. L., Hechtman, L., Hoza, B., Jensen, P. S., March, J. S., Newcorn, J. H., Owens, E. B., Pelham, W. E., Schiller, E., Severe, J. B., Simpson, S., Vitiello, B., Wells, K., Wigal, T., & Wu, M. (2001). Clinical relevance of the primary findings of the MTA: Success rates based on severity of ADHD and ODD symptoms at the end of treatment. *Journal of the American Academy of Child and Adolescent Psychiatry, 40*, 168–179.

Swensen, A. (2001, October). Direct and indirect costs for ADHD patients and family members. *Scientific Proceedings of the American Academy of Child and Adolescent Psychiatry*, 75.

Volkow, N. D., Wang, G. J., Fowler, J. S., Gatler, S. J., Logan, J., Ding, Y. S., Hitzemann, R., & Pappas, N. (1998). Dopamine transporter occupancies in the human brain induced by therapeutic doses of oral methylphenidate. *American Journal of Psychiatry, 155*, 1325–1331.

Wade, T. D., & Kendler, K. S. (2000). The genetic epidemiology of parental discipline. *Psychological Medicine, 30*, 1303–1313.

Waldman, I. D., Rowe, D. C., Abramowitz, A., Kozel, S. T., Mohr, J. H., Sherman, S. L., Cleveland, H. H., Sanders, M. L., Gard, J. M. C., & Stever, C. (1998). Association and linkage of the dopamine transporter gene and attention-deficit hyperactivity disorder in children: Heterogeneity owing to diagnostic subtype and severity. *American Journal of Human Genetics, 63*, 1767–1776.

Wells, K. C., Epstein, J. N., Hinshaw, S. P., Conners, C. K., Klaric, J., Abikoff, H. B., Abramowitz, A., Arnold, L. E., Elliot, G., Greenhill, L. L., Hechtman, L., Hoza, B., Jensen, P. S., March, J. S., Pelham, W. E., Pfiffner, L., Severe, J., Swanson, J., Vitiello, B., & Wigal, T. (2000). Parenting and family stress treatment outcomes in attention deficit hyperactivity disorder (ADHD): An empirical analysis in the MTA study. *Journal of Abnormal Child Psychology, 28*, 543–553.

Wildman, B. G., Kizilbash, A. H., & Smucker, W. D. (1999). Physicians attention to parents' concerns about the psychosocial functioning of their children. *Archives of Family Medicine, 8*, 440–444.

Willcutt, E. G., & Pennington, B. F. (2000). Psychiatric comorbidity in children and adolescents with reading disability. *Journal of Child Psychology and Psychiatry and Allied Disciplines, 8*, 1039–1048.

Winsburg, B. G., & Comings, D. E. (1999). Association of the dopamine-transporter gene (DAT 1) with poor methylphenidate response. *Journal of the American Academy of Child and Adolescent Psychiatry, 38*, 1474–1477.

Zima, B. T., Bussing, R., Crecelius, G. M., Kaufman, A., & Belin, T. R. (1999). Psychotropic medication use among children in foster care: Relationship to severe psychiatric disorders. *American Journal of Public Health, 89*, 1732–1735.

Appendix A

National Institutes of Health Consensus Statement

Diagnosis and Treatment of Attention Deficit Hyperactivity Disorder (ADHD)

(National Institutes of Health Consensus Statement Online 1998 Nov 16–18; 16(2): 1–37.)
[Note: NIH Consensus Statements are prepared by a nonadvocate, non-Federal panel of experts, based on (1) presentations by investigators working in areas relevant to the consensus questions during a 2-day public session; (2) questions and statements from conference attendees during open discussion periods that are part of the public session; and (3) closed deliberations by the panel during the remainder of the second day and morning of the third. This statement is an independent report of the panel and is not a policy statement of the NIH or the Federal Government.]

Abstract

Objective

The objective of this NIH Consensus Statement is to inform the biomedical research and clinical practice communities of the results of the NIH Consensus Development Conference on Diagnosis and Treatment of Attention Deficit Hyperactivity Disorder (ADHD). The statement provides state-of-the-art information regarding effective treatments for ADHD and presents the conclusions and recommendations of the consensus panel regarding these issues. In addition, the statement identifies those areas of study that deserve further investigation. Upon completion of this educational activity, the reader should possess a clear working clinical knowledge of the state of the art regarding this topic. The target audience of clinicians for this statement includes, but is not limited to, psychiatrists, family practitioners, pediatricians, internists, neurologists psychologists, and behavioral medicine specialists.

Participants

Participants were a non-Federal, nonadvocate, 13-member panel representing the fields of psychology, psychiatry, neurology, pediatrics, epidemiology, biostatistics, education and the public. In addition, 31 experts from these same fields presented data to the panel and a conference audience of 1215.

Evidence

The literature was searched through Medline and an extensive bibliography of references was provided to the panel and the conference audience. Experts prepared abstracts with relevant citations from the literature. Scientific evidence was given precedence over clinical anecdotal experience.

Consensus Process

The panel, answering predefined questions, developed their conclusions based on the scientific evidence presented in open forum and the scientific literature. The panel composed a draft statement that was read in its entirety and circulated to the experts and the audience for comment. Thereafter, the panel resolved conflicting recommendations and released a revised statement at the end of the conference. The panel finalized the revisions within a few weeks after the conference. The draft statement was made available on the World Wide Web immediately following its release at the conference and was updated with the panel=s final revisions.

Conclusions

Attention deficit hyperactivity disorder or ADHD is a commonly diagnosed behavioral disorder of childhood that represents a costly major public health problem. Children with ADHD have pronounced impairments and can experience long-term adverse effects on academic performance, vocational success, and social-emotional development which have a profound impact on individuals, families, schools, and society. Despite progress in the assessment, diagnosis, and treatment of ADHD, this disorder and its treatment have remained controversial, especially the use of psychostimulants for both short and long-term treatment.

Although an independent diagnostic test for ADHD does not exist, there is evidence supporting the validity of the disorder. Further research is needed on the dimensional aspects of ADHD, as well as the comorbid (coexisting) conditions present in both childhood and adult forms.

Studies, (primarily short term, approximately three months) including randomized clinical trials, have established the efficacy of stimulants and psychosocial treatments for alleviating the symptoms of ADHD and associated aggressiveness and have indicated that stimulants are more effective than psychosocial therapies in treating these symptoms. Because of the lack of consistent improvement beyond the core symptoms and the paucity of long term studies (beyond 14 months), there is a need for longer term studies with drugs and behavioral modalities and their combination. Although trials are underway, conclusive recommendations concerning treatment for the long term cannot be made presently.

There are wide variations in the use of psychostimulants across communities and physicians, suggesting no consensus regarding which ADHD patients should be treated with psychostimulants. These problems point to the need for improved assessment, treatment, and follow-up of ADHD patients. A more consistent set of diagnostic procedures and practice guidelines is of utmost importance. Furthermore, the lack of insurance coverage preventing the appropriate diagnosis and treatment of ADHD and the lack of integration with educational services are substantial barriers and represent considerable long-term costs for society.

Finally, after years of clinical research and experience with ADHD, our knowledge about the cause or causes of ADHD remain largely speculative. Consequently, we have no documented strategies for the prevention of ADHD.

Introduction

Attention deficit hyperactivity disorder (ADHD) is the most commonly diagnosed behavioral disorder of childhood, estimated to affect 3 to 5 percent (Q 1) of school-age children. Its core symptoms include developmentally inappropriate levels of attention, concentration, activity, distractibility, and impulsivity. Children with ADHD usually have functional impairment across multiple settings including home, school, and peer relationships. ADHD has also been shown to have long-term adverse effects on academic performance, vocational success, and social-emotional development.

Despite the progress in the assessment, diagnosis, and treatment of children and adults with ADHD, the disorder has remained controversial. The diverse and conflicting opinions about ADHD have resulted in confusion for families, care providers, educators, and policymakers. The controversy raises questions concerning the literal existence of the disorder, whether it can be reliably diagnosed, and, if treated, what interventions are the most effective.

One of the major controversies regarding ADHD concerns the use of psychostimulants to treat the condition. Psychostimulants, including amphetamine, methylphenidate, and pemoline, are by far the most widely researched and commonly prescribed treatments for ADHD. Because psychostimulants are more readily available and are being prescribed more frequently, concerns have intensified over their potential overuse and abuse.

This 2 day conference brought together national and international experts in the fields of relevant medical research and health care as well as representatives from the public. After 12 days of presentations and audience discussion, an independent, non-Federal consensus panel chaired by Dr. David J. Kupfer, Thomas Detre Professor and Chair, Department of Psychiatry, University of Pittsburgh, weighed the scientific evidence and wrote a draft statement that was presented to the audience on the third day.

The consensus statement addressed the following key questions:

- What is the scientific evidence to support ADHD as a disorder?

- What is the impact of ADHD on individuals, families, and society?

- What are the effective treatments for ADHD?

- What are the risks of the use of stimulant medication and other treatments?

- What are the existing diagnostic and treatment practices, and what are the barriers to appropriate identification, evaluation, and intervention?

- What are the directions for future research?

The primary sponsors of this conference were the National Institute on Drug Abuse, the National Institute of Mental Health, and the National Institutes of Health (NIH) Office of Medical Applications of Research. The conference was cosponsored by the National Institute of Environmental Health Sciences, the National Institute of Child Health and Human Development, the U.S. Food and Drug Administration, and the Office of Special Education Programs, U.S. Department of Education.

1. What is the Scientific Evidence to Support ADHD as a Disorder?

The diagnosis of ADHD can be made reliably using well-tested diagnostic interview methods. However, as of yet, there is no independent valid test for ADHD. Although research has suggested a central nervous system basis for ADHD, further research is necessary to firmly establish ADHD as a brain disorder. This is not unique to ADHD, but applies as well to most psychiatric disorders, including disabling diseases such as schizophrenia. Evidence supporting the validity of ADHD includes the long-term developmental course of ADHD over time, cross-national studies revealing similar risk factors, familial aggregation of ADHD (which may be genetic or environmental), and heritability.

Additional efforts to validate the disorder are needed: careful description of the cases, use of specific diagnostic criteria, repeated followup studies, family studies (including twin and adoption studies), epidemiologic studies, and long-term treatment studies. To the maximum extent possible, such studies should include various controls, including normal subjects and those with other clinical disorders. Such studies may provide suggestions about subgrouping of patients that will turn out to be associated with different outcomes, responses to different treatment, and varying patterns of familial characteristics and illnesses.

Certain issues about the diagnosis of ADHD have been raised that indicate the need for further research to validate diagnostic methods.

1) Clinicians who diagnose this disorder have been criticized for merely taking a percentage of the normal population who have the most evidence of inattention and continuous activity and labeling them as having a disease. In fact, it is unclear whether the signs of ADHD represent a bimodal distribution in the population or one end of a continuum of characteristics. This is not unique to ADHD as other medical diagnoses, such as essential hypertension and hyperlipidemia, are continuous in the general population, yet the utility of diagnosis and treatment have been proven. Nevertheless, related problems of diagnosis include differentiating this entity from other behavioral problems and determining the appropriate boundary between the normal population and those with ADHD.

2) ADHD often does not present as an isolated disorder, and comorbidities (coexisting conditions) may complicate research studies, which may account for some of the inconsistencies in research findings.

3) Although the prevalence of ADHD in the United States has been estimated at about 3 to 5 percent, a wider range of prevalence has been reported across studies. The reported rate in some other countries is much lower. This indicates a need for a more thorough study of ADHD in different populations and bet-

ter definition of the disorder.

4) All formal diagnostic criteria for ADHD were designed for diagnosing young children and have not been adjusted for older children and adults. Therefore, appropriate revision of these criteria to aid in the diagnosis of these individuals is encouraged.

5) In summary, there is validity in the diagnosis of ADHD as a disorder with broadly accepted symptoms and behavioral characteristics that define the disorder.

2. What is the Impact of ADHD on Individuals, Family, and Society?

Children with ADHD experience an inability to sit still and pay attention in class and the negative consequences of such behavior. They experience peer rejection and engage in a broad array of disruptive behaviors. Their academic and social difficulties have far-reaching and long-term consequences. These children have higher injury rates. As they grow older, children with untreated ADHD in combination with conduct disorders experience drug abuse, antisocial behavior, and injuries of all sorts. For many individuals, the impact of ADHD continues into adulthood.

Families who have children with ADHD, as with other behavioral disorders and chronic diseases, experience increased levels of parental frustration, marital discord, and divorce. In addition, the direct costs of medical care for children and youth with ADHD are substantial. These costs represent a serious burden for many families because they frequently are not covered by health insurance.

In the larger world, these individuals consume a disproportionate share of resources and attention from the health care system, criminal justice system, schools, and other social service agencies. Methodologic problems preclude precise estimates of the cost of ADHD to society. However, these costs are large. For example, additional national public school expenditures on behalf of students with ADHD may have exceeded $3 billion in 1995. Moreover, ADHD, often in conjunction with coexisting conduct disorders, contributes to societal problems such as violent crime and teenage pregnancy.

Families of children impaired by the symptoms of ADHD are in a very difficult position. The painful decision-making process to determine appropriate treatment for these children is often made substantially worse by the media war between those who overstate the benefits of treatment and those who overstate the dangers of treatment.

3. What Are the Effective Treatments for ADHD?

A wide variety of treatments have been used for ADHD including, but not limited to, various psychotropic medications, psychosocial treatment, dietary management, herbal and homeopathic treatments, biofeedback, meditation, and perceptual stimulation/training. Of these treatment strategies, stimulant medications and psychosocial interventions have been the major foci of research. Studies on the efficacy of medication and psychosocial treatments for ADHD have focused primarily on a condition equivalent to DSM-IV combined type, meeting criteria for Inattention and Hyperactivity/Impulsivity. Until recently, most randomized clinical trials have been short term, up to approximately 3 months. Overall, these studies support the efficacy of stimulants and psychosocial treatments for ADHD and the superiority of stimulants relative to psychosocial treatments. However, there are no long-term studies testing stimulants or psychosocial treatments lasting several years. There is no information on the long-term outcomes of medication-treated ADHD individuals in terms of educational and occupational achievements, involvement with the police, or other areas of social functioning.

Short-term trials of stimulants have supported the efficacy of methylphenidate (MPH) (Q 6) dextroamphetamine, and pemoline in children with ADHD. Few, if any, differences have been found among these stimulants on average. However, MPH is the most studied and the most often used of the stimulants. These short-term trials have found beneficial effects on the defining symptoms of ADHD and associated aggressiveness as long as medication is taken. However, stimulant treatments may not "normalize" the entire range of behavior problems, and children under treatment may still manifest a higher level of some behavior problems than normal children. Of concern are the consistent findings that despite the improvement in core symptoms, there is little improvement in academic achievement or social skills.

Several short-term studies of antidepressants show that desipramine produces improvements over placebo in parent and teacher ratings of ADHD symptoms. Results from studies examining the efficacy of imipramine are inconsistent. Although a number of other psychotropic medications have been used to treat ADHD, the extant outcome data from these studies do not allow for conclusions regarding their efficacy.

Psychosocial treatment of ADHD has included a number of behavioral strategies such as contingency management (e.g., point/token reward systems, timeout, response cost) that typically is conducted in the classroom, parent training (where the parent is taught child management skills), clinical behavior therapy (parent, teacher, or both are taught to use contingency management procedures), and cognitive-behavioral treatment (e.g., self-monitoring, verbal self-instruction, problem-solving strategies, self-reinforcement). Cognitive-behavioral treatment has not been found to yield beneficial effects in children with ADHD. In contrast, clinical behavior therapy, parent training, and contingency management have produced beneficial effects. Intensive direct interventions in children with ADHD have produced improvements in key areas of functioning. However, no randomized control trials have been conducted on some of these intensive interventions alone or in combination with medication. Studies that compared stimulants with psychosocial treatment consistently reported greater efficacy of stimulants.

Emerging data suggest that medication using systematic titration and intensive monitoring methods over a period of approximately 1 year is superior to an intensive set of behavioral treatments on core ADHD symptoms (inattention, hyperactivity/impulsivity, aggression). Combined medication and behavioral treatment added little advantage overall, over medication alone, but combined treatment did result in more improved social skills, and parents and teachers judged this treatment more favorably. Both systematically applied medication (monitored regularly) and combined treatment were superior to routine community care, which often involved the use of stimulants. An important potential advantage for behavioral treatment is the possibility of improving functioning with reduced dose of stimulants. This possibility was not tested.

There is a long history of a number of other interventions for ADHD. These include dietary replacement, exclusion, or supplementation; various vitamin, mineral, or herbal regimens; biofeedback; perceptual stimulation; and a host of others. Although these interventions have generated considerable interest and there are some controlled and uncontrolled studies using various strategies, the state of the empirical evidence regarding these interventions is uneven, ranging from no data to well-controlled trials. Some of the dietary elimination strategies showed intriguing results suggesting the need for future research.

The current state of the empirical literature regarding the treatment of ADHD is such that at least five important questions cannot be answered. First, it cannot be determined if the combination of stimulants and psychosocial treatments can improve functioning with reduced dose of stimulants. Second, there are no data on the treatment of ADHD, Inattentive type, which might include a high percentage of girls. Third, there are no conclusive data on treatment in adolescents and adults with ADHD. Fourth, there is no information on the effects of long-term treatment (treatment lasting more than 1 year), which is indicated in this persistent disorder. Finally, given the evidence about the cognitive problems associated with ADHD, such as deficiencies in working memory and language processing deficits, and the demonstrated ineffectiveness of current treatments in enhancing academic achievement, there is a need for application and development of methods targeted to these weaknesses.

4. What Are the Risks of the Use of Stimulant Medication and Other Treatments?

Although little information exists concerning the long-term effects of psychostimulants, there is no conclusive evidence that careful therapeutic use is harmful. When adverse drug reactions do occur, they are usually related to dose. Effects associated with moderate doses may include decreased appetite and insomnia. These effects occur early in treatment and may decrease with continued dosing. There may be negative effects on growth rate, but ultimate height appears not to be affected.

It is well known that psychostimulants have abuse potential. Very high doses of psychostimulants, particularly of amphetamines, may cause central nervous system damage, cardiovascular damage, and hypertension. In addition, high doses have been associated with compulsive behaviors and, in certain vulnerable individuals, movement disorders. There is a rare percentage of children and adults treated at high doses who have hallucinogenic responses. Drugs used for ADHD other than psychostimulants have their own adverse reactions: tricyclic antidepressants may induce cardiac arrhythmias, bupropion at high doses can cause seizures, and pemoline is associated with liver damage.

The degree of assessment and followup by primary care physicians varies significantly. This variance may contribute to the marked differences in appropriate prescribing practices. Adequate followup is required for any prescribed medications, especially for higher doses of psycho-stimulants.

Although an increased risk of drug abuse and cigarette smoking is associated with childhood ADHD (see Question 2), existing studies come to conflicting conclusions as to whether use of psychostimulants increases or decreases the risk of abuse. A major limitation of inferences from observational databases is the inability to examine independently the use of stimulant medication, the diagnosis and severity of ADHD, and the effect of coexisting conditions.

The increased availability of stimulant medications may pose risks for society. The threshold of drug availability that can lead to oversupply and consequent illicit use is unknown. There is little evidence that current levels of production have had a substantial effect on abuse. However, there is a need to be vigilant in monitoring the national indices of use and abuse of stimulants among high school seniors. One of the indices is the Drug Abuse Warning Network (DAWN).

5. What Are the Existing Diagnostic and Treatment Practices, and What Are the Barriers to Appropriate Identification, Evaluation, and Intervention?

The American Academy of Child and Adolescent Psychiatry has published practice parameters for the assessment and treatment of ADHD. The American Academy of Pediatrics has formed a subcommittee to establish parameters for pediatricians, but those guidelines are not available at this time. *[Editors' note: treatment guidelines have in fact now been published by the American Academy of Pediatrics, and are available: American Academy of Pediatrics: Treatment of the school-age child with attention-deficit/hyperactivity disorder. Pediatrics 2001, 108:1033–44].* Primary care and developmental pediatricians, family practitioners, (child) neurologists, psychologists, and psychiatrists are the providers responsible for assessment, diagnosis, and treatment of most children with ADHD. There is wide variation among types of practitioners with respect to frequency of diagnosis of ADHD. Data indicate that family practitioners diagnose more quickly and prescribe medication more frequently than psychiatrists or pediatricians. This may be due in part to the limited time spent making the diagnosis. Some practitioners invalidly use response to medication as a diagnostic criterion, and primary care practitioners are less likely to recognize comorbid (coexisting) disorders. The quickness with which some practitioners prescribe medications may decrease the likelihood that more educationally relevant interventions will be sought.

Diagnoses may be made in an inconsistent manner with children sometimes being overdiagnosed and sometimes underdiagnosed. However, this does not affect the validity of the diagnosis when appropriate guidelines are used. Some practitioners do not use structured parent questionnaires, rating scales, or teacher or school input. Pediatricians, family practitioners, and psychiatrists tend to rely on parent rather than teacher input. There appears to be a "disconnect" between developmental or educational (school-based) assessments and health-related (medical practice-based) services. There is often poor communication between diagnosticians and those who implement and monitor treatment in schools. In addition, followup may be inadequate and fragmented. This is particularly important to ensure monitoring and early detection of any adverse effect of therapy. School-based clinics with a team approach that includes parents, teachers, school psychologists, and other mental health specialists may be a means to remove these barriers and improve access to assessment and treatment. Ideally, primary care practitioners with adequate time for consultation with such school teams should be able to make an appropriate assessment and diagnosis, but they should also be able to refer to mental health and other specialists when deemed necessary.

Studies identify a number of barriers to appropriate identification, evaluation, and treatment. Barriers to identification and evaluation arise when central screening programs limit access to mental health services. The lack of insurance coverage for psychiatric or psychological evaluations, behavior modification programs, school consultation, parent management training, and other specialized programs presents a major barrier to accurate classification, diagnosis, and management of ADHD. Substantial cost barriers exist in that diagnosis results in out-of-pocket costs to families for services not covered by managed care or other health insurance. Mental health benefits are carved out of many policies offered to families, and thus access to treatment other than medication might be severely limited. Parity for mental health conditions in insurance plans is essential. Another cost implication lies in the fact that there is no funded special education category specifically for ADHD, which leaves these students underserved, and there is currently no tracking or monitoring of children with ADHD who are served outside of special education. This results in educational and mental health service sources disputing responsibility for coverage of special educational services.

Barriers exist in relationship to gender, race, socioeconomic factors, and geographical distribution of physicians who identify and evaluate patients with ADHD.

Other important barriers include those perceived by patients, families, and clinicians. These include lack of information, concerns about risks of medications, loss of parental rights, fear of professionals, social stigma, negative pressures from families and friends against seeking treatment, and jeopardizing jobs and military service. For health care providers, the lack of specialists and difficulties obtaining insurance coverage as outlined above present significant obstacles to care.

6. What Are the Directions for Future Research?

Basic research is needed to better define ADHD. This research includes the following: (1) studies of cognitive development, cognitive processing, and attention/inattention in ADHD and (2) brain imaging studies before the initiation of medication and following the individual through young adulthood and middle age.

Further research should be conducted with respect to the dimensional aspects of this disorder, as well as the comorbid (coexisting) conditions present in both childhood and adult ADHD. Therefore, an important research need is the investigation of standardized age- and gender-specific diagnostic criteria.

The impact of ADHD should be determined. Studies in this regard include (1) the nature and severity of the impact on individuals, families, and society of adults with ADHD beyond the age of 20 and (2) determination of the financial costs related to diagnosis and care of children with ADHD.

Additional studies are needed to develop a more systematized treatment strategy. These include:

- Studies of the Inattentive type of ADHD, especially since it might include a higher proportion of girls than the subtypes with hyperactivity/impulsivity.

- Studies of long-term treatment (treatment lasting longer than 1 year), which are needed because of the persistence of the disorder.

- Prospective controlled studies, up to adulthood, of the risks and benefits associated with childhood treatment with psychostimulants.

- Studies to determine the effects of psychotropic therapy on cognitive function and school performance.

- Studies of the effects of instructional treatments on the academic achievement of children with ADHD.

- Studies to determine whether the combination of stimulants and psychosocial treatments can improve functioning with a reduced dose of stimulants.

- Studies to determine the risks and benefits associated with treating children younger than age 5 with stimulants.

- Studies of the effects of various stimulants in adolescents and adults.

Greater attention should be given to developing integrated programs for diagnosis and treatment. These include:

- Model projects to demonstrate methods of training teachers to recognize and provide appropriate special programs for children with ADHD.

- Incorporation of classroom strategies to effectively serve a greater variety of students and thereby reduce the need for ADHD referral and diagnosis.

- Determination of the extent to which individuals with ADHD are being served in postsecondary education and, if so, where they are being served, with what types of accommodations, and with what level of success.

Conclusions

Attention deficit hyperactivity disorder or ADHD is a commonly diagnosed behavioral disorder of childhood that represents a major public health problem. Children with ADHD usually have pronounced difficulties and impairments resulting from the disorder across multiple settings. They can also experience long-term adverse effects on academic performance, vocational success, and social-emotional development.

Despite progress in the assessment, diagnosis, and treatment of ADHD, this disorder and its treatment have remained controversial in many public and private sectors. The major controversy regarding ADHD continues to be the use of psychostimulants both for short-term and long-term treatment.

Although an independent diagnostic test for ADHD does not exist, evidence supporting the validity of the disorder can be found. Further research will need to be conducted with respect to the dimensional aspects of ADHD, as well as the comorbid (coexisting) conditions present in both childhood and adult ADHD. Therefore, an important research need is the investigation of standardized age- and gender-specific diagnostic criteria.

The impact of ADHD on individuals, families, schools, and society is profound and necessitates immediate attention. A considerable share of resources from the health care system and various social service agencies is currently devoted to individuals having ADHD. Often the services are delivered in a nonintegrated manner. Resource allocation based on better cost data leading to integrated care models needs to be developed for individuals with ADHD.

Effective treatments for ADHD have been evaluated primarily for the short term (approximately 3 months). These studies have included randomized clinical trials that have established the efficacy of stimulants and psychosocial treatments for alleviating the symptoms of ADHD and associated aggressiveness and have indicated that stimulants are more effective than psychosocial therapies in treating these symptoms. Lack of consistent improvement beyond the core symptoms leads to the need for treatment strategies that utilize combined approaches. At the present time, there is a paucity of data providing information on long-term treatment beyond 14 months. Although trials combining drugs and behavioral modalities are underway, conclusive recommendations concerning treatment for the long term cannot be made easily.

The risks of treatment, particularly the use of stimulant medication, are of considerable interest. Substantial evidence exists of wide variations in the use of psychostimulants across communities and physicians, suggesting no consensus among practitioners regarding which ADHD patients should be treated with psychostimulants. As measured by attention/activity indices, patients with varying levels and types of problems (and even possibly unaffected individuals) may benefit from stimulant therapy. However, there is no evidence regarding the appropriate ADHD diagnostic threshold above which the benefits of psychostimulant therapy outweigh the risks.

Existing diagnostic and treatment practices, in combination with the potential risks associated with medication, point to the need for improved awareness by the health service sector concerning an appropriate assessment, treatment, and followup. A more consistent set of diagnostic procedures and practice guidelines is of utmost importance. Current barriers to evaluation and intervention exist across the health and education sectors. The cost barriers and lack of coverage preventing the appropriate diagnosis and treatment of ADHD and the lack of integration with educational services represent considerable long-term cost for society. The lack of information and education about accessibility and affordability of services must be remedied.

Finally, after years of clinical research and experience with ADHD, our knowledge about the cause or causes of ADHD remains speculative. Consequently, we have no strategies for the prevention of ADHD.

Consensus Development Panel

David J. Kupfer, M.D.
Panel and Conference Chairperson

Thomas Detre
Professor and Chair of Psychiatry
Western Psychiatric Institute and Clinic
Department of Psychiatry
University of Pittsburgh
Pittsburgh, Pennsylvania

Robert S. Baltimore, M.D.
Professor of Pediatrics, Epidemiology, and Public Health

Division of Infectious Diseases
Department of Pediatrics
Yale University School of
    Medicine
New Haven, Connecticut

Donald A. Berry, Ph.D.
Professor
Institute of Statistics and Decision
Sciences
Duke University Medical Center
Durham, North Carolina

Naomi Breslau, Ph.D.
Director of Research
Department of Psychiatry
Henry Ford Health System
Detroit, Michigan

Everett H. Ellinwood, M.D.
Professor of Psychiatry and
Pharmacology
Duke University Medical Center
Durham, North Carolina

Janis Ferre
Past Chair
Utah Governor's Council for People
With Disabilities
Salt Lake City, Utah

Donna M. Ferriero, M.D.
Associate Professor of Neurology
Division of Child Neurology
Department of Neurology
University of California, San Francisco
San Francisco, California

Lynn S. Fuchs, Ph.D.
Professor
Department of Special Education
Peabody College
Vanderbilt University
Nashville, Tennessee

Samuel B. Guze, M.D.
Spencer T. Olin Professor of Psychiatry
Department of Psychiatry
Washington University School of
Medicine
St. Louis, Missouri

Beatrix A. Hamburg, M.D.
Visiting Professor
Department of Psychiatry
Cornell University Medical College
New York, New York

Jane McGlothlin, Ph.D.
Assistant Superintendent for Curriculum
and Instruction
Scottsdale Unified School District
Phoenix, Arizona

Samuel M. Turner, Ph.D., ABPP
Professor of Psychology
Director of Clinical Training
Department of Psychology
University of Maryland
College Park, Maryland

Mark Vonnegut, M.D.
Pediatrician
Milton Pediatrics
Quincy, Massachusetts

Lead Organizations

Office of Medical Applications of
Research, John H. Ferguson, M.D.,
Director

National Institute on Drug Abuse, Alan
I. Leshner, Ph.D., Director
National Institute of Mental Health,
Steven E. Hyman, M.D., Director

Supporting Organizations
National Institute of Environmental
Health Sciences, Kenneth Olden, Ph.D.,
Director

National Institute of Child Health and
Human Development, Duane Alexander,
M.D., Director

U.S. Food and Drug Administration,
Michael A. Friedman, M.D., Acting
Commissioner

Office of Special Education Programs,
U.S. Department of Education, Thomas
Hehir, Ed.D., Director

Appendix B

Bibliography

Aaron, P. G. (1997). The impending demise of the discrepancy formula. *Review of Educational Research, 67*, 461–502.

Abel, E. L., & Sokol, R. J. (1987). Incidence of fetal alcohol syndrome and economic impacy of FAS-related anomalies. *Drug and Alcohol Dependence, 19*, 51–79.

Abikoff, H. (1985). Efficacy of cognitive training interventions in hyperactive children: A critical review. *Clinical Psychology Review, 5*, 479–512.

Abikoff, H. (1987). An evaluation of cognitive behavior therapy for hyperactive children. In B. B. Lahey & A. E. Kazdin (Eds.), *Advances in clinical child psychology* (pp. 171–216). New York: Plenum Press.

Abikoff, H. (1991). Cognitive training in ADHD children: Less to it than meets the eye. *Journal of Learning Disabilities, 24*, 205–209.

Abikoff H., Ganeles D., Reiter G., Blum C., Foley C., & Klein, R. (1988). Cognitive training in academically deficient ADDH boys receiving stimulant medication. *Journal of Abnormal Child Psychology, 16*(4), 411–432.

Abikoff, H., & Gittelman, R. (1984). Does behavior therapy normalize the classroom behavior of hyperactive children? *Archives of General Psychiatry, 41*, 449–454.

Abikoff, H., & Gittelman, R. (1985). Hyperactive children treated with stimulants: Is cognitive training a useful adjunct? *Archives of General Psychiatry, 42*, 953–961.

Abikoff, H., & Gittelman-Klein, R. (1985). The normalizing effects of methylphenidate on the classroom behavior of hyperactive children. *Journal of Abnormal Child Psychology, 13*, 33–44.

Abikoff, H., & Hechtman, L. (1996). Multimodal therapy and stimulants in the treatment of children with attention deficit hyperactivity disorder. In E. D. Hibbs & P. S. Jensen (Eds.), *Psychosocial treatments for child and adolescent disorders: Empirically based strategies for clinical practice* (pp. 341–369). Washington, DC: American Psychological Association.

Abikoff, H., & Hechtman, L. (1998). *Multimodal treatment for children with ADHD: Effects on ADHD and social behavior and diagnostic status.* Unpublished manuscript.

Abino, P. D., & Pandarinath, S. (1977). Methylphenidate (Ritalin) abuse. *Journal of the Medical Society of New Jersey, 74*, 1061–1062.

Abiuso, P. D. (1977). Methylphenidate (Ritalin) abuse. *Journal of the Medical Society of New Jersey, 74*, 1061–1062.

Abramowicz, M. (1990). Sudden death in children treated with tricyclic antidepressant. *The Medical Letter on Drugs and Therapeutics, The Medical Letter, 32*, 37–40.

Abramowitz, A. J., Eckstrand, D., O'Leary, S. G., & Dulcan, M. K. (1992). ADHD children's responses to stimulant medication and two intensities of a behavioral intervention. *Behavior Modification, 16*, 193–203.

Abramowitz, A. J., & O'Leary, S. G. (1990). Effectiveness of delayed punishment in an applied setting. *Behavior Therapy, 21*, 231–239.

Abramowitz, A. J., O'Leary, S. G., & Futtersak, M. W. (1988). The relative impact of long and short reprimands on children's off-task behavior in the classroom. *Behavior Therapy, 19*, 243–247.

Abramowitz, A. J., O'Leary, S. G., & Rosen, L. A. (1987). Reducing off-task behavior in the classroom: A comparison of encouragement and reprimands. *Journal of Abnormal Child Psychology, 15*, 153–163.

Achenbach, T., & Edelbrock, L. (1983). *Manual for the Child Behavior Checklist and Revised Child Behavior Profile.* Burlington, VT: University of Vermont.

Achenbach, T. M., Howell, C. T., McConaughy, C. H., & Stanger, C. (1995). Six-year predictors of problems in a national sample of children and youth: Cross-informant syndromes. *Journal of the American Academy of Child and Adolescent Psychiatry, 34*, 336–347.

Acker, M. M., & O'Leary, S. G. (1987). Effects of reprimands and praise on appropriate social behavior in the classroom. *Journal of Abnormal Child Psychology, 5*, 549–557.

Acker, M. M., & O'Leary, S. G. (1988). Effects of consistent and inconsistent feedback on inappropriate child behavior. *Behavior Therapy, 19*, 619–624.

Ackerman, P. T., Anhalt, J. M., Holcomb, P. J., & Dykman, R. A. (1986). Presumably innate and acquired automatic processes in children with attention and/or reading disorders. *Journal of Child Psychology and Psychiatry, 27*, 513–529.

ADHD [Special issue]. (1997). *Teacher Education in Special Education, 20*(2), 87–188.

Adler, L., Resnick, S., Kunz, M., Devinsky, O. (1995). *Open-label trial of venlafaxine in attention deficit disorder.* Orlando, FL: New Clinical Drug Evaluation Unit Program.

Agget, P. J., & Harries, J. T. (1979). Current status of zinc in health and disease states. *Archives of Disease in Childhood, 54*, 909–917.

Ahmad, S., Dasgupta, A., & Kenny, M. A. (1989). Fatty acid abnormalities in hemodialysis patients: Effect of l-carnitine administration. *Kidney International, 36*(Suppl. 27), S-243–S-246.

Aigner, T. G., & Balster, R. L. (1979). Rapid substitution procedure for intravenous drug self-administration studies in rhesus monkeys. *Pharmacology, Biochemistry, and Behavior, 10*, 105–112.

Aleman, S. R. (1991, December 5). *Special education for children with attention deficit disorder: Current issues* (Report No. 91–862 EPW). Washington, DC: Congressional Research Service.

Algozzine, R. (1980). The disturbing child: A matter of opinion. *Behavioral Disorders, 5*, 112–115.

Alpert, J. E., Maddocks, A., Nierenberg, A. A., O'Sullivan, R., Pava, J. A., Worthington III, J. J., Biederman, J., Rosenbaum, M., & Fava, M. (1996). Attention deficit hyperactivity disorder in childhood among adults with major depression. *Psychiatry Research, 62*, 213–219.

Aman, C. J., Roberts, R. J., & Pennington, B. F. (1998). A neuropsychological examination of the underlying deficit in attention deficit hyperactivity disorder: Frontal lobe versus right parietal lobe theories. *Developmental Psychology, 34*, 956–969.

Aman, M. G., Kern, R. A., McGhee, D. E., & Arnold, L. E. (1993). Fenfluramine and methylphenidate in children with mental retardation and ADHD: Clinical and side effects. *Journal of the American Academy of Child and Adolescent Psychiatry, 32*, 851–859.

Aman, M., Marks, R., Turbott S., Wilsher, C., & Merry, S. (1991). Methylphenidate and thioridazine in intellectually subaverage children. Effects on cognitive-motor performance. *Journal of the American Academy of Child and Adolescent Psychiatry, 30*, 816–824.

Aman, M. G., Mitchell, E. A., & Turbott, S. H. (1987). The effects of essential fatty acid supplementation by

Efamol in hyperactive children. *Journal of Abnormal Child Psychology, 15*, 75–90.

Aman, M., & Turbott, S. (1991). Prediction of clinical response in children taking methylphenidate. *Journal of Autism and Developmental Disorders, 21*, 211–228.

Aman, M. G., Turbott, S. H., Wilsher, C. P., & Merry, S. N. (1991). The clinical effects of methylphenidate and thioridazine in intellectually subaverage children. *Journal of the American Academy of Child and Adolescent Psychiatry, 30*, 246–256.

American Academy of Child and Adolescent Psychiatry. (1997). Practice parameters for the assessment and treatment of children, adolescents, and adults with attention-deficit/hyperactivity disorder. *Journal of the American Academy of Child and Adolescent Psychiatry, 36*(Suppl.), 85S–121S.

American Academy of Child and Adolescent Psychiatry. (1998). Practice parameters for the assessment and treatment of children and adolescents with language and learning disorders. *Journal of the American Academy of Child and Adolescent Psychiatry, 37*(Suppl.), 46S–62S.

American Academy of Pediatrics Task Force on Pediatric Education. (1978). *The future of pediatrics.* Evanston, IL: American Academy of Pediatrics.

American Psychiatric Association. (1968). *Diagnostic and statistical manual of mental disorders* (2nd ed.). Washington, DC: Author.

American Psychiatric Association. (1980). *Diagnostic and statistical manual of mental disorders* (3rd ed.). Washington, DC: Author.

American Psychiatric Association. (1987). *Diagnostic and statistical manual of mental disorders* (3rd ed., rev.). Washington, DC: Author.

American Psychiatric Association. (1994). *Diagnostic and statistical manual of mental disorders* (4th ed.). Washington, DC: Author

Anastopoulos, A. D., Shelton, T. L., DuPaul, G. J., & Guevremont, D. C. (1993). Parent training for attention-deficit hyperactivity disorder: Its impact on parent functioning. *Journal of Abnormal Child Psychology, 21*, 581–596.

Anastopoulos, A. D., Spisto, M. A., & Maher, M. (1994). The WISC-III Freedom From Distractibility factor: Its utility in identifying children with attention deficit hyperactivity disorder. *Psychological Assessment, 6*, 368–371.

Anderson, C. A., Hinshaw, S. P., & Simmel, C. (1994). Mother-child interactions in ADHD and comparison boys: Relationships to overt and covert externalizing behavior. *Journal of Abnormal Child Psychology, 22*, 247–265.

Anderson J. (1996). Is childhood hyperactivity the product of western culture? *The Lancet, 348*, 73–74.

Anderson, J., Williams, S., McGee, R., & Silva, P. (1987). DSM-III disorders in pre-adolescent children. *Archives of General Psychiatry, 44*, 69–76.

Andreasen, N. C., Grove, W. M., Shapiro, K. W., Keller, M. B., Hirschfeld, R. M., & McDonald Scott, P. (1981). Reliability of lifetime diagnosis. A multicenter collaborative perspective. *Archives of General Psychiatry, 38*, 400–405.

Angold, A., Erkanli, A., Egger, H. L., & Costello, E. J. (2000). Stimulant treatment for children: A community perspective. *Journal of the American Academy of Child and Adolescent Psychiatry, 39*, 975–984.

Angold, A., Erkanli, A., Egger, H. L., & Costello, E. J. (2000). Stimulant treatment for children: A community perspective. *Journal of the American Academy of Child and Adolescent Psychiatry, 39*(8), 975–984.

Angold, A., Messer, S. C., Stangl, D., Farmer, E. M. Z., Costello, E. J., & Burns, B. J. (1998). Perceived parental burden and service use for child and adolescent psychiatric disorders. *American Journal of Public Health, 88*, 75–80.

Anonymous. (1984). Vitamin B6 toxicity: A new megavitamin syndrome. *Nutrition Reviews, 42*, 44–46.

Applegate, B., Lahey, B. B., Hart, E. L., Biederman, J., Hynd, G. W., Barkley, R. A., Ollendick, T., Frick, P. J., Greenhill, L., McBurnett, K., Newcorn, J. H., Kerdyk, L., Garfinkel, B., Waldman, I., & Shaffer, D. (1997). Validity of the age of onset criterion for attention-deficit/hyperactivity disorder: A report from the DSM-IV field trials. *Journal of the American Academy of Child and Adolescent Psychiatry, 36*, 1211–1221.

Arcia, E., & Conners, C. K. (1998). Gender differences in ADHD? *Journal of Developmental and Behavioral Pediatrics, 19*, 77–83.

Arduini, A., Denisova N., Virmani A., Avrova, N., Federici, G., & Arrigoni-Martelli, E. (1994). Evidence for the involvement of carnitine-dependent long-chain acyltransferases in neuronal triglyceride and phospholipid fatty acid turnover. *Journal of Neurochemistry, 62*, 1530–1538.

Arnett, E. N., Battle, W. E., Russo, J. V., & Roberts, W. C. (1976). Intravenous injection of talc-containing drugs intended for oral use. *American Journal of Medicine, 60*, 711–718.

Arnold, E. H., O'Leary, S. G., & Edwards, G. H. (1997). Father involvement and self-reported parenting of children with attention deficit-hyperactivity disorder. *Journal of Consulting and Clinical Psychology, 65*, 337–342.

Arnold, L. E. (1995). Some nontraditional (unconventional and/or innovative) psychosocial treatments for children and adolescents: Critique and proposed screening principles. *Journal of Abnormal Child Psychology, 23*(1), 125–140.

Arnold, L. E., Abikoff, H. B., Cantwell, D. P., Conners, C. K., Elliott, G., Greenhill, L. L., Hechtman, L., Hinshaw, S. P., Hoza, B., Jensen, P. S., Kraemer, H., March, J., Newcorn, J., Pelham, W. E., Richters, J., Severe, J. B., Schiller, E., Swanson, J. M., Vereen, D., & Wells, K. (1997). National Institute of Mental Health Collaborative Multimodal Treatment Study of Children with ADHD (MTA): Design challenges and choices. *Archives of General Psychiatry, 54*, 865–870.

Arnold, L. E., Barnebey, N., McManus, J., Smeltzer, D., Conrad, A., Winer, G., & Desgranges, L. (1977). Prevention by specific perceptual remediation for vulnerable first-graders: Controlled study and follow-up of lasting effects. *Archives of General Psychiatry, 34*, 1279–1294.

Arnold, L. E., Christopher, J., Huestis, R. D., & Smeltzer, D. J. (1978). Megavitamins for minimal brain dysfunction: A placebo-controlled study. *Journal of the American Medical Association, 240*(24), 2642–2643.

Arnold, L. E., Clark, D. L., Sachs, L. A., Jakim, S., & Smithies, C. (1985). Vestibular and visual rotational stimulation as treatment for attention deficit and hyperactivity. *American Journal of Occupational Therapy, 39*(2), 84–91.

Arnold, L. E., Kleykamp, D., Votolato, N., Gibson, R. A., & Horrocks, L. (1994). Potential link between dietary intake of fatty acids and behavior: Pilot Exploration of Serum lipids in ADHD. *Journal of Child and Adolescent Psychopharmacology, 4*(3), 171–180.

Arnold, L. E., Kleykamp, D., Votolato, N. A., Taylor, W. A., Kontras, S. B., & Tobin, K. (1989). Gamma-linolenic acid for attention-deficit hyperactivity disorder: Placebo controlled comparison to d-amphetamine. *Biological Psychiatry, 25*, 222–228.

Arnold, L. E., Votolato, N. A., Kleykamp, D., Baker, G. B., & Bornstein, R. A. (1990). Does hair zinc predict amphetamine improvement of ADHD/Hyperactivity? *International Journal of Neuroscience, 50*, 103–107.

Arnold, L. E., Wender, P. W., McCloskey, K., & Snyder, S. H. (1972). Levoamphetamine and dextroamphetamine: Comparative efficacy in the hyperkinetic syndrome. *Archives of General Psychiatry, 27*(6), 816–824.

Arnsten, A. F., Steere, J. C., & Hunt, R. D. (1996). The contribution of alpha 2-noradrenergic mechanisms to prefrontal cortical cognitive function. *Archives of General Psychiatry, 53*, 448–455.

Aronson, H., & Gilbert, A. (1963). Preadolescent sons of male alcoholics. *Archives of General Psychiatry, 8*, 235–241.

Asarnow, J. (1988). Peer status and social competence in child psychiatric inpatients: A comparison of children with depressive, externalizing, and depressive and externalizing disorders. *Journal of Abnormal Child Psychology, 16*, 151–162.

Ascher, B. A., Farmer, E. M. Z., Burns, B. J., & Angold, A. (1998). The Child and Adolescent Services

Assessment (CASA): Description and psychometric. *Journal of Emotional and Behavioral Disorders, 4,* 12–20.

Atkins, M. S., & Pelham, W. E. (1991). School-based assessment of attention deficit-hyperactivity disorder. *Journal of Learning Disabilities, 24,* 197–204.

Atkins, M. S., Pelham, W. E., & White, K. J. (1989). Hyperactivity and attention deficit disorders. In M. Hersen (Ed.), *Psychological aspects of developmental and physical disabilities: A casebook* (pp. 137–156). Thousand Oaks, CA: Sage.

August, G. J. (1987). Production deficiencies in free recall: A comparison of hyperactive, learning disabled, and normal children. *Journal of Abnormal Child Psychology, 15,* 429–440.

August, G. J., Realmuto, G. M., MacDonald, A. W., Nugent, S. M., & Crosby, R. (1996). Prevalence of ADHD and comorbid disorders among elementary school children screened for disruptive behavior. *Journal of Abnormal Child Psychology, 24,* 571–595.

August, G. J., Stewart, M. A., & Holmes, C. S. (1983). A four-year follow-up of hyperactive boys with and without conduct disorder. *British Journal of Psychiatry, 143,* 192–198.

Ayllon, T., Layman, D., & Kandel, H. J. (1975). A behavioral-educational alternative to drug control of hyperactive children. *Journal of Applied Behavior Analysis, 8,* 137–146.

Aylward, E. H., Reiss, A. L., Reader, M. J., Singer, H. S., Brown, J. E., & Denckla, M. B. (1996). Basal ganglia volumes in children with attention-deficit hyperactivity disorder. *Journal of Child Neurology, 11,* 112–115.

Bailey, J. N., Palmer, C. G. S., Ramsey, C., Cantwell, D., Kim, K., Woodward, J. A., McGough, J., Asarnow, R. F., Nelson, S., Smalley, S. L.. (1997). DRD4 gene and susceptibility to attention deficit hyperactivity disorder: Differences in familial and sporadic cases. *American Journal of Medical Genetics, Neuropsychiatric Genetics, 74,* 623.

Baker, G. B., Bornstein, R. A., Rouget, A. C., Therrien, S., & van Muyden, J. (1991). Phenylethylaminergic mechanisms in attention-deficit disorder. *Biological Psychiatry, 29,* 15–22.

Ball, S. A., Carroll, K. M., , & Rounsaville, B. J. (1994). Sensation seeking, substance abuse, and psychopathology in treatment-seeking and community cocaine abusers. *Journal of Consulting and Clinical Psychology, 62,* 1053–1057.

Bandura, A. (1969). *Principles of behavior modification.* New York: Holt, Rinehart & Winston.

Barkley, R. A. (1977). A review of stimulant drug research with hyperactive children. *Journal of Child Psychology and Psychiatry, 18,* 137–165.

Barkley, R. A. (1987). *Defiant children: Parent-teacher assignments.* New York: Guilford Press.

Barkley, R. A. (1990). *Attention-deficit hyperactivity disorder. A handbook for diagnosis and treatment.* New York: Guilford Press.

Barkley, R. A. (1995). *Taking charge of ADHD: The complete, authoritative guide for parents.* New York: Guilford Press.

Barkley, R. A. (1997). Advancing age, declining ADHD. *American Journal of Psychiatry, 154,* 1323–1324.

Barkley, R. A. (1997). *ADHD and the nature of self-control.* New York: Guilford Press.

Barkley, R. A. (1997). Behavioral inhibition, sustained attention, and executive functions: Constructing a unifying theory of ADHD. *Psychological Bulletin, 121,* 65–94.

Barkley, R. A. (1998). Attention deficit hyperactivity disorder. *Scientific American, 279,* 66–71.

Barkley, R. A. (1998). *Attention-deficit hyperactivity disorder: A handbook for diagnosis and treatment* (2nd ed.). New York: Guilford Press.

Barkley, R. A. (1998). The prevalence of ADHD, Is it just a U.S. disorder? *The ADHD Report, 6*(2), 1–6.

Barkley, R. A., Anastopoulos, A. D., Guevremont, D. C., & Fletcher, K. E. (1991). Adolescents with ADHD: Patterns of behavioral adjustment, academic functioning, and treatment utilization. *Journal of the American Academy of Child and Adolescent Psychiatry, 30,* 752–761.

Barkley, R. A., Anastopoulos, A. D., Guevremont, D. G., & Fletcher, K. F. (1992). Adolescents with attention-deficit hyperactivity disorder: Mother-adolescent interactions, family beliefs and conflicts, and maternal psychopathology. *Journal of Abnormal Child Psychology, 20,* 263–288.

Barkley, R. A., & Biederman, J. (1997). Toward a broader definition of the age-of-onset criterion for attention-deficit hyperactivity disorder. *Journal of the American Academy of Child and Adolescent Psychiatry, 36,* 1201–1210.

Barkley, R. A., Copeland, A. P., & Sivage, C. (1980). A self-control classroom for hyperactive children. *Journal of Autism and Developmental Disorders, 10,* 75–89.

Barkley, R. A., & Cunningham, C. (1979). The effects of methylphenidate on the mother-child interactions of hyperactive children. *Archives of General Psychiatry, 36,* 201–208.

Barkley, R. A., Cunningham, C., & Karlsson, J. (1983). The speech of hyperactive children and their mothers: Comparisons with normal children and stimulant drug effects. *Journal of Learning Disorders, 16,* 105–110.

Barkley, R. A., DuPaul, G. J., & McMurray, M. B. (1990). Comprehensive evaluation of attention deficit disorder with and without hyperactivity as defined by research criteria. *Journal of Consulting and Clinical Psychology, 58,* 775–789.

Barkely, R. A., DuPaul, G. J., & McMurray, M. B. (1991). Attention deficit disorder with and without hyperactivity: Clinical response to three dose levels of methylphenidate. *Pediatrics, 87,* 519–531.

Barkley, R. A., Fischer, M., Edelbrock, C. S., & Smallish, L. (1990). The adolescent outcome of hyperactive children diagnosed by research criteria: I. An 8 year prospective follow-up study. *Journal of the American Academy of Child and Adolescent Psychiatry, 29,* 546–557.

Barkley, R. A., Fischer, M., Fletcher, K., & Smallish, L. (1998). *Young adult outcome of hyperactive children diagnosed by research criteria* (NIMH Grant #42181). Manuscript in preparation.

Barkley, R. A., & Grodinsky, G. M. (1994). Are tests of frontal lobe functions useful in the diagnosis of attention deficit disorders? *The Clinical Neuropsychologist, 8,* 121–139.

Barkley, R. A., Guevremont, D. C., Anastopoulos, A. D., & Fletcher, K. E. (1992). A comparison of three family therapy programs for treating family conflicts in adolescents with attention-deficit hyperactivity disorder. *Journal of Consulting and Clinical Psychology, 60*(3), 450–462.

Barkley, R. A., Karlsson, J., Pollard, S., & Murphy, J. V. (1985). Developmental changes in the mother-child interactions of hyperactive boys: Effects of two dose levels of Ritalin. *Journal of Child Psychiatry and Allied Disciplines, 26,* 705–715.

Barkley, R. A., Karlsson, J., Strzelecki, E., & Murphy, J. V. (1984). Effects of age and ritalin dosage on the mother-child interactions of hyperactive children. *Journal of Consulting and Clinical Psychology, 52,* 739–749.

Barkley, R. A., Koplowicz, S., Anderson, T., & McMurray, M. B. (1998). Sense of time in children with ADHD: Effects of duration, distraction, and stimulant medication. *Journal of the International Neurological Society, 3,* 359–369.

Barkley, R. A., McMurray, M. B., Edelbrock, C. S., & Robbins, K. (1989). The response of aggressive and nonaggressive ADHD children to two doses of methylphenidate. *Journal of the American Academy of Child and Adolescent Psychiatry, 28,* 873–881.

Barkley, R., McMurray, M., Edelbrock, C., & Robbins, K. (1990) Side effects of MPH in children with attention deficit hyperactivity disorder: A systematic placebo-controlled evaluation. *Pediatrics, 86,* 184–192.

Barkley, R. A., Murphy, K. R., & Kwasnik, D. (1996). Psychological adjustment and adaptive impairments in young adults with ADHD. *Journal of Attention Disorders, 1,* 41–54.

Barkley, R. A., Shelton, T. L., Crosswait, C., Moorehouse, M., Fletcher, K., Barrett, S., Jenkins, L., & Metevia, L. (1996). Preliminary findings of an early intervention program with aggressive hyperactive children. *Annals of the New York Academy of Sciences, 794,* 277–289.

Barr, C. L., Wigg, K. G., Bloom, S., Schachar, R., Tannock, R., Roberts, W., Malone, M., & Kennedy, J. L. (2000). Further evidence from haplotype analysis for linkage of the dopamine D4 receptor gene and attention-deficit hyperactivity disorder. *American Journal of Medical Genetics, 96*(3), 262–267.

Barrickman, L., Noyes, R., Kuperman, S., Schumacher, E., & Verda, M. (1991). Treatment of ADHD with fluoxetine: A preliminary trial. *Journal of the American Academy of Child and Adolescent Psychiatry, 30,* 762–767.

Barrickman, L., Perry, P., Allen, A., Kuperman, S., Arndt, S., Herrmann, K., & Schumacher, E. (1995). Bupropion versus methylphenidate in the treatment of attention-deficit hyperactivity disorder. *Journal of the American Academy of Child and Adolescent Psychiatry, 34,* 649–657.

Bauermeister, J. (1992). Factor analysis of teacher ratings of attention-deficit hyperactivity and oppositional defiant symptoms in children aged four through thirteen years. *Journal of Clinical Child Psychology, 21,* 27–34.

Bauermeister, J. J., Alegria, M., Bird, H. R., Rubio-Stipec, M., & Canino, G. (1992). Are attentional-hyperactivity deficits unidimensional or multidimensional syndromes?, Empirical findings from a community survey. *Journal of the American Academy of Child and Adolescent Psychiatry, 31*(3), 423–431.

Bauermeister, J. J., Bird, H. R., Canino, G., Rubio-Stipec, M., Bravo, M., & Alegra, M. (1995). Dimensions of attention deficit hyperactivity disorder: Findings from teacher and parent reports in a community sample. *Journal of Clinical Psychology, 24,* 264–271.

Baumgaertel, A., & Wolraich, M. L. (1998). Practice guideline for the diagnosis and management of attention deficit hyperactivity disorder. *Ambulatory Child Health, 4,* 45–58.

Baumgaertel, A., Wolraich, M. L., & Dietrich, M. (1995). Comparison of diagnostic criteria for attention deficit disorders in a German elementary school sample. *Journal of the American Academy of Child and Adolescent Psychiatry, 34,* 629–638.

Baxley, G. B., & Turner, P. F. (1978). Hyperactive children's knowledge and attitudes concerning drug treatment. *Journal of Pediatric Psychology, 3,* 172–176.

Beck, L., Langford, W., Mackay, M., & Sum, G. (1975). Childhood chemotherapy and later drug abuse and growth curve: A follow-up study of 30 adolescents. *American Journal of Psychiatry, 132*(4), 436–438.

Beck, S. J., Young, G. H., & Tarnowski, K. J. (1990). Maternal characteristics and perceptions of pervasive and situational hyperactives and normal controls. *Journal of the American Academy of Child and Adolescent Psychiatry, 29*, 558–565.

Beery, K. (1982). *Revised administration, scoring, and teaching manual for the developmental test of visual-motor integration.* Cleveland, OH: Modern Curriculum Press.

Befera, M., & Barkley, R. A. (1985). Hyperactive and normal girls and boys: Mother-child interactions, parent psychiatric status, and child psychopathology. *Journal of Child Psychology and Psychiatry, 26*, 439–452.

Bekaroglu, M., Yakup, A., Yusof, G., Orhan, D., Hilal, M., Erol, E., & Caner, K. (1996). Relationships between serum free fatty acids and zinc and ADHD. *Journal of Child Psychology and Psychiatry, 37*, 225–227.

Benezra, E., & Douglas, V. I. (1988). Short-term serial recall in ADD-H, normal and reading-disabled boys. *Journal of Abnormal Child Psychology, 16*, 511–525.

Benson, K., & Hartz, A. J. (2000). A comparison of observational studies and randomized controlled trials. *New England Journal of Medicine, 342*, 1878–1886.

Benton, D., & Buts, J. P. (1990). Vitamin/mineral supplementation and intelligence. *Lancet, 335*, 1158–1160.

Benton, D., & Cook, R. (1991). Vitamin and mineral supplements improve the intelligence scores and concentration of six-year-old children. *Personality and Individual Differences, 12*, 1151–1158.

Berkovitch, M., Pope, E., Phillips, J., & Koren, G. (1995). Pemoline-associated fulminant liver failure: Testing the evidence for causation. *Clinical Pharmacology and Therapeutics, 57*, 696–698.

Bernstein, A. L. (1990). Vitamin B6 in clinical neurology. *Annals of the New York Academy of Sciences, 585*, 250–260.

Bernstein, G. A., Carroll, M. E., Crosby, R. D., Perwien, A. R., Go, F. S., & Benowitz, N. L. (1994). Caffeine effects on learning, performance, and anxiety in normal school-age children. *Journal of the American Academy of Child and Adolescent Psychiatry, 33*, 407–415.

Berquin, P. C., Giedd, J. N., Jacobsen, L. K., Hamburger, S. D., Krain, A. L., Rapoport, J. L., & Castellanos, F. X. (1998). Cerebellum in attention-deficit hyperactivity disorder: A morphometric MRI study. *Neurology, 50*, 1087–93.

Bhatara, V., Clark, D. L., Arnold, L. E., Gonsett, R., & Smeltzer, D. J. (1981). Hyperkinesis treated by vestibular stimulation: An exploratory study. *Biological Psychiatry, 16*(3), 269–279.

Bhatia, M. S., Nigam, V. R., Botua, N., & Malik, S. K. (1991). Attention deficit disorder with hyperactivity among pediatric outpatients. *Journal of Child Psychology and Psychiatry, 32*, 297–306.

Bickett, L., & Milich, R. (1990). First impressions formed of boys with attention deficit disorder. *Journal of Learning Disorders, 23*, 253–259.

Biederman, J., Baldessarini, R., Goldblatt, A., Lapey, K., Doyle, A., & Hesslein P. (1993). A naturalistic study of 24-hour electrocardiographic recordings and echocardiographic finding in children and adolescents treated with desipramine. *Journal of the American Academy of Child and Adolescent Psychiatry, 32*, 805–813.

Biederman, J., Baldessarini, R., Wright, V., Keenan, K., & Faraone, S. (1993). A double-blind placebo controlled study of desipramine in the treatment of attention deficit disorder: III. Lack of impact of comorbidity and family history factors on clinical response. *Journal of the American Academy of Child and Adolescent Psychiatry, 32*, 199–204.

Biederman, J., Baldessarini, R., Wright, V., Knee, D., & Harmatz, J. (1989). A double-blind placebo controlled study of desipramine in the treatment of attention deficit disorder: I. Efficacy. *Journal of the American Academy of Child and Adolescent Psychiatry, 28*, 777–784.

Biederman, J., Faraone, S., Keenan, K., Benjamin, J., Krifcher, B., Moore, C., Sprich-Buckminster, S., Ugaglia, K., Jellinek, M. S., Steingard, R.,Spencer, T., Norman, D., Kolodny, R., Kraus, I., Perrin, J., Keller, M. B., Tsuang, M. T. (1992). Further evidence for family-genetic risk factors in attention deficit hyperactivity disorder: Patterns of comorbidity in probands and psychiatrically and pediatrically referred samples. *Archives of General Psychiatry, 49*, 728–738.

Biederman, J., Faraone, S. V., Keenan, K., Knee, D., & Tsuang, M. T. (1990). Family-genetic and psychosocial risk factors in DSM-III attention deficit disorder. *Journal of the American Academy of Child and Adolescent Psychiatry, 29*, 526–533.

Biederman, J., Faraone, S. V., Mick, E., Spencer, T., Wilens, T., Kiely, K., Guite, J., Ablon, J. S., Reed, E., & Warburton, R. (1995). High risk for attention deficit hyperactivity disorder among children of parents with childhood onset of the disorder: A pilot study. *American Journal of Psychiatry, 152*, 431–435.

Biederman, J., Faraone, S., Milberger, S., Guite, J., Mick, E., Chen, L., Mennin, D., Ouellette, C., Moore, P., Spencer, T., Norman, D., Wilens, T., Kraus, I., & Perrin, J. (1996). A prospective 4-year follow-up study of attention-deficit hyperactivity and related disorders. *Archives of General Psychiatry, 53*, 437–446.

Biederman, J., Faraone, S. V., Spencer, T., Wilens, T., Norman, D., Lapey, K. A., Mick, E., Lehman, B. K., & Doyle, A. (1993). Patterns of psychiatric comorbidity, cognition, and psychosocial functioning in adults with attention deficit hyperactivity disorder. *American Journal of Psychiatry, 150*, 1792–1798.

Biederman, J., Faraone, S. V., Taylor, A., Sienna, M., Williamson, S., & Fine, C. (1998). Diagnostic continuity between child and adolescent ADHD: Findings from a longitudinal clinical sample. *Journal of the American Academy of Child and Adolescent Psychiatry, 37*, 305–313.

Biederman, J., Faraone, S. V., Weber, W., Russell, R. L., Rater, M., & Oark, K. S. (1997). Correspondence between DSM-III-R and DSM-IV attention-deficit/hyperactivity disorder. *Journal of the American Academy of Child and Adolescent Psychiatry, 36*, 1682–1687.

Biederman, J., Gastfriend, D. R., & Jellinek, M. S. (1986). Desipramine in the treatment of children with attention deficit disorder. *Journal of Clinical Psychopharmacology, 6*, 359–363.

Biederman, J., Mick, E., Prince, J., Bostic, J. Q., Wilens, T. E., Spencer, T., Wozniak, J., & Faraone, S. V. (1999). Systematic chart review of the pharmacologic treatment of comorbid attention deficit hyperactivity disorder in youth with mania disorder. *Journal of Child and Adolescent Psychopharmacology, 9*, 247–256.

Biederman, J., Milberger, S., Faraone, S., Kiely, K., Guite, J., Mick, E., Ablon, S., Warburton, R., & Reed, E. (1995). Family environmental risk factors for attention deficit hyperactivity disorder: A test of Rutter's indicators of adversity. *Archives of General Psychiatry, 52*, 464–470.

Biederman, J., Milberger, S., Faraone, S. V., Kiely, K., Guite, J., Mick, E., Ablon, J. S., Warburton, R., Reed, E., & Davis, S. G. (1995). Impact of adversity on functioning and comorbidity in children with attention-deficit hyperactivity disorder. *Journal of the American Academy of Child and Adolescent Psychiatry, 34*, 1495–1503.

Biederman, J., Munir, K., Knee, D., & Habelow, W. (1986). A family study of patients with Attention Deficit Disorder and normal controls. *Journal of Psychiatric Research, 20*, 263–274.

Biederman, J., Newcorn, J., & Sprich, S. (1991). Comorbidity of attention deficit hyperactivity disorder with conduct, depressive, anxiety, and other disorders. *American Journal of Psychiatry, 148*, 564–577.

Biederman, J., Thisted, R., Greenhill, L., & Ryan, N. (1995). Estimation of the association between desipramine and the risk for sudden death in 5- to 14-year-old children. *Journal of Clinical Psychiatry, 56*, 87–93.

Biederman, J., Wilens, T., Mick, E., Faraone, S. V., & Spencer, T. (1998). Does attention deficit hyperactivity disorder impact the developmental course of drug and alcohol abuse and dependence? *Biological Psychiatry, 44*, 269–273.

Biederman, J., Wilens. T., Mick, E., Faraone, S., & Spencer, T. (1999). Pharmacotherapy of ADHD reduces substance abuse in midadolescence: A longitudinal study. *Pediatrics, 104*(2), e20.

Biederman, J., Wilens, T., Mick, E., Faraone, S. V., Weber, W., Curtis, S., Thornell, A., Pfister, K., Jetton, J. G., & Soriano, J. (1997). Is ADHD a risk factor for psychoactive substance use disorders? Findings from a four-year prospective follow-up. *Journal of the American Academy of Child and Adolescent Psychiatry, 36*, 21–29.

Biederman, J., Wilens, T., Mick, E., Milberger, S., Spencer, T. J., & Faraone, S. V. (1995). Psychoactive substance use disorders in adults with attention deficit hyperactivity disorder (ADHD): Effects of ADHD and psychiatric comorbidity. *American Journal of Psychiatry, 152*, 1652–1658.

Biederman, J., Wilens, T., Mick, E., Spencer, T., & Faraone, S. V. (1999, August). Pharmacotherapy of attention-deficit/hyperactivity disorder reduces risk for substance use disorder. *Pediatrics, 104*(2), e20.

Billman, J., & McDevitt, S. C. (1998, October 16). *TACTIC: A measure of temperament, attention, conduct, and emotion for 2–6 year old children in out-of-home settings.* Paper presented at the twelfth Occasional Temperament Conference, Philadelphia.

Bird, H. (1996). Epidemiology of childhood disorders in a cross-cultural context. *Journal of Child Psychology and Psychiatry, 37*(1), 35–49.

Bird, H. R., Canino, G., Rubio-Stipec, M., Gould, M. S., Ribera, J., Sesman, M., Woodbury, M., Huertas, S., Pagan, A., Sanchez-Lacay, A., & Moscoso, M. (1988). Estimates of the prevalence of childhood maladjustment in a community survey in Puerto Rico. *Archives of General Psychiatry, 45*, 1120–1126.

Bird, H. R., Gould, M. S., & Staghezza-Jaramillo, B. M. (1994). The comorbidity of ADHD in a community sample of children aged 6 through 16 years. *Journal of Child and Family Studies, 3*, 365–378.

Birmaher, B. B., Greenhill, L., Cooper, T., Fried, J., & Maminski, B. (1989). Sustained release methylphenidate: Pharmacokinetic studies in ADDH males. *Journal of the American Academy of Child and Adolescent Psychiatry, 28*(5), 768–772.

Blachman, D., & Hinshaw, S. P. (1998). *Friendship patterns in girls with attention-deficit hyperactivity disorder.* Poster presented at the annual meeting of the American Psychological Society, Washington, DC.

Blackburn, W. D., Jr. (1997). Eosinophilia myalgia syndrome. *Seminars in Arthritis and Rheumatism, 26*, 788–793.

Blankstein, A. M., Bullock, L. M., & Copans, S. A. (1998). Special issue: Improving longterm outcomes for children with ADHD. *Journal of Emotional and Behavioral Problems, 2*(2), 2–3.

Bloomquist, M. L., August, G. J., & Ostrander, R. (1991). Effects of a school-based cognitive-behavioral intervention for ADHD children. *Journal of Abnormal Child Psychology, 19*, 591–605.

Blouin, A. G., Bornstein, R. A., & Trites, R. L. (1978). Teenage alcohol use among hyperactive children: A five year follow-up study. *Journal of Pediatric Psychology, 3*, 188–194.

Borcherding, B. G., Keysor, C. S., Cooper, T. B., & Rapoport, J. L. (1989). Differential effects of methylphenidate and dextroamphetamine on the motor activity level of hyperactive children. *Neuropsychopharmacology, 2*, 255–263.

Borcherding, B., Thompson, K., Kruesi, M., & Bartko, J. J. (1988). Automatic and effortful processing in attention deficit/hyperactivity disorder. *Journal of Abnormal Child Psychology, 16*, 333–345.

Boris, M., & Mandel, F. S. (1994). Foods and additives are common causes of the attention deficit hyperactive disorder in children. *Annals of Allergy, 72*, 462–468.

Borland, H. L., & Heckman, H. K. (1976). Hyperactive boys and their brothers: A 25-year follow-up study. *Archives of General Psychiatry, 33*, 669–675.

Bornstein, R. A., Baker, G. B., Carroll, A., King, G., Wong, J. T., & Douglass, A. B. (1990). Plasma amino acids in attention deficit disorder. *Psychiatry Research, 33*, 301–306.

Boudreault, M., Thivierge, J., Cote, R., Boutin, P., Julien, Y., & Bergeron, S. (1988). Cognitive development and reading achievement in pervasive-ADD, situational-ADD and control children. *Journal of Child Psychology and Psychiatry, 29*, 611–619.

Bowyer, J. F., Davies, D. L., Schmued, L., Broening, H. W., Newport, G. D., Slikker, W., Jr., & Holson, R. R. (1994). Further studies of the role of hyperthermia in methamphetamine neurotoxicity. *Journal of Pharmacology and Experimental Therapeutics, 268*, 1571–1580.

Bowyer, J. F., & Holson, R. R. (1995). Methamphetamine and amphetamine neurotoxicity: characteristics, interactions with body temperature and possible mechanisms. In L. W. Chang & R. S. Dyer (Eds.), *Handbook of neurotoxicology* (Vol. II, pp. 845–870). New York: Marcel Dekker.

Boyle, M. H., Offord, D. R., Racine, Y. A., Fleming, J. E., Szatmari, P., & Links, P. S. (1993). Predicting substance use in early adolescence based on parent and teacher assessments of childhood psychiatric disorder: Results from the Ontario child health study follow-up. *Journal of Child Psychology and Psychiatry, 34*, 535–544.

Bradburn, N. M., Rips, L. J., & Shevell, S. K. (1987). Answering autobiographical questions: The impact of memory and inference on surveys. *Science, 236*, 157–161.

Bradley, C. (1937). The behavior of children receiving Benzedrine. *American Journal of Psychiatry, 94*, 577–585.

Brandeis, D., van Leeuwen, T. H., Rubia, K., Vitacco, D., Steger, J., Pascual-Marqui, R. D., & Steinhausen, H-Ch. (1998). Neuroelectric mapping reveals precursor of stop failures in children with attention deficits. *Behavioural Brain Research, 94*, 111–123.

Brandenberg, N. A., Friedman, R. M., & Silver, S. E. (1990). The epidemiology of childhood psychiatric disorders: Prevalence findings from recent studies. *Journal of the American Academy of Child and Adolescent Psychiatry, 29*, 76–83

Breakey, J. (1997). The role of diet and behavior in childhood. *Journal of Pediatrics and Child Health, 33*, 190–194.

Brenner, A. (1979). Trace mineral levels in hyperactive children responding to the Feingold diet. *Journal of Pediatrics, 94*, 44.

Brenner, A. (1982). The effects of megadoses of selected B complex vitamins on children with hyperkinesis; controlled studies with long-term follow-up. *Journal of Learning Disabilities, 15*, 258–264.

Brent, D. A., Kolko, D. J., Birmaher, B., Baugher, M., Bridge, J., Roth, C., & Holder, D. (1998). Predictors of treatment efficacy in a clinical trial of three psychosocial treatments for adolescent depression. *Journal of the American Academy of Child and Adolescent Psychiatry, 37*, 906–914.

Breslau, N., Brown, G. G., Del Dotto, J. E., Kumar, S., Exhuthachan, S., Andreski, P., & Hufnagle, K. G. (1996). Psychiatric sequelae of low birth weight at 6 years of age. *Journal of Abnormal Child Psychology, 24*, 285–300.

Brestan, E. V., & Eyberg, S. M. (1998). Effective psychosocial treatments of conduct-disordered children and adolescents: 29 years, 82 studies, and 5,272 kids. *Journal of Clinical Child Psychology, 27*, 180–189.

Brewer, T., & Colditz, G. A. (1999). Postmarketing surveillance and adverse drug reactions: Current perspectives and future needs. *Journal of the American Medical Association, 281*, 824–829.

British Psychological Society. (1996). *Attention deficit hyperactivity disorder (ADHD): A psychological response to an evolving concept.* Leicester, UK: Author.

Brito, G. N. (1987). The Conners' Abbreviated Teacher Rating Scale, a factor analysis study in Brazil. *Brazilian Journal of Medical and Biological Research, 20*(5), 553–556.

Brito, G. N., Pinto, R. C., & Lins, M. F. (1995). A behavioral assessment scale for attention deficit disorder in Brazilian children based on DSM-IIIR criteria. *Journal of Abnormal Child Psychology, 23*(4), 509–520.

Brock, S. W., & Knapp, P. K. (1996). Reading comprehension abilities of children with attention-deficit/hyperactivity disorder. *Journal of Learning Disabilities, 1*, 173–186.

Broening, H. W., Bacon, L., & Slikker, W. Jr. (1994). Age modulates the long-term but not the acute effects of the serotonergic neurotoxicant, 3,4-methylene-dioxymethampheatmine. *Journal of Pharmacology and Experimental Therapeutics, 271*, 285–293.

Brook, J. S., Whiteman, M., Gordon, A. S., & Cohen, P. (1986). Dynamics of childhood and adolescent personality traits and adolescent drug use. *Developmental Psychology, 22*, 403–414.

Brooks, G. F., O'Donoghue, J. M., Rissing, J. P., Soapes, K., & Smith, J. W. (1974). Eikenella corrodens, a recently recognized pathogen: Infections in medical-surgical patients and in association with methylphenidate abuse. *Medicine, 53*, 325–342.

Brown, A., Mallett, M., Fiser, D., & Arnold, W. C. (1984). Acute isoniazid intoxication: Reversal of CNS symptoms with large doses of pyridoxine. *Pediatric Pharmacology, 4*, 199–202.

Brown, G., Chadwick, O., Shaffer, D., Rutter, M., & Traub, M. (1981). A prospective study of children with head injuries: III. Psychiatric sequelae. *Psychological Medicine, 11*, 63–78.

Brown, G. L., Ebert, M. H., Mikkelsen, E. J., & Hunt, R. D. (1980). Behavior and motor activity response in hyperactive children and plasmas amphetamine levels following a sustained release preparation. *Journal of the American Academy of Child Psychiatry, 19*, 225–239.

Brown, G. L., Hunt, R. D., Ebert, M. H., Bunney, W. E., & Kopin, I. J. (1979). Plasma levels of d-amphetamine in hyperactive children: Serial behavior and motor responses. *Psychopharmacology, 62*, 133–140.

Brown, R. T., Borden, K. A., Wynne, M. E., Schleser, R., & Clingerman, S. R. (1986). Methylphenidate and cognitive therapy with ADD children: A methodologic reconsideration. *Journal of Abnormal Child Psychology, 14*, 481–497.

Brown, R. T., Borden, K. A., Wynne, M. E., Spunt, A. L., & Clingerman, S. R. (1987). Compliance with pharmacological and cognitive treatment for attention deficit disorder. *Journal of the American Academy of Child and Adolescent Psychiatry, 26*, 521–526.

Brown, R. T., & Sexon, S. B. (1989). Effects of methylphenidate on cardiovascular responses in attention deficit hyperactivity disordered adolescents. *Journal of Adolescent Health Care, 10*, 179–183.

Brown, R. T., Wynne, M. E., & Medenis, R. (1985). Methylphenidate and cognitive therapy: A comparison of treatment approaches with hyperactive boys. *Journal of Abnormal Child Psychology, 13*, 69–87.

Brown, W. A. (1977). Psychologic and neuroendocrine response to methylphenidate. *Archives of General Psychiatry, 34*, 1103–1108.

Brown, W. A., Corriveau, D. P., & Ebert, M. H. (1978). Acute psychologic and neuroendocrine effects of dex-troamphetamine and methylphenidate. *Psychopharmacology, 58*, 189–195.

Bruner, A. B., Joffe, A., Duggan, A. K., Casella, F., & Brandt, J. (1996). Randomized study of cognitive effects of iron supplementation in non-anemic iron-deficient girls. *Lancet, 348*(9033), 992–996.

Bryan, V., Franks, L., & Torres, H. (1973) Pseudomonas Aeeruginosa cervical diskis with chondro-osteomyelitis in an intravenous drug abuser. *Surgical Neurology, 1*, 142–144.

Bryant, E., & Shimizu, I. (1988). *Sample design, sampling variance, and estimation procedures for the National Ambulatory Medical Care Survey.* Bethesda, MD: Vital and Health Statistics, Public Health Service.

Bryant, K. J., Rounsaville, B., Spitzer, R. L., & Williams, J. B. W. (1992). Reliability of dual diagnosis substance dependence and psychiatric disorders. *Journal of Nervous Mental Disorders, 180*, 251–257.

Buckner, C. K., Patil, P. N., Tye, A., & Malspeis, L. (1969). Steric aspects of adrenergic drugs. XII. Some peripheral effects of (+/-)-Erythyo-and (+/-)-threo-methylphenidate. *Journal of Pharmacology and Experimental Therapeutics, 166*, 308–319.

Buhrmester, D., Camparo, L., Christensen, A., Gonzalez, L. S., & Hinshaw, S. P. (1992). Mothers and fathers interacting in dyads and triads with normal and hyperactive sons. *Developmental Psychology, 28*, 500–509.

Buitelaar, J., Gary, R., Swaab-Barneveld, H., & Kuiper, M. (1995). Prediction of clinical response to methylphenidate in children with attention deficit hyperactivity disorder. *Journal of the American Academy of Child and Adolescent Psychiatry, 34*, 1025–1032.

Buitelaar, J. K., van der Gagg, R. J., Swaab-Barneveld, H., & Kuiper, M. (1995). Prediction of clinical response to methylphenidate in children with attention-deficit hyperactivity disorder. *Journal of the American Academy of Child and Adolescent Psychiatry, 34*, 1025–1032.

Buitelaar, J., van der Gaag, R., Swaab-Barneveld, H., & Kuiper, M. (1996). Pindolol and methylphenidate in children with attention deficit hyperactivity disorder. *Journal of Child and Adolescent Psychiatry, 36*, 587–595.

Bukstein, O. G., Brent, D. A., & Kaminer, Y. (1989). Comorbidity of substance abuse and other psychiatric disorders in adolescents. *American Journal of Psychiatry, 146*, 1131–1141.

Burattini, M. G., Amendola, F., Aufierio, T., Spano, M., Di Bitonto, G., Del Vecchio, G. C., & De Mattia, D. (1990). Evaluation of the effectiveness of gastro-protected proteoferrin in the therapy of sideropenic anemia in childhood. *Minerva Pediatrica, 42*, 343–347.

Burcham, B., Carlson, L., & Milich, R. (1993). Promising school-based practices for students with attenton deficit disorder. *Exceptional Children, 60*, 174–180.

Burns, B. J., Costello, E. J., Angold, A., Tweed, D., Stangle, D., & Farmer, E. M. Z. (1995). Children's mental health service use across service sectors. *Health Affairs, 124*, 147–159.

Burns, G. L., Walsh, J. A., Owen, S. M., & Snell, J. (1997). Internal validity of attention deficit hyperactivity disorder, oppositional defiant disorder, and overt conduct disorder symptoms in young children: Implications from teacher ratings for a dimensional approach to symptom validity. *Journal of Clinical Child Psychology, 26*, 266–275.

Burns, G. L., Walsh, J. A., Patterson, D. R., Holte, C. S., Sommers-Flanagan, R., & Parker, C. M. (1997). Internal validity of the disruptive behavior disorder symptoms: Implications from parent ratings for a dimensional approach to symptom validity. *Journal of Abnormal Child Psychology, 25*, 307–320.

Bussing, R., Schuhmann, E., Belin, T. R., Widawski, M., & Perwien, A. R. (1998). Diagnostic utility of two commonly used ADHD screening measures among special education students. *Journal of the American Academy of Child and Adolescent Psychiatry, 37*, 74–82.

Bussing, R., Zima, B. T., & Belin, T. R. (1998). Differential access to care for children with ADHD in special education programs. *Psychiatric Services, 49*(9), 1226–1229.

Bussing, R. A., Zima, B. T., & Belin, T. R. (1998). Variations in ADHD treatment among special education students. *Journal of the American Academy of Child and Adolescent Psychiatry, 37*, 968–976.

Bussing, R., Zima, B. T., Belin, T. R., & Forness, S. R. (1998). Children who qualify for LD and SED programs: Do they differ in level of ADHD symptoms and comorbid psychiatric conditions? *Journal of Emotional Disorders, 22*, 85–97.

Bussing, R., Zima, B. T., Perwien, A. R., Belin, T. R., & Widawski, M. (1998). Children in special education programs: Attention deficit hyperactivity disorder, use of services, and unmet needs. *American Journal of Public Health, 88*, 880–886.

Calhoun, G. Jr., & Bolton, J. A. (1986). Hypnotherapy: A possible alternative for treating pupils affected with attention deficit disorder. *Perceptual and Motor Skills, 63*, 1191–1195.

Campbell, S. B. (1990). *Behavior problems in preschool children.* New York: Guilford Press.

Campbell, S. B., Pierce, E. W., Moore, G., & Marakvitz, S. (1996). Boys' externalizing problems at elementary school age: Pathways from early behavior problems, maternal control, and family status. *Developmental Psychopathology, 8*, 701–719.

Cantwell, D. P. (1972). Psychiatric illness in the families of hyperactive children. *Archives of General Psychiatry, 27*, 414–417.

Cantwell, D. P. (1995). Child psychiatry: Introduction and overview. In H. I. Kaplan & B. J. Saddock (Eds.), *Comprehensive textbook of psychiatry-IV* (pp. 2151–2154). Baltimore: Williams & Wilkins.

Cantwell, D. P. (1996). Attention deficit disorder: A review of the past 10 years. *Journal of the American Academy of Child and Adolescent Psychiatry, 35*, 978–987.

Cantwell, D. P., & Baker, L. (1989). Stability and natural history of DSM-III childhood diagnoses. *Journal of the American Academy of Child and Adolescent Psychiatry, 28*, 691–700.

Cantwell, D. P., Swanson, J. M., & Connor, D. F. (1997). Case study: Adverse response to Clonidine. *Journal of the American Academy Child and Adolescent Psychiatry, 36*, 539–544.

Capaldi, D. M. (1991). Co-occurrence of conduct problems and depressive symptoms in adolescent boys: I. Familial factors and general adjustment. *Developmental Psychopathology, 3*, 277–300.

Carey, W. B. (1998). *The relationship between low adaptability and innattention.* Unpublished data.

Carey, W. B. (2000). What the multimodal treatment study of children with attention-deficit/hyperactivity disorder did and did not say about the use of methylphenidate for attention deficits. *Pediatrics, 105*, 863–864.

Carey, W. B., & McDevitt, S. C. (1995). *Coping with children's temperament. A guide for professionals.* New York: Basic Books.

Carey, W. B., McDevitt, S. C., & Baker, D. (1979). Differentiating minimal brain dysfunction and temperament. *Developmental Medicine and Child Neurology, 21*, 765–772.

Carlson, C. L., Lahey, B. B., Frame, C. L., Walker, J., & Hynd, G. (1987). Sociometric status of clinic-referred children with attention deficit disorders with and without hyperactivity. *Journal of Abnormal Child Psychology, 15*, 537–547.

Carlson, C. L., Pelham, W. E., Milich, R., & Dixon, J. (1992). Single and combined effects of methylphenidate and behavior therapy on the classroom performance of children with attention-deficit hyperactivity disorder. *Journal of Abnormal Child Psychology, 20*, 213–232.

Carlson, E. A., Jacobvitz, D., & Sroufe, L. A. (1995). A developmental investigation of inattentiveness and hyperactivity. *Child Development, 66*, 37–54.

Carlson, G. A., & Kelly, K. L. (1998). Manic symptoms in psychiatrically hospitalized children—What do they mean? *Journal of Affective Disorders, 51*, 123–135.

Carlton, P. L., Manowitz, P., McBride, H., Nora, R., Swartzburg, M., & Goldstein, L. (1992). Attention deficit disorder and pathological gambling. *Journal of Clinical Psychiatry, 48*, 487–488.

Caron, C., & Rutter, M. (1991). Comorbidity in child psychopathology: Concepts, issues, and research strategies. *Journal of Child Psychology and Psychiatry, 32*, 1063–1080.

Carroll, K. M., & Rounsaville, B. J. (1993). History and significance of childhood attention deficit disorder in treatment-seeking cocaine abusers. *Comprehensive Psychiatry, 34*, 75–82.

Carroll, K. M., Rounsaville, B. J., & Bryant, K. J. (1993). Alcoholism in treatment-seeking cocaine abusers: clinical and prognostic significance. *Journal of Studies on Alcohol, 54*, 199–208.

Carte, E. T., Nigg, J. T., & Hinshaw, S. P. (1996). Neuropsychological functioning, motor speed, and language processing in boys with and without ADHD. *Journal of Abnormal Child Psychology, 24*, 481–498.

Carter, C. M., Urbanowicz, M., Hemsley, R., Mantilla, L., Strobel, S., Graham, P. J., & Taylor, E. (1993). Effects of a few food diets in attention deficit disorder. *Archives of Disease in Childhood, 69*, 564–568.

Carter, H. S., & Watson, W. A. (1994). IV pentazocine/methylphenidate abuse—The clinical toxicology of another Ts and blues combination. *Clinical Toxicology, 32*(5), 541–547.

Carter, S. (1964). Diagnosis and treatment: management of the child who has had one convulsion. *Pediatrics, 33*, 431–434.

Casat, C. D., Pleasants, D. Z., Schroeder, D. H., & Parler, D. W. (1989). Bupropion in children with attention deficit disorder. *Psychopharmacology, 25*, 198–201.

Casat, C. D., Pleasants, D. Z., & Van Wyck Fleet, J. (1987). A double-blind trial of bupropion in children with attention deficit disorder. *Psychopharmacology, 23*, 120–122.

Casey, B. J., Castellanos, F. X., Giedd, J. N., Marsh, W. L., Hamburger, S. D., Schubert, A. B., Vauss, Y. C., Vaituzis, A. C., Dickstein, D. P., Sarfatti, S. E., & Rapoport, J. L. (1997). Implication of right frontostriatal circuitry in response inhibition and attention-deficit/hyperactivity disorder. *Journal of the American Academy of Child and Adolescent Psychiatry, 36*, 374–383.

Casey, J. E., Rourke, B. P., & DelDotto, J. E. (1996). Learning disabilities in children with attention deficit disorder with and without hyperactivity. *Child Neuropsychology, 2*, 83–98.

Castellanos, F. X. (1997). Toward a pathophysiology of attention-deficit/hyperactivity disorder. *Clinical Pediatrics, 36*, 381–393.

Castellanos, F. X. (2001). Neuroimaging studies of ADHD. In M. V. Solanto, A. F. T. Arnsten, & F. X. Castellanos (Eds.), *Stimulant drugs and ADHD: Basic and clinical neurosciences* (pp. 243–258). New York: Oxford University Press.

Castellanos, F. X., Giedd, J. N., Berquin, P. C., Walter, J. M., Sharp, W., Tran, T., Vaituzis, A. C., Blumenthal, J. D., Nelson, J., Bastain, T. M., Zijdenbos, A., Evans, A. C., & Rapoport, J. L. (2001). A quantitative brain magnetic resonance imaging in girls with attention-deficit/hyperactivity disorder. *Archives of General Psychiatry, 58*, 289–295.

Castellanos, F. X., Giedd, J. N., Eckburg, P., Marsh, W. L., Vaituzis, A. C., Kaysen, D., Hamburger, S. D., & Rapoport, J. L. (1994). Quantitative morphology of the caudate nucleus in attention deficit hyperactivity disorder. *American Journal of Psychiatry, 151*, 1791–1796.

Castellanos, X., Giedd, J., Elia, J., Marsh, W. L., Ritchie, G. F., Hamburger, S. D., & Rapoport, J. L. (1997). Controlled stimulant treatment of ADHD and comorbid Tourette's syndrome: Effects of stimulant and dose. *Journal of the American Academy of Child and Adolescent Psychiatry, 36*, 589–596.

Castellanos, F. X., Giedd, J. N., Marsh, W. L., Hamburger, S. D., Vaituzis, A. C., Dickstein, D. P., Sarfatti, S. E., Vauss, Y. C., Snell, J. W., Lange, N., Kaysen, D., Krain, A. L., Ritchie, G. F., Rajapakse, J. C., & Rapoport, J. L. (1996). Quantitative brain magnetic resonance imaging in attention-deficit hyperactivity disorder. *Archives of General Psychiatry, 53*, 607–616.

Castellanos, F. X., Lau, E., Tayebi, N., Lee, P., Long, B. E., Giedd, J. N., Sharp, W., Marsh, W. L., Walker, J. M., Hamburger, S. D., Ginns, E. I., Rapoport, J. L., & Sidransky, E. (1998). Lack of an association between a dopamine-4 receptor polymorphism and attention-deficit/hyperactivity disorder: Genetic and brain morphometric analyses. *Molecular Psychiatry, 3*(5), 431–434.

Center for Drug Evaluation and Research, U.S. Food and Drug Administration. (1996). The clinical impact of adverse event reporting (*Medwatch* continuing education article, pp. 1–9) [On-line]. Available: http://www.fda.gov/medwatch/articles/med.pdf.

Chait, L. D. (1994). Reinforcing and subjective effects of methylphenidate in humans. *Behavioral Pharmacology, 5*, 281–288.

Chait, L. D., Uhlenhuth, E. H., & Johanson, C. E. (1986). The discriminative stimulus and subjective effects of d-amphetamine, phenmetrazine and fenfluramine in humans. *Psychopharmacology, 89*, 301–306.

Chait, L. D., Uhlenhuth, E. H., & Johanson, C. E. (1986). The discriminative stimulus and subjective effects of phenylpropanolamine, mazindol and d-amphetamine in humans. *Psychopharmacology and Biochemical Behavior, 24*(6), 1665–1672.

Chalkind, S., Danielson, L. C., & Brauen, M. L. (1993). What do we know about the costs of special education? A selected review. *Journal of Special Education, 26*, 344–370.

Chan, Y. P., Swanson, J. M., Soldin, S. S., Thiessen, J. J., & Macleod, S. M. (1983). Methylphenidate hydrochloride given with or before breakfast: II. Effects on plasma concentration of methylphenidate and ritalinic acid. *Pediatrics, 72*(1), 56–59.

Chang, C. H., Wang, Y. M., Yang, A. H., & Chiang, S. S. (2001). Rapidly progressive interstitial renal fibrosis associated with Chinese herbal medications. *American Journal of Nephrology, 21*(6), 441–448.

Chappell, P., Riddle, M., Scahill, L., Lynch, K., Schultz, R., Arnsten, A., Leckman, J., & Cohen, D. (1995). Guanfacine treatment of comorbid attention-deficit hyperactivity disorder and Tourette's syndrome. *Journal of the American Academy of Child and Adolescent Psychiatry, 34*, 1140–1146.

Charles, L., & Schain, R. (1981). A four-year follow-up study of the effects of methylphenidate on the behavior and academic achievement of hyperactive children. *Journal of Abnormal Child Psychology, 9*, 495–505.

Chassin, L., Rogosch, F., & Barrera, M. (1991). Substance use and symptomatology among adolescent children of alcoholics. *Journal of Abnormal Psychology, 100*(4), 449–463.

Chee, P., Logan, G., Schachar, R., Lindsay, P., & Wachsmuth, R. (1989). Effects of event rate and display time on sustained attention in hyperactive, normal and control children. *Journal of Abnormal Child Psychology, 17*, 371–391.

Chess, S., & Thomas, A. (1984). *Origins and evolution of behavior disorders from infancy to early adult life.* New York: Brunner/Mazel.

Chess, S., & Thomas, A. (1996). *Temperament theory and practice.* New York: Brunner/Mazel.

Chilcoat, H. D., & Breslau, N. (1999). Pathways from ADHD to early drug use. *Journal of the American Academy of Child and Adolescent Psychiatry, 38*(11), 1347–1354.

Chillar, R. K., Jackson, A. L., & Alaan, L. (1982). Hemiplegia after intracarotid injection of methylphenidate. *Archives of Neurology, 39*, 598–599.

Claude, D., & Firestone, P. (1995). The development of ADHD boys: A 12-year follow-up. *Canadian Journal of Behavioral Science, 27*, 226–249.

Clements, S. D. (1966). *Minimal brain dysfunction in children: Terminology and identification.* Washington, DC: U.S. Department of Health, Education, and Welfare.

Clements, S., Peters, D., & John, E. (1962). Minimal brain dysfunction in the school-age child: Diagnosis and treatment. *Archives of General Psychiatry, 6*(3), 185–197.

Cobb, D. E., & Evans, J. R. (1981). The use of biofeedback techniques with school-aged children exhibiting behavioral and/or learning problems. *Journal of Abnormal Child Psychology, 9*, 251–281.

Cocores, J. A., Davies, R. K., Mueller, P. S., & Gold, M. S. (1987). Cocaine abuse and adult attention

deficit disorder. *Journal of Clinical Psychiatry, 48*, 376–377.

Cocozza, J. J. (Ed.). (1992). *Responding to the mental health needs of youth in the juvenile justice system.* Seattle: National Coalition for the Mentally Ill in the Criminal Justice System.

Cohen, M. D. (1994). *Children on the boundaries: Challenges posed by children with conduct disorders.* Alexandria, VA: National Association of State Directors of Special Education.

Cohen, N. J., & Thompson, L. (1982). Perceptions and attitudes of hyperactive children and their mothers regarding treatment with methylphenidate. *Canadian Journal of Psychiatry, 27*, 40–42.

Cohen, P., Cohen, J., Kasen, S., Velez, C. N., Hartmark, C., Johnson, J., Rojas, M., Brook, J., & Struening, E. L. (1993). An epidemiological study of disorders in late childhood and adolescence, I. Age and gender-specific prevalence. *Journal of Child Psychology and Psychiatry, 34*(6), 851–867.

Cohen, R. A. (1993). *The neuropsychology of attention.* New York: Plenum Press.

Cohen, S. (1975). Amphetamine abuse. *Journal of the American Medical Association, 231*, 414–415.

Coleman, M., & Gilliam, J. (1983). Disturbing behaviors in the classroom: A survey of teacher attitudes. *Journal of Special Education, 17*, 121–129.

Coleman, M., Steinberg, G., Tippett, J., Bhagavan, H. N., Coursin, D. B., Gross, M., Lewis, C., & DeVeau, L. (1979). A preliminary study of the effect of pyridoxine administration in a subgroup of hyperkinetic children: A double-blind crossover comparison with methylphenidate. *Biological Psychiatry, 14*, 741–751.

Coleman, N., Dexheimer, P., DiMascio, A., Redman, W., & Finnerty, R. (1976). Deanol in the treatment of hyperkinetic children. *Psychosomatics, 17*, 68–72.

Collier, C., Soldin, S., Swanson, J., MacLeod, S., Weinberg, F., & Rochefort, J. (1985). Pemoline pharmacokinetics and long term therapy in children with attention deficit disorder and hyperactivity. *Clinical Pharamcokinetics, 10*, 269–277.

Collins, R. J., Weeks, J. R., Cooper, M. M., Good, P. I., & Russell, R. R. (1984). Prediction of abuse liability of drugs using IV self-administration by rats. *Psychopharmacology, 82*, 6–13.

Colorado Department of Education. (1994). *Attention deficit disorders: A handbook for Colorado educators.* Denver: Colorado Department of Education.

Colpaert, F. C., Niemegeers, C. J. E., & Janssen, P. A. J. (1979). Discriminative stimulus properties of cocaine: Neuropharmacological characteristics as derived from stimulus generalization experiments. *Pharmacology, Biochemistry, and Behavior, 10*, 535–546.

Comings, D., Comings, B., Muhleman, D., Dietz, G., Shahbahrami, B., Tast, D., Knell, E., Kocsis, P., Baumgarten, R., Kovacs, B., Levy, D., Smith, M., Borison, R., Evans, D., Klein, D., MacMurray, J., Tosk, J., Sverd, J., Gysin, R., & Flanagan, S. (1991). The dopamine D2 receptor locus as a modifying gene in neuropsychiatric disorders. *Journal of the American Medical Association, 266*, 1793–1800.

Committee on Children With Disabilities and Committee on Drugs. (1996). Medication for children with attentional disorders. *Pediatrics, 98*, 301–304.

Concato, J., Shah, N., & Horwitz, R. I. (2000). Randomized, controlled trials, observational studies, and the hierarchy of research designs. *New England Journal of Medicine, 342*, 1887–1892.

Connell, P. H. (1968). The use and abuse of amphetamines. *Practitioner, 200*, 234–243.

Conners, C. K. (1973). Rating scales for use in drug studies of children [Special issue]. *Psychopharmacology Bulletin Pharmacotherapy of Children*, pp. 24–29.

Conners, C. K. (1980). *Food additives and hyperactive children*. London: Plenum Press.

Conners, C., Casat, C., Gualtieri, C., Weller, E., Reader, M., Reiss, A., Weller, R., Khayrallah, M., & Ascher, J. (1996). Bupropion hydrochloride in attention deficit disorder with hyperactivity. *Journal of the American Academy of Child and Adolescent Psychiatry, 35*, 1314–1321.

Conners, C. K., Erhardt, D., Epstein, J. N., Parker, J. D. A., Sitarenios, G., & Sparrow, E. (1999). Self-ratings of ADHD symptoms in adults: I. Factor structure and normative data. *Journal of Attention Disorders, 3*, 141–151.

Conners, C. K., Levin, E. D., Sparrow, E., Hinton, S. C., Erhardt, D., Meck, W. H., Rose, J. E., & March, J. (1996). Nicotine and attention in adult attention deficit hyperactivity disorder (ADHD). *Psychopharmacological Bulletin, 32*, 67–73.

Conners, C. K., Sitarenios, G., Parker, J. D. A., & Epstein, J. N. (1998). Revision and restandardization of the Conners Parent Rating Scale (CPRS-R): Factor structure, reliability, and criterion validity. *Journal of Abnormal Child Psychology, 26*, 257–268.

Conners, C. K., Sitarenios, G., Parker, J. D. A., & Epstein, J. N. (1998). Revision and restandardization of the Conners Teacher Rating Scale (CTRS-R): Factor structure, reliability, and criterion validity. *Journal of Abnormal Child Psychology, 26*, 279–291.

Connor, D. F., Barkley, R. A., & Davis, H. T. (2000). A pilot study of methylphenidate, clonidine, or the combination in ADHD comorbid with aggressive oppositional-defiant or conduct disorder. *Clinical Pediatrics, 39*, 15–25.

Connor, D. F., Fletcher, K. E., & Swanson, J. M. (1999). A meta-analysis of clonidine for symptoms of attention-deficit/hyperactivity disorder. *Journal of the American Academy of Child and Adolescent Psychiatry, 38*, 1551–1559.

Connor, D., Ozbayrak, K., Benjamin, S., Ma, Y., & Fletcher, K. (1997). A pilot study of nadolol for overt aggression in developmentally delayed individuals. *Journal of the American Academy of Child and Adolescent Psychiatry, 36*, 826–834.

Cook, E. H., Stein, M. A., Krasowski, M. D., Cox, N. J., Olkon, D. M., Kieffer, J. E., & Leventhal, B. L. (1995). Association of attention deficit disorder and the dopamine transporter gene. *American Journal of Human Genetics, 56*, 993–998.

Cooper, J. R., Czechowicz, D. J., Peterson, R. C., Molinari, S. M. (1992). Prescription drug diversion control and medical practice. *Journal of the American Medical Association, 268*, 1306–1310.

Corkum, P., & Siegel, L. S. (1993). Is the Continuous Performance Task a valuable research tool for use with children with attention-deficit-hyperactivity disorder? *Journal of Child Psychology and Psychiatry, 34*, 1217–1239.

Cornoldi, C., Barbieri, A., Gaiani, C., & Zocchi, S. (1999). Strategic memory deficits in attention deficit disorder with hyperactivity participants: The role of executive processes. *Developmental Neuropsychology, 15*, 53–71.

Costello, E. J., Angold, A., Burns, B. J., Erkanli, A., Stangl, D. K., & Tweed, D. L. (1996). The Great Smoky Mountains Study of Youth: Functional impairment and serious emotional disturbance. *Archives of General Psychiatry, 53*, 1137–1143.

Costello, E. J., Angold, A., Burns, B. J., Stangl, D. K., Tweed, D. L., Erkanli, A., & Worthman, C. M. (1996). The Great Smoky Mountains Study of Youth: Goals, design, methods, and the prevalence of DSM-III-R disorders. *Archives of General Psychiatry, 53*(12), 1129–1136.

Costello, E. J., Costello, A. J., Edelbrock, C., Burns, B. J., Dulcan, M. K., Brent, D., & Janiszewski, S. (1988). Psychiatric disorders in pediatric primary care. *Archives of General Psychiatry, 45*, 1107–1116.

Costello, E. J., Edelbrock, C., Costello, A. J., Dulcan, M. K., Barne, B. J, & Brent, D. (1988). Psychopathology in pediatric primary care: The new hidden morbidity. *Pediatrics, 81*, 415–424.

Costello, E. J., Farmer, M. Z., Angold, A., Burns, B. J., & Erkanli, A. (1997). Psychiatric disorders among American Indian and white youth in Appalachia: The Great Smoky Mountains study. *American Journal of Public Health, 87*(5), 827–832.

Council of Administrators of Special Education. (1992). *Student access: A response guide for educators on Section 504 of the Rehabilitation Act of 1973*. Albuquerque NM: Author.

Council for Exceptional Children. (1992). *Children with ADD: A shared responsibility*. Reston, VA: Author.

Courchesne, E., & Allen, G. (1997). Prediction and preparation, fundamental functions of the cerebellum. *Learning and Memory, 4,* 1–35.

Cox, B. M. (1990). Drug tolerance and physical dependence. In W. B. Pratt & P. Taylor (Eds.), *Principles of drug action: The basis of pharmacology* (pp. 639–690). New York: Churchill Livingstone.

Cox, D. R., & Oakes, D. (1984). *Analysis of survival data.* London: Chapman & Hall.

Cox, W. (1982). An indication for the use of imipramine in attention deficit disorder. *American Journal of Psychiatry, 139,* 1059–1060.

Coyne, J. C., Burchill, S. L., & Stiles, W. B. (1991). Handbook of social and clinical psychology: The health perspective. In C. R. Snyder & D. R. Forsyth (Eds.), *An interactional perspective on depression* (pp. 327–349.) New York: Pergamon Press.

Crandall, M. (1991). A controlled trial of nystatin for the candidiasis hypersensitivity syndrome [Letter to editor]. *New England Journal of Medicine, 323,* 1717–1723.

Crenshaw, T. M., Kavale, K. A., Forness, S. R., & Reeve, R. E. (1999). Attention deficit hyperactivity disorder and the efficacy of stimulation medication: A meta-analysis. In T. Scruggs & M. Mastropieri (Eds.), *Advances in learning and behavioral disabilities* (Vol. 13, pp. 135–165). Greenwich, CT: JAI Press.

Crook, W. G. (1985). Pediatricians, antibiotics, and office practice. *Pediatrics, 76*(1), 139–140.

Crook, W. G. (1989). *The yeast connection* (3rd ed.). Jackson, TN: Professional Books.

Crook, W. G. (1991). A controlled trial of nystatin for the candidiasis hypersensitivity syndrome [Letter to editor]. *New England Journal of Medicine, 323,* 1766–1767.

Cullwood-Brathwaite, D., & McKinney, J. D. (1988, May 9). *Co-occurrence of attention deficit hyperactivity disorder in a school identified sample of students with emotional or behavioral disorders: Implications for educational programming.* Paper presented at the Southwest Regional Conference of the Council for Children with Behavioral Disorders, Gulf Shores, FL.

Cunningham, C. E., Benness, B. B., & Siegel, L. S. (1988). Family functioning, time allocation, and parental depression in the families of normal and ADDH children. *Journal of Clinical Child Psychology, 17,* 169–177.

Cunningham, C. E., Bremner, R., & Secord-Gilbert, M. (1994). *The community parent education (COPE) program: A school based family systems oriented course for parents of children with disruptive behavior disorders.* Unpublished manuscript, McMaster University and Chedoke-McMaster Hospitals.

Daly, J. M., & Fritsch, S. L. (1995). Case study: Maternal residual attention deficit disorder associated with failure to thrive in a two-month-old infant. *Journal of the American Academy of Child and Adolescent Psychiatry, 31,* 55–57.

Danckaerts, M., & Taylor, E. J. (1995). The epidemiology of childhood hyperactivity. In F. C. Verhulst & H. M. Koot (Eds.), *The epidemiology of child and adolescent psychopathology.* New York: Oxford University Press.

Daneman, M., & Merikle, P. M. (1996). Working memory and language comprehension: A meta-analysis. *Psychonomic Bulletin and Review, 3,* 422–433.

Danforth, J., & DuPaul, G. J. (1996). Interrater reliability of teacher rating scales for children with attention deficit hyperactivity disorder. *Journal of Psychopathology and Behavioral Assessment, 18,* 227–237.

Daugherty, T. K., Quay, H. C., & Ramos, L. (1993). Response perseveration, inhibitory control, and central dopaminergic activity in childhood behavior disorders. *Journal of Genetic Psychology, 154,* 177–188.

David, O. J., Hoffman, S. P., Clark, J., Grad, G., & Sverd, J. (1983). The relationship of hyperactivity to moderately elevated lead levels. *Archives of Environmental Health, 38,* 341–346.

David, O. J., Hoffman, S. P., Sverd, J., & Clark, J. (1977). Lead and hyperactivity: Lead levels among hyperactive children. *Journal of Abnormal Child Psychology, 5,* 405–416.

David, O. J., Hoffman, S. P., Sverd, J., Clark, J., & Voeller, K. (1976). Lead and hyperactivity. Behavioral response to chelation: A pilot study. *American Journal of Psychiatry, 133,* 1155–1158.

Davidson, E. S., Finch, J. F., & Schenk, S. (1993). Variability in subjective responses to cocaine: Initial experiences of college students. *Addictive Behavior, 18,* 445–453.

Davidson, L. L., Hughes, S. J., & O'Connor, P. A. (1988). Preschool behavior problems and subsequent risk of injury. *Pediatrics, 90,* 697–702.

Davila, R. R., Williams, M. L., & MacDonald, J. T. (1991, September 16). *Clarification of policy to address the needs of children with attention deficit disorders within general and/or special education.* Washington, DC: U.S. Department of Education, Office of Special Education and Rehabilitation.

Davis, D. L., Bean, G., Schumacher, J., & Stronger, T. (1991). Prevalence of emotional disorders in a juvenile justice institutional population. *American Journal of Forensic Psychology, 9,* 1–13.

De la Garza, R., & Johanson, C. E. (1987). Discriminative stimulus properties of intragastrically administered d-amphetamine and pentobarbital in rhesus monkeys. *Journal of Pharmacology and Experimental Therapeutics, 243,* 955–962.

Del'Homme, M., Kasari, C., Forness, S. R., & Bagley, R. (1996). Prereferral intervention and students at risk for emotional or behavioral disorders. *Education and Treatment of Children, 19*, 272–285.

DeMilio, L. (1989). Psychiatric syndromes in adolescent substance abusers. *American Journal of Psychiatry, 146*, 1212–1214.

Denckla, M. B. (1985). Revised neurological examination for subtle signs. *Psychopharmacological Bulletin, 21*, 773–800.

Denckla, M. B. (1993). The child with developmental disabilities grown up: Adult residua of childhood disorders. *Neurological Clinics, 11*, 105–125.

Denckla, M. B. (1996). Biological correlates of learning and attention: What is relevant to learning disability and attention-deficit hyperactivity disorder? *Journal of Developmental and Behavioral Pediatrics, 17*, 114–119.

Denkowski, K. M., & Denkowski, G. C. (1984). Is group progressive relaxation training as effective with hyperactive children as individual EMG biofeedback? *Biofeedback and Self-Regulation, 9*, 353–364.

Denkowski, K. M., Denkowski, G. C., & Omizo, M. M. (1983). The effects of EMG-assisted relaxation training on the academic performance, locus of control, and self-esteem of hyperactive boys. *Biofeedback and Self-Regulation, 8*, 363–375.

Denkowski, K. M., Denkowski, G. C., & Omizo, M. M. (1984). Predictors of success in the EMG biofeedback training of hyperactive male children. *Biofeedback and Self-Regulation, 9*, 253–264.

De Obaldia, R., Parsons, O. A., & Yohman, R. (1983). Minimal brain dysfunction symptoms claimed by primary and secondary alcoholics: Relation to cognitive functioning. *International Journal of Neuroscience, 20*, 173–182.

Deutsch, C. K., Matthysse, S., Swanson, J. M., & Farkas, L. G. (1990). Genetic latent structure analysis of dysmorphology in attention deficit disorder. *Journal of the American Academy of Child and Adolescent Psychiatry, 29*, 189–194.

De Wit, H., Uhlenhuth, M. D., & Johanson, C. E. (1987). The reinforcing properties of amphetamine in overweight subjects and subjects with depression. *Clinical Pharmacology and Therapeutics, 42*, 127–136.

Diamond, I. R., Tannock, R., & Schachar, R. (1999). Response to methylphenidate in children with ADHD and comorbid anxiety. *Journal of the American Academy of Child and Adolescent* Psychiatry, 38(4), 402–409.

Diener, M. B., & Milich, R. (1997). Effects of positive feedback on the social interactions of boys with attention deficit hyperactivity disorder: A test of the self-protective hypothesis. *Journal of Clinical Child Psychology, 26*, 256–265.

Diener, R. (1991). Toxicology of methylphenidate. In B. Osman & L. L. Greenhill (Eds.), *Ritalin: Theory and patient management* (pp. 435–455). New York: Mary Ann Liebert.

Diller, L. H. (1996). The run on Ritalin: Attention deficit disorder and stimulant treatment in the 1990's. *Hastings Center Report, 26*, 12–18.

Diller, L. H. (1998). *Running on Ritalin. A physician reflects on children, society, and performance in a pill.* New York: Bantam Books.

Dillon, D. C., Salzman, I. J., & Schulsinger, D. A. (1985). The use of imipramine in Tourette's syndrome and attention deficit disorder: Case report. *Journal of Clinical Psychiatry, 46*, 348–349.

Ding, V. C., Chi, H. C., Grady, D. L., Morishima, A., Kidd, J. R., Kidd, K. K., Flodman, P., Spence, M. A., Schuck, S., Swanson, J. M., Zhang, Y. P., & Moyzis, R. K. (2002). Evidence of positive selection acting at the human dopamine receptor D4 gene locus. *Proceedings of the National Academy of Science USA, 99*, 10–12.

Ding, Y. S., Fowler, J., Volkow, N., Dewey, S., Wang, G. J., Logan, J., Gatley, S. J., & Pappas, N. (1997). Clinical drugs: Comparison of the pharmacokinetics of [11C]d-threo and 1-threo-methylphenidate in the human and baboon brain. *Psychopharmacology, 131*, 71–78.

Dismukes, W. E., Wade, J. S., Lee, J. Y., Dockery, B. K., & Hain, J. D. (1990). A randomized double-blind trial of nystatin therapy for the candidiasis hypersensitivity syndrome. *New England Journal of Medicine, 323*, 1717–1723.

Disney, E. R., Elkins, I. J., McGue, M., & Iacono, W. G. (1999). Effects of ADHD, conduct disorder, and gender on substance use and abuse in adolescence. *American Journal of Psychiatry, 156*, 1515–1521.

Dohrn, B., & Leventhal, B. (1997). *Clinical evaluation and services initiative.* Cook County, IL: Juvenile Justice and Child Protection Department.

Dolan, R. J. (1998). Editorial: A cognitive affective role for the cerebellum. *Brain, 121*, 545–546.

Donenberg, G., & Baker, B. L. (1994). The impact of young children with externalizing behaviors on their families. *Journal of Abnormal Child Psychology, 21*, 179–198.

Donnelly, J., Wolraich, M. L., Feurer, I., & Baumgaertel, A. (1998). Evaluating the diagnostic process in determining the presence of attention deficit hyperactivity disorder. Annual meeting of the Society for Developmental and Behavioral Pediatrics, Cleveland, Ohio. *Journal of Developmental and Behavioral Pediatrics, 19*, 383.

Douglas, V. I., Barr, R. G., Amin, K., O'Neill, M. E., & Britton, B. G. (1988). Dose effects and individual responsivity to methylphenidate in attention deficit disorder. *Journal of Child Psychology and Psychiatry, 29,* 453–475.

Douglas, V., Barr, R. G., Desilets, J., & Sherman, E. (1995). Do high doses of stimulants impair flexible thinking in ADHD? *Journal of the American Academy of Child and Adolescent Psychiatry, 34,* 877–885.

Douglas, V. I., & Benezra, E. (1990). Supraspan verbal memory in attention deficit disorder with hyperactivity, normal and reading disabled boys. *Journal of Abnormal Child Psychology, 18,* 617–638.

Douglas, V., & Peter, K. (1979). Toward a clearer definition of the attentional deficit of hyperactive children. In G. Hale & M. Lewis (Eds.), *Attention and the development of cognitive skills* (pp. 173–248), New York: Plenum Press.

Downey, K. K., Stelson, F. W., Pomerleau, O. F., & Giordani, B. (1997). Adult attention deficit hyperactivity disorder: Psychological test profiles in a clinical population. *Journal of Nervous and Mental Disease, 185,* 32–38.

Downs, D. A., Harrigan, S. E., & Wiley, J. N., Robinson, T. E., & Labay, R. J. (1979). Research communications in psychology. *Psychology and Behavior, 4,* 39–49.

Drug Abuse Warning Network. (2000). Detailed emergency department tables [On-line]. Available: http://www.samhsa.gov/oas/DAWN/DetEDT61/2000/text/00DetTbl.pdf.

Drug Enforcement Administration. (1995). *Methylphenidate review document.* Washington, DC: Author.

Drug Enforcement Administration. (1995, October). *Methylphenidate (a background paper).* Washington, DC: Author.

Drug Enforcement Administration. (1995). *Response to petition to transfer methylphenidate from Schedule II to Schedule III.* Washington, DC: Author.

Dubey, D. R., O'Leary, S. G., & Kaufman, K. F. (1983). Training parents of hyperactive children in child management: A comparative outcome study. *Journal of Abnormal Child Psychology, 11,* 229–246.

Dulcan, M. (1997). Practice parameters for the assessment and treatment of attention-deficit / hyperactivity disorder. *Journal of the Academy of Child and Adolescent Psychiatry, 36,* 85s–121s.

Dulcan, M., Dunne, J. E., Ayres, W., Arnold, V., Benson, R. S., Bernet, W., Bukstein, O., Kinlan, J., Leonard, H., Licamele, W., & McClellan, J. (1997). Practice parameters for the assessment and treatment of children, adolescents, and adults with attention-deficit hyperactivity disorder. *Journal of the American Academy of Child and Adolescent Psychiatry, 36,* 85S–121S.

Duncan, B., Forness, S. R., & Hartsough, C. (1995). Students identified as seriously emotionally disturbed in day treatment classrooms: Cognitive, psychiatric, and special education characteristics. *Behavioral Disorders, 20,* 238–252.

Dunn, F. M., & Howell, R. J. (1982). Relaxation training and its relationship to hyperactivity in boys. *Journal of Clinical Psychology, 38,* 92–100.

Dunnick, J. K., & Eustis, S. L. (1991). Decreases in spontaneous tumors in rats and mice after treatment with amphetamine. *Toxicology, 67,* 325–332.

Dunnick, J. K., & Hailey, J. R. (1995). Experimental studies on the long-term effects of methylphenidate hydrochloride. *Toxicology, 103,* 77–84.

DuPaul, G. J. (1991). Parent & teacher ratings of ADHD symptoms: Psychometric properties in a community based sample. *Journal of Clinical Child Psychology, 20,* 242–253.

DuPaul, G. J., Anastopoulos, A. D., McGoey, K. E., Power, T. J., Reid, R., & Ikeda, M. J. (1997). Teacher ratings of attention deficit hyperactivity disorder symptoms: Factor structure and normative data. *Psychological Assessment, 9,* 436–444.

DuPaul, G. J., Anastopoulos, A. D., Power, T. J., Reid, R., Ikeda, M. J., & McGoey, K. E. (1998). Parent ratings of attention-deficit/hyperactivity disorder symptoms: Factor structure and normative data. *Journal of Psychopathology and Behavioral Assessment, 20,* 83–102.

DuPaul, G., Barkley, R., & McMurray, M. (1994). Response of children with ADHD to methylphenidate: Interaction with internalizing symptoms. *Journal of the American Academy of Child and Adolescent Psychiatry, 33*(6), 894–903.

DuPaul, G. J., & Eckert, T. L. (1997). The effects of school-based interventions for attention deficit hyperactivity disorder: A meta-analysis. *School Psychology Review, 26,* 5–27.

DuPaul, G. J., Guevremont, D. C., & Barkley, R. A. (1992). Behavioral treatment of attention-deficit hyperactivity disorder in the classroom: The use of the attention training system. *Behavior Modification, 16,* 204–225.

DuPaul, G. J., & Henningson, P. N. (1993). Peer tutoring effects on the classroom performance of children with ADHD. *School Psychology Review, 22,* 134–143.

DuPaul, G., & Rapport, M. (1993). Does MPH normalize the classroom performance of children with attention deficit disorder? *Journal of the American Academy of Child and Adolescent Psychiatry, 32,* 190–198.

DuPaul, G. J., & Stoner, G. (1996). *ADHD in the schools: Assessment and intervention strategies.* New York: Guilford Press.

Durlach, J., Durlach, V., Bac, P., Bara, M., & Guiet-

Bara, A. (1994). Magnesium and therapeutics. *Magnesium Research, 7*, 313–328.

Dworkin, S. I., Vrana, S. L., Broadbent, J., & Robinson, J. H. (1993). Comparing the reinforcing effects of nicotine, caffeine, methylphenidate, and cocaine. *Medicine and Chemical Research, 2*, 593–602.

Dykman, K. D., & Dykman, R. A. (1998). Effect of nutritional supplements on attentional-deficit hyperactivity disorder. *Integrative Physiological and Behavioral Science, 33*, 49–60.

Dykman, K. D., & McKinley, R. (1997). Effect of glyconutritionals on the severity of ADHD. *Proceedings of the Fisher Institute for Medical Research, 1*(1), 24–25.

Earls, F., Reich, W., Jung, K. G., & Cloninger, C. R. (1988). Psychopathology in children of alcoholic and antisocial parents. *Alcoholism: Clinical and Experimental Research, 12*, 481–487.

Ebstein, R., Novick, O., Umansky, R., Priel, B., Osher, Y., Blaine, D., Bennett, E., Nemanov, L., Katz, M., & Belmaker, R. (1996). Dopamine D4 receptor exon III polymorphism associated with the human personality trait of novelty seeking. *Nature Genetics, 12*, 78–80.

Egeland, J. A., Hostetter, A. M., Pauls, D. L., & Sussex, J. N. (2000). Prodromal symptoms before onset of manic depressive disorder suggested by first hospital admission histories. *Journal of the American Academy of Child and Adolescent Psychiatry, 39*, 1245–1252.

Egger, J., Carter, C. M., Graham, P. J., Gumley, D., & Soothill, J. F. (1985). Controlled trial of oligoantigenic treatment in the hyperkinetic syndrome. *Lancet, 1*(8428), 540–545.

Egger, J., Stolla, A., & McEwen, L. M. (1992). Controlled trial of hyposensitization in children with food-induced hyperkinetic syndrome. *Lancet, 339*(8802), 1150–1153.

Eiraldi, R. B., Power, T. J., & Nezu, C. M. (1997). Patterns of comorbidity association with subtypes of attention-deficit/hyperactivity disorder. *Journal of the American Academy of Child and Adolescent Psychiatry, 36*, 503–514.

Eisenberg, J., Asnis, G. M., van Praag, H. M., & Vela, R. M. (1988). Effect of tyrosine on attention deficit disorder with hyperactivity. *Journal of Clinical Psychiatry, 49*, 193–195.

Elenbaas, R. M., Waeckerle, J. F., & McNabney, W. K. (1976). Abscess formation as a complication of parenteral methylphenidate abuse. *Journal of ACEP, 5*, 977–980.

Elia, J., Ambrosini, P. J., & Rapoport, J. L. (1999). Treatment of attention-deficit-hyperactivity disorder. *New England Journal of Medicine, 340*, 780–788.

Elia, J., Borcherding, B., Rapoport, J., & Keysor, C. (1991). Methylphenidate and dextroamphetamine treatments of hyperactivity: Are there true non-responders? *Psychiatry Research, 36*, 141–155.

Elia, J., Stoff, D. M., & Coccaro, E. F. (1992). Biological correlates of impulsive disruptive behavior disorders: Attention deficit hyperactivity disorder, conduct disorder, and borderline personality disorder. In E. Peschel & R. Peschel (Eds.), *Neurobiological disorders in children and adolescents. New directions for mental health services* [No. 54, Social and Behavioral Sciences Series] (pp. 51–57). San Francisco: Jossey-Bass.

Elkin, I., Gibbons, R. D., Shea, M. T., Sotsky, S. M., Watkins, J. T., Pilkonis, P. A., & Hedeker, D. (1995). Initial severity and differential treatment outcome in the National Institute of Mental Health Treatment of Depression Collaborative Research Program. *Journal of Consulting and Clinical Psychology, 63*, 841–847.

Ellinwood, E. H., & Cohen, S. (1971). Amphetamine abuse. *Science, 171*, 420–421.

Emerit, M. B., Riad, M., & Hamon, M. (1992). Trophic effects of neurotransmitters during brain maturation. *Biology of the Neonate, 62*, 193–201.

Emmett-Oglesby, M. W., & Brewin, A. (1978). Tolerance to the behavioral effects of methylphenidate after daily and intermittent administration. *Journal of the American Osteopathic Association, 78*, 143–144.

Emmett-Oglesby, M. W., & Taylor, K. E. (1981). Role of dose interval in the acquisition of tolerance to methylphenidate. *Neuropharmacology, 20*, 995–1002.

Emmett-Oglesby, M. W., Wurst, M., & Lal, H. (1983). Discriminative stimulus properties of a small dose of cocaine. *Neuropharmacology, 22*, 97–101.

Erhardt, D., & Baker, B. L. (1990). The effects of behavioral parent training on families with young hyperactive children. *Journal of Behavior Therapy and Experimental Psychiatry, 21*, 121–132.

Erhardt, D., & Hinshaw, S. P. (1994). Initial sociometric impressions of attention deficit hyperactivity disorder and comparison boys: Predictions from social behaviors and from nonbehavioral variables. *Journal of Consulting and Clinical Psychology, 62*(4), 833–842.

Erlenmeyer-Kimling, N., & Cornblatt, B. (1978). Attentional measures in a study of children at high-risk for schizophrenia. *Journal of Psychiatric Research, 14*, 93–98.

Ernst, M., Cohen, R. M., Liebenauer, L. L., Jons, P. H., & Zametkin, A. J. (1997). Cerebral glucose metabolism in adolescent girls with attention-deficit/hyperactivity disorder. *Journal of the American Academy of Child and Adolescent Psychiatry, 36*, 1399–1406.

Ernst, M., & Zametkin, A. (1995). The interface of genetics, neuroimaging, and neurochemistry in attention-deficit hyperactivity disorder. In F. Bloom & D. Kupfer (Eds.), *Psychopharmacology: The fourth genera-*

tion of progress (pp. 1643–1652). New York: Raven Press.

Ernst, M., Zametkin, A. J., Matochik, J. A., Pascualvaca, D., Jons, P. H., & Cohen, R. M. (1999). High midbrain [18F]DOPA accumulation in children with attention-deficit hyperactivity disorder. *American Journal of Psychiatry, 156*, 1209–1215.

Eslinger, P. J. (1996). Conceptualizing, describing, and measuring components of executive function, a summary. In G. R. Lyon & N. A. Krasnegor (Eds.), *Attention, memory, and executive function* (pp. 367–396) London: Paul H. Brookes.

Esser, G., Schmidt, M. H., & Woerner, W. (1990). Epidemiology and course of psychiatric disorders in school age children. Results of a longitudinal study. *Journal of Child Psychology and Psychiatry, 31*, 243–263.

Evans, J. H., Ferre, L., Ford, L. A., & Green, J. L. (1995). Decreasing ADHD symptoms utilizing an automated classroom reinforcement device. *Psychology in the Schools, 32*, 210–219.

Evans, S. E., & Johanson, C. E. (1987). Amphetamine-like effects of anorectic and related compounds in pigeons. *Journal of Pharmacology and Experimental Therapeutics, 241*, 817–825.

Evans, S. W., Pelham, W. E., & Grudberg, M. V. (1994). The efficacy of notetaking to improve behavior and comprehension of adolescents with attention deficit hyperactivity disorder. *Exceptionality, 5*, 1–17.

Evans, S. W., Vallano, G., & Pelham, W. (1994). Treatment of parenting behavior with a psychostimulant: A case study of an adult with attention-deficit hyperactivity disorder. *Journal of Child and Adolescent Psychopharmacology, 4*, 64–69.

Everling, S., & Fischer, B. (1998). The antisaccade: A review of basic research and clinical studies. *Neuropsychologia, 36*, 885–899.

Eyre, S. L., Rounsaville, B. J., & Kleber, H. D. (1982). History of childhood hyperactivity in a clinic population of opiate addicts. *Journal of Nervous and Mental Disease, 170*, 522–529.

Faraj, B. A., Israili, Z. H., Perel, J. M., Jenkins, M. L., Holtzman, S. G., Cucinell, S. A., & Dayton, P. G. (1974). Metabolism and disposition of methylphenidate-14C: Studies in man and animals. *Journal of Pharmacology and Experimental Therapeutics, 210*, 422–428.

Faraone, S., & Biederman, J. (1994). Is attention deficit hyperactivity disorder familial? *Harvard Review of Psychiatry, 1*, 271–287.

Faraone, S. V., Biederman, J., Chen, W. J., Krifcher, B., Keenan, K., Moore, C., Sprich, S., & Tsuang, M. T. (1992). Segregation analysis of attention deficit hyperactivity disorder. *Psychiatric Genetics, 2*, 257–275.

Faraone, S. V., Biederman, J., Lehman, B., Keenan, K., Norman, D., Seidman, L. J., Kolodny, R., Kraus, I., Perrin, J., & Chen, W. (1993). Evidence for independent familial transmission of attention deficit hyperactivity disorder and learning disabilities: Results from a family genetic study. *American Journal of Psychiatry, 150*, 891–895.

Faraone, S. V., Biederman, J., Lehman, B. K., Spencer, T., Norman, D., Seidman, L. J., Kraus, I., Perrin, J., Chen, W. J., & Tsuang, M. T. (1993). Intellectual performance and school failure in children with attention deficit hyperactivity disorder and in their siblings. *Journal of Abnormal Psychology, 102*, 616–623.

Faraone, S. V., Biederman, J., Weber, W., & Russell, R. L. (1998). Psychiatric, neuropsychological, and psychosocial features of DSM-IV subtypes of attention-deficit/hyperactivity disorder: Results from a clinically referred sample. *Journal of the American Academy of Child and Adolescent Psychiatry, 37*, 185–193.

Faraone, S., Biederman, J., Weiffenbach, B., Keith, T., Chu, M. P., Weaver, A., Spencer, T. J., Wilens, T. E., Frazier, J., Cleves, M., & Sakai, J. (1999). Dopamine D4 gene 7-repeat allele and attention deficit hyperactivity disorder. *American Journal of Psychiatry, 156*, 768–770.

Farmer, E. M. Z., Angold, A., Burns, B. J., & Costello, E. J. (1994). Reliability of self-reported service use: Test-retest consistency of children's responses to the Child and Adolescent Services Assessment (CASA). *Journal of Child and Family Studies, 3*, 307–325.

Farmer, J. E., & Peterson, L. (1995). Injury risk factors in children with attention deficit hyperactivity disorder. *Health Psychology, 14*, 325–332.

Farwell, J. R., Lee, Y. J., Hirtz, D. G., Sulzbacher, S. I., Ellenberg, J. H., & Nelson, K. B. (1990). Phenobarbital for febrile seizures—Effects on intelligence and on seizure recurrence. *New England Journal of Medicine, 322*, 364–369.

Feingold, B. F. (1975). *Why your child is hyperactive.* New York: Random House.

Feingold, B. F. (1981). Refutes criticism of diet (Reply to nutrition foundation report). *Clinical Psychiatry News, pp.* 2–3.

Felton, R. H., & Wood, F. B. (1989). Cognitive deficits in reading disability and attention deficit disorder. *Journal of Learning Disabilities, 22*, 3–13.

Fergusson, D. M., Harwood, C. J., & Lloyd, M. (1991). Confirmatory factor models of attention deficit and conduct disorder. *Journal of Child Psychology and Psychiatry, 32*, 257–274.

Fergusson, D. M., & Horwood, J. (1995). Predictive validity of categorically and dimensionally scored measures of disruptive childhood behaviors. *Journal of the American Academy of Child and Adolescent Psychiatry, 34*, 477–485.

Fergusson, D. M., & Horwood, L. J. (1993). The structure, stability, and correlations of the trait components of conduct disorder, attention deficit and anxiety/withdrawal reports. *Journal of Child Psychology and Psychiatry, 34*, 749–766.

Fergusson, D. M., Horwood, L. J., & Lynskey, M. T. (1993). Prevalence and comorbidity of DSM-III-R diagnoses in a birth cohort of 15 year olds. *Journal of the American Academy of Child and Adolescent Psychiatry, 32*, 1127–1134.

Fergusson, D. M., Horwood, L. J., & Lynskey, M. T. (1995). The stability of disruptive childhood behaviors. *Journal of Abnormal Child Psychology, 23*, 379–396.

Fergusson, D. M., Lynskey, M. T., & Horwood, L. J. (1997). Attentional difficulties in middle childhood and psychosocial outcomes in young adulthood. *Journal of Child Psychology and Psychiatry, 38*, 633–644.

Feussner, G. (1996). Actual abuse data: State surveys. In *Conference report: Stimulant use in the treatment of ADHD* (pp. 1–48). Washington, DC: Drug Enforcement Administration, Office of Diversion Control.

Field, T., Ironson, G., Pickens, J., Nawrocki, T., Fox, N., Scafidi, F., Burman, I., & Schanberg, S. (1996). Massage therapy reduces anxiety and enhances EEG pattern of alertness and math computations. *International Journal of Neuroscience, 86*, 197-205.

Field, T. M., Lasko, D., Mundy, P., Henteleff, T., Kabat, S., Talpins, S., & Dowling, M. (1997). Autistic children's attentiveness and responsivity improve after touch therapy. *Journal of Autism., & Developmental Disorders 27*, 333-338.

Field, T., Morrow, C., Valdeon, C., Larson, S., Kuhn, C., & Schanberg, S. (1992). Massage reduces anxiety in child and adolescent psychiatric patients. *Journal of the American Academy of Child and Adolescent Psychiatry, 31*(1), 125–131.

Field, T. M., Quintino, O., Hernandez-Reif, M., & Koslovsky, G. (1998). Adolescents with attention-deficit hyperactivity disorder benefit from massage therapy. *Adolescence 33*(129), 103–108.

Filipek, P. A., Semrud-Clikeman, M., Steingard, R. J., Renshaw, P. F., Kennedy, D. N., & Biederman, J. (1997). Volumetric MRI analysis comparing subjects having attention-deficit hyperactivity disorder with normal controls. *Neurology, 48*, 589–601.

Findling, R. L. (1996). Open-label treatment of comorbid depression and attentional disorders of co-administration of serotonin reuptake inhibitors and psychostimulants in children, adolescents, and adults: A case series. *Journal of Child and Adolescent Psychopharmology, 6*, 165–175.

Findling, R., Schwartz, M., Flannery, D., & Manos, M. (1996). Venlafaxine in adults with ADHD: An open trial. *Journal of Clinical Psychiatry, 57*, 184–189.

Fine, E. W., Yudin, L. W., Holmes, J., & Heinemann, S. (1976). Behavioral disorders in children with parental alcoholism. *Annals of the New York Academy of Science, 273*, 507–517.

Finnegan, L. P. (1976). Clinical effects of pharmacologic agents on pregnancy, the fetus and the neonate. *Annals of the New York Academy of Sciences, 281*, 74–89.

Fiore, T. A., Becker, E. A., & Nero, R. C. (1993). Educational interventions for students with attention deficit disorder. *Focus on Exceptional Children, 60*, 163–173.

Firestone, P., Crowe, D., Goodman, J. T., & McGrath, P. (1986). Vicissitudes of follow-up studies: Differential effects of parent training and stimulant medication with hyperactives. *American Journal of Orthopsychiatry, 56*, 184–194.

Firestone, P., Kelly, M. J., Goodman, J. T., & Davey, J. (1981). Differential effects of parent training and stimulant medication with hyperactives. *Journal of the American Academy of Child Psychiatry, 20*, 135–147.

Firestone, P., Musten, L. M., Pisterman, S., Mercer, J., & Bennett, S. (1998). Short-term side effects of stimulant medication are increased in preschool children with attention-deficit/hyperactivity disorder: a double-blind placebo-controlled study. *Journal of Child and Adolescent Psychopharmacology, 8*, 13–25.

Fischer, K. W., & Rose, S. P. (1996). Dynamic growth cycles of brain and cognitive development. In R. W. Thatcher, G. R. Lyon, J. Rumsey, & N. Krasnegor (Eds.), *Developmental neuroimaging: Mapping the development of brain and behavior* (pp. 263–279). San Diego: Academic Press.

Fischer, M. (1990). Parenting stress and the child with attention deficit hyperactivity disorder. *Journal of Clinical Child Psychology, 19*, 337–346.

Fischer, M. (1997). The persistence of ADHD into adulthood: It depends on whom you ask. *The ADHD Report, 5*(4), 8–10.

Fischer, M., Barkley, R. A., Edelbrock, C. S., & Smallish, L. (1990). The adolescent outcome of hyperactive children diagnosed by research criteria: II. Academic, attentional, and neuropsychological status. *Journal of Consulting and Clinical Psychology, 58*, 580–588.

Fischer, M., Barkley, R., Fletcher, K., & Patel, L. (2001, October). Young adult outcomes of childhood ADHD: Costs to society. *Scientific Proceedings of the American Academy of Child and Adolescent Psychiatry*, 75.

Fisher, J. B., Schumaker, J. B., & Deshler, D. D. (1995). Seaching for validated inclusive practices: A review of the literature. *Focus on Exceptional Children, 28*, 1–20.

Fisher, P. A., Gunnar, M. R., Chamberlain, P., & Reid, J. B. (2000). Preventive intervention for maltreated preschool children: Impact on children's behavior, neuroendocrine activity, and foster-parent functioning. *Journal of the American Academy of Child and Adolescent Psychiatry, 39*, 1356–1364.

Fisher, P. W., Shaffer, D., Piacentini, J. C., Lapkin, J., Kafantaris, V., Leonard, H., & Herzog, D. B. (1993). Sensitivity of the Diagnostic Interview Schedule for Children, 2nd Edition (DISC 2.1) for specific diagnoses of children and adolescents. *Journal of the American Academy of Child and Adolescent Psychiatry, 32*, 666–673.

Fitzpatrick, P., Klorman, R., Brumaghim, J., & Borgstedt, A. (1992). Effects of sustained-release and standard preparations of methylphenidate on attention deficit disorder. *American Academy of Child and Adolescent Psychiatry, Scientific Proceedings of the Annual Meeting, 31*(2), 226–234.

Fleming, R., Leventhal, H., Glynn, K., & Ershler, J. (1989). The role of cigarettes in the initiation and progression of early substance use. *Addictive Behaviors, 14*, 261-272.

Fletcher, A. P. (1991). Spontaneous adverse drug reporting vs. event monitoring: A comparison. *Journal of the Royal Society of Medicine, 84*, 341–346.

Fletcher, K., Fischer, M., Barkley, R. A., & Smallish, L. (1996). A sequential analysis of the mother-adolescent interactions of ADHD, ADHD/ODD, and normal teenagers during neutral and conflict discussions. *Journal of Abnormal Child Psychology, 24*, 271–297.

Flink, E. B. (1981). Magnesium deficiency. Etiology and clinical spectrum. *Acta Medica Scandinavica, 647*(Suppl.), 125–137.

Foley, H., Carlton, C., & Howell, R. (1996). The relationship of attention deficit hyperactivity disorder and conduct disorder to juvenile delinquency: Legal implications. *Bulletin of American Academy of Psychiatry Law, 243*, 333–345.

Foote, S. L., Aston-Jones, G., & Bloom, F. E. (1980), Impulse activity of locus coeruleus neurons in awake rats and monkeys is a function of sensory stimulation and arousal. *Proceedings of the National Academy of Science USA, 77*, 3033–3037.

Forehand, R., & Long, N. (1996). *Parenting the strong-willed child.* Chicago: Contemporary Books.

Forehand, R. E., & McMahon, R. J. (1981). *Helping the noncompliant child. A clinician's guide to parent training.* New York: Guilford Press.

Forgatch, M., & Patterson, G. R. (1989). *Parents and adolescents living together: Part 2: Family problem solving.* Eugene, OR: Castalia.

Forness, S. (1990). Subtyping in learning disabilities: Introduction to the issues. In H. L. Swanson & B. Keogh (Eds.), *Learning disabilities: Theoretical and research issues* (pp. 195–200). Hillsdale, NJ: Erlbaum.

Forness, S. R., & Kavale, K. A. (1994). The Balkanization of special education: Proliferation of categories for new behavioral disorders. *Education and Treatment of Children, 17*, 215–227.

Forness, S. R., & Kavale, K. A. (1997). Defining emotional and behavioral disorders in school and related services. In J. W. Lloyd, E. J. Kameenui, & D. Chard (Eds.), *Issues in educating students with disabilities* (pp. 45–61). Hillsdale, NJ: Erlbaum.

Forness, S. R., Kavale, K. A., Blum, I., & Lloyd, J. W. (1997). Mega-analysis of meta-analyses: What works in special education and related services. *Teaching Exceptional Children, 29*(6), 4–9.

Forness, S. R., Kavale, K. A., & Crenshaw, T. M. (1999). Stimulant medication revisited: Effective treatment of children with ADHD. *Journal of Emotional and Behavioral Problems, 7*, 230–235.

Forness, S. R., Kavale, K. A., King, B. H., & Kasari, C. (1993). Conduct disorders in school: Special education eligibility and co-morbidity. *Journal of Emotional and Behavioral Disorders, 1*, 101–108.

Forness, S. R., Kavale, K. A., King, B. H., & Kasari, C. (1994). Simple versus complex conduct disorders: Identification and phenomenology. *Behavioral Disorders, 19*, 306–312.

Forness, S. R., Sweeney, D. P., & Wagner, S. R. (1998). Learning strategies and social skills training for students with ADHD. *Journal of Emotional and Behavioral Problems, 2*(2), 41–44.

Forness, S. R., & Walker, H. M. (1994). *Special education and children with ADD/ADHD.* Mentor, OH: National Attention Deficit Disorder Association.

Forness, S. R., Youpa, D., Hanna, G. L., Cantwell, D. P., & Swanson, J. M. (1992). Classroom instructional characteristics in attention deficit hyperactivity disorder: Comparison of pure and mixed subgroups. *Behavioral Disorders, 17*, 115–125.

Forsyth, P. D., & Davies, J. M. (1995). Pure white cell aplasia and health food products. *Postgraduate Medical Journal, 71*, 557–558.

Fox, N. A., Henderson, H. A., Rubin, K. H., Calkins, S. D., & Schmidt, L. A. (2001). Continuity and discontinuity of behavioral inhibition and exuberance: Psychophysiological and behavioral influences across the first four years of life. *Child Development, 72*, 1–21.

Fox, N. A., Rubin, K. H., Calkins, S. D., Marshall, T. R., Coplan, R. J., Porges, S. W., Long, J. M., & Stewart, S. (1995). Frontal activation asymmetry and social competence at four years of age. *Child Development, 66*, 1770–1784.

Frazier, J., Meyer, M., Biederman, J., Wozniak, J., Wilens, T., Spencer, T., & Shapiro, S. (1999). Risperidone treatment for juvenile bipolar disorder: A case series. *Journal of the American Academy of Child and Adolescent Psychiatry, 38*, 960–965.

Freeman, J. M. (1980). Febrile seizures: A consensus of their significance, evaluation, and treatment. *Pediatrics, 66*, 1009–1012.

Frick, P. J., Kamphaus, R. W., Lahey, B. B., Loeber, R., Christ, M. A. G., Hart, E. L., & Tannenbaum, L. E. (1991). Academic underachievement and the disruptive behavior disorders. *Journal of Consulting and Clinical Psychology, 59*, 289–294.

Frick, P. J., Lahey, B. B., Christ, M. G., Loeber, R., & Green, S. (1991). History of childhood behavior problems in biological relatives of boys with attention-deficit hyperactivity disorders and conduct disorder. *Journal of Clinical Child Psychology, 20*, 445–451.

Fried, J., Greenhill, LL., Torres, D., Martin, J., & Solomon, M. (1987). Sustained-release methylphenidate: Long-term clinical efficacy in ADDH males. *American Academy of Child and Adolescent Psychiatry, Scientific Proceedings of the Annual Meeting, 3*, 47.

Friedman, R. M., Katz-Leavy, J., Mandersheid, R., & Sondheimer, D. L. (1996). *Prevalence of serious emotional and developmental challenges.* New York: McGraw-Hill.

Fritz, G. K., & Bergman, A. S. (1985). Child psychiatrists seen through pediatrician's eyes: Results of a national study. *Journal of Child Psychiatry, 24*, 81–86.

Fuchs, D., & Fuchs, L. S. (1989). Exploring effective and efficient prereferral interventions: A component analysis of behavioral consultation. *School Psychology Review, 18*, 260–283.

Fuchs, D., & Fuchs, L. S. (1994). Inclusive schools movement and the radicalization of special education reform. *Exceptional Children, 60*, 294–309.

Fuller, R. W., Perry, K. W., Bymaster, F. P., & Wong, D. T. (1978). Comparative effects of pemoline, amfonelic acid and amphetamine on dopamine uptake and release in vitro and on brain 3,4-dihydroxyphenylacetic acid concentration in spiperone-treated rats. *Journal of Pharmacy and Pharmacology, 30*(3), 197–198.

Fulton, A., & Yates, W. R. (1988). Family abuse of methylphenidate. *American Family Physician, 38*, 143–145.

Fung, Y. K. (1988). Postnatal behavioural effects of maternal nicotine exposure in rats. *Journal of Pharmacy and Pharmacology, 40*, 870–872.

Fung, Y. K., & Lau, Y. S. (1989). Effects of prenatal nicotine exposure on rat striatal dopaminergic and nicotinic systems. *Pharmacology, Biochemistry and Behavior, 33*, 1–6.

Fuster, J. M. (1989). *The prefrontal cortex: Anatomy, physiology, and neuropsychology of the frontal lobe* (2nd ed.). New York: Raven Press.

Gadow, K. D., Nolan, E. E., & Sverd, J. (1992). Methylphenidate in hyperactive boys with comorbid tic disorder: II. Short-term behavioral effects in school settings. *Journal of the American Academy of Child and Adolescent Psychiatry, 31*, 462–471.

Gadow, K. D., Nolan, E. E., Sverd, J., Sprafkin, J., & Paolicelli, L. (1990). Methylphenidate in aggressive-hyperactive boys: I. Effects on peer aggression in public school settings. *Journal of the American Academy of Child and Adolescent Psychiatry, 29*(5), 710–718.

Gadow, K., Sverd, J., Sprafkin, J., Nolan, E., & Ezor, S. (1995). Efficacy of methylphenidate for attention deficit hyperactivity in children with tic disorder. *Archives of General Psychiatry, 52*, 444–455.

Gadow, K. D., Sverd, J., Sprafkin, J., Nolan, E., & Grossman, S. (1999). Long-term methylphenidate therapy in children with comorbid attention-deficit hyperactivity disorder and chronic multiple tic disorder. *Archives of General Psychiatry, 56*, 330–336.

Galanter, C. A., Carlson, G. A., Jensen, P. S., Greenhill, L. L., Elliott, G. R., Chuang, S. Z., Davies, M., Li, W., & MTA Cooperative Group. (2002). *Response to methylphenidate in children with attention deficit hyperactivity disorder and manic symptoms: Results from the MTA titration trial.* Manuscript submitted for review.

Gallucci, F., Bird, H. R., Berardi, C., Gallai, V., Pfanner, P., & Weinberg, A. (1993). Symptoms of ADHD in an Italian school sample, findings of a pilot study. *Journal of the American Academy of Child and Adolescent Psychiatry, 32*(5), 1051–1058.

Gardill, M. C., DuPaul, G. J., & Kyle, K. E. (1996). Classroom strategies for managing students with attention-deficit/hyperactivity disorder. *Intervention in School and Clinic, 32*(2), 89–94.

Gardner, W., Kelleher, K. J., Wasserman, R., Childs, G., Nutting, P., Lillienfield, H., & Pajer, K. (2000). Primary care treatment of pediatric psychosocial problems: A study from pediatric research in office settings and ambulatory sentinel practice network. *Pediatrics, 106*(4), E44.

Garfinkel, B. D., Wender, P. H., Sloman, L., & O'Neill, I. (1983). Tricyclic antidepressant and methylphenidate treatment of attention deficit disorder in children. *Journal of the American Academy of Child and Adolescent Psychiatry, 22*, 343–348.

Garland, A. F., Hough, R. L., McCabe, K. M., Yeh, M., Wood, P. A., & Aarons, G. A. (2001). Prevalences of psychiatric disorders in youths across five sectors of care. *Journal of the American Academy of Child and Adolescent Psychiatry, 40*, 409–418.

Garland, E. J. (1998). Intranasal abuse of prescribed methylphenidate. *Journal of the American Academy of Child and Adolescent Psychiatry, 37*, 573–574.

Gastfriend, D. R., Biederman, J., & Jellinek, M. S.

(1985). Desipramine in the treatment of attention deficit disorder in adolescents. *Psychopharmacology, 21,* 144–145.

Gaub, M., & Carlson, C. L. (1997). Behavioral characteristics of DSM-IV ADHD subtypes in a school-based population. *Journal of Abnormal Child Psychology, 25,* 103–111.

Gaub, M., & Carlson, C. L. (1997). Gender differences in ADHD: A meta-analysis and critical review. *Journal of the American Academy of Child and Adolescent Psychiatry, 36,* 1036–1045.

Gawin, F. H., & Ellinwood, E. H . (1988). Cocaine and other stimulants. *New England Journal of Medicine, 318,* 1173–1182.

Gawin, F. H., & Kleber, H. (1986). Pharmacologic treatments of cocaine abuse. *Psychiatric Clinics of North America, 9,* 573–583.

Geller, B., Warner, K., Williams, M., & Zimmerman, B. (1998). Prepubertal and young adolescent bipolarity versus ADHD. Assessment and validity using the Wash-U-KSADS, CBCL, and TRF. *Journal of Affective Disorders, 51,* 93–100.

Geller, S. J. (1960). Comparison of a tranquillizer and psychic energizer used in treatment of children with behavior disorders. *Journal of the American Medical Association, 174,* 481–484.

Gerring, J. P., Brady, K. D., Chen, A., Vasa, R., Grados, M., Bandeen-Roche, K. J., Bryan, R. N., & Denckla, M. B. (1998). Premorbid prevalence of ADHD and development of secondary ADHD after closed head injury. *Journal of the American Academy of Child and Adolescent Psychiatry, 37,* 647–654.

Ghose, K. (1983). L-tryptophan in hyperactive child syndrome associated with epilepsy: A controlled study. *Neuropsychobiology, 10,* 111–114.

Giedd, J. N., Castellanos, F. X., Casey, B. J., Kozuch, P., King, A. C., Hamburger, S. D., & Rapoport, J. L. (1994). Quantitative morphology of the corpus callosum in attention deficit hyperactivity disorder. *American Journal of Psychiatry, 151,* 665–669.

Giedd, J. N., Snell, J. W., Lange, N., Rajapakse, J. C., Casey, B. J., Kozuch, P. L., Vaituzis, A. C., Vauss, Y. C., Hamburger, S. D., Kaysen, D., & Rapoport, J. L. (1996). Quantitative magnetic resonance imaging of human brain development: Ages 4–18. *Cerebral Cortex, 6,* 551–560.

Gill, M., Daly, G., Heron, S., Hawl, Z., & Fitzgerald, M. (1997). Confirmation of association between attention deficit hyperactivity disorder and a dopamine transporter polymorphism. *Molecular Psychiatry, 2,* 311–313.

Gillberg, C., Melander, H., von Knorring, A., Janols, L. O., Thernlund, G., Hagglof, B., Eidevall-Wallin, L., Gustafsson, K., & Kopp, S. (1997). Long-term central stimulant treatment of children with attention-deficit hyperactivity disorder. A randomized double-blind placebo-controlled trial. *Archives of General Psychiatry, 54,* 857–864.

Gillberg, C., Rasmussen, P., Carlstrom, G., Svenson, B., & Waldenstrom, E. (1982). Perceptual, motor and attentional deficits in six-year-old children. Epidemiological aspects. *Journal of Child Psychology and Psychiatry, 23,* 131–144.

Gittelman, K. (1987). Pharmacotherapy of childhood hyperactivity: An update. In H. Y. Meltzer (Ed.), *Psychopharmacology: The third generation of progress* (pp. 1215–1224). New York: Raven Press.

Gittelman, R. (1980). Childhood disorders. In D. Klein, F. Quitkin, A. Rifkin, & R. Gittelman (Eds.), *Drug treatment of adult and child psychiatric disorders* (pp. 576–756.) Baltimore: Williams & Wilkins.

Gittelman, R., Abikoff, H., Pollack, E., Klein, D. F., Katz, S., & Mattes, J. (1980). A controlled trial of behavior modification and methylphenidate in hyperactive children. In C. K. Whalen & B. Henker (Eds.), *Hyperactive children: The social ecology of identification and treatment* (pp. 221–243). New York: Academic Press.

Gittelman, R., & Eskanazi, B. (1983). Lead and hyperactivity revisited: An investigation of nondisadvantaged children. *Archives of General Psychiatry, 40,* 827–833.

Gittelman, R., & Mannuzza, S. (1988). Hyperactive boys almost grown up: III. Methylphenidate effects on ultimate height. *Archives of General Psychiatry, 45,* 1131–1134.

Gittelman, R., Mannuzza, S., Shenker, R., & Bonagura, N. (1985). Hyperactive boys almost grown up: I. Psychiatric status. *Archives of General Psychiatry, 42,* 937–947.

Gittelman-Klein, R. (1974). Pilot clinical trial of imipramine in hyperkinetic children. In C. Conners (Ed.), *Clinical use of stimulant drugs in children* (pp. 192–201). The Hague, Netherlands: Excerpta Medica.

Gittelman-Klein, R., Klein, D. F., Abikoff, H., Katz, S., Gloisten, A. C., & Kates, W. (1976). Relative efficacy of methylphenidate and behavior modification in hyperkinetic children: An interim report. *Journal of Abnormal Child Psychology, 4,* 361–379.

Gittelman-Klein, R., Landa, B., Mattes, J. A., & Klein, D. F. (1988). Methylphenidate and growth in hyperactive children. *Archives of General Psychiatry, 45,* 1127–1130.

Gjone, H., Stevenson, J., & Sundet, J. M. (1996). Genetic influence on parent-reported attention-related problems in a Norwegian general population twin sample. *Journal of the American Academy of Child and Adolescent Psychiatry, 35,* 588–596.

Gold, J. M., Carpenter, C., Randolph, C., Goldberg, T. E., & Weinberger, D. R. (1997). Auditory working memory and Wisconsin Card Sorting Test Performance in Schizophrenia. *Archives of General Psychiatry, 54*, 159–165.

Goldberg, I. D., Roughmann, K. J., McInerny, T. K., & Burke, J. D., Jr. (1984). Mental health problems among children seen in pediatric practice: Prevalence and management. *Pediatrics, 73*, 278–293.

Goldman, J. A., Lerman, R. H., Contois, J. H., & Udall, J. N., Jr. (1986). Behavioral effects of sucrose on preschool children. *Journal of Abnormal Child Psychology, 14*, 565–577.

Goldman, L. S., Genel, M., Bezman, R. J., & Slanetz, P. J. (1998). Diagnosis and treatment of attention-deficit/hyperactivity disorder in children and adolescents. Council on Scientific Affairs, American Medical Association. *Journal of the American Medical Association, 279*, 1100–1107.

Goldman-Rakic, P. S. (1987). Development of cortical circuitry and cognitive function. *Child Development, 58*, 601–622.

Goldstein, S., & Goldstein, M. (1990). *Managing attention disorders in children.* New York: Wiley.

Gong, Z., & Evans, H. L. (1997). Effect of chelation with meso-dimercaptosuccinic acid (DMSA) before and after the appearance of lead-induced neurotoxicity in the rat. *Toxicology and Applied Pharmacology, 144*, 205–214.

Goodman, R. (1989). Genetic factors in hyperactivity: Account for about half of the explainable variance. *British Medical Journal, 298*, 1407–1408.

Goodman, R., & Stevenson, J. (1989). A twin study of hyperactivity: I. An examination of hyperactivity scores and categories derived from Rutter teacher and parent questionnaires. *Journal of Child Psychology and Psychiatry, 30*, 671–689.

Goodman, R., & Stevenson, J. (1989). A twin study of hyperactivity: II. The aetiological role of genes, family relationships, and perinatal adversity. *Journal of Child Psychology and Psychiatry, 30*, 691–709.

Goodman, S. H., Hoven, C. W., Narrow, W. E., Cohen, P., Fielding, B., Alegria, M., Leaf, P. J., Kandel, D., Horwitz, S. M., Bravo, M., Moore, R., & Dulcan, M. K. (1998). Measurement of risk for mental disorders and competence in a psychiatric epidemiologic community survey: The National Institute of Mental Health Methods for the Epidemiology of Child and Adolescent Mental Disorders (MECA) Study. *Social Psychiatry and Psychiatric Epidemiology, 33*, 162–173.

Goodman, S. H., Lahey, B. B., Fielding, B., Dulcan, M., Narrow, W., & Regier, D. (1997). Representativeness of clinical samples of youths with mental disorders: A preliminary population-based study. *Journal of Abnormal Psychology, 106*, 3–14.

Goodwin, D. W., Schulsinger, F., Hermansen, L., Guze, S., & Winokur, G. (1975). Alcoholism and the hyperactive child syndrome. *Journal of Nervous and Mental Disease, 160*, 349–353.

Gordon, N. G. (1983). The Gordon diagnostic system. DeWitt, NY: Gordon Systems.

Goyer, P. F., Davis, G. C., & Rapoport, J. L. (1979). Abuse of prescribed stimulant medication by a 13-year-old hyperactive boy. *Journal of the American Academy of Child Psychiatry, 18*, 170–175.

Grandin, T. (1992). Calming effects of deep touch pressure in patients with autistic disorder, college students, and animals. *Journal of Child and Adolescent Psychopharmacology, 2*(1), 63–72.

Green, L. A., Wood, M., Becker, L., Farley, E. S., Freeman, W. L., Froom, J., Hames, C., Niebauer, L. J., Rosser, W. W., & Seifert, M. (1984). The Ambulatory Sentinel Practice Network: Purpose, methods, and policies. *Journal of Family Practice, 18*, 275–280.

Greenberg, L., Yellin, A., Spring, C., & Metcalf, M. (1975). Clinical effects of imipramine and methylphenidate in hyperactive children. *International Journal of Mental Health, 4*, 144–156.

Greenberg, M. T., Speltz, M. L., & DeKlyen, M. (1993). The role of attachment in the early development of disruptive behavior problems. *Developmental Psychopathology, 5*, 191–213.

Greene, R. W., Biederman, J., Faraone, S. V., Ouellette, C. A., Penn, C., & Griffin, S. M. (1996). Toward a new psychometric definition of social disability in children with attention-deficit hyperactivity disorder. *Journal of the American Academy of Child and Adolescent Psychiatry, 35*, 571–578.

Greene, R., Biederman, J., Faraone, S. V., Sienna, M., & Garcia-Jetton, J. (1997). Adolescent outcome of boys with attention-deficit/hyperactivity disorder and social disability: Results from a 4-year follow-up study. *Journal of Consulting and Clinical Psychology, 65*, 758–767.

Greenfield, B., Hechtman, L., & Weiss, G. (1988). Two subgroups of hyperactives as adults: Correlations of outcome. *Canadian Journal of Psychiatry, 33*, 505–508.

Greenhill L.L. (1995). Attention-deficit hyperactivity disorder: The stimulants. *Child and Adolescent Psychiatry Clinics of North America, 4*, 123–168.

Greenhill, L. (1998). Childhood attention deficit hyperactivity disorder: Pharmacological treatments. In P. E. Nathan & J. M. Gorman (Eds.), *A guide to treatments that work* (pp. 42–64). New York: Oxford University Press.

Greenhill, L. (2002). Childhood attention deficit hyperactivity disorder: Pharmacological treatments. In P. E. Nathan & J. Gorman (Eds.), *Treatments that work* (pp. 25–55). Philadephia: Saunders.

Greenhill, L. L., Abikoff, H. B., Arnold, L. E., Cantwell, D. P., Conners, C. K., Elliott, G., Hechtman, L.,

Hinshaw, S. P., Hoza, B., Jensen, P. S., March, J. S., Newcorn, J., Pelham, W. E., Severe, J. B., Swanson, J. M., Vitiello, B., & Wells, K. (1996). Medication treatment strategies in the MTA study: Relevance to clinicians and researchers. *Journal of the American Academy of Child and Adolescent Psychiatry, 35*, 1304–1313.

Greenhill, L. L., Halperin, J. M., & Abikoff, H. (1999). Stimulant medications. *Journal of the American Academy of Child and Adolescent Psychiatry, 38*, 503–512.

Gresham, F. M., MacMillan, D. L., Bocian, K., Ward, S. L., & Forness, S. R. (1998). Comorbidity of hyperactivity-impulsivity-inattention + conduct problems: Risk factors in social, affecrtive, and academic domains. *Journal of Abnormal Child Psychology, 26*, 393–406.

Griffith, D. R., Azuma, S. D., & Chasnoff, I. J. (1994). Three-year outcome of children exposed prenatally to drugs. *Journal of the American Academy of Child and Adolescent Psychiatry, 33*, 20–27.

Grodinsky, G. M., & Diamond, J. (1992). Frontal lobe functioning in boys with attention deficit hyperactivity disorder. *Developmental Neuropsychology, 8*, 427–446.

Gross, M. (1973). Imipramine in the treatment of minimal brain dysfunction in children. *Psychosomatics, 14*, 283–285.

Gualtieri, C. T., & Evans, R. W. (1988). Motor performance in hyperactive children treated with imipramine. *Perceptual Motion, 66*, 763–769.

Guevara, J., Lozano, P., Wickizer, T., Mell, L., & Gephart, H. (2001). Utilization and cost of health care services for children with attention-deficit/hyperactivity disorder. *Pediatrics, 108*, 71–78.

Gunby, P. (1979). Methylphenidate abuse produces retinopathy. *Journal of the American Medical Association, 241*, 546.

Gunning, B. (1992). *A controlled trial of clonidine in hyperkinetic children.* Doctoral thesis, Department of Child and Adolescent Psychiatry, Academic Hospital Rotterdam-Sophia Children's Hospital Rotterdam, The Netherlands.

Hadders-Algra, M., & Groothuis, A. M. (1999). Quality of general movements in infancy as related to neurological dysfunction, ADHD, and aggressive behaviour. *Developmental Medicine and Child Neurology, 41*, 381–391.

Hagerman, R. J., & Falkenstein, A. R. (1987). An association between recurrent otitis media in infancy and hyperactivity. *Clinical Pediatrics, 26*, 253–257.

Haglund, R. M., & Howerton, L. L. (1982). Ritalin: Consequences of abuse in a clinical population. *International Journal of Addiction, 17*, 349–356.

Halas, E. S., & Sandstead, H. H. (1975). Some effects of prenatal zinc deficiency on behavior of the adult rat. *Pediatric Research, 9*, 94–97.

Halikas, J. A., Meller, J., Morse, C., & Lyttle, M. D. (1990). Predicting substance abuse in juvenile offenders: Attention deficit disorder versus aggressivity. *Child Psychiatry and Human Development, 21*, 49–55.

Halperin, J. M., & McKay, K. E. (1998). Psychological testing for child and adolescent psychiatrists: A review of the past 10 years. *Journal of the American Academy of Child and Adolescent Psychiatry, 37*, 575–584.

Halperin, J. M., McKay, K. E., Matier, K., & Sharma, V. (1994). Attention, response inhibition and activity level in children: Developmental neuropsychological perspectives. In M. G. Tramontana & S. R. Hooper (Eds.), *Advances in child neuropsychology* (Vol. 2, pp. 1–54). New York: Springer-Verlag.

Halperin, J. M., Wolf, L. E., Greenblatt, E. R., & Young, J. G. (1991). Subtype analysis of commission errors on the continuous performance test in children. *Developmental Neuropsychology, 7*, 207–217.

Hamazaki, T., Sawazaki, S., Itomura, M., Asaoka, E., Nagao, Y., Nishimura, N., Yazawa, K., Kuwamori, T., & Kobayashi, M. (1996). The effect of docosohexaenoic acid on aggression in young adults. A placebo-controlled double-blind study. *Journal of Clinical Investigation, 97*, 1129–1133.

Handen, B. J., Janosky, K., McAuliffe, S., Breaux, A. M., & Feldman, H. (1994). Prediction of response to methylphenidate among children with ADHD and mental retardation. *Journal of the American Academy of Child and Adolescent Psychiatry, 33*, 1185–1193.

Handen, B. L., Feldman, H. M., Lurier, A., & Murray, P. J. (1999). Efficacy of methylphenidate among preschool children with developmental disabilities and ADHD. *Journal of the American Academy of Child and Adolescent Psychiatry, 38*, 805–812.

Hart, E. L., Lahey, B. B., Loeber, R., Applegate, B., Green, S. M., & Frick, P. J. (1995). Developmental change in attention-deficit hyperactivity disorder in boys: A four-year longitudinal study. *Journal of Abnormal Child Psychology, 23*, 729–749.

Hartsough, C. S., Babinski, L. M., & Lambert, N. M. (1996). Tracking procedures and attrition containment in a long-term follow-up of a community-based ADHD sample. *Journal of Child Psychology and Psychiatry, 37*, 705–713.

Hartsough, C. S., & Lambert N. M. (1985). Medical factors in hyperactive and normal children: Prenatal, developmental, and health history findings. *American Journal of Orthopsychiatry, 55*, 190–210.

Hartsough, C. S., & Lambert, N. M. (1987). Pattern and progression of drug use among hyperactives and controls: A prospective short-term longitudinal study. *Journal of Child Psychology and Psychiatry, 28*, 543–553.

Hartup, W. W. (1996). The company they keep: Friendships and their developmental significance. *Child Development, 67*, 1–13.

Haslam, R. H. A., Dalby, J. T., & Rademaker, A. W. (1984). Effects of Megavitamin therapy on children with attention deficit disorders. *Pediatrics, 74*, 103–111.

Hauger, R. L., Angel, L., Janowsky, A., Berger, P., & Hulihan-Gibin, B. (1990). Brain recognition sites for methylphenidate and amphetamines. In S. Deutsch, A. Weizman, & R. Weizman (Eds.), *Application of basic neuroscience to child psychiatry* (pp. 77–100). New York: Plenum Press.

Hauser, P., Soler, R., Brucker-Davis, F., & Weintraub, B. D. (1997). Thyroid hormones correlate with symptoms of hyperactivity but not inattention in ADHD. *Psychoneuroendocrinology, 22*, 107–114.

Hauser, W. A. (1991). The natural history of febrile seizures. In K. B. Nelson & J. H. Ellenberg (Eds.), *Febrile seizures* (pp. 5–17). New York: Raven Press.

Hawkins, J. D., Catalano, R. F., & Miller, J. Y. (1982). Risk and protective factors for alcohol and other drug problems in adolescence and early adulthood: Implications for substance abuse prevention. *Psychological Bulletin, 112*, 64–105.

Hazall, P., McDowell, M. J., & Walton, J. M. (1996). Management of children prescribed psychostimulant medication for attention deficit hyperactivity disorder in the Hunter region of NSW. *Medical Journal of Australia, 165*, 477–480.

Healey, J. M., Newcorn, J. H., Halperin, J. M., Wolf, L. E., Pascualvaca, D. M., Schmeidler, J., & O'Brien, J. D. (1993). The factor structure of ADHD items in DSM-III-R, internal consistency and external validation. *Journal of Abnormal Child Psychology, 21*(4), 441–453.

Hechtman, L. (1985). Adolescent outcome of hyperactive children treated with stimulants in childhood: A review. *Psychopharmacology Bulletin, 21*(2), 178–191.

Hechtman, L. (1992). Long-term outcome in attention-deficit hyperactivity disorder. *Psychiatric Clinics of North America, 1*, 553–565.

Hechtman, L. (1996). Families of children with attention deficit hyperactivity disorder: A review. *Canadian Journal of Psychiatry, 41*, 350–360.

Hechtman, L., & Abikoff, H. (1995, October). *Multimodal treatment plus stimulants vs. stimulant treatment in ADHD children: Results from a two-year comparative treatment study.* Paper presented at the annual meeting of the American Academy of Child and Adolescent Psychiatry, New Orleans, LA.

Hechtman, L., & Weiss, G. (1986). Controlled prospective 15-year follow-up of hyperactives as adults: Non-medical drug and alcohol use and anti-social behaviour. *Canadian Journal of Psychiatry, 31*, 557–567.

Hechtman, L., Weiss, G., & Perlman, T. (1984). Hyperactives as young adults: Past and current substance abuse and antisocial behavior. *American Journal of Orthopsychiatry, 54*, 415–425.

Hechtman, L., Weiss, G., & Perlman, T. (1984). Young adult outcomes of hyperactive children who received long-term stimulant treatment. *Journal of the American Academic of Child Psychiatry, 23*(3), 261–269.

Hechtman, L., Weiss, G., Perlman, T., & Amsel, R. (1984). Hyperactives as young adults: Initial predictors of adult outcome. *Journal of the American Academy of Child Psychiatry, 23*, 250–260.

Hechtman, L., Weiss, G., Perlman, T., Hopkins, J., & Wener, A. (1981). Hyperactive children in young adulthood: A controlled, prospective, ten-year follow-up. In M. Gittleman (Ed.), *Strategic interventions for hyperactive children* (pp. 186–201), Armonk, NY: M.E. Sharpe.

Heimann, S. W. (1999). Pycnogenol for ADHD? *Journal of the American Academy of Child and Adolescent Psychiatry, 38*, 357-358.

Hellgren, L., Gillberg, I. C., Bagenholm, A., & Gillberg, C. (1994). Children with deficits in attention, motor control and perception (DAMP) almost grown up: Psychiatric and personality disorders at age 16 years. *Journal of Child Psychology and Psychiatry, 35*, 1255–1271.

Henggeler, S. W., Rowland, M. D., Randall, J., Ward, D. M., Pickerel, S., Cunningham, P. B., Miller, S. L., Edwards, J., Zealberg, J. J., Hand, L. D., & Santos, A. B. (1999). Home-based multisystemic therapy as an alternative to the hospitalization of youths in psychiatric crisis: Clinical outcomes. *Journal of the American Academy of Child and Adolescent Psychiatry, 38*(11), 1331–1339.

Henningfield, J. E., Clayton, R., & Pollin, W. (1990). Involvement of tobacco in alcoholism and illicit drug use. *British Journal of Addiction, 85*, 279–291.

Henningfield, J. E., Cohen, C., & Slade, J. D. (1991). Is nicotine more addictive than cocaine? Special Issue: Future directions in tobacco research. *British Journal of Addiction, 86*, 565–569.

Herrero, M. E., Hechtman, L., & Weiss, G. (1994). Antisocial disorders in hyperactive subjects from childhood to adulthood: predictive factors and characterization of subgroups. *American Journal of Orthopsychiatry, 64*, 510–521.

Hertzig, M. E. (1983). Temperament and neurological status. In M. Rutter (Ed.), *Developmental neuropsychiatry* (pp. 164–180). New York: Guilford Press.

Hibbeln, J. R., Umhau, J. C., Linnoila, M., George, D. T., Ragan, P. W., Shoaf, S. E., Vaughan, M. R., Rawlings, R., & Salem, N. Jr. (1998). Essential fatty acids predict metabolistes of serotonin and dopamine in cerebrospinal fluid among healthy control subjects, and early-and late-onset alcoholics. *Biological Psychiatry, 44*(4), 243–349.

Hill, J. C., & Schoener, E. P. (1996). Age-dependent decline of attention deficit hyperactivity disorder. *American Journal of Psychiatry, 153*, 1143–1146.

Hinshaw, S. P. (1987). On the distinction between attentional deficits/hyperactivity and conduct problems/aggression in child psychopathology. *Psychological Bulletin, 101*, 443–463.

Hinshaw, S. P. (1991). Stimulant medication and the treatment of aggression in children with attentional deficits. *Journal of Clinical Child Psychology, 20*, 301–312.

Hinshaw, S. P. (1992). Externalizing behavior problems and academic underachievement in childhood and adolescence: Causal relationships and underlying mechanisms. *Psychological Bulletin, 111*, 127–155.

Hinshaw, S. P. (1994). *Attention deficits and hyperactivity in children.* Thousand Oaks, CA: Sage.

Hinshaw, S. P. (1999). Psychosocial intervention for childhood ADHD: Etiologic and developmental themes, comorbidity, and integration with pharmacotherapy. In D. Cicchetti & S. L. Toth (Eds.), *Rochester Symposium on Developmental Psychopathology (Vol. 9): Developmental approaches to prevention and intervention* (pp. 221–270). Rochester, NY: University of Rochester Press.

Hinshaw, S. P. (2001). *Preadolescent girls with attention-deficit/hyperactivity disorder: Background characteristics, comorbidity, cognitive and social functioning, and parenting practices.* Unpublished manuscript, University of California, Berkeley.

Hinshaw, S., Abikoff, H., & Klein, R. (1998). Psychosocial treatments for attention-deficit hyperactivity disorder. In P. E. Nathan & J. Gorman (Eds.), *Treatments that work* (pp. 21–40). Philadelphia: Saunders.

Hinshaw, S. P., & Erhardt, D. (1991). Attention-deficit hyperactivity disorder. In P. Kendall (Ed.), *Child and adolescent therapy: Cognitive-behavioral procedures* (pp. 98–128). New York: Guilford Press.

Hinshaw, S., Heller, T., & McHale, J. (1992). Covert antisocial behavior in boys with attention-deficit hyperactivity disorder: External validation and effects of methylphendiate. *Journal of Consulting and Clinical Psychology, 60*, 274–281.

Hinshaw, S. P., Henker, B., & Whalen, C. K. (1984). Self-control in hyperactive boys in anger-inducing situations: Effects of cognitive-behavioral training and of methylphenidate. *Journal of Abnormal Child Psychology, 12*, 55–77.

Hinshaw, S. P., Klein, R. G., & Abikoff, H. (1998). Childhood attention deficit hyperactivity disorder: Nonpharmacological and combination treatments. In P. E. Nathan & J. M. Gorman (Eds.), *A guide to treatments that work* (pp. 26–41). New York: Oxford University Press.

Hinshaw, S. P., & Melnick, S. M. (1995). Peer relationships in boys with attention-deficit hyperactivity disorder with and without comorbid aggression. *Development and Psychopathology, 7*, 627–647.

Hinshaw, S. P., Owens, E. B., Wells, K. C., Kraemer, H. C., Abikoff, H. B., Arnold, L. E., Conners, C. K., Elliott, G., Greenhill, L. L., Hechtman, L., Hoza, B., Jensen, P. S., March, J. S., Newcorn, J. H., Pelham, W. E., Swanson, J. M., Vitiello, B., & Wigal, T. (2000). Family processes and treatment outcome in the MTA: Negative/ineffective parenting practices in relation to multimodal treatment. *Journal of Abnormal Child Psychology, 28*, 555–568.

Hinshaw, S. P., Zupan, B. A., Simmel, C., Nigg, J. T., & Melnick, S. M. (1997). Peer status in boys with and without ADHD: Predictions from overt and covert antisocial behavior, social isolation, and authoritative parenting beliefs. *Child Development, 64*, 880–896.

Ho, T. P., Leung, P. W., Luk, E. S., Taylor, E., Bacon-Shone, J., & Mak, F. L. (1996). Establishing the constructs of childhood behavioral disturbances in a Chinese population: A questionnaire study. *Journal of Abnormal Child Psychology, 24*(4), 417–431.

Hoagwood, K., Hibbs, E., Brent, D., & Jensen, P. (1995). Introduction to the special section: Efficacy and effectiveness in studies of child and adolescent psychotherapy. *Journal of Consulting and Clinical Psychology, 63*, 683–687.

Hoagwood, K., Jensen, P. S., Feil, M., Vitiello, B., & Bhatara, V. S. (2000). Medication management of stimulants in pediatric-practice settings: A national perspective. *Developmental and Behavioral Pediatrics, 21*, 322–331.

Hochman, L. B. (1922). Post-encephalitic behavior disorder in children. *Johns Hopkins Hospital Bulletin, 33*, 372–375.

Hocutt, A. M., McKinney, J. D., & Montague, M. (1993). Issues in the education of students with attention deficit disorder: Introduction to the special issue. *Exceptional Children, 60*, 103–108.

Hodapp, R. M., & Dykens, E. M. (1992). The role of etiology in education of children with mental retardation. *McGill Journal of Education, 27*, 165–173.

Hoffman, H. (1848). *Der Struwwelpeter.* Germany.

Hoge, S. K., & Biederman, J. (1986). A case of Tourette's syndrome with symptoms of attention deficit disorder treated with desipramine. *Journal of Clinical Psychiatry, 47*, 478–479.

Holborow, P. L., & Berry, P. S. (1986). Hyperactivity and learning difficulties. *Journal of Learning Disabilities, 19*, 426–431.

Holborow, P., & Berry, P. (1986). A multinational, cross-cultural perspective on hyperactivity. *American Journal of Orthopsychiatry, 56*(2), 320–322.

Hops, H., Walker, H. M., Fleischman, D. H., Nagoshi, J. T., Omura, R. T., Skindrud, K., & Taylor, J. (1978). CLASS: A standardized in-class program for acting-out children: II. Field test evaluations. *Journal of Educational Psychology, 70*, 636–644.

Horger, B. A., Giles, M. K., & Schenk, S. (1992). Preexposure to amphetamine and nicotine predisposes rats to self-administer a low dose of cocaine. *Psychopharmacology, 107*, 271–276.

Horn, W. F., Ialongo, N. S, Greenberg, G., Packard, T., & Smith-Winberry, C. (1990). Additive effects of behavioral parent training and self-control therapy with ADHD children. *Journal of Clinical Child Psychology, 19*, 98–110.

Horn, W. F., Ialongo, N. S., Pascoe, J. M., Greenberg, G., Packard, T., Lopez, M., Wagner, A., & Puttler, L. (1991). Additive effects of psychostimulants, parent training, and self-control therapy with ADHD children. *Journal of the American Academy of Child and Adolescent Psychiatry, 30*(2), 233–240.

Horn, W. F., Ialongo, N. S, Popovich, S., & Peradotto, D. (1987). Behavioral parent training and cognitive-behavioral self-control therapy with ADD-H children: Comparative and combined effects. *Journal of Clinical Child Psychology, 16*, 57–68.

Horn, W., Parker, H., Evans, J., & Portnoy, E. (1994). *Petition for rulemaking to reclassify methylphenidate from Schedule II to Schedule III controlled substance and alternatively to eliminate all likely future methylphenidate shortages.* Unpublished manuscript.

Horner, B. R., & Scheibe, K. E. (1997). Prevalence and implications of attention-deficit hyperactivity disorder among adolescents in treatment for substance abuse. *Journal of the American Academy of Child and Adolescent Psychiatry, 36*, 30–36.

Horner, B., Scheibe, K., & Stine, S. (1996). Cocaine abuse and attention-deficit hyperactivity disorder: Implications of adult symptomatology. *Psychology of Addictive Behaviors, 10*, 55–60.

Hornig-Rohan, M., & Amsterdam, J. (1995). *Venlafaxine vs. stimulant therapy in patients with dual diagnoses of ADHD and depression.* Orlando, FL: New Clinical Drug Evaluation Unit Program.

Horrigan, J. P., & Barnhill, L. J. (1995). Guanfacine for treatment of attention-deficit hyperactivity disorder in boys. *Journal of Child and Adolescent Psychophamacology, 5*, 215–223.

Horwitz, S. M., Leaf, P. J., Leventhal, J. M., Forsyth, B.,

& Speechley, K. N. (1992). Identification and management of psychosocial and developmental problems in community-based, primary care pediatric practices. *Pediatrics, 89*, 480–485.

Houben, G. F., & Penninks, A. H. (1994). Immunotoxicity of the colour additive caramel colour III: A review on complicated issues in the safety evaluation of a food additive. *Toxicology, 91*, 289–302.

Hovens, J. G., Cantwell, D. P., & Kiriakos, R. (1994). Psychiatric comorbidity in hospitalized adolescent substance abusers. *Journal of the American Academy of Child and Adolescent Psychiatry, 33*(4), 476–483.

Hoza, B., Pelham, W. E., Milich, R., Pillow, D., & McBride, K. (1993). The self perceptions and attributions of attention deficit hyperactive disordered and nonreferred boys. *Journal of Abnormal Child Psychology 21*(3), 271–286.

Hoza, B., Pelham, W. E., Sams, S. E., & Carlson, C. (1992). An examination of the dosage effects of both behavior therapy and methylphenidate on the classroom performance of two ADHD children. *Behavior Modification, 16*, 164–192.

Huang, J. T., & Ho, B. T. (1974). Discriminative stimulus properties of d-amphetamine and related compounds in rat. *Pharmacology, Biochemistry and Behavior, 2*, 669–673.

Hudziak, J. J., Heath, A. C., Madden, P. F., Reich, W., Bucholz, K. K., Slutske, W., Beirut, L. J., Neuman, R. J., & Todd, R. D. (1998). Latent class and factor analysis of DSM-IV ADHD: A twin study of female adolescents. *Journal of the American Academy of Child and Adolescent Psychiatry, 37*, 848–857.

Hudziak, J. J., Wadsworth, M. E., Heath, A. C., & Achenbach, T. M. (1999). Latent class analysis of child behavior checklist attention problems. *Journal of the American Academy of Child and Adolescent Psychiatry, 38*, 985–991.

Huessy, H., & Wright, A. (1970). The use of imipramine in children's behavior disorders. *Acta Paedopsychiatrie, 37*, 194–199.

Huey, L. Y., Janowsky, D. S., Judd, L. L., Roitman, N. A., Clopton, P. L., Segal, D., Hall, L., & Parker, D. (1980). The effects of naloxone on methylphenidate-induced mood and behavioral changes: A negative study. *Psychopharmacology, 67*, 125–130.

Hughes, J. R. (1997). Substance abuse and ADHD. *American Journal of Psychiatry, 154*, 132.

Hunt, P., & Goetz, L. (1997). Research on inclusive educational programs, practices, and outcomes for students with severe disabilities. *Journal of Special Education, 31*, 329.

Hunt, R. D. (1987). Treatment effects of oral and trans-dermal clonidine in relation to methylphenidate: An open pilot study in ADD-H. *Psychopharmacology, 23,* 111–114.

Hunt, R., Arnsten, A., & Asbell, M. (1995). An open trial of guanfacine in the treatment of attention-deficit hyperactivity disorder. *Journal of the American Academy of Child and Adolescent Psychiatry, 34,* 50–54.

Hunt, R. D., Minderaa, R. B., & Cohen, D. J. (1985). Clonidine benefits children with attention deficit disorder and hyperactivity: Report of a double-blind placebo-crossover therapeutic trial. *Journal of the American Academy of Child Psychiatry, 24,* 617–629.

Hynd, G. W., Hern, K. L., Novey, E. S., & Eliopulos, D. (1993). Attention deficit-hyperactivity disorder and asymmetry of the caudate nucleus. *Journal of Child Neurology, 8,* 339–343.

Hynd, G. W., Lorys, A. R., Semrud-Clikeman, M., Nieves, N., Huettner, M. I. S., & Lahey, B. B. (1991). Attention deficit disorder without hyperactivity: A distinct behavioral and neurocognitive syndrome. *Journal of Child Neurology, 6*(Suppl.), S37–S41.

Hynd, G. W., Semrud-Clikeman, M., Lorys, A. R., & Novey, E. S. (1990). Brain morphology in developmental dyslexia and attention deficit disorder/hyperactivity. *Archives of Neurology, 47,* 919–926.

Hynd, G. W, Semrud-Clikeman, M., Lorys, A. R., & Novey, E. S. (1991). Corpus callosum morphology in attention deficit-hyperactivity disorder: Morphometric analysis of MRI. *Journal of Learning Disabilities, 24,* 141–146.

Iaboni, F., Douglas, V. I., & Baker, A. G. (1995). Effects of reward and response costs on inhibition in ADHD children. *Journal of Abnormal Psychology, 104,* 232–240.

Ialongo, N. S., Horn, W. F., Pascoe, J. M., Greenberg, G., Packard, T., Lopez, M., Wagner, A., & Puttler, L. (1993). The effects of a multimodal intervention with attention-deficit hyperactivity disorder children: A 9-month follow-up. *Journal of the American Academy of Child and Adolescent Psychiatry, 32,* 182–189.

Ialongo, N. S., Lopez, M., Horn, W. F., Pascoe, J. M., & Greenberg, G. (1994). Effects of psychoactive medication on self-perceptions of competence, control, and mood in children with attention deficit hyperactivity disorder. *Journal of Clinical Child Psychology, 23,* 161–173.

Imamura, K. N., Weiss, P., & Parham, D. (1990). The effects of hug machine usage on behavioral organization of children with autism and autism-like characteristics. *Sensory Integration Quarterly, 27,* 1–5.

Increasing morbidity and mortality associated with abuse of methamphetamine—United States, 1991–1994. (1995). *Morbidity and Mortality Weekly Report, 1, 44*(47), 882–886.

Individuals with Disabilities Education Act of 1990, 20 U.S.C. §§1400 et seq.

Interactive metronome [On-line]. (1998). Available: http://www.interactivemetronome.com/adhd.htm.

Ironson, G., Field, T. M., Scafidi, F., Kumar, M., Patarca, R., Price, A., Goncalves, A., Hashimoto, M., Kumar, A., Burman, I., Tetenman, C., & Fletcher, M. A. (1996). Massage therapy is associated with enhancement of the immune system's cytotoxic capacity. *International Journal of Neuroscience, 84,* 205-218.

Irving, W. C. III (1987). A comparison of biofeedback-assisted relaxation and psychostimulants in treating children with attention deficit disorder with hyperactivity. *Dissertation Abstracts International, 48*(04), 0876A.

Iversen, S. D., & Dunnett, S. B. (1990). Functional organization of striatum as studied with neural graphs. *Neuropsychologia, 28,* 601–626.

Izenwasser, S. E., Garcia-Valdez, K., & Kantak, K. M. (1986). Stimulant-like effects of magnesium on aggression in mice. *Pharmacology, Biochemistry, and Behavior, 25,* 1195–1199.

Jacobson, N. S., & Truax, P. (1991). Clinical significance: A statistical approach to defining meaningful change in psychotherapy research. *Journal of Consulting and Clinical Psychology, 59,* 12–19.

Jacobvitz, D., Sroufe, L. A., Stewart, M., & Leffert, N. (1990). Treatment of attentional and hyperactivity problems in children with sympathomimetic drugs: A comprehensive review. *Journal of the American Academy of Child and Adolescent Psychiatry, 29*(5), 677–688.

Jadad, A., & Atkins, D. (2000). *The treatment of attention-deficit/hyperactivity disorder: An evidence report* (Technology Assessment No. 11). Prepared by McMaster University under contract 290–97–007.

Jaffe, R. B., & Koschmann, E. B. (1970). Intravenous drug abuse: Pulmonary, cardiac, and vascularcomplications. *American Journal of Roentgenology, 109,* 107–120.

Jaffe, S. L. (1991). Intranasal abuse of prescribed methylphenidate by an alcohol and drug abusing adolescent with ADHD. *Journal of the American Academy of Child and Adolescent Psychiatry, 30,* 773–775.

Javorsky, J. (1996). An examination of youth with attention-deficit/hyperactivity disorder and language learning disabilities: A clinical study. *Journal of Learning Disabilities, 29,* 247–258.

Jensen, P. S. (2002). From ivory towers to earthen trenches: Issues and obstacles in effectiveness studies. *Report on Emotional and Behavioral Disorders in Youth,2,* 25–26, 47.

Jensen, P. S., & Abikoff, H. (2000). Tailoring treatment interventions for individuals with ADD. In T. Brown

(Ed.), *Attention deficit disorders and comorbidities in children, adolescents, and adults* (pp. 637–652). Washington, DC: American Psychiatric Press.

Jensen, P. S., Bhatara, V. S., Vitiello, B., Hoagwood, K., Feil, M., & Burke, L. B. (1999). Psychoactive medication prescribing practices for U.S. children: Gaps between research and clinical practice. *Journal American Academy of Child and Adolescent Psychiatry, 38*, 557–565.

Jensen, P. S., Hinshaw, S. P., Kraemer, H. C., Lenora, N., Newcorn, J. H., Abikoff, H. B., March, J. S., Arnold, L. E., Cantwell, D. P., Conners, C. K., Elliott, G. R., Greenhill, L. L., Hechtman, L., Hoza, B., Pelham, W. E., Severe, J. B., Swanson, J. M., Wells, K. C., Vitiello, B., & Wigal, T. (2001). ADHD comorbidity findings from the MTA study: Comparing comorbid subgroups. *Journal of the American Academy of Child and Adolescent Psychiatry, 40*, 147–158.

Jensen, P. S., Hinshaw, S. P., Swanson, J. M., Greenhill, L. L., Conners, C. K., Arnold, L. E., Abikoff, H. B., Elliott, G., Hechtman, L., Hoza, B., March, J. S., Newcorn, J. H., Pelham, W. E., Severe, J. B., Vitiello, B., Wells, K., & Wigal, T. (2001). Findings from the NIMH multimodal treatment study of ADHD (MTA). *Journal of Developmental and Behavioral Pediatrics, 22*, 1–14.

Jensen, P. S., Kettle, L., Roper, M., Sloan, M., Dulcan, M., Hoven, C., & Bauermeister, J. (1999). Are stimulants overprescribed? Treatment of ADHD in 4 US communities. *Journal of the American Academy of Child and Adolescent Psychiatry, 38*, 797–804.

Jensen, P. S., Kettle, L., Roper, M., Sloan, M. T., Dulcan, M. K., Hoven, C., Bird, H. R., Bauermeister, J. J., & Payne, J. D. (1999). Are stimulants overprescribed? Treatment of ADHD in 4 U.S. communities *Journal of the American Academy of Child and Adolescent Psychiatry, 38*(7), 797–804.

Jensen, P. S., Martin, D., & Cantwell, D. P. (1997). Comorbidity in ADHD: Implications for research, practice, and DSM-V. *Journal of the American Academy of Child and Adolescent Psychiatry, 36*, 1065–1079.

Jensen, P. S., Mrazek, D., Knapp, P. K., Steinberg L., Pfeffer, C., Schowalter, J., & Shapiro, T. (1997). Evolution and revolution in child psychiatry: ADHD as a disorder of adaptation. *Journal of the American Academy of Child and Adolescent Psychiatry, 36*, 1672–1679.

Jensen, P., Rubio-Stipec, M., Canino, G., Bird, H., Dulcan, M., Schwab-Stone, M., & Lahey, B. (1999). Parent and child contributions to child psychiatric diagnosis: Are both informants always needed? *Journal of the American Academy of Child and Adolescent Psychiatry, 38*, 1569–1579.

Jensen, P. S., Watanabe, H. K., Richters, J. E., Cortes, R., Roper, M., & Liu, S. (1995). Prevalence of mental disorder in military children and adolescents, Findings from a two-stage community survey. *Journal of the American Academy of Child and Adolescent Psychiatry, 34*, 1514–1524.

Jensen, P., Xenakis, S. N., Shervette, R. E., Bain, M. W., & Davis, H. (1989). Diagnosis and treatment of attention deficit disorder in two general hospital clinics. *Hospital and Community Psychiatry, 40*, 708–712.

Jerome, L., Gordon, M., & Hustler, P. (1994). A comparison of American and Canadian teachers' knowledge and attitudes towards attention deficit hyperactivity disorder (ADHD). *Canadian Journal of Psychiatry, 39*, 563–567.

Jessor, R., & Jessor, S. (1980). A social-psychological framework for studying drug use. In D. J. Letteri, M. Sayers, & H. W. Pearson (Eds.), *Theories on drug abuse: Selected contemporary perspectives* (pp. 95–101), Rockville, MD: National Institute on Drug Abuse.

Johanson, C. E., & Schuster, C. R. (1975). A choice procedure for drug reinforcers: Cocaine and methylphenidate in the rhesus monkey. *Journal of Pharmacology and Experimental Therapeutics, 193*, 676–688.

Johns, J. M., Louis, T. M., Becker, R. F., & Means, L. W. (1982). Behavioral effects of prenatal exposure to nicotine in guinea pigs. *Neurobehavioral Toxicology and Teratology, 4*, 365–369.

Johnson, R. C., & Rosen, L. A. (2000). Sports behavior of ADHD children. *Journal of Attention Disorders, 4*, 150–160.

Johnston, C., & Pelham, W. E. (1990). Maternal characteristics, ratings of child behavior, and mother-child interactions in families of children with externalizing disorders. *Journal of Abnormal Child Psychology, 18*, 407–417.

Johnston, L. D., O'Malley, P. M., & Bachman, J. G. (1998). Trends in prevalence rates for specific drugs within general classes. In *National survey results on drug use from Monitoring the Future Study, 1975–1997. Volume I, Secondary school students*. Washington, DC: U.S. Government Printing Office.

Jones, G., Sahakian, B., Levy, R., Warburton, D., & Gray, J. (1992). Effects of acute subcutaneous nicotine on attention, information and short-term memory in Alzheimer's disease. *Psychopharmacology, 108*, 485–494.

Kahn, C. A., Kelly, P. C., & Walker, W. O., Jr. (1995). Lead screening in children with ADHD and developmental delay. *Clinical Pediatrics, 34*, 498–501.

Kaminer, Y. (1992). Clinical implications of the relationship between attention-deficit hyperactivity disorder and psychoactive substance use disorders. *American Journal on Addictions, 1*, 257–264.

Kanbayashi, Y., Nakata, Y., Fujii, K., Kita, M., & Wada, K. (1994). ADHD-related behavior among non-referred children: Parents' ratings of DSM-III-R symptoms. *Child Psychiatry and Human Development, 25,* 13–29.

Kandel, D., & Faust, R. (1975). Sequence and stages in patterns of adolescent drug use. *Archives of General Psychiatry, 32,* 923–932.

Kandel, D. B., Kessler, R. C., & Margulies, R. A. (1978). Antecedents of adolescent initiation into stages of drug use: A developmental analysis. *Journal of Youth and Adolescence, 7,* 13–40.

Kandel, D. B., & Logan, J. A. (1984). Patterns of drug use from adolescence to young adulthood: I. Periods of risk for initiation, continued use, and discontinuation. *American Journal of Public Health, 74,* 660–666.

Kandel, D. B., Yamaguchi, K., & Chen, K. (1992). Steps in the progression in drug involvement from adolescence to adulthood: Further evidence for the gateway theory. *Journal of Studies in Alcohol, 53,* 447–457.

Kaneto, H., & Hori, A. (1988). Pharmacological interactions between dependence-liable drugs. *Japan Journal of Psychophamacology, 8,* 405–415.

Kaplan, B. J., Dewey, D., Crawford, S. G., & Fischer, G. C. (1998). Deficits in long-term memory are not characteristic of ADHD. Attention Deficit Hyperactivity Disorder. *Journal of Clinical and Experimental Neuropsychology, 20,* 518–528.

Kaplan, B. J., McNicol, J., Conte, R. A., & Moghadam, H. K. (1989). Dietary replacement in preschool-aged hyperactive boys. *Pediatrics, 83,* 7–17.

Kaplan, B. J., McNicol, J., Conte, R. A., & Moghadam, H. K. (1989). Overall nutrient intake of preschool hyperactive and normal boys. *Journal of Abnormal Child Psychology, 17,* 127.

Karetekin, C., & Asarnow, R. F. (1998). Working memory deficits in childhood-onset schizophrenia and attention-deficit/hyperactivity disorder. *Psychiatry Research, 80,* 165–176.

Kashani, J. H., Beck, N. C., Hoeper, E. W., Fallahi, C., Corcoran, M. A., McAllister, J. A., Rosenberg, T. K., & Reid, J. C. (1987). Psychiatric disorders in a community sample of adolescents. *American Journal of Psychiatry, 144,* 584–589.

Katz, L. J., Goldstein, G., & Geckle, M. (1998). Neuropsychological and personality differences between men and women with ADHD. *Journal of Attention Disorders, 2,* 239–247.

Kauffman, J. M., & Hallahan, D. P. (Eds.). (1995). *The illusion of full inclusion: A comprehensive critique of a current special education bandwagon.* Austin, TX: Pro-Ed.

Kaufman, G. (1996). Epidemiology of methylphenidate in the U.S. In *Conference report: Stimulant use in the treatment of ADHD* (pp. 19–20). Washington, DC: U.S. Department of Justice, Drug Enforcement Administration.

Kavale, K. (1982). The efficacy of stimulant drug treatment for hyperactivity: A meta-analysis. *Journal of Learning Disabilities, 15,* 280–289.

Kavale, K. A., & Forness, S. R. (1983). Hyperactivity and diet treatment: A meta-analysis of the Feingold hypothesis. *Journal of Learning Disabilities, 16,* 324–330.

Kavale, K. A., & Forness, S. R. (1996). Learning disabilities grows up: Rehabilitation issues for individuals with learning disabilities. *Journal of Rehabilitation, 62,* 34–41.

Kavale, K. A., & Forness, S. R. (2000). Policy decisions in special education. The role of meta-analysis. In R. M. Gersten & E. P. Schiller (Eds.), *Contemporary special education research: Synthesis of knowledge in critical interactional issues* (pp. 281–326). Mahwah, NJ: Erlbaum.

Kazdin, A. E. (1996). Problem solving and parent management in treating aggressive and antisocial behavior. In E. D. Hibbs & P. S. Jensen (Eds.), *Psychosocial treatments for child and adolescent disorders: Empirically based strategies for clinical practice* (pp. 377–408), Washington, DC: American Psychological Association.

Kazdin, A. E., & Weisz, J. R. (1998). Identifying and developing empirically supported child and adolescent treatments. *Journal of Consulting and Clinical Psychology, 66,* 19–36.

Keeley, K. A., & Light, A. L. (1985). Gradual vs. abrupt withdrawal of methylphenidate in two older dependent males. *Journal of Substance Abuse Treatment, 2,* 123–123.

Kellam, S. G., Ensminger, M. E., & Simon, M. B. (1980). Mental health in first grade and teenage drug, alcohol, and cigarette use. *Drug and Alcohol Dependence, 5,* 273–304.

Kelleher, K. J. (Principal Investigator). (1994, June 1–1998, April 30). *Management of psychosocial problems in primary care* (Grant No. MH 50629). Rockville, MD: National Institute of Mental Health.

Kelleher, K. J., Childs, G. E., Wasserman, R. C., McInerny, T. K., Nutting, P. A., & Gardner, W. P. (1997). Insurance status and recognition of psychosocial problems: A report from the Pediatric Research in Office Settings and the Ambulatory Sentinel Practice Networks. *Archives of Pediatrics and Adolescent Medicine, 151,* 1109–1115.

Kelleher, K. J., Hohmann, A. A., & Larson, D. B. (1989). Prescription of psychotropics to children in office-based practice. *American Journal of Diseases of Children, 143,* 855–859.

Kelleher, K. J., McInerny, T., Gardner, W., Childs, G.,

Wasserman, R., & Nutting, P. (2000). Increasing identification of psychosocial problems: 1979–1997. *Pediatrics, 105*, 1313–1321.

Kelleher, K. J., & Starfield, B. (1990). Use of health care by children receiving mental health treatment. *Pediatrics, 185*(1), 114–118.

Kelley, M. L., & McCain, A. P. (1995). Promoting academic performance in inattentive children: The relative efficacy of school-home notes with and without response-cost. *Behavior Modification, 19*, 357–375.

Kendall, P. C. (1994). Treating anxiety disorders in children: Results of a randomized clinical trial. *Journal of Consulting and Clinical Psychology, 62*, 100–110.

Kendall, P. C., Flannery-Schroeder, E., Panichelli-Mindel, S. M., Southam-Gerow, M., Henin, A., & Warman, M. (1997). Therapy for youths with anxiety disorders: A second randomized clinical trial. *Journal of Consulting and Clinical Psychology, 65*, 366–380.

Kendall, P. C., & Gosch, E. A. (1994). Cognitive-behavioral interventions. In T. H. Ollendick, N. J. King, & W. Yule (Eds.), *International handbook of phobic and anxiety disorders in children and adolescents* (pp. 415–438). New York: Plenum Press.

Kendler, K. S., Thornton, L. M., & Pedersen, N. L. (2000). Tobacco consumption in Swedish twins reared apart and reared together. *Archives of General Psychiatry, 57*, 886–892.

Kennedy, J. L., Richter, P., Swanson, J. M., Wigal, S. B., LaHoste, G. J., & Sunohara, G. (1997). *Association of dopamine D4 receptor gene and ADHD.* Paper presented at the annual meeting of the American Psychiatric Association, San Diego, CA.

Kent, R. N., & O'Leary, K. D. (1976). A controlled evaluation of behavior modification with conduct problem children. *Journal of Consulting and Clinical Psychology, 44*, 586–596.

Kent, R. N., & O'Leary, K. D. (1977). Treatment of conduct problem children: BA and/or PhD therapists. *Behavior Therapy, 8*, 653–658.

Keogh, B. K. (1989). Applying temperament research to school. In G. A. Kohnstamm, J. E. Bates, & M. K. Rothbart (Eds.), *Temperament in childhood* (pp. 437–450). New York: Wiley.

Kershner, J., & Hawke, W. (1979). Megavitamins and learning disorders: A controlled double-blind experiment. *Journal of Nutrition, 159*, 819–826.

Kessel, J. B., & Zimmerman, M. (1993). Reporting errors in studies of the diagnostic performance of self-administered questionnaires: Extent of the problem, recommendations for standardized presentation of results, and implications for the peer review process. *Psychological Assessment, 5*, 395–399.

Kessler, R. C., McGonagle, K. A., Zhao, S., Nelson, C.

B., Hughes, M., Eshleman, S., Wittchen, H., & Kendler, K. S. (1994). Lifetime and 12-month prevalence of DSM-III-R psychiatric disorders in the United States. *Archives of General Psychiatry, 51*, 8–19.

Khantzian, E. J. (1983). An extreme case of cocaine dependence and marked improvement with methylphenidate treatment. *American Journal of Psychiatry, 140*, 784–785.

Khantzian, E. J. (1985). The self-medication hypothesis of addictive disorders: Focus on heroin and cocaine dependence. *American Journal of Psychiatry, 142*, 1259–1264.

Khantzian, E. J. (1997). The self-medication hypothesis of substance use disorders: A reconsideration and recent applications. *Harvard Review of Psychiatry, 4*, 231–244.

King-Sears, M. E. (1997). Best academic practices for inclusive classrooms. *Focus on Exceptional Children, 29*(7), 1–22.

Kishorekumar, R., Yagnik, P., & Dhopesh, V. (1985). Acute myopathy in a drug abuser following an attempted neck vein injection. *Journal of Neurological and Neurosurgical Psychiatry, 48*, 843–844.

Klasen, H., & Goodman, R. (2000). Parents and GPs at cross purposes over hyperactivity: A qualitative study of possible barriers to treatment. *British Journal of General Practice, 50*, 199–202.

Kleber, H., & Gawin, F. H. (1986). Psychopharmacological trials in cocaine abuse treatment. Annual meeting of the American Psychiatric Association (1985, Dallas, TX). *American Journal of Drug and Alcohol Abuse, 12*, 235–246.

Klein, D. (1980). Treatment of anxiety, personality, somatoform and factitious disorders. In D. Klein, R. Gittelman, F. Quitkin, & A. Rifkin (Eds.), *Diagnosis and drug treatment of psychiatric disorders: Adults and children* (pp. 539–573). Baltimore: Williams & Wilkins.

Klein, R. G. (1993). Clinical efficacy of methylphenidate in children and adolescents. *Encephale, 19*, 89–93.

Klein, R. G., & Abikoff, H. (1997). Behavior therapy and methylphenidate in the treatment of children with ADHD. *Journal of Attention Disorders, 2*, 89–114.

Klein, R., Abikoff, H., Klass, E., Ganales, D., Seese, L., & Pollack, S. (1997). Clinical efficacy of methylphenidate in conduct disorder with and without attention deficit hyperactivity disorder. *Archives of General Psychiatry, 54*, 1073–1080.

Klein, R., Klass, E., & Abikoff, H. (1994). Controlled trial of methylphenidate, lithium, and placebo in children and adolescents with conduct disorders. *Proceedings of the annual meeting of the Society for Research in Child and Adolescent Psychopathology* (Vol. 3). London, UK.

Klein, R. G., & Mannuzza, S. (1991). Long-term outcome of hyperactive children: A review. *Journal of the American Academy of Child and Adolescent Psychiatry, 30,* 383–387.

Klein, R. G., & Mannuzza, S. (1999). The importance of childhood hyperactivity in the development of substance use disorders. In D. Bailly & J. Venisse (Eds.), *Addictions et psychiatrie* (pp. 107–122). Paris, France: Editions Masson.

Klorman, R., Brumagham, J., Fitzpatrick, P., & Burgstedt, A. (1990). Clinical effects of a controlled trial of methylphenidate on adolescents with Attention Deficit Disorder. *Journal of the American Academy of Child and Adolescent Psychiatry, 29,* 702–709.

Klorman, R., Brumaghim, J. T., Salzman, L. F., Strauss, J., Borgstedt, A. D., McBride, M. C., & Loeb, S. (1988). Effects of methylphenidate on Attention-Deficit Hyperactivity Disorder with and without aggressive/noncompliant features. *Journal of Abnormal Psychology, 97,* 413–422.

Kolta, M. G., Shreve, P., De Souza, V., & Uretsky, N. J. (1985). Time course of the development of the enhanced behavioral and biochemical responses to amphetamine after pretreatment with amphetamine. *Neuropharmacology, 24,* 823–829.

Kolta, M., Shreve, P., & Uretsky, N. J. (1985). Effects of methylphenidate pretreatment on the behavioral and biochemical response to amphetamine. *European Journal of Pharmacology, 117,* 279–282.

Konkol, R., Fischer, M., & Newby, R. (1990). Double-blind, placebo-controlled stimulant trial in children with Tourette's syndrome and ADHD: Abstract. *Annals of Neurology, 28,* 424.

Koriath, U., Gualtieri, C. T., van Bourgondien, M. E., Quade, D., & Werry, J. S. (1985). Construct validity of clinical diagnosis in pediatric psychiatry: Relationship among measures. *Journal of the American Academy of Child Psychiatry, 24*(4), 429–436.

Korkman, M., & Pesonen, A. E. (1994). A comparison of neuropsychological test profiles of children with attention deficit-hyperactivity disorder and/or learning disabilities. *Journal of Learning Disabilities, 27,* 383–392.

Kozielec, T., & Starobrat-Hermelin, B. (1997). Assessment of magnesium levels in children with ADHD. *Magnesium Research, 10,* 143–148.

Kozielec, T., Starobrat-Hermelin, B., & Kotkowiak, L. (1994). Deficiency of certain trace elements in children with hyperactivity. *Psychiatria Polska, 28,* 345–53.

Kramer, J., & Loney, J. (1982). Childhood hyperactivity and substance abuse: A review of the literature. *Advances in Learning and Behavioral Disabilities, 1,* 225–259.

Kramer, J., Loney, J., & Whaley-Klahn, M. A. (1981). *The role of prescribed medication in hyperactive*

youths' substance use. Paper presented at the 1981 annual meeting of the American Psychological Association, Los Angeles.

Kratter, J. (1983). The use of meditation in the treatment of attention deficit disorder with hyperactivity. *Dissertation Abstracts International, 44,* 1965.

Krieger, G. D. R. (1985). Reduction of hyperactivity using progressive muscle relaxation imagery and autogenic exercises with electromyographic biofeedback. *Dissertation Abstracts International, 46*(10), 3617B.

Kruesi, M. J., Rapoport, J. L., Berg, C., Stables, G., & Bou, E. (1987). Seven-day carbohydrate and other nutrient intakes of preschool boys alleged to be behavior-responsive to sugar and their peers. In W. B. Essman (Ed.), *Nutrients and brain function* (pp. 133–137). Basel, Switzerland: Karger.

Krummel, D. A., Seligson, F. H., & Guthrie, H. A. (1996). Hyperactivity: Is candy causal? *Critical Reviews in Food Science and Nutrition, 36,* 31–47.

Kugel, R. B., & Alexander, T. (1963, April). The effect of a central nervous system stimulant (deanol) on behavior. *Pediatrics,* 651-655.

Kuhne, M., Schachar, R., & Tannock, R. (1997). Impact of comorbid oppositional or conduct problems on attention-deficit hyperactivity disorder. *Journal of the American Academy of Child and Adolescent Psychiatry, 36,* 1715–1725.

Kuperman, S., Johnson, B., Arndt, S., Lindgren S., & Wolraich, M. (1996). Quantitative EEG differences in a nonclinical sample of children with ADHD and undifferentiated ADD. *Journal of the American Academy of Child and Adolescent Psychiatry, 35,* 1009–1017.

Kupietz, S. S., & Balka, E. B. (1976). Alterations in the vigilance performance of children receiving amitriptyline and methylphenidate pharmacotherapy. *Psychopharmacology, 50,* 29–33.

Kwasman, A., Tinsley, B. J., & Lepper, H. S. (1995). Pediatrician's knowledge and attitudes concerning the diagnosis and treatment of attention deficit and hyperactivity disorders. A national survey approach. *Archives of Pediatrics and Adolescent Medicine, 149,* 1211–1216.

Lahey, B. B., Applegate, B., McBurnett, K., Biederman, J., Greenhill, L., Hynd, G. W., Barkley, R. A., Newcorn, J., Jensen, P., Richters, J., Garfinkel, B., Kerdyk, L., Frick, P. J., Ollendick, T., Perez, D., Hart, E. L., Waldman, I., & Shaffer, D. (1994). DSM-IV Field Trials for attention deficit hyperactivity disorder in children and adolescents. *American Journal of Psychiatry, 151,* 1673–1685.

Lahey, B. B., Carlson, C. L., & Frick, P. J. (1997). Attention deficit disorder without hyperactivity: A review of research relevant to DSM-IV. In T. A. Widiger, A. J. Frances, W. Davis, & M. First (Eds.), *DSM-IV sourcebook* (Vol. 1, pp. 163–188). Washington, DC: American Psychiatric Press.

Lahey, B. B., Flagg, E. W., Bird, H. R., Schwab-Stone, M. E., Canino, G., Dulcan, M. K., Leaf, P. J., Davies, M., Brogan, D., Bourdon, K., Horwitz, S. M., Rubio-Stipec, M., Freeman, D. H., Lichtman, J. H., Shaffer, D., Goodman, S. H., Narrow, W. E., Weissman, M. M., Kandel, D. B., Jensen, P. S., Richters, J. E., & Regier, D. A. (1996). The NIMH methods for the epidemiology of child and adolescent mental disorders (MECA) study: Background and methodology. *Journal of the American Academy of Child and Adolescent Psychiatry, 35*, 855–864.

Lahey, B. B., McBurnett, K., & Loeber, R. (2000). Are attention-deficit hyperactivity disorder and oppositional defiant disorder developmental precursors to conduct disorder? In M. Lewis & A. Sameroff (Eds.), *Handbook of developmental psychopathology* (pp. 431–446). New York: Plenum Press.

Lahey, B., McBurnett, K., Piacentinit, J., Hartdagen, S., Walker, J., Frick, P., & Hynd, G. (1987). Agreement of parent and teacher rating scales with comprehensive clinical assessments of attention deficit disorder with hyperactivity. *Journal of Psychological Behavioral Assessment, 9*, 429–439.

Lahey, B. B., Miller, T. L., Gordon, R. A., & Riley, A. (1999). Developmental epidemiology of the disruptive behavior disorders. In H. Quay & A. Hogan (Eds.), *Handbook of the disruptive behavior disorders* (pp. 23–48). New York: Kluwers Academic.

Lahey, B. B., Pelham, W. E., Schaughency, E. A., Atkins, M. S., Murphy, H. A., Hynd, G. W., Russo, M., Hartdagen, S., & Lorys-Vernon, A. (1988). Dimensions and types of attention deficit disorder. *Journal of the American Academy of Child and Adolescent Psychiatry, 27*, 330–335.

Lahey, B. B., Pelham, W. E., Stein, M. A., Loney, J., Trapani, C., Nugent, K., Kipp, H., Schmidt, E., Lee, S., Cale, M., Gold, E., Hartung, C. M., Willcutt, E., & Baumann, B. (1998). Validity of DSM-IV attention-deficit/ hyperactivity disorder for younger children. *Journal of the American Academy of Child and Adolescent Psychiatry, 37*(7), 695–702.

LaHoste, G. J., Swanson, J. M., Wigal, S. B., Glabe, C., Wigal, T., King, N., & Kennedy, J. L. (1996). Dopamine D4 receptor gene polymorphism is associated with attention deficit hyperactivity disorder. *Molecular Psychiatry, 1*, 121–124.

Lambert, N. M. (1982). Temperament profiles of hyperactive children. *American Journal of Orthopsychiatry, 52*, 458–467.

Lambert, N. M. (1988). Adolescent outcomes for hyperactive children: Perspectives on general and specific patterns of childhood risk for adolescent educational, social, and mental health problems. *American Psychologist, 43*, 786–799.

Lambert, N. M. (1998). *Stimulant treatment as a risk factor for nicotine use and stimulant abuse* [abstract].

Paper presented at NIH Consensus Development Conference on Diagnosis and Treatment of Attention Deficit Hyperactivity Disorder, Bethesda, MD.

Lambert, N. M., & Hartsough, C. S. (1987). The measurement of attention deficit disorder with behavior ratings of parents. *American Journal of Orthopsychiatry, 57*, 361–370.

Lambert, N. M., & Hartsough, C. S. (1998). Prospective study of tobacco smoking and substance dependencies among samples of ADHD and non-ADHD subjects. *Journal of Learning Disabilities, 31*, 533–544.

Lambert, N. M., Hartsough, C. S., & Sandoval, J. (1990). *Children's Attention and Adjustment Survey home and school versions.* Circle Pines, MN: American Guidance Service.

Lambert, N. M., Hartsough, C. S., Sassone, S., & Sandoval, J. (1987). Persistence of hyperactive symptoms from childhood to adolescence and associated outcomes. *American Journal of Orthopsychiatry, 57*, 22–32.

Lambert, N. M., Sandoval, J., & Sassone, D. (1978). Prevalence of hyperactivity in elementary school children as a function of social system definers. *American Journal of Orthopsychiatry, 48*, 446–463.

Lambert, N. M., Sandoval, J., & Sassone D. (1979). Prevalence of treatment regimens of children considered to be hyperactive. *American Journal of Orthopsychiatry, 49*, 482–490.

Lambert, N. M., Sandoval, J., & Sassone, D. M. (1981). Prevalence of hyperactivity and related treatments among elementary school children. In K. D. Gadow & J. Loney (Eds.), *Psychosocial aspects of drug treatment for hyperactivity* [AAAS Selected Symposium Series] (pp. 249–294). Boulder, CO: Westview Press.

Lamminaki, T. A., Narhi, V., Lyytinen, H., & Todd de Barra, H. (1995). Attention deficit hyperactivity disorder subtypes: Are there differences in academic problems? *Developmental Neuropsychology, 11*, 297–310.

Lanau, F., Zenner, M., Civelli, O., & Hartman, D. (1997). Epinephrine and norepinephrine act as potent agonists at the recombinant human dopamine D4 receptor. *Journal of Neurochemistry, 68*, 804–812.

Langer, D. H., Sweeney, K. P., Bartenbach, D. E., Davis, P. M., & Menander, K. B. (1986). Evidence of lack of abuse or dependence following pemoline treatment: Results of a retrospective survey. *Drug and Alcohol Dependency, 17*, 213–227.

Laucht, M., Esser, G., Baving, L., Gerhold, M., Hoesch, I., Ihle, W., Steigleider, P., Stock, B., Stoehr, R. M., Weindrich, D., & Schmidt, M. H. (2000). Behavioral sequelae of perinatal insults and early family adversity at eight years of age. *Journal of the American Academy of Child and Adolescent Psychiatry, 39*, 1229–1237.

Lauder, J. M. (1983). Hormonal and humoral influences

on brain development. *Psychoneuroendocrinology, 8,* 121–155.

Lauder, J. M. (1988). Neurotransmitters as morphogens. *Progress in Brain Research, 73,* 365–387.

Laufer, M., & Denhoff, E. (1957). Hyperkinetic behavior syndrome in children. *Journal of Pediatrics, 50,* 463–474.

Lavange, L. M., Stearns, S. C., Lafata, J. E., Koch, G. G., & Shah, B. V. (1996). Innovative strategies using SUDAAN for analysis of health surveys with complex samples. *Statistical Methods in Medical Research, 5,* 311–329.

Law, S., & Schachar, R. (1999). Do typical clinical doses of methylphenidate cause tics in children treated for ADHD? *Journal of the American Academy of Child and Adolescent Psychiatry, 38,* 944–951.

Leaf, P. J., Alegria, M., Cohen, P., Goodman, S. H., Horwitz, S. M., Hoven, C. W., Narrow, W. E., Vaden-Kiernan, M., & Regier, D. A. (1996). Mental health service use in the community and schools: Results from the four-community MECA study. *Journal of the American Academy of Child and Adolescent Psychiatry, 35,* 889–897.

Lee, S. W. (1991). Biofeedback as a treatment for childhood hyperactivity: A critical review of the literature. *Psychological Reports,* pp. 163–192.

LeFever, G. B., Dawson, K. V., & Morrow, A. L. (1999). The extent of drug therapy for attention deficit-hyperactivity disorder among children in public schools. *American Journal of Public Health, 89,* 1359–1364.

Leibson, C., Katusic, S., Barbaresi, W., Ransom, J., & O'Brien, P. (2001). Use and costs of medical care for children and adolescents with and without attention-deficit/hyperactivity disorder. *Journal of the American Medical Association, 285,* 60–66.

Leith, N. J., & Barrett, R. J. (1981). Self-stimulation and amphetamine: Tolerance to d and l isomers and cross tolerance to cocaine and methylphenidate. *Psychopharmacology, 74,* 23–28.

Lester, M. L., Thatcher, R. W., & Monroe-Lord, L. (1982). Refined carbohydrate intake, hair cadmium levels, and cognitive functioning in children. *Nutrition and Behavior, 1,* 3–13.

Lett, B. W. (1989). Repeated exposures intensify rather than diminish the rewarding effects of amphetamine, morphine and cocaine. *Psychopharmacology, 98,* 357–362.

Leung, P. W. L., & Connolly, K. J. (1997). Test of two views of impulsivity in hyperactive and conduct-disordered children. *Developmental Medicine and Child Neurology, 39,* 574–582.

Leung, P. W., Luk, S. L., Ho, T. P., Taylor, E., Mak, F. L., & Bacon-Shone, J. (1996). The diagnosis and prevalence of hyperactivity in Chinese schoolboys. *British Journal of Psychiatry, 168*(4), 486–496.

Levin, E., Conners, C., Sparrow, E., Hinton, S., Erhardt, D., Meck, W., Rose, J., & March, J. (1996). Nicotine effects on adults with attention-deficit/hyperactivity disorder. *Psychopharmacology, 123,* 55–63.

Levin, F., Evans, S. M., Lugo, L., Seham, J., Baird, D., & Kleber, H. (1996). *ADHD in cocaine abusers: Psychiatric comorbidity and pattern of drug use.* Paper presented at the annual meeting of College on Problems of Drug Dependence, San Juan, Puerto Rico.

Levin, F., Evans, S., McDowell, D., Brooks, D., Rhum, M., & Kleber, H. (1998). *Bupropion treatment for adult ADHD and cocaine abuse.* Paper presented at the annual meeting of College on Problems of Drug Dependence, Scottsdale, AZ.

Levin, F. R., Evans, S. M., McDowell, D., & Kleber, H. D. (1997). Methylphenidate treatment for cocaine abusers with adult attention-deficit/hyperactivity disorder: A pilot study. *Journal of Clinical Psychiatry, 58,* 1–21.

Levin, F. R., Evans, S. M., Rosenthal, M., & Kleber, H. D. (1997). *Psychiatric comorbidity in cocaine abusers in outpatient settings or a therapeutic community.* Paper presented at the annual meeting of College on Problems of Drug Dependence, Nashville, TN.

Levin, F. R., & Kleber, H. D. (1995). Attention-deficit hyperactivity disorder and substance abuse: Relationships and implications for treatment. *Harvard Review of Psychiatry, 2,* 246–258.

Levine, B., Caplan, Y. H., & Kauffman, G. (1986) Fatality resulting from methylphenidate overdose. *Journal of Analytical Toxicology, 10,* 209–210.

Levine, M. D. (1994). *Educational care.* Cambridge MA: Educators Publishing.

Levine, M. D. (1999). Attention and dysfunctions of attention. In M. D. Levine, W. B. Carey, & A. C. Crocker (Eds.), *Developmental-behavioral pediatrics* (3rd ed., pp. 499–519). Philadelphia: Saunders.

Levine, M. D., Busch, B., & Aufseeser, C. (1982). The dimension of inattention among children with school problems. *Pediatrics, 29*(7), 387–395.

Levy, F. (1991). The dopamine theory of attention deficit hyperactivity disorder (ADHD). *The Australian and New Zealand Journal of Psychiatry, 25,* 277–283.

Levy, F., Hay, D. A., McStephen, M., Wood, C., & Waldman, I. (1997), Attention-deficit hyperactivity disorder: a category or a continuum? Genetic analysis of a large-scale twin study. *Journal of the American Academy of Child and Adolescent Psychiatry, 36,* 737–744.

Lewinsohn, P. M., Hops, H., Roberts, R. E., Seeley, J.

R., & Andrews, J. A. (1993). Adolescent psychopathology, I. Prevalence and incidence of depression and other DSM-III-R disorders in high school students. *Journal of Abnormal Psychology, 102*, 133–144.

Lewis, J. A., & Young, R. (1975). Deanol and methylphenidate in minimal brain dysfunction. *Clinical Pharmacology and Therapeutics, 17*, 534-540.

Lewman, L. V. (1972). Fatal pulmonary hypertension from intravenous injection of methylphenidate (Ritalin) tablets. *Human Pathology, 3*, 67–70.

Lezak, M. D. (1995). *Neuropsychological assessment* (3rd ed.). New York: Oxford University Press.

Li, X. R., Su, L. Y., Townes, B. D., & Varley, C. K. (1989). Diagnosis of attention deficit disorder with hyperactivity in Chinese boys. *Journal of the American Academy of Child and Adolescent Psychiatry, 28*(4), 497–500.

Lilienfeld, S. O., & Waldman, I. D. (1990). The relation between childhood attention-deficit hyperactivity disorder and adult antisocial behavior reexamined: The problem of heterogeneity. *Clinical Psychology Review, 10*, 699–725.

Lindell, T. D., Porter, J. M., & Langstron, C. (1972). Intra-arterial injections of oral medications: Complications of drug addition. *New England Journal of Medicine, 287*, 1132–1133.

Linden, M., Habib, T., & Radojevic, V. (1996). A controlled study of the effects of EEG biofeedback on cognition and behavior of children with attention deficit disorder and learning disabilities. *Biofeedback and Self-Regulation, 21*, 35–49.

Lindgren, S., Wolraich, M. L., Stromquist, A., Davis, C., Milich, R., & Watson, D. (1989). *Diagnosis of attention deficit hyperactivity disorder by primary care physicians.* Paper presented at a research conference for Mental Health Services for Children and Adolescents in Primary Care Settings, New Haven, CT.

Lindgren, S., Wolraich, M. L., Stromquist, A., Davis, C., Milich, R., & Watson, D. (1990). *Diagnostic heterogeneity in attention deficit hyperactivity disorder.* Paper presented at the fourth annual NIMH International Research Conference on the Classification and Treatment of Mental Disorders in General Medical Settings, Bethesda, MD.

Lipsky, D. K., & Gartner, A. (1996). Inclusion, school restructuring, and the remaking of the American society. *Harvard Education Review, 66*, 762–796.

Lipton, M. A., & Mayo, J. P. (1983). Diet and hyperkinesis—An update. *Journal of the American Dietetic Association, 83*, 132–134.

Lloyd, J. W., Forness, S. R., & Kavale, K. A. (1998). Some methods are more effective than others. *Intervention in School and Clinic, 33*, 195–200.

Lochman, J. E. (1992). Cognitive-behavioral intervention with aggressive boys: Three-year follow up and preventive effects. *Journal of Consulting and Clinical Psychology, 60*, 426–432.

Lochman, J. E., & Lenhart, L. A. (1993). Anger coping intervention for aggressive children: Conceptual models and outcome effects. *Clinical Psychology Review, 13*, 785–805.

Loeber, R., & Farrington, D. (Eds.). (1998). *Serious and violent juvenile offenders: Risk factors and successful interventions.* Thousand Oaks, CA: Sage.

Loeber, R., & Stouthamer-Loeber, M. (1998). Development of juvenile aggression and violence: Some common misconceptions and controversies. *American Psychologist, 53*, 242–259.

Logan, G. D. (1994). On the ability to inhibit thought and action: A user's guide to the stop signal paradigm. In D. Dagenbach & T. H. Carr (Eds.), *Inhibitory processes in attention, memory, and language* (pp. 189–239). San Diego: Academic Press.

Logan, G. D., & Cowan, W. B. (1984). On the ability to inhibit thought and action: A theory of an act of control. *Psychological Review, 91*, 295–327.

Loney, J. (1980). The Iowa theory of substance abuse among hyperactive adolescents. In D. J. Letteri, M. Sayers, & H. W. Pearson (Eds.), *Theories on drug abuse: Selected contemporary perspectives* (pp. 131–136), Rockville, MD: National Institute on Drug Abuse.

Loney, J. (1988). Substance abuse in adolescents: Diagnostic issues derived from studies of attention deficit disorder with hyperactivity. *NIDA Research Monograph, 77*, 19–26.

Loney, J., Kramer, J., & Milich, R. (1981). The hyperkinetic child grows up: Predictors of symptoms, delinquency, and achievement at follow-up. In K. Gadow & J. Loney (Eds.), *Psychosocial aspects of drug treatment for hyperactivity* (pp. 381–415). Boulder, CO: Westview Press.

Loney, J., & Milich, R. (1982). Hyperactivity, inattention, and aggression in clinical practice. In M. Wolraich & D. K. Routh (Eds.), *Advances in developmental behavioral pediatrics* (Vol. 2, pp. 113–147), Greenwich, CT: JAI Press.

Loney, J., Paternite, C. E., Schwartz, J. E., & Roberts, M. A. (1997). Associations between clinic-referred boys and their fathers on childhood inattention-overactivity and aggression dimensions. *Journal of Abnormal Child Psychology, 25*, 499–510.

Loney, J., Weissenberger, F. E., Woolson, R. F., & Lichty, E. C. (1979). Comparing psychological and pharmacological treatments for hyperkinetic boys and their classmates. *Journal of Abnormal Child Psychology, 7*, 133–143.

Loney, J., Whaley-Klahn, M. A., Kosier, T., & Conboy, J. (1983). Prospective studies of crime and delinquency

In K. T. Van Dusen & S. A. Mednick (Eds.), *Hyperactive boys and their brothers at 21: Predictors of aggressive and antisocial outcome* (pp. 181–207). Boston: Kluwer-Nijhoff.

Long, N., Rickert, V. I., & Ashcraft, E. W. (1993). Bibliotherapy as an adjunct to stimulant medication in the treatment of attention-deficit hyperactivity disorder. *Journal of Pediatric Health Care, 7*, 82–88.

Lonigan, C. J., Elbert, J. C., & Johnson, S. B. (1998). Empirically supported psychosocial interventions for children: An overview. *Journal of Clinical Child Psychology, 27*, 138–145.

Lopez, M., Forness, S. R., MacMillan, D. L., Bocian, K., & Gresham, F. M. (1996). Children with attention deficit hyperactivity disorder and emotional and behavioral disorders in the primary grades: Inappropriate placement in the LD category. *Education and Treatment of Children, 19*, 286–299.

Losier, B. J., McGrath, P. J., & Klein, R. M. (1996). Error patterns on the Continuous Performance Test in non-medicated and medicated samples of children with and without ADHD: A meta-analytic review. *Journal of Child Psychology and Psychiatry, 37*, 971–987.

Lou, H. C. (1996). Etiology and pathogenesis of attention-deficit hyperactivity disorder (ADHD): Significance of prematurity and perinatal hypoxic-haemodynamic encephalopathy. *Acta Paediatrica, 85*, 1266–1271.

Lou, H. C., Henriksen, L., & Bruhn, P. (1984). Focal cerebral hypoperfusion in children with dysphasia and/or attention deficit disorder. *Archives of Neurology, 41*(8), 825–829.

Lou, H. C., Henriksen, L., & Bruhn, P. (1990). Focal cerebral dysfunction in developmental learning disabilities. *Lancet, 335*(8680), 8–11.

Lou, H. C., Henriksen, L., Bruhn, P., Borner, H., & Nielsen, J. B. (1989), Striatal dysfunction in attention deficit and hyperkinetic disorder. *Archives of Neurology, 46*, 48–52.

Lubar, J. F. (1991). Discourse on the development of EEG diagnostics and biofeedback for attention-deficit/hyperactivity disorders. *Biofeedback and Self-Regulation, 16*, 201–225.

Lubar, J. F., & Shouse, M. N. (1977). Use of biofeedback in the treatment of seizure disorders and hyperactivity. In B. B. Lahey & A. E. Kazdin (Eds.), *Advances in clinical child psychology* (Vol. 1, pp. 203–265). New York: Plenum Press.

Lubar, J. F., Swartwood, M. O., Swartwood, J. N., & O'Donnell, P. H. (1995). Evaluation of the Effectiveness of EEG Neurofeedback training for ADHD in a clinical setting as measured by changes in TOVA scores, behavior ratings, and WISC-R performance. *Biofeedback and Self-Regulation 20,* 83–99.

Luh, J., Pliszka., S., Olvers, R., & Tatum, R. (1996). *An open trial of venlafaxine in the treatment of attention deficit hyperactivity disorder: A pilot study.* San Antonio: University of Texas Health Science Center.

Luk, S. L., Leung, P. W., & Lee, P. L. (1988). Conners' Teacher Rating Scale in Chinese children in Hong Kong. *Journal of Child Psychology and Psychiatry, 29*(2), 165–174.

Lundquest, D. E., Young, W. K., & Edland, J. F. (1987). Maternal death associated with intravenous methylphenidate (Ritalin) and pentazocine (Talwin) abuse. *Journal of Forensic Science, 32*, 798–801.

Lynskey, M. T., & Fergusson, D. M. (1995). Childhood conduct problems, attention deficit behaviors, and adolescent alcohol, tobacco, and illicit drug use. *Journal of Abnormal Child Psychology, 23*, 281–302.

Lyon, G. (1994). Learning disabilities. In K. L. Freiberg (Ed.), *Educating exceptional children* (10th ed.). Guilford, CT: Dushkin-McGraw-Hill.

Lytton, H. (1990). Child and parent effects in boys' conduct disorder: A reinterpretation. *Developmental Psychology, 26*, 683–697.

Maag, J. W., & Reid, R. (1994). Attention-deficit hyperactivity disorder: A functional approach to assessment and treatment. *Behavioral Disorders, 35*, 1237–1246.

MacMillan, D. L., Gresham, F. M., & Bocian, K. (1998). Discrepancy between definition of learning disabilities and school practices: An empirical investigation. *Journal of Learning Disabilities, 31*(4), 314–326.

MacMillan, D. L., Gresham, F. M., & Forness, S. R. (1996). Full inclusion: An empirical perspective. *Behavioral Disorders, 21*, 146–160.

Magnusson, P., Smari, J., Gretarsdottie, H., & Prandardottir, H. (1999). Attention-deficit/hyperactivity symptoms in Icelandic schoolchildren: Assessment with the attention deficit/hyperactivity rating scale IV. *Scandinavian Journal of Psychology, 40*(4), 301–306.

Malhotra, S., & Santosh, P. J. (1998). An open clinical trial of buspirone in children with attention deficit/hyperactivity disorder. *Journal of the American Academy of Child and Adolescent Psychiatry, 37*, 364–371.

Mann, C. A., Lubar, J. F., Zimmerman, A. W., Miller, C. A., & Muenchen, R. A. (1992). Quantitative analysis of EEG in boys with attention-deficit-hyperactivity disorder: Controlled study with clinical implications. *Pediatric Neurology, 8*(1), 30–36.

Mann, E. M., Ikeda, Y., Mueller, C. W., Takahashi, A., Tao, K. T., Humris, E., Li, B. L., & Chin, D. (1992). Cross-cultural differences in rating hyperactive-disruptive behaviors in children. *American Journal of Psychiatry, 149*(11), 1539–1542.

Mannuzza, S., & Gittelman, R. (1986). Informant variance in the diagnostic assessment of hyperactive children as young adults. In J. E. Barrett & R. M. Rose (Ed.), *Mental disorders in the community* (pp. 243–254), New York: Guilford Press.

Mannuzza, S., Gittelman-Klein, R., Bessler, A., Malloy, P., & LaPadula, M. (1993). Adult outcome of hyperactive boys: Educational achievement, occupational rank, and psychiatric status. *Archives of General Psychiatry, 50,* 565–576.

Mannuzza, S., Gittelman-Klein, R., Bonagura, N., Malloy, P., Giampino, T. L., & Addalli, K. A. (1991). Hyperactive boys almost grown up: V. Replication of psychiatric status. *Archives of General Psychiatry, 48,* 77–83.

Mannuzza, S., Gittelman-Klein, R., Konig, P. H., & Giampino, T. L. (1989). Hyperactive boys almost grown up: IV. Criminality and its relationship to psychiatric status. *Archives of General Psychiatry, 46,* 1073–1079.

Mannuzza, S., & Klein, R. G. (1999). Adolescent and adult outcomes in attention-deficit/hyperactivity disorder. In H. L. Quay (Ed.), *Handbook of disruptive behavior disorders* (pp. 279–294). New York: Kluwer Academic/Plenum Press.

Mannuzza, S., & Klein, R. G. (2000). Long-term prognosis in attention-deficit/hyperactivity disorder. *Child and Adolescent Psychiatric Clinics of North America, 9,* 711–726.

Mannuzza, S., Klein, R. G., & Addalli, K. A. (1991). Young adult mental status of hyperactive boys and their brothers: A prospective follow-up study. *Journal of the American Academy of Child and Adolescent Psychiatry, 30,* 743–751.

Mannuzza, S., Klein, R. G., Bessler, A., Malloy, P., & Hynes, M. E. (1997). Educational and occupational outcome of hyperactive boys grown up. *Journal of the American Academy of Child and Adolescent Psychiatry, 36,* 1222–1227.

Mannuzza, S., Klein R. G., Bessler, A., Malloy, P., & LaPadula, M. (1993). Adult outcome of hyperactive boys: Educational achievement, occupational rank, and psychiatric status. *Archives of General Psychiatry, 50,* 565–576.

Mannuzza, S., Klein, R. G., Bessler, A., Malloy, P., & LaPadula, M. (1998). Adult psychiatric status of hyperactive boys grown up. *American Journal of Psychiatry, 155,* 493–498.

Mannuzza, S., Klein, R. G., Bonagura, N., Malloy, P., Giampino, T. L., & Addalli, K. A. (1991). Hyperactive boys almost grown up: V. Replication of psychiatric status. *Archives of General Psychiatry, 48,* 77–83.

Manos, M. J., Short, E. J., & Findling, R. L. (1999). Differential effectiveness of methylphenidate and adderall in school-age youths with attention-deficit hyperactivity disorder. *Journal of the American Academy of Child and Adolescent Psychiatry, 38,* 813–819.

Manshadi, M., Lippmann, S., O'Daniel, R. G., & Blackman, A. (1983). Alcohol abuse and attention deficit disorder. *Journal of Clinical Psychiatry, 44,* 379–380.

Marakovitz, S. E., & Campbell, S. B. (1998). Inattention, impulsivity, and hyperactivity from preschool to school age: Performance of hard-to-manage boys on laboratory measures. *Journal of Child Psychology and Psychiatry, 39,* 841–851.

Marchetti, A., Magar, R., Lau, H., Murphy, E. L., Jensen, P. S., Conners, C. K., Findling, R., Wineburg, E., Carotenuto, I., Einarson, T. R., & Iskedjian, M. (2001). Pharmacotherapies for attention-deficit/hyperactivity disorder: Expected cost analysis. *Clinical Therapeutics, 23,* 1–18.

Marcus, S. C., Robins, L. N., & Bucholz, K. K. (1990). *Quick Diagnostic Interview Schedule, III-R* [computer program]. Department of Psychiatry, Washington University School of Medicine. St. Louis, MO.

Mariani, M. A., & Barkley, R. A. (1997). Neuropsychological and academic functioning in preschool boys with attention deficit disorder. *Developmental Neuropsychology, 13,* 111–129.

Marotta, P. J., & Roberts, E. A. (1998). Pemoline hepatotoxicity in children. *Journal of Pediatrics 132,* 894–897.

Marshall, R. M., Hynd, G. W., Handwerk, M. J., & Hal, J. (1997). Academic underachievement in ADHD subtypes. *Journal of Learning Disabilities, 30,* 635–642.

Martin, R. P. (1989). Activity level, distractibility and persistence: Critical characteristics in early schooling. In G. A. Kohnstamm, J. E. Bates, & M. K. Rothbart (Eds.), *Temperament in childhood* (pp. 451–462). New York: Wiley.

Martin, W. R., Sloan, J. W., Sapira, B. D., & Jasinski, D. R. (1971). Physiologic, subjective, and behavioral effects of amphetamine, methamphetamine, ephedrine, phenmetrazine, and methylphenidate in man. *Clinical Pharmacology and Therapeutics, 12,* 245–258.

Masand, P. S., & Tesar, G. E. (1996). Use of stimulants in the medically ill. *Psychiatric Clinics of North America, 19,* 515–547.

Mash, E. J., & Dozois, D. J. A. (1996). Child psychopathology: A developmental systems perspective. In E. J. Mash & R. A. Barkley (Eds.), *Child psychopathology* (pp. 3–60). New York: Guilford Press.

Mash, E. J., & Johnston, C. (1982). A comparison of the mother-child interactions of younger and older hyperactive and normal children. *Child Development, 52,* 1371–1381.

Mash, E. J., & Johnston, C. (1983). Parental perceptions of child behavior problems, parenting self-esteem, and mothers' reported stress in younger and older hyperactive and normal children. *Journal of Consulting and Clinical Psychology, 51,* 86–99.

Mash, E. J., & Johnston, C. (1990). Determinants of parenting stress: Illustrations from families of hyperactive children and families of physically abused children. *Journal of Clinical Child Psychology, 19*, 313–328.

Matheny, A. P., & Fisher, J. E. (1984). Behavioral perspectives on children's accidents. In M. L. Wolraich & D. K. Routh (Eds.), *Advances in developmental and behavioral pediatrics* (Vol. 5, pp. 221–264). Greenwich, CT: JAI Press.

Mathew, R. J., Wilson, W. H., Blazer, D. G., & George, L. K, (1993). Psychiatric disorders in adult children of alcoholics: Data from the epidemiologic catchment area project. *American Journal of Psychiatry, 150*(5), 793–800.

Mathias, R. (1997). Marijuana and tobacco use up again among 8th and 10th graders. *NIDA Notes, 12*(2), 12–19.

Matier-Sharma, K., Perachio, N., Newcorn, J. H., Sharma, V., & Halperin, J. M. (1995). Differential diagnosis of ADHD: Are objective measures of attention, impulsivity, and activity level helpful? *Child Neuropsychology, 1*, 118–127.

Matochik, J. A., Liebenauer, L. L., King, A. C., Szymanski, H. V., Cohen, R. M., & Zametkin, A. J. (1994). Cerebral glucose metabolism in adults with attention deficit hyperactivity disorder after chronic stimulant treatment. *American Journal of Psychiatry, 151*, 658–664.

Matochik, J. A., Nordahl, T. E., Gross, M., Semple, W. E., King, A. C., Cohen, R. M., & Zametkin, A. J. (1993). Effects of acute stimulant medication on cerebral metabolism in adults with hyperactivity. *Neuropsychopharmacology, 8*, 377–386.

Mattes, J. A. (1983). The Feingold diet: A current reappraisal. *Journal of Learning Disabilities, 16*, 319–323.

Mattes, J. A. (1986). Propranolol for adults with temper outbursts and residual attention deficit disorder. *Journal of Clinical Psychopharmacology, 6*, 299–302.

Mattison, R. E., & Felix, B. C. (1997). The course of elementary and secondary school students with SED through their special education experience. *Journal of Emotional and Behavioral Disorders, 5*, 107–117.

Mattison, R. E., & Forness, S. R. (1995). Mental health system involvement in special education placement decisions. In J. M. Kauffman, J. W. Lloyd, D. Hallahan, & T. A. Astuto (Eds.), *Issues in educational placement of children with emotional or behavioral disorders* (pp. 197–211). Hillsdale, NJ: Erlbaum.

Mattison, R. E., Lynch, J. C., Kales, H., & Gamble, A. D. (1993). Checklist identification of elementary schoolboys for clinical referral or evaluation of eligibility for special education. *Behavioral Disorders, 18*, 218–227.

Mattison, R. E., Morales, J., & Bauer, M. A. (1993).

Adolescent scholboys in SED classes: Implications for child psychiatry. *Journal of the American Academy of Child and Adolescent Psychiatry, 32*, 1223–1228.

Max, J. E., Arndt, S., Castillo, C. S., Bokura, H., Robin, D. A., Lindgren, S. D., Smith, W. L. Jr., Sato, Y., & Mattheis, P. J. (1998). Attention-deficit hyperactivity symptomatology after traumatic brain injury: A prospective study. *Journal of the American Academy of Child and Adolescent Psychiatry, 37*, 841–847.

Mayes, S. D., Calhoun, S. T., & Crowell, E. W. (1998). WISC-III Freedom From Distractibility as a measure of attention in children with and without attention deficit hyperactivity disorder. *Journal of Attention Disorders, 2*, 217–227.

Mayes, S. D., Crites, D. L., Bixler, E. O., Humphrey, F. J., & Mattison, R. E. (1994). Methylphenidate and ADHD: Influence of age, IQ and neurodevelopmental status. *Developmental Medicine and Child Neurology, 36*, 1099–1107.

Maziade, M (1989). Should adverse temperament matter to the clinician? An empirically based answer. In G. A. Kohnstamm, J. E. Bates, & M. K. Rothbart (Eds.), *Temperament in childhood* (pp. 421–436). New York: Wiley.

Maziade, M. (1994). Temperament research and practical implications for clinicians. In W. B. Carey & S. C. McDevitt (Eds.), *Prevention and early intervention* (pp. 69–80). New York: Brunner/Mazel.

McBurnett, K., Harris S. M., Swanson, J. M., Pfiffner, L. J., Tamm, L., & Freeland, D. (1993). Neuropsychological and psychophysiological differentiation of inattention/overactivity and aggression/defiance symptom groups. *Journal of Clinical Child Psychology, 22*, 165–171.

McBurnett, K., Pfiffner, L. J., Wilcutt, E., Tamm, L., Lerner, M., Ottolini, Y. L., & Furman, M. B. (1999). Experimental cross-validation of DSM-IV types of attention-deficit hyperactivity disorder. *Journal of the American Academy of Child and Adolescent Psychiatry, 38*(1), 17–24.

McCain, A. P., & Kelley, M. L. (1993). Managing the classroom behavior of an ADHD preschooler: The efficacy of a school-home note intervention. *Child and Family Behavior Therapy, 15*, 33–44.

McConaughy, S. H., Mattison, R. E., & Peterson, R. (1994). Behavioral/emotional problems of children with serious emotional disturbance and learning disabilities. *School Psychology Review, 23*, 81–98.

McCormick, T. C., & McNeel, T. W. (1963). Case report: Acute psychosis and Ritalin abuse. *Texas Journal of Medicine, 59*, 99–100.

McCrady, B. S., & Epstein, E. E. (1995). Directions for research on alcoholic relationships: Marital- and individual-based models of heterogeneity. *Psychology of Addictive Behaviors, 9*, 157–166.

McDermott, S. P. (2000). Cognitive and emotional impediments to treating the adult with ADHD: A cognitive therapy perspective. In T. Brown (Eds.), *Subtypes of attention deficit disorders in children, adolescents, and adults* (pp. 569–606). Washington, DC: American Psychiatric Press.

McDevitt, S. C., & Carey, W. B. (1978). The measurement of temperament in 3–7 year old children. *Journal of Child Psychology and Psychiatry, 19,* 245–253.

McGee, R. A., Clark, S. E., & Symons, D. K. (2000). Does the Conners' continuous performance test aid in ADHD diagnosis? *Journal of Abnormal Child Psychology, 28,* 415–424.

McGee, R., Feehan, M., Williams, S. M., Partridge, F., Silva, P. A., & Kelly, J. (1990). DSM-III disorders in a large sample of adolescents. *Journal of the American Academy of Child and Adolescent Psychiatry, 29,* 611–619.

McGee, R., Partridge, F., Williams, S., & Silva, P. A. (1991). A twelve-year follow-up of preschool hyperactive children. *Journal of the American Academy of Child and Adolescent Psychiatry, 30,* 224–232.

McGee, R., Williams, S., Anderson, J., McKenzie-Parnell, J. M., & Silva, P. A. (1990). Hyperactivity and serum and hair zinc levels in 11-year-old children from the general population. *Biological Psychiatry, 28,* 165–168.

McGee, R., Williams, S., Moffit, T., & Anderson, J. (1989). A comparison of 13-year-old boys with Attention Deficit and/or reading disorder on neuropsychological measures. *Journal of Abnormal Child Psychology, 17,* 37–53.

McGee, R., Williams, S., & Silva, P. A. (1985). Factor structure and correlates of ratings of inattention, hyperactivity and antisocial behavior in a large sample of 9 year old children from the general population. *Journal of Consulting Child Psychology, 53,* 480–490.

McKenna, M. L., & Ho, B. T. (1980). The role of dopamine in the discriminative stimulus properties of cocaine. *Neuropharmacology, 19,* 297–303.

McKinney, J. D., Montague, M., & Hocutt, A. M. (1993). Educational assessment of students with attention deficit disorder. *Exceptional Children, 60,* 125–131.

McMaster University Evidence-Based Practice Center. (1998). *The treatment of attention-deficit/hyperactivity disorder: An evidence report* (Contract No. 290–97–0017). Rockville, MD: Agency for Health Care Policy and Research.

McNamara, C. G., Davidson, E. S., & Shenk, S. A. (1993). Comparison of the motor-activating effects of acute and chronic exposure to amphetamine and methylphenidate. *Pharmacology, Biochemistry, and Behavior, 45,* 729–732.

Mealer, C., Morgan, S., & Luscomb, R. (1998).

Cognitive functioning of ADHD and non-ADHD boys on the WISC-III and WRAML: An analysis within a memory model. *Journal of Attention Disorder, 3,* 133–145.

Means, C. D., Stewart, S. L., & Dowler, D. L. (1997). Job accommodations that work: A follow-up study of adults with attention deficit disorder. *Journal of Applied Rehabilitation Counseling, 28,* 13–17.

Meck, W., & Church, R. (1987). Cholinergic modulation of the content of temporal memory. *Behavioral Neurocience, 101,* 457–464.

Mehta, H., Murray, B., & LoIudice, T. A. (1984). Hepatic dysfunction due to intravenous abuse of methylphenidate hydrochloride. *Journal of Clinical Gastroenterology, 6,* 149–151.

Mehta, M. A., Owen, A. M., Sahakian, B. J., Mavaddat, N., Pikard, J. D., & Robbins, G. W. (2000). ethylphenidate enhances working memory by modulating discrete frontal and parietal lobe regions in the human brain. *Journal of Neuroscience, 20,* 1–6.

Meichenbaum, D., & Goodman, J. (1971). Training impulsive children to talk to themselves: A means of developing self-control. *Journal of Abnormal Psychology, 77,* 115–126.

Mellins, C. A., Gatz, M., & Baker, L. (1996). Children's methods of coping with stress: A twin study of genetic and environmental influences. *Journal of Child Psychology and Psychiatry, 37,* 721–730.

Melnick, S. M., & Hinshaw, S. P. (1996). What they want and what they get: The social goals of boys with ADHD and comparison boys. *Journal of Abnormal Child Psychology, 24,* 169–185.

Melnick, S. M., & Hinshaw, S. P. (2000). Emotion regulation and parenting in ADHD and comparison boys. Linkages with social behaviors and peer preference. *Journal of Abnormal Child Psychology, 28,* 73–86.

Meltzer, H., & Arora, R. (1991). Platelet serotonin studies in affective disorders: evidence for a serotonergic abnormality? In M. Sandler., A. Coppen., & S. Harnett (Eds.), *5-Hydroxytryptamine in Psychiatry: A spectrum of ideas* (pp. 23–55). New York: Oxford University Press.

Mendelson, W., Johnson, N., & Stewart, M. A. (1971). Hyperactive children as teenagers: A follow-up study. *Journal of Nervous and Mental Disease, 153,* 273–279.

Mercer, C. D., Jordan, L., Allsopp, D. H., & Mercer, A. R. (1996). Learning disabilities definitions and criteria used by state eduction departments. *Learning Disabilities Quarterly, 19,* 217–232.

Mereu, G., Yoon, K., Gessa, G., Naes, L., & Westfall, T. (1987). Preferential stimulation of ventral tegmental area dopaminergic neurons by nicotine. *European Journal of Pharmacology, 141,* 395–399.

Mesulam, M. M. (1990). Large-scale neural networks

and distributed processing for attention, language, and memory. *Annals of Neurology, 19*, 320–325.

Meyer, D. E., & Keiras, D. E. (1997). A computational theory of executive cognitive processes and multiple-task performance: Part 1. Basic processes. *Psychological Review, 104*, 3–65.

Milberger, S., Biederman, J., Faraone, S. V., Chen, L., & Jones, J. (1996). Is maternal smoking during pregnancy a risk factor for attention deficit hyperactivity disorder in children? *American Journal of Psychiatry, 153*, 1138–1142.

Milberger, S., Biederman, J., Faraone, S. V., Chen, L., & Jones, J. (1997). ADHD is associated with early initiation of cigarette smoking in children and adolescents. *Journal of the American Academy of Child and Adolescent Psychiatry, 36*, 37–44.

Milberger, S., Biederman, J., Faraone, S. V., Chen, L., & Jones, J. (1997). Further evidence of an association between attention-deficit/hyperactivity disorder and cigarette smoking. *American Journal of Addiction, 6*, 205–217.

Milberger, S., Biederman, J., Faraone, S. V., Guite, J., & Tsuang, M. T. (1997). Pregnancy delivery and infancy complications and ADHD: Issues of gene-environment interactions. *Biological Psychiatry, 41*, 65–75.

Milberger, S., Biederman, J., Faraone, S. V., Wilens, T., & Chu, M. P. (1997). Associations between ADHD and psychoactive substance use disorders. *American Journal of Addiction, 6*, 318–329.

Milberger, S., Biederman, J., Faraone, S. V., Wilens, T., & Chu, M. P. (1997). Longitudinal study of high-risk siblings of ADHD children. *American Journal of Addiction, 6*, 318–329.

Milberger, S., Faraone, S., Biederman J., Chu, M., & Wilens, T. (1998). Famililal risk analysis of the association between ADHD and psychoactive substance use disorders. *Archives of Pediatric and Adolescent Medicine, 152*, 945–951.

Milich, R., Hartung C. M., Martin C. A., & Haigler, E. D. (1994). Behavioral disinhibition and underlying processes in adolescents with disruptive behavior disorders. In D. K. Routhm (Ed.), *Disruptive behavior disorders in childhood* (pp. 109–138). New York: Plenum Press.

Milich, R., & Landau, S. (1982). Socialization and peer relations in hyperactive children. In K. D. Gadow & I. Bialer (Eds.), *Advances in learning and behavioral disabilities* (Vol. 1, pp. 283–339). Greenwich, CT: JAI Press.

Milich, R., & Landau, S. (1989). The role of social status variables in differentiating subgroups of hyperactive children. In L. M. Bloomingdale & J. M. Swanson (Eds.), *Attention deficit disorder* (Vol. 4, pp. 1–16). Oxford: Pergamon Press.

Milich, R., Licht, B., & Murphy, D. (1989). Attention-deficit hyperactivity disordered boys evaluations of and attributions for task performance on medication versus placebo. *Journal of Abnormal Psychology, 98*, 280–284.

Milin, R., Halikas, J. A., Meller, J. E., & Morse, C. (1991). Psychopathology among substance abusing juvenile offenders. *Journal of the American Academy of Child and Adolescent Psychiatry, 30*(4), 569–574.

Milin, R., Loh, E., Chow, J., & Wilson, A. (1997). Assessment of symptoms of attention-deficit hyperactivity disorder in adults with substance use disorders. *Psychiatric Services, 48*, 1378–1380.

Miller, A. (1999). Appropriateness of psychostimulant prescription to children: theoretical and empirical perspectives. *Canadian Journal of Psychiatry, 44*, 1017–1024.

Miller, D. B., & O'Callaghan, J. P. (1994). Environment-, drug- and stress-induced alterations in body temperature affect the neurotoxicity of substituted amphetamines in the C57BL/6J mouse. *Journal of Pharmacology and Experimental Therapeutics, 270*, 752–760.

Miller, D. B., & O'Callaghan, J. P. (1996). Neurotoxicity of d-amphetamine in the C57BL/6J and CD-1 mouse; interactions with stress and the adrenal system. *Annals of the New York Academy of Sciences, 801*, 148–167.

Miller, G. E., & Prinz, R. J. (1990). Enhancement of social learning family interventions for childhood conduct disorder. *Psychological Bulletin, 108*, 291–307.

Millichap, J. G. (1973). Drugs in the management of minimal brain dysfunction. *Annals of New York Academy of Sciences, 205*, 321-334.

Millstein, R. B., Wilens, T. E., Biederman, J., & Spencer, T. J. (1997). Presenting ADHD symptoms and subtypes in clinically referred adults with ADHD. *Journal of Attention Disorders, 2*, 159–166.

Minskoff, E., Sautter, S., Hoffmann, F. J., & Hawks, R. (1987). Employer attitudes toward hiring the learning disabled. *Journal of Learning Disorders, 20*, 53–57.

Mitchell, E. A., Aman, M. G., Turbott, S. H., & Manku, M. (1987). Clinical characteristics and serum essential fatty acid levels in hyperactive children. *Clinical Pediatrics, 26*, 406–411.

Mitchell, E. A., Lewis, S., & Cutler, D. R. (1983). Essential fatty acids and maladjusted behavior in children. *Prostaglandins Leukotrienes & Medicine, 12*, 281–287.

Moffitt, T. E. (1990). Juvenile delinquency and attention-deficit disorder: Developmental trajectories from age 3 to 15. *Child Development, 61*, 893–910.

Moffitt, T. E., & Henry, B. (1988). Neuropsychological assessment of executive functions in self-reported delinquents. *Development and Psychopathology, 1*, 105–118.

Moffitt, T. E., & Silva, P. (1988). Self-reported delinquency, neuropsychological deficit, and history of attention deficit disorder. *Journal of Abnormal Child Psychology, 16*, 553–569.

Montague, M., & Warger, C. (1997). Helping students with attention deficit hyperactivity disorder succeed in the classroom. *Focus on Exceptional Children, 30*(4), 1–16.

Moretti-Altuna, G. (1987). The effects of meditation versus medication in the treatment of attention deficit disorder with hyperactivity. *Dissertation Abstracts International, 47*, 46–58.

Morgan, A. E., Hynd, G. W., Riccio, C. A., & Hall, J. (1996). Validity of DSM-IV ADHD predominantly inattentive and combined type: Relationship to previous DSM diagnoses/subtype differences. *Journal of the American Academy of Child and Adolescent Psychiatry, 35*, 325–333.

Morrison, J. (1980). Adult psychiatric disorders in parents of hyperactive children. *American Journal of Psychiatry, 137*, 825–827.

Morrison, J. R. (1980). Childhood hyperactivity in an adult psychiatric population: Social factors. *Journal of Clinical Psychiatry, 41*, 40–43.

Morrison, J. R., & Stewart, M. A. (1971). A family study of the hyperactive child syndrome. *Biological Psychiatry, 3*, 189–195.

Moser, S., & Kallail, K. J. (1995). Attention-deficit hyperactivity disorder: Management by family physicians. *Archives of Family Medicine, 4*, 241–244.

Mostofsky, S. H., Reiss, A. L., Lockhart, P., & Denckla, M. B. (1998). Evaluation of cerebellar size in attention-deficit hyperactivity disorder. *Journal of Child Neurology, 13*, 434–439.

Mrazek, P. J., & Haggerty, R. J. (Ed.). (1994). *Reducing risks for mental disorders: Institute of Medicine.* Washington, DC: National Academy Press.

MTA Cooperative Group. (1999). A 14-month randomized clinical trial of treatment strategies for attention-deficit/hyperactivity disorder: Multimodal Treatment Study of Children with ADHD. *Archives of General Psychiatry, 56*(12), 1073–1086.

MTA Cooperative Group. (1999). Moderators and mediators of treatment response for children with attention-deficit/hyperactivity disorder. *Archives of General Psychiatry, 56*, 1088–1096.

Mueller, K., & Hsiao, S. (1980). Pemoline-induced self-biting in rats and self-mutilation in the deLange syndrome. *Pharmacology and Biochemical Behavior, 13*(5), 627–631.

Mulligan, S. (1996). An analysis of score patterns of children with attention disorders on the sensory integration and praxis tests. *American Journal of Occupational Therapy, 50*, 647–654.

Munoz, D. P., Hampton, K. A., Moore, K. D., &

Goldring, J. E. (1999). Control of purposive saccadic eye movements and visual fixation in children with attention deficit hyperactivity disorder. In W. Becker, H. Deubel, & T. Mergner (Eds.), *Current occulomotor research: Physiological and psychological aspects* (pp. 415–423). New York: Plenum Press.

Murphy, K., & Barkley, R. A. (1996). Attention deficit hyperactivity disorder adults: Comorbidities and adaptive impairments. *Comprehensive Psychiatry, 37*, 393–401.

Murphy, K., & Barkley R. A. (1996). Prevalence of DSM-IV symptoms of ADHD in adult licensed drivers: Implications for clinical diagnosis. *Journal of Attention Disorders, 1*, 147–161.

Murphy, K. R., & Gordon, M. (1998). Assessment of adults with ADHD. In R. A. Barkley (Ed.), *Attention-deficit hyperactivity disorder: A handbook for diagnosis and treatment* (2nd ed., pp. 345–369). New York: Guilford Press.

Musser, C. J., Ahmann, P. A., Theye, F. W., Mundt, P., Broste, S. K., & Mueller-Rizner, N. (1998). Stimulant use and the potential for abuse in Wisconsin as reported by school administrators and longitudinally followed children. *Journal of Developmental and Behavioral Pediatrics, 19*, 187–192.

Musten, L., Firestone, P., Pisterman, S., Bennett, S., & Mercer, J. (1997). Effects of methylphenidate on preschool children with ADHD: Cognitive and behavioral functions. *Journal of the American Academy of Child and Adolescent Psychiatry, 36*, 1407–1415.

Nada-Raja, S., Langley, J. D., McGee, R., Williams, S. M., Begg, D. J., & Reeder, A. I. (1997). Inattentive and hyperactive behaviors and driving offenses in adolescence. *Journal of the American Academy of Child and Adolescent Psychiatry, 36*, 515–522.

Narhi, V., & Ahonen, T. (1995). Reading disability with and without attention deficit hyperactivity disorder: Do attentional problems make a difference? *Developmental Neuropsychology, 11*, 337–350.

National Ambulatory Medical Care Survey. (1994). Summary. National Center for Health Statistics. *Vital Health Statistics 13*, 116.

National Institute on Drug Abuse. (1998). *pidemiologic trends in drug abuse, Community Epidemiology Work Group; Vol II: Proceedings, June 1997* (NIH Publication No. 98-4208A). Washington, DC: Author.

National Institute on Drug Abuse. (1998). *National survey results on drug use from the Monitoring the Future Study, 1975–1997* (NIH Publication No. 98-4345). Washington, DC: Author.

National Institutes of Health. (1981). Consensus development conference on febrile seizures, National Institutes of Health, May 19–21, 1980. *Epilepsia, 22*, 377–381.

National Institutes of Health. (1982). NIH consensus

development conference: Defined diets and childhood hyperactivity. *Clinical Pediatrics, 21*, 627–630.

National Institutes of Health Consensus Development Conference Statement. (1999). Diagnosis and treatment of attention-deficit/hyperactivity disorder (ADHD). *Journal of the American Academy of Child and Adolescent Psychiatry*, 39, 182–188.

National Institute of Mental Health. (1996). *Alternative pharmacology of ADHD.* Washington, DC: Author.

Needleman, H. L., Gunnoe, C., Leviton, A., Reed, R., Peresie, H., Maher, C., & Barrett, P. (1979). Deficits in psychologic and classroom performance of children with elevated dentine lead levels. *New England Journal of Medicine, 300*, 689–695.

Nehra, A., Mullick, F., Ishak, K. G., & Zimmerman, H. J. (1990). Pemoline-associated hepatic injury. *Gastroenterology, 99*, 1517–1519.

Nemzer, E., Arnold, L. E., Votolato, N. A., & McConnell, H. (1986). Amino acid supplementation as therapy for attention deficit disorder (ADD), *Journal of the American Academy of Child and Adolescent Psychiatry, 25*(4), 509–513.

Neuringer, M. (1998, September 2–3). *Overview of omega-3 fatty acids in infant development: Visual, cognitive, and behavioral outcomes.* Paper presented at NIH Workshop on Omega-3 Essential Fatty Acids and Psychiatric Disorders, Bethesda, MD.

Newby, R. F., Recht, D. R., Caldwell, J., & Schaefer, J. (1993). Comparison of WISC-III and WISC-R IQ changes over a 2-year time span in a sample of children with dyslexia. In B. A. Bracken & R. S. McCalum (Eds.), *Journal of Psychoeducational Assessment WISC-III Monograph.*

Nickerson, K. J., Helms, J. E., & Terrell, F. (1994). Cultural mistrust and black students' attitudes toward seeking psychological help from white counselors. *Journal of Counseling Psychology*, 41, 378–385.

Nielsen, J. A., Duda, N. J., Mokler, D. J., & Moore, K. E. (1984). Self-administration of central stimulants by rats: A comparison of the effects of d-amphetamine, methylphenidate and McNeil 4612. *Pharmacology, Biochemistry, and Behavior, 20*, 227–232.

Nigg, J. T. (1999). The ADHD response-inhibition deficit as measured by the stop task: Replication with DSM-IV combined type, extension, and qualification. *Journal of Abnormal Child Psychology, 27*, 393–402.

Nigg, J. T., Hinshaw, S. P., Carte, E. T., & Treuting, J. J. (1998). Neuropsychological correlates of childhood attention deficit hyperactivity disorder: Explainable by comorbid disruptive behavior or reading problems? *Journal of Abnormal Psychology, 107*, 468–480.

Nigg, J. T., Swanson, J. M., & Hinshaw, S. P. (1997). Covert visual spatial attention in boys with attention deficit hyperactivity disorder: lateral effects, methylphenidate response and results for parents. *Neuropsychologia, 35*, 165–176.

Nsouli, T. M., Nsouli, S. M., Linde, R. E., O'Mara, F., Scanlon, R. T., & Bellanti, J. A. (1994). Role of food allergy in serous otitis media. *Annals of Allergy, 73*, 215–219.

Oades, R. D., Dittmann-Balcar, A., Schepker, R., & Eggers, C. (1996). Auditory event-related potentials (ERPs) and mismatch negativity (MMN) in healthy children and those with attention-deficit or Tourette/tic symptoms. *Biological Psychology, 43*, 163–185.

O'Callaghan, J. P., & Miller, D. B. (1994). Neurotoxicity profiles of substituted amphetamines in the C57BL/6J mouse. *Journal of Pharmacology and Experimental Therapeutics, 270*, 741–751.

O'Callaghan, J. P., & Miller, D. B. (in press). Neurotoxic effects of substituted amphetamines in rats and mice: Challenges to current dogma. In E. Massaro & P. A. Broderick (Eds.), *Handbook of neurotoxicity* (Vol. 2). New York: Humana Press.

Office of National Drug Control Policy. (1998). *Pulse check: National trends in drug abuse, summer 1998* (NCJ-171664). Washington, DC: Office of Programs, Budget, Research and Evaluation.

Offord, D. R., Boyle, M. H., Szatmari, P., Rae-Grant, N. I., Links, P. S., Cadman, D. T., Byles, J. A., Crawford, J. W., Blum, H. M., Byrne, C., Thomas, H., & Woodward, C. A. (1987). Ontario child health study. II. Six-month prevalence of disorder and rates of service utilization. *Archives of General Psychiatry, 44*, 832–836.

O'Leary, K. D., & Becker, W. C. (1967). Behavior modification of an adjustment class: A token reinforcement program. *Exceptional Children, 33*, 637–642.

O'Leary, K. D., Kaufmann, K. F., Kass, R. E., & Drabman, R. S. (1970). The effects of loud and soft reprimands on the behavior of disruptive students. *Exceptional Children, 37*, 145–155.

O'Leary, K. D., Pelham, W. E., Rosenbaum, A., & Price, G. (1976). Behavioral treatment of hyperkinetic children: An experimental evaluation of its usefulness. *Clinical Pediatrics, 15*, 510–515.

O'Leary, S. G., & Pelham, W. E. (1978). Behavior therapy and withdrawal of stimulant medication with hyperactive children. *Pediatrics, 61*, 211–217.

Olfson, M., Marcus, S. C., Weissman, M. M., & Jensen, P. J. (2002). National trends in the use of psychotropic medications by children. *Journal of the American Academy of Child and Adolescent Psychiatry.*

Omizo, M. M., & Michael, W. B. (1982) Biofeedback-induced relaxation training and impulsivity, attention to task, and locus of control among hyperactive boys. *Journal of Learning Disabilities, 15*, 414–416.

Oosterlaan, J., Logan, G. D., & Sergeant, J. A. (1998). Response inhibition in AD/HD, CD, comorbid

AD/HD+CD, anxious and control children: A meta-analysis of studies with the stop task. *Journal of Child Psychology and Psychiatry, 39*, 411–426.

Orvaschel, H. (1985). Psychiatric interviews suitable for use in research with children and adolescents. *Psychopharmacology Bulletin, 21*, 737–748.

Orvaschel, H. (1995). *Schedule for Affective Disorders and Schizophrenia for School-Age Children, Version 5.* Fort Lauderdale, FL: Nova Southeastern University.

Ostrander, R., Weinfurt, K. P., Yarnold, P. R., & August, G. J. (1998). Diagnosing attention deficit disorders with the Behavioral Assessment System for Children and the Child Behavior Checklist: Test and construct validity analyses using optimal discriminant classification trees. *Journal of Consulting and Clinical Psychology, 66*, 600–672.

Ottenbacher, J., & Cooper, H. (1983). Drug treatment of hyperactivity in children. *Developmental Medicine and Child Neurology, 25*, 358–366.

Overmeyer, S., Simmons, A., Santosh, J., Andrew, C., Williams, S. C. R., Taylor, A., Chen, W., & Taylor, E. (2000). Corpus colossum may be similar in children with ADHD and siblings of children with ADHD. *Developmental Medicine and Child Neurology, 42*, 8–13.

Overmeyer, S., Taylor, E., Blanz, B., & Schmidt, M. H. (1999). Psychosocial adversities underestimated in hyperkinetic children. *Journal of Child Psychology and Psychiatry, 40*, 259–263.

Overton, D. A. (1982) Comparison of the degree of discriminability of various drugs using a T-maze drug discrimination paradigm. *Psychopharmacology, 76*, 385–395.

Page, J. G., Bernstein, J. E., Janicki, R. S., & Michelli, F. A. (1974). A multicenter trial of pemoline (cylert) in childhood hyperkinesis. In C. K. Conners (Ed.), *Clinical use of stimulant drugs in children* (p. 98). The Hague, Netherlands: Excerpta Medica.

Painter, M. J., & Gaus, L. M. (1995). Phenobarbital: Clinical use. In R. H. Levy, R. H. Mattson, & B. S. Meldrum (Eds.), *Anti-epileptic drugs* (pp. 401–407). New York: Raven Press.

Pakes, G. E. (1978). Death and liquid protein. *American Pharmacy, 18*, 4–5.

Palacios, H. J. (1976). Hypersensitivity as a cause of dermatologic and vaginal moniliasis resistant to topical therapy. *Annals of Allergy, 37*, 110–113.

Palacios, H. J. (1977). Desensitization for monilial hypersensitivity. *Virginia Medical Journal, 104*, 393–395.

Parker, H. C. (1989). *Education position paper: Children with attention deficit disorder.* Plantation, FL: Ch.A.D.D. (Children with Attention Deficit Disorder).

Parker, J. G., & Asher, S. R. (1987). Peer relations and later personal adjustment: Are low-accepted children at risk? *Psychological Bulletin, 102*, 357–389.

Parks, A., Antonoff, S., Drake, C., Skiba, W., & Soberman, J. (1987). A survey of programs and services for learning disabled students in graduate and professional schools. *Journal of Learning Disorders, 20*, 181–187.

Parran, T. V. Jr., & Jasinski, D. R. (1991). Intravenous methylphenidate abuse. Prototype for prescription drug abuse. *Archives of Internal Medicine, 151*, 781–783.

Parrott, A. C., & Winder, G. (1989). Nicotine chewing gum (2 mg, 4 mg) and cigarette smoking: Comparative effects upon vigilance and heart rate. *Psychopharmacology, 97*, 257–261.

Paternite, C. E., Loney, J., & Roberts, M. A. (1996). A preliminary validation of subtypes of DSM-IV attention-deficit/hyperactivity disorder. *Journal of Attention Disorders, 1*, 70–86.

Paternite, C. E., Jr., Loney, J., Salisbury, H., & Whaley, M. A. (1999). Childhood inattention-overactivity, aggression, and medication history as predictors of young adult outcomes. *Journal of Child and Adolescent Psychopharmacology, 9*(3), 169–184.

Patrick, K. S., Mueller, R. A., Gualtieri, C. T., & Breese, G. R. (1987). Pharmocokinetics and actions of methyphenidate. In H. Y. Meltzer (Ed.), *Psychopharmacology: A third generation of progress* (pp. 1387–1395). New York: Raven Press.

Patterson, G. R. (1974). Intervention for boys with conduct problems: Multiple settings, treatment, and criteria. *Journal of Consulting and Clinical Psychology, 42*, 471–481.

Patterson, G. R. (1975). *Families: Application of social learning to family life.* Champaign, IL: Research Press.

Patterson, G. R. (1982). *Coercive family process.* Eugene, OR: Castalia.

Patterson, G. R., Reid, J. B., & Dishion, T. J. (1992). *A social interactional approach: Vol. 4: Antisocial boys.* Eugene, OR: Castalia.

Paule, M. G., Rowland, A. S., Ferguson, S. A., Chelonis, J. J., Tannock, R., Swanson, J. M., & Castellanos, F. X. (2000) Attention deficit/hyperactivity disorder: Characteristics, interventions, and models. *Neurotoxicology and Teratology, 22*, 631–651.

Pearson, D. A., Yaffee, L. S., Loveland, K. A., & Norton, A. M. (1995). Covert visual attention in children with attention deficit hyperactivity disorder: Evidence for developmental immaturity? *Development and Psychopathology, 7*, 351–167.

Peeke, S., & Peeke, H. (1984). Attention, memory, and cigarette smoking. *Psychopharmacology, 84*, 205–216.

Pelham, W. E. (1977). Withdrawal of a stimulant drug

and concurrent behavioral intervention in the treatment of a hyperactive child. *Behavior Therapy, 8*, 473–479.

Pelham, W. E. (1989). Behavior therapy, behavioral assessment and psychostimulant medication in the treatment of attention deficit disorders: An interactive approach. In J. Swanson & L. Bloomingdale (Eds.), *Attention deficit disorder: 4. Emerging trends in the treatment of attention and behavioral problems in children* (pp. 169–195). London: Pergamon.

Pelham, W. E., Aronoff, H. R., Midlam, J. K., Shapiro, C. J., Gnagy, E. M., Chronis, A. M., Onyango, A. N., Forehand, G., Nguyen, A., & Waxmonsky, J. (1999). A comparison of Ritalin and Adderall: Efficacy and time-course in children with attention-deficit hyperactivity/disorder. *Pediatrics, 103*, e43.

Pelham, W. E., & Bender, M. E. (1982). Peer relationships in hyperactive children: Description and treatment. In K. D. Gadow & I. Bialer (Eds.), *Advances in learning and behavioral disabilities* (Vol. 1, pp. 365–436). Greenwich, CT: JAI Press.

Pelham, W. E., Carlson, C., Sams, S. E., Vallano, G., Dixon, M. J., & Hoza, B. (1993). Separate and combined effects of methylphenidate and behavior modification on boys with ADHD in the classroom. *Journal of Consulting and Clinical Psychology, 61*(3), 506–515.

Pelham, W. E., Evans, S. W., Gnagy, E. M., & Greenslade, K. E. (1992). Teacher ratings of DSM-III-R symptoms for the disruptive behavior disorders: Prevalence, factor analyses, and conditional probabilities in a special education sample. *School Psychology Review, 21*, 285–299.

Pelham, W. E., Gnagy, E. M., Greenslade, K. E., & Milich, R. (1992). Teacher ratings of DSM-III-R symptoms for the disruptive behavior disorders. *Journal of the American Academy of Child and Adolescent Psychiatry, 31*, 210–218.

Pelham, W. E., Greenslade, K. E., Vodde-Hamilton, M. A., Murphy, D. A., Greenstein, J. J., Gnagy, E. M., Guthrie, K. J., Hoover, M. D., & Dahl, R. E. (1990). Relative efficacy of long-acting stimulants on ADHD children: A comparison of standard methylphenidate, Ritalin-SR, Dexedrine spansule, and pemoline. *Pediatrics, 86*, 226–237.

Pelham, W. E., Greiner, A. R., & Gnagy, E. M. (1997). *Children's summer treatment program manual*. Buffalo, NY: Comprehensive Treatment for Attention Deficit Disorder.

Pelham, W. E., Greiner, A. R., Gnagy, E. M., Hoza, B., Martin, L., Sams, S. E., & Wilson, T. (1996). A summer treatment program for children with ADHD. In M. Roberts & A. LaGreca (Eds.), *Model programs for service delivery for child and family mental health* (pp. 193–212). Hillsdale, NJ: Erlbaum.

Pelham, W. E., & Hoza, B. (1996). Intensive treatment: A summer treatment program for children with ADHD. In E. Hibbs & P. Jensen (Eds.), *Psychosocial treatments for child and adolescent disorders: Empirically based strategies for clinical practice* (pp. 311–340). New York: American Psychological Association Press.

Pelham, W., Hoza, B., Sturges, J., Schmidt, C., Bijlsma, J., & Moorer, S. (1987). Sustained release and standard methylphenidate effects on cognitive and social behavior in children with attention deficit disorder. *Pediatrics, 80*, 491–501.

Pelham, W. E., Lang, A. R., Atkeson, B., Murphy, D. A., Gnagy, E. M., Greiner, A. R., Vodde-Hamilton, M., & Greenslade, K. E. (1998). Effects of deviant child behavior on parental alcohol consumption: Stress-induced drinking in parents of ADHD children. *American Journal of Addictions, 7*, 103–114.

Pelham, W. E., & Milich, R. (1991). Individual differences in response to Ritalin in classwork and social behavior. In L. L. Greenhill & B. Osman (Eds.), *Ritalin: Theory and patient management* (pp. 203–222). New York City: Mary Ann Liebert.

Pelham, W. E., & Murphy, H. A. (1986). Attention deficit and conduct disorder. In M. Hersen (Ed.), *Pharmacological and behavioral treatment: An integrative approach* (pp. 108–148). New York: Wiley.

Pelham, W., & Murphy, H. (1986). Behavioral and pharmacological treatment of hyperactivity and attention deficit disorders. In M. Hersen & J. Breuning (Eds.), *Pharmacological and behavioral treatment: An integrative approach* (pp. 108–147). New York: Wiley.

Pelham, W. E., Schnedler, R. W., Bender, M. E., Miller, J., Nilsson, D., Budrow, M., Ronnei, M., Paluchowski, C., & Marks, D. (1988). The combination of behavior therapy and methylphenidate in the treatment of hyperactivity: A therapy outcome study. In L. Bloomingdale (Ed.), *Attention deficit disorders* (Vol. 3, pp. 29–48). London: Pergamon Press.

Pelham, W. E., Schnedler, R. W., Bologna, N., & Contreras, A. (1980). Behavioral and stimulant treatment of hyperactive children: A therapy study with methylphenidate probes in a within-study design. *Journal of Applied Behavioral Analysis, 13*, 221–236.

Pelham, W. E., Jr., & Smith, B. H. (2000). Prediction and measurement of individual responses to Ritalin by children and adolescents with ADHD. In L. Greenhill & B. Osman (Eds.), *Ritalin: Theory and patient management* (2nd ed.). New York: Mary Ann Liebert.

Pelham, W. E., Sturges, J., Hoza, J., Schmidt, C., Biilsma, J. J., Milich, R., & Moorer, S. (1989). The effects of sustained release 20 and 10 mg Ritalin bid on cognitive and social behavior in children with attention deficit disorder. *Pediatrics, 80*, 491–501.

Pelham, W., Swanson, J., Furman, M., & Schwint, H. (1995). Pemoline effects on children with ADHD: A time response by dose-response analysis on classroom measures. *Journal of the American Academy of Child and Adolescent Psychiatry, 34*, 1504–1514.

Pelham, W. E., & Waschbusch, D. A. (1999). Behavioral intervention in ADHD. In H. C. Quay & A. E. Hogan (Eds.), *Handbook of disruptive behavior disorders* (pp. 255–278), New York: Plenum Press.

Pelham, W. E., Wheeler, T., & Chronis, A. (1998). Empirically supported psychosocial treatments for ADHD. *Journal of Clinical Child Psychology, 27*, 190–205.

Pemoline. (1999). *Physician's desk reference* (pp. 416–417). Montvale, NJ: Medical Economics.

Pennington, B. F. (1997). Dimensions of executive functions in normal and abnormal development. In N. Krasnegor, R. Lyon, & P. Goldman-Rakic (Eds.), *Development of the prefrontal cortex: Evolution, neurobiology, and behavior* (pp. 265–291). Baltimore: Paul H. Brookes.

Pennington, B. F., Groisser, D., & Welsh, M. C. (1993). Contrasting cognitive deficits in attention deficit hyperactivity disorder versus reading disability. *Developmental Psychology, 29*, 511–523.

Pennington, B. F., & Ozonoff, S. (1991). A neuroscientific perspective on continuity and discontinuity in developmental psychopathology. In D. Cicchetti (Ed.), *Rochester Symposium on developmental psychopathology* (Vol. III, pp. 117–159). Rochester, NY: University of Rochester Press.

Pennington, B. F., & Ozonoff, S. (1996). Executive functions and developmental psychopathology. *Journal of Child Psychology and Psychiatry, 37*, 51–87.

Perel, J. W., & Dayton, P. (1976). Methylphenidate. In E. Usdin & I. Forrest (Eds.), *Psychotherapeutic drugs. Part II* (p. 1287). New York: Marcel Dekker.

Perkins, A. N., Eckerman, D. A., & McPhail, R. C. (1991). Discriminative stimulus properties of triadimefon: Comparison with methylphenidate. *Pharmacology, Biochemistry, and Behavior, 40*, 757–761.

Perlmutter, S. J., Leitman, S. F., Garvey, M. A., Hamburger, S., Feldman, E., Leonard, H. L., & Swedo, S. E. (1999). Therapeutic plasma exchange and intravenous immunoglobulin for obsessive-compulsive and tic disorders in childhood. *Lancet, 354*(9185), 1153–1158.

Peterson, B. S. (1995). Neuroimaging in child and adolescent neuropsychiatric disorders. *Journal of the American Academy of Child and Adolescent Psychiatry, 34*, 1560–1576.

Petrides, M., Aliviasatos, B., Meyer, E., & Evans, A. C. (1993). Functional activation of the human frontal cortex during performance of verbal working memory tasks. *Proceedings of the National Academy of Science, 90*, 878–882.

Pfiffner, L. J., & McBurnett, K. (1997). Social skills training with parent generalization: Treatment effects for children with ADD/ADHD. *Journal of Consulting and Clinical Psychology, 65*, 749–757.

Pfiffner, L. J., & O'Leary, S. G. (1987). The efficacy of all-positive management as a function of the prior use of negative consequences. *Journal of Applied Behavior Analysis, 20*, 265–271.

Pfiffner, L. J., O'Leary, S. G., Rosen, L. A., & Sanderson, W. C., Jr. (1985). A comparison of the effects of continuous and intermittent response-cost and reprimands in the classroom. *Journal of Clinical Child Psychology, 14*, 348–352.

Pfiffner, L. J., Rosen, L. A., & O'Leary, S. G. (1985). The efficacy of an all-positive approach to classroom management. *Journal of Applied Behavior Analysis, 18*, 257–261.

Phillippi, R. (1998). *Attention deficit disorder among Tenncare enrollees: A report of prevalence and medication.* Nashville, TN: Bureau of TennCare–Department of Health.

Piazza, P. V., Deminiere, J. M., Lemma, M., & Simon, H. (1989). Factors that predict individual vulnerability to amphetamine self-administration. *Science, 245*, 1511–1513.

Piazza, P. V., Deminiere, J. M., LeMoal, M., & Simon, H. (1990). Stress and pharmacologically-induced behavioral sensitization increases vulnerability to aquisition of amphetamine self-administration. *Brain Research, 514*, 22–26.

Piazza, P. V., Deroche, V., Rouge-Pont, F., & Le Moal, M. (1993). Behavioral and biological factors associated with individual vulnerability to psychostimulant abuse. In *Laboratory behavioral studies of vulnerability to drug abuse* (NIDA Monograph No. 169) (pp. 105–133). Rockville, MD: U.S. Government Printing Office.

Pierce, J., & Burns, D. (1990). *California Smoking Baseline Survey: Adult attitudes and practices.* Unpublished survey, University of California, San Diego, CA.

Pillow, D. R., Pelham, W. E., Hoza, B., Molina, B. S. G., & Stultz, C. H. (1998). Confirmatory factor analyses examining attention deficit hyperactivity disorder symptoms and other childhood disruptive behavior disorders. *Journal of Abnormal Child Psychology, 26*, 293–309.

Pincus, H. A., Taneilian, T. L., Marcus, S. C., Olfson, M., Zarin, D. A., Thompson, J., & Zito, J. M. (1998). Prescribing trends in psychotropic medications: primary care, psychiatry, and other medical specialties. *Journal of the American Medical Association, 279*, 526–531.

Pisecco, S., Baker, D. B., Silva, P. A., & Brooke, M. (1996). Behavioral distinctions in children with reading disabilities and/or ADHD. *Journal of the American Academy of Child and Adolescent Psychiatry, 35*, 1477–1484.

Pisterman, S., Firestone, P., McGrath, P., Goodman, J. T., Webster, I., Mallory, R., & Goffin, B. (1992). The role of parent training in treatment of preschoolers with

ADD-H. *American Journal of Orthopsychiatry, 62*, 397–408.

Pisterman, S., Firestone, P., McGrath, P., Goodman, J. T., Webster, I., Mallory, R., & Goffin, B. (1992). The effects of parent training on parenting stress and sense of competence. *Canadian Journal of Behavioural Science, 24*, 41–58.

Pisterman, S., McGrath, P., Firestone, P., Goodman, J. T., Webster, I., & Mallory, R. (1989). Outcome of parent-mediated treatment of preschoolers with attention deficit disorder with hyperactivity. *Journal of Consulting and Clinical Psychology, 57*, 628–635.

Pliszka, S. R. (1987). Tricyclic antidepressants in the treatment of children with Attention Deficit Disorder. *Journal of the American Academy of Child and Adolescent Psychiatry, 26*, 127–132.

Pliszka, S. R. (1989). Effect of anxiety on cognition, behavior, and stimulant response in ADHD. *Journal of the American Academy of Child and Adolescent Psychiatry, 28*, 882–887.

Pliszka, S. R. (1992). Comorbidity of attention-deficit hyperactivity disorder and overanxious disorder. *Journal of the American Academy of Child and Adolescent Psychiatry, 31*(2), 197–203.

Pliszka, S. R., Liotti, M., & Woldorff, M. G. (2000). Inhibitory control in children with attention-deficit/hyperactivity disorder: Event-related potentials identify the processing component and timing of an impaired right frontal response-inhibition mechanism. *Biologic Psychiatry, 48*, 238–246.

Pliszka, S. R., McCracken, J. T., & Maas, J. W. (1996), Catecholamines in attention-deficit hyperactivity disorder: Current perspectives. *Journal of the American Academy of Child and Adolescent Psychiatry, 35*, 264–272.

Plomin, R., Owen, M. J., & McGuffin, P. (1994). The genetic basis of complex human behaviors. *Science, 264*, 1733–1739.

Pollard, S., Ward, E. M., & Barkley, R. A. (1983). The effects of parent training and Ritalin on the parent-child interactions of hyperactive boys. *Child and Family Behavior Therapy, 5*, 51–69.

Pollock, I., & Warner, J. O. (1990). Effect of artificial food colors on childhood behavior. *Archives of Disease in Childhood, 65*, 74–77.

Pomerleau, O. F., Downey, K. K., Stelson, F. W., & Pomerleau, C. S. (1995). Cigarette smoking in adult patients diagnosed with attention deficit hyperactivity disorder. *Journal of Substance Abuse, 7*, 373–378.

Porrino, L. J., Rapoport, J. L., Behar, D., Sceery, W., Ismond, D. R., & Bunney, W. E. (1983). A naturalistic assessment of the motor activity of hyperactive boys, I. Comparison with normal controls. *Archives of General Psychiatry, 40*, 681–687.

Porsolt, R. D., Pawelec, C., & Jalfre, M. (1982) Use of drug discrimination procedures to detect amphetamine-like effects of antidepressants. In F. C. Colpaert & J. L. Slangen (Eds.), *Drug discrimination: Applications in CNS pharmacology* (pp. 193–202). Amsterdam: Elsevier Biomedical Press.

Posner, M. I., & Raichle, M. E. (1994). *Images of mind.* New York: Freeman.

Posner, M. I., & Raichle, M. (1996). *Images of mind* (rev.). Washington, DC: Scientific American Books.

Prendergast, M., Taylor, E., Rapoport, J. L., Bartko, J., Donnelly, M., Zametkin, A., Ahearn, M. B., Dunn, G., & Wieselberg, H. M. (1988). The diagnosis of childhood hyperactivity, A U.S.-U.K. cross-national study of DSM-III and ICD-9. *Journal of Child Psychology and Psychiatry, 29*(3), 289–300.

Previc, F. H. (1993). Do the organs of the labyrinth differentially influence the sympathetic and parasympathetic systems? *Neuroscience and Biobehavioral Reviews, 17*, 397–404.

Prifitera A., Weiss L. G., & Saklofske D. H. (1998). The WISC-III in Context. In A. Prifitera & D. H. Saklofske (Eds.), *WISC-III Clinical use and interpretation: Scientist-practitioner perspectives* (pp. 1–38). New York: Academic Press.

Prince, J., Wilens, T., Biederman, J., Spencer, T., Millstein, R., Polisner, D., & Bostic, J. *A controlled study of nortriptyline in children and adolescents with attention deficit hyperactivity disorder.* Manuscript submitted for publication.

Prinz, R. J., Roberts, W. A., & Hantman, E. (1980). Dietary correlates of hyperactive behavior in children. *Journal of Consulting and Clinical Psychology, 6*, 760–769.

Prior, M., & Sanson, A. (1986). Attention deficit disorder with hyperactivity: A critique. *Journal of Child Psychology and Psychiatry, 27*, 307–319.

Pu, C., & Vorhees, C. V. (1993). Developmental dissociation of methamphetamine-induced depletion of dopaminergic terminals and astrocyte reaction in rat striatum. *Brain Research: Developmental Brain Research, 72*, 325–328.

Purcell, R., Maruff, P., Hyrios, M., & Pantelis, C. (1998). Neuropsychological deficits in obsessive-compulsive disorder: A comparison with unipolar depression, panic disorder, and normal controls. *Archives of General Psychiatry, 55*, 415–423.

Purvis, K., & Tannock, R. (2000). Phonological processing, not inhibitory control differentiates ADHD and reading disability. *Journal of the American Academy of Child and Adolescent Psychiatry, 39*, 485–494.

Quay, H. C., & Peterson, D. R. (1983). *Interim manual of the revised Behavior Problem Checklist.* Miami, FL: Authors.

Quinn, P. O., & Rapoport, J. L. (1975). One-year follow-up of hyperactive boys treated with imipramine or methylphenidate. *American Journal of Psychiatry, 132,* 241–245.

Rapoport, J. L., Buchsbaum, M. S., Weingartner, H., Zahn, T. P., Ludlow, C., & Mikkelsen, E. J. (1980). Dextroamphetamine. Its cognitive and behavioral effects in normal and hyperactive boys and normal men. *Archives of General Psychiatry, 37,* 933–943.

Rapoport, J. L., Buchsbaum, M. S., Zahn, T. P., Weingartner, H., Ludlow, C., & Mikkelsen, E. J. (1978). Dextroamphetamine: Cognitive and behavioral effects on normal prepubertal boys. *Journal of the American Academy of Child and Adolescent Psychiatry, 199,* 560–563.

Rapoport, J. L., Quinn, P., Bradbard, G., Riddle, D., & Brooks, E. (1974). Imipramine and methylphenidate treatment of hyperactive boys: A double-blind comparison. *Archives of General Psychiatry, 30,* 789–793.

Rappley, M. D. (1995). The descriptive epidemiology of methylphenidate in Michigan. *Archives of Pediatric and Adolescent Medicine, 149,* 675–679.

Rappley, M. D., Gardiner, J. C., Jetton, J. R., & Houang, R. T. (1995). The use of methylphenidate in Michigan. *Archives of Pediatrics and Adolescent Medicine, 149,* 675–679.

Rappley, M. D., Mullan, P. B., Alvarez, F. J., Ihouma, U. E., Wang, J., & Gardiner, J. C. (1999). Diagnosis of attention-deficit/hyperactivity disorder and the use of psychotropic medication in very young children. *Archives of Pediatrics and Adolescent Medicine, 153,* 1039–1045.

Rapport, M., Carlson, G., Kelly, K., & Pataki, C. (1993). Methylphenidate and desipramine in hospitalized children: I. Separate and combined effects on cognitive function. *Journal of the American Academy of Child and Adolescent Psychiatry, 32,* 333–342.

Rapport, M., Denney, C., DuPaul G., & Gardner, M. (1994). Attention deficit disorder and methylphenidate: Normalization rates, clinical effectiveness and response prediction in 76 children. *Journal of the American Academy of Child and Adolescent Psychiatry, 33*(6), 882–893.

Rapport, M. D., DuPaul, G. J., & Kelly, K. L. (1989). Attention deficit hyperactivity disorder and methylphenidate: The relationship between gross body weight and drug response in children. *Psychopharmacology Bulletin, 25*(2), 285–290.

Rapport, M. D., Murphy, A., & Bailey, J. S. (1980). The effects of a response-cost treatment tactic on hyperactive children. *Journal of School Psychology, 18,* 98–111.

Rapport, M. D., Murphy, H. A., & Bailey, J. S. (1982). Ritalin vs. response-cost in the control of hyperactive children: A within-subjects comparison. *Journal of Applied Behavior Analysis, 15,* 205–216.

Rapport, M., Stoner, G., DuPaul, G., Kelly, K., Tucker, S., & Schoder, T. (1988). Attention deficit disorder and methylphenidate: A multi-step analysis of dose-response effects on children's impulsivity across settings. *Journal of the American Academy of Child and Adolescent Psychiatry, 27,* 60–69.

Rasmussen, P., & Gillberg, C. (2000). Natural outcome of ADHD with developmental coordination disorder at age twenty-two years: A controlled, longitudinal, community-based study. *Journal of the American Academy of Child and Adolescent Psychiatry, 39,* 1424–1431.

Ratey, J., Greenberg, M., & Lindem, K. (1991). Combination of treatments for attention deficit disorders in adults. *Journal of Nervous and Mental Disorders, 176,* 699–701.

Reader, M. J., Harris, E. L., Schuerholz, L. J., & Denckla, M. B. (1994). Attention deficit hyperactivity disorder and executive dysfunction. *Developmental Neuropsychology, 11,* 493–512.

Reason, R. (1999). ADHD: A psychological response to an evolving concept. Report of a Working Party of the British Psychological Society. *Journal of Learning Disabilities, 32,* 85–91.

Rehabilitation Act of 1973, 29 U.S.C. §§ 701 et seq.

Reid, R. (1996). Three faces of attention-deficit hyperactivity disorder. *Journal of Child and Family Studies, 5,* 249–265.

Reid, R., DuPaul, G. J., Power, T. J., Anastopoulos, A. D., Rogers-Adkinson, D., Noll, M. B., & Riccio, C. (1998). Assessing culturally different students for attention deficit hyperactivity disorder using behavior rating scales. *Journal of Abnormal Child Psychology, 26*(3), 187–198.

Reid, R., & Maag, J. W. (1994). How many fidgets in a pretty much: A critique of behavior rating scales for identifying students with ADHD. *Journal of School Psychology, 32,* 339–354.

Reid, R., Maag, J. W., & Vasa, S. F. (1993). Attention deficit hyperactivity disorder as a disability category: A critique. *Exceptional Children, 60,* 198–214.

Reimherr, F., Hedges, D., Strong, R., & Wender, P. (1995). *An open-trial of venlaxine in adult patients with attention deficit hyperactivity disorder.* Orlando, FL: New Clinical Drug Evaluation Unit Program.

Reimherr, F. W., Wender, P. H., Wood, D. R., & Ward, M. (1987). An open trial of l-tyrosine in the treatment of attention deficit disorder, residual type. *American Journal of Psychiatry, 144,* 1071–1073.

Reinecke, M. A., Beebe, D. W., & Stein, M. A. (1999). The third factor of the WISC-III: It's (probably) not freedom from distractibility. *Journal of the American Academy of Child and Adolescent Psychiatry, 38,* 322–328.

Ricciolini, R., Scalibastri, M., Kelleher, J. K., Carminati, P., Calvani, M., & Arduini, A. (1998). Role of acetyl-l-carnitine in rat brain lipogenesis: Implications for polyunsaturated fatty acid synthesis. *Journal of Neurochemistry, 71*, 2510-2517.

Richardson, G. A., & Day, N. L. (1994). Detrimental effects of prenatal cocaine exposure: Illusion or reality? *Journal of the American Academy of Child and Adolescent Psychiatry, 33*, 28–34.

Richters, J. E., Arnold, L. E., Jensen, P. S., Abikoff, H., Conners, C. K., Greenhill, L. L., Hechtman, L., Hinshaw, S. P., Pelham, W. E., & Swanson, J. M. (1995). NIMH collaborative multisite multimodal treatment study of children with ADHD: I. Background and rationale. *Journal of the American Academy of Child and Adolescent Psychiatry, 34*, 987–1000.

Riddle, M. A., Bernstein, G. A., Cook, E. H., Leonard, H. L., March, J. S., & Swanson, J. M. (1999). Anxiolytics, adrenergic agents, and naltrexone. *Journal of the American Academy of Child and Adolescent Psychiatry, 38*, 546–556.

Riddle, M. A., Hardin, M. T., Cho, S. C., Woolston, J. L., & Leckman, J. F. (1988). Desipramine treatment of boys with attention-deficit hyperactivity disorder and tics: Preliminary clinical experience. *Journal of the American Academy of Child and Adolescent Psychiatry, 27*, 811–814.

Riddle, M. A., Labellarte, M. J., & Walkup, J. T. (1998). Pediatric psychopharmacology: problems and prospects. *Journal of Child and Adolescent Psychopharmacology, 8*, 87–97.

Riggs, P. (1998). Clinical approach to treatment of ADHD in adolescents with substance use disorders and conduct disorder. *Journal of the American Academy of Child and Adolescent Psychiatry, 37*(3), 331–332.

Riggs, P., Leon, S. L., Mikulich, S. K., & Pottle, L. C. (1998). An open trial of bupropion for ADHD in adolescents with SUDs and conduct disorder. *Journal of the American Academy of Child and Adolescent Psychiatry, 37*, 1271–1278.

Riggs, P. D., Thompson, L. L., Mikulich, S. K., Whitmore, E. A., & Crowley, T. J. (1996). An open trial of pemoline in drug dependent delinquents with attention deficit hyperactivity disorder. *Journal of the American Academy of Child and Adolescent Psychiatry, 35*, 1018–1024.

Rimland, B. (1983). The Feingold diet: An assessment of the reviews by Mattes, by Kavale, & Forness, and others. *Journal of Learning Disabilities, 16*, 45–49.

Rioux, B. (1960). Is Ritalin an addiction-producing drug? *Diseases of the Nervous System, 21*, 346–349.

Rippere, V. (1983). Food additives and hyperactive children: A critique of Conners. *British Journal of Clinical Psychology, 22*(pt. 1), 19–32.

Risner, M. E., & Jones, B. E. (1975). Self-administra-

tion of CNS stimulants by dogs. *Psychopharmacology, 43*, 207–213.

Risner, M. E., & Jones, B. E. (1976). Characteristics of unlimited access to self-administered stimulant infusion in dogs. *Biological Psychiatry, 11*, 625–634.

Roberts, S., Harbison, R., Roth, L., & James, R. (1994). Methylphenidate-induced hepatoxicity in mice and its potentiation by beta-adrenergic agonist drugs. *Life Sciences, 55*, 269–281.

Robins, E., & Guze, S. B. (1970). Establishment of diagnostic validity in psychiatric illness: Its application to schizophrenia. *American Journal of Psychiatry, 126*, 983–987.

Robins, L. N. (1990).The natural history of drug abuse. In D. J. Letteri, M. Sayers, & H. W. Pearson (Eds.), *Theories on drug abuse: Selected contemporary perspectives* (pp. 215–224), Rockville, MD: National Institute on Drug Abuse.

Robins, P. M. (1992). A comparison of behavioral and attentional functioning in children diagnosed as hyperactive or learning-disabled. *Journal of Abnormal Child Psychology, 20*, 65–82.

Robinson, P. W., Newby, T. J., & Ganzell, S. L. (1981). A token system for a class of underachieving hyperactive children. *Journal of Applied Behavior Analysis, 14*, 307–315.

Robinson, T. E., & Berridge, K. C. (1993). The neural basis of drug craving: An incentive-sensitization theory of addiction. *Brain Research Review, 18*, 247–291.

Robinson, T. N., Wilde, M. L., Navracruz, L. C., Haydel, K. F., & Varady, A. (2001). Effects of reducing children's television and video-game use on aggressive behavior. *Archives of Pediatrics and Adolescent Medicine, 155*, 17–23.

Robison, L. M., Sclar, D. A., Skaer, T. L., & Galin, R. S. (1999). National trends in the prevalence of attention-deficit/hyperactivity disorder and the prescribing of methylphenidate among school-age children 1990–1995. *Clinical Pediatrics, 38*, 209–217.

Rooney, K. J. (1993). Classroom interventions for students with attention deficit disorders. *Focus Exceptional Children, 26*(4), 1–16.

Rosen, J. R., Young, A. M., Beuthin, F. C., & Louis-Ferdinand, R. T. (1986). Discriminative stimulus properties of amphetamine and other stimulants in lead-exposed and normal rats. *Pharmacology, Biochemistry, and Behavior, 24*, 211–215.

Rosen, L. A., O'Leary, S. G., Joyce, S. A., Conway, G., & Pfiffner, L. J. (1984). The importance of prudent negative consequences for maintaining the appropriate behavior of hyperactive students. *Journal of Abnormal Child Psychology, 12*, 581–604.

Rosenbaum, A., O'Leary, S. G., & Jacob, R. G. (1975).

Behavioral intervention with hyperactive children: Group consequences as a supplement to individual contingencies. *Behavior Therapy, 6,* 315–323.

Rosh, J. R., Dellert, S. F., Narkewicz, M., Birnbaum, A., & Whitington, G. (1998). Four cases of severe hepatotoxicity associated with pemoline; possible autoimmune pathogenesis. *Pediatrics, 101,* 921–923.

Ross, H. E., Glaser, F. B., & Germanson, T. (1988). The prevalence of psychiatric disorders in patients with alcohol and other drug problems. *Archives of General Psychiatry, 45,* 1023–1031.

Ross, R. G., Hommer, D., Breiger, D., Varley, C., & Radant, A. C. (1994). Eye movement task related to frontal lobe functioning in children with attention deficit disorder. *Journal of the American Academy of Child and Adolescent Psychiatry, 33,* 869–874.

Rothlind, J. C., Posner, M. I., & Schaughency, E. A. (1991). Lateralized control of eye movements in attention deficit hyperactivity disorder. *Journal of Cognitive Neuroscience, 3,* 377–381.

Rounsaville, B. J., Anton, S. F., Carroll, K., Budde, D., Prusoff, B. A., & Gawin, F. (1991). Psychiatric diagnoses of treatment-seeking cocaine abusers. *Archives of General Psychiatry, 48,* 43–51.

Rounsaville, B. J., Kleber, H. D., Wilber, C., Rosenberger, D., & Rosenberger, P. (1981). Comparison of opiate addicts' reports of psychiatric history with reports of significant-other informants. *American Journal of Drug and Alcohol Abuse, 8,* 51–69.

Rovet, J., & Alvarez, M. (1996). Thyroid hormone and attention in school-age children with congenital hypothyroidism. *Journal of Child Psychology and Psychiatry, 37,* 579–585

Rowe, D. C., Stever, C., Giedinghagen, L. N., Gard, J. M., Cleveland, H. H., Terris, S. T., Mohr, J. H., Sherman, S., Abramowitz, A., & Waldman, I. D. (1998). Dopamine DRD4 receptor polymorphism and attention deficit hyperactivity disorder. *Molecular Psychiatry, 3,* 419–426.

Rowe, K. S. (1988). Synthetic food colorings and hyperactivity: A double-blind crossover study. *Australian Pediatric Journal, 24,* 143–147.

Rowe, K. S., & Rowe, K. J. (1994). Synthetic food coloring and behavior: A dose-response effect in a double-blind, placebo-controlled, repeated-measures study. *Journal of Pediatrics 125,* 691-698.

Roy, P., Rutter, M., & Pickles, A. (2000). Institutional care: Risk from family background or pattern of rearing? *Journal of Child Psychology and Psychiatry, 41,* 139–149.

Roy-Byrne, P., Scheele, L., Brinkley, J., Ward, N., Wiatrack, C., Russo, J., Townes, B., & Varley, C. (1997). Adult attention-deficit hyperactivity disorder: Assessment guidelines based on clinical presentation to a specialty clinic. *Comprehensive Psychiatry, 38,* 133–140.

Rucklidge, J. J., & Kaplan, B. J. (1997). Psychological functioning of women identified in adulthood with attention-deficit/hyperactivity disorder. *Journal of Attention Disorders, 2,* 167–176.

Ruel, J. M., & Hickey, P. (1992). Are too many children being treated with methylphenidate? *Canadian Journal of Psychiatry, 37,* 570–572.

Rutter, M. L. (1983). Behavioral studies: Questions and findings on the concept of a distinctive syndrome. In M. L. Rutter (Ed.), *Developmental neuropsychiatry* (p. 267). New York: Guilford Press.

Rutter, M. L. (1983). Issues and prospects in developmental neuropsychiatry. In M. L. Rutter (Ed.), *Developmental neuropsychiatry* (pp. 577–593). New York: Guilford Press.

Rutter, M. L. (1997). Motivation and delinquency. In *Nebraska Symposium on Motivation* (Vol. 44, p. 73). Lincoln: University of Nebraska Press.

Saccar, C. L. (1978). Drug therapy in the treatment of minimal brain dysfunction. *American Journal of Hospital Pharmacy, 35,* 554-552.

Sachs, R. M., & Bortnichak, E. A. (1986). An evaluation of spontaneous adverse drug reaction monitoring systems. *American Journal of Medicine, 81,* 49–55.

Safer, D. (1994). The impact of eight law suits on methylphenidate sales. *American Academy of Child and Adolescent Psychiatry, Scientific Proceedings of the Annual Meeting, 9,* 46.

Safer, D. J. (1997). Changing patterns of psychotropic medication prescribed by child psychiatrists in the 1990's. *Journal of Child and Adolescent Psychopharmacology, 7,* 267–274.

Safer, D. J., & Krager, J. M. (1985). Prevalence of medication treatment for hyperactive adolescents. *Psychopharmacology Bulletin, 21,* 212–215.

Safer, D. J., & Krager, J. M. (1988). A survey of medication treatment for hyperactive/inattentive students. *Journal of the American Medical Association, 260,* 2256–2258.

Safer, D. J., & Krager, J. M. (1992). Effect of a media blitz and a threatened lawsuit in stimulant treatment. *Journal of the American Medical Association, 268,* 1004–1007.

Safer, D. J., & Krager, J. M. (1994). The increased rate of stimulant treatment for hyperactive/inattentive students in secondary schools. *Pediatrics, 94,* 462–464.

Safer, D. J., & Zito, J. M. (1999). Psychotropic Medication for ADHD. *Mental Retardation and Developmental Disabilities: Research Reviews, 5,* 237–242.

Safer, D. J., Zito, J. M., & Fine, E. M. (1996). Increased methylphenidate usage for attention deficit disorder in the 1990s. *Pediatrics, 98,* 1084–1088.

Sage, D. D., & Burrello, L. C. (1994). *Leadership in educational reform: An administrators guide to changes in special education.* Baltimore: Paul H. Brookes.

Saklofske, D. H., Schwean, V. L., Yackalic, R. A., & Quinn, D. (1994). WISC-III and SB:FE performance of children with Attention Deficit Disorder. *Canadian Journal of School Psychology, 10,* 167–171.

Sallee, F., Stiller, R., & Perel, J. (1992). Pharmacodynamics of pemoline in attention deficit disorder with hyperactivity. *Journal of the American Academy of Child and Adolescent Psychiatry, 31*(2), 244–251.

Samuel, V. J., George, P., Thornell, A., Curtis, S., Taylor, A., Brome, D., Mick, E., Faraone, S. V., & Biederman, J. (1999). A pilot controlled family study of DSM-III-R and DSM-IV ADHD in African-American children. *Journal of the American Academy of Child and Adolescent Psychiatry, 38,* 34–39.

Sandberg, S. T., Rutter, M., & Taylor, E. (1978). Hyperkinetic disorder in psychiatric clinic attenders. *Developmental Medicine and Child Neurology, 20,* 279–299.

Sandberg, S., Weiselberg, M., & Shaffer, D. (1980). Hyperkinetic and conduct problem children in a primary school population: Some epidemiological considerations. *Journal of Child Psychology and Psychiatry, 21,* 293–311.

Sanders, M. R., Montgomery, D. T., & Brechman-Toussaint, M. L. (2000). The mass media and the prevention of childhood behavior problems: The evaluation of a television series to promote positive outcomes for parents and their children. *Journal of Child Psychology and Psychiatry and Allied Disciplines, 41,* 939–948.

Sandoval, J., Lambert, N. M., & Yandell, W. (1979). Current medical practice and hyperactive children. *American Journal of Orthopsychiatry, 46,* 323–324.

Sandstead, H. H., Fosmire, G. J., Halas, E. S., Jacob, R. A., Strobel, D. A., & Marks, E. O. (1977). Zinc deficiency: Effects on brain and behavior of rats and Rhesus monkeys. *Teratology, 16,* 229–234.

Sandyk, R. (1990). Zinc deficiency in attention-deficit/hyperactivity disorder. *International Journal of Neuroscience, 52,* 239–241.

Sannerud, C., & Feussner, G. (1999). Is methylphenidate a Schedule II stimulant? In B. Osman & L. Greenhill (Eds.), *Ritalin: Theory and practice* (2nd ed., pp. 27–42). New York: Mary Ann Liebert.

Sato, K., Taguchi, H., Maeda, T., & Yoshikawa, K. (1993). Pyridoxine toxicity to cultured fibroblasts cause by near-ultraviolet light. *Journal of Investigative Dermatology, 100,* 266–270.

Satterfield, J. H., Cantwell, D. P., & Satterfield, B. T. (1979). Multimodality treatment: A one-year follow-up of 84 hyperactive boys. *Archives of General Psychiatry, 36,* 965–974.

Satterfield, J., Hoppe, C. M., & Schell, A. M. (1982). A prospective study of delinquency in 110 adolescent boys with attention deficit disorder and 88 normal adolescent boys. *American Journal of Psychiatry, 139,* 795–798.

Satterfield, J. H., Satterfield, B. T., & Cantwell, D. P. (1981). Three-year multimodality treatment study of 100 hyperactive boys. *Journal of Pediatrics, 98,* 650–655.

Satterfield, J. H., Satterfield, B. T., & Schell, A. M. (1987). Therapeutic interventions to prevent delinquency in hyperactive boys. *Journal of the American Academy of Child and Adolescent Psychiatry, 26,* 56–64.

Satterfield, J. H., & Schell, A. (1997). A prospective study of hyperactive boys with conduct problems and normal boys: Adolescent and adult criminality. *Journal of the American Academy of Child and Adolescent Psychiatry, 36,* 1726–1735.

Satterfield, J. H., Schell, A. M., & Barb, S. D. (1980). Potential risk of prolonged administration of stimulant medication for hyperactivity. *Journal of Developmental and Behavioral Pediatrics, 1,* 102–107.

Satterfield, J., Swanson, J. M., Schell, A., & Lee, F. (1994). Prediction of antisocial behavior in attention-deficit hyperactivity disorder boys from aggression/defiance scores. *Journal of the American Academy of Child and Adolescent Psychiatry, 33,* 185–190.

Scahill, L., Schwab-Stone, M., Merikangas, K. R., Leckman, J. F., Zhang, H., & Kasl, S. (1999). Psychosocial and clinical correlates of ADHD in a community sample of school-age children. *Journal of the American Academy of Child and Adolescent Psychiatry, 38,* 976–984.

Schachar, R. (1998). *Treatment of ADHD with methylphenidate and parent programs.* Unpublished manuscript.

Schachar, R., & Logan, G. D. (1990). Impulsivity and inhibitory control in normal development and childhood psychopathology. *Developmental Psychology, 26,* 710–720.

Schachar, R., Rutter, M., & Smith, A. (1981). The characteristics of situationally and pervasively hyperactive children: Implications for syndrome definition. *Journal of Child Psychology and Psychiatry, 22,* 375–392.

Schachar, R., & Tannock, R. (1993). Childhood hyperactivity and psychostimulants: A review of extended treatment studies. *Journal of Child and Adolescent Psychopharmacology, 3,* 81–97.

Schachar, R., & Tannock, R. (1995). A test of four hypotheses for the comorbidity of attention deficit hyperactivity disorder and conduct disorder. *Journal of the American Academy of Child and Adolescent Psychiatry, 34,* 639–648.

Schachar, R., Tannock, R., & Cunningham, C. (1996). Treatment. In S. Sandberg (Ed.), *Hyperactivity disor-*

ders of childhood (pp. 433–476). Cambridge: Cambridge University Press.

Schachar, R. J., Tannock, R., Cunningham, C., & Corkum, P. V. (1997). Behavioral, situational, and temporal effects of treatment of ADHD with methylphenidate. *Journal of the American Academy of Child and Adolescent Psychiatry, 36,* 754–763.

Schachar, R., Tannock, R., Marriott, M., & Logan, G. (1995). Deficient inhibitory control in attention deficit hyperactivity disorder. *Journal of Abnormal Child Psychology, 23,* 411–437.

Schachar, R., & Wachsmuth, R. (1990). Hyperactivity and parental psychopathology. *Journal of Child Psychology and Psychiatry, 31,* 381–392.

Schaumburg, H., Kaplan, J., Windebank, A., Vick, N., Rasmus, S., Pleasure, D., & Brown, M. J. (1983). Sensory neuropathy from pyridoxine abuse: A new megavitamin syndrome. *New England Journal of Medicine, 309,* 445–448.

Schechter, M., & Keuezer, E. (1985). Learning in hyperactive children: Are there stimulant-related and state-dependent effects? *Journal of Clinical Pharmacology, 25,* 276–280.

Scheel-Kruger, J. (1971). Comparative studies of various amphetamine analogues demonstrating different interactions with the metabolism of catecholamines in the brain. *European Journal of Pharmacology, 14,* 47–59.

Schenk, S., & Davidson, E. S. (1993). Stimulant preexposure sensitizes rats and humans to the rewarding effects of cocaine. In *Laboratory behavioral studies of vulnerability to drug abuse* (NIDA Monograph No. 169) (pp. 56–82). Rockville, MD: U.S. Government Printing Office.

Schenk, S., & Partridge, B. (1997). Sensitization and tolerance in psychostimulant self-administration. *Pharmacology, Biochemistry, and Behavior, 57,* 543–550.

Schenk, S., & Partridge, B. (1999). Cocaine-seking produced by experimenter-administered drug injections: Dose-effect relationships in rats. *Psychopharmacology, 147,* 285–290.

Schenk, S., Valadez, A., McNamara, C., House, D., Higely, D., Bankson, M. T., Gibbs, S., & Horger, B. A. (1993). Development and expression of sensitization to cocaine's reinforcing properties: Role of NMDA receptors. *Psychopharmacology, 111,* 332–338.

Schiorring, E. (1979). Social isolation and other behavioral changes in groups of adult vervet monkeys produced by low, nonchronic doses of d-amphetamine. *Psychopharmacology, 64,* 297–304.

Schmahmann, J. D., & Sherman, J. C. (1998). The cerebellar cognitive affective syndrome. *Brain, 121,* 61–579.

Schmidt, M. H., Mocks, P., Lay, B., Eisert, H. G., Fojkar, R., Fritz-Sigmund, D., Marcus, A., & Musaeus,

B. (1997). Does oligoantigenic diet influence hyperactive/conduct-disordered children—A controlled trial. *European Child and Adolescent Psychiatry, 6,* 88–95.

Schubiner, H., Tzelepis, A., Isaacson, H., Warbasse, L. H., Sacharek, M., & Musial, J. (1995). The dual diagnosis of attention-deficit/hyperactivity disorder and substance abuse: Case reports and literature review. *Journal of Clinical Psychiatry, 56,* 146–150.

Schubiner, H., Tzelepis, A., Schoener, E., Lockhart, N., Kruger, M., & Kelley, B. (1997). *Prevalence of ADHD among substance abusers.* Paper presented at the annual meeting of College on Problems of Drug Dependence, Nashville, TN.

Schuster, C. R., & Thompson, M. H. (1969). Self-administration and behavioral dependence on drugs. *Annual Review of Pharmacology, 9,* 483–502.

Schuster, L., Grace, Y., & Bates, A. (1977) Sensitization to cocaine stimulation in mice. *Psychopharmacology, 52,* 185–190.

Schwab-Stone, M., Shaffer, D., Dulcan, M., Jensen, P., Fisher, P., Bird, H., Goodman, S. H., Lahey, B. B., Lichtman, J. H., Canino, G., Rubio-Stipec, M., & Rae, D. S. (1996). Criterion validity of the NIMH Diagnostic Interview Schedule for Children (DISC 2.3). *Journal of the American Academy of Child and Adolescent Psychiatry, 35,* 878–888.

Schwean, V. L., & Saklofske, D. H. (1998). WISC-III assessment of children with Attention Deficit/ Hyperactivity Disorder. In A. Prifitera & D. Saklofske (Eds.), *WISC-III clinical use and interpretation* (pp. 91–118). San Diego: Academic Press.

Scruggs, T. E., & Mastropieri, M. A. (1996). Teacher perceptions of mainstreaming/inclusion, 1958–1995: A research synthesis. *Exceptional Children, 63,* 59–74.

Seeman, P., & Madras, B. K. (1998). Anti-hyperactivity medication: Methylphenidate and amphetamine. *Molecular Psychiatry, 3,* 386–396.

Seidman, L. J., Biederman, J., Faraone, S. V., Millberger, S., Norman, D., Sieverd, K., Benedict, K., Guite, J., Mick, E., & Kiely, K. (1995). Effects of family history and comorbidity on the neuropsychological performance of children with ADHD: Preliminary findings. *Journal of the American Academy of Child and Adolescent Psychiatry, 34,* 1015–1024.

Seidman, L. J., Biederman, J., Faraone, S. V., Weber W., Mennin, D., & Jones, J. (1997). A pilot study of neuropsychological function in girls with ADHD. *Journal of the American Academy of Child and Adolescent Psychiatry, 36,* 366–373.

Seidman, L. J., Biederman, J., Faraone, S. V., Weber, W., & Ouellette, C. (1997). Toward defining a neuropsychology of attention deficit-hyperactivity disorder: Performance of children and adolescents from a large clinically referred sample. *Journal of Consulting and Clinical Psychology, 65,* 150–160.

Semrud-Clikeman, M., Biederman, J., Sprich-Buckminster, S., Lehman, B. K., Faraone, S. V., & Norman, D. (1992). Comorbidity between ADDH and learning disability: A review and report in a clinically referred sample. *Journal of the American Academy of Child and Adolescent Psychiatry, 31*, 439–448.

Semrud-Clikeman, M., Filipek, P. A., Biederman, J., & Steingard, R. (1994). Attention-deficit hyperactivity disorder: Magnetic resonance imaging morphometric analysis of the corpus callosum. *Journal of the American Academy of Child and Adolescent Psychiatry, 33*, 875–881.

Sergeant, J. A., & Steinhausen H. C. (1992). European perspectives on hyperkinetic disorder. *European Journal of Child Psychiatry, 1*, 34–41.

Sergeant, J. A., & Van der Meere, J. J. (1990). Convergence of approaches in localizing the hyperactivity deficit. In B. B. Lahey & A. E. Kazdin (Eds.), *Advances in clinical psychology* (pp. 207–246). New York: Plenum Press.

Setterberg, S., Bird, H., & Gould, M. (1992). *Parent and Interviewer Version of the Children's Global Assessment Scale.* New York: Columbia University.

Sever, Y., Ashkenazi, A., Tyano, S., & Weizman, A. (1997). Iron treatment in children with ADHD: A preliminary report. *Neuropsychobiology 35*, 178–180.

Shaffer, D. (1994). Attention deficit hyperactivity disorder in adults. *American Journal of Psychiatry, 151*, 633–638.

Shaffer, D., Fisher, P., Dulcan, M. K., Davies, M., Piacentini, J., Schwab-Stone, M. E., Lahey, B. B., Bourdon, K., Jensen, P. S., Bird, H. R., Canino, G., & Regier, D. A. (1996). The NIMH diagnostic interview schedule for children version 2.3 (DISC-2.3): Description, acceptability, prevalence rates, and performance in the MECA study. *Journal of the American Academy of Child and Adolescent Psychiatry, 35*, 865–877.

Sharp, W. S., Walter, J. M., Marsh, W. L., Ritchie, G. F., Hamburger, S. D., & Castellanos, F. X. (1999). ADHD in girls: Clinical comparability of a research sample. *Journal of the American Academy of Child and Adolescent Psychiatry, 38*, 40–47.

Shaw, S. T., Cullen, J. P., McGuire, J. M., & Brickerhoff, L. C. (1995). Operationalizing a definition of learning disabilities. *Journal of Learning Disabilities, 28*, 586–597.

Shaywitz, B. A., Fletcher, J. M., & Shaywitz, S. E. (1995). Defining and classifying learning disabilities and attention-deficit/hyperactivity disorder. *Journal of Child Neurology, 10*, S50–S57.

Shaywitz, B. A., Siegel, N. J., & Pearson, H. A. (1977). Megavitamins for minimal brain dysfunction: A potentially dangerous therapy. *Journal of the American Medical Association, 238*, 1749–1750.

Shaywitz, S. E., & Shaywitz, B. A. (1987). Attention deficit disorder: Current perspectives. *Pediatric Neurology, 3*, 129–135.

Shaywitz, S. E., & Shaywitz, B. A. (1991). Introduction to the special series on attention deficit disorder. *Journal of Learn Disabilities, 24*, 68–72.

Shekim, W. O., Antun, F., Hanna, G. L., & McCracken, J. T. (1990). S-adenosyl-L-methionine (SAM) in adults with ADHD, RS: Preliminary results from an open trial. *Psychopharmacology Bulletin, 26*, 249-253.

Shekim, W. O., Asarnow, R. F., Hess, E., Zaucha, K., & Wheeler, N. (1990). A clinical and demographic profile of a sample of adults with attention deficit hyperactivity disorder, residual state. *Comprehensive Psychiatry, 31*, 416–425.

Shen, Y. C., & Wang, Y. F. (1984). Urinary 3-methoxy-4-hydroxyphenylglycol sulfate excretion in seventy-three schoolchildren with minimal brain dysfunction. *Biological Psychiatry, 19*, 861–870.

Shen, Y. C., Wang, Y. F., & Xan, X. L. (1985). An epidemiological investigation of minimal brain dysfunction in six elementary schools in Beijing. *Journal of Child Psychology and Psychiatry, 26*, 777–788.

Sher, K. J., Walitzer, K. S., Wood, P. K., & Brent, E. E. (1991). Characteristics of children of alcoholics: Putative risk factors., substance use and abuse, and psychopathology. *Journal of Abnormal Psychology, 100*, 427–448.

Sherman, C. B., Hudson, L. D., & Pierson, D. J. (1987). Severe precocious emphysema in intravenous methylphenidate (Ritalin) abusers. *Chest, 92*, 1085–1087.

Sherman, D. K., Iacono, W. G., & McGue, M. K. (1997). Attention-deficit hyperactivity disorder dimensions: A twin study of inattention and impulsivity-hyperactivity. *Journal of the American Academy of Child and Adolescent Psychiatry, 36*, 745–753.

Sherman, M. (1991). Prescribing Practice of methylphenidate: The Suffolk County Study. In B. Osman & L. L. Greenhill (Eds.), *Ritalin: Theory and patient management* (pp. 401–420). New York: Mary Ann Liebert.

Sherman, M., & Hertzig, M. E. (1991). Prescribing practices of Ritalin: The Suffolk County, New York study. In L. L. Greenhill & B. B. Osman (Eds.), *Ritalin: Theory and patient management* (pp. 187–193). New York: Mary Ann Liebert.

Shevell, M., & Schreiber, R. (1997). Pemoline-associated hepatic failure; a critical analysis of the literature. *Pediatric Neurology, 16*, 14–16.

Shippenberg, T. S., & Heidbreder, C. A. (1995). Sensitization to the conditioned rewarding effects of cocaine: Pharmacological and temporal characteristics.

Journal of Pharmocology and Experimental Therapeutics, 273, 808–815.

Shouse, M. N., & Lubar, J. F. (1978). Physiological basis of hyperkinesis treated with methylphenidate. *Pediatrics, 62,* 343–351.

Shue, K. L., & Douglas, V. I. (1992). Attention deficit hyperactivity disorder and the frontal lobe syndrome. *Brain and Cognition, 20,* 104–124.

Sickmund, M. (2000, October). Offenders in juvenile court, 1997. *OJJDP Juvenile Justice Bulletin,* pp. 1–3.

Sidransky, H. (1997). Tryptophan and carcinogenesis: Review and update on how tryptophan may act. *Nutrition and Cancer, 29,* 181–194.

Silberg, J., Rutter, M., Meyer, J., Maes, H., Hewitt, J., Simonoff, E., Pickles, A., & Loeber, R. (1996). Genetic and environmental influences on the covariation between hyperactivity and conduct disturbance in juvenile twins. *Journal of Child Psychology and Psychiatry and Allied Disciplines, 37,* 803–816.

Silbergeld, E. K., & Goldberg, A. M. (1975). Pharmacological and neurochemical investigations of lead-induced hyperactivity. *Neuropharmacology, 14,* 431–444.

Silberstein, R. B., Farrow, M., Levy, F., Pipingas, A., Hay, D. A., & Jarman, F. C. (1998). Functional brain electrical activity mapping in boys with attention-deficit/hyperactivity disorder. *Archives of General Psychiatry, 55,* 1105-1112.

Silva, R., Munoz, D., & Alpert, M. (1996). Carbamazepine use in children and adolescents with features of attention-deficit hyperactivity disorder: A meta-analysis. *Journal of the American Academy of Child and Adolescent Psychiatry, 35,* 352–358.

Silverman, P. B., & Schultz, K. A. (1989). Comparison of cocaine and procaine discriminative stimuli. *Drug Development and Research, 16,* 427–433.

Simpson, D. D., & Nelson, A. L. (1974). Attention training through breathing control to modify hyperactivity. *Journal of Learning Disabilities, 7,* 15–23.

Singer, H. S., Reiss, A. L., Brown, J. E., & Aylward, E. H. (1993). Volumetric MRI changes in basal ganglia of children with Tourette's syndrome. *Neurology, 43,* 950–956.

Singer, S., Brown, J., Quaskey, S., Rosenberg, L., Mellits, E., & Denckla, M. (1994). The treatment of attention-deficit hyperactivity disorder in Tourette's syndrome: A double-blind placebo-controlled study with clonidine and desipramine. *Pediatrics, 95,* 74–81.

Sleator, E., & Ullman, R. K. (1981). Can the physician diagnose hyperactivity in the office? *Pediatrics, 67,* 13–17.

Sloan, M. T., Jensen, P. S., Hoagwood, K., & Kettle, L.

(1999). Assessing the services for children with ADHD: Gaps and opportunities. *Journal of Attention Disorders, 3,* 13–29.

Slomkowski, C., Klein, R. G., & Mannuzza, S. (1995). Is self-esteem an important outcome in hyperactive children? *Journal of Abnormal Child Psychology, 23,* 303–315.

Smalley, S. L., Bailey, J. N., Palmer, C. G., Cantwell, D. P., McGough, J. J., Del-Homme, M. A., Asarnow, J. R., Woodward, J. A., Ramsey, C., & Nelson, S. F. (1998). Evidence that the dopamine D4 receptor is a susceptibility gene in attention deficit hyperactivity disorder. *Molecular Psychiatry, 3,* 427–430.

Smith, R. C., & Davis, J. M. (1977). Comparative effects of d-amphetamine, l-amphetamine, and methylphenidate on mood in man. *Psychopharmacology, 53,* 1–12.

Snodgrass, S. R. (1992). Vitamin neurotoxicity. *Molecular Neurobiology, 6,* 41–73.

Snyder, H. N. (1997). *Juvenile arrests 1996.* Unpublished internal document, U.S. Department of Justice, Office of Juvenile Justice and Delinquency Prevention, Washington, DC.

Snyder, H. N., Sickmund, M., & Poe-Yamagata, E. (1997). *Juvenile offenders and victims: 1997 update on violence.* Unpublished internal document, U.S. Department of Justice, Office of Juvenile Justice and Delinquency Prevention, Washington, DC.

Sobsey, D., & Dreimanis, M. (1993). Integration outcomes: Theoretical models and empirical investigations. *Developmental Disabilities Bulletin, 21*(1), 1–14.

Solanto, M. (1998). Neuropsychopharmacological mechanisms of stimulant drug action in attention-deficit hyperactivity disorder: A review and integration. *Behavioral Brain Research, 94,* 127–152.

Solanto, M. V. (2000), Neuropharmacological mechanisms of stimulant drug action in attention-deficit hyperactivity disorder: A review and integration. *Behavior and Brain Research, 94,* 127–152.

Solanto, M. V., Wender, E. H., & Bartell, S. S. (1997). Effects of methylphenidate and behavioral contingencies on sustained attention in attention-deficit hyperactivity disorder: A test of the reward dysfunction hypothesis. *Journal of Child and Adolescent Psychopharmacology, 7,* 123–136.

Sonuga-Barke, E. J. S., Daley, D., Thompson, M., Laver-Bradbury, C., & Weeks, A. (2001). Parent-based therapies for preschool attention-deficity/hyperactivity disorder: A randomized, controlled trial with a community sample. *Journal of the American Academy of Child and Adolescent Psychiatry, 40,* 402–408.

Sonuga-Barke, E. J. S., Lamparelli, M., Stevenson, J., Thompson, M., & Henry, A. (1994). Behaviour problems and preschool intellectual attainment: The associations of hyperactivity and conduct problems. *Journal of Child Psychology and Psychiatry, 35,* 949–960.

Sonuga-Barke, E. J., Saxton, T., & Hall, M. (1998). The role of interval underestimation in hyperactive children's failure to suppress responses over time. *Behavioral Brain Research, 94,* 45–50.

Sonuga-Barke, E. J. S., Taylor, E., & Hepenstall, E. (1992). Hyperactivity and delay aversion-II: The effects of self versus externally imposed stimulus presentation periods on memory. *Journal of Child Psychology and Psychiatry, 33,* 399–409.

Sonuga-Barke, E. J. S., Williams, E., Hall, M., & Saxton, T. (1996). Hyperactivity and delay aversion III: the effects on cognitive style of imposing delay after errors. *Journal of Child Psychology and Psychiatry, 37,* 189–194.

Spealman, R. D., Madras, B. K., & Bergman, J. (1989). Effects of cocaine and related drugs in non-human primates. II. Stimulant effects on schedule controlled behavior. *Journal of Pharmacology and Experimental Therapeutics, 251,* 142–149.

Spencer, T. (1997, October). *A double-blind, controlled study of desipramine in children with ADHD and tic disorders.* Paper presented at the annual meeting of the American Academy of Child and Adolescent Psychiatry, Toronto.

Spencer, T. J., Biederman, J., Harding, M., O'Donnell, D., Faraone, S. V., & Wilens, T. (1996). Growth deficits in ADHD children revisited: Evidence for disorder-associated growth delays? *Journal of the American Academy of Child and Adolescent Psychiatry, 35,* 1460–1469.

Spencer, T., Biederman, J., Kerman, K., Steingard, R., & Wilens, T. E. (1993). Desipramine in the treatment of children with Tic disorder or Tourette's Syndrome and attention deficit hyperactivity disorder. *Journal of the American Academy of Child and Adolescent Psychiatry, 32,* 354–360.

Spencer, T., Biederman, J., & Wilens, T. (1998). Growth deficits in children with attention deficit hyperactivity disorder. *Pediatrics, 102,* 501–506.

Spencer, T., Biederman, J., Wilens, T., & Faraone, S. V. (1994). Is attention-deficit hyperactivity disorder in adults a valid disorder? *Harvard Review of Psychiatry, 1,* 326–335.

Spencer, T., Biederman, J., Wilens, T., Harding, M., O'Donnell, D., & Griffin, S. (1996). Pharmacotherapy of attention-deficit hyperactivity disorder across the life cycle. *Journal of the American Academy of Child and Adolescent Psychiatry, 35,* 409–432.

Spencer, T., Biederman, J., Wilens, T. E., Prince, J., & Rea, J. (1999, June). *An open, dose ranging study of tomoxetine in children with ADHD.* Paper presented at the scientific proceedings of International Society for Research in Child and Adolescent Psychopathology, Barcelona, Spain.

Spencer, T., Biederman, J., Wilens, T. E., Steingard, R., & Geist, D. (1993). Nortriptyline in the treatment of children with attention deficit hyperactivity disorder and tic disorder or Tourette's syndrome. *Journal of the American Academy of Child and Adolescent Psychiatry, 32,* 205–210.

Spencer, T., Wilens, T. E., & Biederman, J. (1995). *A double-blind, crossover comparison of tomoxetine and placebo in adults with ADHD.* Paper presented at the 12th scientific proceedings of the American Academy of Child and Adolescent Psychiatrists, New Orleans, LA.

Spencer, T., Wilens, T., Biederman, J., Farone, S., Ablen, S., & Lapey, K. (1995). A double-blind., crossover comparison of methylphenidate and placebo in adults with childhood onset ADHD. *Archives of General Psychiatry, 52,* 434–443.

Spensley, J., & Rockwell, D. A. (1972). Psychosis during methylphenidate abuse. *New England Journal of Medicine, 286,* 880–881.

Spier, S. A. (1995). Toxicity and abuse of prescribed stimulants. *International Journal of Psychiatry and Medicine, 25,* 69–79.

Sprague, R. L., & Sleator, E. K. (1977).Methylphenidate in hyperkinetic children: Differences in dose effects on learning and social behavior. *Science, 198,* 1274–1276.

Sroufe, L. A., & Stewart, M. (1999). Treating problem children with stimulant drugs. *New England Journal Medicine, 289,* 407–413.

Stableford, W., Butz, R., Hasazi, J., Leitenberg, H., & Peyser, J. (1976). Sequential withdrawal of stimulant drugs and use of behavior therapy with two hyperactive boys. *American Journal of Orthopsychiatry, 46,* 302–312.

Stainback, W., & Stainback, S. (Eds.) (1996). *Inclusion: A guide for educators.* Baltimore: Paul H. Brookes.

Starobrat-Hermelin, B., & Kozielec, T. (1997). The effects of magnesium physiological supplementation on hyperactivity in children with ADHD: Positive response to magnesium oral loading test. *Magnesium Research, 10,* 149–156.

Stecyk, O., Loludice, T. A., Demeter, S., & Jacobs, J. (1985). Multiple organ failure resulting from intravenous abuse of methylphenidate hydrochloride. *Annals of Emergency Medicine, 14,* 597/113.

Stein, M. A., Szumowski, E., Blondis, T. A., & Roizen, N. J. (1995). Adaptive skills dysfunction in ADD and ADHD children. *Journal of Child Psychology and Psychiatry, 36,* 663–670.

Stein, T. P., & Sammaritano, A. M. (1984). Nitrogen

metabolism in normal and hyperkinetic boys. *American Journal of Clinical Nutrition, 39*, 520–524.

Steingard, R., Biederman, J., Spencer, T., Wilens, T., & Gonzalez, A. (1993). Comparison of clonidine response in the treatment of attention deficit hyperactivity disorder with and without comorbid tic disorders. *Journal of the American Academy of Child and Adolescent Psychiatry, 32*, 350–353.

Steinhausen, H., Gobel, D., & Nestler, V. (1984). Psychopathology in the offspring of alcoholic parents. *Journal of the American Academy of Child and Adolescent Psychiatry, 23*, 465–471.

Steinhausen, H. C., Willms, J., & Spohr, H. L. (1993). Long-term psychopathological and cognitive outcome of children with fetal alcohol syndrome. *Journal of the American Academy of Child and Adolescent Psychiatry, 32*, 990–994.

Sternberg, E. M. (1996). Pathogenesis of L-tryptophan eosinophilia-myalgia syndrome. *Advances in Experimental Medicine and Biology, 398*, 325–330.

Stevens, L. J., Zentall, S. S., Deck, J. L., Abate, M. L., Watkins, B. A., Lipp, S. R., & Burgess, J. R. (1995). Essential fatty acid metabolism in boys with attention-deficit hyperactivity disorder. *American Journal of Clinical Nutrition, 62*, 761–768.

Stevenson, J., Bateman, B., Hutchinson, E., Warner, J., Dean, T., Rowlandson, P., Grant, C., Grundy, J., & Fitzgerald, C. (2001, June 30). *The effects of a double-blind placebo-controlled artificial food colourings and benzoate preservatives challenge on hyperactivity in a general population sample of preschool children.* Poster presented at 10th scientific meeting of the International Society for Research in Child and Adolescent Psychopathology, Vancouver, British Columbia.

Stewart, M. A., DeBlois, C. S., & Cummings, C. (1980). Psychiatric disorder in the parents of hyperactive boys and those with conduct disorder. *Journal of Child Psychology and Psychiatry, 21*, 283–292.

Stewart, M. A., Thach, B. T., & Friedin, M. R. (1970). Accidental poisoning and the hyperactive child syndrome. *Diseases of the Nervous System, 31*, 403–407.

Stiffman, A. R., Chen, Y. W., Elze, D., Dore, P., & Cheng, L. C. (1997). Adolescents' and providers' perspectives on the need for and use of mental health services. *Journal of Adolescent Health, 21*, 335–342.

Stiffman, A. R., Horwitz, S. M., Hoagwood, K., Compton, W., Cottler, L., Bean, D. L., Narrow, W. E., & Weisz, J. R. (2000). The service assessment for children and adolescents (SACA): Child and adult reports. *Journal of the American Academy of Child and Adolescent Psychiatry, 39*(8), 1032–1039.

Still, G. (1902). The Coulstonian lectures on some abnormal physical conditions in children. *Lancet, 1*, 1008–1012.

Strakowski, S. M., & Sax, K. W. (1998). Progressive behavioral response to repeated d-Amphetamine challenge: Further evidence for sensitization in humans. *Biological Psychiatry, 44*, 1171–1177.

Strauss, A. A., & Lethinen, L. E. (1947). *Psychopathology and education of the brain-injured child.* New York: Grune & Stratton.

Stuss, D. T. (1992). Biological and psychological development of executive functions. *Brain and Cognition, 20*, 3–28.

Stuss, D. T., & Benson, D. F. (1984). Neuropsychological functions of the frontal lobes. *Psychological Bulletin, 95*, 3–28.

Substance Abuse and Mental Health Services Administration. (1997). *Year-end preliminary estimates for the 1996 DAWN* (DHHS Publication No. SMA 98-3175). Washington, DC: Office of Applied Studies.

Substance Abuse and Mental Health Services Administration. (1998). *Methodology series: M-2, DAWN sample design and estimation procedures; technical report* (DHHS Publication No. SMA 98-3178). Washington, DC: Office of Applied Studies.

Sullivan, M. A., & O'Leary, S. G. (1990). Maintenance following reward and cost token programs. *Behavior Therapy, 21*, 139–149.

Sun, Y., Wang, Y., Qu, X., Wang, J., Fang, J., & Zhang, L. (1994). Clinical observations and treatment of hyperkinesia in children by traditional Chinese medicine. *Journal of Traditional Chinese Medicine, 14*(2), 105–109.

Sunohara, G., Barr, C., Jain, U., Schachar, R., Roberts, W., Tannock, R., Malone, M., & Kennedy, J. L. (1997). *Association of the D4 receptor gene in individuals with ADHD.* Baltimore: American Society of Human Genetics.

Sunohara, G. A., & Kennedy, J. L. (1998). *The dopamine D4 receptor gene and neuropsychiatric disorders: Dopaminergic disorders.* New York: IBC Press.

Swanson, J. (1992). *School-based assessments and interventions for ADD students.* Irvine, CA: K.C. Publishing. (SNAP-IV also available on-line: www.ADHD.net)

Swanson, J., Castellanos, F. X., Murias, M., LaHoste, G., & Kennedy, J. (1998). Cognitive neuroscience of attention deficit hyperactivity disorder and hyperkinetic disorder. *Current Opinion in Neurobiology, 8*, 263–271.

Swanson, J. M., Flodman, P., Kennedy, J., Spence, M. A., Moyzis, R., Schuck, S., Murias, M., Moriarity, J., Barr, C., Smith, M., & Posner, M. (2000). Dopamine genes and ADHD. *Neuroscience and Biobehavioral Reviews, 24*(1), 21–25.

Swanson, J. M., Gupta, S., Guinta, D., Flynn, D., Agler,

D., Lerner, M., Williams, L., Shoulson, I., & Wigal, S. (1999). Acute tolerance to methylphenidate in the treatment of attention deficit hyperactivity disorder in children. *Clinical Pharmacology and Therapeutics, 66,* 295–305.

Swanson, J., & Kinsbourne, M. (1980, March 28). Food dyes impair performance of hyperactive children on a laboratory learning test. *Science, 207*(4438), 1485–1487.

Swanson, J., Kinsbourne, M., Roberts, W., & Zucker, K. (1978). Time-response analysis of the effect of stimulant medication on the learning ability of children referred for hyperactivity. *Pediatrics, 61,* 21–29.

Swanson, J. M., Kraemer, H. C., Hinshaw, S. P., Arnold, L. E., Conners, C. K., Abikoff, H. B., Clevenger, W., Davies, M., Elliott, G. R., Greenhill, L. L., Hechtman, L., Hoza, B., Jensen, P. S., March, J. S., Newcorn, J. H., Owens, E. B., Pelham, W. E., Schiller, E., Severe, J. B., Simpson, S., Vitiello, B., Wells, K., Wigal, T., & Wu, M. (2001). Clinical relevance of the primary findings of the MTA: Success rates based on severity of ADHD and ODD symptoms at the end of treatment. *Journal of the American Academy of Child and Adolescent Psychiatry, 40,* 168–179.

Swanson, J., Lerner, M., & Williams, L. (1995). More frequent diagnosis of attention deficit-hyperactivity disorder. *New England Journal of Medicine, 333,* 944.

Swanson, J. M., McBurnett, K., Christian, D. L., & Wigal, T. (1995). Stimulant medication and treatment of children with ADHD. In T. H. Ollendick & R. J. Prinz (Eds.), *Advances in clinical child psychology* (Vol. 17, pp. 265–322). New York: Plenum Press.

Swanson, J. M., McBurnett, K., Wigal, T., Pfiffner, L. J., Lerner, M. A., Williams, L., Christian, D. L., Tamm, L., Willcutt, E., Crowley, K., Clevenger, W., Khouzam, N., Woo, C., Crinella, F., & Fisher, T. D. (1993). Effect of stimulant medication on children with attention deficit disorder: A "review of reviews." *Exceptional Children, 60,* 154–162.

Swanson, J. M., Posner, M. I., Potkin, S., Bonforte, S., Youpa, D., Cantwell, D., & Crinella, F. (1991). Activating tasks for the study of visal-spatial attention in ADHD children: A cognitive anatomical approach. *Journal of Child Neurology, 6*(Suppl.), S119–S127.

Swanson, J. M., Sergeant, J. A., Taylor, E., Sonuga-Barke, E. J., Jensen, P. S., & Cantwell, D. P. (1998). Attention-deficit hyperactivity disorder and hyperkinetic disorder. *Lancet, 351,* 429–433.

Swanson, J. M., Sunohara, G. A., Kennedy, J. L., Regino, R., Fineberg, E., Wigal, T., Lerner, M., Williams, L., LaHoste, G. J., & Wigal, S. (1998). Association of the dopamine receptor D4 (DRD4) gene with a refined phenotype of attention deficit hyperactivity disorder (ADHD): A family-based approach. *Molecular Psychiatry, 3,* 38–41.

Swanson, J., Wigal, S., Greenhill, L., Browne, R.,

Waslik, B., Lerner, M., Williams, L., Flynn, D., Agler, D., Crowley, K., Fineberg, E., Baren, M., & Cantwell, D. P. (1998). Analog classroom assessment of Adderall in children with ADHD. *Journal of the American Academy of Child and Adolescent Psychiatry, 37,* 1–8.

Swedo, S. E., Leonard, H. L., Garvey, M., Mittleman, B., Allen, A. J., Perlmutter, S., Dow, S., Zamkoff, J., Dubbert, B. K., & Lougee, L. (1998). Pediatric autoimmune neuropsychiatric disorders associated with streptococcal infections: Clinical description of the first 50 cases. *American Journal of Psychiatry, 155,* 264–271.

Swensen, A. (2001, October). Direct and indirect costs for ADHD patients and family members. *Scientific Proceedings of the American Academy of Child and Adolescent Psychiatry,* 75.

Szatmari, P., Offord, D. R., & Boyle, M. H. (1989). Correlates, associated impairments, and patterns of service utilization of children with attention deficit disorders: Findings from the Ontario Child Health Study. *Journal of Child Psychology and Psychiatry, 30,* 205–217.

Szatmari, P., Offord, D. R., & Boyle, M. H. (1989). Ontario Child Health Study: Prevalence of attention deficit disorder with hyperactivity. *Journal of Child Psychology and Psychiatry, 30,* 219–230.

Tallmadge, J., & Barkley, R. A. (1983). The interactions of hyperactive and normal boys with their mothers and fathers. *Journal of Abnormal Child Psychology, 11,* 565–579.

Tannock, R. (1998). Attention deficit hyperactivity disorder: Advances in cognitive, neurobiological, and genetic research. *Journal of Child Psychology and Psychiatry, 39,* 65–99.

Tannock, R. (1998). *ADHD as a disorder in children, adolescents, and adults—etiology/risk factors: Genetics and pathophysiology.* Paper presented at the National Institutes of Health Consensus Development Conference on Diagnosis and Treatment of Attention Deficit Hyperactivity Disorder (ADHD), Washington, DC.

Tannock, R. (1998). Attention deficit hyperactivity disorder: Advances in cognitive, neurobiological, and genetic research. *Journal of Child Psychology and Psychiatry, 39,* 65–99.

Tannock, R. (2000). Attention deficit disorders with anxiety disorders. In T. E. Brown (Ed.), *Attention deficit disorders and comorvidities in children, adolescents, and adults* (pp. 125–170). Washington, DC: American Psychiatric Press.

Tannock, R., & Brown, T. E. (2000). Attention deficit disorders with learning disorders in children and adolescents. In T. E. Brown (Ed.), *Attention deficit disorders and comorbidities in children, adolescents and adults* (pp. 231–295). Washington, DC: American Psychiatric Press.

Tannock, R., & Ickowicz, A. (1995). Differential effects of methylphenidate on working memory in ADHD children with and without comorbid anxiety. *Journal of the American Academy of Child and Adolescent Psychiatry, 34*, 886–896.

Tannock, R., Ickowicz, A., & Schachar, R. (1995). Differential effects of MPH on working memory in ADHD children with and without comorbid anxiety. *Journal of the American Academy of Child and Adolescent Psychiatry, 34*, 886–896.

Tannock, R., & Marriott, M. (1992). Learning disabilities: Converging evidence of deficits in inhibitory processes [abstract]. *Proceedings of the 39th annual meeting of the American Academy of Child and Adolescent Psychiatry, 8*, 89.

Tannock, R., Martinussen, R., & Frijters, I. (2000). Naming speed performance and stimulant effects Indicate controlled processing deficits in attention-deficit hyperactivity disorder. *Journal of Abnormal Child Psychology, 28*, 237–252.

Tannock, R., & Schachar, R. (1996). Executive dysfunction as an underlying mechanism of behavior and language problems in attention deficit hyperactivity disorder. In J. H. Beitchman, N. Cohen, M. M. Konstantareas, & R. Tannock (Eds.), *Language, learning, and behavior disorders: Developmental, biological, and clinical perspectives* (pp. 128–155). New York: Cambridge University Press.

Tannock, R., Schachar, R., & Ickowicz, A. (1997). *Disentangling the DSM-IV ADHD subtypes.* Paper presented at the annual meeting of the American Psychological Association, Toronto, Canada.

Tannock, R., Schachar, R. J., & Logan, G. (1993). Does methylphenidate induce overfocusing in hyperactive children? *Journal of Clinical Child Psychology, 22*, 28–41.

Tannock, R., Schachar, R., & Logan, G. D. (1995). Methylphenidate and cognitive flexibility: Dissociated dose effects in hyperactive children. *Journal of Abnormal Child Psychology, 23*, 235–267.

Tannock, R., Schachar, R., Logan, G., & Hetherington, R. (1999, June 16–20). *Do deficits in inhibitory control or time perception best characterize ADHD?* Paper presented at the International Society for Research in Child and Adolescent Psychopathology, Barcelona, Spain.

Tarter, R. E., & Edwards, K. (1988). Psychological factors associated with the risk for alcoholism. *Alcoholism: Clinical and Experimental Research, 12*, 471–480.

Tarter, R. E., McBride, H., Buonpane, N., & Schneider, D. U. (1977). Differentiation of alcoholics. *Archives of General Psychiatry, 34*, 761–768.

Taylor, E. (1994). Syndromes of attention deficit and overactivity. In M. L. Rutter, E. Taylor, & L. Hersov (Eds.), *Child and adolescent psychiatry* (3rd ed., pp. 293–299). Oxford, UK: Blackwell Scientific.

Taylor, E., Chadwick, O., Heptinstall, E., & Danckaerts, M. (1996). Hyperactivity and conduct problems as risk

factors for adolescent development. *Journal of the American Academy of Child and Adolescent Psychiatry, 35*, 1213–1226.

Taylor, E., & Sandberg, S. (1984). Hyperactive behavior in English schoolchildren: A questionnaire survey. *Journal of Abnormal Child Psychology, 12*(1), 143–155.

Taylor, E., Sandberg, S., Thorley, G., & Giles, S. (1991). The epidemiology of childhood hyperactivity. *Institute of Psychiatry, Maudsley Monographs* (No. 33). London: Oxford University Press.

Taylor, E., Schachar, R., Thorley, G., Wieselberg, H. M., Everitt, B., & Rutter, M. (1987). Which boys respond to stimulant medication? A controlled trial of methyphenidate in boys with disruptive behavior. *Psychological Medicine, 17*, 121–143.

Taylor, E., Sergeant, J., Doepfner, M., Gunning, B., Overmeyer, S., Mobius, H. J., & Eisert, H. G. (1998). Clinical guidelines for hyperkinetic disorder. *European Child and Adolescent Psychiatry, 7*(4), 184–200.

Teicher, M. H., Ito, Y., Glod, C. A., & Barber, N. I. (1996). Objective measurement of hyperactivity and attentional problems in ADHD. *Journal of the American Academy of Child and Adolescent Psychiatry, 35*, 334–342.

Temple, C. M. (1998). Cognitive neuropsychology and its application to children. *Journal of Child Psychology and Psychiatry, 38*, 27–52.

Teplin, L. (1998). *Assessing the alcohol, drug and mental health service needs in juvenile detainees.* Grant application submitted to National Institute of Mental Health.

Thatcher, R. W. (1996). Neuroimaging of cyclical cortical reorganization during human development. In R. W. Thatcher, G. R. Lyon, J. Rumsey, & N. Krasnegor (Eds.), *Developmental neuroimaging: Mapping the development of brain and behavior* (pp. 91–106). San Diego: Academic Press.

Thomas, A., & Chess, A. (1977). *Temperament and development.* New York: Brunner/Mazel.

Thomas, A., Chess, A., & Birch, H. G. (1968). *Temperament and behavior disorders in children.* New York: New York University Press.

Thompson, L. L., Riggs, P. D., Mikulich, S. K., & Crowley, T. J. (1996). Contribution of ADHD symptoms to substance problems and delinquency in conduct-disordered adolescents. *Journal of Abnormal Child Psychology, 24*, 325–347.

Thurber, S., & Walker, C. (1983). Medication and hyperactivity: A meta-analysis. *Journal of General Psychiatry, 108*, 79–86.

Thurston, L. P. (1979). Comparison of the effects of parent training and of Ritalin in treating hyperactive children. *International Journal of Mental Health, 8*, 121–128.

Tilson, H. A., MacPhail, R. C., & Crofton, K. M.

(1995). Defining neurotoxicity in a decision-making context. *Neurotoxicology, 16*, 363–375.

Timmons-Mitchell, J., Brown, C., Schulz, S. C., Webster, S. E., Underwood, L. A., & Semple, W. E. (1997). Comparing the mental health needs of female and male incarcerated juvenile delinquents. *Behavioral Sciences and the Law, 15*, 195–202.

Tizard, B., & Hodges, J. (1978). The effect of early institutional rearing on the development of eight year old children. *Journal of Child Psychology and Psychiatry, 19*, 99–118.

Tolman, K. G., Freston, J. W., Berenson, M. M., & Sannella, J. J. (1973). Hepatoxicity due to pemoline. Report of two cases. *Digestion, 9*, 532–539.

Topaz, P. M. (1971). Preliminary study of drug abuse and minimal brain dysfunction. *Journal of Learning Disabilities, 4*, 503–505.

Torabi, M. R., Bailey, W. J., & Madj-Jabbari, M. (1993). Cigarette smoking as a predictor of alcohol and other drug use by children and adolescents: Evidence of the gateway drug effect. *Journal of School Health, 63*, 302–305.

Toren, P., Sofia, E., Sela, B. A., Wolmer, L., Weitz, R., Dov, I., Koren, S., Reiss, A., Weizman, R., & Laor, N. (1996). Zinc deficiency in ADHD. *Biological Psychiatry, 40*, 1308–1310.

Torrioli, M. G., Vernacotola, S., Mariotti, P., Bianchi, E., Calvani, M., DeGaetano, A., Chiurazzi, P., & Neri, G. (1999). Double-blind, placebo-controlled study of l-acetylcarnitine for the treatment of hyperactive behavior in fragile X syndrome. *American Journal of Medical Genetics, 87*, 366-368.

Treuting, J., & Hinshaw, S. P. (1998). *Depression and self-esteem in boys with ADHD: Relationships with comorbid aggression and explanatory attributional mechanisms.* Berkeley: University of California Press.

Tripp, G., Luk, S. L., Schaughency, E. A., & Singh, R. (1999). DSM-IV and ICD-10: A comparison of the correlates of ADHD to hyperkinetic disorder. *Journal of the American Academy of Child and Adolescent Psychiatry, 38*(2), 156–164.

Trites, R. L., & Laprade, K. (1983). Evidence for an independent syndrome of hyperactivity. *Journal of Child Psychology and Psychiatry, 24*(4), 573–586.

Trommer, B. L., Hoeppner, J. B., Lorber, R., & Armstrong, K. J. (1988). The go-no-go paradigm in attention deficit disorder. *Annals of Neurology, 2*, 610–614.

Trott, G. E., Friese, H. J., Menzel, M., & Nissen, G. (1991). Wirksamkeit und vertraglichkeit des selektiven MAO-A-Inhibitors moclobemid bei kindern mit hyper-kinetischem syndrom [Use of moclobemide in children with attention deficit hyperactivity disorder] (both English and German versions). *Jugendpsychiatrica, 19*, 248–253.

Truss, C. O. (1991). A controlled trial of nystatin for the candidiasis hypersensitivity syndrome [Letter to editor]. *New England Journal of Medicine, 324*(22), 1592.

Turkewitz, H., O'Leary, K. D., & Ironsmith, M. (1975). Generalization and maintenance of appropriate behavior through self-control. *Journal of Consulting and Clinical Psychology, 43*, 577–583.

Ullman, R., Sleator, E., & Sprague, R. (1984). ADD-H Comprehensive Teacher Rating Scale. Champaign, IL: Metntech.

Umbreit, J. (1995). Functional assessment and intervention in a regular classroom setting for the disruptive behavior of a student with ADHD. *Behavior Disorders, 20*, 267–278.

Underwood, L. A. (1997). *Ohio's systems approach to dealing with its incarcerated mentally ill juvenile offenders.* Unpublished manuscript.

United Nations International Narcotics Control Board. (1995). *Report of the UN International Narcotics Control Board.* New York: UN Publications.

U.S. Department of Education. (1990–1997). *Twelfth through nineteenth annual reports to Congress on the implementation of the Individuals with Disabilities Education Act.* Washington, DC: U.S. Government Printing Office.

U.S. Department of Education. (1994). *Attention deficit disorders: Adding up the facts.* Washington, DC: U.S. Government Printing Office.

U.S. Department of Education. (1998). *20th annual report to Congress on the implementation of the Individuals with Disabilities Education Act.* Washington, DC: Author.

Urman, R., Ickowicz, A., Fulford, P., & Tannock, R. (1995). An exaggerated cardiovascular response to methylphenidate in ADHD children with anxiety. *Journal of Child and Adolescent Psychopharmacology, 5*, 29–37.

Utah State Office of Education Students at Risk Section. (1996). *Utah attention deficit disorder guide.* Salt Lake City: Author.

Vaidya, C. J., Austin, G., Kirkorian, G., Ridlehuber, H. W., Desmond, J. E., Glover, G. H., & Gabrieli, J. D. (1998). Selective effects of methylphenidate in attention deficit hyperactivity disorder: A functional magnetic resonance study. *Proceedings of the National Academy of Sciences of the United States of America, 95*, 14494–14499.

Valadez, A., & Schenk, S. (1994). Persistence of the ability of amphetamine preexposure to facilitate acquisition of cocaine self-administration. *Pharmacology, Biochemistry and Behavior, 47*, 203–205.

Valentine, J., Rossi, E., O'Leary, P., Parry, T. S., Kurinczuk, J. J., & Sly, P. (1997). Thyroid function in a population of children with ADHD. *Journal of Pediatrics and Child Health, 33*, 117–120.

Van der Meere, J. J. (1996). The role of attention. In S. T. Sandberg (Ed.), *Monographs in child and adolescent psychiatry. Hyperactivity disorders of childhood* (pp. 109–146). Cambridge: Cambridge University Press.

van Leeuwen, T. H., Steinhausen, H-Ch., Overtoom, C. C. E., Pascual-Marqui, R. D., van't Klooster, B., Tothenberger, A., Sergeant, J. A., & Brandeis, D. (1998). The continuous performance test revisited with neuroelectric mapping: Impaired orienting in children with attention deficits. *Behavioural Brain Research, 94*, 97–110.

Vargas, S. L., Patrick, C. C., Ayers, G. D., & Hughes, W. T. (1993). Modulating effect of dietary carbohydrate supplementation on Candida albicans colonization and invasion in a neutropenic mouse model. *Infection and Immunity, 61*, 619-626.

Vatz, B. C. (1997, March 16). *Behavioral subtypes of learning disabled children.* Paper presented at the annual convention of the National Association of School Psychologists, San Francisco.

Verhulst, F. C., van der Ende, J., Ferdinand R. F., & Kasius, M. C. (1997). The prevalence of DSM-III-R diagnoses in a national sample of Dutch adolescents. *Archives of General Psychiatry, 54*, 329–336.

Vermont Department of Education Family and Educational Support Team. (1998, January). *Vermont guidelines for identifying students with ADD and ADHD.* Montpelier, VT: Author.

Vezina, P. (1996). DI dopamine receptor activation is necessary for the induction of sensitization by amphetamine in the ventral tegmental area. *Journal of Neuroscience, 16*(7), 2411–2420.

Virginia Policy Design Team. (1994). *Mental health needs of youth in Virginia's juvenile detention centers*, Richmond, VA.

Vitiello, B., & Burke, L. (1998). Generic methylphenidate versus brand Ritalin: Which should be used. In L. Greenhill & B. Osman (Eds.), *Ritalin: Theory and practice* (pp. 221–226). Larchmont, NY: Mary Ann Liebert.

Voelker, S. L., Lachar, D., & Gdowski, L. L. (1983). The personality inventory for children and response to methylphenidate: Preliminary evidence for predictive validity. *Journal of Pediatric Psychology*, 8, 161–169.

Voeller, K. K. S., & Heilman, K. M. (1988). Motor impersistence in children with attention deficit disorder: Evidence for right hemisphere dysfunction [abstract]. *Annals of Neurology, 24*, 323.

Voight, R. G., Liarente, A. M., Jenden, C. L., Fraley, J. K., Berretta, M. C., & Heird, W. C. (2001). A randomized double-blind placebo-controlled trial of docosahexaenoic acid supplementation in children with atten-

tion-deficit/hyperactivity disorder. *Journal of Pediatrics, 139*, 189–196.

Volkow, N. D., Ding, Y-S., Fowler, J. S., Wang, G-J., Logan, J., Gatley, J. S., Dewey, S., Ashby, C., Lieberman, J., Hitzemann, R., et al. (1995). Is methylphenidate like cocaine? Studies on their pharmacokinetics and distribution in the human brain. *Archives of General Psychiatry, 52*, 456–463.

Volkow, N. D., Wang, G. J., Fowler, J. S., Gatler, S. J., Logan, J., Ding, Y. S., Hitzemann, R., & Pappas, N. (1998). Dopamine transporter occupancies in the human brain induced by therapeutic doses of oral methylphenidate. *American Journal of Psychiatry, 155*, 1325–1331.

Volkow, N. D., Wang, G. J., Fowler, J. S., Logan, J., Angrist, B., Hitzemann, R., Lieberman, J., & Pappas, N. (1997). Effects of methylphenidate on regional brain glucose metabolism in humans: Relationship to dopamine D2 receptors. *American Journal of Psychiatry, 154*, 50–55.

Volkow, N. D., Wang, G. J., Gatley, S. J., Fowler, J. S., Ding, Y. S., Logan, J., Hitzeman, R., Angrist, B., & Lieberman, J. (1996). Temporal relationships between the pharmacokinetics of methylphenidate in the human brain and its behavioral and cardiovascular effects. *Psychopharmacology, 123*, 26–33.

Volpe, J. J. (1992). Effect of cocaine use on the fetus. *New England Journal of Medicine, 327*, 399–406.

Wade, T. D., & Kendler, K. S. (2000). The genetic epidemiology of parental discipline. *Psychological Medicine, 30*, 1303–1313.

Wagner, K. R., Elmore, J. G., & Horwitz, R. I. (1996). Diagnostic bias in clinical decision-making: An example of L-tryptophan and the diagnosis of eosinophilia-myalgia syndrome. *Journal of Rheumatology, 23*, 2079–2085.

Wahler, R. G. (1980). The insular mother: Her problems in parent-child treatment. *Journal of Applied Behavior Analysis, 13*, 207–219.

Wakefield, J. C. (1992). The concept of mental disorder: On the boundary between biological facts and social values. *American Psychologist, 47*, 373–388.

Waldman, I. D., Rowe, D. C., Abramowitz, A., Kozel, S. T., Mohr, J. H., Sherman, S. L., Cleveland, H. H., Sanders, M. L., Gard, J. M., & Stever, C. (1998). Association and linkage of the dopamine transporter gene and attention-deficit hyperactivity disorder in children: Heterogeneity owing to diagnostic subtype and severity. *American Journal of Human Genetics, 63*, 1767–1776.

Walker, H. M., Hops, H., & Johnson, S. M. (1975). Generalization and maintenance of classroom treatment effects. *Behavior Therapy, 6*, 188–200.

Wang, G. J., Volkow, N., Fowler, J. S., Ding, Y. S., Logan, J., Gatley, J. S., MacGregor, R., & Wolf, A. (1995). Comparison of two PET radiologands for imaging extrastriatal dopamine transporters in human brain. *Life Science, 57*, 185–191.

Wang, L. H., Li, C. S., & Li, G. Z. (1995). Clinical and experimental studies on tiaoshen liquor for infantile hyperkinetic syndrome. *Chung-Kuo Chung Hsi i Chieh Ho Tsa Chih, 15*, 337-340.

Wang, Y. C., Chong, M. Y., Chou, W. J., & Yang, J. L. (1993). Prevalence of attention deficit hyperactivity disorder in primary school children in Taiwan. *Journal Formosan Medical Association, 92*(2), 133–138 .

Ward, M. F., Wender, P. H., & Reimherr, F. W. (1993). The Wender Utah Rating Scale: an aid in the retrospective diagnosis of childhood attention deficit hyperactivity disorder. *American Journal of Psychiatry, 150*, 885–890.

Wasserman, G. A., & Miller, L. S. (1998). The prevention of serious and violent juvenile offending. In R. Loeber & D. Farrington (Eds.), *Serious and violent juvenile offenders* (pp. 197–247). Thousand Oaks, CA: Sage.

Wasserman, R. C., Kelleher, K. J., Bocian, A., Baker, A., Childs, G. E., Indacochea, F., Stulp, C., & Gardner, W. P. (1999). Identification of attentional and hyperactivity problems in primary care: A report from pediatric research in office settings and the ambulatory sentinel practice network. *Pediatrics, 103*, E38.

Wasserman, R., Slora, E. J., Bocian, A. B., Fleming, G. V., & Kessel, W. (1998). Pediatric research in office settings (PROS): I. A national practice-based research network to improve children's health care. *Pediatrics, 102*(6), 1350–1357.

Watter, N., & Dreyfuss, F. E. (1973). Modifications of hyperkinetic behavior by nortriptyline. *Virginia Medical Monthly, 100*, 123–126.

Wechsler, D. (1991). *Wechsler Intelligence Scale for Children* (3rd ed.). San Antonio, TX: Psychology Corporation.

Weiner, N. (1991). Drugs that inhibit adrenergic nerves and block adrenergic receptors. In A. Gilman & L. Goodman (Eds.), *Norepinephrine., epinephrine and the sympathomimetic amines* (pp. 145–180). New York: Pharmacological Basis of Therapeutics.

Weiss, G. (1992). *Attention-deficit hyperactivity disorder.* Philadelphia: Saunders.

Weiss, G., & Hechtman, L. T. (1993). *Hyperactive children grown up* (2nd ed.). New York: Guilford Press.

Weiss, G., Hechtman, L., Milroy, T., & Perlman, T. (1985). Psychiatric status of hyperactives as adults: A controlled prospective 15-year follow-up of 63 hyperactive children. *Journal of the American Academy of Child Psychiatry, 24*, 211–220.

Weiss, G., Kruger, E., Danielson, U., & Elman, M.

(1975). Effect of long-term treatment of hyperactive children with methylphenidate. *Canadian Medical Association Journal, 112*, 159–165.

Weiss, R. D., Mirin, S. M., Griffin, M. L., & Michael, J. L. (1988). Psychopathology in cocaine abusers. *Journal of Nervous and Mental Disease, 176*, 719–725.

Weiss, R. E., & Stein, M. A. (1999). Thyroid function and attention deficit hyperactivity disorder. In P. Accardo, B. Whitman, T. Blondis, & M. A. Stein (Eds.), *Attention deficits and hyperactivity in children and adults* (2nd ed., pp. 419–430). New York: Marcel Dekker.

Weiss, R. E., Stein, M. A., & Refetoff, S. (1997). Behavioral effects of liothyronine (L-T3) in children with ADHD in the presence and absence of resistance to thyroid hormone *Thyroid, 7*, 389–393.

Weiss, R. E., Stein, M. A., Trommer, B., & Refetoff, S. (1993). Attention-deficit hyperactivity disorder and thyroid function. *Journal of Pediatrics, 123*, 539–545.

Weisz, J. R., Donenberg, G. R., Han, S. S., & Weisz, B. (1995). Bridging the gap between laboratory and clinic in child and adolescent psychotherapy. *Journal of Consulting and Clinical Psychology, 63*, 688–701.

Weisz, J. R., Weiss, B., Han, S. S., Granger, D. A., & Morton, T. (1995). Effects of psychotherapy with children and adolescents revisited: A meta-analysis of treatment outcome studies. *Psychological Bulletin, 117*, 450–468.

Wells, K. C., Epstein, J. N., Hinshaw, S. P., Conners, C. K., Klaric, J., Abikoff, H. B., Abramowitz, A., Arnold, L. E., Elliot, G., Greenhill, L. L., Hechtman, L., Hoza, B., Jensen, P. S., March, J. S., Pelham, W. E., Pfiffner, L., Severe, J., Swanson, J., Vitiello, B., & Wigal, T. (2000). Parenting and family stress treatment outcomes in attention deficit hyperactivity disorder (ADHD): An empirical analysis in the MTA study. *Journal of Abnormal Child Psychology, 28*, 543–553.

Wells, K. C., Pelham, W. E., Swanson, J. M., Kotkin, R. A., Hoza, B., Abikoff, H. B., Abramowitz, A., Arnold, L. E., Cantwell, D. P., Conners, C. K., Elliott, G., Greenhill, L. L., Hechtman, L., Hibbs, E., Hinshaw, S. P., Jensen, P. S., March, J. S., Swanson, J. M., & Schiller, E. (2000). Psychosocial treatment strategies in the MTA study: rationale, methods, and critical issues in design and implementation. *Journal of Abnormal Child Psychology, 28*(6), 483–505.

Wender, P. (1971). *Minimal brain dysfunction in children.* New York: Wiley-Liss.

Wender, P. (1997). Attention deficit hyperactivity disorder in adults: A wide view of a widespread condition. *Psychiatric Annals, 27*, 556–562.

Wender, P. H., & Reimherr, F. W. (1990). Bupropion treatment of attention-deficit hyperactivity disorder in adults. *American Journal of Psychiatry, 147*, 1018–1020.

Wender, P. H., Reimherr, F. W., & Wood, D. R. (1981). Attention deficit disorder ("minimal brain dysfunction") in adults: A replication study of diagnosis and drug treatment. *Archives of General Psychiatry, 38*, 449–456.

Wenwei, Y. (1996). An investigation of adult outcome of hyperactive children in Shanghai. *Chinese Medical Journal, 109*, 877–880.

Werry, J. (1980). Imipramine and methylphenidate in hyperactive children. *Journal of Child Psychology and Psychiatry, 21*, 27–35.

Wesnes, K., & Warburton, D. (1984). The effects of cigarettes of varying yield on rapid information processing performance. *Psychopharmacology, 82*, 338–342.

Wesson, D. R., & Smith, D. E. (1978). A clinical approach to diagnosis and treatment of amphetamine abuse. *Journal of Psychedelic Drugs, 10*, 343–349.

West, S. A., Sax, K. W., Stanton, S. P., Keck, P. E. Jr., McElroy, S. L., & Strakowski, S. M. (1996). Differences in thyroid function studies in acutely manic adolescents with and without ADHD. *Psychopharmacology Bulletin, 32*, 63–66.

Westfall, T., Grant, H., & Perry, H. (1983). Release of dopamine and 5-hydroxytryptamine from rat striatal slices following activation of nicotinic cholinergic receptors. *Genetic Pharmacology, 14*, 321–325.

Weyandt, L. L., Linterman, I., & Rice, J. A. (1995). Reported prevalence of attentional difficulties in a general sample of college students. *Journal of Psychopathology and Behavior Assessment, 17*, 293–364.

Whalen, C. K., & Henker, B. (1985). The social worlds of hyperactive (ADDH) children. *Clinical Psychology Review, 5*, 447–478.

Whalen, C. K., & Henker, B. (1992). The social profiles of attention-deficit hyperactivity disorder: Five fundamental facets. *Child and Adolescent Psychiatric Clinics of North America, 1*, 395–410.

Whalen, C., Henker, B., Buhrmester, D., Hinshaw, S., Huber, A., & Laski, K. (1989). Does stimulant medication improve the peer status of hyperactive children? *Journal of Consulting and Clinical Psychology, 57*, 545–549.

Wheeler, J., & Carlson, C. L. (1994). The social functioning of children with ADD with hyperactivity and ADD without hyperactivity: A comparison of their peer relationships and social deficits. *Journal of Emotional and Behavior Disorders, 2*, 2–12.

Whitaker, A. H., Van Rossem, R., Feldman, J. F., Schonfeld, I. S., Pinto-Martin, J. A., Torre, C., Shaffer,

D., & Paneth, N. (1997). Psychiatric outcomes in low-birth-weight children at age 6 years: Relation to neonatal cranial ultrasound abnormalities. *Archives of General Psychiatry, 54*, 847–856.

Whitehouse, D., Shah, U., & Palmer, F. B. (1980). Comparison of sustained-release and standard methylphenidate in the treatment of minimal brain dysfunction. *Journal of Clinical Psychiatry, 41*(8), 282–285.

Whitmore, E. A., Mikulich, S. K., Thompson, L. L., Riggs, P. D., Aarons, G. A., Crowley, T. J. (1997). Influences on adolescent substance dependence: conduct disorder, depression, attention deficit hyperactivity disorder, and gender. *Drug and Alcohol Dependence, 47*, 87–97.

Wiers, R. W., Gunning, B., & Sergeant, J. A. (1998). Is a mild deficit in executive functions in boys related to childhood ADHD or to parental multigenerational alcoholism? *Journal of Abnormal Child Psychology, 26*, 415–430.

Wildman, B. G., Kizilbash, A. H., & Smucker, W. D. (1999). Physicians attention to parents' concerns about the psychosocial functioning of their children. *Archives of Family Medicine, 8*, 440–444.

Wilens, T. E. (1994). The children and adolescent offspring of alcoholic parents. *Current Opinions in Psychiatry, 7*, 319–323.

Wilens, T., & Biederman, J. (1992). The stimulants. *Psychiatric Clinics of North America, 15*, 191–222.

Wilens, T., & Biederman, J. (1993). Psychopathology in preadolescent children at high risk for substance abuse: A review of the literature. *Harvard Review of Psychiatry, 1*, 207–218.

Wilens, T. E., Biederman, J., Abrantes, A. M., Spencer, T. J. (1996). A naturalistic assessment of protriptyline for attention-deficit hyperactivity disorder. *Journal of the American Academy of Child and Adolescent Psychiatry, 35*, 1485–1490.

Wilens, T. E., Biederman, J., Geist, D. E., Steingard, R., & Spencer, T. (1993). Nortriptyline in the treatment of attention deficit hyperactivity disorder: A chart review of 58 cases. *Journal of the American Academy of Child and Adolescent Psychiatry, 32*, 343–349.

Wilens, T., Biederman, J., & Mick, E. (1998). Does ADHD affect the course of substance abuse? Findings from a sample of adults with and without ADHD. *American Journal on Addictions, 7*, 156–163.

Wilens, T. E., Biederman, J., Mick, E., Faraone, S. V., & Spencer, T. (1997). Attention deficit hyperactivity disorder (ADHD) is associated with early onset substance use disorders. Journal of Nervous and Mental Disease, 185(8), 475–482.

Wilens, T. E., Biederman, J., Mick, E., & Spencer, T.

(1995). A systematic assessment of tricyclic antidepressants in the treatment of adult attention-deficit hyperactivity disorder. *Journal of Nervous and Mental Disorders, 183,* 48–50.

Wilens, T., Biederman, J., Millstein, R., Wozniak, J., Hahesy, A., & Spencer, T. (1999). Risk for substance use disorders in youth with child- and adolescent-onset bipolar disorder. *Journal of the American Academy of Child and Adolescent Psychiatry, 38,* 680–685.

Wilens, T. E., Biederman, J., Prince, J., Spencer, T. J., Faraone, S. V., Warburton, R., Schleifer, D., Harding, M., Linehan, C., & Geller, D. (1996). Six-week, double-blind, placebo-controlled study of desipramine for adult attention deficit hyperactivity disorder. *American Journal of Psychiatry, 153,* 1147–1153.

Wilens, T. E., Biederman, J., & Spencer, T. J. (1996). Attention-deficit hyperactivity disorder and the psychoactive substance use disorders. *Child and Adolescent Clinics of North America, 5,* 73–91.

Wilens, T. E., Biederman J., & Spencer, T. J. (1997). Case study: Adverse effects of smoking marijuana while receiving tricyclic antidepressants. *Journal of the American Academy of Child and Adolescent Psychiatry, 36,* 45–48.

Wilens, T. E., Biederman, J., Spencer, T., Bostic, J., Prince, J., Monuteaux, M., Soriano, J., Fine, C., Abrams, A., Rater, M., & Polisner, D. (1999, December). A pilot controlled clinical trial of ABT-418, a cholinergic agonist, in the treatment of adults with attention deficit hyperactivity disorder. *American Journal of Psychiatry, 156,* 1931–1937.

Wilens, T. E., Biederman, J., Spencer, T. J., & Frances, R. J. (1994). Comorbidity of attention deficit hyperactivity disorder and the psychoactive substance use disorders. *Hospital and Community Psychiatry, 45,* 421–435.

Wilens, T. E., Biederman, J., Spencer, R. J., & Prince, J. (1995). Pharmacotherapy of adult attention deficit/hyperactivity disorder: A review. *Journal of Clinical Psychopharmacology, 5,* 270–279.

Wilens, T., McDermott, S., Biederman, J., Abrantes, A., Hahesy, A., & Spencer, T. (1999). Cognitive therapy for adults with ADHD: A systematic chart review of 26 cases. *Journal of Cognitive Psychotherapy, 13,* 215–226.

Wilens, T. E., Prince, J. B., Biederman, J., Spencer, T. J., & Frances, R. J. (1995). Attention-deficit hyperactivity disorder and comorbid substance use disorders in adults. *Psychiatric Services, 46,* 761–765

Wilens, T. E., & Spencer, T. J. (1999). Combining methylphenidate and clonidine: A clinically sound medication option. *Journal of American Child and Adolescent Psychiatry, 38,* 614–622.

Wilens, T. E., Spencer, T. J., & Biederman, J. (1995).

Are attention-deficit hyperactivity disorder and the psychoactive substance use disorders really related? *Harvard Review of Psychiatry, 3,* 160–162.

Wilens, T. E., Spencer, T., & Biederman, J. (2000). Attention deficit disorder with substance abuse. In T. Brown (Ed.), *Subtypes of attention deficit disorders in children, adolescents, and adults* (pp. 319–340). Washington, DC: American Psychiatric Press.

Wilens, T. E., Spencer, T., Biederman, J., Wozniak, J., & Connor, D. (1995). Combined pharmacotherapy: An emerging trend in pediatric psychopharmacology. *Journal of the American Academy of Child and Adolescent Psychiatry, 34,* 110–112.

Willcutt, E. (1998). *A twin study of the validity of attention-deficit/hyperactivity disorder.* Unpublished doctoral dissertation, University of Denver.

Willcutt, E. G., & Pennington, B. F. (2000). Psychiatric comorbidity in children and adolescents with reading disability. *Journal of Child Psychology and Psychiatry and Allied Disciplines, 8,* 1039–1048.

Willcutt, E. G., Pennington, B. F., Boada, R., Ogline, J. S., Tunick, R. A., Chhabildas, N. A., & Olson, R. K. (2001). A comparison of cognitive deficits in reading disability and attention-deficit/hyperactivity disorder. *Journal of Abnormal Psychology, 110,* 157–172.

Willcut, E. G., Pennington, B. F., DeFries, J. C. (2000). Twin study of the etiology of comorbidity between reading disability and attention-deficit/hyperactivity disorder. *American Journal of Medical Genetics, 96,* 293–301.

Willey, R. F. (1971). Abuse of methylphenidate. *New England Journal of Medicine, 285,* 464.

Williams, A., Levine, M., & Pelham, W. E. (2001). *Prevalence of attention-deficit hyperactivity disorder and related disruptive behavior disorders in non-detainees in the juvenile justice system: A pilot study.* Manuscript in preparation.

Williams, J. I., & Cram, M. C. (1978). Diet in the management of hyperkinesis. *Canadian Psychiatric Association Journal, 23,* 241–248.

Williamson, B. L., Tomlinson, A. J., Mishra, P. K., Gleich, G. J., & Naylor, S. (1998). Structural characterization of contaminants found in commercial preparations of melatonin: Similarities to case-related compounds from L-tryptophan associated with eosinophilia-myalgia syndrome. *Chemical Research in Toxicology, 11,* 234–240.

Wilson, G. T. (1996). Manual-based treatments: The clinical application of research findings. *Behaviour Research and Therapy, 34,* 295–314.

Wilson, J. M., Kalasinsky, K. S., Levey, A. I., Bergeron, C., Reiber, G., Anthony, R. M., Schmunk, G. A., Shannak, K., Haycock, J. W., & Kish, S. J. (1996).

Striatal dopamine nerve terminal markers in human, chronic methamphetamine users. *Nature Medicine, 2,* 699–703.

Wilson, M. C., Hitomi, M., & Schuster, C. R. (1971). Psychomotor stimulant self-administration as a function of dosage per injection in the rhesus monkey. *Psychopharmacology, 22,* 271–281.

Wilson, M. C., & Schuster, C. R. (1972). The effects of chlorpromazine on psychomotor stimulant self-administration in the rhesus monkey. *Psychopharmacology. (Berl.) , 26,* 115–126.

Windle, M. (1993). A retrospective measure of childhood behavior problems and its use in predicting adolescent problem behaviors. *Journal of Studies on Alcohol, 54,* 422–431.

Winsberg, B. G., Bialer, I., Kupietz, S., & Tobias, J. (1972). Effects of imipramine and dextroamphetamine on behavior of neuropsychiatrically impaired children. *American Journal of Psychiatry, 128,* 1425–1431.

Winsberg, B. G., & Comings, D. E. (1999). Association of the dopamine-transporter gene (DAT 1) with poor methylphenidate response. *Journal of the American Academy of Child and Adolescent Psychiatry, 38,* 1474–1477.

Wolf, J., Fein, A., & Fehrenbacher, L. (1978). Eosinophilic syndrome with methylphenidate abuse. *Annals of International Medicine, 89,* 224–225.

Wolraich, M. L. (1996). *The classification of child and adolescent mental conditions in primary care: Diagnostic and statistical manual for primary care (DSM-PC), child and adolescent version.* Elk Grove, IL: American Academy of Pediatrics.

Wolraich, M., Drummond, T., Solomon, M. K., O'Brien, M. L., & Sivage, C. (1978). Effects of methylphenidate alone and in combination with behavior modification procedures on the behavior and academic performance of hyperactive children. *Journal of Abnormal Child Psychology, 6,* 149–161.

Wolraich, M. L., Feurer, I. D., Hannah, J. N., Baumgaertel, A., & Pinnock, T. Y. (1998). Obtaining systematic reports of disruptive behavior disorders utilizing DSM-IV. *Journal of Abnormal Child Psychology, 26*(2), 141–152.

Wolraich, M. L., Hannah, J. N., Baumgaertel, A., & Feurer, I. D. (1998). Examination of DSM-IV criteria for attention deficit/hyperactivity disorder in a county-wide sample. *Journal of Developmental and Behavioral Pediatrics, 19,* 162–168.

Wolraich, M. L., Hannah, J. N., Pinnock, T. Y., Baumgaertel, A., & Brown, J. (1996). Comparison of diagnostic criteria for attention-deficit hyperactivity disorder in a county-wide sample. *Journal of the American Academy of Child and Adolescent Psychiatry, 35,* 319–324.

Wolraich, M. L., Lindgren, S. D., Stromquist, A., Milich, R., Davis, C., & Watson, D. (1990). Stimulant medication use by primary care physicians in the treatment of attention deficit hyperactivity disorder. *Pediatrics, 86,* 95–101.

Wolraich, M. L., Lindgren, S. D., Stumbo, P. J., Stegink, L. D., Appelbaum, M. I., & Kiritsy, M. C. (1994). Effects of diets high in sucrose or aspartame on the behavior and cognitive performance of children. *New England Journal of Medicine, 330,* 301–307.

Wolraich, M. L., Stumbo, P. J., Milch, R., Chenard, C., & Schultz, F. (1986). Dietary characteristics of hyperactive and control boys. *Journal of the American Dietetic Association, 86*(4), 500-504.

Wolraich, M. L., Wilson, D. B., & White, J. W. (1995). The effect of sugar on behavior or cognition in children. *Journal of the American Medical Association, 274,* 1617–1621.

Wood, A. J., Stein, C. M., & Woosley, R. (1998). Making medicines safer—The need for an independent drug safety board. *New England Journal of Medicine, 339,* 1851–1854.

Wood, D. M., & Emmett-Oglesby, M. W. (1988). Substitution and cross-tolerance profiles of anorectic drugs in rats trained to detect the discriminative stimulus properties of cocaine. *Psychopharmacology, 95,* 364–368.

Wood, D. M., Lal, H., & Emmett-Oglesby, M. (1984). Acquisition and recovery of tolerance to the discriminative stimulus properties of cocaine. *Neuropharmacology, 23,* 1419–1423.

Wood, D. R., Reimherr, F. W., & Wender, P. H. (1985). Amino acid precursors for the treatment of attention-deficit disorder, residual type. *Psychopharmacology Bulletin, 21,* 146–149.

Wood, D. R., Reimherr, F. W., & Wender, P. H. (1985). Treatment of attention-deficit disorder with dl-phenylalanine. *Psychiatry Research, 16,* 21–26.

Wood, D., Wender, P. H., & Reimherr, F. W. (1983). The prevalence of attention deficit disorder, residual type, or minimal brain dysfunction, in a population of male alcoholic patients. *American Journal of Psychiatry, 140,* 95–98.

Woodward, L., Dowdney, L., & Taylor, E. (1997). Child and family factors influencing the clinical referral of children with hyperactivity: A research note. *Journal of Child Psychology and Psychiatry, 38,* 479–485.

Woolverton, W. L., & English, J. A. (1997). Effects of some phenylethylamines in rhesus monkeys trained to discriminate (+)-amphetamine from saline. *Drug and Alcohol Dependence, 14,* 79–85

World Health Organization. (1978). *International classification of diseases* (9th rev.). Geneva, Switzerland: Author.

World Health Organization. (1988). *Pemoline. 25th Expert Committee on Drug Dependence report.* Geneva, Switzerland: Author.

World Health Organization. (1992). *International statistical classification of diseases and related health problems* (10th rev.). Geneva, Switzerland: Author.

Wroblewski, B., Leary, J., Phelan, A., Whyte, J., & Manning, K. (1992). Methylphenidate and seizure frequency in brain injured patients with seizure disorders. *Journal of Clinical Psychiatry, 53*, 86–89.

Wyld, D. C. (1997). Attention deficit/hyperactivity disorder in adults: Will this be the greatest challenge for employment discrimination law? *Employee Responsibilities and Rights Journal, 10*, 103–125.

Yager, T., Bird, H. R., Staghezza-Jaramillo, B., Gould, M. S., & Canino, G. (1993). Symptom counts and diagnostic algorithms as measures of five common psychiatric disorders in children. *International Journal of Methods Psychiatric Research, 3*, 177–191.

Yamaguchi, K., & Kandel, D. B. (1984). Patterns of drug use from adolescence to young adulthood: III. Predictors of progression. *American Journal of Public Health, 74*, 673–681.

Yao, K. N., Solanto, M. V., & Wender, E. H. (1988). Prevalence of hyperactivity among newly immigrated Chinese-American children. *Journal Developmental and Behavioral Pediatrics, 9*(6), 367–373.

Yates, B. J. (1992). Vestibular influences on the sympathetic nervous system. *Brain Research Reviews, 17*, 51–59.

Yell, M. L., & Shriver, J. G. (1997). The IDEA amendments of 1997: Implications for special and general teachers, administrators, and teacher trainers. *Focus on Exceptional Children, 30*(1), 1–19.

Yepes, L. E., Balka, E. B., Winsberg, B. G., & Bialer, I. (1977). Amitriptyline and methylphenidate treatment of behaviorally disordered children. *Journal of Child Psychology and Psychiatry, 18*, 39–52.

Zaczek, R., Battaglia, G., Contrera, J. F., Culp, S., & DeSouza, E. B. (1989). Methylphenidate and pemoline do not cause depletion or rat brain monamine markers similar to that observed with methamphetamine. *Toxicology and Applied Pharmacology, 100*, 227–233.

Zahner, G. E. P., Pawel-Kiewicz, W., DeFrancesco, J., & Adnopoz, J. (1992). Children's mental health service needs and utilization patterns in an urban community: An epidemiological assessment. *Journal of the American Academy of Child and Adolesent Psychiatry, 31*, 951–960.

Zametkin, A., & Ernst, M. (1999). Problems in the management of attention-deficit-hyperactivity disorder. *New England Journal of Medicine, 340*, 40–46.

Zametkin, A. J., Ernst, M., & Silver, R. (1998).

Laboratory and diagnostic testing in child and adolescent psychiatry: A review of the past 10 years. *Journal of the American Academy of Child and Adolescent Psychiatry, 37*, 464–472.

Zametkin, A. J., Karoum, F., & Rapoport, J. (1987). Treatment of hyperactive children with d-phenylalanine. *American Journal of Psychiatry, 144*, 792–794.

Zametkin, A. J., Liebenauer, L. L., Fitzgerald, G. A., King, A. C., Minkunas, D. V., Herscovitch, P., Yamada, E. M., & Cohen, R. M. (1993). Brain metabolism in teenagers with attention-deficit hyperactivity disorder. *Archives of General Psychiatry, 50*, 333–340.

Zametkin, A. J., Nordahl, T. E., Gross, M., King, A. C., Semple, W. E., Rumsey, J., Hamburger, S., & Cohen, R. M. (1990). Cerebral glucose metabolism in adults with hyperactivity of childhood onset. *New England Journal of Medicine, 323*, 1361–1366.

Zametkin, A. J., & Rapoport, J. L. (1987). Neurobiology of attention deficit disorder with hyperactivity: Where have we come in 50 years? *Journal of the American Academy of Child and Adolescent Psychiatry, 26*, 676–686.

Zarin, D., Suarez, A. P., Pincus, H. A., Kupersanin, E., & Zito, J. M. (1998). Clinical and treatment characteristics of children with attention-deficit/hyperactivity disorder (ADHD) in psychiatric practice. *Journal of the American Academy of Child and Adolescent Psychiatry, 37*, 1262-1270.

Zemplenyi, J., Colman, M. F. (1984). Deep neck abscesses secondary to methylphenidate (Ritalin) abuse. *Head and Neck Surgery, 6*, 858–860.

Zentall, S. S. (1988). Production deficiencies in elicited language but not in spontaneous verbalizations of hyperactive children. *Journal of Abnormal Child Psychology, 16*, 657–673.

Zentall, S. S. (1990). Fact-retrieval automatization and math problem solving by learning disabled, attention-disordered, and normal adolescents. *Journal of Educational Psychology, 82*, 856–865.

Zentall, S. S., Hall, A. M., & Lee, D. L. (1998). Attentional focus of students with hyperactivity during a word-search task. *Journal of Abnormal Child Psychology, 26*, 335–343.

Zhang, H., & Huang, J. (1990). Preliminary study of traditional Chinese medicine treatment of minimal brain dysfunction: Analysis of 100 cases. *Chung Hsi i Chieh Ho Tsa Chih Chinese Journal of Modern Developments in Traditional Medicine, 10*, 278–279.

Ziedonis, D. M., Rayford, B. S., Bryant, K. J., & Rounsaville, B. J. (1994). Psychiatric comorbidity in white and African-American cocaine addicts seeking substance abuse treatment. *Hospital and Community Psychiatry, 45*, 43–49.

Zima, B. T., Bussing, R., Crecelius, G. M., Kaufman, A., & Belin, T. R. (1999). Psychotropic medication use among children in foster care: Relationship to severe psychiatric disorders. *American Journal of Public Health, 89*, 1732–1735. Zirkel, P. A. (1995). *Section 504 and the schools.* Horsham, PA: LRP.

Zito, J. M., dosReis, S., Safer, D. J., & Bardner, J. (1998, June 11). *Trends in psychotropic prescriptions for youths with Medicaid insturance from a Midwestern state: 1987–1995.* Paper presented at the NIMH New Clinical Drug Evaluation Unit Meeting, Boca Raton, FL.

Zito, J. M., Safer, D. J., dosReis, S., Gardner, J. F., Boles, M., & Lynch, F. (2000). Trends in prescribing of psychotropic medications to preschoolers. *Journal of the American Medical Association, 283*, 1025–1030.

Zito, J. M., Safer, D. J., dosReis, S., Magder, L. S., & Riddle, M. A. (1997). Methylphenidate patterns among Medicaid youths. *Psychopharmacology Bulletin, 30*, 143–147.

Zito, J. M., Safer, D. J., dosReis, S., & Riddle, M. A. (1998). Racial disparity in psychotropic medications prescribed for youths with Medicaid insurance in Maryland. *Journal of the American Academy of Child and Adolescent Psychiatry, 37*, 179–184.

Zito, J. M., Safer, D. J., Riddle, M. A., Johnson, R. E., Speedie, S. M., & Fox, M. (1998). Prevalence variations in psychotropic treatment of children. *Journal of Child and Adolescent Psychopharmacology, 8*, 99–105.

Zito, J. M., Safer, D. J., Riddle M, Speedie, S., dosReis, S. (1996). Racial, geographic and gender differences in methylphenidate use among Medicaid youths. *Pharmacoepidemiology and Drug Safety, 5*, S1–S119.

Index

[References are to pages.]

A

Abbreviated Conners Teacher's Rating Scale (ACTRS), 12-9
ABT-418, 11-9
Academic achievement
  See also Underachievement
  of adolescents with ADHD, 8-7
  of adults with ADHD, 6-3, 6-7–6-10
  of children with ADHD, 5-6–5-7
    assessment of, 8-17–8-18
    comorbidity and, 5-6–5-7
    delays in, 2-11
    discrepancies with intelligence, 1-10
    low productivity and, 8-6
  impact of behavior therapy on, 12-9–12-10
Academic achievement tests, 8-6–8-7
Accidental injury, of ADHD children, 5-13–5-14
Acetylcarnitine, 13-9
ACSMS. *See* ADHD Cost of Services Medicaid Study
ACTRS. *See* Abbreviated Conners Teacher's Rating Scale
Acupuncture, 13-5, 13-13
Adaptive functioning
  low, 3-10–3-11
  overall, 5-14
ADD. *See* attention deficit disorder
Adderall®
  immediate-release formulations, 9-4
  short-term efficacy, 10-5–10-6
S-Adenosyl-l-methionine supplementation, 13-8
ADHD Cost of Services Medicaid Study (ACSMS)
  analysis, 27-10–27-11
  measures, 27-10
  procedures, 27-9–27-10
  sample, 27-9
  setting, 27-9
Adolescents, ADHD
  academic outcome, 8-7
  comorbidity, 4-6–4-7, 19-2
  in juvenile justice system. *See* Juveniles, detained
  substance use disorders
    comorbidity and, 19-2
    methylphenidate misuse/abuse, 20-12, 20-14
    risk of, 19-8
    survey results, 21-8–21-15
    symptom persistence and, 4-5–4-6
Adults, ADHD
  antisocial behavior risk, 4-8–4-9, 6-15–6-16

childhood medication status
  attitudes on legal and illegal drugs, 17-8
  attitudes on prescribed medications, 17-7–7-8
  later involvement in drugs, 17-8–17-11
  psychiatric diagnoses and, 17-11
criminal behavior risk, 4-8–4-9
diagnosis of, 1-14, 6-5–6-6, 6-16–6-17
drug attitudes of, 17-8
family functioning of, 6-13–6-15
female
  inattentive subtype and, 6-6
  psychological problems and, 6-11
identification of, 6-2
impact of ADHD on functioning, 6-6–6-7
  clinical practice recommendations, 6-17–6-18
  educational, 6-7–6-10
  future research recommendations, 6-17–6-18
  vocational, 6-7–6-10
mood disorder risk, 4-10
prevalence of, 6-4–6-5, 6-16
reliability of childhood history, 6-4, 6-6
smoking status of, 18-11
social skills deficits in, 6-13
study methods for, 6-2
substance abuse, childhood stimulant usage and, 17-2–17-3
  California community study, 17-5
  early investigational findings, 17-4
  future research directions, 17-13–17-14
  implications of newer studies, 17-11–17-13
  Iowa study. *See* Iowa study
  theories on, 17-3–17-4
substance use disorder risk, 4-9–4-10, 19-3
symptoms persistence in, 4-7–4-8, 6-3
treatment efficacy
  of bupropion, 11-6
  of desipramine, 11-5
Adverse drug-reporting systems, limits of, 10-8–10-9
Adversity, in close personal relationships, 3-9
Advocacy, 24-16
Affective disorders. *See* Mood disorders
African Americans, stimulant side effects in, 10-9
Age
  cognitive function and, 8-4
  of onset, 1-5–1-6, 1-9–1-11
  of regular smoking, 18-10, 18-12
  treatment choice and, 12-19, 12-21
Agency for Health Care Policy Research, 14-2

[References are to pages.]

Aggression
  academic achievement and, 5-7
  with ADHD
    accidental injury and, 5-13
    in adults, 6-12
    family relationship impairment and, 5-9
    overconfidence and, 5-12
    peer relationships and, 5-10–5-11
  differentiation from ADHD, 6-15
  hyperactivity/impulsivity and, 1-5
  response inhibition deficits and, 8-14
Aging, DSM-IV criteria and, 1-17–1-18
Alcohol use/abuse
  ADHD severity and, 18-6
  adolescent
    ADHD and, 16-12, 19-2–19-3
    retrospective studies, 16-8
  adult
    childhood medication status and, 17-8–17-11
    oppositional and conduct disorder in, 6-11
  risk, ADHD and, 16-9, 16-12
    clinical longitudinal studies, 16-9–16-11
    longitudinal studies, 19-3
    retrospective studies, 16-3–16-5
Alpha-2 noradrenergic agonists, 11-7–11-9
Ambulatory Sentinel Practice Network (ASPN), 22-12,
    27-5
American Academy of Pediatrics, App. A-8
Americans With Disabilities Act, 5-17, 26-8
Amino acid supplementation, 13-4, 13-7–13-8
Amphetamines
  See also Dextroamphetamine
  abuse, 21-14
    by adolescents, 21-10–21-13
    potential for, 21-1
  Adderall®, 9-4, 10-5–10-6
  discriminative stimulus effects in animals, 20-2
  dose-reinforcing effects, 20-2–20-5
  prescriptions, 21-2, 21-3
  production quotas, 21-2, 21-3
  randomized controlled trials
    long-term efficacy, 9-19–9-20
    short-term efficacy, 9-7–9-11
  research needs, future, 10-11
  safety, short-term, 10-7
  sensitization to cocaine, 18-5
  toxicology, 10-4–10-5, 10-11
  usage questions, for MTF project, 21-5–21-6
Antidepressants
  See also specific antidepressants
  for ADHD with SUD, 19-11–19-12
  non-tricyclic, 11-6–11-7
  short-term trials, App. A-6
  tricyclic. See Tricyclic antidepressants
Antifungal therapy, 13-5, 13-17
Antisocial personality disorder (APD)
  in adults with ADHD, 4-11, 6-12
    female, 6-11
    self-medication and, 19-9
  behavior
    ADHD as risk factor for, 2-11
    in adults with ADHD, 6-11
    risk in adulthood, 4-8–4-9

conduct disorder and, 4-10, 25-3
  in juvenile offenders, 25-3
  research needs, 25-3
Anxiety disorder, with ADHD
  in adolescents, 4-6–4-7
  in adult females, 6-11, 6-12
  in children, 23-6
  incidence of, 15-4
  neuropsychological function and, 8-11
  prevalence, 1-13
  stimulant treatment, 11-3, 15-10
    response profile for, 15-4–15-5
    vs. psychosocial treatment, 15-5–15-7
APD. See Antisocial personality disorder
Asian cultures, ADHD in, 2-8–2-9
ASPN. See Ambulatory Sentinel Practice Network
Assessment
  barriers, App. A-8–App. A-9
  in clinical practice, 1-15–1-16
  cognitive correlates and, 8-17–8-18
  instruments
    different, in longitudinal follow-up studies,
      4-2–4-3
    for follow-up studies, differences in, 4-2–4-3
    subjectivity of, 3-9–3-10
  reliability over time, 1-14, 4-3
  school-based, development of, 24-15
  standardized, 1-15–1-16
  state policies, 26-7–26-8
  of treatment by primary care physicians, 23-8–23-9
Attention
  spatial allocation of, 8-15
  sustained, impairments in, 8-13–8-14
Attentional control therapy, 14-5
Attention deficit disorder (ADD), 1-2
Attrition, follow-up studies and, 4-4–4-5
Auditory feedback, 14-6
Autism, 8-12
Automobile accidents, 1-10

B
Barbiturate usage, in adults with childhood medication
    history, 16-9–16-11, 17-8–17-11
Basal ganglia, in ADHD children, 7-5–7-6
Behavioral symptoms. See Symptoms, behavioral
Behavioral therapy
  classroom strategies, 12-6
  with contingency management, 12-12–12-14
  cost-effectiveness, 12-23–12-24
  durability of, 14-6–14-7
  efficacy of
    evidence for, 12-18–12-19
    in home and classroom settings, 12-8–12-9
    impact on school functioning, 12-9–12-10
    studies on, 12-5, 12-25–12-30
  exportability to real-world settings, 12-24
  parent training intervention, 12-7–12-8
  vs. pharmacotherapy, 14-2–14-3, 14-5
    short-term studies, 14-4–14-6
    vs. combined treatment, 14-4
    2 x 3 factorial study of, 14-4
  with pharmacotherapy
    advantages of, 12-15–12-16

[References are to pages.]

dosage effects and, 12-21–12-22
  duration of, 12-22–12-23
  efficacy of, 12-10, 14-7–14-8
  long-term efficacy of, 12-18, 12-24
  long-term impact from, 12-16
  optimum sequence for, 12-22
  parent training and, 12-21–12-22
  research results, positive, 12-16–12-18
  school's role in, 23-8
  shortcomings of, 12-14–12-15
  teacher consultation, 12-7–12-8
Behavior problems, as substance use risk factor, 18-6
Beta blockers, 11-7–11-8
Bidirectional models, of family relationship
    impairment, 5-8
Biofeedback
  EEG, 13-5, 13-13–13-14
  EMG, 13-14
Biological bases
  dopamine hypothesis, 7-4, 7-14–7-15
  norepinephrine hypothesis, 7-14–7-15
Bipolar disorder
  with ADHD
    self-medication and, 19-9
    substance use disorder risk and, 19-5–19-6
  misdiagnosis as ADHD, A-7
Birth-year cohort, 18-12
Blood pressure, stimulants and, 10-9–10-10
Brain, in ADHD, A-3–A-4
  anatomic anomalies, cognitive impairments and,
      8-15–8-16
  damage and, 23-2
  functional imaging, 7-7–7-9, 7-15
  malfunction, lack of evidence on, 3-7–3-8
  neuroanatomical MRI studies, 7-4–7-5
  trauma and, 7-12–7-13
Bupropion, for ADHD
  efficacy of, 11-6, 11-9
  risks, 11-6
  with SUD, 19-11
Buspirone, 11-8

C

CAAS. See Children's Attention and Adjustment Survey
California community study, 17-5, 17-12–17-13
Calmplex, 13-12
Carcinogenicity
  of amphetamines, 10-4
  of methylphenidate, 10-3–10-4
L-Carnitine supplementation, 13-4, 13-9
CBL. See Child Behavior Checklist
Central nervous system stimulants. See Stimulants
Cerebellar cognitive affective syndrome, executive func-
    tion impairments, 8-12
Cerebellar vermis, in ADHD children, 7-5
Cerebral blood flow, in ADHD, 7-8
CEWG. See Community Epidemiology Work Group
C-GAS. See Children's Global Assessment Scale
Channel-specific perceptual training, 13-5, 13-17
Charter schools, 26-6
Child Behavior Checklist (CBL), 15-3, 23-7, 24-3
Child Behavior Study, 22-12–22-13
  analysis, 27-6

  measures, 27-6
  procedures, 27-6
  results, 27-7–27-8
  sample, 27-5
  setting, 27-5
"Child effects" model, of impaired family relations, 5-8
Children, ADHD
  lifelong impact of, 6-9
  longitudinal studies, 16-9–16-12
  medicated
    See also Pharmacotherapy; specific medications
    bupropion efficacy, 11-6
    clinical study implications, 17-11–17-13
    desipramine efficacy, 11-4
    drug usage/attitudes in adulthood, 17-6–17-11
    early investigations, 17-4
    state education policies for, 26-8
    substance use disorder prevention and,
        17-3–17-4
    substance use disorder risk and, 17-3,
        19-3–19-5
  methylphenidate abuse by, 20-12
  substance use disorders in families and, 19-7
  unmedicated, 17-2–17-3
    clinical study implications, 17-11–17-13
    drug usage/attitudes in adulthood, 17-6–17-11
    Iowa study, 17-5
    substance use disorder risk and, 19-4–19-5
Children's Attention and Adjustment Survey (CAAS),
    18-7–18-9
Children's Global Assessment Scale (C-GAS), 1-4
Children's Summer Treatment Program (STP)
  behavioral interventions in, 12-13
  design of, 12-12
  need for long-term intervention, 12-14
  treatment response, 12-13–12-14
"Child with disability," IDEA definition of, 26-5
Chinese herbals, 13-5, 13-12–13-13
Cholinergic drugs, 11-9–11-10
Chronic illness, as risk factor, 2-9
Cigarette smoking. See Smoking
Circularity, 5-15
Classification, diagnostic. See Diagnosis
Clinicians. See Mental health clinicians
Clockwise hysteresis, 9-5
Clomipramine, for ADHD with mood disorder, 15-8
Clonidine, 7-15, 11-7
Cocaine abuse
  by adolescents, 21-10–21-13
  by adults
    with ADHD, 6-12
    childhood medication status and, 17-8–17-11
    retrospective studies, 16-5–16-6
  age at usage, ADHD severity and, 18-6
  by children, 20-12
  by children with ADHD
    clinical longitudinal studies, 16-9–16-11
    community longitudinal studies, 16-11–16-12
  discriminative stimulus effects in animals, 20-2
  dose-reinforcing effects, 20-2–20-5
  morbidity, 21-14
  potential, 21-2
  risk in ADHD, 16-9, 16-12–16-13

[References are to pages.]

Cocaine abuse *(continued)*
    self-medication hypothesis and, 18-4
    in utero exposure, 19-7
Cognitive-behavioral therapy, App. A-6
    as adjunctive therapy, 12-6
    cost-effectiveness, 12-23–12-24
    efficacy, 12-5–12-6, 12-18–12-19
    with medication, vs. medication alone, 14-4–14-5
    shortcomings of, 12-14–12-15
Cognitive function
    age-related effects on, 8-4
    comorbidity effects on, 8-3–8-4
    correlates
        academic achievement. *See* Academic
            achievement
        ADHD validity and, 8-2
        clinical implications, 8-16–8-18
        conceptual/methodological challenges,
            8-3–8-4
        future research implications, 8-18–8-19
        general intellectual function, 8-4–8-5
        information processing, 8-13–8-15
        neuropsychological function. *See*
            Neuropsychological function
        pathophysiological implications, 8-15–8-16
        research, scientific maturity of, 8-4
    gender-related effects on, 8-4
    not directly affected by ADHD, 8-10
    problems, ADHD diagnosis and, 2-11, 3-11–3-12
    stimulants for, 9-9
Cohort drug surveillance large-scale studies, need for,
    10-9–10-10
Combined subtype, 8-7
    academic underachievement and, 1-9, 1-13
    adaptive functioning and, 1-9
    classroom disruption and, 1-9
    conduct disorders and, 1-12
    DSM-III-R vs. DSM-IV criteria and, 1-2–1-3,
        1-5–1-7
    friendship problems and, 1-9
    future research, 1-17
    gender and, 1-12
    intelligence and, 1-12–1-13
    learning problems and, 1-9–1-10
    oppositional defiant disorder and, 1-12
    peer social relations and, 1-9
    social functioning problems and, 1-9–1-10
    unintentional injuries and, 1-13
Communication
    diagnostic multidisciplinary, 23-4
    problems, parent-physician, A-7–A-8
Community Epidemiology Work Group (CEWG), 21-8,
    21-13, 21-14
Comorbidity, P1-1, A-2
    See also specific comorbid disorders
    academic achievement and, 5-6–5-7
    ADHD-related impairment and, 5-15
    in adolescents, 4-6–4-7
    in adults with ADHD, 4-8–4-10, 6-11–6-12
    cigarette smoking and, 19-5–19-6
    cognitive function effects, 8-3–8-4
    epidemiological data, 2-9, 2-11
    frequency, 27-3–27-4

    impairment and, 5-4–5-5
    patterns, impact on treatment, 15-7
    school functioning and, 5-7–5-8
    special education eligibility and, 24-10
    stimulant therapy for
        efficacy of, 11-3
        vs. tricyclic antidepressants, 11-5–11-6
    treatment choice and, 12-21
Comprehensive Motion Apparatus, 13-16
Concurrent validity, of ADHD diagnosis, 1-8–1-10
Conduct disorder
    with ADHD, 19-9, 23-6
    in adolescents, 4-6
    in adults with ADHD, 6-11
    antisocial behavior and, 25-3
    executive function and, 8-12
    hyperactivity and, 4-10
    in juvenile detainees
        juvenile justice system response, 25-3–25-4
        prevalence of, 25-2–25-3
    neuropsychological function and, 8-11–8-12
    punishment for, 12-11
    response inhibition deficits and, 8-14
    risk
        ADHD and, 2-11, 16-2
        in adolescent ADHD, parental SUD and,
            19-8
        substance use disorders and, 16-2
    school functioning and, 5-7
    severity, 18-11
    special education eligibility, 24-10
    substance use disorder risk, 4-11, 17-3
        with ADHD, 16-8–16-9, 16-14–16-15
        pathways associated with ADHD, 19-5–19-6
Conners Abbreviated Parent-Teacher Rating Scale—
    Revised, 3-9
Conners Parent Rating Scale, 4-2
Conners Parent Rating Scale-Revised, 3-9
Conners Teachers Rating Scale-Revised, 3-9
Contingency management
    with behavioral therapy, 12-12–12-14
    cost-effectiveness, 12-23–12-24
    efficacy, 12-11–12-12
    with methylphenidate, vs. without, 14-6
    setting for, 12-10–12-11
    shortcomings of, 12-14–12-15
    using negative consequences, 12-11
Continuous Performance Test, 3-10
Controlled substances, stimulants as, 11-3
Controlled Substances Act (CSA), 20-1
Corpus callosum, in ADHD children, 7-5, 7-6
Cost-benefit analysis, need for, 27-11–27-12
Cost-effectiveness
    psychosocial interventions, 12-23–12-24
    of treatment services, 27-8–27-11
Counseling services
    by provider type, 22-11
    usage trends, 22-10–22-11
Criminal behavior
    ADHD and, 25-3
    in adults with ADHD, 6-12
    conduct disorder and, 25-3
    risk in adulthood, 4-8–4-9

[References are to pages.]

Cross-cultural validity, 2-6, 2-8
CSA. *See* Controlled Substances Act
C subtype. *See* Combined subtype
Cultural differences, in ADHD, 2-8–2-12
Cylert®. *See* Pemoline

D

Daily report cards (DRC), 12-6, 12-8
d-amphetamines. *See* Amphetamines
Databases, national stimulant, 21-4
DAT1 gene
    discovery of, 7-9–7-10
    population and family studies, 7-10–7-11
    replication of studies, 7-12
DAWN. *See* Drug Abuse Warning Network
DEA. *See* Drug Enforcement Administration
DEA Automation of Reports and Consolidated Orders
        System (ARCOS), 20-8–20-9
Deaner®, 13-9–13-10
Deanol, 13-9–13-10
Defendol, 13-12
Definition, diagnostic, P1-1
    circularity, 5-15
    controversy, xvii–xviii
    developmentally based comparisons in,
        4-3–4-4
    diversity/shifting of, 8-3
    DSM-III, 2-2
    DSM-III-R, 1-6, 2-2
        ADD, 1-2, 2-1
        ADHD, 1-2, 2-1, 4-2, 8-3
        DSM-IV definition and, 1-5–1-7
    DSM-IV, 1-2–1-3, 4-2
        DSM-III-R definition and, 1-5–1-7
        ICD-10 definition and, 1-7
        internal validity of, 1-3
    earlier, 2-2
    ICD-9, 2-2
    three-dimensional vs. two-dimensional, 1-2–1-3
Deleading, 13-5, 13-18, 13-19
Delinquency, ADHD as risk factor for, 2-11
Depression, with ADHD
    in adolescents, 4-6–4-7, 4-10–4-11
    in adult females, 6-11
    diagnosis, 23-6
    stimulants and, 11-3
    treatment of, 15-7–15-8
Desipramine
    for ADHD with mood disorder, 15-8
    efficacy, 11-4, 11-9
        in adults, 11-5
        in children, 11-4
    short-term trials, App. A-6
Development
    accidental injury and, 5-13
    childhood stimulant usage and, 9-7, 11-3
    follow-up studies, 4-3–4-4
    issues, in longitudinal follow-up studies, 4-3–4-4
    long-term course, 4-1, 4-10–4-11
        See also Follow-up studies
        adolescence outcome, 4-5–4-7
        adulthood outcome, 4-7–4-10
        of childhood DSM-IV ADHD, 1-8

methodological limitations, 4-2–4-5
        outcome at adolescence, 4-5–4-7
    predictive validity of ADHD, 1-8
    span, impairment and, 5-5
Developmental disorder, ADHD as, 4-3–4-4
Dextroamphetamine (Dexedrine®)
    absorption, 9-4
    abuse potential, 9-7
    administration, 9-5
    dopamine release, 9-3
    dosage, 9-5
    efficacy of, 9-12–9-13
    formulations
        immediate-release, 9-4
        sustained-release, 9-4, 9-12–9-13
    short-term trials
        limitations of, 9-13–9-17
        results, App. A-6
    single therapy vs. cognitive treatment with
            medication, 14-4–14-5
    therapeutic effect, 9-5
Diagnosis, A-1
    in adults, 6-2–6-4, 6-16–6-17
    age-specific criteria, 1-18
    by American-trained vs. British-trained
            psychiatrists, 17-6
    barriers, App. A-8–App. A-9
    behavioral symptoms spectrum, 23-4–23-5
    cognitive correlates and, 8-16
    comorbidity, 23-6–23-7
    conceptualization vs. dimensions, 1-14–1-15
    consensus area for, 3-3–3-4
    criteria
        See also specific diagnostic criteria
        lack of consensus on, 4-2, 6-3
        lack of specificity of, P1-1
        retention of ADHD in adulthood and, 4-10,
            4-11
        shortcomings of, 3-3
        for young children, future research on, 1-17
    debate, P1-1–P1-3
    definition. *See* Definition, diagnostic
    differential, 6-4, 6-15
    vs. dimensional conceptualization, 1-14–1-15
    DSM criteria, 3-2, 23-2
    DSM-II criteria, 1-2, 2-1, 11-2, 23-2
    DSM-III criteria, 8-3, 23-2
        ADD with hyperactivity, 1-11, 2-11
        ADD without hyperactivity, anxiety and,
            1-11–1-12
        methylphenidate response and, 1-13
    DSM-III-R criteria, 1-5–1-7, 23-2
        ADHD outcomes, 2-11
        diagnostic definitions, 1-2, 2-1, 4-2, 8-3
        prediction of adult daily smoking, 18-15–18-17
        psychoactive substance use disorders, 18-11,
            18-15–18-17
    DSM-IV criteria, 23-2
        academic underachievement and, 1-9
        adult vs. child, 6-3
        age of onset, 1-9–1-11
        areas of consensus with ICD-10, 3-3–3-4
        associated features, 3-10–3-12

[References are to pages.]

Diagnosis *(continued)*
    correspondence with DSM-III-R definition,
        1-5–1-7
    defining traits. *See* Hyperactivity; Impulsivity
    diagnostic definition of ADHD, 1-2–1-3,
        4-2
    with emotional disturbance, 24-5
    field trials for disruptive behavior disorders,
        1-4
    impairment and, 5-3
    vs. ICD-10, 2-2–2-3
    lack of clarity in, 3-6–3-7
    overlap with ICD-10 hyperkinetic disorder
        criteria, 7-2–7-3
    vs. previous DSM versions, 8-3
    problems with, 3-15–3-16
    for research classification, 18-7–18-10
    for severity determination, 18-8–18-9
    shortcomings of, 3-3
    subtype. *See* Subtypes; *specific subtypes*
    for symptom onset, 18-8
    symptoms, 1-3
    unresolved classification issues, 2-3
    validity of, 1-10–1-11, 1-17–1-18
  evolution of, 1-2–1-3
  frequency of, xvii
  ICD-10 criteria
    areas of consensus with DSM-IV,
        3-3–3-4
    vs. DSM-IV, 2-2–2-3
  impact, App. A-10
    on family, App. A-5
    on individuals, App. A-5
    on society, App. A-5
  increased, 22-9
  increased frequency of, 3-2, 27-2–27-3
  labeling
    misapplications of, 3-13–3-14
    negative aspects of, 3-12–3-13
    usefulness of, 3-12
  misdiagnosis, A-7
  multidisciplinary communication and, 23-4
  NIH Consensus statement, App. A-1–App. A-12
  overdiagnosis, A-7
  overlap between ADHD and SUD, 19-2–19-3
  persistence rates, 4-10, 4-11
  problems, 3-4–3-5, 3-14–3-16
    absence of evidence for brain malfunction,
        3-7–3-8
    behaviors not distinguishable from temperament
        variations, 3-5–3-7
    cognitive disabilities as, 3-11–3-12
    environmental role, neglect of, 3-8–3-9
    lack of evolutionary perspective, 3-12
    low adaptability as, 3-10–3-11
    nonspecific stimulant effects, 3-14
    subjective questionnaires, 3-9–3-10
  reconceptualization of, 1-2–1-3
  reliability, 6-3–6-4, P1-2
  state policies for, 26-7–26-8
  taxonomies
    current, 2-2–2-3
    future directions for, 1-18

    three-dimensional, 1-2
    two-dimensional
      concurrent mental disorders, differential
        association with, 1-3–1-4
      discriminant validity of, 1-3–1-5
      of DSM-III-R, 1-2
      of DSM-IV, 1-2–1-3
      impairments, differential association with,
        1-4–1-5
    unresolved classification issues, 2-3
    validity. *See* Validity, of ADHD diagnosis
Diagnostic and Statistical Manual of Mental Disorders
  diagnostic criteria. *See under* Diagnosis
Diagnostic services
  by provider type, 22-11
  usage patterns, 22-13–22-14
  usage trends, 22-10
Dimethylaminoethanol (DMAE), 13-4, 13-9–13-10
Dimethylethanolamine, 13-9–13-10
Discriminant validity, of DSM-IV criteria subtypes,
    1-11–1-13
Disruptive behavior disorders
  with ADHD
    methylphenidate for, 15-2–15-3
    psychosocial treatment for, 15-3–15-4
    stimulants for, 9-9, 15-2–15-4
  Freedom from Distractibility and, 8-5
Divorce rate, of adults with ADHD, 6-13
DMAE. *See* Dimethylaminoethanol
Dopamine
  alternative to hypothesis, 7-14–7-15
  blockade
    by methylphenidate, 7-13
    net effect of, controversy on, 7-14
  hypothesis, 7-4, 7-15
  stimulants and, 9-3, 9-4
Dopamine transporter (DAT1), A-4
Dose-reduction hypothesis, 14-5
DRC (daily report cards), 12-6, 12-8
DRD4 gene
  discovery of, 7-9–7-10
  population and family studies, 7-10–7-11
  replication of studies, 7-12, A-4
Driving history, 1-10
Drug abuse. *See* Substance use disorders; *specific drugs*
  of abuse
Drug Abuse Warning Network (DAWN)
  childhood drug abuse and, 20-12
  design, 21-4
  methodology, 21-4–21-5
  results, 21-10–21-13
  sampling procedures, 21-7–21-8
Drug discrimination studies, 20-2
Drug Enforcement Administration (DEA), 9-2
Drug surveillance large-scale studies, need for,
    10-9–10-10
Drug therapy. *See* Pharmacotherapy; *specific*
  therapeutic drugs
DSM diagnostic criteria, 3-2, 23-2
DSM-II criteria, 1-2, 2-1, 11-2, 23-2
DSM-III criteria. *See* Diagnosis, DSM-III criteria
DSM-III-R. *See* Diagnosis, DSM-III-R criteria
DSM-IV criteria. *See* Diagnosis, DSM-IV criteria

[References are to pages.]

E

Educational functioning. *See* Academic achievement
Educational policy, 26-1–26-2
    federal
        history of, 26-2–26-4
        support for research and, 26-3–26-4
    local. *See* Local education agencies
    state. *See* State education agencies
Education of the Handicapped Act Amendments of
    1990, 26-2
Educators, interest in ADHD, 23-2
Electroencephalogram (EEG), 3-7, 3-10
    biofeedback, 13-5, 13-13–13-14
    brain function in ADHD, 7-9
Electromyography biofeedback, 13-14
Elimination diets (few foods diets/oligoantigenic)
    efficacy, 13-2–13-3, 13-19-13-20
    Feingold hypothesis, 13-2
    probable responders to, 13-3
    recent research on, 13-2–13-3
    risks, 13-7
    scientific status of, 13-4
    sugar restriction, 13-4–13-6
EMG biofeedback, 13-14
Emotional disturbance
    with ADHD, 24-4–24-5, 24-7
    school enrollment, 24-6
    special education cost for, 24-8–24-9
    special education eligibility criteria for, 24-2,
        24-7
Emotional lability, in adult ADHD, 6-3
Employment
    adult, impact of ADHD on, 6-7–6-10
    discrimination, 6-9–6-10
Enuresis, of adult ADHD females, 6-11
Environment
    in ADHD diagnosis, 3-8–3-9
    temperament and, P1-1
Enzyme-potentiated desensitization, scientific status of,
    13-4
Eosinophilia-myalgia, 13-8
Epidemiology
    data analysis, 2-9–2-12
    prevalence. *See* Prevalence
    studies, 2-12–2-13
Essential fatty acid supplementation, 13-4, 13-8–
    13-9
Etiology, P2-1–P2-2, A-3–A-5
    biological bases
        dopamine hypothesis, 7-4, 7-14–7-15
        norepinephrine hypothesis, 7-14–7-15
    dopamine theory of, 7-4
    genetic. *See* Genetic basis, for ADHD
    genetic factors, 11-2
    neuroanatomical abnormalities, 7-4–7-5
        consistency of MRI study findings, 7-7
        differences in MRI study findings, 7-6–7-7
        structural differences in ADHD children,
            7-5–7-6
    nongenetic, 7-12–7-13
Evaluation. *See* Assessment
Evening primrose oil supplementation, 13-8–13-9
Evolutionary perspective, lack of, 3-12

Executive function impairments, in ADHD, 6-3,
    8-8–8-9, 8-12
Expulsion, from school, 5-7, 6-7

F

Face validity, of ADHD diagnosis, 1-8
Family association
    of ADHD and SUD, 19-6–19-7, 19-9
    of cigarette smoking, 19-5
    of cigarette smoking and ADHD, 19-5
Family practice physicians
    counseling usage, 22-11
    medication management, 22-11
    psychotherapy usage, 22-11–22-12
Family relationship
    of adults with ADHD, 6-13–6-15
    of children with ADHD, 5-7–5-10, 24-16
        impairments in, 5-7–5-10
        parental ADHD in, 6-14–6-15
    conflict, hyperactive behavior and, 3-9
    impairment, 5-9–5-10
        comorbid aggression and, 5-9
        stimulant trials and, 5-8–5-9
    stimulants and, 12-3
    treatment choice and, 12-21
    variables, accidental injury and, 5-13
Fathers with ADHD, parenting skills of, 6-14–6-15
FDD. *See* Freedom from Distractibility
Federal government, support for research, 26-3–26-4
Feingold diet. *See* Elimination diets
Fetal alcohol syndrome, 19-7
Few-foods diets. *See* Elimination diets
Fluoxetine, 11-7
Follow-up, by primary care physicians, 23-8–23-9
Follow-up studies
    in adolescence, 4-10–4-11
        comorbid disorders and, 4-6–4-7
        persistence of symptoms in, 4-5–4-6
    assessment instruments for, 4-2–4-3
    attrition and, 4-4–4-5
    developmental issues, 4-3–4-4
    diagnostic criteria for, 4-2
    information source shifting in, 4-4
    measurement over time, unreliability of, 4-3
Food colorings, 13-2–13-3
Fragile X syndrome, 13-9
Freedom from Distractibility (FDD), 8-5
Frontal lobes, in ADHD children, 7-5, 7-6
Full inclusion (mainstreaming), 24-12–24-14
Functional impairment. *See* Impairment
Functional magnetic resonance imaging, 7-8

G

Gambling, adults with ADHD and, 6-12
Gamma-linolenic acid supplementation, 13-8–13-9
Gender
    differences in ADHD, 2-9, 18-12
        cognitive function, 8-4
        future research, 1-17
    treatment service usage variations and, 22-6
    treatment variations and, 22-6
Gene-environment interactions, A-5
Genetic basis, for ADHD, A-4–A-5

[References are to pages.]

Genetic basis, for ADHD *(continued)*
  dopamine candidate genes, 7-9–7-10
    family-based studies, 7-10–7-11
    population-based studies, 7-10–7-11
    replication of studies, 7-12
  evidence for, 3-8
  future directions for, 1-18
  twin studies, 7-9, 7-10
Geographic variations
  in stimulant usage, 10-3
  in treatment and treatment services, 22-6
Gingko biloba, 13-12
Gluconutritional supplements, 13-9
Glue sniffing, by adults with childhood medication
    history, 17-8–17-11
Glyconutritional supplementation, 13-4
Growth, childhood stimulant usage and,
    9-7, 11-3
Guanfacine, 7-15, 11-7
Guardians, identification of psychosocial problems,
    27-6

H

Hallucinogens abuse risk, in ADHD, 16-9
Halo effects, 5-4
Health care providers
    See also specific health care providers
    treatment service usage by, 22-11–22-12
Health care system
    increased usage by ADHD children, 27-7
    interest in ADHD, 23-3
Hepatotoxicity, of stimulants, 9-7
Herbal supplementation, 13-5, 13-12–13-13
Heroin abuse, by adults with childhood medication
    history, 17-8–17-11
Historical aspects, of ADHD, 23-2
H-I subtype. *See* Hyperactive-impulsive subtype
Home life, of ADHD-children, 5-7–5-10
Homeopathic treatments, 13-5, 13-12–13-13
Hyperactive-impulsive subtype (H-I)
    academic outcomes, 8-7
    academic underachievement and, 1-13
    accidental injuries and, 1-5
    ADHD-related impairment and, 5-15–5-16
    behavioral problems, 8-7
    classroom disruption and, 1-9
    comorbidities
        in adults, 6-12
        conduct disorder, 1-4, 1-12
    developmental course of, 1-5
    DSM-III-R vs. DSM-IV criteria, 1-3, 1-5–
        1-7
    future research, 1-17
    gender and, 1-12
    intelligence and, 1-12–1-13
    oppositional defiant disorder and, 1-4, 1-12
    peer relationship problems and, 1-5
    prevalence, impairment and, 1-11
    treatment, 15-9
    unintentional injuries and, 1-13
Hyperactivity
    in adult ADHD, 6-3
    conduct disorder and, 4-10

diagnosis, 18-7
    vs. normal temperament variations, 3-5–3-7
Hypericum, 13-12
Hyperkinetic disorder
    behavior, 3-14–3-15, 3-16
    brain dysfunction and, 3-14–3-15
    ICD-10
        correspondence of DSM-IV ADHD, 1-7
        outcomes, 2-11
Hyperkinetic reaction of childhood, DSM-II, 1-2, 2-1,
    11-2, 23-2
Hypnosis, 13-5, 13-14

I

IDEA. *See* Individuals with Disabilities Education Act
IEP. *See* Individualized education program
Illegal drug usage. *See* Substance use disorders
Imipramine, 11-4
Immune therapy, 13-7
Immunoglobulin, intravenous, 13-7
Impairment, ADHD-related, A-3
    accommodation, 5-17
    appraisals, 5-3–5-4
    biased estimates of, 5-3–5-4
    circularity argument, 5-15
    clinic-referred samples and, 5-3–5-4
    comorbidities and, 5-4–5-5, 5-15
    cross-situational, validity of DSM-IV criteria and,
        1-10–1-11
    current evidence of, A-2
    in definitional criterion, 5-3
    developmental span and, 5-5
    development and, 5-16
    documentation, objective, 5-4
    in DSM-IV criteria, 1-15–1-16
    evidence, 5-2–5-3, 5-14–5-17
        from academic achievement, 5-6–5-7, 5-15
        from accidental injury, 5-13–5-14, 5-15
        from family relationships, 5-7–5-10, 5-15
        from home life, 5-7–5-10
        methodological/conceptual issues, 5-3–5-5
        from peer relationships, 5-10–5-12, 5-15
        from school functioning, 5-7–5-8, 5-15
        from self-esteem, 5-12–5-13
        from self-perception, 5-12–5-13, 5-15
    functional, in DSM-IV ADHD, 1-9
    implications, 5-16–5-17
    prevention, 5-17
    subtypes and, 5-5
    treatment risks for, 1-16
Impulsivity
    in adult ADHD, 6-3
    vs. normal temperament variations, 3-5–3-7
Inattention
    academic underachievement and, 1-4
    in adult ADHD, 6-3
    anxiety symptoms and, 1-4
    depression symptoms and, 1-4
    developmental course of, 1-5
    peer relationship problems and, 1-4
    shyness and, 1-4
    social withdrawal and, 1-4
    special education services and, 1-4

[References are to pages.]

Inattentive subtype (I subtype)
    academic problems of, 8-7
    academic underachievement and, 1-9, 1-13
    adult females and, 6-6
    behavioral problems of, 8-7
    conduct disorders and, 1-12
    vs. DSM-III-R criteria, 1-5–1-7
    future research, 1-17
    gender and, 1-12
    intelligence and, 1-12–1-13
    learning problems and, 1-9–1-10
    oppositional defiant disorder and, 1-12
    prevalence, impairment and, 1-11
    social functioning problems and, 1-9–1-10
    treatment, 15-9, 15-11
    unintentional injuries and, 1-13
Independence, 5-14
Indiana, methylphenidate diversion, 20-17
Individualized education program (IEP), 26-5
Individuals with Disabilities Education Act (IDEA)
    adoption of written educational policies and, 26-6
    Amendments of 1997, 26-5–26-6
    disability categories, 24-6
        ED. See Emotional disturbance
        LD. See Learning disability
        OHI. See Other health impairment
    eligibility, 26-2–26-3
    provision of special education services, 23-8, 26-2
Information
    dissemination, for caregivers and children, 22-16
    processing, 8-13–8-15
Inhalant abuse risk, in ADHD, 16-9
Intellectual function, in ADHD assessment, 8-17
Intelligence, 1-10, 5-14, 8-4–8-5
Intelligence quotient (IQ), 2-11, 24-2
Intelligence tests, 8-4–8-5
Interactive Metronome, 13-15
International Statistical Classification of Diseases and
    Related Health Problems (ICD-9), 2-2, 22-8, 27-9
International Statistical Classification of Diseases and
    Related Health Problems (ICD-10)
    vs. DSM scheme, 2-1–2-2
    hyperkinetic disorder criteria, overlap with DSM-IV
        ADHD criteria, 1-7, 3-3–3-4, 7-2–7-3
    unresolved classification issues, 2-3
Interpersonal relationships, stimulants and, 12-3
IOWA Aggression scale, 15-3, 15-5
Iowa study, new, 17-5–17-6
    follow-up review of patient's attitudes, 17-6–17-11
    implications of, 17-11–17-13
    random assignment procedure for, 17-5–17-6
Iron supplementation, 13-4, 13-11

J
Juvenile justice system
    offending trends, 25-1—25-3
    population. See Juveniles, detained
    response, to increased ADHD and conduct disorder,
        25-3–25-4
Juveniles, detained
    ADHD in
        juvenile justice system response to, 25-3–25-4
        prevalence of, 25-2–25-3

conduct disorder in
    juvenile justice system response to, 25-3–25-4
    prevalence of, 25-2–25-3
mental health disorders in, 25-2–25-3
number of, growth in, 25-1–25-2
research needs, 25-3–25-4

L
Labeling
    misapplications, 3-13–3-14
    negative aspects of, 3-12–3-13
    usefulness of, 3-12
Language
    delays, 2-11
    disorders, of adult ADHD females, 6-11
Lead. See Deleading
Learning disability (LD)
    academic achievement and, 5-6
    with ADHD, 23-6, 24-3
    Freedom from Distractibility scores and, 8-5
    minimal brain dysfunction as, 26-2
    prevalence
        with ADHD, 24-3
        in general population, 24-3
    school enrollment, 24-6
    special education cost for, 24-8–24-9
    special education eligibility, 24-2, 24-7
LEAs. See Local education agencies
Liver damage, from pemoline, 9-7, 10-5
Local education agencies (LEAs)
    revised IDEA regulations and, 26-5, 26-6
    special education eligibility determination, 26-4
    written policies, adoption of, 26-8
Longitudinal studies
    of children with ADHD, 16-9–16-12
        clinical, 16-9–16-11
        community, 16-11–16-12
    on educational functioning, 6-7–6-10
    limitations
        attrition, 4-4–4-5
        developmental issues, 4-3–4-4
        different assessment instruments for, 4-2–4-3
        lack of diagnostic consensus and, 4-2
        shifting information sources, 4-4
        unreliability of measurement over time, 4-3
    of substance use disorders, 18-2, 19-3, 19-5
    on vocational functioning, 6-7–6-10
Long-term developmental course. See Development,
    long-term course
Low birthweight, prevention of, 5-17
LSD usage, adults with childhood medication history,
    17-8–17-11

M
Magnesium supplementation, 13-5, 13-12
Magnetic resonance imaging (MRI), of neuroanatomical
    abnormalities in ADHD, 7-4–7-5, 7-8
Mainstreaming (full inclusion), 24-12–24-14
MAOIs (monoamine oxidase inhibitors), 11-6–11-7
Marijuana usage
    by adolescents with ADHD, 19-9
        clinical longitudinal studies, 16-9–16-11
        retrospective studies, 16-8

[References are to pages.]

Marijuana usage *(continued)*
    by adults with childhood medication history,
        17-8–17-11
    age at usage, ADHD severity and, 18-6
    risk, in ADHD, 16-9
Marital discord, in families with ADHD children,
    5-8–5-9
Marital status, of adults with ADHD, 6-13
Massage
    for ADHD, 13-16
    for hyperkinetic behavior in autism, 13-15–13-16
    by parents, 13-20
    scientific status of, 13-5
MBD. *See* Minimal brain dysfunction
McMaster University Evidence-Based Practice Center,
    14-2
Medicaid, 22-4–22-5
Medical service usage, by ADHD children, 27-4–27-5
Medication Attitude Interview, 17-6–17-11
Medications. *See* Pharmacotherapy; *specific medication*
    or type of medication
Meditation, 13-5, 13-15, 13-20
Megadosing, of vitamins, 13-10–13-11, 13-19
Megavitamin supplements, 13-10–13-11
Memory
    anxiety disorder with ADHD and, 8-11
    long-term, 8-10
    short-term, 8-10
Mental disorders
    See also specific mental disorders
    with ADHD, 1-13–1-14
Mental health clinicians
    identification of psychosocial problems, 27-6
    role in treating ADHD, 23-3–23-4
    speciality training, 22-16
Mental health counseling
    by provider type, 22-11
    usage trends, 22-11
Mental health disorders, prevalence in juvenile justice
    system, 25-2–25-3
Mental health service usage, by ADHD children,
    27-4–27-5
Mental retardation, with ADHD, 15-8–15-9, 15-11
Methamphetamine
    abuse, 20-10–21-14
    morbidity, 21-14
3-Methoxy-4-hydroxyphenylglycol, urinary, 13-13
Methylphenidate (MPH; Ritalin®), P1-2
    absorption, 9-4–9-5
    abuse, 9-2, 20-6
        by adolescents, 20-12, 20-14, 21-10–21-13
        availability and, 21-15
        by children, 20-12
        with narcotics, 20-10–20-11
        potential for, 9-7, 21-1
    abuse liability, 20-2–20-6, 21-2
        amphetamine-and cocaine-like effects, 20-2
        disruptive effects, 20-5–20-6
        dose-reinforcing effects, 20-2–20-5
        stimulus effects, 20-5–20-6
    for ADHD with anxiety disorder, 15-4–15-7
    for ADHD with disruptive behavior disorder,
        15-2–15-4

    for ADHD with SUD, 19-11
    administration schedule, 9-5
    adverse drug effects, 20-6
    animal studies, 9-3
    with behavioral therapy
        efficacy of, 12-10
        long-term efficacy, 12-18
        research results, positive, 12-16–12-18
    blood pressure and, 10-9–10-10
    brain effects, 9-3
    carcinogenicity, 10-3–10-4
    chemical structure, 9-3–9-4
    with clonidine, 11-7
    cocaine sensitization and, 18-5
    comparison studies
        auditory feedback, 14-6
        behavior treatment, 14-5
        contingency management, 14-6
        psychosocial treatment, 15-3–15-4
    diversion, 20-9–20-11
        of children's prescribed medications, 20-14–
            20-15
        contributing factors, 20-16–20-17
        methods of, 20-14
        three-state survey findings, 20-15–20-17
    dopamine blockade, 7-13–7-14
    dosage, 9-5
    dose-reduction study, 14-5
    drug sensitization from, 17-5
    early exposure, predisposition to substance use,
        18-6
    early investigations, 17-4
    efficacy
        short-term, 10-5–10-6
        of sustained-release formulations, 9-12–
            9-13
    immediate-release formulations, 9-4
    manufacturing/production quotas, 20-7–
        20-8
    median lethal dose, 9-6
    metabolism, 9-5
    misuse of, 9-2–9-3
    morbidity, 21-2, 21-4, 21-14–21-15
    mortality, 21-2, 21-4
    nonmedical usage, 21-14
    nonspecific effects, 3-14
    pharmacology, 9-3–9-4
    prescriptions, 21-2, 21-3
        increases in, 10-2, 22-4–22-5
        patterns, 9-2
    prevalence of usage, 9-2, 10-2–10-3
    production of, 9-2, 21-2–21-3
    vs. psychosocial treatment, 15-5–15-7
    randomized control trials, short-term efficacy,
        9-7–9-11
    research needs, future, 10-11
    response
        DSM-III subtypes and, 1-13
        DSM-IV subtypes and, 1-13
    safety, short-term, 10-7
    sales, increased, 20-7–20-8
    Schedule II classification, 20-1
    sensitization, 18-4–18-5

[References are to pages.]

short-term trials
limitations of, 9-13–9-14, 9-16–9-17
results, App. A-6
side effects, 10-9
single therapy, vs. cognitive treatment with
medication, 14-4–14-5
site of action, 7-4, 7-15
sustained-release formulations, 9-4, 9-12–9-13
therapeutic effect, 9-5
toxicology, 9-6, 10-3–10-4, 10-11
trafficking, 20-9–20-11
usage
based on ADHD diagnosis, 9-2–9-3
disparities in, 20-8–20-9
increased, 9-2
Milwaukee study, 4-7–4-8
Mineral supplements, 13-11–13-12
Minimal brain dysfunction (MBD)
ADHD/HKD and, 7-12–7-13
lack of evidence in ADHD, 3-7–3-8
use of term, 1-2, 3-11
Mirror feedback, 13-5, 13-15, 13-20
Mixed substance use disorders, retrospective studies,
16-6–16-7
Monitoring the Future (MTF)
design, 21-4–21-5
methodology, 21-5
questions for, 21-5–21-6
results, 21-8–21-10
sampling procedures, 21-5
Monoamine oxidase inhibitors (MAOIs), 11-6–
11-7
Montreal Longitudinal Study, 6-7
Mood disorders, with ADHD
See also Depression, with ADHD
in adolescence, 4-6–4-7
in adults, 6-11–6-12
risk at adulthood follow-up, 4-10
treatment of, 15-7–15-8, 15-11
Mothers with ADHD, parenting skills of, 6-14–6-15
Motor development delays, 2-11
Motor inhibition deficits, 8-9
Motor planning deficits, 8-9
Motor response inhibition deficits, 8-12
Motor vehicle accidents, 1-10
MPH. See Methylphenidate
MRI. See Magnetic resonance imaging
MTA Study. See Multimodal Treatment Study
MTF. See Monitoring the Future
Multimodal Treatment Study (MTA)
answers, to treatment questions, 9-18–9-19
design of, 9-14–9-15, 9-18, 15-2
impact of comorbidity patterns, 15-7
long-term effectiveness of medication, 10-6
outcome, 9-18
stimulant therapy
with behavioral therapy, 12-16–12-18
vs. psychosocial treatment for ADHD with
anxiety disorder, 15-6–15-7
treatment indications
for ADHD with anxiety, 15-10
psychosocial, 15-10–15-11
Multivitamin supplements, 13-10

N

National Ambulatory Medical Care Survey (NAMCS)
increased identification of ADHD, 22-9
methods
data assessment, 22-8–22-9
data set, 22-8
treatment services
by provider type, 22-11–22-12
trends, 22-9–22-11
treatment trends, 22-9–22-11
National Household Survey (NHS), 21-4
National Institute of Mental Health (NIMH),
Multimodal Treatment Study. See Multimodal
Treatment Study
National Institutes of Health Consensus Statement,
App. A-1–App. A-12
NDA. See New Drug Application
Neuroanatomy
MRI studies, 7-4–7-5
structural differences in ADHD children, 7-5–
7-6
Neurobiological basis, for ADHD diagnosis
cross-cultural findings, 2-11
lack of evidence for, 3-7–3-8
long-term findings, 2-11
for pharmacological treatment, 7-13–7-14
Neuropsychological function
in ADHD assessment, 8-17–8-18
assessment methods, 8-8
cognitive correlates, specificity of, 8-12–8-13
impact of comorbidity on, 8-10–8-12
impairments
in executive functioning, 8-8–8-9
other, 8-9–8-10
latent traits, 8-8
primary deficits, 8-8
Neuropsychological tests, 8-8, 8-9
Neurotoxicity, of amphetamines, 10-4
Neurotransmitters, amphetamines and, 10-4
New Drug Application (NDA), Phases I, II, and III
studies for stimulants, 9-13–9-14
New York Longitudinal Study, 6-8
NHS. See National Household Survey
Nicotine hypothesis, 11-8–11-9
Nicotine usage, clinical longitudinal studies, 16-11–
16-12
Nicotinic drugs, 11-9
NIMH. See National Institute of Mental Health
Nonmedical use, definition of, 21-7
Norepinephrine, stimulants and, 9-3
Norepinephrine hypothesis, 7-14–7-15
Nortriptyline, 11-5, 11-9
Nosological systems, 2-1–2-2, 11-2
See also specific systems
Nutritional supplements
amino acids, 13-7–13-8
L-carnitine, 13-9
dimethylaminoethanol, 13-9–13-10
essential fatty acids, 13-8–13-9
gluconutritional, 13-9
minerals, 13-11–13-12
vitamins, 13-10–13-11
Nystatin, 13-17

[References are to pages.]

O

Obsessive-compulsive disorder
  executive function impairments, 8-12
  immune therapy for, 13-7
OCR. *See* Office of Civil Rights
ODD. *See* Oppositional defiant disorder
Office of Civil Rights (OCR), 26-4
Office of Special Education and Rehabilitative
    Services (OSERS), 26-4
Office of Special Education Programs (OSEP),
    26-4
OHI. *See* Other health impairment
Oligoantigenic diets. *See* Elimination diets
Opiate abuse, with ADHD
  in adults with childhood medication history,
      17-8–17-11
  clinical longitudinal studies, 16-9–16-12
  retrospective studies, 16-6
  risk of, 16-9
Oppositional defiant disorder (ODD)
  with ADHD, 4-11, 23-6
      accidental injury and, 5-13
      in adolescence, 4-6
      in adults, 6-9, 6-11
      prevalence of, 1-13
  differentiation from ADHD, 6-15
  neuropsychological function and, 8-11–8-12
  response inhibition deficits and, 8-14
  school functioning and, 5-7
  special education eligibility, 24-10
  substance use disorder and, 17-3
OSEP. *See* Office of Special Education Programs
OSERS. *See* Office of Special Education and
    Rehabilitative Services
Other health impairment (OHI)
  ADHD as, 24-5–24-10
  definition of, 26-2–26-3
  school enrollment, 24-6–24-7
  special education cost for, 24-8–24-9
  special education criteria for, 24-2
  special education eligibility, 24-7, 26-6
Outcome
  at adolescence, 4-5–4-7
  at adulthood, 4-7–4-10
  research, 24-15
Overconfidence, 5-12
Overdiagnosis, A-7

P

PANDAS. *See* Pediatric autoimmune neuropsychiatric
    disorders associated with group A beta-hemolytic
    infection
Parenting
  by adults with ADHD, 6-14–6-15
  distress, in families with ADHD children, 5-8
Parents
  abuse of children's MPH medication, 20-14
  contact with primary care physician, 23-5
  identification of psychosocial problems, 27-6
  impact of labeling on, 3-13
  information, in ADHD diagnosis, 23-5–23-6
  interactions with children, in family with ADHD
      children, 5-8

psychiatric help-seeking, 23-4
training, combined therapy and, 12-21–12-22
Pathological gambling, adults with ADHD and,
    6-12
Pathophysiology, 8-15–8-16, A-3–A-5
  genetic. *See* Genetic basis, for ADHD
  neuroanatomical, 7-4–7-9
  neurobiological
      dopamine hypothesis, 7-4–7-15
      norepinephrine hypothesis, 7-14–7-15
Pediatric autoimmune neuropsychiatric disorders
    associated with group A beta-hemolytic infection
    (PANDAS), 13-7
Pediatricians
  counseling usage, 22-11
  diagnostic service usage, 22-11
  increased diagnosis of ADHD, 27-2–27-3
  as initial medical contact, 23-3–23-4
  medication management, 22-11
  mental health counseling usage, 22-11
Pediatric research in office settings (PROS), 22-12,
    27-5
Peer relationships, 5-12
  comorbid aggression and, 5-10–5-11
  problems, as risk factor, 1-10, 2-9
  rejection, 5-10
      ADHD subtypes and, 5-11
      aggression and, 5-10–5-11
  social competence and, 5-11
Pemoline (Cylert®)
  abuse, 21-14
  abuse potential, 9-7, 21-1–21-2
  for ADHD with SUD, 19-11
  administration, 9-5
  adverse events, 9-7
  dosage, 9-5
  efficacy, short-term, 10-5
  hepatotoxicity, 10-7–10-8
  liver damage from, 9-7, 10-5
  metabolism, 9-5
  prescriptions, 21-2–21-3
  randomized control trials, short-term efficacy,
      9-7–9-11
  safety, short-term, 10-7–10-8
  short-term trials
      limitations of, 9-13–9-14, 9-16–9-17
      results, App. A-6
  single therapy, vs. cognitive treatment with
      medication, 14-4–14-5
  sustained-release preparations, efficacy of,
      9-21
  therapeutic effect, 9-5–9-6
  toxicology, 10-5
Pencillamine, 13-18
Perceptual stimulation/training, 13-15
Persistence of childhood ADHD, 4-3, 19-2
Personal variables, accidental injury and, 5-13
PET. *See* Positron emission tomography
Pharmacotherapy
  See also specific pharmacotherapeutic agents
  for ADHD with substance use disorder, 19-11–
      19-12
  auditory feedback and, 14-6

[References are to pages.]

vs. behavioral therapy, 14-2–14-3
    vs. combined treatment, 14-4
    short-term studies, 14-4–14-6
with behavioral therapy
    advantages of, 12-15–12-16
    dosage effects and, 12-21–12-22
    duration of, 12-22–12-23
    efficacy of, 14-7–14-8
    long-term effectiveness, 12-24
    long-term impact, 12-16
    optimum sequence for, 12-22
    parent training and, 12-21–12-22
    research results, positive, 12-16–12-18
childhood, adult attitudes on, 17-7–7-11
contingency management and, 14-6
dependence on, 7-8
dosage
    combined therapy and, 12-21–12-22
    reduction of, 14-5
durability of, 14-6–14-7
efficacy of, 14-7–14-8
financial interests and, P1-2
limitations of, 12-3–12-4
long-term effects, App. A-7–App. A-8
neurobiological bases for, 7-13–7-14
new, development of, A-6
nonstimulant
    alpha-2 noradrenergic agonists, 11-7–11-9
    future research needs, 11-10
    non-tricyclic antidepressants, 11-6–11-7
    tricyclic antidepressants, 11-4–11-6
    viability of, 11-9
predisposition to drug abuse, 17-3
prescriptions
    increased levels of, 22-4–22-5
    trends in, 22-4–22-5
prevention of drug abuse, 17-3–17-4
    pharmacological, 17-4
    psychological, 17-4
vs. psychosocial treatment, 14-4, App. A-6
trends, 22-10
usage trends, 22-10
Phenobarbital
    behavioral side effects, 10-10–10-11
    treatment risks, 10-10–10-11
Phenotype, ADHD/HKD, 7-17
Phenylalanine supplementation, 13-8
Phenylethylamines, 21-2
Physical dependence, 21-7
Placebo, vs. stimulant response, 9-9, 9-12
Plasma exchange, 13-7
Positron emission tomography (PET)
    functional imaging studies of ADHD, 7-8, 7-9
    methylphenidate site-of-action, 7-13
Predictive validity, of ADHD diagnosis in childhood, 1-8
Pregnancy, maternal smoking during, 11-8
Prevalence
    of ADHD
        in adults, 6-4–6-5, 6-16
        with anxiety disorder, 1-13
        DSM-III-R, 1-5–1-6, 2-3–2-7
        with emotional disturbances, 24-3–24-4

        in juvenile justice system, 25-2–25-3
        with learning disabilities, 24-3–24-4
        with other health impairments, 24-3–24-4
        in primary care setting, 27-2–27-4
        in states, 26-8
    of attentional problems, 22-3–22-4
    of conduct disorders, in juvenile justice system, 25-2–25-3
    in cross-cultural contexts, P1-2
    of DSM-III ADD, 2-3–2-7, 23-3
    of DSM-III-R, 23-3
    of DSM-IV ADHD, 2-6, 2-7
        C type, 1-5–1-6
        H-I type, 1-5–1-6
        I type, 1-5–1-6
    of ICD-9 hyperkinesis, 2-5–2-6
    of ICD-10 hyperkinesis, 2-5–2-7
    of mental health disorders, in juvenile justice system, 25-2–25-3
    of oppositional defiant disorder with ADHD, 1-13
    of stimulant usage for ADHD, 10-2–10-3, 22-5
Prevention, public policy and, 1-16
Primary care physicians
    comorbidity frequency, 27-3–27-4
    contact
        with parent, 23-5
        with teacher, 23-5–23-6
    decision-making, research findings and, 9-19–9-20
    demographic changes, 27-3
    diagnosis of ADHD, increased, 27-2–27-3
    follow-up, 23-8–23-9
    practical value of labels for, 3-13
    role in treating ADHD, 23-3–23-4
    training, 22-16
    treatment assessment, 23-8–23-9
Primary care setting
    cost-benefit analysis, need for, 27-11–27-12
    service initiation, 27-12–27-13
Problem behavior, as substance use disorder risk factor, 18-6, 18-19–18-20
Processing Speed index, 8-5
Productivity, low, 8-6
Propranolol, 11-7–11-8
PROS (Pediatric Research in Office Settings), 22-12, 27-5
PSUDs. *See* Psychoactive substance use disorders
Psychedelics, clinical longitudinal studies, 16-9–16-11
Psychiatric disorders, validation stages, 71-7-2
Psychiatrists
    counseling usage, 22-11
    diagnostic service usage, 22-11
    medication management, 22-11
    mental health counseling usage, 22-11
    psychotherapy usage, 22-11–22-12
Psychic effects, 21-7
Psychoactive substance use disorders (PSUDs)
    in adolescents with ADHD, 4-7
    DSM-III-R diagnosis, 18-11, 18-12
Psychological functioning impairments, of adults with ADHD, 6-11–6-13
Psychological immunization process, medications and, 17-4
Psychological predisposition, to drug abuse, 17-3, 17-4

[References are to pages.]

Psychologists, practical value of labels for, 3-13
Psychopathology exposure, hyperactive behavior and, 3-9
Psychosocial adversity, ADHD/HKD and, 7-13
Psychosocial interventions
    for ADHD with disruptive behavior disorder, 15-3–15-4
    categories of, 12-4–12-5
    clinical behavior therapy. *See* Behavioral therapy
    cognitive-behavioral treatment, 12-5–12-6
    contingency management, 12-10–12-12
    cost-effectiveness, 12-23–12-24
    efficacy, 12-2, 12-18–12-19, App. A-5–App. A-6
    exportability to real-world settings, 12-24
    historical aspects, 12-2
    indications, 15-10–15-11
    ineffective, 12-2
    intensive, 12-12–12-14
    interventions, App. A-6–App. A-7
    long-term efficacy of, 9-19, 12-24
    vs. pharmacotherapy, 14-4, App. A-6
    shortcomings of, 12-14–12-15
    vs. stimulant therapy, 15-3–15-4
    studies, 12-5, 12-25–12-30
Psychosocial problems
    in primary care setting, 23-6–23-7
    risk factors, 19-9–19-10
Psychostimulants. *See* Stimulants
Psychotherapy
    for ADHD with substance use disorder, 19-11
    usage
        by provider type, 22-11–22-12
        trends, 22-11
Psychotropic drugs, usage trends, 22-5, 22-10, 23-7
Public health implications
    safety/efficacy of stimulants and, 10-12
        See also specific stimulants
    of substance abuse precursor identification, 16-12–16-15
Public Law 101-476. *See* Individuals with Disabilities Education Act
Public Law 105-17, 26-5– 26-6
Public policy, prevention/treatment of ADHD and, 1-16
Punishment, for conduct disorder, 12-11
Pycnogenol, 13-12
Pyridoxine, 13-11

Q

Questionnaire subjectivity, diagnostic, 3-9–3-10

R

Race
    treatment service usage variations and, 22-6
    treatment variations and, 22-6
RCMAS. *See* Revised Children's Manifest Anxiety Scale
Reading comprehension, 8-7–8-7
Reading disorder, with ADHD, 8-10–8-11
Referrals, 23-9
"Refined phenotype," A-2
Rehabilitation Act of 1973, 23-8, 24-2, 24-9, 24-13, 26-3
Relaxation therapy, 13-5

Relaxation training, 13-14
Relocation of subjects, follow-up studies and, 4-4–4-5
Research
    federal support for, 26-3–26-4
    future recommendations
        cognitive correlates and, 8-18–8-19
        directions for, App. A-9–App. A-10
        on nonstimulant drug therapy, 11-10
        target areas for, 1-16–1-18
        treatment alternatives, 13-20–13-21
        treatment services, 22-16–22-17
        treatment strategies, 15-11–15-12
    statistical analysis
        dependent variables in, 18-10–18-11
        independent variables in, 18-11–18-12
Response inhibition deficits, 8-14–8-15
Restlessness, in adult ADHD, 6-3
Retrospective studies
    of ADHD individuals
        with alcohol-related disorders, 16-3–16-5
        with cocaine abuse, 16-5–16-6
        with mixed substance use disorders, 16-6–16-7
        with opiate abuse, 16-6
        with substance use disorders, 16-3–16-7
    of drug use/abuse
        in adolescents, 16-8
        in adult ADHD, 16-7–16-8
Revised Children's Manifest Anxiety Scale (RCMAS), 15-5
Right-hemisphere deficits, P1-1–P1-2
Risk factors, epidemiological data, 2-9, 2-11
Ritalin®. *See* Methylphenidate

S

Saccadic eye movements, 8-15
Schizophrenia, executive function impairments, 8-12
School
    break-ins and theft of methylphenidate, 20-14–20-15
    classroom adaptations/interventions, outcome from, 24-15
    classroom interventions, 24-10
    district challenges, 26-8–26-9
    educational policy. *See* Educational policy
    enrollment
        for emotionally disturbed children, 24-6
        for learning disabled children, 24-6
        for other health impaired children, 24-6–24-7
    factors contributing to methylphenidate diversion, 20-16–20-17
    failure, as risk factor, 2-9
    functioning, 5-7–5-8
    impact of labeling on, 3-13
    information, in ADHD diagnosis, 23-5–23-6
    instructional methods, adapting to ADHD children, 24-15–24-16
    interventions for ADHD, 24-13–24-15
    mainstream classrooms, 24-12–24-14
    mental health services, usage rates, 22-5–22-6
    practice and policy, 24-16
    role, in nondrug therapies, 23-8
    segregated classrooms, 24-10–24-11

[References are to pages.]

special education services, eligibility for,
    24-1–24-2
student medications, state education policies for,
    26-8
treatment concerns, 23-7–23-8
School functioning. *See* Academic achievement
Sedatives
    abuse risk, in ADHD, 16-9
    in ADHD children, clinical longitudinal studies,
        16-9–16-11
Selective serotonin reuptake inhibitors, 11-7
Self-care skills, 5-14
Self-concept problems, in adult ADHD, 6-3
Self-control, hyperactivity/impulsivity and, 1-5
Self-esteem
    of ADHD children, 5-12
    low, as risk factor, 2-9, 2-11
Self-medication hypothesis
    smoking and substance use by ADHD individuals,
        18-3–18-4
    stimulant usage and, 16-2
    SUD in ADHD adolescents and, 19-8–19-9
    support for, 18-17–18-18
    unmedicated individuals and, 17-11
Self-perception, 5-12–5-13
Self-reports, in longitudinal follow-up studies, 4-4
Sensitization hypothesis, support for, 18-18–18-19
Sensory perception, 8-10
Services for ADHD children. *See* Treatment services
Set switching deficits, 8-9
Severity of ADHD
    age of regular smoking and, 18-2–18-3
        childhood stimulant treatment, adult smoking
            and, 18-15
        self-medicating hypothesis support and,
            18-17–18-18
        sensitization hypothesis and, 18-18–18-19
        survival analysis of delay in onset of regular
            smoking, 18-12–18-15
        tobacco gateway hypothesis, partial support for,
            18-19
    levels, 18-11
Smoking
    ADHD and, 19-5–19-6
        clinical longitudinal studies, 16-9–16-11
        self-medication hypothesis and, 18-3–18-4
    in adolescents, retrospective studies, 16-8
    adult
        status, definition of, 18-11
        substance use disorder predictions, 18-15–18-17
    age of, 18-6, 18-10
    retrospective studies, 16-8
    risk, ADHD and, 16-9, 18-3
Social context, of ADHD, 5-16–5-17
Social functioning
    of adults with ADHD, 6-10–6-15
    of children with ADHD, 5-11
Social preference, 5-10
Social relations disorder, 3-15–3-16
Social skills
    deficits, in adults with ADHD, 6-13
    training, 23-8
Soft neurological abnormalities, 2-11

South Carolina, methylphenidate diversion, 20-17
Special education services
    ADHD overrepresentation in, 5-7–5-8
    cost estimates, 24-8–24-9
    criteria
        for emotional disturbance, 24-2
        for other health impairments category, 24-2
    delayed, 24-10
    eligibility
        for ADHD children, 24-7
        categories. *See specific categories*
        under IDEA, 26-2–26-3
        under rehabilitation act, 26-3
    learning disability category, 24-2
    placement, outcome from, 24-15
SPECT, 7-8
Speech disorders, of adult females with ADHD, 6-11
State education agencies
    adoption of written policies, 26-6–26-7
    disability categories, ADHD in, 26-7
    policies
        for ADHD identification, 26-7–26-8
        for assessment of ADHD, 26-7–26-8
        for medication of ADHD students, 26-8
    survey of 1998, 26-8
Stigmatization, from labeling, 3-13
Stimulants
    See also specific stimulants
    absorption, 9-4–9-6
    abuse risk, in ADHD, 16-9
    for ADHD
        with aggression, 15-10
        clinical longitudinal studies, 16-9–16-11
        with conduct disorder, 15-10
        with disruptive behavior disorder, 15-3–15-4
        with ODD, 15-10
        phenobarbital analogy and, 10-10–10-11
        vs. psychosocial treatment, 15-3–15-4
        substance use disorder risk and, 19-3–19-5
    administration, 11-2
    adult usage, childhood medication status and,
        17-8–17-11
    adverse events, 9-6
    age of usage, ADHD severity and, 18-6
    with behavioral therapy
        advantages of, 12-15–12-16
        efficacy of, 12-10
        long-term efficacy, 12-18
        long-term impact, 12-16
        research results, positive, 12-16–12-18
    benefits
        amelioration of disruptive behavior, 9-9
        cognitive functioning, 9-9
    with beta blockers, 11-7–11-8
    blood pressure and, 10-9–10-10
    childhood usage, 18-11–18-12
        age of regular smoking and, 18-12
        severity of ADHD, adult smoking and, 18-15
        survival analysis, 18-13–18-15
        for very young children, 22-14
    compliance, long-term, 12-4
    compliance problems, 11-2
    controlled nature of, 11-3

[References are to pages.]

Stimulants *(continued)*
    controversy, 23-7
    databases, national, 21-4
    disadvantages of, 11-2–11-3
    dose-response curve, 9-6
    dosing issues, 9-20–9-21
    drug abuse, hypothetical rationale for, 16-2
    drug abuse and
        California study, 17-5, 17-12
        early investigational findings, 17-4
        future research directions, 17-13–17-14
        Iowa study, 17-5–17-6
        theories on, 17-3–17-4
    drug holidays, 9-6–9-7
    duration of therapy, smoking risk and, 18-2
    effect on family relationship impairment, 5-8–5-9
    efficacy, 17-13, App. A-5–App. A-6
        future research needs, 10-11–10-12
        long-term, 10-6–10-7, 10-12
        short-term, 9-7–9-11, 10-5–10-6, 10-12
        of sustained-release preparations, 9-12–9-13
        vs. tricyclic antidepressants, 11-5–11-6
    family functioning and, 12-3
    future research needs, 10-11–10-12
    growth/development and, 11-3
    immediate-release preparations, with SR
        preparations, 9-21
    individual differences in response, 12-3
    interpersonal relationships and, 12-3
    limitations of, 9-20–9-21
    long-acting, 11-2–11-3
    long-term effects, 17-2, 17-13, App. A-7–App. A-8
    long-term randomized controlled trials, 9-14
        MTA Study, 9-14–9-15, 9-18–9-19
        other, 9-19–9-20
    for maternal ADHD, 6-14–6-15
    metabolism, 9-4–9-6
    New Drug Application Phases I, II, and III studies,
        9-13–9-14
    nonmedical usage, reasons for, 21-8–21-10
    nonresponders, 9-8–9-9, 9-20–9-21
    nonspecific effects, 3-14
    pharmacology, 9-3–9-4
    preclinical abuse liability studies, 21-2
    predisposition to drug abuse, 17-3
    prescriptions
        geographic differences in, 10-3
        increased levels of, 22-4–22-5
        increase in, 10-2
        patterns, 9-2, 10-2
    prevalence for ADHD treatment, 10-2–10-3
    prevalence of, 10-2–10-3
    prognosis, long-term, 12-4
    vs. psychosocial treatment, 15-5–15-7
    randomized controlled trials
        long-term, 9-14–9-15, 9-18–9-19
        short-term efficacy, 9-7–9-11
    recommendations, 9-21
    research findings, effect on clinical practice,
        9-19–9-20
    research needs, future, 10-11
    response, vs. placebo, 9-9, 9-12, 9-20–9-21
    risk-benefit, 9-21

    risks, 9-6–9-7, App. A-7–App. A-8
    safety
        drug surveillance studies, need for, 10-9–10-11
        future research needs, 10-12
        large-scale cohort studies, need for, 10-9–10-11
        long-term, 10-8–10-11
        short-term, 10-7–10-8
    sensitization, substance use disorders and, 18-4–
        18-5
    shortages of, 9-2
    short-term effects, 17-13
        clinical trials, App. A-6
        limitations of trials, 9-13–9-14, 9-16–9-17
    sites of action
        alternative, 7-14–7-15
        dopamine pathways as, 7-4
    substance use disorder risk and, 17-2, 18-1–18-20
        data collection procedures, 18-9–18-10
        diagnostic proxies, development of, 18-7–18-8
        DSM-IV ADHD classification vs. original
            classification of subjects, 18-9
        hypothesis, 18-6–18-7
        onset of symptoms, DSM-IV criteria for, 18-8
        severity criteria for ADHD, 18-8–18-9
        statistical analysis, variables in, 18-10–18-12
        study interpretations, 17-2–17-3
        study participants, 18-7
        study results, 18-12–18-20
    sustained-release preparations
        efficacy of, 9-21
        with IR preparations, 9-21
    toxicology, 9-6, 10-3–10-5, 10-11
    usage, 23-7
        geographic variation in, 10-3
        prevalence of, 22-5
        trends, 22-10
Stimulant sensitization hypothesis, 18-6
STP. *See* Children's Summer Treatment Program
Substance use disorders (SUDs)
    See also Alcohol use/abuse
    with ADHD, 19-2, 19-12, 21-2
        differential diagnosis, 19-10
        evaluation of, 19-10
        hypothetical rationale, 16-2
        pharmacotherapy, 19-11–19-12
        psychotherapeutic interventions, 19-11
        research implications, 19-7–19-10
        retrospective studies, 16-3–16-7
        self-medication hypothesis and, 18-3–18-4
        stabilization of addiction and, 19-10–19-11
    ADHD as risk factor for, longitudinal studies, 19-3
    with adolescent ADHD, 19-2–19-3
        self-mediation hypothesis and, 19-8–19-9
    adult ADHD, 6-12, 19-3
        childhood medication history and, 17-8–17-11
        childhood medication status and, 17-8–17-11
        female, 6-11
        retrospective studies, 16-7–16-8
    conduct disorder and, 16-8–16-9
    data collection procedure, 18-9–8-10
    diagnostic overlap with ADHD, 19-2–19-3
    familial association, with ADHD, 19-6–19-7
    longitudinal studies, 19-5

[References are to pages.]

in medicated vs. unmedicated ADHD children, 17-2
ongoing studies, MTF. *See* Monitoring the Future
parental, as adolescent ADHD/conduct disorder risk
    factor, 19-8
pathways associated with ADHD, 19-5–19-6
precursor identification
    clinical implications, 16-12–16-15
    problems in drawing inferences from multiple
        studies, 16-13–16-14
    public health implications, 16-12–16-15
    retrospective studies, 16-13
predictions, adult daily smoking and, 18-15–18-17
predisposition
    pharmacological, 17-3
    psychological, 17-3
protection
    pharmacological, 17-4
    psychological, 17-4
psychosocial risk factors and, 19-9–19-10
retrospective studies, in adolescents, 16-8
risk
    in ADHD, 16-8–16-9, 18-3, 19-1–19-2
    in ADHD adolescents, 19-8
    in adulthood follow-up, 4-9–4-10
    childhood stimulant usage and, 9-7
    clinical longitudinal studies, 16-9–16-11
    community longitudinal studies,
        16-11–16-12
    conduct disorder and, 16-14–16-15
    from long-term stimulant usage,
        App. A-7–App. A-8
risk factors
    problem behavior, 18-6
    stimulant therapy for ADHD, 19-3–19-5
    tobacco usage, 18-5–18-6
stimulant usage and, 17-2
    California study, 17-5, 17-12
    early investigational findings, 17-4
    future research directions, 17-13–17-14
    Iowa study, new, 17-5–17-6
    theories of, 17-3–17-4
Subtypes, P1-1
based on DSM-IV and ICD-10 criteria, 7-2–7-3
cognitive correlates and, 8-19
DSM-IV criteria, 11-2
    discriminant validity of, 1-11–1-13
    intelligence differences and, 8-5–8-6
    methylphenidate response and, 1-13
H-I. *See* Hyperactive-impulsive subtype
I. *See* Inattentive subtype
impairment and, 5-5
peer rejection and, 5-11
refined phenotype, 7-3
restricted phenotype, 7-2–7-3
treatment alternatives and, 13-21
treatment response, 15-9
Sugar
chronic intake, 13-17
elimination from diet, 13-4–13-6
Suspension, school, 5-7
Sympathomimetics, 9-3
    noncatecholamine. *See* Stimulants
Symptom Checklist 90—Revised, 6-11

Symptoms
See also specific symptoms
in adults, 6-3, 6-4–6-5
assessment instruments, for follow-up studies,
    4-2–4-3
behavioral
    vs. normal temperament variations, 3-5–3-7
    predisposition, 3-11
    spectrum of, 23-4–23-5
    stimulants vs. tricyclic antidepressants, 11-
        5–11-6
from brain malfunction, lack of evidence on, 3-7–
    3-8
causes, 3-1–3-2
changes in, A-3
developmentally inappropriate, 2-3
in DSM-IV, dimensions of, 1-3
hyperactivitiy/impulsivity, 1-3
inattention, 1-3
in normal-abnormal continuum, P1-1
onset, DSM-IV criteria for, 18-8
parental reports, in follow-up studies, 4-4
persistence, 2-3
    in adolescence, 4-5–4-6
    in adulthood, 4-7–4-8
self-reports, in follow-up studies, 4-4
severity, DSM-IV criteria for, 18-8–18-9
in SUD, 19-10

T

TCAs. *See* Tricyclic antidepressants
Teachers
attitudes toward children with behavioral problems,
    23-8
contact with primary care physician, 23-5–23-6
full-inclusion model and, 24-12
information, in ADHD diagnosis, 23-5–23-6
practical value of labels for, 3-13
training, in detecting ADHD, 24-15
Temperament
difficult, 3-8–3-9, 3-15
DSM system and, 3-15
environmental impact on, 3-8–3-9, P1-1
normal variations, vs. ADHD behaviors, 3-5–
    3-7
Temperamental hypothesis of ADHD, P1-1–P1-3
Thyroid hormone therapy, 13-5, 13-17–13-18
Tic disorders, 11-3
Tobacco gateway hypothesis, 18-19, 19-5–19-6
Tobacco usage
See also Smoking
adult, childhood medication history and, 17-8–
    17-11
age, ADHD severity and, 18-6
data collection procedure, 18-9–8-10
as substance use risk factor, 18-5–18-6
Tomoxetine, 11-7
Tourette's syndrome, with ADHD, 8-12, 11-3, 23-6
Toxicology, future research needs, 10-11
"T–R," 20-11
Tranquilizers
adult, childhood medication history and,
    17-8–17-11

[References are to pages.]

Tranquilizers (continued)
    for children with ADHD, clinical longitudinal
        studies, 16-11–16-12
Transactional models, of family relationship
    impairment, 5-8
Traumatic brain injury, ADHD/HKD and, 7-12–7-13
Treatment, A-6
    alternatives, 13-2
        acupuncture, 13-13
        antifungal therapy, 13-17
        approaches for, 13-20
        channel-specific perceptual training, 13-17
        deleading, 13-18–13-19
        EEG biofeedback, 13-13–13-14
        elimination diets, 13-2–13-7
        EMG biofeedback, 13-14
        future research recommendations, 13-20–13-21
        herbal/homeopathic, 13-12–13-13
        hypnosis, 13-14
        immune therapy, 13-7
        ineffective/unsafe, 13-19
        massage, 13-15–13-16, 13-20
        meditation, 13-15, 13-20
        mirror feedback, 13-15, 13-20
        nutritional supplements, 13-7–13-12, 13-19–
            13-20
        perceptual stimulation/training, 13-15
        proven efficacy, 13-19–13-20
        relaxation training, 13-14
        scientific status of, 13-4–13-5
        thyroid hormone therapy, 13-17–13-18
        unproven, 13-18–13-19
        vestibular stimulation, 13-16, 13-20
        worth trying despite limited evidence of
            efficacy, 13-20
    assessment, by primary care physicians, 23-8–23-9
    barriers, 22-6–22-7, 22-13, 22-15, App. A-8–
        App. A-9
    behavioral. See Behavioral therapy
    choice
        age of child and, 12-19, 12-21
        comorbidity and, 12-21
        family factors and, 12-21
    clinical practice recommendations, 15-9–15-11
    cognitive correlates and, 8-17–8-18
    comprehensive approach, 14-2, 23-9
        vs. behavioral therapy, 14-4
        components of, 12-19, 12-20
        vs. pharmacotherapy, 14-4
    controversy, 23-3
    diversity, 23-3
    drug. See Pharmacotherapy
    durability of, 14-6–14-7
    efficacy, 14-2
    impact of comorbidity patterns on, 15-7
    long-term studies, 14-8–14-10
    matching to patient, 15-1–15-2
    mental health clinician role in, 23-3–23-4
    multimodal. See Multimodal Treatment Study
    NIH Consensus statement on, App. A-5–App. A-19
    nonstimulant drugs. See Pharmacotherapy, nonstim-
        ulant
    primary care physician role in, 23-3–23-4
    psychosocial. See Psychosocial interventions
    public policy and, 1-16
    rationale for, 5-16
    risks, 1-16, A-6–A-7
    school-based interventions, 23-8, 24-13–24-15
    school system concerns, 23-7–23-8
    short-term studies, 14-4–14-8
    small-sample studies, short-term, 14-4–14-6
    stimulant. See Stimulants
    trends, 22-9–22-11
Treatment services
    availability, for attentional problems, 22-3–22-4
    barriers to care, 22-6–22-7, 22-13, 22-15
    costs, 27-8–27-11
    fragmentation of, A-7–A-8
    future research recommendations, 22-16–22-17
    in juvenile justice system, 25-3–25-4
    location, 22-15–22-16
    mix, 22-2, 22-13, 22-15
    need vs. usage, 22-14–22-15
    patterns, 22-13–22-15
    by provider type, 22-11–22-12
    surveys
        Child Behavior Study, 22-12–22-13
        NAMCS. See National Ambulatory Medical
            Care Survey
        results of, 22-7–22-8
    trends, 22-9–22-11
    usage
        by ADHD children, 27-4–27-5
        in primary care, predictors of, 27-7–27-8
    variations in usage, 22-6
Tricyclic antidepressants (TCAs)
    for ADHD with mood disorder, 15-8, 15-11
    advantages of, 11-4
    efficacy, 11-9
        of desipramine, 11-4–11-5
        of imipramine, 11-4
        of nortriptyline, 11-5
        vs. stimulants, 11-5–11-6
    safety, 11-6
Tryptophan supplementation, 13-8
Twin studies, 7-9, 7-10
Tyrosine supplementation, 13-8

U
Underachievement
    as ADHD risk factor, 2-9
    in adult ADHD, 6-3
    DSM-IV ADHD and, 1-9
    evidence of, 8-6–8-7
Undifferentiated attention deficit disorder, 1-2
U.S. Department of Education, 26-1, 26-2, 26-4–
    26-5
U.S. Drug Enforcement Administration (DEA), 9-2
Utah, ADHD resource guide, 26-8

V
Validity, of ADHD diagnosis, 5-16, P1-1–P1-2, A-1
    clinical practice implications, 1-15–1-16
    cognitive correlates and, 8-2
    concurrent, 1-8–1-10, 1-17
    cross-cultural, 2-6, 2-8

[References are to pages.]

discriminant, 1-11–1-13, 1-17
   of DSM-IV criteria, 3-14–3-15
      across life span, 1-17–1-18
      subtypes, 1-11–1-13
   face, 1-8
   future research targets and, 1-16–1-18
   predictive, 1-8, 1-17
   public policy implications, 1-16
   supporting scientific evidence for, App. A-4–
      App. A-5
Verbal memory deficits, 8-9
Vermont, ADHD identification policy, 26-8
Vestibular stimulation, 13-5, 13-16, 13-19
Visual-spatial working memory deficits, 8-9
Visuospatial orienting system dysfunction, 8-15
Vitamin supplements
   megadosing, 13-10–13-11
   multivitamins, 13-10
   recommendations for clinical practice, 13-19
   scientific status of, 13-4
Vocational functioning, adult, 6-7–6-10

W

Werry-Weiss-Peters Activity Rating Scale, 4-2
Weschler Intelligence Scale for Children—Third
   Edition (WISC-III), 8-5
Wisconsin, methylphenidate diversion, 20-17
Working memory deficits, 8-12

Y

Yizhi wit-increasing syrup, 13-13

Z

Zinc supplementation, 13-4, 13-11–13-12